PEARSON ALWAYS LEARNING

Alaska Law for Business I

Contemporary Business Law

A Custom Edition for University of Alaska Anchorage Volume I

Additional Alaska Law Cases Selected
by Clayton Trotter

Taken from:
Business Law: Legal Environment, Online Commerce, Business Ethics, and International Issues, Ninth Edition
by Henry Cheeseman

Cover Art: Courtesy of evenfh/Fotolia and md3d/Fotolia

Taken from:

Business Law: Legal Environment, Online Commerce, Business Ethics, and International Issues, Ninth Edition
by Henry Cheeseman

New York, New York 10013

Pearson Learning Solutions, 330 Hudson Street, New York, New York 10013
A Pearson Education Company
www.pearsoned.com

Printed in the United States of America

2 3 4 5 6 7 8 9 10 V0UD 19 18 17 16 15

000200010271963576

ML/KE

ISBN 10: 1-323-11331-2
ISBN 13: 978-1-323-11331-8

BRIEF CONTENTS

CONTENTS

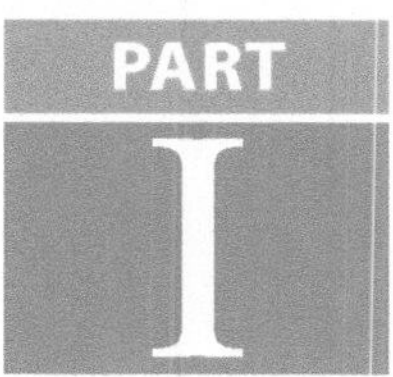

Legal Environment of Business and Online Commerce

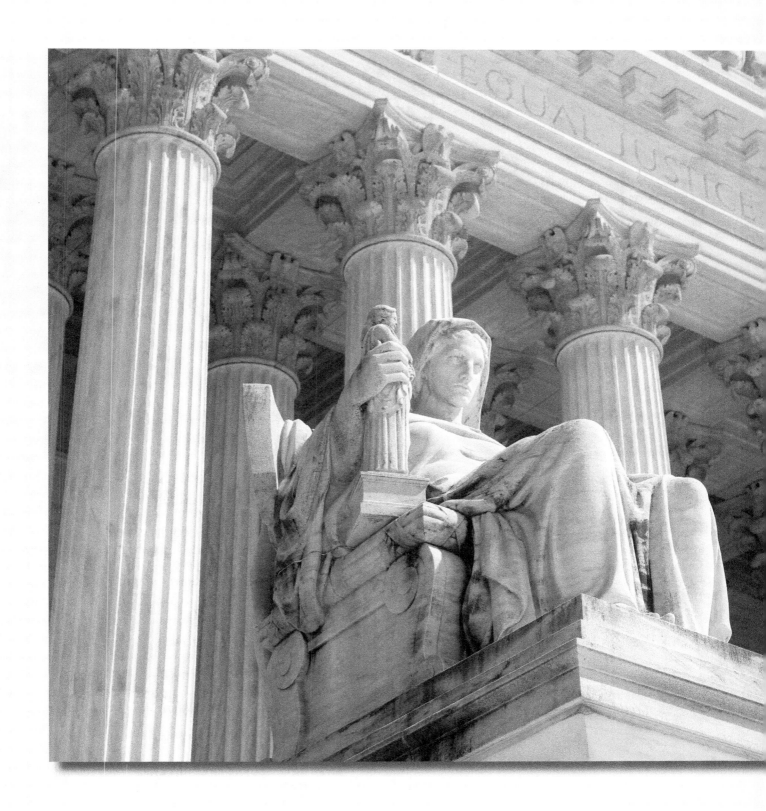

CHAPTER

1 Legal Heritage and the Digital Age

STATUE OF LIBERTY, NEW YORK HARBOR

The Statue of Liberty stands majestically in New York Harbor. During the American Revolution, France gave the colonial patriots substantial support in the form of money for equipment and supplies, officers and soldiers who fought in the war, and ships and sailors who fought on the seas. Without the assistance of France, it is unlikely that the American colonists would have won their independence from Britain. In 1886, the people of France gave the Statue of Liberty to the people of the United States in recognition of friendship that was established during the American Revolution. Since then, the Statue of Liberty has become a symbol of liberty and democracy throughout the world.

Learning Objectives

After studying this chapter, you should be able to:

1. Define *law.*
2. Describe the functions of law.
3. Explain the development of the U.S. legal system.
4. List and describe the sources of law in the United States.
5. Discuss the importance of the U.S. Supreme Court's decision in *Brown v. Board of Education*.

Chapter Outline

> "*Where there is no law, there is no freedom.*"
>
> —*John Locke*
> *Second Treatise of Government, Sec. 57*

Introduction to Legal Heritage and the Digital Age

In the words of Judge Learned Hand, "Without law we cannot live; only with it can we insure the future which by right is ours. The best of men's hopes are enmeshed in its success."[1] Every society makes and enforces laws that govern the conduct of the individuals, businesses, and other organizations that function within it.

Although the law of the United States is based primarily on English common law, other legal systems, such as Spanish and French civil law, also influence it. The sources of law in this country are the U.S. Constitution, state constitutions, federal and state statutes, ordinances, administrative agency rules and regulations, executive orders, and judicial decisions by federal and state courts.

> *Human beings do not ever make laws; it is the accidents and catastrophes of all kinds happening in every conceivable way that make law for us.*
>
> Plato
> *Laws IV, 709*

Businesses that are organized in the United States are subject to its laws. They are also subject to the laws of other countries in which they operate. Businesses organized in other countries must obey the laws of the United States when doing business here. In addition, businesspeople owe a duty to act ethically in the conduct of their affairs, and businesses owe a responsibility not to harm society.

This chapter discusses the nature and definition of law, theories about the development of law, and the history and sources of law in the United States.

What is Law?

The law consists of rules that regulate the conduct of individuals, businesses, and other organizations in society. It is intended to protect persons and their property against unwanted interference from others. In other words, the law forbids persons from engaging in certain undesirable activities. Consider the following passage:

> *Hardly anyone living in a civilized society has not at some time been told to do something or to refrain from doing something, because there is a law requiring it, or because it is against the law. What do we mean when we say such things?*
>
> *At the end of the 18th century, Immanuel Kant wrote of the question "What is law?" that it "may be said to be about as embarrassing to the jurist as the well-known question 'What is truth?' is to the logician."*[2]

> *A lawyer without history or literature is a mechanic, a mere working mason: if he possesses some knowledge of these, he may venture to call himself an architect.*
>
> Sir Walter Scott
> *Guy Mannering, Ch. 37 (1815)*

Definition of *Law*

The concept of **law** is broad. Although it is difficult to state a precise definition, *Black's Law Dictionary* gives one that is sufficient for this text:

> *Law, in its generic sense, is a body of rules of action or conduct prescribed by controlling authority, and having binding legal force. That which must be obeyed and followed by citizens subject to sanctions or legal consequences is a law.*[3]

law
That which must be obeyed and followed by citizens, subject to sanctions or legal consequences; a body of rules of action or conduct prescribed by controlling authority and having binding legal force.

Functions of the Law

Commercial law lies within a narrow compass, and is far purer and freer from defects than any other part of the system.

Henry Peter Brougham
House of Commons, February 7, 1828

The law is often described by the function it serves in a society. The primary *functions* served by the law in this country are the following:

1. Keeping the peace

   Example Some laws make certain activities crimes.

2. Shaping moral standards

   Example Some laws discourage drug and alcohol abuse.

3. Promoting social justice

   Example Some laws prohibit discrimination in employment.

4. Maintaining the status quo

   Example Some laws prevent the forceful overthrow of the government.

5. Facilitating orderly change

   Example Laws are enacted only after considerable study, debate, and public input.

6. Facilitating planning

   Example Well-designed commercial laws allow businesses to plan their activities, allocate their productive resources, and assess the risks they take.

7. Providing a basis for compromise

   Example Laws allow for the settlement of cases prior to trial. Approximately 95 percent of all lawsuits are settled in this manner.

8. Maximizing individual freedom

   Example The rights of freedom of speech, religion, and association are granted by the First Amendment to the U.S. Constitution.

CONCEPT SUMMARY

FUNCTIONS OF THE LAW

1. Keep the peace	5. Facilitate orderly change
2. Shape moral standards	6. Facilitate planning
3. Promote social justice	7. Provide a basis for compromise
4. Maintain the status quo	8. Maximize individual freedom

Fairness of the Law

The law, in its majestic equality, forbids the rich as well as the poor to sleep under bridges.

Anatole France

On the whole, the U.S. legal system is one of the most comprehensive, fair, and democratic systems of law ever developed and enforced. Nevertheless, some misuses and oversights of our legal system—including abuses of discretion and mistakes by judges and juries, unequal applications of the law, and procedural mishaps—allow some guilty parties to go unpunished.

Example In *Standefer v. United States*,[4] Chief Justice Warren Burger of the U.S. Supreme Court stated, "This case does no more than manifest the simple, if discomforting, reality that different juries may reach different results under any criminal statute. That is one of the consequences we accept under our jury system."

Flexibility of the Law

U.S. law evolves and changes along with the norms of society, technology, and the growth and expansion of commerce in the United States and the world. The following quote by Judge Jerome Frank discusses the value of the adaptability of law:

> *The law always has been, is now, and will ever continue to be, largely vague and variable. And how could this be otherwise? The law deals with human relations in their most complicated aspects. The whole confused, shifting helter-skelter of life parades before it—more confused than ever, in our kaleidoscopic age.*
>
> *The constant development of unprecedented problems requires a legal system capable of fluidity and pliancy. Our society would be straight-jacketed were not the courts, with the able assistance of the lawyers, constantly overhauling the law and adapting it to the realities of ever-changing social, industrial, and political conditions; although changes cannot be made lightly, yet rules of law must be more or less impermanent, experimental and therefore not nicely calculable.*
>
> *Much of the uncertainty of law is not an unfortunate accident; it is of immense social value.*[5]

A landmark U.S. Supreme Court case—*Brown v. Board of Education*—is discussed in the following feature. This case shows the flexibility of the law because the U.S. Supreme Court overturned a past decision of the U.S. Supreme Court.

Law must be stable and yet it cannot stand still.

Roscoe Pound
Interpretations of Legal History (1923)

Critical Legal Thinking

Are there any benefits for the law being "vague and variable"? Are bright-line tests possible for the law? Explain the statement, "Much of the uncertainty of law is not an unfortunate accident; it is of immense social value."

LANDMARK U.S. SUPREME COURT CASE Equal Protection

Brown v. Board of Education

"We conclude that in the field of public education the doctrine of 'separate but equal' has no place."

—Warren, Justice

Slavery was abolished by the Thirteenth Amendment to the Constitution in 1865. The Fourteenth Amendment, added to the Constitution in 1868, contains the Equal Protection Clause, which provides that no state shall "deny to any person within its jurisdiction the equal protection of the laws." The original intent of this amendment was to guarantee equality to freed African Americans. But equality was denied to African Americans for years. This included discrimination in housing, transportation, education, jobs, service at restaurants, and other activities.

In 1896, the U.S. Supreme Court decided the case *Plessy v. Ferguson*.[6] In that case, the state of Louisiana had a law that provided for separate but equal accommodations for African American and white railway passengers. The Supreme Court held that the "separate but equal" state law did not violate the Equal Protection Clause of the Fourteenth Amendment. The "separate but equal" doctrine was then applied to all areas of life, including public education. Thus, African American and white children attended separate schools, often with unequal facilities.

It was not until 1954 that the U.S. Supreme Court decided a case that challenged the "separate but equal" doctrine as it applied to public elementary and high schools. In ***Brown v. Board of Education***, a consolidated case that challenged the separate school systems of four states—Kansas, South Carolina, Virginia, and Delaware—the Supreme Court decided to revisit the "separate but equal" doctrine announced by its forbearers in another century. This time, a unanimous Supreme Court, in an opinion written by Chief Justice Earl Warren, reversed prior precedent and held that the separate but equal doctrine violated the Equal Protection Clause of the Fourteenth Amendment to the Constitution. In its opinion, the Court stated,

> *Today, education is perhaps the most important function of state and local governments. We conclude that in the field of public education the doctrine of "separate but equal" has no place. Separate educational facilities are inherently unequal. Therefore, we hold that the plaintiffs and others similarly situated for whom actions have been brought are, by reason of the segregation complained of, deprived of the equal protection of the laws guaranteed by the Fourteenth Amendment.*

(case continues)

After *Brown v. Board of Education* was decided, it took court orders as well as U.S. army enforcement to integrate many of the public schools in this country. *Brown v. Board of Education*, 347 U.S. 483, 74 S.Ct. 686, 1954 U.S. Lexis 2094 (Supreme Court of the United States, 1954)

Critical Legal Thinking Questions
It has been said that the U.S. Constitution is a "living document"—that is, one that can adapt to changing times. Do you think this is a good policy? Or should the U.S. Constitution be interpreted narrowly and literally, as originally written?

Schools of Jurisprudential Thought

WEB EXERCISE
To view court documents related to *Brown v. Board of Education*, go to **www.loc.gov/exhibits/brown/brown-brown.html.**

jurisprudence
The philosophy or science of law.

The law is not a series of calculating machines where definitions and answers come tumbling out when the right levers are pushed.

William O. Douglas
Dissent, A Safeguard of Democracy (1948)

The philosophy or science of the law is referred to as **jurisprudence**. There are several different philosophies about how the law developed, ranging from the classical natural theory to modern theories of law and economics and critical legal studies. Classical legal philosophies are discussed in the following paragraphs.

Natural Law School

The **Natural Law School** of jurisprudence postulates that the law is based on what is "correct." Natural law philosophers emphasize a **moral theory of law**—that is, law should be based on morality and ethics. Natural law is "discovered" by humans through the use of reason and choosing between good and evil.

Examples Documents such as the U.S. Constitution, the Magna Carta, and the United Nations Charter reflect this theory.

The following U.S. Supreme Court case involves the moral theory of law and the issue of ethics.

CASE 1.1 *U.S. SUPREME COURT CASE Moral Theory of Law and Ethics*

POM Wonderful LLC v. Coca-Cola Company

134 S.Ct. 2228, 2014 U.S. Lexis 4165 (2014)
Supreme Court of the United States

"Lanham Act suits provide incentives for manufacturers to behave well."
—Kennedy, Justice

Facts

POM Wonderful, LLC (POM) is a grower of pomegranates, a fruit, and a maker and distributor of pomegranate juice and juice blends. POM produces and sells a pomegranate-blueberry juice blend that consists of 85% pomegranate and 15% blueberry juices.

The Coca-Cola Company's Minute Maid Division makes a juice blend sold with a label that, in describing the contents, displays the words "pomegranate blueberry" with far more prominence than other words on the label. In truth, Coca-Cola's pomegranate blueberry juice is made of five different juices, and contains but 0.3% pomegranate, 0.2% blueberry juice, and 0.1% raspberry juice. The Coca-Cola pomegranate blueberry juice is actually made with 99.4% apple and grape juices.

Despite the minuscule amount of pomegranate and blueberry juices in the blend, the front label of the Coca-Cola product displays the words "POMEGRANATE" and "BLUEBERRY" in all capital letters on two separate lines. Below those words, Coca-Cola placed the phrase "flavored blend of 5 juices" in much smaller type. And below that phrase, in still smaller type, were the words "from concentrate with added ingredients"—and, with a line break before the final phrase—"and other natural flavors." Coca-Cola's front label also displays a vignette of blueberries, grapes, and raspberries in front of a halved pomegranate and a halved apple.

POM sued Coca-Cola under Section 43 of the federal Lanham Act, which allows one competitor to sue another to recover damages for unfair competition

(case continues)

arising from false and misleading product descriptions. Coca-Cola tried to avoid POM's lawsuit by asserting that the Federal Food, Drug, and Cosmetic Act (FDCA), a federal statute that protects the safety of food products, did not require any different labeling. The U.S. district court and the U.S. court of appeals held in favor of Coca-Cola. POM appealed to the U.S. Supreme Court.

Issue

Can a private party bring an unfair competition lawsuit under the Lanham Act against a competitor that challenges the truthfulness of a food label?

Language of the U.S. Supreme Court

The Lanham Act creates a cause of action for unfair competition through misleading advertising and labeling. Coca-Cola is incorrect that the best way to harmonize the statutes is to bar POM's Lanham Act claim. By serving a distinct compensatory function that may motivate injured persons to come forward, Lanham Act suits provide incentives for manufacturers to behave well.

Decision

The U.S. Supreme Court held that the POM may proceed with its Lanham Act unfair competition lawsuit against Coca-Cola and remanded the case for further proceedings.

Ethics Questions

Do you think that Coca-Cola was trying to trick consumers into buying cheap apple-grape juice by labeling it pomegranate blueberry juice? Do you think Coca-Cola acted ethically in this case?

Historical School

The **Historical School** of jurisprudence believes that the law is an aggregate of social traditions and customs that have developed over the centuries. It believes that changes in the norms of society will gradually be reflected in the law. To these legal philosophers, the law is an evolutionary process.

Example Historical legal scholars look to past legal decisions (precedent) to solve contemporary problems.

Analytical School

The **Analytical School** of jurisprudence maintains that the law is shaped by logic. Analytical philosophers believe that results are reached by applying principles of logic to the specific facts of a case. The emphasis is on the logic of the result rather than on how the result is reached.

Example If the U.S. Constitution would have freed the slaves or granted females the right to vote, it would not have been ratified by the states in 1788.

Sociological School

The **Sociological School** of jurisprudence asserts that the law is a means of achieving and advancing certain sociological goals. The followers of this philosophy, known as *realists*, believe that the purpose of law is to shape social behavior. Sociological philosophers are unlikely to adhere to past law as precedent.

Even when laws have been written down, they ought not always to remain unaltered.

Aristotle

Examples Laws that make discrimination in employment illegal and laws that impose penalties for drunk driving reflect this theory.

Command School

The philosophers of the **Command School** of jurisprudence believe that the law is a set of rules developed, communicated, and enforced by the ruling party rather than a reflection of the society's morality, history, logic, or sociology. This school maintains that law changes when the ruling class changes.

Example During certain military conflicts, such as World War II and the Vietnam War, the federal government has enacted draft laws that require men of a certain age to serve in the military if they meet certain physical and other requirements.

Critical Legal Studies School

The **Critical Legal Studies School** proposes that legal rules are unnecessary and are used as an obstacle by the powerful to maintain the status quo. Critical legal theorists argue that legal disputes should be solved by applying arbitrary rules that are based on broad notions of what is "fair" in each circumstance. Under this theory, subjective decision making by judges would be permitted.

Example This school postulates that rape laws often make it difficult for women to prove legally that they have been raped because these laws have mostly been drafted from a male's perspective. Therefore, says this school, these laws should be ignored and the judge should be free to decide whether rape has occurred in his or her subjective decision making.

Law and Economics School

The **Law and Economics School** believes that promoting market efficiency should be the central goal of legal decision making. This school is also called the **Chicago School**, named after the University of Chicago, where it was first developed.

Example Proponents of the law and economics theory suggest that the federal government's policy of subsidizing housing—by a law that permits a portion of interest paid on mortgage loans to be deducted from an individual borrower's federal income taxes and laws that created government-sponsored enterprises (Fannie Mae and Freddie Mac) that purchase low-rate interest mortgages made by banks and other lending institutions—provide incentives so that too many homes are built. If these laws did not exist, then the free market would determine the exact number of homes that should be built.

CONCEPT SUMMARY
SCHOOLS OF JURISPRUDENTIAL THOUGHT

School	Philosophy
Natural Law	Postulates that law is based on what is "correct." It emphasizes a moral theory of law—that is, law should be based on morality and ethics.
Historical	Believes that law is an aggregate of social traditions and customs.
Analytical	Maintains that law is shaped by logic.
Sociological	Asserts that the law is a means of achieving and advancing certain sociological goals.
Command	Believes that the law is a set of rules developed, communicated, and enforced by the ruling party.
Critical Legal Studies	Maintains that legal rules are unnecessary and that legal disputes should be solved by applying arbitrary rules based on fairness.
Law and Economics	Believes that promoting market efficiency should be the central concern of legal decision making.

The following feature discusses the Command School of jurisprudence of Cuba.

Global Law

Command School of Jurisprudence of Cuba

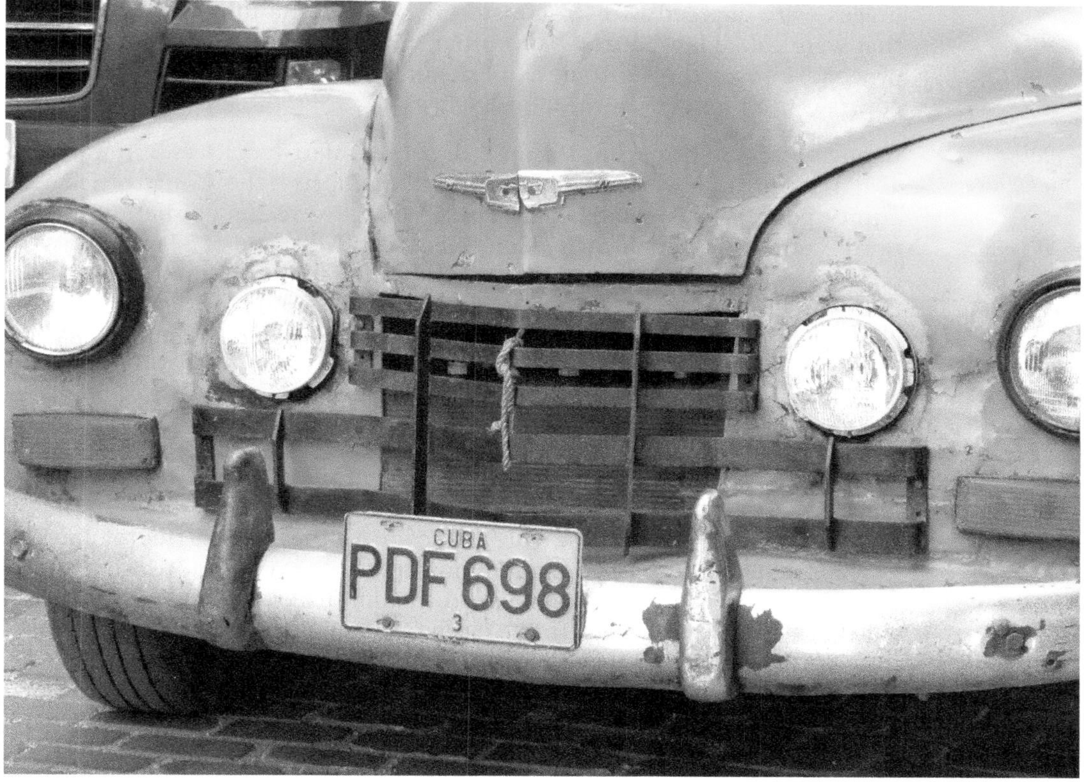

HAVANA, CUBA

Cuba is an island nation located in the Caribbean Sea less than 100 miles south of Key West, Florida. In 1959, Fidel Castro led a revolution that displaced the existing dictatorial government. Castro installed a communist government that expropriated and nationalized much private property. The communist government installed a one-party rule over the country and installed a command economy and system of jurisprudence. More than one million Cubans fled the island to the United States where many created a thriving community and economy in Miami, Florida. Under a state-controlled planned economy based on socialist principles, the production of goods and food items in Cuba fell substantially, and major shortages of houses, medical supplies, and other goods and services occurred. After more than five decades of a command economy, Cuba is permitting limited free-market measures, but 90 percent of workers are still employed by the government.

History of American Law

When the American colonies were first settled, the English system of law was generally adopted as the system of jurisprudence. This was the foundation from which American judges developed a common law in America.

English Common Law

English common law was law developed by judges who issued their opinions when deciding cases. The principles announced in these cases became *precedent* for later judges deciding similar cases. The English common law can be divided into cases decided by the *law courts*, *equity courts*, and *merchant courts*.

English common law
Law developed by judges who issue their opinions when deciding a case. The principles announced in these cases became precedent for later judges deciding similar cases.

Law Courts Prior to the Norman Conquest of England in 1066, each locality in England was subject to local laws, as established by the lord or chieftain in control of a local area. There was no countrywide system of law. After 1066, William the Conqueror and his successors to the throne of England began to replace the various local laws with one uniform system of law. To accomplish this, the king or queen appointed loyal followers as judges in all local areas. These judges were charged with administering the law in a uniform manner, in courts that were called **law courts**. Law at that time tended to emphasize the form (legal procedure) over the substance (merit) of a case. The only relief available at law courts was a monetary award for damages.

Two things most people should never see made: sausages and laws.

An old saying

Chancery (Equity) Courts Because of some unfair results and limited remedies available in the law courts, a second set of courts—the **Court of Chancery** (or **equity court**)—was established. These courts were under the authority of the Lord Chancellor. Persons who believed that the decision of a law court was unfair or believed that the law court could not grant an appropriate remedy could seek relief in the Court of Chancery. Rather than emphasize legal procedure, the chancery court inquired into the merits of the case. The chancellor's remedies were called *equitable remedies* because they were shaped to fit each situation. Equitable orders and remedies of the Court of Chancery took precedence over the legal decisions and remedies of the law courts.

Merchant Courts As trade developed during the Middle Ages, merchants who traveled about England and Europe developed certain rules to solve their commercial disputes. These rules, known as the "law of merchants," or the **Law Merchant**, were based on common trade practices and usage. Eventually, a separate set of courts was established to administer these rules. This court was called the **Merchant Court**. In the early 1900s, the Merchant Court was absorbed into the regular law court system of England.

The following feature discusses the adoption of English common law in the United States.

Landmark Law

Adoption of English Common Law in the United States

All the states—except Louisiana—of the United States of America base their legal systems primarily on the English common law. In the United States, the law, equity, and merchant courts have been merged. Thus, most U.S. courts permit the aggrieved party to seek both legal and equitable orders and remedies.

The importance of common law to the American legal system is described in the following excerpt from Justice Douglas's opinion in the 1841 case *Penny v. Little*:

> *The common law is a beautiful system, containing the wisdom and experiences of ages. Like the people it ruled and protected, it was simple and crude in its infancy and became enlarged, improved, and polished as the nation advanced in civilization, virtue, and intelligence. Adapting itself to the conditions and circumstances of the people and relying upon them for its administration, it necessarily improved as the condition of the people was elevated. The inhabitants of this country always claimed the common law as their birthright, and at an early period established it as the basis of their jurisprudence.*[7]

Currently, the law of the United States is a combination of law created by the judicial system and by congressional legislation.

The following feature discusses the development of the civil law system in Europe.

Global Law

Civil Law System of France and Germany

One of the major legal systems that developed in the world in addition to the Anglo-American common law system is the **Romano-Germanic civil law system.** This legal system, which is commonly called the **civil law**, dates to 450 BCE, when Rome adopted the Twelve Tables, a code of laws applicable to the Romans. A compilation of Roman law, called the *Corpus Juris Civilis* ("Body of Civil Law"), was completed in CE 534. Later, two national codes—the **French Civil Code of 1804 (the Napoleonic Code)** and the **German Civil Code of 1896**—became models for countries that adopted civil codes.

In contrast to the Anglo-American law, in which laws are created by the judicial system as well as by congressional legislation, the civil code and parliamentary statutes are the sole sources of the law in most civil law countries. Thus, the adjudication of a case is simply the application of the code or the statutes to a particular set of facts. In some civil law countries, court decisions do not have the force of law.

Many countries in Europe still follow the civil law system.

Sources of Law in the United States

In the more than 200 years since the founding of the United States and adoption of the English common law, the lawmakers of this country have developed a substantial body of law. The *sources of modern law* in the United States are discussed in the paragraphs that follow.

Constitutions

The **Constitution of the United States of America** is the *supreme law of the land.* This means that any law—whether federal, state, or local—that conflicts with the U.S. Constitution is unconstitutional and therefore unenforceable.

Constitution of the United States of America
The supreme law of the United States.

The principles enumerated in the U.S. Constitution are extremely broad because the founding fathers intended them to be applied to evolving social, technological, and economic conditions. The U.S. Constitution is often referred to as a "living document" because it is so adaptable.

The U.S. Constitution established the structure of the federal government. It created three branches of government and gave them the following powers:

- The **legislative branch (Congress)** has the power to make (enact) the law.
- The **executive branch (president)** has the power to enforce the law.
- The **judicial branch (courts)** has the power to interpret and determine the validity of the law.

The Constitution of the United States is not a mere lawyers' document: it is a vehicle of life, and its spirit is always the spirit of age.

Woodrow Wilson
Constitutional Government in the United States (1927)

Powers not given to the federal government by the Constitution are reserved for the states. States also have their own constitutions. **State constitutions** are often patterned after the U.S. Constitution, although many are more detailed. State constitutions establish the legislative, executive, and judicial branches of state government and establish the powers of each branch. Provisions of state constitutions are valid unless they conflict with the U.S. Constitution or any valid federal law.

Treaties

The U.S. Constitution provides that the president, with the advice and consent of two-thirds of the Senate, may enter into **treaties** with foreign governments. Treaties become part of the supreme law of the land. With increasing international economic relations among nations, treaties will become an even more important source of law that will affect business in the future.

treaty
A compact made between two or more nations.

U.S. CONGRESS, WASHINGTON DC
The U.S. Congress, which is a bicameral system made up of the U.S. Senate and the U.S. House of Representatives, creates federal law by enacting statutes. Each state has two senators and is allocated a certain number of representatives based on population.

Federal Statutes

statute
Written law enacted by the legislative branch of the federal and state governments that establishes certain courses of conduct that covered parties must adhere to.

Statutes are written laws that establish certain courses of conduct that covered parties must adhere to. The U.S. Congress is empowered by the Commerce Clause and other provisions of the U.S. Constitution to enact **federal statutes** to regulate foreign and interstate commerce.

Examples The federal Clean Water Act regulates the quality of water and restricts water pollution. The federal Securities Act of 1933 regulates the issuance of securities. The federal National Labor Relations Act establishes the right of employees to form and join labor organizations.

Federal statutes are organized by topic into **code books**. This is often referred to as **codified law**. Federal statutes can be found in these hardcopy books and online.

The following feature describes how a bill becomes law.

Contemporary Environment

How a Bill Becomes Law

The **U.S. Congress** is composed of two chambers, the **U.S. House of Representatives** and the **U.S. Senate**. Thousands of **bills** are introduced in the U.S. Congress each year, but only a small percentage of them become law. The process of legislation at the federal level is as follows:

1. A member of the U.S. House of Representatives or U.S. Senate introduces a bill in his or her **chamber**. The bill is assigned a number: "H.R. [number]" for House bills and "S [number]" for Senate bills. The bill is printed in the public *Congressional Record*. The bill is available in hard copy and on the Internet. All bills for raising revenue must originate in the U.S. House of Representatives.
2. The bill is referred to the appropriate **committee** for review and study. The committee can do the following: (1) reject the bill; (2) report it to the full chamber for vote; (3) simply not act on it, in which case the bill is said to have died in committee—many bills meet this fate; or (4) send the bill to a **subcommittee** for further study. A subcommittee can let the bill die or report it back to the full committee.
3. Bills that receive the vote of a committee are reported to the full chamber, where they are debated and voted on. If the bill receives a majority vote of the chamber, it is sent to the other chamber, where the previously outlined process is followed. Bills originated in one chamber often die in the other chamber. If the second chamber makes no changes in the original bill, the bill is reported for vote by that chamber. If the second chamber makes significant changes to the bill, a **conference committee** that is made up of members of both chambers will try to reconcile the differences.

If a compromised version is agreed to by the conference committee, the bill is reported for vote.

4. A bill that is reported to a full chamber must receive the majority vote of the chamber, and if it receives this vote, it is forwarded to the other chamber. If a majority of the second chamber approves the bill, it is then sent to the president's desk.
5. If the president signs a bill, it becomes law. If the president takes no action for ten days, the bill automatically becomes law. If the president vetoes the bill, the bill can be passed into law if two-thirds of the members of the House and two-thirds of the members of the Senate vote to override the veto and approve the bill. Many bills that are vetoed by the president do not obtain the necessary two-thirds vote to override the veto.

Because of this detailed and political legislative process, few of the many bills that are submitted by members of the U.S. House of Representatives or U.S. Senate become law.

State Statutes

State legislatures enact **state statutes**. Such statutes are placed in code books. State statutes can be assessed in these hardcopy code books or online.

Critical Legal Thinking
Why is the process of the U.S. Congress enacting statutes so complex? What checks and balances are built into the system before a bill can become law?

Examples The state of Florida has enacted the Lake Okeechobee Protection Act to protect Lake Okeechobee and the northern Everglades ecosystem. The Nevada Corporations Code outlines how to form and operate a Nevada corporation. The Texas Natural Resources Code regulates oil, gas, mining, geothermal, and other natural resources in the state.

Ordinances

State legislatures often delegate lawmaking authority to local government bodies, including cities and municipalities, counties, school districts, and water districts. These governmental units are empowered to adopt **ordinances**. Ordinances are also codified.

ordinance
Law enacted by local government bodies, such as cities and municipalities, counties, school districts, and water districts.

Examples The city of Mackinac Island, Michigan, a city of 1800s Victorian houses and buildings, has enacted ordinances that keep the island car free, keep out fast-food chains, and require buildings to adhere to era-specific aesthetic standards. Other examples of city ordinances include zoning laws, building codes, and sign restrictions.

Executive Orders

The executive branch of government, which includes the president of the United States and state governors, is empowered to issue **executive orders**. This power is derived from express delegation from the legislative branch and is implied from the U.S. Constitution and state constitutions.

executive order
An order issued by a member of the executive branch of the government.

Example When the United States is at war with another country, the president of the United States usually issues executive orders prohibiting U.S. companies from selling goods or services to that country.

Regulations and Orders of Administrative Agencies

The legislative and executive branches of federal and state governments are empowered to establish **administrative agencies** to enforce and interpret statutes enacted by Congress and state legislatures. Many of these agencies regulate business.

administrative agencies
Agencies (such as the Securities and Exchange Commission and the Federal Trade Commission) that the legislative and executive branches of federal and state governments are empowered to establish.

Examples Congress has created the Securities and Exchange Commission (SEC) to enforce federal securities laws and the Federal Trade Commission (FTC) to enforce consumer protection statutes.

Congress or the state legislatures usually empower these agencies to adopt **administrative rules and regulations** to interpret the statutes that the agency is authorized to enforce. These rules and regulations have the force of law.

Administrative agencies usually have the power to hear and decide disputes. Their decisions are called **orders**. Because of their power, administrative agencies are often informally referred to as the "fourth branch of government."

Judicial Decisions

judicial decision
A decision about an individual lawsuit issued by a federal or state court.

When deciding individual lawsuits, federal and state courts issue **judicial decisions**. In these written opinions, a judge or justice usually explains the legal reasoning used to decide the case. These opinions often include interpretations of statutes, ordinances, and administrative regulations and the announcement of legal principles used to decide the case. Many court decisions are reported in books that are available in law libraries.

precedent
A rule of law established in a court decision. Lower courts must follow the precedent established by higher courts.

Doctrine of Stare Decisis Based on the common law tradition, past court decisions become **precedent** for deciding future cases. Lower courts must follow the precedent established by higher courts. That is why all federal and state courts in the United States must follow the precedents established by U.S. Supreme Court decisions.

The courts of one jurisdiction are not bound by the precedent established by the courts of another jurisdiction, although they may look to each other for guidance.

Example State courts of one state are not required to follow the legal precedent established by the courts of another state.

stare decisis
Latin for "to stand by the decision." Adherence to precedent.

Adherence to precedent is called the doctrine of ***stare decisis*** ("to stand by the decision"). The doctrine of *stare decisis* promotes uniformity of law within a jurisdiction, makes the court system more efficient, and makes the law more predictable for individuals and businesses. A court may later change or reverse its legal reasoning if a new case is presented to it and change is warranted. The doctrine of *stare decisis* is discussed in the following excerpt from Justice Musmanno's decision in *Flagiello v. Pennsylvania*:

Critical Legal Thinking
Why was the doctrine of *stare decisis* developed? What would be the consequences if the doctrine of *stare decisis* was not followed?

> *Without* stare decisis*, there would be no stability in our system of jurisprudence.* Stare decisis *channels the law. It erects lighthouses and flies the signal of safety. The ships of jurisprudence must follow that well-defined channel which, over the years, has been proved to be secure and worthy.*[8]

CONCEPT SUMMARY
SOURCES OF LAW IN THE UNITED STATES

Source of Law	Description
Constitutions	The U.S. Constitution establishes the federal government and enumerates its powers. Powers not given to the federal government are reserved to the states. State constitutions establish state governments and enumerate their powers.
Treaties	The president, with the advice and consent of two-thirds of the Senate, may enter into treaties with foreign countries.
Codified law: statutes and ordinances	Statutes are enacted by Congress and state legislatures. Ordinances are enacted by municipalities and local government bodies. They establish courses of conduct that covered parties must follow.
Executive orders	Issued by the president and governors of states. Executive orders regulate the conduct of covered parties.

Source of Law	Description
Regulations and orders of administrative agencies	Administrative agencies are created by the legislative and executive branches of government. They may adopt rules and regulations that regulate the conduct of covered parties as well as issue orders.
Judicial decisions	Courts decide controversies. In doing so, a court issues an opinion that states the decision of the court and the rationale used in reaching that decision.

Priority of Law in the United States

As mentioned previously, the U.S. Constitution and treaties take precedence over all other laws in the United States. Federal statutes take precedence over federal regulations. Valid federal law takes precedence over any conflicting state or local law. State constitutions rank as the highest state law. State statutes take precedence over state regulations. Valid state law takes precedence over local laws.

The following feature discusses law in the digital age.

Where law ends, there tyranny begins.

William Pitt, first Earl of Chatham

Digital Law

Law in the Digital Age

In a span of about three decades, computers have revolutionized society. Computers, once primarily used by businesses, have permeated the lives of most families as well. In addition to computers, many other digital devices are commonly in use, such as smart phones, tablets, televisions, digital cameras, and electronic game devices. In addition to the digital devices, technology has brought new ways of communicating, such as e-mail and texting, as well as the use of social networks.

The electronic age arrived before new laws were written that were unique and specific to this environment. Courts have applied existing laws to the new digital environment by requiring interpretations and applications. In addition, new laws have been written that apply specifically to this new environment. The U.S. Congress has led the way, enacting many new federal statutes to regulate the digital environment.

Critical Legal Thinking

The U.S. Supreme Court, comprised of nine justices chosen from the brightest legal minds in the country, often reach 5–4 decisions or other nonunanimous decisions. Why? It is because each justice has analyzed the facts of a case and the legal issue presented, applied critical legal thinking to reason through the case, and come up with his or her own conclusion. But is one side right and the other wrong? No. It just means that each justice has done his or her best in examining, analyzing, evaluating, and interpreting the law and facts and deciding the case based on his or her unique sociological, political, educational, personal, and legal background.

The key is that each justice applied critical thinking in reaching his or her conclusion. Critical thinking is important to all subjects taken by college and university students, no matter what their major or what course is taken. But critical thinking in law courses—referred to as *critical legal thinking*—is of particular significance because in the law there is not always a bright-line answer; in fact, there seldom is. This is where the famous "gray area" of the law appears. Thus, the need for critical thinking becomes especially important in solving legal disputes.

Defining *Critical Legal Thinking*

Critical Legal Thinking
A method of thinking that consists of investigating, analyzing, evaluating, and interpreting information to solve a legal issue or case.

What is critical legal thinking? **Critical legal thinking** consists of investigating, analyzing, evaluating, and interpreting information to solve simple or complex legal issues or cases. Critical legal thinking improves a person's problem-solving skills and helps him or her make clear, logical, rational, and well-reasoned conclusions and judgments.

Critical legal thinking requires intellectually disciplined thinking. This requires a person to recognize and identify problems, engage in logical inquiry and reasoning, evaluate information and appraise evidence, consider alternative perspectives, question assumptions, identify unjustified inferences and irrelevant information, evaluate opposing positions and arguments, and assess one's own thinking and conclusions.

Your professor has a deep understanding of critical legal thinking, that he or she has developed during years of study in law school, in teaching and scholarship, and often in private practice or government employment as well. Over the course of the semester, he or she will impart to you not only his or her knowledge of the law but also a unique and intelligent way of thinking through and solving complex problems. Critical legal thinking can serve twenty-first-century students and leaders.

Socratic Method

socratic method
A process that consists of a series of questions and answers and a give-and-take inquiry and debate between a professor and students.

In class, many law professors use the **Socratic method** when discussing a case. The Socratic method consists of the professor asking students questions about a case or legal issue to stimulate critical thinking by the students. This process consists of a series of questions and answers and a give-and-take inquiry and debate between a professor and the students. The Socratic method stimulates class discussions. Good teachers recognize and focus on the questions and activities that stimulate the mind. Discussing current events using the Socratic method is also often used in the classroom setting.

Critical legal thinking requires special application in the digital age. Juries and judges are often called on to apply laws enacted prior to the digital age to cases and legal issues that arise in the electronic environment and that had not been contemplated when the law was enacted. Critical legal thinking must also be used by the U.S. Congress and state legislatures as they enact new laws that specifically address new issues of the digital environment.

IRAC Method

Legal cases are usually examined using the following critical legal thinking method. First, the *facts* of the case must be investigated and understood. Next, the *legal issue* that is to be answered must be identified and succinctly stated. Then the *law* that is to be applied to the case must be identified, read, and understood. Once the facts, law, and legal issue have been stated, critical thinking must be used in applying the law to the facts of the case. This requires that the decision maker—whether a judge, juror, or student—*analyze*, examine, evaluate, interpret, and apply the law to the facts of the case. Last, the critical legal thinker must reach a *conclusion* and state his or her judgment. In the study of law, this process is often referred to as the **IRAC method** (an acronym that stands for **issue, rule, application, and conclusion**) as outlined in the following:

IRAC method
A method used to examine a law case. *IRAC* is an acronym that stands for *issue, rule, application,* and *conclusion.*

I = What is the legal *issue* in the case?
R = What is the *rule* (law) of the case?
A = What is the court's *analysis* and rationale?
C = What was the *conclusion* or outcome of the case?

This tex—whether in its print or electronic version—offer students ample opportunities to develop and apply critical legal thinking. The text contains real-world cases in which actual disputing parties have become embroiled. The law cases are real, the parties are real, and the decisions reached by juries and judges are real. Some cases are easier to decide than others, but all provide a unique set of facts that require critical legal thinking to solve.

U.S. Supreme Court Case

So, let us examine how critical legal thinking is applied by the U.S. Supreme Court. Following is the Supreme Court's decision of an important voting rights case.

CASE 1.2 *U.S. SUPREME COURT CASE Voting Rights Act*

Shelby County, Texas v. Holder

133 S.Ct. 2612, 2013 U.S. Lexis 4917 (2013)
Supreme Court of the United States

"The Act has proved immensely successful at redressing racial discrimination and integrating the voting process."

—Roberts, Chief Justice, delivered the opinion of the Court, in which Justices Scalia, Kennedy, Thomas, and Alito joined.

Facts

The Fifteenth Amendment was added to the U.S. Constitution in 1870, following the Civil War. It provides that the right of citizens of the United States to vote shall not be denied or abridged by the federal or state governments on account of race, color, or previous conditions of servitude and gives Congress the power to enact laws to enforce the amendment.

During the first century after the Fifteenth Amendment, congressional enforcement of the Amendment was a complete failure. Many states enacted literacy and knowledge tests, enforced good moral character requirements, created the need for vouchers from registered voters, and intimidated voters to prevent minority citizens from qualifying to vote or prevent them from voting should they meet the requirements. Based on these impairments, voting by minority citizens, particularly African Americans, was substantially lower than it was for white voters.

In 1965, Congress enacted the Voting Rights Act. Section 2 forbids any standard, practice, or procedure that denies or abridges the right of any citizen to vote on account of race or color. Section 4(b) provides a coverage formula that identified six states—Alabama, Georgia, Louisiana, Mississippi, South Carolina, and Virginia—that maintained illegal voting requirements that substantially reduced minority voter turnout. Section 5 stipulates that the covered states could not make any changes to voting districts or voting procedures without clearance from federal authorities in Washington DC. Portions of other states, including Texas, were added to the list of covered jurisdictions.

The Voting Rights Act, which was originally enacted for five years, had been reauthorized by Congress for more than forty years. In 2006, Congress reauthorized the Voting Rights Act for 25 years. Shortly after the 2006 reauthorization, a Texas voting district challenged the constitutionality of the special coverage provision of the Voting Rights Act. The U.S. district court and the U.S. court of appeals upheld this provision. The U.S. Supreme Court agreed to hear the appeal.

Issue

Is the coverage provision of the Voting Rights Act that singles out several states for the federal clearance requirement constitutional?

Language of the U.S. Supreme Court

Census Bureau data from the most recent election indicate that African-American voter turnout exceeded white voter turnout in five of the six States originally covered by Section 5, with a gap in the sixth State of less than one half of one percent. There is no doubt that these improvements are in large part because of the Voting Rights Act. The Act has proved immensely successful at redressing racial discrimination and integrating the voting process.

(*case continues*)

> *A statute's current burdens must be justified by current needs, and any disparate geographic coverage must be sufficiently related to the problem that it targets. The coverage formula met that test in 1965, but no longer does so. Coverage today is based on decades-old data and eradicated practices.*

Decision

The U.S. Supreme Court held that the coverage provision of the Voting Rights Act that requires clearance by the federal government for covered states to make changes to voting districts and other voting requirements is unconstitutional.

Dissenting Opinion

Ginsburg, Justice, filed a dissenting opinion, in which Justices Breyer, Sotomayor, and Kagan joined.

> *Thanks to the Voting Rights Act, progress once the subject of a dream has been achieved and continues to be made. After exhaustive evidence-gathering and deliberative process, Congress reauthorized the Voting Rights Act, including the coverage provision, with overwhelming bipartisan support. In my judgment, the Court errs egregiously by overriding Congress' decision.*

Ethics Questions

When Congress enacted the Voting Rights Act in 1965, was there sufficient justification to do so? Was it ethical for states to adopt impairments to minority voters? Was the special requirement for designated states to seek federal approval before making voting changes necessary in 1965? Do you think that such a requirement is necessary today?

Key Terms and Concepts

Administrative agencies (13)
Administrative rules and regulations (13)
Analytical School (7)
Bill (12)
Brown v. Board of Education (5)
Chamber (12)
Civil law (11)
Code book (12)
Codified law (12)
Command School (7)
Committee (12)
Conference committee (12)
Constitution of the United States of America (11)
Court of Chancery (equity court) (10)
Critical Legal Studies School (8)
Critical legal thinking (16)
English common law (9)
Executive branch (president) (11)
Executive order (13)
Federal statute (12)
Fourth Amendment to the U.S. Constitution (000)
French Civil Code of 1804 (the Napoleonic Code) (11)
German Civil Code of 1896 (11)
Historical School (7)
IRAC method (16)
Judicial branch (courts) (11)
Judicial decision (14)
Jurisprudence (6)
Law (3)
Law and Economics School (Chicago School) (8)
Law courts (10)
Law Merchant (10)
Legislative branch (Congress) (11)
Merchant Court (10)
Moral theory of law (6)
Natural Law School (6)
Order (14)
Ordinance (13)
Precedent (14)
Romano-Germanic civil law system (11)
Sociological School (7)
Socratic method (16)
Stare decisis (14)
State constitution (11)
State statute (13)
Statute (12)
Subcommittee (12)
Treaty (11)
U.S. Congress (12)
U.S. House of Representatives (12)
U.S. Senate (12)

Critical Legal Thinking Cases

1.1 Fairness of the Law In 1909, the state legislature of Illinois enacted a statute called the Woman's Ten-Hour Law. The law prohibited women who were employed in factories and other manufacturing facilities from working more than 10 hours per day. The law did not apply to men. W. C. Ritchie & Co., an employer, brought a lawsuit that challenged the statute as being unconstitutional, in violation of the equal protection clause of the Illinois constitution. In upholding the statute, the Illinois Supreme Court stated,

> *It is known to all men (and what we know as men we cannot profess to be ignorant of as judges) that woman's physical structure and the performance of maternal functions place her at a great disadvantage in the battle of life; that while a man can work for more than 10 hours a day without injury to himself, a woman, especially when the burdens of motherhood are upon her, cannot; that while a man can work standing upon his feet for more than 10 hours a day, day after day, without injury to himself, a woman cannot; and that to require a woman to stand upon her feet for more than 10 hours in any one day and perform severe manual labor while thus standing, day after day, has the effect to impair her health, and that as weakly and sickly women cannot be mothers of vigorous children.*
>
> *We think the general consensus of opinion, not only in this country but in the civilized countries of Europe, is, that a working day of not more than 10 hours for women is justified for the following reasons: (1) the physical organization of women, (2) her maternal function, (3) the rearing and education of children, (4) the maintenance of the home; and these conditions are, so far, matters of general knowledge that the courts will take judicial cognizance of their existence.*
>
> *Surrounded as women are by changing conditions of society, and the evolution of employment which environs them, we agree fully with what is said by the Supreme Court of Washington in the Buchanan case; "law is, or ought to be, a progressive science."*

Is the statute fair? Would the statute be lawful today? Should the law be a "progressive science"? *W. C. Ritchie & Co. v. Wayman, Attorney for Cook County, Illinois*, 244 Ill. 509, 91 N.E. 695, 1910 Ill. Lexis 1958 (Supreme Court of Illinois)

Ethical

Ethics Cases

1.2 Ethics Case When the Constitution was ratified by the original colonies in 1788, it delegated to the federal government the exclusive power to regulate commerce with Native American tribes. During the next 100 years, as the colonists migrated westward, the federal government entered into many treaties with Native American nations. One such treaty was with the Ojibwe Indians in 1837, whereby the Ojibwe sold land located in the Minnesota territory to the United States. The treaty provided, "The privilege of hunting, fishing, and gathering wild rice, upon the lands, the rivers and the lakes included in the territory ceded, is guaranteed to the Indians." The state of Minnesota was admitted into the Union in 1858.

In 1990, the Mille Lacs Band of the Ojibwe tribe sued the state of Minnesota, seeking declaratory judgment that they retained the hunting, fishing, and gathering rights provided in the 1837 treaty and an injunction to prevent Minnesota from interfering with those rights. The state of Minnesota argued that when Minnesota entered the Union in 1858, those rights were extinguished. Are the hunting, fishing, and gathering rights guaranteed to the Ojibwe in the 1837 treaty still valid and enforceable? Did the state of Minnesota act ethically when it asserted that the Ojibwe's hunting, fishing, and gathering rights no longer were valid? *Minnesota v. Mille Lacs Band of Chippewa Indians*, 526 U.S. 172, 119 S.Ct. 1187, 1999 U.S. Lexis 2190 (Supreme Court of the United States)

1.3 Ethics Case In 1975, after the war in Vietnam, the U.S. government discontinued draft registration for men in this country. In 1980, after the Soviet Union invaded Afghanistan, President Jimmy Carter asked Congress for funds to reactivate draft registration. President Carter suggested that both males and females be required to register. Congress allocated funds only for the registration of males. Several men who were subject to draft registration brought a lawsuit that challenged the law as being unconstitutional, in violation of the Equal Protection Clause of the U.S. Constitution. The U.S. Supreme Court upheld the constitutionality of the draft registration law, reasoning as follows:

> *The question of registering women for the draft not only received considerable national attention and was the subject of wide-ranging public debate, but also was extensively considered by Congress in hearings, floor debate, and in committee. The foregoing clearly establishes that the decision to exempt women from registration was not the "accidental by-product of a traditional way of thinking about women."*
>
> *This is not a case of Congress arbitrarily choosing to burden one of two similarly situated groups, such as would be the case with an all-black or all-white, or an all-Catholic or all-Lutheran, or an all-Republican or all-Democratic registration. Men and women are simply not similarly situated for purposes of a draft or registration for a draft.*

Justice Marshall dissented, stating,

> *The Court today places its imprimatur on one of the most potent remaining public expressions of "ancient canards about the proper role of women." It upholds a statute that requires males but not females to register for the draft, and which thereby categorically excludes women from a fundamental civil obligation. I dissent.*

What arguments did the U.S. Supreme Court assert to justify requiring males but not females to register for the draft? Is the law, as determined by the U.S. Supreme Court, fair? Do you agree with the dissent? *Rostker, Director of Selective Service v. Goldberg*, 453 U.S. 57, 101 S.Ct. 2646, 1981 U.S. Lexis 126 (Supreme Court of the United States)

Notes

1. *The Spirit of Liberty*, 3rd ed. (New York: Alfred A. Knopf, 1960).
2. "Introduction," in *The Nature of Law: Readings in Legal Philosophy*, M. P. Golding (New York: Random House, 1966).
3. *Black's Law Dictionary*, 5th ed. (St. Paul, Minnesota: West).
4. 447 U.S. 10, 100 S.Ct. 1999, 1980 U.S. Lexis 127 (Supreme Court of the United States).
5. *Law and the Modern Mind* (New York: Brentano's, 1930).
6. 163 U.S. 537, 16 S.Ct. 1138, 1896 U.S. Lexis 3390 (Supreme Court of the United States, 1896).
7. 4 III. 301, 1841 Ill. Lexis 98 (Ill.).
8. 417 Pa. 486, 208 A.2d 193, 1965 Pa. Lexis 442 (Supreme Court of Pennsylvania).

CHAPTER 2

Courts and Jurisdiction

U.S. DISTRICT COURT, LAS VEGAS, NEVADA

This is the Lloyd D. George United States District Court for the District of Nevada, which is located in Las Vegas, Nevada. This federal trial court, along with the other U.S. district courts located throughout the country, hears and decides lawsuits concerning matters over which it has jurisdiction. State; Washington DC; and U.S. territory courts hear and decide matters over which they have jurisdiction. The process of bringing and defending lawsuits, preparing for court, and the trial itself is complicated, time consuming, and expensive.

Learning Objectives

After studying this chapter, you should be able to:

1. Describe state court systems.
2. Describe the federal court system.
3. List and describe the types of decisions that are issued by the U.S. Supreme Court.
4. Compare the jurisdiction of state courts with that of federal courts.
5. Define *personal jurisdiction*, *standing to sue*, and *venue*.

Chapter Outline

> "*I was never ruined but twice; once when I lost a lawsuit, and once when I won one.*"
>
> —*Voltaire*

Introduction to Courts and Jurisdiction

The glorious uncertainty of law.

Thomas Wilbraham
A toast at a dinner of judges and counsel at Serjeants' Inn Hall, 1756

There are two major court systems in the United States: (1) the federal court system and (2) the court systems of the 50 states; Washington DC (District of Columbia); and territories of the United States. Each of these systems has jurisdiction to hear different types of lawsuits. This chapter discusses the various court systems and the jurisdiction of different courts to hear and decide cases.

State Court Systems

Each state; Washington DC; and each territory of the United States has its own separate court system (hereafter collectively referred to as **state courts**). State courts resolve more than 95 percent of the lawsuits brought in this country. Most state court systems include the following: *limited-jurisdiction trial courts, general-jurisdiction trial courts, intermediate appellate courts,* and a *highest state court*.

Limited-Jurisdiction Trial Courts

limited-jurisdiction trial court (inferior trial court)
A court that hears matters of a specialized or limited nature.

State **limited-jurisdiction trial courts**, which are sometimes referred to as **inferior trial courts**, hear matters of a specialized or limited nature.

Examples Traffic courts, juvenile courts, justice-of-the-peace courts, probate courts, family law courts, and courts that hear misdemeanor criminal law cases are limited-jurisdiction courts in many states.

Because limited-jurisdiction courts are trial courts, evidence can be introduced and testimony can be given. Most limited-jurisdiction courts keep records of their proceedings. A decision of such a court can usually be appealed to a general-jurisdiction court or an appellate court.

WEB EXERCISE
Use **www.google.com** or another Internet search engine and find if your state has a small claims court. If so, what is the dollar-amount limit for cases to qualify for small claims court?

Many states have also created **small claims courts** to hear civil cases involving small dollar amounts (e.g., $5,000 or less). Generally, the parties must appear individually and cannot have lawyers represent them. The decisions of small claims courts are often appealable to general-jurisdiction trial courts or appellate courts.

General-Jurisdiction Trial Courts

general-jurisdiction trial court (court of record)
A court that hears cases of a general nature that is not within the jurisdiction of limited-jurisdiction trial courts. Testimony and evidence at trial are recorded and stored for future reference.

Every state has a **general-jurisdiction trial court**. These courts are often referred to as **courts of record** because the testimony and evidence at trial are recorded and stored for future reference. These courts hear cases that are not within the jurisdiction of limited-jurisdiction trial courts, such as felonies or civil cases involving more than a certain dollar amount.

Some states divide their general-jurisdiction courts into two divisions, one for criminal cases and the other for civil cases. Evidence and testimony are given at general-jurisdiction trial courts. The decisions handed down by these courts are appealable to an intermediate appellate court or the state supreme court, depending on the circumstances.

Intermediate Appellate Courts

intermediate appellate court (appellate court or court of appeals)
A court that hears appeals from trial courts.

In many states, **intermediate appellate courts** (also called **appellate courts** or **courts of appeals**) hear appeals from trial courts. They review the trial court record to determine whether there have been any errors at trial that would require reversal or modification of the trial court's decision. Thus, an appellate court reviews either pertinent parts or the whole trial court record from the lower court. No new evidence or testimony is permitted.

The parties usually file legal *briefs* with the appellate court stating the law and facts that support their positions. Appellate courts usually grant a brief oral hearing to the parties. Appellate court decisions are appealable to the state's highest court. In sparsely populated states that do not have an intermediate appellate court, trial court decisions can be appealed directly to the state's highest court.

Highest State Court

Each state has a **highest state court** in its court system. Many states call this highest court the **state supreme court**. Some states use other names for their highest courts. The function of a state's highest court is to hear appeals from intermediate appellate state courts and certain trial courts. No new evidence or testimony is heard. The parties usually submit pertinent parts of or the entire lower court record for review. The parties also submit legal briefs to the court and are usually granted a brief oral hearing. Decisions of highest state courts are final unless a question of law is involved that is appealable to the U.S. Supreme Court.

highest state court
The highest court in a state court system; it hears appeals from intermediate appellate state courts and certain trial courts.

Exhibit 2.1 portrays a typical state court system. **Exhibit 2.2** lists the websites for the court systems of 50 states; Washington DC; and territories associated with the United States.

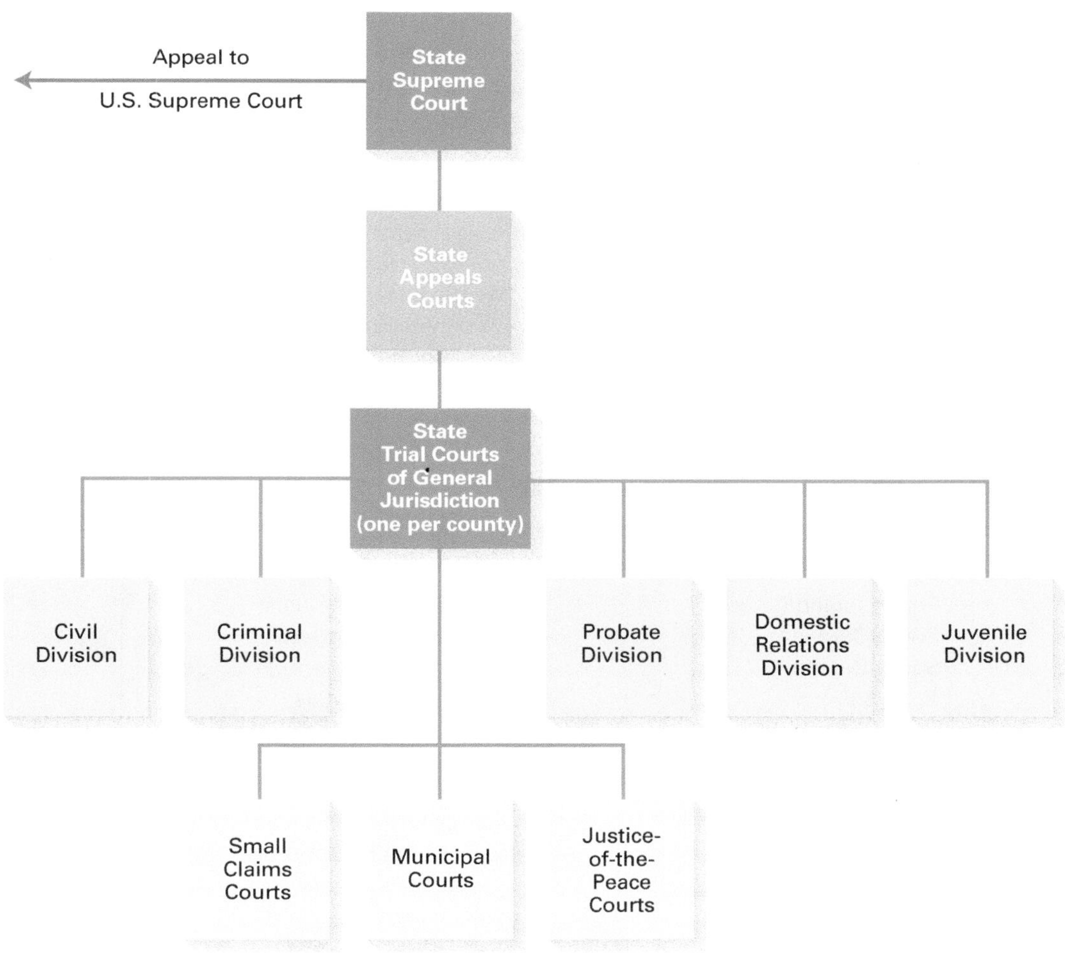

Exhibit 2.1 **TYPICAL STATE COURT SYSTEM**

Exhibit 2.2 WEBSITES FOR STATE; WASHINGTON DC; AND TERRITORY COURT SYSTEMS

State, District, or Territory	Website
Alabama	www.judicial.state.al.us
Alaska	www.state.ak.us/courts
Arizona	www.supreme.state.az.us
Arkansas	www.courts.state.ar.us
California	www.courtinfo.ca.gov/courts
Colorado	www.courts.state.co.us
Connecticut	www.jud.state.ct.us
Delaware	www.courts.state.de.us
District of Columbia	www.dccourts.gov
Florida	www.flcourts.org
Georgia	www.georgiacourts.org
Guam	www.guamsupremecourt.com
Hawaii	www.courts.state.hi.us
Idaho	www.isc.idaho.gov
Illinois	www.state.il.us/court
Indiana	www.in.gov/judiciary
Iowa	www.judicial.state.ia.us
Kansas	www.kscourts.org
Kentucky	www.courts.ky.gov
Louisiana	www.lasc.org
Maine	www.courts.state.me.us
Maryland	www.courts.state.md.us
Massachusetts	www.mass.gov/courts
Michigan	www.courts.michigan.gov
Minnesota	www.courts.state.mn.us
Mississippi	www.mssc.state.ms.us
Missouri	www.courts.mo.gov
Montana	www.montanacourts.org
Nebraska	www.court.nol.org
Nevada	www.nvsupremecourt.us
New Hampshire	www.courts.state.nh.us
New Jersey	www.judiciary.state.nj.us
New Mexico	www.nmcourts.com
New York	www.courts.state.ny.us
North Carolina	www.nccourts.org
North Dakota	www.ndcourts.com
Ohio	www.sconet.state.oh.us
Oklahoma	www.oscn.net/oscn/schome
Oregon	www.ojd.state.or.us
Pennsylvania	www.courts.state.pa.us
Puerto Rico	www.tribunalpr.org
Rhode Island	www.courts.state.ri.us
South Carolina	www.judicial.state.sc.us
South Dakota	www.sdjudicial.com
Tennessee	www.tsc.state.tn.us
Texas	www.courts.state.tx.us
Utah	www.utcourts.gov
Vermont	www.vermontjudiciary.org
Virginia	www.courts.state.va.us
Virgin Islands	www.visuperiorcourt.org
Washington	www.courts.wa.gov
West Virginia	www.wv.gov
Wisconsin	www.wicourts.gov
Wyoming	www.courts.state.wy.us

The following feature discusses special business courts.

Business Environment

Delaware Courts Specialize in Business Disputes

In most states, business and commercial disputes are heard by the same courts that hear and decide criminal, landlord–tenant, matrimonial, medical malpractice, and other non-business-related cases. One major exception to this standard has been the state of Delaware, where a special chancery court hears and decides business litigation. The **Delaware Court of Chancery**, which decides cases involving corporate governance, fiduciary duties of corporate officers and directors, mergers and acquisitions, and other business issues, has earned a reputation for its expertise in handling and deciding corporate matters. Perhaps the existence of this special court and a corporation code that tends to favor corporate management are the primary reasons that more than 50 percent of the corporations listed on the New York Stock Exchange and the NASDAQ stock exchange are incorporated in Delaware.

Businesses tend to favor special commercial courts because the judges have the expertise to decide complex business lawsuits. The courts are also expected to be more efficient in deciding business-related cases, thus saving time and money for the parties. Other states are also establishing courts that specialize in commercial matters.

COUNTY COURTHOUSE, GEORGIA

This is a county courthouse of the state of Georgia. Each state, the District of Columbia, and territories administered by the United States have their own court system. Most counties or parishes (in Louisiana) have a general-jurisdiction trial court. State courts resolve more than 95 percent of the lawsuits brought in these jurisdictions.

WEB EXERCISE

Go to the website of the Delaware Court of Chancery at **www.courts.delaware.gov/chancery**. Read the brief description of the court on the homepage.

Federal Court System

Article III of the U.S. Constitution provides that the federal government's judicial power is vested in one "Supreme Court." This court is the U.S. Supreme Court. Article III authorizes Congress to establish "inferior" federal courts. Pursuant to its Article III power, Congress has established the U.S. district courts, the U.S. courts of appeals, and the U.S. bankruptcy courts. Pursuant to other authority in the Constitution, the U.S. Congress has established other federal courts. Federal judges of the U.S. Supreme Court, U.S. courts of appeals, and U.S. district courts are appointed for life by the president, with the advice and consent of the Senate. Judges of other courts are not appointed for life but are appointed for various periods of time (e.g., bankruptcy court judges are appointed for 14-year terms).

Special Federal Courts

special federal courts
Federal courts that hear matters of specialized or limited jurisdiction.

The **special federal courts** established by Congress have limited jurisdiction. They include the following:

- **U.S. Tax Court.** The **U.S. Tax Court** hears cases that involve federal tax laws. Website: **www.ustaxcourt.gov**.
- **U.S. Court of Federal Claims.** The **U.S. Court of Federal Claims** hears cases brought against the United States. Website: **www.uscfc.uscourts.gov**.
- **U.S. Court of International Trade.** The **U.S. Court of International Trade** handles cases that involve tariffs and international trade disputes. Website: **www.cit.uscourts.gov**.
- **U.S. Bankruptcy Court.** The **U.S. Bankruptcy Court** hears cases that involve federal bankruptcy laws. Website: **www.uscourts.gov/bankruptcycourts.html**.
- **U.S. Court of Appeals for the Armed Forces.** The **U.S. Court of Appeals for the Armed Forces** exercises appellate jurisdiction over members of the armed services. Website: **www.armfor.uscourts.gov**.
- **U.S. Court of Appeals for Veterans Claims.** The **U.S. Court of Appeals for Veterans Claims** exercises jurisdiction over decisions of the Department of Veterans Affairs. Website: **www.uscourts.cavc.gov**.

The following feature discusses a controversial court of the federal court system.

Contemporary Environment

Foreign Intelligence Surveillance Court

In 1978, Congress created the **Foreign Intelligence Surveillance (FISA) Court**, which is located in Washington DC. The FISA Court hears requests by federal law enforcement agencies, such as the Federal Bureau of Investigation and National Security Agency (NSA), for warrants, called **FISA warrants**, to conduct physical searches and electronic surveillance of Americans or foreigners in the United States who are deemed a threat to national security. The application for a surveillance warrant is heard by one of the eleven judges who sit on the court. The judges of the FISA court are appointed by the Chief Justice of the United States. It is rare for an application for a warrant to be rejected by the FISA court. If the FISA court denies a government application for a FISA warrant, the government may appeal the decision to the **U.S. Foreign Intelligence Surveillance Court of Review (FISCR)**.

The FISA court is a "secret court" because its hearings are not open to the public and its decisions are classified. The court rarely releases documents, and when it does, the documents are usually highly redacted; that is, certain sensitive information is either removed or obscured before release.

The nature and extent of FISA court operations came to light in 2013 when a government insider disclosed that the NSA had obtained a warrant requiring a subsidiary of Verizon to provide daily electronic data of all cell phone and other telephone call records to the NSA. Although the alleged purpose was to gather foreign intelligence information, most of the call records consisted of domestic calls. It is expected that legislation will be enacted to protect the public from general sweeps of their electronic data by FISA court warrants.

U.S. District Courts

The **U.S. district courts** are the federal court system's trial courts of *general jurisdiction*. There are 94 U.S. district courts. There is at least one federal district court in each state and the District of Columbia, and heavily populated states have more than one district court. The geographical area served by each court is referred to as a **district**. The federal district courts are empowered to impanel juries, receive evidence, hear testimony, and decide cases. Most federal cases originate in federal district courts.

U.S. district courts
The federal court system's trial courts of general jurisdiction.

U.S. Courts of Appeals

The **U.S. courts of appeals** are the federal court system's intermediate appellate courts. There are 13 circuits in the federal court system. The first 12 are geographical. Eleven are designated by numbers, as the "First Circuit," "Second Circuit," and so on. The geographical area served by each court is referred to as a **circuit**. The 12th circuit court, located in Washington DC, is called the **U.S. District of Columbia Circuit**.

U.S. courts of appeals
The federal court system's intermediate appellate courts.

Congress created the 13th court of appeals in 1982. It is called the **U.S. Court of Appeals for the Federal Circuit** and is located in Washington DC. This court has special appellate jurisdiction to review the decisions of the Court of Federal Claims, the Patent and Trademark Office, and the Court of International Trade. This court was created to provide uniformity in the application of federal law in certain areas, particularly patent law.

U.S. Court of Appeals for the Federal Circuit
A U.S. Court of Appeals in Washington DC, that has special appellate jurisdiction to review the decisions of the Court of Federal Claims, the Patent and Trademark Office, and the Court of International Trade.

As an appellate court, each of these courts hears appeals from the district courts located in its circuit as well as from certain special courts and federal administrative agencies. An appellate court reviews the record of the lower court or administrative agency proceedings to determine whether there has been any error that would warrant reversal or modification of the lower court decision. No new evidence or testimony is heard. The parties file legal briefs with the court and are given a short oral hearing. The number of judges of various U.S. courts of appeals range from approximately 6 to 30. Appeals are usually heard by a three-judge panel. After a decision is rendered by the three-judge panel, a petitioner can request an *en banc* **review** by the full appeals court.

Exhibit 2.3 shows a map of the 13 federal circuit courts of appeals. **Exhibit 2.4** lists the websites of the 13 U.S. courts of appeals.

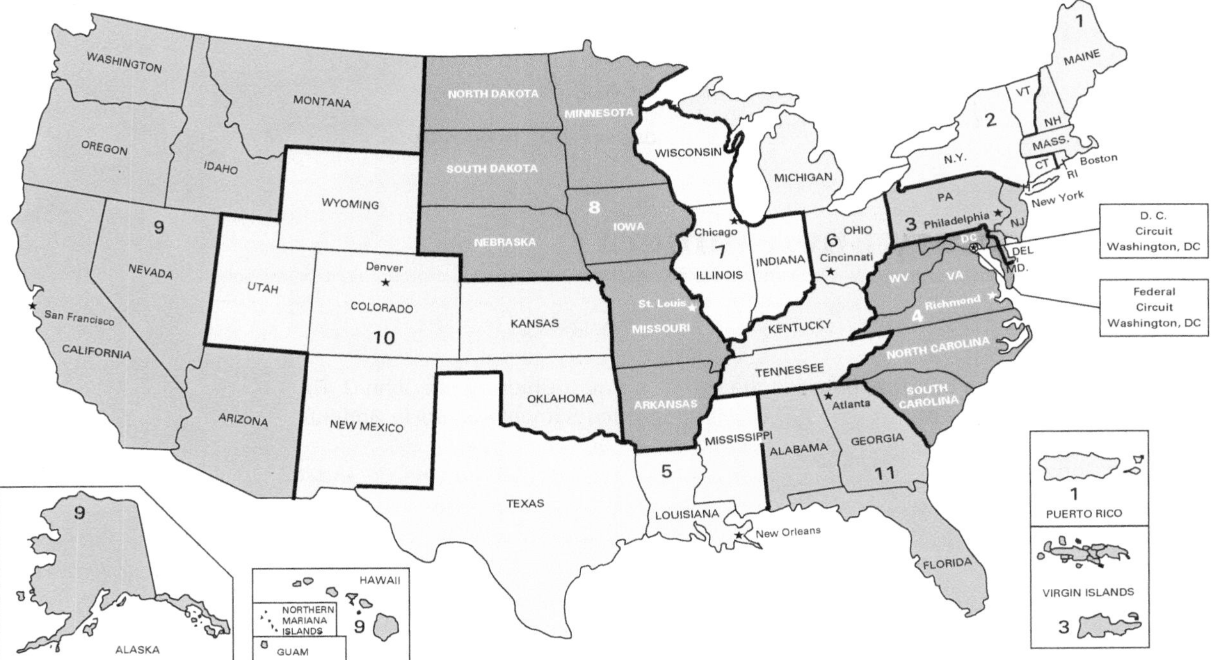

Exhibit 2.3 **MAP OF THE FEDERAL CIRCUIT COURTS**

Exhibit 2.4 WEBSITES FOR THE FEDERAL COURTS OF APPEAL

U.S. Court of Appeals	Main Office	Website
First Circuit	Boston, Massachusetts	www.ca1.uscourts.gov
Second Circuit	New York, New York	www.ca2.uscourts.gov
Third Circuit	Philadelphia, Pennsylvania	www.ca3.uscourts.gov
Fourth Circuit	Richmond, Virginia	www.ca4.uscourts.gov
Fifth Circuit	Houston, Texas	www.ca5.uscourts.gov
Sixth Circuit	Cincinnati, Ohio	www.ca6.uscourts.gov
Seventh Circuit	Chicago, Illinois	www.ca7.uscourts.gov
Eighth Circuit	St. Paul, Minnesota	www.ca8.uscourts.gov
Ninth Circuit	San Francisco, California	www.ca9.uscourts.gov
Tenth Circuit	Denver, Colorado	www.ca10.uscourts.gov
Eleventh Circuit	Atlanta, Georgia	www.ca11.uscourts.gov
District of Columbia	Washington, D.C.	www.dcd.uscourts.gov
Court of Appeals for the Federal Circuit	Washington DC	www.cafc.uscourts.gov

Supreme Court of the United States

Supreme Court of the United States (U.S. Supreme Court) The highest court in the United States, located in Washington DC. The Supreme Court was created by Article III of the U.S. Constitution.

The highest court in the land is the **Supreme Court of the United States**, also called the **U.S. Supreme Court**, which is located in Washington DC. The Court is composed of nine justices who are nominated by the president and confirmed by the Senate. The president appoints one justice as the **Chief Justice of the U.S. Supreme Court**, who is responsible for the administration of the Court. The other eight justices are **Associate Justices of the U.S. Supreme Court**.

Following is Alexis de Tocqueville's 1840 description of the Supreme Court's role in U.S. society:

> *The peace, the prosperity, and the very existence of the Union are vested in the hands of the justices of the Supreme Court. Without them, the Constitution would be a dead letter: the executive appeals to them for assistance against the encroachments of the legislative power; the legislature demands their protection against the assaults of the executive; they defend the Union from the disobedience of the states, the states from the exaggerated claims of the Union; the public interest against private interests, and the conservative spirit of stability against the fickleness of the democracy.*[1]

The following feature discusses the process of choosing a U.S. Supreme Court justice.

Contemporary Environment

Process of Choosing a U.S. Supreme Court Justice

In an effort to strike a balance of power between the executive and legislative branches of government, Article II, Section 2, of the U.S. Constitution gives the president the power to appoint Supreme Court justices "with the advice and consent of the Senate." This means that the majority of the 100 senators must approve the president's nominee in order for that nominee to become a justice of the U.S. Supreme Court.

President George W. Bush, a Republican, while in office from 2001 to 2009, placed two justices on the Supreme Court, Chief Justice John G. Roberts Jr. and Associate Justice Samuel A. Alito Jr. Both justices were confirmed by the Senate.

President Barack Obama was inaugurated as president in January 2009. Within months after taking office, he had the opportunity to nominate a justice for the U.S. Supreme Court. President Obama nominated Sonia Sotomayor for the seat. Sotomayor was born in the Bronx, New York City, and is of Puerto Rican descent. As a child, she was raised in public housing projects. Sotomayor, who graduated from

Yale Law School, served as a U.S. district court judge and a U.S. court of appeals justice. Sotomayor was confirmed to the Supreme Court by a majority vote of the U.S. Senate, becoming the first Hispanic person to be a justice and the third female appointed to the Court.

In 2010, President Obama had a second opportunity to nominate another justice to the Supreme Court. The president nominated Elena Kagan, the U.S. solicitor general. Kagan, although not a judge, had been a constitutional law professor at the University of Chicago and Harvard University law schools. Kagan was confirmed by a majority vote of the U.S. Senate.

A president who is elected to one or two four-year terms in office may have the opportunity to nominate justices to the U.S. Supreme Court who, if confirmed, may serve many years after the president leaves office.

Jurisdiction of the U.S. Supreme Court

The Supreme Court, which is an appellate court, hears appeals from federal circuit courts of appeals and, under certain circumstances, from federal district courts, special federal courts, and the highest state courts. No new evidence or testimony is heard. As with other appellate courts, the lower court record is reviewed to determine whether there has been an error that warrants a reversal or modification of the decision. Legal briefs are filed, and the parties are granted a brief oral hearing. The Supreme Court's decision is final.

The federal court system is illustrated in **Exhibit 2.5**.

Critical Legal Thinking

Is the U.S. Supreme Court apolitical? Explain the difference between a policy-oriented Supreme Court and an original constructionist Supreme Court. Why are U.S. Supreme Court justices appointed for life?

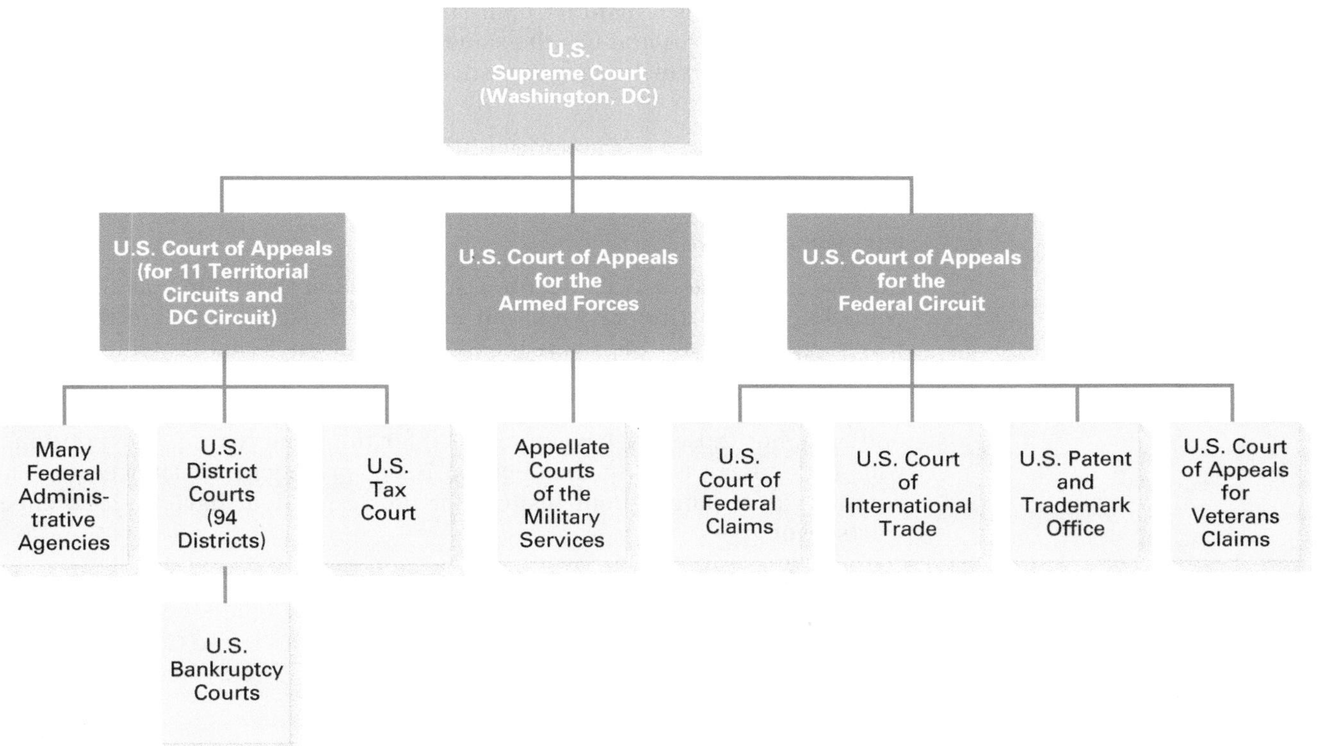

Exhibit 2.5 **FEDERAL COURT SYSTEM**

Decisions of the U.S. Supreme Court

The U.S. Constitution gives Congress the authority to establish rules for the appellate review of cases by the Supreme Court, except in the rare case in which mandatory review is required. Congress has given the Supreme Court discretion to decide what cases it will hear.[2]

petition for certiorari
A petition asking the Supreme Court to hear a case.

writ of certiorari
An official notice that the Supreme Court will review a case.

Sancho: But if this is hell, why do we see no lawyers?

Clarindo: They won't receive them, lest they bring lawsuits here.

Sancho: If there are no lawsuits here, hell's not so bad.

Lope de Vega
The Star of Seville,
Act 3, Scene 2

A petitioner must file a **petition for certiorari**, asking the Supreme Court to hear the case. If the Court decides to review a case, it issues a **writ of certiorari**. Because the Court issues only about 100 opinions each year, writs are usually granted only in cases involving constitutional and other important issues.

Each justice of the Supreme Court, including the chief justice, has an equal vote. The Supreme Court can issue several types of decisions:

1. **Unanimous decision.** If all the justices voting agree as to the outcome and reasoning used to decide a case, it is a **unanimous decision**. Unanimous decisions are precedent for later cases.

   Example If all nine justices hear a case and all nine agree to the outcome (e.g., the petitioner wins) and the reason why (e.g., the Equal Protection Clause of the U.S. Constitution had been violated), it is a unanimous decision. This unanimous decision becomes precedent for later cases.

2. **Majority decision.** If a majority of the justices agree as to the outcome and reasoning used to decide a case, it is a **majority decision**. Majority decisions are precedent for later cases. A majority decision occurs if five, six, seven, or eight justices vote for the same outcome for the same reason.

   Example If all nine justices hear a case and five of them agree as to the outcome (e.g., the petitioner wins) and all of these five justices agree to the same reason why (e.g., the Equal Protection Clause of the U.S. Constitution has been violated), it is a majority opinion. The majority opinion becomes precedent for later cases and has the same force of law as a unanimous decision. The votes of the remaining four justices for the respondent have no legal effect whatsoever.

3. **Plurality decision.** If a majority of the justices agree as to the outcome of a case but not as to the reasoning for reaching the outcome, it is a **plurality decision**. A plurality decision settles the case but is not precedent for later cases.

   Example If all nine justices hear a case and five of them agree as to the outcome (e.g., the petitioner wins) but not all of these five agree to the reason why (e.g., three base their vote on a violation of the Equal Protection Clause and two base their vote on a violation of the Due Process Clause of the U.S. Constitution), it is a plurality decision. Five justices have agreed to the same outcome, but those five have not agreed for the same reason. The petitioner wins his or her case, but the decision is not precedent for later cases. The votes of the remaining four justices for the respondent have no legal effect whatsoever.

4. **Tie decision.** Sometimes the Supreme Court sits without all nine justices being present. This could happen because of illness, conflict of interest, or a justice not having been confirmed to fill a vacant seat on the Court. If there is a **tie decision**, the lower court decision is affirmed. Such votes are not precedent for later cases.

   Example A petitioner wins his or her case at the U.S. court of appeals. At the Supreme Court, only eight justices hear the case. Four justices vote for the petitioner, and four justices vote for the respondent. This is a tie vote. The petitioner remains the winner because he or she won at the court of appeals. This decision of the Supreme Court sets no precedent for later cases.

WEB EXERCISE
Go to the website **www.supremecourt.gov/about/biographies.aspx**. Who are the current members of the Supreme Court? Who is the chief justice? Pick a justice and read his or her biography.

A justice who agrees with the outcome of a case but not the reason proffered by other justices can issue a **concurring opinion** that sets forth his or her reasons for deciding the case. A justice who does not agree with a decision can file a **dissenting opinion** that sets forth the reasons for his or her dissent.

The following feature discusses the process for having a case heard by the U.S. Supreme Court.

Contemporary Environment

"I'll Take You to the U.S. Supreme Court!"

In reality, having a case heard by the U.S. Supreme Court is rare. Each year, approximately 10,000 petitioners ask the Supreme Court to hear their cases. In recent years, the Supreme Court has accepted fewer than 100 of these cases for full review each term.

The nine Supreme Court justices meet once a week to discuss what cases merit review. The votes of four justices are necessary to grant an appeal and schedule an oral argument before the Court; this is called the **rule of four**. The decision and written opinions by the justices are usually issued many months later.

So what does it take to win a review by the Supreme Court? The U.S. Supreme Court usually decides to hear cases involving major constitutional questions, such as freedom of speech, freedom of religion, equal protection, and due process. The Supreme Court also hears many cases involving the interpretation of federal statutes enacted by Congress. The Court rarely decides day-to-day legal issues, such as breach of contract, tort liability, or corporations law, unless they involve more important constitutional or federal law questions.

So the next time you hear someone say, "I'll take you to the U.S. Supreme Court!" just say, "Not!"

Jurisdiction of Federal Courts

Article III, Section 2, of the U.S. Constitution sets forth the jurisdiction of federal courts. Federal courts have *limited jurisdiction* to hear cases involving a *federal question* or *diversity of citizenship*. Each of these topics is discussed in the following paragraphs.

Federal Question

The federal courts have subject matter jurisdiction to hear cases involving "federal questions." **Federal question cases** are cases arising under the U.S. Constitution, treaties, and federal statutes and regulations. There is no dollar-amount limit on federal question cases that can be brought in federal court.[3]

federal question case
A case arising under the U.S. Constitution, treaties, or federal statutes and regulations.

Example A defendant is sued by a plaintiff for engaging in insider trading, in violation of the Securities Exchange Act of 1934, which is a federal statute. This lawsuit involves a federal question, a federal statute, and therefore qualifies to be brought in federal court.

Diversity of Citizenship

A case may be brought in federal court even though it involves a nonfederal subject matter question, which would usually be heard by state; Washington DC; or territory courts, if there is diversity of citizenship. **Diversity of citizenship** occurs if a lawsuit involves (1) citizens of different states or (2) a citizen of a state and a citizen or subject of a foreign country.

diversity of citizenship
A means for bringing a lawsuit in federal court that involves a nonfederal question if the parties are (1) citizens of different states or (2) a citizen of a state and a citizen or subject of a foreign country.

If there is diversity of citizenship, the plaintiff may bring the case in either state or federal court. If a plaintiff brings a diversity of citizenship case in federal court, it remains there. If the plaintiff brings a diversity of citizenship case in state court, it will remain there unless the defendant removes the case to federal court. Federal courts must apply the relevant state law to diversity of citizenship cases.

The original reason for providing diversity of citizenship jurisdiction to federal courts was to prevent state court bias against nonresidents, although this reason has been questioned as irrelevant in modern times. The federal court must apply the appropriate state's law in deciding the case. The dollar amount of the controversy must exceed the sum or value of $75,000.[4] If this requirement is not met, action must be brought in the appropriate state; Washington DC; or territory court.

Critical Legal Thinking

What was the original reason for the doctrine of diversity of citizenship? Do you think that this reason is valid today?

Example Henry, a resident of the state of Idaho, is driving his automobile in Idaho when he negligently hits an automobile driven by Mary, a resident of the state of New York. Mary is injured in the accident. There is no federal question involved in this case; it is an automobile accident that involves state negligence law. However, there is diversity of citizenship in this case because the parties are residents of different states. Therefore, Mary can sue Henry and bring her case in federal court in Idaho, and, if she does, the case will remain in federal court. If she brings the case in Idaho state court, the case will remain in Idaho state court unless Henry has the case removed to federal court. If this case is heard by a federal court, the court must apply Idaho law to the case.

A corporation is considered to be a citizen of the state in which it is incorporated and the state in which its principal place of business, such as its headquarters, is located. Thus, if a plaintiff who is a resident of one of these states sues the corporation in the same state, there is no diversity of citizenship, and the case will be heard in state court. However, if a plaintiff who is a resident of one state sues the corporation in any state in which the corporation is not a citizen, there is diversity of citizenship; the case will be heard in a U.S. district court if the plaintiff brings the case in federal court or if the corporate defendant moves the case to federal court should the plaintiff have brought the case in state court. A corporation could be incorporated and have its principal place of business in one state, therefore making it a citizen of only one state.

Example Game Company, Inc., is incorporated in Delaware and has its principal place of business in California. If a plaintiff who is a resident of Florida sues the corporation in Florida, there is diversity of citizenship, and the case will be heard by a federal court if the defendant corporation wants it to be heard there or if the plaintiff has chosen to bring the lawsuit in federal court rather than state court.

Federal courts have **exclusive jurisdiction** to hear cases involving federal crimes, antitrust, bankruptcy, patent and copyright, suits against the United States, and most admiralty cases. State courts cannot hear these cases.

CONCEPT SUMMARY
JURISDICTION OF FEDERAL COURTS

Type of Jurisdiction	Description
Federal question	Cases arising under the U.S. Constitution, treaties, and federal statutes and regulations. There is no dollar-amount limit for federal question cases that can be brought in federal court.
Diversity of citizenship	Cases between citizens of different states or between a citizen of a state and a citizen or subject of a foreign country. Federal courts must apply the appropriate state law in such cases. The controversy must exceed the dollar limit of $75,000 for the federal court to hear the case.

Jurisdiction of State Courts

State courts and the courts of Washington DC, and the territories of the United States have jurisdiction to hear cases that federal courts do not have jurisdiction to hear. These usually involve laws of states; Washington DC; territories; and local governments (e.g., cities and counties).

Examples Cases involving real estate, corporations, partnerships, limited liability companies, contracts, sales and lease contracts, and negotiable instruments are usually state law subject matters.

State courts have **concurrent jurisdiction** with federal courts to hear cases involving diversity of citizenship and federal questions over which federal courts do not have exclusive jurisdiction. If a case involving concurrent jurisdiction is brought by a plaintiff in federal court, the case remains in federal court. If the plaintiff brings a case involving concurrent jurisdiction in state court, the defendant can either let the case be decided by the state court or remove the case to federal court. If a case does not qualify to be brought in federal court, it must be brought in the appropriate state court.

Standing to Sue, Jurisdiction, and Venue

Not every court has the authority to hear all types of cases. First, to bring a lawsuit in a court, the plaintiff must have *standing to sue*. In addition, the court must have *personal jurisdiction* or other jurisdiction to hear the case, and the case must be brought in the proper *venue*. These topics are discussed in the following paragraphs.

Standing to Sue

To bring a lawsuit, a plaintiff must have **standing to sue**. This means the plaintiff must have some stake in the outcome of the lawsuit.

standing to sue
Having some stake in the outcome of a lawsuit.

Example Linda's friend Jon is injured in an accident caused by Emily. Jon refuses to sue. Linda cannot sue Emily on Jon's behalf because she does not have an interest in the result of the case.

A few states now permit investors to invest money in a lawsuit for a percentage return of any award of judgment. Courts hear and decide actual disputes involving specific controversies. Hypothetical questions will not be heard, and trivial lawsuits will be dismissed.

In Personam Jurisdiction

A court's jurisdiction over a person is called ***in personam* jurisdiction**, or **personal jurisdiction**. A *plaintiff*, by filing a lawsuit with a court, gives the court *in personam* jurisdiction over him- or herself. The court must also have *in personam* jurisdiction over the *defendant*, which is usually obtained by having a summons served to that person within the territorial boundaries of the state (i.e., **service of process**). Service of process is usually accomplished by personal service of the summons and complaint on the defendant.

***in personam* jurisdiction (personal jurisdiction)**
Jurisdiction over the parties to a lawsuit.

service of process
A summons being served on a defendant to obtain personal jurisdiction over him or her.

If personal service is not possible, alternative forms of notice, such as mailing or e-mailing of the summons and complaint or publication of a notice in a newspaper, may be permitted. A corporation is subject to personal jurisdiction in the state in which it is incorporated, has its principal office, or is doing business.

A party who disputes the jurisdiction of a court can make a *special appearance* in that court to argue against imposition of jurisdiction. Service of process is not permitted during such an appearance.

The following case is an example of an alternative form of service of process.

CASE 2.1 *FEDERAL COURT CASE Service of Process*

Chanel, Inc. v. Zhixian

2010 U.S. Dist. Lexis 50745 (2010)
United States District Court for the Southern District of Florida

"Thus, in this instance, service by e-mail satisfies due process."

—Cohn, District Judge

Facts

Chanel, Inc. is engaged in the business of manufacturing and distributing throughout the world various luxury goods, including handbags, wallets, and numerous other products under the federally registered trademark "Chanel" and monogram marks. Its principal place of business is in New York City. Chanel filed a lawsuit in the U.S. district court against defendant Liu Zhixian, a resident of China, doing business through the following websites: chanel2u.com, chanel4u.com, chanel-belts.com, chanelbikini.com, chanel-rings.com, chanel-sandals.com, chanel-scarf .com, chanelswimwear.com, and chaneltalk.com. Chanel alleges trademark infringement by the defendant. Chanel's agent in China could not locate the defendant for service of process because the defendant used false, incomplete, or invalid addresses and phone numbers to register the domain names. However, e-mail addresses that the defendant provided when registering the domain names are currently active. Plaintiff Chanel made a motion for an order authorizing service of the summons and complaint on the defendant via electronic mail to these e-mail addresses.

Issue

Should the court grant plaintiff Chanel authority to serve the defendant by e-mail?

Language of the Court

The court is reasonably satisfied that service upon defendant via e-mail is reasonably calculated to notify defendant of the pendency of this action and provide him with an opportunity to present objections. Thus, in this instance, service by e-mail satisfies due process. In the abundance of caution, the court will require plaintiff to serve defendant via public announcement in accordance with Civil Procedure Law of the People's Republic of China.

Decision

The U.S. district court granted plaintiff Chanel's motion for alternative service of process on the defendant.

Ethics Questions

Is it ethical for a person to infringe on the trademarks of others? Is it likely that the defendant, if served by e-mail, will defend this case?

Long-Arm Statute

long-arm statute
A statute that extends a state's jurisdiction to nonresidents who were not served a summons within the state.

In most states, a state court can obtain jurisdiction in a civil lawsuit over persons and businesses located in another state or country through the state's **long-arm statute**. These statutes extend a state's jurisdiction to nonresidents who are not served a summons within the state. The nonresident defendant in the civil lawsuit must have had some **minimum contact** with the state such that the maintenance of that lawsuit in that state does not offend traditional notions of *fair play* and *substantial justice*.

Following is the landmark U.S. Supreme Court case that established the minimum contacts standard.

LANDMARK U.S. SUPREME COURT CASE Minimum Contacts

International Shoe Company v. State of Washington

". . . have certain minimum contacts with [the state] such that the maintenance of that suit does not offend traditional notions of fair play and substantial justice."

—Stone, Chief Justice

How far can a state go to require a person or business to defend him-, her-, or itself in a court of law in that state? That question was presented to the Supreme Court of the United States in the landmark case *International Shoe Company v. State of Washington*.

The International Shoe Company was a Delaware corporation that had its principal place of business in St. Louis, Missouri. The company manufactured and distributed shoes throughout the United States and it maintained a sales force throughout the United States. In the state of Washington, its sales representative did not have a specific office but sold the shoes door-to-door and sometimes at temporary locations.

The state of Washington assessed an unemployment tax on International Shoe for the sales representative it had in the state. When International Shoe failed to pay, Washington served personal service on a sales representative of the company in Washington and mailed the service of process to the company's headquarters in St. Louis. International Shoe appeared specially to argue that it did not do sufficient business in Washington to warrant having to pay unemployment taxes in that state. Eventually, the Supreme Court of Washington ruled against International Shoe. International Shoe appealed to the U.S. Supreme Court. In its decision, the U.S. Supreme Court stated,

> *Due process requires only that in order to subject a defendant to a judgment in personam, if he be not present within the territory of the forum, he have certain minimum contacts with it such that the maintenance of that suit does not offend traditional notions of fair play and substantial justice.*

Applying this standard, the U.S. Supreme Court held that International Shoe was subject to the lawsuit in Washington. Thus, the famous "minimum contacts" test and "traditional notions of fair play and substantial justice" establish when a state may require a person or business to appear in its courtrooms. Obviously, this is not a bright-line test, so battles of *in personam* jurisdiction abound to this day.*International Shoe Company v. State of Washington*, 326 U.S. 310, 66 S.Ct. 154, 1945 U.S. Lexis 1447 (Supreme Court of the United States, 1945).

Critical Legal Thinking Questions

Is it difficult determining when a party has had the minimum contacts with a state? How does one determine what constitutes "traditional notions of fair play and substantial justice"?

The exercise of long-arm jurisdiction is generally permitted over nonresidents who have (1) committed torts within the state (e.g., caused an automobile accident in the state), (2) entered into a contract either in the state or that affects the state (and allegedly breached the contract), or (3) transacted other business in the state that allegedly caused injury to another person.

In the following case, the court applied a state's long-arm statute.

CASE 2.2 *FEDERAL COURT CASE Long-Arm Statute*

MacDermid, Inc. v. Deiter

702 F.3d 725, 2012 U.S. App. Lexis 26382 (2012)
United States Court of Appeals for the Second Circuit

"We conclude that the Connecticut district court had long-arm jurisdiction."

—Parker, Circuit Judge

Facts

MacDermid, Inc. is a chemical company with its principal place of business in Waterbury, Connecticut. Jackie Deiter, a Canadian citizen, lives near Toronto, Canada, and was employed by MacDermid's Canadian subsidiary located in Canada. MacDermid stores proprietary and electronic data on computer servers located in Waterbury, Connecticut. Deiter was aware that MacDermid housed its e-mail system and its confidential and proprietary information on these servers. Deiter had to access MacDermid's Waterbury computer servers both to obtain and to e-mail files. Deiter had signed an employment contract with MacDermid whereby she agreed to safeguard MacDermid's confidential information and agreed not to misuse or misappropriate this information. MacDermid decided to terminate Deiter's employment. Deiter became aware of her impending termination and, just prior to it, forwarded from her MacDermid e-mail account to her personal e-mail account confidential and proprietary MacDermid data files. MacDermid sued Deiter in U.S. district court located in Connecticut, asserting that the Connecticut long-arm statute permitted jurisdiction over Deiter for unauthorized access and misuse of a computer system and misappropriation of trade secrets. MacDermid brought the suit in U.S. district court rather than Connecticut state court because there was diversity of citizenship between the parties—MacDermid was a U.S. corporation, and Deiter was a Canadian citizen. Deiter made a motion for the U.S. district court to dismiss the lawsuit, alleging that the court did not have jurisdiction over her because she lived in Canada and committed the allegedly illegal acts in Canada. The district court granted Deiter's motion and dismissed the case for lack of personal jurisdiction. MacDermid appealed.

Issue

Does the U.S. district court in Connecticut have personal jurisdiction over Deiter?

Language of the Court

We conclude that the Connecticut district court had long-arm jurisdiction. Deiter purposefully availed herself of the privilege of conducting activities within Connecticut because she was aware of the centralization and housing of the companies' email system and storage of confidential, proprietary information and trade secrets in Waterbury, Connecticut, and she used that email system and its Connecticut servers in retrieving and emailing confidential files. She directed her allegedly tortuous conduct towards MacDermid, a Connecticut corporation. Accordingly, we conclude that jurisdiction is reasonable in this case.

Decision

The U.S. court of appeals held that the U.S. district court in Connecticut had personal jurisdiction over Deiter and allowed the case to go to trial in Connecticut.

Ethics Questions

Did the defendant act ethically in this case? Was it fair to require the defendant to defend herself in a court in Connecticut?

In Rem Jurisdiction

***in rem* jurisdiction**
Jurisdiction to hear a case because of jurisdiction over the property of the lawsuit.

A court may have jurisdiction to hear and decide a case because it has jurisdiction over the property of the lawsuit. This is called ***in rem* jurisdiction** ("jurisdiction over the thing").

Example A state court would have jurisdiction to hear a dispute over the ownership of a piece of real estate located within the state. This is so even if one or more of the disputing parties live in another state or states.

Quasi In Rem Jurisdiction

Sometimes, a plaintiff who obtains a judgment against a defendant in one state will try to collect the judgment by attaching property of the defendant that is located in another state. This is permitted under ***quasi in rem* jurisdiction**, or **attachment jurisdiction**. Under the **Full Faith and Credit Clause** of the U.S. Constitution (Article IV, Section 1), a judgment of a court of one state must be given "full faith and credit" by the courts of another state.

quasi in rem **jurisdiction (attachment jurisdiction)**
Jurisdiction that allows a plaintiff who obtains a judgment in one state to try to collect the judgment by attaching the defendant's property in another state.

Example A plaintiff wins a dollar judgment against a defendant in California court. The defendant owns property in Ohio. If the defendant refuses to pay the judgment, the plaintiff can file a lawsuit in Ohio to enforce the California judgment and collect against the defendant's property in Ohio.

CONCEPT SUMMARY

***IN PERSONAM, IN REM,* AND *QUASI IN REM* JURISDICTION**

Type of Jurisdiction	Description
In personam jurisdiction	With *in personam* jurisdiction, a court has jurisdiction over the parties to the lawsuit. The plaintiff submits to the jurisdiction of the court by filing the lawsuit there. Personal jurisdiction is obtained over the defendant through *service of process* to that person.
In rem jurisdiction	With *in rem* jurisdiction, a court has jurisdiction to hear and decide a case because it has jurisdiction over the property at issue in the lawsuit (e.g., real property located in the state).
Quasi in rem jurisdiction	A plaintiff who obtains a judgment against a defendant in one state may utilize the court system of another state to attach property of the defendant that is located in the second state.

Venue

Venue requires lawsuits to be heard by the court of the court system that has jurisdiction to hear the case that is located nearest to where the incident occurred, where witnesses and evidence are available, and such other relevant factors.

venue
A concept that requires lawsuits to be heard by the court with jurisdiction that is nearest the location in which the incident occurred or where the parties reside.

Example Harry, a resident of the state of Georgia, commits a felony crime in Los Angeles County, California. The California Superior Court system has jurisdiction to hear the case. The superior court located in the county of Los Angeles is the proper venue because the crime was committed in Los Angeles, the witnesses are probably from the area, and so on. Although Harry lives in Georgia, the state of Georgia is not the proper venue for this case.

Occasionally, pretrial publicity may prejudice jurors located in the proper venue. In such cases, a **change of venue** may be requested so that a more impartial jury can be found. The courts generally frown on **forum shopping** (i.e., looking for a favorable court without a valid reason).

Forum-Selection and Choice-of-Law Clauses

One issue that often comes up when parties from different states or countries have a legal dispute is which jurisdiction's court will be used. Also, sometimes there is a dispute as to which jurisdiction's laws apply to a case. When the parties have not agreed in advance, courts must make the decision about which court has jurisdiction and what law applies. This situation causes ambiguity, and resolving it will cost the parties time and money.

forum-selection clause (choice-of-forum clause) A contract provision that designates a certain court to hear any dispute concerning nonperformance of the contract.

choice-of-law clause A contract provision that designates a certain state's or country's law that will be applied in any dispute concerning nonperformance of the contract.

Therefore, parties sometimes agree in their contract as to what state's courts, what federal court, or what country's court will have jurisdiction to hear a legal dispute should one arise. Such clauses in contracts are called **forum-selection clauses** or **choice-of-forum clauses**. Of course, the selected court must have jurisdiction to hear the case.

In addition to agreeing to a forum, the parties also often agree in contracts as to what state's law or country's law will apply in resolving a dispute. These clauses are called **choice-of-law clauses**. The selected law may be of a jurisdiction that does not have jurisdiction to hear the case.

Example Export Company, located in Shanghai, China, enters into a contract with Import Company, located in San Francisco, California, United States, whereby Export Company agrees to deliver designated goods to Import Company. In their contract, the parties agree that, if there is a dispute, the Superior Court of California, located in San Francisco, will hear the case and that the United Nations Convention on Contracts for the International Sale of Goods (CISG) will be the contract law that will be applied in resolving the dispute.

In the following case, the court had to decide whether to enforce a forum-selection clause.

CASE 2.3 *FEDERAL COURT CASE Forum-Selection Clause*

Fteja v. Facebook, Inc.

841 F.Supp.2d 829, 2012 U.S. Dist. Lexis 12991 (2012)
United States District Court for the Southern District of New York

"While new commerce on the Internet has exposed courts to many new situations, it has not fundamentally changed the principles of contract."

—Holwell, District Judge

Facts

Facebook, Inc. is a Delaware corporation with its principal place of business in Palo Alto, California. Facebook operates the world's largest social networking website. During the Facebook sign-up process, an applicant is asked to fill out several fields containing personal and contact information. The user is asked to click a button that reads "Sign Up." The user is asked to enter more information, and then a page displays a second "Sign Up" button where the following sentence appears: "By clicking Sign Up, you are indicating that you have read and agree to the Terms of Service." A hyperlink is available that may be clicked to find Facebook's terms of service agreement. The agreement contains a forum-selection clause that stipulates that any disputes between Facebook and the user will be brought exclusively in a state or federal court located in Santa Clara County, California.

Mustafa Fteja, a resident of Staten Island, New York, was an active user of facebook.com. To have obtained a Facebook account, Fteja would have followed Facebook's sign-up procedure. Fteja alleges that defendant Facebook disabled his Facebook account without justification and for discriminatory reasons because he is a Muslim. Fteja alleges that Facebook has caused him harm in all his personal relationships and ability to communicate, and thus caused emotional distress and assaulted his good reputation among his friends and family. Fteja filed an action in New York Supreme Court in New York County against Facebook, Inc. Because of diversity of citizenship of the parties—Fteja is a resident of New York, and Facebook is a corporation incorporated in Delaware with principal offices in California—Facebook moved the case to the U.S. district court for the southern district of New York. Facebook made a motion to transfer this action to the U.S. district court for the northern district of California pursuant to the forum-selection clause.

Issue

Is the forum-selection clause in the Facebook agreement enforceable?

(case continues)

Language of the Court

While new commerce on the Internet has exposed courts to many new situations, it has not fundamentally changed the principles of contract. There is no reason why the outcome should be different because Facebook's Terms of Use appear on another screen rather than another sheet of paper. The court concludes that Fteja assented to the Terms of Use and therefore to the forum-selection clause therein. Fteja agreed to litigate all disputes regarding his Facebook account exclusively in a state or federal court located in Santa Clara County, California.

Decision

The U.S. district court for the southern district of New York enforced the forum-selection clause of Facebook's Terms of Service and transferred Fteja's case against Facebook to the U.S. district court for the northern district of California.

Ethics Questions

Is it ethical for Facebook to require its users to bring lawsuits against it in Santa Clara County, California? If you have a Facebook account, have you read Facebook's terms of service agreement?

Jurisdiction in Cyberspace

Obtaining personal jurisdiction over a defendant in another state has always been difficult for courts. Today, with the advent of the Internet and the ability of persons and businesses to reach millions of people in other states electronically, particularly through websites, modern issues arise as to whether courts have jurisdiction in cyberspace. For example, if a person in one state uses the website of an Internet seller located in another state, can the user sue the Internet seller in his or her state under that state's long-arm statute?

One seminal case that addressed jurisdiction in cyberspace was ***Zippo Manufacturing Company v. Zippo Dot Com, Inc.***[5] Zippo Manufacturing Company (Zippo) manufactures its well-known line of tobacco lighters in Bradford, Pennsylvania, and sells them worldwide. Zippo Dot Com, Inc. (Dot Com), which was a California corporation with its principal place of business and its servers located in Sunnyvale, California, operated an Internet website that transmitted information and sexually explicit material to its subscribers.

Zippo Manufacturing Company v. Zippo Dot Com, Inc.
An important case that established a test for determining when a court has jurisdiction over the owner or operator of an interactive, semi-interactive, or passive website.

Three thousand of Dot Com's 140,000 paying subscribers worldwide were located in Pennsylvania. Zippo sued Dot Com in U.S. district court in Pennsylvania for trademark infringement. Dot Com defended, alleging that it was not subject to personal jurisdiction in Pennsylvania because the "minimum contacts" and "traditional notions of fair play and substantial justice" standards were not met and therefore did not permit Pennsylvania to assert jurisdiction over it. In addressing jurisdiction, the court created a "sliding scale" in order to measure the nature and quality of the commercial activity effectuated in a forum state through a website:

> *At one end of the spectrum are situations where a defendant clearly does business over the Internet. If the defendant enters into contracts with residents of a foreign jurisdiction that involve the knowing and repeated transmission of computer files over the Internet, personal jurisdiction is proper. At the opposite end are situations where a defendant has simply posted information on an Internet Web site which is accessible to users in foreign jurisdictions. A passive Web site that does little more than make information available to those who are interested in it is not grounds for the exercise of personal jurisdiction. The middle ground is occupied*

The Internet is becoming the town square for the global village of tomorrow.
Bill Gates

by interactive Web sites where a user can exchange information with the host computer. In these cases, the exercise of jurisdiction is determined by examining the level of interactivity and commercial nature of the exchange of information that occurs on the Web site.

In applying this standard, the court found that the case involved doing business over the Internet. The court held that Dot Com was subject to personal jurisdiction under the Pennsylvania long-arm statute and ordered Dot Com to defend itself in Pennsylvania.

The following feature compares the legal systems of Japan and the United States.

Global Law

Judicial System of Japan

Much of the difference is cultural: Japan nurtures the attitude that confrontation should be avoided, and the Japanese bias against courtroom solutions is strong. Thus, companies often avoid battle in court and instead opt for private arbitration of many of their disputes.

Other differences are built into the legal system itself. Plaintiffs usually must pay their lawyers a large up-front fee to represent them. Plaintiffs must pay a filing fee with the court, which is based on amount claimed rather than a flat fee. And contingency fees are not available in many cases.

In the past, few law schools existed in Japan to become a bengoshi, or lawyer, and the government restricted the number of new lawyers that were admitted to Japan's exclusive legal club each year. However, with globalization and increasing business and personal disputes, the Japanese government has decided that more lawyers are necessary to represent business and personal clients in court.

JAPAN

Businesses often complain that there are too many lawyers and there is too much litigation in the United States. There are currently more than 1 million lawyers and approximately 20 million civil lawsuits filed per year in this country. On the other hand, in Japan, a country with about 40 percent of the population of the United States, there are approximately 25,000 lawyers and much less litigation.

Key Terms and Concepts

Article III of the U.S. Constitution (26)
Associate Justices of the U.S. Supreme Court (28)
Change of venue (37)
Chief Justice of the U.S. Supreme Court (28)
Choice-of-law clause (38)
Circuit (27)
Concurrent jurisdiction (33)
Concurring opinion (30)
Delaware Court of Chancery (25)
Dissenting opinion (30)
District (27)
District of Columbia (27)
Diversity of citizenship (31)
En banc review (27)
Exclusive jurisdiction (32)
Federal question case (31)
FISA warrant (26)
Forum-selection clause (choice-of-forum clause) (38)
Forum shopping (37)
Full Faith and Credit Clause (37)
General-jurisdiction trial court (court of record) (22)
Highest state court (23)
In personam jurisdiction (personal jurisdiction) (33)
In rem jurisdiction (36)
Intermediate appellate court (appellate court or court of appeals) (22)
International Shoe Company v. State of Washington (35)
Limited-jurisdiction trial court (inferior trial court) (22)
Long-arm statute (34)
Majority decision (30)
Minimum contact (35)
Petition for certiorari (30)
Plurality decision (30)
Quasi in rem jurisdiction (attachment jurisdiction) (37)
Rule of four (31)
Service of process (33)
Small claims court (22)
Special federal courts (26)
Standing to sue (33)
State courts (22)
State supreme court (23)
Supreme Court of the United States (U.S. Supreme Court) (28)
Tie decision (30)
Unanimous decision (00)
U.S. Bankruptcy Court (26)
U.S. Court of Appeals (27)
U.S. Court of Appeals for the Armed Forces (26)
U.S. Court of Appeals for the Federal Circuit (27)
U.S. Court of Appeals for Veterans Claims (26)
U.S. Court of Federal Claims (26)
U.S. Court of International Trade (26)
U.S. district courts (27)
U.S. District of Columbia Circuit (27)
U.S. Foreign Intelligence Surveillance Court of Review (FISCR) (26)
U.S. Foreign Intelligence Surveillance (FISA) Court) (26)
U.S. Tax Court (26)
Venue (37)
Writ of certiorari (30)
Zippo Manufacturing Company v. Zippo Dot Com, Inc. (39)

Critical Legal Thinking Cases

2.1 Personal Jurisdiction Richtone Design Group LLC (Richtone) is a New York limited liability company (LLC) that owns the copyright to the Pilates Teacher Training Manual and licenses fitness instructors to teach pilates exercise programs. Live Siri Art, Inc. is a California corporation owned by Siri Galliano. Richtone learned that Live Siri Art and Galliano were selling the pilates manual over a website for profit without permission. They sold several copies of the manual to New York residents, making only about $1,000 in sales in New York from 2000 to 2012. Defendants have no office, property, or bank accounts in New York. Richtone brought a copyright infringement lawsuit against Live Siri Art and Galliano in U.S. district court in New York, alleging that the defendants were subject to personal jurisdiction in New York based on New York's long-arm statute. The defendants Live Siri Art and Galliano defended, alleging that they were not subject to suit in New York because they were residents of California, that they did not have the requisite minimum contacts with New York to be subject to suit in that state, and that to make them defend the lawsuit in New York violated their due process rights. The defendants made a motion to dismiss the New York lawsuit based on lack of personal jurisdiction. Are the defendants subject to lawsuit in New York? *Richtone Design Group, LLC v. Live Art, Inc.*, 2013 U.S. Dist. Lexis 157781 (United States District Court for the Southern District of New York, 2013)

2.2 Service of Process Facebook, Inc. filed a complaint in the U.S. district court against numerous defendants alleging that the named defendants engaged in trademark infringement, cybersquatting, and false designation of origin. Facebook seeks to enjoin the defendants from engaging in typosquatting schemes whereby the defendants register Internet domain names that are confusingly similar to facebook.com (e.g., facebock.com); thus potential users of Facebook's website who enter a typographical error are diverted to the typesquatter's website, which is designed to look strikingly similar in appearance to Facebook's website, to trick users into thinking that they are using Facebook's website. Facebook served all of the defendants except fourteen, who Facebook has not been able to serve personally, by mail, or by telephone. Facebook made a motion to the U.S. district court to be permitted to serve these defendants by sending an e-mail notice to the defendants' websites. May Facebook use alternative service of process by sending e-mail notices to the defendants' websites? *Facebook, Inc. v. Banana Ads LLC*, 2013 U.S. Dist. Lexis 65834 (2013) (United States District Court for the Northern District of California, 2012)

2.3 Standing to Sue Four friends, John Bertram, Matt Norden, Scott Olson, and Tony Harvey, all residents of Ohio, traveled to the Upper Peninsula of Michigan to go snowmobiling. On their first day of snowmobiling, after going about 135 miles, the lead snowmobiler, Olson, came to a stop sign on the snowmobile trail where it intersected a private driveway. As Olson approached the sign, he gave the customary hand signal and stopped his snowmobile. Harvey, second in line, was going too fast to stop, so Olson pulled his snowmobile to the right side of the private driveway. Harvey, to avoid hitting Olson, pulled his snowmobile to the left and went over a 5- or 6-foot snow embankment. Bertram, third in line, going about 30 miles per hour, slammed on his brake, turned 45 degrees, and slammed into Olson's snowmobile. Bertram was thrown from his snowmobile. Norden, fourth in line, could not stop, and his snowmobile hit Bertram's leg. Bertram's tibia and fibula were both fractured and protruded through his skin. Bertram had to undergo surgery to repair the broken bones.

Bertram filed a lawsuit against Olson, Harvey, and Norden in a trial court in Ohio, claiming that each of his friends was liable to him for their negligent snowmobile operation. A Michigan statute specifically stated that snowmobilers assumed the risks associated with snowmobiling. Ohio law did not contain an assumption of the risk rule regarding snowmobiling. The three defendants made a motion for summary judgment. Does Michigan or Ohio law apply to this case? *Bertram v. Norden, et al.*, 159 Ohio App.3d 171, 823 N.E.2d 478, 2004 Ohio App. Lexis 550 (Court of Appeals of Ohio, 2004)

2.4 Long-Arm Statute Casino Queen, Inc. operates a gambling and hotel establishment in East St. Louis, Illinois. Casino Queen's location places it within a large metropolitan area comprised of East St. Louis, Illinois, and St. Louis, Missouri, and several other cities in both Illinois and Missouri. Casino Queen advertises through print, radio, and television media in Missouri. Mark Myers is a resident of St. Louis County, Missouri. Myers went to Casino Queen to gamble and won $17,500. He cashed out his winnings and took a cab to Missouri. Two individuals who saw him cash out his winnings at the casino followed Myers in a cab to Missouri, where they beat and robbed him of his winnings. Myers sued Casino Queen in a Missouri court, alleging that the casino was negligent in not providing Myers warnings of such illegal activities and protecting him from such activities. Casino Queen, an Illinois corporation, made a motion to have the lawsuit dismissed by the Missouri court, alleging that the Missouri court did not have personal jurisdiction over the Illinois casino. Myers argued that Missouri's long-arm statute gave it personal jurisdiction over Casino Queen. Does the Missouri court have personal jurisdiction over the Illinois casino based on Missouri's long-arm statute? *Myers v. Casino Queen, Inc.*, 689 F.3d 904 (United States Court of Appeals for the Eighth Circuit, 2012)

2.5 Standing to Sue McDonald's Corporation owns, operates, and franchises fast-food restaurants. Over the years, McDonald's ran promotional games such as Monopoly Game at McDonald's, Who Wants to be a Millionaire, and other games where high-value prizes, including vehicles and cash up to $1 million, could be won. A person could win by collecting certain games pieces distributed by McDonald's. McDonald's employed Simon Marketing, Inc. (Simon) to operate the promotional games. An investigation by the Federal Bureau of Investigation(FBI) uncovered a criminal ring led by Jerome Jacobson, director of security at Simon, whereby he embezzled games pieces and diverted them to "winners" who collected more than $20 million in high-value prizes. After being caught, Jacobson and other members of the ring entered guilty pleas in connection with the conspiracy.

The Burger King Corporation, a competitor of McDonald's, owns, operates, and franchises fast-food restaurants. One franchisee is Phoenix of Broward, Inc. (Phoenix), which operates a Burger King restaurant in Fort Lauderdale, Florida. Phoenix brought a class action lawsuit in U.S. District Court on behalf of Burger King franchises against McDonald's, alleging that McDonald's engaged in false advertising in violation of the federal Lanham Act when it advertised that players had an equal chance of winning high-value prizes, when in fact they did not because of the Jacobson's criminal conspiracy. Phoenix alleged that it suffered injuries of lost sales because of McDonald's false advertising claims. McDonald's filed a motion to dismiss Phoenix's lawsuit, asserting that Phoenix had no standing to sue. Did plaintiff Phoenix have standing to sue McDonald's? *Phoenix of Broward, Inc. v. McDonald's Corporation*, 441 F.Supp.2d 1241, 2006 U.S. Dist. Lexis 55112 (United States District Court for the Northern District of Georgia, 2006)

2.6 U.S. Supreme Court Decision Two brothers were shot and killed in their Houston home. The police found shotgun shells at the scene of the crime. Witness testimony led the police to consider Genovevo Salinas to be a person of interest. Police found Salinas at his home, where he agreed to turn over his shotgun for ballistics testing and accompanied the officers to the police station for questioning. The interview with the police was custodial: It lasted approximately one hour, and Salinas was not read his *Miranda* rights. For most of the interview, Salinas answered the officers's questions. However, when asked whether his shotgun would match the shells recovered at the scene of the murder, Salinas declined to answer and remained silent. The police let Salinas go. Eventually, after more evidence was obtained, the government brought murder charges against Salinas. At trial, over Salinas's objection, the police witnesses testified that when Salinas was asked whether the shotgun shells found at the scene would match Salinas's shotgun, he grew silent and refused to answer that question. The jury found Salinas guilty, and he received a 20twenty-year sentence. Salinas appealed, alleging that the evidence that he remained silent when asked the question regarding his shotgun and the shells at the scene of crime should not have been admitted at trial. His appeal reached the U.S. Supreme Court.

Three Supreme Court justices upheld the verdict of guilty, finding that the admission of Salinas's silence when asked about the shotgun shells did not violate his Fifth Amendment privilege not to testify against him because a defendant normally does not invoke the privilege by remaining silent during a noncustodial interview. Two other justices upheld the verdict of guilty but did so based on another reason, that the Fifth Amendment does not prohibit a prosecutor from commenting on a defendant's silence during a precustodial interview. Four justices filed a dissenting opinion, finding that the evidence of the defendant's silence at a precustodial interview should not be admitted into evidence. What kind of decision is this U.S. Supreme Court decision? Does this decision establish precedent? *Salinas v. Texas*, 133 S.Ct. 2174, 2012 U.S. Lexis 4697 (Supreme Court of the United States, 2012)

Ethics Cases

Ethical

2.7 Ethics Case Chanel, Inc. is a corporate entity duly organized under the laws of the state of New York, with its principal place of business in New York City. Chanel is engaged in the business of manufacturing and distributing throughout the world various luxury goods, including handbags, wallets, and numerous other products under the federally registered trademark "Chanel" and monogram marks. Chanel filed a lawsuit in the U.S. district court in Maryland against defendant Ladawn Banks, a resident of Florida. Chanel alleged that Banks owned and operated the fully interactive website www.lovenamebrands.com, through which she sold handbags and wallets bearing counterfeit trademarks identical to the registered Chanel marks. The goods at issue in this case were sold over the Internet to a resident of Maryland. The court had to address the issue of whether Maryland had personal jurisdiction under its long-arm statute over the Florida defendant Banks. Does the Maryland court have personal jurisdiction over the Florida defendant? Did defendant Banks act ethically in this case? *Chanel, Inc. v. Banks*, 2010 U.S. Dist. Lexis 135374 (United States District Court for Maryland, 2010)

2.8 Ethics Case Hertz Corporation is incorporated in the state of Delaware and has its headquarters in the state of New Jersey. Melinda Friend, a California citizen, sued the Hertz Corporation in California state court seeking damages for Hertz's alleged violation of California's wage and hour laws. Hertz filed notice to move the case from state court to U.S. district court, a federal court, asserting diversity of citizenship between the parties. Friend argued that because Hertz operated more than 270 rental car locations and had more than 2,000 employees in California, it was a citizen of California; thus diversity of citizenship did not apply and the case could not be moved to federal court but should be decided by a California state court. Is Hertz Corporation a citizen of California and subject to suit in state court? Was it ethical for Hertz to deny citizenship in California when it had such a large presence in California with its 270 rental car locations and more than 2,000 employees in California? *Hertz Corporation v. Friend*, 130 S.Ct. 1181, 2010 U.S. Lexis 1897 (Supreme Court of the United States, 2010)

Notes

1. Book I, Chapter 8, *Democracy in America*.
2. Effective September 25, 1988, mandatory appeals were all but eliminated, except for reapportionment cases and cases brought under the Civil Rights Act and Voting Rights Act, antitrust laws, and the Presidential Election Campaign Fund Act.
3. Prior to 1980, there was a minimum dollar-amount controversy requirement of $10,000 to bring a federal question action in federal court. This minimum amount was eliminated by the Federal Question Jurisdictional Amendment Act of 1980, Public Law 96--486.
4. The amount was raised to $75,000 by the 1996 Federal Courts Improvement Act. Title 28 U.S.C. Section 1332(a).
5. 952 F.Supp. 1119 (U.S. District Court, Western District of Pennsylvania).

CHAPTER

3 Judicial, Alternative, and E-Dispute Resolution

OLD COURTHOUSE, ST. LOUIS, MISSOURI
This is the old state courthouse located in St. Louis, Missouri. It is now part of the national monument.

Learning Objectives

After studying this chapter, you should be able to:

1. Describe the pretrial litigation process.
2. Describe how a case proceeds through trial.
3. Describe how a trial court decision is appealed.
4. Explain the use of arbitration and other methods of alternative dispute resolution.
5. Describe e-courts and e-dispute resolution.

Chapter Outline

Chapter Contents *(continued)*

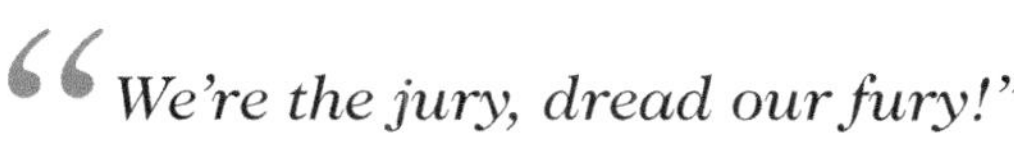
"We're the jury, dread our fury!"

—*William S. Gilbert*
Trial by Jury

Introduction to Judicial, Alternative, and E-Dispute Resolution

The process of bringing, maintaining, and defending a lawsuit is called *litigation*. It is also called *judicial dispute resolution* because courts are used to decide the case. Litigation is a difficult, time-consuming, and costly process that must comply with complex procedural rules. Although it is not required, most parties employ a lawyer to represent them when they are involved in a lawsuit.

Several forms of *nonjudicial dispute resolution* have developed in response to the expense and difficulty of bringing a lawsuit. These methods, collectively called *alternative dispute resolution*, are being used more and more often to resolve contract and commercial disputes.

Pieces of evidence, each by itself insufficient, may together constitute a significant whole and justify by their combined effect a conclusion.

Lord Wright
Grant v. Australian Knitting Mills, Ltd. (1936)

The computer, e-mail, the Internet, and electronic devices are now heavily used in resolving legal disputes. Many courts either allow or mandate that documents be submitted to the court electronically. Lawyers often correspond with each other, hold depositions, and do various other tasks using electronic means. In addition, electronic arbitration and mediation is often used to resolve legal disputes. The resolution of legal disputes using electronic means is often referred to as *e-dispute resolution*.

How many a dispute could have been deflated into a single paragraph if the disputants had dared to define their terms.

Aristotle

This chapter discusses the judicial litigation process, alternative dispute resolution, and e-dispute resolution.

Pretrial Litigation Process

The bringing, maintaining, and defending of a lawsuit is generally referred to as the *litigation process*, or **litigation**. The pretrial litigation process can be divided into the following major phases: *pleadings*, *discovery*, *pretrial motions*, and *settlement conference*. Each of these phases is discussed in the paragraphs that follow.

litigation
The process of bringing, maintaining, and defending a lawsuit.

Pleadings

The paperwork that is filed with the court to initiate and respond to a lawsuit is referred to as the **pleadings**. The major pleadings are the *complaint*, the *answer*, the *cross-complaint*, and the *reply*.

pleadings
The paperwork that is filed with the court to initiate and respond to a lawsuit.

plaintiff
The party who files a complaint.

complaint
The document a plaintiff files with the court and serves on the defendant to initiate a lawsuit.

Complaint and Summons

To initiate a lawsuit, the party who is suing (the **plaintiff**) must file a **complaint** in the proper court. The complaint names the parties to the lawsuit, alleges the ultimate facts and law violated, and contains a "prayer for relief" (for a remedy to be awarded by the court). The complaint can be as long as necessary, depending on the case's complexity. A sample complaint appears in **Exhibit 3.1**.

Exhibit 3.1 SAMPLE COMPLAINT

In the United States District Court for the District of Idaho

John Doe
Plaintiff

v.

Jane Roe

Defendant

Civil No. 2-1001

COMPLAINT

The plaintiff, by and through his attorney, alleges:

1. The plaintiff is a resident of the State of Idaho, the defendant is a resident of the State of Washington, and there is diversity of citizenship between the parties.
2. The amount in controversy exceeds the sum of $75,000, exclusive of interest and costs.
3. On January 10, 2016, plaintiff was exercising reasonable care while walking across the intersection of Sun Valley Road and Main Street, Ketchum, Idaho when defendant negligently drove her car through a red light at the intersection and struck plaintiff.
4. As a result of the defendant's negligence, plaintiff has incurred medical expenses of $104,000 and suffered severe physical injury and mental distress.

WHEREFORE, plaintiff claims judgment in the amount of $1,000,000 interest at the maximum legal rate, and costs of this action.

By ______________________
Edward Lawson
Attorney for Plaintiff
100 Main Street
Ketchum, Idaho

summons
A court order that directs the defendant to appear in court and answer the complaint.

Once a complaint has been filed with the court, the court issues a summons. A **summons** is a court order directing the defendant to appear in court and answer the complaint. The complaint and summons are served on the defendant. This is called **service of process**. Usually this is accomplished by a sheriff, another government official, or a private process server personally serving the complaint and summons on the defendant. If personal service has been tried and is unsuccessful, the court may permit alternative forms of service, such as by mail, fixing the complaint on the last known address of the defendant, or e-mail.

defendant
The party who files an answer.

answer
The defendant's written response to a plaintiff's complaint that is filed with the court and served on the plaintiff.

Answer

The party who is being sued (the **defendant**) must file an **answer** to the plaintiff's complaint. The defendant's answer is filed with the court and served on the plaintiff. In the answer, the defendant admits or denies the allegations contained in the plaintiff's complaint. A judgment is entered against a defendant who admits all of the allegations in the complaint. The case proceeds if the defendant denies all or some of the allegations.

If the defendant does not answer the complaint, a **default judgment** is entered against him or her. A default judgment establishes the defendant's liability. The plaintiff then has only to prove damages.

In addition to answering the complaint, a defendant's answer can assert **affirmative defenses**.

Examples If a complaint alleges that the plaintiff was personally injured by the defendant, the defendant's answer could state that he or she acted in self-defense. Another affirmative defense would be an assertion that the plaintiff's lawsuit is barred because the *statute of limitations* (time within which to bring the lawsuit) has expired.

Cross-Complaint and Reply

A defendant who believes that he or she has been injured by the plaintiff can file a **cross-complaint** against the plaintiff in addition to an answer. In the cross-complaint, the defendant (now the **cross-complainant**) sues the plaintiff (now the **cross-defendant**) for damages or some other remedy. The original plaintiff must file a **reply** (answer) to the cross-complaint. The reply, which can include affirmative defenses, must be filed with the court and served on the original defendant.

cross-complaint
A document filed by the defendant against the plaintiff to seek damages or some other remedy.

reply
A document filed by the original plaintiff to answer the defendant's cross-complaint.

CONCEPT SUMMARY
PLEADINGS

Type of Pleading	Description
Complaint	A document filed by a plaintiff with a court and served with a *summons* on the defendant. It sets forth the basis of the lawsuit.
Answer	A document filed by a defendant with a court and served on the plaintiff. It usually denies most allegations of the complaint.
Cross-complaint and reply	A document filed and served by a defendant if he or she countersues the plaintiff. The defendant is the *cross-complainant*, and the plaintiff is the *cross-defendant*. The cross-defendant must file and serve a *reply* (answer).

Intervention and Consolidation

If other persons have an interest in a lawsuit, they may *intervene* and become parties to the lawsuit. This is called **intervention**.

Example A bank that has made a secured loan on a piece of real estate can intervene in a lawsuit between parties who are litigating ownership of the property.

If several plaintiffs have filed separate lawsuits stemming from the same fact situation against the same defendant, the court can *consolidate* the cases into one case if doing so would not cause undue prejudice to the parties. This is called **consolidation**.

Example If a commercial airplane crashes, killing and injuring many people, the court could consolidate all the lawsuits against the defendant airplane company. This is because the deaths and injuries all relate to the same fact situation.

intervention
The act of others to join as parties to an existing lawsuit.

consolidation
The act of a court to combine two or more separate lawsuits into one lawsuit.

Class Action

class action
A lawsuit where a group of plaintiffs with common claims collectively bring a lawsuit against a defendant.

If certain requirements are met, a lawsuit can be brought as a **class action**. A class action occurs when a group of plaintiffs collectively bring a lawsuit against a defendant. Usually, one or several named plaintiffs file a lawsuit against a defendant on behalf of her- himself, or themselves and other similarly situated alleged aggrieved parties.

To maintain a class action lawsuit, a class must be *certified* by the appropriate federal or state court. A class can be certified if the legal and factual claims of all the parties are common, it is impracticable for individual claimants to bring multiple lawsuits against the defendant, the claims and defenses are typical for the plaintiffs and the defendant, and the representative parties will adequately protect the interests of the class. A class will not be certified if there is not sufficient commonality among the plaintiffs' claims or if the court otherwise finds that a class action is not suitable to the facts of the case.

Example Three individual employees of Wal-Mart Stores, Inc., brought a class action lawsuit against Wal-Mart alleging that it systematically engaged in sex discrimination against females in violation of federal employment law. The U.S. Supreme Court refused to grant certification because the class would consist of more than 1.5 million claimants spread over more than 3,400 stores in a multitude of different jobs involving thousands of supervisors over varying time periods. The U.S. Supreme Court stated, "Walmart is entitled to individualized determinations of each employee's eligibility for backpay."[1]

Critical Legal Thinking
What is the purpose of a class action lawsuit? Would some plaintiffs be denied redress for grievances if class action lawsuits were not permitted?

If a court certifies a class, notice of the class action must be sent, published, or broadcast to class members. Class members have the right to opt out of the class action and pursue their own legal process against the defendant. If a class action lawsuit is won or a settlement is obtained from the defendant, the members of the class share the proceeds as determined by the court.

Attorneys are often more likely to represent a class of plaintiffs, with aggregate monetary claims, than an individual plaintiff with a small claim. Where appropriate, class action lawsuits increase court efficiency and lower the costs of litigation. Class actions are usually disfavored by defendants.

In the following case, the court had to decide whether a class action was proper.

CASE 3.1 *FEDERAL COURT CASE Class Action*

Matamoros v. Starbucks Corporation

699 F.3d 129, 2012 U.S. App. Lexis 23185 (2012)
United States Court of Appeals for the First Circuit

"Consideration of fairness and judicial economy are well-served by resolving the baristas' claims in a class action."

—Selya, Circuit Judge

Facts

Starbucks Corporation operates a national chain of upscale coffee houses including outlets in Massachusetts. Employees are divided into four subcategories: store managers, assistant managers, shift supervisors, and baristas. Baristas are frontline employees who serve food and beverages to customers, are paid wages for hours worked, and have no management responsibilities. Starbucks stores maintain tip containers in which customers may deposit tips. The accumulated tips are distributed weekly to baristas and shift supervisors within the store in proportion to the number of hours worked that week by each individual. Massachusetts Tips Act, applicable to the restaurant industry, stipulates that wait-staff employees shall not be required to share tips with anyone who is not a wait-staff employee. Starbucks baristas filed a class action lawsuit against Starbucks

(case continues)

alleging that Starbucks's policy of permitting shift supervisors to share in pooled tips violated the Tips Act. The plaintiffs alleged that their class consists of baristas who worked during an identified class period of six years. The U.S. district court certified the class, found that Starbucks had violated the Tips Act, and awarded damages of $14 million to the baristas plus prejudgment interest of 12 percent. Starbucks appealed, alleging that the court erred by certifying the class action.

Issue

Was the case properly certified as class action?

Language of the Court

The civil rules establish four elements that must be present in order to obtain class certification: number of claims, commonality of legal or factual questions, typicality of representative claims, and adequacy of representation. Consideration of fairness and judicial economy are well-served by resolving the baristas' claims in a class action. We conclude, therefore, that a class action is superior to other alternative ways of adjudicating this controversy.

Decision

The U.S. court of appeals upheld the U.S. district court's decision certifying the class action and the award of $14 million to the class of baristas. Because the shift supervisors who shared in the tips were not made defendants in the case, they were not required to reimburse any funds that they had received from the tip pools.

Ethics Questions

Did Starbucks act ethically in paying money to its shift supervisors from customers' tips? Why did Massachusetts pass the Tips Act?

Statute of Limitations

A **statute of limitations** establishes the period during which a plaintiff must bring a lawsuit against a defendant. If a lawsuit is not filed within this time period, the plaintiff loses his or her right to sue. A statute of limitations begins to "run" at the time the plaintiff first has the right to sue the defendant (e.g., when the accident happens or when the breach of contract occurs).

statute of limitations
A statute that establishes the period during which a plaintiff must bring a lawsuit against a defendant.

Federal and state governments have established statutes of limitations for each type of lawsuit. Most are from one to four years, depending on the type of lawsuit.

Example The state of Idaho has a two-year statute of limitations for personal injury actions. On July 1, 2016, Otis negligently causes an automobile accident in Sun Valley, Idaho, in which Cha-Yen is injured. Cha-Yen has until July 1, 2018, to bring a negligence lawsuit against Otis. If she waits longer than that, she loses her right to sue him.

Discovery

The legal process provides for a detailed pretrial procedure called **discovery**. During discovery, each party engages in various activities to discover facts of the case from the other party and witnesses prior to trial. Discovery serves several functions, including preventing surprises, allowing parties to prepare thoroughly for trial, preserving evidence, saving court time, and promoting the settlement of cases. The major forms of discovery are discussed in the following paragraphs.

discovery
A legal process during which each party engages in various activities to discover facts of the case from the other party and witnesses prior to trial.

deposition
Oral testimony given by a party or witness prior to trial. The testimony is given under oath and is transcribed.

deponent
A party who gives his or her deposition.

Deposition

A **deposition** is oral testimony given by a party or witness prior to trial. The person giving a deposition is called the **deponent**. A *party* to the lawsuit must give a deposition if called on by the other party to do so. The deposition of a *witness* can be given voluntarily or pursuant to a subpoena (court order). The deponent can be required to bring documents to the deposition. Most depositions are taken at the office of one of the attorneys. The deponent is placed under oath and then asked questions orally by one or both of the attorneys. The questions and answers are recorded in written form by a court reporter. Depositions can also be video-recorded. The deponent is given an opportunity to correct his or her answers prior to signing the deposition. Depositions are used to preserve evidence (e.g., if the deponent is deceased, ill, or not otherwise available at trial) and impeach testimony given by witnesses at trial.

Interrogatories

interrogatories
Written questions submitted by one party to another party. The questions must be answered in writing within a stipulated time.

Interrogatories are written questions submitted by one party to a lawsuit to another party. The questions can be very detailed. In addition, certain documents might be attached to the answers. A party is required to answer interrogatories in writing within a specified time period (e.g., 60 to 90 days). An attorney usually helps with the preparation of the answers. The answers are signed under oath.

Production of Documents

production of documents
A request by one party to another party to produce all documents relevant to the case prior to the trial.

Often, particularly in complex business cases, a substantial portion of a lawsuit may be based on information contained in documents (e.g., memorandums, correspondence, and company records). One party to a lawsuit may request that the other party produce all documents that are relevant to the case prior to trial. This is called **production of documents**. If the documents sought are too voluminous to be moved or are in permanent storage or if their movement would disrupt the ongoing business of the party that is to produce them, the requesting party may be required to examine the documents at the other party's premises.

Physical or Mental Examination

physical or mental examination
A court-ordered examination of a party to a lawsuit before trial to determine the extent of the alleged injuries.

In cases that concern the physical or mental condition of a party, a court can order the party to submit to certain **physical or mental examinations** to determine the extent of the alleged injuries. This would occur, for example, where the plaintiff has been injured in an accident and is seeking damages for physical injury and mental distress.

The following case involves the issue of discovery.

CASE 3.2 *STATE COURT CASE Discovery*

Averyt v. Wal-Mart Stores, Inc.

265 P.3d 456, 2011 Colo. Lexis 857 (2011)
Supreme Court of Colorado

"Rather, any prejudice that the jury may have harbored was due to Wal-Mart's initial refusal to produce evidence of or admit the evidence of the grease spill."

—Rice, Justice

Facts

Holly Averyt, a commercial truck driver, slipped in grease while making a delivery to Walmart store number 980 in Greeley, Colorado. As a result of the fall, Averyt ruptured a disc in her spine and injured her shoulder and neck. These injuries left her unable to perform many daily functions. Averyt sued Wal-Mart Stores, Inc. (Walmart), alleging claims of negligence and premises liability.

Averyt's attorney sought evidence from Walmart documenting the grease spill, but Walmart denied the existence of the grease spill and did not turn over documents to Averyt. During opening statements

(case continues)

on the first day of trial, Walmart denied the existence of the grease spill. On that day, Averyt's attorney contacted the government of the City of Greeley and discovered a memorandum that referenced the grease spill and documentation of the cleanup of the spill. Averyt impeached a Walmart witness' statements using the Greeley report.

The next morning, Walmart informed the court and Averyt that it had located an assistant manager who remembered the grease spill and disclosed numerous documents that confirmed the existence of the spill, including documents from three companies that were involved in cleaning up the spill. From that point forward, Walmart ceased to deny the existence of the grease spill and instead asserted that it had exercised reasonable care to clean up the spill.

The jury found in Averyt's favor and awarded her $15 million in damages. The trial court judge applied a legal cap on damages, reducing the award to approximately $11 million. Walmart made a motion for a new trial, alleging nondisclosure of the Greeley report by plaintiffs before being introduced at trial and unfair prejudice of the jury. The trial court granted Walmart's motion for a new trial. Averyt appealed.

Issue

Was the jury unduly prejudiced against Walmart?

Language of the Court

Discovery is not required of public documents. In short, the report is a publicly available record that Averyt's attorney obtained from the City of Greeley. Averyt and Wal-Mart were on equal footing with regard to the ability to obtain the report. Any prejudice that the jury may have harbored was due to Wal-Mart's initial refusal to produce evidence of or admit the evidence of the grease spill. We do not find that the jury's award was the result of unfair prejudice. There is also adequate support in the record to justify the jury's award.

Decision

The supreme court of Colorado reversed the trial court's order granting a new trial, thus upholding the $11 million award to plaintiff Averyt.

Ethics Questions

Do you think that Walmart willfully did not disclose the evidence of the grease spill? Did the jury consider Walmart's conduct when it reached its verdict?

CONCEPT SUMMARY

DISCOVERY

Type	Description
Deposition	Oral testimony given by a *deponent*, either a party or witness Depositions are transcribed.
Interrogatories	Written questions submitted by one party to the other party of a lawsuit They must be answered within a specified period of time.
Production of documents	Copies of all relevant documents obtained by a party to a lawsuit from another party on order of the court
Physical or mental examination	Court-ordered examination of a party where injuries are alleged that could be verified or disputed by such examination

Pretrial Motions

Parties to a lawsuit can make several **pretrial motions** to try to resolve or dispose of all or part of a lawsuit prior to trial. The two pretrial motions are *motion for judgment on the pleadings* and *motion for summary judgment*.

pretrial motion
A motion a party can make to try to dispose of all or part of a lawsuit prior to trial.

Motion for Judgment on the Pleadings

motion for judgment on the pleadings
A motion that alleges that if all the facts presented in the pleadings are taken as true, the party making the motion would win the lawsuit when the proper law is applied to these asserted facts.

A **motion for judgment on the pleadings** can be made by either party once the pleadings are complete. This motion alleges that if all the facts presented in the pleadings are true, the party making the motion would win the lawsuit when the proper law is applied to these facts. In deciding this motion, the judge cannot consider any facts outside the pleadings.

Example A plaintiff files a complaint alleging that the defendant breached an oral contract and allegedly owes the plaintiff damages. If the state's statute of limitations requires that a lawsuit be brought within two years from the date that an oral contract was breached and the pleadings show that the lawsuit has been filed after the two-year period has expired, the defendant can make a motion to have the plaintiff's lawsuit dismissed based on the facts alleged in the pleadings.

Motion for Summary Judgment

motion for summary judgment
A motion that asserts that there are no factual disputes to be decided by the jury and that the judge can apply the proper law to the undisputed facts and decide the case without a jury. These motions are supported by affidavits, documents, and deposition testimony.

The trier of fact (i.e., the jury or, if there is no jury, the judge) determines factual issues. A **motion for summary judgment** asserts that there are no factual disputes to be decided by the jury and that the judge should apply the relevant law to the undisputed facts and decide the case. Thus, the case can be decided before trial by a judge who comes to a conclusion and issues a summary judgment in the moving party's favor. Motions for summary judgment, which can be made by either party, are supported by evidence outside the pleadings. Affidavits from the parties and witnesses, documents (e.g., a written contract between the parties), depositions, and so on are common forms of evidence.

If, after examining the evidence, the court finds no factual dispute, it can decide the issue or issues raised in the summary judgment motion. It may then dispense with the entire case or with part of the case. If the judge finds that a factual dispute exists, the motion will be denied, and the case will go to trial.

The following case involves the issue of summary judgment.

CASE 3.3 *STATE COURT CASE Summary Judgment*

Murphy v. McDonald's Restaurants of Ohio

2010 Ohio App. Lexis 402 (2010)
Court of Appeals of Ohio

"The existence of snow deposited on an elevated island situated in defendants' parking lot/drive-thru does not constitute negligence."
—Froelich, Judge

Facts

In February, Elijah Murphy drove to a McDonald's restaurant in New Carlisle, Ohio, and parked his vehicle in the parking area. The front of his vehicle faced a four-inch-high, 30-inch-long concrete median that divided the parking area from the restaurant's drive-through lane. The median was covered with snow that had been plowed from the drive-through lane and the parking area. On leaving the restaurant, Murphy walked across the drive-through lane and the median. As he stepped down from the median onto the pavement next to his vehicle, Murphy slipped on the icy pavement and fell. Murphy's left foot ended up underneath the front wheel of the pickup truck parked next to his vehicle.

(case continues)

Murphy suffered severe ankle dislocation that required surgery.

Murphy sued McDonald's to recover damages for negligence. After several depositions were taken, McDonald's moved for summary judgment. The trial court found that no genuine issue of material fact existed, applied the law to the facts of the case, and granted summary judgment to McDonald's. Murphy appealed.

Issue

Is there a genuine issue of material fact that would deny a grant of summary judgment?

Language of the Court

Snow and ice are part of wintertime life in Ohio. The existence of snow deposited on an elevated island situated in defendants' parking lot/drive-thru does not constitute negligence. Upon review of the record before us, we find no evidence that the placement of the snow on the McDonald's median created an increased hazard, i.e., an "unnatural" accumulation of ice. We find that the presence of the ice where Murphy fell was an open and obvious hazard.

Decision

The court of appeals held that there was no genuine issue of material fact and affirmed the trial court's grant of summary judgment to McDonald's.

Ethics Questions

Do you think that Murphy had a very good case against McDonald's? What are the major reasons for permitting judges to grant summary judgments?

Settlement Conference

Federal court rules and most state court rules permit the court to direct the attorneys or parties to appear before the court for a **settlement conference**, or **pretrial hearing**. One of the major purposes of such hearings is to facilitate the settlement of a case. Pretrial conferences are often held informally in the judge's chambers. If no settlement is reached, the pretrial hearing is used to identify the major trial issues and other relevant factors. More than 95 percent of all cases are settled before they go to trial.

The following feature discusses the cost–benefit analysis of a lawsuit.

settlement conference (pretrial hearing)
A hearing before a trial in order to facilitate the settlement of a case.

Critical Legal Thinking

Why are so many cases settled before trial? What would be the consequences if most cases actually went to trial?

Contemporary Environment

Cost–Benefit Analysis of a Lawsuit

The choice of whether to bring or defend a lawsuit should be analyzed like any other business decision. This includes performing a **cost–benefit analysis** of the lawsuit. For the plaintiff, it may be wise not to sue. For the defendant and the plaintiff, it may be wise to settle the case. The following factors should be considered in deciding whether to bring or settle a lawsuit:

- The probability of winning or losing
- The amount of money to be won or lost
- Lawyers' fees and other costs of litigation
- Loss of time by managers and other personnel
- The long-term effects on the relationship and reputation of the parties
- The amount of prejudgment interest provided by law
- The aggravation and psychological costs associated with a lawsuit
- The unpredictability of the legal system and the possibility of error
- Other factors peculiar to the parties and lawsuit

COURTROOM
This is a typical American courtroom. When people think of resolving disputes, courtrooms often come to mind, although there are nonjudicial ways to resolve disputes other than by trial.

Trial

trier of fact
The jury in a jury trial; the judge when there is not a jury trial.

Pursuant to the Seventh Amendment to the U.S. Constitution, a party to a civil action at law is guaranteed the right to a **jury trial** in a case in federal court.[2] Most state constitutions contain a similar guarantee for state court actions. If either party requests a jury, the trial will be by jury. If both parties waive their right to a jury, the trial will occur without a jury. The judge sits as the **trier of fact** in non-jury trials. At the time of trial, each party usually submits to the judge a **trial brief** that contains legal support for its side of the case.

A trial can last less than one day to many months, depending on the type and complexity of the case. A typical trial is divided into stages. The stages of a trial are discussed in the following paragraphs.

Jury Selection

voir dire
The process whereby the judge and attorneys ask prospective jurors questions to determine whether they would be biased in their decisions.

The pool of potential jurors is usually selected from voter or automobile registration lists. Individuals are selected to hear specific cases through a process called ***voir dire*** ("to speak the truth"). Lawyers for each party and the judge can ask prospective jurors questions to determine whether they would be biased in their decisions. Biased jurors can be prevented from sitting on a particular case.

Once the appropriate number of jurors is selected (usually six to twelve jurors, depending on the jurisdiction), they are **impaneled** to hear the case and are sworn in. Several *alternative jurors* are usually also selected to replace jurors who cannot complete the trial because of sickness or other reason. The trial is ready to begin. A jury can be **sequestered** (i.e., separated from family and so on) in important cases.

Opening Statements

A jury consists of twelve persons chosen to decide who has the better lawyer.
Robert Frost

Each party's attorney is allowed to make an **opening statement** to the jury at the beginning of a trial. During opening statements, an attorney usually summarizes the main factual and legal issues of the case and describes why he or she believes the client's position is valid. The information given in this statement is not considered as evidence.

The Plaintiff's Case

A plaintiff bears the **burden of proof** to persuade the trier of fact of the merits of his or her case. This is called the **plaintiff's case**. The plaintiff's attorney calls witnesses to give testimony. After a witness has been sworn in, the plaintiff's attorney examines (i.e., questions) the witness. This is called **direct examination**. Documents and other evidence can be introduced through each witness. After the plaintiff's attorney has completed his or her questions, the defendant's attorney can question the witness. This is called **cross-examination**. The defendant's attorney can ask questions only about the subjects that were brought up during the direct examination. After the defendant's attorney completes his or her questions, the plaintiff's attorney can ask questions of the witness. This is called **re-direct examination**.

The Defendant's Case

The **defendant's case** proceeds after the plaintiff has concluded his or her case. The defendant's case must (1) rebut the plaintiff's evidence, (2) prove any affirmative defenses asserted by the defendant, and (3) prove any allegations contained in the defendant's cross-complaint. The defendant's witnesses are examined by the defendant's attorney. The plaintiff's attorney can cross-examine each witness. This is followed by re-direct examination by the defendant and re-cross-examination by the plaintiff.

Rebuttal and Rejoinder

After the defendant's attorney has finished calling witnesses, the plaintiff's attorney can call witnesses and put forth evidence to rebut the defendant's case. This is called a **rebuttal**. The defendant's attorney can call additional witnesses and introduce other evidence to counter the rebuttal. This is called the **rejoinder**.

WEB EXERCISE
Go to **www.eff.org/IP/digitalradio/XM_complaint.pdf** to view a copy of a complaint filed in a U.S. district court.

Closing Arguments

At the conclusion of the presentation of the evidence, each party's attorney is allowed to make a **closing argument** to the jury. Each attorney tries to convince the jury to render a verdict for his or her client by pointing out the strengths in the client's case and the weaknesses in the other side's case. Information given by the attorneys in their closing statements is not evidence.

Jury Instructions, Deliberation, and Verdict

Once the closing arguments are completed, the judge reads **jury instructions** (or **charges**) to the jury. These instructions inform the jury about what law to apply when they decide the case.

jury instructions (charges)
Instructions that the judge gives to the jury that inform the jurors of the law to be applied in the case.

Example In a criminal trial, the judge reads the jury the statutory definition of the crime charged (e.g., first-degree murder). In an unintentional automobile accident case, the judge reads the jury the legal definition of *negligence*.

After the judge reads the jury instructions, the jury retires to the jury room to consider the evidence and attempt to reach a decision. This is called **jury deliberation**, which can take from a few minutes to many weeks. After deliberation, the jury reaches a **verdict**. In civil cases, the jury assesses damages against the defendant if they have held in favor of the plaintiff. In criminal cases, if the jury finds the defendant guilty, the jury may assess penalties on the defendant in some jurisdictions or cases.

Entry of Judgment

judgment
The official decision of the court.

After the jury has returned its verdict, in most cases the judge enters a **judgment** to the successful party, based on the verdict. This is the official decision of the court.

The court may overturn the verdict, however, if it finds bias or jury misconduct. This is called a **judgment notwithstanding the verdict** (or **judgment n.o.v.** or **j.n.o.v.**)

In a civil case, the judge may reduce the amount of monetary damages awarded by the jury if he or she finds the jury to have been biased, emotional, or inflamed. This is called **remittitur**.

The trial court usually issues a **written memorandum** that sets forth the reasons for the judgment. This memorandum, together with the trial transcript and evidence introduced at trial, constitutes the permanent **record** of the trial court proceeding.

E-Courts

The Internet, e-mail, websites, and other digital technologies have radically changed how lawyers and courts operate. They have enabled many normal communications between lawyers and courts to be conducted electronically.

When litigation takes place, the clients, lawyers, and judges involved in the case are usually buried in papers. These papers include pleadings, interrogatories, documents, motions, briefs, and memorandums. By the time a case is over, reams of paper are stored in dozens, if not hundreds, of boxes. In addition, court appearances, for even a very small matter, must be made in person.

Example Lawyers often wait hours for a 10-minute scheduling conference or another conference with a judge. The time it takes to drive to and from court also has to be taken into account, which in some areas may amount to hours.

electronic court (e-court)
A court that either mandates or permits the electronic filing of pleadings, briefs, and other documents related to a lawsuit. Also called a *virtual courthouse*.

electronic filing (e-filing)
The electronic filing of pleadings, briefs, and other documents with the court.

Today, because of the Internet and other technologies, **electronic courts**, or **e-courts**, also referred to as **virtual courthouses**, are used more and more often by courts. Technology allows for the **electronic filing—e-filing—**of pleadings, briefs, and other documents related to a lawsuit. In addition, technology allows for the scanning of evidence and documents into a computer for storage and retrieval and for e-mailing correspondence and documents to the court, the opposing counsel, and clients. Scheduling and other conferences with the judge or opposing counsel are held via telephone conferences and e-mail.

Many courts have instituted electronic document filing and tracking. In some courts, e-filing of pleadings and other documents is now mandatory. Companies such as Microsoft and LexisNexis have developed systems to manage e-filings of court documents.

Appeal

appeal
The act of asking an appellate court to overturn a decision after the trial court's final judgment has been entered.

In a civil case, either party can **appeal** the trial court's decision once a **final judgment** is entered. Only the defendant can appeal in a criminal case. The appeal is made to the appropriate appellate court. A **notice of appeal** must be filed by a party within a prescribed time after judgment is entered (usually within 60 or 90 days).

The appealing party is called the **appellant**, or **petitioner**. The responding party is called the **appellee**, or **respondent**. The appellant is often required to post bond (e.g., one and one-half times the judgment) on appeal.

appellant (petitioner)
The appealing party in an appeal.

appellee (respondent)
The responding party in an appeal.

The parties may designate all or relevant portions of the trial record to be submitted to the appellate court for review. The appellant's attorney usually must file an **opening brief** with the court that sets forth legal research and other information to support his or her contentions on appeal. The appellee can file a **responding brief** that answers the appellant's contentions. Appellate courts usually permit a brief oral argument at which each party's attorney is heard.

An appellate court will reverse a lower court decision if it finds an **error of law** in the record.

Examples Errors of law occur if prejudicial evidence was admitted at trial when it should have been excluded, prejudicial evidence was admitted that was obtained through an unconstitutional search and seizure, the jury was instructed improperly by the judge, and the like.

An appellate court will not reverse a **finding of fact** made by a jury, or made by a judge if there is no jury, unless such finding is unsupported by the evidence or is contradicted by the evidence. Very few trial court decisions are reversed because most findings of fact are supported by the evidence. On rare occasions, an appellate court will overturn a jury verdict if the appellate court cannot, from the record of the trial court, find sufficient evidence to support the trier of fact's findings.

In the following U.S. Supreme Court case, the Court reviewed an appellate court decision.

Courts of appeals should be constantly alert to the trial judge's firsthand knowledge of witnesses, testimony, and issues; in other words, appellate courts should give due consideration to the first-instance decision maker's "feel" for the overall case.

Justice Ginsburg
Weisgram v. Marley Company
528 U.S. 440, 120 S.Ct. (2000)

CASE 3.4 U.S. SUPREME COURT CASE Appeal

Cavazos, Acting Warden v. Smith

132 S.Ct. 2, 2011 U.S. Lexis 7603 (2011)
Supreme Court of the United States

"In light of the evidence presented at trial, the Ninth Circuit plainly erred in concluding that the jury's verdict was irrational."

—Per Curiam

Facts

Tomeka put her seven-week-old son Etzel to sleep on a sofa before going to sleep herself in another room. Shirley Smith, Tomeka's mother, slept on the floor next to Etzel. Several hours later, Smith ran into Tomeka's room, holding Etzel, who was limp. By the time emergency personnel arrived, Etzel was not breathing and had no heartbeat and was pronounced dead. After an autopsy, the coroner concluded that the cause of death was shaken baby syndrome (SBS). In an interview with the police several days later, Smith admitted that she had shaken Etzel.

Smith was arrested and charged with the crime of assault on a child resulting in death. At trial in a California court, the prosecution offered the testimony of the medical examiner for the coroner who supervised Etzel's autopsy and of two other medical experts, all of whom testified that Etzel's death was the result of SBS. The jury found Smith guilty and the court sentenced her to 15 years to life in prison.

Smith eventually appealed to the U.S. Court of Appeals for the Ninth Circuit, which determined that there was no evidence to permit an expert conclusion regarding death by SBS. The case was appealed to the U.S. Supreme Court.

Issue

Can an appellate court substitute its judgment of facts introduced at trial for that of the jury?

(*case continues*)

Language of the U.S. Supreme Court

In light of the evidence presented at trial, the Ninth Circuit plainly erred in concluding that the jury's verdict was irrational. Doubts about whether Smith is in fact guilty are understandable. But it is not the job of this Court and was not that of the Ninth Circuit, to decide whether the State's theory was correct. The jury decided that question, and its decision is supported by the record.

Decision

The U.S. Supreme Court reversed the decision of the U.S. court of appeals and let the jury verdict stand.

Ethics Questions

Do you think jurors are competent to understand expert medical testimony? Did the U.S. court of appeals have the right to substitute its judgment for that of the jury?

The following feature discusses the British legal system.

Global Law

British Legal System

LONDON, ENGLAND

The court system of England consists of trial courts that hear criminal and civil cases and appellate courts. The House of Lords, in London, is the supreme court of appeal. The legal profession of England is divided into two groups, solicitors and barristers. Solicitors are lawyers who have direct contact with clients and handle legal matters for clients other than appearing in court. Barristers are engaged to appear in court on behalf of a client.

Alternative Dispute Resolution

The use of the court system to resolve business and other disputes can take years and cost thousands or even millions of dollars in legal fees and expenses. In commercial litigation, the normal business operations of the parties are often disrupted. To avoid or reduce these problems, businesses and individuals are increasingly turning to methods of **nonjudicial dispute resolution** where disputes are resolved outside the court judicial system. This is often referred to as **alternative dispute resolution (ADR)**. The most common form of ADR is *arbitration*. Other forms of ADR are *negotiation, mediation, mini-trial, fact-finding*, and using a *judicial referee*.

alternative dispute resolution (ADR)
Methods of resolving disputes other than litigation.

Negotiation

The simplest form of alternative dispute resolution is engaging in negotiations between the parties to try to settle a dispute. **Negotiation** is a procedure whereby the parties to a legal dispute engage in discussions to try to reach a voluntary settlement of their dispute. Negotiation may take place either before a lawsuit is filed, after a lawsuit is filed, or before other forms of alternative dispute resolution are used.

negotiation
A procedure whereby the parties to a dispute engage in discussions and bargaining to try to reach a voluntary settlement of their dispute.

In a negotiation, the parties, who are often represented by attorneys, negotiate with each other to try to reach an agreeable solution to their dispute. During negotiation proceedings, the parties usually make offers and counteroffers to one another. The parties or their attorneys also may provide information to the other side in order to assist the other side in reaching an amicable settlement.

Many courts require that the parties to a lawsuit engage in settlement discussions prior to trial to try to negotiate a settlement of the case. In these instances, the judge must be assured that a settlement of the case is not possible before he or she permits the case to go to trial. A judge may convince the parties to engage in further negotiations if he or she determines that the parties are not too far apart in the negotiations of a settlement.

If a settlement of a dispute is reached through negotiation, a settlement agreement is drafted that contains the terms of the agreement. A **settlement agreement** is an agreement that is voluntarily entered into by the parties to a dispute that settles the dispute. Each side must sign the settlement agreement for it to be effective. The settlement agreement is usually submitted to the court, and the case will be dismissed based on the execution of the settlement agreement.

Arbitration

In **arbitration**, the parties choose an impartial third party to hear and decide the dispute. This neutral party is called the **arbitrator**. Arbitrators are usually members of the American Arbitration Association (AAA) or another arbitration association. Labor union agreements, franchise agreements, leases, employment contracts, and other commercial contracts often contain **arbitration clauses** that require disputes arising out of the contract to be submitted to arbitration. If there is no arbitration clause, the parties can enter into a **submission agreement** whereby they agree to submit a dispute to arbitration after the dispute arises.

Critical Legal Thinking

What are the benefits and detriments of arbitration versus a lawsuit? Are you currently subject to any arbitration agreements?

Congress enacted the *Federal Arbitration Act* to promote the arbitration of disputes. Many states have adopted the **Uniform Arbitration Act**, which promotes the arbitration of disputes at the state level. Many federal and state courts have instituted programs to refer legal disputes to arbitration or another form of ADR.

ADR services are usually provided by private organizations or individuals who qualify to hear and decide certain disputes. A landmark federal arbitration statute is discussed in the following feature.

arbitration
A form of alternative dispute resolution in which the parties choose an impartial third party to hear and decide the dispute.

arbitration clause
A clause in a contract that requires disputes arising out of the contract to be submitted to arbitration.

Landmark Law

Federal Arbitration Act

"By agreeing to arbitrate a statutory claim, a party does not forgo the substantive rights afforded by the statute, it only submits to their resolution in an arbitral, rather than a judicial, forum."

—Blackmun, Justice, Supreme Court of the United States *Mitsubishi Motors Corporation v. Soler Chrysler-Plymouth, Inc. 473 U.S. 614 (1985)*

The **Federal Arbitration Act (FAA)**[3] was enacted in 1925 to reverse long-standing judicial hostility to arbitration agreements. The FAA provides that arbitration agreements involving commerce are valid, irrevocable, and enforceable contracts, unless some grounds exist at law or equity (e.g., fraud or duress) to revoke them. The FAA permits one party to obtain a court order to compel arbitration if the other party has failed or refused to comply with an arbitration agreement.

Since the FAA's enactment, the courts have wrestled with the problem of which types of disputes should be arbitrated. Breach of contract is subject to arbitration if there is a valid arbitration agreement. In addition, the U.S. Supreme Court has enforced arbitration agreements that call for the resolution of disputes arising under federal statutes. The Supreme Court has stated, "By agreeing to arbitrate a statutory claim, a party does not forgo the substantive rights afforded by the statute, it only submits to their resolution in an arbitral, rather than a judicial, forum."[4]

Federal Arbitration Act (FAA)
A federal statute that provides for the enforcement of most arbitration agreements.

Arbitration Procedure

An arbitration agreement often describes the specific procedures that must be followed for a case to proceed to and through arbitration. If one party seeks to enforce an arbitration clause, that party must give notice to the other party. The parties then select an arbitration association or arbitrator, as provided in the agreement. The parties usually agree on the date, time, and place of the arbitration (e.g., at the arbitrator's office or some other agreed-on location).

At the arbitration, the parties can call witnesses to give testimony and introduce evidence to support their case and refute the other side's case. Rules similar to those followed by federal courts are usually followed at an arbitration hearing. Each party often pays a filing fee and other fees for the arbitration. Sometimes the agreement provides that one party will pay all the costs of the arbitration. Arbitrators are paid by the hour, day, or other agreed-on method of compensation.

After an arbitration hearing is complete, the arbitrator reaches a decision and issues an award. The parties often agree in advance to be bound by the arbitrator's decision and remedy. This is called **binding arbitration**. In this situation, the decision and award of the arbitrator cannot be appealed to the courts. If the arbitration is not binding, the decision and award of the arbitrator can be appealed to the courts. This is called **nonbinding arbitration**. Courts usually give great deference to an arbitrator's decision and award.

WEB EXERCISE
Go to the website of the American Arbitration Association at **www.adr.org/sp.asp?id=28749** and read the information on arbitration.

If an arbitrator has rendered a decision and an award but a party refuses to abide by the arbitrator's decision, the other party may file an action in court to have the arbitrator's decision enforced.

In the following U.S. Supreme Court case, the Court addressed the issue of arbitration.

CASE 3.5 *U.S. SUPREME COURT CASE Arbitration*

Nitro-Lift Technologies, L.L.C. v. Howard

133 S.Ct. 500, 2012 U.S. Lexis 8897 (2012)
Supreme Court of the United States

"The Oklahoma Supreme Court must abide by the Federal Arbitration Act, which is the 'Supreme Law of the Land.'"

—Per Curiam

Facts

Eddie Howard and Shane D. Schneider worked as employees of Nitro-Lift Technologies, L.L.C. Howard and Schneider entered into a noncompetition

(case continues)

agreement with Nitro-Lift whereby they agreed that they would not work for a competitor of Nitro-Lift's for a stated period of time after they left Nitro-Lift's employment. The agreement contained an arbitration clause wherein the parties agreed to submit any contract dispute to arbitration.

When Howard and Schneider quit and began working for Nitro-Lift's competitors, Nitro-Lift served the two men with a demand for arbitration to enforce the noncompetition agreement. Howard and Schneider filed a lawsuit in Oklahoma state court asking the court to declare the noncompetition agreement null and void. The supreme court of Oklahoma held that the state court and not an arbitrator should hear and decide the dispute. Defendant Nitro-Lift appealed to the U.S. Supreme Court.

Issue

Is the contract dispute between the parties subject to arbitration?

Language of the U.S. Supreme Court

State courts rather than federal courts are most frequently called upon to apply the Federal Arbitration Act (FAA), including the Act's national policy favoring arbitration. The Oklahoma Supreme Court must abide by the FAA, which is "the Supreme Law of the Land."

Decision

The U.S. Supreme Court held that the contract dispute in the case was to be heard by the arbitrator and not by the Oklahoma state court.

Ethics Questions

Why do companies place arbitration clauses in their employment contracts? Why did the plaintiffs want their case heard in state court?

Mediation

Mediation is a form of negotiation in which a neutral third party assists the disputing parties in reaching a settlement of their dispute. The neutral third party is called a **mediator**. The mediator is usually a person who is an expert in the area of the dispute or a lawyer or retired judge. The mediator is selected by the parties as provided in their agreement or as otherwise agreed by the parties. Unlike an arbitrator, however, a mediator does not make a decision or an award.

mediation
A form of alternative dispute resolution in which the parties use a mediator to propose a settlement of their dispute.

A mediator's role is to assist the parties in reaching a settlement. The mediator usually acts as an intermediary between the parties. In many cases, the mediator meets with the two parties at an agreed-on location, often the mediator's office or one of the offices of the parties. The mediator then meets with both parties, usually separately, to discuss each side of the case.

After discussing the facts of the case with both sides, the mediator will encourage settlement of the dispute and transmits settlement offers from one side to the other. In doing so, the mediator points out the strengths and weaknesses of each party's case and gives his or her opinion to each side about why the parties should decrease or increase their settlement offers.

If the parties agree to a settlement, a settlement agreement is drafted that expresses their agreement. Execution of the settlement agreement ends the dispute. The parties, of course, must perform their duties under the settlement agreement. If an agreement is not reached, the parties may proceed to a judicial resolution of their case.

Example Parties to a divorce action often use mediation to try to help resolve the issues involved in the divorce, including property settlement, payment of alimony and child support, custody of children, and visitation rights.

In the following critical legal thinking case, the U.S. Supreme Court issued an important decision regarding plaintiffs' ability to sue corporations.

Critical Legal Thinking Case

Class Action Waiver

"Arbitration is poorly suited to the higher stakes of class litigation."

—Scalia, Justice

Class actions allow many complainants to join together to challenge legally a defendant whom they believe has harmed them under similar circumstances. Class actions have been hailed as a means for the average citizen to get redress against large corporations who engage in illegal activities. To curtail class actions in arbitration, many companies put **class action waivers** in their arbitration agreements. This prevents defendants subject to the class action waiver from joining together to pursue a single defendant in an arbitration proceeding.

AT&T Mobility LLC (AT&T) includes such an arbitration agreement and class action waiver in their consumer contracts. When a customer brought a class action against AT&T for allegedly cheating him out of $30.22 in the purchase of a phone, the U.S. Supreme Court upheld the class action waiver in the arbitration agreement as legal, thus denying the consumer class status. Therefore, consumers must arbitrate their claims against businesses that include class action waivers in their contracts individually and not within a class of consumers. *AT&T Mobility LLC v. Concepcion*, 131 S.Ct. 1740, 2011 U.S. Lexis 3367 (Supreme Court of the United States, 2011)

Critical Legal Thinking Questions

Why do employers place class action waivers in their arbitration agreements? How important is this U.S. Supreme Court decision?

E-Dispute Resolution

electronic dispute resolution (e-dispute resolution) The use of online alternative dispute resolution services to resolve a dispute.

Electronic technologies have made it possible to settle disputes online. This is referred to as **electronic dispute resolution**, or **e-dispute resolution**. Many ADR providers offer electronic arbitration, or e-arbitration services. Most of these services allow a party to a legal dispute to register the dispute with the service and then notify the other party by e-mail of the registration of the dispute. The parties may be represented by attorneys if they so choose.

electronic arbitration (e-arbitration) The arbitration of a dispute using online arbitration services.

Most online arbitration, called **electronic arbitration** or **e-arbitration**, requires the registering party to submit an amount that the party is willing to accept or pay to the other party in the online arbitration. The other party is afforded the opportunity to accept the offer. If that party accepts the offer, a settlement has been reached; However, the other party may return a counteroffer. The process continues until a settlement is reached or one or both parties remove themselves from the online ADR process.

electronic mediation (e-mediation) The mediation of a dispute using online mediation services.

Several websites offer online mediation, called **electronic mediation** or **e-mediation**. In an online mediation, the parties sit before their computers and sign on to the website. A chat room is assigned to each party and the mediator, and another is set aside for both parties and the mediator. The individual chat rooms are used for private conversations with the online mediator, and the other chat room is for conversations between both parties and the mediator.

Online arbitration and online mediation services charge fees, but the fees are reasonable. In an online arbitration or online mediation, a settlement can be reached rather quickly, without paying substantial lawyers' fees and court costs. The parties also act through a more objective online process rather than meet face-to-face or negotiate over the telephone, either of which could involve verbal arguments.

If a legal dispute is not settled using e-arbitration or e-mediation, the parties may pursue their case in the courts.

The following feature discusses local dispute resolution in another country.

Global Law

Solving Tribal Disputes, Mali, West Africa

MALI, WEST AFRICA
These are mask dancers of the Dogon tribe who live primarily in Mali, West Africa. The Dogon are organized in villages. In resolving disputes, the Dogon usually do not go to government courts. Instead, a council of elders from the village hears and decides disputes between members of the village and administers justice in the local area.

Key Terms and Concepts

Affirmative defense (47)
Alternative dispute resolution (ADR) (59)
Answer (46)
Appeal (56)
Appellant (petitioner) (57)
Appellee (respondent) (57)
Arbitration (59)
Arbitration clause (59)
Arbitrator (59)
Binding arbitration (60)
Burden of proof (55)
Class action (48)
Class action waiver (62)
Closing argument (55)
Complaint (46)
Consolidation (47)
Cost–benefit analysis (53)
Cross-complainant (47)
Cross-complaint (47)
Cross-defendant (47)
Cross-examination (55)
Default judgment (47)
Defendant (46)
Defendant's case (55)
Deponent (49)
Deposition (49)
Direct examination (55)
Discovery (49)
Electronic arbitration (e-arbitration) (62)
Electronic court (e-court) (56)
Electronic dispute resolution (e-dispute resolution) (62)
Electronic filing (e-filing) (56)
Electronic mediation (e-mediation) (62)
Error of law (57)
Final judgment (56)
Finding of fact (57)
Impanel (54)
Interrogatories (50)
Intervention (47)
Judgment (56)
Judgment notwithstanding the verdict (judgment n.o.v. or j.n.o.v.) (56)
Jury deliberation (55)
Jury instructions (charges) (55)
Jury trial (54)
Litigation (45)
Mediation (61)
Mediator (61)
Motion for judgment on the pleadings (52)
Motion for summary judgment (52)
Negotiation (59)
Nonbinding arbitration (60)
Nonjudicial dispute resolution (59)
Notice of appeal (56)
Opening brief (57)

Critical Legal Thinking Cases

3.1 Summary Judgment Deborah Daughetee consumed multiple bags of microwave popcorn daily for approximately 5 years. Deborah recalled eating more than 10 different brands of buttered popcorn. After removing a bag of butter-flavored microwave popcorn from the microwave, Deborah would open the bag and draw the buttery smell into her nose and lungs. She testified that she "liked the smell of opening a bag near my face." Diacetyl is a food chemical that is an ingredient used to produce the "buttery" taste and smell of buttered microwave popcorn. Chr. Hansen, Inc., Symrise, Inc., and Firmenich, Inc. (defendants) are corporations that produce butter flavoring that contains diacetyl. Defendants sold their butter flavoring to microwave popcorn manufacturers who produced the various brands of buttered popcorn eaten by Deborah. On opening a microwave popcorn bag with butter flavoring, diacetyl vapors are released. After several industry studies found that extended exposure to diacetyl vapors could cause lung disease, many popcorn manufacturers adopted a number of safety precautions in their microwave popcorn plants to protect workers from overexposure to butter flavoring vapors. However, the popcorn makers made no changes to their products' packaging. Deborah sued the defendants claiming that she had developed respiratory injury—known as popcorn lung—by smelling the microwave popcorn that contained the buttered flavoring made by the defendants. The defendant corporations made motions for summary judgment. Should the defendants' motions for summary judgment be granted? *Daughetee v. Chr. Hansen, Inc.*, 2013 U.S. Dist. Lexis 50804 (2013) (United States District Court for the Northern District of Iowa, 2013)

3.2 Service of Process Jon Summervold purchased a remote-controlled toy watercraft from the Walmart store located in Aberdeen, South Dakota. The plaintiff sued Wal-Mart, Inc. for alleged defective design and failure to warn that arose out of the trauma he suffered when the toy watercraft exploded when he was handling it. Nine days before the three-year statute of limitations was to run on the plaintiff's claim, the plaintiff had a process server serve his complaint and summons against Walmart. The process server served the complaint and summons on Josh Hehn, a Walmart assistant manager in charge of the apparel department at Walmart's Aberdeen, South Dakota, store. The assistant manager and the manager of the store were physically available at the store at the time of service. South Dakota law requires that service of process be made on the president, officer, director, or registered agent of a defendant corporation. Walmart had designated a registered agent, whose name was publicly available at a state government office as required by law, to accept service of process for South Dakota lawsuits. Walmart challenged the plaintiff's service of process on an assistant manager at a Walmart store rather than on its resident agent, asserting that the plaintiff's service violated South Dakota's statute for service of process against corporations. The three-year statute of limitations on Summervold's claim had run before Walmart's challenge to the legality of the service of process was heard by the court. Has plaintiff properly served defendant Walmart? *Sommervold v. Wal-Mart, Inc.*, 709 F.3d 1234, 2013 U.S. App. Lexis 4972 (United States Court of Appeals for the Eighth Circuit, 2013)

3.3 Summary Judgment Sandra Primrose, who was 73 years old, was shopping in a Walmart store owned and operated by Wal-Mart Stores, Inc. (Walmart). She picked up a watermelon from a large display stand and as she took several steps around the display to reach her shopping cart, she tripped over a corner of the display. Primrose sustained a concussion and other serious injuries as a result of the accident. Primrose sued Walmart for negligence to recover damages, alleging that Walmart "created a trap" for her. Evidence showed that the watermelon display had been used for more than four years without incident, and photographs showed that the four corners of the display were visibly marked with "Watch Step" warning signs. Walmart noted that the area in question was open and obvious. Walmart, alleging that no material facts were in dispute, made a motion for summary judgment, which plaintiff Primrose objected to. Should Walmart be granted summary judgment? *Primrose v. Wal-Mart Stores, Inc.*, 127 So.3d 13, 2013 La. App. Lexis 1985 (Court of Appeals of Louisiana, 2013)

3.4 Class Certification Zurn Pex, Inc., and Zurn Industries, Inc. (Zurn), manufactures and markets a home plumbing system that uses Pex tubing, an alternative to traditional copper water pipes. Pex tubing systems are marketed as easier to install, cheaper, and longer lasting than copper plumbing systems. The Zurn Pex systems have been installed in homes throughout the United States. Zurn has sold its Pex systems with a 25-year limited warranty. Pex tubes are joined together using a brass fitting and crimp. Many home owners have alleged that the brass fittings used in these systems have leaked because of their susceptibility to corrosion. The corrosion increases over time and has caused costly water damage to homes. Zurn argues that corrosion is not an inherent defect in its product but that it is instead caused by a variety of factors, including improper installation and overly corrosive water. Home owners in Minnesota who have installed Zurn's Pex systems, including those who have had leaks and those who have not yet experienced such leaks, seek to bring a class action against Zurn to enforce its warranties and to have the Pex systems repaired or replaced according to the warranty. The class is defined as "All persons and entities that own a structure located within the State of Minnesota that contains a Zurn Pex plumbing system with Zurn brass crimp fittings." Zurn argues that the class should not be certified. Should the class be certified? *In re Zurn Pex Plumbing Products Liability Litigation*, 644 F.3d 604, 2011 U.S. App. Lexis 13663 (United States Court of Appeals for the Eighth Circuit, 2011)

3.5 Summary Judgment Bad Boy Enterprises LLC (BBE) designs and manufactures the Bad Boy Classic vehicle, an electric four-wheel-drive vehicle that is built on a golf cart chassis. The buggy is designed primarily for off-road use and is marketed mostly to hunters and outdoor enthusiasts. Mark Silver purchased a Bad Boy Classic vehicle. Mr. Silver taught his daughter, Elle, who was 13 years old, how to drive the vehicle and gave her permission to drive it. Elle drove the vehicle with Elle's friend Brittany Peacock and Elle's little sister as passengers. When Elle was driving the vehicle around a looping gravel driveway, she noticed that the vehicle would, at times, go fast as if she had pressed harder on the accelerator even though she was keeping steady pressure on the accelerator. Brittany, who had also driven the vehicle that day, also stated that the vehicle had an unintended acceleration problem. Elle, while driving the vehicle, felt the vehicle surge as she approached a curve. Elle took her foot off the gas and applied the brake, and the vehicle slowed down a little. The vehicle started tilting, tipped over, and came to rest on the driver's side. The vehicle was traveling between 10 and 13 miles per hour when the accident happened. As a result of the accident, Elle's left foot and part of her left leg were severed. In the past, BBE had recalled several types of its vehicles to repair them for unintended acceleration problems. Elle's parents brought a product liability action against BBE, alleging that the buggy was defectively designed because it would accelerate without any input from the driver, that it had a propensity to roll over, and that it was not crashworthy. At trial, Elle planned on calling Brittany, her sister and parents, and employees of BBE as witnesses as well as calling expert witnesses. BBE filed a motion for summary judgment, alleging that there were no facts to be decided by a jury and that the court could decide the case on a summary judgment motion. Elle opposed the motion, asserting that there were sufficient facts for the jury to decide at trial that would prevent the granting of a summary judgment. Must the court grant defendant BBE's motion for summary judgment? *Silver v. Bad Boy Enterprises*, 2013 U.S. Dist. Lexis 117562 (United States District Court for the Middle District of Georgia, 2013)

3.6 Summary Judgment Plaintiff Phyllis Toote filed a lawsuit against Pathmark Stores, Inc., a grocery store, and Canada Dry Bottling Company of New York, a bottler and distributor of soda. In her complaint, the plaintiff alleged that the defendants were liable for negligence for injuries she suffered when she fell over cases of soda that were stacked on the floor of the supermarket when she was shopping at the supermarket.

Defendant Pathmark took plaintiff Toote's deposition, in which she stated that she had entered the supermarket and, on entering the store, immediately walked to the soda aisle. Toote stated that she did not see the soda stacked on the floor before she fell over the soda. In the deposition, Toote stated that she did not know how long the soda had been on the floor before she tripped and fell. Pathmark made a motion for summary judgment, alleging that plaintiff Toote could not establish how long the soda had been on the floor before she fell. The motion court denied Pathmark's motion for summary judgment, finding that there were questions of fact to be decided by the jury. Pathmark appealed. Should the court grant Pathmark's motion for summary judgment? *Toote v. Canada Dry Bottling Company of New York, Inc. and Pathmark Stores, Inc.*, 7 A.D.3d 251, 776 N.Y.S.2d 42, 2004 N.Y. App. Div. Lexis 6470 (Supreme Court of New York, Appellate Division, 2004)

Ethical

Ethics Cases

3.7 Ethics Case BMW North America, LLC, and Rolls-Royce Motor Cars NA, LLC, distribute luxury automobiles, automobile parts, and lifestyle items in the United States. These companies and their parent and affiliate companies own various trademarks bearing the "BMW" and "Roll-Royce" trademarks. These companies (plaintiffs) discovered that counterfeit products bearing their trademarks were being advertised and sold from certain websites. After further investigation, it was determined that DinoDirect Corporation, a Delaware corporation; DinoDirect China Ltd., a Hong Kong limited liability company; and B2CForce International Corporation, a California corporation (corporate defendants) were involved with the production and distribution of these counterfeit items in the United States. Kevin Feng is the president or founder of these corporations. The plaintiffs sued the corporate defendants and Feng in U.S. district court in California for trademark infringement. The defendants were served the complaint and summons in the case. The defendants sent various e-mails to the court but never appeared in court or filed an answer to the complaint. The court gave the defendants several opportunities to do so, but no answers were ever filed. The court granted the plaintiffs a default judgment against the defendants. Is the issuance of a default judgment against the defendants warranted in this case? Did the defendants act ethically in this case? *BMW of North America v. Dinodirect Corporation*, 2012 U.S. Dist. Lexis 170667 (United States District Court for the Northern District of California, 2012)

3.8 Ethics Case Johnson Controls, Inc., is a Wisconsin company that manufactures building equipment and management systems, and distributes its products worldwide through direct sales, contractors, and distributors. Edman Controls, Inc. is a distribution company incorporated in the British Virgin Islands. Johnson and Edman entered into an agreement that awarded Edman the exclusive rights to distribute Johnson products in the country of Panama. The agreement provided that any dispute arising from the parties' arrangement would be resolved through arbitration using Wisconsin law and that the losing party would have to pay the prevailing party's attorney's fees and costs. Under this arrangement, Edman developed relationships with builders in Panama and distributed Johnson's products to these builders. Three years later, Edman discovered that Johnson was circumventing Edman by selling its products directly to Panamanian developers, including some that had previously purchased Johnson's products from Edman. Edman initiated arbitration proceedings against Johnson for breach of contract. The arbitrator found that Johnson had breached its agreement with Edman and awarded Edman $733,341 in lost profits and damages, $252,127 in attorney's fees, $39,958 in costs, and $23,042 in prejudgment interest. Johnson did not accept this result and filed a motion with the U.S. district court asking the court to vacate the arbitrator's award. The court refused to do so and confirmed the arbitrator's award. Still not satisfied, Johnson appealed the case to the U.S. court of appeals, asking the court to vacate the arbitrator's award. Should the U.S. court of appeals vacate the arbitrator's award? Did Johnson Controls act ethically in this case? *Johnson Controls, Inc. v. Edman Controls, Inc.*, 712 F.3d 1021, 2013 U.S. App. Lexis 5583 (United States Court of Appeals for the Seventh Circuit, 2013)

Notes

1. *Wal-Mart Stores, Inc. v. Dukes*, 131 S.Ct. 2541, 2011 U.S. Lexis 4567 (Supreme Court of the United States, 2011).
2. There is no right to a jury trial for actions in equity (e.g., injunctions, specific performance).
3. 9 U.S.C. Section 1 et seq.
4. *Gilmer v. Interstate/Johnson Lane Corporation*, 500 U.S. 20, 111 S.Ct. 1647, 1991 U.S. Lexis 2529 (Supreme Court of the United States).

CHAPTER

4 Constitutional Law for Business and E-Commerce

CONSTITUTION OF THE UNITED STATES OF AMERICA
The U.S. Constitution was adopted in 1787 and was ratified by each state in the name of "the people." Ratification by the required number of states was completed on June 21, 1788. The U.S. Constitution establishes the federal government and delegates certain powers to the federal government.

Learning Objectives

After studying this chapter, you should be able to:

1. Describe the concept of federalism and the doctrine of separation of powers.
2. Define and apply the Supremacy Clause of the U.S. Constitution.
3. Explain the federal government's authority to regulate interstate commerce and foreign commerce.
4. Explain how the freedoms of speech, assembly, religion, and the press are protected by the First Amendment and how commercial speech may be limited.
5. Explain the doctrines of equal protection and due process.

Chapter Outline

Chapter Outline *(continued)*

"We the People of the United States, in Order to form a more perfect Union, establish Justice, insure domestic Tranquility, provide for the common defense, promote the general Welfare, and secure the Blessings of Liberty to ourselves and our Posterity, do ordain and establish this Constitution for the United States of America."

—*Preamble to the Constitution of the United States of America*

Introduction to Constitutional Law for Business and E-Commerce

The nation's armour of defence against the passions of men is the Constitution. Take that away, and the nation goes down into the field of its conflicts like a warrior without armour.

Henry Ward Beecher
Proverbs from Plymouth Pulpit, 1887

Prior to the American Revolution, each of the 13 original colonies operated as a separate sovereignty under the rule of England. In September 1774, representatives of the colonies met as a Continental Congress. In 1776, the colonies declared independence from England, and the American Revolution ensued. The **Declaration of Independence** was the document that declared the American colonies independence from England.

This chapter examines the major provisions of the U.S. Constitution and the amendments that have been added to the Constitution. Of particular importance, this chapter discusses how these provisions affect the operations of business in this country. The Constitution, with amendments, is set forth as Appendix A to this text.

WEB EXERCISE
Go to **www.ushistory.org/declaration/document/index.htm** for the text of the Declaration of Independence. Read the first two paragraphs of the Declaration of Independence.

Constitution of the United States of America

In 1778, the Continental Congress formed a **federal government** and adopted the **Articles of Confederation**. The Articles of Confederation created a federal Congress composed of representatives of the 13 new states. The Articles of Confederation was a particularly weak document that gave limited power to the newly created federal government. It did not provide Congress with the power to levy and collect taxes, to regulate commerce with foreign countries, or regulate interstate commerce.

The **Constitutional Convention** was convened in Philadelphia in May 1787. The primary purpose of the convention was to strengthen the federal government. After substantial debate, the delegates agreed to a new **U.S. Constitution**. The Constitution was reported to Congress in September 1787. State ratification of the Constitution was completed in 1788. Many amendments, including the Bill of Rights, have been added to the Constitution since that time.

U.S. Constitution
The fundamental law of the United States of America. It was ratified by the states in 1788.

The U.S. Constitution, as amended, serves two major functions:

1. It creates the three branches of the federal government (i.e., the legislative, executive, and judicial branches) and allocates powers to these branches.
2. It protects individual rights by limiting the government's ability to restrict those rights.

The Constitution itself provides that it may be amended to address social and economic changes. Some important constitutional concepts are discussed in the following paragraphs.

Federalism and Delegated Powers

Our country's form of government is referred to as **federalism**, which means that the federal government and the 50 state governments share powers.

federalism
The U.S. form of government in which the federal government and the 50 state governments share powers.

When the states ratified the Constitution, they *delegated* certain powers—called **enumerated powers**—to the federal government.

enumerated powers
Certain powers delegated to the federal government by the states.

Example The federal government is authorized to regulate interstate commerce and foreign affairs.

Any powers that are not specifically delegated to the federal government by the Constitution are reserved to the state governments. These are called **reserved powers**. State governments are empowered to deal with local affairs.

Examples States enact laws that provide for the formation and regulation of partnerships and corporations. Cities adopt zoning laws that designate certain portions of the city as residential areas and other portions as business and commercial areas.

Doctrine of Separation of Powers

As mentioned previously, the federal government is divided into three branches:

1. **Article I: Legislative branch.** **Article I of the U.S. Constitution** establishes the **legislative branch** of the federal government. The legislative branch is responsible for making federal law. This branch is **bicameral**; that is, it consists of the U.S. Senate and the U.S. House of Representatives. Collectively, they are referred to as the **U.S. Congress** or simply **Congress**.[1] Each state has two senators in the **U.S. Senate**. The number of representatives to the **U.S. House of Representatives** is determined according to the population of each state. The current number of representatives is determined by the most recent national census.
2. **Article II: Executive branch.** **Article II of the U.S. Constitution** establishes the **executive branch** of the federal government by providing for the election of the president and vice-president. The president is not elected by popular vote but instead is selected by the **Electoral College**, whose representatives are appointed by state delegations.[2] The executive branch is responsible for enforcing federal law.
3. **Article III: Judicial branch.** **Article III of the U.S. Constitution** establishes the **judicial branch** of the federal government by establishing the U.S. Supreme Court and providing for the creation of other federal courts by Congress.[3] The judicial branch of the government is responsible for interpreting the U.S. Constitution and federal law.

legislative branch
The part of the U.S. government that makes federal laws. It is known as Congress (the Senate and the House of Representatives).

executive branch
The part of the U.S. government that enforces the federal law; it consists of the president and vice president.

judicial branch
The part of the U.S. government that interprets the law. It consists of the Supreme Court and other federal courts.

Checks and Balances

Certain **checks and balances** are built into the Constitution to ensure that no one branch of the federal government becomes too powerful.

checks and balances
A system built into the U.S. Constitution to prevent any one of the three branches of the government from becoming too powerful.

Example The *judicial* branch has authority to examine the acts of the other two branches of government and determine whether those acts are constitutional.[4]

Example The *executive* branch can enter into treaties with foreign governments only with the advice and consent of the Senate.

Example The *legislative* branch is authorized to create federal courts and determine their jurisdiction and to enact statutes that change judicially made law.

Example The president has *veto power* over bills passed by Congress. If a bill has been vetoed by the president, the bill goes back to Congress, where a vote of two-thirds of each the Senate and the House of Representatives is required to override the president's veto.

Example The House of Representatives has the power to *impeach* the president for certain activities, such as treason, bribery, and other crimes. The Senate has the power to try an impeachment case. A two-thirds vote of the Senate is required to impeach the president.

CONCEPT SUMMARY
BASIC CONSTITUTIONAL CONCEPTS

Concept	Description
Federalism	The Constitution created the federal government. The federal government; the 50 state governments; and Washington DC, share powers in this country.
Delegated powers	When the states ratified the Constitution, they delegated certain powers to the federal government. These are called *enumerated powers*.
Reserved powers	Those powers not granted to the federal government by the Constitution are reserved to the state governments.
Separation of powers	Each branch of the federal government has separate powers. These powers are the following: a. Legislative branch—power to make the law. b. Executive branch—power to enforce the law. c. Judicial branch—power to interpret the law.
Checks and balances	Certain checks and balances are built into the Constitution to ensure that no one branch of the federal government becomes too powerful.

SUPREME COURT OF THE UNITED STATES, WASHINGTON DC
The highest court in the land is the Supreme Court of the United States, located in Washington DC. The U.S. Supreme Court decides the most important constitutional law cases and other important issues it deems ripe for review and decision. The Supreme Court's unanimous and majority decisions are precedent for all the other courts in the country.

Supremacy Clause

The **Supremacy Clause** establishes that the U.S. Constitution and federal treaties, laws, and regulations are the supreme law of the land.[5] State and local laws that conflict with valid federal law are unconstitutional. The concept of federal law taking precedence over state or local law is commonly called the **preemption doctrine**.

Congress may expressly provide that a particular federal statute *exclusively* regulates a specific area or activity. No state or local law regulating the area or activity is valid if there is such a statute. Often, though, federal statutes do not expressly provide for exclusive jurisdiction. In these instances, state and local governments have *concurrent jurisdiction* to regulate the area or activity. However, any state or local law that "directly and substantially" conflicts with valid federal law is preempted under the Supremacy Clause.

The following U.S. Supreme Court case involves the Supremacy Clause.

Supremacy Clause
A clause of the U.S. Constitution that establishes that the U.S. Constitution and federal treaties, laws, and regulations as the supreme law of the land.

preemption doctrine
A doctrine that provides that federal law takes precedence over state or local law.

CASE 4.1 *U.S. SUPREME COURT CASE Supremacy Clause*

Mutual Pharmaceutical Company, Inc. v. Bartlett

133 S.Ct. 2466, 2013 U.S. Lexis 4702 (2013)
Supreme Court of the United States

"But sympathy for respondent does not relieve us of the responsibility of following the law."

—Alito, Justice

Facts

In 1978, the Food and Drug Administration (FDA), a federal government agency, approved a nonsteroidal anti-inflammatory pain reliever called sulindac under the brand name Clinoril. At the time, the FDA approved the labeling of the prescription drug, which contained warnings of specific side effects of the drug. When the Clinoril patent expired, the law permitted other pharmaceutical companies to sell generic versions of sulindac under their own brand names. Federal law requires that generic sellers of drugs use the exact labeling as required on the original drug, without alteration.

Mutual Pharmaceutical Company, Inc. (Mutual), manufactured and sold a generic brand of sulindac. Karen L. Bartlett was prescribed sulindac for shoulder pain, and a pharmacist dispensed Mutual's generic brand of sulinac to her. Bartlett soon developed an acute case of toxic epidermal necrolysis. The results were horrific. Sixty percent of the surface of her body deteriorated and burned off. She spent months in a medically induced coma, underwent 12 eye surgeries, and was tube-fed for a year. She is now severely disfigured, has a number of physical disabilities, and is nearly blind. The original patented drug's label—and therefore Mutual's generic brand label—did not refer to the possible side effect of toxic epidermal necrolysis.

The law in the state of New Hampshire required stricter warnings on prescription drugs than did federal laws. Bartlett sued Mutual for product liability under New Hampshire law. The jury of the U.S. district court found Mutual liable and awarded Bartlett more than $21 million in damages, and the U.S. court of appeals affirmed the award. Mutual appealed to the U.S. Supreme Court, asserting that the federal labeling law preempted New Hampshire law under the Supremacy Clause.

Issue

Does the federal drug labeling law preempt a stricter state drug labeling law?

Language of the U.S. Supreme Court

Under the Supremacy Clause, state laws that require a private party to violate federal law are pre-empted and, thus, are "without effect." In the instant case, it was impossible for Mutual to comply with both its state-law duty to strengthen the warnings on sulindac's label and its federal-law duty not to alter sulindac's label. Accordingly, the state law is pre-empted. The dreadful injuries from which products liabilities cases arise often engender passionate responses. But sympathy for respondent does not relieve us of the responsibility of following the law.

(case continues)

Decision

The U.S. Supreme Court held that federal drug labeling law preempted New Hampshire's stricter labeling law under the Supremacy Clause of the U.S. Constitution. The Supreme Court reversed the U.S. court of appeal's decision that was in favor of Bartlett.

Ethics Questions

What is the public policy for having the Supremacy Clause? Do you think that pharmaceutical companies supported the passage of the federal drug labeling statute? Was it ethical for Mutual to deny liability in this case?

Critical Legal Thinking

Why was the Supremacy Clause added to the U.S. Constitution? What would be the result if there were no Supremacy Clause?

Commerce Clause
A clause of the U.S. Constitution that grants Congress the power "to regulate commerce with foreign nations, and among the several states, and with Indian tribes."

Commerce Clause

The **Commerce Clause** of the U.S. Constitution grants Congress the power "to regulate commerce with foreign nations, and among the several states, and with Indian tribes."[6] Because this clause authorizes the federal government to regulate commerce, it has a greater impact on business than any other provision in the Constitution. Among other things, this clause is intended to foster the development of a national market and free trade among the states.

The U.S. Constitution grants the federal government the power to regulate three types of commerce:

1. Commerce with Native American tribes
2. Foreign commerce
3. Interstate commerce

Each of these is discussed in the following paragraphs.

Commerce with Native Americans

Before Europeans arrived in the "New World," the land had been occupied for thousands of years by people we now refer to as Native Americans. There were many different Native American tribes, each having its own independent and self-governing system of laws.

When the United States was first founded more than 200 years ago, it consisted of the original 13 colonies, all located in the east, primarily on the Atlantic Ocean. At that time, these colonies (states), in the U.S. Constitution, delegated to the federal government the authority to regulate commerce with the Native American tribes—in both the original 13 states and the territory that was to eventually become the United States of America.

Under its Commerce Clause powers, the federal government entered into treaties with many Native American nations. Most tribes, in the face of white settlers' encroachment on their land and federal government pressure, were forced to sell their lands to the federal government. The Native Americans received money and goods for land. The federal government obtained many treaties through unscrupulous means, cheating the Native Americans of their land. These tribes were then relocated to other, smaller pieces of land called *reservations*, often outside their typical tribal lands. The federal government eventually broke many of the treaties.

Once Native Americans came under U.S. authority, they lost much of their political power. Most tribes were allowed to keep their own governments but were placed under the "protection" of the U.S. government. In general, the United States treats Native Americans as belonging to separate nations, similarly to the way it treats Spain or France; however, it still considers Native Americans "domestic dependent" nations with limited sovereignty.

Today, many Native Americans live on reservations set aside for various tribes. Others live and work outside reservations.

Indian Gaming Regulatory Act In the late 1980s, the federal government authorized Native American tribes to operate gaming facilities. Congress passed the **Indian Gaming Regulatory Act**,[7] a federal statute that establishes the requirements for conducting casino gambling and other gaming activities on tribal land. This act allows Native Americans to negotiate with the states for gaming compacts and ensures that the states do so in good faith. If a state fails to do so, the tribe can bring suit in federal court, forcing the state to comply. Today, casinos operated by Native Americans can be found in many states. Profits from the casinos have become an important source of income for members of certain tribes.

Let our last sleep be in the graves of our native land!

Osceola

Foreign Commerce

The Commerce Clause of the U.S. Constitution gives the federal government the *exclusive power* to regulate commerce with foreign nations. This is called the **Foreign Commerce Clause**. Direct and indirect regulation of foreign commerce by state or local governments that *unduly burdens* foreign commerce violates the Foreign Commerce Clause and is therefore unconstitutional.

Foreign Commerce Clause Commerce with foreign nations. The Commerce Clause grants the federal government the authority to regulate foreign commerce.

Examples The federal government could enact a law that forbids another country from doing business in the United States if that country engages in activities that are not condoned by the United States. A state, however, could not enact a law that forbids a foreign country from doing business in that state if that country engages in activities that are not condoned by that state.

Example The state of Michigan is the home of General Motors Company, Ford Motor Company, and Chrysler Corporation, three large automobile manufacturers. Suppose the Michigan state legislature enacts a law that imposes a 100 percent tax on any automobile imported from a foreign country that is sold in Michigan but does not impose the same tax on domestic automobiles sold in Michigan. The Michigan tax violates the Foreign Commerce Clause and is therefore unconstitutional and void. However, the federal government could enact a 100 percent tax on all foreign automobiles sold in the United States but not on domestic automobiles sold in the United States, and that law would be valid.

Interstate Commerce

The Commerce Clause gives the federal government the authority to regulate **interstate commerce**. Originally, the courts interpreted this clause to mean that the federal government could regulate only commerce that moved *in* interstate commerce, that is, commerce that is conducted across state borders. The modern rule, however, allows the federal government to regulate activities that *affect* interstate commerce.

interstate commerce Commerce that moves between states or that affects commerce between states.

Under the **effects on interstate commerce test**, the regulated activity does not itself have to be in interstate commerce. Thus, any local (*intrastate*) activity that has an effect on interstate commerce is subject to federal regulation. Theoretically, this test subjects a substantial amount of business activity in the United States to federal regulation.

Example In the famous case ***Wickard, Secretary of Agriculture v. Filburn***,[8] a federal statute limited the amount of wheat that a farmer could plant and harvest for home consumption. Filburn, a farmer, violated the law. The U.S. Supreme Court upheld the federal statute on the grounds that it involved interstate commerce because the statute was designed to prevent nationwide surpluses and shortages of wheat. The Court reasoned that wheat grown for home consumption would affect the supply of wheat available in interstate commerce.

The American Constitution is, so far as I can see, the most wonderful work ever struck off at a given time by the brain and purpose of man.

W. E. Gladstone
Kin beyond Sea (1878)

In the following landmark U.S. Supreme Court case, the Court decided the scope of interstate commerce.

LANDMARK U.S. SUPREME COURT CASE Interstate Commerce

Heart of Atlanta Motel v. United States

"One need only examine the evidence which we have discussed . . . to see that Congress may . . . prohibit racial discrimination by motels serving travelers, however 'local' their operations may appear."

—Clark, Justice

The Heart of Atlanta Motel, which was located in the state of Georgia, had 216 rooms available to guests. The motel was readily accessible to motorists using U.S. interstate highways 75 and 85 and Georgia state highways 23 and 41. The motel solicited patronage from outside the state of Georgia through various national advertising media, including magazines with national circulation. Approximately 75 percent of the motel's registered guests were from out of state. The Heart of Atlanta Motel refused to rent rooms to blacks.

Congress enacted the **Civil Rights Act of 1964**, which made it illegal for motels, hotels, and other public accommodations to discriminate against guests based on their race. After the act was passed, the Heart of Atlanta Motel continued to refuse to rent rooms to blacks. The owner-operator of the motel brought a declaratory relief action in U.S. district court, ***Heart of Atlanta Motel v. United States***, to have the Civil Rights Act of 1964 declared unconstitutional. The plaintiff argued that Congress, in passing the act, had exceeded its powers to regulate interstate commerce under the Commerce Clause of the U.S. Constitution.

The U.S. Supreme Court held that the provisions of the Civil Rights Act of 1964 that prohibited discrimination in accommodations properly regulated interstate commerce. In reaching its decision, the U.S. Supreme Court stated,

> *The power of Congress over interstate commerce is not confined to the regulation of commerce among the states. It extends to those activities intrastate which so affect interstate commerce or the exercise of the power of Congress over it as to make regulation of them appropriate means to the attainment of a legitimate end, the exercise of the granted power of Congress to regulate interstate commerce. One need only examine the evidence which we have discussed above to see that Congress may—as it has—prohibit racial discrimination by motels serving travelers, however "local" their operations may appear.*

The U.S. Supreme Court held that the challenged provisions of the Civil Rights Act of 1964 were constitutional as a proper exercise of the commerce power of the federal government. *Heart of Atlanta Motel v. United States*, 379 U.S. 241, 85 S.Ct. 348, 1964 U.S. Lexis 2187 (Supreme Court of the United States)

Critical Legal Thinking Questions

Why was this case so important? Why did the U.S. Supreme Court develop the "effects on interstate commerce" test? Is most commerce considered "interstate commerce" that can be regulated by the federal government?

State Police Power

The states did not delegate all power to regulate business to the federal government. They retained the power to regulate **intrastate commerce** and much of the interstate commerce that occurs within their borders. This is commonly referred to as states' **police power**.

police power
Power that permits states and local governments to enact laws to protect or promote the public health, safety, morals, and general welfare.

Police power permits states (and, by delegation, local governments) to enact laws to protect or promote the *public health, safety, morals, and general welfare*. This includes the authority to enact laws that regulate the conduct of business.

Example State real property laws, personal property laws, and state environmental laws are enacted under state police power.

Dormant Commerce Clause

If the federal government has chosen not to regulate an area of interstate commerce that it has the power to regulate under its Commerce Clause powers, this area of commerce is subject to what is referred to as the **Dormant Commerce Clause**. A state, under its police power, can enact laws to regulate that area of commerce. However, if a state enacts laws to regulate commerce that the federal government has the power to regulate but has chosen not to regulate, the Dormant Commerce Clause prohibits the state's regulation from **unduly burdening interstate commerce**.

Dormant Commerce Clause
A situation in which the federal government has the Commerce Clause power to regulate an area of commerce but has chosen not to regulate that area of commerce.

Example The federal government, under its interstate commerce powers, could, if it wanted to, regulate corporations. However, the federal government has chosen not to. Thus, states regulate corporations. Assume that one state's corporation code permits only corporations from that state but from no other state to conduct business in that state. That state's law would unduly burden interstate commerce and would be unconstitutional.

unduly burdening interstate commerce
A concept that says states may enact laws which protect or promote the public health, safety, morals, and general welfare, as long as the laws do not unduly burden interstate commerce.

E-Commerce and the Constitution

The advent of the Internet has caused a revolution in how commerce is conducted. The Internet and other computer networks permit parties to obtain website domain names and conduct business electronically. This is usually referred to as **electronic commerce** or **e-commerce**. Some businesses that conduct e-commerce over the Internet do not have any physical location, whereas many brick-and-mortar businesses augment their traditional sales with e-commerce sales. Currently, a significant portion of the sales of goods, licensing of intellectual property, and sales of services are accomplished through e-commerce. Because e-commerce is commerce, it is subject to the Commerce Clause of the U.S. Constitution.

The following feature discusses a U.S. Supreme Court case that applies the Commerce Clause to e-commerce.

Critical Legal Thinking
Can the law keep up with the changes brought by e-commerce and electronic devices? Are new laws required to apply to the digital environment?

Digital Law

E-Commerce and the Commerce Clause

"State bans on interstate direct shipping represent the single largest regulatory barrier to expanded e-commerce in wine."

—Kennedy, Justice

In this information age, federal and state governments have had to grapple with how to regulate the Internet and e-commerce. The federal government seems to be taking the upper hand in passing laws that regulate business conducted in cyberspace, thus creating laws that apply uniformly across the country. However, states have also enacted laws that regulate the Internet and e-commerce. State laws that unduly burden interstate e-commerce are unconstitutional, however. Consider the following case.

The state of Michigan regulates the sale of wine within its boundaries. Michigan law permits in-state wineries to sell wine directly to consumers, including by mail, Internet, and other means of sale. Michigan law prohibits out-of-state wineries from selling wine directly to Michigan consumers, including over the Internet. Michigan instead requires out-of-state wineries to sell their wine to Michigan wholesalers, who then sell the wine to Michigan retailers, who then sell the wine to Michigan consumers.

Domaine Alfred, a small winery located in San Luis Obispo, California, and several other out-of-state wineries that were prohibited from selling wine directly to Michigan consumers sued Michigan. The plaintiff wineries alleged that the Michigan law caused an undue burden on interstate e-commerce in violation of the Commerce Clause of the U.S. Constitution.

The U.S. Supreme Court held that the Michigan state law that discriminated against out-of-state wineries in favor of in-state wineries caused an undue burden on interstate e-commerce, in violation of the Commerce

(continued)

Clause of the U.S. Constitution. The U.S. Supreme Court stated, "Technological improvements, in particular the ability of wineries to sell wine over the Internet, have helped make direct shipments an attractive sales channel. State bans on interstate direct shipping represent the single largest regulatory barrier to expanded e-commerce in wine." In this case, the U.S. Supreme Court saved e-commerce from a discriminatory state law. *Granholm, Governor of Michigan v. Heald*, 544 U.S. 460, 125 S.Ct. 1885, 2005 U.S. Lexis 4174 (Supreme Court of the United States, 2005)

Bill of Rights and Other Amendments to the U.S. Constitution

The U.S. Constitution provides that it may be amended. Currently, there are 27 **amendments to the U.S. Constitution**.

Bill of Rights
The first 10 amendments to the Constitution that were added to the U.S. Constitution in 1791.

In 1791, the 10 amendments that are commonly referred to as the **Bill of Rights** were approved by the states and became part of the U.S. Constitution. The Bill of Rights guarantees certain fundamental rights and protects these rights from intrusive government action.

Examples Fundamental rights guaranteed in the **First Amendment** include *freedom of speech*, *freedom to assemble*, *freedom of the press*, and *freedom of religion*. Most of these rights have also been found applicable to so-called artificial persons (i.e., corporations).

In addition to the Bill of Rights, 17 other amendments have been added to the Constitution. These amendments cover a variety of issues.

I disapprove of what you say, but I will defend to the death your right to say it.
Voltaire

Example The additional 17 amendments to the Constitution have abolished slavery, prohibited discrimination, authorized the federal income tax, given women the right to vote, and specifically recognized that persons 18 years of age and older have the right to vote.

Originally, the Bill of Rights limited intrusive action by the *federal government* only. Intrusive actions by state and local governments were not limited until the *Due Process Clause of the Fourteenth Amendment* was added to the Constitution in 1868. The Supreme Court has applied the **incorporation doctrine** and held that most of the fundamental guarantees contained in the Bill of Rights are applicable to *state and local government* action. The amendments to the Constitution that are most applicable to business are discussed in the sections that follow.

PROTEST, LOS ANGELES, CALIFORNIA
The Freedom of Speech Clause of the First Amendment to the U.S. Constitution protects the right to engage in political speech. Freedom of speech is one of Americans' most highly prized rights.

Freedom of Speech

One of the most honored freedoms guaranteed by the Bill of Rights is the **freedom of speech** of the First Amendment. Many other constitutional freedoms would be meaningless without it. The First Amendment's Freedom of Speech Clause protects speech only, not conduct. The U.S. Supreme Court places speech into three categories: (1) *fully protected*, (2) *limited protected*, and (3) *unprotected speech*. These types of speech are discussed in the following paragraphs.

freedom of speech
The right to engage in oral, written, and symbolic speech protected by the First Amendment.

Fully Protected Speech

Fully protected speech is speech that the government cannot prohibit or regulate. The government cannot prohibit or regulate the content of fully protected speech.

fully protected speech
Speech that cannot be prohibited or regulated by the government.

Example Political speech is an example of fully protected speech. Thus, the government could not enact a law that forbids citizens from criticizing the current president.

The First Amendment protects oral, written, and symbolic speech.

Example Burning the American flag in protest of a federal government military action is protected symbolic speech.

In the following U.S. Supreme Court case, the Court decided an important freedom of speech issue.

CASE 4.2 *U.S. SUPREME COURT CASE Free Speech and Video Games*

Brown, Governor of California v. Entertainment Merchants Association

131 S.Ct. 2729, 2011 U.S. Lexis 4802 (2011)
Supreme Court of the United States

"And whatever the challenges of applying the Constitution to ever-advancing technology, the basic principles of freedom of speech and the press, like the First Amendment's command, do not vary when a new and different medium for communication appears."

—Scalia, Justice

Facts

Video games are played by millions of youth and adults. The dollar sales of video games exceed the receipts of the movie industry. Some of the games contain violent content. The state of California enacted a state statute that prohibits the sale or rental of "violent video games" to minors. The act covers games "in which the range of options available to a player includes killing, maiming, dismembering, or sexually assaulting an image of a human being, if those acts are depicted" in a manner that "a reasonable person, considering the game as a whole, would find appeals to a deviant or morbid interest of minors"; that is "patently offensive to prevailing standards in the community as to what is suitable for minors"; and that "causes the game, as a whole, to lack serious literary, artistic, political, or scientific value for minors." Violation of the act is punishable by a civil fine of up to $1,000.

Members of the video game and software industries challenged the enforcement of the act. The U.S. district court concluded that the act violated the First Amendment and permanently enjoined its enforcement. The U.S. court of appeals affirmed the decision. California appealed to the U.S. Supreme Court.

Issue

Does the California act that restricts violent video games violate the First Amendment?

Language of the U.S. Supreme Court

Whatever the challenges of applying the Constitution to ever-advancing technology, the basic principles of freedom of speech and the press, like the First Amendment's command,

(case continues)

do not vary when a new and different medium for communication appears.

Certainly the books we give children to read—or read to them when they are younger—contain no shortage of gore. As her just deserts for trying to poison Snow White, the wicked queen is made to dance in red hot slippers "till she fell dead on the floor, a sad example of envy and jealousy." Cinderella's evil stepsisters have their eyes pecked out by doves. And Hansel and Gretel (children!) kill their captor by baking her in an oven.

Here, California has singled out the purveyors of video games for disfavored treatment—at least when compared to booksellers, cartoonists, and movie producers—and has given no persuasive reason why. Even where the protection of children is the object, the constitutional limits on governmental action apply.

Decision

The U.S. Supreme Court held that the California act violated the First Amendment to the U.S. Constitution.

Ethics Questions

Does the majority have the right to legislate what the minority should see and hear? Do video game producers act ethically in producing violent video games?

Limited Protected Speech

limited protected speech Speech that the government may not prohibit but that is subject to time, place, and manner restrictions.

offensive speech Speech that is offensive to many members of society. It is subject to time, place, and manner restrictions.

The Supreme Court has held that certain types of speech have only *limited protection* under the First Amendment. The government cannot forbid this type of speech, but it can subject this speech to *time, place, and manner of restrictions*. Two major forms of **limited protected speech** are *offensive speech* and *commercial speech*.

Offensive speech is speech that offends many members of society. (It is not the same as obscene speech, however.) The Supreme Court has held that the content of offensive speech may not be forbidden but that it may be restricted by the government under time, place, and manner restrictions.

Example The Federal Communications Commission (FCC) is a federal administrative agency that regulates radio, television, and cable stations. Under its powers, the FCC has regulated the use of offensive language on television by limiting such language to time periods when children would be unlikely to be watching (e.g., late at night).

commercial speech Speech used by businesses, such as advertising. It is subject to time, place, and manner restrictions.

Commercial speech, such as advertising, was once considered unprotected by the First Amendment. Today, because of U.S. Supreme Court decisions, however, the content of commercial speech is protected but is also subject to time, place, and manner restrictions.

Example In *Virginia State Board of Pharmacy v. Virginia Citizens Consumer Council, Inc.*,[9] the U.S. Supreme Court held that a state statute that prohibited a pharmacist from advertising the price of prescription drugs was unconstitutional because it violated the Freedom of Speech Clause. The U.S. Supreme Court held that this was commercial speech that was protected by the First Amendment.

Example A city can prohibit billboards along its highways for safety and aesthetic reasons if other forms of advertising (e.g., print media) are available. This is a lawful place restriction.

The following case involves a contemporary issue of free speech.

CASE 4.3 U.S. SUPREME COURT CASE Free Speech

McCullen v. Coakley, Attorney General of Massachusetts

134 S.Ct. 2518, 2014 U.S. Lexis 4999 (2014)
Supreme Court of the United States

"It is no accident that public streets and sidewalks have developed as venues for the exchange of ideas."
—Roberts, Chief Justice

Facts

The state of Massachusetts enacted a statute that makes it a crime to knowingly stand on a public way or sidewalk within 35 feet of an entrance or driveway to any place, other than a hospital, where abortions are formed. The petitioners are individuals who approach and talk to women outside such facilities who attempt to dissuade them from having abortions. The petitioners sued, alleging that the Massachusetts statute violates their free speech rights guaranteed by the First Amendment to the U.S. Constitution. The U.S. district court and the U.S. court of appeals upheld the Massachusetts statute. Petitioners appealed to the U.S. Supreme Court.

Issue

Does the Massachusetts statute violate the free speech rights of the First Amendment?

Language of the U.S. Supreme Court

The Massachusetts Act regulates access to public ways and sidewalks. Such areas occupy a special position in terms of First Amendment protection because of their historic role as sites for discussion and debate. It is no accident that public streets and sidewalks have developed as venues for the exchange of ideas. The buffer zones impose serious burdens on petitioner's speech.

Decision

The U.S. Supreme Court held that the Massachusetts statute violates the First Amendment.

Ethics Questions

What are the competing interests of the parties in this case? What will be the effects of removing the 35 foot barrier?

Unprotected Speech

The U.S. Supreme Court has held that certain speech is **unprotected speech** that is not protected by the First Amendment and may be forbidden totally by the government. The Supreme Court has held that the following types of speech are unprotected speech:

unprotected speech
Speech that is not protected by the First Amendment and may be forbidden by the government.

1. **Dangerous speech**

   Example Yelling "fire" in a crowded theater when there is no fire is not protected speech.

2. **Fighting words that are likely to provoke a hostile or violent response from an average person**[10]

   Example Walking up to a person and intentionally calling that person names because of race or ethnicity would not be protected speech if it would likely cause the person being called the names to respond in a hostile manner.

3. **Speech that incites the violent or revolutionary overthrow of the government.** However, the mere abstract teaching of the morality and consequences of such action is protected.[11]
4. **Defamatory language**[12]

Critical Legal Thinking

Why has the U.S. Supreme Court designated some speech as being not protected by the First Amendment? Do you think that these exceptions are warranted?

Examples Committing libel or slander by writing or telling untrue statements about another person or committing product disparagement or trade libel by writing or telling untrue statements about a company's products or services is not protected speech, and the injured party may bring a civil lawsuit to recover damages.

5. **Child pornography**[13]

Example Selling material depicting children engaged in sexual activity is unprotected speech.

obscene speech
Speech that (1) appeals to the prurient interest; (2) depicts sexual conduct in a patently offensive way; and (3) lacks serious literary, artistic, political, or scientific value.

6. **Obscene speech.**[14] If speech is considered **obscene speech**, it has no protection under the Freedom of Speech Clause of the First Amendment and can be banned by the government.

Examples Movies, videos, music, and other forms of speech that are obscene are unprotected speech.

The definition of *obscenity* has plagued the courts. The definition of *obscene speech* is quite subjective. One Supreme Court justice stated, "I know it when I see it."[15] In ***Miller v. California***, the U.S. Supreme Court determined that speech is obscene when:

The Constitution of the United States is not a mere lawyers' document: It is a vehicle of life, and its spirit is always the spirit of the age.

Woodrow Wilson
Constitutional Government in the United States (1908)

1. The average person, applying contemporary community standards, would find that the work, taken as a whole, appeals to the *prurient interest*.
2. The work depicts or describes, in a patently offensive way, sexual conduct specifically defined by the applicable state law.
3. The work, taken as a whole, lacks serious literary, artistic, political, or scientific value.[16]

States are free to define what constitutes obscene speech. Movie theaters, magazine publishers, and so on are often subject to challenges that the materials they display or sell are obscene and therefore not protected by the First Amendment. Over the years, the content of material that has been found to be obscene has shifted to a more liberal view as the general norms of society have become more liberal. Today, fewer obscenity cases are brought than was true in the past.

In the following U.S. Supreme Court case, the Court had to decide if certain contemptuous speech was protected by the First Amendment.

CASE 4.4 U.S. SUPREME COURT CASE Free Speech

Snyder v. Phelps

131 S.Ct. 1207, 2011 U.S. Lexis 1903 (2011)
Supreme Court of the United States

"Speech is powerful. It can stir people to action, move them to tears of both joy and sorrow, and—as it did here—inflict great pain. On the facts before us, we cannot react to that pain by punishing the speaker."
—Roberts, Chief Justice

Facts

Fred Phelps founded the Westboro Baptist Church in Topeka, Kansas. The church's congregation believes that God hates and punishes the United States for its tolerance of homosexuality, particularly in America's military. The church frequently communicates its views by picketing at military funerals. In more than 20 years, the members of Westboro Baptist have picketed at nearly 600 funerals.

Lance Corporal Matthew Snyder, a member of the U.S. Marines, was killed in Iraq in the line of duty. Lance Corporal Snyder's father, Albert Snyder, selected the Catholic church in the Snyders' hometown of Westminster, Maryland, as the site for his son's funeral.

Phelps decided to travel to Maryland with six other Westboro Baptist parishioners—two of his daughters and four of his grandchildren—to picket at Lance Corporal Snyder's funeral service. The Westboro congregation members picketed while standing on

(case continues)

public land adjacent to a public street approximately 1,000 feet from the church. They carried placards that read "God Hates the USA/Thank God for 9/11," "America Is Doomed," "Don't Pray for the USA," "Thank God for Dead Soldiers," and "You're Going to Hell." The picketers sang hymns and recited Bible verses. The funeral procession passed within 200 to 300 feet of the picket site.

Albert Snyder filed a lawsuit against Phelps, Phelps's daughters, and the Westboro Baptist Church (collective "Westboro") in U.S. district court. Snyder alleged intentional infliction of emotional distress and other state law tort claims. Westboro argued that their speech was protected by the First Amendment. The jury found for Snyder and held Westboro liable for $2.9 million in compensatory damages and $8 million in punitive damages. The U.S. district court remitted the punitive damages to $2.1 million. The U.S. court of appeals held that the First Amendment protected Westboro's speech and reversed the judgment. Snyder appealed to the U.S. Supreme Court.

Issue

Does the Free Speech Clause of the First Amendment shield church members from tort liability for their picketing speech at funerals?

Language of the U.S. Supreme Court

Given that Westboro's speech was at a public place on a matter of public concern, that speech is entitled to "special protection" under the First Amendment. Such speech cannot be restricted simply because it is upsetting or arouses contempt. Speech is powerful. It can stir people to action, move them to tears of both joy and sorrow, and—as it did here—inflict great pain. On the facts before us, we cannot react to that pain by punishing the speaker. As a Nation we have chosen a different course—to protect even hurtful speech on public issues to ensure that we do not stifle public debate. That choice requires that we shield Westboro from tort liability for its picketing in this case.

Decision

The U.S. Supreme Court held that the First Amendment protected Westboro's speech in this case. The U.S. Supreme Court held that Mr. Snyder could not recover tort damages for the emotional distress he suffered because of Westboro's speech.

Ethics Questions

Did the Westboro picketers know that they were causing personal grief to Mr. Snyder who had lost his son? Should they have let Mr. Snyder bury his son in peace?

Freedom of Religion

Freedom of religion is a key concept addressed by the First Amendment. The First Amendment contains two separate religion clauses, the *Establishment Clause* and the *Free Exercise Clause*. These two clauses are discussed in the following paragraphs.

Establishment Clause

The U.S. Constitution requires federal, state, and local governments to be neutral toward religion. The **Establishment Clause** prohibits the government from either establishing a government-sponsored religion or promoting one religion over another. Thus, it guarantees that there will be no state-sponsored religion.

Establishment Clause
A clause of the First Amendment that prohibits the government from either establishing a state religion or promoting one religion over another.

Example The U.S. Supreme Court ruled that an Alabama statute that authorized a one-minute period of silence in school for "meditation or voluntary prayer" was invalid.[17] The Court held that the statute endorsed religion.

Free Exercise Clause

The **Free Exercise Clause** prohibits the government from interfering with the free exercise of religion in the United States. Generally, this clause prevents the

Free Exercise Clause
A clause of the First Amendment that prohibits the government from interfering with the free exercise of religion in the United States.

government from enacting laws that either prohibit or inhibit individuals from participating in or practicing their chosen religions.

Examples Federal, state, or local governments cannot enact a law that prohibits all religions. The government cannot enact a law that prohibits churches, synagogues, mosques, or temples. The government cannot prohibit religious practitioners from celebrating their major holidays and high holy days.

I am for freedom of religion and against all maneuvers to bring about a legal ascendancy of one sect over another.

Thomas Jefferson

Example In *Church of Lukumi Babalu Aye, Inc. v. City of Hialeah, Florida*,[18] the U.S. Supreme Court held that a city ordinance that prohibited ritual sacrifices of chickens during church service violated the Free Exercise Clause and that such sacrifices should be allowed.

Of course, the right to be free from government intervention in the practice of religion is not absolute.

Example Human sacrifices are unlawful and are not protected by the First Amendment.

The following U.S. Supreme Court case involves an issue of freedom of religion.

CASE 4.5 *U.S. SUPREME COURT CASE Freedom of Religion*

Burwell v. Hobby Lobby Stores, Inc.

134 S.Ct. 2751, 2014 U.S. Lexis 4505 (2014)
Supreme Court of the United States

"The contraceptive mandate, as applied to closely held corporations, violates RFRA."

—Alito, Justice

Facts

The Religious Freedom Restoration Act of 1993 (RFRA) prohibits the government from substantially burdening a person's exercise of religion. David and Barbara Green and their children are Christians who own and operate a nationwide chain of arts-and-crafts stores called Hobby Lobby. Hobby Lobby has more than 500 stores and more than 13,000 employees. Hobby Lobby is organized as a for-profit closely held corporation owned by the Greens.

Pursuant to power granted by the Patient Protection and Affordable Care Act of 2010, the U.S. Department of Health and Human Services (HHS), a federal government agency, adopted a regulation that requires for-profit corporations to provide contraceptive methods to employees, including methods that are considered abortifacients, that is, drugs that would prevent an already fertilized egg from developing any further.

The Greens believe that human life begins at conception, and that therefore the HHS regulation violates their religious beliefs. Hobby Lobby and the Greens sued HHS for violating RFRA and sought an injunction against the enforcement of the regulation. The U.S. district court denied the injunction. The U.S. court of appeals held that for-profit closely held corporations are persons covered by RFRA and that HHS had failed to demonstrate a compelling government interest for interfering with the Greens' religious beliefs. HHS appealed to the U.S. Supreme Court.

Issue

Do owners of closely held corporations have to provide health insurance coverage to their employees for methods of contraception that violate the owners' sincerely held religious beliefs?

Language of the U.S. Supreme Court

We reject HHS's argument that the owners forfeited all RFRA protection when they decided to organize their businesses as corporations. By requiring the Greens and their company to arrange for such coverage, the HHS mandate demands that they engage in conduct that seriously violates their religious beliefs. The contraceptive mandate, as applied to closely held corporations, violates RFRA.

Decision

The U.S. Supreme Court held that owners of closely held corporations do not have to provide health insurance coverage to their employees for methods

(case continues)

of contraception that violate the owners' sincerely held religious beliefs.

Ethics Questions

The U.S. Supreme Court's decision only applies to closely held corporations and not to publicly held corporations. Do you see a justification for this distinction?

Note

Under federal law, women who are employed by Hobby Lobby and by other closely held corporations with owners who share similar religious beliefs, as well as employees of nonprofit religious affiliated corporations, are entitled to Food and Drug Administration (FDA) approved contraceptives, including abortifacients, without cost sharing.

CONCEPT SUMMARY

FREEDOM OF RELIGION

Clause	Description
Establishment Clause	Prohibits the government from establishing a government-sponsored religion and from promoting one religion over other religions.
Free Exercise Clause	Prohibits the government from enacting laws that either prohibit or inhibit individuals from participating in or practicing their chosen religions.

Equal Protection

The **Fourteenth Amendment** was added to the U.S. Constitution in 1868. Its original purpose was to guarantee equal rights to all persons after the Civil War. The **Equal Protection Clause** of the Fourteenth Amendment provides that a state cannot "deny to any person within its jurisdiction the equal protection of the laws." Although this clause expressly applies to state and local government action, the Supreme Court has held that it also applies to federal government action.

This clause prohibits state, local, and federal governments from enacting laws that classify and treat "similarly situated" persons differently. Artificial persons, such as corporations, are also protected. Note that this clause is designed to prohibit invidious discrimination: It does not make the classification of individuals unlawful per se.

Fourteenth Amendment
An amendment added to the U.S. Constitution in 1868 that contains the Due Process, Equal Protection, and Privileges and Immunities clauses.

Equal Protection Clause
A clause that provides that a state cannot "deny to any person within its jurisdiction the equal protection of the laws."

Standards of Review

The Supreme Court, over years of making decisions involving the Equal Protection Clause, has held that the government can treat people or businesses differently from one another if the government has sufficient justification for doing so. The Supreme Court has adopted three different standards of review for deciding whether the government's different treatment of people or businesses violates or does not violate the Equal Protection Clause:

1. **Strict scrutiny test.** Any government activity or regulation that classifies persons based on a **suspect class** (e.g., **race**, **national origin**, and **citizenship**) or involves **fundamental rights** (e.g., **voting**) is reviewed for lawfulness using a **strict scrutiny test**. This means that the government must have an exceptionally important reason for treating persons differently because of their race in order for such unequal treatment to be lawful. Under this standard, many government classifications of persons based on race are found to be unconstitutional. Others are found lawful.

   Example A government rule that permits persons of one race but not of another race to receive government benefits such as Medicaid would violate this test.

strict scrutiny test
A test that is applied to determine the constitutionality of classifications by the government that are based on a suspect class (e.g., race) or a fundamental right (e.g., voting rights).

2. **Intermediate scrutiny test.** The lawfulness of government classifications based on a **protected class** other than a suspect class or a fundamental right, such as a classification based on **gender**, is examined using an **intermediate scrutiny test**. This means that the government must have an important reason for treating persons differently because of their sex in order for such unequal treatment to be lawful. Applying this standard, many government classifications of persons based on sex are found to be unconstitutional. Under this standard, the courts must determine whether the government classification is "reasonably related" to a legitimate government purpose.

intermediate scrutiny test
A test that is applied to determine the constitutionality of classifications based on a protected class other than a suspect class or a fundamental right (e.g., gender).

Example The federal government's requirement that males (upon reaching the age of 18) must register for a military draft but that females do not have to register for the draft has been held to be constitutional by the U.S. Supreme Court.[19]

3. **Rational basis test.** The lawfulness of all government classifications that do not involve suspect or protected classes is examined using a **rational basis test**. Under this test, the courts uphold government regulation as long as there is a justifiable reason for the law. This standard permits much of the government regulation of business.

rational basis test
A test that is applied to determine the constitutionality of classifications by the government that do not involve a suspect class, a fundamental right, or a protected class (e.g., age).

Example Providing government subsidies to farmers but not to those in other occupations is permissible.

Example The federal government's Social Security program, which pays benefits to older members of society but not to younger members of society, is lawful. The reason is that older members of society have earned this right during the course of their lifetimes.

In the following case, the U.S. Supreme Court addressed the constitutionality of a federal statute that applied differently to same-sex married couples and heterosexual married couples.

CASE 4.6 U.S. SUPREME COURT CASE Equality

United States v. Windsor

133 S.Ct. 2675, 2013 U.S. Lexis 4921 (2013)
Supreme Court of the United States

"DOMA [Defense of Marriage Act] seeks to injure the very class New York seeks to protect. By doing so it violates basic due process and equal protection principles applicable to the Federal Government."

—Kennedy, Justice

Facts

Edith Windsor and Thea Spyer were same-sex partners who resided in the state of New York. They began their long-term relationship in 1963. In 2007, Windsor and Spyer traveled to Canada, where they were lawfully married. They continued to live in New York. The state of New York recognized the marriage of Windsor and Spyer. Spyer died in 2009 and left her entire estate to Windsor.

In 1996, Congress enacted the Defense of Marriage Act (DOMA). Section 3 of this federal statute defined *marriage* as a legal union between a husband and wife and defined *spouse* as a person of the opposite sex who is a husband or wife. Because of these definitions, DOMA denies same-sex married partners benefits allowed to heterosexual married couples in more than 1,000 federal statues and thousands of federal regulations. Thus, same-sex partners are denied Social Security benefits if a partner dies, are not allowed to file joint federal tax returns, and are denied countless other federal benefits allowed to heterosexual married couples.

When Spyer died, Winsor sought to claim the federal tax exemption for surviving spouses. This would have saved Windsor $363,053 in federal estate taxes. However, DOMA barred her from obtaining this exemption. Windsor paid the taxes but filed a lawsuit in U.S. district court alleging that Section 3 of DOMA violated the guarantee of equal protection provided

(case continues)

by the U.S. Constitution. The U.S. district court and the U.S. court of appeals ruled that the challenged provision of DOMA was unconstitutional and ordered the United States to pay Windsor a tax refund. The U.S. Supreme Court agreed to hear the appeal.

Issue

Is Section 3 of DOMA unconstitutional?

Language of the U.S. Supreme Court

DOMA writes inequality into the entire United States Code. By creating two contradictory marriage regimes within the same State, DOMA forces same-sex couples to live as married for the purpose of state law but unmarried for the purpose of federal law. This places same-sex couples in an unstable position of being in a second-tier marriage. DOMA divests married same-sex couples of the duties and responsibilities that are an essential part of married life.

Decision

The U.S. Supreme Court held that Section 3 of DOMA was unconstitutional, thus making federal benefits equally available to same-sex married couples and heterosexual married couples.

Ethics Questions

Because not all states recognize same-sex marriages, however, federal benefits are available only to same-sex partners in states that do recognize same-sex marriages. Does this result create another form of discrimination? In a future case, could the U.S. Supreme Court decide that all state laws that prohibit same-sex marriage violates the Equal Protection Clause of the U.S. Constitution?

In the following case, the U.S. Supreme Court addressed the constitutionality of a state law that prohibits affirmative action in college admissions.

CASE 4.7 *U.S. SUPREME COURT CASE Equal Protection Clause*

Schuette, Attorney General of Michigan v. Coalition to Defend Affirmative Action

134 S.Ct. 1623, 2014 U.S. Lexis 2932 (2014)
Supreme Court of the United States

"Our Constitution is color-blind, and neither knows nor tolerates classes among citizens."

—Harlan, Justice (1896)

Facts

The trustees and administrative decision makers at the University of Michigan, Michigan State University, and other public universities and colleges in Michigan used affirmative action programs that granted race-based preferences for minority applicants for admission. In 2006, the voters of Michigan adopted Proposal 2 which amended the state's constitution to prohibit state and other governmental entities in Michigan from granting race-based preferences. Under the terms of the amendment, which is now Article I, Section 26 of the Michigan constitution, race-based preferences cannot be part of the admissions process of public universities and colleges. The amendment passed by a margin of 58 percent to 42 percent of the voters.

Various organizations and groups that support affirmative action sued Michigan, alleging that the constitutional amendment that eliminates race-based preferences in state college admissions violates the Equal Protection Clause of the U.S. Constitution. The U.S. district court upheld the Michigan amendment. The U.S. court of appeals held that the amendment violated the Equal Protection Clause of the U.S. Constitution. The case was appealed to the U.S. Supreme Court.

Issue

Does the amendment to the Michigan constitution that eliminates race-based preferences in college admissions violate the Equal Protection Clause of the U.S. Constitution?

Language of the U.S. Supreme Court

—Kennedy, Justice

Government action that classifies individuals on the basis of race is inherently suspect and carries the danger of perpetuating the very racial divisions the polity seeks to transcend.

(case continues)

The electorate's instruction to governmental entities not to embark upon the course of race-defined and race-based preferences was adopted because the voters deemed a preference system to be unwise, on account of what voters may deem its latent potential to become itself a source of the very resentments and hostilities based on race that this Nation seeks to put behind it.

— Scalia, Justice – Concurring Opinion

The Equal Protection Clause cannot mean one thing when applied to one individual and something else when applied to a person of another color. If both are not accorded the same protection it is not equal. As Justice Harlan observed over a century ago, "Our Constitution is color-blind, and neither knows nor tolerates classes among citizens."

Decision

In a plurality decision of 6 to 2, the U.S. Supreme Court held that Michigan's constitutional amendment that eliminates race-based affirmative action in public college admission decisions does not violate the Equal Protection Clause of the U.S. Constitution.

Note

The case holds that states may enact laws that prohibit race-based affirmative action programs in college admissions. The case does not prohibit states from using race-based affirmative action programs in college admissions where no law prohibits such practice.

Ethics Questions

Do affirmative action programs in college admissions promote an important government and societal interest? Do affirmative action programs impair certain individuals' interests?

Due Process

Due Process Clause
A clause that provides that no person shall be deprived of "life, liberty, or property" without due process of the law.

The Fifth and Fourteenth Amendments to the U.S. Constitution contain a **Due Process Clause**. These clauses provide that no person shall be deprived of "life, liberty, or property" without due process of the law. The Due Process Clause of the Fifth Amendment applies to federal government action; that of the Fourteenth Amendment applies to state and local government action. It is important to understand that the government is not prohibited from taking a person's life, liberty, or property. However, the government must follow due process to do so. There are two categories of due process: *substantive* and *procedural*.

Substantive Due Process

substantive due process
A category of due process that requires government statutes, ordinances, regulations, or other laws be clear on their face and not overly broad in scope.

The **substantive due process** category of due process requires that government statutes, ordinances, regulations, and other laws be clear on their face and not overly broad in scope. The test of whether substantive due process is met is whether a "reasonable person" could understand the law to be able to comply with it. Laws that do not meet this test are declared *void for vagueness*.

Example A city ordinance making it illegal for persons to wear "clothes of the opposite sex" would be held unconstitutional as void for vagueness because a reasonable person could not clearly determine whether his or her conduct violates the law.

Most government laws, although often written in "legalese," are considered not to violate substantive due process.

Procedural Due Process

procedural due process
A category of due process that requires that the government give a person proper notice and hearing of the legal action before that person is deprived of his or her life, liberty, or property.

The **procedural due process** form of due process requires that the government give a person proper *notice* and *hearing* of legal action before that person is deprived of his or her life, liberty, or property.

Example If the federal government or a state government brings a criminal lawsuit against a defendant for the alleged commission of a crime, the government must notify the person of its intent (by charging the defendant with a crime) and provide the defendant with a proper hearing (a trial).

LINCOLN MEMORIAL, WASHINGTON DC

The United States has had many blemishes on its citizen's constitutional rights. For example, during World War II, Japanese Americans were involuntarily placed in camps. During the McCarthy hearings of the 1950s, citizens who were communists or associated with communists were "blacklisted" from their occupations, most notably in the film industry. Women did not get the right to vote until the Nineteenth Amendment was added to the U.S. Constitution in 1920. Prohibitions against interracial marriage were not made illegal until 1967.[20] And it was not until the mid-1960s that equal opportunity laws outlawed discrimination in the workplace based on race and sex.

Privileges and Immunities

The purpose of the U.S. Constitution is to promote nationalism. If the states were permitted to enact laws that favored their residents over out-of-state residents, the concept of nationalism would be defeated.

Article IV of the Constitution contains the **Privileges and Immunities Clause**, which provides that "The Citizens of each State shall be entitled to all Privileges and Immunities of Citizens in the several states." The Fourteenth Amendment contains the **Privileges or Immunities Clause**, which provides that "No State shall make or enforce any law that shall abridge the privileges or immunities of the citizens of the United States."

Privileges and Immunities Clauses
Constitutional provisions that prohibit states from enacting laws that unduly discriminate in favor of their residents.

Collectively, the clauses prohibit states from enacting laws that unduly discriminate in favor of their residents. Note that the clauses apply only to citizens; they do not protect corporations or aliens.

Example A state cannot enact a law that prevents residents of other states from owning property or businesses in that state.

Example Residents of one state have the right to travel freely to other states.

Courts have held that certain types of discrimination that favor state residents over nonresident are lawful.

Examples State universities are permitted to charge out-of-state residents higher tuition than in-state residents. States are also permitted to charge higher fees to nonresidents for hunting and fishing licenses.

Human rights violations are discussed in the following feature.

Global Law

Human Rights Violations in Myanmar

MYANMAR
The country of Myanmar (also called Burma) is ruled by a junta composed of its military generals. The country has been accused of human rights violations, including using child labor and forced labor, eliminating political dissidents, and following strict censorship. The United Nations has consistently censored Myanmar for human rights violations. Recently, because of improved conditions in Myanmar, the United States lifted some sanctions against trading with Myanmar.

Key Terms and Concepts

Amendments to the U.S. Constitution (76)
Article I of the U.S. Constitution (69)
Article II of the U.S. Constitution (69)
Article III of the U.S. Constitution (69)
Articles of Confederation (68)
Bicameral (69)
Bill of Rights (76)
Checks and balances (69)
Citizenship (83)
Civil Rights Act of 1964 (74)
Commerce Clause (72)
Commercial speech (78)
Constitutional Convention (68)
Declaration of Independence (68)
Dormant Commerce Clause (75)
Due Process Clause (86)
Effects on interstate commerce test (73)
Electoral College (69)
Electronic commerce (e-commerce) (75)
Enumerated powers (69)
Equal Protection Clause (83)
Establishment Clause (81)
Executive branch (69)
Federal government (68)
Federalism (69)
First Amendment (76)
Foreign Commerce Clause (73)
Fourteenth Amendment (83)
Free Exercise Clause (81)
Freedom of religion (81)
Freedom of speech (77)
Fully protected speech (77)
Fundamental right (83)
Gender (84)
Heart of Atlanta Motel v. United States (74)
Incorporation doctrine (76)
Indian Gaming Regulatory Act (73)
Intermediate scrutiny test (84)
Interstate commerce (73)
Intrastate commerce (74)
Judicial branch (69)
Legislative branch (69)
Limited protected speech (78)
Miller v. California (80)
National origin (83)
Obscene speech (80)
Offensive speech (78)
Police power (74)
Preemption doctrine (71)

Critical Legal Thinking Cases

4.1 Supremacy Clause The military regime of the country of Myanmar (previously called Burma) has been accused of major civil rights violations, including using forced and child labor, imprisoning and torturing political opponents, and harshly repressing ethnic minorities. These inhumane actions have been condemned by human rights organizations around the world. The state legislators of the state of Massachusetts were so appalled at these actions that they enacted a state statute banning the state government from purchasing goods and services from any company that did business with Myanmar.

In the meantime, the U.S. Congress enacted a federal statute that delegated power to the president of the United States to regulate U.S. dealings with Myanmar. The federal statute (1) banned all aid to the government of Myanmar except for humanitarian assistance, (2) authorized the president to impose economic sanctions against Myanmar, and (3) authorized the president to develop a comprehensive multilateral strategy to bring democracy to Myanmar.

The National Foreign Trade Council—a powerful Washington DC–based trade association with more than 500 membercompanies—filed a lawsuit against Massachusetts to have the state law declared unconstitutional. The council argued that the Massachusetts "anti-Myanmar" statute conflicted with the federal statute and that under the Supremacy Clause that makes federal law the "supreme law of the land" the state statute was preempted by the federal statute. Does the Massachusetts anti-Myanmar statute violate the Supremacy Clause of the U.S. Constitution? *Crosby, Secretary of Administration and Finance of Massachusetts v. National Foreign Trade Council*, 530 U.S. 363, 120 S.Ct. 2288, 2000 U.S. Lexis 4153 (Supreme Court of the United States, 2000)

4.2 Establishment Clause McCreary County and Pulaski County (the counties), Kentucky, placed in their courthouses a large, gold-framed copy of the Ten Commandments. In both courthouses, the Ten Commandments were prominently displayed so that visitors could see them. The Ten Commandments hung alone, not with other paintings and such. The American Civil Liberties Union (ACLU) of Kentucky sued the counties in U.S. district court, alleging that the placement of the Ten Commandments in the courthouses violated the Establishment Clause of the U.S. Constitution. The U.S. district court granted a preliminary injunction ordering the removal of the Ten Commandments from both courthouses. The counties added copies of the Magna Carta, the Declaration of Independence, the Bill of Rights, and other nonreligious items to the display of the Ten Commandments. The U.S. district court reissued the injunction against this display, and the U.S. court of appeals affirmed. The counties appealed to the U.S. Supreme Court. Does the display of the Ten Commandments in the counties' courthouses violate the Establishment Clause? *McCreary County, Kentucky v. American Civil Liberties Union of Kentucky*, 545 U.S. 844, 125 S.Ct. 2722, 2005 U.S. Lexis 5211 (Supreme Court of the United States, 2005)

4.3 Supremacy Clause The Clean Air Act, a federal statute, establishes national air pollution standards for fleet vehicles such as buses, taxicabs, and trucks. The South Coast Air Quality Management District (South Coast) is a political entity of the state of California. South Coast establishes air pollution standards for the Los Angeles, California, metropolitan area. South Coast enacted fleet rules that prohibited the purchase or lease by public and private fleet operators of vehicles that do not meet stringent air pollution standards set by South Coast. South Coast's fleet emission standards are more stringent than those set by the federal Clean Air Act. The Engine Manufacturers Association (Association), a trade association that represents manufacturers and sellers of vehicles, sued South Coast, claiming that South Coast's fleet rules are preempted by the federal Clean Air Act. The U.S. District Court and the U.S. Court of Appeals upheld South Coast's fleet rules. The Association appealed to the U.S. Supreme Court. Are South Coast's fleet rules preempted by the federal Clean Air Act? *Engine Manufacturers Association v. South Coast Air Quality Management District*, 541 U.S. 246, 124 S.Ct. 1756, 2004 U.S. Lexis 3232 (Supreme Court of the United States, 2004)

4.4 Due Process The Federal Communications Commission (FCC) is a federal administrative agency that regulates television and radio. The FCC is authorized to restrict indecent material on television during the hours of 6:00 A.M. to 10:00 P.M. In 2001, the FCC issued guidelines stating that material that dwelled on or repeated at length offensive descriptions or depictions violated federal communications laws. In both the 2002 and 2003 Billboard Music Awards program televised live by Fox Television Stations, Inc. (Fox), a person used the f*** word once in each broadcast. In 2003, an episode of *NYPD Blue*, a regular television show broadcast by ABC Television Network (ABC), showed the nude buttocks of an adult female for approximately seven seconds as she entered a shower.

In 2004, the FCC issued guidelines that stipulated that fleeting expletives and momentary nudity on television was a violation of federal communications law. The FCC applied the 2004 guidelines retroactively and issued orders finding that both Fox and ABC violated communications law by showing fleeting expletives and momentary nudity on television in 2002 and 2003. The FCC assessed a $1.24 million penalty on ABC. Fox and ABC challenged the orders, alleging that there had been a violation of the Fifth Amendment's Due Process Clause because they had not been notified prior to the events occurring that fleeting expletives and momentary nudity violated communications law. Did the FCC violate the Fifth Amendment's due process rights of Fox and ABC? *Federal Communications Commission v. Fox Television Stations, Inc.*, 132 S.Ct. 2307, 2012 U.S. Lexis 4661 (Supreme Court of the United States, 2012)

4.5 Commerce Clause State departments of motor vehicles (DMVs) register automobiles and issue driver's licenses. State DMVs require automobile owners and drivers to provide personal information—including a person's name, address, telephone number, vehicle description, Social Security number, medical information, and a photograph—as a condition for registering an automobile or obtaining a driver's license. Many states' DMVs sold this personal information to individuals, advertisers, and businesses. These sales generated significant revenues for the states.

After receiving thousands of complaints from individuals whose personal information had been sold, the U.S. Congress enacted the Driver's Privacy Protection Act (DPPA) of 1994. This federal statute prohibits a state from selling the personal information of a person unless the state obtains that person's affirmative consent to do so. South Carolina sued the United States, alleging that the federal government violated the Commerce Clause by adopting the DPPA. Was the Driver's Privacy Protection Act properly enacted by the federal government pursuant to its Commerce Clause power? *Reno, Attorney General of the United States v. Condon, Attorney General of South Carolina*, 528 U.S. 141, 120 S.Ct. 666, 2000 U.S. Lexis 503 (Supreme Court of the United States, 2000)

Ethics Cases

Ethical

4.6 Ethics Case Vaccines are biological preparations usually containing an agent that resembles a disease-causing microorganism, which is often administered by needle and which improves immunity to a particular disease. Vaccines are subject to federal premarket approval of the federal Food and Drug Administration (FDA). The elimination of communicable diseases through vaccination became one of the greatest achievements of public health in the twentieth century. However, harm caused by sideeffects to some individuals led to a massive increase in vaccine-related tort litigation against the manufacturers of vaccines. One group of manufacturers that was subject to such lawsuits was the manufacturers who made the vaccine against diphtheria, tetanus, and pertussis (DTP). Because of the lawsuits, two of the three domestic manufacturers of DTP withdrew from the market. In response, the U.S. Congress enacted the National Childhood Vaccine Injury Act (NCVIA) of 1986. One of the provisions of the act stated,

No vaccine manufacturer shall be liable in a civil action for damages arising from a vaccine-related injury or death associated with the administration of a vaccine after October 1, 1988, if the injury or death resulted from side effects that were unavoidable even though the vaccine was properly prepared and was accompanied by proper directions and warnings.

When Hanna Bruesewitz was one year old, her pediatrician administered doses of DTP vaccine that was manufactured by Lederle Laboratories (later purchased by Wyeth LLC). Hanna immediately started to experience seizures and has suffered seizures since being vaccinated. Hanna's parents filed a lawsuit against Lederle, alleging that the company was liable for strict liability and negligent design of the vaccine. The U.S. District Court granted Wyeth summary judgment, holding that Bruesewitz's causes of action was preempted by the NCVIA. The U.S. Court of Appeals affirmed the judgment. Bruesewitz appealed to the U.S. Supreme Court. Does the preemption provision in the federal NCVIA bar state law design-defect product liability claims against vaccine manufacturers? Is it ethical for vaccine manufacturers to be absolved from liability by federal law? What is the public policy underlying the federal law? *Bruesewitz v. Wyeth LLC*, 131 S.Ct. 1068, 2011 U.S. Lexis 1085 (Supreme Court of the United States, 2011)

4.7 Ethics Case Pursuant to enabling statutes, two federal administrative agencies—the Federal Trade Commission (FTC) and the Federal Communications Commission (FCC)—created the national do-not-call registry. The national do-not-call registry is a list that contains the personal telephone numbers of telephone users who have voluntarily placed themselves on this list, indicating that they do not want to receive unsolicited calls from commercial telemarketers. Commercial telemarketers are prohibited from calling phone numbers that have been placed on the do-not-call registry. Telemarketers must pay an annual fee to access the phone numbers on the registry so that they can delete those numbers from their solicitation lists. The national do-not-call registry restrictions apply only to telemarketers' calls made by or on behalf of sellers of goods or services. Charitable and fund-raising calls are exempt from the do-not-call registry's restrictions. Persons who do not voluntarily place their phone numbers on the do-not-call registry may still receive unsolicited telemarketers' calls.

Mainstream Marketing Services, Inc., and other telemarketers sued the FTC and the FCC in several lawsuits, alleging that their free speech rights were violated and that the do-not-call registry was unconstitutional. The FTC and FCC defended the list, arguing that unsolicited telemarketing calls constituted commercial speech that could properly be regulated by the government's do-not-call registry's restrictions. The separate lawsuits were consolidated for appeal. Is unsolicited telemarketing calls commercial speech that is constitutionally regulated by the do-not-call registry restrictions? Do telemarketers act ethically in calling persons with their promotions and sales pitches? Did the telemarketers act ethically in challenging the law? *Mainstream Marketing Services, Inc. v. Federal Trade Commission and Federal Communications Commission*, 358 F.3d 1228, 2004 U.S. App. Lexis 2564 (United States Court of Appeals for the Tenth Circuit, 2004)

Notes

1. To be elected to Congress, an individual must be a U.S. citizen, either naturally born or granted citizenship. To serve in the Senate, a person must be 30 years of age or older. To serve in the House of Representatives, a person must be 25 years of age or older.
2. To be president, a person must be 35 years of age or older and a natural citizen of the United States. According to the Twenty-Second Amendment to the Constitution, a person can serve only two full terms as president.
3. Federal court judges and justices are appointed by the president, with the consent of the Senate.
4. The principle that the U.S. Supreme Court is the final arbiter of the U.S. Constitution evolved from *Marbury v. Madison*, 1 Cranch 137, 5 U.S. 137, 1803 U.S. Lexis 352 (Supreme Court of the United States, 1803). In that case, the Supreme Court held that a judiciary statute enacted by Congress was unconstitutional.
5. Article VI, Section 2.
6. Article I, Section 8, clause 3.
7. 25 U.S.C. Sections 2701–2721.
8. 317 U.S. 111, 63 S.Ct. 82, 1942 U.S. Lexis 1046 (Supreme Court of the United States).
9. 425 U.S. 748, 96 S.Ct. 1817, 1976 U.S. Lexis 55 (Supreme Court of the United States).
10. *Chaplinsky v. New Hampshire*, 315 U.S. 568, 62 S.Ct. 766, 1942 U.S. Lexis 851 (Supreme Court of the United States).
11. *Brandenburg v. Ohio*, 395 U.S. 444, 89 S.Ct. 1827, 1969 U.S. Lexis 1367 (Supreme Court of the United States).
12. *Beauharnais v. Illinois*, 343 U.S. 250, 72 S.Ct. 725, 1952 U.S. Lexis 2799 (Supreme Court of the United States).
13. *New York v. Ferber*, 458 U.S. 747, 102 S.Ct. 334, 1982 U.S. Lexis 12 (Supreme Court of the United States).
14. *Roth v. United States*, 354 U.S. 476, 77 S.Ct. 1304, 1957 U.S. Lexis 587 (Supreme Court of the United States).
15. Justice Stewart in *Jacobellis v. Ohio*, 378 U.S. 184, 84 S.Ct. 1676, 1964 U.S. Lexis 822 (Supreme Court of the United States).
16. 413 U.S. 15, 93 S.Ct. 2607, 1973 U.S. Lexis 149 (Supreme Court of the United States).
17. *Wallace v. Jaffree*, 472 U.S. 38, 105 S.Ct. 2479, 1985 U.S. Lexis 91 (Supreme Court of the United States).
18. 508 U.S. 520, 113 S.Ct. 2217, 1993 U.S. Lexis 4022 (Supreme Court of the United States).
19. *Rostker v. Goldberg*, 453 U.S. 57, 101 S.Ct. 2646, 1981 U.S. Lexis 126 (Supreme Court of the United States).
20. *Loving v. Virginia*, 388 U.S. 1, 87 S.Ct. 1817 (Supreme Court of the United States).

CASE Statute of Limitations or Laches?

Moffitt v. Moffitt

3PA-06-01070 CI, 6936 August 8, 2014
Supreme Court of Alaska
Before: Fabe, Chief Justice, Winfree, Stowers, Maassen, and Bolger, Justices
Opinion by, Bolger, Justice

Introduction

Linda Moffitt filed a lawsuit as her mother's guardian and conservator and the successor trustee of her parents' living trusts, seeking to rescind or reform a deed they executed in 1995 and a contract they signed in 1998. The superior court dismissed Linda's claims, reasoning that the statutes of limitations had run before Linda filed her lawsuit in 2005. The primary question in this appeal is whether the superior court properly applied the statutes of limitations. We conclude that Linda's mostly equitable claims are subject to the defense of laches, and the statutes of limitations do not apply to these claims.

Facts and Proceedings

In 1992 Leonard and Betty Moffitt created two trusts to provide lifetime support for the surviving spouse, and then to pass the trusts' assets to their children. In 1995 Leonard and Betty agreed to sell their family farm to their son, Tracy, and his wife, Kathy, and deeded part of the property to Tracy and Kathy. In 1998 Leonard and Betty signed a contract memorializing the 1995 agreement and providing that the rest of the farm would be sold to Tracy and Kathy after Leonard and Betty died. Leonard died in 2000 and Betty was diagnosed with dementia in 2001. Their daughter, Linda Moffitt, became personal representative of Leonard's estate, Betty's guardian and conservator, and successor trustee of Leonard's and Betty's trusts.

In 2005 Linda, in her capacity as guardian, conservator, and trustee, brought a civil suit against Tracy and Kathy seeking damages and rescission of the contract. In 2009 Linda filed an amended complaint, adding an alternate request for reformation and containing five counts: conversion, diminished capacity, undue influence, unconscionability, and unjust enrichment. In Leonard's probate proceeding, Linda petitioned the court for the sale of the real property free of contract. The probate court denied the petition. In 2010 Linda moved to consolidate the civil case with the probate case, but the motion was denied.

The superior court ultimately dismissed part of the civil case on summary judgment, concluding that, although the limitations periods were tolled during Leonard's and Betty's disabilities, Linda's claims were barred by the two-year tort statute of limitations and the three-year contract statute of limitations. The court noted Linda may retain claims for certain profits received by Tracy and Kathy and for repayment of an allegedly unpaid loan, and it denied summary judgment as to those collateral matters. The superior court awarded Tracy and Kathy \$80,025.75 in attorney's fees and \$9,523.08 in costs. Linda appealed. Betty died before oral argument in the fall of 2013.

Standard of Review

"We review a grant or denial of summary judgment de novo."[1] "[W]e review de novo questions regarding the applicable statute of limitations, the interpretation of that statute, and whether that statute bars a claim."[2] We review the denial of a motion to consolidate for abuse of discretion.[3]

Discussion

The Laches Defense Applies to Linda's Equitable Claims

Linda's claims are equitable claims

Linda's main claims are for rescission or reformation of the 1995 deed and the 1998 agreement due to diminished capacity, undue influence, and unconscionability. She argued that the deed and the agreement are invalid and asked that the superior court declare these transactions "null and void or voidable" or reform them "to correct any unconscionable terms and to avoid unjust enrichment."

A claim for rescission may be either legal or equitable. "Rescission *at law* is a suit based upon rescission already accomplished."[4] "Rescission at law occurs where at least one of the parties to a contract rescinds the contract and then turns to a court for enforcement of that rescission and an award of damages."[5] In contrast, "rescission in equity occurs only upon a court's decree. In those cases, the court must intervene both to rescind the agreement and to award damages."[6] In other words: "Rescission is equitable if the complaint asks the court to order

(case continues)

rescission of the contract, and is legal if the court is asked to enforce a completed rescission."[7]

Here, Linda had not rescinded the contract when she filed her claim. Rather, she asked the court for an order declaring both transactions null and void, that is, rescinded. And Linda alleged adequate grounds for rescission: undue influence[8] and diminished capacity.[9] Thus, it appears that she has pleaded claims for equitable rescission.

Linda's complaint also requested the remedy of reformation. "Reformation is an equitable remedy by which a court alters the terms of a written instrument to make the writing conform with the meaning that the parties agreed upon."[10] As noted above, Linda's complaint specifically requested that the court reform the 1995 deed and the 1998 agreement. Linda's reformation claims are also equitable in nature.

Linda's equitable claims are not subject to a statute of limitations, but are subject to laches

Equitable claims for rescission or reformation of a contract may be barred by the doctrine of laches.[11] This doctrine "creates an equitable defense when a party delays asserting a claim for an unconscionable period."[12] To apply this defense, "[a] court must find both an unreasonable delay in seeking relief and resulting prejudice to the defendant."[13]

Several courts have held that statutes of limitations do not control the time limit for asserting equitable claims.[14] For example, the Pennsylvania Supreme Court stated: "[B]ecause statutes of limitation are not controlling in equity, but only provide guidance in determining the reasonableness of any delay, this Court has allowed suits in equity to proceed despite significant delays in bringing the action."[15] Similarly, the South Carolina Supreme Court noted "that the statute of limitations does not apply to actions in equity."[16]

This rule was applied by the Ninth Circuit to a dispute in the Alaska territorial court around the time of statehood.[17] And it is consistent with our determination in the inverse situation that the defense of laches does not apply to a legal claim governed by a statute of limitations.[18] We are not aware of any statutory provision that would conflict with our decision to apply the defense of laches to this case. We therefore conclude that Linda's equitable claims for reformation and rescission are controlled by the doctrine of laches. The laches defense should also apply to any associated restitution claims.[19]

In the superior court, Tracy and Kathy moved for summary judgment based on the statutes of limitations for tort and contract claims. In response, Linda asserted that these statutes did not apply to her equitable claims. But neither party raised the issue of laches in the motion papers, so the superior court did not have the occasion to address this doctrine. And we cannot determine on appeal whether there are factual issues that may preclude summary judgment on the laches defense. We must therefore reverse the summary judgment order as to the equitable claims and remand this case for further proceedings.

The Contract and Tort Statutes of Limitations Apply to Linda's Legal Claims

Some of Linda's claims are clearly legal claims—particularly her claim for punitive damages.[20] Linda argues that her complaint asserts claims regarding the ownership and possession of the property. Thus, she contends the real property statutes of limitations apply. But Alaska law prevents the application of real property statutes of limitations to this case.

In *Bauman v. Day*,[21] the superior court set aside a foreclosure where the defaulting plaintiff buyers argued their original land sale agreement with the defendant sellers was invalid.[22] We affirmed that decision but rejected the plaintiffs' argument that their separate action contesting the validity of the sales contract fell under a statute of limitations for real property.[23] We reasoned that the salient issue there was "not the ownership interest itself but improprieties in the bargaining that resulted in the conveyance of that interest to the Baumans."[24] Here, as in *Bauman*, Linda's claim is not subject to a real property statute of limitations because, as discussed above, her claim attacks the legality of the land sale contracts.

We thus affirm the superior court's decision that the tort and contract statutes of limitations apply to Linda's legal claims. We note that in 1997 the statute of limitations for contract cases changed from six years to three years under the newly adopted AS 09.10.053.[25]

Finally, while there are substantial questions about the operation of the tolling statute, AS 09.10.140(a), they were not adequately addressed in the briefing on appeal. We thus do not decide whether the cases applying the tolling statute to a minor's claims, even when the minor has competent parents,[26] also apply to toll an incompetent plaintiff's claims after appointment of a guardian.

It Was Not an Abuse of Discretion for the Superior Court to Decline to Consolidate this Case with the Probate Proceedings

Linda points out that she attempted to sell the farm in probate court, but the probate court denied her motion. The superior court also denied her motion to consolidate, and Linda argues that this ruling was

(case continues)

an abuse of discretion. In *C.L. v. P.C.S.*, however, we found no abuse of discretion in the trial court's denial of a motion to consolidate the probate case with the civil case where the moving party was not prejudiced and the trial court had reasonably considered the moving party's arguments.[27]

The superior court denied Linda's motion to consolidate, reasoning that: (1) the motion was procedurally defective because venue of the probate case had not yet been changed from Anchorage to Palmer; (2) consolidation was not appropriate because the probate proceedings involved issues beyond the dispute over the family farm; and (3) denying consolidation posed little risk of delay or duplicative litigation. These reasons are sufficient to support the superior court's decision, and Linda has not explained how she has been prejudiced. We conclude that the superior court did not abuse its discretion when it denied the motion for consolidation.

Conclusion

The superior court's order of dismissal is VACATED. The attorney's fees and costs awards are therefore also VACATED. In view of our disposition, it is not necessary to address the other issues raised in this appeal.

---

1. *Alaska Civil Liberties Union v. State*, 122 P.3d 781, 785 (Alaska 2005) (citations omitted).
2. *Gefre v. Davis Wright Tremaine, LLP*, 306 P.3d 1264, 1271 (Alaska 2013) (citing *Weimer v. Cont'l Car & Truck, LLC*, 237 P.3d 610, 613 (Alaska 2010)).
3. *C. L. v. P.C.S.*, 17 P.3d 769, 772 (Alaska 2001) (citing *Foltz-Nelson Architects v. Kobylk*, 749 P.2d 1347, 1349 n.2 (Alaska 1988)).
4. *Knaebel v. Heiner*, 663 P.2d 551, 554 (Alaska 1983) (emphasis in original).
5. *Commercial Recycling Ctr., Ltd. v. Hobbs Indus., Inc.*, 228 P.3d 93, 98 (Alaska 2010) (citation omitted).
6. *Id.* at 99 (citation omitted).
7. 12A C.J.S. *Cancellation of Instruments* § 5 (2014) (citation omitted).
8. *Id.* § 46 ("Alone, or accompanied by other inequitable circumstances, undue influence is a ground for the cancellation of instruments.").
9. *Id.* § 62 ("As a general rule, total incapacity to contract because of unsoundness of mind constitutes a ground for the rescission and cancellation of contracts executed by persons in that condition.").
10. *Wasser & Winters Co. v. Ritchie Bros. Auctioneers (Am.)*, 185 P.3d 73, 77 (Alaska 2008) (citing Restatement (Second) of Contracts § 155 cmt. a (1981)).
11. *Cf. Vockner v. Erickson*, 712 P.2d 379, 384 (Alaska 1986) (evaluating laches defense to a claim for reformation where no prejudice from delay was shown).
12. *Offshore Sys.-Kenai v. State, Dep't of Transp. & Pub. Facilities*, 282 P.3d 348, 354 (Alaska 2012) (quoting *State, Dep't of Commerce & Econ. Dev. v. Schnell*, 8 P.3d 351, 358–59 (Alaska 2000) (internal quotation marks omitted)).
13. *Id.* (alteration in original) (quoting *Schnell*, 8 P.3d at 358–59) (internal quotation marks omitted).
14. *E.g., Holmberg v. Armbrecht*, 327 U.S. 392, 396 (1946) ("Traditionally and for good reasons, statutes of limitation are not controlling measures of equitable relief."); *Castner v. First Nat'l Bank of Anchorage*, 278 F.2d 376, 385 (9th Cir. 1960); *see also* 30A C.J.S. *Equity* § 164 (2014) (citations omitted) ("Statutes of limitations, . . . as ordinarily enacted, apply only to actions at law, and do not in terms apply to suits in equity.").
15. *United Nat'l Ins. Co. v. J.H. France Refractories Co.*, 668 A.2d 120, 124 (Pa. 1995) (citations and internal quotation marks omitted).
16. *Dixon v. Dixon*, 608 S.E.2d 849, 855 (S.C. 2005).
17. *Castner*, 278 F.2d at 385 (holding that the statute of limitations did not apply to an equitable claim).
18. *Kodiak Elec. Ass'n, Inc. v. DeLaval Turbine, Inc.*, 694 P.2d 150, 157 (Alaska 1984) ("The defense of laches is inapplicable to an action at law.").
19. *See* Restatement (Third) of Restitution and Unjust Enrichment § 70 (2011).
20. *See Loomis Elec. Prot., Inc. v. Schaefer*, 549 P.2d 1341, 1344 (Alaska 1976) (holding action for damages is an action at law).
21. 892 P.2d 817 (Alaska 1995).
22. *Id.* at 822–23.
23. *Id.* at 824–25.
24. *Id.* at 825.
25. The three-year contract statute of limitations applies to all claims arising on or after August 7, 1997, and the prior six-year statute of limitations applies to claims arising before that date. *See* ch. 26, § 55, SLA 1997; 1997 House Journal 1796.
26. *See Grober v. State, Dep't of Revenue*, 956 P.2d 1230, 1233 (Alaska 1998) (quoting *Hanson v. Kake Tribal Corp.*, 939 P.2d 1320, 1326 (Alaska 1997)); *see also Sands ex rel. Sands v. Green*, 156 P.3d 1130, 1133 (Alaska 2007).
27. 17 P.3d 769, 773 (Alaska 2001).

CASE *Bush Planes, LLC*

RBG Bush Planes, LLC v. Kirk

3AN-12-10793 CI, 6978 January 9, 2015
Supreme Court of Alaska
Before: Winfree, Stowers, and Bolger, Justices
Opinion by, Bolger, Justice

Introduction

Robert Gillam and two of his business ventures (collectively, Gillam) filed suit, alleging that the Alaska Public Offices Commission should not be allowed to investigate and decide whether Gillam had committed certain campaign finance violations. Gillam alleged that both the Executive Director and the Chair of the Commission were biased and that further consideration by the Commission would violate his right to due process protected by the Alaska and federal constitutions and his Alaska constitutional right to a fair investigation. The superior court concluded that Gillam's claims are not ripe and that Gillam has failed to exhaust his administrative remedies. We agree that there is an administrative recusal procedure for Gillam's state law claims and that Gillam must exhaust that remedy before bringing his state law claims to court. We also agree that Gillam's federal due process claim is not ripe because the recusal procedure may resolve that claim.

Facts and Proceedings

The Alaska Public Offices Commission is appointed by the governor[1] and charged with interpreting and enforcing Alaska's campaign finance laws.[2] In that capacity, the Commission investigates and adjudicates claims that those laws have been violated. There are five commissioners[3] who appoint a chairperson[4] and who may employ an executive director, as well as any additional staff they require.[5]

A person who suspects a violation of campaign finance laws may file a complaint with the Commission, and the complaint must satisfy several formal requirements.[6] When the Commission receives the complaint, its staff determines whether the complaint satisfies those formal requirements, and, if so, the staff investigates the complaint and prepares a report of its findings.[7] Finally, the Commission holds a hearing and issues a decision,[8] which is appealable to the superior court.[9]

In August 2012 Joel Natwick filed a complaint with the Commission against the three appellants: Gillam, RBG Bush Planes, and McKinley Capital Management. The Commission staff accepted the complaint over Gillam's objection that it failed to meet the formal requirements mentioned above, and it asked Gillam to produce several documents for purposes of an investigation. The Commission requested that an Administrative Law Judge (ALJ) be assigned to oversee the Natwick proceedings, and one was assigned.

In September 2012 there was apparently a meeting between Curtis Thayer, a Deputy Commissioner of the Department of Administration, and appellee Paul Dauphinais, the Executive Director of the Commission. Thayer later testified in a deposition that, at the meeting, Dauphinais asked for a budget increase so the Commission could investigate and thus "get" and "ruin" Gillam. At the same meeting, Dauphinais allegedly mentioned a conversation he had with the Securities and Exchange Commission (SEC) regarding purported wrongdoing that "would bring Mr. Gillam's business down."

Gillam filed suit in superior court in November 2012 against Elizabeth Hickerson, in her capacity as Chair of the Commission, and Paul Dauphinais, in his capacity as Executive Director of the Commission.[10] Gillam invoked 42 U.S.C. §§ 1983 and 1988, as well as provisions of the federal and Alaska constitutions, claiming his constitutional rights were being violated in the Natwick matter due to bias on the part of the Commission. Gillam asked that the court enjoin the Commission from being involved in any way with the Natwick complaint and appoint a special investigator to investigate the matter. He also asked that an independent ALJ or the superior court conduct any hearing to adjudicate the complaint.

Hickerson and Dauphinais moved to dismiss under Alaska Civil Rule 12(b)(6). They also moved to stay discovery pending the court's decision on dismissal. Gillam opposed the motions to dismiss and moved for a preliminary injunction to stay the Natwick proceedings. Gillam attached to his motion a portion of the transcript of Thayer's deposition testimony as

(case continues)

well as an affidavit from former Commission staff member Vullnet Greva to demonstrate the Commission's alleged bias against Gillam.

The superior court granted Gillam leave to submit supplemental briefing in response to the motions to dismiss and to address all pending discovery motions. Gillam submitted briefing, to which he appended additional evidence—notes from an interview with a former Commission attorney. The superior court then informed the parties that, because of the evidence that had been introduced post-pleading, it would convert the Rule 12(b)(6) motion to dismiss to a Alaska Civil Rule 56 motion for summary judgment. The superior court granted summary judgment to Hickerson and Dauphinais. Gillam now appeals to this court.

Standard of Review

"We review grants of summary judgment de novo, 'draw[ing] all factual inferences in favor of, and view[ing] the facts in the light most favorable to, the party against whom summary judgment was granted.' "[11] "We will affirm the grant of summary judgment when the record presents no genuine issues of material fact and the movant was entitled to judgment as a matter of law."[12]

"Whether a type of claim generally requires exhaustion of administrative remedies is a legal question that we review *de novo*."[13] But "[w]e review for abuse of discretion a superior court's determination of whether a plaintiff exhausted those remedies or whether the failure to exhaust should be excused."[14] Questions of ripeness are reviewed de novo.[15] An Alaska Civil Rule 56(f) decision is reviewed for abuse of discretion.[16]

Discussion

The superior court granted summary judgment to Hickerson for three reasons: (1) failure to exhaust administrative remedies; (2) lack of ripeness; and (3) failure to allege "facts sufficient to overcome the presumption of integrity to which Ms. Hickerson and the other commissioners [were] entitled." The court also granted summary judgment to Dauphinais, noting that although the allegations against him were "more troubling," judicial intervention was nonetheless "improper" based on the claim's lack of ripeness.

As noted above, Gillam alleged claims under 42 U.S.C. § 1983 and the Alaska Constitution.[17] Specifically, he argued that the Commission violated the Fourteenth Amendment to the United States Constitution and article I, section 7 of the Alaska Constitution. Both constitutional provisions protect one's right not to be deprived of life, liberty, or property without due process of law,[18] but the Alaska Constitution additionally protects "[t]he right of all persons to fair and just treatment in the course of legislative and executive investigations."[19]

With respect to Gillam's state constitutional claim, we agree with the superior court that Gillam failed to exhaust his administrative remedies. As to the federal constitutional claim, we conclude that although exhaustion of remedies was not required, the claim was not ripe for review. Thus, we affirm the superior court's grant of summary judgment against Gillam.[20]

Exhaustion of Administrative Remedies

To determine "whether a complaint was correctly dismissed for failure to exhaust administrative remedies, we must decide whether (a) exhaustion of remedies was required; (b) the complainant exhausted those remedies; and (c) the failure to exhaust remedies was excused."[21]

Gillam was required to exhaust administrative remedies only with respect to his state constitutional claim

As a general matter, "[e]xhaustion is required if a statute or regulation provides for administrative review."[22] "[C]ertain 'pure issues of law,' most notably constitutional issues [and] certain questions of statutory validity, are 'within the special expertise' of the court, ... [but] only the purest legal questions, requiring no factual context, are exempt from the exhaustion requirement."[23] In other words, "exhaustion may be required when non-constitutional issues are present or when a factual context is needed for deciding the constitutional issue."[24]

In Commission proceedings,[25] the Alaska Administrative Procedure Act (APA) provides that "[a] party may request the disqualification of a hearing officer or agency member by filing an affidavit, before the taking of evidence at a hearing, stating with particularity the grounds upon which it is claimed that a fair and impartial hear cannot be accorded."[26] The resolution of Gillam's state constitutional claim would benefit from the type of factual record developed in an administrative resolution of such a request.[27] We thus conclude that Gillam would generally be required to exhaust this remedy before seeking judicial intervention.[28]

But because Gillam raised a federal constitutional claim under section 1983, our analysis does not end here. In *Patsy v. Board of Regents*, the

(case continues)

United States Supreme Court held that a plaintiff need not exhaust state administrative remedies before filing a section 1983 suit in federal court,[29] and in *Felder v. Casey*, the Court expanded that holding to litigation commenced in state courts.[30] This court applied that rule in *Diedrich v. City of Ketchikan*, concluding that "federal law does not permit states to require exhaustion of administrative remedies as a prerequisite to the maintenance of a section 1983 claim."[31]

We disagree with the superior court's conclusion that a departure from *Diedrich* is warranted because Gillam's alleged injury involves a biased tribunal, thus raising the question of "whether and how [the injury] may be avoided in the first place." The superior court cited two Ninth Circuit decisions, *Flangas v. State Bar of Nevada*[32] and *Stivers v. Pierce*,[33] as establishing that a section 1983 plaintiff alleging bias "has a duty to avail himself of agency recusal procedures if they are provided for by statute." But neither case so decisively supports this proposition.

First, the decision in *Flangas* was based on the doctrine of abstention, under which a federal court "must refrain from hearing constitutional challenges to state action under certain circumstances in which a federal action is regarded as an improper intrusion on the right of a state to enforce its laws in its own courts."[34] Under this doctrine, such intrusion may nonetheless be warranted under "exceptional circumstances."[35] In *Flangas*, an attorney had sued in federal district court under section 1983, alleging bias on the part of the Nevada Supreme Court justices involved in a disciplinary proceeding against him.[36] The Ninth Circuit concluded that because the attorney "fail[ed] to utilize Nevada's disqualification procedures," the court was "unable to determine" whether the case presented "exceptional circumstances" necessary to warrant a federal injunction of the pending state court proceeding.[37] *Flangas* thus stands for the proposition that exhaustion of remedies may be required to enjoin a state court proceeding; it does not show that exhaustion of state administrative remedies can be required to *bring* a section 1983 claim in state court.

Stivers is similarly inapposite. In that case, the Ninth Circuit considered whether a section 1983 plaintiff had waived the issue of tribunal bias by failing to ask for recusal of the allegedly biased tribunal member before the tribunal adjudicated the underlying matter.[38] Citing only cases dealing with abstention, the court noted that "[w]here state law provides a mechanism for seeking recusal, the litigant *may* be required to avail himself of that mechanism."[39] But the court found that no recusal procedures existed,[40] and accordingly, it had no occasion to address the special protection afforded section 1983 claims under *Patsy* and its progeny.[41] Based on the clear rule articulated in this United States Supreme Court precedent,[42] we conclude that Gillam's federal constitutional claim is saved from dismissal on exhaustion grounds because it was brought under section 1983.[43]

Based on our decision in *Diedrich*, however, we also conclude that Gillam's state constitutional claim may be separated from his section 1983 claim for purposes of exhaustion. In *Diedrich*, the plaintiff challenged the termination of his employment with the City of Ketchikan under both section 1983 and other grounds.[44] In particular, he alleged that the City "had breached the covenant of good faith and fair dealing implied in his employment contract," that his discharge was retaliatory, and "that the City had violated his constitutional rights to substantive due process (premised in part on 42 U.S.C. § 1983) by offering a pretext for his termination."[45] The superior court treated the suit as an administrative appeal, holding that it was untimely under the applicable statute of limitations, which is 30 days.[46] On appeal, this court held that although the plaintiff's section 1983 claim could not be dismissed for lack of timeliness, the plaintiff's suit was nonetheless "properly considered an administrative appeal" with respect to the *non*-section 1983 claims, which were "appropriately dismissed as untimely."[47]

Thus, under *Diedrich*, Gillam was required to exhaust his administrative remedies with respect to his state constitutional claims, even though they are presented in the same action as his section 1983 claim.

The APA provides for administrative review of Gillam's bias claims

Gillam contends that exhaustion was not required because no administrative remedies existed. But as noted above, a party to a Commission proceeding "may request the disqualification of a hearing officer or agency member by filing an affidavit, before the taking of evidence at a hearing, stating with particularity the grounds upon which it is claimed that a fair and impartial hearing cannot be accorded."[48]

As an initial matter, we reject Gillam's contention that "ruling on whether the Commissioners and Staff are biased is outside the [Commission's] statutory authority." Alaska Statute 44.62.450(c) explicitly provides the Commission with the statutory

(case continues)

authority to address allegations of bias within its ranks. Gillam is correct that the Commission was not created for the purpose of "investigating bias and managing compliance with due process requirements," but it is still statutorily authorized to do so when necessary. Gillam argues that he cannot be forced to submit to the Commission's disqualification proceeding without suffering constitutional injury because "the [Commission] is a biased tribunal."[49] However, Gillam's claim that the Commission is biased has not yet been adjudicated on the merits, so his argument is unavailing.[50]

Similarly, Gillam argues that the APA at AS 44.62.560(e) authorizes the court to "enjoin agency action in excess of constitutional or statutory authority at any stage of an agency proceeding."[51] But we cannot determine whether the Commission has acted in excess of its authority until Gillam has exhausted his administrative remedies by pursing the APA's procedure for disqualification.[52]

Gillam also argues that "the legislature contemplated circumstances where the superior court will hear administrative complaints normally subject to the [Commission's] primary jurisdiction." He points to two statutory provisions, each of which addresses a situation in which the Commission has failed to timely proceed on a complaint.[53] Because Gillam does not claim that the Commission failed to take timely action on the Natwick complaint, his proffered authority does not apply to this situation and cannot be used to support his argument that exhaustion should not have been required.

Contrary to Gillam's contention, moreover, the statutory disqualification procedures were available to him even before staff had completed its investigation and issued its report.[54] Gillam argues that had such a report been completed, it would have "serve[d] as an accusation, that would cause reputational and financial harm to [him], as previous Staff Reports have." But there is no apparent reason why Gillam could not have filed an affidavit, per the statutory procedure, as early as he suspected Commission bias—so long as he did so at some time "before the taking of evidence at a hearing."[55]

Additionally, Gillam asserts "the trial court fundamentally erred in its assumption that [he was] seeking a remedy confined to the *Natwick* complaint." But the scope of the remedy sought in Gillam's complaint is limited to the Natwick proceedings. He asked only that the Commission be disqualified from having any further involvement in that matter.

Finally, the disqualification procedure outlined in AS 44.62.450(c) represents an administrative remedy to Dauphinais's allegedly biased conduct. Even if the statutory procedure does not expressly address improper staff conduct, it nonetheless provides Gillam with an opportunity to prove how Dauphinais's alleged bias has tainted the other Commissioners, thus allowing the Commission to formulate a response. This response may include not only recusal of a Commissioner but also restrictions as to staff involvement in the Natwick matter.

Exhaustion of administrative remedies would not be futile

Gillam points out that "the failure to exhaust administrative remedies is excused ... where the pursuit of the administrative remedy would be futile due to the certainty of an adverse decision."[56] He argues that exhaustion of administrative remedies would have been futile here because "the evidence showed that the Commissioners and Staff were biased against" him. The superior court disagreed, distinguishing Gillam's case from one in which a regulatory commission refused to hear the plaintiff's claims at all, thus rendering exhaustion of administrative remedies "manifestly futile."[57]

The superior court instead compared Gillam's case to one in which a tribunal—the Department of Revenue—had received a memorandum from the Attorney General suggesting that the plaintiff's claim was untenable.[58] There, the Department wrote a letter to the plaintiff, stating "[i]t would take a rare and unusual situation to disregard" the Attorney General's opinion, but also stressing the importance of the Department's formal review process.[59] This court acknowledged it was "highly possible" that the Department would ultimately defer to the Attorney General's opinion and find against the plaintiff, but "a decision adverse to [the plaintiff's] interests [still did] not appear to be a 'certainty.'"[60]

Gillam argues that his case is more similar to one in which this court affirmed the superior court's decision to excuse exhaustion on futility grounds because the Department of Revenue refused to address the plaintiffs' constitutional challenge.[61] He also offers a similar case in which exhaustion was deemed futile because an employee attempting to sue regarding a collective bargaining agreement was prevented by his union representative from utilizing the proper administrative procedures.[62] But those cases are distinguishable because the Commission has never refused to address Gillam's bias contentions. Gillam's argument that, here, the Commission has "effectively refused" to address his claims because it is biased is unavailing for the reasons explained above.[63]

(case continues)

Finally, Gillam notes this court's holding that failure to exhaust may be excused "where the administrative procedures are ineffective because of ... bias ... or the possibility that the claimant could face irreparable harm if the administrative process is followed."[64] To this end, he asserts: (1) "[s]ubmission to a fatally biased decision making process is in itself a constitutional injury ... "[65] and (2) the Commission will use the time required to exhaust administrative remedies to injure Gillam. But the superior court only found fault with Gillam's failure to utilize the available administrative *recusal* procedures. As explained above, those procedures anticipate situations in which bias may necessitate recusal, but they still require the agency itself to make that determination.[66] Gillam's second contention is purely speculative.

Thus, the superior court did not abuse its discretion when it held Gillam had failed to show that exhaustion of administrative remedies was certain to be futile. We therefore affirm the superior court's dismissal of Gillam's Alaska constitutional claim for failure to exhaust administrative remedies.

The Superior Court did not Err by Granting Summary Judgment for Lack of Ripeness as to Gillam's Federal Constitutional Claim

The superior court also granted summary judgment for lack of ripeness, reasoning that Gillam's injury is merely prospective. Ripeness "depends on 'whether ... there is a substantial controversy, between parties having adverse legal interests, of sufficient immediacy and reality to warrant the issuance of a declaratory judgment.'"[67] In particular, this court "examine[s] 'the fitness of the issues for judicial decision' and 'the hardship to the parties of withholding court consideration.'"[68]

Only Gillam's federal constitutional claim remains after our exhaustion analysis. Accordingly, our ripeness inquiry applies only to interests protected by the Fourteenth Amendment to the United States Constitution—namely, the right not to be deprived of life, liberty, or property without due process of law.[69] Gillam is correct to point out that "[s]ubmission to a fatally biased decisionmaking process is in itself a constitutional injury."[70] Indeed, "[a] fair trial in a fair tribunal is a basic requirement of due process."[71] In evaluating a procedural due process claim, a court must therefore examine "the procedural safeguards built into the statutory or administrative procedure of effecting the deprivation, and any remedies for erroneous deprivations provided by statute or tort law."[72] Here, no hearing has occurred, and thus Gillam's injury—for federal due process purposes—is purely prospective.[73]

The Ninth Circuit's decision in *Standard Alaska Production Company v. Schaible* is directly relevant to evaluating the ripeness of Gillam's federal constitutional claim.[74] There, the State of Alaska filed suit in state court against a group of oil producers, seeking to recover from an alleged underpayment of royalties owed to the State.[75] The producers filed suit in federal court under section 1983 for injunctive and declaratory relief against the state court proceedings, alleging that they would be deprived of their right to an impartial tribunal because, as Permanent Fund Dividend recipients, all potential judges and jurors in the state courts would have a direct interest in the case's outcome.[76] The federal district court dismissed the oil producers' case on ripeness grounds, and the Ninth Circuit affirmed, noting that the producers had not attempted to use Alaska's judicial disqualification procedures to avoid potential conflicts and had not demonstrated that the procedures were "inadequate to resolve the issue of bias."[77]

Like the plaintiffs in *Standard Alaska Production*, Gillam has not taken advantage of the procedures available to prevent his "[s]ubmission to a fatally biased tribunal" from occurring.[78] The APA expressly provides for situations where, as here, "it is claimed that a fair and impartial hearing cannot be accorded."[79] Similarly, the Commission's regulations provide for disqualification of a Commissioner who is "unable to participate in a decision in an unbiased manner so as to reach a fair and impartial decision."[80] Accordingly, Gillam's procedural due process claim is only ripe if he can show that this procedure is "inadequate to resolve the issue of bias."[81]

Gillam raises various arguments as to why the APA's disqualification process is inadequate. For instance, Gillam argues that the Commission will be an ineffective investigator because "the Commissioners do not have any specialized knowledge with regard to personnel issues." But AS 44.62.450(c) charges all agencies under the purview of the APA with deciding recusal issues as they arise, regardless of the agencies' standard functions.

Similarly, Gillam argues that because of the Commissioners' bias, they "necessarily cannot decide if they, and the Staff carrying out their policy, are biased." But as discussed above, the statutory scheme anticipates precisely the kind of allegation at issue here, and does not allow a Commissioner to vote on a request for his or her own disqualification.[82] And although, as Gillam points out, the APA may not specifically

(case continues)

address staff misconduct, Gillam has presented no evidence that the Commissioners are unwilling to evaluate his allegations regarding Dauphinais's bias. Because Gillam has not shown the disqualification process to be facially inadequate, the superior court cannot know whether the process will be inadequate as applied until it has been given a chance to work.

Finally, we share the superior court's concerns regarding the lack of factual development, which the administrative process would help address.[83] As the superior court explained:

> *[F]urther factual development will be valuable should a court need to address the issues again on appeal. For example, Mr. Dauphinais denies that the conversation which forms the basis for much of Mr. Gillam's complaint occurred as Mr. Gillam claims. The [Commission] has the time, resources, and expertise to quickly investigate this matter. ... Likewise, the commissioners deny that Mr. Dauphinais pursued his alleged bias with their encouragement, approval, or even knowledge. Allowing the commissioners the opportunity to consider and rule on the matter and then inspecting that administrative record is preferable, in this court's view, to hauling the commissioners into court at the outset as a means to test their impartiality.*

Gillam argues that "[t]he factual development desired by the trial court was possible, and should have been obtained, by ruling on the pending discovery motions, a continuance to allow further discovery, and an evidentiary hearing." But this argument does not address the view that the facts would be better developed at the agency level.[84]

Gillam has not been subject to a hearing in the Natwick matter and has not availed himself of the process for ensuring that he receives a "fair trial in a fair tribunal."[85] Because Gillam has not shown that process to be inadequate, his claim of tribunal bias is not fit for judicial decision. We therefore affirm the superior court's decision to dismiss Gillam's section 1983 claim for lack of ripeness.

The Superior Court did not Err by Failing to Consider and Grant Gillam's Request to Conduct Additional Discovery

Gillam argues the superior court should not have granted summary judgment when there was a pending request for additional discovery.[86] Gillam's argument relies on Alaska Rule of Civil Procedure 56(f), which states: "Should it appear from the affidavits of a party opposing the motion [for summary judgment] that the party cannot for reasons stated present by affidavit facts essential to justify the party's opposition, the court may refuse the application for judgment," order a continuance, or take similar such action. But to benefit from the rule, a party "must unambiguously request relief on Rule 56(f) grounds."[87]

Here, Gillam "reserve[d] the right to seek an ARCP 56(f) continuance" but appears never to have followed through. He argues that he "made it clear [he] was seeking a continuance to conduct necessary discovery to defend against summary judgment," but points to nothing in the record to support his claim. The superior court cannot have abused its discretion where Gillam failed to invoke Rule 56(f).

Conclusion

The judgment of the superior court is AFFIRMED.

---

1. AS 15.13.020.
2. AS 15.13.030; *see also Alaska Right to Life Comm. v. Miles*, 441 F.3d 773, 776 (9th Cir. 2006).
3. AS 15.13.020(a).
4. AS 15.13.020(g).
5. AS 15.13.020(i). Neither the executive director nor any other Commission employee may vote on matters decided by the Commission. *Id.*
6. 2 Alaska Administrative Code (AAC) 50.870 (2013). The complaint must be in writing, signed "under oath and upon penalty of perjury" and notarized, and must contain certain information such as the facts constituting the alleged violation and the basis for the complainant's knowledge of those facts. *Id.*
7. 2 AAC 50.875.
8. 2 AAC 50.875(e); 2 AAC 50.891.
9. AS 15.13.380(g).
10. The current chair of the Commission, Kenneth Kirk, has recently been substituted in place of Elizabeth Hickerson.
11. *Charles v. Stout*, 308 P.3d 1138, 1140 (Alaska 2013) (alteration in original) (quoting *Interior Cabaret, Hotel, Rest. & Retailers Ass'n v. Fairbanks N. Star Borough*, 135 P.3d 1000, 1002 (Alaska 2006)).
12. *Id.* (citing *Smith v. State*, 282 P.3d 300, 303 (Alaska 2012)).
13. *Winterrowd v. State, Dep't of Admin., Div. of Motor Vehicles*, 288 P.3d 446, 449 (Alaska 2012) (emphasis in original) (quoting *Smart v. State, Dep't of Health & Soc. Servs.*, 237 P.3d 1010, 1014 (Alaska 2010)).
14. *Id.* (quoting *Smart*, 237 P.3d at 1014).
15. *State v. Am. Civil Liberties Union of Alaska*, 204 P.3d 364, 368 (Alaska 2009) (citations omitted).
16. *Mitchell v. Teck Cominco Alaska Inc.*, 193 P.3d 751, 757 (Alaska 2008) (citing *Hymes v. DeRamus*, 119 P.3d 963, 965 (Alaska 2005)).
17. 42 U.S.C. § 1983 (2012) provides, in relevant part:

    > Every person who, under color of any statute, ordinance, regulation, custom, or usage, of any State ... subjects, or causes to be subjected, any citizen of the United States ... to the deprivation of any rights, privileges, or immunities secured by the Constitution and laws, shall

(case continues)

be liable to the party injured in an action at law, suit in equity, or other proper proceeding for redress.

Section 1983 offers "a uniquely federal remedy against incursions under the claimed authority of state law upon rights secured by the Constitution and laws of the Nation." *Mitchum v. Foster*, 407 U.S. 225, 239 (1972).

18. U.S. CONST. amend. XIV, § 1; Alaska Const. art. I, § 7.
19. Alaska Const. art. I, § 7.
20. Because we affirm on exhaustion and ripeness grounds, we need not address the superior court's dismissal on the alternative, presumption-of-integrity ground. *See Winterrowd v. State, Dep't of Admin., Div. of Motor Vehicles*, 288 P.3d 446, 449-50 (Alaska 2012).
21. *Id.* at 450 (citation omitted).
22. *Id.*
23. *Doubleday v. State, Commercial Fisheries Entry Comm'n*, 238 P.3d 100, 107 (Alaska 2010) (citation omitted) (quoting *Moore v. State, Dep't of Transp. & Pub. Facilities*, 875 P.2d 765, 767 (Alaska 1994)).
24. *Ben Lomond, Inc. v. Municipality of Anchorage*, 761 P.2d 119, 122 (Alaska 1988) (citing 4 KENNETH CULP DAVIS, ADMINISTRATIVE LAW TREATISE § 26:6 (2d ed. 1983)) (also noting that "successful pursuit of a claim through the administrative process could obviate the need for judicial review of the constitutional issues" and that "it is axiomatic to our system of justice that we have a factual context within which to review a case.").
25. *See* AS 44.62.330(a)(23).
26. AS 44.62.450(c).
27. *Cf. Voigt v. Snowden*, 923 P.2d 778, 782 (Alaska 1996) (noting that the administrative termination process could have allayed an employee's fears of a biased decision-maker); *Eufemio v. Kodiak Island Hosp.*, 837 P.2d 95, 99 (Alaska 1992) (noting that a hospital peer review committee could "identify unfair or arbitrary processes, such as a biased tribunal, and correct the deficiency to avoid litigation").
28. Gillam raises various arguments as to why, despite this statutory procedure, no remedy existed. We address these arguments in the following sub-section.
29. 457 U.S. 496, 516 (1982).
30. 487 U.S. 131, 146-47, 153 (1988).
31. 805 P.2d 362, 368 (Alaska 1991).
32. 655 F.2d 946 (9th Cir. 1981).
33. 71 F.3d 732 (9th Cir. 1995).
34. 655 F.2d at 948 (citing *Younger v. Harris*, 401 U.S. 37 (1971)).
35. *Id.* at 949 (citing *Rosenthal v. Carr*, 614 F.2d 1219, 1220 (9th Cir. 1980)).
36. *Id.* at 947–48.
37. *Id.* at 949–50.
38. 71 F.3d at 748.
39. *Id.* (emphasis added) (citing *Partington v. Gedan*, 880 F.2d 116, 127 (9th Cir.1989) (noting recusal procedures in assessing whether "exceptional circumstances" existed); *Flangas*, 655 F.2d at 950).
40. *Id.*
41. *See Patsy v. Board of Regents*, 457 U.S. 496, 516 (1982) (concluding "that exhaustion of state administrative remedies should not be required as a prerequisite to bringing an action pursuant to § 1983"); *Felder v. Casey*, 487 U.S. 131, 147 (1988) (concluding that given the goals of section 1983, Congress could not have "contemplated that those who sought to vindicate their federal rights in state courts could be required to seek redress in the first instance from the very state officials whose hostility to those rights precipitated their injuries.").
42. *See id.*
43. As we discuss in Part IV.B, however, we affirm the superior court's decision on the alternative ground that Gillam's section 1983 claim is not ripe.
44. 805 P.2d 362, 364–65 (Alaska 1991).
45. *Id.*
46. *Id.* at 365, 368; *see also* Alaska R. App. P. 602(a)(2).
47. *Diedrich*, 805 P.2d at 366, 368–69.
48. AS 44.62.450(c).
49. Along a similar vein, Gillam argues that the statutory disqualification procedures are not available because it would require an allegedly biased agency member to rule on his or her own disqualification. But the Commission has five members, and the statute provides that where a disqualification request "concerns an agency member," the disqualification issue "shall be determined by the *other* members of the agency." AS 44.62.450(c) (emphasis added).
50. Gillam argues that for purposes of summary judgment, the court was required to assume the Commission was biased against him. This is accurate. However, even if we assume the Commission is biased against Gillam, the Commission should still be allowed the opportunity to recuse itself or some of its members, given the fact that recusal is proper in exactly such a situation—that is, where bias exists. Indeed, AS 44.62.450(c) provides for disqualification where a party states "with particularity" why "a fair and impartial hearing cannot be accorded."
51. Gillam makes this and the following argument in the ripeness portion of his brief, but they appear to be more relevant to exhaustion. We thus address them here.
52. *See* AS 44.62.450(c).
53. Alaska Statute 15.13.380(h) allows an administrative complainant to file in superior court if the Commission has failed to take action on a complaint within 90 days of filing; Alaska Statute 44.62.305(a) allows a party to an administrative proceeding to sue in superior court if "the state agency has unreasonably delayed the progress of the administrative proceeding."
54. *See* AS 44.62.450(c) ("A party may request the disqualification of a hearing officer or agency member by filing an affidavit, before the taking of evidence at a hearing . . . . ").
55. *Id.*
56. *See Bruns v. Municipality of Anchorage*, 32 P.3d 362, 371 (Alaska 2001) (internal quotation marks omitted).
57. *See Matanuska Elec. Ass'n, Inc. v. Chugach Elec. Ass'n, Inc.*, 99 P.3d 553, 560–61 (Alaska 2004).
58. *Standard Alaska Prod. Co. v. State, Dep't of Revenue*, 773 P.2d 201, 208–09 (Alaska 1989).
59. *Id.* at 209.
60. *Id.* (quoting *Municipality of Anchorage v. Higgins*, 754 P.2d 745, 747–48 (Alaska 1988) (holding that an exception to the rule would be unwarranted absent a showing that exhaustion "would so certainly result in an adverse decision as to render the remedy futile" (internal quotation marks omitted)).
61. *State, Dep't of Revenue v. Andrade*, 23 P.3d 58, 67 (Alaska 2001).
62. *Beard v. Baum*, 796 P.2d 1344, 1349 (Alaska 1990).
63. *See supra* note 50.
64. *Hymes v. DeRamus*, 222 P.3d 874, 883 (Alaska 2010) (quoting *Bruns v. Municipality of Anchorage*, 32 P.3d 362, 371 n.46 (Alaska 2001)).
65. *United Church of the Med. Ctr. v. Med. Ctr. Comm'n*, 689 F.2d 693, 701 (7th Cir. 1982).
66. *See supra* note 50.

(case continues)

67. *State v. Am. Civil Liberties Union of Alaska*, 204 P.3d 364, 369 (Alaska 2009) (alteration in original) (quoting *Brause v. State, Dep't of Health & Soc. Servs.*, 21 P.3d 357, 359 (Alaska 2001)).
68. *Id.* (quoting *Brause*, 21 P.3d at 359).
69. U.S. Const. amend. XIV, § 1; *see also Zinermon v. Burch*, 494 U.S. 113, 126 (1990) ("In procedural due process claims, the deprivation by state action of a constitutionally protected interest in life, liberty, or property is not in itself unconstitutional; what is unconstitutional is the deprivation of such an interest *without due process of law*." (emphasis in original) (internal quotation marks omitted)).
70. *See United Church of the Med. Ctr.*, 689 F.2d at 701.
71. *Stivers v. Pierce*, 71 F.3d 732, 741 (9th Cir. 1995) (quoting *In re Murchison*, 349 U.S. 133, 136 (1955)) (internal quotation marks omitted).
72. *Zinermon*, 494 U.S. at 126.
73. Gillam asserts that his alleged injuries are not merely prospective, but have already occurred or are ongoing. In particular, he contends that: (1) the Commission staff accepted the Natwick complaint even though it was technically deficient; (2) during the Natwick investigation, the Commission staff made unreasonable document requests; and (3) the Commission staff has already contacted the SEC in an attempt to ruin Gillam and his business. But these injuries relate solely to the investigative stage of the Natwick matter, and accordingly, are relevant only in the context of Gillam's Alaska constitutional claim regarding "fair and just treatment in the course of legislative and executive investigations." Alaska Const. art. I, § 7.
74. 874 F.2d 624 (9th Cir. 1989).
75. *Id.* at 625.
76. *Id.* at 625–26.
77. *Id.* at 629; *see also id.* at 626, 630.
78. *See United Church of the Med. Ctr.*, 689 F.2d at 701.
79. AS 44.62.450(c).
80. 2 AAC 50.835.
81. *Standard Alaska Prod. Co.*, 874 F.2d at 629; *see also District of Columbia v. Craig*, 930 A.2d 946, 966-67 (D.C. Cir. 2007) (holding that procedural due process claims regarding tax assessments were unripe because plaintiffs still were in the administrative review process and "ha[d] not yet allowed the statutorily-prescribed process to run its course").
82. *See supra* notes 49 & 50 and accompanying text.
83. As we noted in *Brause*, among the factors we look to in evaluating the ripeness of a claim is "the need for further factual development to aid decision." 21 P.3d 357, 360 (Alaska 2001) (internal quotation marks omitted).
84. Gillam also argues the court improperly "considered potential delay to the Natwick investigation due to continued proceedings before the [s]uperior [c]ourt." But the superior court merely noted its fear that, over the course of judicial proceedings, "the facts giving rise to the initial complaint may be obscured." This is a reasonable concern, and one that does not evidence any desire on the part of the superior court to "rush" the Natwick proceeding, but rather to preserve its adjudicability.
85. *See Stivers v. Pierce*, 71 F.3d 732, 741 (9th Cir. 1995) (quoting *In re Murchison*, 349 U.S. 133, 136 (1955)) (internal quotation marks omitted).
86. Gillam also takes issue with Hickerson's and Dauphinais's requests to stay discovery but provides no argument as to why their requests were improper.
87. *Mitchell v. Teck Cominco Alaska Inc.*, 193 P.3d 751, 758 (Alaska 2008).

CASE *Bristol Bay Mining I*

Hughes v. Treadwell

4FA-13-01296 CI, 6981 January 30, 2015
Supreme Court of Alaska
Before: Winfree, Stowers, Maassen, and Bolger, Justices
Opinion by, STOWERS, Justice

Introduction

Richard Hughes, the Alaska Miners Association, and the Council of Alaska Producers (collectively referred to as "Hughes") challenged Lieutenant Governor Mead Treadwell's certification of a ballot initiative that would require final legislative approval for any large-scale metallic sulfide mining operation located within the Bristol Bay watershed. Hughes argued that the initiative violates the constitutional prohibitions on appropriation and enacting local or special legislation by initiative. Following oral argument we issued an order affirming the superior court's summary judgment order in favor of the State and the initiative sponsors, and allowing preparation of ballots to proceed.[1] This opinion explains our reasoning.[2]

Facts and Proceedings

In October 2012 Lieutenant Governor Mead Treadwell received an application for an initiative entitled "Bristol Bay Forever"; the Division of Elections denominated the initiative "12BBAY." The stated purpose of the initiative was to enact law "providing for [the] protection of Bristol Bay wild salmon and waters within or flowing into the existing 1972 Bristol Bay Fisheries Reserve." Section 1 of the initiative would add the following new section to AS 38.05:

(case continues)

Sec. 38.05.142. Legislative Approval Required for Certain Large Scale Mines

(a) In addition to permits and authorizations otherwise required by law, a final authorization must be obtained from the legislature for a large-scale metallic sulfide mining operation located within the watershed of the Bristol Bay Fisheries Reserve designated in AS 38.05.140(f). This authorization shall take the form of a duly enacted law finding that the proposed large-scale metallic sulfide mining operation will not constitute danger to the fishery within the Bristol Bay Fisheries Reserve.
(b) The commissioner may adopt regulations under AS 44.62 to implement this section.
(c) In this section, "large-scale metallic sulfide mining operation" means a specific mining proposal to extract metals, including gold and copper, from sulfide-bearing rock that would directly disturb 640 or more acres of land.

Section 2 would amend the "uncodified law of the State of Alaska" to make findings recognizing the ecological and economic importance of the Bristol Bay Fisheries Reserve and the potential adverse effects of metallic sulfide mining.[3] After review by the Department of Law—which concluded that the initiative did not make an appropriation or enact local or special legislation and violated no other constitutional provisions—the Lieutenant Governor certified 12BBAY.

In January 2013 Hughes challenged 12BBAY's certification in superior court, arguing that the initiative "constitutes impermissible local and special legislation and violates the separation of powers doctrine." Hughes amended his complaint several times, joining the Alaska Miners Association and the Council of Alaska Producers as plaintiffs. Initiative sponsors Christina Salmon, Mark Niver, and John H. Holman moved to intervene as defendants; the superior court granted their unopposed motion. In February the initiative sponsors moved for summary judgment. They then filed a separate answer to the amended complaint in March. In August Hughes cross-moved for summary judgment. In January 2014 Hughes filed a third amended complaint, adding a claim that 12BBAY would unconstitutionally appropriate state assets, and again moved for summary judgment.

Considering his motions for summary judgment together, Hughes argued that 12BBAY would: (1) enact local or special legislation in violation of article XI, section 7 of the Alaska Constitution; (2) violate separation of powers under article XII, section 11 of the Alaska Constitution; and (3) appropriate state assets in violation of article XI, section 7 of the Alaska Constitution. The superior court concluded that 12BBAY would not enact local or special legislation, would not clearly violate separation of powers, and would not appropriate public assets. The court granted summary judgment in favor of the State and the initiative sponsors and declined to enjoin placement of 12BBAY on the ballot. Hughes appeals to this court, challenging the superior court's conclusions that 12BBAY would not make an unconstitutional appropriation of public assets or enact local or special legislation.

Standard of Review

We review a superior court's summary judgment decision de novo, reading the record in the light most favorable to, and drawing all reasonable inferences in favor of, the non-moving party.[4] Ballot initiatives are subject to pre-election review only "where the initiative is challenged on the basis that it does not comply with the state constitutional and statutory provisions regulating initiatives" or "where the initiative is clearly unconstitutional or clearly unlawful."[5] The constitutionality of a ballot initiative is a question of law, which we review using our independent judgment, "adopting the rule of law that is most persuasive in light of precedent, reason, and policy."[6] We "construe voter initiatives broadly so as to preserve them whenever possible."[7] And "we liberally construe constitutional and statutory provisions that apply to the initiative process."[8] However, whether an initiative complies with article XI, section 7's limits on the right of direct legislation requires careful consideration.[9]

Discussion

Article XI, section 1 of the Alaska Constitution provides that "[t]he people may propose and enact laws by the initiative." But article XI, section 7 creates several specific restrictions on this power: "The initiative shall not be used to dedicate revenues, make or repeal appropriations, create courts, define jurisdiction of courts or prescribe their rules, or enact local or special legislation." Here, Hughes argues that 12BBAY violates article XI, section 7's prohibition on appropriation by initiative and on enacting local or special legislation by initiative. We conclude that 12BBAY would not appropriate state assets or enact local or special legislation.

(case continues)

12BBAY Does Not Violate Article XI, Section 7's Anti-Appropriation Clause

Hughes argues that 12BBAY violates the anti-appropriation clause of article XI, section 7 because it impermissibly interferes with the legislature's appropriation authority. Hughes contends that "12BBAY would set aside the entire Bristol Bay Watershed for the purpose of propagating salmon" and "would immediately ban new large-scale hardrock mining in this vast area without any further legislative action." The State and sponsors respond that 12BBAY is not an appropriation because it regulates rather than allocates resources, expressly leaving final authority to allocate state resources with the legislature.

We employ a two-part inquiry to determine whether an initiative makes an appropriation of state assets in violation of article XI, section 7.[10] First we must determine "whether the initiative deals with a public asset."[11] Second, if the initiative deals with a public asset, then we must determine "whether the initiative would appropriate that asset."[12] None of the parties dispute the superior court's conclusion that "12BBAY concerns a 'public asset.'" As the superior court noted, "[w]hether the initiative is construed as one that affects fish, waters of the state or state lands, each of these resources is a public asset."[13] The issue here is whether 12BBAY appropriates fish, waters of the state, or state lands.

In evaluating whether an initiative that deals with a state asset appropriates that asset, we look to "two core objectives" of the prohibition against appropriation by initiative.[14] Those objectives are (1) "to prevent give-away programs that appeal to the self-interest of voters and endanger the state treasury,"[15] and (2) "to preserve legislative discretion by ensur[ing] that the legislature, and *only* the legislature, retains control over the allocation of state assets among competing needs."[16] Hughes does not challenge the superior court's conclusion that 12BBAY is not a give-away program. And that conclusion is clearly correct: 12BBAY does not give away state resources to voters or to any particular group, person, or entity.[17] Thus, the only remaining question is whether 12BBAY impermissibly interferes with the legislature's control over allocation of state assets.

Hughes argues that because the legislature delegated the allocation of mineral leases to the Department of Natural Resources (DNR), 12BBAY impermissibly limits legislative discretion by forcing the legislature itself to make final allocation decisions and thus violates the anti-appropriation clause. The superior court concluded that 12BBAY does not limit legislative control over state assets because it expressly leaves final authority for appropriating state resources in the hands of the legislature. The superior court rejected Hughes's argument that the second objective of the anti-appropriation clause is violated when an initiative affects the process of making appropriations.

We have previously stated that an initiative "narrows the legislature's range of freedom to make allocation decisions in a manner sufficient to render the initiative an appropriation"[18] when "the initiative 'would set aside a certain specified amount of money or property for a specific purpose or object in such a manner that is executable, mandatory, and reasonably definite with no further legislative action.'"[19] Several of our decisions regarding whether particular initiatives would make an appropriation illuminate this principle.

In *McAlpine v. University of Alaska* we considered an initiative that would have established a state community college system and required the University of Alaska to transfer certain property to the new system.[20] We upheld the initiative's provisions creating and funding an independent community college system, but struck the initiative's third sentence, which provided: "The amount of property transferred shall be commensurate with that occupied and operated by the Community Colleges on November 1, 1986."[21] We concluded that this language impermissibly "designat[ed] the use of an ascertainable and definite amount of state assets"—that amount in use by the community colleges on November 1, 1986.[22] We noted that a key consideration supporting this conclusion was that "no further legislative action would be necessary to require the University to transfer property to the community college system, or to specify the amount of property the University must transfer."[23] But we concluded that the initiative's second sentence, which provided that "[t]he University of Alaska shall transfer to the Community College System of Alaska such real and personal property as is necessary to the independent operation and maintenance of the Community College System,"[24] was not an appropriation because the legislature would maintain "all the discretion it needs with respect to appropriations for community colleges."[25] We reasoned that the legislature's discretion would be limited only to the extent that the legislature could not eliminate all appropriations for community colleges, and we saw no realistic danger that the legislature would attempt to do so.[26]

(case continues)

In *City of Fairbanks v. Fairbanks Convention & Visitors Bureau* we considered a local ballot initiative that would have amended a municipal ordinance governing the use of funds from the city's hotel tax by allowing revenue from the tax to be used for non-tourist and entertainment purposes and eliminating the requirement that a certain percentage of the tax go to the Fairbanks Convention and Visitors Bureau.[27] We concluded that the initiative did not repeal an appropriation because the ordinance it amended was not an "appropriation" as the legislature used the term in AS 29.35.100—"that is as an act which accompanies the approval of the annual budget or is supplemental to that act."[28] We further concluded that the initiative was not an appropriation in its own right because it would not "reduce the [city] council's control over the appropriations process. Instead, the initiative [would] allow the council *greater* discretion in appropriating funds than [did] the current law."[29]

In *Pullen v. Ulmer* we considered an initiative that would direct allocation of the salmon harvest among competing users and would create preferences for subsistence, personal, and recreational users.[30] After determining that wild salmon were a state asset,[31] we held that the initiative would impermissibly appropriate that asset.[32] We concluded that the initiative was a giveaway, both because it was "designed to appeal to the self-interests of sport, personal and subsistence fishers" and would "significantly reduce the legislature's and Board of Fisheries' control of and discretion over allocation decisions, particularly in the event of stock-specific or region-specific shortages of salmon between the competing needs of users."[33] We distinguished *McAlpine* by emphasizing that the initiative at issue could significantly limit the Board of Fisheries' discretion to make allocation decisions in times of shortages and that "there is a very realistic danger that such shortages will occur."[34]

In *Alaska Action Center, Inc. v. Municipality of Anchorage* we considered an initiative that would have limited development on municipal property.[35] We concluded that the initiative was distinguishable from the permissible section of the initiative in *McAlpine* because it "'designat[ed] the use of' specified amounts of public assets in a way that encroaches on the legislative branch's exclusive 'control over the allocation of state assets among competing needs.'"[36] We rejected Alaska Action Center's argument that the initiative was distinguishable from the one at issue in *McAlpine* because it did not mandate a transfer of property: "*McAlpine* did not rest . . . on the fact that the initiative at issue there would have required a formal land transfer; the ruling focused on the fact that the initiative directed a specific amount of property to be used for a specified purpose."[37] We also emphasized that the prohibition against appropriations is meant to keep "control of the appropriation process *in the legislative body*"[38] and concluded that the initiative would intrude on legislative control by "limiting the mechanism for future change to another initiative process."[39]

In *Staudenmaier v. Municipality of Anchorage* we considered whether two initiatives that would have directed the municipality to sell utility assets would impermissibly appropriate assets.[40] The first initiative would have required the municipality to sell Anchorage Municipal Light & Power Utility and its assets and would have granted Chugach Electric Association a right of first refusal.[41] The second initiative would have required the municipality to sell the Anchorage Municipal Refuse Collection Utility to the highest bidder.[42] We concluded that the municipal clerk properly rejected the initiative petitions because, by requiring the sale of public assets, they violated article XI, section 7's prohibition on appropriating by initiative.[43] We explained that the line between an unobjectionable initiative that deals with a public asset and one that is an impermissible appropriation is crossed "where an initiative controls the use of public assets such that the voters essentially usurp the legislature's resource allocation role."[44]

In *Pebble Ltd. Partnership ex rel. Pebble Mines Corp. v. Parnell* we considered an initiative that would have regulated large-scale metallic mines for the purpose of protecting water quality.[45] We concluded that the initiative dealt with a public asset—waters of the state—but that the initiative would not appropriate that asset.[46] As in this case, no party argued that the initiative was a "give-away program."[47] Instead, the primary question was "whether the initiative narrow[ed] the legislature's range of freedom to make allocation decisions in a manner sufficient to render the initiative an appropriation."[48] We concluded that because the initiative was properly read as "preclud[ing] only discharges of toxic chemicals and other mine waste that cause 'adverse effects' to humans, salmon, and waters used for human consumption or as salmon habitat," it did not make an appropriation.[49] We stated that "the prohibition against initiatives that appropriate public assets does not extend to prohibit

(case continues)

initiatives that regulate public assets, so long as the regulations do not result in the allocation of an asset entirely to one group at the expense of another."[50] We further observed that the initiative left the Department of Environmental Conservation and Department of Natural Resources the discretion to determine specific amounts of toxic pollutants that may be discharged and did not exhibit any "explicit preference among potential users."[51]

In *Alliance of Concerned Taxpayers, Inc. v. Kenai Peninsula Borough* we considered a ballot initiative passed by voters that required voter approval for all Borough capital projects with a total cost in excess of one million dollars.[52] We concluded that requiring voter approval for a specific class of Borough expenditures was an appropriation, and, therefore, the initiative was invalid.[53] We explained that "an initiative may make an impermissible appropriation not only when it designates public assets for some particular use, but also when it allocates those assets *away from* a particular group."[54] We concluded that the voters would not invariably approve all capital projects placed on the ballot as a result of the initiative, and thus the initiative would allocate assets away from those capital projects meeting the voter-approval threshold.[55]

Most recently in *Municipality of Anchorage v. Holleman* we considered, among other things, whether a referendum to repeal a municipal ordinance was an appropriation.[56] The ordinance at issue made a number of changes to the employee relations chapter of the Anchorage Municipal Code, including limiting overtime compensation, prohibiting strikes, and placing new restrictions on collective bargaining.[57] The municipality argued that by repealing an ordinance intended to save money on labor costs, the referendum would effectively appropriate public assets that the municipal assembly could direct to other priorities.[58] We rejected that argument, noting that "we have never held that any effect on public resources triggers the prohibition on direct legislation; nearly all legislation involves public assets to some degree."[59] We observed that "the referendum [did] not compel or restrict the expenditure of public funds, the approval of labor contracts, or any particular level of employee compensation," and that "the economic effects of the ordinance are indirect and presently unknowable."[60] Thus, we concluded that the referendum was not an "'executable, mandatory, and reasonably definite' set-aside [of money or property] that our case law requires before we will find that an initiative or referendum makes an appropriation."[61]

Read together, these cases create a relatively detailed outline of when an initiative or referendum impermissibly limits legislative discretion to allocate state assets in violation of article XI, section 7. An initiative or referendum may: (1) mandate a non-appropriative allocation of property—including a transfer of property from a specific government entity—sufficient to accomplish a particular purpose;[62] (2) repeal a legislative enactment that designates the use of government funds, as long as the statute or ordinance is not an "appropriation" as the legislature used the term in AS 29.35.100;[63] (3) increase the legislative body's discretion in making appropriations by changing existing law;[64] (4) regulate the use of public assets;[65] or (5) repeal a legislative enactment intended to reduce government expenditures in a particular area of the budget.[66]

But an initiative or referendum may not: (1) require the allocation of "an ascertainable and definite amount of state assets";[67] (2) set aside specified property for a particular use, especially where the initiative "limit[s] the mechanism for future change to another initiative process";[68] (3) set preferences among user groups of a particular public resource;[69] (4) require the sale of specified public assets;[70] or (5) require voter approval for any public expenditure of funds within a particular class.[71] Additionally, an initiative that regulates the use of public assets may not "result in the allocation of an asset entirely to one group at the expense of another."[72] These cases also suggest that a limitation on legislative discretion is only an "appropriation" where the limitation would restrict a plausible legislative choice.[73]

The effect of 12BBAY is similar to that of the initiative at issue in *City of Fairbanks* in that it ultimately gives the legislature more discretion whether to approve a particular mining project. In *City of Fairbanks* an existing ordinance allocated the use of hotel tax revenue and the initiative would have returned complete control of that revenue to the City Council.[74] In the present case an extensive set of statutes and regulations governs mining, and the legislature has delegated permitting decisions to DNR. 12BBAY would alter that scheme by returning final decision-making authority to the legislature for proposed "large-scale metallic sulfide mining operation[s] located within the watershed of the Bristol Bay Fisheries Reserve."

12BBAY is also distinguishable from each case where this court has invalidated an initiative on the basis that it interferes with the legislature's control over resource allocation. Unlike the initiative at issue in *McAlpine*, 12BBAY would not direct the use of "an

(case continues)

ascertainable and definite amount of state assets."[75] While 12BBAY would regulate resource use in an identified geographic area, it does not set that area aside for a particular use as the initiative in *Alaska Action Center* would have.[76] 12BBAY does not require the sale of any public assets and does not require voter approval for any expenditure of public funds.[77] Finally, contrary to Hughes's assertion, 12BBAY does not attempt to allocate any state assets to one user group to the exclusion of another.[78] Adding an additional regulatory step for large-scale mining projects may or may not benefit the fishing industry and burden a segment of the mining industry, but it certainly does not "result in the allocation of an asset entirely to one group at the expense of another."[79] And, ultimately, the legislature retains the discretion to make the necessary findings and decisions.

12BBAY undeniably would alter the legislature's existing scheme for allocating and regulating the use of the state's mineral resources. But this court concluded in *Pebble Limited Partnership* that there is no prohibition on initiatives altering existing public resource regulations.[80] An initiative violates the anti-appropriation clause of article XI, section 7 only when it "controls the use of public assets such that the voters essentially usurp the legislature's resource allocation role."[81] 12BBAY does not cross that line. Because the legislature would retain ultimate control over allocation of state assets, 12BBAY is not an appropriation.

12BBAY Does Not Violate Article XI, Section 7's Local And Special Legislation Clause

Hughes argues that 12BBAY violates the local and special legislation clause of article XI, section 7 of the Alaska Constitution. He asserts that there is no legitimate basis for 12BBAY's narrow geographic scope. The State responds that 12BBAY is not unconstitutional under this court's interpretation of article XI, section 7's local and special legislation prohibition as articulated in *Pebble Limited Partnership*.

Both article XI, section 7 of the Alaska Constitution and AS 15.45.010 prohibit enacting local or special legislation by initiative. This prohibition is absolute. Article XI, section 7 provides that "[t]he initiative shall not be used to . . . enact local or special legislation."[82] We apply a "two-stage analysis for determining whether proposed legislation is 'local or special legislation' barred by article XI, section 7."[83] We first consider "whether the proposed legislation is of general, statewide applicability."[84] If the initiative is generally applicable, the initiative will not enact local or special legislation and the inquiry ends.[85] If the initiative is not generally applicable, we move on to consider whether the initiative nevertheless "bears a fair and substantial relationship to legitimate purposes." [86] We have explained that this standard is analogous to our most deferential standard of equal protection review.[87]

The parties agree that 12BBAY is not generally applicable. We agree and therefore next consider whether 12BBAY "bears a fair and substantial relationship to legitimate purposes."[88] 12BBAY's purpose is to protect "Bristol Bay wild salmon and waters within or flowing into the existing 1972 Bristol Bay Fisheries Reserve." We conclude there is no serious question that requiring legislative approval of large-scale metallic sulfide mining operations in the Bristol Bay watershed bears a fair and substantial relationship to that purpose.[89] Thus, we must consider only whether protecting "Bristol Bay wild salmon and waters within or flowing into the existing 1972 Bristol Bay Fisheries Reserve" comprises a legitimate purpose. We conclude that it does.

The superior court determined that protecting the Bristol Bay fishery is legitimate because the legislation creating the Bristol Bay Fisheries Reserve had the same purpose and applied to the same geographic area as 12BBAY. The court stated that "[i]n effect . . . , [Hughes's] attack on 12BBAY as local and special legislation is really a misdirected attack on the creation of the fisheries reserve in 1972" and that "[t]here is nothing in Alaska constitutional jurisprudence that authorizes a collateral constitutional attack on an existing statute in the guise of a pre-election challenge to an initiative that does not seek to revise the existing statute."

Hughes argues that the superior court erred by concluding that AS 38.05.140(f) justified 12BBAY's special treatment of the Bristol Bay watershed. He suggests that the correct question is "whether the narrow classification drawn by the legislation that is actually at issue is fairly and substantially justified." As discussed above, the issue here is whether protecting the Bristol Bay fishery comprises a legitimate purpose, not whether it is "fairly and substantially justified." While we conclude that AS 38.05.140 is relevant to whether 12BBAY's purpose is legitimate, we reject the superior court's conclusion that AS 38.05.140 is dispositive of that question. Under the court's reasoning, the purpose of any initiative that relies on the unchallenged classification or geographic scope of an existing and unchallenged statute with a similar purpose would be per se legitimate. Nothing in our jurisprudence supports such a rule.

(case continues)

Hughes argues there is no legitimate economic or biological basis for limiting 12BBAY to the Bristol Bay watershed. His argument suggests that the initiative's geographic scope must be justified by detailed economic or scientific findings. But such a requirement would not be consistent with our deferential "legitimate purpose" test. In *State v. Lewis* it was sufficient that legislation allowing a specific land transfer was "designed to facilitate statewide land use management and to resolve a host of pressing legal issues arising in the context of [the Alaska Native Claims Settlement Act]."[90] In *Baxley v. State* it was sufficient that the oil and gas leases singled out for modification had unique characteristics that could incentivize lessees to abandon the fields before extracting all of the oil, thus implicating the state's interest in maximizing oil production.[91]

As the superior court discussed in its decision in this case, the legislature recognized the importance of the Bristol Bay fishery by establishing the Bristol Bay Fisheries Reserve in AS 38.05.140(f). This statute mandates that oil and gas leases or exploration licenses may "not be issued on state owned or controlled land [within the reserve] until the legislature by appropriate resolution specifically finds that the entry will not constitute danger to the fishery."[92] The record in this case also indisputably establishes that the Bristol Bay watershed has unique ecological, geographic, and economic characteristics; that the fishery has significant statewide importance; and that metallic sulfide mining poses potential water quality risks. For example, the initiative sponsors provided a report extensively documenting the economic importance of the Bristol Bay salmon industry, which concluded that Bristol Bay has the world's most valuable wild salmon fishery. The initiative sponsors also provided a report discussing the potentially significant impacts of a proposed large-scale mining project on the Bristol Bay wild salmon ecosystem.

Hughes's argument and the expert reports that he relies on paint a picture of the Bristol Bay fishery as comparatively less economically and biologically important than several other fisheries in the state. But even if this were correct, the Bristol Bay fishery does not need to be the most important or best fishery in the state to justify targeted legislation. Rather, it merely needs to have some unique statewide importance that justifies geographically limited legislation.[93] Even Hughes's economist, Dr. Michael Taylor, points to factors that distinguish Bristol Bay from the state's other salmon-producing regions and also show its significance to the state as a whole. For example, Bristol Bay possesses a particularly high incidence of sockeye salmon relative to other salmon species.[94] Its salmon enter the supply chain through different markets than other state fisheries—particularly Japan, China, and Russia—thus contributing to Alaska's Asian-Russian export market. Bristol Bay has a significantly compressed harvest window,[95] with correspondingly low employment stability. Dr. Taylor states that "[c]ompared to other regions in Alaska, the Bristol Bay salmon fishery is an economic engine," even though much of the economic benefit favors non-residents. The total annual average (2008–2012) of gross earnings by salmon permit holders was approximately $143,000,000 for Bristol Bay, $94,000,000 for Southeast Alaska, and $93,000,000 for Prince William Sound. Excluding gross earnings by non-resident permit holders, the annual averages for these three regions were approximately $61,000,000 (Bristol Bay), $56,000,000 (Southeast Alaska), and $71,000,000 (Prince William Sound).

According to a report prepared by the University of Alaska Anchorage's Institute of Social and Economic Research titled "The Economic Importance of the Bristol Bay Salmon Industry," the Bristol Bay sockeye fishery "is the world's most valuable wild salmon fishery, and typically supplies almost half of the world's wild sockeye salmon." The report states that in 2010 "harvesting, processing, and retailing Bristol Bay salmon and the multiplier effects of these activities created $1.5 billion in output or sales value across the United States." "Between 2005 and 2010, Bristol Bay averaged 67% of total sockeye salmon harvests (by volume) . . . . " In 2010, Bristol Bay salmon fishing and processing employed an estimated 4,369 Alaska residents.

We conclude that Bristol Bay's unique and significant biological and economic characteristics are of great interest not just to the Bristol Bay region but to the state as a whole. We also conclude that 12BBAY's purpose—to protect "Bristol Bay wild salmon and waters"—is legitimate. And we conclude that 12BBAY bears a fair and substantial relationship to the initiative's legitimate purpose.

The sponsors of 12BBAY certainly could have proposed an initiative of statewide application, but instead they chose to focus on a very important fishery in a single region. As we explained in *Pebble Limited Partnership*, however, "legislatures routinely must draw lines and create classifications."[96] As in the equal protection context, "we are guided by the familiar principles that a statute is not invalid under the Constitution because it might have gone farther than it did, that a legislature need not strike at all evils at the same time, and that reform may take one step at a time, addressing itself to the phase of the problem which seems most acute to the legislative mind."[97] Applying these principles, we conclude that

(case continues)

12BBAY permissibly distinguishes the Bristol Bay watershed and its salmon fishery and does not violate the Alaska Constitution's prohibition on local or special legislation.

Conclusion

For the reasons discussed above, we AFFIRM the superior court's summary judgment order in favor of the State and the initiative sponsors.

---

1. *Hughes v. Treadwell*, 328 P.3d 1037 (Alaska 2014).
2. The initiative was passed by a majority of the voters in the November 4, 2014 general election.
3. Sections 3–5 of the initiative are not important to this appeal. Section 3 is a grandfather clause that would protect existing mining operations. Section 4 is a severability provision. Section 5 proposes an effective date.
4. *Pebble Ltd. P'ship ex rel. Pebble Mines Corp. v. Parnell*, 215 P.3d 1064, 1072 (Alaska 2009) (citing *Anchorage Citizens for Taxi Reform v. Municipality of Anchorage*, 151 P.3d 418, 422 (Alaska 2006)).
5. *Alaskans for Efficient Gov't, Inc. v. State*, 153 P.3d 296, 298 (Alaska 2007) (quoting *State v. Trust the People*, 113 P.3d 613, 614 n.1 (Alaska 2005)).
6. *Pebble Ltd. P'ship*, 215 P.3d at 1072 (citing *Anchorage Citizens for Taxi Reform*, 151 P.3d at 422).
7. *Id.* at 1073 (quoting *Anchorage Citizens for Taxi Reform*, 151 P.3d at 422) (internal quotation marks omitted).
8. *Kodiak Island Borough v. Mahoney*, 71 P.3d 896, 898 (Alaska 2003) (citing *Brooks v. Wright*, 971 P.2d 1025, 1027 (Alaska 1999); *Interior Taxpayers Ass'n v. Fairbanks North Star Borough*, 742 P.2d 781, 782 (Alaska 1987)).
9. *Pebble Ltd. P'ship*, 215 P.3d at 1073 ("[I]nitiatives touching upon the allocation of public revenues and assets require careful consideration because the constitutional right of direct legislation is limited by the Alaska Constitution." (quoting *Anchorage Citizens for Taxi Reform*, 151 P.3d at 422) (internal quotation marks omitted)).
10. *Id.* (citing *Anchorage Citizens for Taxi Reform*, 151 P.3d at 422).
11. *Id.* (quoting *Anchorage Citizens for Taxi Reform*, 151 P.3d at 422) (internal quotation marks omitted).
12. *Id.* (quoting *Anchorage Citizens for Taxi Reform*, 151 P.3d at 423) (internal quotation marks omitted).
13. *See id.* at 1073–74 (holding that "the waters of the state are a public asset," and noting that "[this court has] previously determined that public land, public revenue, a municipally-owned utility, and wild salmon are all public assets that cannot be appropriated by initiative" (footnotes omitted)).
14. *Id.* at 1074–75 (citing *Anchorage Citizens for Taxi Reform*, 151 P.3d at 423).
15. *Id.* (quoting Anchorage Citizens for Taxi Reform, 151 P.3d at 423).
16. *Id.* (emphasis in original) (quoting *McAlpine v. Univ. of Alaska*, 762 P.2d 88 (Alaska 1988)) (internal quotation marks omitted).
17. *See City of Fairbanks v. Fairbanks Convention & Visitors Bureau*, 818 P.2d 1153, 1157 (Alaska 1991) (concluding that an initiative was not a give-away program because "[n]o particular group or person or entity [was] targeted to receive state money or property, nor [was] there any indication that by passing [the] initiative, the voters would be voting themselves money").
18. *Pebble Ltd. P'ship*, 215 P.3d at 1075 (citing *Pullen v. Ulmer*, 923 P.2d 54, 64 n.15 (Alaska 1996)).
19. *Id.* (quoting *Staudenmaier v. Municipality of Anchorage*, 139 P.3d 1259, 1262 (Alaska 2006)).
20. 762 P.2d 81, 87–88 (Alaska 1988).
21. *Id.* at 83, 95–96.
22. *Id.* at 89–90.
23. *Id.* at 91.
24. *Id.* at 87.
25. *Id.* at 91.
26. *Id.*
27. 818 P.2d 1153, 1154–55 (Alaska 1991).
28. *Id.* at 1157.
29. *Id.* (emphasis added).
30. 923 P.2d 54, 55 (Alaska 1996).
31. *Id.* at 61.
32. *Id.* at 63–64.
33. *Id.* at 63.
34. *Compare id.* at 64 *with McAlpine v. Univ. of Alaska*, 762 P.2d 81, 91 (Alaska 1988) (upholding limitation on legislature's discretion to eliminate all funding for community colleges because there was "no realistic danger that the legislature would attempt to do so").
35. 84 P.3d 989, 990–91 (Alaska 2004).
36. *Id.* at 994 (quoting *McAlpine*, 762 P.2d at 89; *Pullen*, 923 P.2d at 63) (footnote omitted).
37. *Id.*
38. *Id.* (emphasis in original) (quoting *City of Fairbanks v. Fairbanks Convention & Visitors Bureau*, 818 P.2d 1153, 1156 (Alaska 1991)) (internal quotation marks omitted).
39. *Id.* at 994–95.
40. 139 P.3d 1259, 1260 (Alaska 2006).
41. *Id.* at 1260–61.
42. *Id.* at 1261.
43. *Id.* at 1263.
44. *Id.* (citing *Alaska Action Ctr. v. Municipality of Anchorage*, 84 P.3d 989, 994 (Alaska 2004)).
45. 215 P.3d 1064, 1069–70 (Alaska 2009).
46. *Id.* at 1074–77.
47. *Id.* at 1075.
48. *Id.* (citing *Pullen v. Ulmer*, 923 P.2d 54, 64 n.15 (Alaska 1996)).
49. *Id.* at 1077.
50. *Id.*
51. *Id.*
52. 273 P.3d 1128, 1130 (Alaska 2012).
53. *Id.* at 1137–38.
54. *Id.* at 1138 (emphasis added) (citing *Pullen v. Ulmer*, 923 P.2d 54, 64 (Alaska 1996)).
55. *Id.*
56. 321 P.3d 378, 380 (Alaska 2014).
57. *Id.* at 380–81.
58. *Id.* at 384.
59. *Id.*
60. *Id.* at 385.
61. *Id.* (quoting *Alliance of Concerned Taxpayers, Inc. v. Kenai Peninsula Borough*, 273 P.3d 1128, 1136 (Alaska 2012)).
62. *See McAlpine v. Univ. of Alaska*, 762 P.2d 81, 87, 96 (Alaska 1988) (approving initiative's requirement that the University of Alaska transfer to an independent community college

(case continues)

system "such real and personal property as is necessary to the independent operation and maintenance of the Community College System").
63. *See City of Fairbanks v. Fairbanks Visitors & Convention Bureau*, 818 P.2d 1153, 1157 (Alaska 1991) (concluding that initiative amending a city ordinance that designated the use of the city's hotel tax did not repeal an appropriation).
64. *See id.* (concluding that initiative could not be an appropriation if it expanded the legislature's authority to allocate funds).
65. *Pebble Ltd. P'ship ex rel. Pebble Mines Corp. v. Parnell*, 215 P.3d 1064, 1077 (Alaska 2009) (concluding that an initiative precluding discharge of mining waste that causes "'adverse effects' to humans, salmon, and waters used for human consumption or as salmon habitat" was not an appropriation).
66. *Holleman*, 321 P.3d at 381–85 (upholding referendum that would repeal municipal ordinance intended to reduce the Municipality of Anchorage's labor costs).
67. *See McAlpine*, 762 P.2d at 87–91 (striking from initiative a provision requiring the University of Alaska to transfer the amount of property "commensurate with that occupied and operated by the Community Colleges on November 1, 1986").
68. *See Alaska Action Ctr., v. Municipality of Anchorage*, 84 P.3d 989, 994–95 (Alaska 2004) (invalidating initiative limiting the use of a particular area of municipal land).
69. *See Pullen v. Ulmer*, 923 P.2d 54, 64 (Alaska 1996) (invalidating initiative establishing preferences for subsistence, personal, and recreational users in salmon fishery).
70. *See Staudenmaier v. Municipality of Anchorage*, 139 P.3d 1259, 1260–63 (Alaska 2006) (upholding municipality's rejection of initiative requiring the municipality to sell specified public utility assets).
71. *See Alliance of Concerned Taxpayers, Inc. v. Kenai Peninsula Borough*, 273 P.3d 1128, 1137–38 (Alaska 2012) (invalidating initiative requiring voter approval for all Borough capital expenditures in excess of one million dollars).
72. *Pebble Ltd. P'ship ex rel. Pebble Mines Corp. v. Parnell*, 215 P.3d 1064, 1077 (Alaska 2009).
73. *See Pullen*, 923 P.2d at 64 (holding that initiative setting user preferences in salmon fishery was an appropriation because it would limit the Board of Fisheries' discretion to make allocation decisions in times of shortage and "there is a very realistic danger that such shortages will occur"); *McAlpine v. Univ. of Alaska*, 762 P.2d 81, 91 (Alaska 1988) (concluding that limiting legislature's discretion to eliminate all appropriations for community colleges was permissible because there was no realistic danger that the legislature would attempt to do so).
74. 818 P.2d 1153, 1154–55 (Alaska 1991).
75. 762 P.2d at 89.
76. 84 P.3d 989, 995–96 (Alaska 2004).
77. *See Staudenmaier v. Municipality of Anchorage*, 139 P.3d 1259, 1263 (Alaska 2006); *Alliance of Concerned Taxpayers, Inc. v. Kenai Peninsula Borough*, 273 P.3d 1128, 1137–38 (Alaska 2012).
78. *See Pullen*, 923 P.2d at 64 (invalidating initiative that would have established preferences for subsistence, personal, and recreational users in salmon fishery).
79. *See Pebble Ltd. P'ship ex rel. Pebble Mines Corp. v. Parnell*, 215 P.3d 1064, 1077 (Alaska 2009) (citing *Pullen*, 923 P.2d at 63–64).
80. *Id.*
81. *Staudenmaier*, 139 P.3d at 1263 (citing *Alaska Action Ctr.*, 84 P.3d at 994–95).
82. This contrasts with article II, section 19, under which a legislative act that is "local or special" may still be constitutional, so long as a general act could not have been made applicable. Hughes argues that 12BBAY is local or special legislation because the initiative could have been drafted to apply statewide. But neither article XI, section 7, nor any other source of authority in Alaska, suggests that an initiative would enact local or special legislation simply because it could have been drafted to apply statewide. Article II, section 19 implies that local or special legislation may be permissible where a general act could not have been made applicable, but that provision does not apply to initiatives. While the substantive provisions of these two constitutional provisions differ, the analysis they use to determine whether particular legislation is "local or special" is the same.
83. *Pebble Ltd. P'ship*, 215 P.3d at 1078.
84. *Id.* (citing *Boucher v. Engstrom*, 528 P.2d 456, 461 (Alaska 1974), *overruled on other grounds by McAlpine v. Univ. of Alaska*, 762 P.2d 81, 85 (Alaska 1988)).
85. *Id.*
86. *Id.* at 1079 (quoting *State v. Lewis*, 559 P.2d 630, 643 & n.44 (Alaska 1977)) (internal quotation marks omitted).
87. *Id.* (citing *Boucher*, 528 P.2d at 461).
88. *Id.* (internal quotation marks omitted).
89. The record indicates that large-scale metallic sulfide mining has real potential to affect water quality and fisheries.
90. 559 P.2d 630, 643–44 (Alaska 1977).
91. 958 P.2d 422, 430–31 (Alaska 1998).
92. AS 38.05.140(f).
93. *See Baxley*, 958 P.2d at 430–31.
94. Bristol Bay also has the vast majority of sockeye (red) salmon statewide; chum and pink salmon represent the majority of the harvest in Prince William Sound and Southeast Alaska. A significant loss of salmon in Bristol Bay would therefore particularly affect the state's sockeye salmon population.
95. The commercial fishing season is six to eight weeks in Bristol Bay, but most of the run occurs in just two weeks. This contrasts with fisheries in Prince William Sound and Southeast Alaska, where the harvest windows are longer by a month or more. Other fisheries that have higher incidence of coho or chum salmon may have several months more of harvest as well.
96. *Pebble Ltd. P'ship ex rel. Pebble Mines Corp. v. Parnell*, 215 P.3d 1064, 1081 (Alaska 2009) (internal quotation marks omitted).
97. *Id.* (internal quotation marks omitted).

CASE *Bristol Bay Mining II*

Hughes, et al v. Treadwell, et al

S-15468, Order of June 23, 2014
Supreme Court of Alaska
Before: Winfree, Stowers, Maassen, and Bolger, Justices

In October 2012 Lieutenant Governor Mead Treadwell received an application for an initiative entitled "Bristol Bay Forever"; the Division of Elections denominated the initiative "12BBAY." 12BBAY would require final legislative authorization for any new large-scale metallic sulfide mining operations in the watershed of the Bristol Bay Fisheries Reserve. After review by the Department of Law, the Lieutenant Governor certified the initiative application and directed the Division of Elections to prepare petition booklets.

In January 2013 Richard Hughes filed suit in the superior court challenging the Lieutenant Governor's certification of 12BBAY. The Alaska Miners Association and the Council of Alaska Producers later joined as plaintiffs,[1] and initiative sponsors Christina Salmon, Mark Niver, and John H. Holman intervened as defendants. While litigation was pending in the superior court, the Division of Elections determined that the sponsors had gathered sufficient signatures, and the Lieutenant Governor issued a Notice of Proper Filing allowing the Division of Elections to place 12BBAY on the ballot.[2]

Hughes moved for summary judgment, arguing that 12BBAY would: (1) enact local or special legislation in violation of article XI, section 7 of the Alaska Constitution; (2) violate separation of powers under article XII, section 11 of the Alaska Constitution; and (3) appropriate state assets in violation of article XI, section 7 of the Alaska Constitution. Superior Court Judge Paul R. Lyle concluded that 12BBAY would not enact local or special legislation, would not clearly violate separation of powers, and would not appropriate public assets. Judge Lyle granted summary judgment in favor of the State and the initiative sponsors and declined to enjoin placement of 12BBAY on the ballot. Hughes appealed to this court, challenging Judge Lyle's conclusions that 12BBAY would not make an unconstitutional appropriation of public assets or enact local or special legislation.[3] We heard oral argument on June 11, 2014.

Because an expedited decision is needed by September 3, 2014 so that the Division of Elections can know whether to include 12BBAY on the November ballot, we issue the following order.

It is Ordered:

1. 12BBAY would not make an appropriation of state assets in violation of article XI, section 7 of the Alaska Constitution.
2. 12BBAY would not enact local or special legislation in violation of article XI, section 7 of the Alaska Constitution.
3. Accordingly, we AFFIRM the superior court's decision granting summary judgment to the State and the initiative sponsors and declining to enjoin placement of 12BBAY on the ballot.
4. We will issue a written opinion at a future date explaining the reasons for this result, but preparation of the ballots to include 12BBAY shall proceed without awaiting our opinion.

---

1. We refer to the plaintiffs/appellants collectively as "Hughes."
2. Letter from Mead Treadwell, Lieutenant Governor, State of Alaska, to John Holman, Initiative Sponsor (December 23, 2013) (on file with State of Alaska, Division of Elections), *available at* http://www.elections.alaska.gov/petitions/12BBAY/12BBAY-Notice-of-Proper-Filing.pdf.
3. Hughes does not appeal Judge Lyle's conclusion that 12BBAY would not clearly violate separation of powers principles.

CASE *The Fire in Fairbanks*

Brewer v. Alaska

4FA-10-02618 CI, 6968 November 28, 2014
Supreme Court of Alaska
Before: Fabe, Chief Justice, Stowers, Maassen, and Bolger, Justices
Opinion by, MAASSEN, Justice

Introduction

Major forest fires swept through areas south of Fairbanks in the summer of 2009 and approached properties owned by the appellants (the landowners). In an effort to save the landowners' structures, firefighters working under the direction of the State Department of Forestry intentionally set fire to the landowners' vegetation. The burnouts deprived the advancing wildfires of fuel and saved the structures. But the landowners sued the State, bringing a takings claim under the eminent domain provision of the Alaska Constitution, article I, section 18 (the Takings Clause), and tort claims for negligence and intentional misconduct. We affirm the superior court's dismissal of the tort claims because of governmental immunity; we reverse its dismissal of the constitutional claim, remanding it to the superior court for further consideration of whether the specific exercise of the State's police powers at issue here was justified by the doctrine of necessity.

Facts and Proceedings

Facts

During the summer of 2009, wildfires that came to be known as the Railbelt Complex developed in Interior Alaska, ultimately engulfing over 600,000 acres.[1] The appellant landowners owned property in subdivisions known as Teklanika Channel Lake, Dune Lake, and Totek Lake, about 45 miles southwest of Fairbanks. Their properties are on land designated by the State's "Alaska Interagency Wildland Fire Management Plan" (the Plan) as a "Full Management Option" fire protection area, meaning that the State anticipated an "aggressive initial attack dependent upon the availability of suppression resources."[2] The landowners and the State agree that, as the fires approached, firefighters acting under State authority entered the landowners' property and set fire to vegetation surrounding their structures; these fires were pushed out to meet the oncoming wildfires. The tactic, called backfires or burnouts, is used to deprive an oncoming fire of fuel.[3] According to the State, the Railbelt Complex fires passed through the subdivisions without damaging the landowners' structures; the landowners do not appear to dispute it.

Proceedings

Landowners William Brewer II and Donna Brewer, William Brewer III and Stephanie Brewer, Charles and Margaret Gray, and Cindy Walker[4] all filed suit against the State in 2010. Each suit alleged a takings claim under article I, section 18 of the Alaska Constitution and tort claims alleging negligent and intentional acts. The suits were consolidated in December 2010. Allen Gray filed suit in March 2011, asserting identical harms and legal theories, and his suit was consolidated with the others.

The landowners moved for partial summary judgment, contending that the burnouts constituted a compensable taking as a matter of law and that the State's actions were intentional, making it liable in tort. According to the landowners, the only remaining question of fact was the amount of just compensation they were due. The State cross-moved for summary judgment, claiming governmental immunity and advancing a number of arguments against liability for a taking.

In subsequent filings the landowners elaborated on their claims. They asserted that, in contravention of its stated policy of Full Management Option protection, the State made no attempt to minimize or suppress the wildfires, instead opting to burn "as much wildland forest as possible," impliedly for purposes of "fuels management." The landowners offered affidavits alleging that the State conducted the burnouts even though there was no "imminent threat of fire damage" to their properties and the State could have "undertaken . . . the damaging fire suppression activities on bordering State-owned lands" instead.

The superior court granted summary judgment to the State. As for the constitutional claim, the superior court decided that the State's actions did not constitute a taking because they were a valid exercise of its police powers. As for the tort claims, the superior court concluded that the State was entitled to immunity under both AS 09.50.250 and AS 41.15.045.

The landowners filed this appeal.

(case continues)

Standards of Review

We review a grant of summary judgment de novo, affirming if there is no genuine dispute of material fact and the undisputed facts demonstrate that the moving party is entitled to judgment as a matter of law.[5] We review the facts in the light most favorable to the non-moving parties and draw all reasonable inferences in their favor.[6] We review the Alaska Constitution and Alaska statutes de novo, "adopting rules of law that best reflect precedent, reason, and policy."[7]

Discussion

It Was Error to Dismiss the Landowners' Takings Claims

Article I, section 18 of the Alaska Constitution—entitled "Eminent Domain" and commonly known as the Takings Clause—states that "[p]rivate property shall not be taken or damaged for public use without just compensation."[8] The landowners contend that the State damaged their private property for public use, entitling them to just compensation under the Constitution.

"We liberally interpret Alaska's Takings Clause in favor of property owners, whom it protects more broadly than the federal Takings Clause."[9] This protection applies to personal as well as real property and allows compensation for temporary as well as permanent takings.[10] Takings claims are not based in tort and do not require that the government act with any particular mental state.[11] The viability of a constitutional takings claim thus is unaffected by tort immunity, which is not constitutional but statutory.[12]

The landowners allege a taking for public use

For the landowners to state a claim entitling them to just compensation under the Takings Clause, they must show that the State damaged their property and did so for a public use. There is no dispute in this case that the landowners' property was damaged, nor that the damage was caused by the State. The parties do dispute, however, whether the damage was for a public use.

The landowners concede that the burnouts were intended to protect their structures; their quarrel is with when and where the State set the burnouts. They argue that the burnouts could have been conducted before the structures were directly threatened and could have been set on State-owned land instead of their private land. In the landowners' view, the burnouts damaged their property for a public use because "the State encouraged the burn off of the wildlands between the Kantishna and Teklanika rivers as far south as possible as a public project to rejuvenate the wildlands," an action which "obviously serves to benefit the public demand for, *inter alia*, game animals for human consumption." They allege a second public use as well: "to forestall the spread of the fire to State-owned lands, e.g. the Tanana Valley State Forest and other commercial forests."

The State takes two arguably contradictory positions in response to the landowners' takings claim. In support of its argument that it acted within the lawful exercise of its police powers, the State asserts "that the burnouts were part of the larger fire management effort, and that public purposes of promoting the general health, safety, and welfare of the public animate the police powers." On the other hand, the State argues that the burnouts were "not necessary to the overall fire suppression effort" and were conducted solely to prevent the destruction of the landowners' private structures—not a public use at all.

We find more persuasive the State's first argument—that it acted within the lawful exercise of its police powers. The United States Supreme Court has described the public use requirement of the federal Takings Clause as "coterminous with the scope of a sovereign's police powers."[13] One important aspect of the police power is the suppression and prevention of fires; indeed, "[p]erhaps the most striking application of the police power is the destruction of buildings to prevent the spread of a conflagration."[14]

In Alaska, the State's entry upon private land "for the purpose of preventing, suppressing, or controlling a wildland fire" is explicitly authorized by statute.[15] The legislature further emphasized the public nature of such activities in its enactment of a specific statutory immunity for actions taken while fighting wildfires (discussed below).[16] Implicit in these provisions is the accepted wisdom that fighting wildfires, even on private property, is of benefit to the public as a whole regardless of whether only individual landowners are immediately benefitted. In this case, putting aside the issues of whether the burnouts were set at the right time and in the right place, there is no dispute that they were part of the State's efforts to contain and direct the Railbelt Complex fires. Because the burnouts were set in the exercise of the State's police powers, the damage they caused was for a public use for purposes of the Takings Clause.

We therefore need not reach the landowners' arguments that the public use can be found in alleged State purposes to maximize forage for wildlife or to protect forests that were commercially valuable. And we reject the State's argument that there is no public

(case continues)

benefit or use in conducting burnouts on private land to prevent the destruction of private structures.

On this point, the United States Supreme Court's decision in *Hawaii Housing Authority v. Midkiff*[17] is helpful. One issue was whether the condemnation of private property was for a public use when it was made under a Hawaii law that transferred ownership to other private parties, the long-term lessees, in an effort to break up historic oligarchies. According to the Supreme Court, "[t]he mere fact that property taken outright by eminent domain is transferred in the first instance to private beneficiaries does not condemn that taking as having only a private purpose."[18] It quoted its earlier decisions for the propositions that "[i]t is not essential that the entire community, nor even any considerable portion, . . . directly enjoy or participate in any improvement in order [for it] to constitute a public use";[19] and "what in its immediate aspect [is] only a private transaction may . . . be raised by its class or character to a public affair."[20] The Court also noted the great deference courts show to the legislature's determination that certain measures involve a public use.[21]

Here, too, the State's argument that the individual landowners benefitted—and perhaps solely benefitted—from the burnouts on their property does not dilute the evident public purpose of the State's firefighting activity. A similar issue was presented in *Town of Gila Bend v. Walled Lake Door Co.*[22] The Arizona Supreme Court considered an argument that a town's contract to construct a water main to a factory building violated a state constitutional provision prohibiting public investment in private corporations. The court rejected the argument, observing in part that "the fact that the Company stands to be directly benefited in the event that a fire should occur at its plant and will be indirectly benefited by reduced fire insurance premiums is of absolutely no consequence."[23] The court concluded, "There can be no doubt but that the supplying of water for purposes of preserving and protecting lives and property is a 'public purpose' and one which will provide a direct benefit to the public at large."[24]

We recognize that precedent can lead us in different directions. In *National Board of YMCA v. United States*, the Supreme Court created what came to be known as the "intended beneficiary" rule, by which government action taken primarily to defend private property from damage does not result in a compensable taking.[25] During riots in the Panama Canal Zone, the Army occupied the petitioners' buildings, which were heavily damaged during the fighting that followed.[26] Although the petitioners argued that the Army used their buildings "as part of a general defense of the Zone as a whole," the Court concluded that "[t]he stipulated record . . . demonstrates that the troops were acting primarily in defense of petitioners' buildings."[27]

Relying on the purpose of the federal Just Compensation Clause—"to bar Government from forcing some people alone to bear public burdens which, in all fairness and justice, should be borne by the public as a whole"—the Supreme Court held that the clause did not apply to the petitioners' losses.[28] It acknowledged that "any protection of private property also serves a broader public purpose."[29] But it went on to say that

> *where, as here, the private party is the particular intended beneficiary of the governmental activity, 'fairness and justice' do not require that losses which may result from that activity 'be borne by the public as a whole,' even though the activity may also be intended incidentally to benefit the public. Were it otherwise, governmental bodies would be liable under the Just Compensation Clause to property owners every time policemen break down the doors of buildings to foil burglars thought to be inside.*[30]

That the petitioners' damage was not directly caused by the government made no difference to the Court's analysis: "[P]etitioners would not have a claim for compensation under the Fifth Amendment even if they could show that damage inflicted by rioters occurred because of the presence of the troops."[31]

We do not believe that *YMCA*'s "intended beneficiary" test adequately reflects the broad protection of Alaska's Takings Clause.[32] A New Jersey appellate court recently identified several of the test's shortcomings, most importantly that it "forces courts to be 'caught up in an identification and evaluation of the primary beneficiary,' when, in reality, 'the intended beneficiary of police activity is always the general public.'"[33] We note further that the danger the Supreme Court identified in recognizing a right to compensation under the Fifth Amendment when a private party is "the particular intended beneficiary of the government activity"—that it would make the government liable to the owners "every time policemen break down the doors of buildings to foil burglars thought to be inside"[34]—ignores the doctrine of necessity, discussed below.

In this case, when the State conducted burnouts on the landowners' properties, it was exercising an essential aspect of its police power. We conclude that this is sufficient to show a public use, whether the burnouts were intended to benefit primarily other

(case continues)

State lands, as the landowners allege, or primarily the landowners, as the State alleges.

The burnouts conducted by the state do not constitute a compensable taking if they were justified by the doctrine of necessity

Regardless of whether the State damaged the landowners' property for a public use, the landowners have no constitutional right to just compensation if the State's actions were justified by the doctrine of necessity. But given the broad protections of Alaska's Takings Clause, we decline to hold that every valid exercise of the police power is justified by the doctrine of necessity and results in a noncompensable taking.

In granting summary judgment to the State on the takings claims, the superior court found in effect that necessity was implicit in the State's exercise of its police power. The court reasoned that it was pursuant to the State's police power that the legislature enacted AS 41.15.040, the statute granting firefighters access to private property for the purpose of fighting fires,[35] and that the State acted pursuant to this statutory authority when it set burnouts on the landowners' property. The court reasoned: "Wildfire suppression activities such as those authorized by AS 41.15.040 are clear examples of the valid exercise of state police power for the protection of its citizenry and natural resources, and therefore no compensation is due when property is damaged pursuant to the prevention, suppression, or control of wildland fires." The State essentially adopts the superior court's analysis on this appeal.

Firefighting is undoubtedly an exercise of the State's police power, as we acknowledge above. But we decline to hold that the police power is coextensive with the doctrine of necessity, i.e., that because firefighting is an exercise of the police power, all damage caused during the State's firefighting activities is per se necessary and therefore not compensable under the takings clause. We agree with an observation of a federal claims court: "If the police power exception to just compensation is limited only by the sovereign power of the Government, . . . it becomes the exception which swallows the rule, an intolerable result."[36] In the context of firefighting, as we explain below, the doctrine of necessity requires that there be an imminent danger and an actual emergency giving rise to actual necessity; otherwise, damage may be compensable under the Takings Clause even though it is caused by the State's otherwise valid exercise of the police power.

We have held that "[t]he distinction between eminent domain and the state's police power is well established legal doctrine."[37] Where one ends and the other begins, however, may be difficult to define. Eminent domain is "the right of a government to take and appropriate private property to public use whenever the public exigency requires it; which can be done only on condition of providing a reasonable compensation therefor,"[38] whereas the police power may allow the State "consistently with constitutional requirements [to] acquire private property interests in a manner that does not constitute a taking,"[39] i.e., without having to provide reasonable compensation.[40] In *Waiste v. State*, for example, we held that the "government seizure of property suspected of having been used to break the law falls squarely within the police power" and "is not an exercise of the State's constitutional taking power for which the Takings Clause triggers the requirement of just compensation."[41]

But the distinction between eminent domain (compensable) and a valid exercise of the police power (not compensable) is not a sharp one.[42] The United States Supreme Court has repeatedly recognized that there are limits beyond which a state's otherwise valid exercise of its police power may require compensation.[43] Defining those limits in the context of firefighting activities is our immediate task; we do so by reference to the doctrine of necessity, which has a long history in the common law.[44]

Public necessity acts as a defense to property torts such as trespass and conversion and allows a person to enter land and destroy property where there is "[a] necessity that involves the public interest."[45] Public necessity "completely excuses the defendant's liability."[46] While the privilege of public necessity is an individual one, state officials can exercise it.[47] Thus, the state generally does not have to pay compensation where "the destruction or damage was, or reasonably appeared to be, necessary to prevent an impending or imminent public disaster from fire, flood, disease, or riot."[48] Almost all cases that discuss public necessity note that it generally includes the destruction of buildings or land to stop the spread of a fire.[49]

When the United States and state constitutions were adopted, courts continued to use public necessity as an implicit exception to the requirement of just compensation.[50] A seminal case is *Bowditch v. City of Boston*, in which the Supreme Court explained the common law roots of the necessity doctrine: "At the common law every one had the right to destroy real and personal property, in cases of actual necessity, to prevent the spreading of a fire, and there was no responsibility on the part of such destroyer, and no remedy for the owner."[51] It went on: "In these cases the common law adopts

(case continues)

the principle of the natural law, and finds the right and the justification in the same imperative necessity."[52] Later cases affirmed the common law foundations of the necessity defense under similar circumstances.[53]

The Federal Circuit recently discussed the necessity doctrine in *TrinCo Investment Co. v. United States*.[54] Wildfires were burning parts of the Shasta-Trinity National Forest in California. The Forest Service intentionally lit fires on and adjacent to TrinCo's properties in order to deprive the fires of fuel, thereby destroying nearly two thousand acres of TrinCo's timber, worth over $6 million. TrinCo sued the United States, alleging a taking, though unlike the landowners here they alleged that the fires would never have reached their property at all were it not for government intervention.[55]

The federal claims court granted the United States' motion to dismiss, reasoning that "the doctrine of necessity absolves the Government from liability for any taking or destruction of property in efforts to fight fires."[56] On appeal, however, the Federal Circuit held that the lower court had "misapprehended the reach of the doctrine of necessity."[57] It held that "extend[ing] the doctrine of necessity to automatically absolve the Government's action in any case involving fire control stretches the doctrine too far."[58]

The Federal Circuit found no law directly on point, but it concluded that Supreme Court precedent required "that the doctrine of necessity may be applied only when there is an imminent danger and an actual emergency giving rise to actual necessity."[59] It noted that in *Bowditch*, the City of Boston was not liable when its firefighters demolished a building "at a place of danger in the immediate vicinity [of a fire], to arrest the spreading of the fire," and "the measure . . . stopped the progress of the fire."[60] It noted that in *Caltex*, the United States was not liable for the Army's destruction of privately owned oil facilities in Manila "in the face of their impending seizure by the enemy," where Japanese troops were marching into the city and their planes were bombing the area.[61] It cited another wartime seizure case, *Mitchell v. Harmony*, involving the Army's confiscation and loss of a trader's goods during the war with Mexico:[62] "[F]or a taking to be justified during wartime the 'danger must be immediate and impending' or the 'necessity urgent . . . such as will not admit delay' because 'it is the emergency that gives the right [to the Government to take private property], and emergency must be shown to exist before the taking can be justified.'"[63]

Applying the test for necessity that it extrapolated from this case law—"imminent danger and an actual emergency giving rise to actual necessity"—the Federal Circuit reversed the dismissal of TrinCo's takings claim.[64] It noted that the facts as alleged in TrinCo's complaint did not demonstrate "the kind of imminent danger and actual emergency posed by a fire burning in a populated city, as in *Bowditch*, or an invading enemy army, as in *Caltex*."[65] It held that "[i]t is certainly plausible that the Iron Complex fire did not pose an imminent danger or actual emergency necessitating the destruction of such a sizable portion of TrinCo's property," and that discovery could show "why the Plaintiff's property had to be sacrificed, as opposed to other property, including other portions of the National Forest itself."[66] It concluded: "It would be a remarkable thing if the Government is allowed to take a private citizen's property without compensation if it could just as easily solve the problem by taking its own."[67]

We agree with the analysis in *TrinCo*. Here, the superior court considered only whether the State's actions were taken within the context of its general police power. But a taking of private property does not escape application of the Takings Clause simply because it occurs in the course of the State's fire-fighting activities; to be noncompensable, the taking must be justified by the doctrine of necessity. The doctrine applies only if the State demonstrates the existence of "imminent danger and an actual emergency giving rise to actual necessity," an inquiry that is fact-specific.[68]

This inquiry should not devolve into an after-the-fact evaluation of the wisdom of the fire fighting policies and tactical choices that preceded the taking, decisions that in a tort action are immunized by AS 41.15.045. Whether a taking is necessary must be judged at the time the taking occurs. The essence of the doctrine is that the government is acting "under pressure of public necessity and to avert impending peril" and chooses to damage private property as the lesser of two evils.[69] It is that choice, in that moment, for which necessity may provide a defense.

The facts of this case may support applying the doctrine of necessity. But the parties' evidence must be evaluated in the context of whether there was an "imminent danger and an actual emergency giving rise to actual necessity," a task we leave to the superior court in the first instance. We reverse the grant of summary judgment to the State on the landowners' claim under the Takings Clause of the Alaska Constitution and remand it to the superior court for further consideration; but in so doing we do not decide whether the evidence already in the record would preclude another grant of summary judgment for the State.

(case continues)

The Superior Court Did Not Err in Dismissing the Landowners' Tort Claims

The landowners argue that the superior court also erred in dismissing their tort claims against the State, but on this issue we affirm the judgment of the superior court, finding the claims barred by statutory immunity.

Alaska statute 41.15.045, not AS 09.50.250, controls whether the state's firefighting activities are immune from tort liability

The superior court conducted a two-step analysis of the State's governmental immunity defense, addressing first the discretionary immunity provided by AS 09.50.250 and then addressing the specific firefighting immunity provided by AS 41.15.045. We hold that the latter statute controls.[70]

Alaska Statute 09.50.250 precludes tort claims against the State that are "based upon the exercise or performance or the failure to exercise or perform a discretionary function or duty on the part of a state agency or an employee of the state, whether or not the discretion involved is abused." We discussed this statute in the context of fighting wildfires in *Angnabooguk v. State*, in which we specifically rejected the State's claim that all such activities were immune as necessarily involving policy choices or some other exercise of discretion.[71] Focusing on AS 09.50.250, our analysis began with the well-established distinction between planning (that is, discretionary) and operational decisions for purposes of determining whether statutory immunity applies.[72] We noted our consistent holdings that "the State's decision to engage in an activity is an immune 'planning' decision, while the decisions undertaken in implementing the activity are operational, as long as the implementation does not involve the consideration of policy factors."[73] We noted that "certain on-the-scene firefighting tactical decisions may be considered discretionary because they entail resource allocation decisions or considered decisions of firefighting policy that are properly vested in the officials in charge," and we gave as one example the setting of backfires.[74] On the other hand, we noted that decisions considered operational could include the State's failure to prevent employees from working under the influence of drugs or alcohol, failure to build a firewall, failure to post lookouts during a burnout, and failure to conduct an adequate mop-up.[75] We remanded the case to the superior court for further factual development as to which of the tactical firefighting decisions at issue were operational and which were planning and therefore immune.[76]

Following *Angnabooguk*, the legislature enacted an immunity statute that provides broad tort immunity for firefighting activities without regard to the "planning/operational" distinction drawn in the context of the more general immunity statute, AS 09.50.250. The new statute, AS 41.15.045(a), provides immunity to the State and other governmental entities from any "civil action for damages for death, personal injury, or property damage that results from an act or omission in performing or failing to perform activities or duties arising out of prevention, monitoring, control, or suppression of fires authorized to be performed under AS 41.15.010–41.15.170 [addressing wildland and forest fires]." The new statute's only exception is for actions for damages resulting from "intentional misconduct within the course and scope of employment or agency and with complete disregard for the safety and property of others."[77]

Legislative history shows that AS 41.15.045 was adopted in direct response to our decision in *Angnabooguk* and the law of governmental immunity as we applied it to firefighting activities in that case.[78] The governor's sponsor statement, and his letter transmitting the proposed bill to the legislature, reported that two of this court's 2001 decisions[79] "ruled that the State of Alaska may be sued and held liable for tort claims for losses due to fire suppression efforts" and that "[t]hese decisions open the door to significant financial exposure to the state for losses due to fires."[80] The transmittal letter and sponsor statement stated that "[d]ecisions regarding forest management related to fire control and suppression should be prompted by sound forestry and firefighting principles, rather than concerns regarding possible tort liability," and that "[l]itigation of such claims inherently disrupts the division of forestry's day-to-day operations and diverts substantial state resources to defend such lawsuits."[81] The proposed bill was intended to correct this perceived problem; in a contemporaneous sectional analysis of the bill, the Department of Law observed that the broad firefighting immunity provision was included in order to "override the decision of the Alaska Supreme Court in *Angnabooguk* . . . that, because the state legislature had not explicitly made all firefighting activities and decisions immune from suit, both the state and individual firefighters could be held liable for damage caused by a wildfire."[82]

In sum, as we held in *Angnabooguk*, AS 09.50.250 immunizes tactical firefighting activities only to the extent they may be categorized as discretionary planning decisions; it does not immunize firefighting activities that are operational.[83] Alaska Statute 41.15.045, on the other hand, immunizes *all* firefighting activities regardless of the planning/operational

(case continues)

distinction, with a limited exception for intentional misconduct. As the two statutes conflict, we apply the one that is both more specific and later in time—AS 41.15.045, the 2003 law that addresses firefighting activities specifically.[84]

The state's conduct does not fall within the "intentional misconduct" exception of AS 41.15.045(B)

Focusing on the firefighter immunity statute, the landowners argue that their claims satisfy its exception for "intentional misconduct within the course and scope of employment or agency and with complete disregard for the safety and property of others."[85] The landowners argue that (1) the State acted intentionally in conducting the burnouts on their properties; and (2) burnouts in violation of the State's Full Management Option protection policy—which applies to the landowners' properties under the interagency fire protection plan—constitute misconduct. The Full Management Option protection policy has as its stated objectives (1) to control fires on the designated property "at the smallest acreage reasonably possible on initial attack without compromising fire fighter safety"; (2) to protect the property from the spread of fires "burning in a lower priority management option"; and (3) to minimize damage on the property "commensurate with the values at risk."

The landowners acknowledge that the "Plan was developed to enable appropriate fire suppression decisions 'within the constraints of policy and land management objectives.' " The landowners recognize that the objectives the State faces may be competing ones: for example, the minimization of burning on properties given Full protection status and the maximization of burning for ecological purposes. The landowners complain, however, that the State made the wrong choice between these objectives: "the State's maximum acreage goal was prioritized and realized to its fullest extent by means of deliberately damaging the Full fire protection properties." Under the landowners' theory, the State's deliberate election of one policy objective over another constitutes misconduct.

As we observed in *Angnabooguk*, "we have consistently held that, for all State activities, the State's decision to engage in an activity is an immune 'planning' decision, while the decisions undertaken in implementing the activity are operational, *as long as the implementation does not involve the consideration of policy factors*."[86] When analyzing cases under AS 09.50.250, we "have recognized that if decisions require the state to balance 'the detailed and competing elements of legislative or executive policy,' they nearly always deserve protection by discretionary function immunity."[87] Furthermore, " '[d]ecisions about how to allocate scarce resources' will ordinarily be immune from judicial review."[88]

The decision on which the landowners base their misconduct argument—allegedly a decision to prioritize a "maximum acreage goal" over the Full protection policy expressed in the interagency fire management plan—inescapably involves both balancing executive policies and allocating limited resources. Under AS 09.50.250, these decisions would be immune as discretionary planning activities. Given that AS 41.15.045 clearly expands the range of firefighting activities for which the State is immune, it would be unreasonable for us to conclude that activities that would be immune under AS 09.50.250 lost their immunity with the enactment of AS 41.50.045 because of the "intentional misconduct" exception. And because the landowners cannot show intentional misconduct, we need not address the other elements of the exception: whether the alleged misconduct occurred "within the course and scope of employment or agency and with complete disregard for the safety and property of others."

Conclusion

We AFFIRM the superior court's dismissal of the landowners' tort claims and REVERSE the dismissal of their claims for just compensation under the Takings Clause of the Alaska Constitution. We REMAND for further proceedings consistent with this opinion.

---

1. *See* Alaska Interagency Coordination Ctr. Predictive Servs. Section, Alaska Fire Season 2009: Wildland Fire Summary & Statistics Annual Report 18 (2009), *available at* http://fire.ak.blm.gov/content/aicc/stats/archive/2009.pdf.
2. The Plan sets four levels of fire management—Critical, Full, Modified, and Limited—with different planned responses and objectives for each. The listed objectives for the Full Management Option are these:
   1. Control all wildland fires occurring within this management option at the smallest acreage reasonably possible on initial attack without compromising fire fighter safety.
   2. Protect sites or areas designated as Full management from the spread of wildland fires burning in a lower priority management option.
   3. Minimize damage from wildland fires to the resources identified for protection within the Full management designation commensurate with values at risk.
3. The State explains that "backfire" refers primarily to a fire set to attack and suppress an oncoming wildfire, whereas "burnout" refers primarily to a fire set in defense of designated areas behind control lines. The State asserts that it set the fires at issue primarily to protect structures rather than to suppress

(case continues)

the wildfire complex; we therefore use the term "burnout" in this opinion.

4. Walker was released from the suit before summary judgment.
5. *Waiste v. State*, 10 P.3d 1141, 1144 (Alaska 2000).
6. *Id.* at 1144–45.
7. Id. at 1144.
8. We recognize that when the government takes private property for public use without paying just compensation and the property owner brings suit, the claim is not for eminent domain but for inverse condemnation. *See Mt. Juneau Enters., Inc. v. City & Borough of Juneau*, 923 P.2d 768, 773 (Alaska 1996). The constitutional provision on which such a suit is grounded, however—the Takings Clause—is entitled "Eminent Domain."
9. *Waiste*, 10 P.3d at 1154.
10. *Id.*
11. *Cannone v. Noey*, 867 P.2d 797, 801 n.7 (Alaska 1994) ("If an owner is denied productive use of his or her property, that may be a taking regardless of the mental state of the involved government official, whether it be malicious, negligent, non-negligent but mistaken, or non-negligent and not mistaken.").
12. *State, Dep't of Health & Soc. Servs. v. Planned Parenthood of Alaska, Inc.*, 28 P.3d 904, 914 (Alaska 2001) ("[W]e cannot defer to the legislature when infringement of a constitutional right results from legislative action." (quoting *Valley Hosp. Ass'n v. Mat-Su Coalition for Choice*, 948 P.2d 963, 972 (Alaska 1997)) (internal quotation marks omitted)). *See also Thousand Trails, Inc. v. Cal. Reclamation Dist. No. 17*, 21 Cal. Rptr. 3d 196, 204 (Cal. App. 2004) ("The inverse condemnation action is independent of any right to sue under traditional tort theories.").
13. *Haw. Housing Auth. v. Midkiff*, 467 U.S. 229, 240 (1984); *see also Ruckelshaus v. Monsanto Co.*, 467 U.S. 986, 1014 (1984).
14. *Northwestern Fertilizing Co. v. Vill. of Hyde Park*, 97 U.S. 659, 669 (1878).
15. AS 41.15.040.
16. AS 41.15.045.
17. 467 U.S. at 243–44.
18. *Id.*
19. *Id.* at 244 (second and third alterations in original) (quoting *Rindge Co. v. Los Angeles Cnty.*, 262 U.S. 700, 707 (1923)) (internal quotation marks omitted).
20. *Id.* (alterations in original) (quoting *Block v. Hirsh*, 256 U.S. 135, 155 (1921)) (internal quotation marks omitted).
21. *Id. See also Mountain Water Co. v. Mont. Dep't of Pub. Serv. Regulation*, 919 F.2d 593, 599–600 (9th Cir. 1990) (explaining *Hawaii Housing* and noting that "[a] taking satisfies the constitutional public use requirement if it advances a 'conceivable public purpose' and regardless of whether it succeeds in realizing that purpose").
22. 490 P.2d 551 (Ariz. 1971).
23. *Id.* at 555–56.
24. *Id.* at 556. *See also Concerned Citizens for Responsible Gov't v. W. Pt. Fire Prot. Dist.*, 127 Cal. Rptr. 3d 783, 791 (Cal. App. 2011), review granted, 262 P.3d 853 (Cal. 2011) ("Fire suppression, like bus transportation or police protection, is a classic example of a service that confers general benefits on the community as a whole."); *Verizina v. City of Hartford*, 138 A. 145, 146 (Conn. 1927) ("A fire department engaged in extinguishing fires is performing a governmental duty for the general good.").
25. 395 U.S. 85 (1969).
26. *Id.* at 87–88.
27. *Id.* at 90.
28. *Id.* at 89.
29. *Id.* at 92.
30. *Id.* (citations omitted).
31. *Id.* at 89.
32. "We liberally interpret Alaska's Takings Clause in favor of property owners, whom it protects more broadly than the federal Takings Clause." *Waiste v. State*, 10 P.3d 1141, 1154 (Alaska 2000); *see also Vanek v. State, Bd. of Fisheries*, 193 P.3d 283, 288 (Alaska 2008) ("The Alaska Constitution contains a broader conception of compensable takings" than the Fifth Amendment of the federal constitution.).
33. *Simmons v. Loose*, 13 A.3d 366, 389 (N.J. Super. App. Div. 2011) (quoting C. Wayne Owen, Jr., *Everyone Benefits, Everyone Pays: Does the Fifth Amendment Mandate Compensation When Property is Damaged During the Course of Police Activities?*, 9 Wm. & Mary Bill Rts. J. 277, 295 (2000)).
34. *Nat'l Bd. of YMCA*, 395 U.S. at 92.
35. The statute provides:
Upon approval by the commissioner or an authorized agent, an employee of the division of lands, or of any organization authorized to prevent, control, or suppress a fire or a destructive agent, and others assisting in the control or suppression of a fire upon request of an officer or employee of the United States or the state may at any time enter upon any land, whether publicly or privately owned, for the purpose of preventing, suppressing, or controlling a wildland fire or a destructive agent.
36. *Morton Thiokol, Inc. v. United States*, 4 Cl. Ct. 625, 630 (1984).
37. *Waiste v. State*, 10 P.3d 1141, 1155 (Alaska 2000).
38. *Wernberg v. State*, 516 P.2d 1191, 1195 (Alaska 1973) (quoting *Commonwealth v. Alger*, 61 Mass. (7 Cush.) 53, 85 (1851)) (internal quotation marks omitted).
39. *Waiste*, 10 P.3d at 1155 (quoting *Hughes v. State*, 838 P.2d 1018, 1037 (Or. 1992)) (internal quotation marks omitted).
40. *R & Y, Inc. v. Municipality of Anchorage*, 34 P.3d 289, 297–98 (Alaska 2001).
41. *Waiste*, 10 P.3d at 1155.
42. *See Penn. Coal Co. v. Mahon*, 260 U.S. 393, 416 (1922) ("[T]his is a question of degree—and therefore cannot be disposed of by general propositions.").
43. *Lucas v. S. C. Coastal Council*, 505 U.S. 1003, 1021–28 (1992) (tracing the judicial development of the distinction between compensable takings for public use and attempts to proscribe uses of property without compensation through the police power, and making note of "*Mahon*'s affirmation of limits to the noncompensable exercise of the police power"); *Mahon*, 260 U.S. at 413 ("[O]bviously the implied limitation [of the police power] must have its limits or the contract and due process clauses [of the Constitution] are gone.").
44. *See generally* Derek T. Muller, *"As Much Upon Tradition As Upon Principle": A Critique of the Privilege of Necessity Destruction Under the Fifth Amendment*, 82 Notre Dame L. Rev. 481 (2006).
45. Black's Law Dictionary 1131 (9th ed. 2009).
46. *Id.*
47. 1 Julius L. Sackman, Nichols on Eminent Domain §1.43[2] (3d ed. 2014) ("If the individual who enters and destroys private property happens to be a public officer whose duty it is to avert an impending calamity, the rights of the owner of the property to compensation are no greater than in the case of a private individual.")
48. *City of Rapid City v. Boland*, 271 N.W.2d 60, 66 (S.D. 1978) (citations omitted).
49. *See, e.g., Ralli v. Troop*, 157 U.S. 386, 405 (1895) ("By our law, indeed, either public officers or private persons may raze houses to prevent the spreading of a conflagration. But this right rests on public necessity, and no one is bound to compensate

(case continues)

for or to contribute to the loss, unless the town or neighborhood is made liable by express statute."); *Field v. City of Des Moines*, 39 Iowa 575, 577 (1874) ("That any persons may 'raze houses to the ground to prevent the spreading of a conflagration,' without incurring any liability for the loss to the owner of the houses destroyed, is a doctrine well established in the common law."); *Hale v. Lawrence*, 21 N.J.L. 714, 730 (N.J. 1848) ("[I]n a densely populated town, all may unite in destroying a building to stop a conflagration which threatens destruction to the rest."); *Respublica v. Sparhawk*, 1 U.S. (1 Dall.) 357, 363 (Pa. 1788) ("Houses may be razed to prevent the spreading of fire, because [of] the public good."); *The Case of the King's Prerogative in Saltpetre*, (1606) 77 Eng. Rep. 1294 (K.B.) (analogizing taking saltpeter from a private landowner during wartime to destruction to prevent the spread of fire).

50. *See* Muller, *supra* note 44, at 508–10; *see also Lucas v. S.C. Coastal Council*, 505 U.S. 1003, 1029 n.16 (1992) (recognizing that there is no compensable taking when the state's destruction of property is done "'in cases of actual necessity, to prevent the spreading of a fire' or to forestall other grave threats to the lives and property of others").
51. 101 U.S. 16, 18 (1879).
52. *Id.* at 19.
53. *See, e.g., Lucas*, 505 U.S. at 1029 n.16 (citing with approval *Bowditch*, 101 U.S. at 18–19); *United States v. Caltex (Phil.), Inc.*, 344 U.S. 149, 154 (1952) ("[T]he common law ha[s] long recognized that in times of imminent peril—such as when fire threatened a whole community—the sovereign could, with immunity, destroy the property of a few that the property of many and the lives of many more could be saved."); *TrinCo Inv. Co. v. United States*, 722 F.3d 1375, 1377 (Fed. Cir. 2013) ("This principle, absolving the State . . . of liability for the destruction of real and personal property in cases of actual necessity, to prevent . . . or forestall . . . grave threats to the lives and property of others, is commonly referred to as 'the doctrine of necessity' or the 'necessity defense.'" (omissions in original) (internal quotation marks omitted) (quoting *Lucas*, 505 U.S. at 1029 n.16); *see also State v. Olsen*, 299 N.W.2d 632, 634 (Wis. App. 1980) (An example of the doctrine of necessity is "[a] person who, seeking to stop the spread of a fire, razes a building in order to save a town." (citing W. LAFAVE & A. SCOTT, JR., HANDBOOK ON CRIMINAL LAW at 384 (Hornbook Series 1972))).
54. 722 F.3d at 1377–80.
55. *Id.* at 1377.
56. *Id.*
57. *Id.* at 1378.
58. *Id.*
59. *Id.* (citing *Bowditch v. City of Boston*, 101 U.S. 16, 16-19 (1879); *Ralli v. Troop*, 157 U.S. 386, 405 (1895); *United States v. Caltex (Phil.), Inc.*, 344 U.S. 149, 151–56 (1952); *Mitchell v. Harmony*, 54 U.S. 115, 135 (1851)).
60. *Id.* (alterations in original) (quoting *Bowditch*, 101 U.S. at 16) (internal quotation marks omitted).
61. *Id.* at 1378–79 (citing *Caltex*, 344 U.S. at 151).
62. *Mitchell*, 54 U.S. at 129.
63. *TrinCo*, 722 F.3d at 1379 (alteration in original) (quoting *Mitchell*, 54 U.S. at 135).
64. *Id.* at 1378, 1380.
65. *Id.* at 1380.
66. *Id.*
67. *Id.*
68. *See United State v. Caltex (Phil.), Inc.*, 344 U.S. 149, 156 (1952) ("No rigid rules can be laid down to distinguish compensable losses from noncompensable losses. Each case must be judged on its own facts."); *Mitchell*, 54 U.S. at 134 ("It is impossible to define the particular circumstances of danger or necessity in which this power may be lawfully exercised. Every case must depend on its own circumstances.").
69. *Customer Co. v. City of Sacramento*, 895 P.2d 900, 910 (Cal. 1995) (quoting *Holtz v. Superior Court*, 475 P.2d 441, 446 (Cal. 1970)).
70. Because we conclude that only AS 41.15.045 applies, we reject the State's argument that the landowners waived the immunity issue by not appealing from the superior court's holding that the State was also protected by AS 09.50.250.
71. *See* 26 P.3d 447, 454–55 (Alaska 2001).
72. *See id.* at 455–56.
73. *Id.* at 456.
74. *Id.* at 459.
75. *Id.*
76. *Id.*
77. AS 41.15.045(b).
78. Sectional Analysis of Committee Substitute for H.B. 245, 23d Leg., 1st Sess., *available at* Alaska Leg. Microfiche Collection No. 10825.
79. Besides *Angnabooguk*, the letter apparently refers to *Bartek v. State, Dep't of Natural Res., Div. of Forestry*, 31 P.3d 100, 101 (Alaska 2001), which we observed in *Bartek* was "closely related" to *Angnabooguk* and presented the same immunity issues. Because we decided those issues in *Angnabooguk*, in *Bartek* we decided only issues of class certification. *See also* State of Alaska, Dep't of Law, Op. Att'y Gen., 2003 WL 22718859 (June 2, 2003) at *4 ("These sections are intended to overrule holdings of the Alaska Supreme Court in the cases of *Angnabooguk* . . . and *Bartek* . . . that the State is not immune and may be sued for its firefighting activities.").
80. 2003 House Journal 782–83.
81. *Id.*
82. Sectional Analysis of Committee Substitute for H.B. 245, 23d Leg., 1st Sess., *available at* Alaska Leg. Microfiche Collection No. 10825. *See also* STATE OF ALASKA, DEP'T OF LAW, OP. ATT'Y GEN., 2003 WL 22718859 (June 2, 2003) at *4 (The immunity provisions "reassert the State of Alaska's sovereign immunity from claims arising out of fire fighting and related activities and are intended to immunize the entire class of fire fighting activities, with the limited exception of a civil action for damages as a result of intentional misconduct within the course and scope of employment or agency and with complete disregard for the safety and property of others.").
83. 26 P.3d 447, 458–59 (Alaska 2001).
84. *See Nelson v. Municipality of Anchorage*, 267 P.3d 636, 642 (Alaska 2011) ("If one statutory 'section deals with a subject in general terms and another deals with a part of the same subject in a more detailed way, the two should be harmonized, if possible; but if there is a conflict, the specific section will control over the general.'. . . '[I]f two statutes conflict, then the later in time controls over the earlier.'" (quoting *In re Hutchinson's Estate*, 577 P.2d 1074, 1075 (Alaska 1978); *Allen v. Alaska Oil & Gas Conservation Comm 'n*, 147 P.3d 664, 668 (Alaska 2006))).
85. AS 41.15.045(b).
86. *Angnabooguk v. State, Dep't of Natural Res., Div. of Forestry*, 26 P.3d 447, 456 (Alaska 2001) (emphasis added).
87. *Guerrero ex rel. Guerrero v. Alaska Hous. Fin. Corp.*, 123 P.3d 966, 977 (Alaska 2005) (quoting *Indus. Indem. Co. v. State*, 669 P.2d 561, 563 (Alaska 1983)).
88. *Id.* (quoting *Adams v. City of Tenakee Springs*, 963 P.2d 1047, 1051 (Alaska 1998)).

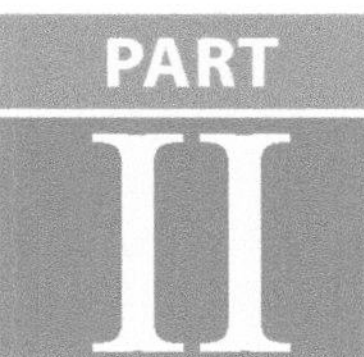

Torts, Crimes, and Intellectual Property

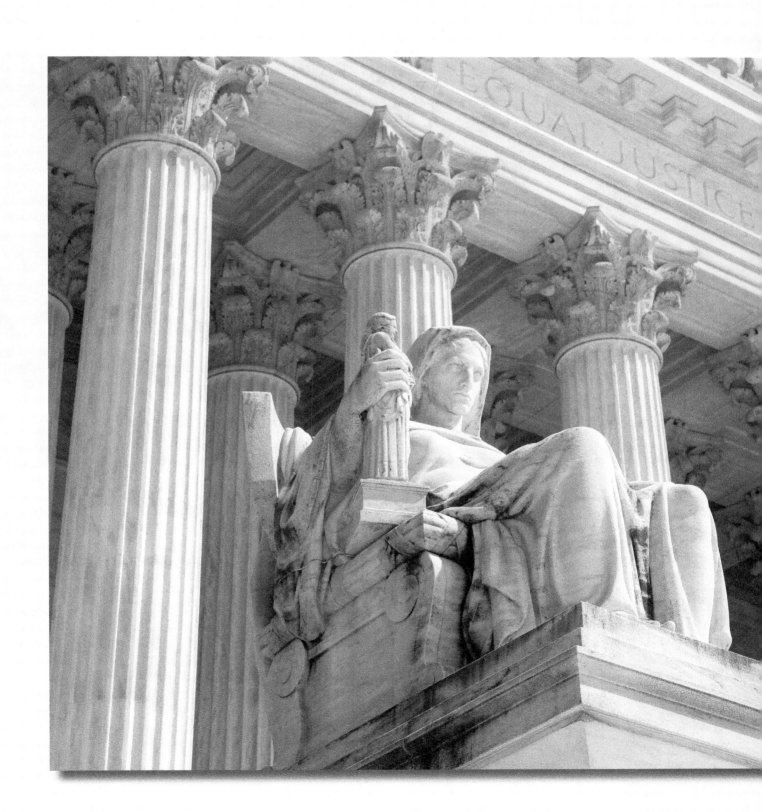

CHAPTER 5

Intentional Torts and Negligence

CHILDREN'S THRILL RIDE
In this children's thrill ride, the children are strapped in with their feet left dangling. The car goes up a 100-foot tower and then free-falls down, giving the riders a feeling of weightlessness. Operators of thrill rides carry liability insurance to cover any possible accidents that may occur.

Learning Objectives

After studying this chapter, you should be able to:

1. List and describe intentional torts against persons.
2. List and explain the elements necessary to prove negligence.
3. Describe the business-related torts of disparagement and fraud.
4. Describe special negligence doctrines.
5. Define and apply the doctrine of strict liability.

Chapter Outline

> *"Negligence is not actionable unless it involves the invasion of a legally protected interest, the violation of a right. Proof of negligence in the air, so to speak, will not do."*
>
> —*Chief Judge Cardozo*
> *Palsgraf v. Long Island Railroad Co. 248 N.Y. 339, 162 N.E. 99, 1928 N.Y. Lexis 1269 (1928)*

Introduction to Intentional Torts and Negligence

Tort is the French word for "a wrong." The law provides remedies to persons and businesses that are injured by the tortious actions of others. Under tort law, an injured party can bring a *civil lawsuit* to seek compensation for a wrong done to the party or to the party's property. Many torts have their origin in common law. The courts and legislatures have extended tort law to reflect changes in modern society. Most torts are either intentional torts or unintentional torts, such as negligence. These are based on the concept of fault. In many jurisdictions, the law recognizes the doctrine of *strict liability*. Under this doctrine, in certain circumstances, defendants may be held liable without fault.

tort
A wrong. There are three categories of torts: (1) intentional torts, (2) unintentional torts (negligence), and (3) strict liability.

Tort damages are monetary damages that are sought from the offending party. They are intended to compensate the injured party for the injury suffered. Such injury may consist of past and future medical expenses, loss of wages, pain and suffering, mental distress, and other damages caused by the defendant's tortious conduct. If the victim of a tort dies, his or her beneficiaries can bring a *wrongful death action* to recover damages from the defendant.

> *Thoughts much too deep for tears subdue the Court.*
> *When I assumpsit bring, and God-like waive a tort.*
>
> J. L. Adolphus
> *The Circuiteers (1885)*

This chapter discusses intentional torts, negligence, special tort doctrines, and the doctrine of strict liability.

Intentional Torts

The law protects a person from unauthorized touching, restraint, or other contact. In addition, the law protects a person's reputation and privacy. Violations of these rights are actionable as torts. **Intentional torts** against persons are discussed in the paragraphs that follow.

intentional tort
A category of torts that requires that the defendant possessed the intent to do the act that caused the plaintiff's injuries.

Assault

Assault is (1) the threat of immediate harm or offensive contact or (2) any action that arouses reasonable apprehension of imminent harm. Actual physical contact is unnecessary. Threats of future harm are not actionable.

assault
(1) The threat of immediate harm or offensive contact or (2) any action that arouses reasonable apprehension of imminent harm. Actual physical contact is unnecessary.

Examples Suppose a 6-foot-5-inch, 250-pound person makes a fist and threatens to punch a 5-foot, 100-pound person. If the threatened person is afraid that he or she will be physically harmed, that person can sue the threatening person to recover damages for the assault.

Battery

Battery is unauthorized and harmful or offensive physical contact with another person that causes injury. Basically, the interest protected here is each person's reasonable sense of dignity and safety. Direct physical contact, such as intentionally hitting someone with a fist, is battery.

battery
Unauthorized and harmful or offensive direct or indirect physical contact with another person that causes injury.

Indirect physical contact between the victim and the perpetrator is also battery, as long as injury results.

Examples Throwing a rock, shooting an arrow or a bullet, knocking off a hat, pulling a chair out from under someone, and poisoning a drink are all instances of actionable battery. The victim need not be aware of the harmful or offensive contact (e.g., it may take place while the victim is asleep).

Assault and battery often occur together, although they do not have to (e.g., the perpetrator hits the victim on the back of the head without any warning).

transferred intent doctrine
Under this doctrine, the law transfers the perpetrator's intent from the target to the actual victim of the act.

Transferred Intent Doctrine Sometimes a person acts with the intent to injure one person but actually injures another. The **transferred intent doctrine** applies to such situations. Under this doctrine, the law transfers the perpetrator's intent from the target to the actual victim of the act. The victim can then sue the defendant.

False Imprisonment

false imprisonment
The intentional confinement or restraint of another person without authority or justification and without that person's consent.

The intentional confinement or restraint of another person without authority or justification and without that person's consent constitutes **false imprisonment**. The victim may be restrained or confined by physical force, barriers, threats of physical harm, or the perpetrator's false assertion of legal authority (i.e., false arrest). A threat of future harm or moral pressure is not considered false imprisonment. The false imprisonment must be complete.

Examples A person who locks the doors in a house or automobile and does not let another person leave is liable for false imprisonment. Merely locking one door to a building when other exits are not locked is not false imprisonment. However, a person is not obliged to risk danger or an affront to his or her dignity by attempting to escape.

Shoplifting and Merchant Protection Statutes

merchant protection statutes (shopkeeper's privilege)
Statutes that allow merchants to stop, detain, and investigate suspected shoplifters without being held liable for false imprisonment if (1) there are reasonable grounds for the suspicion, (2) suspects are detained for only a reasonable time, and (3) investigations are conducted in a reasonable manner.

Shoplifting causes substantial losses to retail and other merchants each year. Suspected shoplifters are often stopped by the store employees, and their suspected shoplifting is investigated. These stops sometimes lead to the merchant being sued for false imprisonment because the merchant detained the suspect.

Almost all states have enacted **merchant protection statutes**, also known as the **shopkeeper's privilege**. These statutes allow merchants to stop, detain, and investigate suspected shoplifters without being held liable for false imprisonment if:

1. There are *reasonable grounds* for the suspicion.
2. Suspects are detained for only a *reasonable time*.
3. Investigations are conducted in a *reasonable manner*.

Proving these elements is sometimes difficult. The following case applies the merchant's protection statute.

CASE 5.1 *STATE COURT CASE False Imprisonment*

Wal-Mart Stores, Inc. v. Cockrell

61 S.W.3d 774, 2001 Tex. App. Lexis 7992 (2001)
Court of Appeals of Texas

"He made me feel like I was scum. That I had no say-so in the matter, that just made me feel like a little kid on the block, like the bully beating the kid up."
—Karl Cockrell

Facts

Karl Cockrell and his parents went to the layaway department at a store owned by Wal-Mart Stores, Inc. (Walmart). Cockrell stayed for about five minutes and decided to leave. As he was going out the front door, Raymond Navarro, a Walmart loss-prevention officer, stopped him and requested that Cockrell follow him to the manager's office. Once in the office, Navarro told him to pull his pants down. Cockrell put his hands between his shorts and underwear, pulled them out, and shook them. Nothing fell out. Next Navarro told him to take off his shirt. Cockrell

(case continues)

raised his shirt, revealing a large bandage that covered a surgical wound on the right side of his abdomen. Cockrell had recently had a liver transplant. Navarro asked him to take off the bandage despite Cockrell's explanation that the bandage maintained a sterile environment around his surgical wound. On Navarro's insistence, Cockrell took down the bandage, revealing the wound. Navarro let Cockrell go. Cockrell sued Walmart to recover damages for false imprisonment. Walmart defended, alleging that the shopkeeper's privilege protected the store from liability. The trial court found in favor of Cockrell and awarded Cockrell $300,000 for his mental anguish. Walmart appealed.

Issue

Does the shopkeeper's privilege protect Walmart from liability under the circumstances of the case?

Language of the Court

Navarro claimed he had reasons to suspect Cockrell of shoplifting. He said that Cockrell was acting suspiciously, because he saw him in the women's department standing very close to a rack of clothes and looking around. We conclude that a rational jury could have found that Navarro did not "reasonably believe" a theft had occurred and therefore lacked authority to detain Cockrell. Navarro's search was unreasonable in scope, because he had no probable cause to believe that Cockrell had hidden any merchandise under the bandage. Removal of the bandage compromised the sterile environment surrounding the wound.

Decision

The court of appeals upheld the trial court's finding that Walmart had falsely imprisoned Cockrell and had not proved the shopkeeper's privilege. The court of appeals upheld the trial court's judgment that awarded Cockrell $300,000 for mental anguish.

Ethics Questions

Did Navarro, the Walmart employee, act responsibly in this case? Did Walmart act ethically in denying liability in this case?

Misappropriation of the Right to Publicity

Each person has the exclusive legal right to control and profit from the commercial use of his or her name and identity during his or her lifetime. This is a valuable right, particularly to well-known persons such as sports figures and movie stars. Any attempt by another person to appropriate a living person's name or identity for commercial purposes is actionable. The wrongdoer is liable for the tort of **misappropriation of the right to publicity** (also called the **tort of appropriation**).

In such cases, the plaintiff can (1) recover the unauthorized profits made by the offending party and (2) obtain an injunction preventing further unauthorized use of his or her name or identity. Many states provide that the right to publicity survives a person's death and may be enforced by the deceased's heirs.

misappropriation of the right to publicity (tort of appreciation)
An attempt by another person to appropriate a living person's name or identity for commercial purposes.

Example Megan Fox is a famous movie star. If an advertising agency places Megan Fox's likeness (e.g., photo) on a billboard advertising a product without Megan Fox's permission, it has engaged in the tort of misappropriation of the right to publicity. Megan Fox could sue and recover the profits made by the offending party as well as obtain an injunction to prevent unauthorized use of her likeness by the offending party.

Invasion of the Right to Privacy

The law recognizes each person's right to live his or her life without being subjected to unwarranted and undesired publicity. A violation of this right constitutes the tort of **invasion of the right to privacy**. If a fact is public information, there is no claim to privacy. However, a fact that was once public (e.g., commission of a crime) may become private after the passage of time.

invasion of the right to privacy
The unwarranted and undesired publicity of a private fact about a person. The fact does not have to be untrue.

Examples Secretly taking photos of another person with a cell phone camera in a men's or women's locker room constitutes invasion of the right to privacy. Reading someone else's mail, wiretapping someone's telephone, and reading someone else's e-mail without authorization to do so are also examples of invasion of the right to privacy.

Placing someone in a "false light" constitutes an invasion of privacy.

Example Sending an objectionable telegram to a third party and signing another's name would place the purported sender in a false light in the eyes of the receiver.

Defamation of Character

A person's reputation is a valuable asset. Therefore, every person is protected from false statements made by others during his or her lifetime. This protection ends upon a person's death. The tort of **defamation of character** requires a plaintiff to prove that:

1. The defendant made an *untrue statement of fact* about the plaintiff.
2. The statement was intentionally or accidentally *published* to a third party. In this context, *publication* simply means that a third person heard or saw the untrue statement. It does not require appearance in newspapers, magazines, or books.

defamation of character
False statement(s) made by one person about another. In court, the plaintiff must prove that (1) the defendant made an untrue statement of fact about the plaintiff and (2) the statement was intentionally or accidentally published to a third party.

A false statement that appears in writing or other fixed medium is **libel**. An oral defamatory statement is **slander**.

libel
A false statement that appears in a letter, newspaper, magazine, book, photograph, movie, video, and so on.

slander
Oral defamation of character.

Examples False statements that appear in a letter, newspaper, magazine, book, photograph, movie, video, and the like, are libel. If a person verbally makes an untrue statement of fact about another person to a third person, such oral statement constitutes slander. Most courts hold that defamatory statements in radio and television broadcasts are considered libel because of the permanency of the media.

The publication of an untrue statement of fact is not the same as the publication of an *opinion*. The publication of opinions is usually not actionable. Because defamation is defined as an untrue statement of fact, truth is an absolute defense to a charge of defamation.

Examples The statement "My lawyer is lousy" is an opinion and is not defamation. The statement "My lawyer has been disbarred from the practice of law," when she has not been disbarred, is an untrue statement of fact and is actionable as defamation.

Hard cases make bad law.
Legal maxim

Public Figures as Plaintiffs In ***New York Times Co. v. Sullivan***,[1] the U.S. Supreme Court held that *public officials* cannot recover for defamation unless they can prove that the defendant acted with "actual malice." Actual malice means that the defendant made the false statement knowingly or with reckless disregard of its falsity. This requirement has since been extended to **public figure** plaintiffs, such as movie stars, sports personalities, and other celebrities.

Disparagement

Business firms rely on their reputation and the quality of their products and services to attract and keep customers. That is why state unfair-competition laws protect businesses from disparaging statements made by competitors or others. A disparaging statement is an untrue statement made by one person or business about the products, services, property, or reputation of another business.

To prove **disparagement**, which is also called **trade libel**, **product disparagement**, and **slander of title**, the plaintiff must show that the defendant (1) made an untrue statement about the plaintiff's products, services, property, or business reputation; (2) published that untrue statement to a third party; (3) knew the

disparagement
False statements about a competitor's products, services, property, or business reputation.

statement was not true; and (4) made the statement maliciously (i.e., with intent to injure the plaintiff).

Example If a competitor of John Deere tractors told a prospective customer that "John Deere tractors often break down" when in fact they rarely do, that would be product disparagement.

Intentional Misrepresentation (Fraud)

One of the most pervasive business torts is **intentional misrepresentation**. This tort is also known as **fraud** or **deceit**. It occurs when a wrongdoer deceives another person out of money, property, or something else of value. A person who has been injured by intentional misrepresentation can recover damages from the wrongdoer. Four elements are required to find fraud:

intentional misrepresentation (fraud or deceit)
The intentional defrauding of a person out of money, property, or something else of value.

1. The wrongdoer made a false representation of a material fact.
2. The wrongdoer had knowledge that the representation was false and intended to deceive the innocent party.
3. The innocent party justifiably relied on the misrepresentation.
4. The innocent party was injured.

He that's cheated twice by the same man, is an accomplice with the Cheater.
Thomas Fuller
Gnomologia (1732)

Item 2, which is called *scienter*, refers to intentional conduct. It also includes situations in which the wrongdoer recklessly disregards the truth in making a representation that is false. Intent or recklessness can be inferred from the circumstances.

Example Matt, a person claiming to be a minerals expert, convinces 100 people to invest $10,000 each with him so that he can purchase, on their behalf, a gold mine he claims is located in the state of North Dakota. Matt shows the prospective investors photographs of a gold mine to substantiate his story. The investors give Matt their money. There is no gold mine. Instead, Matt runs off with the investors' money. Matt intended to steal the money from the investors. This is an example of fraud: (1) Matt made a false representation of fact (there was no gold mine, and he did not intend to invest their money to purchase the gold mine), (2) Matt knew that his statements were false and intended to steal the investors' money, (3) the investors relied on Matt's statements, and (4) the investors were injured by losing their money.

Intentional Infliction of Emotional Distress

In some situations, a victim may suffer mental or emotional distress without first being physically harmed. The *Restatement (Second) of Torts* provides that a person whose *extreme and outrageous* conduct intentionally or recklessly causes severe emotional distress to another is liable for that emotional distress.[2] This is called the tort of **intentional infliction of emotional distress**, or the **tort of outrage**.

intentional infliction of emotional distress (tort of outrage)
A tort that says a person whose extreme and outrageous conduct intentionally or recklessly causes severe emotional distress to another person is liable for that emotional distress.

The plaintiff must prove that the defendant's conduct was "so outrageous in character and so extreme in degree as to go beyond all possible bounds of decency, and to be regarded as atrocious and utterly intolerable in a civilized society."[3] The tort does not require any publication to a third party or physical contact between the plaintiff and defendant.

An indignity, an annoyance, rough language, or an occasional inconsiderate or unkind act does not constitute outrageous behavior. However, repeated annoyances or harassment coupled with threats are considered outrageous.

The mental distress suffered by the plaintiff must be severe. Many states require that this mental distress be manifested by some form of physical injury, discomfort, or illness, such as nausea, ulcers, headaches, or miscarriage. This requirement is intended to prevent false claims. Some states have abandoned this requirement.

Examples Shame, humiliation, embarrassment, anger, fear, and worry constitute severe mental distress.

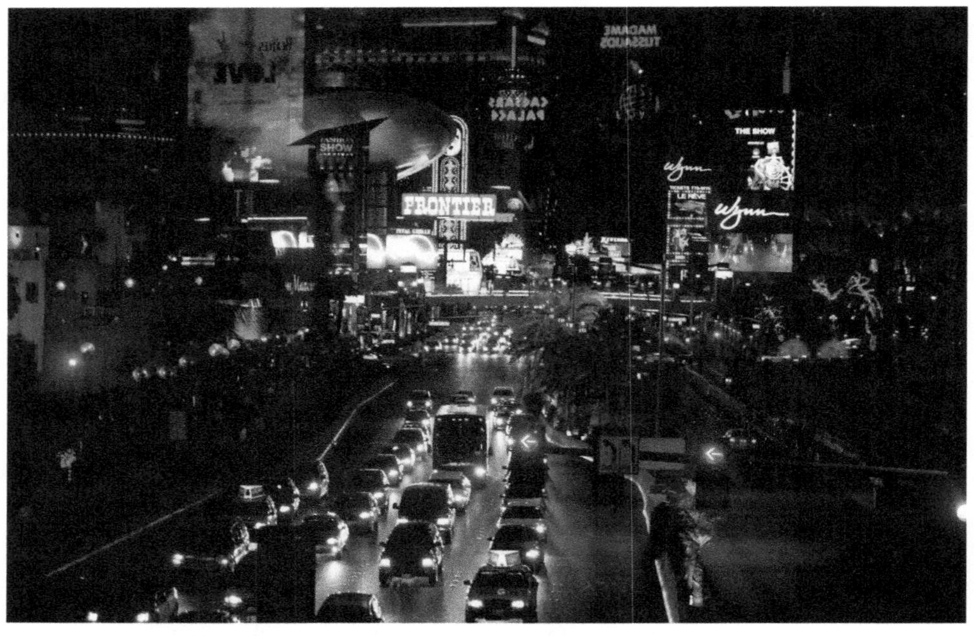

LAS VEGAS, NEVADA
Automobile accidents are a primary cause of injury and death in the United States. Most states require automobile owners to carry liability insurance, but the required amount is often low.

Malicious Prosecution

Businesses and individuals often believe they have a reason to sue someone to recover damages or other remedies. If the plaintiff has a legitimate reason to bring the lawsuit and does so but the plaintiff does not win the lawsuit, he or she does not have to worry about being sued by the person whom he or she sued. But a losing plaintiff does have to worry about being sued by the defendant in a second lawsuit for **malicious prosecution** if certain elements are met. In a lawsuit for malicious prosecution, the original defendant sues the original plaintiff. In this second lawsuit, which is a *civil* action for damages, the original defendant is the plaintiff and the original plaintiff the defendant. To succeed in a malicious prosecution lawsuit, the courts require the plaintiff to prove all of the following:

malicious prosecution
A lawsuit in which the original defendant sues the original plaintiff. In the second lawsuit, the defendant becomes the plaintiff and vice versa.

1. The plaintiff in the original lawsuit (now the defendant) instituted or was responsible for instituting the original lawsuit.
2. There was no *probable cause* for the first lawsuit (i.e., it was a frivolous lawsuit).
3. The plaintiff in the original action brought it with *malice*. (Caution: This is a very difficult element to prove.)
4. The original lawsuit was terminated in favor of the original defendant (now the plaintiff).
5. The current plaintiff suffered injury as a result of the original lawsuit.

The courts do not look favorably on malicious prosecution lawsuits because they feel that such lawsuits inhibit the original plaintiff's incentive to sue.

Critical Legal Thinking

Should defendants that lose cases and plaintiffs that do not win cases have to pay the other side's legal expenses? What would be the consequences of such a rule?

Example One student actor wins a part in a play over another student actor. To get back at the winning student, the rejected student files a lawsuit against the winning student, alleging intentional infliction of emotional distress, defamation, and negligence. The lawsuit is unfounded, but the winning student must defend the lawsuit. The jury returns a verdict exonerating the defendant. The defendant now can sue the plaintiff for malicious prosecution and has a very good chance of winning the lawsuit.

Unintentional Torts (Negligence)

Under the doctrine of **unintentional tort**, commonly referred to as **ordinary negligence** or **negligence**, a person is liable for harm that is the *foreseeable consequence* of his or her actions. *Negligence* is defined as "the omission to do something which a reasonable man would do, or doing something which a prudent and reasonable man would not do."[4]

To be successful in a negligence lawsuit, the plaintiff must prove that (1) the defendant owed a *duty of care* to the plaintiff, (2) the defendant *breached* this duty of care, (3) the plaintiff suffered *injury*, (4) the defendant's negligent act was the *actual cause* of plaintiff's injury, and (5) the defendant's negligent act was the *proximate cause* of the plaintiff's injuries. Each of these elements is discussed in the paragraphs that follow.

unintentional tort (negligence)
A doctrine that says a person is liable for harm that is the foreseeable consequence of his or her actions.

1. Duty of Care

To determine whether a defendant is liable for negligence, it must first be ascertained whether the defendant owed a **duty of care** to the plaintiff. *Duty of care* refers to the obligation people owe each other—that is, the duty not to cause any unreasonable harm or risk of harm.

duty of care
The obligation people owe each other not to cause any unreasonable harm or risk of harm.

Examples Each person owes a duty to drive his or her car carefully, not to push or shove on escalators, not to leave skateboards on the sidewalk, and the like. Businesses owe a duty to make safe products, not to cause accidents, and so on.

The courts decide whether a duty of care is owed in specific cases by applying a **reasonable person standard**. Under this test, the courts attempt to determine how an *objective, careful, and conscientious person would have acted in the same circumstances* and then measure the defendant's conduct against that standard. The defendant's subjective intent ("I did not mean to do it") is immaterial in assessing liability. Certain impairments do not affect the reasonable person standard.

Defendants with a particular expertise or competence are measured against a **reasonable professional standard**. Applying this test, the courts attempt to determine how an objective, careful, and conscientious equivalent professional would have acted in the same circumstances and then measure the defendant professional's conduct against that standard.

reasonable person standard
A test used to determine whether a defendant owes a duty of care. This test measures the defendant's conduct against how an objective, careful, and conscientious person would have acted in the same circumstances.

No court has ever given, nor do we think ever can give, a definition of what constitutes a reasonable or an average man.

Lord Goddard C.J.R.
Regina v. McCarthy, 2 Q.B. 105 (1954)

Examples A brain surgeon is measured against a reasonable brain surgeon standard. A general practitioner doctor who is the only doctor who serves a small community is measured against a reasonable small-town general practitioner standard.

2. Breach of the Duty of Care

Once a court finds that the defendant actually owed the plaintiff a duty of care, it must determine whether the defendant breached that duty. A **breach of the duty of care** is the failure to exercise care. In other words, it is the failure to act as a reasonable person would act. A breach of this duty may consist of an action.

breach of the duty of care
A failure to exercise care or to act as a reasonable person would act.

Example Throwing a lit match on the ground in the forest and causing a fire is a breach of a duty of care.

A breach of duty may also consist of a failure to act when there is a duty to act.

Example A firefighter who refuses to put out a fire when her safety is not at stake breaches her duty of care for failing to act when she has a duty to act.

Passersby are generally not expected to rescue others gratuitously to save them from harm. However, most states require certain relatives—parents to children or children to parents if the children are old enough—to try to save their relatives from harm.

Negligence is the omission to do something which a reasonable man would do, or doing something which a prudent and reasonable man would not do.

B. Alderson
Blyth v. Birmingham Waterworks Co. (1856)

The following ethics feature discusses a classic case involving the issue of negligence.

Ethics

Ouch! McDonald's Coffee Is Too Hot!

McDonald's Corporation found itself embroiled in one of the most famous negligence cases of modern times. Stella Liebeck, a 79-year-old resident of Albuquerque, New Mexico, visited a drive-through window of a McDonald's restaurant with her grandson Chris. Her grandson, the driver of the vehicle, placed the order for breakfast. When breakfast came at the drive-through window, Chris handed a hot cup of coffee to Stella. Chris pulled over so that Stella could put cream and sugar in her coffee. Stella took the lid off the coffee cup she held in her lap, and the hot coffee spilled in her lap. The coffee spilled all over Stella, who suffered third-degree burns on her legs, thighs, groin, and buttocks. Stella was driven to the emergency room and was hospitalized for seven days. She required medical treatment and later returned to the hospital to have skin grafts. She suffered permanent scars from the incident.

Stella's medical costs were $11,000. Stella asked McDonald's to pay her $20,000 to settle the case, but McDonald's offered only $800. Stella refused this settlement and sued McDonald's in court for negligence for selling coffee that was too hot and for failing to warn her of the danger of the hot coffee it served. At trial, McDonald's denied that it had been negligent and asserted that Stella's own negligence—opening a hot coffee cup on her lap—had caused her injuries. The jury heard the following evidence:

- McDonald's enforces a quality-control rule that requires its restaurants and franchises to serve coffee at 180 to 190 degrees Fahrenheit.
- Third-degree burns occur on skin in just two to five seconds when coffee is served at 185 degrees.
- McDonald's coffee temperature was 20 degrees hotter than coffee served by competing restaurant chains.
- McDonald's coffee temperature was approximately 40 to 50 degrees hotter than normal house-brewed coffee.
- McDonald's had received more than 700 prior complaints of people who had been scalded by McDonald's coffee.
- McDonald's did not place a warning on its coffee cups to alert patrons that the coffee it served was exceptionally hot.

Based on this evidence, the jury concluded that McDonald's acted recklessly and awarded Stella $200,000 in compensatory damages, which was then reduced by $40,000 because of her own negligence, and $2.7 million in punitive damages. The trial court judge reduced the amount of punitive damages to $480,000, which was three times the amount of compensatory damages. McDonald's now places a warning on its coffee cups that its coffee is hot. *Liebeck v. McDonald's Restaurants, P.T.S., Inc.* (New Mexico District Court, Bernalillo County, New Mexico, 1994)

Ethics Questions Do you think that McDonald's properly warned Stella Liebeck of the dangers of drinking McDonald's hot coffee? Do you think McDonald's acted ethically in offering Stella an $800 settlement? Was the award of punitive damages justified in this case? Why or why not?

3. Injury to Plaintiff

injury
A plaintiff's personal injury or damage to his or her property that enables him or her to recover monetary damages for the defendant's negligence.

Even though a defendant's negligent act may have breached a duty of care owed to the plaintiff, this breach is not actionable unless the plaintiff suffers **injury** or injury to his or her property. That is, the plaintiff must have suffered some injury before he or she can recover any damages. The damages recoverable depend on the effect of the injury on the plaintiff's life or profession.

Examples Suppose that a man injures his hand when a train door malfunctions. The train company is found negligent. If the injured man is a star professional basketball player who makes $5 million per year, with an expected seven years of good playing time left, this plaintiff can recover multiple millions of dollars because he can no longer play professional basketball. If the injured man is a college professor with 15 years until retirement who is making only one-fortieth per year of what the basketball player makes, he can recover some money for his injuries. However, because he makes a lot less per year than the professional basketball player and because he can continue working, albeit with more difficulty, the professor can recover much less for the same injury.

The following case involves the issues of injury and damages.

CASE 5.2 *STATE COURT CASE Negligence*

Jones v. City of Seattle, Washington

314 P.3d 380, 2013 Wash. Lexis 955 (2013)
Supreme Court of Washington

"The trial judge characterized the city's motion as an attempt to get a 'second bite of the apple.'"

—McCloud, Justice

Facts

Mark Jones was a firefighter for the city of Seattle, Washington. He was assigned to Station 33 firehouse, where he remained on duty for long shifts, including staying overnight. Mark slept in quarters on the second floor of the firehouse. One of the common features of many firehouses, including the one Mark worked in, is the pole hole in the second floor with a pole leading to the first floor. When called to action, firefighters slide down the pole to reach the first floor and their firefighting equipment and vehicles. One night, around 3:00 A.M., Mark fell 15 feet through the fire station's pole hole. Mark told a responding medic that he had awoken to use the bathroom, which was next to the pole hole. Mark sustained both serious physical and cognitive impairments as a result of his fall. Because of his permanent impaired mental and physical injuries, Mark's sister Meg was appointed his guardian. Meg, on behalf of Mark, sued the city of Seattle for injuries caused to Mark by the accident, alleging that the city had been negligent in failing to block accidental access to the pole hole. The jury found that the city's negligence was the sole cause of Mark's injuries and awarded Mark $12.75 million in damages. Seattle made a motion for a new trial, which the trial court denied. The court of appeals upheld the verdict and damages. Seattle appealed to the supreme court of Washington, seeking a new trial regarding damages.

Issue

Is the award of damages proper?

Language of the Court

The first two weeks of trial were devoted to testimony by Mark's treating physicians, various witnesses who spoke to the general condition and layout of Station 33, to the city's ability to prevent accidents like Mark's, and to Mark's demeanor, habits, and capabilities since the accident. The various physicians and therapists who took the stand uniformly testified that Mark had significant and permanent cognitive impairments. Further, the judge permitted the city to cross-examine Meg and Mark on Mark's ability to perform physical tasks. The trial judge characterized the city's motion as an attempt to get a "second bite of the apple" after its strategic choices proved unwise.

Decision

The supreme court of Washington upheld the damage award to the plaintiff against the city of Seattle.

Ethics Questions

Do traditional pole holes in fire stations pose a risk to firefighters? Should pole holes be eliminated? Was the award in this case warranted?

4. Actual Cause

A defendant's negligent act must be the **actual cause** (also called **causation in fact**) of the plaintiff's injuries. The test is this: "But for" the defendant's conduct, would the accident have happened? If the defendant's act caused the plaintiff's injuries, there is causation in fact.

actual cause (causation in fact)
The actual cause of negligence. A person who commits a negligent act is not liable unless actual cause can be proven.

Example Suppose a corporation negligently pollutes the plaintiff's drinking water. The plaintiff dies of a heart attack unrelated to the polluted water. Although the corporation has acted negligently, it is not liable for the plaintiff's death. There were a negligent act and an injury, but there was no cause-and-effect relationship between them. If, instead, the plaintiff had died from the polluted drinking water, there would have been causation in fact, and the polluting corporation would have been liable.

If two (or more) persons are liable for negligently causing the plaintiff's injuries, both (or all) can be held liable to the plaintiff if each of their acts is a substantial factor in causing the plaintiff's injuries.

5. Proximate Cause

Under the law, a negligent party is not necessarily liable for all damages set in motion by his or her negligent act. Based on public policy, the law establishes a point along the damage chain after which the negligent party is no longer responsible for the consequences of his or her actions. This limitation on liability is referred to as **proximate cause** (also called **legal cause**). The general test of proximate cause is *foreseeability*. A negligent party who is found to be the actual cause—but not the proximate cause—of the plaintiff's injuries is not liable to the plaintiff. Situations are examined on a case-by-case basis.

proximate cause (legal cause)
A point along a chain of events caused by a negligent party after which this party is no longer legally responsible for the consequences of his or her actions.

Example A person is walking on a public sidewalk. When he finishes smoking a cigarette, which is still lit, he negligently tosses it and it lands close to a house. The cigarette causes a fire that burns down the house. In this instance, the smoker is the proximate cause of the damage because it is reasonably foreseeable that his action could burn down the house. If the fire jumps and burns down the adjacent house, the smoker is still the proximate cause. If the third house in the row burns, he is probably still the proximate cause. However, if the fire spreads and burns down 100 houses before it is put out (the smoker is the *actual cause* of the damage under the "but for" test), the smoker would not be the *proximate cause* of burning the one-hundredth house because it would not be reasonably foreseeable that his action of throwing a lit cigarette would burn down so many houses. Where does one draw the line of liability? At the 4th house? The 20th house? The 40th house? This decision is left up to the jury.

The following critical legal thinking case discusses the issue of proximate cause.

Critical Legal Thinking Case

Proximate Cause

"Proof of negligence in the air, so to speak, will not do."
—Cardozo, Justice

The landmark case establishing the doctrine of proximate cause is ***Palsgraf v. The Long Island Railroad Company***, a New York case decided in 1928. Helen Palsgraf was standing on a platform waiting for a passenger train. The Long Island Railroad Company owned and operated the trains and employed the station guards. As a man carrying a package wrapped in a newspaper tried to board the moving train, railroad guards tried to help him. In doing so, the package was dislodged from the man's arm, fell to the railroad tracks, and exploded. The package contained hidden fireworks. The explosion shook the railroad platform, causing a scale located on the platform to fall on Helen Palsgraf, injuring her. Palsgraf sued the railroad for negligence.

Justice Benjamin Cardozo denied Palsgraf's recovery, finding that the railroad was not the proximate cause of her injuries, and was therefore not liable to Palsgraf for negligence. In his decision, Justice Cardozo eloquently addressed the issue of proximate cause:

> *The conduct of the defendant's guard, if a wrong in its relation to the holder of the package, was not a wrong in its relation to the plaintiff, standing far away. Relatively to her it was not negligence at all. Nothing in the situation gave notice that the falling package had in it the potency of peril to persons thus removed. Negligence is not actionable unless it involves the invasion of a legally protected interest, the violation of a right. Proof of negligence in the air, so to speak, will not do.*

Palsgraf v. The Long Island Railroad Company, 248 N.Y. 339, 162 N.E. 99, 1928 N.Y. Lexis 1269 (Court of Appeals of New York, 1928)

Critical Legal Thinking Questions
How does *actual cause* differ from *proximate cause*? Why does the law recognize the doctrine of proximate cause?

CONCEPT SUMMARY
ELEMENTS OF NEGLIGENCE

1. The defendant owed a *duty of care* to the plaintiff.
2. The defendant *breached this duty*.
3. The plaintiff suffered *injury*.
4. The defendant's negligent act was the *actual cause* (or *causation in fact*) of the plaintiff's injuries.
5. The defendant's negligent act was the *proximate cause* (or *legal cause*) of the plaintiff's injuries. The defendant is liable only for the *foreseeable* consequences of his or her negligent act.

In the following case, the court had to decide if the elements of negligence had been proven.

CASE 5.3 *FEDERAL COURT CASE Duty of Care*

James v. Meow Media, Inc.

300 F.3d 683, 2002 U.S. App. Lexis 16185 (2002)
United States Court of Appeals for the Sixth Circuit

"Our inquiry is whether the deaths of James, Steger, and Hadley were the reasonably foreseeable result of the defendants' creation and distribution of their games, movie, and Internet sites."

—Boggs, Circuit Judge

Facts

Michael Carneal was a 14-year-old freshman student in high school in Paducah, Kentucky. Carneal regularly played violent interactive video and computer games that involved the player shooting virtual opponents with computer guns and other weapons. Carneal also watched violent video-recorded movies and Internet sites. Carneal took a .22-caliber pistol and five shotguns into the lobby of his high school and shot several of his fellow students, killing three and wounding many others. The three students killed were Jessica James, Kayce Steger, and Nicole Hadley.

The parents of the three dead children sued the producers and distributors of the violent video games and movies that Carneal had watched previous to the shooting. The parents sued to recover damages for wrongful death, alleging that the defendants were negligent in producing and distributing such games and movies to Carneal. The U.S. district court applied Kentucky law and held that the defendants did not owe or breach a duty to the plaintiffs and therefore were not liable for negligence. The plaintiffs appealed to the U.S. Court of appeals.

Issue

Are the video and movie producers liable to the plaintiffs for selling and licensing violent video games and movies to Carneal, who killed the plaintiffs' three children?

Language of the Court

Our inquiry is whether the deaths of James, Steger, and Hadley were the reasonably foreseeable result of the defendants' creation and distribution of their games, movie, and Internet sites. It appears simply impossible to predict that these games, movie, and Internet sites would incite a young person to violence. We find that it is simply too far a leap from shooting characters on a video screen (an activity undertaken by millions) to shooting people in a classroom (an activity undertaken by a handful, at most) for Carneal's actions to have been reasonably foreseeable to the manufacturers of the media that Carneal played and viewed.

Decision

The U.S. court of appeals held that the defendant video game and movie producers and distributors were not liable to the plaintiffs.

Ethics Questions

Do producers and distributors owe a duty to society not to produce and distribute violent games and movies? Are any free speech issues involved in this case?

Special Negligence Doctrines

The courts have developed many *special negligence doctrines*. The most important of these are discussed in the paragraphs that follow.

Professional Malpractice

Professionals, such as doctors, lawyers, architects, accountants, and others, owe a duty of ordinary care in providing their services. This duty is known as the *reasonable professional standard*. A professional who breaches this duty of care is liable for the injury his or her negligence causes. This liability is commonly referred to as **professional malpractice**.

professional malpractice
The liability of a professional who breaches his or her duty of ordinary care.

Examples A doctor who accidently leaves a medical instrument in a patient after an operation has been completed is liable for *medical malpractice*. A lawyer who fails to file a document with the court on time, thus causing the client's case to be dismissed, is liable for *legal malpractice*.

Negligent Infliction of Emotional Distress

negligent infliction of emotional distress
A tort that permits a person to recover for emotional distress caused by the defendant's negligent conduct.

Some jurisdictions have extended the tort of emotional distress to include the **negligent infliction of emotional distress**. Here, a person who is not physically injured by the defendant's negligence suffers emotional distress because of the defendant's action and can recover damages from the defendant for emotional distress.

The most common example of negligent infliction of emotional distress involves bystanders who witness the injury or death of a relative that is caused by another's negligent conduct. Under this tort, the bystander, even though not physically injured personally, may be able to recover damages against the negligent party for his or her own mental suffering. Many states require that the following elements are proved in bystander cases:

1. A close relative was killed or injured by the defendant.
2. The plaintiff suffered severe emotional distress.
3. The plaintiff's mental distress resulted from a sensory and contemporaneous observance of the accident.

Some states require that the plaintiff's mental distress be manifested by some physical injury; other states have eliminated this requirement.

Example A father is walking his young daughter to school when a driver of an automobile negligently runs off the road and onto the sidewalk, hitting the girl but not her father. Suppose that the young daughter dies from her injuries. The father suffers severe emotional distress by seeing his daughter die and manifests his distress by suffering physically. The father can recover damages for negligent infliction of emotional distress for the severe distress he suffered by seeing his daughter die.

Negligence *Per Se*

negligence *per se*
A tort in which the violation of a statute or an ordinance constitutes the breach of the duty of care.

Statutes often establish duties owed by one person to another. The violation of a statute that proximately causes an injury is **negligence *per se***. The plaintiff in such an action must prove that (1) a statute existed, (2) the statute was enacted to prevent the type of injury suffered, and (3) the plaintiff was within a class of persons meant to be protected by the statute.

Example Most cities have an ordinance that places the responsibility for fixing public sidewalks in residential areas on the home owners whose homes front the sidewalks. A home owner is liable if he or she fails to repair a damaged sidewalk in front of his or her home if a pedestrian trips and is injured because of the unrepaired sidewalk. The injured party does not have to prove that the home owner owed the duty because the statute establishes that.

Res Ipsa Loquitur

If a defendant is in control of a situation in which a plaintiff has been injured and has superior knowledge of the circumstances surrounding the injury, the plaintiff might have difficulty proving the defendant's negligence. In such a situation, the law applies the doctrine of ***res ipsa loquitur*** (Latin for "the thing speaks for itself"). This doctrine raises a presumption of negligence and switches the burden to the defendant to prove that he or she was not negligent. *Res ipsa loquitur* applies in cases where the following elements are met:

1. The defendant had exclusive control of the instrumentality or situation that caused the plaintiff's injury.
2. The injury would not have occurred ordinarily but for someone's negligence.

res ipsa loquitur
A tort in which the presumption of negligence arises because (1) the defendant was in exclusive control of the situation and (2) the plaintiff would not have suffered injury but for someone's negligence. The burden switches to the defendant to prove that he or she was not negligent.

Examples Haeran goes in for major surgery and is given anesthesia to put her to sleep during the operation. Sometime after the operation, it is discovered that a surgical instrument was left in Haeran during the operation. She suffers severe injury because of the instrument left in her body. Haeran has no way to identify which doctor or nurse carelessly left the instrument. In this case, the court can apply the doctrine of *res ipsa loquitur* and place the presumption of negligence on the defendants. Any defendant who can prove that he or she did not leave the instrument in Haeran escapes liability; any defendant who does not disprove his or her negligence is liable. Other typical *res ipsa loquitur* cases involve commercial airplane crashes, falling elevators, and the like.

Gross Negligence

A person can be liable for injury and damage caused by their **gross negligence**. Gross negligence is extreme when compared with ordinary negligence. Gross negligence has often been defined as either a want of even scant care or an extreme departure from the ordinary standard of conduct. In most jurisdictions, gross negligence requires a finding that the defendant engaged in willful misconduct or reckless behavior. A person who engages in wanton and reckless conduct usually has no intent to cause harm to others. However, she or he performs an act that she or he knows or should have known is so unreasonable and dangerous that it is likely to cause harm. Because the definition of gross negligence is vague, a claim for gross negligence is often difficult to prove. The determination of whether a party's conduct is ordinary negligence or gross negligence depends on the unique circumstances of the case.

gross negligence
A doctrine that says a person is liable for harm that is caused by his or her willful misconduct or reckless behavior. Punitive damages may be assessed.

A person who injures someone by his or her gross negligence is liable for compensatory damages suffered by the injured party, including actual losses such as medical costs and also for pain and suffering. If gross negligence is found, *punitive damages* may also be awarded.

Example If an automobile driver runs a stop sign by mistake and hits another car, causing injury to its occupants, the driver is liable for ordinary negligence. If that driver had been drinking alcohol before running the stop sign and his alcohol levels are well above the legal limit, and he causes the same accident, the driver would be found liable for gross negligence because of his reckless disregard for the safety of others, which is caused by his excessive drinking and then driving.

Example If a person is texting while driving and causes an accident in which other persons are injured or killed, that person is most likely liable for gross negligence. It is well known that texting while driving causes the driver to take her or his eyes off the road to use an electronic texting device. Texting while driving is a conscious disregard for the safety of others.

Critical Legal Thinking
How does gross negligence differ from ordinary negligence? What is the advantage for a plaintiff to try to prove gross negligence rather than ordinary negligence?

The following case involves the issue of gross negligence.

CASE 5.4 *STATE COURT CASE Gross Negligence*

Aleo v. SLB Toys USA, Inc.

995 N.E.2d 740, 2013 Mass. Lexis 709 (2013)
Supreme Judicial Court of Massachusetts

"We conclude that the circumstances of this case exhibit a substantial degree of reprehensibility."

—Lenk, Judge

Facts

Toys "R" Us, a toy retailer, purchased Banzai Falls In-Ground Pool Slides from a vendor in China. The slide is made of a tent-like fabric with a rubber-coated sliding surface and is sold with an electric unit to inflate it. The slide is intended to be installed adjacent to an in-ground swimming pool so that a person using the slide may descend the slide ramp into the pool. Sarah Letsky purchased a Banzai Pool Slide from Toys "R" Us using the Internet. She and her husband installed the slide beside the swimming pool at their home. One day the Letskys had family and friends over, including Robin and Michael Aleo. Robin, who weighed 140 pounds, climbed to the top of the slide and descended head first. The bottom part of the slide collapsed, and Robin's head struck the pool ledge through the fabric of the slide. Robin died from the accident. The slide had not been tested to ensure that it complied with federal safety standards requiring pool slides be capable of supporting 350 pounds and be safe for head-first sliding. Michael, Robin's husband, sued Toys "R" Us to recover damages for gross negligence. The jury found Toys "R" Us liable for gross negligence and awarded $2,640,000 in compensatory damages and $18 million in punitive damages. Toys "R" Us appealed.

Issue

Was Toys "R" Us grossly negligent?

Language of the Court

Gross negligence is substantially and appreciably higher in magnitude than ordinary negligence, the element of culpability which characterizes all negligence magnified to a high degree. The judge instructed the jury that it was deemed admitted that the slide was not tested or certified prior to being imported and sold. On this evidence, the jury could have determined that Toys "R" Us's conduct evinced want of even scant care as to the safety of its customers. We conclude that the circumstances of this case exhibit a substantial degree of reprehensibility. Accordingly, the evidence was sufficient to support the jury's finding of gross negligence.

Decision

The appellate court upheld the trial court's finding of gross negligence on the part of Toys "R" Us and the award of compensatory and punitive damages.

Ethics Questions

What is gross negligence? What distinguishes it from ordinary negligence? Was the award of $18 million in punitive damages warranted in this case?

Attractive Nuisance Doctrine

attractive nuisance doctrine
A tort rule that imposes liability on a landowner to children who have been attracted onto the landowner's property by an attractive nuisance and who are killed or injured on the property.

The **attractive nuisance doctrine** is a special tort rule that imposes liability on a landowner to children who have trespassed onto his or her property with the intent to play on the attractive nuisance and are killed or injured while doing so. The underlying reason for this doctrine is that children, due to their youth, do not understand the potential risk associated with the hazard. To find the landowner liable to the child, the attraction must pose an unreasonable risk of death or serious bodily harm.

Examples Attractive nuisances include machinery, abandoned refrigerators and freezers, junk yards, open pits, and unguarded pools.

The landowner owes a duty to remove the dangerous condition or take steps to prevent children from reaching the dangerous object.

Example A home owner owes a duty to place a fence and locked gate around a swimming pool in his or her yard.

Good Samaritan Laws

In the past, liability exposure made many doctors, nurses, and other medical professionals reluctant to stop and render aid to victims in emergency situations, such as highway accidents. Almost all states have enacted **Good Samaritan laws** that relieve medical professionals from liability for injury caused by their ordinary negligence in such circumstances. Good Samaritan laws protect medical professionals only from liability for their *ordinary negligence*, not for injuries caused by their gross negligence or reckless or intentional conduct. Most Good Samaritan laws protect licensed doctors, nurses, and laypersons certified in cardiopulmonary resuscitation (CPR). Laypersons not trained in CPR are not generally protected by Good Samaritan statutes—that is, they are liable for injuries caused by their ordinary negligence in rendering aid.

Good Samaritan law
A statute that relieves medical professionals from liability for ordinary negligence when they stop and render aid to victims in emergency situations.

Examples Sam is injured in an automobile accident and is unconscious in his automobile alongside the road. Doctor Pamela Heathcoat, who is driving by the scene of the accident, stops, pulls Sam from the burning wreckage, and administers first aid. In doing so, Pamela negligently breaks Sam's shoulder. If Pamela's negligence is *ordinary negligence*, she is not liable to Sam because the Good Samaritan law protects her from liability; if Pamela was *grossly negligent* or *reckless* in administering aid to Sam, she is liable to him for the injuries she caused. It is a question of fact for the jury to decide whether a doctor's conduct was ordinary negligence or gross negligence or recklessness.

Critical Legal Thinking
What is the purpose of relieving medical personnel from liability for ordinary negligence when rendering aid? Do persons who do not qualify for protection under the Good Samaritan law run a risk of liability if they choose to render aid?

Example If, in the prior example Pamela was not a doctor or otherwise protected by the Good Samaritan law, she would be liable for any injuries caused to Sam by her *ordinary negligence* (or gross negligence or recklessness) while rendering aid to Sam.

Thus, there is some liability exposure when a person renders aid to another person.

Defenses Against Negligence

A defendant in a negligence lawsuit may raise several defenses to the imposition of liability. These defenses are discussed in the following paragraphs.

Superseding or Intervening Event

Under negligence, a person is liable only for foreseeable events. Therefore, an original negligent party can raise a **superseding event** or an **intervening event** as a defense to liability.

superseding event (intervening event)
An event for which a defendant is not responsible. The defendant is not liable for injuries caused by the superseding or intervening event.

Example Assume that an avid golfer negligently hits a spectator with a golf ball, knocking the spectator unconscious. While lying on the ground, waiting for an ambulance to come, the spectator is struck by a bolt of lightning and killed. The golfer is liable for the injuries caused by the golf ball. He is not liable for the death of the spectator, however, because the lightning bolt was an unforeseen intervening event.

Assumption of the Risk

If a plaintiff knows of and voluntarily enters into or participates in a risky activity that results in injury, the law recognizes that the plaintiff assumed, or took on, the risk involved. Thus, the defendant can raise the defense of **assumption of the risk** against the plaintiff. This defense assumes that the plaintiff (1) had knowledge of the specific risk and (2) voluntarily assumed that risk.

assumption of the risk
A defense that a defendant can use against a plaintiff who knowingly and voluntarily enters into or participates in a risky activity that results in injury.

Example Under assumption of the risk, a race-car driver assumes the risk of being injured or killed in a crash.

In the following case, the court had to decide whether there was an obvious danger.

CASE 5.5 *STATE COURT CASE Obvious Danger*

Martinez v. Houston McLane Company, LLC

414 S.W.3d 219, 2013 Tex. App. Lexis 2420 (2013)
Court of Appeals of Texas

"The risk of injury from a ball is considered an inherent risk of the game."

—Brown, Justice

Facts

The Houston Astros is a professional baseball team that plays its games in Minute Maid Park, a baseball stadium in Houston, Texas. The Houston Astros are owned and operated by Houston McLane Company, LLC. Shirley and Richard Martinez, along with five young children they were caring for, attended a Houston Astros baseball game. Their seats were in the bleachers behind the right-field wall, which is an area where a fly ball hit during the game would be a home run. The baseball field contains almost 41,000 seats, of which about 5,000 seats located behind home plate are shielded by a protective screen. The rest of the seats, including those in the right-field bleachers where Martinez sat, were open and did not have a protective screen. Prior to the game, teams were practicing on the field, including taking batting practice. When Shirley Martinez was walking on the steps near her seats carrying a young child, she heard someone yell a warning that a fly ball was coming toward her. She shielded the child with her arms and was struck in the face by the ball. She suffered an orbital fracture and corneal laceration. Martinez sued Houston McLane Company, LLC, to recover damages for negligence. Houston asserted in defense the "baseball rule," which holds that spectators at baseball games attend at their own risk. The trial court granted Houston's motion for summary judgment. Martinez appealed.

Issue

Is the defendant baseball owner liable for negligence?

Language of the Court

The baseball rule establishes a standard of care for injuries caused by errant balls at baseball stadiums by accounting for the open and obvious nature of the risk that batted balls pose to fans. The risk of injury from a ball is considered an inherent risk of the game. Fans who attend games are aware that objects may leave the playing field with the potential to cause injury. We conclude that the baseball rule applies to the facts presented here.

Decision

The court of appeals upheld the trial court's decision that the owner of the Houston Astros was not negligent.

Ethics Questions

Was it ethical for the baseball team owners not to pay Martinez for her injuries? Do baseball spectators assume the risk of being hit by flying baseballs?

Contributory and Comparative Negligence

Sometimes a plaintiff is partially liable for causing his own injuries. In such cases, the law usually penalizes the plaintiff for his negligence. States apply one of the two following standards:

contributory negligence
A doctrine that says that a plaintiff who is partially at fault for his or her own injury cannot recover against the negligent defendant.

- **Contributory negligence.** Some states apply the doctrine of **contributory negligence**, which holds that a plaintiff who is partially at fault for his or her own injury cannot recover against the negligent defendant.

  Example Suppose a driver who is driving over the speed limit negligently hits and injures a pedestrian who is jaywalking against a red "Don't Walk" sign. Suppose the jury finds that the driver is 80 percent responsible for the accident and that the jaywalker is 20 percent responsible. The pedestrian suffered $100,000 in injuries. Under the doctrine of contributory negligence, the pedestrian cannot recover any damages from the driver.

- **Comparative negligence.** Many states have replaced the doctrine of contributory negligence with the doctrine of **comparative negligence**, also called **comparative fault**. Under this doctrine, damages are apportioned according to fault.

  Example When the comparative negligence rule is applied to the previous example in which the pedestrian suffered $100,000 of injuries, the result is much fairer. The plaintiff-pedestrian, who was 20 percent at fault for causing his own injuries, can recover 80 percent of his damages (or $80,000) from the negligent defendant-driver.

comparative negligence (comparative fault)
A doctrine under which damages are apportioned according to fault.

Critical Legal Thinking
What is the difference between contributory negligence and comparative negligence? Which rule is the fairest rule?

Several states have adopted **partial comparative negligence**, which provides that a plaintiff must be less than 50 percent responsible for causing his or her own injuries to recover under comparative negligence; otherwise, contributory negligence applies.

Strict Liability

Strict liability, another category of torts, is *liability without fault*. That is, a participant in a covered activity will be held liable for any injuries caused by the activity, even if he or she was not negligent. This doctrine holds that (1) there are certain activities that can place the public at risk of injury even if reasonable care is taken and that (2) the public should have some means of compensation if such injury occurs. Strict liability is imposed for **abnormally dangerous activities** that cause injury or death.

strict liability
Liability without fault.

Activities such as crop dusting, blasting, fumigation, burning of fields, storage of explosives, and the keeping of animals and pets are usually considered activities to which strict liability applies.

Example Ellison has owned a dog for years. The dog has shown no dangerous propensities and has never bitten anyone. Ellison goes out of town on a business trip and has his neighbor take care of the dog while he is gone. While Ellison is gone, the neighbor, while walking the dog, lets the dog off of her leash to play with a child who has asked to play with the dog. When the child hits the dog in the eye, the dog bites the child, injuring the child. Here, Ellison is strictly liable for the injuries caused by his dog even though he has committed no negligence himself.

Key Terms and Concepts

Abnormally dangerous activities (139)
Actual cause (causation in fact) (131)
Assault (123)
Assumption of the risk (137)
Attractive nuisance doctrine (136)
Battery (123)
Breach of the duty of care (129)
Comparative negligence (comparative fault) (139)
Contributory negligence (138)
Defamation of character (126)
Disparagement (trade libel, product disparagement, and slander of title) (126)
Duty of care (129)
False imprisonment (124)
Good Samaritan law (137)
Gross negligence (135)
Injury (130)
Intentional infliction of emotional distress (tort of outrage) (127)
Intentional misrepresentation (fraud or deceit) (127)
Intentional tort (123)
Invasion of the right to privacy (125)
Libel (126)
Malicious prosecution (128)
Merchant protection statute (shopkeeper's privilege) (124)
Misappropriation of the right to publicity (tort of appropriation) (125)
Negligence *per se* (134)

Negligent infliction of emotional distress (134)
New York Times Co. v. Sullivan (126)
Ordinary negligence (negligence) (129)
Palsgraf v. The Long Island Railroad Company (132)
Partial comparative negligence (139)
Professional malpractice (134)
Proximate cause (legal cause) (132)
Public figure (126)
Reasonable person standard (129)
Reasonable professional standard (129)
Res ipsa loquitur (135)
Scienter (127)
Slander (126)
Strict liability (139)
Superseding event (intervening event) (137)
Tort (123)
Transferred intent doctrine (124)
Unintentional tort (negligence) (129)

Critical Legal Thinking Cases

5.1 Assumption of the Risk The Greater Gulf State Fair, Inc. operated the Gulf State Fair in Mobile County, Alabama. One of the events at the fair was a mechanical bull ride, and participants paid money to ride the mechanical bull. A mechanical bull is a ride where the rider sits on a motorized device shaped like a real bull and the ride simulates a real bull ride as the mechanical bull turns, twists, and bucks. The challenge is to stay on the bull and not be thrown off it. A large banner above the ride reads "Rolling Thunder."

John Lilya and a friend watched a rider being thrown from the mechanical bull. Lilya also watched as his friend paid and rode the bull and was also thrown off. Lilya then paid the $5 admission charge and boarded the mechanical bull. He was immediately thrown off onto a soft pad underneath the bull. Lilya reboarded the bull for a second ride. The bull ride began again and became progressively faster, spinning and bucking to the left and right until Lilya fell off the bull. On the fall, Lilya landed on his head and shoulders, and he suffered a fractured neck. Lilya sued Gulf State Fair to recover damages for his severe injuries. Was riding the mechanical bull an open and obvious danger for which Lilya had voluntarily assumed the risk? *Lilya v. The Greater Gulf State Fair, Inc.*, 855 So.2d 1049, 2003 Ala. Lexis 57 (Supreme Court of Alabama, 2003)

5.2 Negligence Three teenagers, Sarah Mitchell, Adam Jacobs, and David Messer, were driving in Mitchell's car at 2:30 A.M. in Indianapolis, Indiana. Mitchell was driving the car, Jacobs was in the front passenger seat, and Messer was in the back seat. Jacobs suggested that they "jump the hills" on Edgewood Avenue, where the speed limit was 40 miles per hour. Mitchell speeded up her car to jump the "big hill" on Edgewood Avenue. The car crested the hill at 80 miles per hour, went airborne, and landed on the road. Mitchell lost control of the car, which sideswiped a Bell Telephone Company utility pole and spun clockwise until the car slammed into an Indianapolis Power & Light Company utility pole. Messer escaped from the burning wreckage but Mitchell and Jacobs died. The utility poles were legally placed twenty-five feet from Edgewood Avenue at the far edge of the companies' easement right of way. Susan Carter, the personal representative of the estate of Adam Jacobs, sued both utility companies, alleging that the companies were negligent in the placement of their utility poles along Edgewood Avenue. Are the utility companies negligent? *Carter v. Indianapolis Power & Light Company and Indiana Bell Telephone Company, Inc.*, 837 N.E.2d 509, 2005 Ind. App. Lexis 2129 (Court of Appeals of Indiana, 2005)

5.3 Proximate Cause One evening, Andrea Filer and her daughter were riding their horses along Riley Hill Road, a public highway in the Town of Salem, New York. At the same time, Megan Adams was jogging along the same road with her son in a stroller and two dogs by her side. Filer noticed that her horse's ears flickered and stiffened, apparently hearing sounds from behind. Filer turned and saw Adams. When Adams observed that Filer was having difficulty controlling her horse, she slowed to a walk. While Adams was still about 50 yards behind the riders, one of her dogs barked and the horses both abruptly broke into a canter or a run. Filer, who was not wearing a helmet, fell from her horse seconds later and sustained serious injuries. Plaintiff Filer sued Adams, alleging that Adams was negligent in following the horse riders too closely and letting her dogs bark, which she claimed spooked the horses. Defendant Adams asserted that Filer, an experienced rider, should have had control of her horse. Adams stated that she was a far enough distance from Filer and that walking with the stroller and the dog's bark were not the proximate cause of Filer's accident. Were Adams's activities the proximate cause of Filer's riding accident? *Andrea v. Adams*, 966 N.Y.S.2d 553, 106 A.D.3d 1417, 2013 N.Y. App. Div. Lexis 3831 (Appellate Division of the Supreme Court of New York, 2013)

5.4 Disparagement Zagat Survey, LLC, publishes the famous Zagat series of dining, travel, and leisure guides for different cities and locations. The Zagat restaurant guides lists and ranks each reviewed restaurant from 0 to 30 for categories such as food, décor, and service. These ratings are calculated from surveys of customers of the restaurants, and the Zagat guide often quotes anonymous consumer comments.

Lucky Cheng's is a restaurant owned by Themed Restaurants, Inc., that is located in Manhattan, New York. Lucky Cheng's is a theme restaurant with a drag queen cabaret where female impersonators are both waiters and performers, and customer participation contributes to the entertainment. The *Zagat Survey of New York City Restaurants* rated the food at Lucky Cheng's as 9 and rated the décor and service as 15. The Zagat guide then stated,

> *God knows "you don't go for the food" at this East Village Asian-Eclectic—rather you go to "gawk" at the "hilarious" "cross-dressing" staff who "tell dirty jokes", perform "impromptu floor shows" and offer "lap dances for dessert"; obviously, it "can be exhausting", and weary well-wishers suggest they "freshen up the menu—and their makeup."*

Themed Restaurants sued Zagat for disparagement. Zagat defended, arguing that the ratings and comments about Lucky Cheng's restaurant that appeared in the Zagat guide were opinions and not statements of fact and were, therefore, not actionable as disparagement. Were the statements made in Zagat's restaurant guide statements of fact or statements of opinion? Is Zagat liable for disparagement? *Themed Restaurants, Inc., Doing Business as Lucky Cheng's v. Zagat Survey, LLC*, 801 N.Y.S.2d 38, 2005 N.Y. App. Div. Lexis 9275 (Supreme Court of New York, Appellate Division, 2005)

5.5 Negligence Curtis R. Wilhelm owned beehives and kept the hives on property he owned. John Black, who operated a honeybee business, contracted to purchase some beehives from Wilhelm. Black employed Santos Flores Sr. to help him pick up the beehives from Wilhelm. Black provided Flores with a protective suit to wear while picking up the beehives. Neither Wilhelm nor Black informed Flores of the danger of working with bees. After picking up beehives from Wilhelm's home, Black and Flores drove to remote property owned by Wilhelm to pick up other beehives. Flores opened the veil on his protective suit. After loading one beehive onto the truck, Flores started staggering and yelling for help. Flores sustained several bee stings, suffered anaphylactic shock reaction, and died before an ambulance could reach him. Flores's wife and children sued Wilhelm and Black for negligence for failing to warn Flores of the dangers of working with beehives and the possibility of dying of anaphylactic shock if stung by a bee. Did Wilhelm act negligently by failing to warn Flores of the dangers of working with beehives? *Wilhelm v. Flores*, 133 S.W.3d 726, 2003 Tex. App. Lexis 9335 (Court of Appeals of Texas, 2003)

5.6 Negligence One morning, after working at night, Tim Clancy was driving a Chevrolet S-10 pickup truck on State Road 231. Clancy fell asleep at the wheel of the truck. Robert and Dianna Goad, husband and wife, were riding separate motorcycles on the other side of the road. Clancy's truck crossed the center line of the road and collided with Dianna's motorcycle. The collision immediately severed Dianna's leg above the knee, and she was thrown from her motorcycle into a water-filled ditch at the side of the road. Clancy was awakened by the sound of the impact, and the truck veered into the ditch as well. Robert stopped his motorcycle, ran back to the scene of the accident, and held Dianna's head out of the water-filled ditch. Clancy called 911, and when the paramedics arrived, Dianna was taken to the hospital. Dianna remained in a coma for two weeks. Her leg had to be amputated. In addition, Dianna suffered from a fractured pelvic bone, a fractured left elbow, and a lacerated spleen, which had to be removed. Dianna endured multiple skin graft procedures. At the time of the trial, Dianna had undergone seven surgeries, she had taken more than 6,800 pills, and her medical expenses totaled more than $368,000. Furthermore, Dianna's medical expenses and challenges continue and are expected to continue indefinitely. In addition, Dianna has been fitted with a C-leg, a computerized prosthetic leg. A C-leg needs to be replaced every three to five years, at full cost. Dianna sued Clancy to recover damages based on his negligence. Has Clancy been negligent? If so, what amount of damages should be awarded to Dianna? *Clancy v. Goad*, 858 N.E.2d 653, 2006 Ind. App. Lexis 2576 (Court of Appeals of Indiana, 2006)

Ethics Cases

Ethical

5.7 Ethics Case LaShawna Goodman went to a local Walmart store in Opelika, Alabama, to do some last-minute holiday shopping. She brought along her two young daughters and a telephone she had purchased earlier at Walmart to exchange. She presented the telephone and receipt to a Walmart employee, who took the telephone. Unable to find another telephone she wanted, Goodman retrieved the previously purchased telephone from the employee, bought another item, and left. Outside, Goodman was stopped by Walmart security personnel and was accused of stealing the phone. Goodman offered to show the Walmart employees the original receipt, but the Walmart employees detained her and called the police. Goodman was handcuffed in front of her children. Walmart filed criminal charges against Goodman.

At the criminal trial, Goodman was acquitted of all charges. Goodman then filed a civil lawsuit against Walmart Stores, Inc., to recover damages for falsely accusing her of stealing the telephone and false imprisonment. Walmart asserted the defense that it was within its rights to have detained Goodman as it did and to have prosecuted her based on its investigation. Walmart asserted that the merchant protection statute protected its actions in this case. Was Walmart's conduct ethical? Did Walmart act responsibly by bringing criminal charges against Goodman? Did Walmart present sufficient evidence to prove that it should be protected by the merchant protection statute? *Walmart Stores, Inc. v. Goodman*, 789 So.2d 166, 2000 Ala. Lexis 548 (Supreme Court of Alabama, 2000)

5.8 Ethics Case Shortly after 2:00 A.M. one summer night, 12-year-old Denise Colbert and several friends took a motor boat out on Lake Tapps, in Washington state. Denise had been drinking. Skier's Choice, Inc. had manufactured the Moomba brand boat they were using. Denise and several of her friends jumped off the boat into the water and held onto the boat's rear platform as the boat drove slowly toward shore. When the boat neared 200 yards from shore, Denise and Lindsay Lynam began swimming to shore. Sometime between 3:00 and 3:30 A.M., Lindsay noticed that Denise had disappeared beneath the water's surface. The friends called 911 and began searching for Denise. One of the friends called Denise's father, Jay Colbert, and told him that Denise had fallen off the boat and they could not find her.

Police and other rescuers arrived around 3:45 A.M., and Mr. Colbert arrived sometime thereafter. Mr. Colbert went to a friend's dock, where he could watch the rescuers search for Denise. The rescuers searched with boats, spotlights, and divers. Sometime after 6:00 A.M., the rescuers found Denise's body. About 10 minutes later, Mr. Colbert saw the rescuers, about 100 yards away, pull a body out of the water and onto a boat. The rescuers wrapped the body in a blanket and placed the body in an ambulance while Mr. Colbert looked on. The medical examiner reported the cause of Denise's death as drowning. The examiner noted two other significant conditions: high levels of carbon monoxide and ethanol toxicity that would come from a boat's engine.

Thereafter, Mr. Colbert saw a psychologist, who later testified that Mr. Colbert was suffering from severe emotional distress caused by the death of his daughter. Mr. Colbert sued Skier's Choice, Inc., the manufacturer of the boat, to recover damages under the doctrine of negligent infliction of emotional distress. The trial court dismissed Mr. Colbert's claim. Mr. Colbert appealed. Is the defendant liable to Mr. Colbert under the legal theory of negligent infliction of emotional distress in this case? Did the defendant act ethically by denying liability in this case? *Colbert v. Moomba Sports, Inc. and Skier's Choice, Inc.*, 135 P.3d 485, 2006 Wash. App. Lexis 975 (Court of Appeals of Washington, 2006)

Notes

1. 376 U.S. 254, 84 S.Ct. 710, 1964 U.S. Lexis 1655 (Supreme Court of the United States, 1964).
2. *Restatement (Second) of Torts*, Section 46.
3. *Restatement (Second) of Torts*, Section 46, Comment d.
4. Justice B. Anderson, *Blyth v. Birmingham Waterworks Co.*, 11 Exch. 781, 784 (Court of Exchequer, 1856).

CHAPTER 6 Product and Strict Liability

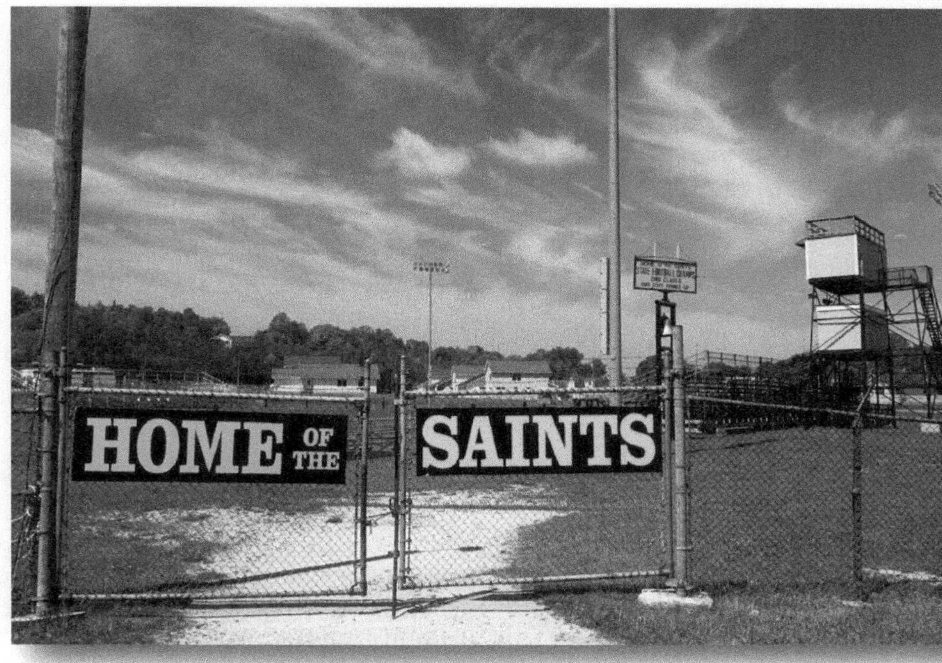

FOOTBALL FIELD
Football helmets and other sports equipment are usually designed to be as safe as possible. However, many manufacturers have discontinued making football helmets because of the exposure to product liability lawsuits.

Learning Objectives

After studying this chapter, you should be able to:

1. Describe and distinguish among the several legal theories of product liability.
2. Define the doctrine of *strict liability*.
3. Identify and describe defects in manufacture and design.
4. Identify and describe defects of failure to warn and in packaging.
5. Describe the damages recoverable in a product liability lawsuit.

Chapter Outline

"*A manufacturer is strictly liable in tort when an article he places on the market, knowing that it is to be used without inspection for defects, proves to have a defect that causes injury to a human being.*"

—*Traynor, Justice*
Greenman v. Yuba Power Products, Inc., 59 Cal.2d 57, 27 Cal.Rptr. 697, 1963 Cal. Lexis 140 (1963)

Introduction to Product and Strict Liability

An injustice anywhere is an injustice everywhere.
Samuel Johnson

If a product defect causes injury or death to purchasers, lessees, users, or bystanders, the injured party or the heirs of a deceased person may bring legal actions and recover damages under certain tort doctrines. These tort doctrines include negligence, misrepresentation, and the modern theory of strict liability. The liability of manufacturers, sellers, lessors, and others for injuries caused by defective products is commonly referred to as **product liability**.

product liability
The liability of manufacturers, sellers, and others for the injuries caused by defective products.

These tort doctrines include negligence and the modern theory of strict liability. Under the doctrine of strict liability, a plaintiff may also recover punitive damages if the defendant's conduct has been reckless or intentional.

The various tort principles that permit injured parties to recover damages caused by defective products are discussed in this chapter.

Product Liability: Negligence

Often, the plaintiff who brings a product liability action relies on the traditional tort theory of **negligence**. Negligence requires the defendant to be *at fault* for causing the plaintiff's injuries. To be successful, the plaintiff must prove that the defendant breached a duty of due care to the plaintiff and thereby caused the plaintiff's injuries. In other words, the plaintiff must prove that the defendant was at fault for causing his or her injuries.

negligence
A tort related to defective products in which the defendant has breached a duty of due care and caused harm to the plaintiff.

Failure to exercise due care includes failing to assemble a product carefully, negligent product design, negligent inspection or testing of a product, negligent packaging, failure to warn of the dangerous propensities of a product, and so forth. It is important to note that in a negligence lawsuit, only a party who was actually negligent is liable to the plaintiff.

Example Assume that the purchaser of a motorcycle is injured in an accident. The accident occurred because a screw was missing from the motorcycle. How does the buyer prove who was negligent? Was it the manufacturer, which left out the screw during the assembly of the motorcycle? Was it the retailer, who negligently failed to discover the missing screw while preparing the motorcycle for sale? Was it the mechanic, who failed to replace the screw after repairing the motorcycle? To be successful, the plaintiff must prove that the defendant breached a duty of due care to the plaintiff and thereby caused the plaintiff's injuries. In other words, the plaintiff must prove that the defendant was at fault for causing his or her injuries. Negligence remains a viable yet sometimes difficult theory on which to base a product liability action.

Product Liability: Misrepresentation

A buyer or lessee who is injured because a seller or lessor fraudulently misrepresented the quality of a product can sue the seller for the tort of **intentional misrepresentation**, or **fraud**. Recovery is limited to persons who were injured because they relied on the misrepresentation.

intentional misrepresentation (fraud)
A tort in which a seller or lessor fraudulently misrepresents the quality of a product and a buyer is injured thereby.

Intentional misrepresentation occurs when a seller or lessor either (1) affirmatively misrepresents the quality of a product or (2) conceals a defect in it.

Because most reputable manufacturers, sellers, and lessors do not intentionally misrepresent the quality of their products, fraud is not often used as the basis for product liability actions.

Product Liability: Strict Liability

In the landmark case ***Greenman v. Yuba Power Products, Inc.***,[1] the California Supreme Court adopted the doctrine of **strict liability** in tort as a basis for product liability actions. Most states have now adopted this doctrine as a basis for product liability actions. The doctrine of strict liability removes many of the difficulties for the plaintiff associated with other theories of product liability. This section examines the special features of the doctrine of strict liability.

strict liability
A tort doctrine that makes manufacturers, distributors, wholesalers, retailers, and others in the chain of distribution of a defective product liable for the damages caused by the defect, *regardless of fault*.

Liability Without Fault

Unlike negligence, strict liability does not require the injured person to prove that the defendant breached a duty of care. Strict liability is **liability without fault**. A seller or lessor can be found strictly liable even though he or she has exercised all possible care in the preparation and sale or lease of his or her product. Strict liability may not be disclaimed.

The doctrine of strict liability applies to sellers and lessors of products who are engaged in the business of selling and leasing products. Casual sales and transactions by nonmerchants are not covered. Thus, a person who sells a defective product to a neighbor in a casual sale is not strictly liable if the product causes injury.

Strict liability applies only to products, not services. In hybrid transactions that involve both services and products, the dominant element of the transaction dictates whether strict liability applies.

Example In a medical operation that requires a doctor to insert an electronic pacemaker to help a patient's heart pump blood regularly, the surgical operation would be the dominant element and the provision of the pacemaker would not be the dominant element. Therefore, the doctor would not be liable for strict liability if the pacemaker is defective and fails, causing injury to the patient. However, the manufacturer and seller of the defective pacemaker (a product) would be strictly liable.

All in the Chain of Distribution Are Liable

All parties in the **chain of distribution** of a defective product are strictly liable for the injuries caused by that product. Thus, all manufacturers, distributors, wholesalers, retailers, lessors, and subcomponent manufacturers may be sued and assessed liability under the doctrine of strict liability in tort. This view is based on public policy. First, the injured party will have more parties from whom to recover damages for injuries. This is particularly important if the negligent party is out of business or does not have the money to pay the judgment. Second, lawmakers presume that sellers and lessors insure against the risk of a strict liability lawsuit and spread the cost to their consumers by raising the price of their products. Third, parties in the chain of distribution may be more careful about the products they distribute.

chain of distribution
All manufacturers, distributors, wholesalers, retailers, lessors, and subcomponent manufacturers involved in a transaction.

A defendant who has not been negligent but who is made to pay a strict liability judgment can bring a separate action against the negligent party in the chain of distribution to recover losses.

Critical Legal Thinking
What is the public policy for holding parties in the chain of distribution of a product strictly liable *without fault*? Can they protect against liability for some other party's negligence?

Example Suppose a subcomponent manufacturer produces a defective tire and sells it to a truck manufacturer. The truck manufacturer places the defective tire on one of its new-model trucks. The truck is sold to a retail car dealership. Ultimately, the car dealership sells the truck to a buyer. The defective tire

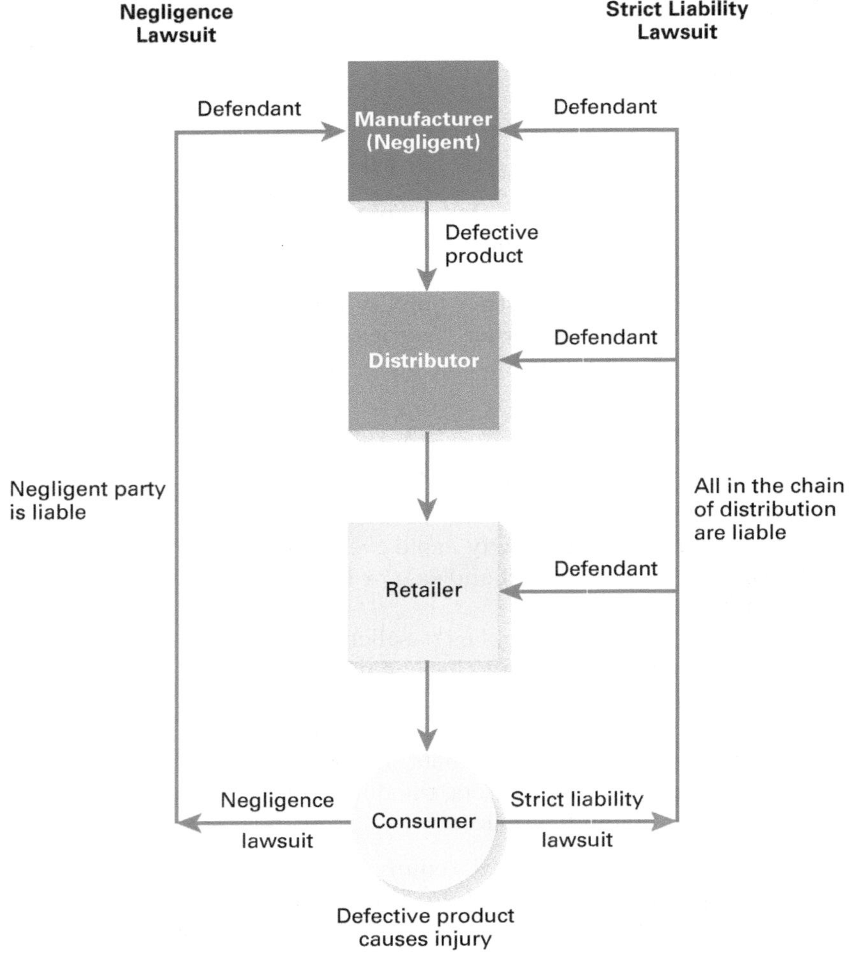

Exhibit 6.1 **NEGLIGENCE AND STRICT LIABILITY COMPARED**

Nobody has a more sacred obligation to obey the law than those who make the law.
Sophocles

causes an accident in which the buyer is injured. All the parties in the tire's chain of distribution can be sued by the injured party; in this case, the liable parties are the subcomponent manufacturer, the truck manufacturer, and the car dealership.

Exhibit 6.1 compares the doctrines of negligence and strict liability.

Parties Who Can Recover for Strict Liability

Because strict liability is a tort doctrine, **privity of contract** between the plaintiff and the defendant is not required. In other words, the doctrine applies even if the injured party had no contractual relations with the defendant. Thus, manufacturers, distributors, sellers, and lessors of a defective product are liable to the consumer who purchased the product and any user of the product. Users include the purchaser or lessee, family members, guests, employees, customers, and persons who passively enjoy the benefits of the product (e.g., passengers in automobiles).

The manufacturer, distributor, seller, and lessor of a defective product are also liable to third-party bystanders injured by the defective product. The courts have stated that bystanders who are injured by a defective product should be entitled to the same protection as consumers or users. Bystanders and nonusers do not have the opportunity to inspect products for defects that have caused their injury.

Damages Recoverable for Strict Liability

The damages recoverable in a strict liability action vary by jurisdiction. Damages for personal injuries are recoverable in all jurisdictions that have adopted the doctrine of strict liability, although some jurisdictions limit the dollar amount of the award. Property damage is recoverable in most jurisdictions, but economic loss (e.g., lost income) is recoverable in only a few jurisdictions.

In product liability cases, a court can award **punitive damages** if it finds that the defendant's conduct was committed with intent or with reckless disregard for human life. Punitive damages are meant to punish the defendant and to send a message to the defendant (and other companies) that such behavior will not be tolerated.

punitive damages
Monetary damages that are awarded to punish a defendant who either intentionally or recklessly injured the plaintiff.

Example An automobile manufacturer realizes that one of its models of vehicles has a defect in the braking mechanism. If the automobile manufacturer does not notify the owners of this type of vehicle of the defect and someone is injured because of the defect, the manufacturer will be liable for compensatory damages for the injuries caused to the injured party. The automobile manufacturer will most likely be assessed punitive damages for its callous disregard for the safety of the public.

Critical Legal Thinking

What are punitive damages? Why are they assessed? Do they serve a public purpose?

Product Defects

To recover for strict liability, the injured party must show that the product that caused the injury was somehow *defective*. (Remember that the injured party does not have to prove who caused the product to become defective.) Plaintiffs can allege multiple **product defects** in one lawsuit. A product can be found to be defective in many ways. The most common types of defects are:

- Defect in manufacture
- Defect in design
- Failure to warn
- Defect in packaging
- Failure to provide adequate instructions

These defects are discussed in the following paragraphs.

product defect
Something wrong, inadequate, or improper in the manufacture, design, packaging, warning, or instructions about a product.

Defect in Manufacture

A **defect in manufacture** occurs when the manufacturer fails to (1) assemble a product properly, (2) test a product properly, or (3) check the quality of a product adequately.

defect in manufacture
A defect that occurs when a manufacturer fails to (1) assemble a product properly, (2) test a product properly, or (3) check the quality of the product adequately.

Example American Ladder Company designs, manufactures, and sells ladders. While manufacturing a ladder, a worker at the company fails to insert one of the screws that would support one of the steps of the ladder. The ladder is sold to Weingard Distributor, a wholesaler, which sells it to Reynolds Hardware Store, which sells the ladder to Heather, a consumer. When Heather is on the ladder painting her house, the step of the ladder breaks because of the missing screw, and Heather falls and is injured. The missing screw is an example of a defect in manufacture. Under the doctrine of strict liability, American Ladder Company, Weingard Distributor, and Reynolds Hardware Store are liable for Heather's injury.

The following case is a classic example involving a defect in manufacture.

CASE 6.1 STATE COURT CASE Defect in Manufacture

Shoshone Coca-Cola Bottling Company v. Dolinski

82 Nev. 439, 420 P.2d 855, 1966 Nev. Lexis 260
Supreme Court of Nevada

"In the case at hand, Shoshone contends that insufficient proof was offered to establish that the mouse was in the bottle of 'Squirt' when it left Shoshone's possession."
—Thompson, Justice

Facts

Leo Dolinski purchased a bottle of Squirt, a soft drink, from a vending machine at a Sea and Ski plant, his place of employment. Dolinski opened the bottle and consumed part of its contents. He immediately became ill. On examination, it was found that the bottle contained the decomposed body of a mouse, mouse hair, and mouse feces. Dolinski suffered physical and mental distress from consuming the decomposed mouse and thereafter possessed an aversion to soft drinks. The Shoshone Coca-Cola Bottling Company (Shoshone) had manufactured and distributed the Squirt bottle. Dolinski sued Shoshone, basing his lawsuit on the doctrine of strict liability. The trial court adopted the doctrine of strict liability, and the jury returned a verdict in favor of the plaintiff. Shoshone appealed.

Issue

Was there a defect in the manufacture of the Squirt bottle that caused the plaintiff's injuries?

Language of the Court

In our view, public policy demands that one who places upon the market a bottled beverage in a condition dangerous for use must be held strictly liable to the ultimate user for injuries resulting from such use, although the seller has exercised all reasonable care. The plaintiff offered the expert testimony of a toxicologist who examined the bottle and contents on the day the plaintiff drank from it. It was his opinion that the mouse "had been dead for a long time" and that the dark stains (mouse feces) that he found on the bottom of the bottle must have been there before the liquid was added.

Decision

The supreme court of Nevada adopted the doctrine of strict liability and held that the evidence supported the trial court's finding that there was a defect in manufacture. The supreme court affirmed the trial court's decision in favor of plaintiff Dolinski.

Ethics Questions

Was it ethical for Shoshone to argue that it was not liable to Dolinski? Could this case have been "faked"?

Defect in Design

defect in design
A defect that occurs when a product is designed improperly.

A **defect in design** can support a strict liability action. A defect in design occurs when a product is designed incorrectly. In this case, not just one item has a defect but all of the products are defectively designed and can cause injury.

Examples Design defects that have supported strict liability awards include toys designed with removable parts that could be swallowed by children, machines and appliances designed without proper safeguards, and trucks and other vehicles designed with defective parts.

In evaluating the adequacy of a product's design, a court may apply a **risk–utility analysis**. This requires the court to consider the gravity of the danger posed by the design, the likelihood that injury will occur, the availability and cost of producing a safer alternative design, the social utility of the product, and other factors. Some courts apply a **consumer expectation test**, which requires a showing that the product is more dangerous than the ordinary consumer would expect.

Example An action figure doll for children is designed, manufactured, and sold to consumers, but the toys are defective because they contain lead paint, which can cause injury. This is a design defect because *all* of the toys are improperly designed using lead paint. Children who are injured by the lead paint can recover damages for their injuries. Here, all of the parties in the chain of distribution—the manufacturer of the defective toy, and the distributors, wholesalers, and retailers who sold the toy—are strictly liable.

The following critical legal thinking case applies the doctrine of strict liability.

Business Environment

Strict Liability: Defect in Design

"Evidence of the blind spot was clear and showed that a person of the decedent's height could not be seen by the driver from head to toe until he was standing over fifty-two feet in front of the truck."

—Decuir, Judge

Russel Domingue, Charles Judice, and Brent Gonsoulin, who were employed by M. Matt Durand, Inc. (MMD), were stockpiling barite ore at a mine site. Judice and Gonsoulin were operating Cameco 405-B articulating dump trucks (ADTs) that were manufactured by Cameco Industries, Inc. Each of the trucks weighed over 25 tons and could carry a load of more than 20 metric tons. Domingue was using a bulldozer to push the barite onto a growing pile of ore.

Gonsoulin, who was new to the job, had trouble dumping a large load of barite. Domingue, who was an experienced ADT operator, got off the bulldozer and walked to Gonsoulin's ADT to give his coworker advice on how to dump a heavy load. Meanwhile, Judice made another trip to dump ore and turned his ADT around to return to the barge. At the same time, Domingue was walking back to his bulldozer. Judice testified that he then saw "a pair of sunglasses and cigarettes fly." Judice immediately stopped his ADT and discovered Domingue's body, which he had run over. Domingue died from the accident. Domingue's widow, on behalf of herself and her children, filed a strict liability lawsuit against Cameco, alleging that a design defect in the ADT caused a forward blind spot for anyone operating an ADT. Cameco could have spent $5,000 to reduce greatly or eliminate the blind spot.

The trial court found that the forward blind spot on Cameco's 405-B dump truck was a design defect and held Cameco responsible for causing Domingue's death. Damages were set at $1,101,050. Cameco appealed. The court of appeals upheld the trial court judgment. The court of appeals stated, "Evidence of the blind spot was clear and showed that a person of the decedent's height could not be seen by the driver from head to toe until he was standing over fifty-two feet in front of the truck." *Domingue v. Cameco Industries, Inc.*, 936 So.2d 282, 2006 La. App. Lexis 1593 (Court of Appeal of Louisiana, 2006).

Crashworthiness Doctrine

Often, when an automobile is involved in an accident, the driver or passengers are not injured by the blow itself. Instead, they are injured when their bodies strike something inside their own automobile (e.g., the dashboard or the steering wheel). This is commonly referred to as the "second collision." The courts have held that automobile manufacturers are under a duty to design automobiles to take into account the possibility of this second collision. This is called the **crashworthiness doctrine**.

crashworthiness doctrine
A doctrine that says that automobile manufacturers are under a duty to design automobiles so that they take into account the possibility of harm from a person's body striking something inside the automobile in the case of a car accident.

Example Failure of an automobile manufacturer to design an automobile to protect occupants from foreseeable dangers caused by a second collision when the automobile is involved in an accident subjects the manufacturer and car dealer who sold the vehicle to strict liability.

Failure to Warn

Certain products are inherently dangerous and cannot be made any safer and still accomplish the purpose for which they are designed. Many such products have risks and side effects caused by their use. Manufacturers and sellers owe a duty to warn consumers and users about the dangers of using these products. A proper and conspicuous warning placed on the product insulates the manufacturer and others in the chain of distribution from strict liability. **Failure to warn** of these dangerous propensities is a defect that supports a strict liability action.

failure to warn
A defect that occurs when a manufacturer does not place a warning on the packaging of products that could cause injury if the danger is unknown.

Example Prescription medicine must contain warnings of its *side effects*. That way, a person can make an informed decision whether to use the medicine. If a manufacturer produces a prescription medicine but fails to warn about its known side effects, any person who uses the medicine and suffers from the side effects can sue and recover damages based on failure to warn.

The following case involves the issue of failure to warn.

CASE 6.2 *STATE COURT CASE Failure to Warn*

Patch v. Hillerich & Bradsby Company

257 P.3d 383, 2011 Mont. Lexis 214 (2011)
Supreme Court of Montana

"The risk of harm accompanying the bat's use extends beyond the player who holds the bat in his or her hands."

—Selley, Justice

Facts

While pitching in an American Legion baseball game, 18-year-old Brandon Patch was struck in the head by a batted ball hit by a batter using a model CB-13 aluminum bat manufactured by Hillerich & Bradsby Company (H&B). Brandon died from his injuries. A baseball hit by an aluminum bat travels at a higher velocity than a ball hit by a traditional wooden baseball bat, thus increasing an infielders' required reaction time.

Brandon's parents, individually and as representatives of Brandon's estate, sued H&B for strict liability, asserting that H&B failed to warn Brandon of the alleged defect in the aluminum bat, that is, the increased speed of a ball hit by H&B's bat. In defense, H&B alleged, first, that there was no defect of failure to warn and, second, that it did not have a duty to warn a nonuser of the bat. The jury found failure to warn and awarded the plaintiffs $850,000 against H&B. H&B appealed.

Issue

Did H&B fail to warn Brandon of the increased risk of injury caused by its aluminum bat?

Language of the Court

The bat is an indispensable part of the game. The risk of harm accompanying the bat's use extends beyond the player who holds the bat in his or her hands. A warning of the bat's risks to only the batter standing at the plate inadequately communicates the potential risk of harm posed by the bat's increased exit speed. H&B is subject to liability to all players in the game, including Brandon, for the physical harm caused by its bat's increased exit speed.

Decision

The supreme court of Montana upheld the jury's finding of failure to warn by H&B and affirmed the award of $850,000 damages.

Ethics Questions

Do you think that H&B should have been found liable in this case? Do baseball leagues and teams owe an ethical duty to ban the use of aluminum bats?

Defect in Packaging

Manufacturers owe a duty to design and provide safe packages for their products. This duty requires manufacturers to provide packages and containers that are tamperproof or that clearly indicate whether they have been tampered with. Certain manufacturers, such as drug manufacturers, owe a duty to place their products in containers that cannot be opened by children. A manufacturer's failure to meet this duty—a **defect in packaging**—subjects the manufacturer and others in the chain of distribution of the product to strict liability.

defect in packaging
A defect that occurs when a product has been placed in packaging that is insufficiently tamperproof.

Example A manufacturer of salad dressing fails to put tamperproof seals on its salad dressings (i.e., caps that have seals that show whether they have been opened). A person purchases several bottles of the salad dressing from a grocery store, opens the caps, places the poison cyanide in the dressings, replaces the caps, and places the bottles back on the grocery store shelves. Consumers who purchase and use the salad dressing suffer injuries and death. Here, the salad dressing manufacturer would be strictly liable for failing to place a tamperproof seal on its products.

Other Defects

Sellers are responsible for providing adequate instructions for the safe assembly and use of the products they sell. **Failure to provide adequate instructions** for the safe assembly and use of a product is a defect that subjects the manufacturer and others in the chain of distribution to strict liability.

failure to provide adequate instructions
A defect that occurs when a manufacturer does not provide detailed directions for safe assembly and use of a product.

Example Mother goes to a retailer and buys her 4-year-old daughter Lia a tricycle that has been manufactured by Bicycle Corporation. The tricycle comes in a box with many parts that need to be assembled. The instructions for assembly are vague and hard to follow. Mother puts together the tricycle, using these instructions. The first time Lia uses the tricycle, a pedal becomes loose, and Lia's tricycle goes into the street, where she is hit and injured by an automobile. In this case, Mother could sue Bicycle Corporation and the retailer on behalf of Lia for strict liability to recover damages for failing to provide adequate instructions.

Other defects that support a finding of product liability based on strict liability include inadequate testing of products, inadequate selection of component parts or materials, and improper certification of the safety of a product. The concept of "defect" is an expanding area of the law.

Defenses to Product Liability

Defendant manufacturers and sellers in negligence and strict liability actions may raise certain defenses to the imposition of liability. Some of the most common defenses are:

- **Generally known danger.** Certain products are inherently dangerous and are known to the general population to be so. Manufacturers and sellers are not strictly liable for failing to warn of **generally known dangers**.

  Example Because it is a known fact that guns shoot bullets, manufacturers and sellers of guns do not have to place a warning on the barrel of a gun warning of this generally known danger.

- **Government contractor defense.** Defense and other contractors that manufacture products to government specifications are not usually liable if such a product causes injury. This is called the **government contractor defense**.

  Example A manufacturer that produces a weapon to U.S. Army specifications is not liable if the weapon is defective and causes injury.

- **Abnormal misuse of a product.** A manufacturer or seller is relieved of product liability if the plaintiff has been injured by an **abnormal misuse of a product**.

  Example A manufacturer or seller of a power lawn mower is not liable if a consumer lifts a power lawn mower on its side to cut hedge and is injured when the lawn mower falls and cuts him.

- **Supervening event.** The manufacturer or seller is not liable if a product is materially altered or modified after it leaves the seller's possession and the alteration or modification causes an injury. Such alteration or modification is called a **supervening event**.

generally known dangers
A defense that acknowledges that certain products are inherently dangerous and are known to the general population to be so.

government contractor defense
A defense that provides that contractors that manufacture products to government specifications are not usually liable if such a product causes injury.

abnormal misuse of a product
A defense that relieves a seller of product liability if the user misused a product *abnormally*.

supervening event
An alteration or a modification of a product by a party in the chain of distribution that absolves all prior sellers from strict liability.

Example A seller is not liable if a consumer purchases a truck and then replaces the tires with large off-road tires that cause the truck to roll over, injuring the driver or another person.

- **Assumption of the risk.** The doctrine of **assumption of the risk** can be asserted as a defense to a product liability action. For this defense to apply, the defendant must prove that (1) the plaintiff knew and appreciated the risk and that (2) the plaintiff voluntarily assumed the risk.

  Example A prescription drug manufacturer warns of the dangerous side effects of taking a prescription drug. A user is injured by a disclosed side effect. The user assumed the disclosed risk and therefore the manufacturer is not liable for product liability.

The following case illustrates a claim of supervening event.

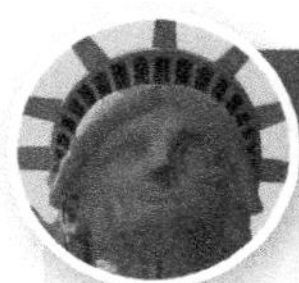

CASE 6.3 *FEDERAL COURT CASE Supervening Event*

Cummins v. BIC USA, Inc.

727 F.3d 506, 2013 U.S. App. Lexis 16800 (2013)
United States Court of Appeals for the Sixth Circuit

"But [the lawyer's] various comments were neither inaccurate nor inflammatory."

—Keague, Circuit Judge

Facts

The minor victim, referred to simply as "CAP," sustained serious burns when he was three years old. CAP had just returned to his mother Amy Cowles's home after an overnight visit with his father Thor Polley. CAP found a cigarette lighter on the floor in his father's truck as he returned to his mother's home. After arriving home, CAP lit the lighter, his shirt caught on fire, and he was burned from the waist up. CAP was taken to the hospital, where he received treatment for second- and third-degree burns to his face and chest and underwent several skin graft surgeries. A black BIC cigarette lighter was found at the scene of the fire and delivered to Police Chief John Brady. The lighter was admitted into evidence at trial, where Chief Brady testified that the lighter was worn and that the legally required child safety guard had been removed from the lighter when it was given to him. CAP's father Thor acknowledged that he usually bought BIC lighters and customarily removed the child-resistant guards from them to make them easier to use. He later denied that he had removed the child-resistant guard from the lighter in question. The conservator for CAP sued BIC USA, Inc., the manufacturer of the lighter, to recover damages for the injuries suffered by CAP. BIC defended, alleging that the BIC lighter was not defective because of a supervening event, namely, that someone had removed the child safety guard from the lighter. In closing arguments to the jury, BIC's lawyer Edward H. Stopher made the following remarks:

> *Presumably, if this was the lighter, presumably that lighter was disabled by Thor Polley. He made an intentional adult choice to disable that lighter. And by his testimony, he disabled it not because it is easy to deactivate it or override it, he disabled it because he said it made it easier to light. It is undisputed that no one can make a fool-proof lighter. No one based on the evidence that we have heard can make a Thorproof lighter.*

The trial court judge admonished the jury to disregard this last remark as inappropriate. The jury found that the lighter was not defective because the child-resistant guard had been removed from the lighter before the accident and held that BIC was not liable for CAP's injuries. The plaintiff appealed for a new trial, alleging that BIC's lawyer's remarks prejudiced the jury.

Issue

Did the BIC's lawyer's remarks in the closing statement prejudice the jury?

(case continues)

Language of the Court

Granted, implying that CAP's father was "foolish" for presumably removing the child resistant guard from the lighter that presumably caused the fire was unnecessary and inappropriate. But Stopher's various comments were neither inaccurate nor inflammatory.

Decision

The U.S. court of appeals affirmed the judgment in favor of defendant BIC.

Ethics Questions

Was it ethical for the BIC's lawyer to make the comments he did? Was the use of the term "Thorproof" effective?

Statute of Limitations and Statute of Repose

Most states have **statutes of limitations** that require an injured person to bring an action within a certain number of years from the time that he or she was injured by a defective product. If the plaintiff does not bring the lawsuit in the allotted time, he or she loses the right to sue.

statute of limitations
A statute that requires an injured person to bring an action within a certain number of years from the time that he or she was injured by a defective product.

Example Assume that a state statute of limitations for strict liability is two years. The plaintiff is injured by a defective product on May 1, 2016. The plaintiff must sue the defendant by May 1, 2018. However, after that date, the plaintiff loses his right to sue the defendant.

Some states have enacted **statutes of repose**, which limit a manufacturer's and seller's liability to a certain number of years from the date when the product was first sold. The period of repose varies from state to state.

statute of repose
A statute that limits the seller's liability to a certain number of years from the date when the product was first sold.

Example Assume that a state statute of repose for strict liability is seven years. If a purchaser purchases a product on May 1, 2016, the statute of repose expires May 1, 2023. If the product is defective but does not cause injury until after that date, the manufacturer and sellers are relieved of liability.

CONCEPT SUMMARY
STATUTE OF LIMITATION AND STATUTE OF REPOSE

Statute	Begins to Run
Statute of limitations	When the plaintiff suffers injury
Statute of repose	When the product is first sold

Plaintiff Partially at Fault

Sometimes a person who is injured by a defective product is negligent and contributes to his or her own injuries. States have adopted either of the following two defenses where a plaintiff is partially at fault:

1. **Contributory negligence.** Under the defense of **contributory negligence**, a party who is partially at fault for causing her own injuries is barred from recovering damages from the defendant in a product liability action.

   Example An automobile manufacturer produces a car with a hidden defect, and a consumer purchases the car from an automobile dealer. The consumer is injured in an automobile accident in which the defect is found to be 75 percent responsible for the accident, and the consumer's reckless driving

contributory negligence
A defense that says that a person who is injured by a defective product but has been negligent and has contributed to his or her own injuries cannot recover from the defendant.

is found to be 25 percent responsible. Under the doctrine of contributory negligence, the plaintiff cannot recover damages from the defendant.

comparative negligence (comparative fault) A doctrine that applies to strict liability actions that says that a plaintiff who is contributorily negligent for his or her injuries is responsible for a proportional share of the damages.

2. **Comparative negligence.** Many states apply the doctrine of **comparative negligence**, also known as **comparative fault**, to product liability actions. Under this doctrine, where a plaintiff has been partially responsible for causing his own injuries, liability is assessed *proportionately* to the degree of fault of each party. In other words, the damages are apportioned proportionally between the plaintiff and the defendant.

   Example An automobile manufacturer produces a car with a hidden defect, and a consumer purchases the car from an automobile dealer. The consumer is injured in an automobile accident in which the defect is found to be 75 percent responsible for the accident, and the consumer's reckless driving is found to be 25 percent responsible. The plaintiff suffers $1 million worth of injuries. Under the doctrine of comparative negligence, the plaintiff would recover $750,000 from the defendants (75 percent of $1 million).

CONCEPT SUMMARY

CONTRIBUTORY NEGLIGENCE AND COMPARATIVE FAULT

Doctrine	Description
Contributory negligence	A person who is partially responsible for causing his or her own injuries may not recover anything from the manufacturer or seller of a defective product.
Comparative negligence	A person who is partially responsible for causing his or her own injuries is responsible for a proportional share of the damages. The manufacturer or seller of the defective product is responsible for the remainder of the plaintiff's damages.

Key Terms and Concepts

Abnormal misuse of a product (151)
Assumption of the risk (152)
Chain of distribution (145)
Comparative negligence (comparative fault) (154)
Consumer expectation test (148)
Contributory negligence (153)
Crashworthiness doctrine (149)
Defect in design (148)
Defect in manufacture (147)
Defect in packaging (150)
Failure to provide adequate instructions (151)
Failure to warn (150)
Generally known dangers (151)
Government contractor defense (151)
Greenman v. Yuba Power Products, Inc. (145)
Intentional misrepresentation (fraud) (144)
Liability without fault (145)
Negligence (144)
Privity of contract (146)
Product defects (147)
Product liability (144)
Punitive damages (147)
Risk–utility analysis (148)
Statute of limitations (153)
Statute of repose (153)
Strict liability (145)
Supervening event (151)

Critical Legal Thinking Cases

6.1 Defect in Design Victoria Berridge, Robert Cook, Robert Walsh, and the pilot, Scott Cowan, boarded a Twin Otter airplane for a skydiving expedition. Shortly after takeoff, the right engine failed, and the airplane crashed. All four persons aboard the airplane died because of the crash. Plaintiffs, the decedents' parents, filed a strict liability lawsuit for wrongful death against Doncasters, Inc., a company that manufactured the blades used in the turbine engines of the airplane. Plaintiffs introduced evidence at trial that showed that the blades manufactured by Doncasters were defective because the aluminide coating and base metal alloy used in the blades made the blades unsafe for use in the airplanes engine. Plaintiffs' expert witnesses testified that the coating used by Doncasters was prone to cracking and that the base metal alloy had low oxidation resistance, both which made Doncastors' blades defective. Other evidence showed that the blades had never passed a required 150-hour endurance test before they were installed. The parents sought compensatory damages for each of the deceased parties as well as punitive damages against Doncastors. Is Doncasters, Inc., strictly liable for the death of the deceased parties of the airplane crash because of a defect in design of the blades used in the engine of the crashed airplane? Is Doncasters liable for punitive damages? *Delacroix v. Doncasters, Inc.*, 407 S.W.3d 13, 2013 Mo. App. Lexis 567 (Missouri Court of Appeals, 2013)

6.2 Defect in Manufacture Western Manufacturing, Incorporated, manufactures a mobile pump for the commercial application of stucco to buildings. The pump consists of a diesel engine, a mixer for the stucco, a batch hopper, a pumping mechanism, and a hose, all mounted on a two-wheel trailer that can be hitched to a truck. The pump pulls slurry from the hopper into a thick 250-foot-long rubber hose for application. The slurry is made with cement and water in the mixer and then added to the hopper. A fitting lock attaches the hose in place. Dorel Roman is a stucco subcontractor. About 15 minutes after one of Roman's workers had started using the pump to spray stucco on a building, the high-pressure hose dislodged and struck Roman, who was 20 feet from the hose, causing severe injuries to Roman's legs. Roman sued Western for strict liability to recover damages for his injuries. Roman alleged that the mobile pump contained a defect in construction when it was produced by Western that caused the hose to dislodge, thus causing Roman's injuries. Roman introduced expert witnesses who testified that the pump had been improperly manufactured by Western and that there was a defect in manufacture. Is Western Manufacturing strictly liable for Roman's injuries based on a defect in manufacture? *Roman v. Western Manufacturing, Incorporated*, 691 F.3d 686, 2012 U.S. App. Lexis 17353 (United States Court of Appeals for the Fifth Circuit, 2012)

6.3 Design Defect Dwayne Maddox and his wife, Amanda, were driving home on a highway in their Nissan Pathfinder SUV. Dwayne, who was driving the vehicle, weighed 170 pounds, and Amanda, who was sitting in the passenger seat, weighed 240 pounds. Amanda had previously had a gastric bypass surgery to help control her weight. Both were wearing their seat belts. Another driver, Edward Sapp, who was greatly intoxicated, drove his vehicle on the wrong side of the highway and collided head-on with Maddox's SUV. Sapp died at the scene. Dwayne was able to exit the SUV and suffered a shattered right heel. Amanda, however, was trapped inside the front passenger seat, and rescuers needed to extricate her from the vehicle with hydraulic equipment. Amanda was transported to a medical center. Amanda's seat belt did not properly protect her and had caused her bypass surgery to rupture. Amanda's injuries were extensive. She suffered fractures of her sternum, several ribs, vertebrae, and hip. Amanda was hospitalized for 139 days, had 75 surgical procedures, was unable to eat food for seven months, and was medically required to keep an open abdominal wound—with her internal organs visible—during part of the time she was hospitalized. Amanda sued Nissan Motor Company, Ltd., the company that manufactured the Nissan Pathfinder SUV that she and her husband were in at the time of the accident, to recover damages for strict liability based on an alleged defect in design of the seat belt restraint system of the SUV. Amanda alleged that Nissan designed its seat belt restraint system to protect persons weighing approximately 171 pounds, that the restraint system was not properly designed to protect a person of her weight, and that Nissan should be found strictly liable for a design defect for not designing its seat belt restraint system to safely protect persons of her weight. Is Nissan strictly liable for failing to design a seat belt restraint system to safely protect heavier persons in vehicle collisions? *Nissan Motor Company, Ltd. v. Maddox*, 2013 Ky. App. Lexis 133 (Court of Appeals of Kentucky, 2013)

6.4 Supervening Event Cincinnati Incorporated (Cincinnati) manufactures a hydraulic press brake, a machine tool commonly used to shape sheet metal. The tool consists of a hydraulic ram that presses the metal and a die onto which the metal is pressed. The operator feeds sheet metal between the die and the ram, and the ram descends to bend the sheet metal. The press is operated by a foot pedal, known as a foot switch. As originally sold by Cincinnati, the press was equipped with a foot switch that had a front flap, or gate, to prevent accidental depression. The operator had to lift the gate with his foot to access the enclosed pedal. The press also came equipped with two foot switches, each of which had to be depressed simultaneously by two different operators in order to trigger the ram. When the press was first sold by Cincinnati 20 years ago to a company named Steelgard, the safety equipment was in place. The press had been sold several times to other companies before Ventaire, Inc. acquired it. Sometime between the press's original sale and its sale to Ventaire, the original foot switches were removed and replaced with ones that did not have a gate. Also, one of the foot switches had been disabled so that the press could be operated with a single foot switch unprotected by any gate. The press still contained the original conspicuous signs that warned the operator not to place his or her hands in the press and that his or her fingers or hands could be crushed if he or she did so.

While Derek Braswell, an employee of Ventaire, was operating the press, Braswell reached into the die area with his right hand to remove a jammed piece of metal. While doing so, he accidentally stepped on the foot switch, triggering the ram's descent and crushing his right arm, which was later amputated. Braswell filed a strict liability lawsuit against Cincinnati to recover damages for his injuries, alleging that Cincinnati's press was designed defectively. In defense, Cincinnati asserted that the press was designed properly and equipped with safety features when the press was first sold, which would have prevented this type of accident, and that the removal and disabling of the safety features was a supervening event and that it is not responsible for plaintiff Braswell's injuries. Is Cincinnati liable in strict liability for a design defect? *Braswell v. Cincinnati Incorporated*, 731 F.3d 1081, 2013 U.S. App. Lexis 19451 (United States Court of Appeals for the Tenth Circuit, 2013)

6.5 Failure to Warn Taser International, Inc., manufactures a product commonly known as a "taser." Tasers have prongs or cords that emit high-voltage electrical currents that, when they touch a person's body, immobilize the person. Tasers are often used by police forces to subdue criminal suspects. Usually, because the amperage of the taser is very low, no serious or permanent injury is inflicted. Darryl Wayne Turner, age seventeen, who the police believed was engaging in a dispute and refused to comply with the police officer's directives, was shot with a taser by an officer. The taser hit Turner near the chest area and immobilized him. However, the taser shock caused Turner to suffer cardiac arrest, from which he died. Turner had been shot with a model X26 taser made by Taser. Evidence showed that the officer used the taser as he had been trained and in compliance with the manual that accompanied the X26. The X26 taser had been subject to several academic studies that showed that the device posed a risk of ventricular fibrillation, a cause of cardiac arrest, especially when the electrical current from the taser was applied near the subject's heart. Taser did not warn users to avoid deploying the taser's electrical current in proximity to the heart. Turner's mother, Tammy Lou Fontenot, sued Taser for product liability based on negligence to recover damages, alleging that Taser failed to warn of the dangers of deploying the X26 taser to a suspect's chest. Was Taser negligent in failing to warn the police of the dangers of discharging the Taser X26 at a suspect's chest? *Fontenot v. Taser International, Inc.*, 736 F.3d 318, 2013 U.S. App. Lexis 23510 (United States Court of Appeals for the Fourth Circuit, 2013)

6.6 Design Defect Intex Recreation Corporation designed and sold the Extreme Sno-Tube II. This snow tube is ridden by a user down snow-covered hills and can reach speeds of 30 miles per hour. The snow tube has no steering device, and therefore a rider may end up spinning and going down a hill backward. Dan Falkner bought an Extreme Sno-Tube II and used it for sledding the same day. During Falkner's second run, the tube rotated him backward about one-quarter to one-third of the way down the hill. A group of parents, including Tom Higgins, stood near the bottom of the hill. Higgins saw 7-year-old Kyle Potter walking in the path of Falkner's speeding Sno-Tube. Higgins ran and grabbed Potter to save him from harm, but while he was doing so, the Sno-Tube hit Higgins and threw him into the air. Higgins landed on his forehead, which snapped his head back. The impact severed Higgins's spinal cord and left him quadriplegic. Higgins sued Intex for damages based on strict liability. Is the snow tube defective? *Higgins v. Intex Recreation Corporation*, 199 P.3d 421, 2004 Wash. App. Lexis 2424 (Court of Appeals of Washington, 2004)

Ethical

Ethics Cases

6.7 Ethics Case Jolie Glenn placed her 3-year-old daughter, Brittany, in a car with the engine running while it was parked in her garage with the garage door closed. Glenn went back into the house, sat down, and fell asleep. When she awoke, she realized that Brittany was not with her. Jolie went into the garage and saw that the garage door was closed. Brittany was in the car and had died as a result of carbon monoxide poisoning. Overhead Door Corporation had manufactured the garage door and the garage door opener used by Jolie to open and close the garage door.

Malcolm Glenn, Jolie's ex-husband and Brittany's father, sued Overhead Door for strict liability, alleging design defect and failure to warn. Glenn argued that Overhead Door should have designed its garage door opener with a sensor that would determine when carbon monoxide had gotten too high in a garage and then alert the car owner. Glenn also alleged that Overhead Door had failed to warn a user of its garage door opener that if the car was left running and the garage door was closed, carbon monoxide could build up to dangerous levels in the garage. Was Overhead Door liable for strict liability for either design defect or failure to warn? Did

Glenn act ethically in suing Overhead Dorr Corporation? *Glenn v. Overhead Door Corporation*, 935 S.2d 1074, 2006 Miss. App. Lexis 60 (Court of Appeals of Mississippi, 2006)

6.8 Ethics Case Barbara K. Thompson purchased a Sunbeam brand food hand mixer. The mixer was made by Simatelex, a company located in Hong Kong, China, marketed in the United States by Sunbeam Products, Inc., and purchased by Thompson at a Walmart store. Thompson was familiar with electric hand mixers and had owned previous mixers for about twenty years before purchasing the Sunbeam mixer. The box for the Sunbeam mixer included an instruction booklet, which included the heading "IMPORTANT SAFEGUARDS" in enlarged capital letters. Under this section the booklet stated "Unplug from outlet while not in use, before putting on or taking off parts and before cleaning." Under the section entitled in enlarged capital letters "INSTALLING ATTACHMENTS" the manual stated, "Make sure the speed control is in the 'OFF' position and unplugged from an electrical outlet. Insert attachments one at a time by placing stem end into the opening on the bottom of the mixer." Under the section entitled in enlarged capital letters "EJECTING BEATERS" the manual stated, "Make sure the speed control is in the 'OFF' position and unplugged from an electrical outlet prior to ejecting beaters." Thompson took the mixer out of the box, inserted the beaters, and turned on the mixer. When she thought one of the beaters was loose, Thompson held the mixer in one hand and tried to push the beater back into place with her other hand while the mixer was still on. One of Thompson's fingers was pulled into the two moving beaters. She called her husband for assistance, was taken to the hospital and had her finger amputated. Thompson sued Simatelex, Sunbeam, and Walmart for strict liability for failure to warn. Are the defendants strictly liable to Thompson? Did Thompson act ethically in this case? *Thompson v. Sunbeam Products, Inc.*, 2012 U.S. App. Lexis 22530 (United States Court of Appeals for the Sixth Circuit, 2012)

Note

1. 59 Cal.2d 57, 377 P.2d 897, 27 Cal. Rptr. 697, 1963 Cal. Lexis 140 (Supreme Court of California).

CHAPTER 7

Intellectual Property and Cyber Piracy

COPYRIGHT

The owners of copyright material such as books, movies, CDs, DVDs, and video games; the owners of trademarks such as McDonald's Corporation and Starbucks Corporation; the creators of patents such as Microsoft Corporation and Intel Corporation; the owners of trade secrets such as the Coca-Cola Corporation; and the owners of other intellectual property lose substantial revenues caused by the sale of knockoffs of their intellectual property. Computers and software programs have helped increase cyber piracy of intellectual property. Intellectual property is protected by a variety of civil and criminal laws.

Learning Objectives

After studying this chapter, you should be able to:

1. Describe the business tort of misappropriating a trade secret.
2. Describe how an invention can be patented under federal patent laws and the penalties for patent infringement.
3. List the items that can be copyrighted and describe the penalties of copyright infringement.
4. Define *trademark* and *service mark* and describe the penalties for trademark infringement.
5. Define *cyber piracy* and describe the penalties for engaging in cyber-infringement of intellectual property rights.

Chapter Outline

Chapter Outline *(continued)*

> *"The Congress shall have the power . . . to promote the Progress of Science and useful Arts, by securing for limited Times to Authors and Inventors the exclusive Right to their respective Writings and Discoveries."*
>
> —*Article 1, Section 8, Clause 8 of the U.S. Constitution*

Introduction to Intellectual Property and Cyber Piracy

The U.S. economy is based on the freedom of ownership of property. In addition to real estate and personal property, *intellectual property rights* have value to both businesses and individuals. This is particularly the case in the modern era of the information age, computers, and the Internet.

Federal law provides protections for intellectual property rights, such as patents, copyrights, and trademarks. Certain federal statutes provide for either civil damages or criminal penalties or both to be assessed against infringers of patents, copyrights, and trademarks. Trade secrets form the basis of many successful businesses, and such trade secrets are protected from misappropriation. State law imposes civil damages and criminal penalties against persons who misappropriate trade secrets.

This chapter discusses trade secrets, patents, copyrights, and trademarks and how to protect them from infringement, misappropriation, and cyber piracy.

> *And he that invents a machine augments the power of a man and the well-being of mankind.*
>
> Henry Ward Beecher
> *Proverbs from Plymouth Pulpit (1887)*

Intellectual Property

Intellectual property is a term that describes property that is developed through an intellectual and creative process. Intellectual property falls into a category of property known as *intangible rights*, which are not tangible physical objects.

intellectual property
Patents, copyrights, trademarks, and trade secrets. Federal and state laws protect intellectual property rights from misappropriation and infringement.

Most persons are familiar with the fact that intellectual property includes patents, copyrights, and trademarks. It also includes trade secrets. For patents, think of Microsoft's patents on its operating system. Microsoft has obtained more than 10,000 patents. For copyrights, think of music, movies, books, and video games. Nike's slogan "Just Do It" and Swoosh logo, and McDonald's Big Mac and "I'm lovin' it" Are recognizable trademarks. For trade secrets, think of Coca-Cola Company's secret recipe for making Coca-Cola. Patents, trademarks, and copyrights give their owners or holders monopoly rights for specified periods of time. Trade secrets remain valuable as long as they are not easily discovered.

Intellectual property is of significant value to companies in the United States and globally as well. Over one-half of the value of large companies in the United

Where a new invention promises to be useful, it ought to be tried.

Thomas Jefferson

States is related to their intangible property rights. Some industries are intellectual property–intensive, such as the music and movie industries. Other industries that are not intellectual property–intensive, such as the automobile and food industries, are still highly dependent on their intellectual property rights.

Because of their intangible nature, intellectual property rights are more subject to misappropriation than is tangible property. It is almost impossible to steal real estate, and it is often difficult to steal tangible property, such as equipment, furniture, and other personal property. However, intellectual property rights are much easier to misappropriate. Think of illegally downloaded copyrighted music, movies, and video games, and fake designer purses. In addition, computers and cyber piracy make it easier to steal many forms of intellectual property. The misappropriation of intellectual property rights is one of the major threats to companies today.

Trade Secret

trade secret
A product formula, pattern, design, compilation of data, customer list, or other business secret.

Many businesses are successful because their **trade secrets** set them apart from their competitors. Trade secrets may be product formulas, patterns, designs, compilations of data, customer lists, or other business secrets. Many trade secrets do not qualify to be—or simply are not—patented, copyrighted, or trademarked. Many states have adopted the **Uniform Trade Secrets Act** to give statutory protection to trade secrets.

State unfair competition laws allow the owner of a trade secret to bring a lawsuit for *misappropriation* against anyone who steals a trade secret. For the lawsuit to be actionable, the defendant (often an employee of the owner or a competitor) must have obtained the trade secret through unlawful means, such as theft, bribery, or industrial espionage. No tort has occurred if there is no misappropriation.

The owner of a trade secret is obliged to take all reasonable precautions to prevent that secret from being discovered by others. If the owner fails to take such actions, the secret is no longer subject to protection under state unfair competition laws. Precautions to protect a trade secret may include fencing in buildings, placing locks on doors, hiring security guards, and the like.

Examples The most famous trade secret is the formula for Coca-Cola. This secret recipe, which is referred to by the code name Merchandise 7X, is kept in a bank vault in Atlanta, Georgia. The formula is supposedly known by only two executives who have signed nondisclosure agreements. Another secret recipe that is protected as a trade secret is KFC's secret recipe of eleven herbs and spices for the batter used on the Colonel's Original Recipe Kentucky Fried Chicken.

Reverse Engineering

WEB EXERCISE
Go to **www.usatoday.com/money/industries/food/2005-07-22-kfc-secret-recipe_x.htm** and read about how KFC protects its secret recipe.

A competitor can lawfully discover a trade secret by **reverse engineering** (i.e., taking apart and examining a rival's product or re-creating a secret recipe). A competitor who has reverse engineered a trade secret can use the trade secret but not the trademarked name used by the original creator of the trade secret.

Example An inventor invents a new formula for a perfume. The inventor decides not to get a patent for her new formula (because patent protection is good for only twenty years). Instead, the inventor chooses to try to protect it as a trade secret, which gives her protection for as long a period of time as she can successfully keep it a secret. Another party purchases the perfume, chemically analyzes it, and discovers the formula. The trade secret has been reverse engineered, and the second party may begin producing a perfume using the inventor's formula.

Misappropriation of a Trade Secret

The owner of a trade secret can bring a *civil lawsuit* under state law against anyone who has misappropriated a trade secret through unlawful means, such as theft, bribery, or industrial espionage. Generally, a successful plaintiff in a **misappropriation of a trade secret** action can (1) recover the *profits* made by the offender from the use of the trade secret, (2) recover for *damages*, and (3) obtain an *injunction* prohibiting the offender from divulging or using the trade secret.

Economic Espionage Act

Congress enacted the federal **Economic Espionage Act (EEA)**,[1] which makes it a federal *crime* to steal another's trade secrets. Under the EEA, it is a federal crime for any person to convert a trade secret to his or her benefit or for the benefit of others, knowing or intending that the act would cause injury to the owner of the trade secret. The definition of *trade secret* under the EEA is very broad and parallels the definition used under the civil laws of misappropriating a trade secret.

Economic Espionage Act A federal statute that makes it a crime for any person to convert a trade secret for his or her own or another's benefit, knowing or intending to cause injury to the owners of the trade secret.

One of the major reasons for the passage of the EEA was to address the ease of stealing trade secrets through computer espionage and use of the Internet. Confidential information can be downloaded onto a flash drive, placed in a pocket, and taken from the legal owner. Computer hackers can crack into a company's computers and steal customer lists, databases, formulas, and other trade secrets. The EEA is a very important weapon in addressing computer and Internet espionage and penalizing those who commit it.

The EEA provides severe criminal penalties. The act imposes prison terms on individuals of up to fifteen years per criminal violation. An organization can be fined up to $10 million per criminal act. The criminal prison term for individuals and the criminal fine for organizations can be increased if the theft of a trade secret was made to benefit a foreign government.

The following ethics feature discusses the misappropriation of a trade secret.

Ethics

Coca-Cola Employee Tries to Sell Trade Secrets to Pepsi-Cola

"What if you knew the markets Coca-Cola was going to move into and out of and beat them to the punch."

—Letter to PepsiCo

PepsiCo received a letter sent to the company by an employee of Coca-Cola Company that offered to sell PepsiCo trade secrets of Coca-Cola. The letter stated, "What if you knew the markets Coca-Cola was going to move into and out of and beat them to the punch." The letter proposed selling trade secrets regarding a proposed Coke product code-named Project Lancelot for $1.5 million.

PepsiCo notified Coca-Cola officials and federal authorities. The Federal Bureau of Investigation (FBI) initiated an investigation into the matter. The federal government brought criminal charges against Coca-Cola secretary Joya Williams. During trial, prosecutors produced the letter as well as a video-recording of Williams putting confidential documents and samples of Coke products that were still in development into her bag.

Williams was convicted by a federal jury of conspiring to steal Coca Cola trade secrets and attempting to sell them to archrival PepsiCo. The trial court judge sentenced Williams to 8 years in jail. The U.S. court of appeals upheld the decision. Two other co-conspirators were arrested and pled guilty. *United States v. Williams*, 526 F.3d 1312, 2008 U.S. App. Lexis 6073 (United States Court of Appeals for the Eleventh Circuit, 2008)

Ethics Question Did Williams act loyally in this case? Did PepsiCo do what it was supposed to do in this case? How likely is it that PepsiCo would have paid Williams and her co-conspirators the money they demanded?

Patent

When drafting the Constitution of the United States of America, the founders of the United States provided for protection of the work of inventors and writers. Article I, Section 8, of the Constitution provides, "The Congress shall have Power . . . To promote the Progress of Science and useful Arts, by securing for limited Times

Critical Legal Thinking

Why did the founders of the United States place protections for inventors and writers in Article I of the U.S. Constitution? Have these protections become even more important in the current digital age?

to Authors and Inventors the exclusive Right to their respective Writings and Discoveries." Pursuant to the express authority granted in the U.S. Constitution, Congress enacted the **Federal Patent Statute** of 1952 to provide for obtaining and protecting patents.[2]

Federal Patent Statute
A federal statute that establishes the requirements for obtaining a patent and protects patented inventions from infringement.

patent
A grant by the federal government to the inventor of an invention for the exclusive right to use, sell, or license the invention for a limited amount of time.

A **patent** is a grant by the federal government to the inventor of an invention for the exclusive right to use, sell, or license the invention for a limited amount of time.

Patent law is intended to provide an incentive for inventors to invent and make their inventions public and to protect patented inventions from infringement. Federal patent law is exclusive; there are no state patent laws. Applications for patents must be filed with the **U.S. Patent and Trademark Office (PTO)** in Washington DC. The PTO grants approximately 250,000 patents each year.

U.S. Court of Appeals for the Federal Circuit

U.S. Court of Appeals for the Federal Circuit
A special federal appeals court that hears appeals from the Board of Patent Appeals and Interferences and federal court concerning patent issues.

The **U.S. Court of Appeals for the Federal Circuit** in Washington DC, was created in 1982. This is a special federal appeals court that hears appeals from the Patent Trial and Appeal Board of the U.S. Patent and Trademark Office and U.S. district courts concerning patent issues. This court of appeals was created to promote uniformity in patent law.

Patent Application

To obtain a patent, a **patent application** must be filed with the PTO in Washington DC. The PTO provides for the online submission of patent applications and supporting documents through its EFS-Web system. A patent application must contain a written description of the invention. Patent applications are complicated. Therefore, an inventor should hire a patent attorney to assist in obtaining a patent for an invention.

The PTO must make a decision whether to grant a patent within three years from the date of filing a patent application. For the payment of approximately $5,000, inventors can move their patent application to the top of the list of other patent applications for review by the PTO and receive an answer within one year. The PTO can grant priority to patent applications for products, processes, or technologies that are important to the national economy or national competiveness.

provisional application
An application that an inventor may file with the PTO to obtain 3 months to prepare a final patent application.

An inventor may file a **provisional application** with the PTO. This provisional right gives an inventor 3 months to prepare and file a final and complete patent application.

Third parties may file a **pre-issuance challenge** to a pending patent application by submitting prior art references that assert that the sought-after patent is not patentable. There is also a nine-month period after the issuance of a patent for a third party to seek **post-grant review** of a patent by submitting prior art references and other information that assert that the patent holder's claim is not patentable.

The **Patent Trial and Appeal Board (PTAB)**, a section within the PTO, reviews adverse decisions by patent examiners, reviews reexaminations, conducts post-grant reviews, and conducts other patent challenge proceedings. By permitting pre-issuance and post-grant challenges within the PTO, the law attempts to have disputes resolved within the PTO before reaching the litigation stage.

Patent Number

If a patent is granted, the invention is assigned a **patent number**. Patent holders usually affix the word *patent* or *pat.* and the patent number on the patented article. A patent holder may mark an item "Patent" or "Pat" and direct a party to a freely accessible Web address that identifies the product covered by the patent number. If a patent application is filed but a patent has not yet been issued, the applicant usually places the words **patent pending** on the article.

The patent system added the fuel of interest to the fire of genius.

Abraham Lincoln

Exhibit 7.1 shows the abstract from the patent application for the Facebook social networking system (U.S. Patent 20070192299).

Exhibit 7.1 PATENT APPLICATION FOR THE FACEBOOK SOCIAL NETWORKING SYSTEM

Systems and Methods for Social Mapping

Abstract

A system, method, and computer program for social mapping is provided. Data about a plurality of social network members is received. A first member of the plurality of social network members is allowed to identify a second member of the plurality of social network members with whom the first member wishes to establish a relationship. The data is then sent to the second member about the first member based on the identification. Input from the second member is received in response to the data. The relationship between the first member and the second member is confirmed based on the input in order to map the first member to the second member.

Subject Matter That Can Be Patented

Most patents are **utility patents**; that is, they protect the functionality of the item. The term *patent* is commonly used in place of the words *utility patent*. Only certain subject matter can be patented. Federal patent law recognizes categories of innovation that can be patented, including:

utility patent
A patent that protects the functionality of the invention.

- Machines
- Processes
- Compositions of matter
- Improvements to existing machines, processes, or compositions of matter
- Designs for an article of manufacture
- Asexually reproduced plants
- Living material invented by a person

Patent law prohibits the issuance of a patent encompassing a human organism. The law also bans the ability to patent tax strategies. Abstractions and scientific principles cannot be patented unless they are part of the tangible environment.

Example Einstein's theory of relativity ($E = mc^2$) cannot be patented.

For centuries, most patents involved tangible inventions and machines, such as the telephone and the lightbulb. Next, chemical and polymer inventions were patented. Then biotechnology patents were granted. More recently, subject matter involving the computer, Internet, and e-commerce has been added to what can be patented.

Requirements for Obtaining a Patent

To be patented, an invention must be (1) *novel*, (2) *useful*, and (3) *nonobvious*. An invention must meet all three of these requirements. If an invention is found not to meet any one of these requirements, it cannot be patented:

requirements for obtaining a patent
To be patented, an invention must be (1) novel, (2) useful, and (3) nonobvious.

1. **Novel.** An invention is **novel** if it is new and has not been invented and used in the past. If an invention has been used in "prior art," it is not novel and cannot be patented.

   Example College and professional football games are often shown on television. It is often difficult, however, for a viewer to tell how far the offensive team must go to get a first down and keep possession of the football. Inventors invented a system whereby a yellow line is digitally drawn across the football field at the distance that a team has to go to obtain a first down. This yellow line qualified for a patent because it was novel.

2. **Useful.** An invention is **useful** if it has some practical purpose. If an invention has only theoretical benefit and no useful purpose, it cannot be patented.

   Example A cardboard or heavy paper sleeve that can be placed over the outside of a paper coffee cup so that the cup will not be too hot to hold serves a useful purpose. Many coffee shops use these sleeves. The sleeve serves a useful purpose and therefore qualifies to be patented.

3. **Nonobvious.** If an invention is **nonobvious**, it qualifies for a patent; if it is obvious, then it does not qualify for a patent.

   Example An invention called "Forkchops" was found to be nonobvious and was granted a patent. Forkchops consist of chopsticks with a spoon on one end of one of the chopsticks and a fork on one end of the other chopstick. Thus, when eating, a user can use either the chopstick ends or the spoon and fork ends.

   Example An inventor filed for a patent for a waffle fry, which is a fried slice of potato with a waffle shape that is not as thick as a typical french fry but is thicker than a potato chip. Thus, the thickness of a waffle fry is somewhere between the thickness of a french fry and a potato chip. The court rejected a patent for the waffle fry because it was obvious that a potato could be sliced into different sizes.

CONCEPT SUMMARY

REQUIREMENTS FOR OBTAINING A PATENT

1. **Novel.** An invention is **novel** if it is new and has not been invented and used in the past. If an invention has been used in "prior art," it is not novel and cannot be patented.
2. **Useful.** An invention is **useful** if it has some practical purpose. If an invention has only theoretical benefit and no useful purpose, it cannot be patented.
3. **Nonobvious.** If an invention is **nonobvious**, it qualifies for a patent; if it is obvious, then it does not qualify for a patent.

The following U.S. Supreme Court case involves the question of what is patentable subject matter.

CASE 7.1 *U.S. SUPREME COURT CASE Patent*

Association for Molecular Pathology v. Myriad Genetics, Inc.

133 S.Ct. 2107, 2013 U.S. Lexis 4540 (2013)
Supreme Court of the United States

"Laws of nature, natural phenomena, and abstract ideas are not patentable."

—Thomas, Justice

Facts

After substantial research and expenditure of money and resources, Myriad Genetics, Inc. (Myriad), discovered the precise location and sequence of two naturally occurring segments of deoxyribonucleic acid (DNA) known as BRCA1 and BRCA2. Mutations in these genes can dramatically increase a female's risk of developing breast and ovarian cancer. The average American woman has a 12 to 13 percent risk of developing breast cancer, but in a woman with the genetic mutations discovered by Myriad, the risk can range between 50 and 80 percent for breast cancer

(case continues)

and between 20 and 50 percent for ovarian cancer. Before Myriad's discovery of the BRCA1 and BRCA2 genes, scientists knew that heredity played a role in establishing a woman's risk of developing breast and ovarian cancer, but they did not know which genes were associated with those cancers. For women who are tested and found to have the dangerous mutations of BRCA1 and BRCA2, medical measures can be taken to reduce the risks of breast and ovarian cancer developing.

Myriad obtained a patent from the U.S. Patent and Trademark Office based on its discovery. The Association for Molecular Pathology sued Myriad, seeking a declaration that Myriad's patent was invalid. The U.S. district court held that Myriad's claim was invalid because it covered a product of nature and was therefore unpatentable. The Federal Circuit Court of Appeals held that the isolated DNA was patent eligible. The U.S. Supreme Court granted review.

Issue

Is a naturally occurring segment of DNA patent eligible?

Language of the U.S. Supreme Court

Laws of nature, natural phenomena, and abstract ideas are not patentable. It is undisputed that Myriad did not create or alter any of the genetic information encoded in the BRCA1 and BRCA2 genes. The location and order of the nucleotides existed in nature before Myriad found them. Nor did Myriad create or alter the genetic structure of DNA. Instead, Myriad's principal contribution was uncovering the precise location and genetic sequence of the BRCA1 and BRCA2 genes. Myriad did not create anything. To be sure, it found an important and useful gene, but separating that gene from its surrounding genetic material is not an act of invention.

Decision

The U.S. Supreme Court held that a naturally occurring DNA segment is a product of nature and not patent eligible merely because it has been isolated. The U.S. Supreme Court reversed the decision of the Federal Circuit Court of Appeals on this issue.

Ethics Questions

Will the Supreme Court's decision affect the amount of research that is conducted to find naturally occurring disease-causing DNA sequences? Should Myriad be compensated by the government for its research costs?

Patent Period

In 2011, Congress passed the **Leahy-Smith America Invents Act (AIA)**.[3] The act stipulates a **first-to-file rule** for determining the priority of a patent. This means that the first party to file a patent on an invention receives the patent even though some other party was the first to invent the invention. Previously, the United States followed the **first-to-invent rule**, whereby the party that first invented the invention was awarded the patent even if another party had previously filed for and received the patent. The adoption of the first-to-file rule is a major change in U.S. patent law.

Leahy-Smith America Invents Act (AIA)
A federal statute that significantly amended federal patent law.

Utility patents for inventions are valid for *20 years*. The patent term begins to run from the date the patent application is *filed*.

After the patent period runs out, the invention or design enters the **public domain**, which means that anyone can produce and sell the invention without paying the prior patent holder.

Example On January 12, 2016, an inventor invents a formula for a new prescription drug. On March 1, 2016, the inventor files for and is eventually granted a twenty-year patent for this invention. Twenty years after the filing of the patent application, on March 1, 2036, the patent expires. The next day, the patent enters the public domain, and anyone can use the formula to produce exactly the same prescription drug.

In the following case, the U.S. Supreme Court had to decide whether a financial model was patentable.

WEB EXERCISE

Go to **www.uspto.gov**. Go to the left column titled "Patents." Click on number 2 "Search." Toward the middle of the page that appears, find the term "Patent Number Search." Click on this term. In the open line under the term "Query," type in the patent number 3741662. Click on the term "Search." Read the information about this patent.

CASE 7.2 U.S. SUPREME COURT CASE Patent

Alice Corporation v. CLS Bank International

134 S.Ct. 2347, 2014 U.S. Lexis 4303 (2014)
Supreme Court of the United States

"The abstract ideas category embodies the longstanding rule than an idea itself is not patentable."

—Thomas, Justice

Facts

Alice Corporation owns several patents that use computers to calculate the intermediated settlement risk that a party to an agreed-upon financial exchange will satisfy its obligation. CLS Bank International, which operates a network that facilitates financial transactions, filed a lawsuit against Alice Corporation seeking a declaratory judgment that Alice Corporation's patents are invalid. The U.S. district court held that claims were patent ineligible because they merely use computers directed to the abstract idea of minimizing risk. The en banc U.S. court of appeals affirmed the judgment. Alice Corporation appealed to the U.S. Supreme Court.

Issue

Are the claims patent eligible, or are they patent ineligible abstract ideas?

Language of the U.S. Supreme Court

The abstract ideas category embodies the longstanding rule than an idea itself is not patentable. The concept of intermediated settlement is a fundamental economic practice long prevalent in our system of commerce. Viewed as a whole, petitioner's method claims simply recite the concept of intermediated settlement as performed by a generic computer. Under our precedents, that is not enough to transform an abstract idea into a patent eligible invention.

Decision

The U.S. Supreme Court held that Alice Corporation's claims of using generic computer implementation adds nothing of substance to the underlying abstract idea of intermediate settlement and are therefore patent ineligible.

Ethics Questions

Do companies sometimes overreach in their patent claims? Why do they do this?

Patent Infringement

patent infringement
Unauthorized use of another's patent. A patent holder may recover damages and other remedies against a patent infringer.

Patent holders own exclusive rights to use and exploit their patents. **Patent infringement** occurs when someone makes unauthorized use of another's patent. Patent infringement claims must be brought in the U.S. district court that has jurisdiction to hear the case. Patent decisions of the U.S. district courts can be appealed to the **U.S. Court of Appeals for the Federal Circuit.**

In a suit for patent infringement, a successful plaintiff can recover (1) money damages equal to a reasonable royalty rate on the sale of the infringed articles, (2) other damages caused by the infringement (e.g., loss of customers), (3) an order requiring the destruction of the infringing article, and (4) an injunction preventing the infringer from such action in the future. The court has the discretion to award up to treble damages if the infringement was intentional. It costs between several hundred thousand dollars to several million dollars to bring an infringement case to trial.

Design Patent

design patent
A patent that may be obtained for the ornamental nonfunctional design of an item.

In addition to utility patents, a party can obtain a design patent. A **design patent** is a patent that may be obtained for the ornamental nonfunctional design of an item. A design patent is valid for 14 years.

Examples The design of a chair, a doorknob, a perfume bottle, and the outside of a computer are examples of design patents.

STATUE OF LIBERTY
The Statue of Liberty is one of the most famous design patents. It was patented in the United States by Auguste Bartholdi on February 18, 1879. Patent No. 11,023.

Copyright

Article I, Section 8, of the Constitution of the United States of America authorizes Congress to enact statutes to protect the works of writers for limited times.

Pursuant to this authority, Congress has enacted copyright statutes that establish the requirement for obtaining a copyright. **Copyright** is a legal right that gives the author of qualifying subject matter and who meets other requirements established by copyright law the exclusive right to publish, produce, sell, license, and distribute the work.

copyright
A legal right that gives the author of qualifying subject matter, who meets other requirements established by copyright law, the exclusive right to publish, produce, sell, license, and distribute the work.

The **Copyright Revision Act** of 1976 currently governs copyright law.[4] The act establishes the requirements for obtaining a copyright and protects copyrighted works from infringement. Federal copyright law is exclusive; there are no state copyright laws. Federal copyright law protects the work of authors and other creative persons from the unauthorized use of their copyrighted materials and provides a financial incentive for authors to write, thereby increasing the number of creative works available in society. Copyrights can be sold or licensed to others, whose rights are then protected by copyright law.

Copyright Revision Act
A federal statute that (1) establishes the requirements for obtaining a copyright and (2) protects copyrighted works from infringement.

Tangible Writing

Only **tangible writings**—writings that can be physically seen—are subject to copyright registration and protection. The term *writing* has been broadly defined.

Examples Books, periodicals, and newspapers; lectures, sermons, addresses, and poems; musical compositions; plays, motion pictures, and radio and television productions; maps; works of art, including paintings, drawings, jewelry, glassware, tapestry, and lithographs; architectural drawings and models; photographs, including prints, slides, and filmstrips, greeting cards, and picture postcards; photoplays, including feature films, cartoons, newsreels, travelogues, and training films; and sound recordings published in the form of CDs and MP3 files qualify for copyright protection.

Registration of Copyrights To be protected under federal copyright law, a work must be the original work of the author. A copyright is automatically granted the moment a work is created and fixed in tangible form.

Example When a student writes a term paper for his class, he owns a copyright to his work.

In 1989, the United States signed the **Berne Convention**, an international copyright treaty. This law eliminated the need to place the symbol © or the word

Berne Convention
An international copyright treaty.

copyright or *copr.* on a copyrighted work. However, it is still advisable to place the copyright notice ©, the year of publication, and the author's name on many copyrighted works because it notifies the world that the work is protected by a copyright, identifies the owner of the copyright, and shows the year of its publication. This helps eliminate a defendant's claim of innocent copyright.

Example Copyright © 2017 Henry Richard Cheeseman.

Published and unpublished works may be registered with the **U.S. Copyright Office** in Washington DC. Registration of a copyright is permissive and voluntary and can be effectuated at any time during the term of the copyright. Copyright registration creates a public record of the copyrighted work. A **copyright registration certificate** is issued to the copyright holder. Registration permits a holder to obtain statutory damages for copyright infringement, which may be greater than actual damages, and attorney's fees.

Copyright Period

The law in respect to literature ought to remain upon the same footing as that which regards the profits of mechanical inventions and chemical discoveries.

William Wordsworth
Letter (1838)

The **Copyright Term Extension Act** of 1998 extended copyright protection to the following:[5]

1. Individuals are granted copyright protection for their lifetime plus 70 years.
2. Copyrights owned by businesses are protected for the shorter of either:
   a. 120 years from the year of creation, or
   b. 95 years from the year of first publication

After the copyright period runs out, the work enters the **public domain**, which means that anyone can publish the work without paying the prior copyright holder.

Example If an author publishes a novel on April 1, 2015, and lives until August 1, 2040, his heirs will own the copyright until August 1, 3010.

CONCEPT SUMMARY
COPYRIGHT PERIOD

Type of Holder	Copyright Period
Individual	Life of the author plus 70 years beyond the author's life
Business	The shorter of either 95 years from the year of first publication or 120 years from the year of creation

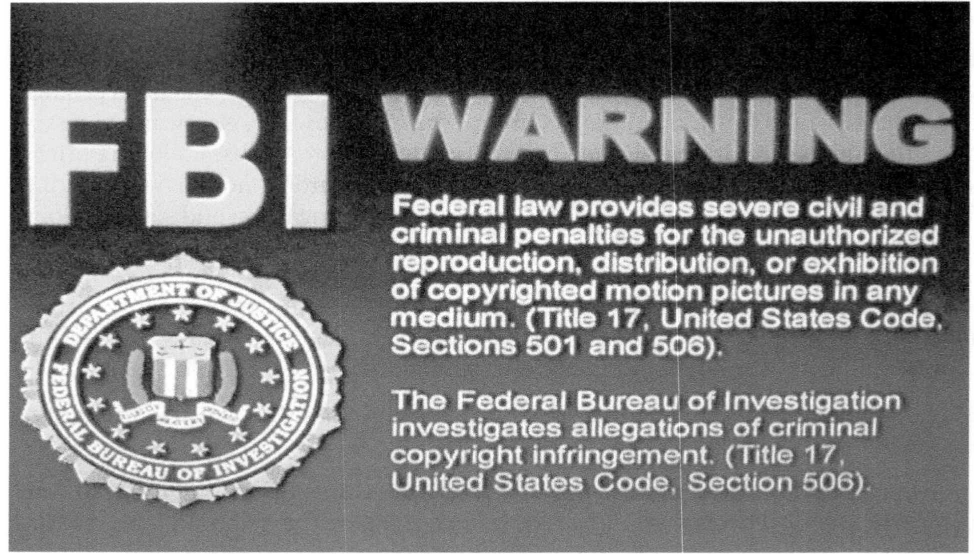

FBI WARNING
The Federal Bureau of Investigation (FBI), a federal government agency, is authorized to investigate violations of copyright law. An FBI warning concerning copyright infringement usually appears at the beginning of a DVD and before a feature movie or television program is shown. The FBI warning was developed to deter illegal piracy and increase awareness of the criminal penalties associated with piracy.

Civil Copyright Law: Copyright Infringement

Copyright infringement occurs when a party copies a substantial and material part of the plaintiff's copyrighted work without permission. The copying does not have to be either word for word or the entire work. A plaintiff can bring a civil action against the alleged infringer and, if successful, recover (1) the profit made by the defendant from the copyright infringement, (2) damages suffered by the plaintiff, (3) an order requiring the impoundment and destruction of the infringing works, and (4) an injunction preventing the defendant from infringing in the future. The court, at its discretion, can award statutory damages for willful infringement in lieu of actual damages.

copyright infringement
An infringement that occurs when a party copies a substantial and material part of a plaintiff's copyrighted work without permission. A copyright holder may recover damages and other remedies against the infringer.

The federal government can bring criminal charges against a person who commits copyright infringement. Criminal copyright infringement, including infringement committed without monetary gain, is punishable by up to five years in federal prison.

In the following case, the court had to decide whether copyright infringement had occurred.

CASE 7.3 *FEDERAL COURT CASE Copyright Infringement*

Broadcast Music, Inc. v. McDade & Sons, Inc.

928 F.Supp.2d 1120, 2013 U.S. Dist. Lexis 30211 (2013)
United States District Court for Arizona

"The record reflects that defendants' infringements were knowing and willful."

—Bade, United States Magistrate Judge

Facts

Norton's Country Corner (Norton's) is a cowboy bar located in Queen Creek, Arizona. The bar is owned by McDade & Sons, Inc., which is owned 100 percent by Nancy McDade. McDade is its sole officer and director. Live bands play country-and-western music at Norton's on various nights of the week. Certain copyright owners of music have authorized Broadcast Music, Inc. (BMI), to license the use of their copyright songs to broadcasters and to owners of concert halls, restaurants, and nightclubs for live performances of the copyrighted music. BMI attends public performances of music to determine whether any copyrights it is authorized to license are being performed without such license.

One night, a BMI representative attended a live band performance at Norton's bar and recorded the songs played by the band that night. The audio recording showed that 13 copyrighted songs that BMI was authorized to license were played by the band at Norton's without the required license. The songs included classics originally sung by famous artists, such as "All My Ex's Live in Texas" (George Strait), "Baby Don't Get Hooked on Me" (Mac Brown), "Brown Eyed Girl" (Van Morrison), and "Ring of Fire" (Johnny Cash). BMI sued McDade & Sons, Inc. and Nancy McDade in U.S. district court for trademark infringement. The defendants argued they had not committed trademark infringement and that trademark law did not apply to owners of small establishments.

Issue

Are the defendants liable for trademark infringement?

Language of the Court

The Copyright Act gives the owner of a copyright the exclusive right to publicly perform, or authorize others to perform, the copyrighted work. Any person who violates this exclusive right is an infringer. Lack of authorization is established by the undisputed fact that defendants were not licensed by BMI to perform plaintiffs' copyrighted musical compositions. Defendants contend that the copyright laws are unfair to small bar owners "struggling to get by week by week." Defendants seek an exemption from complying with the Copyright Act, but have not cited any authority for such an exemption. The record reflects that defendants' infringements were knowing and willful.

(case continues)

Decision

The U.S. district court held that the defendants had engaged in copyright infringement and awarded $39,000 in damages, attorney's fees, and costs to the plaintiffs, and issued a permanent injunction against the defendants' infringement of copyrighted musical compositions licensed by Broadcast Music, Inc.

Ethics Questions

Should small-business owners of bars and other establishments be free from copyright laws? How many restaurants, bars, and other establishments play copyrighted music without the copyright owner's permission?

The following case involves the issue of digital copyright infringement.

CASE 7.4 *U.S. SUPREME COURT CASE Digital Copyright Infringement*

American Broadcasting Companies, Inc. v. Aereo, Inc.

134 S.Ct. 2498, 2014 U.S. Lexis 4496 (2014)
Supreme Court of the United States

"The Copyright Act gives a copyright owner the exclusive right to perform the copyrighted work publicly."
—Breyer, Justice

Facts

For a monthly fee Aereo, Inc. offers subscribers broadcast television programming over the Internet virtually as the programs are being broadcast on television. Most of the programming is made up of copyrighted works. Aereo's system is made up of thousands of tiny dime-sized antennas housed in a central warehouse. A subscriber visits Aereo's website and selects a television show that he or she wishes to watch which is currently being broadcast. One of Aereo's thousands of small antennas is assigned to the subscriber, a server tunes the small antenna to the over-the-air broadcast carrying the show, and an Aero transcoder translates the signals into data that is then transmitted over the Internet to the subscriber's digital device.

American Broadcasting Companies, Inc. and other television broadcasters, producers, marketers, distributers (petitioners) who own the copyrights to the programs Aereo streams sued Aereo for copyright infringement and sought an injunction against Aereo. Aereo argued that it does not perform the copyrighted programs publicly because it streams programs to each subscriber individually from tiny individual antennas. The U.S. district court denied the injunction and the U.S. court of appeals affirmed. The petitioners appealed to the U.S. Supreme Court.

Issue

Has Aereo engaged in copyright infringement?

Language of the U.S. Supreme Court

The Copyright Act gives a copyright owner the exclusive right to perform the copyrighted work publicly. We must decide whether Aereo infringes this exclusive right by selling its subscribers a technologically complex service that allows them to watch television programs over the Internet at about the same time as the programs are broadcast over the air. We conclude that it does.

Decision

The U.S. Supreme Court held that Aereo engaged in copyright infringement.

Ethics Questions

Why did Aereo use thousands of tiny dime-size antennas rather than using one big antenna to recover petitioners' over-the-air broadcasts? Did Aereo act ethically in adopting this business model?

fair use doctrine
A doctrine that permits certain limited use of a copyright by someone other than the copyright holder without the permission of the copyright holder.

Fair Use Doctrine

A copyright holder's right in a work is not absolute. The law permits certain limited unauthorized use of copyrighted materials under the **fair use doctrine**. The following uses are protected under this doctrine: (1) quotation of the copyrighted work for review or criticism or in a scholarly or technical work, (2) use in a parody or satire, (3) brief quotation in a news report, (4) reproduction by a teacher or student of a small part of the work to illustrate a lesson, (5) incidental reproduction of a work in a newsreel or broadcast of an event being reported, and (6) reproduction of a work in a legislative or judicial proceeding. The copyright holder cannot recover for copyright infringement where fair use is found.

Examples A student is assigned to write a paper in class about a certain subject matter. The student conducts research and writes her paper. In her paper, the student uses two paragraphs from a copyrighted book and places these paragraphs in quotation marks and properly cites the source and author in a footnote. This is fair use for academic purposes. However, if the student copies and uses three pages from the book, this would not be fair use and would constitute copyright infringement whether she cites the author and his or her work in a footnote or not.

Critical Legal Thinking

Has copyright infringement become endemic? Is illegal downloading of copyrighted music, movies, and video games "stealing"? Can copyright law and enforcement keep up with digital piracy?

Example A comedy television show that performs parodies and satires on famous celebrities is an example of *parody fair use*.

In the following case, the court addresses the doctrine of fair use.

CASE 7.5 *FEDERAL COURT CASE Fair Use*

Faulkner Literary Rights, LLC v. Sony Pictures Classics, Inc.

953 F.Supp.2d 701, 2013 U.S. Dist. Lexis 100625 (2013)
United States District Court for the Northern District of Mississippi

"The court considers it relevant that the copyrighted work is a serious piece of literature lifted for use in a speaking part in a movie comedy."
—Mills, Chief District Judge

Facts

William Faulkner was a great American author who wrote novels, short stories, poetry, and screenplays, including the novels *A Fable*, *The Reivers*, *As I Lay Dying*, and *The Sound and the Fury*. Faulkner won the Noble Prize in Literature. One of Faulkner's novels was *Requiem for a Nun* (*Requiem*), published in 1950, which is a murder mystery set in the South in which one of the main characters uses the famous line "The past is never dead. It's not even past." Faulkner died in 1962. Faulkner Literary Rights, LLC (Faulkner) owns the copyrights to Faulkner's works. Woody Allen is an iconic American screenwriter, actor, playwright, and director who stars in many of his films, which have included *Annie Hall*, *Manhattan*, and *Hannah and Her Sisters*. Allen has been nominated 24 times for Academy Awards and has won 3 for best original screenplay and one for best director. One of his films, *Midnight in Paris* (*Midnight*), was released in 2011, for which Allen won the Academy Award for Best Original Screenplay. *Midnight* is a romantic comedy set in Paris, France, in which a major character says the line "The past is not dead! Actually, it's not even past. You know who said that? Faulkner. And he was right." The line lasts 8 seconds. Sony Pictures Classics, Inc. (Sony) produced and distributed *Midnight* and owns the copyright to the movie. Faulkner sued Sony for copyright infringement for using the paraphrased version of the famous line from Faulkner's book *Requiem* in Allen's movie *Midnight*. Sony defends, arguing that the use qualifies as fair use and is not copyright infringement.

Issue

Is the paraphrased use of Faulkner's quote from his book *Requiem* in Allen's movie *Midnight* fair use?

Language of the Court

At issue in this case is whether a single line from a full-length novel singly paraphrased and attributed to the original author in a full-length Hollywood film can be considered a copyright infringement. In this case, it cannot. The court considers it relevant that the copyrighted work is a serious piece of literature

(case continues)

lifted for use in a speaking part in a movie comedy. Moreover, it should go without saying that the quote at issue is of miniscule quantitative importance to the work as a whole. The court is highly doubtful that any relevant markets have been harmed by the use in Midnight.

Decision

The U.S. district court held that Sony's use of Faulkner's paraphrased quotation from his book *Requeim* in the movie *Midnight* is *de minimus* (minimal) and fair use and not copyright infringement. The court dismissed the lawsuit.

Ethics Questions

What is the public policy behind the doctrine of fair use? Should Sony have voluntarily paid some money to Faulkner for the use of its copyrighted material?

Criminal Copyright Law: No Electronic Theft Act

No Electronic Theft Act (NET Act)
A federal statute that makes it a crime for a person to infringe willfully on a copyright.

In 1997, Congress enacted the **No Electronic Theft Act (NET Act)**, a federal statute that *criminalizes* certain copyright infringement.[6] The NET Act prohibits any person from willfully infringing a copyright for the purpose of either commercial advantage or financial gain or by reproduction or distribution even without commercial advantage or financial gain, including by electronic means. Thus, the NET Act makes it a federal crime to reproduce, share, or distribute copyrighted electronic works, including movies, songs, software programs, and video games.

Examples Violations of the NET Act include distributing copyrighted works without permission of the copyright holder over the Internet, uploading such works to a website, and posting information about the availability of such uploaded electronic works.

Criminal penalties for violating the act include imprisonment for up to five years and fines of up to $250,000. Subsequent violators may be fined and imprisoned for up to 10 years. The creation of the NET Act adds a new law that the federal government can use to attack criminal copyright infringement and curb digital piracy.

The NET Act also permits copyright holders to sue violators in a civil lawsuit and recover monetary damages of up to $150,000 per work infringed.

The following feature discusses a federal law designed to protect digital copyright material.

Digital Law

Digital Millennium Copyright Act

The Internet makes it easier than ever before for people to copy and distribute copyrighted works illegally. To combat this, software and entertainment companies have developed digital wrappers and **encryption technology** to protect their copyrighted works from unauthorized access. Not to be outdone, software pirates have devised ways to crack these wrappers and protection devices.

Software and entertainment companies lobbied Congress to enact federal legislation to make the cracking of their wrappers and selling of technology to do so illegal. In response, Congress enacted the **Digital Millennium Copyright Act (DMCA)**,[7] a federal statute that does the following:

- Prohibits unauthorized access to copyrighted *digital works* by circumventing the wrapper or encryption technology that protects the intellectual property.
- Prohibits the manufacture and distribution of technologies, products, or services primarily designed for the

purpose of circumventing wrappers or encryption technology protecting digital works.

Congress granted exceptions to DMCA liability to (1) software developers to achieve compatibility of their software with the protected work; (2) federal, state, and local law enforcement agencies conducting criminal investigations; (3) parents who are protecting children from pornography or other harmful materials available on the Internet; (4) Internet users who are identifying and disabling cookies and other identification devices that invade their personal privacy rights; and (5) nonprofit libraries, educational institutions, and archives that access a protected work to determine whether to acquire the work.

The DMCA imposes civil and criminal penalties.

Trademark

Businesses often develop company names, as well as advertising slogans, symbols, and commercial logos, to promote the sale of their goods and services. Companies such as Nike, Microsoft, Louis Vuitton, and McDonald's spend millions of dollars annually promoting their names, slogans, symbols, and logos to gain market recognition from consumers. The U.S. Congress has enacted trademark laws to provide legal protection for these names, slogans, and logos.

A **mark** is any trade name, symbol, word, logo, design, or device used to identify and distinguish goods of a manufacturer or seller or services of a provider from those of other manufacturers, sellers, or providers.

In 1946, Congress enacted the **Lanham (Trademark) Act**,[8] commonly referred to as the **Lanham Act**, to provide federal protection to trademarks, service marks, and other marks. This act, as amended, is intended to (1) protect the owner's investment and goodwill in a mark and (2) prevent consumers from being confused about the origin of goods and services.

Digital Millennium Copyright Act (DMCA)
A federal statute that prohibits unauthorized access to copyrighted digital works by circumventing encryption technology or the manufacture and distribution of technologies designed for the purpose of circumventing encryption protection of digital works.

mark
Any trade name, symbol, word, logo, design, or device used to identify and distinguish goods of a manufacturer or seller or services of a provider from those of other manufacturers, sellers, or providers.

Registration of a Mark

Marks can be registered with the U.S. Patent and Trademark Office (PTO) in Washington DC. A registrant must file an application with the PTO wherein the registrant designates the name, symbol, slogan, or logo that he is requesting to be registered. A registrant must either prove that he has used the intended mark in commerce (e.g., actually used the mark in the sale of goods or services) or state that he intends to use the mark in commerce within six months from the filing of the application. In the latter case, if the proposed mark is not used in commerce within this six-month period, the applicant loses the right to register the mark. However, the applicant may file for a six-month extension to use the mark in commerce, which is often granted by the PTO.

The PTO provides for either the paper filing or the electronic filing of the application through its **Trademark Electronic Application System (TEAS)**. A party other than the registrant can submit an *opposition* to a proposed registration of a mark.

The PTO registers a mark if it determines that the mark does not infringe any existing marks, the applicant has paid the registration fee (approximately $375), and other requirements for registering the mark have been met.

Once the PTO has issued a registration of the mark, the owner is entitled to use the registered mark symbol ® in connection with a registered trademark or service mark. The symbol ® is used to designate marks that have been registered with the PTO. The use of the symbol ® is not mandatory, although it is wise to use the ® symbol to put others on notice that the trademark or service mark is registered with the PTO. Once a mark is registered, the mark is given nationwide effect, serves as constructive notice that the mark is the registrant's personal property, and provides that federal lawsuits may be brought to protect the mark. The original registration of a mark is valid for 10 years, and it can be renewed for an unlimited number of 10-year periods.

WEB EXERCISE
Go to **www.coca-cola.com** to see trademarks of the Coca-Cola Corporation.

Lanham (Trademark) Act
A federal statute that (1) establishes the requirements for obtaining a federal mark and (2) protects marks from infringement.

®
A symbol that is used to designate marks that have been registered with the U.S. Patent and Trademark Office.

While the application is pending with the PTO, the registrant cannot use the symbol ®. However, during the application period, a registrant can use the symbol **TM** for goods or **SM** for services to alert the public to his or her legal claim. TM and SM may also be used by parties who claim a mark for goods or services but have not filed an application with the PTO to register the mark. In summary, TM and SM are used to designate unregistered trademarks and service marks, respectively.

TM
A symbol that designates an owner's legal claim to an unregistered mark that is associated with a product.

SM
A symbol that designates an owner's legal claim to an unregistered mark that is associated with a service.

A party who sells goods and services using brand names and product or service names is not required to register these names with the PTO. The party who does not register a name with the PTO still has legal rights in the name and can sue to prevent others from using the name. The lawsuit will be in state court, however. A party can use the symbols TM and SM with his or her goods or services, respectively, even if there is no application pending at the PTO.

A party may file for the *cancelation* of a previously registered mark if the party believes that the registrant did not meet the requirements for being issued the mark or if a mark has been abandoned.

CONCEPT SUMMARY

MEANING OF SYMBOLS USED IN ASSOCIATION WITH MARKS

Symbol	Meaning
TM	Unregistered mark used with goods
SM	Unregistered mark used with services
®	Registered mark

Types of Marks

The word *mark* collectively refers to *trademarks*, *service marks*, *certification marks*, and *collective membership marks*:

trademark
A distinctive mark, symbol, name, word, motto, or device that identifies the goods of a particular business.

- **Trademark.** A **trademark** is a distinctive mark, symbol, name, word, motto, or device that identifies the *goods* of a particular business.

  Examples *Coca-Cola* (The Coca-Cola Company), *Big Mac* (McDonald's Corporation), *Mac* (Apple Computer), *Intel Inside* (Intel Corporation), *Better Ingredients. Better Pizza.* (Papa John's Pizza), and *Harley* (Harley-Davidson Motor Company) are trademarks.

service mark
A mark that distinguishes the services of the holder from those of its competitors.

- **Service mark.** A **service mark** is used to distinguish the *services* of the holder from those of its competitors.

  Examples *FedEx* (FedEx Corporation), *The Friendly Skies* (United Airlines, Inc.), *Big Brown* (UPS Corporation), *Weight Watchers* (Weight Watchers International, Inc.), and *Citi* (Citigroup, Inc.) are service marks.

certification mark
A mark that certifies that a seller of a product or service has met certain geographical location requirements, quality standards, material standards, or mode of manufacturing standards established by the owner of the mark.

- **Certification mark.** A **certification mark** is a mark usually owned by a nonprofit cooperative or association. The owner of the mark establishes certain geographical location requirements, quality standards, material standards, or mode of manufacturing standards that must be met by a seller of products or services in order to use the certification mark. If a seller meets these requirements, the seller applies to the cooperative or association to use the mark on its products or in connection with the sale of services. The owner of the certification mark usually licenses sellers who meet the requirements to use the mark. A party does not have to be a member of the organization to use the mark.

  Examples A *UL* mark certifies that products meet safety standards set by Underwriters Laboratories, Inc. The *Good Housekeeping Seal of Approval* certifies that products meet certain quality specifications set by *Good Housekeeping* magazine (Good Housekeeping Research Institute). Other certification marks are *Certified Maine Lobster*, which indicates lobster or lobster products originating in the coastal waters of the state of Maine (Maine Lobster Promotion Council); *100% Napa Valley*, which is associated with grape wine from the Napa Valley, California (Napa Valley Vintners Association); and *Grown in Idaho*, which indicates potatoes grown in the state of Idaho (State of Idaho Potato Commission).

- **Collective membership mark.** A **collective membership mark** is owned by an organization (such as an association) whose members use it to identify themselves with a level of quality or accuracy or other characteristics set by the organization. Only members of the association or organization can use the mark. A collective membership mark identifies membership in an organization but does not identify goods or services.

  collective membership mark
  A mark that indicates that a person has met the standards set by an organization and is a member of that organization.

  Examples *CPA* is used to indicate that someone is a member of the Society of Certified Public Accountants, *Teamster* is used to indicate that a person is a member of The International Brotherhood of Teamsters (IBT) labor union, and *Realtor* is used to indicate that a person is a member of the National Association of Realtors. Other collective marks are *Boy Scouts of America*, *League of Women Voters*, and *National Honor Society*.

Certain marks cannot be registered. They include (1) the flag or coat of arms of the United States, any state, municipality, or foreign nation; (2) marks that are immoral or scandalous; (3) geographical names standing alone (e.g., "South"); (4) surnames standing alone (note that a surname can be registered if it is accompanied by a picture or fanciful name, such as *Smith Brothers cough drops*); and (5) any mark that resembles a mark already registered with the federal PTO.

CONCEPT SUMMARY
TYPES OF MARKS

1. **Trademark.** A distinctive mark, symbol, name, word, motto, or device that identifies the *goods* of a particular business.
2. **Service mark.** A mark used to distinguish the *services* of the holder from those of its competitors.
3. **Certification mark.** A mark that establishes certain geographical location requirements, quality standards, material standards, or mode of manufacturing standards that must be met by a seller of products or services in order to use the certification mark.
4. **Collective membership mark.** A mark owned by an organization whose members use it to identify themselves with a level of quality or accuracy or other characteristics set by the organization.

Distinctiveness or Secondary Meaning

To qualify for federal protection, a mark must be either (1) **distinctive** or (2) have acquired a **secondary meaning**:

distinctive
Being unique and fabricated.

secondary meaning
A brand name that has evolved from an ordinary term.

- **Distinctive.** A distinctive mark would be a word or design that is unique. It therefore qualifies as a mark. The words of the mark must not be ordinary words or symbols.

  Examples Words such a *Xerox* (Xerox Corporation), *Acura* (Honda Motor Corporation), *Google* (Google Inc.), *Exxon* (Exxon Mobil Corporation), and *Pinkberry* (Pinkberry, Inc.) are distinctive words and therefore qualify as marks.

- **Secondary meaning.** Ordinary words or symbols that have taken on a secondary meaning can qualify as marks. These are words or symbols that have an established meaning but have acquired a secondary meaning that is attached to a product or service.

  Examples *Just Do It* (Nike Corporation), *I'm lovin' it* (McDonald's Corporation), *Windows* (Microsoft Corporation), and *Ben & Jerry's Ice Cream* (Unilever) are ordinary words that have taken on a secondary meaning when used to designate the products or services of the owners of the marks.

Words that are descriptive but have no secondary meaning cannot be trademarked.

Trademark Infringement

trademark infringement
Unauthorized use of another's mark. The holder may recover damages and other remedies from the infringer.

The owner of a mark can sue a third party for the unauthorized use of the mark. To succeed in a **trademark infringement** case, the owner must prove that (1) the defendant infringed the plaintiff's mark by using it in an unauthorized manner and (2) such use is likely to cause confusion, mistake, or deception of the public as to the origin of the goods or services.

A successful plaintiff can recover (1) the profits made by the infringer through the unauthorized use of the mark, (2) damages caused to the plaintiff's business and reputation, (3) an order requiring the defendant to destroy all goods containing the unauthorized mark, and (4) an injunction preventing the defendant from such infringement in the future. The court has discretion to award up to *treble* damages where intentional infringement is found.

WEB EXERCISE
Go to **www.videojug.com/film/how-to-spot-a-fake-louis-vuitton-bag** and watch the video "How to Spot a Fake Louis Vuitton Bag."

The following case involves trademark infringement.

Ethics

Knockoff of Trademark Goods

"When the manufacturer of knockoff goods offers a consumer a cheap knockoff copy . . . there is infringement."

—Sack, Circuit Judge

Louis Vuitton is a French fashion house that manufactures and distributes luxury consumer goods, including leather goods, purses, handbags, jewelry, shoes, and other high-end fashion apparel. Louis Vuitton owns many registered trademarks, including its well-known stylized, overlapping "LV" monogram. Louis Vuitton spends millions of dollars each year to advertise and market its trademarked goods.

Chong Lam and Joyce Chan engaged in a large-scale operation involving the importation and sale of counterfeit luxury goods in the United States bearing trademarks owned by Louis Vuitton and others. Most of the goods were made in and imported from China. Lam and Chan used a variety of companies to facilitate the distribution of the counterfeit goods to retailers and vendors in the United States. Customs officials seized tens of thousands of counterfeit items in Houston, Los Angeles, Newark, New York, Norfolk, and elsewhere that were imported by the defendants. It is alleged that the defendants imported more than 300,000 handbags, wallets, and other knockoff products showing Louis Vuitton and other luxury brand trademarks.

Louis Vuitton brought suit against Lam and Chan and their related companies in U.S. district court, alleging trademark infringement by the defendants. The district court granted summary judgment to plaintiff Louis Vuitton on its claims of trademark counterfeiting and infringement, awarded Louis Vuitton damages of $3 million and more than $500,000 in attorney's fees and costs, and issued a permanent injunction barring the defendants from infringing Louis Vuitton's trademarks. The U.S. court of appeals upheld the judgment. The court stated, "When the manufacturer of knockoff goods offers a consumer a cheap knockoff copy of the original manufacturer's more expensive product, allowing the buyer to acquire the prestige of owning what appears to be the more expensive product, there is infringement." *Louis Vuitton Malletier S.A. v. LY USA, Inc.*, 676 F.3d 83, 2012 U.S. App. Lexis 6391 (United States Court of Appeals for the Second Circuit, 2012)

Ethics Questions Did the defendants act unethically? How prevalent do you think selling counterfeit goods is? Have you ever knowingly purchased a knockoff good?

Generic Names

Critical Legal Thinking
More than 5 percent of global trade is comprised of illegal knockoffs of clothing, handbags, toys, pharmaceuticals, and other products.. Can such counterfeiting be curtailed successfully?

When filing for a trademark, if a word, name, or slogan is too generic, it cannot be registered as a trademark. If a word is not generic, it can be trademarked.

Examples The word *apple* cannot be trademarked because it is a generic name or word. However, the brand name *Apple Computer* is permitted to be trademarked because it is not a generic name. The word *secret* cannot be trademarked because it is a generic name or word. However, the brand name *Victoria's Secret* is permitted to be trademarked because it is not a generic name.

Once a company has been granted a trademark or service mark, the company usually uses the mark as a brand name to promote its goods or services. Obviously, the owner of the mark wants to promote its brand so that consumers and users will easily recognize the brand name.

However, sometimes a company may be *too* successful in promoting a mark, and at some point in time, the public begins to use the brand name as a common name to denote the type of product or service being sold rather than as the trademark or service mark of the individual seller. A trademark that becomes a common term for a product line or type of service is called a **generic name**. Once a trademark becomes a generic name, the term loses its protection under federal trademark law.

generic name
A term for a mark that has become a common term for a product line or type of service and therefore has lost its trademark protection.

Example Sailboards are boards that have sails mounted on them that people use to ride on water such as oceans and lakes. There were many manufacturers and sellers of sailboards. However, the most successful manufacturer of these sailboards used the trademarked brand name Windsurfer. However, the word *windsurfer* was used so often by the public for all brands of sailboards that the trademarked name Windsurfer was found to be a generic name, and its trademark was canceled.

Exhibit 7.2 lists names that at one time were trademarked but lost trademark protection because the trademarked names became overused and generic. **Exhibit 7.3** lists trademarked names that are at some risk of becoming generic names.

Exhibit 7.2 **GENERIC NAMES**

The following once-trademarked names have been so overused to designate an entire class of products that they have been found to be generic and have lost their trademark status.

Windsurfer	Frisbee
Laser	Trampoline
Escalator	Cornflakes
Kerosene	Yo-yo
Aspirin	Raisin bran
Thermos	Tollhouse cookies
Linoleum	Nylon
Cellophane	Zipper

Exhibit 7.3 **NAMES AT RISK OF BECOMING GENERIC NAMES**

Certain trademark and service marks are often used improperly and have some risk in the future of becoming generic names. Several of these marks are listed below, with their proper use and typical misuse also noted:

Mark	Proper Use	Misuse
Xerox	"Copy this document on a Xerox brand copier."	"Go xerox this."
Google	"Use the Google search engine to find information about him.	"Just google him."
FedEx	"Use FedEx overnight delivery service to send this package."	"Please fedex this."
Rollerblade	"Let's go inline skating on our Rollerblade inline skates."	"Let's go rollerblading."

CONCEPT SUMMARY
TYPES OF INTELLECTUAL PROPERTY PROTECTED BY FEDERAL LAW

Type	Subject Matter	Term
Patent	Inventions (e.g., machines, processes, compositions of matter, designs for articles of manufacture, and improvements to existing machines and processes). Invention must be novel, useful, and nonobvious. *Public use doctrine:* Patent is not granted if the invention was used in public for more than one year prior to the filing of the patent application.	Patents on articles of manufacture and processes: 20 years; design patents: 14 years.
Copyright	Tangible writing (e.g., books, magazines, newspapers, lectures, operas, plays, screenplays, musical compositions, maps, works of art, lithographs, photographs, postcards, greeting cards, motion pictures, newsreels, sound recordings, computer programs, and mask works fixed to semiconductor chips). Writing must be the original work of the author. The *Fair use doctrine:* Permits the use of copyrighted material without consent for limited uses (e.g., scholarly work, parody or satire, and brief quotation in news reports).	Individual holder: life of author plus 70 years. Corporate holder: the shorter of either 120 years from the year of creation or 95 years from the year of first publication.
Trademark	Marks (e.g., name, symbol, word, logo, or device). Marks include trademarks, service marks, certification marks, and collective marks. Mark must be distinctive or have acquired a secondary meaning. *Generic name*: A mark that becomes a common term for a product line or type of service loses its protection under federal trademark law.	Original registration: 10 years. Renewal registration: unlimited number of renewals for ten-year terms.

Dilution

Many companies that own trademarks spend millions of dollars each year advertising and promoting the quality of the goods and services sold under their names. Many of these become household names that are recognized by millions of consumers, such as Coca-Cola, McDonald's, Microsoft, and Nike.

Traditional trademark law protected these marks where an infringer used the mark and confused consumers as to the source of the goods or services. For example, if a knockoff company sold athletic shoes and apparel under the name Nike, there would be trademark infringement because there would be confusion as to the source of the goods.

Often, however, a party uses a name similar to, or close to but not exactly identical to, a holder's trademark name and sells other goods or services or misuse the name. Because there was no direct competition, the trademark owner often could not win a trademark infringement case.

Federal Trademark Dilution Act (FTDA)
A federal statute that protects famous marks from dilution, erosion, blurring, or tarnishing.

To address this problem, Congress enacted the **Federal Trademark Dilution Act (FTDA)** of 1995 to protect famous marks from **dilution**.[9] The FTDA provides that owners of marks have a valuable property right in their marks that should not be *diluted*, *blurred*, *tarnished*, or *eroded* in any way by another.

Dilution is broadly defined as the lessening of the capacity of a famous mark to identify and distinguish its holder's goods and services, regardless of the presence or absence of competition between the owner of the mark and the other party. The two most common forms of dilution are blurring and tarnishment:

- **Blurring** occurs where a party uses another party's famous mark to designate a product or service in another market so that the unique significance of the famous mark is weakened.

  Examples Examples of blurring include Rolex skateboards or eBay toiletries.

- **Tarnishment** occurs where a famous mark is linked to products of inferior quality or is portrayed in an unflattering, immoral, or reprehensible context likely to evoke negative beliefs about the mark's owner.

  Example An example of tarnishment is using the mark Gucci on a deck of playing cards depicting sexually explicit graphics.

Congress revised the FTDA when it enacted the **Trademark Dilution Revision Act** of 2006.[10] This act provides that a dilution plaintiff does not need to show that it has suffered actual harm to prevail in its dilution lawsuit but instead only needs to show that there would be the *likelihood of dilution*. The FTDA, as amended, has three fundamental requirements that the holder of the senior mark must prove:

Trademark Dilution Revision Act
A federal statute that states that a plaintiff must only show that there is a *likelihood of dilution* to prevail in a dilution lawsuit against a defendant.

1. Its mark is famous.
2. The use by the other party is commercial.
3. The use by the other party causes *a likelihood of dilution* of the distinctive quality of the mark.

The following case involves the dilution of a famous mark.

CASE 7.6 *FEDERAL COURT CASE Dilution of a Trademark*

V Secret Catalogue, Inc. and Victoria's Secret Stores, Inc. v. Moseley

605 F.3d 382, Web 2010 U.S. App. Lexis 10150 (2010)
United States Court of Appeals for the Sixth Circuit

"The phrase 'likely to cause dilution' used in the new statute significantly changes the meaning of the law from 'causes actual harm' under the preexisting law."

—Merritt, Circuit Judge

Facts

Victoria's Secret is a successful worldwide retailer of women's lingerie, clothing, and beauty products that owns the famous trademark "Victoria's Secret." A small store in Elizabethtown, Kentucky, owned and operated by Victor and Cathy Moseley, used the business names "Victor's Secret" and "Victor's Little Secret." The store sold adult videos, novelties, sex toys, and racy lingerie. Victoria's Secret sued the Moseleys, alleging a violation of the Federal Trademark Dilution Act of 1995. The case eventually was decided by the U.S. Supreme Court in favor of the Moseleys when the Court found that there was no showing of *actual dilution* by the junior marks, as required by the statute. Congress overturned the Supreme Court's decision by enacting the Trademark Dilution Revision Act of 2006, which requires the easier showing of a *likelihood of dilution* by the senior mark. On remand, the U.S. district court applied the new likelihood of confusion test, found a presumption of tarnishment of the Victoria's Secret mark that the Moseleys failed to rebut, and held against the Moseleys. The Moseleys appealed to the U.S. court of appeals.

(case continues)

Issue

Is there tarnishment of the Victoria's Secret senior mark by the Moseleys' use of the junior marks Victor's Secret and Victor's Little Secret?

Language of the Court

The phrase "likely to cause dilution" used in the new statute significantly changes the meaning of the law from "causes actual harm" under the preexisting law. In the present case, the Moseleys have had two opportunities in the District Court to offer evidence that there is no real probability of tarnishment and have not done so. The defendants have given us no basis to reverse the judgment of the District Court.

Decision

The U.S. court of appeals affirmed the U.S. district court's judgment in favor of Victoria's Secret.

Ethics Questions

Do you think the Moseleys were trading off the famous Victoria's Secret name? Do you think that the Moseleys had a legitimate claim to their business names because the husband's name was Victor?

The following feature discusses international treaties that protect intellectual property rights.

Global Law

International Protection of Intellectual Property

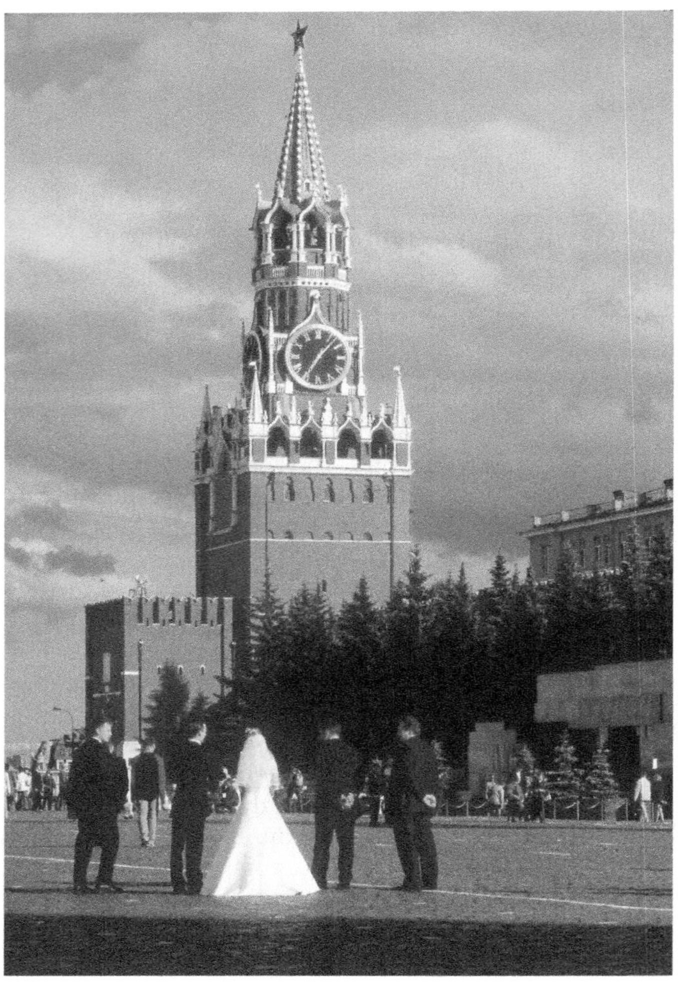

RED SQUARE, MOSCOW

There are many treaties that protect intellectual property rights internationally. Signatory countries to an intellectual property treaty must abide by the provisions of the treaty. In the copyright area, two major treaties are the Berne Convention and the WIPO Copyright Treaty. In the patent area, two major treaties are the Paris Convention and the Patent Cooperation Treaty (PCT). In the trademark area, major treaties include the Paris Convention, the Madrid Agreement and Protocol, and the Nice Agreement.

The Agreement on Trade-Related Aspects of Intellectual Property Rights (TRIPS) protects patents, copyrights, trademarks, and other intellectual property rights internationally. Members of the World Trade Organization (WTO), of which there are more than 150 member nations, are subject to the provisions of TRIPS.

Key Terms and Concepts

© (167)
® (173)
Berne Convention (167)
Blurring (179)
Certification mark (174)
Collective membership mark (175)
Copyright (167)
Copyright infringement (169)
Copyright registration certificate (168)
Copyright Revision Act (167)
Copyright Term Extension Act (168)
Design patent (166)
Digital Millennium Copyright Act (DMCA) (173)
Dilution (178)
Distinctive (175)
Economic Espionage Act (EEA) (161)
Encryption technology (172)
Fair use doctrine (170)
Federal Patent Statute (162)
Federal Trademark Dilution Act (FTDA) (178)
First-to-file rule (165)
First-to-invent rule (165)
Generic name (177)
Intellectual property (159)
Lanham (Trademark) Act (Lanham Act) (173)
Leahy-Smith America Invents Act (AIA) (165)
Mark (173)
Misappropriation of a trade secret (161)
No Electronic Theft Act (NET Act) (172)
Nonobvious (164)
Novel (163)
Patent (162)
Patent application (162)
Patent infringement (166)
Patent number (162)
Patent pending (162)
Patent Trial and Appeal Board (PTAB) (162)
Post-grant review (162)
Pre-issuance challenge (162)
Provisional application (162)
Public domain (for copyright) (168)
Public domain (for patent) (165)
Requirements for obtaining a patent (163)
Reverse engineering (160)
Secondary meaning (175)
Service mark (174)
SM (174)
Tangible writings (167)
Tarnishment (179)
TM (174)
Trade secret (160)
Trademark (174)
Trademark Dilution Revision Act (179)
Trademark Electronic Application System (TEAS) (173)
Trademark infringement (176)
Uniform Trade Secrets Act (160)
U.S. Copyright Office (168)
U.S. Court of Appeals for the Federal Circuit (162)
U.S. Patent and Trademark Office (PTO) (162)
Useful (164)
Utility patent (163)

Critical Legal Thinking Cases

7.1 Patent Bernard Bilski and Rand Warsaw filed a patent application with the U.S. Patent and Trademark Office (PTO). The application sought patent protection for a claimed invention that explains how buyers and sellers of commodities in the energy market can hedge against the risk of price changes. The key claims are claims 1 and 4. Claim 1 describes a series of steps instructing how to hedge risk. Claim 4 puts the concept articulated in claim 1 into a simple mathematical formula. The remaining claims describe how claims 1 and 4 can be applied to allow energy suppliers and consumers to minimize the risks resulting from fluctuations in market demand for energy. The PTO rejected the patent application, holding that it merely manipulates an abstract idea and solves a purely mathematical problem. Bilski and Warsaw brought their case to the U.S. Supreme Court, arguing that their claimed invention deserved a patent. Is the claimed invention patentable? *Bilski v. Kappos, Director, Patent and Trademark Office*, 561 U.S. 593, 130 S.Ct. 3218, 2010 U.S. Lexis 5521 (Supreme Court of the United States, 2010)

7.2 Trademark Zura Kazhiloti sold jewelry bearing the luxury brand names "Cartier" and "Van Cleef & Arpels" to jewelry stores. The retailers then sold the jewelry through their brick-and-mortar stores, through websites, and through the Internet auction site eBay. The jewelry was high-quality counterfeits, however, that Kazhiloti sold at high prices and made hundreds of thousands of dollars in revenues. Each piece of fake Cartier jewelry bore the Cartier stylized "C" design trademark and other Cartier design trademarks. Each piece of fake Van Cleef & Arpels jewelry bore the Van Cleef & Arpels or "VCA" design trademark and other Van Cleef & Arpels design trademarks. The counterfeit jewelry used stones of inferior quality, and inferior cuts, chains, and clasps compared to the authentic pieces. The counterfeit jewelry contained serial numbers similar to those used by Cartier and Van Cleef & Arpels. Kazhiloti supplied fake certificates of authenticity with each piece of jewelry. Eventually, Kazhiloti's scheme was uncovered. In total, 24 pieces of counterfeit Cartier and 83 pieces of Van Cleef & Arpels jewelry were purchased or seized from the jewelry stores. Cartier International AG and Van Cleef & Arpels S.A. brought suit against Kazhiloti for trademark infringement. The plaintiffs sought a permanent injunction against Kazhiloti engaging in such activity and to recover monetary damages.

Kazhiloti asserted his Fifth Amendment constitutional right against self-incrimination and refused to speak to authorities or produce any documents. Is Kazhiloti liable for trademark infringement? *Cartier International A.G. and Van Cleef & Arpels S.A. v. Kazhiloti*, 2013 U.S. Dist. Lexis 145278 (United States District Court for the District of New Jersey, 2013)

7.3 Copyright James W. Newton Jr. is an accomplished avant-garde jazz composer and flutist. Newton wrote a composition for the song "Choir," a piece for flute and voice that incorporated elements of African American gospel music. Newton owns the copyright to the composition "Choir." The Beastie Boys, a rap and hip-hop group, used six seconds of Newton's "Choir" composition in their song "Pass the Mic" without obtaining a license from Newton to do so. Newton sued the Beastie Boys for copyright infringement. The Beastie Boys defended, arguing that their use of six seconds of Newton's song was *de minimis* (minimal) and therefore fair use. Does the incorporation of a short segment of a copyrighted musical composition into a new musical recording constitute fair use, or is it copyright infringement? *Newton v. Beastie Boys*, 349 F.3d 591, 2003 U.S. App. Lexis 22635 (United States Court of Appeals for the Ninth Circuit, 2003)

7.4 Trademark Kraft Foods Group Brands LLC (Kraft) is a well-known manufacture of food products sold in more than 15,000 grocery stores located throughout the United States. Many of its packaged cheeses that are sold in outlets are available under Kraft's trademarked "Cracker Barrel" label. Kraft has been selling cheeses in grocery stores under the Cracker Barrel trademark for more than 50 years. Cracker Barrel Old Country Store, Inc. (CBOCS), operates a well-known chain of more than 600 low-price restaurants. On learning that CBOCS planned to sell a variety of food products in grocery stores under the logo "Cracker Barrel Old Country Store," Kraft filed a lawsuit for trademark infringement. Kraft argues that consumers will be confused by the similarity of the names and alleges that it will be hurt financially. Kraft filed for an injunction to prevent CBOCS from selling product containing the "Cracker Barrel" name in grocery stores. Will CBOCS's use of the Cracker Barrel name on the food products it proposes to sell in grocery stores infringe on the Kraft's Cracker Barrel trademark? *Kraft Foods Group Brands LLC v. Cracker Barrel Old Country Store, Inc.*, 735 F.3d 735, 2013 U.S. App. Lexis 23124 (United States Court of Appeals for the Seventh Circuit, 2013)

7.5 Copyright Dodger Productions, Inc. and Dodger Theatricals, Ltd. (Dodger) produced a stage musical called *Jersey Boys*. The musical is a historical dramatization about the American 1960s rock 'n' roll singing group called the Four Seasons and the lives of its members. The musical contains hit songs of the Four Seasons, including "Sherry," "Big Girls Don't Cry," "Rag Doll," "Stay," "Working My Way Back to You," "Dawn," and other songs. Each band member narrates one of the play's four acts and offers his take on the group's history. *The Ed Sullivan Show* was a weekly television show from 1948 to 1971 that highlighted many singing groups. The Four Seasons appeared and sang on *The Ed Sullivan Show* on January 2, 1966. SOFA Entertainment, Inc. (SOFA) owns copyrights to the entire run of *The Ed Sullivan Show*, including the appearance of the Four Seasons.

At the end of the first act of *Jersey Boys*, a seven-second clip is shown on a screen hanging over the center of the stage of the Four Seasons television appearance on *The Ed Sullivan Show*. The clip shows Ed Sullivan assuming his signature pose and introducing the band to his studio and television audiences, saying, "Now ladies and gentlemen, here, for all of the youngsters in the country, the Four Seasons." Ed Sullivan turns, and with an extended arm and open palm, directs the attention of the theater audience to the stage. At this point in the *Jersey Boys* production, the screen goes dark, and the singers perform a rendition of the Four Seasons song "Dawn." SOFA sued Dodger for copyright infringement. Dodger asserted the defense of fair use. Was Dodger's use of the seven-second clip from *The Ed Sullivan Show* in its *Jersey Boys* musical production fair use of a copyrighted work? *SOFA Entertainment, Inc. v. Dodger Productions, Inc.*, 709 F.3d 1273, 2013 U.S. App. Lexis 4830 (United States Court of Appeals for the Ninth Circuit, 2013)

7.6 Copyright Cecilia Gonzalez downloaded more than 1,300 copyrighted songs on her computer using a file-sharing network during a few weeks, and she kept them on her computer until she was caught. BMG Music, which owns the copyrights on many of the songs she downloaded, sued Gonzalez for copyright infringement of 30 of these songs. Gonzalez defended, arguing that her downloading of these copyrighted songs was lawful. Gonzalez's position was that she was just sampling music to determine what she liked enough to buy at retail. She also defended by arguing that other persons were greater offenders than she was. Is Gonzalez liable for copyright infringement? *BMG Music v. Gonzalez*, 430 F.3d 888, 2005 U.S. App. Lexis 26903 (United States Court of Appeals for the Seventh Circuit, 2005)

Ethical

Ethics Cases

7.7 Ethics Case Intel Corporation is a large company that distributes its entire line of products and services under the registered trademark and service mark INTEL. The company also owns numerous marks that incorporate its INTEL marks as a permanent component, such as the marks INTEL INSIDE, INTEL SPEEDSTEP, INTEL XEON, and INTEL NETMERGE. Intelsys Software, LLC, which is owned by another party, develops software applications for network utilities and wireless applications. Intelsys uses the mark Intelsys Software and maintains a website at www.intelsys.com. Intel Corporation brought an action in U.S. district court against Intelsys Software, LLC, alleging that Intelsys infringed on Intel's trademarks and service marks, in violation of the Lanham Act. Intel filed a motion for judgment and a permanent injunction against Intelsys's use of the mark INTEL in any of its company, product, or service names. Is there trademark infringement that warrants the issuance of a permanent injunction against Intelsys? Did Intelsys act ethically in this case? *Intel Corporation v. Intelsys Software, LLC*, 2009 U.S. Dist. Lexis 14761 (United States District Court for the Northern District of California, 2009)

7.8 Ethics Case Elvis Presley, a rock 'n' roll singer, became a musical icon during a career that spanned more than twenty years, until he died at the age of 42. Many companies and individuals own copyrights to Presley's songs, lyrics, photographs, movies, and appearances on television shows. Millions of dollars of Elvis Presley–related copyrighted materials are sold or licensed annually.

Passport Video produced a video documentary titled *The Definitive Elvis*, comprising sixteen one-hour episodes. The producers interviewed more than 200 people regarding virtually all aspects of Elvis's life. Passport sold the videos commercially for a profit. Approximately 5 to 10 percent of the videos were composed of copyrighted music and appearances of Presley on television and in movies owned by copyright holders other than Passport. Passport did not obtain permission to use those copyrighted works. Elvis Presley Enterprises, Inc., and other companies and individuals that owned copyrights to the Presley works used by Passport sued Passport for copyright infringement. Passport defended, arguing that its use of the copyrighted materials was fair use. The U.S. district court held in favor of the plaintiff copyright holders and enjoined Passport from further distribution of its documentary videos. Passport appealed.

Did Passport act ethically in including the Elvis Presley copyrighted material in its video? Why do you think Passport Video did so? Has there been fair use in this case, or has there been copyright infringement? *Elvis Presley Enterprises, Inc. v. Passport Video*, 349 F.3d 622, 2003 U.S. App. Lexis 22775 (United States Court of Appeals for the Ninth Circuit, 2003)

Notes

1. 18 U.S.C. Sections 1831–1839.
2. 35 U.S.C. Section 10 et seq.
3. Public Law 112–129.
4. 17 U.S.C. Section 101 et seq.
5. Public Law 105–298.
6. Public Law 105–147.
7. 17 U.S.C. Section 1201.
8. 15 U.S.C. Section 1114 et seq.
9. 15 U.S.C. Section 1125.
10. Public Law No. 109-312, 15 U.S.C. Section 1125(c).

CHAPTER 8

Criminal Law and Cybercrime

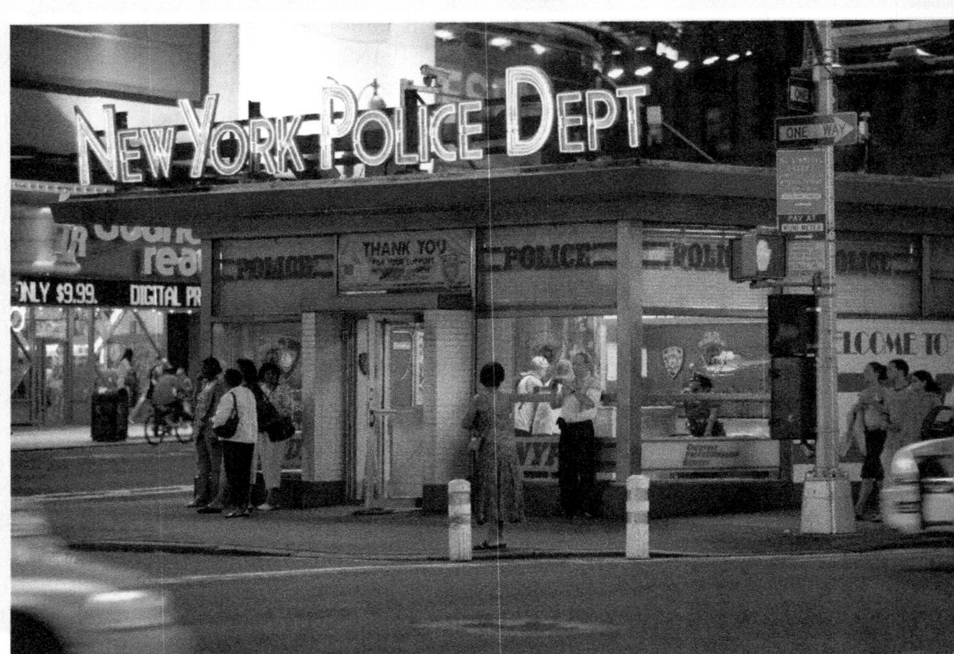

NEW YORK POLICE DEPARTMENT, TIMES SQUARE, NEW YORK CITY
Criminal cases make up a large portion of cases tried in U.S. courts. Criminal cases are bought against persons for violating federal, state, and local laws. Suspected criminals are given many rights by the U.S. Constitution and state constitutions. Parties in the United States are free from unreasonable searches and seizures of evidence, and any evidence obtained illegally is considered tainted evidence and cannot be used in court. People who are suspected of a criminal act may assert their right of privilege against self-incrimination and may choose not to testify at any pretrial proceedings or at trial. Parties have a right to a public trial by a jury of their peers. In addition, if convicted of a crime, the criminal is free from cruel and unusual punishment.

Learning Objectives

After studying this chapter, you should be able to:

1. List and describe the essential elements of a crime.
2. Describe criminal procedure, including arrest, indictment, arraignment, and the criminal trial.
3. Identify and define business and white-collar crimes.
4. List and describe cybercrimes.
5. Explain the constitutional safeguards provided by the Fourth, Fifth, Sixth, and Eighth Amendments to the U.S. Constitution.

Chapter Outline

Chapter Outline *(continued)*

"It is better that ten guilty persons escape than that one innocent suffer."

—*Sir William Blackstone*
Commentaries on the Law of England (1765)

Introduction to Criminal Law and Cybercrime

For members of society to coexist peacefully and for commerce to flourish, people and their property must be protected from injury by other members of society. Federal, state, and local governments' **criminal laws** are intended to afford this protection by providing an incentive for persons to act reasonably in society and imposing penalties on persons who violate the laws.

There can be no equal justice where the kind of trial a man gets depends on the amount of money he has.

Justice Black
Griffin v. Illinois 351 U.S. 12, 76 S.Ct. 585, 1956 U.S. Lexis 1059 (1956)

The United States has one of the most advanced and humane criminal law systems in the world. It differs from other criminal law systems in several respects. Under many other countries' legal systems, a person accused of a crime is presumed guilty unless the person can prove he or she is not. A person charged with a crime in the United States is **presumed innocent until proven guilty**. The **burden of proof** in a criminal trial is on the government to prove that the accused is guilty of the crime charged. Further, the accused must be found guilty **beyond a reasonable doubt**. Conviction requires unanimous jury vote. A person charged with a crime in the United States is also provided with substantial constitutional safeguards during the criminal justice process.

Many crimes are referred to as *white-collar crimes* because they are most often committed by business managers and employees. These crimes include fraud, bribery, and other such crimes. In addition, in the information age, many *cybercrimes* are committed using computers and the Internet.

The jury, passing on the prisoner's life, May, in the sworn twelve, have a thief or two Guiltier than him they try.

William Shakespeare
Measure for Measure

This chapter discusses criminal procedure, crimes, business and white-collar crimes, cybercrimes, and constitutional safeguards afforded criminal defendants.

Definition of a Crime

A **crime** is defined as any act done by an individual in violation of those duties that he or she owes to society and for the breach of which the law provides that the wrongdoer shall make amends to the public. Many activities have been considered crimes through the ages, whereas other crimes are of recent origin.

crime
A violation of a statute for which the government imposes a punishment.

Penal Codes and Regulatory Statutes

Statutes are the primary source of criminal law. Most states have adopted comprehensive **penal codes** that define in detail the activities considered to be crimes within their jurisdictions and the penalties that will be imposed for their commission. A comprehensive federal criminal code defines federal crimes.[1]

penal code
A collection of criminal statutes.

Examples Each state has a criminal penal code that lists and defines the activities that are illegal in that state. These crimes include first-degree murder, burglary, robbery, arson, rape, and other crimes.

regulatory statutes
Statutes such as environmental laws, securities laws, and antitrust laws that provide for criminal violations and penalties.

In addition, state and federal **regulatory statutes** often provide for criminal violations and penalties. The state and federal legislatures are continually adding to the list of crimes.

Example Federal securities statutes are regulatory statutes that establish rules for disclosure of information before securities can be sold to the public. These federal statutes also make it a crime for an issuer of securities to defraud investors.

The penalty for committing a crime may consist of the imposition of a fine, imprisonment, both, or some other form of punishment (e.g., probation). Generally, imprisonment is imposed to (1) incapacitate the criminal so he or she will not harm others in society, (2) provide a means to rehabilitate the criminal, (3) deter others from similar conduct, and (4) inhibit personal retribution by the victim.

Parties to a Criminal Action

Law cannot persuade where it cannot punish.
Thomas Fuller
Gnomologia (1732)

In a **criminal lawsuit**, the **government** (not a private party) is the **plaintiff**. The government is represented by a lawyer called the **prosecutor** or **prosecuting attorney**. The accused, which is usually an individual or a business, is the **defendant**. The accused is represented by a **defense attorney**. Sometimes the accused will hire a private attorney to represent him or her if he or she can afford to do so. If the accused cannot afford a private defense lawyer, the government will provide one free of charge. This government defense attorney is often called a **public defender**.

Classification of Crimes

Crimes are classified from serious to minor. A crime is usually classified as one of the following:

felony
The most serious type of crime; an inherently evil crime. Most crimes against persons and some business-related crimes are felonies.

- **Felony. Felonies** are the most serious kinds of crimes. Felonies include crimes that are ***mala in se***—that is, inherently evil. Felonies are usually punishable by imprisonment. In some jurisdictions, certain felonies (e.g., first-degree murder) are punishable by death. Federal law[2] and some state laws require mandatory sentencing for specified crimes. Many statutes define different degrees of crimes (e.g., first-, second-, and third-degree murder). Each degree earns different penalties. Serious violations of regulatory statutes are also felonies.

  Examples Most crimes against persons (e.g., murder, rape) and certain business-related crimes (e.g., embezzlement, bribery) are felonies in most jurisdictions.

misdemeanor
A crime that is less serious than a felony; a crime that is not inherently evil but prohibited by society. Many crimes against property are misdemeanors.

- **Misdemeanor. Misdemeanors** are less serious than felonies. They are crimes ***mala prohibita***; that is, they are not inherently evil but are prohibited by society. Misdemeanors carry lesser penalties than felonies. They are usually punishable by fines and/or imprisonment for one year or less.

  Examples Many crimes committed against property, such as robbery, burglary, and less serious violations of regulatory statutes, are classified as misdemeanors in most jurisdictions.

violation
A crime that is neither a felony nor a misdemeanor that is usually punishable by a fine.

- **Violation. Violations** are the least serious of crimes. These crimes are generally punishable by fines. Occasionally, one day or a few days of imprisonment is imposed.

  Examples Crimes such as traffic violations and jaywalking are usually classified as violations.

CONCEPT SUMMARY
CLASSIFICATION OF CRIMES

Classification	Description
Felony	The most serious kinds of crimes. They are *mala in se* (inherently evil) and are usually punishable by imprisonment.
Misdemeanor	Crimes that are less serious than felonies. They are *mala prohibita* (prohibited by society) and are usually punishable by fine and/or imprisonment for less than one year.
Violation	Crimes that are neither felonies nor misdemeanors. Violations are generally punishable by a fine.

Intent Crimes

Most crimes require **criminal intent** to be proven before the accused can be found guilty of the defined crime. Two elements must be proven for a person to be found guilty of an **intent crime**: (1) criminal act (*actus reus*) and (2) criminal intent (*mens rea*):

intent crime
A crime that requires the defendant to be found guilty of committing a criminal act (*actus reus*) with criminal intent (*mens rea*).

actus reus
"Guilty act"—the actual performance of a criminal act.

1. **Criminal act (*actus reus*).** The defendant must have actually performed the prohibited act. The actual performance of the criminal act is called the ***actus reus*** (guilty act). Sometimes, the omission of an act can constitute the requisite *actus reus*.

   Examples Killing someone without legal justification constitutes a criminal act (*actus reus*) because the law forbids persons from killing one another. If a taxpayer who is under a legal duty to file income tax returns and to pay income taxes that are due the government fails to do so, there is the requisite criminal act (*actus reus*). A person who commits auto theft has engaged in a criminal act.

2. **Criminal intent (*mens rea*).** To be found guilty of an intent crime, the accused must be found to have possessed the requisite state of mind when the act was performed. This is called ***mens rea*** (evil intent). Juries may infer a defendant's intent from the facts and circumstances of the case. Many jurisdictions have defined intent crimes as either *general intent* crimes or *specific intent* crimes:

   mens rea
   "Evil intent"—the possession of the requisite state of mind to commit a prohibited act.

   a. **Specific intent crime. Specific intent crimes** require that the perpetrator intended to achieve a specific result from his or her illegal act.

   specific intent crime
   A crime that requires that the perpetrator intended to achieve a specific result from his or her illegal act.

   Examples Premeditated murder is a specific intent crime because the perpetrator intends a specific result, the death of the victim. Arson, forgery, and fraud are other examples of specific intent crimes.

   b. **General intent crime. General intent crimes** require that the perpetrator either knew or should have known that his or her actions would lead to harmful results. The government does not have to prove that the accused intended the precise harm that resulted from his or her actions.

   general intent crime
   A crime that requires that the perpetrator either knew or should have known that his or her actions would lead to harmful results.

   Examples Assault and battery are usually considered general intent crimes because the perpetrator intends to commit the crime but does not know the actual result of the crime in advance.

Individual criminal statutes state whether the crime requires a showing of specific or general intent. Some jurisdictions have eliminated the distinction between specific and general crimes.

There is no such crime as a crime of thought; there are only crimes of action.
Clarence Darrow

Merely thinking about committing a crime is not a crime because no action has been taken. Thus, merely thinking about killing someone or evading taxes and not actually doing so is not a crime.

CONCEPT SUMMARY

ELEMENTS OF AN INTENT CRIME

Element	Description
Actus reus	Guilty act
Mens rea	Evil intent

Nonintent Crimes

nonintent crime
A crime that imposes criminal liability without a finding of *mens rea* (intent).

Most states have enacted laws that define certain unintended conduct as a crime. These are called **nonintent crimes**. Nonintent crimes are often imposed for reckless or grossly negligent conduct that causes injury to another person.

The following feature discusses how criminal acts may also be the basis for civil tort actions by an injured victim or a deceased victim's relatives.

Contemporary Environment

Criminal Acts as the Basis for Tort Actions

An injured victim of a crime or the relatives of a deceased victim of a crime may bring a **civil action** against a wrongdoer who has caused injury or death during the commission of a criminal act. Civil lawsuits are separate from the government's criminal action against the wrongdoer. In a civil lawsuit, the plaintiff usually wants to recover monetary damages from the wrongdoer.

Example A person commits the crime of battery and physically injures the victim. In this case, the government can prosecute the perpetrator for the crime of battery. In addition, the victim may sue the perpetrator in a civil lawsuit to recover monetary damages for the injuries the victim suffers because of the attack.

In many cases, a person injured by a criminal act does not sue the criminal to recover civil damages because the criminal is often **judgment proof**—that is, the criminal does not have the money to pay a civil judgment.

Criminal and civil law differ in the following ways:

Issue	Civil Law	Criminal Law
Party who brings the action	The plaintiff	The government
Trial by jury	Yes, except actions for equity	Yes
Burden of proof	Preponderance of the evidence	Beyond a reasonable doubt
Jury vote	Judgment for plaintiff requires specific jury vote (e.g., 9 of 12 jurors)	Conviction requires unanimous jury vote
Sanctions and penalties	Monetary damages and equitable remedies (e.g., injunction, specific performance)	Imprisonment, capital punishment, fine, probation

Criminal Procedure

Critical Legal Thinking

Compare a criminal case with a civil case. Why is there such a difference in the burden of proof? Why is there a difference in the required jury vote?

The procedure for initiating and maintaining a criminal action is quite detailed. It includes both pretrial procedures and the actual trial.

Arrest

arrest warrant
A document for a person's detainment, based on a showing of probable cause that the person committed a crime.

Before the police can **arrest** a person for the commission of a crime, they usually must obtain an **arrest warrant** based on a showing of probable cause. The police go before a judge and present the evidence they have for arresting the suspect. If the judge finds that there is *probable cause* to issue the warrant, he or she will do so. The police will then use the arrest warrant to arrest the suspect. **Probable cause** is defined as the substantial likelihood that a person either committed or is about to commit a crime.

Example The police have obtained information from a reliable informant about the criminal activity of an individual; they further investigate the situation and arrive at the conclusion that the individual who is the target of their investigation is involved in the illegal selling of drugs. The police can take this evidence, place it before a judge, and request that the judge issue an arrest warrant. If the judge believes there is probable cause, the judge will issue an arrest warrant. The police can then arrest the suspect pursuant to the arrest warrant.

probable cause
Evidence of the substantial likelihood that a person either committed or is about to commit a crime.

An arrest can be made without obtaining an arrest warrant if there is no time to obtain one or it is otherwise not feasible to obtain a warrant prior to the arrest. **Warrantless arrests** must be based on probable cause.

warrantless arrest
An arrest that is made without obtaining an arrest warrant. The arrest must be based on probable cause and a showing that it was not feasible to obtain an arrest warrant.

Examples The police can make a warrantless arrest if they arrive during the commission of a crime, when a person is fleeing from the scene of a crime, or when it is likely that evidence will be destroyed.

Example In *Atwater v. Lago Vista, Texas,*[3] the U.S. Supreme Court held that a police officer may make a warrantless arrest pursuant to a minor criminal offense. Gail Atwater was driving her pickup truck in Lago Vista, Texas, with her 3-year-old son and 5-year-old daughter in the front seat. None of them were wearing seat belts. Bart Turek, a Lago Vista police officer, observed the seat belt violation and pulled Atwater over. A friend of Atwater's arrived at the scene and took charge of

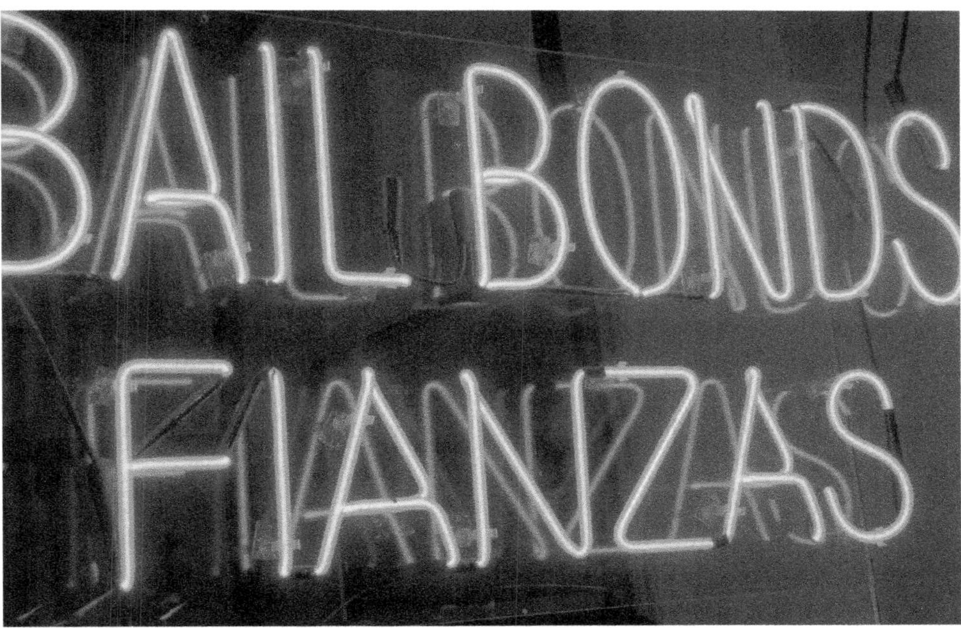

BAIL BOND
When a person is arrested, a ***bail*** *amount is usually set by the court. If the court sets a bail amount and the arrested person posts bail (pays the bail amount), he or she can be released from prison. If he or she does not post bail, the arrestee may be kept in jail for some period of time and, in serious crimes, until the date of trial. The arrested person can post the bail him- or herself by paying the court the set bail amount, which will be returned to him or her if he or she shows up for trial. More often, the arrestee (or a relative or friend) pays a bail bonds professional who operates a bail bonds business to post a* ***bail bond*** *with the court. Bail bonds professionals usually require payment of 10 percent of the bail in order to post bond. For example, if the bail is set at \$100,000, then the arrestee pays the bail bonds professional \$10,000 to post bail. The bail bonds professional keeps this \$10,000 payment. The bail bonds professional guarantees the court that he or she will pay the court \$100,000 if the arrestee does not show up for trial. If this happens, the bail bonds professional attempts to obtain the amount of the bond—here, \$100,000—from the arrestee. Bail bonds professionals often require collateral (e.g., title to an automobile, second mortgage on a house) before they issue a bail bond.*

the children. Turek handcuffed Atwater, placed her in his squad car, and drove her to the police station. Atwater was booked, her mug shot was taken, and she was placed in a jail cell for about one hour until she was released on $310 bond. Atwater ultimately pleaded no contest to the misdemeanor seat belt offenses and paid a $50 fine. Atwater sued the City of Lago Vista and the police officer for compensatory and punitive damages for allegedly violating her Fourth Amendment right to be free from unreasonable seizure. The U.S. Supreme Court ruled against Atwater, finding that the Fourth Amendment permits police officers to make a warrantless arrest pursuant to a minor criminal offense.

WEB EXERCISE
Go to *www.fbi.gov* and click on "Most Wanted" and then "Ten Most Wanted Fugitives." Who is the number-one fugitive listed, and what crime is he or she wanted for?

After a person is arrested, he or she is taken to the police station to be booked. **Booking** is the administrative procedure for recording an arrest, fingerprinting the suspect, taking a photograph of the suspect (often called a mug shot), and so on.

Indictment or Information

indictment
The charge of having committed a crime (usually a felony), based on the judgment of a grand jury.

information
The charge of having committed a crime (usually a misdemeanor), based on the judgment of a judge (magistrate).

An accused person must be formally charged with a crime before he or she can be brought to trial. This is usually done through an **indictment** issued by a grand jury or an **information** statement issued by a magistrate.

Evidence of serious crimes, such as murder, is usually presented to a **grand jury**. Most grand juries are comprised of between 6 and 24 citizens who are charged with evaluating the evidence presented by the government. Grand jurors sit for a fixed period of time, such as one year. If the grand jury determines that there is sufficient evidence to hold the accused for trial, it issues an indictment. Note that the grand jury does not determine guilt. If an indictment is issued, the accused will be held for later trial.

For lesser crimes (e.g., burglary, shoplifting), the accused is brought before a **magistrate** (judge). A magistrate who finds that there is enough evidence to hold the accused for trial issues an information statement.

The case against the accused is dismissed if neither an indictment nor an information statement is issued.

Arraignment

arraignment
A hearing during which the accused is brought before a court and is (1) informed of the charges against him or her and (2) asked to enter a plea.

If an indictment or information is issued, the accused is brought before a court for an **arraignment** proceeding during which the accused is (1) informed of the charges against him or her and (2) asked to enter a **plea**. The accused may plead **guilty** or **not guilty**.

Example Peter has been arrested for the crime of automobile theft. At the arraignment, Peter is asked how he pleads. Peter replies, "Not guilty." Peter has pleaded not guilty rather than guilty. The majority of accused persons plead not guilty at their arraignment.

Nolo Contendere A party may enter a plea of *nolo contendere*, whereby the accused agrees to the imposition of a penalty but does not admit guilt. The government has the option of accepting a *nolo contendere* plea or requiring the defendant to plead guilty or not guilty. If the government agrees to accept the *nolo contendere* plea, the accused and the government usually enter into a plea bargain in which the accused agrees to the imposition of a penalty but does not admit guilt. A *nolo contendere* plea cannot be used as evidence of liability against the accused at a subsequent civil trial. Corporate defendants often enter this plea.

Example The government brings charges against a corporation for criminally violating environmental pollution laws. The government and the corporation enter into an agreement whereby the corporation pleas *nolo contendere* and agrees to pay a fine of $5 million but does not plead guilty to the violation.

Plea Bargain

Sometimes the accused and the government enter into **plea bargain** negotiations prior to trial with the intent of avoiding a trial. If an agreement is reached, the government and the accused execute a **plea bargaining agreement** that sets forth the terms of their agreement.

plea bargain agreement
An agreement in which the accused admits to a lesser crime than charged. In return, the government agrees to impose a lesser sentence than might have been obtained had the case gone to trial.

Example An accused is charged with first-degree murder, which, if proven, carries a penalty of life imprisonment. The government and the accused engage in plea bargaining, and an agreement is reached whereby the accused agrees to plead guilty to the crime of second-degree murder, which carries a maximum penalty of 20 years in jail. Therefore, a trial is avoided.

The government engages in plea bargaining to save costs, avoid the risks of a trial, and prevent further overcrowding of the prisons. In return, the government agrees to impose a lesser penalty or sentence on the accused than might have been obtained had the case gone to trial and the accused found guilty. The accused often agrees to a plea bargain to avoid the risks of trial, where, if he or she were found guilty, he or she would be subject to a greater penalty than the penalty imposed by the plea bargain he or she has agreed to with the government. Approximately 95 percent of criminal cases are plea bargained and do not go to trial. Of those that go to trial, the government wins a conviction in approximately 75 percent of these cases.

Critical Legal Thinking
Why does the government offer plea bargains rather than go to trial? Is there any reason why an innocent person may agree to a plea bargain of criminal charges?

Criminal Trial

At a criminal trial, all jurors must *unanimously* agree before the accused is found *guilty* of the crime charged. If even one juror disagrees (i.e., has reasonable doubt) about the guilt of the accused, the accused cannot be found guilty of the crime charged. If all the jurors agree that the accused did not commit the crime, the accused is found *not guilty* of the crime charged. After trial, the following rules apply:

- If the defendant is found guilty, he or she may appeal.
- If the defendant is found not guilty, the government cannot appeal.
- If the jury cannot come to a **unanimous decision** about the defendant's guilt one way or the other, the jury is considered a **hung jury**. In this situation, the government may choose to retry the case before a new judge and jury.

hung jury
A jury that cannot come to a unanimous decision about the defendant's guilt. In the case of a hung jury, the government may choose to retry the case.

Example A defendant is tried for the crime of murder. A 12-person jury hears the case. If 10 jurors find the defendant guilty but 2 jurors find the defendant not guilty, then there is a hung jury. The government may retry the defendant and often does so with such a vote. However, if the vote had been four jurors voting guilty and eight jurors voting not guilty, it is highly unlikely the government would retry the case.

Common Crimes

Many **common crimes** are committed against persons and property. Some of the most important common crimes against persons and property are discussed in the following paragraphs.

Murder

Murder is defined as the unlawful killing of a human being by another person without justification. In most states, there are several degrees of murder—usually defined as *first-degree murder*, *second-degree murder*, *voluntary manslaughter*, and *involuntary manslaughter*:

murder
The unlawful killing of a human being by another person without justification.

1. **First-degree murder. First-degree murder** is the intentional unlawful killing of a human being by another person with premeditation, malice aforethought, and willful act. When a person can be executed for committing the murder, it is referred to as **capital murder**.

first-degree murder
The intentional unlawful killing of a human being by another person with premeditation, malice aforethought, and willful act.

Example A person purchases a weapon for the purpose of killing someone, lies in wait to kill that person, and then carries out the murder.

second-degree murder
The intentional unlawful killing of a human being by another person that is not premeditated or planned in advance.

2. **Second-degree murder. Second-degree murder** is the intentional unlawful killing of a human being by another person that is not premeditated or planned in advance. Second-degree murder involves some deliberation but not long-term planning.

   Example Two persons who are at a bar get into an unplanned fight, and one of the combatants kills the other.

voluntary manslaughter
The intentional unlawful killing of a human being by another person that is not premeditated or planned in advance and that is committed under circumstances that would cause a reasonable person to become emotionally disturbed.

3. **Voluntary manslaughter. Voluntary manslaughter** is the intentional unlawful killing of a human being by another person that is not premeditated or planned in advance and that is committed under circumstances that would cause a person to become emotionally upset. Some states refer to this crime as *third-degree murder*.

   Example A spouse comes home unexpectedly; finds his or her spouse committing infidelity; and in the heat of passion "snaps" and kills the spouse, the lover, or both.

involuntary manslaughter
The unintentional unlawful killing of a human being by another person that is caused from a reckless or negligent act.

4. **Involuntary manslaughter. Involuntary manslaughter** is the unintentional unlawful killing of a human being by another person that is caused from a reckless or negligent act. Some states refer to this crime as *negligent homicide*.

   Example A drunk driver unintentionally causes another person's death.

The first three crimes are intent crimes. The fourth is a nonintent crime. The penalties assessed against persons found to have committed these crimes differ by state.

Felony Murder Rule Sometimes a murder is committed during the commission of another crime even though the perpetrator did not originally intend to commit murder. Most states hold the perpetrator liable for the crime of murder in addition to the other crime. This is called the **felony murder rule**. The intent to commit the murder is inferred from the intent to commit the other crime. Many states also hold accomplices liable under this doctrine.

The following case involves the crime of murder.

Ethics

Murder Conviction Upheld on Appeal

"In determining whether a verdict is against the manifest weight of the evidence, the appellate court acts as a 'thirteenth juror.'"

—Sadler, Judge

Gregory O. Wilson, who had been arguing earlier in the day with his girlfriend, Melissa Spear, approached a parked car within which Ms. Spear was seated and poured gasoline from a beer bottle over her head. When Ms. Spear exited the car, Wilson ignited her with his cigarette lighter, setting her body on fire. As Ms. Spear became engulfed in flames, Wilson walked away.

Ms. Spear was transported to a hospital. When she arrived, she had third-degree burns over most of her body. She remained in a coma for 45 days, during which time she underwent 10 surgeries. She was subsequently transferred to a rehabilitation facility and then home. Nine months after the incident and five days before her 30th birthday, Ms. Spear's seven-year-old son found her lying dead in her bed.

The state of Ohio brought murder charges against Wilson. Wilson argued that he was not liable for murder because there was not sufficient causation between Wilson's act of setting Ms. Spear on fire and Ms. Spear's death nine months later to warrant a conviction for murder. The jury disagreed and convicted Wilson of aggravated murder, and he was sentenced to prison for 30 years to life. The court of appeals upheld the conviction and sentence. The court stated, "In determining whether a verdict is against the manifest weight of the evidence, the appellate court acts as a 'thirteenth juror.' A defendant is not relieved of culpability for the natural consequences of inflicting serious wounds on another merely because the victim later died of complications brought on by the injury." *State of Ohio v. Wilson*, 2004 Ohio 2838, 2004 Ohio App. Lexis 2503 (Court of Appeals of Ohio, 2004)

Ethics Questions Do you think Wilson's legal argument on appeal was justified? If you were a juror in this case, what sentence would you have imposed on Wilson?

Robbery

In common law, **robbery** is defined as the taking of personal property from another person or business by the use of fear or force. Robbery with a deadly weapon is generally considered aggravated robbery (or armed robbery) and carries a harsher penalty.

robbery
The taking of personal property from another person by the use of fear or force.

Examples If a person threatens to shoot another person with a gun unless the victim gives her purse to that person, this constitutes the crime of robbery. If a person picks a wallet from someone's pocket, it is not robbery because there has been no use of force or fear. This is a theft.

Burglary

In common law, **burglary** is defined as "breaking and entering a dwelling at night" with the intent to commit a felony. Modern penal codes have broadened this definition to include daytime thefts from homes, offices, commercial buildings, and other buildings. In addition, the "breaking-in" element has been abandoned by most modern definitions of burglary. Thus, unauthorized entering of a building through an unlocked door is sufficient. Aggravated burglary (or armed burglary) carries stiffer penalties.

burglary
The taking of personal property from another's home, office, or commercial or other type of building.

Example Harold breaks into Sibyl's home and steals jewelry and other items. Harold is guilty of the crime of burglary because he entered a dwelling and committed theft.

Larceny

In common law, **larceny** is defined as the wrongful and fraudulent taking of another person's personal property that is not robbery or burglary. Most personal property—including tangible property, trade secrets, computer programs, and other business property—is subject to larceny. Neither the use of force nor the entry of a building is required. Some states distinguish between grand larceny and petit larceny. This distinction depends on the value of the property taken.

larceny
The taking of another's personal property other than from his or her person or building.

Examples Stealing automobiles and stealing satellite radios from automobiles are considered larcenies.

Theft

Some states have dropped the distinction among the crimes of robbery, burglary, and larceny. Instead, these states group these crimes under the general crime of **theft**. Most of these states distinguish between grand theft and petit theft. The distinction depends on the value of the property taken, a dollar amount that varies from one state to the next.

Receiving Stolen Property

A person commits the crime of **receiving stolen property** if he or she (1) knowingly receives stolen property and (2) intends to deprive the rightful owner of that property. Knowledge and intent can be inferred from the circumstances. The stolen property can be any tangible property (e.g., personal property, money, negotiable instruments, stock certificates).

receiving stolen property
A crime that involves (1) knowingly receiving stolen property and (2) intending to deprive the rightful owner of that property.

Example David is walking down the street and is approached by a man who offers to sell David a Rolex watch "at a bargain price." David looks at the 20 Rolex watches that the man displays, chooses one that would normally sell in a retail store for $1,000, and pays $200 for it. It is an authentic Rolex watch. David is guilty of the crime of receiving stolen property because it could easily be proven by circumstantial evidence that he had knowledge that the watch was stolen property.

Arson

arson
The willful or malicious burning of a building.

In common law, **arson** is defined as the malicious or willful burning of the dwelling of another person. Modern penal codes have expanded this definition to include the burning of all types of private, commercial, and public buildings.

Examples An owner of a motel burns down the motel to collect fire insurance proceeds. The owner is guilty of the crime of arson. In this case, the insurance company does not have to pay the proceeds of any insurance policy on the burned property to the arsonist-owner. On the other hand, if a third-party arsonist burned down the motel without the knowledge or assistance of the owner, the third party is the arsonist, and the owner is entitled to recover the proceeds of any fire insurance he had on the property.

Business and White-Collar Crimes

white-collar crime
Crimes that are often committed by businesspeople.

Certain types of crimes are prone to being committed by businesspeople. These crimes are often referred to as **white-collar crimes**. Such crimes usually involve cunning and deceit rather than physical force. Many of the most important white-collar crimes are discussed in the paragraphs that follow.

Forgery

forgery
The fraudulent making or alteration of a written document that affects the legal liability of another person.

The crime of **forgery** occurs if a written document is fraudulently made or altered and that change affects the legal liability of another person. Counterfeiting, falsifying public records, and materially altering legal documents are examples of forgery.

Example Signing another person's signature to a check or changing the amount of a check without the owner's permission is forgery.

Note that signing another person's signature without intent to defraud is not forgery.

Example Forgery has not been committed if one spouse signs the other spouse's payroll check for deposit in a joint checking or savings account at the bank.

Embezzlement

embezzlement
The fraudulent conversion of property by a person to whom that property was entrusted.

The crime of **embezzlement** is the fraudulent conversion of property by a person to whom that property was entrusted. Typically, embezzlement is committed by an employer's employees, agents, or representatives (e.g., accountants, lawyers, trust officers, treasurers). Embezzlers often try to cover their tracks by preparing false books, records, or entries.

The key element here is that the stolen property was *entrusted* to the embezzler. This differs from robbery, burglary, and larceny, where property is taken by someone not entrusted with the property.

Examples A bank entrusts a teller to take deposits from its customers and deposit them into the customers' accounts at the bank. Instead, the bank teller absconds with the money. This is embezzlement. A lawyer who steals money from a trust fund that has been entrusted to him or her to administer commits the crime of embezzlement.

Bribery

Bribery is one of the most prevalent forms of white-collar crime. A bribe can be money, property, favors, or anything else of value. The crime of commercial bribery entails the payment of bribes to private persons and businesses. This type of bribe is often referred to as a **kickback**, or **payoff**. Intent is a necessary element of this crime. The offeror of a bribe commits the crime of bribery when the bribe is tendered. The offeree is guilty of the crime of bribery when he or she accepts the bribe. The offeror can be found liable for the crime of bribery even if the person to whom the bribe is offered rejects the bribe.

bribery
A crime in which one person gives another person money, property, favors, or anything else of value for a favor in return. A bribe is often referred to as a *payoff* or *kickback*.

Example Harriet Landers is the purchasing agent for the ABC Corporation and is in charge of purchasing equipment to be used by the corporation. Neal Brown, the sales representative of a company that makes equipment that can be used by the ABC Corporation, offers to pay her a 10 percent kickback if she buys equipment from him. She accepts the bribe and orders the equipment. Both parties are guilty of bribery.

Modern penal codes also make it a crime to bribe public officials.

Example If a real estate developer who is constructing an apartment building offers to pay the building inspector to overlook a building code violation, this is bribery.

Extortion

The crime of **extortion** involves the obtaining of property from another, with his or her consent, induced by wrongful use of actual or threatened force, violence, or fear. Extortion occurs when a person threatens to expose something about another person unless that other person gives money or property. The truth or falsity of the information is immaterial. Extortion of private persons is commonly referred to as **blackmail**. Extortion of public officials is called **extortion under color of official right**.

extortion
A threat to expose something about another person unless that other person gives money or property. Often referred to as *blackmail*.

Example A person knows that an executive who works for a company has been engaged in a physical altercation with another person. The person who knows this information threatens the executive that he will disclose this fact to the company unless the executive pays him money. The person who makes the threat of exposure has committed the crime of extortion even though the fact he or she threatens to divulge is true.

Criminal Fraud

Obtaining title to property through deception or trickery constitutes the crime of **false pretenses**. This crime is commonly referred to as **criminal fraud** or **deceit**.

criminal fraud (false pretenses or deceit)
A crime that involves obtaining title to property through deception or trickery.

Example Bob, a stockbroker, promises Mary, a prospective investor, that he will use any money she invests with him to purchase interests in oil wells. Based on this promise, Mary decides to make the investment. Bob never intended to invest the money. Instead, he uses the money for his personal needs. This is criminal fraud.

Mail Fraud and Wire Fraud

Federal law prohibits the use of mail or wires (e.g., telephone, television, radio, computer) to defraud another person. These crimes are called **mail fraud**[4] and **wire fraud**,[5] respectively. The government often includes these crimes in a criminal charge against a defendant who is charged with committing another crime but who also used the mail or wires to further her crime. Sometimes the government prosecutes a suspect under these statutes if there is insufficient evidence to prove

There are some frauds so well conducted that it would be stupidity not to be deceived by them.

C. C. Colton
Lacon, Volume 1 (1820)

the real crime that the criminal was attempting to commit or did commit. Persons convicted of mail or wire fraud are subject to imprisonment and the imposition of monetary fines.

Money Laundering

When criminals make money from illegal activities, they are often faced with the problem of having large sums of money and no record of how this money was earned. This could easily tip off the government to their illegal activities. To "wash" the money and make it look as though it was earned legitimately, many criminals purchase legitimate businesses and run the money through those businesses to "clean" it before they "receive" the money from the so-called legitimate business. The legitimate business has "cooked" books, which show faked expenditures and receipts, and is the repository for the "buried" illegal money. Restaurants, motels, and other cash businesses make excellent money laundries.

Money Laundering Control Act
A federal statute that makes it a crime to (1) engage knowingly in a *money transaction* through a financial institution involving property from an unlawful activity worth more than $10,000 and (2) engage knowingly in a *financial transaction* involving the proceeds of an unlawful activity.

To address the problem of **money laundering**, the federal government enacted the **Money Laundering Control Act**.[6] This act makes it a crime to:

- Engage knowingly in a *monetary transaction* through a financial institution involving property from an unlawful activity worth more than $10,000.

  Examples Monetary transactions through a financial institution include making deposits; making withdrawals; conducting transactions between accounts; or obtaining monetary instruments, such as cashiers' checks, money orders, and travelers' checks, from a bank or another financial institution for more than $10,000.

- Engage knowingly in a *financial transaction* involving the proceeds of an unlawful activity.

  Examples Financial transactions involving the proceeds of an illegal activity include buying real estate, automobiles, personal property, intangible assets, or anything else of value with money obtained from illegal activities.

Thus, money laundering itself is now a federal crime. The money that is washed could have been made from illegal gambling operations, drug dealing, fraud, or other crimes, including white-collar crimes. Persons convicted of money laundering can be fined up to $500,000 or twice the value of the property involved, whichever is greater, and sentenced to up to 20 years in federal prison. In addition, violation of the act subjects any property involved in or traceable to the offense to forfeiture to the government.

Racketeer Influenced and Corrupt Organizations Act (RICO)

Racketeer Influenced and Corrupt Organizations Act (RICO)
A federal act that provides for both criminal and civil penalties for racketeering.

Organized crime has a pervasive influence on many parts of the U.S. economy. To combat this activity, Congress enacted the Organized Crime Control Act. The **Racketeer Influenced and Corrupt Organizations Act (RICO)** is part of this act.[7] Originally, RICO was intended to apply only to organized crime. However, the broad language of the RICO statute has been used against non–organized crime defendants as well. RICO, which provides for both criminal and civil penalties, is one of the most important laws affecting business today.

Criminal RICO RICO makes it a federal crime to acquire or maintain an interest in, use income from, or conduct or participate in the affairs of an enterprise through a pattern of racketeering activity. An *enterprise* is defined as a corporation, a partnership, a sole proprietorship, another business or organization, or the government.

Racketeering activity consists of a number of specifically enumerated federal and state crimes, including activities such as gambling, arson, robbery, counterfeiting, and dealing in narcotics. Business-related crimes, such as bribery, embezzlement, mail fraud, and wire fraud, are also considered racketeering. To prove a *pattern of racketeering*, at least two of these acts must be committed by the defendant within a 10-year period. Commission of the same crime twice within this 10-year period also constitutes **criminal RICO** as well.

Individual defendants found criminally liable for RICO violations can be fined, imprisoned for up to 20 years, or both. In addition, RICO provides for the *forfeiture* of any property or business interests (even interests in a legitimate business) that were gained because of RICO violations. This provision allows the government to recover investments made with monies derived from racketeering activities. The government may also seek civil penalties for RICO violations, which include injunctions, orders of dissolution, reorganization of business, and divestiture of the defendant's interest in an enterprise.

The criminal is to go free because the constable has blundered. Chief Judge Cardozo

People v. Defore (1926)

Civil RICO Persons injured by a RICO violation can bring a private **civil RICO** action against the violator to recover damages for injury to business or property. A successful plaintiff may recover *treble damages* (three times the actual loss) plus attorney's fees.

Criminal Conspiracy

A **criminal conspiracy** occurs when two or more persons enter into an *agreement* to commit a crime. To be liable for a criminal conspiracy, a person must commit an *overt act* to further the crime. The crime itself does not have to be committed, however. The government usually brings criminal conspiracy charges if (1) the defendants have been thwarted in their efforts to commit the substantive crime or (2) there is insufficient evidence to prove the substantive crime.

criminal conspiracy
A crime in which two or more persons enter into an agreement to commit a crime and an overt act is taken to further the crime.

Example Two securities brokers agree over the telephone to commit a securities fraud. They obtain a list of potential victims and prepare false financial statements necessary for the fraud. Because they entered into an agreement to commit a crime and took an overt act, the brokers are guilty of the crime of criminal conspiracy, even if they never carry out the securities fraud.

The following feature discusses the criminal liability of corporations for the acts of its officers, directors, and employees.

Business Environment

Corporate Criminal Liability

A *corporation* is a fictitious legal person that is granted legal existence by the state when certain requirements are met. A corporation cannot act on its own behalf. Instead, it must act through *agents*, such as a board of directors, officers, and employees.

Originally, under the common law, it was generally held that corporations lacked the criminal mind (*mens rea*) to be held criminally liable. Modern courts, however, impose **corporate criminal liability**. These courts have held that corporations are criminally liable for the acts of their directors, officers, and employees. Because corporations cannot be put in prison, they are usually sanctioned with fines, loss of a license or franchise, and the like.

Corporate directors, officers, and employees are individually liable for crimes that they commit on behalf of or to further the interests of the corporation. In addition, under certain circumstances, a corporate manager can be held criminally liable for the criminal activities of his or her subordinates. To be held criminally liable, the manager must have failed to supervise the subordinates appropriately. This is an evolving area of the law.

Critical Legal Thinking Questions

Why is criminal liability imposed on a corporation? Do you think that the penalties (e.g., jail time) that are imposed on corporate executives for white-collar crimes are sufficient?

Cybercrimes

The development of computers, e-mail, and the Internet has made it easier for criminals to perpetrate many existing crimes and has created the ability for them to commit crimes that did not exist before the digital age. These are commonly referred to as **cybercrimes**. The government has had to apply existing laws to these new media and develop new laws to attack digital crimes.

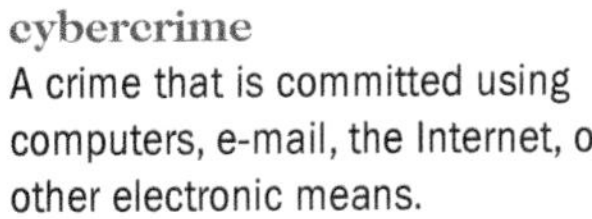

cybercrime
A crime that is committed using computers, e-mail, the Internet, or other electronic means.

One of the most pervasive monetary crimes today is Internet fraud. The following feature discusses the crime of cyber identity theft.

Digital Law

The Internet and Identity Theft

The advent of the computer, the Internet, and digital devices have made one type of crime—identity theft—easier to commit. Identity theft was around long before the computer was invented, but computers and the Internet have made it much easier for criminals to obtain the information they need to commit identity theft. In **identity theft**—or **ID theft**—one person steals information about another person to pose as that person and take the innocent person's money or property or to purchase goods and services using the victim's credit information.

To commit ID theft, thieves must first obtain certain information about the victim. This could be the victim's name, Social Security number, credit card numbers, bank account information, and other personal information. With the use of computers, criminals can obtain the information they need to commit ID theft more easily. Credit card fraud is one of the crimes most commonly committed by ID thieves. An ID thief may use a victim's existing credit card or open new credit card accounts in the victim's name and purchase goods and services with these credit cards, often using the Internet.

To address the growing problem of ID theft, Congress enacted the **Identity Theft and Assumption Deterrence Act.**[8] This statute makes it a federal crime to transfer or use, without authority, the identity of another person knowingly and with the intent to commit any unlawful activity as defined by federal law and state and local felony laws. Violators can be sentenced to prison for up to 15 years and have any property used in the commission of ID theft forfeited to the government.

Identity Theft and Assumption Deterrence Act
A federal act that makes it a crime to transfer or use, without authority, the identity of another person knowingly and with the intent to commit any unlawful activity as defined by federal law and state and local felony laws.

Information Infrastructure Protection (IIP) Act
A federal act that makes it a crime for anyone to access and acquire information intentionally from a protected computer without authorization.

Information Infrastructure Protection Act (IIP Act)

The Internet and the information age ushered in a whole new world for education, business, and consumer transactions. It also made cybercrimes possible. Prosecutors and courts have wrestled with questions about how to apply existing laws written before the digital age to new Internet-related abuses.

Congress responded by enacting the **Information Infrastructure Protection (IIP) Act.**[9] The act addresses computer-related crimes as distinct offenses. The IIP Act provides protection for any computer attached to the Internet.

The IIP Act makes it a federal crime for anyone to access and acquire information intentionally from a protected computer without authorization. The IIP Act does not require that the defendant accessed a protected computer for commercial benefit. Thus, persons who transmit a computer virus over the Internet or hackers who trespass into Internet-connected computers may be criminally prosecuted under the IIP Act. Even merely observing data on a protected computer without authorization is sufficient to meet the requirement that the defendant has accessed a protected computer. Criminal penalties for violating the IIP Act include imprisonment and fines.

The IIP Act gives the federal government a much-needed weapon for directly prosecuting cyber crooks, hackers, and others who enter, steal, destroy, or look at others' computer data without authorization.

Counterfeit Access Device and Computer Fraud and Abuse Act

The **Counterfeit Access Device and Computer Fraud and Abuse Act (CFAA)**, as amended, makes it a federal crime to access a computer knowingly to obtain

(1) restricted federal government information, (2) financial records of financial institutions, or (3) consumer reports of consumer reporting agencies. The act also makes it a crime to use counterfeit or unauthorized access devices, such as cards or code numbers, to obtain things of value, transfer funds, or traffic in such devices.[10]

The following case involves computer crimes.

CASE 8.1 *FEDERAL COURT CASE Computer Crime*

United States v. Barrington

648 F.3d 1178, 2011 U.S. App. Lexis 16535 (2011)
United States Court of Appeals for the Eleventh Circuit

"We have no hesitation in concluding that the Government's theory rested on a legally cognizable theory of conspiracy to defraud by wire and computer."
—Whittemore, Judge

Facts

Marcus Barrington, Christopher Jacquette, and Lawrence Secrease were undergraduate students at Florida A&M University (FAMU). They concocted a scheme to access FAMU's Internet-based grading system. They went to the registrar's office and surreptitiously installed keylogger software on FAMU's computers. The keylogger software recorded the keystrokes made by registrar employees as they signed into their computers, capturing their usernames and passwords. That data was automatically transmitted to various email accounts, including Barrington's personal e-mail address.

With the usernames and passwords, Barrington and the others, using their own computers and FAMU's computers, accessed FAMU's grading system and changed course grades for themselves and other students. Barrington received approximately 30–35 grade changes, Jacquette approximately 43, and Secrease approximately 36. Ultimately, the group made in excess of 650 unauthorized grade changes for at least 90 students, including fraternity brothers. Eventually, a professor uncovered the scheme, and the FAMU police and the Federal Bureau of Investigation were notified.

Barrington, Jacquette, and Secrease were indicted and charged with the federal crimes of conspiring to commit wire fraud using a protected computer, fraud using a protected computer, and identity theft. Jacquette and Secrease entered into a plea agreement and were each sentenced to 22 months in prison. Barrington went to trial and denied involvement in the scheme. Jacquette was a witness against Barrington at Barrington's trial. Barrington was convicted on all counts and was sentenced to 7 years in prison. Barrington appealed his conviction and sentence.

Issue

Was Barrington guilty of the crimes charged and was the prison sentence appropriate?

Language of the Court

There was an adequate basis for the jury to find that Barrington actually committed the extrinsic acts. Jacquette's uncorroborated testimony was sufficient, since he had personal knowledge of Barrington's conduct. We have no hesitation in concluding that the Government's theory rested on a legally cognizable theory of conspiracy to defraud by wire and computer. The evidence was sufficient to support Barrington's convictions for aggravated identity theft. Barrington's lack of remorse, coupled with his false trial testimony, obstructive conduct during the investigation, and what the district court described as his "arrogance and contempt for the law," certainly justified the sentence imposed.

Decision

The U.S. court of appeals affirmed Barrington's conviction and prison sentence.

Ethics Questions

Should Barrington have entered into a plea deal before trial? Did Jacquette act ethically by being a witness against Barrington? Was the seven-year prison sentence warranted?

Fourth Amendment Protection Against Unreasonable Search and Seizure

In many criminal cases, the government relies on information obtained from searches of individuals and businesses. The **Fourth Amendment** to the U.S. Constitution protects persons and corporations from overzealous investigative activities by the government. It protects the rights of the people from **unreasonable search and seizure** by the government. It permits people to be secure in their persons, houses, papers, and effects.

unreasonable search and seizure
Protection granted by the Fourth Amendment for people to be free from unreasonable search and seizure by the government.

search warrant
A warrant issued by a court that authorizes the police to search a designated place for specified contraband, articles, items, or documents. A search warrant must be based on probable cause.

Reasonable search and seizure by the government is lawful. **Search warrants** based on *probable cause* are necessary in most cases. Such a warrant specifically states the place and scope of the authorized search. General searches beyond the specified area are forbidden. **Warrantless searches** are permitted only (1) incident to arrest, (2) where evidence is in "plain view," or (3) in exigent circumstances such as when it is likely that evidence will be destroyed. Warrantless searches are judged by the probable cause standard.

Example The police obtained a search warrant to attach a Global Positioning System (GPS) to a suspect's automobile, and the warrant stated that the device be installed within 10 days; however, the police did not install the device until the 11th day. The U.S. Supreme Court held that this was an unconstitutional search and that the evidence obtained from the search be excluded from evidence.[11]

The following case involves the issue of search and seizure of evidence.

CASE 8.2 *U.S. SUPREME COURT CASE Search*

Navarette v. California

134 S.Ct. 1683, 2014 U.S. Lexis 2930 (2014)
Supreme Court of the United States

"A mere 'hunch' does not create reasonable suspicion."

—Thomas, Justice

Facts

A driver of a vehicle called 911 and reported that a truck had run her off the road. She gave a description of the vehicle and its license number to the 911 dispatcher. The dispatcher relayed the information to California Highway Patrol officers, who located and stopped the truck. As two officers approached the truck they smelled marijuana. A search of the truck bed revealed 30 pounds of marijuana. The officer arrested the driver, Lorenzo Prado Navarette, and the passenger, José Prado Navarette (petitioners). The petitioners moved to suppress the evidence, arguing that the traffic stop violated the Fourth Amendment because the officers lacked reasonable suspicion of criminal activity. The California trial court denied their motion and the petitioners were sentenced to 90 days in jail plus three years of probation. The California court of appeals affirmed. The petitioners appealed to the U.S. Supreme Court.

Issue

Did the stop and search of the truck violate the Fourth Amendment?

Language of the U.S. Supreme Court

A mere "hunch" does not create reasonable suspicion. But under appropriate circumstances an anonymous tip can demonstrate sufficient indicia of reliability to provide reasonable suspicion to make an investigatory stop. The caller necessarily claimed eyewitness knowledge of the alleged dangerous driving. Another indicator of veracity is the caller's use of the 911 emergency system. The stop was therefore proper.

(case continues)

Decision

The U.S. Supreme Court held that the stop and search of the truck based on the caller's tip comported with the requirements of the Fourth Amendment and was therefore lawful.

Ethics Questions

Is there a possibility that someone might make a false report of criminal activity? How much specificity is required for the tip to justify a lawful search?

Exclusionary Rule

Evidence obtained from an unreasonable search and seizure is considered tainted evidence ("fruit of a tainted tree"). Under the **exclusionary rule**, such evidence can generally be prohibited from introduction at a trial or an administrative proceeding against the person searched. However, this evidence is freely admissible against other persons.

The U.S. Supreme Court created a *good faith exception* to the exclusionary rule.[12] This exception allows evidence obtained illegally to be introduced as evidence against the accused if the police officers who conducted the unreasonable search reasonably believed that they were acting pursuant to a lawful search warrant.

In the following case, the U.S. Supreme Court had to decide whether a search was reasonable.

exclusionary rule
A rule that says evidence obtained from an unreasonable search and seizure can generally be prohibited from introduction at a trial or an administrative proceeding against the person searched.

Critical Legal Thinking
Does the exclusionary rule allow some guilty parties to go free? Is this an acceptable result when balanced against the protections afforded by the Fourth Amendment?

CASE 8.3 U.S. SUPREME COURT CASE Search

Maryland v. King

133 S.Ct. 1958, 2013 U.S. Lexis 4165 (2013)
Supreme Court of the United States

"The advent of DNA technology is one of the most significant scientific advancements of our era."
—Kennedy, Justice

Facts

In 2003, a man concealing his face and armed with a gun broke into a woman's home in Salisbury, Maryland, and then raped her. The police were unable to identify or apprehend the assailant, but they did obtain from the victim a sample of the perpetrator's DNA (deoxyribonucleic acid).

In 2009, Alonzo King was arrested in Maryland and charged with first- and second-degree assault for menacing a group of people with a shotgun. As part of the booking procedure for serious offenses, a DNA sample was taken from King by applying a cotton swab—known as a buccal swab—to the inside of his cheeks. His DNA was found to match the DNA taken from the Salisbury rape victim. King was tried and convicted of the 2003 rape. King alleged that the DNA taken when he was booked in 2009 violated the Fourth Amendment as an unreasonable search and seizure and therefore could not be used to convict him of the 2003 rape. The court of appeals of Maryland agreed and set the rape conviction aside. The U.S. Supreme Court granted review.

Issue

Did Maryland's collection of King's DNA during the booking procedure in 2009 constitute an unreasonable search and seizure?

Language of the U.S. Supreme Court

The advent of DNA technology is one of the most significant scientific advancements of our era. It can be agreed that using a buccal swab on the inner tissues of a person's cheek in order to obtain DNA samples is a search. The Court concludes that DNA identification of arrestees is a reasonable search that can be considered part of a routine booking procedure. When officers make an arrest supported by probable cause to hold for a serious offense and they bring the suspect to the station to be detained in custody, taking and analyzing a cheek swab of the arrestee's DNA is, like fingerprinting and photographing, a legitimate police booking procedure that is reasonable under the Fourth Amendment.

(*case continues*)

Decision

The U.S. Supreme Court held that the taking of the DNA from King at the time of booking was a reasonable search and seizure and reversed the judgment of the court of appeals of Maryland.

Ethics Questions

Why did King want his DNA kept out of his criminal trial for the 2003 rape charge? Should law enforcement and the courts rely on DNA evidence as much as they do?

The following case involves the issue of searching cell phones.

CASE 8.4 *U.S. SUPREME COURT CASE Search of Cell Phones*

Riley v. California and United States v. Wurie

134 S.Ct. 2473, 2014 U.S. Lexis 4497 (2014)
Supreme Court of the United States

"Our answer to the question of what police must do before searching a cell phone seized incident to an arrest is accordingly simple—get a warrant."

—Roberts, Chief Justice

Facts

Two cases were combined for decision by the U.S. Supreme Court. In the first case, David Riley was stopped for driving with expired registration tags. A search of the car turned up two concealed and loaded firearms. The police confiscated Riley's smart phone and went through it and found gang related information and a photograph of Riley in front of a car they suspected to be involved in a shooting a few weeks earlier. Based on the information retrieved from the cell phone Riley was charged in connection with that earlier shooting, with firing at an occupied vehicle, assault with a semiautomatic weapon, and attempted murder. Riley was convicted of all charges and was sentenced to 15 years in prison.

In the second case, police observed Brima Wurie making an apparent drug sale from a car. The officers arrested Wurie and seized two cell phones from him. After monitoring the calls made to the cell phones, police determined the location of the calls, which was Wurie's apartment. The police went to the apartment and searched the apartment and found and seized crack cocaine, marijuana, drug paraphernalia, a firearm and ammunition, and cash. Wurie was charged with distributing crack cocaine and being a felon in possession of a firearm. Wurie was convicted and sentenced to 262 months in prison.

Prior to their trials, Riley and Wurie moved to suppress all the evidence the police obtained from their cell phones, alleging that the information obtained from their cell phones were the fruits of an unconstitutional search in violation of the Fourth Amendment. The courts in each case denied their requests. After appeals, the U.S. Supreme Court granted certiorari to hear these combined cases.

Issue

Can the police, without a warrant, search digital information on a cell phone from an individual who has been arrested?

Language of the U.S. Supreme Court

These cases require us to decide how the search incident to arrest doctrine applies to modern cell phones. Courts have approved searches of a variety of personal items carried by an arrestee (e.g., billfolds, address books, wallets, and purses). The government parties assert that a search of all data stored on a cell phone is materially indistinguishable from searches of these sorts of physical items.

Cell phones differ in both a quantitative and qualitative sense from other objects that might be kept on an arrestee's person. Before cell phones, a search of a person was limited by physical realities and tended as a general matter to constitute only a narrow intrusion on privacy. But the possible intrusion on privacy is not limited in the same way when it comes to cell phones.

(case continues)

Today, it is no exaggeration to say that many of the more than 90% of American adults who own a cell phone keep on their person a digital record of nearly every aspect of their lives—from the mundane to the intimate. Allowing the police to scrutinize such records on a routine basis is quite different from allowing them to search a personal item or two in the occasional case.

Modern cell phones are not just another technological convenience. With all they contain and all they may reveal, they hold for many Americans "the privacies of life." Our answer to the question of what police must do before searching a cell phone seized incident to an arrest is accordingly simple—get a warrant.

Decision

The U.S. Supreme Court held that police cannot, without a warrant, search digital information on a cell phone from an individual who has been arrested.

Ethics Question

Does the Supreme Court's decision protect privacy rights? Did the Supreme Court justices evidence an understanding of the digital world in their opinion?

Searches of Business Premises

Generally, the government does not have the right to search business premises without a search warrant.[13] However, certain hazardous and regulated industries are subject to warrantless searches if proper statutory procedures are met.

Examples Sellers of firearms, liquor stores and bars that sell alcohol, coal mines, and the like are businesses subject to warrantless searches.

The criminal is to go free because the constable has blundered.

Chief Judge Cardozo
People v. Defore 242 N.Y. 13, 150 N.E. 585, 1926 N.Y. Lexis 956 (1926)

Fifth Amendment Privilege Against Self-Incrimination

The **Fifth Amendment** to the U.S. Constitution provides that no person "shall be compelled in any criminal case to be a witness against himself." Thus, a person cannot be compelled to give testimony against him- or herself. A person who asserts this right is described as "taking the Fifth." This protection applies to federal cases and is extended to state and local criminal cases through the Due Process Clause of the Fourteenth Amendment. The right established by the Fifth Amendment is referred to as the **privilege against self-incrimination**.

privilege against self-incrimination
The Fifth Amendment provision that a person may not be required to be a witness against him- or herself in a criminal case. This is called the *Privilege against self-incrimination*.

Nontestimonial evidence (e.g., fingerprints, body fluids) may be obtained without violating the Fifth Amendment.

The protection against **self-incrimination** applies only to natural persons who are accused of crimes. Therefore, artificial persons (e.g., corporations, partnerships) cannot raise this protection against incriminating testimony.[14] Thus, business records of corporations and partnerships are not generally protected from disclosure, even if they incriminate individuals who work for the business. However, certain "private papers" of businesspersons (e.g., personal diaries) are protected from disclosure.

Critical Legal Thinking
What is the policy behind adding the privilege against self-incrimination to the U.S. Constitution? What percentage of criminal defendants "take the Fifth" and do not take the witness stand?

Miranda Rights

Many people have not read and memorized the provisions of the U.S. Constitution. The U.S. Supreme Court recognized this fact when it decided the landmark case *Miranda v. Arizona* in 1966.[15] In this case, the Supreme Court held that the Fifth Amendment privilege against self-incrimination is not useful unless a criminal suspect has knowledge of this right. Therefore, the Supreme Court required that the following warning—colloquially called the ***Miranda* rights**—be read to a

***Miranda* rights**
Rights that a suspect must be informed of before being interrogated so that the suspect will not unwittingly give up his or her Fifth Amendment right.

criminal suspect before he or she is interrogated by the police or other government officials:

- You have the right to remain silent.
- Anything you say can and will be used against you.
- You have the right to consult a lawyer and to have a lawyer present with you during interrogation.
- If you cannot afford a lawyer, a lawyer will be appointed free of charge to represent you.

Many police departments read an accused a more detailed version of the *Miranda* rights (see **Exhibit 8.1**). This is designed to cover all issues that a detainee might encounter while in police custody. A detainee may be asked to sign a statement acknowledging that the *Miranda* rights have been read to him or her.

Exhibit 8.1 **MIRANDA RIGHTS**

POLICE DEPARTMENT
PINE SHORES, MICHIGAN

- You have the right to remain silent and refuse to answer questions. Do you understand?
- Anything you say may be used against you in a court of law. Do you understand?
- You have the right to consult an attorney before speaking to the police and to have an attorney present during questioning now or in the future. Do you understand?
- If you cannot afford an attorney, one will be appointed for you before any questioning if you wish. Do you understand?
- If you decide to answer questions now without an attorney present, you will still have the right to stop answering at any time until you talk to an attorney. Do you understand?
- Knowing and understanding your rights as I have explained them to you, are you willing to answer my questions without an attorney present?

Any statements or confessions obtained from a suspect before he or she has been read the *Miranda* rights can be excluded from evidence at trial. In 2000, the U.S. Supreme Court upheld *Miranda* in *Dickerson v. United States*.[16] In that opinion, Chief Justice Rehnquist stated, "We do not think there is justification for overruling *Miranda*. *Miranda* has become embedded in routine police practice to the point where the warnings have become part of our national culture."

In the following case, the court had to decide if *Miranda* rights had been given properly to a criminal suspect.

CASE 8.5 ***STATE COURT CASE Miranda Rights***

Ragland v. Commonwealth of Kentucky

191 S.W.3d 569, 2006 Ky. Lexis 251 (2006)
Supreme Court of Kentucky

"*Miranda* does not require a 'talismanic incantation' as long as the warnings adequately advise the suspect of his *Miranda* rights."

—Cooper, Justice

Facts

One night, Trent DiGiuro, a student-athlete at the University of Kentucky, was sitting in a chair on the front porch of his residence celebrating his twenty-first

(case continues)

birthday with friends when he was shot and killed. Fragments of the bullet were recovered from DiGiuro's body, and a firearms expert discovered that the bullet had been fired from a .243-caliber rifle.

Six years elapsed after the murder, which was not solved. At that time, Shane Layton Ragland's ex-girlfriend informed the police that Ragland confessed to her that he killed DiGiuro because DiGiuro had caused Ragland to be blackballed by a college fraternity. The witness also told police that Ragland had shown her the rifle he had used to shoot DiGiuro and that he told her he hid the rifle at his mother's residence. Pursuant to a search warrant, the police recovered a Wetherby Vanguard .243-caliber rifle from Ragland's mother's residence with three unspent .243-caliber bullets in the chamber. A police metallurgist fired several recovered bullets and found that they were indistinguishable in metallurgical composition with the bullet that had killed DiGiuro.

Ragland was taken into police custody, was interrogated and answered police questions until he eventually asked for an attorney. Ragland stood trial for the murder of Trent DiGiuro. After substantial evidence was produced, including the statements made by Ragland to the police during his interrogation, Ragland was convicted by a jury of murder and was sentenced to 30 years in prison. Ragland appealed, asserting that the statements he made during the interrogation should have been suppressed because he (1) received an inadequate *Miranda* warning, (2) never waived any of his *Miranda* rights, and (3) asserted the right to counsel.

Issue

Was defendant Ragland properly given his Miranda rights?

Language of the Court

After obtaining preliminary identification information, Sergeant Barnard of the Lexington police, the lead interrogator, advised appellant of his rights under Miranda v. Arizona.

Miranda *does not require a "talismanic incantation" as long as the warnings adequately advise the suspect of his* Miranda *rights. Nor do the warnings have to be in writing, much less audiotaped or videotaped. The trial court's finding that appellant voluntarily waived his* Miranda *rights was supported by substantial evidence.*

Later in the interrogation, appellant did request an attorney, and the trial court properly suppressed any statements he made after that request.

Decision

The supreme court of Kentucky held that appellant Ragland had been read his *Miranda* rights properly and had waived his right to an attorney. Thus, any statements he made during the interrogation, up until the time he clearly asked for an attorney, constituted evidence that was properly admissible at his trial.

Note

Trent's father, Michael DiGiuro, on behalf of his son's estate, filed a civil lawsuit for the tort of wrongful death against Ragland. After a jury trial and appeal, DiGiuro was awarded $3,341,708 in compensatory damages and $30,000,000 in punitive damages against Ragland.

Ethics Questions

Do you think that Ragland understood his *Miranda* rights when he answered the interrogators' questions? Do you think many suspects answer questions during interrogation when they should have pleaded the Fifth Amendment privilege to avoid incriminating themselves and demanded a lawyer? What have you learned from this case?

Attorney–Client Privilege and Other Privileges

To obtain a proper defense, an accused should tell his lawyer the truth so that the lawyer can prepare the best defense she can for him. However, the accused must be able tell his attorney facts about his case without fear that the attorney will be called as a witness against him. This information is protected from disclosure by the **attorney–client privilege**, which is recognized by the Fifth Amendment. Either the client or the attorney can raise this privilege. For the privilege to apply, the information must be told to the attorney in his or her capacity as an attorney and not as a friend or neighbor or such.

attorney–client privilege
A rule that says a client can tell his or her lawyer anything about the case without fear that the attorney will be called as a witness against the client.

Example Cedric is accused of murder and employs Gloria, a renowned criminal attorney, to represent him. During the course of their discussions, Cedric confesses to the murder. Gloria cannot be a witness against Cedric at his criminal trial.

The Fifth Amendment has also recognized the following privileges under which an accused may keep the following individuals from being witnesses against him or her:

- **Psychiatrist/psychologist–patient privilege** so that the accused may tell the truth in order to seek help for his or her condition.
- **Priest/rabbi/minister/imam–penitent privilege** so that the accused may tell the truth in order to repent, be given help, and seek forgiveness for his or her deed.
- **Spouse–spouse privilege** so that the family will remain together.
- **Parent–child privilege** so that the family will remain together.

At the present time in this country there is more danger that criminals will escape justice than that they will be subjected to tyranny.

Justice Holmes, Dissenting Opinion, *Kepner v. United States 195 U.S. 100, 24 S.Ct. 797, 1904 U.S. Lexis 820 (1904)*

A spouse or child who is injured by a spouse or parent (e.g., domestic abuse) may testify against the accused. In addition, if the accused discloses that he or she is planning to commit a crime in the future (e.g., murder), the accused's lawyer; psychiatrist or psychologist; or priest, rabbi, minister, or imam is required to report this to the police or other relevant authorities.

The U.S. Supreme Court has held that there is no accountant–client privilege under federal law.[17] Thus, an accountant can be called as a witness in cases involving federal securities laws, federal mail or wire fraud, or other federal crimes. Approximately 20 states have enacted special statutes that create an **accountant–client privilege**. An accountant cannot be called as a witness against a client in a court action in a state where these statutes are in effect. However, federal courts do not recognize this privilege.

Immunity from Prosecution

On occasion, the government may want to obtain information from a suspect who has asserted his or her Fifth Amendment privilege against self-incrimination. The government can often achieve this by offering the suspect **immunity from prosecution**. Immunity from prosecution means that the government agrees not to use against a person granted immunity any evidence given by that person. Once immunity is granted, the suspect loses the right to assert his or her Fifth Amendment privilege.

immunity from prosecution The government's agreement not to use against a person granted immunity any evidence given by that person.

Example Grants of immunity are often given when the government wants a suspect to give information that will lead to the prosecution of other, more important criminal suspects.

Partial grants of immunity are also available. A suspect must agree to a partial grant of immunity in order for it to occur.

In serious cases, the government can place a witness in a government protective program whereby, after the trial, the witness and her or his family are moved permanently to an undisclosed location, given a new identity, and provided monetary assistance. Such a witness is also usually protected prior to trial.

Other Constitutional Protections

Besides those already discussed in this chapter, many other provisions in the U.S. Constitution and its amendments guarantee and protect certain other rights in the criminal process. Several of these additional rights are described in the paragraphs that follow.

Fifth Amendment Protection Against Double Jeopardy

The **Double Jeopardy Clause** of the Fifth Amendment protects persons from being tried twice for the same crime.

Critical Legal Thinking

Why was the Double Jeopardy Clause added to the U.S. Constitution? What does it prevent the government from doing?

Double Jeopardy Clause
A clause of the Fifth Amendment that protects persons from being tried twice for the same crime.

Example If a state tries a suspect for the crime of murder and the suspect is found not guilty, the state cannot bring another trial against the accused for the same crime. This is so even if more evidence later surfaces that would lead to conviction. The government is given the opportunity to bring its case against an accused once and cannot keep retrying the same case.

If the same act violates the laws of two or more jurisdictions, each jurisdiction may try the accused.

Example If an accused kidnaps a person in one state and brings the victim across a state border into another state, the act violates the laws of two states and the federal government. Thus, three jurisdictions can prosecute the accused without violating the Double Jeopardy Clause.

If an accused is tried once and the jury reaches a *hung jury* decision—that is, the verdict is not unanimously either guilty or not guilty—the government can retry the case against the accused without violating the Double Jeopardy Clause.

Sixth Amendment Right to a Public Jury Trial

The **Sixth Amendment** guarantees that a criminal defendant has the **right to a public jury trial**. This includes the rights to (1) be tried by an impartial jury of the state or district in which the alleged crime was committed, (2) confront (cross-examine) the witnesses against the accused, (3) have the assistance of a lawyer, and (4) have a speedy trial.

The **Speedy Trial Act** is a federal statute that requires that a criminal defendant in a federal case be brought to trial within 70 days after indictment.[18] Continuances may be granted by the court to serve the "ends of justice" and are often granted.

Eighth Amendment Protection Against Cruel and Unusual Punishment

The **Eighth Amendment** protects criminal defendants from **cruel and unusual punishment**. For example, it prohibits the torture of criminals. However, this clause does not prohibit capital punishment.[19] The U.S. Supreme Court has held that in capital punishment cases, death by lethal injection is not cruel and unusual punishment.[20]

WEB EXERCISE
Go to *http://usdoj.gov/usao* and read the Mission Statement of U.S. Attorneys of the United States Department of Justice.

Example The U.S. Supreme Court has held that the imposition of life imprisonment without the possibility of parole on a juvenile defendant convicted of murder violates the Eighth Amendment's prohibition against cruel and unusual punishment.[21]

The following feature examines how France handles the issue of the death penalty.

Global Law

France Does Not Impose the Death Penalty

EIFFEL TOWER, PARIS, FRANCE

The majority of the states and the federal government in the United States permit the death penalty to be imposed for many heinous crimes. France, however, has abolished the death penalty in all cases. Most developed countries have extradition treaties with each other whereby one country can, through an official procedure, request and obtain a person located in another country to be returned to stand trial in the country seeking the extradition. France, however, will not extradite a person already in France to the United States or elsewhere where the death penalty could be imposed. Over 120 countries in the world, by either law or practice, do not impose the death penalty. The death penalty remains a controversial issue in the United States as well as many foreign countries.

Key Terms and Concepts

Accountant–client privilege (206)
Actus reus (criminal act, guilty act) (187)
Arraignment (190)
Arrest (190)
Arrest warrant (188)
Arson (194)
Attorney–client privilege (205)
Bail (189)
Bail bond (189)
Beyond a reasonable doubt (185)
Blackmail (195)
Booking (190)
Bribery (195)
Burden of proof (185)
Burglary (193)
Capital murder (191)
Civil action (188)
Civil RICO (197)
Common crime (191)
Corporate criminal liability (197)
Counterfeit Access Device and Computer Fraud and Abuse Act (CFAA) (198)
Crime (185)
Criminal conspiracy (197)
Criminal fraud (false pretenses or deceit) (195)
Criminal intent (187)
Criminal law (185)
Criminal RICO (197)
Cruel and unusual punishment (207)
Cybercrime (198)
Defendant (186)
Defense attorney (186)
Double Jeopardy Clause (207)
Eighth Amendment (207)
Embezzlement (194)
Exclusionary rule (201)
Extortion (195)
Extortion under color of official right (195)
Felony (186)
Felony murder rule (192)
Fifth Amendment (203)
First-degree murder (187)
Forgery (194)
Fourth Amendment (200)
General intent crime (187)
Grand jury (190)
Guilty (190)
Hung jury (191)
Identity theft (ID theft) (198)
Identity Theft and Assumption Deterrence Act (198)
Immunity from prosecution (206)
Indictment (190)
Information (190)
Information Infrastructure Protection Act (IIP Act) (198)
Intent crime (187)
Involuntary manslaughter (192)
Kickback (payoff) (195)
Larceny (193)
Magistrate (190)
Mail fraud (195)
Mala in se (186)
Mala prohibita (186)
Mens rea (criminal intent, evil intent) (186)

Critical Legal Thinking Cases

8.1 Search and Seizure Bernardo Garcia had served time in jail for methamphetamine (meth) offenses. On release from prison, a person reported to the police that Garcia had brought meth to her and used it with her. Another person told police that Garcia bragged that he could manufacture meth in front of a police station without being caught. A store's security video system recorded Garcia buying ingredients used in making meth. From someone else, the police learned that Garcia was driving a Ford Tempo.

The police found the car parked on the street near where Garcia was staying. The police placed a GPS (global positioning system) tracking device underneath the rear bumper of the car so the device could receive and store satellite signals that indicate the device's location. Using the device, the police learned that Garcia had been visiting a large tract of land. With permission of the owner of the land, the police conducted a search and discovered equipment and materials to manufacture meth. While the police were there, Garcia arrived in his car. The police had not obtained a search warrant authorizing them to place the GPS tracker on Garcia's car.

The government brought criminal charges against Garcia. At Garcia's criminal trial in U.S. district court, the evidence the police obtained using the GPS was introduced. Based on this evidence, Garcia was found guilty of crimes related to the manufacture of meth. Garcia appealed to the U.S. court of appeals, arguing that the use of the GPS tracking device by the police was an unreasonable search, in violation of the Fourth Amendment to the Constitution. Does the police officers' use of the GPS without first obtaining a search warrant constitute an unreasonable search in violation of the Fourth Amendment? *United States of America v. Garcia*, 474 F.3d 994, 2007 U.S. App. Lexis 2272 (United States Court of Appeals for the Seventh Circuit, 2007)

8.2 Cruel and Unusual Punishment One night in 2003, Evan Miller, who was 14 years old, was smoking marijuana with another juvenile and an adult, Cole Cannon, at Cannon's trailer. When Cannon passed out, Miller stole his wallet, splitting about $300 with the other juvenile. When Miller tried to put the wallet back into Cannon's pocket, Cannon awoke and grabbed Miller. Miller grabbed a baseball bat and repeatedly struck Cannon with it. Miller placed a sheet over Cannon's head, told him "I am God, I've come to take your life," and delivered one more blow. Cannon was not dead. Miller and his accomplice set Cannon's trailer on fire. Cannon died from his injuries and smoke inhalation. Miller was caught and was tried as an adult as permitted by Alabama law. Miller was convicted of murder in the course of arson. Under Alabama law, the crime carried a mandatory minimum punishment of life in prison without the possibility of parole, which was assessed against Miller. Miller challenged the sentence, alleging that a minimum sentence of life in prison without the possibility of parole assessed against a juvenile constitutes cruel and unusual punishment in violation of the Fifth Amendment to the U.S. Constitution.

Does Alabama's mandatory sentencing requirement of life imprisonment without the possibility of parole as applied to juvenile defendants constitute cruel and unusual punishment in violation of the Fifth Amendment? *Miller v. Alabama*, 132 S.Ct. 2455, 2012 U.S. Lexis 4873 (Supreme Court of the United States, 2012)

8.3 Search Kentucky undercover police officers set up a controlled buy of cocaine outside an apartment complex. After the deal took place, uniformed police moved in on the suspect. The suspect ran to a breezeway of an apartment building. As the officers arrived in the area, they heard a door shut. At the end of the breezeway were two apartments, one on the left and one on the right. The officers smelled marijuana smoke emanating from the apartment on the left.

The officers banged on the door as loudly as they could, while yelling "Police!" As soon as the officers started banging on the door, they heard people moving inside and things being moved inside the apartment. These noises led the officers to believe that drug-related evidence was about to be destroyed. At that point, the officers kicked in the door and entered the apartment, where they found three people, including Hollis King, his girlfriend, and a guest. The officers saw marijuana and powder cocaine in plain view. A further search turned up crack cocaine, cash, and drug paraphernalia. Police eventually entered the apartment on the right side of the breezeway and found the suspect who was the initial target of their investigation.

King was indicted for criminal violations, including trafficking in marijuana, trafficking in controlled substances, and persistent felony offender status. King filed a motion to have the evidence suppressed as the fruits of an illegal warrantless search in violation of the Fourth Amendment. The government argued that the search was a valid warrantless search that was justified by exigent circumstances. Is the warrantless search constitutional? *Kentucky v. King*, 131 S.Ct. 1849, 2011 U.S. Lexis 3541 (Supreme Court of the United States, 2011)

8.4 Search William Wheetley, a police officer, was on a routine patrol in his police car with Aldo, a German shepherd dog trained to detect certain narcotics (methamphetamine, marijuana, cocaine, heroin, and ecstasy). Wheetley stopped Clayton Harris's truck because it had an expired license plate. On approaching the driver's side door, Wheetley saw that Harris was visibly nervous, shaking, and breathing rapidly. Wheetley also noticed an open can of beer in the truck's cup holder. Wheetley asked Harris for consent to search the truck, but Harris refused. Wheetley then retrieved Aldo from the patrol car and walked him around Harris's truck. Aldo stopped and alerted at the driver's-side door, signaling that he had smelled drugs there. Wheetley concluded, based principally on Aldo's alert, that he had probable cause to search the truck. The search revealed 200 loose pseudoephedrine pills, 8,000 matches, a bottle of hydrochloric acid, two containers of antifreeze, and a coffee filter full of iodine crystals—all ingredients for making methamphetamine. Wheetley arrested Harris, and the state of Florida charged Harris with possession of pseudoephedrine for use in manufacturing methamphetamine. At trial, Harris moved to suppress the evidence found in his truck on the grounds that Aldo's alert had not given Wheetley probable cause for the search and therefore the evidence against Harris was inadmissible under the Fourth Amendment protection against unreasonable search and seizure. The trial court permitted the evidence to be submitted at trial. Did Aldo's alert give Wheetley probable cause to search Harris's truck? *Florida v. Harris*, 133 S.Ct. 1050, 2013 U.S. Lexis 1121 (Supreme Court of the United States, 2013)

8.5 Search and Seizure Government agents suspected that marijuana was being grown in the home of Danny Kyllo, who lived in a triplex building in Florence, Oregon. Indoor marijuana growth typically requires high-intensity lamps. To determine whether an amount of heat was emanating from Kyllo's home consistent with the use of such lamps, federal agents used a thermal imager to scan the triplex. Thermal imagers detect infrared radiation and produce images of the radiation. The scan of Kyllo's home, which was performed from an automobile on the street, showed that the roof over the garage and a side wall of Kyllo's home were "hot." The agents used this scanning evidence to obtain a search warrant authorizing a search of Kyllo's home. During the search, the agents found an indoor growing operation involving more than 100 marijuana plants.

Kyllo was indicted for manufacturing marijuana, a violation of federal criminal law. Kyllo moved to suppress the imaging evidence and the evidence it led to, arguing that it was an unreasonable search that violated the Fourth Amendment to the U.S. Constitution. Is the use of a thermal-imaging device aimed at a private home from a public street to detect relative amounts of heat within the home a "search" within the meaning of the Fourth Amendment? *Kyllo v. United States*, 533 U.S. 27, 121 S.Ct. 2038, 2001 U.S. Lexis 4487 (Supreme Court of the United States, 2001)

8.6 Search and Seizure The police of the city of Indianapolis, Indiana, began to operate vehicle roadblock checkpoints on Indianapolis roads in an effort to interdict unlawful drugs. Once a car had been stopped, police questioned the driver and passengers and conducted an open-view examination of the vehicle from the outside. A narcotics detection dog walked around outside each vehicle. The police conducted a search and seizure of the occupants and vehicle only if particular suspicion developed from the initial investigation. The overall "hit rate" of the program was approximately 9 percent.

James Edmond and Joel Palmer, both of whom were attorneys who had been stopped at one of the Indianapolis checkpoints, filed a lawsuit on behalf of themselves and the class of all motorists who had been stopped or were subject to being stopped at such checkpoints. They claimed that the roadblocks violated the Fourth Amendment's prohibition against unreasonable search and seizure. Does the Indianapolis highway checkpoint program violate the Fourth Amendment to the U.S. Constitution? *City of Indianapolis v. Edmond*, 531 U.S. 32, 121 S.Ct. 447, 2000 U.S. Lexis 8084 (Supreme Court of the United States, 2000)

Ethical

Ethics Cases

8.7 Ethics Case Detective William Pedraja of the Miami-Dade Police Department received a Crime Stoppers unverified tip that one of the tipper's neighbors, Joelis Jardines, was growing marijuana in his house. Detective Pedraja and Detective Bartelt and his drug detection dog, Franky, went to Jardines's home. There were no cars in the driveway, and the window blinds were closed. The two detectives and Franky went onto Jardines's porch. Franky sniffed the base of the front door and sat, alerting the detectives of the smell of drugs.

Based on this investigation, the detectives obtained a search warrant to search Jardines's home. The search revealed marijuana plants. Jardines was arrested for the crime of trafficking in marijuana. At trial, Jardines made a motion to suppress the marijuana plants as evidence on the grounds that the detectives and Franky's investigation was an unreasonable search in violation of the Fourth Amendment to the U.S. Constitution. The Florida trial court and the Florida Supreme Court held that there was an unreasonable search and suppressed the evidence. The case was appealed to the U.S. Supreme Court. Was the canine investigation an unreasonable search? Is it ethical for a defendant to assert the Fourth Amendment to suppress evidence when he knows he is guilty of the crime charged? *Florida v. Jardines*, 133 S.Ct. 1409, 2013 U.S. Lexis 2542 (Supreme Court of the United States, 2013)

8.8 Ethics Case Acting on an anonymous tip that a residence was being used to sell drugs, Tucson, Arizona, police officers knocked on the front door of the residence. Rodney Gant opened the door, and the police asked to speak to the owner. Gant identified himself and stated that the owner was expected to return later. The police officers then left the residence. Later, the police conducted a records search that revealed that there was an outstanding warrant for Gant's arrest for driving with a suspended license.

When the police officers returned to the house that evening, Gant drove up in an automobile, parked in the driveway, got out of his car, and shut the door. One of the police officers called to Gant, and he walked toward the officer. When Gant was about 10 to 12 feet from the car, the officer arrested Gant, handcuffed him, and locked him in the backseat of a patrol car.

The police officers searched Gant's car and found a gun and a bag of cocaine in the passenger compartment. Gant was charged with possession of a narcotic drug for sale. At the criminal trial, Gant moved to suppress the evidence seized from the car on the ground that the warrantless search violated the Fourth Amendment. The Arizona trial court held that the search was permissible as a search incident to an arrest and admitted the evidence. The jury found Gant guilty, and he was sentenced to prison. Gant appealed to the U.S. Supreme Court. Was the search of Gant's car a reasonable search? Was it ethical for Gant to protest that the evidence was not admissible against him? *Arizona v. Gant*, 129 S.Ct. 1710, 2009 U.S. Lexis 3120 (Supreme Court of the United States, 2009)

Notes

1. Title 18 of the U.S. Code contains the federal criminal code.
2. Sentencing Reform Act of 1984, 18 U.S.C. Section 3551 et seq.
3. 532 U.S. 318, 121 S.Ct. 1536, 2001 U.S. Lexis 3366 (Supreme Court of the United States, 2001).
4. 18 U.S.C. Section 1341.
5. 18 U.S.C. Section 1343.
6. 18 U.S.C. Section 1957.
7. 18 U.S.C. Sections 1961–1968.
8. 18 U.S.C. Section 1028.
9. 18 U.S.C. Section 1030.
10. 18 U.S.C. Section 1030.
11. *United States v. Jones*, 132 S.Ct. 945, 2012 U.S. Lexis 1063 (Supreme Court of the United States, 2012).
12. *United States v. Leon*, 468 U.S. 897, 104 S.Ct. 3405, 1984 U.S. Lexis 153 (Supreme Court of the United States).
13. *Marshall v. Barlow's Inc.*, 436 U.S. 307, 98 S.Ct. 1816, 1978 U.S. Lexis 26 (Supreme Court of the United States).
14. *Bellis v. United States*, 417 U.S. 85, 94 S.Ct. 2.179, 1974 U.S. Lexis 58 (Supreme Court of the United States)
15. 384 U.S. 436, 86 S.Ct. 1602, 1966 U.S. Lexis 2817 (Supreme Court of the United States).
16. 530 U.S. 428, 120 S.Ct. 2326, 2000 U.S. Lexis 4305 (Supreme Court of the United States, 2000).
17. 409 U.S. 322, 93 S.Ct. 611, 1973 U.S. Lexis 23 (Supreme Court of the United States).
18. 18 U.S.C. Section 316(c) (1).
19. *Baldwin v. Alabama*, 472 U.S. 372, 105 S.Ct. 2727, 1985 U.S. Lexis 106 (Supreme Court of the United States).
20. *Baze v. Rees*, 128 S.Ct. 1520, 2008 U.S. Lexis 3476 (Supreme Court of the United States. 2008)
21. *Miller v. Alabama*, 132 S.Ct. 2455, 2012 U.S. Lexis 4873 (Supreme Court of the United States, 2012).

CASE *Suing GEICO*

Bush v. Elkins

3KN-10-01140 CI, 6980 January 23, 2015
Supreme Court of Alaska
Before: Fabe, Chief Justice, Winfree, Stowers, Maassen, and Bolger, Justices
Opinion by, FABE, Chief Justice

Introduction

An adult passenger in a car was injured in a single-car accident. The passenger and his family brought suit against the vehicle's unlicensed minor driver, the minor's mother, the owner of the car, the insurance policy holder, the insurer, and the insurance adjuster who handled the claims arising from the accident. The passenger's father attempted to raise a contractual interference claim, but the superior court concluded that the complaint did not state such a claim on his behalf. The superior court dismissed the father's only other claim—intentional infliction of emotional distress—removed the father's name from the case caption, and ordered the father to cease filing pleadings on behalf of other parties.

After the superior court judge dismissed him from the action, the passenger's father attempted to file a first amended complaint, which expressly stated his contractual interference claim on the theory that he was a third-party beneficiary of the contracts between his son and his son's doctors. But the superior court denied the father leave to amend the complaint because the father had already been dismissed from the case. Following a settlement among all of the other plaintiffs and defendants—a settlement in which the father did not join—the superior court granted final judgment to the insurer. The insurer moved for attorney's fees against the father under Alaska Civil Rule 82, but the father never responded to that motion. The superior court granted the award without soliciting a response from the father, and the father appeals.

We affirm the superior court's order dismissing the father's claims and denying leave to amend the complaint because the proposed first amended complaint was futile. But because the superior court had barred the father from filing any further pleadings in the case and had removed his name from the caption, the superior court had a responsibility to inform the self-represented father that he was permitted to file an opposition to the motion for attorney's fees. We thus vacate the fee award and remand to the superior court to afford the father an opportunity to respond to the insurer's motion for reasonable attorney's fees.

Facts and Proceedings

The Accident and Initial Complaint

This action arises out of a single-car accident in early July 2010. The driver was 16-year-old Bradley Luke, who was not licensed to drive in Alaska. Bradley crashed a car owned by Monte Luke, which was insured by Government Employees Insurance Company (GEICO) under a policy held by Coral Frank. Craig Elkins is the GEICO employee in Alaska who handled claims arising from the accident. Frank Bush, an adult passenger in the car, suffered severe injuries in the accident.

Frank Bush, his mother, his father, and his sister filed a civil complaint against Bradley Luke as the driver of the car and against Bradley's mother Arlene Luke; Monte Luke, the owner of the car; Coral Frank, the policy holder; GEICO, the insurer; and its employee, Elkins. The plaintiffs proceeded without representation. Frank Bush's father, James Bush, is the sole appellant in this case.

The complaint alleged seven causes of action including four claims against Bradley Luke, Arlene and Monte Luke, and Coral Frank (collectively, "the Luke defendants") for negligent driving, negligent supervision, negligent entrustment, and negligent infliction of emotional distress. The complaint also alleged three claims against GEICO and its employee Elkins for contractual interference, intentional infliction of emotional distress, and negligent supervision. On the claim of contractual interference, the complaint alleged that GEICO "improperly interfered with contractual relations betwee[n] the plaintiff(s) and various health care providers," resulting in increased physical and economic injuries to Frank Bush and "sever[e] emotional distress and anxiety" to "the plaintiff(s)." Whether this language effectively pleaded a claim for contractual interference on James's behalf is central to the subsequent proceedings before the superior court and to this appeal.

(case continues)

Procedural History: Motion to Dismiss, Motions for Summary Judgment, and Motions to Amend the Complaint

GEICO answered the complaint and moved to dismiss all claims raised against it for failure to state a claim. It admitted that the vehicle involved in the accident was insured by GEICO and argued that it could not, as a matter of law, be held directly liable for the wrongdoing of the Luke defendants. GEICO contended that the three causes of action brought against it—intentional infliction of emotional distress, negligent supervision, and contractual interference—were "really claims handling type claims" that might apply were the plaintiffs insured by GEICO but could not apply absent a contractual relationship between GEICO and Frank Bush, his parents, or his sister.

The plaintiffs responded that GEICO was misreading the three causes of action, arguing that those claims against GEICO were for torts whose viability is unaffected by the existence of a contractual relationship. The superior court granted in part and denied in part GEICO's motion to dismiss. The order specified that the "direct actions against [the Luke defendants] ... may not be brought against [GEICO] based on its role as the insurer for these individuals." But the superior court denied GEICO's motion to dismiss the claim for intentional interference with contractual relations, reasoning that the claim provided GEICO with "fair notice of the grounds on which Plaintiffs' claim rests," and it denied GEICO's motion to dismiss the negligent supervision claim, noting that it did not "fully understand the basis" of the claim and that the claim might better be addressed after it was "more fully developed." Finally, the superior court denied GEICO's motion to dismiss the intentional infliction of emotional distress claim, "except for that portion pertaining to GEICO's failure to contact James Bush" which it granted because "fail[ing] to contact Plaintiff James Bush as the family's designee ... is not outrageous and is not actionable." Thus, the superior court's ruling on GEICO's motion dismissed James's only individual claim: intentional infliction of emotional distress. The other plaintiffs—Frank Bush, his mother, and his sister—retained their first four claims against the Luke defendants, as well as their three claims against GEICO.

Before resolution of its motion to dismiss, GEICO moved for summary judgment on all remaining claims against it and its claims handler, Elkins, reiterating the arguments raised in its motion to dismiss. The Luke defendants moved for summary judgment against James because he "ha[d] not stated a claim against the defendants," requested that James's "name [be] removed from the caption," and requested "an order prohibiting him from the unauthorized practice of law," stating their view that James "should not be allowed to continue to sign any type of pleading on behalf of any of the parties or make appearances in court for the parties" once dismissed from the lawsuit.

GEICO joined the Luke defendants' motion for summary judgment against James and their motion for an order removing James from the case caption. In response to these motions, James acknowledged that he "[brought] no claim against [the Lukes]." In his response to GEICO's motions for summary judgment, James for the first time stated, with regard to the contractual interference claim, his view that he "was ... a third-party beneficiary to the contracts involved" and that he remained "a viable party" in that claim. He further argued that the motions were "insufficient as a matter of law" because "[n]owhere in any of the pleadings proffered by GEICO ... do they allege [James Bush] would not be a proper party to the action against them under a theory of intentional interference with contractual relations."

In June 2012 the superior court granted the defendants' motions for summary judgment against James. The superior court read the complaint as indicating that James had brought a single claim for intentional infliction of emotional distress against GEICO and that this claim had been rejected when the superior court granted GEICO's motion to dismiss. The superior court also concluded that "James Bush should be removed from the caption of this case and is not allowed to file pleadings on behalf of other parties, as he is not a licensed attorney in the State of Alaska."

On the same day that it granted complete summary judgment against James, the superior court granted some of the remaining plaintiffs' motions for leave to amend their complaint. Frank Bush, his parents, and his sister had each moved to amend their complaint. All four motions were identical, asking only to add a defendant and two plaintiffs to the action.[1] The Luke defendants did not oppose the motions, and the superior court granted the motions made by Frank's mother and sister, while overlooking Frank's and James's identical motions.[2]

Shortly after the superior court granted the motions for summary judgment, James filed a motion "seeking clarification and/or reconsideration upon the issue of his status as a plaintiff." He argued that the superior court's order denying GEICO's motion to dismiss as to the contractual interference claim had "ruled that all plaintiffs," including

(case continues)

James, "may have an actionable complaint against [GEICO] for interference with contractual relations," and he reiterated the position he took in his opposition to the motion for summary judgment that he was "a third party beneficiary" of Frank's attempts to contract with health care providers because he "was paying all costs associated with achieving performance of these contracts." Accordingly, James argued that the court had no authority to remove his name from the caption and that the removal would improperly interfere with James's right to appeal.

The superior court denied James's motion for clarification and reconsideration, explaining that its order granting GEICO's motion to dismiss entirely disposed of James's role in the case by dismissing his intentional infliction of emotional distress claim. The superior court ruled that "[t]he original complaint d[id] not set forth" a claim by James for contractual interference and did not allege that James "is a third party beneficiary to contracts entered by Frank Bush."

After denial of James's motion, the plaintiffs, including James, submitted a first amended complaint. Along with adding another defendant and two new plaintiffs, the amended complaint also revised the contractual interference claim to state that James "invest[ed] personal funds for the express purpose of obtaining medical care for his son," that James "invested these funds with the expressed intent ... of assisting [Frank] in contracting with various health care providers to receive treatment," that James "sought no other, no[r] did he receive any other, consideration for having provided these funds," and that "to date [James] has not received the contractual consideration he had expected when investing these funds and as a result has sustained economic loss and personal injury in the form of emotional distress."

The superior court rejected James's first amended complaint, ruling that James "can't be added back in; I've already dismissed him out." The superior court returned the amended complaint for re-filing without James as a plaintiff.

Settlements, Final Judgment, and Attorney's Fees

All of the plaintiffs and defendants, except James, reached a settlement and agreed to dismiss the action with prejudice and bear their own litigation expenses. James separately agreed to dismiss with prejudice any claims against the Luke defendants, but he did not agree to a settlement with GEICO. Having failed to reach a settlement, GEICO filed a motion for entry of final judgment against James, which the superior court granted in light of its prior orders dismissing all of James's claims.

GEICO then moved for attorney's fees from James pursuant to Alaska Civil Rule 82. GEICO stated that its actual costs were $24,700 and sought an award of $7,410.[3] James did not respond to the motion for attorney's fees. Instead, in his points on appeal filed with this court a month before the superior court's order awarding attorney's fees to GEICO, James expressed his view that the superior court erred by "removing [James's] name from the caption" while "continu[ing] to accept and rule upon pleadings offered by other parties seeking procedural decisions and judgments against [him] and not permitting him to file any sort of responsive pleadings."

GEICO filed a motion requesting a ruling on its motion for an award of attorney's fees, and the superior court awarded GEICO $3,533.68 in attorney's fees from James, noting that it had deducted fees incurred after James's claims were dismissed, and that it awarded only 20% of the actual reasonable fees, per Rule 82(b)(2), because the case did not go to trial.

Standards of Review

"We review for abuse of discretion a trial court's decisions concerning whether to inform a pro se litigant of the specific defects in a pleading and whether to provide an opportunity to remedy those defects. 'We will find an abuse of discretion if our review of the record leaves us with a definite and firm conviction that the [trial court] made a mistake[.]' "[4] Similarly, "[w]e review a superior court's denial of a motion to amend a complaint for abuse of discretion."[5] However, "[i]t is within a trial court's discretion to deny such a motion where amendment would be futile because it advances a claim or defense that is legally insufficient on its face."[6] "We consider with independent judgment whether a proposed amended complaint could survive dismissal; if we conclude that it could not, we will hold that the superior court did not abuse its discretion by denying the motion for leave to amend."[7] "We review rulings on motions for summary judgment de novo."[8] "When applying the de novo standard of review, we apply our 'independent judgment to questions of law, adopting the rule of law most persuasive in light of precedent, reason, and policy.' "[9] Finally, "[t]his court reviews an award of attorney's fees for an abuse of discretion. Under this standard, the trial court has broad discretion in awarding attorney's fees; this court will not find an abuse of discretion absent a showing that the award was arbitrary, capricious, manifestly unreasonable, or stemmed from improper motive."[10]

Discussion

On appeal, James raises arguments related to the dismissal of his claims at summary judgment and the superior court's award of attorney's fees against him.[11] We address each in turn.

(case continues)

The Superior Court's Grant of Summary Judgment and Refusal to Grant Leave to Amend the Complaint

James argues first that summary judgment was improperly granted because he had raised a contractual interference claim in the original complaint and GEICO failed to satisfy its burden to establish no genuine issue of material fact under Alaska Civil Rule 56(c).[12] Alternatively, James argues that the superior court should either have informed him of the need to amend his complaint before granting summary judgment against him or adopted the first proposed amended complaint submitted to the court after his dismissal from the case. Because James ultimately filed an amended complaint, which clearly articulated his contractual interference claim, any error regarding the superior court's interpretation of the original complaint or its failure to instruct James regarding the need to amend his complaint was cured, leaving the superior court's decision not to grant leave to amend as the only potential source of error.

In rejecting James's first amended complaint, the superior court reasoned only that it could not add James back in after it had "already dismissed him out." Ordinarily, under Alaska Civil Rule 15(a), leave to amend "shall be freely given."[13] We have elaborated on this rule, recognizing that absent an "apparent or declared reason—such as undue delay, bad faith or dilatory motive on the part of the movant, repeated failure to cure deficiencies by amendments previously allowed, undue prejudice to the opposing party by virtue of allowance of the amendment, futility of amendment, etc.—the leave sought should, as the rules require, be freely given."[14] Although the superior court did not undertake any analysis of whether leave to amend should have been freely given or whether there was basis to deny leave under Rule 15(a), we conclude that the proposed amendment to the complaint was futile and would not have survived a motion for summary judgment.[15]

Even if the proposed amended complaint had been adopted, James's contractual interference claim would have failed as a matter of law because James did not allege that he was a direct party to any of the contracts with Frank's healthcare providers, and he was not a third-party beneficiary to those contracts as a matter of law. "In determining whether a third party is an intended beneficiary of a contract, we refer to the Restatement (Second) of Contracts [§ 302]."[16] We look to the intent of the promisee, in this case Frank Bush, "to give the beneficiary the benefit of the promised performance."[17] In doing so, we look for objective manifestations of intent rather than subjective motives.[18] Applying this standard, the proposed amended complaint would not have survived summary judgment because it did not allege that Frank intended for his contracts with health care providers to benefit James. Rather, the proposed amended complaint states only that James gave money to Frank with the intent that Frank use it to obtain medical care. Moreover, the benefit of the promised performance—medical care—did not run to James. It was directed entirely to Frank, the patient undergoing treatment. Because the proposed amendment did not state a valid claim for relief, it was futile and we affirm the superior court's refusal to permit James to amend his complaint.

The Superior Court's Award of Attorney's Fees to GEICO

Following James's dismissal and GEICO's settlement with the remaining plaintiffs, GEICO sought and obtained entry of final judgment against James. GEICO then moved for attorney's fees as the prevailing party pursuant to Alaska Civil Rule 82.[19] James did not respond to the motion in superior court. Instead he filed points on appeal in this court indicating that the superior court had "not permitted him to file any sort of responsive pleadings." James's belief that he was not permitted to file responsive pleadings may have derived from a combination of factors including his dismissal from the case, the removal of his name from the case caption, and the superior court's instruction to cease filing "pleadings on behalf of other parties." Following GEICO's renewed request for a ruling on its motion for attorney's fees, and without receiving a response from James, the superior court granted an award of $3,533.68, or 20% of the reasonable fees incurred while James was still a party to the case.[20] James argues on appeal that the superior court lacked authority to remove his name from the case caption and abused its discretion in granting GEICO's motion for attorney's fees while simultaneously prohibiting him from filing a response.

We need not address the superior court's authority to amend the caption because that question relates primarily to James's argument that he was unconstitutionally denied access to the court and that he was unaware that he was allowed to file an opposition to GEICO's motion for attorney's fees. We vacate the attorney's fee award on the ground that the superior court erred by failing to inform James that he was permitted to file a response to GEICO's motion

(case continues)

despite the court's earlier direction that James not file further pleadings. Thus we do not address the superior court's unusual decision to remove James's name from the caption.

Turning to the superior court's duty to self-represented litigants, trial court judges must strike an appropriate balance between their role as a neutral and impartial decision maker[21] and their affirmative duty to advise self-represented litigants.[22] We first addressed this balancing act in *Breck v. Ulmer*, which established a duty to "inform a *pro se* litigant of the proper procedure for the action he or she is obviously attempting to accomplish."[23] Since *Breck*, we have delineated the contours of this obligation.[24] We have also acknowledged that while the rules of court "may be models of clarity to one schooled in the law, a pro se litigant might not find them so."[25] Thus while "open-ended participation by the court [that] would be difficult to contain" is outside the scope of the superior court's duty to self-represented litigants,[26] where a self-represented litigant is obviously attempting to accomplish a discrete action and his procedural failing is the result of "a lack of familiarity with the rules rather than gross neglect or lack of good faith,"[27] the superior court retains an obligation to inform that litigant of the proper procedure for that action.[28] Although the superior court has no general duty to inform a self-represented litigant of the opportunity or need to file a responsive pleading,[29] here a duty to inform James of his ability to file a response to GEICO's motion arose from the superior court's actions in removing James's name from the case caption and instructing James to cease filing pleadings on behalf of other parties once he had been dismissed and his name was no longer listed in the caption as a party to the case.

We emphasize that this holding is limited to the unique facts presented. The dismissal of James from the case, the removal of his name from the case caption, and most importantly the instruction to cease filing "pleadings on behalf of other parties" left James with the belief that he was not permitted to file responsive pleadings in the matter arising out of his son's injuries. The superior court was on notice of this misunderstanding. In his response to GEICO and the Luke defendants' motions for summary judgment James expressed his belief that the removal of his name from the case caption, and the prohibition against filing pleadings, would impermissibly curtail his access to the court system and right to an appeal. James's misunderstanding reflects "a lack of familiarity with the rules rather than gross neglect or lack of good faith."[30] Such a lack of familiarity, particularly here where James had actively engaged with the litigation process up to the point of being instructed to cease filing pleadings, required the superior court to inform James of his ability to respond to the motion for attorney's fees. This error is not harmless. Because the superior court failed to clarify that James was permitted to respond, he was not afforded an opportunity to dispute the reasonableness of the fees or the reasonableness of using the total fees incurred against all of the plaintiffs as the base for applying the Rule 82 percentage for an award against him, or to argue for a downward deviation from the default 20% fee award at the discretion of the superior court under Civil Rule 82(b)(3).[31] To grant an award without notice of the opportunity to respond to the motion for attorney's fees requires that we vacate the superior court's order granting an award of attorney's fees to GEICO and remand to provide James leave to file a response to GEICO's attorney's fees motion.

Conclusion

We AFFIRM the grant of summary judgment and AFFIRM the superior court's order denying leave to amend because the proposed amendment to the complaint was futile. We VACATE the fee award and REMAND to the superior court to afford James Bush an opportunity to respond to the insurer's motion for reasonable attorney's fees.

1. James contends that he sought leave to amend "to add additional parties and to solidify his third-party beneficiary claim." The record on appeal does not support this assertion. He sought leave to amend only to add additional parties.
2. James contends that the superior court "granted his motion seeking leave to amend the complaint." Once again, the record on appeal does not support this assertion.
3. GEICO argued that it was the prevailing party and therefore was entitled to 30% of reasonable actual fees, despite the fact that the case did not go to trial.
4. *Genaro v. Municipality of Anchorage*, 76 P.3d 844, 845 (Alaska 2003) (alteration in original) (quoting *Hughes v. Bobich*, 875 P.2d 749, 755 (Alaska 1994)).
5. *Krause v. Matanuska-Susitna Borough*, 229 P.3d 168, 174 (Alaska 2010).
6. *Id.* (internal quotation marks omitted).
7. *Id.* at 177.
8. *ConocoPhillips Alaska, Inc. v. Williams Alaska Petroleum, Inc.*, 322 P.3d 114, 122 (Alaska 2014) (citing *Witt v. State, Dep't of Corr.*, 75 P.3d 1030,1033 (Alaska 2003)).
9. *Id.* (quoting *Russell ex rel. J.N. v. Virg-In*, 258 P.3d 795, 802 (Alaska 2011)).
10. *Id.* at 137 (quoting *Ware v. Ware*, 161 P.3d 1188, 1192 (Alaska 2007)) (internal quotation marks omitted).
11. James raised an additional argument in his points on appeal related to a discovery dispute with GEICO. But James did not

(case continues)

discuss the issue in his brief on appeal. Therefore the issue is forfeited despite GEICO's briefing on the issue and James's response in his reply brief. *See Lyman v. State*, 824 P.2d 703, 706 (Alaska 1992) ("Generally, points on appeal not briefed are considered abandoned.").

12. Civil Rule 56(c) provides in part that "[t]here must ... be served and filed with each motion a memorandum showing that there is no genuine issue as to any material fact and that the moving party is entitled to judgment as a matter of law."
13. Alaska R. Civ. P. 15(a).
14. *Miller v. Safeway, Inc.*, 102 P.3d 282, 294 (Alaska 2004) (quoting *Betz v. Chena Hot Springs Group*, 742 P.2d 1346, 1348 (Alaska 1987)) (internal quotation marks omitted).
15. *See Krause v. Matanuska-Susitna Borough*, 229 P.3d 168, 177 (Alaska 2010) ("We consider with independent judgment whether a proposed amended complaint could survive dismissal; if we conclude that it could not, we will hold that the superior court did not abuse its discretion by denying the motion for leave to amend.").
16. *Rathke v. Corr. Corp. of Am., Inc.*, 153 P.3d 303, 310 (Alaska 2007). The Restatement (Second) of Contracts § 302 provides:
    (1) Unless otherwise agreed between promisor and promisee, a beneficiary of a promise is an intended beneficiary if recognition of a right to performance in the beneficiary is appropriate to effectuate the intention of the parties and either
        (a) the performance of the promise will satisfy an obligation of the promisee to pay money to the beneficiary; or
        (b) the circumstances indicate that the promisee intends to give the beneficiary the benefit of the promised performance.
17. Restatement (Second) of Contracts § 302(1)(b) (1979).
18. *Rathke*, 153 P.3d at 310.
19. Alaska R. Civ. P. 82(a) ("[T]he prevailing party in a civil case shall be awarded attorney's fees calculated under this rule.").
20. *Id.* 82(b)(2) ("In cases in which the prevailing party recovers no money judgment, the court shall ... award the prevailing party in a case resolved without trial 20 percent of its actual attorney's fees which were necessarily incurred.").
21. *See Bauman v. State, Div. of Family & Youth Servs.*, 768 P.2d 1097, 1099 (Alaska 1989) ("To require a judge to instruct a pro se litigant as to each step in litigating a claim would compromise the court's impartiality in deciding the case by forcing the judge to act as an advocate for one side.").
22. *See Breck v. Ulmer*, 745 P.2d 66, 74 (Alaska 1987).
23. *Id.*
24. For instance, "the trial court ha[s] no obligation to be lenient with a pro se litigant who ha[s] made 'no effort to cooperate with the trial court or to request assistance in complying with its orders.' " *Genaro v. Municipality of Anchorage*, 76 P.3d 844, 846 (Alaska 2003) (quoting *Coffland v. Coffland*, 4 P.3d 317, 321 (Alaska 2000)).
25. *Collins v. Arctic Builders*, 957 P.2d 980, 982 (Alaska 1998).
26. *Bauman*, 768 P.2d at 1099. We have also noted that open-ended participation by the court would tax limited judicial resources and impair judicial efficiency. *See Greenway v. Heathcott*, 294 P.3d 1056, 1072 (Alaska 2013).
27. *Wagner v. Wagner*, 299 P.3d 170, 174 (Alaska 2013) (quoting *Kaiser v. Sakata*, 40 P.3d 800, 803 (Alaska 2002)) (internal quotation marks omitted).
28. *See Breck*, 745 P.2d at 74.
29. *See Capolicchio v. Levy*, 194 P.3d 373, 379 (Alaska 2008) (declining to require a trial court judge to inform a pro se litigant of the need to file an opposition to a motion for summary judgment).
30. *Wagner*, 299 P.3d at 174 (quoting *Kaiser*, 40 P.3d at 803) (internal quotation marks omitted).
31. Civil Rule 82(b)(3) provides discretion to the superior court to deviate downward from the 20% default award based on factors such as "the extent to which a given fee award may be so onerous to the non-prevailing party that it would deter similarly situated litigants from the voluntary use of the courts," "the extent to which the fees incurred by the prevailing party suggest that they had been influenced by considerations apart from the case at bar," and "other equitable factors deemed relevant."

CASE *The "Two Moose"*

Christensen v. Alaska Sales & Service, INC.

3AN-10-07948 CI, 6959 October 10, 2014
Supreme Court of Alaska
Before: Fabe, Chief Justice, Winfree, Stowers, Maassen, and Bolger, Justices
Opinion by, WINFREE, Justice

Introduction

Four years after a couple purchased a new car, it collided with two moose on the Parks Highway. The couple sued the car dealership for product liability, alleging that the car's seat belt failed to restrain the driver in the accident. The superior court granted summary judgment to the dealership, concluding that "no reasonable jury could find that the Plaintiffs have proven that the seat belt...was defective." The couple appeals, arguing that the superior court applied an incorrect summary judgment standard and that genuine issues of material fact made summary judgment inappropriate. Because we conclude that the couple has raised genuine issues of material

(case continues)

fact regarding a seat belt defect and causation of the driver's injury, we reverse the superior court's grant of summary judgment.

Facts and Proceedings

Facts

In spring 2004 Ramona Christensen and Jack Scott purchased a new 2004 Buick from Alaska Sales & Service, Inc. In June 2008 Christensen was driving the Buick on the Parks Highway when she collided with two moose. Other than Christensen, there were no witnesses to the accident. Photographs taken after the accident show damage to the Buick's front driver's side.

After the collision Christensen called the police to report the accident and called Scott to come pick her up at the scene. When Scott arrived Christensen said she felt nauseated, and Scott noticed a red mark on her forehead. Christensen could not remember many details of the collision, including whether she hit her head on something inside the car.

During the days following the accident, Christensen reported feeling lightheaded and dizzy. Christensen's speech became disfluent and broken, and her gait became unsteady, causing her to fall repeatedly. About one week after the accident, Christensen sought medical attention to address her worsening symptoms. A neurologist examined Christensen and ordered an MRI spectroscopy. The spectroscopy showed evidence of bilateral frontal lobe brain damage. Since 2008 numerous other physicians and psychiatrists have examined and treated Christensen for her continuing speech, short-term memory, and mobility problems.

Shortly after the accident Scott took the Buick to a repair shop. Scott suspected that Christensen's seat belt failed to work properly during the crash. Prior to the accident Scott had noticed that the seat belts in the Buick seemed different than what he was accustomed to—the Buick's seat belts sometimes had not retracted on their own or locked when suddenly pulled forward. When Scott asked the repair shop to repair the driver's seat belt, the repair shop responded that both the driver's and passenger's seat belts were not working properly. The repair shop contacted Alaska Sales & Service, but it refused to pay for seat belt replacements. Scott's insurance company agreed to pay for the replacements, and the repair shop replaced both seat belts. The original seat belts were not returned to Scott.

Proceedings

In 2010 Christensen and Scott filed suit against Alaska Sales & Service, claiming that the Buick's seat belt failed to work properly during the crash. After receiving answers to interrogatories, taking depositions of Christensen and Scott, and obtaining an expert affidavit, Alaska Sales & Service filed a motion for summary judgment. Alaska Sales & Service argued that Christensen and Scott had not presented enough evidence that the Buick's seat belt was defective or that a seat belt failure caused Christensen's injuries. The superior court granted summary judgment to Alaska Sales & Service. Christensen and Scott filed a motion to reconsider; the superior court denied reconsideration and set out its reasons for granting summary judgment to Alaska Sales & Service. The court described the evidence presented, including the absence of the original seat belts, and concluded that "no reasonable jury could find that [Christensen and Scott] have proven that the seat belt . . . was defective."

Christensen and Scott appeal.

Standard of Review

We review grants of summary judgment de novo.[1]

Discussion

The Summary Judgment Standard in Alaska

The superior court dismissed Christensen and Scott's case on the ground that "no reasonable jury could find that [Christensen and Scott] have proven that the seat belt ... was defective." Christensen and Scott argue that to survive the motion for summary judgment, they only had to show they could present admissible evidence to raise a genuine issue of material fact for trial. Alaska Sales & Service responds that the correct summary judgment test is whether "even if everything [Christensen and Scott] said was true . . . a reasonable jury ... *could* find in their favor," and that the superior court actually meant and used this standard. (Emphasis in original.) Christensen and Scott are more correct: a non-moving party does not need to *prove* anything to defeat summary judgment. But a non-moving party cannot create a genuine issue of material fact merely by offering admissible evidence—the offered evidence must not be too conclusory, too speculative, or too incredible to be believed, and it must directly contradict the moving party's evidence. We take this opportunity to clarify and reaffirm Alaska's longstanding summary judgment standard.

Alaska Civil Rule 56 provides for judgment to be granted to a party where "there is no genuine issue as to any material fact" and "the moving party is entitled to judgment as a matter of law."[2] One of our earliest cases involving Rule 56 illustrated the meaning of "genuine issue" by affirming a grant of summary judgment against a party who had pointed to no

(case continues)

evidence supporting his position. *Gilbertson v. City of Fairbanks* involved a dispute over unpaid utility bills between the city-owned utility and a hotel owner whose hotel had been destroyed in a fire.[3] The city filed a motion for summary judgment, submitting an affidavit from the city comptroller detailing the hotel owner's unpaid heat, electric, water, and telephone bills.[4] The hotel owner responded by submitting his deposition testimony: " 'I am sure my bills w[ere] paid as my cancelled checks show .... [S]o far as I know. I could have lost some checks in the fire.' "[5] The superior court granted summary judgment to the city.[6]

We affirmed the superior court's decision because the hotel owner had not pointed to any evidence actually disputing the city comptroller's testimony.[7] We noted the hotel owner's assertion that he " 'could have lost some checks in the fire' " was contradicted by the physical evidence: "All of the checks produced ... plainly indicated that his utility bills were not fully paid.... From the cancelled checks produced for every month preceding the fire, and including the month of the fire, the fair inference was that no checks were lost."[8] And during his deposition, when the city's lawyer asked the hotel owner whether an audit of his checks would show an unpaid utility bill balance, the hotel owner refused to answer.[9] That question "went to the very heart of the issue—where an unequivocal straightforward answer might well have raised an issue of fact."[10] The city had met its summary judgment burden of putting forth evidence showing the lack of genuine issues of material fact, and the hotel owner had failed to "clearly stat[e] his defense of payment and [show] the court how he planned to support that defense with facts which would be admissible in evidence at the trial."[11] We affirmed the grant of summary judgment on the ground that no genuine issue of material fact remained for trial.[12]

Gilbertson exemplifies the summary judgment standard we consistently have followed. "[A] party seeking summary judgment has the initial burden of proving, through admissible evidence, that there are no [genuine] disputed issues of material fact and that the moving party is entitled to judgment as a matter of law."[13] Once the moving party has made that showing, the burden shifts to the non-moving party "to set forth specific facts showing that he could produce evidence reasonably tending to dispute or contradict the movant's evidence and thus demonstrate that a material issue of fact exists."[14]

In *Gilbertson* we observed that Alaska Civil Rule 56 mirrors Federal Rule of Civil Procedure 56,[15] and for the first 29 years of statehood we followed the federal courts' approach to summary judgment.[16] Then in 1986 the U.S. Supreme Court announced a new interpretation of the federal summary judgment standard,[17] incorporating the substantive evidentiary burdens applicable at trial into the summary judgment determination.[18]

In *Anderson v. Liberty Lobby, Inc.* a citizens group filed libel claims against a magazine and its publisher for portraying the group's members as racists.[19] The magazine moved for summary judgment in federal district court, submitting a reporter's affidavit stating that he believed the information published about the group was true.[20] If accepted as true, the reporter's statement would have negated an essential element of the group's libel claim.[21] The group responded with allegations that the reporter had relied on clearly unbelievable sources—allegations the group claimed disputed the reporter's statement of belief that the information was true.[22] The group argued that it had raised a genuine issue of material fact, but the federal district court disagreed and granted summary judgment to the magazine.[23]

The U.S. Supreme Court's analysis began with a discussion of summary judgment standards and the appropriate weight to give conflicting evidentiary claims.[24] The Court clarified the meaning of Federal Rule 56 "genuine issues" of material fact, defining a "genuine" issue as one from which a "reasonable jury could return a verdict for the nonmoving party."[25] By defining "genuine issues" in terms of a jury outcome, the Court incorporated the substantive evidentiary burdens on the parties at the summary judgment stage: "[T]here is no issue for trial unless there is sufficient evidence favoring the nonmoving party for a jury to return a verdict for that party."[26] "Sufficient" evidence requires more than "a scintilla of evidence" supporting the non-moving party's position.[27]

The *Liberty Lobby* Court equated summary judgment with the existing standard for deciding directed verdict motions under Federal Rule 50.[28] The Court explained that "the inquiry involved in a ruling on a motion for summary judgment or for a directed verdict necessarily implicates the substantive evidentiary standard of proof that would apply at the trial on the merits."[29] Thus, both federal summary judgment and directed verdict standards required federal courts to inquire "whether the evidence presents a sufficient disagreement to require submission to a jury or whether it is so one-sided that one party must prevail as a matter of law."[30]

In *Moffatt v. Brown* we considered whether to follow *Liberty Lobby*'s new approach to summary judgment, but ultimately rejected it.[31] In that case, a physician sued a newsletter publisher for defamation related to allegedly false statements about the physician's abortion procedures.[32] The publisher moved for

(case continues)

summary judgment, arguing that the superior court should apply the *Liberty Lobby* test for summary judgment and determine there was not sufficient evidence to raise a genuine issue of material fact because no reasonable jury would find for the physician.[33] The superior court denied the publisher's motion.[34]

We affirmed the denial of summary judgment, concluding that Alaska Civil Rule 56 does not require a trial court to apply substantive evidentiary standards.[35] We rejected *Liberty Lobby*'s summary judgment reformulation and declined "to incorporate the applicable substantive evidentiary standard into this state's summary judgment practice."[36] Summary judgment does not require the non-moving party to prove factual issues according to the applicable evidentiary standard, and does not allow trial judges to predict how a reasonable jury would decide the case—we explained that weighing and evaluating evidence "'intrudes into the province of the jury.'"[37]

Since *Moffatt* we consistently have interpreted Rule 56 to require only "'a showing that a genuine issue of material fact exists to be litigated, and not a showing that a party will ultimately prevail'" at trial.[38] There are two important aspects to this requirement. First, a material fact is one upon which resolution of an issue turns.[39] Second, because the existence of a dispute over a material fact is a question of law,[40] the determination is objectively based and employs a reasonableness standard.[41] Although we occasionally have described the reasonableness standard as whether "reasonable jurors could disagree on the resolution of a factual issue,"[42] our perhaps inartful use of the term "reasonable jurors" was not meant to suggest use of the federal summary judgment standard. We require only that the evidence proposed for trial must not be based entirely on "unsupported assumptions and speculation"[43] and must not be "too incredible to be believed by reasonable minds."[44] After the court makes reasonable inferences from the evidence in favor of the non-moving party,[45] summary judgment is appropriate only when no reasonable person could discern a genuine factual dispute on a material issue.[46]

Alaska's summary judgment standard does not allow trial courts, on the limited evidence presented at the summary judgment stage, to make trial-like credibility determinations, conduct trial-like evidence weighing,[47] or decide whether a non-moving party has proved its case. Although a trial court initially must determine whether the evidence could be believed by a reasonable person, that decision is not based on whether the court actually believes the evidence or whether it believes the moving party has better evidence.[48] The trier of fact ultimately may find against the non-moving party after evaluating credibility and applying the substantive evidentiary standards of proof at trial. But the only questions to be answered at the summary judgment stage are whether a reasonable person could believe the non-moving party's assertions and whether a reasonable person could conclude those assertions create a genuine dispute as to a material fact.[49]

We reiterate that ours is a "lenient standard for withstanding summary judgment."[50] The low standard for surviving summary judgment serves the important function of preserving the right to have factual questions resolved by a trier of fact only after following the procedures of a trial. Alaska's traditional standard for summary judgment is more protective of this right than the federal standard.[51] We see no reason to deviate from our long-established summary judgment standard today.

Genuine Issues of Material Fact Precluded Summary Judgment

To prevail on their design-defect claim of strict liability, Christensen and Scott ultimately must prove at trial that the Buick's seat belt was defective and that the defect caused Christensen some compensable injury.[52] The superior court granted summary judgment on the issue of defect, but Alaska Sales & Service also argues that there is no evidence for causation, presumably as an alternative ground for upholding summary judgment. Construing all of the evidence in the light most favorable to Christensen and Scott and making all reasonable factual inferences in their favor, we conclude that there are genuine issues of material fact with respect to both the seat belt defect and causation.

Evidence exists reasonably suggesting a defect in the seat belt

Christensen and Scott presented evidence that is not too incredible to be believed and, taking all reasonable inferences in their favor, raises a discernible dispute whether the driver's seat belt was defective at the time of the accident. Christensen and Scott produced evidence indicating an unbroken chain of custody of the Buick and that the seat belts as originally sold had not been altered in any way. Scott stated that before the accident he tested the seat belts by quickly pulling them forward and that sometimes the mechanism would not lock or retract the belts. After the accident the seat belts were replaced but, according to Scott, the new seat belts failed in the same manner as the previous belts. Scott testified that the new seat belts would also sometimes not lock in place following a sudden forward movement. This evidence

(case continues)

supports the inference that the driver's seat belt may not have worked as intended in the accident.

Christensen said she always wears her seat belt and was wearing it at the time of the accident. Christensen also said that after hitting the moose she was not pinned against her seat and that she had no bruising or marks on her body other than a red mark on her forehead. The absence of bruising from the seat belt supports an inference that it did not restrain Christensen during the collision, and the forehead marking supports the inference that her body went forward far enough to contact something in the car; both support the inference that the seat belt may not have restrained her as intended.

Alaska Sales & Service points to the lack of specific pieces of evidence in the record supporting a seat belt defect. According to Alaska Sales & Service, summary judgment was warranted because Christensen and Scott could not produce the seat belts in question, a description of the seat belt's performance during the crash, evidence of occupant contact marks within the vehicle, or any police report describing the collision. Although these evidentiary gaps may play a role in the resolution of the case at trial, the evidence in the record and reasonable inferences drawn from the evidence raise a genuine issue of material fact as to the seat belt defect.

Evidence exists reasonably suggesting Christensen's injury was caused by the seat belt defect

Christensen and Scott also produced evidence that is not too incredible to be believed and, taking all reasonable inferences in their favor, raises a discernible dispute whether the allegedly defective seat belt caused her injury. Christensen and Scott said that after the accident Christensen had a mark on her forehead. Christensen said she could not remember some of the events immediately before, during, or after the collision. Christensen's ongoing post-accident symptoms include dizziness, impaired speech, and difficulty walking.

Christensen and Scott presented evidence from medical specialists diagnosing a "closed head injury" and "bilateral frontal damage" to her brain. A neurologist noted that Christensen's symptoms "started after the accident," and although none of the treating physicians could yet conclude with certainty that the accident caused Christensen's brain injury, the neurologist stated that "there is no other explanation."

Alaska Sales & Service argues that Christensen and Scott cannot establish causation without an expert who can examine the seat belt and link Christensen's brain injury to the seat belt defect. But the evidence and reasonable inferences that can be drawn from it support Christensen and Scott's allegation that Christensen suffered a head injury. The mark on Christensen's head and her memory loss support an inference that she hit her head during the accident hard enough to lose consciousness. Christensen's and Scott's testimony about symptom onset, along with the neurologist's statements describing Christensen's symptoms as beginning after the accident and noting "there is no other explanation," support an inference that her symptoms resulted from the accident.[53]

Summary judgment was inappropriate

Christensen and Scott raised genuine issues of material fact with respect to both seat belt defect and causation. The evidence they presented goes well beyond assumption and speculation, is not too incredible to be believed, and relates directly to the material issues in the case. Taking all reasonable inferences from that evidence in their favor, genuine factual disputes as to defect and causation are reasonably discernable. Whether Christensen and Scott ultimately will prevail at trial under the appropriate evidentiary standard is irrelevant—at the summary judgment stage courts do not weigh evidence or predict how a jury will decide the case. Christensen and Scott were not required to "prove" their case; rather, they were required to and did demonstrate the existence of genuine issues of material fact to be litigated at trial. Thus, it was error to grant summary judgment.

Conclusion

We REVERSE the superior court's grant of summary judgment to Alaska Sales & Service and REMAND for further proceedings.

---

1. *Hurn v. Greenway*, 293 P.3d 480, 483 (Alaska 2013) (citing *State, Dep't of Health & Soc. Servs., Div. of Family & Youth Servs. v. Sandsness*, 72 P.3d 299, 301 (Alaska 2003)).
2. Alaska R. Civ. P. 56(c).
3. 368 P.2d 214, 214–15 (Alaska 1962).
4. *Id.*
5. *Id.* at 215.
6. *Id.* at 214.
7. *Id.* at 216–17.
8. *Id.* at 215–16.
9. *Id.* at 216.
10. *Id.*
11. *Id.* at 216–17.
12. *Id.*

(case continues)

13. *Mitchell v. Teck Cominco Alaska Inc.*, 193 P.3d 751, 760 n.25 (Alaska 2008); *see also Alakayak v. B.C. Packers, Ltd.*, 48 P.3d 432, 447–48 (Alaska 2002) ("The movant bears the initial burden of proving through admissible evidence (1) the absence of genuine fact disputes, and (2) its entitlement to judgment as a matter of law." (citing *Philbin v. Matanuska-Susitna Borough*, 991 P.2d 1263, 1265 (Alaska 1999))); *Shade v. Co & Anglo Alaska Serv. Corp.*, 901 P.2d 434, 437 (Alaska 1995) ("[I]t is the moving party that bears the initial burden of proving, through admissible evidence, the absence of genuine factual disputes and its entitlement to judgment."); *Gilbertson*, 368 P.2d at 216.
14. *State, Dep't of Highways v. Green*, 586 P.2d 595, 606 n.32 (Alaska 1978); *see also Gilbertson*, 368 P.2d at 216–17.
15. 368 P.2d at 214 ("The rules are identical in every aspect with which we are here concerned.").
16. *See Moffatt v. Brown*, 751 P.2d 939, 943–44 (Alaska 1988) (rejecting new federal summary judgment standard); *Bentley Family Trust, Bank of Cal. v. Lynx Enters., Inc.*, 658 P.2d 761,765 n.11 (Alaska 1983) (citing federal summary judgment decisions); *Palzer v. Serv-U-Meat Co.*, 419 P.2d 201, 205 (Alaska 1966) (following federal summary judgment approach).
17. *See Anderson v. Liberty Lobby, Inc.*, 477 U.S. 242, 251 (1986).
18. *Id.*; *see also* Samuel Issacharoff & George Loewenstein, *Second Thoughts About Summary Judgment*, 100 YALE L.J. 73, 85 (1990).
19. 477 U.S. at 244–45.
20. *Id.* at 245.
21. *See id.* at 244 (noting the requirement for actual malice in libel claims).
22. *Id.* at 246.
23. *Id.*
24. *Id.* at 247–52.
25. *Id.* at 248.
26. *Id.* at 249.
27. *Id.* at 252 ("The mere existence of a scintilla of evidence in support of the plaintiff's position will be insufficient; there must be evidence on which the jury could reasonably find for the plaintiff.").
28. *Id.* at 250–51; *see* Fed. R. Civ. P. 50(a)(1) ("If a party has been fully heard on an issue during a jury trial and the court finds that a reasonable jury would not have a legally sufficient evidentiary basis to find for the party on that issue, the court may ... (B) grant a motion for judgment as a matter of law against the party ....").
29. *Liberty Lobby*, 477 U.S. at 252; *see also id.* at 249 ("[T]here is no issue for trial unless there is sufficient evidence favoring the nonmoving party for a jury to return a verdict for that party.").
30. *Id.* at 251–52 ("The 'primary difference between the two motions is procedural .... In essence, though, the inquiry under each is the same ....' " (quoting *Bill Johnson's Rests., Inc. v. Nat'l Labor Relations Bd.*, 461 U.S. 731, 745 n.11 (1983))).
31. 751 P.2d 939, 942–43 (Alaska 1988).
32. *Id.* at 940.
33. *Id.* at 940–41.
34. *Id.* at 941.
35. *Id.* at 943.
36. *Id.*
37. *Id.* at 944 (quoting *Dairy Stores, Inc. v. Sentinel Publ'g Co.*, 516 A.2d 220, 235–36 (N.J. 1986)).
38. *E.g., Lockwood v. Geico Gen. Ins. Co.*, 323 P.3d 691, 697 (Alaska 2014) (quoting *Moffatt*, 751 P.2d at 943–44); *DeNardo v. Bax*, 147 P.3d 672, 684 (Alaska 2006).
39. *Sonneman v. State*, 969 P.2d 632, 635 (Alaska 1998) ("A factual issue will not be considered material if, even assuming the factual situation to be as the non-moving party contends, he or she would still not have a factual basis for a claim for relief against the moving party." (citing *Whaley v. State*, 438 P.2d 718, 720 (Alaska 1968))).
40. *ConocoPhillips Alaska, Inc. v. Williams Alaska Petroleum, Inc.*, 322 P.3d 114, 122 (Alaska 2014) ("Whether the evidence presented a genuine issue of material fact is a question of law that we independently review." (quoting *Kalenka v. Jadon, Inc.*, 305 P.3d 346, 349 (Alaska 2013)) (internal quotation marks omitted)).
41. *See Yurioff v. Am. Honda Motor Co.*, 803 P.2d 386, 389 (Alaska 1990) ("To prevent summary judgment, [the non-movant] was required to rebut this prima facie showing with evidence 'reasonably tending to dispute or contradict' [the movant's] evidence." (quoting *State, Dep't of Highways v. Green*, 586 P.2d 596, 606 n.32 (Alaska 1978))); *Semlek v. Nat'l Bank of Alaska*, 458 P.2d 1003, 1007 (Alaska 1969) ("[I]t was incumbent upon the appellants to set forth facts showing that they could produce admissible evidence which reasonably would tend to dispute the appellees' evidence and demonstrate that a triable issue existed."); *Isler v. Jensen*, 382 P.2d 901, 902 (Alaska 1963) ("[T]o prevent the entry of a summary judgment, [non-movants must] set forth facts showing that they could produce admissible evidence which reasonably would tend to dispute or contradict [movants'] evidence ....").
42. *E.g., Kalenka*, 305 P.3d at 349 (quoting *Burnett v. Covell*, 191 P.3d 985, 990 (Alaska 2008)) (internal quotation marks omitted); *McGee Steel Co. v. State ex rel. McDonald Indus. Alaska, Inc.*, 723 P.2d 611, 614 (Alaska 1986); *accord Green v. N. Publ'g Co.*, 655 P.2d 736, 743 (Alaska 1982).
43. *Peterson v. State, Dep't of Natural Res.*, 236 P.3d 355, 367 (Alaska 2010) (quoting *Perkins v. Doyon Universal Servs., LLC*, 151 P.3d 413, 416 (Alaska 2006)) (internal quotation marks omitted); *Mahan v. Arctic Catering, Inc.*, 133 P.3d 655, 661 (Alaska 2006) (quoting *French v. Jadon, Inc.*, 911 P.2d 20, 25 (Alaska 1996)) (internal quotation marks omitted).
44. *Wilson v. Pollet*, 416 P.2d 381, 384 (Alaska 1966).
45. *Lockwood v. Geico Gen. Ins. Co.*, 323 P.3d 691, 696 (Alaska 2014) (quoting *Lum v. Koles*, 314 P.3d 546, 552 (Alaska 2013)). An inference is a "conclusion reached by considering other facts and deducing a logical consequence from them." BLACK'S LAW DICTIONARY 897 (10th ed. 2014).
46. *See supra* note 41.
47. *Kelly v. Municipality of Anchorage*, 270 P.3d 801, 804 (Alaska 2012) ("Courts do not weigh evidence or witness credibility on summary judgment."); *accord Gudenau & Co. v. Sweeney Ins., Inc.*, 736 P.2d 763, 765 (Alaska 1987).

    In *Braund, Inc. v. White* we recognized the complexity of the court's task in evaluating evidence at the summary judgment stage: "The most difficult determinations lie in the area of credibility. The question of when summary judgment should be denied because of credibility is difficult to determine." 486 P.2d 50, 53 n.3 (Alaska 1971). But evidence or assertions should be rejected based on credibility only when it is "too incredible to be believed by reasonable minds." *Wilson*, 416 P.2d at 384.
48. *See Wilson*, 416 P.2d at 384 ("The court is not to resolve any existing genuine issues as to material facts in determining a summary judgment motion.").

(case continues)

49. *Cf. Sharp v. Fairbanks N. Star Borough*, 569 P.2d 178, 183–84 (Alaska 1977) ("Although the issue of 'proximate cause' is normally left for the trier of fact where unresolved fact questions remain, it becomes a question of law where the evidence is such that reasonable minds cannot differ." (footnote omitted)); *Otis Elevator Co. v. McLaney*, 406 P.2d 7, 9–10 (Alaska 1965) ("Review of the record convinces us that a jury question was presented as to the issues ... because fair-minded jurors could differ as to the conclusions of fact that might be drawn from the evidence which was presented as to these questions.").

We reiterate that our summary judgment standard is not the same as the standard for deciding post-trial motions for directed verdict. *Compare* Alaska R. Civ. P. 56(c), *with* Alaska R. Civ. P. 50(a). *See Murray E. Gildersleeve Logging Co. v. N. Timber Corp.*, 670 P.2d 372, 377 (Alaska 1983) ("[A] directed verdict will be granted when reasonable jurors could not differ in their resolution of a disputed issue of fact."). To the extent that we have equated the summary judgment and directed verdict standards, *see, e.g., Cameron v. Chang-Craft*, 251 P.3d 1008, 1017 & n.16 (Alaska 2011); *Braund, Inc.*, 486 P.2d at 53, we disavow those misleading statements.

50. *Shaffer v. Bellows*, 260 P.3d 1064, 1069 (Alaska 2011) (citing *Estate of Milos v. Quality Asphalt Paving, Inc.*, 145 P.3d 533, 537 (Alaska 2006)); *see also Hammond v. State, Dep't of Transp. & Pub. Facilities*, 107 P.3d 871, 881 (Alaska 2005) ("It is well established that 'the evidentiary threshold necessary to preclude an entry of summary judgment is low.' " (quoting *John's Heating Serv. v. Lamb*, 46 P.3d 1024, 1032 (Alaska 2002))).

51. *See DeNardo v. Bax*, 147 P.3d 672, 683–84 (Alaska 2006) ("The standard for granting and upholding summary judgments in Alaska is therefore more rigorous than the federal standard."); *Moffatt v. Brown*, 751 P.2d 939, 944 (Alaska 1988) (recognizing that the federal summary judgment standard "inevitably implicates a weighing of the evidence, an exercise that intrudes into the province of the jury" (quoting *Dairy Stores, Inc. v. Sentinel Publ'g Co.*, 516 A.2d 220, 236 (N.J. 1986))); *cf. Anderson v. Liberty Lobby, Inc.*, 477 U.S. 242, 266 (1986) (Brennan, J., dissenting) ("[T]he Court's opinion is also full of language which could surely be understood as an invitation—if not an instruction—to trial courts to assess and weigh evidence much as a juror would ....").

52. *See Dura Corp. v. Harned*, 703 P.2d 396, 405–06 (Alaska 1985), *superseded on other grounds by statute*, Tort Reform Act, ch. 139, § 1, SLA 1986.

53. *See Thompson v. Cooper*, 290 P.3d 393, 399–400 (Alaska 2012) (acknowledging that causation could be inferred from symptoms beginning after an accident); *John's Heating Serv.*, 46 P.3d at 1036 (noting "temporal relationship between the symptoms" and alleged source of injury bolsters credibility of expert's causation testimony).

CASE *Convict of Just One Offense*

Moreno v. Alaska

2BA-09-00239 CR, 6982 January 30, 2015
Supreme Court of Alaska
Before: Fabe, Chief Justice, Winfree, Stowers, and Maassen, Justices
Opinion by, STOWERS, Justice

Introduction

"Trial errors to which the parties did not object are reviewed for plain error."[1] In *Adams v. State* we held that plain error is "an error that (1) was not the result of intelligent waiver or a tactical decision not to object; (2) was obvious; (3) affected substantial rights; and (4) was prejudicial."[2] These consolidated cases require us to clarify the standard for determining when a defendant intelligently waived an objection or made a tactical decision not to object.

Defendants in two criminal cases failed to object to errors at trial: in *Moreno v. State*, the admission of improper testimony regarding Jorge Moreno's exercise of his right to be free from compelled self-incrimination;[3] in *Hicks v. State*, the lack of a jury unanimity instruction when the prosecutor directed the jury that it could find Mary Hicks guilty of either of two episodes of allegedly driving under the influence of alcohol. [4] Moreno and Hicks each sought plain error review, and in each case the court of appeals held that the defendant failed to show that the error was not the result of defense counsel's tactical decision not to object.[5] In *Moreno*, the court of appeals also applied a presumption that where the record is silent or ambiguous, defense counsel's inaction is tactical and precludes plain error review.[6]

Moreno and Hicks filed petitions for hearing before this court, arguing that the burden of proof should be on the State to show that their counsels' failures to object were the result of tactical decisions. They also contended that the court of appeals erroneously speculated on the purported tactical benefits they received due to their attorneys' lack of objections. Finally, they each requested an evidentiary hearing to develop the record on this issue.

(case continues)

We granted review to determine whether to apply an evidentiary presumption or to place a burden of proof on a party to establish that a defendant's lack of objection at trial was or was not the result of defense counsel's intelligent waiver or tactical decision not to object.[7] But we conclude that our case law compels neither result. Today we hold that defense counsel's tactical reason for failing to object, or counsel's intelligent waiver of an objection, should be plainly obvious from the record before foreclosing the reviewing court's consideration of the remaining plain error elements. We therefore reverse the court of appeals' decisions on this issue. But we conclude that Moreno suffered no prejudice despite the error in his case, and we affirm the court of appeals' decision upholding Moreno's conviction on this alternate ground. We remand Hicks's case to the court of appeals for further proceedings consistent with this opinion.

Facts and Proceedings

Moreno v. State

Jorge Moreno was charged with possession and delivery of methamphetamine and illegal sale of alcohol in a local option community.[8] At trial, Moreno's attorney asked the investigating officer whether the police had been able to verify that Moreno owned a jacket that contained a methamphetamine pipe.[9] The officer replied that Moreno had refused to speak to the police.[10] Moreno's attorney did not object to the officer's statement; instead, the attorney interrupted the officer and directed the officer to reply "[y]es or no."[11] Moreno was convicted, and he appealed arguing that the officer's reference to his silence was impermissible.[12]

The court of appeals concluded that Moreno's attorney's question elicited the officer's testimony and that counsel "apparently made a tactical decision not to object to the officer's answer."[13] Both the State and the court of appeals identified potential reasons why Moreno's counsel failed to object.[14] The State argued that Moreno likely sought "to impeach the police investigation and to lay a foundation for arguing that the [S]tate had not proved that Moreno knowingly possessed the pipe."[15] The court also offered its own possible explanations: that the defense attorney perceived the officer had made an inadmissible comment and chose to preserve "at least one colorable issue" on appeal or that the attorney recognized an objection would have focused the jury's attention on Moreno's silence.[16]

The court of appeals additionally examined whether Moreno had suffered any prejudice from his counsel's failure to object.[17] The court of appeals interpreted *Adams* as holding that a reviewing court should consider the following factors in determining whether a prosecutor's comments on a defendant's silence resulted in harmless error:

> *(1) [W]hether the conviction depended primarily on resolution of conflicting witness testimony; (2) whether any comments on the defendant's silence were made during the prosecutor's closing argument; (3) whether the reference was "express" rather than "brief and passing"; and (4) whether the evidence was "directly elicited by the prosecutor's questioning."*[18]

The court of appeals examined these factors and concluded that the alleged error in Moreno's case was harmless beyond a reasonable doubt.[19]

Moreno petitioned the court of appeals for rehearing, arguing that the court improperly placed the burden on him to prove that his counsel did not make a tactical decision to withhold an objection to the officer's testimony.[20] The court of appeals denied his petition, reasoning that the plain error doctrine required the court to "focus on ... a serious potential for tactical inaction."[21] The court relied on its decision in *Borchgrevink v. State*, which held that "when the record is silent or ambiguous ... [an appellate court] appl[ies] a presumption that the defense attorney's action (or, more precisely, inaction) was tactical."[22]

Moreno petitioned this court for hearing. We granted the petition and consolidated it with Hicks's petition.[23]

Hicks v. State

Mary Hicks was arrested for and convicted of driving under the influence.[24] At her trial a village public safety officer testified that, while responding to a report that Hicks was driving under the influence, he located Hicks's truck parked in a spot at her friend's house that he knew had recently been vacant.[25] He also testified to observing Hicks enter the truck and start the engine.[26] He stated that Hicks then exited the truck and ran back inside the friend's house.[27] The officer spoke with Hicks at the friend's house, determined that she was intoxicated, and arrested her.[28] During closing arguments at Hicks's trial, the prosecutor told the jury that it could find Hicks guilty of either of the two distinct driving or operating incidents: driving to the friend's house or starting the parked truck in front of the friend's house.[29]

This was obvious error under the Alaska Constitution's due process clause,[30] which we have interpreted to bestow on a criminal defendant the "right to have jurors 'all agree that the defendant committed a single offense.' "[31] Hicks did not object to the prosecutor's statement or ask the court to instruct the jury that it had to unanimously agree on one offense

(case continues)

to return a guilty verdict.[32] The jury convicted Hicks of driving under the influence.[33]

Hicks appealed, arguing plain error. Before the court of appeals, the State proffered two possible tactical reasons for Hicks's failure to object.[34] First, the State asserted that "had she raised the issue in the trial court, the State might have sought to amend the indictment to charge her with two separate felony offenses."[35] Second, the State argued that Hicks's defense focused on attacking the strength of the evidence of the second incident when the officer observed Hicks start her engine.[36] The court of appeals concluded that Hicks's attorney made a tactical decision not to object because an objection would have emphasized that the jury could convict Hicks based solely on the evidence of her driving under the influence, which did not rely on the officer's disputed testimony.[37]

Hicks filed a petition for hearing. We granted Hicks's petition and consolidated it with Moreno's petition.[38]

Standard of Review

These consolidated petitions present only questions of law to which we apply our independent judgment.[39] We will adopt the rule of law that "is most persuasive in light of precedent, reason, and policy."[40]

Discussion

It was Error to Apply a Presumption on a Silent or Ambiguous Record that Defense Counsel Made a Tactical Decision Not to Object and to Place the Burden on Defendant to Disprove this Presumption

In *Johnson v. State*, we explained why a general rule requiring a party in trial to object to a perceived error is necessary to preserve that error as a point on appeal:

> *Typically, a litigant or defendant must raise an objection in the trial court in order to preserve that argument for appeal. This general preservation rule is a prudential gate-keeping doctrine adopted by the courts to serve important judicial policies: ensuring that there is "a ruling by the trial court that may be reviewed on appeal,... afford[ing] the trial court the opportunity to correct an alleged error," and creating a sufficient factual record "so that appellate courts do not decide issues of law in a factual vacuum."*[41]

"But the general preservation rule is not absolute, and it is subject to [certain] exceptions, such as the plain error doctrine."[42] The plain error doctrine allows an appellate court to review issues not otherwise preserved where "there was [an] obvious and prejudicial error below affecting substantial rights that did not result from 'intelligent waiver or a tactical decision not to object.' "[43]

Under Alaska Criminal Rule 47(b), "[p]lain errors or defects affecting substantial rights may be noticed [sua sponte by the trial court][44] although they were not brought to the attention of the court." When the trial court fails to correct an error on its own initiative, however, plain error review on appeal operates "to mitigate ... the harsh effects of a rigid application of the adversary method of trial."[45]

We use a four-part test when determining whether to review a defendant's claim of plain error.[46] The appellate court must find the error "(1) was not the result of intelligent waiver or a tactical decision not to object; (2) was obvious; (3) affected substantial rights; and (4) was prejudicial."[47] Plain error review operates as a safety valve allowing an appellate court to review unobjected-to errors "involv[ing] such egregious conduct as to undermine the fundamental fairness of the trial and contribute to a miscarriage of justice."[48]

These consolidated cases concern the tactical-decision prong of the plain error test announced in *Adams*.[49] While the remainder of the plain error test involves substantive requirements an appellate court must conclude are present to reverse on the basis of plain error, the tactical-decision prong acts as a bar to substantive review, preventing defense counsel from deliberately bypassing the contemporaneous-objection rule as part of a trial strategy.[50] We will not afford a defendant an after-the-fact review of a claim of error when defense counsel made a tactical decision not to object or engaged in strategic gamesmanship to avoid the trial court's correction of the error in the first instance.[51]

In *Hicks*, the court of appeals concluded that "Hicks ha[d] not shown that she did not make a tactical decision to forgo a jury unanimity instruction" because (1) it "appear[ed] that the defense attorney tried to focus on the weakness in the State's proof" of one of the incidents; and (2) had Hicks raised the issue earlier, "the trial court might have allowed the State to add a second count of driving under the influence."[52] In *Moreno*, the court of appeals reasoned that "when the record is silent or ambiguous ... [the court] appl[ies] a presumption that the defense attorney's ... inaction ... was tactical."[53] The court also speculated as to Moreno's counsel's reasons for not objecting[54] and stated that the test was whether, based on the record, "there is a serious potential for tactical inaction."[55] As explained below,

(case continues)

neither approach accords with our prior case law up to and including *Adams*.[56]

The tactical-decision case law from 1960-1980

In *Rank v. State*, we examined whether allowing trial testimony regarding the defendant's failure to take a lie detector test was reversible error where defense counsel did not object to this evidence at trial.[57] We reviewed the trial transcript and concluded that Rank's counsel "went into the subject [of his client's failure to take the test] in great detail in his cross-examination of a [S]tate witness and when [Rank] testified in his own defense."[58] Based on this clear indication in the record of defense counsel's tactics, we reasoned that "Rank had presumably taken the position that to explore the subject in detail would be advantageous to his cause."[59] But on appeal Rank "adopt[ed] the totally inconsistent position that he ha[d] suffered a grave disadvantage."[60] We held that Rank was "bound by the choice he first made in the court below. He ha[d] waived any error that might otherwise have occurred when testimony regarding the polygraph was first brought into the case by a [S]tate witness."[61]

In *Noffke v. State*, the trial judge received a question from the jury and responded by giving the jury a supplemental instruction without contemporaneously notifying the defendant and his counsel of the question or the court's answer.[62] Unlike in *Rank*, we noted "[t]here [was] nothing in the record to show that appellant's trial counsel had any knowledge ... of the fact that the trial judge had given the jury this supplemental instruction" and consequently held that "it would work an injustice to appellant to hold that he is now precluded from questioning the propriety of the supplementary instruction" by not contemporaneously objecting to preserve the issue for appellate review.[63] In both *Rank* and *Noffke*, we focused on whether the record on its face clearly indicated defense counsel's obvious knowledge of the error.

In *Hammonds v. State*, defense counsel failed to object when a police officer testified to statements the defendant made after an inadequate *Miranda* warning.[64] Similar to *Rank* and *Noffke*, the issue before us was "not merely one of a technical failure to object in the trial court."[65] The trial record plainly indicated that defense counsel was aware of the requirements of *Miranda* and that he could have excluded his client's statements by objecting, but chose not to object because the statements were potentially exculpatory.[66] We concluded that there was "a clear intimation of a *deliberate* design to knowingly [forgo] a constitutional claim" and "[s]uch a deliberate act on the part of counsel amount[ed] to a waiver of appellant's constitutional right."[67] In other words, because counsel's failure to object was "an *intelligent* waiver of a known right,"[68] Hammonds could not complain on appeal that his Fifth Amendment privilege against self-incrimination was infringed upon because the record indicated that his counsel was aware of the requirements of *Miranda* and allowed the admission of his client's statements despite the constitutional violation.

Then in *Gafford v. State*, another lie detector case, the record revealed that Gafford's counsel had informed the court that he had decided not to request an instruction on the inadmissibility of information about the lie detector test because he "did not want 'to underline' the lie detector answer" elicited during cross examination.[69] We held "In view of the decision made at trial by his counsel,... appellant is now precluded from asserting that it was error for the trial court not to have instructed the jury to disregard [the witness's] reference to a lie detector [test]."[70]

Finally, in *Pulakis v. State*, the trial court, without objection from defense counsel, admitted testimony regarding two lie detector tests the defendant took.[71] We considered Pulakis's counsel's actions throughout the course of trial and concluded they "present[ed] a more compelling factual situation for finding an intelligent waiver of a known right than existed in *Rank*."[72] For example, defense counsel (1) questioned prospective jurors intensively on the subject of polygraph examinations; (2) elicited responses favorable to Pulakis's position; (3) minimized the importance of the polygraph evidence in his opening statement and closing argument; and (4) made no objection to the qualifications of the expert witness on the results of the polygraph examination or to the admissibility of that testimony.[73] We noted that "[i]n fact, counsel stated explicitly that there was no objection to the admission of the written report of the expert witness," and "[o]n cross-examination,... counsel obtained significant admissions from the expert about the unreliability of the polygraph test."[74] Defense counsel also requested highly favorable jury instructions on the issue, which were given by the superior court.[75] We concluded "that this entire pattern of events demonstrate[d] a clear, intelligent waiver of any privilege to exclude this evidence" based on defense counsel's trial strategy, thus precluding plain error review.[76]

These cases make clear that for an appellate court to decline plain error review because defense counsel made a tactical decision, it must be plainly obvious from the record on its face: (1) that counsel had an obvious awareness or knowledge of the error,

(case continues)

and (2) that counsel made an intentional or tactical decision not to object to the error. Our case law has remained consistent on this point.

The tactical-decision case law from 1980-2000

In *Owens v. State*, the prosecution arranged for a radio broadcast on Sitka's only radio station in an effort to locate an anonymous caller to testify.[77] Unfortunately, the station broadcast the message during the morning hours before jurors were due to report for the trial.[78] Owens brought the broadcast to the court's attention the next day, but opposed the prosecution's suggestion that the court make a general inquiry of the jurors.[79] The superior court noted on the record that "it would respect Owens'[s] request not to have the jury queried in a general manner, but pointed out that Owens, by his tactical decision, was depriving the court of the ability to take any actions necessary to cure the harm caused by jury exposure to the inadmissible evidence."[80] The superior court "indicated that it considered Owens to be waiving the jury exposure issue by objecting to a general inquiry of the jurors."[81] On appeal we stressed that because Owens objected to a procedure that would have cured any possible prejudice, he waived his right to raise this issue on appeal under plain error review.[82] It was Owens's attorney's intentional decision not to cure the error in the first instance that barred further plain error review.

In *Moss v. State*, a defense witness refused to testify and defense counsel asked that the witness be held in contempt.[83] The court took a short recess, during which defense counsel was permitted to confer with the witness.[84] Following the recess, defense counsel did not renew his attempt to compel the witness to testify under threat of contempt, made no further mention of the witness or counsel's proposed line of inquiry, and instead rested Moss's case.[85] On appeal Moss argued that the trial court should have compelled the witness to testify, that its failure to do so violated Moss's constitutional rights to due process and to confrontation, and that the court's failure to hold a hearing concerning the proposed testimony was plain error.[86] We summarily dismissed these contentions, concluding:

> *[W]e believe that[,] given the tactical reasons that may have supported a decision to withdraw the witness, it was incumbent upon counsel to renew his attempt to obtain the witness['s] testimony following the recess. During the recess counsel may have learned that the witness would not testify in a manner helpful to the defense and thus have decided not to proceed further with him.... [C]ounsel's decision to rest his case at that point is inconsistent with the present claim of error.*[87]

In other words, we concluded that Moss's counsel made a tactical decision when he chose to forgo asking the court to compel the witness's testimony after speaking to the witness. While speculating somewhat on counsel's rationale for this particular trial strategy, we were careful to point out that the record reflected counsel's *intentional choice* not to go forward with this witness.[88] Thus, *Moss* is distinguishable from *Moreno* and *Hicks* where, on a silent or ambiguous record, the court of appeals applied a presumption that defense counsels' inaction was tactical.[89] In *Moss*, the record reflected that defense counsel made an affirmative decision to withdraw a witness and rest his client's case after conferring with the witness.[90] We did not apply a presumption that defense counsel's *inaction* was tactical; rather, we recognized that defense counsel's *action* of withdrawing the witness was tactical.

In *Dorman v. State*, we discussed the distinction between cases where defense counsel deliberately injects error at trial or makes a tactical decision not to object, and cases where defense counsel's lack of objection could have no tactical benefit.[91] During closing arguments at Dorman's trial, the prosecutor commented that the jury should infer guilt from the fact that Dorman remained silent between the time of his arrest and the time he was advised of his *Miranda* rights.[92] Dorman's counsel failed to object.[93] We noted that Dorman's counsel (1) failed to object to identical testimony during trial; (2) mentioned Dorman's *Miranda* rights during cross-examination; (3) asked for no curative instruction at the time; and (4) made no motion for a mistrial.[94]

Despite Dorman's counsel's awareness of *Miranda*, we held the failure to object was not tactical because Dorman had not "injected the issue of his silence into the case" and there could be no benefit to him in letting the potentially incriminating silence into evidence.[95] In addressing whether counsel may have been inviting error, we concluded:

> *There is no basis for the inference that defense counsel was trying to further Dorman's case by failing to object to the final argument comment, unless it is implied that defense counsel invited error for the purpose of obtaining a reversal on appeal.* That conclusion, however, is not one which should be lightly inferred in any case, for it would preclude review of the most fundamental defects under the plain error doctrine .... [96]

(case continues)

In other words, we explicitly refrained from construing counsel's inaction as a tactical decision absent a clear indication in the record. Without an affirmative act by counsel indicating his awareness of the existence of a known right and some indication in the record of a conscious failure to preserve the issue, we conducted the remainder of the plain error analysis.[97]

Finally, in *Raphael v. State*, the prosecutor told the trial judge at an ex parte hearing that the State's key witness was likely to recant, was intoxicated, and should be incarcerated until she testified.[98] Without first notifying Raphael or his attorney of the prosecutor's statements, the trial judge granted the prosecutor's request, jailing the key witness and placing her children in protective custody.[99] Raphael was convicted and appealed, arguing that the trial court denied him due process given the potentially coercive effect of the witness's incarceration on her testimony and his right to be present at the hearing.[100] The State responded that Raphael abandoned his right to appeal his absence from the ex parte hearing (and the hearing's allegedly coercive effect on the key witness's testimony) because his attorney failed to object to, and thus preserve, these alleged errors during trial.[101] The State argued that the tactical-decision prong should bar further review because Raphael's failure to object might have been tactical and Raphael could have obtained a benefit from his failure to object.[102]

We rejected such speculation because it "assume[d] that Raphael's attorney had a sufficiently accurate view of the scope of the error and deliberately chose to waive any objection."[103] We compared the situation in *Raphael* to *Noffke v. State*, where we held that defense counsel's failure to object was not a tactical decision because the record failed to demonstrate that defense counsel was aware of the error asserted on appeal.[104] And we noted that we had requested that both parties search the trial record for "*any* evidence,... of [Raphael's attorney's] knowledge of the ex parte hearing and the surrounding circumstances," but that "[n]either party found any such references."[105]

Based on the lack of support in the record for the conclusion that defense counsel knew the full extent of the constitutional errors and deliberately chose not to object, we could not say that Raphael's attorney's decision not to object was tactical.[106] Because plain error review was not foreclosed by any tactical decision not to object, we held that the error complained of (1) was obvious; (2) was substantially prejudicial; and (3) undermined the fundamental fairness of the trial and contributed to a miscarriage of justice.[107] Concluding there was plain error, we remanded Raphael's case for a new trial.[108]

In sum, these cases consistently demonstrate our reluctance to foreclose plain error review on tactical-decision grounds. Evidence of a tactical decision not to object to a trial error must be plainly obvious from the record to persuade an appellate court that a defendant's otherwise meritorious substantive claim of error should not trigger appellate review.[109] This rule was further underscored in *Adams v. State*.[110]

The tactical-decision analysis in *Adams v. State*, 2011

All parties agree that our decision in *Adams* governs the outcome of the present cases. Moreno and Hicks argue that *Adams*'s reliance on *Dorman*, *Owens*, *Pulakis*, and *Hammonds* indicates that we intended defense counsel's tactical decisions to operate as implied waivers of future appeals, with the State bearing the burden of proving that a decision was tactical. Moreno and Hicks also read *Adams* as precluding plain error review where the benefit conferred on the defendant is readily apparent on the record.[111]

The State does not read *Adams* as requiring proof of an express or implied waiver or a discernable benefit on the defendant. According to the State, nothing in *Adams* suggests that these are the only types of tactical decisions that will preclude plain error review. The State instead attempts to factually distinguish *Adams* and the cases it relied on to convince us to adopt the court of appeals' line of cases.[112]

Adams began its analysis of the plain error rule by discussing how our cases "have consistently held that plain error does not exist where the right at issue was intelligently waived or the defendant's decision not to object to the error was strategic or tactical."[113] We underscored our analysis in *Dorman* that where there is "no evidence" that defendant's failure to object was strategic, there is "no basis for inferring that the failure to object was tactical 'unless it is implied that defense counsel invited error for the purpose of obtaining a reversal on appeal.' "[114] And we stated that this implication "*is not one which should be inferred lightly*, for it would preclude review of the most fundamental defects under the plain error doctrine."[115] This statement recognized the central focus of plain error review:

> *[The rule] [is] intended to ensure that litigants have a means for the prompt redress of miscarriages of justice, and it applies only when the error was so plain that the trial court and prosecutor were derelict in countenancing it, even absent the defendant's timely assistance in detecting it. It also reflects a careful balancing between the Court's intention of*

(case continues)

> *encourag[ing] all trial participants to seek a fair and accurate trial the first time around and the Court's insistence that obvious injustice be promptly redressed.*[116]

In *Adams*, we cautioned that appellate courts should concentrate on the substantive requirements of plain error review: the obvious nature of the error, the substantial rights the error affected, and the prejudice that resulted from the error.[117] Inferring a tactical decision or intelligent waiver of a known right on a silent or ambiguous record would serve only to impede substantive review of the error.

Adams and the cases it relied upon thus stand at odds with the court of appeals' conclusion in *Moreno* that "when the record is silent or ambiguous[,] ... [the court] appl[ies] a presumption that the defense attorney's ... inaction ... was tactical."[118] It was also error to place the burden on the defendant to negate the possibility that his attorney's failure to object was tactical.[119]

The same error was made in *Hicks*, where the court of appeals held that "Hicks must ... show that the error was not the result of her attorney's tactical decision not to object."[120] We have never placed this burden on the defendant. *Hicks* cited our analysis in *Khan v. State*,[121] but *Khan* only reaffirmed the "*Adams* rule" that "includ[es] an inquiry into whether the defendant's non-objection was tactical, [which] better respects the trial process and the role of counsel."[122]

Whether the defendant made a tactical decision not to object or intelligently waived an opportunity to object must be plainly obvious from the face of the record, not presumed in the face of a silent or ambiguous record. The records in *Moreno* and *Hicks* do not reveal plainly obvious evidence of tactical decisions not to object by defense counsel. Because the court of appeals improperly placed the burden on Moreno and Hicks to prove that their attorneys did not make tactical decisions, and because the court of appeals improperly applied a presumption of tactical inaction in the case of a silent or ambiguous record in *Moreno*, we reverse the court of appeals' conclusions regarding the tactical-decision determination in both cases.[123]

We Affirm the Court of Appeals' Conclusion that the Error in Moreno's Case was not Prejudicial

In *Moreno*, the court of appeals also addressed the prejudice prong of plain error review. The court held that admitting the arresting officer's statement regarding Moreno's decision to remain silent did not result in prejudice because admitting the statement was harmless beyond a reasonable doubt.[124] Moreno argues that the court of appeals erred in reaching that conclusion.

Adams considered what would constitute prejudice and held that

> *[a] constitutional violation will always affect substantial rights and will be prejudicial unless the State proves that it was harmless beyond a reasonable doubt. An error that is not constitutional in nature will be prejudicial if the defendant proves that there is a reasonable probability that it affected the outcome of the proceeding.*[125]

We identified several factors that a reviewing court must consider in determining whether a trial court's failure to take remedial action regarding a prosecutor's comments on a defendant's silence constituted harmless error. These include (1) whether the conviction depended primarily on conflicting witness testimony; (2) whether the comment occurred during closing argument; (3) whether the comment was "express" rather than "brief and passing"; and (4) whether the evidence was "directly elicited by the prosecutor's questioning."[126]

Moreno was convicted at trial of delivery and possession of methamphetamine.[127] On cross-examination, Moreno's defense attorney asked the investigating officer whether the officer had been able to identify the owner of a jacket that contained a methamphetamine pipe. The officer replied that there were "no identifying items [in the jacket] *and the defendant refused to speak to us about it*, but we did photograph where that—that came out of," at which point the defense attorney interrupted and directed the officer to answer yes or no. (Emphasis added.) This was the only reference in the entire course of trial implicating Moreno's constitutional right to be free from self-incrimination.[128]

By comparison, in *Adams*, the prosecutor made two remarks on cross-examination that directly addressed Adams's post-arrest silence:

> [PROSECUTOR]: And then you refused to talk to police any further. Correct?
> [ADAMS]: That's right.
> [PROSECUTOR]: Okay. Until today?
> [ADAMS]: I was exercising my right.[129]

And then again:

> [PROSECUTOR]: Now, new information that we heard from you today is

(case continues)

everything that happened in your apartment, correct? Would you agree to that? From your perspective?

[ADAMS]: What do you mean by everything?

[PROSECUTOR]: Well, we didn't know anything about what happened in your apartment from you, because you didn't talk to police, until after hearing all the evidence so far in the case.[130]

And during closing argument, the prosecutor again pointed to Adams's silence to argue that Adams's testimony was less credible than the victim's.[131]

The prosecution's conduct in *Adams* was egregious, continued over a protracted period, and went to the core of the prosecution's theory of the case, namely, that Adams was not credible and "changed his decision not to talk when he learned about the DNA evidence indicating that he had sex with [the underage victim]."[132] The facts in *Moreno* are far less compelling: the officer's comment was elicited by defense counsel; it was made in passing; and the prosecutor did not refer to it during his closing argument.

Accordingly, we agree with the court of appeals that the officer's testimony "had little impact on Moreno's trial" and was "harmless beyond a reasonable doubt" under the four factors of *Adams* that a reviewing court considers when determining whether a court's failure to address a prosecutor's comments on a defendant's silence was harmless error.[133] We thus affirm the court of appeals' decision in *Moreno* on this alternate ground.

Conclusion

We REVERSE the court of appeals' decisions foreclosing plain error review in both *Hicks* and *Moreno*, but we AFFIRM the court of appeals' decision in *Moreno* on the alternate ground that the error was not prejudicial. We REMAND *Hicks* for further proceedings consistent with this opinion.

---

1. *Khan v. State*, 278 P.3d 893, 896 (Alaska 2012) (citing *Adams v. State*, 261 P.3d 758, 764 (Alaska 2011)).
2. *Adams*, 261 P.3d at 764.
3. *Moreno v. State*, Mem. Op. & J. No. 5819, 2013 WL 120907, at *1 (Alaska App. Jan. 9, 2013), *reh'g denied*, 2013 WL 120907, at *5 (Alaska App. Feb. 7, 2013).
4. *Hicks v. State*, Mem. Op. & J. No. 5911, 2013 WL 203264, at *1 (Alaska App. Jan. 16, 2013).
5. *Moreno*, 2013 WL 120907, at *2–3; *Hicks*, 2013 WL 203264, at *3–4.
6. *Moreno*, 2013 WL 120907, at *5 (concluding that when a litigant pursues a claim of plain error on a silent or ambiguous record, the court will "focus on *whether there is a serious potential for* tactical inaction" because where "an attorney makes a conscious decision not to object to inadmissable evidence in order to gain a tactical advantage . . . the attorney is unlikely to make this decision a matter of record" (emphasis added)).
7. *Moreno v. State*, Nos. S-15067/15070 (Alaska Supreme Court Order, June 10, 2013).
8. *Moreno*, 2013 WL 120907, at *1. A local option community is one that has elected to prohibit the sale, importation, or possession of alcoholic beverages. *See* AS 04.11.491.
9. *Id.* at *1–2 (discussing the defense attorney's question: "And at no point during your investigation did you determine who that jacket belonged to?" and the officer's reply: "Correct, ma'am. There [were] no identifying items [in the jacket] and the defendant refused to speak to us about it, but we did photograph where that—that came out of . . . ." (emphasis omitted)).
10. *Id.* at *1.
11. *Id.* at *1–2.
12. We have held that questions or comments by the State about a defendant's pre-arrest silence are generally inadmissible under Alaska Rule of Evidence 403 and that questions or comments by the State on a defendant's post-arrest silence are prohibited by article I, section 9 of the Alaska Constitution. *Adams v. State*, 261 P.3d 758, 765–67 (Alaska 2011). It is unclear whether Moreno had been arrested when police questioned him about the jacket. *Moreno*, 2013 WL 120907, at *2.
13. *Moreno*, 2013 WL 120907, at *1.
14. *Id.* at *2–3.
15. *Id.* at *2
16. *Id.* at *3.
17. *Id.*
18. *Id.*
19. *Id.*
20. *Id.* at *5.
21. *Id.*
22. *Id.* at *5 (omissions in original) (quoting *Borchgrevink v. State*, 239 P.3d 410, 421 (Alaska App. 2010)).
23. *Moreno v. State*, Nos. S-15067/15070 (Alaska Supreme Court Order, June 10, 2013).
24. *See Hicks v. State*, Mem. Op. & J. No. 5911, 2013 WL 203264, at *1 (Alaska App. Jan. 16, 2013).
25. *Id.*
26. *Id.*
27. *Id.*
28. *Id.* at *1–2.
29. *Id.* at *3.
30. Alaska Const. art. I, § 7 ("No person shall be deprived of life, liberty, or property without due process of law.").
31. *Khan v. State*, 278 P.3d 893, 899 (Alaska 2012) (quoting *State v. James*, 698 P.2d 1161, 1167 (Alaska 1985)).
32. *Hicks*, 2013 WL 203264, at *3.
33. *Id.* at *1.
34. *Id.* at *4.
35. *Id.*
36. *Id.*
37. *Id.* at *1, *4.
38. *Moreno v. State*, Nos. S-15067/15070 (Alaska Supreme Court Order, June 10, 2013).
39. *State v. Doe A*, 297 P.3d 885, 887 (Alaska 2013), *as modified on denial of reh'g* (Apr. 10, 2013).
40. *Id.* (quoting *Ford v. Municipality of Anchorage*, 813 P.2d 654, 655 (Alaska 1991)) (internal quotation marks omitted).

(case continues)

41. 328 P.3d 77, 82 (Alaska 2014) (alteration in original) (footnotes omitted) (quoting *Alexander v. State*, 611 P.2d 469, 478 (Alaska 1980) and *Pierce v. State*, 261 P.3d 428, 433 (Alaska App. 2011)).
42. *Id.*
43. *Id.* (quoting *Adams v. State*, 261 P.3d 758, 764 (Alaska 2011)).
44. *Cf. Adams*, 261 P.3d at 764 (noting that "Alaska Criminal Rule 47(b) allows *appellate* courts to notice '[p]lain errors or defects affecting substantial rights ... although they were not brought to the attention of the court' " without restricting the rule's application to appellate proceedings (alterations in original) (emphasis added) (quoting Alaska R. Crim. P. 47(b))). We recently clarified in *Johnson* that plain error is a "prudential exception" to the general preservation rule; in other words, we retain inherent discretion to hear such appeals under the rubric of plain error as a common law doctrine. *Johnson*, 328 P.3d at 82 & n.24.
45. *Dorman v. State*, 622 P.2d 448, 459 (Alaska 1981) (alteration in original) (quoting *Bargas v. State*, 489 P.2d 130, 133 (Alaska 1971)) (internal quotation marks omitted).
46. *Adams*, 261 P.3d at 764.
47. *Id.*
48. *Id.* (alteration in original) (quoting *Raphael v. State*, 994 P.2d 1004, 1015 (Alaska 2000)) (internal quotation marks omitted).
49. We recently revisited the plain error test in *Johnson v. State*, 328 P.3d 77 (Alaska 2014), where we reiterated *Adams*'s holding that "we will review unpreserved claims for plain error and reverse the trial court where there was obvious and prejudicial error below affecting substantial rights that did not result from 'intelligent waiver or a tactical decision not to object.' " *Id.* at 82 (quoting *Adams*, 261 P.3d at 764).
50. *E.g., Hammonds v. State*, 442 P.2d 39, 42, and 43 n.16 (Alaska 1968) ("There is here a clear intimation of a deliberate design to knowingly [forgo] a constitutional claim. Such a deliberate act on the part of counsel amounts to a waiver of appellant's constitutional right which is binding on appellant.").
51. *Id.* at 42–43.
52. *Hicks v. State*, Mem. Op. & J. No. 5911, 2013 WL 203264, at *3–4 (Alaska App. Jan. 16, 2013).
53. *Moreno v. State*, Mem. Op. & J. No. 5819, 2013 WL 120907, at *5 (Alaska App. Jan. 9, 2013), *reh'g denied*, 2013 WL 120907, at *5 (Alaska App. Feb. 7, 2013) (omissions in original) (alterations added) (quoting *Borchgrevink v. State*, 239 P.3d 410, 421 (Alaska App. 2010)).
54. *Id.* at *2–3.
55. *Id.* at *5.
56. We divide our discussion of the tactical-decision case law into three categories: (1) cases from 1960 to 1980; (2) cases from 1980 to 2000; and (3) the tactical-decision analysis in *Adams v. State*, 261 P.3d 758 (Alaska 2011). We discern no significant changes in our tactical-decision analysis from one period to the next but have divided our discussion into these sections to assist the reader.
57. 373 P.2d 734, 735 (Alaska 1962), *overruled in part on other grounds by Shafer v. State*, 456 P.2d 466 (Alaska 1969).
58. *Id.* at 736.
59. *Id.*
60. *Id.*
61. *Id.*
62. 422 P.2d 102, 103 (Alaska 1967).
63. *Id.* at 106–07.
64. 442 P.2d 39, 40–41 (Alaska 1968).
65. *Id.* at 43.
66. *Id.* at 42 (referring to *Miranda v. Arizona*, 384 U.S. 436 (1966), which held that statements obtained from defendants during interrogation in a police-dominated atmosphere, without full warning of constitutional rights, were inadmissible in violation of their Fifth Amendment privileges against self-incrimination).
67. *Id.* (emphasis added).
68. *Id.* at 43 (emphasis added).
69. 440 P.2d 405, 410 (Alaska 1968), *overruled on other grounds by Fields v. State*, 487 P.2d 831 (Alaska 1971).
70. *Id.*
71. 476 P.2d 474, 477 (Alaska 1970).
72. *Id.* at 480.
73. *Id.*
74. *Id.*
75. *Id.*
76. *Id.*
77. 613 P.2d 259, 260 (Alaska 1980).
78. *Id.*
79. *Id.*
80. *Id.*
81. *Id.*
82. *Id.* at 262 ("We conclude that the trial court here could have cured any possible prejudice with an instruction to the jury that they were to determine guilt or innocence solely on the basis of the evidence admitted at trial. Because Owens objected to this procedure, he has waived his right to raise on appeal this issue." (footnote omitted)). We note that the trial judge in *Owens* did a commendable job making a clear record on this issue. Best practices for trial judges who become aware of an attorney's probable tactical decision not to object (or not to request a curative instruction) include making an inquiry and findings on the record outside the presence of the jury.
83. 620 P.2d 674, 677 (Alaska 1980).
84. *Id.*
85. *Id.*
86. *Id.*
87. *Id.* at 677–78.
88. *Id.*
89. *Hicks v. State*, Mem. Op. & J. No. 5911, 2013 WL 203264, at *4 (Alaska App. Jan. 16, 2013); *Moreno v. State*, Mem. Op. & J. No. 5819, 2013 WL 120907, at *5 (Alaska App. Jan. 9, 2013), *reh'g denied*, 2013 WL 120907, at *5 (Alaska App. Feb. 7, 2013).
90. *Moss*, 620 P.2d at 677–78.
91. 622 P.2d 448, 457–58 (Alaska 1981) (comparing *Davis v. State*, 501 P.2d 1026 (Alaska 1972) and *Hammonds v. State*, 442 P.2d 39 (Alaska 1968) with *Bargas v. State*, 489 P.2d 130 (Alaska 1971)).
92. *Id.* at 456. There had also been testimony regarding Dorman's reactions to questions *after* he had been informed of his *Miranda* rights, despite Dorman's counsel's objections. *Id.* at 452. The trial court prohibited the prosecutor from referencing that testimony during closing arguments. *Id.*
93. *Id.* at 457.
94. *Id.*
95. *Id.* at 458.
96. *Id.* at 458 (emphasis added). We also noted Dorman's counsel's "many objections" to testimony regarding Dorman's silence *after* receiving a *Miranda* warning compared to Dorman's counsel's failure to object to testimony regarding Dorman's silence *before* receiving a *Miranda* warning. *Id.* We stated that this discrepancy further indicated that counsel's

(case continues)

failure to object to evidence of Dorman's pre-*Miranda*-warning silence was not invited error. *Id.*

97. *Id.* ("Thus, since the failure to object to the final comment has not been shown to have been a tactical or strategic decision, the [S]tate's argument does not compel us to disregard the error. We must still, of course, determine whether this remark constituted plain error.").
98. 994 P.2d 1004, 1006 (Alaska 2000).
99. *Id.*
100. *Id.*
101. *Id.* at 1015.
102. *Id.* ("Specifically, the State contends that Raphael could have hoped that [the complaining witness's] incarceration would make her hostile toward the prosecution and cause her to slant her testimony in his favor.").
103. *Id.*
104. *Id.* at 1016 (citing *Noffke v. State*, 422 P.2d 102, 106–07 (Alaska 1967)).
105. *Id.* at 1016 n.53 (emphasis added) (explaining our request that the parties provide supplemental briefing on whether the record contained any evidence of defense counsel's knowledge of the hearing, apart from the trial court's limited description of it).
106. *Id.*
107. *See id.* at 1015.
108. *Id.* at 1015–16.
109. *See, e.g., Hammonds v. State*, 442 P.2d 39, 42–43 (Alaska 1968).
110. 261 P.3d 758, 773 (Alaska 2011).
111. Moreno and Hicks cite *Adams*'s discussion of *Dorman*, where we explained: "[W]here a defendant 'neither injected the issue of his silence into the case nor obtained a benefit from the prosecutor's inculpatory comment,' there [was] no basis for inferring that the failure to object was tactical 'unless it is implied that defense counsel invited error for the purpose of obtaining a reversal on appeal.' " *Adams*, 261 P.3d at 773 (quoting *Dorman v. State*, 622 P.2d 448, 458 (Alaska 1981)).
112. The State argues that we should explicitly adopt the court of appeals' standard for deciding whether a failure to object was tactical. Under this standard, the court of appeals reviews the trial court record for any "plausible" tactical reason for defense counsel's failure to object, *Borchgrevink v. State*, 239 P.3d 410, 422 (Alaska App. 2010), and "unless the record precludes the possibility that counsel's actions may have been tactical, a finding of plain error is rarely appropriate." *Massey v. State*, 771 P.2d 448, 453 (Alaska App. 1989). Under the court of appeals' approach, if the court can divine a conceivable tactical reason or the record is silent or ambiguous, that court applies a presumption that the defense attorney's decision was tactical, and then the burden shifts to the defendant to prove that counsel's decision was not tactical. *Borchgrevink*, 239 P.3d at 421.
113. *Adams*, 261 P.3d at 770.
114. *Id.* at 773 (quoting *Dorman*, 622 P.2d at 458).
115. *Id.* (emphasis added) (quoting *Dorman*, 622 P.2d at 458) (internal quotation marks omitted).
116. Larry Cunningham, *Appellate Review of Unpreserved Questions in Criminal Cases: An Attempt to Define the "Interest of Justice,"* 11 J. APP. PRAC. & PROCESS 285, 298 (2010) (third alteration in original) (footnote omitted) (quoting *United States v. Frady*, 456 U.S. 152, 163 (1982)) (internal quotation marks omitted).
117. *Adams*, 261 P.3d at 770, 773 (noting that "our [earlier] cases ... consistently define[d] plain error as error that affects substantial rights and is obviously prejudicial," but noting that three substantive requirements must now be met: there "must be error ... ; the error must be obvious, meaning that it should have been apparent to any competent judge or lawyer; ... the error must affect substantial rights, meaning that it must pertain to the fundamental fairness of the proceeding; and ... the error must be prejudicial").
118. *Moreno v. State*, Mem. Op. & J. No. 5819, 2013 WL 120907, at *5 (Alaska App. Jan. 9, 2013), *reh'g denied*, 2013 WL 120907, at *5 (Alaska App. Feb. 7, 2013) (quoting *Borchgrevink*, 239 P.3d 410, 421 (Alaska App. 2010)).
119. *Id.*
120. *Hicks v. State*, Mem. Op. & J. No. 5911, 2013 WL 203264, at *4 (Alaska App. Jan. 16, 2013) (citing *Khan v. State*, 278 P.3d 893, 901 (Alaska 2012)).
121. *Id.* at *4 (citing *Khan*, 278 P.3d at 901).
122. *Khan*, 278 P.3d at 901.
123. We note that the court of appeals recently discussed the tactical-decision principle in *Anderson v. State*, 337 P.3d 534, 543–44 (Alaska App. 2014). We had previously remanded the *Anderson* case to the court of appeals for its reconsideration of this issue in that case. The court of appeals decided not to reconsider its earlier determination of the tactical decision in that case in light of its alternative holding that the jury instruction error in *Anderson* was harmless beyond a reasonable doubt. *Id.* at 544.
124. *Moreno*, 2013 WL 120907, at *3.
125. *Adams v. State*, 261 P.3d 758, 773 (Alaska 2011).
126. *Id.* at 774–75 (quoting *Van Hatten v. State*, 666 P.2d 1047, 1056 (Alaska App. 1983)).
127. *Moreno*, 2013 WL 120907, at *1.
128. *See* Alaska Const. art. I, § 9 ("No person shall be compelled in any criminal proceeding to be a witness against himself."); *Moreno*, 2013 WL 120907, at *2 ("Evidence of a defendant's post-arrest silence in response to police questioning is generally inadmissible under Article I, section 9 of the Alaska Constitution. In addition, a defendant's pre-arrest silence will usually be inadmissible under Alaska Evidence Rule 403 because its probative value is inherently low and the danger of unfair prejudice is inherently high." (footnote omitted)).

    We note that the court of appeals did not explicitly determine whether Moreno was under arrest when he was questioned about the jacket, but assumed that he was, at the very least, detained when the questioning occurred. *Moreno,* 2013 WL 120907, at *2. The court of appeals therefore analyzed the officer's comment under the higher "harmless beyond a reasonable doubt" standard employed when the alleged error implicates a constitutional right. *See id.; see also Adams*, 261 P.3d at 771. Because our decision to affirm the court of appeals' conclusion in Moreno regarding the lack of prejudice would be the same under either the pre- or post-arrest standard as stated in Adams, 261 P.3d at 773, whether Moreno was under arrest at the time of his statement is irrelevant.
129. *Adams*, 261 P.3d at 770.
130. *Id.*
131. *Id.* at 762.
132. *Id.*
133. *Moreno*, 2013 WL 120907, at *3.

CASE *The Irate Sam's Club Shopper*

Garibay v. State of Alaska, Department of Administration, Division of Motor Vehicles

4FA-11-01772 CI, 6970 November 28, 2014
Supreme Court of Alaska
Before: Fabe, Chief Justice, Winfree, Stowers, Maassen, and Bolger, Justices
Opinion by, MAASSEN, Justice

Introduction

After a woman reported having an altercation with Joe Garibay in a store, the police stopped him, then arrested him for driving under the influence of alcohol. The Department of Motor Vehicles revoked Garibay's driver's license for 90 days, and the superior court affirmed the revocation. Garibay appeals, arguing that the police stop constituted an unconstitutional search and seizure requiring that evidence of his drinking be excluded from the license revocation proceedings. We affirm on the basis of our prior cases, which hold that the exclusionary rule applies in license revocation proceedings only in exceptional circumstances not present here.

Facts and Proceedings

Joe Garibay was at the Sam's Club in Fairbanks when he collided with a woman's shopping cart, waking her baby.[1] The woman demanded an apology, but Garibay swore at her instead. Assuming he was drunk because of the beer in his cart and his threatening manner, the woman called the police, then followed Garibay out to the parking lot to get his license plate number. When a police officer arrived a few minutes later, the woman told him that Garibay was "maybe ... a drunk," that he had threatened her in front of her children, and that she wanted him charged with assault. Informed that an assault charge was unlikely, the woman asked that the police at least "find that guy to make sure he's not drunk." The officer assured her that they would try to find Garibay and "make sure he's not, you know, drunk driving, something like that."

The police located Garibay's empty vehicle shortly afterward in a nearby parking lot. Officer Fett parked behind it and activated his emergency lights. When Garibay returned, he attempted to back out of the parking space despite the police car behind him; he apparently did not notice he was blocked in until Officer Fett knocked on his window. Another officer arrived, and both officers spoke with Garibay. Although he told them he had not consumed any alcohol that day, the officers observed that he swayed, had bloodshot and watery eyes, and smelled strongly of alcohol. He failed three field sobriety tests and blew .128 on the preliminary breath test. The officers arrested him for driving under the influence of alcohol and for possessing firearms while in an impaired state.[2] They then tested him again using the Datamaster breath testing machine, which showed a breath alcohol content of .111. As a result, the Department of Motor Vehicles (DMV) revoked Garibay's license for 90 days.

Garibay appealed the license revocation, and the DMV held an administrative hearing. Garibay was represented by counsel, who cross-examined both police officers involved in the arrest. It was Garibay's position that the officers' conduct in approaching his vehicle constituted an illegal investigative stop. But the hearing officer, citing prior decisions of this court,[3] instructed Garibay's attorney not to inquire about the stop's legality. The hearing officer concluded that the legality of the stop was not relevant in a license revocation proceeding, that there was probable cause to believe Garibay was operating a motor vehicle while under the influence of alcohol, and that the Datamaster breath test demonstrated that Garibay's breath alcohol limit was over the legal limit—thus satisfying the requirements of the revocation statute, AS 28.15.166(g).[4] The hearing officer therefore affirmed the 90-day license revocation.

Garibay appealed the agency decision to the superior court, arguing again that the investigative stop was illegal. Like the hearing officer, the superior court held that the legality of the stop was irrelevant in license revocation proceedings and therefore affirmed the revocation of Garibay's license.

Garibay appeals, arguing again that the investigative stop was illegal and that this divested the DMV of jurisdiction to revoke his license. He also argues that the exclusionary rule should apply in civil license revocation proceedings, and alternatively that the exclusionary rule should at least apply to his case because the police conduct was shocking.

(case continues)

Standards of Review

We set out the standards of review relevant here in our earlier decisions involving the application of the exclusionary rule in license revocation proceedings:

> *We review license revocation hearings under AS 28.15.166(m), which provides that the court may reverse the department's determination if the court finds that the department misinterpreted the law, acted in an arbitrary and capricious manner, or made a determination unsupported by the evidence in the record. Where the superior court acts as an intermediate court of appeals, we independently review the hearing officer's decision. For legal questions not involving agency expertise, we apply the substitution of judgment standard. We also review constitutional questions de novo, and will adopt the rule of law that is most persuasive in light of precedent, reason, and policy.*[5]

Discussion

The Exclusionary Rule Generally Does not Apply in License Revocation Proceedings

Under the exclusionary rule, "evidence obtained from an unconstitutional search or seizure is inadmissible and must be excluded."[6] In *Nevers v. State* we considered for the first time whether the exclusionary rule should apply to search and seizure violations in license revocation proceedings.[7] Citing *State v. Sears*,[8] we balanced the costs of applying the rule against its benefits.[9] On the cost side, we noted that "application of the exclusionary rule to license revocation hearings will in some cases frustrate the important state interest in keeping drunk drivers off the road by excluding pertinent evidence"; "will significantly increase the administrative burden of what is intended to be an informal process," particularly given that "hearing officers in Alaska need not even be lawyers"; and will likely "result in longer and more complicated hearings in many cases."[10] On the benefit side, we considered the likelihood that applying the rule in license revocation proceedings would "deter unlawful police conduct," concluding that the effect would be insignificant "because the police are already sufficiently deterred from such unlawful conduct by the applicability of the exclusionary rule to all criminal cases that may result from their investigations."[11] Finding that the costs significantly outweighed the potential benefits, we held that the exclusionary rule was inapplicable to license revocation proceedings—with a few exceptions, discussed below.[12]

In a subsequent case, *Alvarez v. State, Department of Administration, Division of Motor Vehicles*, we affirmed a hearing officer's decision to preclude cross-examination of the arresting officer about "details leading up to the initial stop."[13] We agreed with the hearing officer "that only [the arresting officer's] observations *after* pulling Alvarez over were relevant to the statutory inquiry whether [the arresting officer] had probable cause to arrest Alvarez for driving while intoxicated."[14] We explained that "whether or not [the arresting officer] had reasonable suspicion to stop Alvarez is irrelevant in a license suspension proceeding."[15]

Applying *Nevers* and *Alvarez* in this case, the hearing officer was correct to rule that the exclusionary rule did not apply to Garibay's license revocation hearing.

The Exceptions Noted in Nevers do not Apply to this Case

In *Nevers* we did note certain exceptional circumstances that would justify application of the exclusionary rule in license revocation proceedings. We held that the rule would apply if there is "police misconduct which shocks the conscience, or is of a nature that calls for the judiciary, as a matter of judicial integrity, to disassociate itself from benefits derivable therefrom."[16] In a footnote we set out another exception relevant here: "where a Fourth Amendment violation stems from a lack of probable cause for a DWI arrest,... because probable cause is an affirmative statutory element of the offense of refusal and is an affirmative element for proof in the license revocation proceeding."[17] Garibay argues that these exceptions allow him to challenge the legality of the investigative stop at the license revocation hearing, but we disagree.

First, we reject Garibay's argument that "the police action in this case was shocking misconduct, because of the completely speculative basis for the police officer's investigative stop." The investigative stop was based on the report of the woman at Sam's Club, who suspected from Garibay's actions and demeanor that he was drunk. Garibay did not present any facts to indicate that the officers who stopped him acted deliberately to violate his constitutional rights[18] or that they engaged in any other shocking behavior. We see no basis for applying the exception to this case.

Also inapplicable is the exception that requires exclusion of evidence where the DUI arrest is not based on probable cause. Garibay frames the relevant time as the moment of the investigative stop rather than the arrest. But his argument is precluded by our decision in *Alvarez*, where we affirmed the hearing officer's determination that "only [the arresting officer's] observations *after* pulling Alvarez over were relevant to the statutory inquiry whether [the arresting

(case continues)

officer] had probable cause to arrest Alvarez for driving while intoxicated."[19] Here, after stopping Garibay in his attempt to back out of his parking space, the officers observed that he had bloodshot, watery eyes, smelled strongly of alcohol, had balance issues, failed several field sobriety tests, and had a preliminary breath test result significantly over the legal limit. These observations "would warrant a prudent person in believing"[20] that Garibay had committed the offense of operating a vehicle while under the influence of alcohol.[21] Because the officers had probable cause to arrest Garibay at the relevant moment—the moment of his arrest for DUI—the second *Nevers* exception does not apply here either.[22]

The DMV had Jurisdiction to Revoke Garibay's License

Under the implied consent statute, AS 28.35.031(a), "[a] person who operates or drives a motor vehicle in this state ... shall be considered to have given consent" to a test to determine the person's blood or breath alcohol concentration, if that person is "lawfully arrested" for driving under the influence of alcohol. Garibay argues that this "lawful arrest" component of the implied consent statute must be read into AS 28.15.166(g), the statute providing for administrative review of a license revocation, such that the DMV lacks the authority to revoke a license absent a "lawful arrest." We reject this argument too as inconsistent with our prior cases.

In *Javed v. Department of Public Safety, Division of Motor Vehicles*, we explained that although AS 28.15.166(g)(1) cites the implied consent statute, its focus "is clearly on the result of the test or the fact of refusal to take the test."[23] Our explanation continued:

> *Reading subsection .166(g)(1)–(3) to encompass an inquiry into the underlying facts that justify administration of the test would render the first part of subsection .166(g), regarding the issue of whether the law enforcement officer had reasonable grounds to believe that the person was operating a motor vehicle, almost meaningless. The statute offers very precise limiting language for the issues that are to be considered. There is no reason to believe that the reference to the implied consent statutes is anything more than a descriptive tool used to identify the "chemical test" named in each instance.*[24]

The statute thus does not require an inquiry into the lawfulness of the investigative stop at the administrative review hearing.

For his contrary reading of the statute, Garibay relies on the dissent in *Hartman v. State, Department of Administration, Division of Motor Vehicles*.[25] The dissent concluded that the investigative stop in *Hartman* was unlawful, and that therefore "[t]he ensuing arrest was also unlawful because [the trooper] established probable cause to arrest Hartman with information gathered during the unlawful stop."[26]

But the dissent in *Hartman* is not the law in Alaska, and it conflicts with *Nevers*, which is the law in Alaska. The police unlawfully entered Nevers's home, questioned him, and gave him a preliminary breath test that showed he was intoxicated.[27] They then arrested him. Nevers tried to exclude the results of the breath test because of the police's unlawful entry.[28] We held, however, that the results could not be suppressed because the exclusionary rule does not apply to license revocation proceedings.[29] Nevers's arrest was based on probable cause; the problem was that the probable cause was the result of an unlawful entry into his home. In a criminal proceeding, under the exclusionary rule, the police's illegal conduct would invalidate the breath test and the subsequent arrest.[30] But in a license revocation proceeding, because the exclusionary rule does not apply, illegal police conduct prior to arrest does not invalidate the arrest unless it "shocks the conscience."[31] As the dissent in *Hartman* recognized, it is the exclusionary rule that acts to invalidate an arrest by taking out of the equation some evidence on which probable cause to arrest was based;[32] without the exclusionary rule, the evidence stays in and the arrest stands.

Because the exclusionary rule does not apply to Garibay's case, his argument that he was unlawfully arrested fails. The DMV had the authority to revoke his license.

Conclusion

We AFFIRM the hearing officer's decision upholding the revocation of Garibay's license.

---

1. The facts of this altercation are the subject of police reports but were not adjudicated; they are recited here only to place the actions of the police in the context of what they had been told.
2. *See* AS 11.61.210(a)(1) (defining fourth-degree weapons misconduct to include a person's possession of a firearm "when the person's physical or mental condition is impaired as a result of the introduction of an intoxicating liquor").
3. *See Alvarez v. State, Dep't of Admin., Div. of Motor Vehicles*, 249 P.3d 286, 296 (Alaska 2011) (holding, in part, that whether the police have reasonable suspicion to stop a driver is irrelevant in a license suspension proceeding because the exclusionary rule does not apply); *Nevers v. State, Dep't of Admin., Div. of Motor Vehicles*, 123 P.3d 958, 966 (Alaska 2005) (holding that the exclusionary rule does not apply to license revocation hearings as a general rule).

(case continues)

4. As relevant here, the statute states that administrative review of a revocation decision "shall be limited to the issues of whether the law enforcement officer had probable cause to believe ... that the person was operating a motor vehicle ... while under the influence of an alcoholic beverage" and had chemical test results that violated the statutory limits.
5. *Alvarez*, 249 P.3d at 290–91 (quoting *Nevers*, 123 P.3d at 961) (internal quotation marks omitted).
6. *Nevers*, 123 P.3d at 962 (citing *Ellison v. State*, 593 P.2d 640, 718 (Alaska 1979)).
7. *Id.* at 962 n.16.
8. 553 P.2d 907, 912–14 (Alaska 1976).
9. *Nevers*, 123 P.3d at 963–64.
10. *Id.* at 963.
11. *Id.* at 964.
12. *Id.*
13. 249 P.3d 286, 295 (Alaska 2011).
14. *Id.* at 296 (emphasis in original).
15. *Id.*
16. *Nevers*, 123 P.3d at 964 (quoting *State v. Sears*, 553 P.2d 907, 914 (Alaska 1976)) (internal quotation marks omitted).
17. *Id.* at 964 n.21.
18. *See Fraiman v. State, Dep't of Admin., Div. of Motor Vehicles*, 49 P.3d 241, 245 (Alaska 2002).
19. *Alvarez*, 249 P.3d at 296 (emphasis in original).
20. *State v. Blank*, 90 P.3d 156, 162 n.38 (Alaska 2004) (citing *Schmid v. State*, 615 P.2d 565, 574 (Alaska 1980)).
21. AS 28.35.030(a).
22. "Probable cause to arrest exists if the facts and circumstances known to the officer would warrant a prudent person in believing that the defendant had committed an offense." *Blank*, 90 P.3d at 162 n.38 (citing *Schmid*, 615 P.2d at 574).
23. 921 P.2d 620, 625 (Alaska 1996).
24. *Id.*
25. 152 P.3d 1118, 1126–30 (Alaska 2007) (Eastaugh, J., dissenting).
26. *Id.*
27. *Nevers v. State, Dep't of Admin., Div. of Motor Vehicles*, 123 P.3d 958, 960–61 (Alaska 2005).
28. *Id.*
29. *Id.* at 963.
30. *See id.* at 962.
31. *Id.* at 964.
32. *Hartman v. State, Dep't of Admin., Div. of Motor Vehicles*, 152 P.3d 1118, 1130 (Alaska 2007) (Eastaugh, J., dissenting) ("[A]n unlawful stop may 'invalidate' an ensuing arrest ... through the exclusion of evidence garnered from the stop." (alterations in original)).

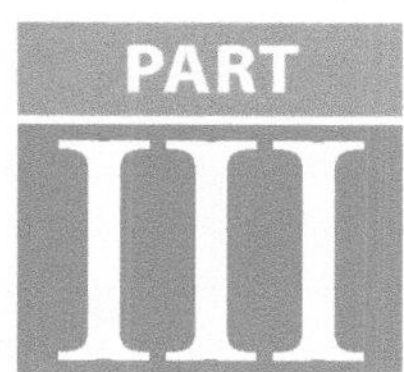

Contracts and E-Commerce

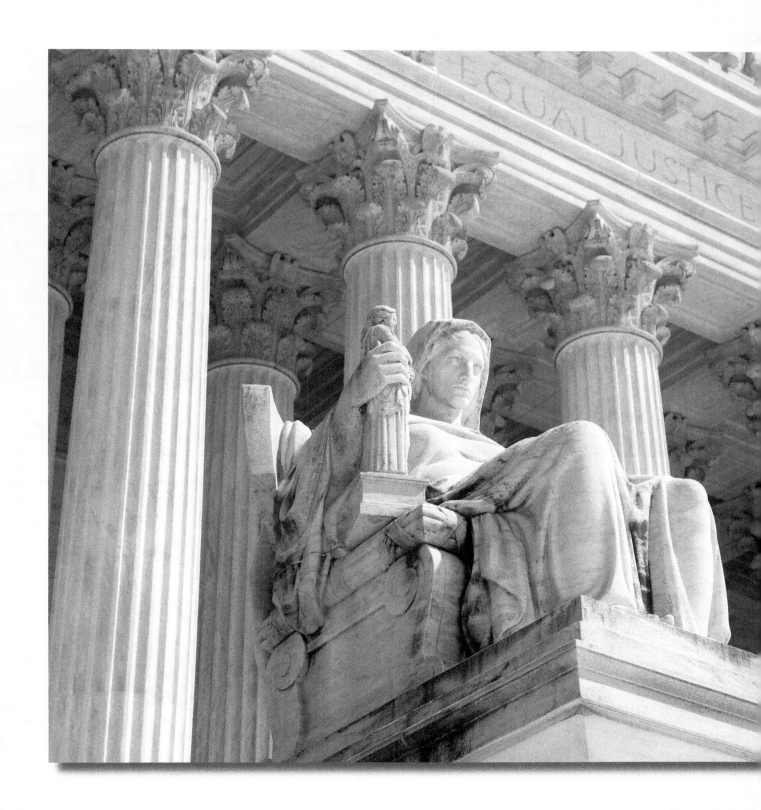

CHAPTER 9

Nature of Traditional and E-Contracts

NEW YORK CITY

New York City is the largest city in the United States. It is an international center of business, commerce, industry, and finance. Commerce in New York City and worldwide relies on business contracts. Contracts are the basis of many of our daily activities. They provide the means for individuals and businesses to sell and otherwise transfer property, services, and other rights. The purchase of goods is based on sales contracts; the hiring of employees is based on service contracts; the lease of an apartment, office, and commercial buildings is based on a rental contract; and the sale of goods and services over the Internet is based on electronic contracts. The list is almost endless. Without enforceable contracts, commerce would collapse.

Learning Objectives

After studying this chapter, you should be able to:

1. Define *contract*.
2. List the elements necessary to form a valid contract.
3. Distinguish between bilateral and unilateral contracts.
4. Describe and distinguish between express and implied-in-fact contracts.
5. Describe and distinguish among valid, void, voidable, and unenforceable contracts.

Chapter Outline

> *"The movement of the progressive societies has hitherto been a movement from status to contract."*
>
> —*Sir Henry Maine*
> *Ancient Law, Chapter 5*

Introduction to Nature of Traditional and E-Contracts

Contracts are voluntarily entered into by parties. The terms of a contract become *private law* between the parties. One court has stated that "the contract between parties is the law between them and the courts are obliged to give legal effect to such contracts according to the true interests of the parties."[1]

Most contracts are performed without the aid of the court system. This is usually because the parties feel a moral duty to perform as promised. Although some contracts, such as illegal contracts, are not enforceable, most are **legally enforceable**.[2] Thus, if a party fails to perform a contract, the other party may call on the courts to enforce the contract.

This chapter introduces the study of **traditional contract law** and **electronic contract law (e-contract law)**. Topics such as the definition of *contract*, requirements for forming a contract, sources of contract law, and the various classifications of contracts are discussed.

Contracts must not be the sports of an idle hour, mere matters of pleasantry and badinage, never intended by the parties to have any serious effect whatever.

Lord Stowell
Dalrymple v. Dalrymple (1811)

legally enforceable contract
A contract in which if one party fails to perform as promised, the other party can use the court system to enforce the contract and recover damages or other remedy.

Definition of a Contract

A **contract** is an agreement that is enforceable by a court of law or equity. A simple and widely recognized definition of *contract* is provided by the *Restatement (Second) of Contracts*: "A contract is a promise or a set of promises for the breach of which the law gives a remedy or the performance of which the law in some way recognizes a duty."[3]

Parties to a Contract

Every contract involves at least two parties. The **offeror** is the party who makes an offer to enter into a contract. The **offeree** is the party to whom the offer is made (see **Exhibit 9.1**). In making an offer, the offeror promises to do—or to refrain from doing—something. The offeree then has the power to create a contract by accepting the offeror's offer. A contract is created if the offer is accepted. No contract is created if the offer is not accepted.

offeror
The party who makes an offer to enter into a contract.

offeree
The party to whom an offer to enter into a contract is made.

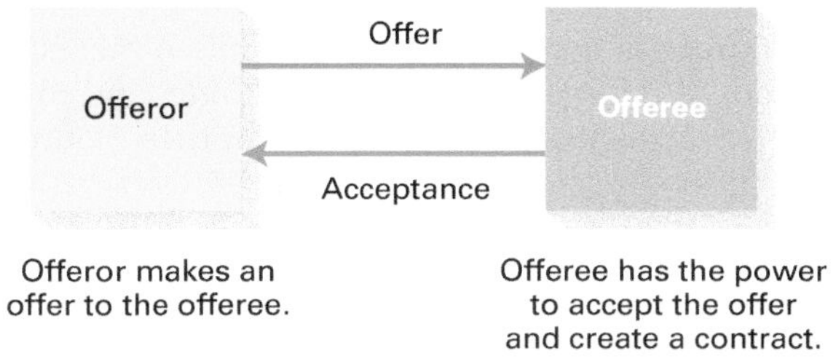

Offer

Offeror

Offeree

Acceptance

Offeror makes an offer to the offeree.

Offeree has the power to accept the offer and create a contract.

Exhibit 9.1 PARTIES TO A CONTRACT

Example Ross makes an offer to Elizabeth to sell his automobile to her for $10,000. In this case, Ross is the offeror, and Elizabeth is the offeree.

Elements of a Contract

Justice is the end of government. It is the end of civil society. It ever has been, and ever will be pursued, until it be obtained, or until liberty be lost in the pursuit.

James Madison
The Federalist No. 51 (1788)

For a contract to be enforceable, the following four basic requirements must be met:

1. **Agreement.** To have an enforceable contract, there must be an **agreement** between the parties. This requires an **offer** by the offeror and an **acceptance** of the offer by the offeree. There must be mutual assent by the parties.
2. **Consideration.** A promise must be supported by a bargained-for **consideration** that is legally sufficient. Money, personal property, real property, provision of services, and the like, qualify as consideration.
3. **Contractual capacity.** The parties to a contract must have **contractual capacity** for the contract to be enforceable against them. Contracts cannot be enforced against parties who lacked contractual capacity when they entered into the contracts.
4. **Lawful object.** The object of a contract must be lawful. Most contracts have a **lawful object**. However, contracts that have an illegal object are void and cannot be enforced.

CONCEPT SUMMARY
ELEMENTS OF A CONTRACT

1. Agreement	3. Contractual capacity
2. Consideration	4. Lawful object

Defenses to the Enforcement of a Contract

Two *defenses* may be raised to the enforcement of contracts:

1. **Genuineness of assent.** The consent of the parties to create a contract must be **genuine**. If the consent is obtained by duress, undue influence, or fraud, there is no real consent.
2. **Writing and form.** The law requires that certain contracts be in **writing** or in a certain **form**. Failure of such a contract to be in writing or to be in proper form may be raised against the enforcement of the contract.

The requirements to form an enforceable contract and the defenses to the enforcement of contracts are discussed in this chapter and the following chapters on contract law.

Sources of Contract Law

There are several sources of contract law in the United States, including the *common law of contracts*, the *Uniform Commercial Code*, and the *Restatement (Second) of Contracts*. The following paragraphs explain these sources in more detail.

Common Law of Contracts

common law of contracts
Contract law developed primarily by state courts.

A major source of contract law is the **common law of contracts**, which developed from early court decisions that became precedent for later decisions. There is a limited federal common law of contracts that applies to contracts made by the federal government. The larger and more prevalent body of common law has been developed from state court decisions. Thus, although the general principles remain the same throughout the country, there is some variation from state to state.

Uniform Commercial Code (UCC)

Another major source of contract law is the **Uniform Commercial Code (UCC)**. The UCC, which was first drafted by the National Conference of Commissioners on Uniform State Laws in 1952, has been amended several times. Its goal is to create a uniform system of commercial law among the 50 states. The provisions of the UCC normally take precedence over the common law of contracts. (The provisions of the UCC are discussed in chapters 18–25 and 27 in this book.)

Uniform Commercial Code (UCC)
A comprehensive statutory scheme that includes laws that cover aspects of commercial transactions.

The UCC is divided into nine main articles. Every state has adopted at least part of the UCC. In the area of contract law, two of the major provisions of the UCC are:

- **Article 2 (Sales).** **Article 2 (Sales)** prescribes a set of uniform rules for the creation and enforcement of contracts for the sale of goods. These contracts are often referred to as **sales contracts**.

  Examples The sale of equipment, automobiles, computers, clothing, and such involve sales contracts subject to Article 2 of the UCC.

- **Article 2A (Leases).** **Article 2A (Leases)** prescribes a set of uniform rules for the creation and enforcement of contracts for the lease of goods. These contracts are referred to as **lease contracts**.

  Examples Leases of automobiles, leases of aircraft, and other leases involving goods are subject to Article 2A of the UCC.

The Restatement of the Law of Contracts

In 1932, the American Law Institute, a group comprised of law professors, judges, and lawyers, completed the ***Restatement of the Law of Contracts***. The *Restatement* is a compilation of contract law principles as agreed on by the drafters. The *Restatement*, which is currently in its second edition, is cited in this book as the ***Restatement (Second) of Contracts***. Note that the *Restatement* is not law. However, lawyers and judges often refer to it for guidance in contract disputes because of its stature.

Restatement of the Law of Contracts
A compilation of model contract law principles drafted by legal scholars. The *Restatement* is not law.

Objective Theory of Contracts

The intent to enter into a contract is determined using the **objective theory of contracts**—that is, whether a reasonable person viewing the circumstances would conclude that the parties intended to be legally bound.

Critical Legal Thinking
Why is the objective theory of contracts applied in determining whether a contract has been created? Why is the subjective intent of the parties not considered?

Example The statement "I will buy your building for $2 million" is a valid offer because it indicates the offeror's present intent to contract.

Example A statement such as "Are you interested in selling your building for $2 million?" is not an offer. It is an invitation to make an offer or an invitation to negotiate.

objective theory of contracts
A theory stating that the intent to contract is judged by the reasonable person standard and not by the subjective intent of the parties.

Offers that are made in jest, anger, or undue excitement do not include the necessary objective intent.

Example The owner of Company A has lunch with the owner of Company B. In the course of their conversation, Company A's owner exclaims in frustration, "For $200, I'd sell the whole computer division!" An offer such as that cannot result in a valid contract.

In the following case, the court enforced a contract.

CASE 9.1 *FEDERAL COURT CASE Contract*

Facebook, Inc. v. Winklevoss

640 F.3d 1034, 2011 U.S. App. Lexis 7430 (2011)
United States Court of Appeals for the Ninth Circuit

"At some point, litigation must come to an end. That point has now been reached."

—Kozinski, Circuit Judge

Facts

Mark Zuckerberg, Cameron Winklevoss, Tyler Winklevoss, and Divya Narendra were schoolmates at Harvard University. The Winklevoss twins, along with Narendra, started a company called ConnectU. They alleged that Zuckerberg stole their idea and created Facebook, and in a lawsuit they filed claims against Facebook and Zuckerberg. The court ordered the parties to mediate their dispute. After a day of negotiations, the parties signed a handwritten, one-and-one-third-page "Term Sheet & Settlement Agreement." In the agreement, the Winklevosses agreed to give up their claims in exchange for cash and Facebook stock. The Winklevosses were to receive $20 million in cash and $45 million of Facebook stock, valued at $36 per share.

The parties stipulated that the settlement agreement was confidential and binding and "may be submitted into evidence to enforce it." The agreement granted all parties mutual releases. The agreement stated that the Winkelvosses represented and warranted that "they have no further right to assert against Facebook" and have "no further claims against Facebook and its related parties." Facebook became an extremely successful social networking site, with its value exceeding over $30 billion at the time the next legal dispute arose.

Subsequently, in a lawsuit, the Winklevosses brought claims against Facebook and Zuckerberg, alleging that Facebook and Zuckerberg had engaged in fraud at the time of forming the settlement agreement. The Winklevosses alleged that Facebook and Zuckerberg had misled them into believing that Facebook shares were worth $36 per share at the time of settlement, when in fact an internal Facebook document valued the stock at $8.88 per share for tax code purposes. The Winklevosses sought to rescind the settlement agreement. The U.S. district court enforced the settlement agreement. The Winklevosses appealed.

Issue

Is the settlement agreement enforceable?

Language of the Court

The Winklevosses are sophisticated parties who were locked in a contentious struggle over ownership rights in one of the world's fastest-growing companies. They brought half-a-dozen lawyers to the mediation. When adversaries in a roughly equivalent bargaining position and with ready access to counsel sign an agreement to "establish a general peace," we enforce the clear terms of the agreement.

There are also very important policies that favor giving effect to agreements that put an end to the expensive and disruptive process of litigation. For whatever reason, the Winklevosses now want to back out. Like the district court, we see no basis for allowing them to do so. At some point, litigation must come to an end. That point has now been reached.

Decision

The U.S. court of appeals upheld the decision of the U.S. district court that enforced the settlement agreement.

Ethics Questions

Should the Winklevosses have had their claims of fraud decided by the court? Did anyone act unethically in this case?

electronic commerce (e-commerce)
The sale and lease of goods and services and other property and the licensing of software over the Internet or by other electronic means.

E-Commerce

During the last few decades, a new economic shift brought the United States and the rest of the world into the information age. Computer technology and the use of the Internet increased dramatically. A new form of commerce—**electronic commerce**, or **e-commerce**—is flourishing. All sorts of goods and services are now sold over the Internet. You can purchase automobiles and children's toys, participate in auctions, purchase airline tickets, make hotel reservations, and purchase other goods and services over the Internet. Companies such as Microsoft Corporation, Google Inc., Facebook, Inc., and other technology companies license the use of their software over the Internet.

Much of the new cyberspace economy is based on **electronic contracts (e-contracts)** and **electronic licenses (e-licenses)**. Electronic licensing is usually of computer and software information. E-commerce has created problems for forming e-contracts over the Internet, enforcing e-contracts, and providing consumer protection. In many situations, traditional contract rules apply to e-contracts. Many states have adopted rules that specifically regulate e-commerce transactions. The federal government has also enacted several laws that regulate e-contracts. Contract rules that apply to e-commerce are discussed in this and the following chapters.

The following feature discusses a uniform law that provides rules for the formation and performance of computer information contracts.

electronic contract (e-contract)
A contract that is formed electronically.

Uniform Computer Information Transactions Act (UCITA)
A model act that establishes uniform legal rules for the formation and enforcement of electronic contracts and licenses.

Digital Law

Electronic Contracts and Licenses

The National Conference of Commissioners on Uniform State Laws (a group of lawyers, judges, and legal scholars) drafted the **Uniform Computer Information Transactions Act (UCITA)**.

The UCITA establishes uniform legal rules for the formation and enforcement of electronic contracts and licenses. The UCITA addresses most of the legal issues that are encountered while conducting e-commerce over the Internet.

The UCITA is a model act that does not become law until a state legislature adopts it as a statute for the state. Although most states have not adopted the UCITA, the UCITA has served as a model for states that have enacted their own statutes that govern e-commerce. Because of the need for uniformity of e-commerce rules, states are attempting to adopt uniform laws to govern the creation and enforcement of cyberspace contracts and licenses.

Classifications of Contracts

There are several types of contracts. Each differs somewhat in formation, enforcement, performance, and discharge. The different types of contracts are discussed in the following paragraphs.

Bilateral and Unilateral Contracts

Contracts are either *bilateral* or *unilateral*, depending on what the offeree must do to accept the offeror's offer. The language of the offeror's promise must be carefully scrutinized to determine whether it is an offer to create a bilateral or a unilateral contract. If there is any ambiguity as to which it is, it is presumed to be a bilateral contract.

A contract is **bilateral contract** if the offeror's promise is answered with the offeree's promise of acceptance. In other words, a bilateral contract is a "promise for a promise." This exchange of promises creates an enforceable contract. No act of performance is necessary to create a bilateral contract.

bilateral contract
A contract entered into by way of exchange of promises of the parties; "a promise for a promise."

Example Mary, the owner of the Chic Dress Shop, says to Peter, a painter, "If you promise to paint my store by July 1, I will pay you $3,000." Peter says, "I promise to do so." A *bilateral contract* was created at the moment Peter promised to paint the dress shop (a promise for a promise). If Peter fails to paint the shop, Mary can sue Peter and recover whatever damages result from his breach of contract.

Similarly, Peter can sue Mary if she refuses to pay him after he has performed as promised.

unilateral contract
A contract in which the offeror's offer can be accepted only by the performance of an act by the offeree; a "promise for an act."

A contract is a **unilateral contract** if the offeror's offer can be accepted only by the performance of an act by the offeree. There is no contract until the offeree performs the requested act. An offer to create a unilateral contract cannot be accepted by a promise to perform. It is a "promise for an act."

Example Mary, the owner of the Chic Dress Shop, says to Peter, a painter, "If you paint my shop by July 1, I will pay you $3,000." This offer creates a *unilateral contract*. The offer can be accepted only by the painter's performance of the requested act. If Peter does not paint the shop by July 1, there has been no acceptance, and Mary cannot sue Peter for damages. If Peter paints the shop by July 1, Mary owes Peter $3,000. If Mary refuses to pay, Peter can sue Mary to collect payment.

Incomplete or Partial Performance Problems can arise if the offeror in a unilateral contract attempts to revoke an offer after the offeree has begun performance. Generally, an offer to create a unilateral contract can be revoked by the offeror any time prior to the offeree's performance of the requested act. However, the offer cannot be revoked if the offeree has begun or has substantially completed performance.

A man must come into a court of equity with clean hands.

C. B. Eyre
Dering v. Earl of Winchelsea (1787)

Example Suppose Alan Matthews tells Sherry Levine that he will pay her $5,000 if she finishes the Boston Marathon. Alan cannot revoke the offer once Sherry starts running the marathon.

Formal and Informal Contracts

Contracts may be classified as either *formal* or *informal*.

formal contract
A contract that requires a special form or method of creation.

Formal Contracts **Formal contracts** are contracts that require a special form or method of creation. The *Restatement (Second) of Contracts* identifies the following types of formal contracts[4]:

- **Negotiable instruments. Negotiable instruments**, which include checks, drafts, notes, and certificates of deposit, are special forms of contracts recognized by the UCC. They require a special form and language for their creation and must meet certain requirements for transfer.
- **Letters of credit.** A **letter of credit** is an agreement by the issuer of the letter to pay a sum of money on the receipt of an invoice and other documents. Letters of credit are governed by the UCC.
- **Recognizance.** In a **recognizance**, a party acknowledges in court that he or she will pay a specified sum of money if a certain event occurs.
- **Contracts under seal.** This type of contract is one to which a seal (usually a wax seal) is attached. Although no state currently requires contracts to be under seal, a few states provide that no consideration is necessary if a contract is made under seal.

informal contract (simple contract)
A contract that is not formal. Valid informal contracts are fully enforceable and may be sued upon if breached.

Informal Contracts All contracts that do not qualify as formal contracts are called **informal contracts** (or **simple contracts**). The term is a misnomer. Valid informal contracts (e.g., leases, sales contracts, service contracts) are fully enforceable and may be sued on if breached. They are called *informal contracts* only because no special form or method is required for their creation. Thus, the parties to an informal contract can use any words they choose to express their contract. The majority of the contracts entered into by individuals and businesses are informal contracts.

Valid, Void, Voidable, and Unenforceable Contracts

Contract law places contracts in the following categories:

1. **Valid contract.** A **valid contract** meets all the essential elements to establish a contract. In other words, it (1) consists of an agreement between the parties, (2) is supported by legally sufficient consideration, (3) is between parties with contractual capacity, and (4) accomplishes a lawful object. A valid contract is enforceable by at least one of the parties.
2. **Void contract.** A **void contract** has no legal effect. It is as if no contract had ever been created. A contract to commit a crime is void. If a contract is void then neither party is obligated to perform the contract and neither party can enforce the contract.
3. **Voidable contract.** A **voidable contract** is a contract in which at least one party has the *option* to void his or her contractual obligations. If the contract is voided, both parties are released from their obligations under the contract. If the party with the option chooses to ratify the contract, both parties must fully perform their obligations.

   With certain exceptions, contracts may be voided by minors; insane persons; intoxicated persons; and persons acting under duress, undue influence, or fraud; and in cases involving mutual mistake.
4. **Unenforceable contract.** With an **unenforceable contract**, there is some legal defense to the enforcement of the contract. If a contract is required to be in writing under the Statute of Frauds but is not, the contract is unenforceable. The parties may voluntarily perform a contract that is unenforceable.

valid contract
A contract that meets all the essential elements to establish a contract; a contract that is enforceable by at least one of the parties.

void contract
A contract that has no legal effect; a nullity.

voidable contract
A contract in which one or both parties have the option to void their contractual obligations. If a contract is voided, both parties are released from their contractual obligations.

unenforceable contract
A contract in which the essential elements to create a valid contract are met but there is some legal defense to the enforcement of the contract.

Executory and Executed Contracts

A contract that has not been performed by both sides is called an **executory contract**. Contracts that have been fully performed by one side but not by the other are classified as executory contracts.

executory contract
A contract that has not been fully performed by either or both sides.

Examples Suppose Elizabeth signs a contract to purchase a new BMW automobile from Ace Motors. She has not yet paid for the car, and Ace Motors has not yet delivered the car to Elizabeth. This is an executory contract because the contract has not yet been performed. If Elizabeth has paid for the car but Ace Motors has not yet delivered the car to Elizabeth, there is an executory contract because Ace Motors has not performed the contract.

A completed contract—that is, one that has been fully performed on both sides—is called an **executed contract**.

executed contract
A contract that has been fully performed on both sides; a completed contract.

Example If in the prior example Elizabeth has paid for the car and Ace Motors has delivered the car to Elizabeth, the contract has been fully performed by both parties and is an executed contract.

Express and Implied Contracts

An **actual contract** may be either *express* or *implied-in-fact*. These are described in the following paragraphs.

Express Contract

An **express contract** is stated in oral or written words. Most personal and business contracts are express contracts.

express contract
An agreement that is expressed in written or oral words.

Examples A written agreement to buy an automobile from a dealership is an express contract because it is in written words. An oral agreement to purchase a neighbor's bicycle is an express contract because it is in oral words.

Implied-in-Fact Contract

implied-in-fact contract
A contract in which agreement between parties has been inferred from their conduct.

Implied-in-fact contracts are implied from the conduct of the parties. The following elements must be established to create an implied-in-fact contract:

1. The plaintiff provided property or services to the defendant.
2. The plaintiff expected to be paid by the defendant for the property or services and did not provide the property or services gratuitously.
3. The defendant was given an opportunity to reject the property or services provided by the plaintiff but failed to do so.

In the following case, the court had to decide whether there was an implied-in-fact contract.

CASE 9.2 *FEDERAL COURT CASE Implied-in-Fact Contract*

Wrench LLC v. Taco Bell Corporation

256 F.3d 446, 2001 U.S. App. Lexis 15097 (2001)
United States Court of Appeals for the Sixth Circuit

"The district court found that appellants produced sufficient evidence to create a genuine issue of material fact regarding whether an implied-in-fact contract existed between the parties."

—Graham, Circuit Judge

Facts

Thomas Rinks and Joseph Shields created the Psycho Chihuahua cartoon character, which they promote, market, and license through their company, Wrench LLC. Psycho Chihuahua is a clever, feisty cartoon character dog with an attitude, a self-confident, edgy, cool dog who knows what he wants and will not back down. Rinks and Shields attended a licensing trade show in New York City, where they were approached by two Taco Bell employees, Rudy Pollak, a vice president, and Ed Alfaro, a creative services manager. Taco Bell owns and operates a nationwide chain of fast-food Mexican restaurants. Pollak and Alfaro expressed interest in the Psycho Chihuahua character for Taco Bell advertisements because they thought his character would appeal to Taco Bell's core consumers, males ages 18 to 24. Pollak and Alfaro obtained some Psycho Chihuahua materials to take back with them to Taco Bell's headquarters.

Later, Alfaro contacted Rinks and asked him to create art boards combining Psycho Chihuahua with the Taco Bell name and image. Rinks and Shields prepared art boards and sent them to Alfaro, along with Psycho Chihuahua T-shirts, hats, and stickers. Alfaro showed these materials to Taco Bell's vice president of brand management as well as to Taco Bell's outside advertising agency. Rinks suggested to Alfaro that Taco Bell should use a live Chihuahua dog manipulated by computer graphic imaging that had the personality of Psycho Chihuahua and a love for Taco Bell food. Rinks and Shields gave a formal presentation of their concept of using an animated dog to Taco Bell's marketing department. Taco Bell would not enter into an express contract with Wrench LLC, Rinks, or Shields.

Just after Rinks and Shields's presentation, Taco Bell hired a new outside advertising agency, Chiat/Day. Taco Bell gave Chiat/Day materials received from Rinks and Shields regarding Psycho Chihuahua. Three months later, Chiat/Day proposed using a Chihuahua in Taco Bell commercials. Chiat/Day says that it conceived this idea by itself. Taco Bell aired its Chihuahua commercials in the United States, and they became an instant success and the basis of its advertising. Taco Bell paid nothing to Wrench LLC or to Rinks and Shields. Plaintiffs Wrench LLC, Rinks, and Shields sued defendant Taco Bell to recover damages for breach of an implied-in-fact contract. On this issue, the U.S. district court agreed with the plaintiffs. The decision was appealed.

Issue

Have the plaintiffs Wrench LLC, Rinks, and Shields stated a cause of action for the breach of an implied-in-fact contract?

(case continues)

Language of the Court

The district court found that appellants produced sufficient evidence to create a genuine issue of material fact regarding whether an implied-in-fact contract existed between the parties. On appeal, Taco Bell argues that this conclusion was erroneous, and asserts that the record contains no evidence of an enforceable contract. We agree with the district court's finding that appellants presented sufficient evidence to survive summary judgment on the question of whether an implied-in-fact contract existed under Michigan law.

Decision

The U.S. court of appeals held that the plaintiffs had stated a proper cause of action against defendant Taco Bell for breach of an implied-in-fact contract. The court of appeals remanded the case for trial.

Note

The U.S. Supreme Court denied review of the decision in this case. In 2003, a federal court jury ordered Taco Bell to pay $30 million to plaintiffs Thomas Rinks and Joseph Shields for stealing their idea for the Psycho Chihuahua commercials. Later, the court awarded an additional $11.8 million in prejudgment interest, bringing the total award to more than $42 million.

Ethics Questions

Did Taco Bell act ethically in this case? Did Chiat/Day act ethically in this case?

Implied-in-Law Contract (Quasi Contract)

The equitable doctrine of **implied-in-law contract**, also called **quasi contract**, allows a court to award monetary damages to a plaintiff for providing work or services to a defendant even though no actual contract existed between the parties. Recovery is generally based on the reasonable value of the services received by the defendant.

The doctrine of quasi contract is intended to prevent *unjust enrichment* and *unjust detriment*. It does not apply where there is an enforceable contract between the parties. A quasi contract is imposed where (1) one person confers a benefit on another, who retains the benefit, and (2) it would be unjust not to require that person to pay for the benefit received.

implied-in-law contract (quasi contract)
An equitable doctrine whereby a court may award monetary damages to a plaintiff for providing work or services to a defendant even though no actual contract existed. The doctrine is intended to prevent unjust enrichment and unjust detriment.

Example Heather is driving her automobile when she is involved in a serious accident in which she is knocked unconscious. She is rushed to Metropolitan Hospital, where the doctors and other staff members perform the necessary medical procedures to save her life. Heather comes out of her coma and, after recovering, is released from the hospital. Subsequently, Metropolitan Hospital sends Heather a bill for its services. The charges are reasonable. Under the doctrine of quasi contract, Heather is responsible for any charges that are not covered by her insurance.

WEB EXERCISE
Go to **www.youtube.com/watch?v=BOoEwOIMLXI** for a video clip of Taco Bell's Chihuahua commercial.

Critical Legal Thinking
Why does the law recognize quasi contracts? Are they difficult to prove?

CONCEPT SUMMARY
CLASSIFICATIONS OF CONTRACTS

Formation	1. **Bilateral contract.** A promise for a promise. 2. **Unilateral contract.** A promise for an act. 3. **Express contract.** A contract expressed in oral or written words. 4. **Implied-in-fact contract.** A contract inferred from the conduct of the parties. 5. **Implied-in-law contract (quasi contract).** A contract implied by law to prevent unjust enrichment. 6. **Formal contract.** A contract that requires a special form or method of creation. 7. **Informal contract.** A contract that requires no special form or method of creation.

Enforceability	1. **Valid contract.** A contract that meets all the essential elements of establishing a contract. 2. **Void contract.** No contract exists. 3. **Voidable contract.** A contract in which at least one party has the option of voiding the contract. 4. **Unenforceable contract.** A contract that cannot be enforced because of a legal defense.
Performance	1. **Executed contract.** A contract that is fully performed on both sides. 2. **Executory contract.** A contract that is not fully performed by one or both parties.

Equity

equity
A doctrine that permits judges to make decisions based on fairness, equality, moral rights, and natural law.

Recall that two separate courts developed in England: the courts of law and the Chancery Court (or courts of equity). The equity courts developed a set of maxims based on fairness, equality, moral rights, and natural law that were applied in settling disputes. **Equity** was resorted to when (1) an award of money damages "at law" would not be the proper remedy or (2) fairness required the application of equitable principles. Today, in most states of the United States, the courts of law and equity have been merged into one court. In an action "in equity," the judge decides the equitable issue; there is no right to a jury trial in an equitable action. The doctrine of equity is sometimes applied in contract cases.

The following critical legal thinking case illustrates the application of the doctrine of equity.

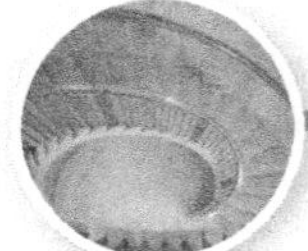

Critical Legal Thinking Case

Equity

"There is only minimal delay in giving notice, the harm to the lessor is slight, and the hardship to the lessee is severe."

—Abbe, Judge

A landlord leased a motel he owned to lessees for a 10-year period. The lessees had an option to extend the lease for an additional 10 years. To do so, they had to give written notice to the landlord three months before the first 10-year lease expired.

For almost 10 years, the lessees devoted most of their assets and a great deal of their energy to building up the business. During this time, they transformed a disheveled, unrated motel into an AAA three-star operation. With the landlord's knowledge, the lessees made extensive long-term improvements that greatly increased the value of both the property and the business.

Prior to three months before the end of the lease, the lessees told the landlord orally that they intended to extend the lease. The lessees instructed their accountant to give the landlord written notice of the option to extend the lease for another 10 years. Despite reminders from the lessees, the accountant failed to give the written notice within three months of the expiration of the lease. As soon as they discovered the mistake, the lessees personally delivered a written notice of renewal of the option to the landlord, 13 days too late. The landlord rejected it as late and instituted a lawsuit to evict the lessees.

The trial and appellate courts held in favor of the lessees. The courts rejected the landlord's argument for strict adherence to the deadline for giving written notice of renewal of the lease. Instead, the courts granted equitable relief and permitted the late renewal notice. The court reasoned that "there is only minimal delay in giving notice, the harm to the lessor is slight, and the hardship to the lessee is severe." *Romasanta v. Mitton*, 189 Cal.App.3d 1026, 234 Cal.Rptr. 729, 1987 Cal. App. Lexis 1428 (Court of Appeal of California)

Critical Legal Thinking Questions

Why does the law recognize the doctrine of *equity*? Should the court have applied the doctrine of equity and saved the lessees from their mistake? Did the landlord act ethically in this case?

Key Terms and Concepts

Acceptance (240)
Actual contract (245)
Agreement (240)
Article 2 (Sales) (241)
Article 2A (Leases) (241)
Bilateral contract (243)
Common law of contracts (240)
Consideration (240)
Contract (239)
Contractual capacity (240)
Electronic commerce (e-commerce) (242)
Electronic contract (e-contract) (243)
Electronic contract law (e-contract law) (239)
Electronic license (e-license) (243)
Equity (248)
Executed contract (245)
Executory contract (245)
Express contract (245)
Form (240)
Formal contract (244)
Genuine (240)
Genuineness of assent (240)
Implied-in-fact contract (246)
Implied-in-law contract (quasi contract) (247)
Informal contract (simple contract) (244)
Lawful object (240)
Lease contract (241)
Legally enforceable (239)
Letter of credit (244)
Negotiable instrument (244)
Objective theory of contracts (241)
Offer (240)
Offeree (239)
Offeror (239)
Recognizance (244)
Restatement of the Law of Contracts (241)
Restatement (Second) of Contracts (241)
Sales contract (241)
Traditional contract law (239)
Unenforceable contract (245)
Uniform Commercial Code (UCC) (241)
Uniform Computer Information Transactions Act (UCITA) (243)
Unilateral contract (244)
Valid contract (245)
Void contract (245)
Voidable contract (245)
writing (240)

Critical Legal Thinking Cases

9.1 Implied-in-Fact Contract Selchow & Richter Company (S&R) owns the trademark to the famous board game Scrabble. Mark Landsberg wrote a book on strategy for winning at Scrabble and contracted S&R to request permission to use the Scrabble trademark. In response, S&R requested a copy of Landsberg's manuscript, which he provided. After prolonged negotiations between the parties regarding the possibility of S&R's publication of the manuscript broke off, S&R brought out its own Scrabble strategy book. No express contract was ever entered into between Landsberg and S&R. Landsberg sued S&R for damages for breach of an implied contract. Is there an implied-in-fact contract between the parties? *Landsberg v. Selchow & Richter Company*, 802 F.2d 1193, 1986 U.S. App. Lexis 32453 (United States Court of Appeals for the Ninth Circuit)

9.2 Bilateral or Unilateral Contract G. S. Adams Jr., vice president of the Washington Bank & Trust Co., met with Bruce Bickham. An agreement was reached whereby Bickham agreed to do his personal and corporate banking business with the bank, and the bank agreed to loan Bickham money at 7.5 percent interest per annum. Bickham would have ten years to repay the loans. For the next two years, the bank made several loans to Bickham at 7.5 percent interest. Adams then resigned from the bank. The bank notified Bickham that general economic changes made it necessary to charge a higher rate of interest on both outstanding and new loans. Bickham sued the bank for breach of contract. Was the contract a bilateral or a unilateral contract? Does Bickham win? *Bickham v. Washington Bank & Trust Company*, 515 So.2d 457, 1987 La. App. Lexis 10442 (Court of Appeal of Louisiana)

9.3 Implied-in-Fact Contract For six years, Lee Marvin, an actor, lived with Michelle Marvin. They were not married. At the end of six years, Lee Marvin compelled Michelle Marvin to leave his household. He continued to support her for another year but thereafter refused to provide further support. During their time together, Lee Marvin earned substantial income and acquired property, including motion-picture rights worth more than $1 million. Michelle Marvin brought an action against Lee Marvin, alleging that an implied-in-fact contract existed between them and that she was entitled to half of the property that they had acquired while living together. She claimed that she had given up a lucrative career as an entertainer and singer to be a full-time companion, homemaker, housekeeper, and cook. Can an implied-in-fact contract result from the conduct of unmarried persons who live together? *Marvin v. Marvin*, 18 Cal.3d 660, 557 P.2d 106, 134 Cal. Rptr. 815, 1976 Cal. Lexis 377 (Supreme Court of California)

9.4 Objective Theory of Contracts Al and Rosemary Mitchell owned a small secondhand store. The Mitchells attended Alexander's Auction, where they frequently shopped to obtain merchandise for their business. While at the auction, they purchased a used safe for $50. They were told by the auctioneer that the inside compartment of the safe was locked and that no key could be found to unlock it. The safe was part of the Sumstad Estate. Several days after the auction, the Mitchells took the safe to a locksmith to have the locked compartment opened. When the locksmith opened the compartment, he found $32,207 in cash. The locksmith called the City of Everett Police, who impounded the money. The City of Everett commenced an action against the Sumstad Estate and the Mitchells to determine who owns the cash that was found in the safe. Who owns the money found in the safe? *City of Everett, Washington v. Mitchell*, 631 P.2d 366, 1981 Wash. Lexis 1139 (Supreme Court of Washington)

Ethical

Ethics Cases

9.5 Ethics Case The Lewiston Lodge of Elks sponsored a golf tournament at the Fairlawn Country Club in Poland, Maine. For promotional purposes, Marcel Motors, an automobile dealership, agreed to give any golfer who shot a hole-in-one a new Dodge automobile. Fliers advertising the tournament were posted in the Elks Club and sent to potential participants. On the day of the tournament, the new Dodge automobile was parked near the clubhouse, with one of the posters conspicuously displayed on the vehicle. Alphee Chenard Jr., who had seen the promotional literature regarding the hole-in-one offer, registered for the tournament and paid the requisite entrance fee. While playing the 13 hole of the golf course, in the presence of the other members of his foursome, Chenard shot a hole-in-one. When Marcel Motors refused to tender the automobile, Chenard sued for breach of contract. Was the contract a bilateral or a unilateral contract? Does Chenard win? Is it ethical for Marcel Motors to refuse to give the automobile to Chenard? *Chenard v. Marcel Motors*, 387 A.2d 596, 1978 Me. Lexis 911 (Supreme Judicial Court of Maine)

9.6 Ethics Case Loren Vranich, a doctor practicing under the corporate name Family Health Care, P.C., entered into a written employment contract to hire Dennis Winkel. The contract provided for an annual salary, insurance benefits, and other employment benefits. Another doctor, Dr. Quan, also practiced with Dr. Vranich. About 9 months later, when Dr. Quan left the practice, Vranich and Winkel entered into an oral modification of their written contract whereby Winkel was to receive a higher salary and a profit-sharing bonus. During the next year, Winkel received the increased salary. However, a disagreement arose, and Winkel sued to recover the profit-sharing bonus. Under Montana law, a written contract can be altered only in writing or by an executed oral agreement. Dr. Vranich argued that the contract could not be enforced because it was not in writing. Does Winkel receive the profit-sharing bonus? Is it ethical of Dr. Vranich to raise the defense that the contract is not in writing? *Winkel v. Family Health Care, P.C.*, 668 P.2d 208, 1983 Mont. Lexis 785 (Supreme Court of Montana)

Notes

1. *Rebstock v. Birthright oil & Gas Co.*, 406 So.2d 636, 1981 La.App. Lexis 5242 (Court of Appeal of Louisiana).
2. *Restatement (Second) of Contracts*, Section 1.
3. *Restatement (Second) of Contracts*, Section 1.
4. *Restatement (Second) of Contracts*, Section 6.

CHAPTER

10 Agreement

HOUSE FOR SALE

The owner of this house has offered the house for sale. The owner's offer lists the price and other terms that the owner wishes to be met before he will sell the house. An interested buyer can purchase the house by agreeing to those terms. Most likely, the interested buyer will make a counteroffer whereby she offers a lower price or possibly other terms that she wants met before she is obligated to purchase the house. If the parties eventually come to a mutual agreement about a price and other terms, a contract has been formed. There has been an offer and an acceptance, therefore creating an enforceable contract. Consideration has been paid by both parties: The seller has sold his property—the house—and the buyer paid money.

Learning Objectives

After studying this chapter, you should be able to:

1. Define *agreement*, *offer*, and *acceptance*.
2. Describe the required terms of an offer.
3. Define special forms of offers, including internet auctions.
4. Define *counteroffer* and describe the effects of a counteroffer.
5. Describe how offers are terminated by acts of the parties and by operation of law.

Chapter Outline

> *"When I use a word," Humpty Dumpty said, in rather a scornful tone, "it means just what I choose it to mean—neither more nor less."*
>
> *"The question is," said Alice, "whether you can make words mean so many different things."*
>
> *"The question is," said Humpty Dumpty, "which is to be master—that's all."*
>
> —*Lewis Carroll*
> *Alice's Adventures in Wonderland (1865)*

Introduction to Agreement

Contracts are voluntary agreements between the parties. One party makes an offer to sell, purchase, or lease a good or to provide or obtain services from another party. The other party may accept the terms of the offer, and if he or she does so, a contract is created. Thus, an offer and an acceptance form the agreement. Assent may be expressly evidenced by the oral or written words of the parties or implied from the conduct of the parties. Without mutual assent, there is no contract.

A party to whom an offer is made may take actions different than accepting the contract. That party may reject the offer, make a counteroffer, or take other actions that do not constitute assent. Sometimes, an offer is terminated before it has been accepted, and this may be by action of the parties or operation of law.

Topics such as offer, acceptance, agreement, and termination of offers are discussed in this chapter.

Agreement

agreement
The manifestation by two or more persons of the substance of a contract.

The words *agreement* and *contract* are often used interchangeably. An **agreement** is a voluntary exchange of promises between two or more legally competent persons to do or to refrain from doing an act. An agreement requires a "meeting of the minds" of the parties—that is, their **mutual assent** to perform current or future contractual duties. A **contract** is an agreement that meets certain additional legal criteria (to be discussed in this and the following chapters) and is enforceable in a court of law. To begin with, a contract requires an *offer* and an *acceptance*.

Offer

offeror
The party who makes an offer.

offeree
The party to whom an offer has been made.

offer
"The manifestation of willingness to enter into a bargain, so made as to justify another person in understanding that his assent to that bargain is invited and will conclude it" (Section 24 of the *Restatement (Second) of Contracts*).

The process of reaching an agreement begins when one party makes an offer to another party to sell or lease property or provide services to another party. Often, prior to entering into a contract, the parties engage in preliminary negotiations about price, time of performance, and so on. At some point, one party makes an offer to the other party. The person who makes the offer is called the **offeror**, and the person to whom the offer is made is called the **offeree**. The offer sets forth the terms under which the offeror is willing to enter into the contract. The offeree has the power to create an agreement by accepting the offer.

Section 24 of the *Restatement (Second) of Contracts* defines an **offer** as "the manifestation of willingness to enter into a bargain, so made as to justify another person in understanding that his assent to that bargain is invited and will conclude it." The following three elements are required for an offer to be effective:

1. The offeror must *objectively intend* to be bound by the offer.
2. The terms of the offer must be definite or reasonably *certain*.
3. The offer must be *communicated* to the offeree.

Generally, an offer is not effective until it is actually received by the offeree. The making of an offer is shown in **Exhibit 10.1**.

Exhibit 10.1 **OFFER**

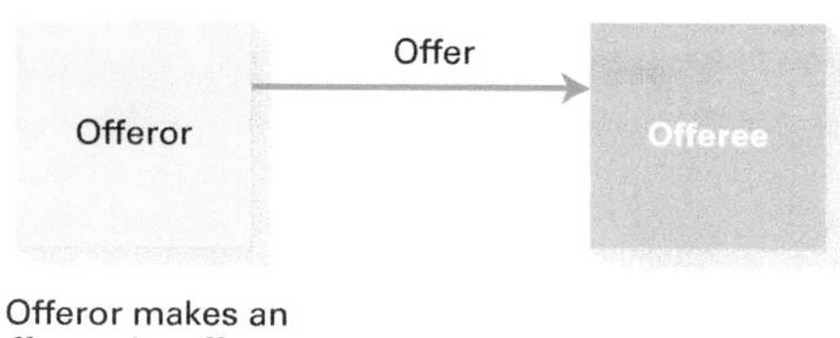
Offer
Offeror
Offeree
Offeror makes an offer to the offeree.

Express Terms

The terms of an offer must be clear enough for the offeree to be able to decide whether to accept or reject the terms of the offer. To be considered definite, an offer (and contract) generally must contain the following terms: (1) identification of the parties, (2) identification of the subject matter and quantity, (3) consideration to be paid, and (4) time of performance. Complex contracts usually state additional terms.

WEB EXERCISE
Go to **www.zenfulcreations.com/resources/worksheets/design_contract.htm**. Read the Web Site Design Contract.

Most offers and contracts set forth **express terms** that identify the parties, the subject matter of the contract, the consideration to be paid by the parties, and the time of performance as well as other terms of the offer and contract.

If the terms are indefinite, the courts usually cannot enforce the contract or determine an appropriate remedy for its breach. However, the law permits some terms to be implied.

Implied Terms

The common law of contracts required an exact specification of contract terms. If one essential term was omitted, the courts held that no contract had been made. This rule was inflexible.

The modern law of contracts is more lenient. The *Restatement (Second) of Contracts* merely requires that the terms of the offer be "reasonably certain."[1] Accordingly, the court can supply a missing term if a reasonable term can be implied.[2] The definition of *reasonable* depends on the circumstances. Terms that are supplied in this way are called **implied terms**.

implied term
A term in a contract that can reasonably be supplied by the courts.

Generally, time of performance can be implied. Price can be implied if there is a market or source from which to determine the price of the item or service (e.g., the "blue book" for an automobile price).

The parties or subject matter of the contract usually cannot be implied if an item or a service is unique or personal, such as the construction of a house or the performance of a professional sports contract.

Communication of an Offer

An offer cannot be accepted if it is not communicated to the offeree by the offeror or a representative or an agent of the offeror.

A contract is a mutual promise.

William Paley
The Principles of Moral and Political Philosophy (1784)

Example Mr. Jones, the CEO of Ace Corporation, wants to sell a manufacturing division to Baker Corporation. He puts the offer in writing, but he does not send it. Mr. Griswald, the CFO of Baker Corporation, visits Mr. Jones and sees the written offer lying on Jones's desk. Griswald tells his CEO about the offer. Because Mr. Jones never communicated the offer to Baker Corporation, there is no offer to be accepted.

In the following case, the court applied the adage "A contract is a contract is a contract."

CASE 10.1 *FEDERAL COURT CASE Contract*

Marder v. Lopez

450 F.3d 445, 2006 U.S. App. Lexis 14330 (2006)
United States Court of Appeals for the Ninth Circuit

". . . . In hindsight the agreement appears to be unfair to Marder—she only received $2,300 in exchange for a release of all claims relating to a movie that grossed over $150 million. . . ."

—Pregerson, Circuit Judge

Facts

The movie *Flashdance* tells a story of a woman construction worker who performs at night as an exotic dancer. Her goal is to obtain formal dance training at a university. The movie is based on the life of Maureen Marder, a nightclub dancer. Paramount Pictures Corporation used information from Marder to create the screenplay for the movie. Paramount paid Marder $2,300, and Marder signed a general release contract that provided that Marder "releases and discharges Paramount Picture Corporation of and from each and every claim, demand, debt, liability, cost and expense of any kind or character which have risen or are based in whole or in part on any matters occurring at any time prior to the date of this Release."

Paramount released the movie *Flashdance*, which grossed more than $150 million in box office receipts and is still shown on television and distributed through DVD rentals. Marder brought a lawsuit in U.S. district court against Paramount, seeking a declaration that she had rights as a coauthor of *Flashdance* and a co-owner with Paramount of the copyright to *Flashdance*. The district court dismissed Marder's claims against Paramount. Marder appealed.

Issue

Is the general release Marder signed an enforceable contract?

Language of the Court

The Release's language is exceptionally broad and we hold that it is fatal to each of Marder's claims against Paramount. Accordingly, the law imputes to Marder an intention corresponding to the reasonable meaning of her words and acts. Though in hindsight the agreement appears to be unfair to Marder—she only received $2,300 in exchange for a release of all claims relating to a movie that grossed over $150 million—there is simply no evidence that her consent was obtained by fraud, deception, misrepresentation, duress, or undue influence.

Decision

The U.S. court of appeals held that the general release Marder signed was an enforceable contract. The court of appeals affirmed the judgment of the district court that dismissed Marder's complaint against Paramount.

Ethics Questions

Did Marder act unethically in bringing this lawsuit? Did Paramount owe an ethical duty to pay Marder more money after the movie *Flashdance* became a success?

Special Offers

There are several special types of offers. These include *advertisements*, *rewards*, and *auctions*.

Advertisements

advertisement
An invitation to make an offer or an actual offer.

As a general rule, **advertisements** for the sale of goods, even at specific prices, generally are treated as **invitations to make an offer**. This rule is intended to protect advertiser-sellers from the unwarranted breach of contract suits for nonperformance that would otherwise arise if the seller ran out of the advertised goods.

There is one exception to this rule: An advertisement is considered an offer if it is so definite or specific that it is apparent that the advertiser has the present intent to bind himself or herself to the terms of the advertisement.

Example An automobile owner's advertisement to sell a "previously owned white 2014 Toyota Prius automobile, serial no. 3210674, $25,000" is an offer. Because the advertisement identifies the exact automobile for sale, the first person to accept the offer owns the automobile.

Rewards

An offer to pay a **reward** (e.g., for the return of lost property or the capture of a criminal) is an offer to form a unilateral contract. To be entitled to collect the reward, the offeree must (1) have knowledge of the reward offer prior to completing the requested act and (2) perform the requested act.

reward
An award given for performance of some service or attainment. To collect a reward, the offeree must (1) have knowledge of the reward offer prior to completing the requested act and (2) perform the requested act.

Example John Anderson accidentally leaves a briefcase containing $500,000 in negotiable bonds on a subway train. He places newspaper ads stating "$5,000 reward for return of briefcase left on a train in Manhattan on January 10, 2015, at approximately 10:00 A.M. Call 212-555-6789." Helen Smith, who is unaware of the offer, finds the briefcase. She reads the luggage tag containing Anderson's name, address, and telephone number, and she returns the briefcase to him. She is not entitled to the reward money because she did not know about it when she performed the requested act.

Auctions

In an **auction**, the seller offers goods for sale through an auctioneer. Unless otherwise expressly stated, an auction is considered an **auction with reserve**—that is, it is an invitation to make an offer. The seller retains the right to refuse the highest bid and withdraw the goods from sale. A contract is formed only when the auctioneer strikes the gavel down or indicates acceptance by some other means. The bidder may withdraw his or her bid prior to that time.

auction with reserve
An auction in which the seller retains the right to refuse the highest bid and withdraw the goods from sale. Unless expressly stated otherwise, an auction is an auction with reserve.

Example If an auction is an *auction with reserve* and an item is offered at $100,000 but the highest bid is $75,000, the auctioneer does not have to sell the item.

If an auction is expressly announced to be an **auction without reserve**, the participants reverse the roles: The seller is the offeror, and the bidders are the offerees. The seller must accept the highest bid and cannot withdraw the goods from sale. However, if the auctioneer has set a minimum bid that it will accept, the auctioneer has to sell the item only if the highest bid is equal to or greater than the minimum bid.

auction without reserve
An auction in which the seller expressly gives up his or her right to withdraw the goods from sale and must accept the highest bid.

CONCEPT SUMMARY
TYPES OF AUCTIONS

Type	Does the seller offer the goods for sale?
Auction with reserve	No. It is an invitation to make an offer. Because the bidd[illegible] (the offeree) may refuse to sell the goods. An auctior[illegible] otherwise stated.
Auction without reserve	Yes. The seller is the offeror and must sell the goods to [illegible] offeree). An auction is without reserve only if it is stipul[illegible]

Termination of an Offer by Act of the Parties

An offer may be terminated by certain acts of the parties. The **termination of an offer by act of the parties** consists of situations in which one party takes an action that indicates that he is not interested in forming a contract under the terms of the offer. Acts of the parties that terminate an offer are discussed in the following paragraphs.

Revocation of an Offer by the Offeror

revocation
Withdrawal of an offer by the offeror that terminates the offer.

Under the common law, an offeror may revoke (i.e., withdraw) an offer any time prior to its acceptance by the offeree. Generally, an offer can be so revoked even if the offeror promised to keep the offer open for a longer time. The **revocation** may be communicated to the offeree by the offeror or by a third party and made by (1) the offeror's express statement (e.g., "I hereby withdraw my offer") or (2) an act of the offeror that is inconsistent with the offer (e.g., selling the goods to another party). Generally, a revocation of an offer is not effective until it is actually received by the offeree.

Offers made to the public may be revoked by communicating the revocation by the same means used to make the offer.

Example If a reward offer for a lost watch was published in two local newspapers each week for four weeks, notice of revocation must be published in the same newspapers for the same length of time. The revocation is effective against all offerees, even those who saw the reward offer but not the notice of revocation.

Rejection of an Offer by the Offeree

rejection
Express words or conduct by the offeree to reject an offer. Rejection terminates the offer.

An offer is terminated if the offeree *rejects* it. Any subsequent attempt by the offeree to accept the offer is ineffective and is construed as a new offer that the original offeror (now the offeree) is free to accept or reject. A **rejection** may be evidenced by the offeree's express words (oral or written) or conduct. Generally, a rejection of an offer is not effective until it is actually received by the offeror.

Example Ji Eun, a sales manager at Apple Computer, Inc., offers to sell 4,000 iMac computers to Ted, the purchasing manager of General Motors Corporation, for $4,000,000. The offer is made on August 1. Ted telephones Ji Eun to say that he is not interested. This rejection terminates the offer. If Ted later decides that he wants to purchase the computers, an entirely new contract must be formed.

Counteroffer by the Offeree

counteroffer
A response by an offeree that contains terms and conditions different from or in addition to those of the offer. A counteroffer terminates the previous offer.

A **counteroffer** by the offeree simultaneously terminates the offeror's offer and creates a new offer. Offerees' making of counteroffers is the norm in many transactions. A counteroffer terminates the existing offer and puts a new offer into play. The previous offeree becomes the new offeror, and the previous offeror becomes the new offeree. Generally, a counteroffer is not effective until it is actually received by the offeror.

Example Fei says to Harold, "I will sell you my house for $700,000." Harold says, "I think $700,000 is too high; I will pay you $600,000." Harold has made a counteroffer. Fei's original offer is terminated, and Harold's counteroffer is a new offer that Fei is free to accept or reject.

The following case involves the issue of a counteroffer.

CASE 10.2 *STATE COURT CASE Counteroffer*

Ehlen v. Melvin

823 N.W.2d 780, 2012 N.D. Lexis 252 (2012)
Supreme Court of North Dakota

"The parties' mutual assent is determined by their objective manifestations, not their secret intentions."
—Kapsner, Justice

Facts

Paul Ehlen signed a document titled "Purchase Agreement" (Agreement) offering to purchase real estate owned by John M. and LynnDee Melvin (the Melvins) for $850,000, with closing to be within twelve days. Two days after the offer was made by Ehlen, the Melvins modified the terms of the Agreement by correcting the spelling of LynnDee Melvin's name and the description of the property, adding that the property was to be sold "as is," that the mineral rights conveyed by the Melvins were limited to the rights that they owned, and that the property was subject to a federal wetland easement and an agricultural lease. The Melvins handwrote all of the changes on the Agreement, initialed each change, signed the Agreement, and returned it to Ehlen. When the Melvins had not heard from Ehlen on the date of the proposed closing, they notified Ehlen that the transaction was terminated. Ehlen sued the Melvins to enforce the Purchase Agreement as modified by them, alleging that there was a binding and enforceable contract. The trial court held that the Melvins had made a counteroffer that had not been accepted by Ehlen, and therefore there was no contract. Ehlen appealed.

Issue

Was a counteroffer made by the Melvins that was accepted by Ehlen?

Language of the Court

The parties' mutual assent is determined by their objective manifestations, not their secret intentions. We conclude the evidence supports the court's finding that the parties did not agree to the essential terms of the agreement and the Melvins' modifications to the agreement constituted a counteroffer. Ehlen argues he accepted any counteroffer the Melvins made. It is a general rule that silence and inaction do not constitute an acceptance of the offer. Ehlen did not sign the modified agreement or initial the changes. The evidence supports the court's finding that Ehlen did not accept the Melvins' counteroffer.

Decision

The supreme court of North Dakota held that no agreement existed between Ehlen and the Melvins.

Ethics Questions

Did Ehlen act ethically in trying to enforce the purported contract? What would be the consequence if silence were considered acceptance?

CONCEPT SUMMARY

TERMINATION OF AN OFFER BY ACT OF THE PARTIES

Action	Description
Revocation	The offeror *revokes* (withdraws) the offer any time prior to its acceptance by the offeree.
Rejection	The offeree rejects the offer by his or her words or conduct.
Counteroffer	A counteroffer by the offeree creates a new offer and terminates the offeror's offer.

The following feature discusses the use of an option contract to require that an offer be kept open for a specified period of time.

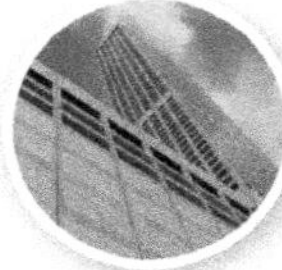

Business Environment

Option Contract

An offeree can prevent the offeror from revoking his or her offer by paying the offeror compensation to keep the offer open for an agreed-on period of time. This creates what is called an **option contract**. In other words, the offeror agrees not to sell the property to anyone except the offeree during the option period. An option contract is a contract in which the original offeree pays consideration (usually money) in return for the original offeror giving consideration (time of the option period). The death or incompetency of either party does not terminate an option contract unless the contract is for the performance of a personal service.

Example Anne offers to sell a piece of real estate to Hal for $1 million. Hal wants time to investigate the property for possible environmental problems and to arrange financing if he decides to purchase the property, so he pays Anne $20,000 to keep her offer open to him for six months. At any time during the option period, Hal may exercise his option and pay Anne the $1 million purchase price. If Hal lets the option expire, however, Anne may keep the $20,000 and sell the property to someone else. Often option contracts are written so that if the original offeree purchases the property, the option amount is applied to the sale price.

Termination of an Offer by Operation of Law

Where law ends, there tyranny begins.

William Pitt, first Earl of Chatham
"Case of Wilkes" (speech, 1805)

An offer can be **terminated by operation of law**. The ways that an offer can be terminated by operation of law are discussed in the following paragraphs.

Destruction of the Subject Matter

An offer terminates if the subject matter of the offer is destroyed through no fault of either party prior to the offer's acceptance.

Example If a fire destroys an office building that has been listed for sale, the offer automatically terminates.

Death or Incompetency of the Offeror or Offeree

Prior to acceptance of an offer, the death or incompetency of either the offeror or the offeree terminates an offer. Notice of the other party's death or incompetence is not a requirement.

Example Suppose that on June 1, Shari offers to sell her house to Damian for $1 million, provided that Damian decides on or before June 15 that he will buy it. Shari dies on June 7, before Damian has made up his mind. The offer automatically terminates on June 7 when Shari dies.

Supervening Illegality

supervening illegality
The enactment of a statute, regulation, or court decision that makes the object of an offer illegal. This action terminates the offer.

If the object of an offer is made illegal prior to the acceptance of the offer, the offer terminates. This situation, which usually occurs when a statute is enacted or a decision of a court is announced that makes the object of the offer illegal, is called a **supervening illegality**.

Example Suppose City Bank offers to loan ABC Corporation $5 million at an 18 percent interest rate. Prior to ABC's acceptance of the offer, the state legislature enacts a statute that sets a usury interest rate of 12 percent. City Bank's offer to ABC Corporation is automatically terminated when the usury statute became effective.

Lapse of Time

lapse of time
A stated time period after which an offer terminates. If no time is stated, an offer terminates after a reasonable time.

An offer expires at the **lapse of time** of an offer. An offer may state that it is effective only until a certain date. Unless otherwise stated, the time period begins to run when the offer is actually received by the offeree and terminates when the stated time period expires.

Example If an offer states, "This offer is good for 10 days," the offer expires at midnight of the 10 day after the offer was made.

Example If an offer states, "This offer must be accepted by January 1, 2017," the offer expires on midnight of January 1, 2017.

If no time is stated in an offer, the offer terminates after a "reasonable time" dictated by the circumstances. A reasonable time to accept an offer to purchase stock traded on a national stock exchange may be a few moments, but a reasonable time to accept an offer to purchase a house may be a week. Unless otherwise stated, an offer made face-to-face or during a telephone call usually expires when the conversation ends.

CONCEPT SUMMARY

TERMINATION OF AN OFFER BY OPERATION OF LAW

Action	Description
Destruction of the subject matter	The subject matter of an offer is destroyed prior to acceptance through no fault of either party.
Death or incompetency	Prior to acceptance of an offer, either the offeror or the offeree dies or becomes incompetent.
Supervening illegality	Prior to the acceptance of an offer, the object of the offer is made illegal by statute, regulation, court decision, or other law.
Lapse of time	An offer terminates on the expiration of a stated time in the offer. If no time is stated, the offer terminates after a "reasonable time."

Acceptance

Acceptance is "a manifestation of assent by the offeree to the terms of the offer in a manner invited or required by the offer as measured by the objective theory of contracts."[3] Recall that generally (1) unilateral contracts can be accepted only by the offeree's performance of the required act and (2) a bilateral contract can be accepted by an offeree who promises to perform (or, where permitted, by performance of) the requested act.

acceptance
"A manifestation of assent by the offeree to the terms of the offer in a manner invited or required by the offer as measured by the objective theory of contracts" (Section 50 of the *Restatement (Second) of Contracts*).

Who Can Accept an Offer?

Only the offeree has the legal power to accept an offer and create a contract. Third persons usually do not have the power to accept an offer. If an offer is made individually to two or more persons, each has the power to accept the offer. Once one of the offerees accepts the offer, it terminates as to the other offeree(s). An offer that is made to two or more persons jointly must be accepted jointly.

The acceptance of an offer is illustrated in **Exhibit 10.2**.

Exhibit 10.2 ACCEPTANCE OF AN OFFER

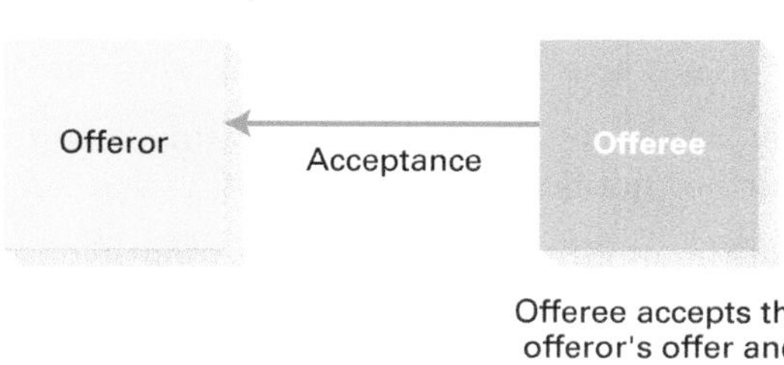
Offeror
Acceptance
Offeree
Offeree accepts the offeror's offer and creates a contract.

Unequivocal Acceptance

An offeree's acceptance must be an **unequivocal acceptance**. That is, the acceptance must be clear and unambiguous, and it must have only one possible meaning. An unequivocal acceptance must not contain conditions or exceptions.

Example Abraham says to Caitlin, "I will sell you my iPad for $300." Caitlin says, "Yes, I will buy your iPad at that price." This is an unequivocal acceptance that creates a contract.

Usually, even a "grumbling acceptance" is a legal acceptance.

Example Jordan offers to sell his computer to Taryn for $450. Taryn says, "Okay, I'll take the computer, but I sure wish you would make me a better deal." This grumbling acceptance creates an enforceable contract because it was not a rejection or a counteroffer.

An **equivocal response** by the offeree does not create a contract.

Example Halim offers to sell his computer to Nicole for $450. Nicole says, "I think I would like it, but I'm not sure." This is equivocation and does not amount to an acceptance.

Mirror Image Rule

For an acceptance to exist, the offeree must accept the terms as stated in the offer. This is called the **mirror image rule**. To meet this rule, the offeree must accept the terms of the offer without modification. Any attempt to accept the offer on different terms constitutes a counteroffer, which rejects the offeror's offer.

mirror image rule
A rule stateing that, for an acceptance to exist, the offeree must accept the terms as stated in the offer.

Critical Legal Thinking

What is the mirror image rule? Why is this rule applied strictly in determining whether a contract has been made?

Examples A seller offers to sell a specific automobile she owns for $30,000. The automobile is a certain brand, model, year, color, and condition. The automobile contains a radio. A buyer accepts the exact terms of the offer. Under the mirror image rule, a contract has been created. On the other hand, if the potential buyer agrees to all of the terms of the seller's offer but demands that an XM satellite radio be installed to replace the regular radio and that a five-year subscription be paid for the satellite service, the mirror image rule has not been met, and no contract is created.

Silence as Acceptance

Silence usually is not considered acceptance, even if the offeror states that it is. This rule is intended to protect offerees from being legally bound to offers because they failed to respond.

Example Coco sends a letter to Dwayne stating, "You have agreed to purchase my motorcycle for $4,000 unless I otherwise hear from you by Friday." Obviously, there is no contract if Dwayne ignores the letter.

Nevertheless, silence *does* constitute acceptance in the following situations:

1. The offeree has indicated that silence means assent.

   Example "If you do not hear from me by Friday, ship the order."

2. The offeree has signed an agreement indicating continuing acceptance of delivery until further notification.

   Example Book-of-the-month and DVD-of-the-month club memberships are examples of such acceptances.

WEB EXERCISE
Go to "Petitioner's Jurisdictional Brief" at **www.floridasupremecourt.org/clerk/briefs/2005/1001-1200/05-1186_Jurislni.pdf**. Scroll to the bottom of page 9 and read "II Strict Application of the 'Mirror Image Rule' Produces Harsh and Inequitable Results" on pages 9 and 10 and the "Conclusion" on page 10.

3. Prior dealings between the parties indicate that silence means acceptance.

   Example A fish wholesaler who delivers 30 pounds of fish to a restaurant each Friday for several years and is paid for the fish can continue the deliveries with expectation of payment until notified otherwise by the restaurant.

Time of Acceptance

Under the common law of contracts, acceptance of a bilateral contract occurs when the offeree *dispatches* the acceptance by an authorized means of communication. This rule is called the **acceptance-upon-dispatch rule** or, more commonly, the **mailbox rule**. Under this rule, the acceptance is effective when it is dispatched, even if it is lost in transmission. If an offeree first dispatches a rejection and then sends an acceptance, the mailbox rule does not apply to the acceptance.[4]

An acceptance sent by an overnight delivery service (e.g., FedEx, UPS) or by fax is governed by the mailbox rule. However, the states are not consistent in applying the mailbox rule to e-mail acceptances. Some states hold that an e-mail acceptance is valid when posted, while others hold that an e-mail acceptance is not valid until received.

The problem of lost acceptances can be minimized by expressly altering the mailbox rule. The offeror can do this by stating in the offer that acceptance is effective only on actual receipt of the acceptance.

Now equity is no part of the law, but a moral virtue, which qualifies, moderates, and reforms the rigor, hardness, and edge of the law, and is a universal truth.

Lord Cowper
Dudley v. Dudley (1705)

acceptance-upon-dispatch rule (mailbox rule)
A rule stating that that an acceptance is effective when it is dispatched, even if it is lost in transmission.

CONCEPT SUMMARY
EFFECTIVE DATES OF COMMUNICATIONS

Type of Communication	Effective When
Offer	Received by offeree
Revocation of offer	Received by offeree
Rejection of offer	Received by offeror
Counteroffer	Received by offeror
Acceptance of offer for a bilateral contract	Dispatched by offeree

Mode of Acceptance

An acceptance must be **properly dispatched**. The acceptance must be properly addressed, packaged in an appropriate envelope or container, and have prepaid postage or delivery charges. Under common law, if an acceptance is not properly dispatched, it is not effective until it is actually received by the offeror.

proper dispatch
The proper addressing, packaging, and posting of an acceptance.

Generally, an offeree must accept an offer by an **authorized means of communication**. Most offers do not expressly specify the means of communication required for acceptance. The common law recognizes certain implied means of communication. Implied authorization may be inferred from what is customary in similar transactions, usage of trade, or prior dealings between the parties. Section 30 of the *Restatement (Second) of Contracts* permits **implied authorization** "by any medium reasonable in the circumstances." Thus, in most circumstances, a party may send an acceptance by mail, overnight delivery service, fax, or e-mail.

implied authorization
A mode of acceptance that is implied from what is customary in similar transactions, usage of trade, or prior dealings between the parties.

An offer can stipulate that acceptance must be by a specified means of communication (e.g., registered mail, telegram). Such stipulation is called **express authorization**. If the offeree uses an unauthorized means of communication to transmit the acceptance, the acceptance is not effective, even if it is received

express authorization
A stipulation in an offer that says the acceptance must be by a specified means of communication.

by the offeror within the allowed time period, because the means of communication was a condition of acceptance.

CONCEPT SUMMARY

RULES OF ACCEPTANCE

Rule	Description
Unequivocal acceptance	An acceptance must be clear and unambiguous, have only one possible meaning, and not contain conditions or exceptions.
Mirror image rule	To create a contract, an offeree must accept the terms as stated in the offeror's offer, without modification. Any attempt to accept the offer on different terms constitutes a counteroffer, which rejects the offeror's offer.
Acceptance-upon-dispatch rule (mailbox rule)	Unless otherwise provided in an offer, acceptance is effective when it is dispatched by the offeree.
Proper dispatch rule	An acceptance must be properly addressed, packaged, and have prepaid postage or delivery charges to be effective when dispatched. Generally, improperly dispatched acceptances are not effective until actually received by the offeror.
Authorized means of communication	Acceptance must be by the express means of communication stipulated in the offer or, if no means is stipulated, then by reasonable means in the circumstances.

Key Terms and Concepts

Acceptance (259)
Acceptance-upon-dispatch rule (mailbox rule) (261)
Advertisement (254)
Agreement (252)
Auction (255)
Auction with reserve (255)
Auction without reserve (255)
Authorized means of communication (261)
Contract (252)
Counteroffer (256)
Equivocal response (260)
Express authorization (261)
Express terms (253)
Implied authorization (261)
Implied terms (253)
Invitation to make an offer (254)
Lapse of time (258)
Mirror image rule (260)
Mutual assent (252)
Offer (252)
Offeree (252)
Offeror (252)
Option contract (258)
Properly dispatched (261)
Rejection (256)
Revocation (256)
Reward (255)
Supervening illegality (258)
Termination of an offer by act of the parties (256)
Termination of an offer by operation of law (258)
Unequivocal acceptance (260)

Critical Legal Thinking Cases

10.1 Mirror Image Rule Norma English made an offer to purchase a house owned by Michael and Laurie Montgomery (Montgomery) for $272,000. In her offer, English also proposed to purchase certain personal property—paving stones and a fireplace screen worth a total of $100—from Montgomery. When Montgomery received English's offer, Montgomery made many changes to English's offer, including deleting the paving stones and fireplace screen from the personal property that English wanted. When English received the Montgomery counteroffer, English accepted and initialed all of Montgomery's changes except that English did not initial the change that deleted the paving stones and fireplace screen from the deal.

Subsequently, Montgomery notified English that because English had not completely accepted the terms of Montgomery's counteroffer, Montgomery was withdrawing from the deal. That same day, Montgomery signed a contract to sell the house to another buyer for $285,000. English sued Montgomery for specific performance of the contract. Montgomery defended, arguing that the mirror image rule was not satisfied because English had not initialed the provision that deleted the paving stones and fireplace screen. Is there an enforceable contract between English and Montgomery? *Montgomery v. English*, 902 So.2d 836, 2005 Fla. App. Lexis 4704 (Court of Appeal of Florida, 2005)

10.2 Agreement Wilbert Heikkila listed eight parcels of real property for sale. David McLaughlin submitted written offers to purchase three of the parcels. Three printed purchase agreements were prepared and submitted to Heikkila, with three earnest-money checks from McLaughlin. Writing on the purchase agreements, Heikkila changed the price of one parcel from $145,000 to $150,000, the price of another parcel from $32,000 to $45,000, and the price of the third parcel from $175,000 to $179,000. Heikkila also changed the closing dates on all three of the properties, added a reservation of mineral rights to all three, and signed the purchase agreements.

McLaughlin did not sign the purchase agreements to accept the changes before Heikkila withdrew his offer to sell. McLaughlin sued to compel specific performance of the purchase agreements under the terms of the agreements before Heikkila withdrew his offer. The court granted Heikkila's motion to dismiss McLaughlin's claim. McLaughlin appealed. Does a contract to convey real property exist between Heikkila and McLaughlin? *McLaughlin v. Heikkila*, 697 N.W.2d 231, 2005 Minn. App. Lexis 591 (Court of Appeals of Minnesota, 2005)

10.3 Solicitation to Make an Offer The U.S. Congress directed the Secretary of the Treasury to mint and sell a stated number of specially minted commemorative coins to raise funds to restore and renovate the Statue of Liberty. The U.S. Mint mailed advertising materials to persons, including Mary and Anthony C. Mesaros, husband and wife that described the various types of coins that were to be issued. Payment could be made by check, money order, or credit card. The materials included an order form. Directly above the space provided on this form for the customer's signature was the following: "YES, Please accept my order for the U.S. Liberty Coins I have indicated."

Mary Mesaros forwarded to the mint a credit-card order of $1,675 for certain coins, including the $5 gold coin. All credit-card orders were forwarded by the Mint to Mellon Bank in Pittsburgh, Pennsylvania, for verification, which took a period of time. Meanwhile, cash orders were filled immediately, and orders by check were filled as the checks cleared. The issuance of 500,000 gold coins was exhausted before Mesaros's credit-card order could be filled. The Mint sent a letter to the Mesaroses, notifying them of this fact. The gold coin increased in value by 200 percent within the first few months of issue. Mary and Anthony C. Mesaros filed a class action lawsuit against the United States, seeking in the alternative either damages for breach of contract or a decree ordering the Mint to deliver the gold coins to the plaintiffs. Is there a contract between the Mesaros and the United States? *Mesaros v. United States*, 845 F.2d 1576, 1988 U.S. App. Lexis 6055 (United States Court of Appeals for the Federal Circuit)

10.4 Counteroffer Glende Motor Company (Glende), an automobile dealership that sold new cars, leased premises from certain landlords. One day, fire destroyed part of the leased premises, and Glende restored the leasehold premises. The landlords received payment of insurance proceeds for the fire. Glende sued the landlords to recover the insurance proceeds. Ten days before the trial was to begin, the defendants jointly served on Glende a document titled "Offer to Compromise Before Trial," which was a settlement offer of $190,000. Glende agreed to the amount of the settlement but made it contingent on the execution of a new lease. The next day, the defendants notified Glende that they were revoking the settlement offer. Glende thereafter tried to accept the original settlement offer. Has there been a settlement of the lawsuit? *Glende Motor Company v. Superior Court*, 159 Cal.App.3d 389, 205 Cal. Rptr. 682, 1984 Cal. App. Lexis 2435 (Court of Appeal of California)

Ethics Case

Ethical

10.5 Ethics Case *Mighty Morphin' Power Rangers* was a phenomenal success as a television series. The Power Rangers battled to save the universe from all sorts of diabolical plots and bad guys. They were also featured in a profitable line of toys and garments bearing the Power Rangers logo. The name and logo of the Power Rangers are known to millions of children and their parents worldwide. The claim of ownership of the logo for the Power Rangers ended up in a battle in a courtroom.

David Dees is a designer who works as d.b.a. David Dees Illustration. Saban Entertainment, Inc. (Saban), which owns the copyright and trademark to Power Rangers figures and the name "Power Ranger," hired Dees as an independent contractor to design a logo for the Power Rangers. The contract signed by the parties was titled "Work-for-Hire/Independent Contractor Agreement." The contract was drafted by Saban with the help of its attorneys; Dees signed the agreement without the representation of legal counsel.

Dees designed the logo currently used for the Power Rangers and was paid $250 to transfer his copyright ownership in the logo. Subsequently, Dees sued Saban to recover damages for copyright and trademark infringement. Saban defended, arguing that Dees was bound by the agreement he had signed. What does the adage "A contract is a contract is a contract" mean? Does the doctrine of equity save Dees from his contract? Does Saban owe an ethical duty to pay Dees more money now that the Power Rangers is a successful brand? Is Dees bound by the contract? *Dees, d/b/a David Dees Illustration v. Saban Entertainment, Inc.*, 131 F.3d 146, 1997 U.S. App. Lexis 39173 (United States Court of Appeals for the Ninth Circuit)

Notes

1. *Restatement (second) of contracts*, Section 204.
2. Section 87(2) of the *Restatement (Second) of Contracts* states that an offer that the offeror should reasonably expect to induce action or forbearance of a substantial character on the part of the offeree before acceptance and that does induce such action or forbearance is binding as an option contract to the extent necessary to avoid injustice.
3. *Restatement (second) of contracts*, Section 50(1).
4. *Restatement (second) of contracts*, Section 40.

CHAPTER

11 Consideration and Promissory Estoppel

BEIJING, CHINA

This is a photograph of the Forbidden City, Beijing, China. In 1999, China dramatically overhauled its contract laws by enacting the ***Unified Contract Law (UCL)****. This new set of laws changed many outdated business and commercial contract laws. The UCL was designed to provide users with a consistent and easy-to-understand set of statutes that more closely resembled international business contracting principles. It also provides for resolution of contract disputes by the application of the rule of law. The UCL covers all the parts of contract law that should be familiar to Western businesses, including the definitions of contract, acceptance, agreement, consideration, breach of contract, and remedies.*

Learning Objectives

After studying this chapter, you should be able to:

1. Define *consideration* and describe the requirements of consideration
2. Define *gift promise* and identify whether gift promises are enforceable.
3. Describe contracts that lack consideration, such as those involving illegal consideration, an illusory promise, a preexisting duty, or past consideration.
4. Define *accord and satisfaction* of a disputed claim.
5. Define and apply the equitable doctrine of *promissory estoppel*.

Chapter Outline

> *"The law has outgrown its primitive stage of formalism when the precise word was the sovereign talisman, and every slip was fatal. It takes a broader view today. A promise may be lacking, and yet the whole writing may be 'instinct with an obligation,' imperfectly expressed."*
>
> —*Cardozo, Justice*
> *Wood v. Duff-Gordon, 222 N.Y.88, 91 (1917)*

Introduction to Consideration and Promissory Estoppel

There is grim irony in speaking of freedom of contract of those who, because of their economic necessities, give their service for less than is needful to keep body and soul together.

Harlan Fiske Stone
Morehead v. New York ex rel. Tipaldo 298 U.S. 587, 56 S.Ct. 918, 1936 U.S. Lexis 1044 (1936)

To be enforceable, a contract must be supported by *consideration*, which is broadly defined as something of legal value. It can consist of money, property, the provision of services, the forbearance of a right, or anything else of value. Most contracts are supported by consideration.

Contracts that are not supported by consideration are usually not enforceable. This means that a party who has not given consideration cannot enforce a contract. The parties may, however, voluntarily perform a contract that is lacking in consideration. If a contract that was lacking in consideration is performed by the parties, the parties cannot subsequently assert lack of consideration to undo the performed contract. *Promissory estoppel* is an equity doctrine that permits a court to order enforcement of a contract that lacks consideration.

This chapter discusses consideration, promises that lack consideration, and equity doctrines that permit promises that lack consideration to be enforced.

Consideration

consideration
Something of legal value given in exchange for a promise.

Consideration must be given before a contract can exist. **Consideration** is defined as something of legal value given in exchange for a promise. Consideration can come in different forms. The most common types consist of either a tangible payment (e.g., money, property) or the performance of an act (e.g., providing legal services). Less usual forms of consideration include the forbearance of a legal right (e.g., accepting an out-of-court settlement in exchange for dropping a lawsuit) and noneconomic forms of consideration (e.g., refraining from "drinking, using tobacco, swearing, or playing cards or billiards for money"[1] for a specified time period).

Written contracts are presumed to be supported by consideration. This rebuttable presumption, however, may be overcome by sufficient evidence. A few states provide that contracts made under seal cannot be challenged for lack of consideration.

Requirements of Consideration

Consideration consists of two elements: (1) Something of *legal value* must be given (i.e., either a legal benefit must be received or legal detriment must be suffered), and (2) there must be a *bargained-for exchange*. Each of these is discussed in the paragraphs that follow:

legal value
Support for a contract when either (1) the promisee suffers a legal detriment or (2) the promisor receives a legal benefit.

bargained-for exchange
Exchange that parties engage in that leads to an enforceable contract.

1. **Legal value.** Under the modern law of contracts, a contract is considered to be supported by **legal value** if (1) the promisee suffers a *legal detriment* or (2) the promisor receives a *legal benefit*.
2. **Bargained-for exchange.** To be enforceable, a contract must arise from a **bargained-for exchange**. In most business contracts, the parties engage in such exchanges. The commercial setting in which business contracts are formed leads to this conclusion.

Gift Promise

Gift promises, also called **gratuitous promises**, are unenforceable because they lack consideration. To change a gift promise into an enforceable promise, the promisee must offer to do something in exchange—that is, in consideration—for the promise. Gift promises cause considerable trouble for persons who do not understand the importance of consideration.

gift promise (gratuitous promise)
A promise that is unenforceable because it lacks consideration.

Example On May 1, Mrs. Colby promises to give her son $10,000 on June 1. When June 1 arrives, Mrs. Colby refuses to pay the $10,000. The son cannot recover the $10,000 because it was a gift promise that lacked consideration. If, however, Mrs. Colby promises to pay her son $10,000 if he earns an A in his business law course and the son earns the A, the contract is enforceable and the son can recover the $10,000.

A completed gift promise cannot be rescinded for lack of consideration.

Example On May 1, Mr. Smith promises to give his granddaughter $10,000 on June 1. If Mr. Smith actually gives the $10,000 to his granddaughter on or before June 1, it is a completed gift promise. Mr. Smith cannot thereafter recover the money from his granddaughter, even if the original promise lacked consideration.

The case that follows involves the issue of whether a giver can recover gifts that he made.

Critical Legal Thinking
Why are gift promises unenforceable if they are not supported by consideration? Do you think that many gift promises are made without the parties realizing that the promise is unenforceable?

CASE 11.1 *STATE COURT CASE Gifts and Gift Promises*

Cooper v. Smith

800 N.E.2d 372, 2003 Ohio App. Lexis 5446 (2003)
Court of Appeals of Ohio

"Many gifts are made for reasons that sour with the passage of time. Unfortunately, gift law does not allow a donor to recover/revoke a gift simply because his or her reasons for giving it have soured."

—Harsha, Judge

Facts

Lester Cooper suffered serious injuries that caused him to be hospitalized for an extended time period. While he was hospitalized, Julie Smith, whom Cooper had met the year before, and Janet Smith, Julie's mother, made numerous trips to visit him. A romantic relationship developed between Cooper and Julie. While in the hospital, Cooper proposed marriage to Julie, and she accepted. Cooper ultimately received an $180,000 settlement for his injuries.

After being released from the hospital, Cooper moved into Janet's house and lived with Janet and Julie. Over the next couple of months, Cooper purchased a number of items for Julie, including a diamond engagement ring, a car, a computer, a tanning bed, and horses. On Julie's request, Cooper paid off Janet's car. Cooper also paid for various improvements to Janet's house, such as having a new furnace installed and having wood flooring laid in the kitchen.

Several months later, the settlement money had run out, and Julie had not yet married Cooper. About six months later, Julie and Cooper had a disagreement, and Cooper moved out of the house. Julie returned the engagement ring to Cooper. Cooper sued Julie and Janet to recover the gifts or the value of the gifts he had given them. The magistrate who heard the case dismissed Cooper's case, and the trial court affirmed the dismissal of the case. Cooper appealed.

Issue

Can Cooper recover the gifts or the value of the gifts he gave to Julie and Janet Smith?

Language of the Court

Unless the parties have agreed otherwise, the donor is entitled to recover the engagement ring (or its value) if the marriage does not occur, regardless of who ended the engagement. Unlike

(case continues)

the engagement ring, the other gifts have no symbolic meaning. Rather, they are merely "tokens of love and affection" which the donor bore for the donee. Many gifts are made for reasons that sour with the passage of time. Unfortunately, gift law does not allow a donor to recover/revoke a gift simply because his or her reasons for giving it have soured. Thus, the gifts are irrevocable gifts and Cooper is not entitled to their return.

Decision

The court of appeals held that the gifts made by Cooper to Julie (other than the engagement ring) and to Janet were irrevocable gifts that he could not recover simply because his engagement with Julie ended. The court of appeals affirmed the judgment of the trial court, allowing Julie and Janet Smith to keep these gifts.

Ethics Questions

Did Julie and Janet Smith act ethically in keeping the gifts Cooper had given them? Did Cooper act ethically in trying to get the gifts back?

Promises That Lack Consideration

Some contracts seem as though they are supported by consideration even though they are not. These contracts *lack consideration* and are therefore unenforceable. Several types of contracts that fall into this category are discussed in the following paragraphs.

Illegal Consideration

illegal consideration
A promise to refrain from doing an illegal act. Such a promise will not support a contract.

A contract cannot be supported by a promise to refrain from doing an illegal act because that is **illegal consideration**. Contracts based on illegal consideration are void.

Example A person threatens a business owner, "I will burn your business down unless you agree to pay me $10,000." Out of fear, the business owner promises to pay the money. This agreement is not an enforceable contract because the consideration given—not to burn a business—is illegal consideration. Thus, the extortionist cannot enforce the contract against the business owner.

Illusory Promise

illusory promise (illusory contract)
A contract into which both parties enter but in which one or both of the parties can choose not to perform their contractual obligations. Thus, the contract lacks consideration.

If parties enter into a contract but one or both of the parties can choose not to perform their contractual obligations, the contract lacks consideration. Such promises, which are known as **illusory promises** (or **illusory contracts**), are unenforceable.

Example A contract that provides that one of the parties has to perform only if he or she chooses to do so is an illusory contract.

Preexisting Duty

preexisting duty
Something a person is already under an obligation to do. A promise lacks consideration if a person promises to perform a preexisting duty.

A promise lacks consideration if a person promises to perform an act or do something he is already under an obligation to do. This is called a **preexisting duty**. The promise is unenforceable because no new consideration has been given.

Example Statutes prohibit police officers from demanding money for investigating and apprehending criminals and prohibit firefighters from demanding payment for fighting fires. If a person agrees to such a demand, she does not have to pay it because public servants are under a preexisting duty to perform their functions.

In the private sector, the preexisting duty rule often arises when one of the parties to an existing contract seeks to change the terms of the contract during the course of its performance. Such midstream changes are unenforceable: The parties have a preexisting duty to perform according to the original terms of the contract.

Sometimes a party to a contract runs into substantial *unforeseen difficulties* while performing his or her contractual duties. If the parties modify their contract to accommodate these unforeseen difficulties, the modification will be enforced even though it is not supported by new consideration.

Past Consideration

Problems of **past consideration** often arise when a party promises to pay someone some money or other compensation for work done in the past. Past consideration is not consideration for a new promise; therefore, a promise based on past consideration is not enforceable.

past consideration
A prior act or performance. Past consideration (e.g., prior acts) do not support a new contract. New consideration must be given.

Example Felipe, who has worked in management for the Acme Corporation for thirty years, is retiring. The president of Acme says, "Because you were such a loyal employee, Acme will pay you a bonus of $100,000." Subsequently, the corporation refuses to pay the $100,000. Unfortunately for Felipe, he has already done the work for which he has been promised to be paid. The contract is unenforceable against Acme because it is based on past consideration.

In the following case, the court had to decide whether there was mutuality of consideration.

CASE 11.2 *FEDERAL COURT CASE Lack of Consideration*

Noohi v. Toll Brothers, Inc.

708 F.3d 599, 2013 U.S. App. Lexis 4188 (2013)
United States Court of Appeals for the Fourth Circuit

"We agree with the district court that the provision binds only plaintiffs to arbitration, and thus lacks mutuality of consideration."

—Davis, Circuit Judge

Facts

Toll Brothers, Inc., is a real estate development company that builds and sells luxury homes across the country. TBI Mortgage, a subsidiary of Toll Brothers, provides mortgages to buyers of Toll Brothers homes. Mehdi Noohi and Soheyla Bolouri, husband and wife (plaintiffs), deposited a total of $77,008 toward the purchase of a Toll Brothers home for $1,006,975 to be built in Maryland. The agreement for sale included an arbitration clause that required the plaintiffs—but not Toll Brothers—to submit to arbitration any disputes regarding the agreement. The agreement of sale required that the plaintiffs seek a mortgage to finance the purchase of the home. The plaintiffs applied for a mortgage from TBI Mortgage and many other lenders but could not get approval for a loan. Toll Brothers had not yet started to build the home and had incurred no costs at the time plaintiffs sought to rescind the agreement and obtain the return of their deposit. When Toll Brothers refused to return the deposit, plaintiffs sued Toll Brothers in U.S. district court for breach of contract individually and on behalf of a class of other prospective buyers who allegedly lost deposits to Toll Brothers in a similar manner. Toll Brothers made a motion to have the case removed for arbitration pursuant to the arbitration clause in the agreement. The district court denied Toll Brothers motion, finding that the arbitration clause was unenforceable because it lacked mutuality of consideration because it required only the buyer—but not the seller—to submit disputes to arbitration. Toll Brothers appealed.

(case continues)

Issue

Was there consideration for the arbitration agreement?

Language of the Court

Under Maryland law an arbitration provision is treated as a severable contract that must be supported by adequate consideration. We agree with the district court that the provision binds only plaintiffs to arbitration, and thus lacks mutuality of consideration. We conclude that the district court correctly held that the arbitration provision was unenforceable for lack of mutual consideration.

Decision

The U.S. court of appeals upheld the U.S. district court's decision that the arbitration clause was unenforceable. The court allowed the plaintiffs to proceed in district court with their class action lawsuit against Toll Brothers.

Ethics Questions

Was it ethical for Toll Brothers to keep the plaintiffs' deposit? Was it ethical for Toll Brothers to bind the plaintiffs to arbitration but not itself?

CONCEPT SUMMARY

CONTRACTS THAT LACK CONSIDERATION

Type of Consideration	Description of Promise
Illegal consideration	Promise to refrain from doing an illegal act.
Illusory promise	Promise in which one or both parties can choose not to perform their obligation.
Preexisting duty	Promise based on the preexisting duty of the promisor to perform.
Past consideration	Promise based on the past performance of the promisee.

Special Business Contracts

Generally, the courts tolerate a greater degree of uncertainty as to the issue of consideration in business contracts than in personal contracts, based on the premise that sophisticated parties know how to protect themselves when negotiating contracts. The law imposes an obligation of good faith on the performance of the parties to requirements and output contracts.

The following paragraphs describe special types of business contracts that allow a greater-than-usual degree of uncertainty concerning consideration.

Output Contract

output contract
A contract in which a seller agrees to sell all of its production to a single buyer.

In an **output contract**, the seller agrees to sell all of its production to a single buyer. Output contracts serve the legitimate business purposes of (1) assuring the seller of a purchaser for all its output and (2) assuring the buyer of a source of supply for the goods it needs.

Example Organic Foods Inc. is a company that operates farms that produce organically grown grains and vegetables. Urban Food Markets is a grocery store chain that sells organically grown foods. Urban Food Markets contracts with Organic Foods Inc. to purchase all the foods Organic Foods Inc. grows organically this year. This is an example of an output contract: Organic Foods Inc. must sell all of its output to Urban Foods Market, and Urban Foods Market must buy all of the output.

Requirements Contract

requirements contract
A contract in which a buyer agrees to purchase all of its requirements for an item from one seller.

A **requirements contract** is a contract in which a buyer agrees to purchase all of its requirements for an item from one seller. Such contracts serve the legitimate business purposes of (1) assuring the buyer of a uniform source of supply and (2) providing the seller with reduced selling costs.

Example The Goodyear Tire & Rubber Company manufactures tires that are used on automobiles. Ford Motor Company manufactures automobiles on which it must place tires before the automobiles can be sold. Assume that Ford Motor Company enters into a contract with Goodyear Tire & Rubber Company to purchase all of the tires it will need this year from Goodyear. This is an example of a requirements contract: Ford Motor Company has agreed to purchase all of the tires it will need from Goodyear. Goodyear may sell tires to other purchasers, however.

Best-Efforts Contract

A **best-efforts contract** is a contract that contains a clause that requires one or both of the parties to use their *best efforts* to achieve the objective of the contract. The courts generally have held that the imposition of the best-efforts duty provides sufficient consideration to make a contract enforceable.

best-efforts contract
A contract that contains a clause that requires one or both of the parties to use their best efforts to achieve the objective of the contract.

Example Real estate listing contracts often require a real estate broker to use his or her best efforts to find a buyer for the listed real estate. Contracts often require underwriters to use their best efforts to sell securities on behalf of their corporate clients. Both of these contracts would be enforceable. Of course, a party can sue another company for failing to use its promised best efforts.

CONCEPT SUMMARY

SPECIAL BUSINESS CONTRACTS

Type of Contract	Description of Contract
Output contract	A contract where the seller agrees to sell all of its production to a single buyer.
Requirements contract	A contract in which a buyer agrees to purchase all of its requirements for an item from one seller.
Best-efforts contract	A contract which contains a clause that requires one or both of the parties to use their *best efforts* to achieve the objective of the contract.

Settlement of Claims

In some situations, one of the parties to a contract believes that he or she did not receive what he or she was due. This party may attempt to reach a compromise with the other party (e.g., by paying less consideration than was provided for in the contract). If the two parties agree to a compromise, a settlement of the claim has been reached. The settlement agreement is called an **accord**. If the accord is performed, it is called a **satisfaction**. This type of settlement is called an **accord and satisfaction**, or a **compromise**.

accord
An agreement whereby the parties agree to accept something different in satisfaction of the original contract.

satisfaction
The performance of an accord.

Example A retailer enters into a contract to license computer software from a technology company for $300,000. This software is to be used to keep track of inventory, accounts receivable, and other financial data. After the software is installed, the computer system works but not as well as promised. The retailer refuses to pay the full amount of the contract. To settle the dispute, the parties agree that $200,000 is to be paid as full and final payment for the software. The retailer pays the $200,000 as agreed. Here, the retailer performed the accord, so there is an accord and satisfaction.

If the accord is not satisfied, the other party can sue to enforce the accord. An accord is enforceable even though no new consideration is given because the parties reasonably disagreed as to the value of the goods or services contracted for. In the alternative, the nonbreaching party to an unperformed accord can choose to enforce the original contract rather than the accord.

Equity: Promissory Estoppel

promissory estoppel (detrimental reliance)
An equitable doctrine that prevents the withdrawal of a promise by a promisor if it will adversely affect a promisee who has adjusted his or her position in justifiable reliance on the promise.

Promissory estoppel (or **detrimental reliance**) is an equity doctrine that permits a court to order enforcement of a contract that lacks consideration. Promissory estoppel is applied to avoid injustice. It is usually used to provide a remedy to a party who has relied on another party's promise but that party has withdrawn its promise and is not subject to a breach of contract action because consideration is lacking.

The doctrine of promissory estoppel **estops** (prevents) the promisor from revoking his or her promise based on lack of consideration. Therefore, the person who has *detrimentally relied* on the promise for performance may sue the promisor for performance or other remedy the court feels is fair to award in the circumstances.

Critical Legal Thinking
What public policy supports the equity doctrine of promissory estoppel to permit the enforcement of a contract that lacks consideration? Are the elements of promissory estoppel difficult to apply?

For the doctrine of promissory estoppel to apply, the following elements must be *shown*:

1. The promisor made a promise.
2. The promisor should have reasonably expected to induce the promisee to reply on the promise.
3. The promisee actually relied on the promise and engaged in an action or forbearance of a right of a definite and substantial nature.
4. Injustice would be caused if the promise were not enforced.

Now equity is no part of the law, but a moral virtue, which qualifies, moderates, and reforms the rigor, hardness, and edge of the law, and is a universal truth.

Lord Cowper
Dudley v. Dudley (1705)

Example XYZ Construction Company, a general contractor, requests bids from subcontractors for work to be done on a hospital building that XYZ plans to submit a bid to build. Bert Plumbing Company, a plumbing subcontractor, submits the lowest bid for the plumbing work, and XYZ incorporates Bert's low bid in its own bid for the general contract. Based on all of the subcontractors' bids, XYZ submits the lowest overall bid to build the hospital and is awarded the contract. Bert Plumbing plans to withdraw its bid. However, the doctrine of promissory estoppel prevents Bert from withdrawing its bid. Since XYZ has been awarded the contract to build the hospital based partially on Bert's Plumbing bid, XYZ can enforce Bert's promise to perform under the doctrine of promissory estoppel. Allowing Bert to withdraw its bid would cause injustice.

Key Terms and Concepts

Accord (271)
Accord and satisfaction (compromise) (271)
Bargained-for exchange (266)
Best-efforts contract (271)
Consideration (266)
Estop (272)
Gift promise (gratuitous promise) (267)
Illegal consideration (268)
Illusory promise (illusory contract) (268)
Legal value (266)
Output contract (270)
Past consideration (269)
Preexisting duty (268)
Promissory estoppel (detrimental reliance) (272)
Requirements contract (270)
Satisfaction (271)
Unified Contract Law (UCL) (265)

Critical Legal Thinking Cases

11.1 Gift Promise Elvis Presley, a singer of great renown and a man of substantial wealth, became engaged to Ginger Alden. He was generous with the Alden family, paying for landscaping the lawn, installing a swimming pool, and making other gifts. When his fiancée's mother, Jo Laverne Alden, sought to divorce her husband, Presley promised to pay off the remaining mortgage indebtedness on the Alden home, which Mrs. Alden was to receive in the divorce settlement. Subsequently, Presley died suddenly, leaving the mortgage unpaid. When the legal representative of Presley's estate refused to pay the mortgage, Mrs. Alden brought an action to enforce Presley's promise. The trial court denied recovery. Mrs. Alden appealed. Is Presley's promise to pay the mortgage enforceable? *Alden v. Presley*, 637 S.W.2d 862, 1982 Tenn. Lexis 340 (Supreme Court of Tennessee)

11.2 Consideration Jack Tallas immigrated to the United States from Greece. He lived in Salt Lake City for nearly 70 years, during which time he achieved considerable success in business, primarily as an insurance agent and landlord. Over a period of 14 years, Peter Dementas, a close personal friend of Tallas's, rendered services to Tallas, including picking up his mail, driving him to the grocery store, and assisting with the management of his rental properties. One day, Tallas met with Dementas and dictated a memorandum to him, in Greek, stating that he owed Dementas $50,000 for his help over the years. Tallas indicated in the memorandum that he would change his will to make Dementas an heir for this amount. Tallas signed the document. Tallas died seven weeks later, without having changed his will to include Dementas as an heir. He left a substantial estate. Dementas filed a claim for $50,000 with Tallas's estate. When the estate denied the claim, Dementas brought this action to enforce the contract. The estate of Tallas argued that Tallas's promise to Dementas lacked consideration and should not be enforced. Is there consideration supporting Tallas's promise to Dementas? *Dementas v. Estate of Tallas*, 764 P.2d 628, 1988 Utah App. Lexis 174 (Court of Appeals of Utah)

Ethics Case

Ethical

11.3 Ethics Case Raymond P. Wirth signed a pledge agreement that stated that in consideration of his interest in education, and "intending to be legally bound," he irrevocably pledged and promised to pay Drexel University the sum of $150,000. The pledge agreement provided that an endowed scholarship would be created in Wirth's name. Wirth died two months after signing the pledge but before any money had been paid to Drexel. When the estate of Wirth refused to honor the pledge, Drexel sued the estate to collect the $150,000. The administrators of the estate alleged that the pledge was unenforceable because of lack of consideration. The surrogate court denied Drexel's motion for summary judgment and dismissed Drexel's claim against the estate. Drexel appealed. Did the administrators of the estate of Wirth act ethically by refusing to honor Mr. Wirth's pledge? Was the pledge agreement supported by consideration and therefore enforceable against the estate of Wirth? *In the Matter of Wirth*, 14 A.D.3d 572, 789 N.Y.S.2d 69, 2005 N.Y. App. Div. Lexis 424 (Supreme Court of New York, Appellate Division, 2005)

Note

1. *Hamer v. Sidwa*, 124 N.Y. 538, 27 N.E. 256, 1891 N.Y. Lexis 1396 (Court of Appeals of New York).

CHAPTER 12

Capacity and Legality

LAS VEGAS, NEVADA
Gambling is illegal in many states. However, the state of Nevada permits lawful gambling. A casino must obtain a license from the Nevada Gaming Commission before it can engage in the gambling business.

Learning Objectives

After studying this chapter, you should be able to:

1. Define and describe the infancy doctrine.
2. Define *legal insanity* and *intoxication* and explain how they affect contractual capacity.
3. Identify illegal contracts that are contrary to statutes and those that violate public policy.
4. Describe covenants not to compete and exculpatory clauses and identify when they are lawful.
5. Define *unconscionable contract* and determine when such contracts are unlawful.

Chapter Outline

"An unconscionable contract is one which no man in his senses, not under delusion, would make, on the one hand, and which no fair and honest man would accept on the other."

—*Fuller, Chief Justice*
Hume v. United States 132 U.S. 406, 10 S.Ct. 134, 1889 U.S. Lexis 1888 (1889)

Introduction to Capacity and Legality

Generally, the law presumes that the parties to a contract have the requisite contractual capacity to enter into the contract. Certain persons do not have this capacity, however, including minors, insane persons, and intoxicated persons. The common law of contracts and many state statutes protect persons who lack contractual capacity from having contracts enforced against them. The party asserting incapacity or his or her guardian, conservator, or other legal representative bears the burden of proof.

An essential element for the formation of a contract is that the object of the contract be lawful. A contract to perform an illegal act is called an *illegal contract*. Illegal contracts are void. That is, they cannot be enforced by either party to the contract. The term *illegal contract* is a misnomer, however, because no contract exists if the object of the contract is illegal. In addition, courts hold that *unconscionable contracts* are unenforceable. An unconscionable contract is one that is so oppressive or manifestly unfair that it would be unjust to enforce it.

Capacity to contract and the lawfulness of contracts are discussed in this chapter.

Minors

Minors do not always have the maturity, experience, or sophistication needed to enter into contracts with adults. Most states have enacted statutes that specify the **age of majority**. The most prevalent age of majority is 18 years of age for both males and females. Any age below the statutory age of majority is called the **period of minority**.

minor
A person who has not reached the age of majority.

Infancy Doctrine

To protect minors, the law recognizes the **infancy doctrine**, which gives minors the right to *disaffirm* (or *cancel*) most contracts they have entered into with adults. This right is based on public policy, which reasons that minors should be protected from the unscrupulous behavior of adults. In most states, the infancy doctrine is an objective standard. If a person's age is below the age of majority, the court will not inquire into his or her knowledge, experience, or sophistication. Generally, contracts for the necessaries of life, which we discuss later in this chapter, are exempt from the scope of this doctrine.

infancy doctrine
A doctrine that allows minors to disaffirm (cancel) most contracts they have entered into with adults.

Under the infancy doctrine, a minor has the option of choosing whether to enforce a contract (i.e., the contract is **voidable** by a minor). The adult party is bound to the minor's decision. If both parties to a contract are minors, both parties have the right to disaffirm the contract.

If performance of the contract favors the minor, the minor will probably enforce the contract. Otherwise, he or she will probably disaffirm the contract. A minor may not affirm one part of a contract and disaffirm another part.

Disaffirmance

disaffirm
The act of a minor to rescind a contract under the infancy doctrine. Disaffirmance may be done orally, in writing, or by the minor's conduct.

A minor can expressly **disaffirm** a contract orally, in writing, or through his or her conduct. No special formalities are required. The contract may be disaffirmed at any time prior to the person's reaching the age of majority plus a "reasonable time." The designation of a reasonable time is determined on a case-by-case basis.

Duties of Restoration and Restitution

If a minor's contract is executory and neither party has performed, the minor can simply disaffirm the contract: There is nothing to recover because neither party has given the other party anything of value. If the parties have exchanged consideration and partially or fully performed the contract by the time the minor disaffirms the contract, however, the issue becomes one of what consideration or restitution must be made. The following rules apply:

- **Minor's duty of restoration.** Generally, a minor is obligated only to return the goods or property he or she has received from the adult in the condition it is in at the time of disaffirmance (subject to several exceptions, discussed later in this chapter), even if the item has been consumed, lost, or destroyed or has depreciated in value by the time of disaffirmance. This rule, called the **duty of restoration**, is based on the rationale that if a minor had to place the adult in status quo on disaffirmance of a contract, there would be no incentive for an adult not to deal with a minor.
- **Competent party's duty of restitution.** If a minor has transferred consideration—money, property, or other valuables—to a competent party before disaffirming the contract, that party must place the minor in status quo. That is, the minor must be restored to the same position he or she was in before the minor entered into the contract. This restoration is usually done by returning the consideration to the minor. If the consideration has been sold or has depreciated in value, the competent party must pay the minor the cash equivalent. This action is called the **duty of restitution**.

duty of restoration
A rule that states that a minor is obligated only to return the goods or property he or she has received from the adult in the condition it is in at the time of disaffirmance.

duty of restitution
A rule that states that if a minor has transferred money, property, or other valuables to the competent party before disaffirming the contract, that party must place the minor in status quo.

Example When Sherry is 17 years old (a minor), she enters into a contract to purchase an automobile costing $10,000 from Bruce, a competent adult. Bruce, who believes that Sherry is an adult and does not ask for verification of her age, delivers ownership of the automobile to Sherry after he receives her payment of $10,000. Subsequently, before Sherry reaches the age of 18 (the age of majority), she is involved in an automobile accident caused by her own negligence. The automobile sustains $7,000 worth of damage in the accident (the automobile is now only worth $3,000). Sherry can disaffirm the contract, return the damaged automobile to Bruce, and recover $10,000 from Bruce. In this result, Sherry recovers her entire $10,000 purchase price from Bruce, and Bruce has a damaged automobile worth only $3,000.

The right of a minor to disaffirm his contract is based upon sound public policy to protect the minor from his own improvidence and the overreaching of adults.

Justice Sullivan
Star Chevrolet v. Green
473 So.2d 157, 1985 Miss. Lexis 2141 (1985)

Most states provide that the minor owes a duty of restitution and must put the adult in status quo on disaffirmance of the contract if the minor's intentional, reckless, or grossly negligent conduct caused the loss of value to the adult's property. On occasion, minors might misrepresent their age to adults when entering into contracts. Most state laws provide that minors who misrepresent their age must place the adult in status quo if they disaffirm the contract.

Examples If in the prior example Sherry had recklessly caused the accident (e.g., by driving 20 miles an hour over the speed limit) or had misrepresented her age when she purchased the car, Sherry can still disaffirm the contract and return the damaged automobile to Bruce, but she can recover only $3,000 from Bruce. In this result, Bruce is made whole (he keeps $7,000 of Sherry's money and has a damaged automobile worth $3,000). Sherry has $3,000.

Ratification

If a minor does not disaffirm a contract either during the period of minority or within a reasonable time after reaching the age of majority, the contract is considered ratified (accepted). Hence, the minor (who is now an adult) is bound by the contract; the right to disaffirm the contract is lost. Note that any attempt by a minor to ratify a contract while still a minor can be disaffirmed just as the original contract can be disaffirmed.

The **ratification**, which relates back to the inception of the contract, can be expressed by oral or written words or implied from the minor's conduct (e.g., after reaching the age of majority, the minor remains silent regarding the contract).

ratification
The act of a minor after the minor has reached the age of majority by which he or she accepts a contract entered into when he or she was a minor.

Parents' Liability for Their Children's Contracts

Generally, parents owe a legal duty to provide food, clothing, shelter, and other necessaries of life for their minor children. Parents are liable for their children's contracts for necessaries of life if they have not adequately provided such items.

The parental duty of support terminates if a minor becomes *emancipated*. **Emancipation** occurs when a minor voluntarily leaves home and lives apart from his or her parents. The courts consider factors such as getting married, setting up a separate household, or joining the military in determining whether a minor is emancipated. Each situation is examined on its merits.

emancipation
The act or process of a minor voluntarily leaving home and living apart from his or her parents.

Necessaries of Life

Minors are obligated to pay for the **necessaries of life** that they contract for. Otherwise, many adults would refuse to sell these items to them. There is no standard definition of what is a necessary of life. The minor's age, lifestyle, and status in life influence what is considered necessary.

necessaries of life
Food, clothing, shelter, medical care, and other items considered necessary to the maintenance of life. Minors must pay the reasonable value of necessaries of life for which they contract.

Examples Items such as food, clothing, shelter, and medical services are generally understood to be necessaries of life.

Examples Goods and services such as automobiles, tools of trade, education, and vocational training have also been found to be necessaries of life in some situations.

The seller's recovery is based on the equitable doctrine of **quasi contract** rather than on the contract itself. Under this theory, the minor is obligated only to pay the reasonable value of the goods or services received. Reasonable value is determined on a case-by-case basis.

The following feature discusses modern statutes that make minors liable on certain contracts.

Contemporary Environment

Special Types of Minors' Contracts

Based on public policy, many states have enacted statutes that make certain specified contracts enforceable against minors—that is, minors cannot assert the infancy doctrine against enforcement for these contracts. These usually include contracts for the following:

- Medical, surgical, and pregnancy care
- Psychological counseling
- Health insurance
- Life insurance
- The performance of duties related to stock and bond transfers, bank accounts, and the like
- Educational loan agreements
- Contracts to support children
- Artistic, sports, and entertainment contracts that have been entered into with the approval of the court

Many statutes mandate that a certain portion of the wages and fees earned by a minor (e.g., 50 percent) based on an artistic, sports, or entertainment contract be put in trust until the minor reaches the age of majority.

Mentally Incompetent Persons

In most contracts, the parties to the contract are mentally competent to enter into the contract. However, in certain other cases, a party to a contract may not have had the requisite mental competence to have entered into an enforceable contract. In those situations, a mentally incompetent party will not be bound to the contract.

Mental incapacity may arise because of mental illness, brain damage, mental retardation, senility, and the like. The law protects people suffering from substantial mental incapacity from enforcement of contracts against them because such persons may not understand the consequences of their actions in entering into a contract.

legal insanity
A state of contractual incapacity, as determined by law.

To be relieved of his or her duties under a contract, a person must have been legally insane at the time of entering into the contract. This state is called **legal insanity**. Most states use the *objective cognitive "understanding" test* to determine legal insanity. Under this test, the person's mental incapacity must render that person incapable of understanding or comprehending the nature of the transaction. Mere weakness of intellect, slight psychological or emotional problems, or delusions does not constitute legal insanity.

Insanity vitiates all acts.
Sir John Nicholl
Countess of Portsmouth v. Earl of Portsmouth (1828)

The law has developed two standards concerning contracts of mentally incompetent persons: (1) adjudged insane and (2) insane but not adjudged insane.

Adjudged Insane

adjudged insane
Declared legally insane by a proper court or administrative agency.
A contract entered into by a person adjudged insane is *void*.

In certain cases, a relative, a loved one, or another interested party may institute a legal action to have someone declared legally (i.e., adjudged) insane. If, after evidence is presented at a formal judicial or administrative hearing, the person is **adjudged insane**, the court will make that person a ward of the court and appoint a guardian to act on that person's behalf. Any contract entered into by a person who has been adjudged insane is **void**. That is, no contract exists. The court-appointed guardian is the only one who has the legal authority to enter into contracts on behalf of the person who has been adjudged insane.

Insane but Not Adjudged Insane

insane but not adjudged insane
Being insane but not having been adjudged insane by a court or an administrative agency. A contract entered into by such person is generally *voidable*. Some states hold that such a contract is void.

If no formal ruling has been made about a person's sanity but the person suffers from a mental impairment that makes him or her legally insane—that is, the person is **insane but not adjudged insane**—any contract entered into by this person is voidable by the insane person. Unless the other party does not have contractual capacity, he or she does not have the option to void the contract.

Some people have alternating periods of sanity and insanity. Any contracts made by such persons during a lucid interval are enforceable. Contracts made while the person was not legally sane can be disaffirmed.

A person who has dealt with an insane person must place that insane person in status quo if the contract is either void or voided by the insane person. Most states hold that a party who did not know he or she was dealing with an insane person must be placed in status quo on voidance of the contract. Insane persons are liable in *quasi contract* to pay the reasonable value for the necessaries of life they receive.

CONCEPT SUMMARY

DISAFFIRMANCE OF CONTRACTS BASED ON LEGAL INSANITY

Type of Legal Insanity	Disaffirmance Rule
Adjudged insane	Contract is void. Neither party can enforce the contract.
Insane but not adjudged insane	Contract is voidable by the insane person; the competent party cannot void the contract.

Intoxicated Persons

Most states provide that contracts entered into by certain **intoxicated persons** are voidable by those persons. The intoxication may occur because of alcohol or drugs. The contract is not voidable by the other party if that party had contractual capacity.

intoxicated person
A person who is under contractual incapacity because of ingestion of alcohol or drugs to the point of incompetence.

Under the majority rule, the contract is voidable only if the person was so intoxicated when the contract was entered into that he or she was incapable of understanding or comprehending the nature of the transaction. In most states, this rule holds even if the intoxication was self-induced. Some states allow the person to disaffirm the contract only if the person was forced to become intoxicated or did so unknowingly.

The amount of alcohol or drugs that must be consumed for a person to be considered legally intoxicated to disaffirm contracts varies from case to case. The factors that are considered include the user's physical characteristics and his or her ability to "hold" intoxicants.

Men intoxicated are sometimes stunned into sobriety.

Lord Mansfield
R. v. Wilkes (1770)

A person who disaffirms a contract based on intoxication generally must be returned to the status quo. In turn, the intoxicated person generally must return the consideration received under the contract to the other party and make restitution that returns the other party to status quo. After becoming sober, an intoxicated person can ratify the contracts he or she entered into while intoxicated. Intoxicated persons are liable in *quasi contract* to pay the reasonable value for necessaries they receive.

Legality

One requirement to have an enforceable contract is that the object of the contract must be lawful. Most contracts that individuals and businesses enter into are **lawful contracts** that are enforceable. These include contracts for the sale of goods, services, real property, and intangible rights; the lease of goods; property leases; licenses; and other contracts.

lawful contract
A contract that has a lawful object.

Some contracts have illegal objects. A contract with an illegal object is *void* and therefore unenforceable. These contracts are called **illegal contracts**. The following paragraphs discuss various illegal contracts.

illegal contract
A contract that has an illegal object. Such contracts are *void*.

Contracts Contrary to Law

Both federal and state legislatures have enacted statutes that prohibit certain types of conduct. Administrative agencies adopt rules and regulations to enforce statutory law. And the president of the United States can issue executive orders making certain conduct illegal. Contracts to perform activities that are prohibited by law are illegal contracts. These are called **contracts contrary to law**.

contract contrary to law
A contract that violates a law.

Examples An agreement between two companies to engage in price fixing in violation of federal antitrust statutes is illegal and therefore void. Thus, neither company to this illegal contract can enforce the contract against the other company.

In the following case, the court addressed the legality of contracts.

CASE 12.1 *FEDERALCOURT CASE Illegal Contract*

Ford Motor Company v. Ghreiwati Auto

2013 U.S. Dist. Lexis 159470 (2013)
United States District Court for the Eastern District of Michigan

"A contract that violates an executive order or law is unlawful and discharges performance of the contract."

—Edmunds, District Judge

Facts

Ford Motor Company manufactures automobiles, trucks, and other vehicles. In 2004, Ford entered into a dealership agreement with Ghreiwati Auto (Auto), a Syrian corporation, whereby Auto would sell and service Ford vehicles in Syria. Auto invested more than $20 million creating a dealer network and brand representation and sold and serviced Ford vehicles in Syria. In 2011, after civil and military hostilities developed in Syria, the president of the United States issued an executive order that imposed widespread sanctions against Syria, including prohibiting American companies from selling products and services in Syria. Violation of the executive order carries both civil and criminal penalties. Pursuant to the executive order, Ford immediately terminated its dealership agreement with Auto. Ford filed an action in U.S. district court, requesting a declaratory judgment that it did not terminate the dealership agreement improperly because the executive order made Ford's performance of the contract illegal. Auto alleged that Ford breached the dealer agreement and was liable for damages.

Issue

Did the presidential executive order make the dealership contract illegal for Ford to perform?

Language of the Court

Ford argues that the executive order renders performance of the agreement illegal, thereby permitting Ford to immediately terminate Auto's dealership agreement and discharges Ford from any duties under the agreement. The Court agrees with Ford and its arguments. A contract that violates an executive order or law is unlawful and discharges performance of the contract.

Decision

The U.S. district court held that the executive order rendered the Ford–Auto dealership agreement illegal and that Ford had therefore terminated the agreement properly.

Ethics Questions

Did Ford have any other course of action in this case? Did Ford have an ethical duty to reimburse Auto for its losses? Would such reimbursement have been legal?

Usury Laws

usury law
A law that sets an upper limit on the interest rate that can be charged on certain types of loans.

State **usury laws** set an upper limit on the annual interest rate that can be charged on certain types of loans. The limits vary from state to state. Lenders who charge a higher rate than the state limit are guilty of usury. These laws are intended to protect unsophisticated borrowers from loan sharks and others who charge exorbitant rates of interest.

Most states provide criminal and civil penalties for making usurious loans. Some states require lenders to remit the difference between the interest rate charged on the loan and the usury rate to the borrower. Other states prohibit lenders from collecting any interest on the loan. Still other states provide that a usurious loan is a void contract, permitting the borrower not to have to pay the interest or the principal of the loan to the lender.

Example Suppose a state has set a usurious rate of interest as any interest rate above 15 percent. Christopher borrows $1,000 from Tony, which requires Christopher to pay $4,000 in one year to pay off the loan. This is a usurious loan because that amount of interest—$3,000—calculates to a 300 percent annual interest rate.

Most usury laws exempt certain types of lenders and loan transactions involving legitimate business transactions from the reach of the law. These exemptions usually include loans made by banks and other financial institutions, loans above a certain dollar amount, and loans made to corporations and other businesses.

WEB EXERCISE
Go to **www.bankrate.com/brm/news/cc/20020320a.asp** to read about credit-card interest rates.

Contracts to Commit Crimes

Contracts to commit criminal acts are void. If the object of a contract becomes illegal after the contract is entered into because the government has enacted a statute that makes it unlawful, the parties are discharged from the contract. The contract is not an illegal contract unless the parties agree to go forward and complete it.

Gambling Statutes

All states either prohibit or regulate gambling, wagering, lotteries, and games of chance via **gambling statutes**. States provide various criminal and civil penalties for illegal gambling. There are many exceptions to wagering laws. Many states have enacted statutes that permit games of chance under a certain dollar amount, bingo games, lotteries conducted by religious and charitable organizations, and the like. Many states also permit and regulate horse racing, harness racing, dog racing, and state-operated lotteries.

gambling statutes
Statutes that make certain forms of gambling illegal.

In 1988, Congress enacted the **Indian Gaming Regulatory Act (IGRA)**,[1] which established the framework for permitting and regulating Native American gaming casinos. There are more than 450 such establishments in the country operated by more than 240 federally recognized tribes. Federal law permits these casinos only if the state permits such gambling.

Effect of Illegality

The **effects of illegality** are as follows: Because illegal contracts are void, the parties cannot sue for nonperformance. Further, if an illegal contract is executed, the court will generally *leave the parties where it finds them*.

effect of illegality
A doctrine that states that the courts will refuse to enforce or rescind an illegal contract and will leave the parties where it finds them.

Certain situations are exempt from the general rule of the effect of finding an illegal contract. If an exception applies, the innocent party may use the court system to sue for damages or to recover consideration paid under the illegal contract. Persons who can assert an exception are as follows:

- Innocent persons who were justifiably ignorant of the law or fact that made the contract illegal.

  Example A person who purchases insurance from an unlicensed insurance company may recover insurance benefits from the unlicensed company.

- Persons who were induced to enter into an illegal contract by fraud, duress, or undue influence.

  Example A shop owner who pays $5,000 "protection money" to a mobster so that his store will not be burned down by the mobster can recover the $5,000.

Critical Legal Thinking

Why is an illegal contract void? Does the rule that the court "will leave the parties where it finds them" ever cause unfair results?

- Persons who entered into an illegal contract who withdraw before the illegal act is performed.

  Example If the president of New Toy Corporation pays $10,000 to an employee of Old Toy Corporation to steal a trade secret from his employer but reconsiders and tells the employee not to do it before he has done it, the New Toy Corporation may recover the $10,000.

- Persons who were less at fault than the other party for entering into the illegal contract. At common law, parties to an illegal contract were considered ***in pari delicto*** (in equal fault). Some states have changed this rule and permit the less-at-fault party to recover restitution of the consideration they paid under an illegal contract from the more-at-fault party.

in pari delicto
A situation in which both parties are equally at fault in an illegal contract.

The following ethics feature analyzes whether a contract was lawful.

Ethical

Ethics

Gambling Contract

"The trial court could not have compelled Ryno to honor his wager by delivering the BMW to Tyra. However, Ryno did deliver the BMW to Tyra and the facts incident to that delivery are sufficient to establish a transfer by gift of the BMW from Ryno to Tyra."

—Farris, Judge

R. D. Ryno Jr. owned Bavarian Motors, an automobile dealership in Fort Worth, Texas. One day, Lee Tyra discussed purchasing a BMW M-1 from Ryno for $125,000. Ryno then suggested a double-or-nothing coin flip to which Tyra agreed. If the Ryno won the coin flip, Tyra would have to pay $250,000 for the car; if Tyra won the coin flip, he would get the car for free. The coin was flipped, and Tyra won the coin flip. Ryno said, "It's yours," and handed Tyra the keys, title, and possession to the car. Tyra drove away in the BMW. A lawsuit ensued as to the ownership of the car.

The court held that when Tyra won the coin toss and Ryno voluntarily gave the keys, title, and possession of the BMW to Tyra, this was a performed illegal gambling contract. The court left the parties where it found them: Tyra had the keys, title, and possession of the BMW; Ryno did not have either the car or payment for the car.

Note: If when Tyra won the coin toss and Ryno had refused to give the BMW to Tyra, Tyra could not have used the courts to compel Ryno to honor his wager. The court would again have left the parties where it found them. Tyra would have won the coin toss but could not obtain the car from Ryno. *Ryno v. Tyra*, 752 S.W.2d 148, 1988 Tex. App. Lexis 1646 (Court of Appeals of Texas)

Ethics Questions Did Ryno act ethically in this case? Did Tyra act ethically in this case? Should the court have lent its help to Ryno to recover the BMW from Tyra? Why or why not?

Contracts Contrary to Public Policy

Certain contracts are illegal because they are contrary to public policy. **Contracts contrary to public policy** are void. Although *public policy* eludes precise definition, the courts have held contracts to be contrary to public policy if they have a negative impact on society or interfere with the public's safety and welfare.

contract contrary to public policy
A contract that has a negative impact on society or that interferes with the public's safety and welfare.

Immoral contracts—that is, contracts whose objective is the commission of an act that society considers immoral—may be found to be against public policy. Judges are not free to define morality based on their individual views. Instead, they must look to the practices and beliefs of society when defining immoral conduct.

immoral contract
A contract whose objective is the commission of an act that society considers immoral.

Example A contract that is based on sexual favors is an immoral contract and void as against public policy.

Special Business Contracts and Licensing Statutes

The issue of the lawfulness of contracts applies to several special business contracts. These include contracts that restrain trade or provide services that require a government license, exculpatory clauses, and covenants not to compete. These contracts are discussed in the following paragraphs.

Contract in Restraint of Trade

The general economic policy of this country favors competition. At common law, **contracts in restraint of trade**—that is, contracts that unreasonably restrain trade—are held to be unlawful.

contract in restraint of trade
A contract that unreasonably restrains trade.

Example It would be an illegal restraint of trade for Toyota, General Motors, and Ford to agree to fix the prices of the automobiles they sell. Their contract would be void and could not be enforced by any of the parties against the other parties.

Licensing Statute

All states have **licensing statutes** that require members of certain professions and occupations to be licensed by the state in which they practice. Lawyers, doctors, real estate agents, insurance agents, certified public accountants, teachers, contractors, hairdressers, and such are among them. In most instances, a license is granted to a person who demonstrates that he or she has the proper schooling, experience, and moral character required by the relevant statute. Sometimes, a written examination is also required.

licensing statute
A statute that requires a person or business to obtain a license from the government prior to engaging in a specified occupation or activity.

Problems arise if an unlicensed person tries to collect payment for services provided to another under a contract. Some statutes expressly provide that unlicensed persons cannot enforce contracts to provide these services. If the statute is silent on the point, enforcement depends on whether it is a *regulatory statute* or a *revenue-raising statute*:

- **Regulatory licensing statute.** Statutes may require persons or businesses to obtain a license from the government to qualify to practice certain professions or engage in certain types of businesses. These statutes, which are enacted to protect the public, are called **regulatory licensing statutes**. Generally, unlicensed persons cannot recover payment for services where he or she does not have the required license.

  regulatory licensing statute
  A licensing statute enacted to protect the public.

  Example State law provides that legal services can be provided only by lawyers who have graduated from law school and passed the appropriate bar exam. Nevertheless, suppose Marie, a first-year law student, agrees to draft a will for Randy for a $350 fee. Because Marie is not licensed to provide legal services, she has violated a regulatory statute. She cannot enforce the contract and recover payment from Randy. Randy, even though receiving services by having his will drafted, does not have to pay Marie $350.

- **Revenue-raising statute.** Licensing statutes enacted to raise money for the government are called **revenue-raising statutes**. A person who provides services pursuant to a contract without the appropriate license required by such a statute can enforce the contract and recover payment for services rendered.

  revenue-raising statute
  A licensing statute with the primary purpose of raising revenue for the government.

  Example A state licensing statute requires licensed attorneys to pay an annual $500 renewal fee without requiring continuing education or other new qualifications. If a lawyer provides legal services but has not paid the annual licensing fee, the lawyer can still recover for her services.

Exculpatory Clause

exculpatory clause (release of liability clause)
A contractual provision that relieves one (or both) of the parties to a contract from tort liability for ordinary negligence. Also known as a *release of liability clause*.

An **exculpatory clause** (also called a **release of liability clause**) is a contractual provision that relieves one (or both) of the parties to a contract from tort liability. An exculpatory clause can relieve a party of liability for ordinary negligence. It cannot be used in a situation involving willful conduct, intentional torts, fraud, recklessness, or gross negligence. Exculpatory clauses are often found in leases, sales contracts, sporting event ticket stubs, parking lot tickets, service contracts, and the like. Such clauses do not have to be reciprocal (i.e., one party may be relieved of tort liability, whereas the other party is not).

Example Jim voluntarily enrolls in a parachute jump course and signs a contract containing an exculpatory clause that relieves the parachute center of liability. After receiving proper instruction, he jumps from an airplane. Unfortunately, Jim is injured when he could not steer his parachute toward the target area. He sues the parachute center for damages. Here, the court would usually enforce the exculpatory clause, reasoning that parachute jumping was a voluntary choice and did not involve an essential service.

Exculpatory clauses that either affect the public interest or result from superior bargaining power are usually found to be void as against public policy. Although the outcome varies with the circumstances of the case, the greater the degree to which the party serves the general public, the greater the chance that the exculpatory clause will be struck down as illegal. The courts will consider such factors as the type of activity involved; the relative bargaining power, knowledge, experience, and sophistication of the parties; and other relevant factors.

Example If a department store had a sign above the entrance stating, "The store is not liable for the ordinary negligence of its employees," this would be an illegal exculpatory clause and would not be enforced.

In the following case, the court had to determine whether a release of liability contract was enforceable.

CASE 12.2 *FEDERAL COURT CASE Release Contract*

Lin v. Spring Mountain Adventures, Inc.

2010 U.S. Dist. Lexis 136090 (2010)
United States District Court for the Eastern District of Pennsylvania

"It is a well established rule that failure to read a contract does not relieve a party of their obligation under such contract . . ."

—Tucker, District Judge

Facts

Dong Lin went skiing at the Spring Mountain ski area in Pennsylvania, which was owned by Spring Mountain Adventures, Inc. (Spring Mountain). Prior to renting her equipment and going skiing, Lin signed a release form that included the following title line on the front page in bold capital print: **"EQUIPMENT RENTAL FORM AND RELEASE FROM LIABILITY."** Above the signature line, the contract stated in capital print, "PLEASE READ THE AGREEMENT ON THE BACK OF THIS FORM BEFORE SIGNING. IT RELEASES US FROM CERTAIN LIABILITY." Directly between the instruction to read the release and the signature line was the following statement: "I, the undersigned, have carefully read and understood the Acceptance of Risk and Liability Release on the back of this paper." Lin did not read the contract before signing it.

As Lin was skiing, she lost control and fell or slid into a padded snowmaking machine that was on the slopes. As a result of her collision, Lin suffered several permanent and many disfiguring injuries to her face and body and injuries to her brain, bones, muscles,

(*case continues*)

and nerves. Lin underwent surgical procedures and incurred medical expenses. Lin sued Spring Mountain in U.S. district court for negligence to recover damages for her injuries, current and future medical costs, pain and suffering, and emotional harm. Spring Mountain made a motion to dismiss the lawsuit based on the release of liability form signed by Lin.

Issue

Is the release of liability form signed by Lin enforceable?

Language of the Court

Plaintiff Lin signed the release form herself, and such form contained the bolded front-page title ***"EQUIPMENT RENTAL FORM AND RELEASE FROM LIABILITY,"*** *giving Plaintiff Lin notice of the form's purpose and intent. At the bottom of the page is the following bolded statement* ***"I have carefully read and understood the Acceptance of Risk and Liability Release and have signed the front of this form."*** *Plaintiff Lin signed the form, which provided her with ample notice of the release terms. It is a well established rule that failure to read a contract does not relieve a party of their obligation under such contract that they sign, and such parties will be bound by the agreement without regard to whether the terms were read and fully understood.*

Decision

The U.S. district court held that the release form signed by Lin was enforceable and granted Spring Mountain's motion to dismiss.

Ethics Questions

Is it ethical for companies to use release of liability forms? What would be the consequences if persons were held not to be bound by contracts they did not read?

The following feature discusses covenants not to compete.

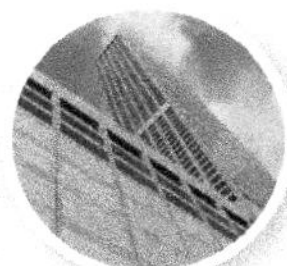

Business Environment

Covenants Not to Compete

Entrepreneurs and others often buy and sell businesses. The sale of a business includes its "goodwill," or reputation. To protect this goodwill after the sale, the seller often enters into an agreement with the buyer not to engage in a similar business or occupation within a specified geographic area for a specified period of time following the sale. This agreement is called a **covenant not to compete**, or a **noncompete clause**.

Employers often do not want an employee who resigns or is terminated to work in a position that competes with the employer for a certain length of time after the employee is gone from the employer. Employers often require an employee, usually before he or she is hired, to sign a noncompete clause, agreeing not to work for another employer or for themselves in a position that would compete with their prior employer for a certain period of time after the employee has left or been terminated by the employer.

Covenants not to compete that are *ancillary* to a legitimate sale of a business or employment contract are lawful if they are reasonable in three aspects: (1) the line of business protected, (2) the geographic area protected, and (3) the duration of the restriction. A covenant that is found to be unreasonable is not enforceable as written. The reasonableness of covenants not to compete is examined on a case-by-case basis. If a covenant not to compete is unreasonable, the courts may either refuse to enforce it or change it so that it is reasonable. Usually, the courts choose the first option.

Examples Stacy is a certified public accountant (CPA) with a lucrative accounting practice in Providence, Rhode Island. Her business includes a substantial amount of goodwill with her clients. Stacy sells her accounting practice to Gregory. When she sells her practice to Gregory, Stacy agrees not to open another accounting practice in the state of Rhode Island for a 20-year period. This covenant not to compete is reasonable in the line of business protected but is unreasonable in geographic scope and duration. It will not be enforced by the courts as written. The covenant not to compete would be reasonable and enforceable if it prohibited Stacy only from practicing as a CPA in the city of Providence for three years.

Some states have severely restricted the use of covenants not to compete in employment contracts.

Unconscionable Contracts

covenant not to compete (noncompete clause)
A contract that provides that a seller of a business or an employee will not engage in a similar business or occupation within a specified geographical area for a specified time following the sale of the business or termination of employment.

The general rule of freedom of contract holds that if the object of a contract is lawful and the other elements for the formation of a contract are met, the courts will enforce a contract according to its terms. Although it is generally presumed that parties are capable of protecting their own interests when contracting, it is a fact of life that dominant parties sometimes take advantage of weaker parties.

In addition, many contracts that a consumer signs are **contracts of adhesion**—that is, they are preprinted forms whose terms the consumer cannot negotiate and that they must sign in order to obtain a product or service. Most adhesion contracts are lawful even though there is a disparity in power of contracting.

Examples Automobile sales contracts and leases, mortgages, and apartment leases are usually contracts of adhesion.

However, when a contract is so oppressive or manifestly unfair as to be unjust, the law has developed the equity doctrine of unconscionability to prevent the enforcement of such contracts. The doctrine of unconscionability is based on public policy. A contract found to be unconscionable under this doctrine is called an **unconscionable contract**.

unconscionable contract
A contract that courts refuse to enforce in part or at all because it is so oppressive or manifestly unfair as to be unjust.

The courts are given substantial discretion in determining whether a contract or contract clause is unconscionable. There is no single definition of *unconscionability*. This doctrine may not be used merely to save a contracting party from a bad bargain.

Elements of Unconscionability

Critical Legal Thinking
What is the policy that permits a court to not enforce a contract because it is unconscionable? Is it difficult to determine when a contract is unconscionable? Are all contracts of adhesion unconscionable?

The following elements must be shown to prove that a contract or a clause in a contract is unconscionable:

- The parties possessed severely unequal bargaining power.
- The dominant party unreasonably used its unequal bargaining power to obtain oppressive or manifestly unfair contract terms.
- The adhering party had no reasonable alternative.

Unconscionable contracts are sometimes found where there is a consumer contract that takes advantage of uneducated, poor, or elderly people who have been persuaded to enter into an unfair contract.

If the court finds that a contract or contract clause is unconscionable, it may (1) refuse to enforce the contract, (2) refuse to enforce the unconscionable clause but enforce the remainder of the contract, or (3) limit the applicability of any unconscionable clause and thus avoid any unconscionable result. The appropriate remedy depends on the facts and circumstances of each case. Note that because unconscionability is a matter of law, the judge may opt to decide the case without a jury trial.

A good judge decides fairly, preferring equity to strict law.

Legal maxim

Example Suppose a door-to-door salesperson sells a poor family a freezer full of meat and other foods for $3,000, with monthly payments for 60 months at 20 percent interest. If the actual cost of the freezer and the food is $1,000, this contract could be found to be unconscionable. The court could either find the entire contract unenforceable or rewrite the contract so that it has reasonable terms.

In the following case, the court found that a provision of a contract was unconscionable.

CASE 12.3 *STATE COURT CASE Unconscionable Contract*

Stoll v. Xiong

241 P.3d 301, 2010 Okla. Civ. App. Lexis 89 (2010)
Court of Civil Appeals of Oklahoma

"The actual price Buyers will pay under the paragraph Stoll included in the land sale contract is so gross as to shock the conscience."

—Hetherington, Judge

Facts

Chong Lor Xiong and Mee Yang are husband and wife. Xiong, who is from Laos, became a refugee due to the Vietnam War. He spent three years in a refugee camp in Thailand before coming to the United States. He understands some English but can read only a few words of English. His wife Yang is a Hmong immigrant from Laos. She received no education in Laos but took a few adult courses in English in the United States.

Ronal Stoll contracted to sell Xiong and Yang (Buyers) a 60-acre parcel of real estate he owned in Delaware County, Oklahoma, for $130,000. The purchase price represented $2,000 per acre plus $10,000 for a road. Nearby land sold for approximately $1,200 per acre. The written land sale contract described the property and the price, but Stoll added a provision that the Buyers were obligated to deliver to Stoll for 30 years the litter from chicken houses that the Buyers had on the property. Stoll then planned on selling the litter.

The Buyers thought they were buying the real estate for $130,000. When the Buyers failed to deliver the litter to Stoll, he sued the Buyers for breach of contract. The Buyers defended, alleging that the 30-year litter provision was unconscionable. The trial court calculated that the value of the litter added more than $3,000 per acre to the original purchase price of the land. The trial court held that the litter provision was unconscionable and therefore unenforceable. Stoll appealed.

Issue

Is the 30-year litter clause unconscionable?

Language of the Court

Here, the consideration actually to be paid under the contract far exceeds that stated. The parties to be surcharged with the extra expense were, due to language and education, unable to understand the nature of the contract. The actual price Buyers will pay under the paragraph Stoll included in the land sale contract is so gross as to shock the conscience.

Decision

The court of appeals affirmed the trial court's finding that the litter provision of the land sale contract was unconscionable and unenforceable. The Buyers owned the real estate free of that provision.

Ethics Questions

Did Stoll act ethically in this case? Were the buyers taken advantage of? Should the buyers have employed a lawyer to represent them to protect against unethical conduct?

Key Terms and Concepts

Adjudged insane (278)
Age of majority (275)
Contract contrary to law (280)
Contract contrary to public policy (282)
Contract in restraint of trade (283)
Contract of adhesion (286)
Contractual capacity (289)
Covenant not to compete (noncompete clause) (285)
Disaffirm (275)
Duty of restitution (276)
Duty of restoration (276)
Effect of illegality (281)
Emancipation (277)
Exculpatory clause (release of liability clause) (284)
Gambling statute (281)
Illegal contract (279)
Immoral contract (282)
In pari delicto (282)
Indian Gaming Regulatory Act (IGRA) (281)
Infancy doctrine (275)
Insane but not adjudged insane (278)
Intoxicated person (279)
Lawful contract (279)

Legal insanity (278)
Licensing statute (283)
Minor (275)
Necessaries of life (277)
Period of minority (275)
Quasi contract (277)
Ratification (277)
Regulatory licensing statute (283)
Revenue-raising statute (283)
Unconscionable contract (286)
Usury law (280)
Void contract (278)
Voidable contract (275)

Critical Legal Thinking Cases

12.1 Minor Harun Fountain, a minor, was shot in the back of the head at point-blank range by a playmate. Fountain required extensive lifesaving medical services from a variety of medical service providers, including Yale Diagnostic Radiology. The expense of the services rendered by Yale to Fountain totaled $17,694. Yale billed Vernetta Turner-Tucker (Tucker), Fountain's mother, for the services. Tucker, however, declared bankruptcy and had Yale's claim against her discharged in bankruptcy. Tucker, on behalf of Fountain, sued the boy who shot Fountain and recovered damages in a settlement agreement. These funds were placed in an estate on Fountain's behalf under the supervision of the probate court.

Yale filed a motion with the probate court for payment of the $17,694 from the estate. The probate court denied the motion. Yale appealed to the trial court, which held in favor of Yale. The trial court held that minors were liable for their necessaries. Fountain's estate appealed. Is Fountain's estate liable to Yale under the doctrine of necessaries? *Yale Diagnostic Radiology v. Estate of Fountain*, 267 Conn. 351, 838 A.2d 179, 2004 Conn. Lexis 7 (Supreme Court of Connecticut, 2004)

12.2 Illegal Contract Andrew Parente had a criminal record. He and Mario Pirozzoli Jr. formed a partnership to open and operate the Speak Easy Café in Berlin, Connecticut, which was a bar that would serve alcohol. The owners were required to obtain a liquor license from the state of Connecticut before operating the bar. Because the state of Connecticut usually would not issue a liquor license to anyone with a criminal record, it was agreed that Pirozzoli would form a corporation called Centerfolds, Inc., to own the bar, sign the real estate lease for the bar in his name, and file for the liquor license in his name only. Pirozzoli did all of these things. Parente and Pirozzoli signed a partnership agreement acknowledging that Parente was an equal partner in the business. The state of Connecticut granted the liquor license, and the bar opened for business. Parente and Pirozzoli shared the profits of the bar. Six years later, Pirozzoli terminated the partnership and kept the business. Parente sued Pirozzoli for breach of the partnership agreement to recover the value of his alleged share of the business. Parente's share would have been $138,000. Pirozzoli defended, arguing that the partnership agreement was an illegal contract that should not be enforced against him. Is the partnership agreement an illegal contract that is void and unenforceable by the court? *Parente v. Pirozzoli*, 866 A.2d 629, 2005 Conn. App. Lexis 25 (Appellate Court of Connecticut, 2005)

12.3 Infancy Doctrine Lindsey Stroupes was 16 years old and a sophomore in high school. Anthony Bradley, the manager of a Finish Line, Inc.'s, store in a mall, offered Lindsey a position as a sales associate that she accepted. Lindsey signed an employment contract that required that all claims against Finish Line be submitted to binding arbitration. Shortly after being hired, Lindsey quit, and she and her parents filed a civil action in U.S. district court against Finish Line, Inc., alleging that Bradley sexually harassed Lindsey in violation of Title VII of the Civil Rights Act of 1964. Finish Line filed a motion to dismiss Lindsey's lawsuit and to compel arbitration of her complaints. Lindsey argued that the arbitration agreement was voidable by her under the infancy doctrine because she was a minor when she signed the contract. Is Finish Line's arbitration agreement voidable by Lindsey under the infancy doctrine? *Stroupes v. The Finish Line, Inc.*, 2005 U.S. Dist. Lexis 6975 (United States District Court for the Eastern District of Tennessee, 2005)

12.4 Capacity to Contract Martha M. Carr suffered from schizophrenia and depression. Schizophrenia is a psychotic disorder that is characterized by disturbances in perception, inferential thinking, delusions, hallucinations, and grossly disorganized behavior. Depression is characterized by altered moods and diminished ability to think or concentrate. Carr was taking prescription drugs for her mental diseases. Carr, a resident of New York, inherited from her mother a 108-acre tract of unimproved land in South Carolina. Carr contacted Raymond C. and Betty Campbell (Campbell), who had leased the property for 30 years, about selling the property to them. Carr asked Campbell how much the property was worth, and Campbell told Carr $54,000. Carr and Campbell entered into a written contract for $54,000. Campbell paid Carr earnest money. Carr subsequently missed the closing day for the sale of the property, returned the earnest money, and refused to sell the property to Campbell. Campbell sued Carr to obtain a court judgment ordering Carr to specifically perform the contract. At trial, evidence and expert witness testimony placed the value of the property at $162,000. Testimony showed that Campbell knew the value of the property exceeded $54,000. Does Carr, because of her mental diseases of schizophrenia and depression, lack the mental capacity to enter into the contract with Campbell? *Campbell v. Carr*, 603 S.E.2d 625, 2004 S.C. App. Lexis 276 (Court of Appeals of South Carolina, 2004)

Ethical

Ethics Cases

12.5 Ethics Case City Segway Tours of Washington DC, LLC (CST), operated tours where customers used Segway personal transportation vehicle to tour the city. Norman Mero and his significant other signed up for such a tour. The contract they signed prior to beginning the tour contained a release of liability clause (exculpatory clause) that stated,

> *I do hereby waive, release, acquit, and forever discharge the CST Indemnitees from any and all losses, claims, suits, causes of actions, etc. for property damages, personal injuries, or death I may suffer or sustain while riding or operating the Segway, whether arising from my own acts, actions, activities and/or omissions of those of others, except only those arising solely from the gross negligence of the CST Indemnitees.*

While riding the Segway, Mero collided with the Segway ridden by his significant other. Mero fell to the ground and fractured his right arm. Mero sued CST for negligence to recover for his injuries. CST asserted that the release of liability clause the Mero signed released it from liability. Mero argued the release of liability clause was not enforceable. Is CST liable to Mero? Did CST act ethically in placing a release of liability clause in its contract? *Mero v. City Segway Tours of Washington DC*, 962 F.Supp.2d 92, 2013 U.S. Dist. Lexis 120304 (United States District Court for the District of Columbia, 2013)

12.6 Ethics Case The United Arab Emirates (UAE), a country in the Middle East, held a competition for the architectural design of a new embassy it intended to build in Washington DC. Elena Sturdza, an architect licensed in Maryland and Texas, entered the competition and submitted a design. After reviewing all of the submitted designs, UAE notified Sturdza that she had won the competition. UAE and Sturdza entered into contract negotiations, and over the next two years, they exchanged multiple contract proposals. During that time, at UAE's request, Sturdza modified her design. She agreed to defer billing UAE for her work until the execution of their contract. At last, UAE sent Sturdza a final agreement. Sturdza informed UAE that she assented to the contract. Without explanation, however, UAE stopped communicating with Sturdza. UAE hired another architect to design the embassy. Sturdza filed suit against UAE to recover damages for breach of contract or, alternatively, under equity, to prevent unjust enrichment to UAE. UAE defended, alleging that because Sturdza did not have an architectural license issued by Washington DC, she could not recover damages. Was there an illegal contract? Was it ethical for UAE not to pay Sturdza? *Sturdza v. United Arab Emirates*, 11 A.3d 251, 2011 D.C. App. Lexis 2 (District of Columbia Court of Appeals, 2011)

Note

1. 25 U.S.C. Section 2701 et. seq.

CHAPTER 13

Genuineness of Assent and Undue Influence

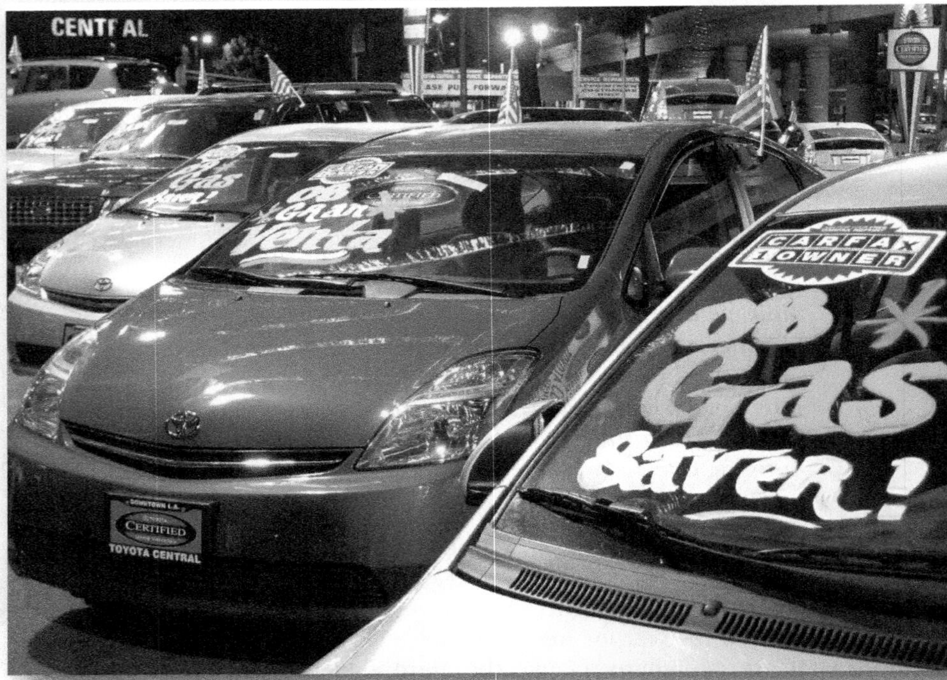

CARS FOR SALE
The history of car sales has generated many cases of contracts tainted by mistake and fraud.

Learning Objectives

After studying this chapter, you should be able to:

1. Explain genuineness of assent.
2. Explain how mutual mistake of fact excuses performance.
3. Describe the elements of intentional misrepresentation (fraud).
4. Describe duress.
5. Define the equitable doctrine of *undue influence*.

Chapter Outline

"*Most of the disputes in the world arise from words.*"

—*Lord Mansfield, Chief Justice*
Morgan v. Jones (1773)

Introduction to Genuineness of Assent and Undue Influence

Voluntary assent by the parties is necessary to create an enforceable contract. Assent is determined by the relevant facts surrounding the negotiation and formation of a contract. Assent may be manifested in any manner sufficient to show agreement, including express words or conduct of the parties.

A contract may not be enforced if the assent of one or both the parties to the contract was not genuine or real. Genuineness of assent may be missing because a party entered into a contract based on *mistake*, *fraudulent misrepresentation*, or *duress*. A court may permit the rescission of a contract based on the equitable doctrine of *undue influence*.

Problems concerning **genuineness of assent** are discussed in this chapter.

genuineness of assent
The requirement that a party's assent to a contract be genuine.

Mistake

A **mistake** occurs where one or both of the parties to a contract have an erroneous belief about the subject matter, value, or some other aspect of the contract. Mistakes may be either *unilateral* or *mutual*. The law permits **rescission** of some contracts made in mistake.

rescission
An action to undo a contract.

Unilateral Mistake

A **unilateral mistake** occurs when only one party is mistaken about a material fact regarding the subject matter of the contract. In most cases of unilateral mistake, the mistaken partyis be permitted to rescind the contract. The contract is enforced on its terms.

unilateral mistake
A mistake in which only one party is mistaken about a material fact regarding the subject matter of a contract.

There are three types of situations in which a contract may not be enforced due to a unilateral mistake:

1. One party makes a unilateral mistake of fact, and the other party knew (or should have known) that a mistake was made.
2. A unilateral mistake occurs because of a clerical or mathematical error that is not the result of gross negligence.
3. The mistake is so serious that enforcing the contract would be unconscionable.[1]

Words are chameleons, which reflect the color of their environment.

Justice Learned Hand
Commissioner v. National Carbide Corporation 167 F.2d 304, 1948 U.S. App. Lexis 3910 (1948)

Example If a buyer contracts to purchase a new automobile while thinking that there is a V-8 engine in the automobile when in fact there is a V-6 engine in the automobile, this unilateral mistake does not excuse the buyer from the contract.

Mutual Mistake of a Material Fact

A party may rescind a contract if there has been a **mutual mistake of a material fact**.[2] A **material fact** is a fact that is important to the subject matter of a contract. An ambiguity in a contract may constitute a mutual mistake of a material fact. An ambiguity occurs where a word or term in the contract is susceptible to more than one logical interpretation. If there has been a mutual mistake, the contract may be rescinded on the grounds that no contract has been formed because there has been no "meeting of the minds" between the parties.

mutual mistake of a material fact
A mistake made by both parties concerning a material fact that is important to the subject matter of a contract.

Example In the celebrated case *Raffles v. Wichelhaus*,[3] which has become better known as the case of the good ship *Peerless*, the parties agreed on a sale of cotton that was to be delivered from Bombay (now Mumbai) by the ship. There were two ships named *Peerless*, however, and each party, in agreeing to the sale, was referring to a different ship. Because the sailing time of the two ships was materially different, neither party was willing to agree to shipment by the other *Peerless*. The court ruled that there was no binding contract because each party had a different ship in mind when the contract was formed.

Mutual Mistake of Value

mutual mistake of value
A mistake that occurs if both parties know the object of the contract but are mistaken as to its value.

A **mutual mistake of value** exists if both parties know the object of the contract but are mistaken as to its value. Here, the contract remains enforceable by either party because the identity of the subject matter of the contract is not at issue. If the rule were different, almost all contracts could later be rescinded by the party who got the "worst" of the deal.

Example Helen cleans her attic and finds a red and green silkscreen painting of a tomato soup can. She has no use for the painting, so she offers to sell it to Qian for $100. Qian, who thinks that the painting is "cute," accepts the offer and pays Helen $100. It is later discovered that the painting is worth $2 million because it was painted by the famous American pop artist Andy Warhol. Neither party knew this at the time they entered into the contract. It is a mistake of value. Helen cannot recover the painting.

Fraud

intentional misrepresentation (fraudulent misrepresentation or fraud)
An event that occurs when one person consciously decides to induce another person to rely and act on a misrepresentation.

A misrepresentation occurs when an assertion is made that is not in accord with the facts.[4] An **intentional misrepresentation** occurs when one person consciously decides to induce another person to rely and act on a misrepresentation. Intentional misrepresentation is commonly referred to as **fraudulent misrepresentation**, or **fraud**. When fraudulent misrepresentation is used to induce another to enter into a contract, the innocent party's assent to the contract is not genuine, and the contract is voidable by the innocent party.[5] The innocent party can either rescind the contract and obtain restitution or enforce the contract and sue for contract damages.

Elements of Fraud

To prove fraud, the following elements must be shown:

1. The wrongdoer made a false representation of material fact.
2. The wrongdoer intended to deceive the innocent party.
3. The innocent party justifiably relied on the misrepresentation.
4. The innocent party was injured.

Each of these elements is discussed in the following list.

1. **Misrepresentation of a material fact.** A **misrepresentation of a material fact** by the wrongdoer may occur by words (oral or written) or by the conduct of a party. To be actionable as fraud, the misrepresentation must be of a past or existing *material fact*. This means that the misrepresentation must have been a significant factor in inducing the innocent party to enter into the contract. It need not have been the sole factor. Statements of opinion or predictions about the future generally do not form the basis for fraud.
2. **Intent to deceive.** To prove that a person intended to deceive an innocent party, the person making the misrepresentation must have either had

knowledge that the representation was false or made it without sufficient knowledge of the truth. This is called ***scienter* ("guilty mind")**. The misrepresentation must have been made with the **intent to deceive** the innocent party. Intent can be inferred from the circumstances.

3. **Reliance on the misrepresentation.** A misrepresentation is not actionable unless the innocent party to whom the misrepresentation was made relied on the misrepresentation and acted on it. An innocent party who acts in **reliance on a misrepresentation** must justify his or her reliance. Justifiable reliance is generally found unless the innocent party knew that the misrepresentation was false or was so extravagant as to be obviously false.
4. **Injury to the innocent party.** To recover damages, the innocent party must prove that the fraud caused him or her **economic injury**. The measure of damages is the difference between the value of the property as represented and the actual value of the property. This measure of damages gives the innocent party the "benefit of the bargain." Instead of suing to recover damages, the buyer can rescind the contract and recover the purchase price.

scienter ("guilty mind")
Knowledge that a representation is false or that it was made without sufficient knowledge of the truth.

A charge of fraud is such a terrible thing to bring against a man that it cannot be maintained in any court unless it is shown that he had a wicked mind.

M. R. Lord Esher
Le Lievre v. Gould (1732)

Individuals must be on guard in their commercial and personal dealings not to be defrauded. Basically, something sounding "too good to be true" is a signal that the situation might be fraudulent. Although the law permits a victim of fraud to rescind the contract and recover damages from the wrongdoer, often the wrongdoer cannot be found or the money has been spent.

Types of Fraud

There are various types of fraud. Several of these are discussed in the following paragraphs.

Fraud in the Inception

Fraud in the inception, or **fraud in the factum**, occurs if a person is deceived as to the nature of his or her act and does not know what he or she is signing. Contracts involving fraud in the inception are void rather than just voidable.

fraud in the inception (fraud in the factum)
Fraud that occurs if a person is deceived as to the nature of his or her act and does not know what he or she is signing.

Example Heather brings her professor a grade card to sign. The professor signs the grade card on the front without reading the grade card. On the front, however, are contract terms that transfer all of the professor's property to Heather. Here, there is fraud in the inception. The contract is void.

Fraud in the Inducement

Many fraud cases concern **fraud in the inducement**. Here, the innocent party knows what he or she is signing or doing but has been fraudulently induced to enter into the contract. Such contracts are voidable by the innocent party.

fraud in the inducement
Fraud that occurs when the party knows what he or she is signing but has been fraudulently induced to enter into the contract.

Example Lyle tells Candice that he is forming a partnership to invest in drilling for oil in an oil field and invites her to invest in this venture. In reality, though, there is no oil field, and Lyle intends to use whatever money he receives from Candice for his personal expenses. Candice relies on Lyle's statements and invests $30,000 with Lyle. Lyle absconds with Candice's $30,000 investment. Here, there has been fraud in the inducement. Candice has been induced to give Lyle $30,000 based on Lyle's misrepresentation of fact. Candice can rescind the contract and recover the money from Lyle, if she can find him and locate his money or property.

In the following case, the court had to decide if fraud had occurred.

CASE 13.1 *FEDERAL COURT CASE Fraud in the Inducement*

Portugués-Santana v. Rekomdiv International, Inc.

725 F.3d 17, 2013 U.S. App. Lexis 15331 (2013)
United States Court of Appeals for the First Circuit

"In the end, Portugués got zilch for his money."
—Thompson, Circuit Judge

Facts

Victor Omar Portugués-Santana wanted to open a Victoria's Secret franchise in Puerto Rico. Richard Domingo, a business broker, told Santana that obtaining a Victoria's Secret franchise was a "done deal" if he hired Domingo's firm, Rekomdiv International, Inc., and hired former United States Senator Birch Bayh's law firm, Venable, LLP, to assist him. Portugués relied on Domingo's representations and entered into retainer agreements with Rekomdiv and Venable. Portugués paid $225,000 to Rekomdiv and $400,000 to Venable. Several months after entering into these agreements and paying the retainers, someone from Venable e-mailed Portugués, telling him that a Victoria's Secret franchise was not available because Victoria's Secret did not use a franchise system but owned and operated its own stores. Portugués sued Domingo and Rekomdiv and Bayh and Venable for breach of contract and *dolo*—Spanish for "fraud." Venable and Bayh settled with Portugués for an undisclosed amount. Portugués's lawsuit against Domingo and Rekomdiv proceeded to trial in U.S. district court in Puerto Rico, where the jury held in favor of Portugués and awarded him $625,000 in damages. The decision was appealed.

Issue

Are Domingo and Rekomdiv liable to Portugués for *dolo*?

Language of the Court

In the end, Portugués got zilch for his money. On the verdict form the jury answered yes to the following question: "Do you find that any of the defendants incurred in dolo?" and listed each defendant's name with a space to the left of each name where the jury could mark an "X". The jury placed an "X" next to "Richard Domingo" and "Rekomdiv Int'l, Inc." When asked on the verdict form, "What damages, if any, did plaintiff sustain as the consequence of defendant's/defendants' dolo," the jury responded the damages amounted to $625,000.

Decision

The U.S. court of appeals affirmed the U.S. district court's finding of fraud and the award of $625,000 in favor of the plaintiff.

Ethics Questions

What is *dolo*? Did Domingo act ethically in this case? Why do defendants settle the lawsuits?

fraud by concealment
Fraud that occurs when one party takes specific action to conceal a material fact from another party.

Whoever is detected in a shameful fraud is ever after not believed even if they speak the truth.

Phaedrus (Thrace of Macedonia)
(c. 15 BCE–c. 50 CE)

Fraud by Concealment

Fraud by concealment occurs when one party takes specific action to conceal a material fact from another party.[6]

Example Steel Inc. contracts to buy used manufacturing equipment from United Inc. United Inc. does not show Steel Inc. the invoices for repairs to the equipment even though Steel Inc. has asked to see all of the repair invoices for the equipment. Relying on the knowledge that the equipment is in good condition and has never been repaired, Steel Inc. purchases the equipment. If Steel Inc. subsequently discovers that a significant repair record has been concealed by United Inc., Steel Inc. can sue United Inc. for fraud by concealment.

CONCEPT SUMMARY
TYPES OF FRAUD

1. **Fraud in the inception (fraud in the factum).** Fraud that occurs if a person is deceived as to the nature of his or her act and does not know what he or she is signing.
2. **Fraud in the inducement.** Fraud that occurs when the party knows what he or she is signing but has been fraudulently induced to enter into the contract.
3. **Fraud by concealment.** Fraud that occurs when one party takes specific action to conceal a material fact from another party.

Silence as Misrepresentation

Generally, neither party to a contract owes a duty to disclose all the facts to the other party. Ordinarily, such silence is not a misrepresentation unless (1) nondisclosure would cause bodily injury or death, (2) there is a fiduciary relationship (i.e., a relationship of trust and confidence) between the contracting parties, or (3) federal and state statutes require disclosure. The *Restatement (Second) of Contracts* specifies a broader duty of disclosure: Nondisclosure is a misrepresentation if it would constitute a failure to act in "good faith."[7]

Examples Some states require that home sellers disclose material facts about their property, such as structural problems, the existence of mold or mildew, water leaks in the foundations or walls, or unresolved disputes with adjacent landowners about the size or survey lines of the property. Some states require disclosure of suicides and other deaths that have occurred on the property within a certain time period prior to listing the property for sale. Nondisclosure of such required facts constitutes silence as misrepresentation and violates the law.

Misrepresentation of Law

Usually, a **misrepresentation of law** is not actionable as fraud. The innocent party cannot generally rescind the contract because each party to a contract is assumed to know the law that applies to the transaction, either through his or her own investigation or by hiring a lawyer. There is one major exception to this rule: The misrepresentation will be allowed as grounds for rescission of the contract if one party to the contract is a professional who should know what the law is and intentionally misrepresents the law to a less sophisticated contracting party.[8]

Innocent Misrepresentation

An **innocent misrepresentation** occurs when a person makes a statement of fact that he or she honestly and reasonably believes to be true even though it is not. Innocent misrepresentation is not fraud. If an innocent misrepresentation has been made, the aggrieved party may rescind the contract but may not sue for damages. Often, innocent misrepresentation is treated as a mutual mistake.

innocent misrepresentation Fraud that occurs when a person makes a statement of fact that he or she honestly and reasonably believes to be true even though it is not.

In the following case, the court found fraud and awarded punitive damages.

CASE 13.2 *STATE COURT CASE Fraud*

Krysa v. Payne

176 S.W.3d 150, 2005 Mo. App. Lexis 1680 (2005)
Court of Appeals of Missouri

"Payne's conduct can only be seen as exhibiting a very high degree of reprehensibility."

—Ellis, Judge

Facts

Frank and Shelly Krysa were shopping for a truck to pull their 18-foot trailer. During the course of their search, they visited Payne's Car Company, a used car dealership owned by Emmett Payne. Kemp Crane, a used car salesman, showed the Krysas around the car lot. The Krysas saw an F-350 truck that they were interested in purchasing. Crane told the Krysas that the truck would tow their trailer and that the truck would make it to 400,000 miles and that it was "a one-owner trade-in." The Krysas took the truck for a test-drive and decided to purchase the truck. The Krysas paid for the truck and took possession.

Later that day, the Krysas noticed that the power locks did not work on the truck. A few days later, the truck took three hours to start. The heater was not working. Mr. Krysa tried to fix some problems and noticed that the radiator was smashed up, the radiator cap did not have a seal, and the thermostat was missing. Mr. Krysa noticed broken glass on the floor underneath the front seats and that the driver's side window had been replaced. Shortly thereafter, Mr. Krysa attempted to tow his trailer, but within two miles, he had his foot to the floor trying to get the truck to pull the trailer. A large amount of smoke was pouring out of the back of the truck. Mr. Krysa also noticed that the truck was consuming a lot of oil. Mr. Krysa obtained a CARFAX report for the truck, which showed that the truck had had 13 prior owners. Evidence proved that the truck was actually two halves of different trucks that had been welded together. An automobile expert told the Krysas not to drive the truck because it was unsafe.

Mr. Krysa went back to the dealership to return the truck and get his money back. Payne would not give Krysa his money back. The Krysas sued Payne for fraudulent nondisclosure and fraudulent misrepresentation, and they sought to recover compensatory and punitive damages. The jury returned a verdict for the Krysas and awarded them $18,449 in compensatory damages and $500,000 in punitive damages. Payne appealed the award of punitive damages.

Issue

Did Payne engage in fraudulent nondisclosure, fraudulent misrepresentation, and reckless disregard for the safety of the Krysas and the public to support the award of $500,000 in punitive damages?

Language of the Court

The record clearly supports a finding that Payne acted indifferently to or in reckless disregard of the safety of the Krysas in selling them a vehicle that he knew or should have known was not safe to drive. The evidence also supported a finding that the harm sustained by Krysas was the result of intentional malice, trickery, or deceit, and was not merely an accident. Payne's conduct can only be seen as exhibiting a very high degree of reprehensibility.

Decision

The court of appeals found that Payne's fraudulent concealment, fraudulent misrepresentation, and reckless disregard for the safety of the Krysas and the public justified the award of $500,000 of punitive damages to the Krysas.

Ethics Questions

Did Payne, the used car dealer, act ethically in this case? Should punitive damages have been awarded in this case?

Duress

duress
A situation in which one party threatens to do a wrongful act unless the other party enters into a contract.

Duress occurs when one party threatens to do some wrongful act unless the other party enters into a contract. If a party to a contract has been forced into making the contract, the assent is not voluntary. Such a contract is not enforceable against the innocent party. Thus, if someone threatens to physically harm another person unless that person signs a contract, this is *physical duress*. If the victim of the duress signs the contract, it cannot be enforced against the victim. Duress can also occur where a threat does not involve physical harm.

Examples The threat to commit extortion unless someone enters into a contract constitutes duress. A threat to bring (or not drop) a criminal lawsuit unless someone enters into a contract constitutes duress even if the criminal lawsuit is well founded.[9] A threat to bring (or not drop) a civil lawsuit, however, does not constitute duress unless such a suit is frivolous or brought in bad faith.

Equitable Doctrine: Undue Influence

The courts may permit the rescission of a contract based on the equitable doctrine of **undue influence**. Undue influence occurs when one person (the **dominant party**) takes advantage of another person's mental, emotional, or physical weakness and unduly persuades that person (the **servient party**) to enter into a contract. The persuasion by the wrongdoer must overcome the free will of the innocent party. A contract that is entered into because of undue influence is voidable by the innocent party.[10]

The following elements must be shown to prove undue influence:

- A fiduciary or confidential relationship must have existed between the parties.
- The dominant party must have unduly used his or her influence to persuade the servient party to enter into a contract.

If there is a confidential relationship between persons—such as a lawyer and a client, a doctor and a patient, a psychiatrist and a patient—any contract made by the servient party that benefits the dominant party is presumed to be entered into under undue influence. This rebuttable presumption can be overcome through proper evidence.

undue influence
A situation in which one person takes advantage of another person's mental, emotional, or physical weakness and unduly persuades that person to enter into a contract; the persuasion by the wrongdoer must overcome the free will of the innocent party.

Example Mr. Johnson, who is 70 years old, has a stroke and is partially paralyzed. He is required to use a wheelchair, and he needs constant nursing care. Prior to his stroke, Mr. Johnson had executed a will, leaving his property on his death equally to his four grandchildren. Edward, a licensed nurse, is hired to care for Mr. Johnson on a daily basis, and Mr. Johnson relies on Edward's care. Edward works for Mr. Johnson for two years before Mr. Johnson passes away. It is later discovered that Mr. Johnson had executed a written contract with Edward three months before he died, deeding a valuable piece of real estate to Edward. If it is shown that Edward has used his dominant and fiduciary position to unduly influence Mr. Johnson to enter into this contract, then the contract is invalid. If no undue influence is shown, the contract with Edward is valid, and Edward will receive the property deeded to him by Mr. Johnson.

Critical Legal Thinking
Is it difficult to determine when undue influence has occurred? Do you think that undetected undue influence occurs very often?

Key Terms and Concepts

Dominant party (297)
Duress (296)
Economic injury (293)
Fraud by concealment (294)
Fraud in the inception (fraud in the factum) (293)
Fraud in the inducement (293)
Fraudulent misrepresentation (fraud) (292)
Genuineness of assent (291)
Innocent misrepresentation (295)
Intent to deceive (293)
Material fact (291)
Misrepresentation of a material fact (292)
Misrepresentation of law (295)
Mistake (291)
Mutual mistake of a material fact (291)
Mutual mistake of value (292)
Reliance on a misrepresentation (293)
Rescission (291)
Scienter ("guilty mind") (293)
Servient party (297)
Undue influence (297)
Unilateral mistake (291)

Critical Legal Thinking Cases

13.1 Unilateral Mistake The County of Contra Costa, California, held a tax sale in which it offered for sale a vacant piece of property located in the city of El Cerrito. Richard J. Schultz, a carpenter, saw the notice of the pending tax sale and was interested in purchasing the lot to build a house. Prior to attending the tax sale, Schultz visited and measured the parcel, examined the neighborhood and found the houses there to be "very nice," and had a title search done that turned up no liens or judgments against the property. Schultz did not, however, check with the city zoning department regarding the zoning of the property.

Schultz attended the tax sale and, after spirited bidding, won with a bid of $9,100 and received a deed to the property. Within one week of the purchase, Schultz discovered that the city's zoning laws prevented building a residence on the lot. In essence, the lot was worthless. Schultz sued to rescind the contract. Can the contract be rescinded? *Schultz v. County of Contra Costa, California*, 157 Cal. App.3d 242, 203 Cal. Rptr. 760, 1984 Cal. App. Lexis 2198 (Court of Appeal of California)

13.2 Fraud James L. "Skip" Deupree, a developer, was building a development of townhouses called Point South in Destin, Florida. All the townhouses in the development were to have individual boat slips. Sam and Louise Butner, husband and wife, bought one of the townhouses. The sales contract between Deupree and the Butners provided that a boat slip would be built and was included in the price of the townhouse. The contract stated that permission from the Florida Department of Natural Resources (DNR) had to be obtained to build the boat slips. It is undisputed that a boat slip adds substantially to the value of the property and that the Butners relied on the fact that the townhouse would have a boat slip.

Prior to the sale of the townhouse to the Butners, the DNR had informed Deupree that it objected to the plan to build the boat slips and that permission to build them would probably not be forthcoming. Deupree did not tell the Butners this information but instead stated that there would be "no problem" getting permission from the state to build the boat slips. The Butners purchased the townhouse. When the DNR would not approve the building of the boat slips for the Butners' townhouse, they sued for damages for fraud. Who wins? *Deupree v. Butner*, 522 So.2d 242, 1988 Ala. Lexis 55 (Supreme Court of Alabama)

13.3 Undue Influence Conrad Schaneman Sr. had eight sons and five daughters. He owned an eighty-acre farm in the Scottsbluff area of Nebraska. Conrad was born in Russia and could not read or write English. All of his children had frequent contact with Conrad and helped with his needs. Subsequently, however, his eldest son, Lawrence, advised the other children that he would henceforth manage his father's business affairs. After much urging by Lawrence, Conrad deeded the farm to Lawrence for $23,500. Evidence showed that at the time of the sale, the reasonable fair market value of the farm was between $145,000 and $160,000.

At the time of the conveyance, Conrad was more than 80 years old, had deteriorated in health, suffered from heart problems and diabetes, had high and uncontrollable blood sugar levels, weighed almost 300 pounds, had difficulty breathing, could not walk more than 15 feet, and had to have a jack hoist lift him in and out of the bathtub. He was for all purposes an invalid, relying on Lawrence for most of his personal needs, transportation, banking, and other business matters. After Conrad died, the conservators of the estate brought an action to cancel the deed transferring the farm to Lawrence. Can the conservators cancel the deed? *Schaneman v. Schaneman*, 206 Neb. 113, 291 N.W.2d 412, 1980 Neb. Lexis 823 (Supreme Court of Nebraska)

13.4 Duress Judith and Donald Eckstein were married and had two daughters. Years later, Judith left the marital abode in the parties' jointly owned Volkswagen van with only the clothes on her back. She did not take the children, who were 6 and 8 years old at the time. She had no funds, and the husband promptly closed the couple's bank account. The wife was unemployed. Shortly after she left, the husband discovered her whereabouts and the location of the van and seized and secreted the van. The husband refused the wife's request to visit or communicate with her children and refused to give her clothing. He told her that she could see the children and take her clothes only if she signed a separation agreement prepared by his lawyer. The wife contacted Legal Aid but was advised that she did not qualify for assistance.

The wife was directed to go to her husband's lawyer's office. A copy of a separation agreement was given to her to read. The separation agreement provided that the wife (1) give custody of the children to her husband, (2) deed her interest in their jointly owned house to the husband, (3) assign her interest in a jointly owned new Chevrolet van to her husband, and (4) waive alimony, support, maintenance, court costs, attorneys' fees, and any right to inheritance in her husband's estate. By the agreement, she was to receive $1,100 cash, her clothes, the Volkswagen van, and any furniture she desired. The wife testified that her husband told her over an interoffice phone in the lawyer's office that if she did not sign the separation agreement, he would get her for desertion, that she would never see her children again, and that she would get nothing—neither her clothes nor the van—unless she signed the agreement.

The wife signed the separation agreement. Immediately thereafter, her clothes were surrendered to her, and she was given $1,100 cash and the keys to the Volkswagen van. The husband filed for divorce. The wife filed an answer seeking to rescind the separation agreement. Can she rescind the separation agreement? *Eckstein v. Eckstein*, 38 Md. App. 506, 379 A.2d 757, 1978 Md. App. Lexis 324 (Court of Special Appeals of Maryland)

Ethics Case

Ethical

13.5 Ethics Case Wells Fargo Credit Corporation (Wells Fargo) obtained a judgment of foreclosure on a house owned by Mr. and Mrs. Clevenger. The total indebtedness stated in the judgment was $207,141. The foreclosure sale was scheduled for 11:00 A.M. on a specified day at the west front door of the Hillsborough County Courthouse. Wells Fargo was represented by a paralegal, who had attended more than 1,000 similar sales. Wells Fargo's handwritten instruction sheet informed the paralegal to make one bid at $115,000, the tax-appraised value of the property. Because the first 1 in the number was close to the dollar sign, the paralegal misread the bid instruction as $15,000 and opened the bidding at that amount.

Harley Martin, who was attending his first judicial sale, bid $20,000. The county clerk gave ample time for another bid and then announced, "$20,000 going once, $20,000 going twice, sold to Harley." The paralegal screamed, "Stop, I'm sorry. I made a mistake!" The certificate of sale was issued to Martin. Wells Fargo filed suit to set aside the judicial sale based on its unilateral mistake. Does Wells Fargo's unilateral mistake constitute grounds for setting aside the judicial sale? Did any party act unethically in this case? *Wells Fargo Credit Corporation v. Martin*, 650 So.2d 531, 1992 Fla. App. Lexis 9927 (Court of Appeal of Florida)

Notes

1. *Restatement (Second) of Contracts*, Section 153.
2. *Restatement (Second) of Contracts*, Section 152.
3. 59 Eng. Rep. 375 (1864).
4. *Restatement (Second) of Contracts*, Section 159.
5. *Restatement (Second) of Contracts*, Sections 163 and 164.
6. *Restatement (Second) of Contracts*, Section 160.
7. *Restatement (Second) of Contracts*, Section 161.
8. *Restatement (Second) of Contracts*, Section 170.
9. *Restatement (Second) of Contracts*, Section 177.
10. *Restatement (Second) of Contracts*, Section 176.

CHAPTER 14

Statute of Frauds and Equitable Exceptions

GOLDEN PAVILION, JAPAN

In some countries of the world, such as Japan, China, Korea, Vietnam, and other countries of Asia, individuals often follow the tradition of using a seal as their signature. The seal is a character or set of characters carved onto one end of a cylinder-shaped stamp—made out of ivory, stone, metal, wood, plastic, or other material. A party places the end bearing the characters in ink and then applies this end to the document to be signed, leaving an ink imprint that serves as the party's signature. Government agencies and corporations often use seals on contracts. Seals are usually registered with the government. Today, however, such seals are being replaced by hand-applied signatures in many commercial transactions.

Learning Objectives

After studying this chapter, you should be able to:

1. List the contracts that must be in writing under the Statute of Frauds.
2. Explain the effect of noncompliance with the Statute of Frauds.
3. Describe how the Statute of Frauds is applicable to the UCC sale of goods and lease of goods.
4. Describe the formality of the writing of contracts and the *parol evidence rule*.
5. Define equitable doctrines of *part performance* and *promissory estoppel*.

Chapter Outline

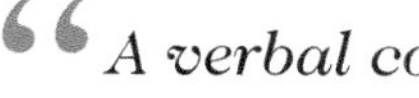

A verbal contract isn't worth the paper it's written on."

—Samuel Goldwyn

Introduction to Statute of Frauds and Equitable Exceptions

Certain types of contracts must be in writing pursuant to the Statute of Frauds. Other issues regarding the form of a contract may arise, such as the form of signature that is required on a written contract, whether a contract can be created by the integration of several documents, whether any previous oral or written agreements between the parties can be given effect, and how contract language should be interpreted. Also, there are several equitable exceptions to the Statute of Frauds—namely, the part performance exception and the doctrine of promissory estoppel.

Statute of Frauds: That unfortunate statute, the misguided application of which has been the cause of so many frauds.

Bacon, Viscount
Morgan v. Washington (1878)

Issues regarding the Statute of Frauds, the formality of the writing of contracts, and equitable doctrines that allow exceptions to the Statute of Frauds are discussed in this chapter.

Statute of Frauds for Common Contracts

In 1677, the English Parliament enacted a statute called "An Act for the Prevention of Frauds and Perjuries." This act required that certain types of contracts had to be in writing and signed by the party against whom enforcement was sought. Today, every U.S. state has enacted a **Statute of Frauds** that requires certain types of contracts to be in *writing*. This statute is intended to ensure that the terms of important contracts are not forgotten, misunderstood, or fabricated. One court stated about the Statute of Frauds, "It is the purpose of the Statute of Frauds to suppress fraud, i.e., cooked-up claims of agreement, sometimes fathered by wish, sometimes imagined in the light of subsequent events, and sometimes simply conjured up."[1]

Statute of Frauds
A state statute that requires certain types of contracts to be in writing.

Writing Requirement

Although the statutes vary slightly from state to state, most states require the following types of contracts to be in writing:[2]

- Contracts involving interests in real property
- Contracts that by their own terms cannot possibly be performed within one year
- Collateral contracts in which a person promises to answer for the debt or duty of another
- Promises made in consideration of marriage
- Contracts for the sale of goods for $500 or more
- Contracts for the lease of goods with payments of $1,000 or more
- Real estate agents' contracts
- Agents' contracts where the underlying contract must be in writing
- Promises to write a will
- Contracts to pay debts barred by the statute of limitations or discharged in bankruptcy
- Contracts to pay compensation for services rendered in negotiating the purchase of a business
- Finder's fee contracts

Generally, an **executory contract** that is not in writing even though the Statute of Frauds requires it to be is unenforceable by either party. The Statute of Frauds is usually raised by one party as a defense to the enforcement of the contract by the other party.

Critical Legal Thinking
What is the purpose of the Statute of Frauds? Why does it not apply to all contracts?

If an oral contract that should have been in writing under the Statute of Frauds is already executed, neither party can seek to **rescind** the contract on the grounds of noncompliance with the Statute of Frauds. That is, the contract may be voluntarily performed by the parties.

Example Edward enters into an oral contract to sell his house to Lana for $400,000, closing of the transaction to be in 30 days. At the time of closing, Edward signs the deed to the property to Lana, and Lana pays Edward the $400,000 purchase price. Under the statute of frauds, this contract for the sale of real estate would have had to be in writing to be enforceable. However, since both parties have performed the oral contract, neither party can raise the statute of frauds to rescind the contract.

Generally, contracts listed in the Statute of Frauds must be in writing to be enforceable. There are several equity exceptions to this rule. The contracts that must be in writing pursuant to the Statute of Frauds, and the exceptions to this rule are discussed in the following paragraphs.

Contracts Involving Interests in Real Property

real property
The land itself, as well as buildings, trees, soil, minerals, timber, plants, crops, fixtures, and other things permanently affixed to the land or buildings.

Under the Statute of Frauds, any contract that transfers an ownership interest in **real property** must be in writing to be enforceable. Real property includes the land itself, buildings, trees, soil, minerals, timber, plants, crops, fixtures, and things permanently affixed to the land or buildings. Certain items of personal property that are permanently affixed to the real property are fixtures that become part of the real property.

Example Built-in cabinets in a house are *fixtures* that become part of the real property.

Other contracts that transfer an ownership interest in land must be in writing under the Statute of Frauds. These interests include the following:

mortgage (deed of trust)
An interest in real property given to a lender as security for the repayment of a loan.

- **Mortgages.** Borrowers often give a lender an interest in real property as security for the repayment of a loan. This action must be done through the use of a written **mortgage** or **deed of trust**.

  Example Ida purchases a house for $500,000. She pays $100,000 toward the payment of the house and borrows $400,000 of the purchase price from Country Bank. Country Bank requires that the house be collateral for the loan and takes a mortgage on the house. Here, the mortgage between Ida and Country Bank must be in writing to be enforceable.

lease
The transfer of the right to use real property for a specified period of time.

life estate
An interest in real property for a person's lifetime; on that person's death, the interest will be transferred to another party.

easement
A right to use someone else's land without owning or leasing it.

- **Leases.** A **lease** is the transfer of the right to use real property for a specified period of time. Most Statutes of Frauds require leases for a term more than one year to be in writing.
- **Life estates.** On some occasions, a person is given a **life estate** in real property. In other words, the person has an interest in the real property for the person's lifetime, and the interest will be transferred to another party on that person's death. A life estate is an ownership interest that must be in writing under the Statute of Frauds.
- **Easements.** An **easement** is a given or required right to use another person's land without owning or leasing it. Easements may be either express or implied. Express easements must be in writing to be enforceable, while implied easements need not be written.

One-Year Rule

According to the Statute of Frauds, an executory contract that cannot be performed by its own terms within one year of its formation must be in writing.[3]

This **one-year rule** is intended to prevent disputes about contract terms that may otherwise occur toward the end of a long-term contract. If the performance of the contract is possible within the one-year period, the contract may be oral.

The extension of an oral contract might cause the contract to violate the Statute of Frauds if the original term and the extension period exceed one year.

one-year rule
A rule stating that an executory contract that cannot be performed by its own terms within one year of its formation must be in writing.

Example Frederick, the owner of a store, hires Anna as the store manager for six months. Assume that after three months, Frederick and Anna agree to extend the contract for an additional 11 months. At the time of the extension, the contract would be for 14 months (the three left on the original contract plus 11 months added by the extension). The modification would have to be in writing because it exceeds the one-year rule.

In the following ethics feature, the court applied the one-year rule.

Ethics

Bonus Lost Because of the Statute of Frauds

"The end result may not seem 'fair' to Sawyer. The Statute of Frauds, by its own terms, can be considered 'harsh' in that it will bar oral agreements between parties under certain conditions. This is simply the nature of the beast."

—Ishmael, Trial Court Judge

Barbara Lucinda Sawyer worked as a paralegal for Melbourne Mills Jr., an attorney at a law firm. Sawyer proposed that Mills and the law firm become engaged in class action lawsuits. Mills agreed to pay Sawyer an unspecified bonus when "the ship comes in." After Sawyer's assistance and persistence, the law firm became involved in pharmaceutical class action litigation. After the law firm received millions of dollars in fees from class action lawsuits, Sawyer and her husband Steve met with Mills to discuss Sawyer's bonus. Mills orally agreed to pay Sawyer $1,065,000 as a bonus to be paid in monthly installments over 107 months. Sawyer secretly tape-recorded the conversation. Mills later refused to sign a written contract conveying the terms of the oral agreement.

After Mills had paid $165,000, he quit making further payments. Sawyer sued Mills to collect the remaining $900,000. Mills defended, arguing that the oral contract exceeded one year and was therefore unenforceable because it was not in writing, as required by the Statute of Frauds. The jury ruled in favor of Sawyer.

Mills made a motion to the trial court judge to refuse to enforce the oral contract against him. The trial court held that the Statute of Frauds required the bonus agreement between Sawyer and Mills to be in writing to be enforceable. Because the oral agreement exceeded one year, the court held that it did not meet the requirements of the Statute of Frauds and was therefore unenforceable. The trial court judge stated,

> *The end result may not seem "fair" to Sawyer. The Statute of Frauds, by its own terms, can be considered "harsh" in that it will bar oral agreements between parties under certain conditions. This is simply the nature of the beast.*

The court of appeals and the supreme court of Kentucky affirmed the trial court's decision holding that Sawyer would not receive the remainder of the promised bonus because of the Statute of Frauds. *Sawyer v. Mills*, 295 S.W.3d 79, 2009 Ky. Lexis 195 (Supreme Court of Kentucky)

Ethics Questions Should Mills honor the oral agreement with Sawyer? Does the Statute of Frauds sometimes assist the commission of fraud?

Guaranty Contract

A **guaranty contract** occurs when one person agrees to answer for the debts or duties of another person. Guaranty contracts are required to be in writing under the Statute of Frauds.[4]

In a guaranty situation, there are at least three parties and two contracts (see **Exhibit 14.1**). The *first contract*, which is known as the **original contract**, or **primary contract**, is between the debtor and the creditor. It does not have to be in writing (unless another provision of the Statute of Frauds requires it to be). The *second contract*, called the *guaranty contract*, is between the person who agrees to pay the debt if the primary debtor does not (i.e., the **guarantor**) and the

guaranty contract
A promise in which one person agrees to answer for the debts or duties of another person. It is a contract between the guarantor and the original creditor.

guarantor
A person who agrees to pay a debt if the primary debtor does not.

Exhibit 14.1 **GUARANTY CONTRACT**

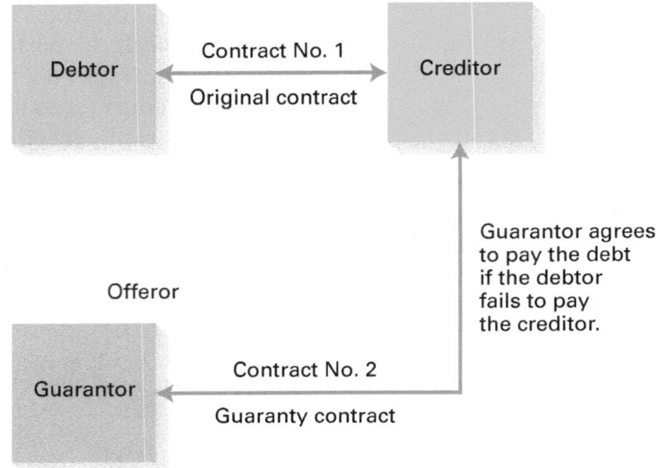

original creditor. The guarantor's liability is secondary because it does not arise unless the party primarily liable fails to perform.

Example Wei, a recent college graduate, offers to purchase a new automobile on credit from a Mercedes-Benz automobile dealership. Because Wei does not have a credit history, the dealer will agree to sell the car to her only if there is a guarantor. If Wei's father signs a written guaranty contract, he becomes responsible for any payments his daughter fails to make. If Wei's father only orally guaranteed Wei's contract, he would not be bound to the guaranty because it was oral and not in writing.

In the following case, the court refused to enforce an oral guaranty contract.

CASE 14.1 *STATE COURT CASE Guaranty Contract*

Page v. Gulf Coast Motors

903 So.2d 148, 2004 Ala. Civ. App. Lexis 982 (2004)
Court of Civil Appeal of Alabama

"A promise to pay the debt of another is barred by the Statute of Frauds unless it is in writing."

—Murdock, Judge

Facts

Glenn A. Page (Glenn) had a long-term friendship with Jerry Sellers, an owner of Gulf Coast Motors. Glenn began borrowing money from Gulf Coast Motors on a recurring basis during a two-year period. There was no evidence as to what Glenn used the loan proceeds for, but evidence showed that he had a gambling problem.

Sellers testified that toward the end of the two-year period of making loans to Glenn, he telephoned Mary R. Page, Glenn's wife, and Mary orally guaranteed to repay Glenn's loans. Mary had significant assets of her own. Mary denied that she had promised to pay any of Glenn's debt, and she denied that Sellers had asked her to pay Glenn's debt. Gulf Coast Motors sued Glenn and Mary to recover payment for the unpaid loans. The trial court entered judgment in the amount of $23,020 in favor of Gulf Coast Motors. Mary appealed.

Issue

Was Mary's alleged oral promise to guarantee her husband's debts an enforceable guaranty contract?

Language of the Court

A promise to pay the debt of another is barred by the Statute of Frauds unless it is in writing. Mary's alleged oral promises are not

(case continues)

enforceable under the Statute of Frauds. We conclude that Mary's alleged promises to guaranty or repay Glenn's debts were within the Statute of Frauds and, therefore, were not enforceable.

Decision

The court of civil appeals held that Mary's alleged oral promises to guarantee her husband's debts were not in writing, as required by the Statute of Frauds. The court remanded the case to the trial court to enter judgment in Mary's favor.

Ethics Questions

What is the public policy for requiring guaranty contracts to be in writing? Did Mary act ethically if she made the oral guaranty promise and did not honor the promise?

The "Main Purpose" Exception If the main purpose of a transaction and an oral collateral contract is to provide pecuniary (i.e., financial) benefit to the guarantor, the collateral contract is treated like an original contract and does not have to be in writing to be enforced.[5] This exception is called the **main purpose exception**, or **leading object exception**, to the Statute of Frauds. This exception is intended to ensure that the primary benefactor of the original contract (i.e., the guarantor) is answerable for the debt or duty.

main purpose exception (leading object exception)
An exception to the Statute of Frauds that states that if the main purpose of a transaction and an oral collateral contract is to provide pecuniary benefit to the guarantor, the collateral contract does not have to be in writing to be enforced.

Example Ethel is president and sole shareholder of Computer Corporation, Inc. Assume (1) that the corporation borrows $100,000 from CityBank for working capital and (2) that Ethel orally guarantees to repay the loan if the corporation fails to pay it. CityBank can enforce the oral guaranty contract against Ethel if the corporation does not meet its obligation because the main purpose of the loan was to benefit her as the sole shareholder of the corporation.

Agents' Contracts

Many state Statutes of Frauds require that **agents' contracts** to sell real property covered by the Statute of Frauds be in writing to be enforceable. The requirement is often referred to as the **equal dignity rule**.

equal dignity rule
A rule stating that agents' contracts to sell property covered by the Statute of Frauds must be in writing to be enforceable.

Example Barney hires Cynthia, a licensed real estate broker, to sell his house. Because a contract to sell real estate must be in writing pursuant to the Statute of Frauds, the equal dignity rule requires that the real estate agents' contract be in writing as well. Some state Statutes of Frauds expressly state that the real estate broker and agents' contracts must be in writing.

Promises Made in Consideration of Marriage

Under the Statute of Frauds, a unilateral promise to pay money or property in consideration for a promise to marry must be in writing.

Example A **prenuptial agreement**, which is a contract entered into by parties prior to marriage that defines their ownership rights in each other's property, must be in writing.

UCC Statutes of Fraud

The **Uniform Commercial Code (UCC)** establishes statutes of fraud for contracts for the sales and lease of *goods*. The UCC statutes of fraud are discussed in the following paragraphs.

UCC: Contract for the Sale of Goods

Section 2-201(1) of the Uniform Commercial Code (UCC)
A section of the Uniform Commercial Code (UCC) stating that sales contracts for the sale of goods priced at $500 or more must be in writing.

Section 2-201(1) of the Uniform Commercial Code (UCC) is the basic Statute of Frauds provision for **sales contracts**. It states that contracts for the sale of goods priced at *$500 or more* must be in writing to be enforceable. If the contract price of an original sales contract is below $500, it does not have to be in writing under the **UCC Statute of Frauds**. However, if a modification of the sales contract increases the sales price to $500 or more, the *modification* has to be in writing to be enforceable.

Example Echo enters into an oral contract to sell James her used car for $10,000, with the delivery date to be May 1. When May 1 comes and James tenders $10,000 to Echo, Echo refuses to sell her car to James. The contract will not be enforced against Echo because it was an oral contract for the sale of goods costing $500 or more, and it should have been in writing.

UCC: Contract for the Lease of Goods

Section 2A-201(1) of the Uniform Commercial Code (UCC)
A section of the Uniform Commercial Code (UCC) stating that lease contracts requiring payments of $1,000 or more must be in writing.

Section 2A-201(1) of the Uniform Commercial Code (UCC) is the Statute of Frauds provision that applies to the lease of goods. It states that **lease contracts** requiring payments of *$1,000 or more* must be in writing. If a lease payment of an original lease contract is less than $1,000, it does not have to be in writing under the UCC Statute of Frauds. However, if a modification of the lease contract increases the lease payment to $1,000 or more, the *modification* has to be in writing to be enforceable.

Equitable Exception: Part Performance

part performance
An equitable doctrine that allows the court to order an oral contract for the sale of land or transfer of another interest in real property to be specifically performed if it has been partially performed and performance is necessary to avoid injustice.

If an oral contract for the sale of land or transfer of other interests in real property has been partially performed, it may not be possible to return the parties to their *status quo*. To solve this problem, the courts have developed the equitable doctrine of **part performance**. This doctrine allows the court to order such an oral contract to be specifically performed if performance is necessary to avoid injustice. For this performance exception to apply, most courts require that the purchaser either pay part of the purchase price and take possession of the property or make valuable improvements on the property.

In the following critical legal thinking case, the court was asked to apply the equity doctrine of part performance.

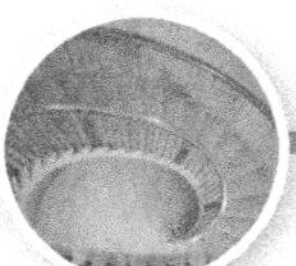

Critical Legal Thinking Case

Doctrine of Part Performance

"The doctrine of part performance by the purchaser is a well-recognized exception to the Statute of Frauds as applied to contracts for the sale of real property."

—Kline, Judge

Arlene and Donald Warner inherited a home at 101 Molimo Street in San Francisco. The Warners obtained a $170,000 loan on the property. Donald Warner and Kenneth Sutton were friends. Donald Warner proposed that Sutton and his wife purchase the residence. His proposal included a $15,000 down payment toward the purchase price of $185,000. The Suttons were to pay all the mortgage payments and real estate taxes on the property for five years, and at any time during the five-year period, they could purchase the house. All this was agreed to orally.

The Suttons paid the down payment and cash payments equal to the monthly mortgage to the Warners. The Suttons paid the annual property taxes on the house. The Suttons also made improvements to the property. Four and one-half years later, the Warners reneged on the oral sales/option agreement. At that time, the house had risen in value to between $250,000 and $320,000. The Suttons sued for specific performance of the sales agreement. The Warners defended, alleging that the oral promise to sell real estate had to be in writing under the Statute of Frauds and was therefore unenforceable.

The trial court applied the equitable doctrine of part performance and ordered the Warners specifically to perform the oral contract for the sale of real estate and transfer ownership of the property to the Suttons. The court of appeal agreed. *Sutton v. Warner*, 12 Cal. App.4th 415, 15 Cal. Rptr.2d 632, 1993 Cal. App. Lexis 22 (Court of Appeal of California)

Critical Legal Thinking Questions

Why was the doctrine of part performance developed? Who would have won if the Statute of Frauds were applied to this case?

Formality of the Writing

Some written commercial contracts are long, detailed documents that have been negotiated by the parties and drafted and reviewed by their lawyers. Others are preprinted forms with blanks that can be filled in to fit the facts of a particular situation.

A written contract does not, however, have to be either drafted by a lawyer or formally typed to be legally binding. Generally, the law requires only a writing containing the essential terms of the parties' agreement. Thus, any writing—including letters, telegrams, invoices, sales receipts, checks, and handwritten agreements written on scraps of paper—can be an enforceable contract under this rule.

Required Signature

The Statute of Frauds and the UCC require a written contract, whatever its form, to be signed *by the party against whom enforcement is sought*. The signature of the person who is enforcing the contract is not necessary. Thus, a written contract may be enforceable against one party but not the other party.

Generally, the signature may appear anywhere on the writing. In addition, it does not have to be a person's full legal name. The person's last name, first name, nickname, initials, seal, stamp, engraving, or other symbol or mark (e.g., an *X*) that indicates the person's intent can be binding. The signature may be affixed by an authorized agent.

If a signature is suspected of being forged, the victim can hire handwriting experts and use modern technology to prove that it is not his or her signature.

WEB EXERCISE
John Hancock's bold signature on the U.S. Declaration of Independence is one of the most famous signatures in history. Go to **www.fotosearch.com/DGT081/cbr002400** to see this signature.

Integration of Several Writings

Both the common law of contracts and the UCC permit several writings to be integrated to form a single written contract. That is, the entire writing does not have to appear in one document to be an enforceable contract. This rule is called **integration**.

Integration may be by an *express reference* in one document that refers to and incorporates another document within it. This procedure is called **incorporation by reference**. Thus, what may often look like a simple one-page contract may actually be hundreds of pages long when the documents that are incorporated by reference are included.

integration
The combination of several writings to form a single contract.

incorporation by reference
Integration made by express reference in one document that refers to and incorporates another document within it.

Example Credit card contracts often incorporate by express reference such documents as the master agreement between the issuer and cardholders, subsequent amendments to the agreement, and such.

Several documents may be integrated to form a single written contract if they are somehow physically attached to each other to indicate a party's intent to show integration. Attaching several documents together with a staple, paper clip, or some other means may indicate integration. Placing several documents in the same container (e.g., an envelope) may also indicate integration. Such an action is called **implied integration**.

The meaning of words varies according to the circumstances of and concerning which they are used.

Justice Blackburn
Allgood v. Blake (1873)

Interpreting Contract Words and Terms

When contracts are at issue in a lawsuit, courts are often called on to interpret the meaning of certain contract words or terms. The parties to a contract may define the words and terms used in their contract. Many written contracts contain a detailed definition section—usually called a **glossary**—that defines many of the words and terms used in the contract.

Counsel Randle Jackson: In the book of nature, my lords, it is written . . . Lord Ellenborough: Will you have the goodness to mention the page, sir, if you please?

Lord Campbell
Lives of the Chief Justices (1857)

If the parties have not defined the words and terms of a contract, the courts apply the following **standards of interpretation**:

- *Ordinary* words are given their usual meaning according to the dictionary.
- *Technical words* are given their technical meaning, unless a different meaning is clearly intended.
- *Specific terms* are presumed to qualify *general terms*. For example, if a provision in a contract refers to the subject matter as "corn" but a later provision refers to the subject matter as "feed corn" for cattle, this specific term qualifies the general term.
- If both parties are members of the same trade or profession, words will be given their meaning as used in the trade (i.e., **usage of trade**). If the parties do not want trade usage to apply, the contract must indicate that.
- Where a preprinted form contract is used, *typed words* in a contract prevail over *preprinted words*. *Handwritten words* prevail over both preprinted and typed words.
- If there is an ambiguity in a contract, the ambiguity will be resolved against the party who drafted the contract.

Parol Evidence Rule

By the time a contract is reduced to writing, the parties usually have engaged in prior or contemporaneous discussions and negotiations or exchanged prior writings. Any oral or written words outside the *four corners* of the written contract are called **parol evidence**. *Parol* means "word."

parol evidence
Any oral or written words outside the four corners of a written contract.

parol evidence rule
A rule stating that if a written contract is a complete and final statement of the parties' agreement, any prior or contemporaneous oral or written statements that alter, contradict, or are in addition to the terms of the written contract are inadmissible in court regarding a dispute over the contract. There are several exceptions to this rule.

The **parol evidence rule** was originally developed by courts as part of the common law of contracts. The UCC has adopted the parol evidence rule for sales and lease contracts.[6] The parol evidence rule states that if a written contract is a complete and final statement of the parties' agreement (i.e., a **complete integration**), any prior or contemporaneous oral or written statements that alter, contradict, or are in addition to the terms of the written contract are inadmissible in any court proceeding concerning the contract.[7] In other words, a completely integrated contract is viewed as the best evidence of the terms of the parties' agreement.

Merger, or Integration, Clause

merger clause (integration clause)
A clause in a contract that stipulates that it is a complete integration and the exclusive expression of the parties' agreement.

The parties to a written contract may include a clause stipulating that the contract is a complete integration and the exclusive expression of their agreement and that parol evidence may not be introduced to explain, alter, contradict, or add to the terms of the contract. This type of clause, called a **merger clause**, or an **integration clause**, expressly reiterates the parol evidence rule.

Exceptions to the Parol Evidence Rule

There are several major exceptions to the parol evidence rule. Parol evidence may be admitted in court if it:

- Shows that a contract is void or voidable (e.g., evidence that the contract was induced by fraud, misrepresentation, duress, undue influence, or mistake).
- Explains ambiguous language.

- Concerns *a prior course of dealing or course of performance* between the parties or a *usage of trade*.[8]
- *Fills in the gaps* in a contract (e.g., if a price term or time of performance term is omitted from a written contract, the court can hear parol evidence to imply the reasonable price or time of performance under the contract).
- Corrects an obvious clerical or typographical error. The court can *reform* the contract to reflect the correction.

Don't get it right, just get it written.

James Thurber

In the following case, the court refused to admit parol evidence and enforced the express terms of a written contract.

CASE 14.2 *STATE COURT CASE Parol Evidence Rule*

Yarde Metals, Inc. v. New England Patriots Limited Partnership

834 N.E.2d 1233, 2005 Mass. App. Lexis 904 (2005)
Appeals Court of Massachusetts

"The purchase of a ticket to a sports or entertainment event typically creates nothing more than a revocable license."

—Greenberg, Judge

Facts

Yarde Metals, Inc. (Yarde), was a season ticket holder to New England Patriots professional home football games. The football team is owned by the New England Patriots Limited Partnership (Patriots). Yarde permitted a business associate to attend a Patriots game. However, the associate was ejected from the game for disorderly conduct. Subsequently, the Patriots sent Yarde a letter terminating his season ticket privileges in the future. Yarde sued the Patriots, claiming that the Patriots had breached his implied contractual right to purchase season tickets. The Patriots countered that the Patriots' written contract with season ticket holders expressly provided that the "purchase of season tickets does not entitle purchaser to renewal in a subsequent year." The Patriots asserted that because the contract with Yarde was an express written contract, Yarde's claim of an implied right to purchase season tickets in the future was parol evidence and was inadmissible to change the express terms of the contract. The trial court dismissed Yarde's case. Yarde appealed.

Issue

Does Yarde have an implied right to purchase Patriots' season tickets?

Language of the Court

The purchase of a ticket to a sports or entertainment event typically creates nothing more than a revocable license. The ticket specifically stated that "purchase of season tickets does not entitle purchaser to renewal in a subsequent year." Parol evidence is not generally admissible to vary the unambiguous terms of the contract. Yarde has articulated no basis on which we can ignore the language on the ticket.

Decision

The appeals court held that there was an express written contract between Yarde and the Patriots and that the parol evidence rule prevented Yarde's alleged implied right to purchase season tickets from becoming part of that contract. The appeals court affirmed the trial court's dismissal of Yarde's case.

Ethics Questions

Was it ethical for the Patriots to terminate Yarde's season ticket privileges? What would be the consequences if there were no parol evidence rule?

Equitable Doctrine: Promissory Estoppel

The doctrine of **promissory estoppel**, or **equitable estoppel**, is another equitable exception to the strict application of the Statute of Frauds. The version of promissory estoppel in the *Restatement (Second) of Contracts* provides that if parties

promissory estoppel (equitable estoppel)
An equitable doctrine that permits enforcement of oral contracts that should have been in writing. It is applied to avoid injustice.

enter into an oral contract that should be in writing under the Statute of Frauds, the oral promise is enforceable against the promisor if three conditions are met: (1) The promise induces action or forbearance of action by another, (2) the reliance on the oral promise was foreseeable, and (3) injustice can be avoided only by enforcing the oral promise.[9] Where this doctrine applies, the promisor is *estopped (prevented)* from raising the Statute of Frauds as a defense to the enforcement of the oral contract.

Key Terms and Concepts

Agents' contract (305)
Complete integration (308)
Easement (302)
Equal dignity rule (305)
Executory contract (301)
Glossary (308)
Guarantor (303)
Guaranty contract (303)
Implied integration (307)
Incorporation by reference (307)
Integration (307)
Lease (302)
Lease contract (306)
Life estate (302)
Main purpose exception (leading object exception) (305)
Merger clause (integration clause) (308)
Mortgage (deed of trust) (302)
One-year rule (303)
Original contract (primary contract) (303)
Parol evidence (308)
Parol evidence rule (308)
Part performance (306)
Prenuptial agreement (305)
Promissory estoppel (equitable estoppel) (309)
Real property (302)
Rescind (302)
Sales contract (306)
Section 2-201(1) of the Uniform Commercial Code (UCC) (306)
Section 2A-201(1) of the Uniform Commercial Code (UCC) (306)
Standards of interpretation (308)
Statute of Frauds (301)
UCC Statute of Frauds (306)
Usage of trade (308)
Uniform Commercial Code (UCC) (305)

Critical Legal Thinking Cases

14.1 Statute of Frauds Fritz Hoffman and Fritz Frey contracted the Sun Valley Company (Company) about purchasing a 1.64-acre piece of property known as the Ruud Mountain Property, located in Sun Valley, Idaho, from Company. Mr. Conger, a representative of Company, was authorized to sell the property, subject to the approval of the executive committee of Company. Conger reached an agreement on the telephone with Hoffman and Frey whereby they would purchase the property for $90,000, payable at 30 percent down, with the balance to be payable quarterly at an annual interest rate of 9.25 percent. The next day, Hoffman sent Conger a letter confirming the conversation.

The executive committee of Company approved the sale. Sun Valley Realty prepared the deed of trust, note, seller's closing statement, and other loan documents. However, before the documents were executed by either side, Sun Valley Company sold all its assets, including the Ruud Mountain property, to another purchaser. When the new owner refused to sell the Ruud Mountain lot to Hoffman and Frey, they brought this action for specific performance of the oral contract. Who wins? *Hoffman v. Sun Valley Company*, 102 Idaho 187, 628 P.2d 218, 1981 Ida. Lexis 320 (Supreme Court of Idaho)

14.2 Guaranty Contract David Brown met with Stan Steele, a loan officer with the Bank of Idaho (now First Interstate Bank), to discuss borrowing money from the bank to start a new business. After learning that he did not qualify for the loan on the basis of his own financial strength, Brown told Steele that his former employers, James and Donna West of California, might be willing to guarantee the payment of the loan. Steele talked to Mr. West, who orally stated on the telephone that he would personally guarantee the loan to Brown. Based on this guaranty, the bank loaned Brown the money. The bank sent a written guarantee to Mr. and Mrs. West for their signatures, but it was never returned to the bank. When Brown defaulted on the loan, the bank filed suit against the Wests to recover on their guaranty contract. Are the Wests liable? *First Interstate Bank of Idaho, N.A. v. West*, 107 Idaho 851, 693 P.2d 1053, 1984 Ida. Lexis 600 (Supreme Court of Idaho)

14.3 Sufficiency of a Writing Irving Levin and Harold Lipton owned the San Diego Clippers Basketball Club, a professional basketball franchise. Levin and Lipton met with Philip Knight to discuss the sale of the Clippers to Knight. After the meeting, they all initialed a three-page handwritten memorandum that Levin had drafted during the meeting. The memorandum outlined the major terms of their discussion, including subject matter, price, and the parties to the agreement. Levin and Lipton forwarded to Knight a letter and proposed sale agreement. Two days later, Knight informed Levin that he had decided not to purchase the Clippers. Levin and Lipton sued Knight for breach of contract. Knight argued in defense that the handwritten memorandum was not enforceable because it did not satisfy the Statute of Frauds. Is he correct? *Levin v. Knight*, 865 F.2d 1271, 1989 U.S. App. Lexis 458 (United States Court of Appeals for the Ninth Circuit)

Ethical

Ethics Case

14.4 Ethics Case Adolfo Mozzetti, who owned a construction company, orally promised his son, Remo, that if Remo would manage the family business for their mutual benefit and would take care of him for the rest of his life, he would leave the family home to Remo. Section 2714 of the Delaware Code requires contracts for the transfer of land to be in writing. Section 2715 of the Delaware Code requires testamentary transfers of real property to be in writing. Remo performed as requested: He managed the family business and took care of his father until the father died. When the father died, his will devised the family home to his daughter, Lucia M. Shepard. Remo brought an action to enforce his father's oral promise that the home belonged to him. The daughter argued that the will should be upheld. Who wins? Did the daughter act ethically in trying to defeat the father's promise to leave the property to the son? Did the son act ethically in trying to defeat his father's will? *Shepard v. Mozzetti*, 545 A.2d 621, 1988 Del. Lexis 217 (Supreme Court of Delaware)

Notes

1. *Elias v. George Sahely & Co.*, 1983 App. Cas. (P.C.) 646, 655.
2. *Restatement (Second) of Contracts*, Section 110.
3. *Restatement (Second) of Contracts*, Section 130.
4. *Restatement (Second) of Contracts*, Section 112.
5. *Restatement (Second) of Contracts*, Section 116.
6. UCC Section 2-202 and UCC Section 2A-202.
7. *Restatement (Second) of Contracts*, Section 213.
8. UCC Sections 1-205, 2-202, and 2-208.
9. *Restatement (Second) of Contracts*, Section 139.

CHAPTER 15 Third-Party Rights and Discharge

PYRAMIDS OF GIZA, EGYPT
In many parts of the world, substantial negotiations occur before the parties devise a contract.

Learning Objectives

After studying this chapter, you should be able to:

1. Describe assignment of contract rights and what contract rights are assignable.
2. Define *intended beneficiary* and describe this person's rights under a contract.
3. Define *covenant*.
4. Distinguish between conditions precedent, conditions subsequent, and concurrent conditions.
5. Explain when the performance of a contract is excused because of objective impossibility.

Chapter Outline

"An honest man's word is as good as his bond."

—Don Quixote de la Mancha
Part II, Book IV, ch. 34 (1615)
Miguel de Cervantes Saavedra

Introduction to Third-Party Rights and Discharge

The parties to a contract are said to be in **privity of contract**. Contracting parties have a legal obligation to perform the duties specified in their contract. A party's duty of performance may be discharged by agreement of the parties, excuse of performance, or operation of law. If one party fails to perform as promised, the other party may enforce the contract and sue for breach.

privity of contract
The state of two specified parties being in a contract.

With two exceptions, third parties do not acquire any rights under other people's contracts. The exceptions include (1) *assignees* to whom rights are subsequently transferred and (2) *intended third-party beneficiaries* to whom the contracting parties intended to give rights under the contract at the time of contracting.

Make fair agreements and stick to them.

Confucius

This chapter discusses the rights of third parties under a contract, conditions to performance, and ways of discharging the duty of performance.

Assignment of a Right

In many cases, the parties to a contract can transfer their rights under the contract to other parties. The transfer of contractual rights is called an **assignment of rights** or just an **assignment**.

assignment of a right (assignment)
The transfer of contractual rights by an obligee to another party.

Form of Assignment

A party who owes a duty of performance under a contract is called the **obligor**. A party who is owed a right under a contract is called the **obligee**. An obligee that transfers the right to receive performance is called an **assignor**. The party to whom the right has been transferred is called the **assignee**. The assignee can assign the right to yet another person (called a **subsequent assignee**, or **subassignee**). **Exhibit 15.1** illustrates these relationships.

assignor
An obligee who transfers a right.

assignee
A party to whom a right has been transferred.

Exhibit 15.1 **ASSIGNMENT OF A RIGHT**

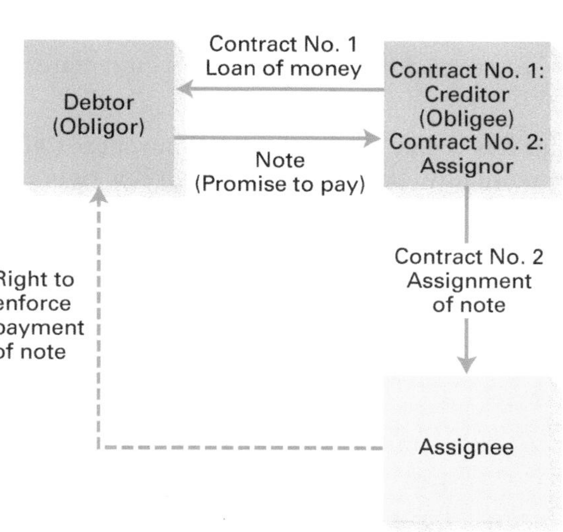

Generally, no formalities are required for a valid assignment of rights. Although the assignor often uses the word *assign*, other words or terms, such as *sell*, *transfer*, *convey*, and *give*, are sufficient to indicate intent to transfer a contract right.

Example A retail clothing store purchases $5,000 worth of goods on credit from a manufacturer. Payment is due in 120 days. If the manufacturer needs cash before the 120-day period expires, the manufacturer (assignor) can sell its right to collect the money to another party (assignee) for some price, let's say $4,000. If the retail store is given proper notice of the assignment, it must pay $5,000 to the assignee when the 120-day period is reached.

In the United States, public policy favors a free flow of commerce. Hence, most contract rights are assignable, including sales contracts and contracts for the payment of money. The following paragraphs discuss types of contracts that present special problems for assignment.

Personal Service Contract

Contracts for the provision of personal services are generally not assignable.[1]

Example A famous actor signs a contract with a movie studio where she agrees to star in a romantic comedy. The movie studio cannot assign the actor's contract to another movie studio because it is a personal service contract.

The parties may agree that a **personal service contract** may be assigned.

Example Many professional sports players agree in their contracts with professional team owners that their contracts may be assigned. Therefore, the professional team that owns a player's contract can trade a player by assigning his or her contract to another team.

Assignment of a Future Right

Usually, a person cannot assign a currently nonexistent right that he or she expects to have in the future (i.e., a **future right**).

If a man will improvidently bind himself up by a voluntary deed, and not reserve a liberty to himself by a power of revocation, this court will not loose the fetters he hath put upon himself, but he must lie down under his own folly.

Lord Chancellor
Lord Nottingham
Villers v. Beaumont (1682)

Example Henrietta, an heiress worth millions of dollars, signs a will, leaving all her property to her granddaughter Brittany. Brittany has only an expected future right, not a current right, to the money. Brittany cannot lawfully assign her expected future right to receive her inheritance. The assignment would be invalid.

Contract Where an Assignment Would Materially Alter the Risk

A contract cannot be assigned if the assignment would materially alter the risk or duties of the obligor.

Example Laura, who has a safe driving record, purchases automobile insurance from an insurance company. Laura cannot assign her rights to be insured to another driver because the assignment would materially alter the risk and duties of the insurance company.

Assignment of a Legal Action

The right to sue another party for a violation of personal rights cannot usually be assigned.

Example Donald is severely injured by Alice in an automobile accident caused by Alice's negligence. Donald can sue Alice for the tort of negligence to recover monetary damages for his injuries. Donald's right to sue Alice is a personal right that cannot be assigned to another person.

A legal right that arises out of a breach of contract may be assigned.

Example Andrea borrows $10,000 from Country Bank with an 8 percent interest rate. The loan is to be repaid in equal monthly installments over a five-year period. If Andrea defaults on the loan, Country Bank may sue Andrea to collect the unpaid amount of the loan. Instead, Country Bank may sell (assign) its legal right to a collection agency to recover the money Andrea still owes on the loan. In this case, Country Bank is the assignor, and the collection agency is the assignee.

Effect of an Assignment of a Right

Where there has been a valid assignment of rights, the assignee "stands in the shoes of the assignor." That is, the assignor is entitled to performance from the obligor. The unconditional assignment of a contract right extinguishes all the assignor's rights, including the right to sue the obligor directly for nonperformance.[2] An assignee takes no better rights under the contract than the assignor had.

Example If the assignor has a right to receive $10,000 from a debtor, the right to receive this $10,000 is all that the assignor can assign to the assignee.

An obligor can assert any defense he or she had against the assignor or the assignee. An obligor can raise the defenses of fraud, duress, undue influence, minority, insanity, illegality of the contract, mutual mistake, or payment by worthless check of the assignor, against enforcement of the contract by the assignee. The obligor can also raise any personal defenses (e.g., participation in the assignor's fraudulent scheme) he or she may have directly against the assignee.

Notice of Assignment

When an assignor makes an assignment of a right under a contract, the assignee is under a duty to notify the obligor that (1) the assignment has been made and (2) performance must be rendered to the assignee. If the assignee fails to provide **notice of assignment** to the obligor, the obligor may continue to render performance to the assignor, who no longer has a right to it. The assignee cannot sue the obligor to recover payment because the obligor has performed according to the original contract. The assignee's only course of action is to sue the assignor for damages.

That what is agreed to be done, must be considered as done.

Lord Chancellor Lord Hardwicke
Guidot v. Guidot (1745)

Example Juan borrows $10,000 from Sam. Juan is to pay Sam the principal amount, with 10 percent interest, over three years in 36 equal monthly payments. After six months of receiving the proper payments from Juan, Sam assigns this right to receive future payments to Heather. Heather, as the assignee, owes a duty to notify Juan that he is to now make the payments to Heather. If Heather fails to give Juan this notice, Juan will continue to pay Sam. In this situation, Heather cannot recover from Juan the money that Juan continued to pay Sam; Heather's only recourse is to recover the money from Sam.

The result changes if the obligor is notified of the assignment but continues to render performance to the assignor. In such situations, the assignee can sue the obligor and recover payment. The obligor will then have to pay twice: once wrongfully to the assignor and then rightfully to the assignee. The obligor's only recourse is to sue the assignor for damages.

Anti-Assignment Clause

Some contracts contain an **anti-assignment clause** that prohibits the assignment of rights under the contract. Such clauses may be used if the obligor does not want to deal with or render performance to an unknown third party. Anti-assignment clauses are usually given effect.

anti-assignment clause
A clause that prohibits the assignment of rights under the contract.

Approval Clause

Some contracts contain an **approval clause**. Such clauses require that the obligor approve any assignment of a contract. Where there is an approval clause, many states prohibit the obligor from unreasonably withholding approval.

BASEBALL PARK
Professional baseball, football, basketball, and other athletes' contracts often provide that their contract can be assigned to a third party—that is, they can be traded to other teams.

Successive Assignments

An obligee (the party who is owed performance, money, a right, or another thing of value) has the right to assign a contract right or a benefit to another party. If the obligee fraudulently makes successive assignments of the same right to a number of assignees, which assignee has the legal right to the assigned right? To answer this question, the following rules apply:

- **American rule (New York Rule).** The **American rule** (or **New York Rule**) provides that the first assignment in time prevails, regardless of notice. Most states follow this rule.

  Example Whitehall (obligor) owes $10,000 to Vinnie. On April 1, Vinnie (assignor) sells (assigns) his right to collect this money to Jackson (first assignee) for the payment of $8,000. On April 15, Vinnie (assignor) sells (assigns) his right to collect this money to Maybell (second assignee) for the payment of $7,000. Maybell notifies Whitehall to make future payments to her. There has been a successive assignment of the same right. Under the American rule, Jackson, the assignee who was first in time, can recover the money from Whitehall. Maybell's only recourse is to sue Vinnie to recover her $7,000.

Critical Legal Thinking

What is a successive assignment of a right or benefit? What is the difference between the American rule and the English rule regarding successive assignments of a right?

- **English rule.** The **English rule** provides that the first assignee to *give notice* to the obligor (the person who owes the performance, money, duty, or other thing of value) prevails.

  Example Millicent (obligor) owes $20,000 to Tony. On August 1, Tony (assignor) sells (assigns) his right to collect this money to Justin (first assignee) for the payment of $15,000. Justin does not notify Millicent of this assignment. On August 20, Tony (assignor) sells (assigns) his right to collect the money from Millicent to Marcia (second assignee) for the payment of $14,000. Marcia notifies Millicent to make future payments to her. There has been a successive assignment of the same right. Under the English rule, Marcia, the second assignee, can recover the money from Millicent because Marcia was the first to give notice of the assignment to Millicent. Justin's only recourse is to sue Tony to recover her $15,000.

- **Possession of tangible token rule.** The **possession of tangible token rule** provides that under either the American or the English rule, if the assignor makes successive assignments of a contract right that is represented by a tangible token, such as a stock certificate or a savings account passbook, the first assignee who receives delivery of the tangible token prevails over subsequent assignees.

The same rules apply if the obligee has mistakenly made successive assignments of the same right to a number of assignees.

CONCEPT SUMMARY
SUCCESSIVE ASSIGNMENTS OF A RIGHT

The following rules apply if there has been a successive assignment of a contract right.

- **American rule (New York rule).** The *American rule* (or *New York rule*) provides that the first assignment in time prevails, regardless of notice. Most states follow this rule.
- **English rule.** The *English rule* provides that the first assignee to *give notice* to the obligor (the person who owes the performance, money, duty, or other thing of value) prevails.
- **Possession of tangible token rule.** The *possession of tangible token rule* provides that the first assignee who receives delivery of the tangible token prevails over subsequent assignees.

Delegation of a Duty

delegation of duties
A transfer of contractual duties by an obligor to another party for performance.

delegator
An obligor who has transferred his or her duty.

delegatee
A party to whom a duty has been transferred.

Unless otherwise agreed, the parties to a contract can generally transfer the performance of their duties under the contract to other parties. This transfer is called the **delegation of a duty**, or just **delegation**.

An obligor who transfers his or her duty is called a **delegator**. The party to whom the duty is transferred is the **delegatee**. The party to whom the duty is owed is the *obligee*. Generally, no special words or formalities are required to create a delegation of duties. **Exhibit 15.2** illustrates the parties to a delegation of a duty.

Exhibit 15.2 **DELEGATION OF A DUTY**

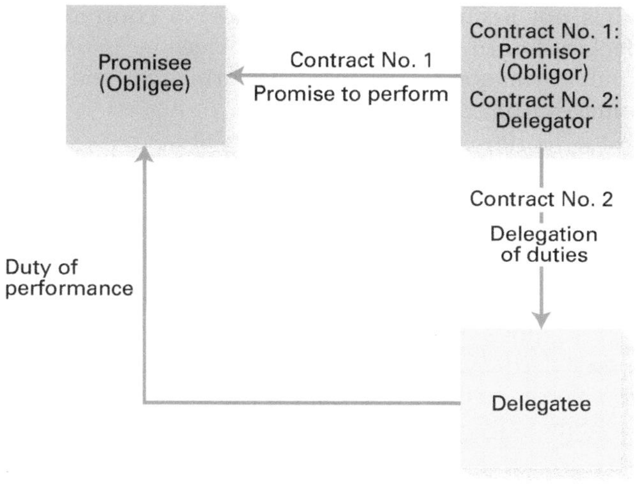

Example A city law imposes a legal duty on home owners to keep the sidewalk in front of their house repaired. The sidewalk in front of a home owner's house is damaged by tree roots. The home owner hires a contractor, who is an independent contractor, to repair the damage. Here, the home owner is the delegator, and the contractor is the delegatee.

Duties That Can and Cannot Be Delegated

If there's no meaning in it, said the King, that saves a world of trouble, you know, we needn't try to find any.

Lewis Carroll
Alice in Wonderland, Chapter 12

If an obligee has a substantial interest in having an obligor perform the acts required by a contract, these duties cannot be transferred.[3] This restriction includes obligations under the following types of contracts:

1. Personal service contracts calling for the exercise of personal skills, discretion, or expertise

   Example If Lady Gaga is hired to give a concert on a college campus, Miley Cyrus cannot appear in her place.

2. Contracts whose performance would materially vary if the obligor's duties were delegated

   Example If a person hires an experienced surgeon to perform a complex surgery, a recent medical school graduate cannot be substituted to perform the operation.

Often, contracts are entered into with companies or firms rather than with individuals. In such cases, a firm may designate any of its qualified employees to perform the contract.

Example If a client retains a firm of lawyers to represent him or her, the firm can **delegate** the duties under the contract to any qualified member of the firm.

Effect of Delegation of Duties

Where there has been a delegation of duties, the liability of the delegatee is determined by the following rules:

assumption of duties
A situation in which a delegation of duties contains the term *assumption, I assume the duties,* or other similar language. In such a case, the delegatee is legally liable to the obligee for nonperformance.

1. **Assumption of duties.** Where a valid delegation of duties contains the term *assumption* or other similar language, there is an **assumption of duties** by the delegatee. Here, the obligee can sue the delegatee and recover damages from the delegatee for nonperformance or negligent performance by the delegatee.
2. **Declaration of duties.** Where there is a valid delegation of duties but the delegatee has not assumed the duties under a contract, the delegation is called a **declaration of duties**. Here, the delegatee is not liable to the obligee for nonperformance or negligent performance, and the obligee cannot recover damages from the delegatee.

In either form of delegation, the delegator remains legally liable for the performance of the contract. If the delegatee does not perform properly, the obligee can sue the obligor-delegator for any resulting damages.

Anti-Delegation Clause

anti-delegation clause
A clause that prohibits the delegation of duties under the contract.

The parties to a contract can include an **anti-delegation clause** indicating that the duties cannot be delegated. Anti-delegation clauses are usually enforced. Some courts, however, have held that duties that are totally impersonal in nature—such as the payment of money—can be delegated despite such clauses.

Assignment and Delegation

An **assignment and delegation** occurs when there is a transfer of both rights and duties under a contract. If the transfer of a contract to a third party contains only language of assignment, the modern view holds that there is corresponding delegation of the duties of the contract.[4]

Third-Party Beneficiary

Third parties sometimes claim rights under others' contracts; these parties are called **third-party beneficiaries**. Such third parties are either *intended* or *incidental beneficiaries*. Each of these designations is discussed here.

Intended Beneficiary

When parties enter into a contract, they can agree that the performance of one of the parties should be rendered to or directly benefit a third party. Under such circumstances, the third party is called an **intended third-party beneficiary**. An intended third-party beneficiary can enforce the contract against the party who promised to render performance.[5]

intended third-party beneficiary
A third party who is not in privity of contract but who has rights under the contract and can enforce the contract against the promisor.

Examples The beneficiary may be expressly named in a contract from which he or she is to benefit ("I leave my property to my son Ben") or may be identified by another means ("I leave my property to all my children, equally").

Intended third-party beneficiaries may be classified as either *donee* or *creditor* beneficiaries. These terms are defined in the following paragraphs. The *Restatement (Second) of Contracts* and many state statutes have dropped this distinction, however, and now refer to both collectively as *intended beneficiaries*.[6]

Donee Beneficiary

The first type of intended beneficiary is the donee beneficiary. When a person enters into a contract with the intent to confer a benefit or gift on an intended third party, the contract is called a **donee beneficiary contract**. The three persons involved in such a contract are the following:

donee beneficiary contract
A contract entered into with the intent to confer a benefit or gift on an intended third party.

1. The **promisee** (the contracting party who directs that the benefit be conferred on another)
2. The **promisor** (the contracting party who agrees to confer performance for the benefit of the third person)
3. The **donee beneficiary** (the third person on whom the benefit is to be conferred)

donee beneficiary
A third party on whom a benefit is to be conferred.

If the promisor fails to perform the contract, the donee beneficiary can sue the promisor directly.

Example Nina goes to Life Insurance Company and purchases a $2 million life insurance policy on her life. Nina names her husband John as the beneficiary of the life insurance policy—that is, he is to be paid the $2 million if Nina dies. John is an intended beneficiary of the Nina–Life Insurance Company contract. Nina makes the necessary premium payments to Life Insurance Company. She dies in an automobile accident. Life Insurance Company does not pay the $2 million life insurance benefits to John. John, as an intended beneficiary, can sue Life Insurance Company to recover the life insurance benefits. Here, John has rights as an intended third-party beneficiary to enforce the Nina–Life Insurance Company contract (see **Exhibit 15.3**).

He who derives the advantage ought to sustain the burden.

Legal maxim

Exhibit 15.3 **DONEE BENEFICIARY CONTRACT**

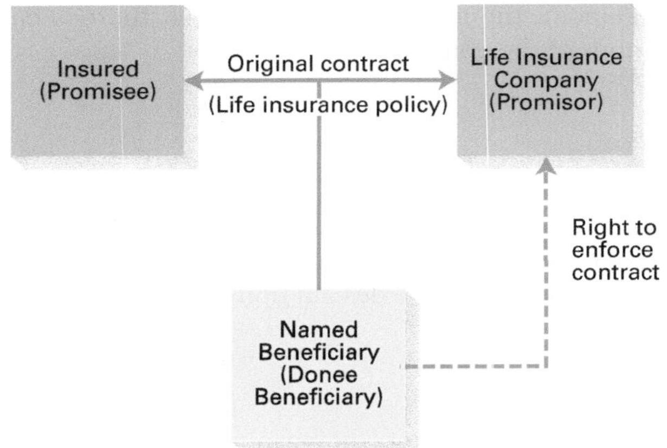

Creditor Beneficiary

creditor beneficiary contract
A contract that arises in the following situation: (1) a debtor borrows money, (2) the debtor signs an agreement to pay back the money plus interest, (3) the debtor sells the item to a third party before the loan is paid off, and (4) the third party promises the debtor that he or she will pay the remainder of the loan to the creditor.

creditor beneficiary
An original creditor who becomes a beneficiary under the debtor's new contract with another party.

The second type of intended beneficiary is the *creditor beneficiary*. A **creditor beneficiary contract** usually arises in the following situation:

1. A debtor (promisor) borrows money from a creditor (promisee) to purchase some item.
2. The debtor signs an agreement to pay the creditor the amount of the loan plus interest.
3. The debtor sells the item to another party before the loan is paid.
4. The new buyer (new promisor) promises the original debtor (new promisee) that he or she will pay the remainder of the loan amount to the original creditor.

The original creditor is now the **creditor beneficiary** of this second contract. The parties to the second contract are the original debtor (promisee of the second contract) and the new party (promisor of the second contract) (see **Exhibit 15.4**).

Exhibit 15.4 **CREDITOR BENEFICIARY CONTRACT**

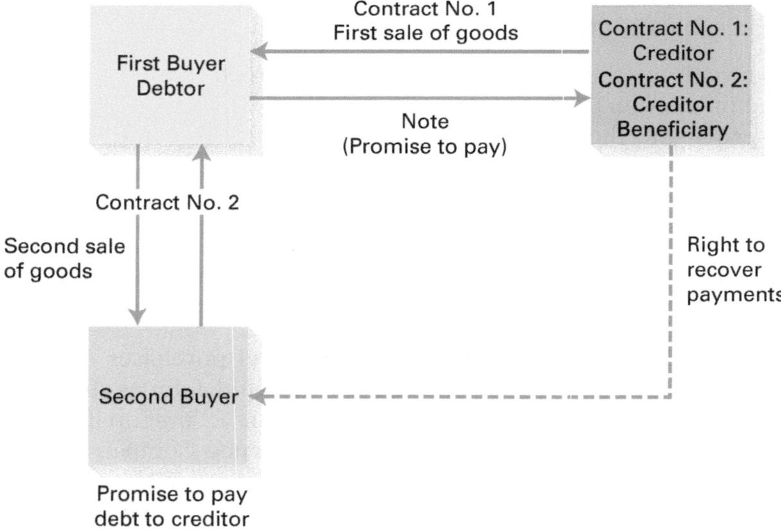

If the new debtor (promisor) fails to perform according to the second contract, the creditor beneficiary may either (1) enforce the original contract against the original debtor-promisor or (2) enforce the new contract against the new debtor-promisor. However, the creditor can collect only once.

Example Big Hotels obtains a loan from City Bank to build an addition to a hotel it owns in Atlanta, Georgia. The parties sign a promissory note requiring Big Hotels (promisor) to pay off the loan in equal monthly installments over a period of 10 years to City Bank (promisee). With six years left before the loan would be paid, Big Hotels sells the hotel to Palace Hotels, another chain of hotels. Palace Hotels (new promisor) agrees with Big Hotels (new promisee) to complete the payments due to City Bank on the loan. If Palace Hotels fails to pay the loan, City Bank has two options: It can sue Big Hotels on the original promissory note to recover the unpaid loan amount, or it can use its status as a creditor beneficiary to sue and recover the unpaid loan amount from Palace Hotels.

Incidental Beneficiary

In many instances, the parties to a contract unintentionally benefit a third party when a contract is performed. In such situations, the third party is referred to as an **incidental beneficiary**. An incidental beneficiary has no rights to enforce or sue under other people's contracts.

incidental beneficiary
A party who is unintentionally benefited by other people's contracts.

Example Heather owns a house on Residential Street. Her house, which is somewhat older, needs a new exterior coat of paint. Her neighbor John owns the house next door. If Heather has her house painted, John will benefit by having a nicer-looking house next door that may actually raise housing values on the street. Heather contracts with George, a painting contractor, to paint her house. George breaches the contract and does not paint Heather's house. Although John may have benefited if Heather's house had been painted, he is merely an incidental beneficiary to the Heather–George contract and has no cause of action to sue George for not painting Heather's house. Heather, of course, can sue George for breach of contract.

Generally, the public and taxpayers are only incidental beneficiaries to contracts entered into by the government on their behalf. As such, they acquire no right to enforce government contracts or to sue parties who breach these contracts.

Often, the courts are asked to decide whether a third party is an intended or an incidental beneficiary, as in the following case.

CASE 15.1 *FEDERAL COURT CASE Third-Party Beneficiary*

Does I-XI, Workers in China, Bangladesh, Indonesia, Swaziland, and Nicaragua v. Wal-Mart Stores, Inc.

572 F.3d. 677, 2009 U.S. App. Lexis 15279 (2009)
United States Court of Appeals for the Ninth Circuit

"We agree with the district court that the language of the Standards does not create a duty on the part of Walmart to monitor the suppliers, and does not provide plaintiffs a right of action against Walmart as third-party beneficiaries."

—Gould, Circuit Judge

Facts

Wal-Mart Stores, Inc. (Walmart) owns and operates a chain of large big-box discount department and warehouse stores and is the largest company in the United States. Walmart is the largest importer in the United States of foreign-produced goods. Walmart developed a code of conduct for its foreign suppliers entitled "Standards for Suppliers" (Standards). These Standards require foreign suppliers to adhere to local law and local industry working conditions, such as pay, hiring forced labor, child labor, and discrimination. These Standards are incorporated into Walmart's supply contracts with foreign suppliers.

(case continues)

The Standards provide that Walmart may make on-site inspections of production facilities and permit Walmart to cancel orders with, or terminate, any foreign supplier that fails to comply with the Standards.

Workers at foreign suppliers in China, Bangladesh, Indonesia, Swaziland, and Nicaragua who produce and sell goods to Walmart sued Walmart in U.S. district court. The foreign workers alleged that they were third-party beneficiaries to Walmart's contract with its foreign suppliers and that they were due damages from Walmart for Walmart's breach of the Standards. They alleged that their employers regularly violated the Standards and that Walmart failed to investigate working conditions at foreign suppliers, knew that the Standards were being violated, and failed to enforce the standards contained in these contracts. The U.S. district court held that the plaintiffs were not intended third-party beneficiaries to Walmart's contracts with its foreign suppliers and dismissed their lawsuit. The plaintiffs appealed.

Issue

Are the foreign workers intended third-party beneficiaries under Walmart's contracts with its foreign suppliers?

Language of the Court

We agree with the district court that the language of the Standards does not create a duty on the part of Walmart to monitor the suppliers, and does not provide plaintiffs a right of action against Walmart as third-party beneficiaries. Plaintiffs' allegations are insufficient to support the conclusion that Walmart and the suppliers intended for plaintiffs to have a right of performance against Walmart under the supply contracts.

Decision

The U.S. court of appeals held that the plaintiff foreign workers were not intended third-party beneficiaries to Walmart's contracts with its foreign suppliers. The U.S. court of appeals affirmed the dismissal of the plaintiff's case.

Ethics Questions

Are Walmart's Standards illusory if it does not consistently enforce them against foreign suppliers? Does Walmart owe a duty to require that its foreign suppliers provide the same protections to their workers as is provided to workers in the United States?

Covenants

covenant
An unconditional promise to perform.

In contracts, parties make certain promises to each other. A **covenant** is an *unconditional* promise to perform. Nonperformance of a covenant is a breach of contract that gives the other party the right to sue. The majority of provisions in contracts are covenants.

Example Seed Company borrows $400,000 from Rural Bank and signs a promissory note to repay the $400,000 plus 10 percent interest in one year. This promise is a covenant. That is, it is an unconditional promise to perform.

Example Michael enters into a written contract with Vivian to sell Vivian his house for $1 million. Closing is to be June 1. These are covenants: Michael owes a duty to deliver the deed to his house to Vivian, and Vivian owes a duty to pay $1 million to Michael. If either of the parties fails to perform, the other party can sue the breaching party for nonperformance of his or her covenant.

Conditions

condition
A qualification of a promise that becomes a covenant if it is met. There are three types of conditions: conditions precedent, conditions subsequent, and concurrent conditions.

Some contract provisions are conditions rather than covenants. A **conditional promise** (or qualified promise) is not as definite as a covenant. The promisor's duty to perform or not perform arises only if the **condition** does or does not occur.[7] A condition becomes a covenant if the condition is met, however.

Generally, contract language such as *if*, *on condition that*, *provided that*, *when*, *after*, and *as soon as* indicates a condition. A single contract may contain numerous conditions that trigger or excuse performance.

There are three primary types of conditions: *conditions precedent*, *conditions subsequent*, and *concurrent conditions*. Each of these is discussed in the following paragraphs.

Condition Precedent

If a contract requires the occurrence (or nonoccurrence) of an event *before* a party is obligated to perform a contractual duty, this is a **condition precedent**. The happening (or nonhappening) of the event triggers the contract or duty of performance. If the event does not occur, no duty to perform the contract arises because there is a failure of condition.

condition precedent
A condition that requires the occurrence or nonoccurrence of an event before a party is obligated to perform a duty under a contract.

Example SoftWare Company offers Joan, a senior who is a computer science major in college, a job. SoftWare and Joan sign a three-year employment contract, but the contract contains a provision that SoftWare Company has to hire Joan only if she graduates from college. This is a condition precedent. If Joan graduates, the condition precedent has been met and a contract is created. If SoftWare Company refuses to hire Joan at that time, she can sue SoftWare Company for breach of contract. If Joan does not graduate from college, however, SoftWare Company is not obligated to hire her because there has been a failure of the condition precedent.

Condition Precedent Based on Satisfaction

Some contracts reserve the right to a party to pay for services provided by the other only if the services meet the first party's "satisfaction." The courts have developed two tests—the *personal satisfaction test* and the *reasonable person test*—to determine whether this special form of condition precedent has been met:

1. **Personal satisfaction test.** The **personal satisfaction test** is a *subjective* test that applies if the performance involves personal taste and comfort (e.g., contracts for interior decorating, contracts for tailoring clothes). The only requirement is that the person given the right to reject the contract acts in good faith.

   personal satisfaction test
   A subjective test that applies to contracts involving personal taste and comfort.

   Example Gretchen employs an artist to paint her daughter's portrait. The contract provides that Gretchen does not have to accept and pay for the portrait unless she is personally satisfied with it. This is a condition precedent based on the personal satisfaction test. Gretchen rejects the painting because she personally dislikes it. This rejection is lawful because it is based on the personal satisfaction test.

2. **Reasonable person test.** The **reasonable person test** is an *objective* test that is used to judge contracts involving mechanical fitness and most commercial contracts. Most contracts that require the work to meet the satisfaction of a third person (e.g., engineer, architect) are judged by this standard.

   reasonable person test
   An objective test that applies to commercial contracts and contracts involving mechanical fitness.

   Example E-Commerce Company hires Einstein to install a state-of-the-art Internet Web page ordering system that will handle its order-entry and record-keeping functions. Einstein installs a state-of-the-art Internet Web page ordering system that meets current industry standards. E-Commerce Company rejects the contract as not meeting its personal satisfaction. This is a breach of contract because the personal satisfaction test does not apply to this contract. Instead, the objective reasonable person test applies, and a reasonable e-commerce company in the same situation would have accepted the system.

The following feature discusses a special type of condition—a "time is of the essence" condition in a contract.

Business Environment

"Time Is of the Essence" Contract

Generally, there is a breach of contract if a contract is not performed when due. Nevertheless, if the other party is not jeopardized by the delay, most courts treat the delay as a minor breach and give the nonperforming party additional time to perform.

Conversely, if a contract expressly provides **"time is of the essence"** or similar language, performance by the stated time is an express condition. There is a breach of contract if the contracting party does not perform by the stated date.

Example Kosko Store, a large discount retail store, contracts to purchase 1,000 bottles of New Spice cologne for men from Old Spice Company. The contract provides for delivery on October 1. If, on October 1, Old Spice Company fails to deliver the cologne but can do so on October 4, which would not cause a significant loss to Kosko Stores, delivery can be made on October 4 without there being a breach of contract.

Example McDonald's Corporation contracts to purchase 100,000 Ronald McDonald dolls to be manufactured by NYManufacturing Company that will be used in a McDonald's promotion to begin October 1. The contract provides that the dolls are to be delivered to McDonald's on September 1 and that "time is of the essence." NYManufacturing does not deliver the dolls to McDonald's on September 1 but can complete and deliver the dolls by October 1. Here, NYManufacturing Company gets no more time. The contract was a "time is of the essence" contract that called for a delivery date of September 1, and since the dolls were not delivered by September 1, NYManufacturing Company is in breach of the contract.

Condition Subsequent

condition subsequent
A condition whose occurrence or nonoccurrence of a specific event automatically excuses the performance of an existing contractual duty to perform.

A **condition subsequent** exists when there is a condition in a contract that provides that the occurrence or nonoccurrence of a specific event automatically excuses the performance of an existing duty to perform. That is, failure to meet the condition subsequent relieves the other party from obligation under the contract.

Example Bill is hired as an employee by Google.com as a Web troubleshooter. The three-year employment contract provides that Google.com can terminate Bill's employment anytime during the three-year employment period if he fails a random drug test. This is a condition subsequent. If Bill fails a random drug test, Google.com can terminate Bill immediately. Bill cannot sue Google.com for breach of contract.

Note that the *Restatement (Second) of Contracts* eliminates the distinction between conditions precedent and conditions subsequent. Both are referred to as "conditions."[8]

Concurrent Conditions

concurrent condition
A condition that exists when the parties to a contract must render performance simultaneously; each party's absolute duty to perform is conditioned on the other party's absolute duty to perform.

Concurrent conditions arise when the parties to a contract agree to render performance simultaneously—that is, when each party's absolute duty to perform is conditioned on the other party's absolute duty to perform.

Example A contract by Samantha's Club to purchase goods from Kid's Toys Inc. provides that payment is due on delivery of the goods. In other words, Samantha's Club's duty to pay and Kid's Toys Inc.'s duty to deliver the goods are concurrent conditions. Recovery of damages is available if one party fails to respond to the other party's performance.

Implied Condition

Any of the previous types of conditions may be further classified as either express or implied conditions. An **express condition** exists if the parties expressly agree on it. An **implied-in-fact condition** is one that can be implied from the circumstances surrounding a contract and the parties' conduct.

implied-in-fact condition
A condition that can be implied from the circumstances surrounding a contract and the parties' conduct.

Example A contract in which a buyer agrees to purchase grain from a farmer implies that there are proper street access to the delivery site, proper unloading facilities, and the like.

CONCEPT SUMMARY

TYPES OF CONDITIONS

Type of Condition	Description
Condition precedent	A specified event must occur or not occur before a party is obligated to perform contractual duties.
Condition subsequent	The occurrence or nonoccurrence of a specified event excuses the performance of an existing contractual duty to perform.
Concurrent condition	The parties to a contract are obligated to render performance simultaneously. Each party's duty to perform is conditioned on the other party's duty to perform.
Implied-in-fact condition	A condition implied from the circumstances surrounding a contract and the parties' conduct.

Discharge of Performance

A party's duty to perform under a contract may be discharged by *mutual agreement* of the parties, by *impossibility of performance*, by *commercial impracticability*, or by *operation of law*. These methods of discharge are discussed in the paragraphs that follow.

Discharge by Agreement

The parties to a contract may mutually agree to discharge their contractual duties under a contract. This is called **discharge by agreement**. The different methods for discharging a contract by mutual agreement are the following:

- **Mutual rescission.** If a contract is wholly or partially executory on both sides, the parties can agree to rescind (i.e., cancel) the contract. **Mutual rescission** requires parties to enter into a second agreement that expressly terminates the first one. **Unilateral rescission** of a contract by one of the parties without the other party's consent is not effective. Unilateral rescission of a contract constitutes a breach of that contract.
- **Substituted contract.** The parties to a contract may enter into a new contract that revokes and discharges an existing contract. The new contract is called a **substituted contract**. If one of the parties fails to perform his or her duties under a substituted contract, the nonbreaching party can sue to enforce its terms against the breaching party. The prior contract cannot be enforced against the breaching party because it has been discharged.
- **Novation.** A **novation agreement** (commonly called **novation**) substitutes a third party for one of the original contracting parties. The new substituted party is obligated to perform a contract. All three parties must agree to the substitution. In a novation, the exiting party is relieved of liability on the contract.
- **Accord and satisfaction.** The parties to a contract may agree to settle a contract dispute by an **accord and satisfaction**. The agreement whereby the parties agree to accept something different in satisfaction of the original contract is called an *accord*.[9] The performance of an accord is called a *satisfaction*. An

novation agreement (novation)
An agreement that substitutes a new party for one of the original contracting parties and relieves the exiting party of liability on the contract.

accord and satisfaction
The settlement of a contract dispute.

accord does not discharge the original contract. It only suspends it until the accord is performed. Satisfaction of the accord discharges both the original contract and the accord. If an accord is not satisfied when it is due, the aggrieved party may enforce either the accord or the original contract.

Discharge by Impossibility

impossibility of performance (objective impossibility)
Nonperformance that is excused if a contract becomes impossible to perform. It must be objective, not subjective, impossibility.

Under certain circumstances, the nonperformance of contractual duties is excused—that is, discharged—because of *impossibility of performance*. **Impossibility of performance** (or **objective impossibility**) occurs if a contract becomes impossible to perform.[10] The impossibility must be objective impossibility ("it cannot be done") rather than subjective impossibility ("I cannot do it"). The following types of objective impossibility excuse nonperformance:

- The death or incapacity of the promisor prior to the performance of a personal service contract[11]

  Example If a professional athlete dies prior to or during a contract period, his or her contract with the team is discharged.

- The destruction of the subject matter of a contract prior to performance[12]

  Example If a building is destroyed by fire, the lessees are discharged from further performance unless otherwise provided in the lease.

- A supervening illegality that makes performance of the contract illegal[13]

  Example An art dealer contracts to purchase native art found in a foreign country. The contract is discharged if the foreign country enacts a law forbidding native art from being exported from the country before the contract is performed.

Force Majeure Clause

***force majeure* clause**
A clause in a contract in which the parties specify certain events that will excuse nonperformance.

The parties may agree in a contract that certain events will excuse nonperformance of the contract. These clauses are called ***force majeure* clauses**.

Example A *force majeure* clause usually excuses nonperformance caused by natural disasters such as floods, tornadoes, and earthquakes. Modern clauses also often excuse performance due to labor strikes, shortages of raw materials, and the like.

Statute of Limitations

statute of limitations
A statute that establishes the time period during which a lawsuit must be brought; if the lawsuit is not brought within this period, the injured party loses the right to sue.

Every state has a **statute of limitations** that applies to contract actions. Under these statutes, if an aggrieved party does not bring suit for breach of contract during a designated period after a breach of contract has occurred, he loses the right to sue. Time periods vary from state to state. The usual period for bringing a lawsuit for breach of contract is one to five years.

Example Assume that a state has a statute of limitations that requires that a lawsuit alleging a breach of a written contract be brought within two years of the breach. If a contract is breached on May 1, 2016, the nonbreaching party has until May 1, 2018, to bring a lawsuit against the breaching party. If a nonbreaching party waits until May 2, 2018, or thereafter to bring the lawsuit, the court will dismiss the lawsuit because it was not brought within the statute of limitations.

Key Terms and Concepts

Accord and satisfaction (325)
American rule (New York Rule) (316)
Anti-assignment clause (315)
Anti-delegation clause (318)
Approval clause (315)
Assignee (313)
Assignment and delegation (318)
Assignment of rights (assignment) (313)
Assignor (313)
Assumption of duties (318)
Concurrent conditions (324)
Condition (322)
Condition precedent (323)
Condition subsequent (324)
Conditional promise (322)
Covenant (322)
Creditor beneficiary (320)
Creditor beneficiary contract (320)
Declaration of duties (318)
Delegate (318)
Delegatee (317)
Delegation of a duty (delegation) (317)
Delegator (317)
Discharge by agreement (325)
Donee beneficiary (319)
Donee beneficiary contract (319)
English rule (316)
Express condition (324)
Force majeure clause (326)
Future right (314)
Implied-in-fact condition (325)
Impossibility of performance (objective impossibility) (326)
Incidental beneficiary (321)
Intended third-party beneficiary (319)
Mutual rescission (325)
Notice of assignment (315)
Novation agreement (novation) (325)
Obligee (313)
Obligor (313)
Personal satisfaction test (323)
Personal service contract (314)
Possession of tangible token rule (317)
Privity of contract (313)
Promisee (319)
Promisor (319)
Reasonable person test (323)
Statute of limitations (326)
Subsequent assignee (subassignee) (313)
Substituted contract (325)
Third-party beneficiary (319)
"Time is of the essence" (324)
Unilateral rescission (325)

Critical Legal Thinking Cases

15.1 Intended or Incidental Beneficiary The Phillies, L.P., the owner of the Philadelphia Phillies professional baseball team (Phillies), decided to build a new baseball stadium called Citizens Bank Park (the Project). The Phillies entered into a contract (Agreement) with Driscoll/Hunt Joint Venture (DH) whereby DH would act as the Construction Manager of the Project. In that capacity, DH entered into multiple contracts with subcontractors to provide material and services in constructing the Project. One such subcontractor was Ramos/Carson/DePaul, Joint Venture (RCD), which was hired to install concrete foundations for the Project. The Project was beset with numerous delays and disruptions, for which RCD claimed it was owed additional compensation from DH and the Phillies. Subcontractor RCD sued the Phillies to recover the alleged compensation, alleging it was an intended beneficiary to the Phillies–DH Agreement, thus giving it rights to recover compensation from the Phillies. The Phillies argued that RCD was merely an incidental beneficiary to the Phillies–DH Agreement and could not recover compensation from the Phillies. Was RCD an intended or an incidental beneficiary of the Phillies–DH Agreement? *Ramos/Carson/DePaul, a Joint Venture v. The Phillies, L.P.*, 2008 Phila. Ct. Com. Pl. Lexis 282 (Common Pleas Court of Philadelphia County, Pennsylvania, 2008)

15.2 Third-Party Beneficiary Eugene H. Emmick hired L. S. Hamm, an attorney, to draft his will. The will named Robert Lucas and others (Lucas) as beneficiaries. When Emmick died, it was discovered that the will was improperly drafted, violated state law, and was therefore ineffective. Emmick's estate was transferred pursuant to the state's intestate laws. Lucas did not receive the $75,000 he would have otherwise received had the will been valid. Lucas sued Hamm for breach of the Emmick–Hamm contract to recover what he would have received under the will. Who wins? *Lucas v. Hamm*, 56 Cal.2d 583, 364 P.2d 685, 15 Cal. Rptr. 821, 1961 Cal. Lexis 321 (Supreme Court of California)

15.3 Assignment William John Cunningham, a professional basketball player, entered into a contract with Southern Sports Corporation, which owned the Carolina Cougars, a professional basketball team. The contract provided that Cunningham was to play basketball for the Cougars for a three-year period. The contract contained a provision that it could not be assigned to any other professional basketball franchise without Cunningham's approval. Subsequently, Southern Sports Corporation sold its assets, including its franchise and Cunningham's contract, to the Munchak Corporation (Munchak). There was no change in the location of the Cougars after the purchase. When Cunningham refused to play for the new owners, Munchak sued to enforce Cunningham's contract. Is Cunningham's contract assignable to the new owner? *Munchak Corporation v. Cunningham*, 457 F.2d 721, 1972 U.S. App. Lexis 10272 (United States Court of Appeals for the Fourth Circuit)

15.4 Delegation of Duties C.W. Milford owned a registered quarter horse named Hired Chico. Milford sold the horse to Norman Stewart. Recognizing that Hired Chico was a good stud, Milford included the following provision in the written contract that was signed by both parties: "I, C.W. Milford, reserve 2 breedings each year on Hired Chico registration #403692 for the life of this stud horse regardless of whom the horse may be sold to." The agreement was filed with the County Court Clerk of Shelby County, Texas. Stewart later sold Hired Chico to Sam McKinnie. Prior to purchasing the horse, McKinnie read the Milford–Stewart contract and testified that he understood the terms of the contract. When McKinnie refused to grant Milford the stud services of Hired Chico, Milford sued McKinnie for breach of contract. Who wins? *McKinnie v. Milford*, 597 S.W.2d 953, 1980 Tex. App. Lexis 3345 (Court of Appeals of Texas)

15.5 Condition Shumann Investments, Inc. (Shumann), hired Pace Construction Corporation (Pace), a general contractor, to build Outlet World of Pasco Country. In turn, Pace hired OBS Company, Inc. (OBS), a subcontractor, to perform the framing, drywall, insulation, and stucco work on the project. The contract between Pace and OBS stipulated, "Final payment shall not become due unless and until the following conditions precedent to final payment have been satisfied . . . (c) receipt of final payment for subcontractor's work by contractor from owner." When Shumann refused to pay Pace, Pace refused to pay OBS. OBS sued Pace to recover payment. Who wins? *Pace Construction Corporation v. OBS Company, Inc.*, 531 So.2d 737, 1988 Fla. App. Lexis 4020 (Court of Appeal of Florida)

Ethical

Ethics Case

15.6 Ethics Case Indiana Tri-City Plaza Bowl (Tri-City) leased a building from Charles H. Glueck for use as a bowling alley. The lease provided that Glueck was to provide adequate paved parking for the building. The lease gave Tri-City the right to approve the plans for the construction and paving of the parking lot. When Glueck submitted paving plans to Tri-City, it rejected the plans and withheld its approval. Tri-City argued that the plans were required to meet its personal satisfaction before it had to approve them. Evidence showed that the plans were commercially reasonable in the circumstances. A lawsuit was filed between Tri-City and Glueck. Who wins? Was it ethical for Tri-City to reject the plans? *Indiana Tri-City Plaza Bowl, Inc. v. Estate of Glueck*, 422 N.E.2d 670, 1981 Ind. App. Lexis 1506 (Court of Appeals of Indiana)

Notes

1. *Restatement (Second) of Contracts*, Sections 311 and 318.
2. *Restatement (Second) of Contracts*, Section 317.
3. *Restatement (Second) of Contracts*, Section 318(2).
4. *Restatement (Second) of Contracts*, Section 328.
5. *Restatement (Second) of Contracts*, Section 302.
6. *Restatement (Second) of Contracts*, Section 302(1)(b).
7. *The Restatement (Second) of Contracts*, Section 224, defines *condition* as "an event, not certain to occur, which must occur, unless its nonperformance is excused, before performance under a contract is due."
8. *Restatement (Second) of Contracts*, Section 224.
9. *Restatement (Second) of Contracts*, Section 281.
10. *Restatement (Second) of Contracts*, Section 261.
11. *Restatement (Second) of Contracts*, Section 262.
12. *Restatement (Second) of Contracts*, Section 263.
13. *Restatement (Second) of Contracts*, Section 264.

CHAPTER

16

Breach of Contract and Remedies

LONDON, ENGLAND

The United Kingdom is a member of the European Union (EU), a regional organization of countries of Western and Eastern Europe. The EU has adopted measures to provide uniform contract law in specific economic sectors. The EU is working on developing a general uniform contract law for member countries.

Learning Objectives

After studying this chapter, you should be able to:

1. Describe complete, substantial, and inferior performance of contractual duties.
2. Describe compensatory, consequential, and nominal damages awarded for the breach of traditional and e-contracts.
3. Explain rescission and restitution.
4. Define the equitable remedies of specific performance, reformation, and injunction.
5. Describe torts associated with contracts.

Chapter Outline

> *"Contracts must not be sports of an idle hour, mere matters of pleasantry and badinage, never intended by the parties to have any serious effect whatsoever."*
>
> —*Lord Stowell*
> *Dalrymple v. Dalrymple* 2 Hag. Con. 54, at 105 (1811)

Introduction to Breach of Contract and Remedies

Men keep their agreements when it is an advantage to both parties not to break them.
Solon
(ca. 600 BCE)

breach of contract
A situation that occurs if one or both of the parties do not perform their duties as specified in the contract.

There are three levels of performance of a contract: *complete, substantial*, and *inferior*. Complete (or strict) performance by a party discharges that party's duties under the contract. Substantial performance constitutes a minor breach of the contract. Inferior performance constitutes a material breach that impairs or destroys the essence of the contract. Various remedies may be obtained by a nonbreaching party if a **breach of contract** occurs—that is, if a contracting party fails to perform an absolute duty owed under a contract.[1]

The most common remedy for a breach of contract is an award of *monetary damages*, often called the "law remedy." Monetary damages include *compensatory, consequential, liquidated*, and *nominal* damages. If a monetary award does not provide adequate relief, however, the court may order any one of several *equitable remedies*, including *specific performance, reformation*, and *injunction*. Equitable remedies are based on the concept of fairness.

This chapter discusses breach of contract and the remedies available to the nonbreaching party.

Performance and Breach

If a contractual duty has not been discharged (i.e., terminated) or excused (i.e., relieved of legal liability), the contracting party owes an absolute duty (i.e., covenant) to perform the duty. As mentioned in the chapter introduction, there are three types of performance of a contract: (1) *complete performance*, (2) *substantial performance* (or minor breach), and (3) *inferior performance* (or material breach). A breach of contract occurs if one or the parties do not perform their duties as specified in the contract. These concepts are discussed in the following paragraphs.

complete performance (strict performance)
A situation in which a party to a contract renders performance exactly as required by the contract. Complete performance discharges that party's obligations under the contract.

tender of performance (tender)
An unconditional and absolute offer by a contracting party to perform his or her obligations under a contract.

substantial performance
Performance by a contracting party that deviates only slightly from complete performance.

minor breach
A breach that occurs when a party renders substantial performance of his or her contractual duties.

Complete Performance

Most contracts are discharged by the **complete performance**, or **strict performance**, of the contracting parties. Complete performance occurs when a party to a contract renders performance exactly as required by the contract. A fully performed contract is called an **executed contract**.

Tender of performance, or **tender**, also discharges a party's contractual obligations. Tender is an unconditional and absolute offer by a contracting party to perform his or her obligations under the contract.

Example Ashley, who owns a women's retail store, contracts to purchase a lot of high-fashion blue jeans from a manufacturer for $75,000. At the time of performance, Ashley tenders the $75,000. Ashley has performed her obligation under the contract once she tenders the $75,000 to the manufacturer. The manufacturer tenders the jeans to Ashley when required to do so and Ashley accepts the jeans. There is a complete performance of the contract.

Substantial Performance: Minor Breach

Substantial performance occurs when there has been a **minor breach** of contract. In other words, it occurs when a party to a contract renders performance that deviates slightly from complete performance. The nonbreaching party may try to convince the breaching party to elevate his or her performance to complete performance. If the breaching party does not correct the breach, the nonbreaching party can sue to recover *damages* by (1) deducting the cost to repair the defect from the contract price and remitting the balance to the breaching party or (2) suing the breaching party to recover the cost to repair the defect if the breaching party has already been paid (see **Exhibit 16.1**).

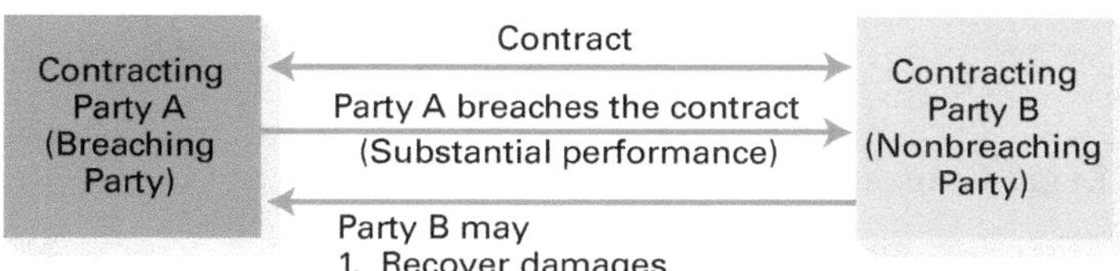

Exhibit 16.1 SUBSTANTIAL PERFORMANCE: MINOR BREACH

Examples Donald Trump contracts with Big Apple Construction Co. to have Big Apple construct an office building for $100 million. The architectural plans call for installation of three-ply windows in the building. Big Apple constructs the building exactly to plan except that it installs two-ply windows. There has been substantial performance. It would cost $5 million to install the correct windows. If Big Apple agrees to replace the windows and does so, its performance is elevated to complete performance, and Trump must pay the entire contract price. However, if Trump has to hire someone else to replace the windows, he may deduct this cost of repair of $5 million from the contract price of $100 million and remit the difference of $95 million to Big Apple. If Trump had already paid the $100 million and Big Apple refuses to install the proper windows, Trump can sue and recover the $5 million.

No cause of action arises from a bare promise.

Legal maxim

Inferior Performance: Material Breach

A **material breach** of a contract occurs when a party renders **inferior performance** of his or her contractual obligations that impairs or destroys the essence of the contract. There is no clear line between a minor breach and a material breach. A determination is made on a case-by-case basis.

Where there has been a material breach of contract, the nonbreaching party may *rescind* the contract and seek restitution of any compensation paid under the contract to the breaching party. The nonbreaching party is discharged from any further performance under the contract.[2] Alternatively, the nonbreaching party may treat the contract as being in effect and sue the breaching party to recover *damages* (see **Exhibit 16.2**).

material breach
A breach that occurs when a party renders inferior performance of his or her contractual duties.

inferior performance
A situation in which a party fails to perform express or implied contractual obligations and impairs or destroys the essence of a contract.

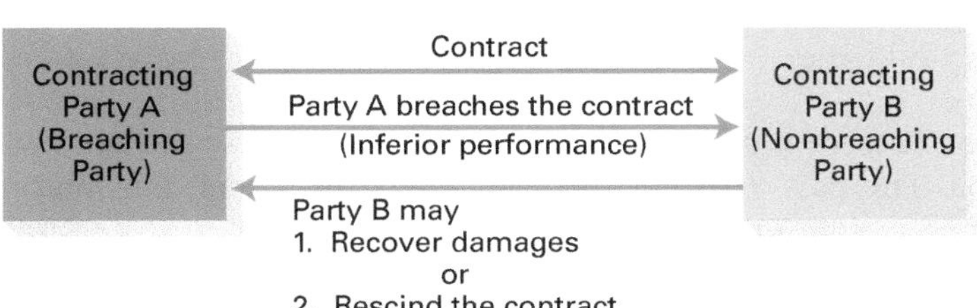

Exhibit 16.2 INFERIOR PERFORMANCE: MATERIAL BREACH

Example A university contracts with a general contractor to build a new three-story classroom building with classroom space for 1,000 students. The contract price is $100 million. However, the completed building cannot support more than 500 students because the contractor used inferior materials. The defect cannot be repaired without rebuilding the entire structure. Because this is a material breach, the university may rescind the contract, recover any money that it has paid to the contractor, and require the contractor to remove the building.

The university is discharged of any obligations under the contract and is free to employ another contractor to rebuild the building. However, the building does meet building codes so that it can be used as an administration building of the university. Thus, as an alternative remedy, the university could accept the building as an administration building, which has a value of $20 million. The university would owe this amount—$20 million—to the contractor.

CONCEPT SUMMARY
TYPES OF PERFORMANCE

Type of Performance	Legal Consequence
Complete performance	The contract is discharged.
Substantial performance (minor breach)	The nonbreaching party may recover damages caused by the breach.
Inferior performance (material breach)	The nonbreaching party may either (1) rescind the contract and recover restitution or (2) affirm the contract and recover damages.

In the following case, the court found a breach of contract.

CASE 16.1 *STATE COURT CASE Breach of Contract*

Turner Broadcasting System, Inc. v. McDavid

693 S.E.2d 873, 2010 Ga. App. Lexis 317 (2010)
Court of Appeals of Georgia

"It is undisputed that the parties intended to sign written documents that memorialized the terms of their oral agreement."

—Bernes, Judge

Facts

Among other assets, Turner Broadcasting System, Inc., owned the Atlanta Hawks professional basketball team, the Atlanta Thrashers professional hockey team, and the Philips Arena located in Atlanta, Georgia (collectively "assets"). Turner Broadcasting publicly announced its intent to sell the assets. David McDavid expressed an interest in purchasing the assets and entered into negotiations with Turner Broadcasting.

On April 30, the parties entered into a "Letter of Intent" outlining the proposed sale terms. The parties held meetings and engaged in telephone conference calls to resolve any outstanding issues. During a conference call on July 30 with McDavid, Turner Broadcasting's chief executive officer (CEO) Phil Kent announced, "We have a deal." On or about August 16, as the drafting process of a final written agreement continued, Turner Broadcasting's executive and principal negotiator, James McCaffrey, told McDavid that the "deal was done" and that "they were ready to close the deal." On August 19, the directors of Time Warner, Inc., Turner Broadcasting's parent company, approved the sale of the assets to McDavid based on the agreed-on terms.

On or about September 12, during a conference call, Turner Broadcasting and McDavid verbally reached a final agreement for the written agreement, and Turner Broadcasting's principal negotiator announced, "The deal is done. Let's get documents we can sign, and we'll meet in Atlanta for a press conference and a closing early next week."

However, Ted Turner, a member of Time Warner's board of directors, opposed the deal. Ted Turner's son-in-law, Rutherford Seydel, approached Turner Broadcasting about purchasing the assets on behalf his company, Atlanta Spirit, LLC. Turner Broadcasting began negotiations with Atlanta Spirit. Turner Broadcasting's principal negotiator signed an agreement to sell the assets to Atlanta Spirit on substantially the same terms agreed on by Turner Broadcasting and McDavid.

McDavid sued Turner Broadcasting for breach of contract. Turner Broadcasting denied the existence of any binding contract with McDavid, arguing that the parties had not executed a final written agreement. Following an eight-week trial, the jury returned a verdict in favor of McDavid, finding that Turner Broadcasting had breached its contract with

(case continues)

McDavid, and awarded $281 million in damages to McDavid. Turner Broadcasting appealed.

Issue

Is there an enforceable contract between McDavid and Turner Broadcasting?

Language of the Court

It is undisputed that the parties intended to sign written documents that memorialized the terms of their oral agreement. McDavid and his advisors testified that in accordance with the customary deal-making process, the parties first had to reach an oral agreement upon the material terms, and then the lawyers were expected to prepare the written documents that memorialized the parties' agreed upon terms. There was evidence from which the jury could conclude that the parties entered into a binding oral agreement with the intent to sign written documents that memorialized the terms, but failed to do so as a result of Turner Broadcasting's breach.

Decision

The court of appeals affirmed the trial court's judgment that found that Turner Broadcasting had breached an oral agreement with McDavid and that awarded $281 million in damages against Turner Broadcasting.

Ethics Questions

Should businesspeople be bound to their oral word? Did Turner Broadcasting act unethically in this case?

Anticipatory Breach

Anticipatory breach (or **anticipatory repudiation**) of a contract occurs when a contracting party informs the other party in advance that he or she will not perform his or her contractual duties when due. This type of material breach can be expressly stated or implied from the conduct of the repudiator. Where there is an anticipatory repudiation, the nonbreaching party's obligations under the contract are discharged immediately. The nonbreaching party also has the right to sue the repudiating party when the anticipatory breach occurs; there is no need to wait until performance is due.[3]

anticipatory breach (anticipatory repudiation)
A breach that occurs when one contracting party informs the other that he or she will not perform his or her contractual duties when due.

Monetary Damages

Where there has been a breach of a contract, the nonbreaching party may recover **monetary damages** from a breaching party. Monetary damages are available whether the breach was minor or material. Monetary damages are sometimes referred to as **dollar damages**. Several types of monetary damages may be awarded. These include *compensatory, consequential, liquidated*, and *nominal damages*. Each is discussed in the following paragraphs.

monetary damages
An award of money.

Compensatory Damages

Compensatory damages are intended to compensate a nonbreaching party for the loss of the bargain. In other words, they place the nonbreaching party in the same position as if the contract had been fully performed by restoring the "benefit of the bargain."

compensatory damages
An award of money intended to compensate a nonbreaching party for the loss of the bargain. Compensatory damages place the nonbreaching party in the same position as if the contract had been fully performed by restoring the "benefit of the bargain."

Examples Lederle Laboratories enters into a written contract to employ Wei as a chief operations officer of the company for three years, at a salary of $20,000 per month. After one year at work, Lederle informs Wei that her employment is terminated. This is a material breach of the contract. If Wei is unable to find a comparable job, Wei can sue Lederle Laboratories and recover $480,000 (24 months × $20,000) as compensatory damages. However, if after six months of being unemployed Wei finds a comparable job that pays $20,000 per month,

Wei can recover $120,000 from Lederle (6 months × $20,000) as compensatory damages. In these examples, the damages awarded to Wei place her in the same situation as if her contract with Lederle had been performed.

It is a vain thing to imagine a right without a remedy: for want of right and want of remedy are reciprocal.

Lord Chief Justice Holt
Ashby v. White (1703)

The amount of compensatory damages that will be awarded for breach of contract depends on the type of contract involved and which party breached the contract. The award of compensatory damages in some special types of contracts is discussed in the following paragraphs.

Sale of a Good

Compensatory damages for a breach of a sales contract involving goods are governed by the Uniform Commercial Code (UCC). The usual measure of damages for a breach of a sales contract is the difference between the contract price and the market price of the goods at the time and place the goods were to be delivered.[4]

Example Revlon, Inc., contracts to buy a piece of equipment from Greenway Supply Co. for $80,000. Greenway does not deliver the equipment to Revlon when it is required to do so. Revlon purchases the equipment from another vendor but has to pay $100,000 because the current market price for the equipment has risen. Revlon can recover $20,000 from Greenway—the difference between the market price paid ($100,000) and the contract price ($80,000)—in compensatory damages.

Construction Contract

Every unjust decision is a reproach to the law or the judge who administers it. If the law should be in danger of doing injustice, then equity should be called in to remedy it. Equity was introduced to mitigate the rigor of the law.

Lord Denning,
Master of the Rolls
Re: Vandervell's Trusts (1974)

A construction contract arises when the owner of real property contracts to have a contractor build a structure or do other construction work. The compensatory damages recoverable for a breach of a construction contract vary with the stage of completion of the project when the breach occurs.

A contractor may recover the profits he or she would have made on the contract if the owner breaches the construction contract before construction begins.

Example RXZ Corporation contracts to have Ace Construction Company build a factory building for $1,200,000. It will cost Ace $800,000 in materials and labor to build the factory for RXZ. If RXZ Corporation breaches the contract before construction begins, Ace can recover $400,000 in "lost profits" from RXZ as compensatory damages.

Example Entel Corporation contracts to have the Beta Construction Company build a factory building for Entel for $1,200,000. It will cost Beta Construction Company $800,000 to construct the building. Thus, Beta Corporation will make $400,000 profit on the contract. Beta begins construction and has spent $300,000 on materials and labor before Entel breaches the contract by terminating Beta. Here, Beta can recover $700,000, which is comprised of $400,000 lost profits ($1,200,000 − $800,000) plus $300,000 expended on materials and labor. The $700,000 of compensatory damages will make Beta Construction Company "whole."

If the builder breaches a construction contract either before or during construction, the owner can recover the increased cost above the contract price that he or she has to pay to have the work completed by another contractor.

Example Ethenol Corporation contracts to have the Sherry Construction Company build a factory building for Ethenol for $1,200,000. Just before Sherry Construction Company is to begin work, it breaches the contract by withdrawing from the project. Ethenol seeks new bids, and the lowest bid to construct the building is $1,700,000. Here, Ethenol can recover $500,000 in compensatory damages from Sherry Construction Company ($1,700,000 [new contract price] − $1,200,000 [Sherry Construction's original price]).

Employment Contract

An employee whose employer breaches an employment contract can recover lost wages or salary as compensatory damages. If the employee breaches the contract, the employer can recover the costs to hire a new employee plus any increase in salary paid to the replacement.

Example EBM Corporation enters into a written contract to employ Mohammad as a chief financial officer of the company for three years at a salary of $30,000 per month. Before Mohammad starts work, EBM informs Mohammad that his employment is terminated. This is a material breach of the contract. If Mohammad is unable to find a comparable job, Mohammad can recover $1,080,000 (36 months × $30,000) as compensatory damages.

Consequential Damages

A nonbreaching party can sometimes recover **consequential damages**, or **special damages**, from the breaching party. Consequential damages are *foreseeable damages* that arise from circumstances outside a contract. To be liable for consequential damages, the breaching party must know or have reason to know that the breach will cause special damages to the other party.

consequential damages (special damages)
Foreseeable damages that arise from circumstances outside a contract. To be liable for these damages, the breaching party must know or have reason to know that the breach will cause special damages to the other party.

Example W-Mart, a major retailer, contracts with Maytell, a major manufacturer of toys, to purchase one million of the new "G.I. Barby Dolls" produced by Maytell at $20 per doll. W-Mart plans to sell these dolls in its stores nationwide at $50 per doll, and Maytell is aware that W-Mart intends to resell the dolls. The popularity of Barby Dolls guarantees that all the dolls purchased by W-Mart will be sold. If Maytell breaches this contract and fails to deliver the dolls to W-Mart, W-Mart cannot purchase the dolls elsewhere because Maytell holds the copyright and trademark on the doll. Therefore, W-Mart can recover the lost profits on each lost sale as consequential damages from Maytell—that is, the difference between the would-be sales price of the dolls ($50) and the purchase price of each doll ($20), or $30 lost profit per doll. In total, W-Mart can recover $30 million in consequential damages from Maytell ($50 − $20 = $30 × 1,000,000).

Disclaimer of Consequential Damages

Consequential damages are often disclaimed in a sales or license agreement. This means that the breaching party is not responsible to pay consequential damages. **Disclaimer of consequential damages** is lawful in most instances.

Example A student installs a new software program on his computer that is licensed from a software company. The license price was $100. The software was installed, but it was defective. The software causes files in the computer, including the student's class notes, PhD dissertation, and other valuable information, to be deleted. These were the only copies of the files. The student suffers a loss by having his only copies of these important materials to be deleted because of the newly installed software. These losses are consequential damages. However, the software license contains a disclaimer stating that the licensor is not liable for consequential damages. Therefore, the student cannot recover monetary damages for his consequential damages. The student can recover $100 in compensatory damages, however, for the license price he paid for the defective software.

Nominal Damages

nominal damages
Damages awarded when the nonbreaching party sues the breaching party even though no financial loss has resulted from the breach. Nominal damages are usually $1 or some other small amount.

A nonbreaching party can sue a breaching party to a contract for nominal damages even if no financial loss resulted from the breach. **Nominal damages** are usually awarded in a small amount, such as $1. Cases involving nominal damages are usually brought on principle. Most courts disfavor nominal damages lawsuits because they use valuable court time and resources.

Example Mary enters into an employment contract with Microhard Corporation. It is a three-year contract, and Mary is to be paid $100,000 per year. After Mary works for one year, Microhard Corporation fires Mary. The next day, Mary finds a better position at Microsoft Corporation, in the same city, paying $125,000 per year on a two-year contract. Mary has suffered no monetary damages but could bring a civil lawsuit against Microhard Corporation because of its breach and recover nominal damages ($1).

Mitigation of Damages

mitigation of damages
A nonbreaching party's legal duty to avoid or reduce damages caused by a breach of contract.

If a contract has been breached, the law places a duty on the innocent nonbreaching party to make reasonable efforts to *mitigate* (i.e., avoid or reduce) the resulting damages. The extent of **mitigation of damages** required depends on the type of contract involved.

If an employer breaches an employment contract, the employee owes a duty to mitigate damages by trying to find substitute employment. The employee is only required to accept *comparable employment*. The courts consider factors such as compensation, rank, status, job description, and geographical location in determining the comparability of jobs.

Example Edith is employed by Software Inc., a software company located in the Silicon Valley of California, as a software manager. Her contract is for three years at $200,000 per year. If Software Inc. terminates Edith after one year, she is under a duty to mitigate the damages that would be owed to her by Software Inc. If Edith finds a job as a software manager at another software company located in the Silicon Valley for the same salary, she is required to take the job. However, if Edith finds a job at a similar salary as a sales manager in the Silicon Valley; or if she is offered a job as a software manager at the same salary at a software company in Los Angeles, California; or if she is offered a job as a software manager at a company in the Silicon Valley but at a salary of $120,000 per year, she is not required to accept any of these job offers because they are not comparable jobs.

Critical Legal Thinking
What is mitigation of damages? Why does the law impose a duty on the nonbreaching party to mitigate damages?

If an employee who has been dismissed improperly accepts a job that is not comparable, the employee can sue the prior employer for damages.

Examples Andrew is employed as a chief financial officer of Financial Company in New York City for a salary of $200,000 per year on a three-year contract. His employer terminates Andrew with two years left on the contract. Andrew accepts employment as a financial analyst at a new employer that pays $150,000 per year. Andrew can sue his prior employer Financial Company and recover $100,000 ($50,000 difference in salary per year for two years).

Liquidated Damages

liquidated damages
Damages that parties to a contract agree in advance should be paid if the contract is breached.

Under certain circumstances, the parties to a contract may agree in advance to the amount of damages payable on a breach of contract. These damages are called **liquidated damages**. To be lawful, the actual damages must be difficult or impracticable to determine, and the liquidated amount must be reasonable in the circumstances.[5] An enforceable **liquidated damages clause** is an exclusive remedy even if actual damages are later determined to be different.

Example Alaska Oil Company discovers a new rich oil field in the northern-most part of Alaska. Alaska Oil contracts to purchase special oil-drilling equipment that is necessary to drill holes in the hard ground in the Alaska tundra from Tundra

Equipment Corporation. The contract states that the equipment is to be delivered by July 1, 2018. The parties know that Alaska Oil cannot start digging the oil holes until it receives this equipment. It is uncertain how great the oil flow will be from the drilled oil holes. The parties place a liquidated damage clause in their contract that states that Tundra Equipment will pay $20,000 per day in liquidated damages for each day after July 1, 2018, that the equipment is not delivered. This is an enforceable liquidated damages clause because actual damages are difficult to determine and the liquidated amount is reasonable in the circumstances. Thus, if Tundra Equipment does not deliver the equipment until July 1, 2019, it owes Alaska Oil $7,300,000 (365 days × $20,000 per day).

Penalty

A liquidated damages clause is considered a **penalty** if actual damages are clearly determinable in advance or if the liquidated damages are excessive or unconscionable. If a liquidated damages clause is found to be a penalty, it is unenforceable. The nonbreaching party may then recover actual damages.

Example Rent-to-Own Store is a store that rents furniture to individuals who are usually poorer, and these individuals take title to the furniture after having paid the cost of the furniture (which is often overpriced with high interest rates). Mable, an elderly person who is poor, has rented and purchased a living room set, a dining room set, and a bedroom set from Rent-to-Own Store. Mable rents a big-screen HD television from Rent-to-Own Store and signs a contract that states that if Mable falls more than three months behind in her television payments, Rent-to-Own Store can recover all of the furniture she had previously purchased from the store as liquidated damages. This is an example of a liquidated damages clause that is a penalty and that would not be enforced.

The following case demonstrates the enforcement of a liquidated damages clause.

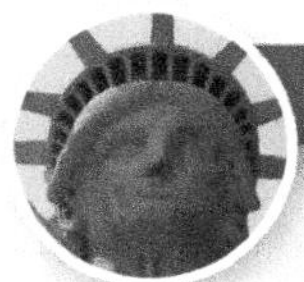

CASE 16.2 *FEDERAL COURT CASE Liquidated Damages*

SAMS Hotel Group, LLC v. Environs, Inc.

716 F.3d 432, 2013 U.S. App. Lexis 11047 (2013)
United States Court of Appeals for the Seventh Circuit

"The general rule of freedom of contract includes the freedom to make a bad bargain."
—Hamilton, Circuit Judge

Facts

Environs, Inc. is an architectural firm that designs commercial and business buildings. SAMS Hotel Group, LLC signed a contract with Environs whereby Environs would provide architectural services for the design of a six-story hotel in Fort Wayne, Indiana, to be built by SAMS. Environs was paid a fee of $70,000 for its work. The contract between the parties limited Environs's liability for breach of contract to $70,000. The hotel structure was nearly complete when serious structural defects were discovered. The county building department condemned the building and the hotel was demolished. SAMS sued Environs, alleging that the defendant had breached its contract by providing negligent architectural services, and sought to recover its loss of more than $4.2 million. The U.S. district court found that Environs had been negligent and breached the contract, but the court enforced the liquidated damages clause and awarded SAMS $70,000. SAMS appealed.

Issue

Is the liquidated damages clause enforceable?

Language of the Court

The undisputed facts show that the negotiating parties were two sophisticated business

(case continues)

entities of equal bargaining power who were aware of the risks involved in designing and building a hotel. They were in the best position to allocate the relevant risks between them, and it is undisputed that they signed the contract with knowledge and understanding of each of its terms. The general rule of freedom of contract includes the freedom to make a bad bargain.

Decision

The U.S. court of appeals affirmed the U.S. district court's enforcement of the liquidated damages clause.

Ethics Questions

Was it ethical for Environs to avoid paying the full claim? How could SAMS have protected itself from the outcome of this case?

CONCEPT SUMMARY

TYPES OF MONETARY DAMAGES

Type of Damage	Description
Compensatory	Damages that compensate a nonbreaching party for the loss of a bargain. It places the nonbreaching party in the same position as if the contract had been fully performed.
Consequential	Damages that compensate a nonbreaching party for foreseeable special damages that arise from circumstances outside a contract. The breaching party must or should have known that these damages would result from the breach.
Nominal	Damages awarded against the breaching party even though the nonbreaching party has suffered no financial loss because of the breach. A small amount (e.g., $1) is usually awarded.
Liquidated	An agreement by the parties in advance that sets the amount of damages recoverable in case of breach. These damages are lawful if they do not cause a penalty.

Rescission and Restitution

rescission
An action to rescind (undo) a contract. Rescission is available if there has been a material breach of contract, fraud, duress, undue influence, or mistake.

restitution
The return of goods or property received from the other party to rescind a contract. If the actual goods or property are not available, a cash equivalent must be made.

Rescission is an action to undo a contract. It is available where there has been a material breach of contract, fraud, duress, undue influence, or mistake. Generally, to rescind a contract, the parties must make **restitution** of the consideration they received under the contract.[6] Restitution consists of returning the goods, property, money, or other consideration received from the other party. If possible, the actual goods or property must be returned. If the goods or property have been consumed or are otherwise unavailable, restitution must be made by conveying a cash equivalent. The rescinding party must give adequate notice of the rescission to the breaching party. Rescission and restitution restore the parties to the positions they occupied prior to the contract.

Example Pralene's Store contracts to purchase $1,000,000 of goods from a clothing manufacturer. Pralene's pays $100,000 as a down payment, and the first $200,000 worth of goods are delivered. The goods are materially defective, and the defect cannot be cured. This breach is a material breach. Pralene's can rescind the contract. Pralene's is entitled to receive its $100,000 down payment back from the manufacturer, and the manufacturer is entitled to receive the goods back from Pralene's.

Enforcement of Remedies

If a nonbreaching party brings a successful lawsuit against a breaching party to a contract, the court will enter a **judgment** in his or her favor. This judgment must then be collected. If the breaching party refuses to pay the judgment, the court may do the following:

- **Issue a writ of attachment.** A **writ of attachment** orders the sheriff or other government officer to seize property in the possession of the breaching party that he or she owns and to sell the property at auction to satisfy the judgment.
- **Issue a writ of garnishment.** A **writ of garnishment** orders that wages, bank accounts, or other property of the breaching party that are in the hands of third parties be paid over to the nonbreaching party to satisfy the judgment. Federal and state laws limit the amount of the breaching party's wages or salary that can be garnished.

writ of attachment
An order of the court that enables a government officer to seize property of the breaching party and sell it at auction to satisfy a judgment.

writ of garnishment
An order of the court that orders that wages, bank accounts, or other property of the breaching party held by third persons be paid to the nonbreaching party to satisfy a judgment.

Equitable Remedies

Equitable remedies are available if there has been a breach of contract that cannot be adequately compensated through a legal remedy. They are also available to prevent unjust enrichment. The most common equitable remedies are *specific performance, reformation*, and *injunction*, which are discussed in the following paragraphs.

equitable remedy
A remedy that is available if there has been a breach of contract that cannot be adequately compensated through a legal remedy or to prevent unjust enrichment.

Specific Performance

An award of **specific performance** orders the breaching party to perform the acts promised in a contract. The courts have the discretion to award this remedy if the subject matter of the contract is *unique*.[7] Specific performance is available to enforce land contracts because every piece of real property is considered to be unique. Works of art, antiques, items of sentimental value, rare coins, stamps, heirlooms, and the like, also fit the requirement for uniqueness. Most other personal property does not.

specific performance
A remedy that orders the breaching party to perform the acts promised in the contract. Specific performance is usually awarded in cases in which the subject matter is unique, such as in contracts involving land, heirlooms, and paintings.

Example On September 1, Won-Suk enters into a contract to purchase a house from Geraldine for $1 million. The closing date is set for November 1. On November 1, Won-Suk brings the money to the closing, but Geraldine does not appear at the closing and thereafter refuses to sell the house to Won-Suk. In this case, because each piece of real estate is considered unique, Won-Suk can bring an action of specific performance against Geraldine and obtain a court judgment ordering Geraldine to sell the house to Won-Suk.

Specific performance of personal service contracts is not granted because the courts would find it difficult or impracticable to supervise or monitor performance of such a contract.

Example A concert hall contracts with a famous rap artist to hold a series of concerts. Later, the rap artist refuses to perform. Here, the concert hall cannot require the rap artist to perform because it is a personal service contract. The concert hall could, however, sue to recover any payments it has made to the rap artist and recover any damages that it may have suffered because of the breach.

Critical Legal Thinking
What is the purpose of the equitable remedy of specific performance? To what types of contracts does this equitable doctrine apply? Why would a buyer seek specific performance of a contract rather than damages?

The court had to decide whether to issue an order of specific performance in the following case.

CASE 16.3 *STATE COURT CASE Specific Performance*

Alba v. Kaufmann

27 A.D.3d 816, 810 N.Y.S.2d 539, 2006 N.Y. App. Div. Lexis 2321 (2006)
Supreme Court of New York, Appellate Division

"The case law reveals that the equitable remedy of specific performance is routinely awarded in contract actions involving real property, on the premise that each parcel of real property is unique."

—Crew, Judge

Facts

Jean-Claude Kaufmann owned approximately 37 acres of real property located in the town of Stephentown, Rensselaer County, New York. The property is located in a wooded area and is improved with a 19th-century farmhouse. Kaufmann and his spouse, Christine Cacace, reside in New York City and use the property as a weekend or vacation home. Kaufmann listed the property for sale for $350,000.

Richard Alba and his spouse (Albas) looked at the property and offered Kaufmann the asking price. The parties executed a contract for sale, and the Albas paid a deposit, obtained a mortgage commitment, and procured a satisfactory home inspection and title insurance. A date for closing the transaction was set. Prior to closing, Cacace sent the Albas an e-mail, indicating that she and Kaufmann had "a change of heart" and no longer wished to go forward with the sale. Albas sent a reply e-mail, stating their intent to go forward with the scheduled closing. When Kaufmann refused to close, the Albas sued, seeking specific performance, and moved for summary judgment. The supreme court of New York denied the motion. The Albas appealed.

Issue

Is an order of specific performance of the real estate contract warranted in this case?

Language of the Court

The Albas plainly discharged that burden here. In short, the record demonstrates that the Albas were ready, willing and able to close and, but for Kaufmann's admitted refusal to do so, would have consummated the transaction. As to the remedy the Albas seek, the case law reveals that the equitable remedy of specific performance is routinely awarded in contract actions involving real property, on the premise that each parcel of real property is unique. Moreover, volitional unwillingness, as distinguished from good faith inability, to meet contractual obligations furnishes neither a ground for cancellation of the contract nor a defense against its specific performance.

Decision

The appellate court, as a matter of law, granted the Albas' motion for summary judgment and ordered Kaufmann specifically to perform the real estate contract.

Ethics Questions

Was it ethical for Kaufman to try to back out of the contract? Was it ethical for the buyer to sue for specific performance when the seller had a "change of heart" and no longer wanted to sell?

Reformation

reformation
An equitable doctrine that permits the court to rewrite a contract to express the parties' true intentions.

Reformation is an equitable doctrine that permits the court to rewrite a contract to express the parties' true intentions. Reformation is usually available to correct clerical errors in contracts.

Example A clerical error is made during the typing of a contract, and both parties sign the contract without discovering the error. If a dispute later arises, the court can reform the contract to correct the clerical error to read as the parties originally intended.

Injunction

An **injunction** is a court order that prohibits a person from doing a certain act. To obtain an injunction, the requesting party must show that he or she will suffer irreparable injury if the injunction is not issued.

injunction
A court order that prohibits a person from doing a certain act.

Example A professional basketball team enters into a five-year employment contract with a basketball player. The basketball player breaches the contract and enters into a contract to play for a competing professional basketball team. Here, the first team can obtain an injunction to prevent the basketball player from playing for the other team during the remaining term of the original contract.

CONCEPT SUMMARY
TYPES OF EQUITABLE REMEDIES

Type of Equitable Remedy	Description
Specific performance	A court orders the breaching party to perform the acts promised in the contract. The subject matter of the contract must be unique.
Reformation	A court rewrites a contract to express the parties' true intentions. This remedy is usually used to correct clerical errors.
Injunction	A court prohibits a party from doing a certain act. Injunctions are available in contract actions only in limited circumstances.

Arbitration of Contract Disputes

Many contract disputes are heard and decided by the court system. In the contract area, however, other contract disputes are heard and decided through **arbitration**. Arbitration is a nonjudicial, private resolution of a contract dispute. An arbitrator, not a judge or jury, renders a decision in the case. Most arbitration agreements stipulate **binding arbitration**; that is, the arbitrator's decision cannot be appealed to the courts. Arbitration occurs if the parties have entered into an **arbitration agreement**, either as part of their contract or as a separate agreement. Many consumer and business contracts contain arbitration clauses.

arbitration
A nonjudicial, private resolution of a contract dispute.

Examples Credit-card agreements, mortgages, sales contracts, automobile leases, employment contracts, electronics contracts, and software licenses (e.g., Facebook, Microsoft).

Critical Legal Thinking
Why do so many form contracts contain arbitration clauses? What percentage of the contracts that you enter into contain arbitration agreements?

The U.S. Congress has enacted the **Federal Arbitration Act**,[8] which promotes the arbitration of contract disputes, whether the dispute involves federal or state law. The U.S. Supreme Court has upheld the act's national policy favoring arbitration and the enforcement of arbitration agreements.[9]

The enforcement of an arbitration agreement is at issue in the following case.

CASE 16.4 *FEDERAL COURT CASE Arbitration of a Contract Dispute*

Mance v. Mercedes-Benz USA

901 F.Supp.2d 1147, 2012 U.S. Dist. Lexis 140778 (2012)
United States District Court for the Northern District of California

"The arbitration provision was highlighted, apparent, and not oppressive, and it should not have taken Mr. Mance by surprise."
—Beeler, Judge

Facts

Demetrius Mance purchased a new Mercedes-Benz E350 automobile from a Mercedes-Benz dealer in Sacramento, California. The automobile was distributed

(case continues)

by Mercedes-Benz USA. To purchase the car, Mance signed a retail installment contract. In the contract, Mercedes-Benz warranted to preserve and maintain the utility and performance of the vehicle. The contract contained an arbitration clause that states that any claim or dispute between the parties will be decided by arbitration and not by a court proceeding. The arbitration clause was highlighted by bold, capitalized text. The arbitration clause provided for binding, nonappealable arbitration.

Mance experienced numerous problems with the automobile, but Mercedes-Benz has not repaired the car satisfactorily according to Mance. Mance filed this lawsuit in U.S. district court against Mercedes-Benz for breach of express and implied warranties, alleging that the arbitration clause was unconscionable. Mercedes-Benz made a motion for an order compelling Mance to arbitrate his claims.

Issue

Is the arbitration clause enforceable?

Language of the Court

The arbitration provision was highlighted, apparent, and not oppressive, and it should not have taken Mr. Mance by surprise. He argues that the binding arbitration would leave him with limited appeal rights, but conclusiveness is one of the primary purposes of arbitration. The arbitration clause provides Mr. Mance with a choice of two common arbitration associations and allows him to suggest an alternative. Mr. Mance's unconscionability argument fails.

Decision

The U.S. district court held that the arbitration clause was enforceable and granted Mercedes-Benz's motion to compel arbitration.

Ethics Questions

Is it ethical for sellers to make consumers go to arbitration rather than to court? Did Mance know that he was subject to the arbitration agreement?

Torts Associated with Contracts

The recovery for breach of contract is usually limited to contract damages. A party who can prove a contract-related **tort**, however, may also recover tort damages. Tort damages include compensation for personal injury, pain and suffering, emotional distress, and possibly punitive damages. Generally, punitive damages are not recoverable for breach of contract. They are recoverable, however, for certain tortious conduct that may be associated with the nonperformance of a contract.

The very definition of a good award is that it gives dissatisfaction to both parties.

Sir Thomas Plumer,
Master of the Rolls
Goodman v. Sayers (1820)

The major torts associated with contracts are *intentional interference with contractual relations* and *breach of the implied covenant of good faith and fair dealing*. These torts are discussed in the following paragraphs.

Intentional Interference with Contractual Relations

intentional interference with contractual relations
A tort that arises when a third party induces a contracting party to breach the contract with another party.

A party to a contract may sue any third person who intentionally interferes with the contract and causes that party injury. The third party does not have to have acted with malice or bad faith. This tort, which is known as the tort of **intentional interference with contractual relations**, usually arises when a third party induces a contracting party to breach a contract with another party. The following elements must be shown:

1. A valid, enforceable contract between the contracting parties
2. Third-party knowledge of this contract
3. Third-party inducement to breach the contract

A third party can contract with the breaching party without becoming liable for this tort if a contracting party has already breached the contract, and thus the third party cannot be held to have induced a breach of the other parties' contract.

Example A professional football player signs a five-year contract to play football for a certain professional football team. Two years into the contract, another professional football team, with full knowledge of the player's contract with the other team, offers the player twice the amount of money that he is currently making to breach his contract and sign and play with the second football team. The player breaches his contract and signs to play for the second team. Here, the second team intentionally interfered with the player's contract with the first team. The first team can recover tort damages—including punitive damages—from the second team for the tort of intentional interference with a contract.

Breach of the Implied Covenant of Good Faith and Fair Dealing

Several states have held that a **covenant of good faith and fair dealing** is implied in certain types of contracts. Under this covenant, the parties to a contract are not only held to the express terms of the contract but also required to act in "good faith" and deal fairly in all respects in obtaining the objective of the contract. A breach of this implied covenant is a tort for which tort damages are recoverable. This covenant is usually implied in contracts where the parties have a special relationship that involves a fiduciary duty.

Examples Contracts between insurance companies and insureds, publishing agreements between publishers and authors, and employment contracts.

This tort, which is sometimes referred to as the **tort of bad faith**, is an evolving area of the law. In the following case, the court had to decide whether a bad faith tort had occurred.

Critical Legal Thinking

Why is the covenant of good faith and fair dealing implied in some contracts? Is it difficult to define *bad faith*?

covenant of good faith and fair dealing
An implied covenant under which the parties to a contract not only are held to the express terms of the contract but also required to act in "good faith" and deal fairly in all respects in obtaining the objective of the contract.

CASE 16.5 *STATE COURT CASE Bad Faith Tort*

Mitchell v. Fortis Insurance Company

686 S.E.2d 176, 2009 S.C. Lexis 451 (2009)
Supreme Court of South Carolina

"First, any court reviewing a punitive damages award should consider the degree of reprehensibility of the defendant's conduct."

—Toal, Chief Justice

Facts

On May 15, 2001, Jerome Mitchell Jr., who was 17 years old, submitted an application for health insurance to Fortis Insurance Company. The application required Mitchell to complete a medical questionnaire, which included the question "Been diagnosed as having or been treated for any immune deficiency disorder by a member of the medical profession?" Mitchell answered "no" to this question. Fortis issued Mitchell a health insurance policy.

In April 2002, Mitchell attempted to donate blood to the Red Cross. On May 13, 2002, the Red Cross notified Mitchell that his blood had screened positive for HIV. On the next day, Mitchell contacted Dr. Michael Chandler, whose tests confirmed that Mitchell was HIV positive. On that day, one of Dr. Chandler's assistants noted on Mitchell's chart "Gave blood in March—got letter yesterday stating blood tested for HIV." The handwritten note was erroneously dated May 14, 2001, rather than May 14, 2002. Dr. Chandler referred Mitchell to Dr. Kevin Shea, an infectious disease specialist, for treatment.

Fortis soon received claims for Mitchell's treatment. Fortis launched an investigation to determine whether Mitchell had failed to disclose a preexisting condition on his insurance policy application. With Mitchell's permission, Fortis obtained Mitchell's medical and billing files from Dr. Chandler and Dr. Shea and Mitchell's blood test results. A Fortis investigator reviewed the files and discovered the erroneously dated note in Dr. Chandler's files. Based on this note, Fortis's rescission committee voted to rescind Mitchell's health insurance policy. Fortis

(*case continues*)

sent Mitchell a letter informing him that his health insurance policy was rescinded due to material misrepresentation.

Mitchell tried to contact the recission committee at Fortis but was told by a representative there was nothing the representative could do about the rescission. Mitchell, who by then was obtaining medical help from the Hope Health free medical clinic, had Hope's health care manager contact Fortis to explain that Mitchell had not tested positive for HIV until after he purchased the Fortis health insurance policy. A Fortis representative told Hope's manager "that there was nothing she could do at this time."

Mitchell hired an attorney, and the attorney filed an appeal with Fortis and sent Fortis all of the medical records that proved that Mitchell was first diagnosed with HIV after he had obtained health insurance from Fortis. Fortis upheld there rescission denying coverage. Mitchell sued Fortis for the bad faith rescission of his health insurance. The jury held in favor of Mitchell and awarded him compensatory damages and $15 million in punitive damages. The court of appeals affirmed this decision. Fortis appealed, challenging the finding of a bad faith tort, and alternatively challenging the award of punitive damages.

Issue

Is Fortis liable for committing a bad faith tort? If so, was the award of punitive damages warranted?

Language of the Court

First, any court reviewing a punitive damages award should consider the degree of reprehensibility of the defendant's conduct.

Turning to the facts of the instant case, we find ample support in the record to establish that Fortis's conduct was reprehensible. This case is unique in that Mitchell's harm—the termination of his health insurance policy—exposed him to great risk of physical danger. It was reasonable to conclude, from the evidence presented, that Fortis was motivated to avoid the losses it would undoubtedly incur in supporting Mitchell's costly medical condition. Based upon this evidence, we find that Fortis was deliberately indifferent to its contractual obligations and to Mitchell's health and wellbeing. We remit the punitive damages award to $10 million, resulting in a ratio of 9.2 to 1. We are also certain that a $10 million award will adequately vindicate the twin purposes of punishment and deterrence that support the imposition of punitive damages.

Decision

The supreme court of South Carolina held that Fortis had committed bad faith rescission of Mitchell's health insurance policy. The court held that the imposition of punitive damages was warranted but reduced the award of punitive damages from $15 million to $10 million.

Ethics Questions

What is a bad faith tort? Does the fear of a finding bad faith and being assessed punitive damages make insurance companies act more ethically?

Key Terms and Concepts

Anticipatory breach (anticipatory repudiation) (333)
Arbitration (341)
Arbitration agreement (341)
Binding arbitration (341)
Breach of contract (330)
Compensatory damages (333)
Complete performance (strict performance) (330)
Consequential damages (special damages) (335)
Covenant of good faith and fair dealing (343)
Disclaimer of consequential damages (335)
Dollar damages (333)
Equitable remedies (339)
Executed contract (330)
Federal Arbitration Act (FAA) (341)
Inferior performance (331)
Injunction (341)
Intentional interference with contractual relations (342)
Judgment (339)
Liquidated damage clause (336)
Liquidated damages (336)
Material breach (331)
Minor breach (330)
Mitigation of damages (336)
Monetary damages (333)
Nominal damages (335)
Penalty (337)
Reformation (340)
Rescission (338)
Restitution (338)
Specific performance (339)
Substantial performance (330)
Tender of performance (tender) (330)
Tort (342)
Tort of bad faith (343)
Writ of attachment (339)
Writ of garnishment (339)

Critical Legal Thinking Cases

16.1 Liquidated Damages The Trump World Tower is a 72-story luxury condominium building constructed at 845 United Nations Plaza in Manhattan, New York. Before the building was constructed, 845 UN Limited Partnership (845 UN) began selling condominiums at the building. The condominium offering plan required a nonrefundable down payment of 25 percent of the purchase price. The purchase contract provided that if a purchaser defaulted and did not complete the purchase, 845 UN could keep the 25 percent down payment as liquidated damages.

Cem Uzan and Hakan Uzan, brothers and Turkish billionaires, each contracted to purchase two condominium units on the top floors of the building. Both Cem and Hakan were represented by attorneys. Over the course of two years, while the building was being constructed, the brothers paid the 25 percent nonrefundable down payment of $8 million. On September 11, 2001, before the building was complete, terrorists attacked New York City by flying two planes into the World Trade Center, the city's two tallest buildings, murdering thousands of people.

Cem and Hakan sent letters to 845 UN, rescinding their purchase agreements because of the terrorist attack that occurred on September 11. Thus, 845 UN terminated the four purchase agreements and kept the 25 percent down payments on the four condominiums as liquidated damages. Cem and Hakan sued 845 UN, alleging that the money should be returned to them. However, 845 UN defended, arguing that the 25 percent nonrefundable down payment was an enforceable liquidated damages clause. Is the liquidated damage clause enforceable? *Uzan v. 845 UN Limited Partnership*, 10 A.D.3d 230, 778 N.Y.S.2d 171, 2004 N.Y. App. Div. Lexis 8362 (Supreme Court of New York, Appellate Division, 2004)

16.2 Specific Performance The California and Hawaiian Sugar Company (C&H), a California corporation, is an agricultural cooperative owned by 14 sugar plantations in Hawaii. It transports raw sugar to its refinery in Crockett, California. Sugar is a seasonal crop, with about 70 percent of the harvest occurring between April and October. C&H requires reliable seasonal shipping of the raw sugar from Hawaii to California. Sugar stored on the ground or left unharvested suffers a loss of sucrose and goes to waste.

After C&H was notified by its normal shipper that it would be withdrawing its services at a specified date in the future, C&H commissioned the design of a large hybrid vessel—a tug of a catamaran design consisting of a barge attached to the tug. After substantial negotiation, C&H contracted with Sun Ship, Inc. (Sun Ship), a Pennsylvania corporation, to build the vessel for $25,405,000. The contract gave Sun Ship one and three-quarter years to build and deliver the ship to C&H. The contract also contained a liquidated damages clause calling for a payment of $17,000 per day for each day that the vessel was not delivered to C&H after the agreed-on delivery date. Sun Ship did not complete the vessel until eight and one-half months after the agreed-on delivery date. On delivery, the vessel was commissioned and christened the *Moku Pahu*.

During the season that the boat had not been delivered, C&H was able to find other means of shipping the crop from Hawaii to its California refinery. Evidence established that actual damages suffered by C&H because of the nonavailability of the vessel from Sun Ship were $368,000. When Sun Ship refused to pay the liquidated damages, C&H filed suit to require payment of $4,413,000 in liquidated damages under the contract. Can C&H recover the liquidated damages from Sun Ship? *California and Hawaiian Sugar Company v. Sun Ship, Inc.*, 794 F.2d 1433, 1986 U.S. App. Lexis 27376 (United States Court of Appeals for the Ninth Circuit)

16.3 Damages Hawaiian Telephone Company entered into a contract with Microform Data Systems, Inc. (Microform), for Microform to provide a computerized assistance system that would handle 15,000 calls per hour with a one-second response time and with a "nonstop" feature to allow automatic recovery from any component failure. The contract called for installation of the host computer no later than mid-February of the next year. Microform was not able to meet the initial installation date, and at that time, it was determined that Microform was at least nine months away from providing a system that met contract specifications. Hawaiian Telephone canceled the contract and sued Microform for damages. Did Microform materially breach the contract? Can Hawaiian Telephone recover damages? *Hawaiian Telephone Co. v. Microform Data Systems Inc.*, 829 F.2d 919, 1987 U.S. App. Lexis 13425 (United States Court of Appeals for the Ninth Circuit)

16.4 Damages Ptarmigan Investment Company (Ptarmigan), a partnership, entered into a contract with Gundersons, Inc. (Gundersons), a South Dakota corporation in the business of golf course construction. The contract provided that Gundersons would construct a golf course for Ptarmigan for a contract price of $1,294,129. Gundersons immediately started work and completed about one-third of the work by about three months later, when bad weather forced cessation of most work. Ptarmigan paid Gundersons for the work to that date. In the following spring, Ptarmigan ran out of funds and was unable to pay for the completion of the golf course. Gundersons sued Ptarmigan and its individual partners to recover the lost profits that it would have made on the remaining two-thirds of the contract. Can Gundersons recover these lost profits as damages?

Gundersons, Inc. v. Ptarmigan Investment Company, 678 P.2d 1061, 1983 Colo. App. Lexis 1133 (Court of Appeals of Colorado)

16.5 Specific Performance Liz Claiborne, Inc. (Claiborne) is a large maker of sportswear in the United States and a well-known name in fashion, with sales of more than $1 billion per year. Claiborne distributes its products through 9,000 retail outlets in the United States. Avon Products, Inc. (Avon) is a major producer of fragrances, toiletries, and cosmetics, with annual sales of more than $3 billion per year. Claiborne, which desired to promote its well-known name on perfumes and cosmetics, entered into a joint venture with Avon whereby Claiborne would make available its names, trademarks, and marketing experience and Avon would engage in the procurement and manufacture of the fragrances, toiletries, and cosmetics. The parties would equally share the financial requirements of the joint venture. During its first year of operation, the joint venture had sales of more than $16 million. In the second year, sales increased to $26 million, making it one of the fastest-growing fragrance and cosmetic lines in the country. One year later, Avon sought to "uncouple" the joint venture. Avon thereafter refused to procure and manufacture the line of fragrances and cosmetics for the joint venture. When Claiborne could not obtain the necessary fragrances and cosmetics from any other source for the fall/Christmas season, Claiborne sued Avon for breach of contract, seeking specific performance of the contract by Avon. Is specific performance an appropriate remedy in this case? *Liz Claiborne, Inc. v. Avon Products, Inc.*, 141 A.D.2d 329, 530 N.Y.S.2d 425, 1988 N.Y. App. Div. Lexis 6423 (Supreme Court of New York)

16.6 Injunction Anita Baker, a then-unknown singer, signed a multiyear recording contract with Beverly Glen Music, Inc. (Beverly Glen). Baker recorded for Beverly Glen a record album that was moderately successful. After having some difficulties with Beverly Glen, Baker was offered a considerably more lucrative contract by Warner Communications, Inc. (Warner). Baker accepted the Warner offer and informed Beverly Glen that she would not complete their contract because she had entered into an agreement with Warner. Beverly Glen sued Baker and Warner, and it sought an injunction to prevent Baker from performing as a singer for Warner. Is an injunction an appropriate remedy in this case? *Beverly Glen Music, Inc. v. Warner Communications, Inc.*, 178 Cal. App.3d 1142, 224 Cal. Rptr. 260, 1986 Cal. App. Lexis 2729 (Court of Appeal of California)

Ethical

Ethics Case

16.7 Ethics Case On Halloween Day, Christine Narvaez drove her automobile onto the parking lot of a busy supermarket. Narvaez had her two-year-old grandchild with her. The youngster was riding, unconstrained, in a booster seat. Narvaez saw a friend and decided to stop for a brief chat. She parked the car and exited the car, leaving the keys in the ignition and the motor running. The youngster crawled behind the wheel, slipped the car into gear, and set it in motion. The car struck Marguerite O'Neill, a woman in her 80s; pinned her between the Narvaez car and another car; and slowly crushed the woman's trapped body.

O'Neill suffered a crushed hip, a broken arm, and four cracked ribs, and she lost more than 40 percent of her blood supply as a result of internal bleeding. She spent one month in a hospital's intensive care unit and had to be placed in a nursing home and was deprived of the ability to live independently.

Narvaez carried the $20,000 minimum amount of liability insurance allowed by law. She was insured by Gallant Insurance Company. O'Neill's medical bills totaled $105,000. O'Neill sued Narvaez and her insurance company, Gallant. O'Neill's attorney demanded the policy limit of $20,000 from Gallant in settlement of O'Neill's claim and offered a complete release from liability for Narvaez. Three Gallant insurance adjusters, its claims manager, and the lawyer of the law firm representing Gallant for the case all stated to John Moss, Gallant's executive vice president, that Gallant should accept the settlement offer. Moss rejected their advice and refused to settle the case.

One year later, on the eve of trial, Moss offered to settle for the $20,000 policy limit, but O'Neill then refused. The case went to trial, and the jury returned a verdict against Narvaez of $731,063. Gallant paid $20,000 of this amount, closed its file, and left Narvaez liable for the $711,063 excess judgment. To settle her debt to

O'Neill, Narvaez assigned her claims against Gallant to O'Neill. O'Neill then sued Gallant for a bad faith tort for breaching the implied covenant of good faith and fair dealing that Gallant owed to Narvaez to settle the case. Is Gallant Insurance Company liable for a bad faith tort? Did Gallant act unethically? *O'Neill v. Gallant Insurance Company*, 769 N.E.2d 100, 2002 Ill. App. Lexis 311 (Appellate Court of Illinois, 2002)

Notes

1. *Restatement (Second) of Contracts*, Section 235(2).
2. *Restatement (Second) of Contracts*, Section 241.
3. *Restatement (Second) of Contracts*, Section 253; UCC Section 2-610.
4. UCC Sections 2-708 and 2-713.
5. *Restatement (Second) of Contracts*, Section 356(1).
6. *Restatement (Second) of Contracts*, Section 370.
7. *Restatement (Second) of Contracts*, Section 359.
8. 9 U.S.C. Section 1 *et seq*.
9. *Nitro-Lift Technologies, L.L.C. v. Howard*, 133 S.Ct. 500 (Supreme Court of the United States, 2012).

CHAPTER 17 Digital Law and E-Commerce

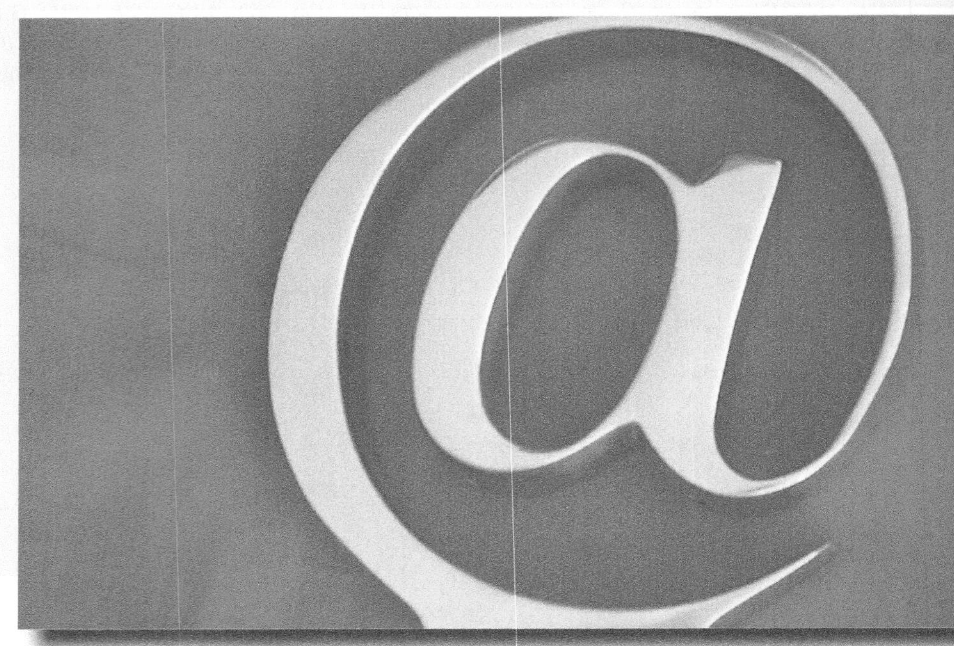

DIGITAL LAW AND E-COMMERCE
The development of the Internet and electronic commerce has required courts to apply existing law to online commerce transactions and e-contracts and spurred the U.S. Congress and state legislatures to enact new laws that governs the formation and enforcement of e-contracts.

Learning Objectives

After studying this chapter, you should be able to:

1. Describe the laws that apply to e-mail contracts, e-commerce, and Web contracts.
2. Describe e-licensing and software law.
3. Describe the provisions of the federal Electronic Signatures in Global and National Commerce Act (E-Sign Act).
4. Describe laws that protect privacy in cyberspace.
5. Define *Internet domain names* and describe how domain names are registered and protected.

Chapter Outline

"Through the use of chat rooms, any person with a phone line can become a town crier with a voice that resonates farther than it could from any soapbox. Through the use of Web pages, mail exploders, and newsgroups, the same individual can become a pamphleteer."

—*Stevens, Justice*
Reno v. American Civil Liberties Union 521 U.S. 844, 117 S.Ct. 2329, 1997 U.S. Lexis 4037 (1997)

Introduction to Digital Law and E-Commerce

The use of the Internet and the World Wide Web and the sale of goods and services through **electronic commerce**, or **e-commerce**, have exploded. Large and small businesses sell goods and services over the Internet through **websites** and registered *domain names*. Consumers and businesses can purchase almost any good or service they want over the Internet, using sites such as Amazon.com, eBay, and others. Businesses and individuals may register domain names to use on the Internet. Anyone who infringes on these rights may be stopped from doing so and is liable for damages.

electronic commerce (e-commerce)
The sale of goods and services by computer over the Internet.

In addition, software and information may be licensed either by physically purchasing the software or information and installing it on a computer or by merely downloading the software or information directly into a computer.

Many legal scholars and lawyers argued that traditional rules of contract law do not meet the needs of Internet transactions and software and information licensing. These concerns led to an effort to create new contract law for electronic transactions. After much debate, the National Conference of Commissioners on Uniform State Laws developed the *Uniform Computer Information Transactions Act (UCITA)*. This model act provides uniform and comprehensive rules for contracts involving computer information transactions and software and information licenses.

The Net is a waste of time, and that's exactly what's right about it.
William Gibson

The federal government has also enacted many federal statutes that regulate the Internet and e-commerce. Federal law has been passed that regulates the Internet and protects personal rights while people are using the Internet.

This chapter covers Internet law, domain names, e-commerce, e-contracts, licensing of software, and other laws that regulate the Internet and e-commerce.

Internet

The **Internet** is a collection of millions of computers that provide a network of electronic connections between the computers. Hundreds of millions of computers are connected to the Internet. The Internet's evolution helped usher in the information age. Individuals and businesses use the Internet for communication of information and data.

Internet
A collection of millions of computers that provide a network of electronic connections between the computers.

World Wide Web

The **World Wide Web**, also called the **Web**, consists of millions of computers that support a standard set of rules for the exchange of information called Hypertext Transfer Protocol (HTTP). Web-based documents are formatted using common coding languages. Businesses and individuals can access the Web by registering with a service provider.

World Wide Web (Web)
An electronic connection of millions of computers that support a standard set of rules for the exchange of information.

Individuals and businesses can have their own websites. A website is composed of electronic documents known as Web pages. Websites and Web pages are stored on servers throughout the world, which are operated by **Internet service providers (ISPs)**. They are viewed by using Web-browsing software such as Microsoft Internet Explorer. Each website has a unique online address.

The Web has made it extremely attractive to conduct commercial activities online. Companies such as Amazon.com and eBay are e-commerce powerhouses that sell all sorts of goods and services. Existing brick-and-mortar companies, such as Walmart, Merrill Lynch, and Dell Computers, sell their goods and services online as well. E-commerce over the Web will continue to grow dramatically each year.

E-Mail Contracts

electronic mail (e-mail)
Electronic written communication between individuals using computers connected to the Internet.

Electronic mail, or **e-mail**, is one of the most widely used applications for communication over the Internet. Using e-mail, individuals around the world can communicate instantaneously in electronic writing with one another. Each person can have an e-mail address that identifies him or her by a unique address. E-mail is replacing telephone and paper communication between individuals and businesses.

electronic mail contract (e-mail contract)
A contract entered into by the parties by use of e-mail.

Controlling the Assault of Non-Solicited Pornography and Marketing Act (CAN-SPAM Act)
A federal statute that places certain restrictions on persons and businesses that send unsolicited commercial advertising (spam) to e-mail accounts, prohibits falsified headers, prohibits deceptive subject lines, and requires spammers to label sexually oriented e-mail as such.

Many contracts are now completed by via e-mail. These are referred to as **electronic mail contracts**, or **e-mail contracts**. E-mail contracts are enforceable as long as they meet the requirements necessary to form a traditional contract, including agreement, consideration, capacity, and lawful object. Traditional challenges to the enforcement of a contract, such as fraud, duress, intoxication, insanity, and other defenses, may be asserted against the enforcement of an e-mail contract. E-mail contracts usually meet the requirements of the Statute of Frauds which requires certain contracts to be in writing, such as contracts of the sale of real estate, contracts for the sale of goods that cost $500 or more, and other contracts listed in the relevant Statute of Frauds.

The use of e-mail communication is often somewhat informal. In addition, an e-mail contract may not have the formality of drafting a paper contract that includes the final terms and conditions of the parties' agreement. The terms of the parties' agreement may have to be gleaned from several e-mails that have been communicated between the parties. In such case, the court can integrate several e-mails in order to determine the terms of the parties' agreement.

The following feature discusses a federal law that regulates spam e-mail.

Digital Law

Regulation of E-Mail Spam

Americans are being bombarded in their e-mail accounts by **spam**—unsolicited commercial advertising. Spammers try to sell people literally anything. Spam accounts for approximately three-quarters of all business e-mail traffic. In addition, many spam messages are fraudulent and deceptive, including misleading subject lines. It takes time and money to sort through, review, and discard unwanted spam.

In 2003, Congress enacted the federal **Controlling the Assault of Non-Solicited Pornography and Marketing Act (CAN-SPAM Act)**.[1] The act (1) prohibits spammers from using falsified headers in e-mail messages, including the originating domain name and e-mail address; (2) prohibits deceptive subject lines that mislead a recipient about the contents or subject matter of the message; and (3) requires that recipients of spam be given the opportunity to opt out and not have the spammer send e-mail to the recipient's address. The Federal Trade Commission (FTC), a federal administrative agency, is empowered to enforce the CAN-SPAM Act.

The act also requires spammers who send sexually oriented e-mail to label it properly as such. The FTC has adopted a rule that requires that sexually explicit spam e-mail contain a warning on the subject line reading "SEXUALLY EXPLICIT." The FTC rule also prohibits the messages themselves from containing graphic material. The graphic material can appear only after the recipient has opened the e-mail message.

In effect, the CAN-SPAM Act does not end spam but instead approves businesses to use spam as long as they do not lie. The act provides a civil right of action to Internet access services that have suffered losses because of spam; However, the act does not provide a civil right of action to individuals who have received unsolicited spam. The CAN-SPAM Act does not regulate spam sent internationally to Americans from other countries. In essence, the CAN-SPAM Act is very weak in helping consumers ward off the spam that deluges them daily.

In the following case, the court was presented with an issue involving spam.

CASE 17.1 *FEDERAL COURT CASE E-Mail Spam*

Facebook, Inc. v. Porembski

2011 U.S. Dist. Lexis 9668 (2011)
United States District Court for the Northern District of California

"The record demonstrates that defendants willfully and knowingly violated the statutes in question by engaging in the circumvention of Facebook's security measures."

—Fogel, District Judge

Facts

Facebook, Inc. owns and operates the social networking website located at http://www.facebook.com. Facebook users must register with the website and agree to Facebook's Statement of Rights and Responsibilities (SRR). Facebook maintains strict policies against spam or any other form of unsolicited advertising by users. Facebook filed a lawsuit in U.S. district court against Philip Porembski and PP Web Services, LLC, which was controlled by Porembski. Facebook alleged that Porembski registered as a Facebook user and was bound by the SRR. Porembski created PP Web Services LLC and was the sole person to act on its behalf. Through fraudulent misrepresentations, Porembski obtained more than 116,000 Facebook users' account information. PP Web Services then sent more than 7.2 million spam messages to these Facebook users. Facebook alleged that the defendants' spamming activities violated the federal CAN-SPAM Act. Facebook sought damages and a permanent injunction against the defendants.

Issue

Did the defendants violate the CAN-SPAM Act?

Language of the Court

The record demonstrates that defendants willfully and knowingly violated the statutes in question by engaging in the circumvention of Facebook's security measures. The court will award statutory damages of $50.00 per violation of the CAN-SPAM Act, for a total award of $360,000,000 under that Act. It is appropriate that defendants be permanently enjoined from accessing and abusing Facebook services. Facebook's request for permanent injunctive relief is granted.

Decision

The U.S. district court held that the defendants had violated the CAN-SPAM Act, awarded Facebook $360,000,000 in damages, and issued a permanent injunction against the defendants.

Ethics Questions

Did Porembski act ethically in this case? Will Facebook recover its awarded damages?

Internet Service Provider (ISP)

Internet service providers (ISPs) are companies that provide consumers and businesses with access to the Internet. ISPs provide e-mail accounts, Internet access, and storage on the Internet to subscribers. ISPs offer a variety of access devices and services, including dial-up, cable, DSL, broadband wireless, Ethernet, satellite Internet access, and other services, to connect users to the Internet. There are also Web-hosting services that allow users to create their own websites and provide storage space for website users.

A provision in the federal **Communications Decency Act** of 1996 provides, "No provider or user of an interactive computer service shall be treated as the publisher or speaker of any information provided by another information content provider."[2] Thus, ISPs are not liable for the content transmitted over their networks by e-mail users and websites.

Communications Decency Act
A federal statute stating that Internet service providers are not liable for the content transmitted over their networks by e-mail users and websites.

E-Commerce and Web Contracts

The Internet and electronic contracts, also called e-contracts, have increased as means of conducting personal and commercial business. Internet sellers, lessors, and licensors use Web addresses to sell and lease goods and services and license software and other intellectual property. Websites such as www.amazon.com, www.dell.com, and www.microsoft.com use the Internet extensively to sell, lease, or license goods, services, and intellectual property. Assuming that all the elements to establish a traditional contract are present, a **Web contract** is valid and enforceable.

Web contract
A contract entered into by purchasing, leasing, or licensing goods, services, software, or other intellectual property from websites operated by sellers, lessors, and licensors.

In the following case, the court considered whether a Web contract was enforceable.

CASE 17.2 *STATE COURT CASE Web Contract*

Hubbert v. Dell Corporation

835 N.E.2d 113, 205 Ill. App. Lexis 808 (2005)
Appellate Court of Illinois

"The blue hyperlinks on the defendant's Web pages, constituting the five-step process for ordering the computers, should be treated the same as a multi-page written paper contract."
—Hopkins, Justice

Facts

Plaintiffs Dewayne Hubbert, Elden Craft, Chris Grout, and Rhonda Byington purchased computers from Dell Corporation online through Dell's website. To make their purchase, each of the plaintiffs completed online order forms on five pages on Dell's website. On each of the five pages, Dell's terms and conditions of sale were accessible by clicking on a blue hyperlink. To find the terms and conditions, the plaintiffs would have had to click on the blue hyperlink and read the terms and conditions of sale. On the last page of the five-page order form, the following statement appeared: "All sales are subject to Dell's Terms and Conditions of Sale."

The plaintiffs filed a lawsuit against Dell, alleging that Dell misrepresented the speed of the microprocessors included in their computers they purchased. Dell made a demand for arbitration, asserting that the plaintiffs were bound by the arbitration agreement that was contained in the terms and conditions of sale. The plaintiffs countered that the arbitration clause was not part of their Web contract because the terms and conditions of sale were not conspicuously displayed as part of their Web contract. The trial court sided with the plaintiffs, finding that the arbitration clause was unenforceable because the terms and conditions of sale were not adequately communicated to the plaintiffs. Dell appealed.

Issue

Were the terms and conditions of sale adequately communicated to the plaintiffs?

Language of the Court

We find that the online contract included the "Terms and Conditions of Sale." The blue hyperlink entitled "Terms and Conditions of Sale" appeared on numerous Web pages the plaintiffs completed in the ordering process. The blue hyperlinks on the defendant's Web pages, constituting the five-step process for ordering the computers, should be treated the same as a multipage written paper contract. The blue hyperlink simply takes a person to another page of the contract, similar to turning the page of a written paper contract. Although there is no conspicuousness requirement, the hyperlink's contrasting blue type makes it conspicuous. Because the "Terms and Conditions of Sale" were a part of the online contract, the plaintiffs were bound by the "Terms and Conditions of Sale," including the arbitration clause.

Decision

The appellate court held that Dell's terms and conditions of sale, accessible by clicking on a blue hyperlink and which included the arbitration clause, were part of the Web contract between the plaintiffs and Dell. The appellate court reversed the decision of the trial court and held in favor of Dell.

Ethics Questions

Did the plaintiffs act ethically in claiming that the terms and conditions of sale were not included in their Web contract? Do you read the terms and conditions of sale when you purchase goods over the Internet?

The following two features discuss a federal statute that established rules for electronic contracts and electronic signatures.

Digital Law

E-SIGN Act: Statute of Frauds and Electronic Contracts

In 2000, the federal government enacted the **Electronic Signatures in Global and National Commerce Act (E-SIGN Act)**,[3] which is a federal statute, enacted by Congress, with national reach. The act is designed to place the world of electronic commerce on a par with the world of paper contracts in the United States.

One of the main features of the E-SIGN Act is that it recognizes electronic contracts as meeting the writing requirement of the Statute of Frauds for most contracts. Statutes of Frauds are state laws that require certain types of contracts to be in writing. The E-SIGN Act provides that electronically signed contracts cannot be denied effect because they are in electronic form or delivered electronically. The act also provides that record retention requirements are satisfied if the records are stored electronically.

The federal law was passed with several provisions to protect consumers. First, consumers must consent to receiving electronic records and contracts. Second, to receive electronic records, consumers must be able to demonstrate that they have access to the electronic records. Third, businesses must tell consumers that they have the right to receive hard-copy documents of their transaction.

Digital Law

E-SIGN Act: E-Signatures and Electronic Contracts

In the past, signatures have been handwritten by the person signing a document. In the electronic commerce world, it is now "What is your mother's maiden name?," "Slide your smart card in the sensor," or "Look into the iris scanner." But are electronic signatures sufficient to form an enforceable contract? The federal Electronic Signatures in Global and National Commerce Act (E-SIGN Act) made the answer clear.

The E-SIGN Act recognizes an **electronic signature**, or **e-signature**. The act gives an e-signature the same force and effect as a handwritten, pen-inscribed signature on paper. The act is technology neutral, however, in that the law does not define or decide which technologies should be used to create a legally binding signature in cyberspace. Loosely defined, a digital signature is some electronic method that identifies an individual. The challenge is to make sure that someone who uses a digital signature is the person he or she claims to be. The act provides that a digital signature can basically be verified in one of three ways:

1. By something the signatory knows, such as a secret password or pet's name
2. By something a person has, such as a smart card, which looks like a credit card and stores personal information
3. By biometrics, which uses a device that digitally recognizes fingerprints or the retina or iris of the eye

The verification of electronic signatures is creating a need for the use of scanners and methods for verifying personal information.

Counteroffers Ineffectual Against Electronic Agent

In today's e-commerce, many Internet sellers have websites that use electronic agents to sell goods and services. An **electronic agent** is any computer system that has been established by a seller to accept orders. Web page order systems are examples of electronic agents.

In the past, when humans dealt with each other face-to-face, by telephone, or in writing, their negotiations might have consisted of an exchange of several offers and counteroffers until agreed-on terms were reached and a contract was formed. Each new counteroffer extinguished the previous offer and became a new viable offer.

Most Web pages use electronic ordering systems that do not have the ability to evaluate and accept counteroffers or to make counteroffers. Thus, counteroffers are not effective against these electronic agents.

Electronic Signatures in Global and National Commerce Act (E-SIGN Act)
A federal statute that (1) recognizes electronic contracts as meeting the writing requirement of the Statute of Frauds and (2) recognizes and gives electronic signatures—e-signatures—the same force and effect as pen-inscribed signatures on paper.

Critical Legal Thinking

Does the Electronic Signatures in Global and National Commerce Act (E-SIGN Act) bring uniformity to electronic contracting? Should additional new federal laws be enacted to bring more uniformity to electronic contracting? Why or why not?

Example Green Company has a website that uses an electronic ordering system for accepting orders for products sold by the company. Freddie accesses the Green Company's website and orders a product costing $1,000. Freddie enters the product code and description, his mailing address and credit-card information, and other data needed to complete the transaction. The Green Company's Web ordering system does not provide a method for a party to submit a counteroffer. After ordering the goods on the website, Freddie sends an e-mail to the Green Company stating, "I will accept the product I ordered if, after two weeks of use, I am satisfied with the product." However, because Freddie has placed the order with an electronic agent, Freddie has ordered the product, and his counteroffer is ineffectual.

E-Licensing of Software and Information Rights

Uniform Computer Information Transactions Act (UCITA)
A model act that creates contract law for the licensing of information technology rights.

Much of the new cyberspace economy is based on electronic contracts and the licensing of computer software and information. E-commerce created problems for forming contracts over the Internet, enforcing e-commerce contracts, and providing consumer protection. To address these problems, in 1999, the National Conference of Commissioners on Uniform State Laws (a group of lawyers, judges, and legal scholars) drafted the **Uniform Computer Information Transactions Act (UCITA)**, which is discussed in the following feature.

Digital Law

Uniform Computer Information Transactions Act

The Uniform Computer Information Transactions Act (UCITA) is a model act that establishes a uniform and comprehensive set of rules that govern the creation, performance, and enforcement of computer information transactions. A computer information transaction is an agreement to create, transfer, or license computer information or information rights [UCITA Section 102(a)(11)].

The UCITA does not become law until a state's legislature enacts it as a state statute. Most states have adopted e-commerce and licensing statutes that are similar to many of the provisions of the UCITA as their law for computer transactions and the licensing of software and information rights. The UCITA will be used in this text as the basis for discussing state laws that affect computer, software, and licensing contracts.

Unless displaced by the UCITA, state law and equity principles, including principal and agent law, fraud, duress, mistake, trade secret law, and other state laws supplement the UCITA [UCITA Section 114]. Any provisions of the UCITA that are preempted by federal law are unenforceable to the extent of the preemption [UCITA Section 105(a)].

License

Intellectual property and information rights are extremely important assets of many individuals and companies. Patents, trademarks, copyrights, trade secrets, data, software programs, and the like, constitute valuable intellectual property and information rights.

license
A contract that transfers limited rights in intellectual property and informational rights.

The owners of intellectual property and information rights often wish to transfer limited rights in the property or information to parties for specified purposes and limited duration. The agreement that is used to transfer such limited rights is called a **license**, which is defined as follows [UCITA Section 102(a)(40)]:

> *License means a contract that authorizes access to, or use, distribution, performance, modification, or reproduction of, information or information rights, but expressly limits the access or uses authorized or expressly grants fewer than all rights in the information, whether or not the transferee has title to a licensed copy. The term includes an access contract, a lease of a computer program, and a consignment of a copy.*

licensor
An owner of intellectual property or information rights who transfers rights in the property or information to the licensee.

The parties to a license are the licensor and the licensee. The **licensor** is the party who owns the intellectual property or information rights and obligates him- or herself to transfer rights in the property or information to the licensee. The **licensee** is the party who is granted limited rights in or access to the intellectual property or information [UCITA Section 102(a)(41), (42)].

A licensing arrangement is illustrated in **Exhibit 17.1**.

licensee
A party who is granted limited rights in or access to intellectual property or information rights owned by a licensor.

Exhibit 17.1 **LICENSING AGREEMENT**

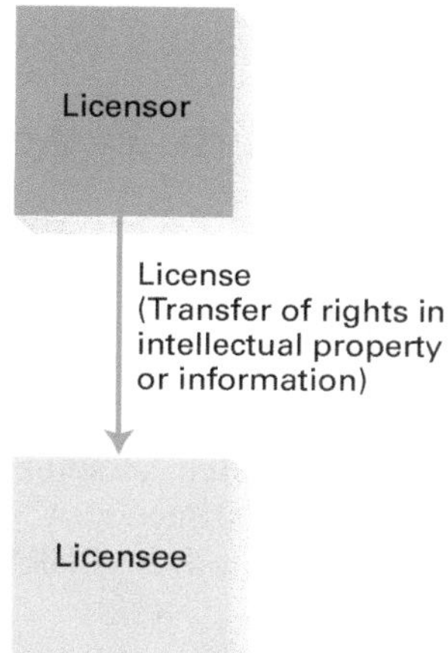

A license grants the contractual rights expressly described in the license and the right to use information rights within the licensor's control that are necessary to perform the expressly described rights [UCITA Section 307(a)]. A license can grant the licensee the exclusive rights to use the information. An **exclusive license** means that for the specified duration of the license, the licensor will not grant to any other person rights to the same information [UCITA Section 307(f)(2)].

exclusive license
A license that grants the licensee exclusive rights to use information rights for a specified duration.

E-License

Most software programs and digital applications are licensed electronically by the owner of the program or application to a user of a computer or digital device. An **electronic license**, or **e-license**, is a contract whereby the owner of a software or a digital application grants limited rights to the owner of a computer or digital device to use the software or a digital application for a limited period and under specified conditions. The owner of the program or application is the **electronic licensor**, or **e-licensor**, and the owner of the computer or digital device to whom the license is granted is the **electronic licensee**, or **e-licensee**.

electronic license (e-license)
A contract whereby the owner of a software or a digital application grants limited rights to the owner of a computer or digital device to use the software or digital application for a limited period and under specified conditions.

Example Dorothy owns a computer and licenses a computer software program from SoftWare Company to use on her computer. Dorothy downloads the software onto her computer from SoftWare Company's website. There is an e-license between the two parties. SoftWare Company is the e-licensor, and Dorothy is the e-licensee.

Licensing Agreement

A licensor and a licensee usually enter into a written **licensing agreement** that expressly states the terms of their agreement. Licensing agreements tend to be very detailed and comprehensive contracts. This is primarily because of the nature of the subject matter and the limited uses granted in the intellectual property or information rights.

licensing agreement
A detailed and comprehensive written agreement between a licensor and a licensee that sets forth the express terms of their agreement.

The parties to a contract for the licensing of information owe a duty to perform the obligations stated in the contract. If a party fails to perform as required, there is a breach of the contract. Breach of contract by one party to a licensing agreement gives the nonbreaching party certain rights, including the right to recover damages or other remedies [UCITA Section 701].

Privacy in Cyberspace

E-mail, computer data, and other electronic communications are sent daily by millions of people using computers and the Internet. Recognizing that the use of computer and other electronic communications raises special issues of privacy, the federal government enacted the **Electronic Communications Privacy Act (ECPA)**.[4]

Electronic Communications Privacy Act (ECPA)
A federal statute that makes it a crime to intercept an electronic communication at the point of transmission, while in transit, when stored by a router or server, or after receipt by intended recipient. There are some exceptions to this law.

Electronic Communications Privacy Act

The ECPA makes it a crime to intercept an electronic communication at the point of transmission, while in transit, when stored by a router or server, or after receipt by the intended recipient. An electronic communication includes any transfer of signals, writings, images, sounds, data, or intelligence of any nature. The ECPA makes it illegal to access stored e-mail as well as e-mail in transmission.

Example Henry owns a computer on which he sends and receives e-mail. Harriet learns Henry's access code to his e-mail account. Harriet opens Henry's e-mail and reads his e-mails. Harriet has violated the ECPA.

Exceptions

The ECPA provides that stored electronic communications may be accessed without violating the law by the following:

1. The party or entity providing the electronic communication service. The primary example would be an employer who can access stored e-mail communications of employees using the employer's service.
2. Government and law enforcement entities that are investigating suspected illegal activity. Disclosure would be required only pursuant to a valid warrant.

Critical Legal Thinking
Is the Electronic Communications Privacy Act (ECPA) sufficient to protect the privacy of electronic communications? Have you ever had your privacy violated while using the Internet or e-mail or texting?

Example John works for the National Paper Corporation. In his job, he has access to a computer on which to conduct work for his employer. John receives and sends e-mail that is work related. John also has access on his computer to the Internet. The National Paper Corporation investigates what John has been viewing and what he has stored on his computer. During its investigation, the National Paper Corporation discovers that John has been viewing and storing child pornography images. The National Paper Corporation fires John for his conduct because it violates company policy of which John is aware. Here, the National Paper Company did not violate ECPA.

The ECPA provides for criminal penalties. In addition, the ECPA provides that an injured party may sue for civil damages for violations of the ECPA.

Domain Names

Most businesses conduct e-commerce by using websites on the Internet. Each website is identified by a unique Internet **domain name**.

domain name
A unique name that identifies an individual's or a company's website.

Examples The domain name for the publisher of this book—Pearson Education, Inc.—is www.pearson.com. The domain name for Microsoft Corporation is www.microsoft.com. The domain name for McDonald's Corporation is www.mcdonalds.com.

Registration of Domain Names

Domain names can be registered. The first step in registering a domain name is to determine whether any other party already owns the name. For this purpose,

InterNIC maintains a database that contains the domain names that have been registered. The InterNIC website can be accessed at www.internic.net.

Domain names can also be registered at Network Solutions, Inc.'s, website, which is located at www.networksolutions.com, as well as at other sites. An applicant must complete a registration form, which can be done online. It usually costs less than $50 to register a domain name for one year, and the fee may be paid online by credit card. Some country-specific domain names are more expensive to register.

Domain Name Extensions

The most commonly used top-level extensions for domain names are listed in **Exhibit 17.2**.

.com	This extension represents the word *commercial* and is the most widely used extension in the world. Most businesses prefer a .com domain name because it is a highly recognized business symbol.
.net	This extension represents the word *network*, and it is most commonly used by ISPs, Web-hosting companies, and other businesses that are directly involved in the infrastructure of the Internet. Some businesses also choose domain names with a .net extension.
.org	This extension represents the word *organization* and is used primarily by nonprofit groups and trade associations.
.info	This extension signifies a resource website. It is an unrestricted global name that may be used by businesses, individuals, and organizations.
.biz	This extension is used for small-business websites.
.us	This extension is for U.S. websites. Many businesses choose this extension, which is a relatively new one.
.mobi	This extension is reserved for websites that are viewable on mobile devices.
.bz	This extension was originally the country code for Belize, but it is now unrestricted and may be registered by anyone from any country. It is commonly used by small businesses.
.name	This extension is for individuals, who can use it to register personalized domain names.
.museum	This extension enables museums, museum associations, and museum professionals to register websites.
.coop	This extension represents the word *cooperative* and may be used by cooperative associations around the world.
.aero	This extension is exclusively reserved for the aviation community. It enables organizations and individuals in that community to reserve websites.
.pro	This extension is available to professionals, such as doctors, lawyers, and consultants.
.edu	This extension is for educational institutions.

Exhibit 17.2 **COMMONLY USED TOP-LEVEL EXTENSIONS FOR DOMAIN NAMES**

WEB EXERCISE

Go to **www.networksolutions.com**. See if your name is available in the .name extension.

WEB EXERCISE

Think of an Internet domain name you would like to use for a business. Go to the Network Solutions website at **www.networksolutions.com** and see if that name is available with the top-level domain **extension .com**.

WEB EXERCISE

Go to **http://rwgusa.net/domain_extension_by_country.php**. Find the domain extension for the following countries: Canada, China, France, India, Israel, Japan, Mexico, and Saudi Arabia. Are there any restrictions for obtaining each domain name?

The following feature discusses the creation of new top-level domain names.

Digital Law

New Top-Level Domain Names

In 2011, the Internet Corporation for Assigned Names and Numbers (ICANN), the organization that oversees the registration and regulation of domain names, issued new rules that permit a party to register a domain name with new **top level domain (TLD)** suffixes that are personalized. The new rules are the biggest change in domain names in more than four decades.

The new rules permit companies to have their own company name TLDs, such as .canon, .google, and . cocacola. In addition, companies can obtain TLDs for specific products, such as .ipad or .prius. Such TLDs will help companies with the branding of their company names and products. New TLDs can also be registered for industries and professions, such as .bank, .food, .basketball, and .dentist.

Under the new rules, cities and other government agencies can register their names, such as .nyc (New York City), .paris (Paris, France), and .quebec (Quebec Province, Canada). Even persons sharing a cultural identity could have their own TLD, such as .kurd (for Kurds living in Iraq and elsewhere) or .ven (Venetian community, Italy). Another important change is that the new rules permit TLDs to be registered in languages other than English. This would include Arabic, Chinese, French, Russian, Spanish, and other languages.

To obtain a new TLD, a party must file a detailed application with ICANN.

Country Domain Names

Countries have specific extensions assigned to the country. Many countries make these domain name extensions available for private purchase for commercial use. Examples of country domain names are listed in **Exhibit 17.3**.

Exhibit 17.3 EXAMPLES OF COUNTRY DOMAIN NAMES

WEB EXERCISE
Pick out a name of a country that is not listed in Exhibit 17.3 and find its domain name extension.

Afghanistan	**.af**
Angola	**.ao**
Argentina	**.ar**
Australia	**.au**
Bangladesh	**.bd**
Bhutan	**.bt**
Brazil	**.br**
Burkina Faso	**.bf**
Canada	**.ca**
Chile	**.cl**
China	**.cn**
Cuba	**.cu**
Egypt	**.eg**
France	**.fr**
Germany	**.de**
Great Britain (UK)	**.gb**
Greece	**.gr**
India	**.in**
Indonesia	**.id**
Iran	**.ir**
Ireland	**.ie**

Israel	.il
Japan	.jp
Kenya	.ke
Madagascar	.mg
Mali	.ml
Mexico	.mx
Mongolia	.mn
New Zealand	.nz
Nigeria	.ng
Pakistan	.pk
Peru	.pe
Russia	.ru
Saudi Arabia	.sa
South Korea	.kr
Turkey	.tr
United States	.us
Venezuela	.ve
Zambia	.zm

Cybersquatting on Domain Names

Sometimes a party registers a domain name of another party's trademarked name or a famous person's name, an act called **cybersquatting**. Often the domain name owner has registered the domain name with the hope of obtaining payment for the name from the trademark holder or the famous person whose name has been registered as a domain name.

Anticybersquatting Consumer Protection Act (ACPA)
A federal statute that permits trademark owners and famous persons to recover domain names that use their names where the domain name has been registered by another person or business in bad faith.

Trademark law was of little help in this area. Either the famous person's name was not trademarked or, even if the name was trademarked, trademark laws required distribution of goods or services to find infringement. Most cybersquatters do not distribute goods or services but merely sit on the Internet domain names.

The following feature discusses an important federal law that restricts cybersquatting.

Digital Law

Anticybersquatting Consumer Protection Act

In 1999, the U.S. Congress enacted the **Anticybersquatting Consumer Protection Act (ACPA)**.[5] The act was specifically aimed at cybersquatters who register Internet domain names of famous companies and people and hold them hostage by demanding ransom payments from the famous company or person.

The act has two fundamental requirements: (1) the name must be famous, and (2) the domain name must have been registered in bad faith. Thus, the law prohibits the act of cybersquatting itself if it is done in bad faith.

The first issue in applying the statute is whether the domain name is someone else's famous name. Trademarked names qualify; nontrademarked names—such as those of famous actors, actresses, singers, sports stars, and politicians—are also protected. The second issue is whether the domain name was registered in bad faith. In determining bad faith, a court may consider the extent to which the domain

(continued)

name resembles the trademark owner's name or the famous person's name, whether goods or services are sold under the name, the holder's offer to sell or transfer the name, whether the holder has acquired multiple Internet domain names of famous companies and persons, and other factors.

The act provides for the issuance of cease-and-desist orders and injunctions against the domain name registrant. The court may order the domain name registrant to turn over the domain name to the trademark owner or famous person. The law also provides for monetary penalties. The ACPA gives owners of trademarks and persons with famous names rights to prevent the kidnapping of Internet domain names by cyberpirates.

The following case involves a domain name dispute.

CASE 17.3 *NATIONAL ARBITRATION FORUM Domain Name*

New York Yankees Partnership d/b/a The New York Yankees Baseball Club

Claim Number FA0609000803277 (2006)
National Arbitration Forum

"Such use by Moniker is indicative of an intent to disrupt the business of the Yankees, and constitutes registration and use of the disputed domain name in bad faith."

—Kalina, Judge, Retired

Facts

The New York Yankees Partnership d/b/a/ The New York Yankees Baseball Club (Yankees) is among the world's most recognized and followed sports teams, having won more than 20 World Series Championships and more than 30 American League pennants. The Yankees own the trademark for the NEW YORK YANKEES (Reg. No. 1,073,346), which was issued to the Yankees by the U.S. Patent and Trademark Office (PTO) on September 13, 1977. Moniker Online Services, Inc. (Moniker) registered the domain name <nyyankees.com>. Moniker operates a commercial website under this domain name where it offers links to third-party commercial websites that sell tickets to Yankee baseball games and sell merchandise bearing the NEW YORK YANKEES trademark without the Yankees' permission. The Yankees filed a complaint with the National Arbitration Forum, alleging that Moniker had registered the domain in bad faith in violation of the **Internet Corporation for Assigned Names and Numbers (ICANN)** Uniform Domain Dispute Resolution Policy and seeking to obtain the domain name from Moniker.

Issue

Did Moniker violate the ICANN's Uniform Domain Dispute Resolution Policy (Policy)?

Language of the Arbitrator

Complainant has sufficiently demonstrated that Moniker's <nyyankees.com> domain name is confusingly similar to complainant's NEW YORK YANKEES mark. There is no evidence in the record to suggest that Moniker is commonly known by the disputed domain name. Such use by Moniker is indicative of an intent to disrupt the business of the Yankees, and constitutes registration and use of the disputed domain name in bad faith.

Decision

The arbitrator held that Moniker violated the ICANN Policy and ordered that the <nyyankees.com> domain name be transferred from Moniker to the Yankees.

Ethics Questions

Did Moniker act ethically in obtaining and using the <nyyankees.com> domain name and website? Do you think that the element of bad faith was shown in this case? Explain your answer.

The following feature discusses the use of the Internet globally.

Global Law

Internet in Foreign Countries

SIEM REAP, CAMBODIA
Far-flung regions of the world are connected by the Internet, e-mail, text messaging, and other electronic communications. Some countries restrict or censure the use of the Internet. Currently, no international law governs the Internet. Although U. S. law may make certain Internet activities illegal, these laws do not reach Internet sources located outside the United States. Many Internet frauds are conducted over the Internet by persons located in other countries, beyond the reach of U.S. criminal laws.

Key Terms and Concepts

.aero (357)
.biz (357)
.bz (357)
.com (357)
.coop (357)
.edu (357)
.info (357)
.mobi (357)
.museum (357)
.name (357)
.net (357)
.org (357)
.pro (357)
.us (357)
Anticybersquatting Consumer Protection Act (ACPA) (359)
Communications Decency Act (351)
Controlling the Assault of Non-Solicited Pornography and Marketing Act (CAN-SPAM Act) (350)
Cybersquatting (359)
Domain name (356)
Electronic agent (353)
Electronic commerce (e-commerce) (349)
Electronic Communications Privacy Act (ECPA) (356)
Electronic license (e-license) (355)
Electronic licensee (e-licensee) (355)
Electronic licensor (e-licensor) (355)
Electronic mail (e-mail) (350)
Electronic mail contract (e-mail contract) (350)
Electronic signature (e-signature) (353)
Electronic Signatures in Global and National Commerce Act (E-SIGN Act) (353)
Exclusive license (355)
Internet (349)
Internet Corporation for Assigned Names and Numbers (ICANN) (360)
Internet service provider (ISP) (349)
License (354)
Licensee (355)
Licensing agreement (355)
Licensor (354)
Spam (350)
Top-level domain name (TLD) (358)
Uniform Computer Information Transactions Act (UCITA) (354)
Web contract (352)
Website (349)
World Wide Web (Web) (349)

Critical Legal Thinking Cases

17.1 Cybersquatting Ernest & Julio Gallo Winery (Gallo) is a famous maker of wines located in California. The company registered the trademark "Ernest & Julio Gallo" in 1964 with the U.S. Patent and Trademark Office. The company has spent more than $500 million promoting its brand name and has sold more than 4 billion bottles of wine. Its name has taken on a secondary meaning as a famous trademark name. Steve, Pierce, and Fred Thumann created Spider Webs Ltd., a limited partnership, to register Internet domain names. Spider Webs registered more than 2,000 Internet domain names, including ernestandjuliogallo.com. Spider Webs is in the business of selling domain names. Gallo filed suit against Spider Webs Ltd. and the Thumanns, alleging violation of the federal Anticybersquatting Consumer Protection Act (ACPA). The U.S. District Court held in favor of Gallo and ordered Spider Webs to transfer the domain name ernestandjuliogallo.com to Gallo. Spider Webs Ltd. appealed. Who wins? *E. & J. Gallo Winery v. Spider Webs Ltd.*, 286 F.3d 270, 2002 U.S. App. Lexis 5928 (United States Court of Appeals for the Fifth Circuit, 2002)

17.2 Internet Service Provider Someone secretly took video cameras into the locker room and showers of the Illinois State football team. Videotapes showing these undressed players were displayed at the website univ.youngstuds.com operated by Franco Productions. The Internet name concealed the name of the person responsible. The GTE Corporation, an ISP, provided a high-speed connection and storage space on its server so that the content of the website could be accessed. The nude images passed over GTE's network between Franco Productions and its customers. The football players sued Franco Productions and GTE for monetary damages. Franco Productions defaulted when it could not be located. Is GTE Corporation liable for damages to the plaintiff football players? *John Doe v. GTE Corporation*, 347 F.3d 655, 2003 U.S. App. Lexis 21345 (United States Court of Appeals for the Seventh Circuit, 2003)

17.3 Domain Name Frances Net, a freshman in college and a computer expert, browses websites for hours each day. One day, she thinks to herself, "I can make money registering domain names and selling them for a fortune." She has recently seen an advertisement for Classic Coke, a cola drink produced and marketed by Coca-Cola Company. Coca-Cola Company has a famous trademark on the term *Classic Coke* and has spent millions of dollars advertising this brand and making the term famous throughout the United States and the world. Frances goes to the website www.networksolutions.com, an Internet domain name registration service, to see if the Internet domain name classiccoke.com has been taken. She discovers that it is available, so she immediately registers the Internet domain name classiccoke.com for herself and pays the $70 registration fee with her credit card. Coca-Cola Company decides to register the Internet domain name classiccoke.com, but when it checks at Network Solutions, Inc.'s, website, it discovers that Frances Net has already registered the Internet domain name. Coca-Cola Company contacts Frances, who demands $500,000 for the name. Coca-Cola Company sues Frances to prevent her from using the Internet domain name classiccoke.com and to recover it from her under the federal Anticybersquatting Consumer Protection Act (ACPA). Who wins?

17.4 E-Mail Contract The Little Steel Company is a small steel fabricator that makes steel parts for various metal machine shop clients. When Little Steel Company receives an order from a client, it must locate and purchase 10 tons of a certain grade of steel to complete the order. The Little Steel Company sends an e-mail message to West Coast Steel Company, a large steel company, inquiring about the availability of 10 tons of the described grade of steel. The West Coast Steel Company replies by e-mail that it has available the required 10 tons of steel and quotes $450 per ton. The Little Steel Company's purchasing agent replies by e-mail that the Little Steel Company will purchase the 10 tons of described steel at the quoted price of $450 per ton. The e-mails are signed electronically by the Little Steel Company's purchasing agent and the selling agent of the West Coast Steel Company. When the steel arrives at the Little Steel Company's plant, the Little Steel Company rejects the shipment, claiming the defense of the Statute of Frauds. The West Coast Steel Company sues the Little Steel Company for damages. Who wins?

17.5 Electronic Signature David Abacus uses the Internet to place an order to license software for his computer from Inet.License, Inc. (Inet), through Inet's electronic website ordering system. Inet's Web-page order form asks David to type in his name, mailing address, telephone number, e-mail address, credit-card information, computer location information, and personal identification number. Inet's electronic agent requests that David verify the information a second time before it accepts the order, which David does. The license duration is two years at a license fee of $300 per month. Only after receiving the verification of information does Inet's electronic agent place the order and send an electronic copy of the software program to David's computer, where he installs the new software program. David later refuses to pay the license fee due Inet because he claims his electronic signature and information were not authentic. Inet sues David to recover the license fee. Is David's electronic signature enforceable against him?

17.6 License Tiffany Pan, a consumer, intends to order three copies of a financial software program from iSoftware, Inc. Tiffany, using her computer, enters iSoftware's website isoftware.com and places an order with the electronic agent taking orders for the website. The license is for three years at $300 per month for each copy of the software program. Tiffany enters the necessary product code and description; her name, mailing address, and credit-card information; and other data necessary to place the order. When the electronic order form prompts Tiffany to enter the number of copies of the software program she is ordering, Tiffany mistakenly types in "30." iSoftware's electronic agent places the order and ships 30 copies of the software program to Tiffany. When Tiffany receives the 30 copies of the software program, she ships them back to iSoftware with a note stating, "Sorry, there has been a mistake. I meant to order only 3 copies of the software, not 30." When iSoftware bills Tiffany for the license fees for the 30 copies, Tiffany refuses to pay. iSoftware sues Tiffany to recover the license fees for 30 copies. Who wins?

Ethical

Ethics Cases

17.7 Ethics Case BluePeace.org is a new environmental group that has decided that the Internet is the best and most efficient way to spend its time and money to advance its environmental causes. To draw attention to its websites, BluePeace.org comes up with catchy Internet domain names. One is macysweaRus.org, another is exxonvaldezesseals.org, and another is generalmotorscrashesdummies.org. The macyswearus.org website first shows beautiful women dressed in mink fur coats sold by Macy's Department Stores and then goes into graphic photos of minks being slaughtered, skinned, and made into the coats. The exxonvaldezesseals.org website first shows a beautiful, pristine bay in Alaska, with the *Exxon Valdez* oil tanker quietly sailing through the waters. Then it shows photos of the ship breaking open and spewing forth oil, followed by seals who are covered with oil, suffocating and dying on the shoreline. The website generalmotorscrashesdummies.org shows a General Motors automobile involved in normal crash tests with dummies, followed by photographs of automobile accident scenes where people and children lay bleeding and dying after an accident involving General Motors automobiles. Macy's Inc., the ExxonMobil Corporation, and the General Motors Corporation sue BluePeace.org for violating the federal Anticybersquatting Consumer Protection Act (ACPA). Who wins? Has BluePeace.org acted unethically in this case?

17.8 Ethics Case Apricot.com is a major software developer that licenses software to be used over the Internet. One of its programs, called Match, is a search engine that searches personal ads on the Internet and provides a match for users for potential dates and possible marriage partners. Nolan Bates subscribes to the Match software program from Apricot.com. The license duration is five years, with a license fee of $200 per month. For each subscriber, Apricot.com produces a separate Web page that shows photos of the subscriber and personal data. Bates posted a photo of himself with his mother, with the caption, "Male, 30 years old, lives with mother, likes quiet nights at home." Bates licenses the Apricot.com Match software and uses it 12 hours each day, searching for his Internet match. Bates does not pay Apricot.com the required monthly licensing fee for any of the three months he uses the software. After using the Match software but refusing to pay Apricot.com its licensing fee, Apricot.com activates the disabling bug in the software and disables the Match software on Bates's computer. Apricot.com does this with no warning to Bates. It then sends a letter to Bates stating, "Loser, the license is canceled!" Bates sues Apricot.com for disabling the Match software program. Who wins? Did Bates act ethically? Did Apricot.com act ethically?

Notes

1. 15 U.S.C. Sections 7701–7713.
2. 47 U.S.C. Section 230 (c)(1).
3. 15 U.S.C. Chapter 96.
4. 18 U.S.C. Section 2510.
5. 15 U.S.C. Section 1125(d).

CASE *Exchange Agreement*

Conocophillips Alaska, Inc. v Williams Alaska Petroleum, Inc

S-14654, S-14674, S-14953 Decided: March 14, 2014
Before: Fabe, Chief Justice, Winfree, Stowers, Maassen, and Bolger, Justices
Opinion by, FABE, Chief Justice

Introduction

Williams Alaska Petroleum owned and operated a refinery, which ConocoPhillips Alaska supplied with crude oil pursuant to an Exchange Agreement. ConocoPhillips demanded that Williams tender a payment of $31 million as adequate assurances of Williams's ability to perform if an ongoing administrative rate-making process resulted in a large retroactive increase in payments that Williams would owe ConocoPhillips under the Exchange Agreement. ConocoPhillips offered to credit Williams with a certain rate of interest on that principal payment against a future retroactive invoice. Williams transferred the principal of $31 million but demanded, among other terms, credit corresponding to a higher rate of interest. Williams stated that acceptance and retention of the funds would constitute acceptance of all of its terms. ConocoPhillips received and retained the funds, rejecting only one particular term in Williams's latest offer but remaining silent as to which rate of interest would apply. Years later, after the conclusion of the regulatory process, ConocoPhillips invoiced Williams retroactively pursuant to the Exchange Agreement. ConocoPhillips credited Williams for the $31 million principal already paid as well as $5 million in interest on that principal calculated using the lower of the two interest rates. Williams sued ConocoPhillips, arguing that a contract had been formed for the higher rate of interest and that it was therefore owed a credit for $10 million in interest on the $31 million principal.

On cross-motions for summary judgment, the superior court initially ruled for Williams, concluding that a contract for the higher rate of interest had formed under the Uniform Commercial Code (UCC) § 2–207(1) when ConocoPhillips retained the $31 million while rejecting one offered term but voicing no objection to Williams's specified interest term. On a motion for reconsideration, the superior court again ruled for Williams, this time determining that a contract for the higher rate of interest had formed based on the behavior of the parties after negotiation under UCC § 2–207(3), or, in the alternative, that Williams was entitled to a credit for a different, third rate of interest in quantum meruit. The superior court also ruled in favor of Williams on all issues related to attorney's fees and court costs.

ConocoPhillips and Williams both appeal. We conclude that the superior court was right the first time and that the parties entered into a contract for the higher rate of interest under UCC § 2–207(1). Thus, it was incorrect for the superior court to rescind its initial summary judgment order as improvidently granted. Accordingly, we do not reach the UCC § 2–207(3) or quantum meruit holdings of the superior court's order on reconsideration. Finally, we affirm all of the superior court's actions with regard to attorney's fees and court costs.

Facts and Proceedings

Facts

The parties and the contract

In December 1999, BP Oil Supply Company and Williams Energy Marketing & Trading Company entered into a contract for the sale of crude oil, called an Exchange Agreement. Within months, the rights and duties of the original parties to this Exchange Agreement were assigned to the parties to the present case: ConocoPhillips and Williams.

Under the Exchange Agreement, ConocoPhillips would provide Williams's refinery at North Pole with crude oil from the Trans–Alaska Pipeline System. Williams would extract valuable components from the crude oil and provide an equal volume of lower-quality crude back to ConocoPhillips, and ConocoPhillips would then return the crude oil to the pipeline. The Trans–Alaska Pipeline System operates a "Quality Bank," which compensates all pipeline shippers for the degradation in the average quality of crude in the pipeline downstream caused by tender of less-valuable crude upstream. The Quality Bank Administrator assesses "degradation charges" to shippers tendering comparatively lower-value crude to the pipeline based on a quality pricing scheme set by the Federal Energy Regulatory Commission (FERC) and the Regulatory Commission of Alaska (RCA). ConocoPhillips, as the shipper tendering lower-quality crude back into the pipeline, would be assessed degradation charges by the Administrator.

(*case continues*)

The Exchange Agreement's pricing provision, on top of a flat per-barrel fee, required Williams to reimburse ConocoPhillips for such degradation charges, including any retroactive adjustments resulting from new FERC regulations.

The Exchange Agreement contained two additional provisions relevant to this case. First, an adequate-assurances clause specified that when one party "has reasonable grounds for insecurity," that party may demand "adequate security for, or assurances of [the other party's] ability to perform, all of its obligations under the Agreement." If adequate security or assurances were not forthcoming within 48 hours, the demanding party would "have the right to liquidate the Agreement" and cease performance of its other obligations under the Exchange Agreement. Second, a signed-writing clause specified that "[n]o changes, alterations, or modifications of the Agreement shall be effective unless agreed to in writing by an authorized representative of the Parties."

The dispute

In 2002, ConocoPhillips believed that it had reasonable grounds for insecurity. The FERC and the RCA initiated a regulatory rate-making process that could result in a retroactive increase in Quality Bank degradation charges to ConocoPhillips for its tender of lower-quality crude back into the pipeline. Under the pricing provision of the Exchange Agreement requiring reimbursement for retroactive degradation charges, Williams could owe ConocoPhillips substantial sums of money, the precise amount of which would depend on the agencies' promulgation of a revised pricing scheme, perhaps years in the future. ConocoPhillips, believing Williams and its parent company to be in a precarious financial position, doubted Williams's ability to pay a large, retroactively assessed charge in the future. Invoking the adequate-assurances provision of the Exchange Agreement, ConocoPhillips sent Williams an initial demand letter on October 4 stating its position that Williams "now owes" $31,268,645 in "Quality Bank adjustments to the price of oil" already exchanged over the prior two years under the contract. ConocoPhillips proposed a range of options for providing adequate financial assurances: a cash payment, a trust with ConocoPhillips as beneficiary, a letter of credit, or a senior security interest in Williams's property. This letter did not mention whether or at what rate ConocoPhillips would credit Williams for interest on any such assurance payment or security.

Following a series of telephone calls, Williams sent ConocoPhillips a letter on October 8. Williams disputed that it was in financial peril or that ConocoPhillips had reasonable grounds for insecurity. Williams also stated its view that potential future Quality Bank adjustments "are not currently due," as ConocoPhillips would have it, but rather "may become due in the future upon resolution of the Quality Bank proceedings." Nonetheless, fearing the harm that would come from ConocoPhillips halting the flow of crude, Williams offered to settle the dispute in a package deal that included, among other terms, wire transfer of $29.01 million to ConocoPhillips. This principal, plus interest that would accrue on the principal "calculated at the LIBOR six-month rate,"[1] would be "held by ConocoPhillips for Williams'[s] account" pending a resolution in the rate-making case, at which point "the advance payments to ConocoPhillips, including all interest thereon, will be applied toward any Quality Bank Amounts so determined to be due from Williams." On October 11, ConocoPhillips responded, saying it might be willing to meet some of Williams's conditions for settlement but demanding a payment of $35,245,181. The letter made no mention of Williams receiving credit for interest on that sum in the future. In a follow-up letter dated October 17, ConocoPhillips proposed that Williams pay $35,245,181 "as a partial preliminary settlement payment" of any retroactively assessed Quality Bank degradation charges. For the first time, ConocoPhillips offered to credit Williams for interest earned on the principal at the LIBOR rate.

On October 18, Williams wired $31,268,645 to ConocoPhillips. Later that day, Williams sent ConocoPhillips a letter stating that the money was intended to "avoid litigation and resolv[e] the disputes" over retroactive price modifications under the Exchange Agreement. Williams specified that "ConocoPhillips'[s] receipt and retention of the $31,268,645 shall constitute ConocoPhillips'[s] agreement with the terms set forth in this letter." The letter's terms included three substantive provisions: (1) that the "full principal amount" already wired to ConocoPhillips receive interest at a "rate prescribed by FERC"[2] and that the principal and interest would be held by ConocoPhillips for Williams's account and later be credited toward any final retroactive assessments; (2) that ConocoPhillips agree to "continue good faith efforts" in "vigorous support" of a preexisting joint-negotiating agreement that would present a united front in the FERC rate-making case; and (3) that the parties agree to keep the agreement "in strictest confidence."

On October 29, ConocoPhillips responded, acknowledging that it had "received and retained the Payment as a preliminary partial settlement," using language mirroring Williams's specification of the mode of acceptance of the terms in its October 18 letter.

(case continues)

ConocoPhillips stated that it "does not agree with all of the terms stated in [Williams's October 18 letter]" and "also do[es] not believe it would prove productive to conduct a letter writing campaign as to what the Payment represents or specific terms and conditions associated with the Payment." ConocoPhillips did object to one term in particular. It noted that it would voluntarily continue to support the joint-negotiating efforts in front of the FERC under the terms of the preexisting agreement on the issue, but it denied "[any] linkage whatsoever between ConocoPhillips['s] right to adequate assurance under the Agreement and ConocoPhillips'[s] performance with respect to" the independent joint-negotiating agreement. ConocoPhillips did not address the issue of whether or at what rate the cash payment would accrue interest.

After ConocoPhillips's October 29 letter, there was no further communication between the parties about the principal payment or accrual of interest until the FERC rate-making case finally came to a close in July 2007. In August 2007, ConocoPhillips invoiced Williams for reimbursement of the retroactively assessed Quality Bank degradation charges amounting to over $167 million, giving Williams credit for the $31 million prepayment as well as accrued interest at the LIBOR rate amounting to an additional $5 million, yielding a final billed amount of $131 million. Williams paid ConocoPhillips about $5 million less than the invoiced amount, claiming it deserved credit on the $31 million prepayment at the (higher) FERC interest rate which would amount to a $10 million interest credit. ConocoPhillips responded by revising its invoice to give no credit for any interest on the $31 million prepayment, claiming that no agreement had been reached on the issue.

Judicial Proceedings and the Superior Court's Holdings

Litigation ensued,[3] and in 2009 both parties moved for summary judgment on the effect of the October 2002 correspondence with respect to interest credits. Both parties agreed that "no issues of material fact prevent [ed] summary resolution of that issue." The superior court applied Ohio's substantive contract law pursuant to the Exchange Agreement's choice-of-law provision and found that there was no conflict with Alaska law because both states had adopted the Uniform Commercial Code.

The superior court granted summary judgment to Williams. The superior court concluded that under the Uniform Commercial Code §§ 2–207(1) & (2)[4] the October 18 and October 29 letters modified the Exchange Agreement and that the resulting contract required ConocoPhillips to credit Williams with interest on the prepayment at the higher FERC interest rate proposed by Williams in its October 18 letter. ConocoPhillips's October 29 reply letter constituted a "definite and seasonable expression of acceptance" of Williams's October 18 offer. Because ConocoPhillips acknowledged receipt and retention of the $31 million prepayment, mirroring the conditions of acceptance in Williams's October 18 offer, and explicitly objected to only one term of the offer, while remaining silent as to interest and otherwise just hinting at unspecified additional quibbles, the court found that ConocoPhillips "grudgingly but definitively assented" to Williams's reasonable proposal of FERC interest.

Neither party had briefed the application of UCC § 2–207. ConocoPhillips moved for reconsideration, and the superior court ordered further briefing. The superior court concluded that it "improvidently granted summary judgment that a contract was formed pursuant to [UCC § 2–207(1)]" because ConocoPhillips's "express rejection of Williams's joint-negotiating provision" renders disputable the material factual inference that ConocoPhillips's letter of October 29, 2002 was a definite and seasonable expression of acceptance. Nevertheless, the court again granted summary judgment for Williams, this time concluding that the parties' behavior after October 2002 created an implied-in-fact contract under UCC § 2–207(3)[5] and that one of the terms of that contract was the FERC interest that Williams had proposed on October 18 and ConocoPhillips had objectively accepted on October 29. In the alternative, the superior court held that, if this court were to reverse summary judgment as to contract formation, Williams would be entitled to recovery in quantum meruit for the benefit to ConocoPhillips of the time-value of the $31 million prepayment, measured by the average market rate for commercial paper during the relevant period.

The superior court granted Williams's motion to enlarge time to file a motion for attorney's fees and subsequently granted Williams full attorney's fees and court costs as the prevailing party under the Dispute Resolution Agreement between Williams and ConocoPhillips.

Arguments on Appeal

Both parties appeal. ConocoPhillips seeks reversal of summary judgment and entry of summary judgment in its own favor on a theory that no contract was formed for any interest rate. It also argues that no interest should be paid to Williams under a theory of quasi-contract or quantum meruit. Williams seeks reversal of the superior court's order on reconsideration rescinding the initial summary judgment order as improvidently granted, arguing that a contract was

(case continues)

formed under UCC §§ 2–207(1) & (2) as the superior court originally held. Williams also seeks reversal of the superior court's alternative quantum meruit holding, arguing that it should receive FERC interest rather than commercial-paper interest awarded in quantum meruit.

As to attorney's fees and court costs, ConocoPhillips argues that the superior court abused its discretion by granting Williams's motion to enlarge time to file a motion for attorney's fees, by enlarging Williams's time to file a cost bill with the Clerk of Court, and by granting full attorney's fees and costs without reducing the award for various reasons.

Standard of Review

We review rulings on motions for summary judgment de novo, "reading the record in the light most favorable to the non-moving party and making all reasonable inferences in its favor."[6] A party is entitled to summary judgment only if there is no genuine issue of material fact and if the party is entitled to judgment as a matter of law.[7] "A genuine issue of material fact exists where reasonable jurors could disagree on the resolution of a factual issue."[8] "Whether the evidence presented a genuine issue of material fact is a question of law that we independently review."[9] Determinations of which legal authorities apply in a case[10] and interpretations of what those legal authorities mean[11] are questions of law subject to de novo review. Contract interpretation is a question of law subject to de novo review.[12] When applying the de novo standard of review, we apply our "independent judgment to questions of law, adopting the rule of law most persuasive in light of precedent, reason, and policy."[13]

Discussion

A. UCC § 2–207 applies to this case to determine whether an original contract for sale of oil has been modified, and the additional requirements of § 2–209 regarding modification have been satisfied or waived.

The parties vigorously dispute which article and sections of the UCC govern this case. We conclude that the superior court correctly held that Article 2 of the UCC and § 2–207 apply to this case, notwithstanding ConocoPhillips's arguments that Article 9 or § 2–209 should govern to the exclusion of § 2–207.

Article 2 of the UCC, rather than Article 9, applies to this case

ConocoPhillips and Williams disagree as to which article of the UCC applies in this case: Article 2, which governs "transactions in goods" but not "any transaction intended to operate only as a security transaction,"[14] or Article 9, which governs transactions that "create a security interest in personal property or fixtures."[15] ConocoPhillips argues that Article 9 should apply because the parties intended to "create an interest in the $31 million to secure Williams'[s] future payment obligations." Williams argues that Article 2 should apply because the parties' correspondence in October 2002 was a modification of the original Exchange Agreement for the sale of goods and the $31 million was a prepayment of a future obligation under that contract.[16]

The superior court concluded that the $31 million was a prepayment as part of a contract modifying the original Exchange Agreement for a sale of goods and was thus covered by the provisions of Article 2. We agree.

First, the superior court concluded that the parties intended the $31 million and subsequent agreement to constitute a "prepayment of an unliquidated account payable" rather than a security transaction. We agree and conclude that there is no genuine issue of material fact on this point. ConocoPhillips styled the payment as a "preliminary partial settlement" in its letter of October 29. ConocoPhillips now argues that it meant to indicate that the payment was a partial settlement of ConocoPhillips's demands for an adequate security interest, but the record supports the superior court's contrary conclusion. The October 29 letter refers to the payment as a preliminary partial settlement, not of ConocoPhillips's demands for an adequate security interest, but rather of a dispute over the pricing provision of the Exchange Agreement with respect to retroactive Quality Bank adjustments.[17] The course of negotiations provides further support for this view. ConocoPhillips's first demand letter argued that Williams "now owes" ConocoPhillips $31 million under the Exchange Agreement's pricing provision due to forthcoming Quality Bank adjustments that would be made retroactive. Williams disagreed, arguing in its letter of October 8 that the money was "not currently due" under the contract. It was this dispute over when the retroactive assessment charges would come due that the parties intended to settle with the wire transfer and subsequent agreement. The superior court correctly interpreted the Exchange Agreement's adequate-assurances provision, not as providing a right to demand security interests, but rather as "invit[ing] a negotiation between the parties regarding the nature and extent of additional consideration for the [continued] sale of goods" with a "contemplated outcome [of] a modification of the original sale contract such that the ground for insecurity be abated or ameliorated." ConocoPhillips

(case continues)

treated the adequate-assurances provision similarly in its initial demand letter of October 4 when it cited the adequate-assurances provision and then laid out a number of options for settling the dispute going beyond mere security interests, including making a cash payment, establishing a trust, providing a letter of credit, and providing a security interest.

Second, as a matter of law, the Ohio courts have held that Article 2's scope, covering "transactions in goods," encompasses far more than just the original contract for sale and also includes subsequent agreements to modify the original contract, such as by establishing new payment schedules.[18] Thus, we conclude that the superior court correctly determined that, due to the parties' intent to modify the original contract for the sale of goods, Article 2 would apply to the question of contract formation in this case.

UCC § 2–207 applies to the contract modification in this case alongside the additional requirements of § 2–209

ConocoPhillips and Williams also disagree as to which specific sections of Article 2 of the UCC, if any, should apply in this case: § 2–209 to the *exclusion* of § 2–207, or § 2–209 in *addition* to § 2–207? We conclude that the superior court correctly held that § 2–209 should apply in addition to § 2–207, and we further conclude that the superior court correctly determined that the additional requirements of § 2–209 have been satisfied in this case.

As relevant here, UCC § 2–209, titled "Modification, Rescission and Waiver," establishes several important rules governing modification of contracts within the scope of Article 2 of the UCC. First, § 2–209(1) abrogates the common law and specifies that "[a]n agreement modifying a contract within [Article 2 of the UCC] needs no consideration to be binding."[19] Second, § 2–209(2) establishes that "[a] signed agreement which excludes modification or rescission except by a signed writing" is enforceable and that the agreement "cannot be otherwise modified or rescinded."[20] Finally, § 2–209(4) states that even if an attempted modification "does not satisfy the requirements of [subsection (2)] it can operate as a waiver."[21]

As discussed in greater detail in section IV.B below, UCC § 2–207, titled "Additional Terms in Acceptance or Confirmation," relaxes the common law mirror-image rule, which held that a contract could be formed only if the acceptance was a "mirror image" of the offer, replicating all of the terms of the offer without adding conflicting or additional terms.[22] Instead of requiring a mirror-image acceptance, UCC § 2–207(1) permits contract formation whenever "[a] definite and seasonable expression of acceptance is sent within a reasonable time even though it states terms additional to or different from those offered or agreed upon, unless acceptance is expressly made conditional on assent to the additional or different terms."[23]

ConocoPhillips argues that, even if Article 2 of the UCC were to apply in this case, UCC § 2–209 should govern to the exclusion of the lenient contract-formation rules of § 2–207.[24] ConocoPhillips reasons that § 2–207 addresses only initial contract formation and that any subsequent modification must satisfy § 2–209. ConocoPhillips contends modifications governed by § 2–209 can gain no help from § 2–207's limited alterations of the common law because § 2–209 leaves untouched the common law mirror-image rule for agreements modifying a contract.[25]

The superior court held that both § 2–209 and § 2–207 apply to the issue of contract modification in this case, and we agree. Precedent indicates that under Ohio law, § 2–207 applies to contract formation as well as subsequent contract modification.[26] Nor is Ohio alone in this conclusion; many other jurisdictions agree.[27] The text of § 2–209 supports this conclusion. It does not purport to supplant any other provisions of Article 2; rather, it is best read as providing five *additional* rules that apply to modifications of preexisting contracts, supplementing other applicable rules elsewhere in the Code. Nothing in § 2–209 purports to restrict the application of § 2–207 to contract modifications, nor does anything in § 2–207 indicate that its scope should be restricted to initial contract formation to the exclusion of subsequent contract formations modifying the initial contract. Therefore, we conclude that § 2–207 may apply alongside § 2–209 to modifications of a preexisting contract, at least under the facts presented in this case.[28]

The additional requirement of § 2–209(2) for a signed writing to modify the Exchange Agreement was satisfied or waived

ConocoPhillips argues that even if § 2–207 applies in this case, no agreement could have been reached to modify the Exchange Agreement because the negotiations in October 2002 did not comply with the signed-writing requirement of the Exchange Contract as made enforceable by § 2–209(2). Section 2–209(2) states that "[a] signed agreement which excludes modification or rescission except by a signed writing cannot be otherwise modified or rescinded,"[29] and the Exchange Agreement specifies that "[n]o changes, alterations, or modifications of the Agreement shall be effective unless agreed to in writing by an authorized representative of the Parties." The superior court concluded that the signed-writing requirement was satisfied in this case because "the parties

(*case continues*)

communicated their offers by signed letters" or, in the alternative, because ConocoPhillips's actions in accepting and retaining the $31 million and behaving "as if a contract had in fact been formed" constituted a waiver of the signed-writing requirement as permitted by § 2–209(4).[30] We agree.

ConocoPhillips argues that a signed writing within the meaning of § 2–209 must include express assent to all proposed terms and that ConocoPhillips never explicitly agreed to FERC interest. But nothing in § 2–209 indicates that a signed writing must include express assent to all proposals, and we have already concluded that § 2–209's requirements are additions to other Article 2 rules such as those in § 2–207. The signed-writing requirement of § 2–209(2) is not a back-door route to reintroduce the common law requirements that are modified by § 2–207.

ConocoPhillips also argues that its October 2002 correspondence could not be found to waive the signed-writing clause, citing *Saydell v. Geppetto's Pizza & Ribs Franchise Systems, Inc.*[31] But, as relevant here, that case indicates only that the delay of a franchisee in requesting the return of his franchise fee from the franchisor will not be held as a waiver of his right to recover the fee under the franchise contract at a later date.[32] Moreover, that case rests on the common law of contract rather than the UCC.[33] We agree with ConocoPhillips that waiver under § 2–209(4) may be accomplished only through affirmative statements or actions indicating intent to waive and not merely by silence or inaction of ambiguous import, but we also agree with the superior court that ConocoPhillips's actions and statements in this case could be construed as a matter of law only as indicating waiver of a signed-writing requirement. The following facts are decisive on this matter: ConocoPhillips's characterization of the payment as a "preliminary partial settlement" of the dispute over the Exchange Agreement's pricing provision, ConocoPhillips's use of the "received and retained" language mirroring the mode of acceptance laid down in Williams's offer, and the entire course of conduct following these negotiations in which the parties indicated their belief that the deal was done and that they could move on to other matters.

The Superior Court did not Err in its Initial Grant of Summary Judgment to Williams Under UCC § 2–207(1) and Should Not Have Rescinded its Order as Improvidently Granted

At common law, a contract could be formed only if the acceptance were a "mirror image" of the offer, replicating all of the terms of the offer without adding conflicting or additional terms.[34] Bowing to the "modern realities of commerce" in which parties exchange non-mirroring writings and nonetheless proceed as if the deal is done, the UCC abrogated the mirror-image rule and replaced it with the provisions of UCC § 2–207.[35] UCC § 2–207(1) permits contract formation whenever "[a] definite and seasonable expression of acceptance is sent within a reasonable time even though it states terms additional to or different from those offered or agreed upon, unless acceptance is expressly made conditional on assent to the additional or different terms."[36] The purpose of UCC § 2–207(1) is to bring commercial practice and legal doctrine closer together: "Under this Article a proposed deal which in commercial understanding has in fact been closed is recognized as a contract."[37]

When a contract is formed under UCC § 2–207(1), the terms of that contract generally include all of the offeror's terms "which are not contradicted by the acceptance."[38] The "additional terms" found in the acceptance "are to be construed as proposals for addition to the contract."[39] UCC § 2–207(2) governs the conditions under which those proposals for additional terms become part of the contract: When the contracting parties are merchants,[40] "the terms become part of the contract unless one of the following applies: (1) The offer expressly limits acceptance to the terms of the offer. (2) They materially alter it. (3) Notification of objection to them has already been given or is given within a reasonable time after notice of them is received."[41]

The superior court initially granted Williams's motion for summary judgment on the grounds that ConocoPhillips's letter of October 29 was a "definite and seasonable expression of acceptance" of the offer contained in Williams's letter of October 18, within the meaning of UCC § 2–207(1), and that the contract that formed included a term for FERC interest.[42] On reconsideration, the superior court concluded that "it should not have ruled summarily that Conoco's letter of October 29, 2002 was a 'definite and seasonable expression of acceptance,' given Conoco's express rejection of Williams's joint-negotiating provision. The court's characterization of Williams's term as non-material constitutes a disputable inference, which defeats summary judgment." We conclude that the superior court correctly granted summary judgment to Williams on the grounds that ConocoPhillips's letter of October 29 was a definite and seasonable expression of acceptance under § 2–207(1), and that its order on reconsideration was an understandable error resulting from an overabundance of caution.

(case continues)

Under UCC § 2–207(1), ConocoPhillips's reply letter of October 29 was a definite and seasonable acceptance leading to contract formation

The superior court correctly held in its grant of summary judgment that ConocoPhillips's letter of October 2943 was a "definite and seasonable expression of acceptance" of the offer made in Williams's letter of October 18, within the meaning of UCC § 2–207(1). In that letter, ConocoPhillips acknowledged that it had "received and retained the Payment as a preliminary partial settlement" of the disagreement over the pricing provision of the oil exchange contract, mirroring the language Williams used in its letter of October 18 specifying the mode of acceptance of its offer: "ConocoPhillips' [s] receipt and retention of the [money] shall constitute ConocoPhillips' [s] agreement with the terms set forth in this letter." ConocoPhillips did not state that its letter was a rejection of and counteroffer to Williams's offer of October 18 but rather indicated that the dispute over the pricing provision of the Exchange Agreement was now settled and that no further negotiation was necessary to close the deal. ConocoPhillips agreed to continue to honor the Exchange Agreement, thus lifting the threat to halt crude oil deliveries and indicating satisfaction with Williams's assurance. Finally, ConocoPhillips closed the letter by indicating that the matter was settled and the parties could move on with their regular business: "ConocoPhillips looks forward to continuing to work with Williams under the parties' various agreements."[44] All of these facts indicate that ConocoPhillips gave Williams a definite and seasonable expression of acceptance of its offer of October 18.

Our conclusion is not altered by the fact that ConocoPhillips's letter of October 29 seemed to object to the joint-negotiating provision,[45] as well as vaguely hint that "ConocoPhillips does not agree with all of the terms stated in your letter." The UCC makes clear that a "definite and seasonable expression of acceptance" results in contract formation "even though it states terms additional to or different from those offered."[46] Indeed, the entire purpose of UCC § 2–207(1) was to abrogate the common law mirror-image rule and allow for non-mirroring acceptances to nonetheless result in contract formation.[47]

To be sure, there is an outer limit to how much a return letter may differ from an offer and still result in contract formation under § 2–207(1), and the contours of that limit are not entirely clear from the Code, the case law, or treatises. UCC § 2–207(2) presupposes that a return document can be an acceptance under § 2–207(1) even though it includes additional terms that "materially alter" the offer,[48] and a respected treatise concludes that "it is clear that a document may be an acceptance and yet differ *substantially* from the offer."[49] A Court of Appeals in Ohio has held in *Alliance Wall Corp. v. Ampat Midwest Corp*. that a return letter does not constitute an acceptance under § 2–207(1) "where the parties disagree as to 'dickered for' terms."[50] The court did not define "dickered-for terms" but cited an example used in the learned treatise: No contract forms when a purchase order requests a certain amount of a commodity at $0 .10 per pound and the acknowledgment proposes $0.15 per pound.[51] Another example comes from *Alliance Wall itself*, where the court concluded that no contract formed under § 2–207(1) when time was of the essence, the parties did not reach agreement on a delivery date, the delivery date was of utmost importance to each party, and the return document struck the offeror's delivery date and inserted its own.[52] We conclude based on these authorities that, whatever the precise boundaries of the dickered-for exception to § 2–207(1) acceptance, the return document will qualify for that exception only if it differs *significantly* (not just materially) from the offer on a *sufficiently important* term.[53]

ConocoPhillips's letter of October 29 is clearly outside of those bounds and results in contract formation under § 2–207(1). First, the joint-negotiating provision was not sufficiently important in the context of the overall transaction to stymie § 2–207(1) contract formation. Unlike the delivery date in *Alliance Wall*, the joint-negotiating provision was not of utmost importance to the parties in this case, subjectively or objectively: From an objective perspective, it would be difficult to conclude that a term merely purporting to reaffirm ConocoPhillips's commitment to a preexisting joint-negotiating agreement is important in the context of the overall settlement. Indeed, the relative unimportance of this provision may explain why the parties indicate little subjective interest in the provision. The joint-negotiating term was first introduced into negotiations in Williams's letter of October 18. That the parties considered this provision to be relatively unimportant is confirmed by the parties' actions indicating that, in their minds, the deal was done following acceptance of the payment notwithstanding ConocoPhillips's objections.[54] Second, the degree of change to the contested term proposed by the October 29 acceptance is also relatively small. Unlike the 50% increase in price in the treatise hypothetical cited in *Alliance Wall*, there is relatively little distance between the offer to reinscribe a preexisting, independent agreement and the return proposal to voluntarily commit to continue performing a preexisting, independent agreement.

Simply put, ConocoPhillips's rejection of Williams's joint-negotiating provision was a relatively

(*case continues*)

unimportant and relatively small discrepancy within the context of the larger deal. The course of negotiation and the parties' post-negotiation behavior indicate that neither party thought the term sufficiently important or the change sufficiently great to require additional negotiation.[55] In short, the parties thought they were done negotiating, and the purpose of § 2–207(1) is to step in to supply a contract in just such a situation.

Finally, ConocoPhillips garners no help from § 2–207(1)'s narrow exception for acceptances "expressly made conditional on assent to the additional or different terms." That exception "has been construed narrowly" by courts[56] to apply "only to an acceptance which clearly reveals that the offeree is unwilling to proceed with the transaction unless he is assured of the offeror's assent to the additional or different terms therein."[57] Here, ConocoPhillips failed to state explicitly in its letter of October 29 that its acceptance was conditioned on Williams's assent to the omission of the joint-negotiating provision from the contract. ConocoPhillips instead appeared eager to proceed with the transaction as concluded and move on to address other issues. As ConocoPhillips told Williams in an email after receiving the $31 million transfer, "We can now focus our efforts on getting [the Quality Bank rate-making case] settled."

Accordingly, we conclude that the superior court's initial grant of summary judgment in favor of Williams under UCC § 2–207(1) was proper.

The terms of the resulting contract included a provision to credit the $31 million prepayment with interest at the FERC rate

When a contract is formed under UCC § 2–207(1), the terms of that contract generally include all of the offeror's terms "which are not contradicted by the acceptance."[58] We have previously held that an offeree's failure to "manifest any objection to the terms" of an offer or to "mak[e] its acceptance of the offer conditional on [the offeror's] assent to different terms" results in the offeror's terms "be[coming] part of the contract."[59] This position is amply supported by persuasive authority in other jurisdictions.[60] It is true that in response to *an entire offer*, mere silence or inaction generally do not indicate assent.[61] But silence *as to one term*, coupled with assent to the offer *as a whole*, cannot defeat inclusion of that term in the resulting contract.

The superior court's order on summary judgment correctly concluded that, on the facts of this case, ConocoPhillips's acceptance of October 29 formed a contract under § 2–207(1), the terms of which included a provision to credit Williams with interest on the $31 million principal prepayment at the rate prescribed by the FERC. ConocoPhillips's letter of October 29 was a definite and seasonable expression of acceptance resulting in contract formation. ConocoPhillips indicated that no further negotiation was necessary, thereby communicating acceptance of all but the explicitly rejected terms. ConocoPhillips did not object to Williams's provision specifying that the principal would accrue interest at the FERC rate but rather objected only to the joint-negotiating provision. Moreover, ConocoPhillips had already proposed that the prepayment would accrue interest (at the LIBOR rate) on October 17, so as a matter of law its silence as to Williams's counteroffer of October 18 for FERC interest constitutes assent to Williams's proposal. Finally, as the superior court correctly noted, "[t]he demand for FERC interest was not an implausible overreach" but rather was a reasonable proposal in light of the deal, such that its inclusion in the resulting contract is proper.[62] We conclude that the contract formed by ConocoPhillips's acceptance includes a term for FERC interest.

The superior court was correct in its first entry of summary judgment, and thus it should not have rescinded its initial order as improvidently granted

After granting Williams's motion for summary judgment and concluding that a contract for FERC interest was formed under § 2–207(1), the superior court granted ConocoPhillips's motion for reconsideration and ordered additional briefing on the UCC § 2–207 issues because the parties had not briefed them before. ConocoPhillips argued: (1) its letter of October 29 was not a definite and seasonable expression of acceptance within the meaning of § 2–207(1); (2) a contract under § 2–207(3) was formed in the course of performance but only for retention of the transferred money; (3) no agreement was reached for interest; and (4) the gap-filling interest provision of UCC § 9–207(3), which does not mandate accrual of interest on cash collateral obtained in a security transaction, governs this case. Williams supported the original grant of summary judgment.

On reconsideration, the court concluded that it had improvidently granted summary judgment because "it should not have ruled summarily that Conoco's letter of October 29, 2002 was a 'definite and seasonable expression of acceptance,' given Conoco's express rejection of Williams's joint-negotiating provision. The court's characterization of Williams's term as non-material constitutes a disputable inference, which defeats summary judgment."[63]

We conclude that the superior court correctly granted Williams summary judgment the first time around and erred in concluding on reconsideration

(*case continues*)

that it had improvidently granted summary judgment.[64] As we have already noted, the superior court's error was understandable, resulting from an abundance of caution. This is a complex case. But as we concluded in section IV.B.1 above, ConocoPhillips's rejection of Williams's joint-negotiating provision was neither a sufficiently large change in that provision nor a sufficiently important part of the overall bargain to vitiate contract formation under § 2–207(1). That conclusion of law is not a disputable inference of fact that could foreclose summary judgment .[65] Indeed, the parties do not dispute any material issues of fact, as the superior court correctly noted in its initial order granting Williams summary judgment. The only remaining disputes were about the legal conclusions to be drawn from those facts. Accordingly, we hold that the superior court's order rescinding summary judgment as improvidently granted was error. We reverse that order and affirm the initial order granting summary judgment on the basis of UCC § 2–207(1).[66]

The Superior Court did not Abuse its Discretion by Granting Attorney's Fees and Court Costs to Williams

ConocoPhillips and Williams agreed in a Dispute Resolution Agreement at the outset of litigation in 2007 that the "prevailing Party shall be entitled to recover reasonable attorney fees and court costs" to be "paid within twenty (20) days after receipt of an invoice for such costs containing documentation reasonably supporting the amounts." Both parties agree that Williams is the prevailing party in this litigation because Williams "obtained the relief it sought." But ConocoPhillips argues that the superior court abused its discretion by granting Williams's motion for leave to enlarge time to file a motion for attorney's fees, extending the time to file a cost bill with the Clerk of Court, and awarding full attorney's fees to Williams while rejecting ConocoPhillips's suggested reductions. We affirm the superior court's actions with regard to attorney's fees and court costs in all respects.

The superior court did not abuse its discretion by granting Williams additional time to file its motion for attorney's fees

Under Alaska Civil Rule 82, in order to recover an "award of attorney's fees pursuant to contract," the prevailing party must file a motion "within 10 days after the date shown in the clerk's certificate of distribution on the judgment" or within "such additional time as the court may allow."[67] Failure to file a timely motion "shall be construed as a waiver of the party's right to recover attorney's fees."[68] Alaska Civil Rule 6(b) further specifies that, where the Alaska Civil Rules require an act "be done at or within a specified time, the court for cause shown may at any time in its discretion upon motion made after the expiration of the specified period permit the act to be done where the failure to act was the result of excusable neglect."[69] Finally, Alaska Civil Rule 94 provides that the Civil Rules "are designed to facilitate business and advance justice" and they "may be relaxed or dispensed with by the court in any case where it shall be manifest to the court that a strict adherence to them will work injustice."[70]

In this case, the clerk's certificate of distribution on the final judgment shows the date February 9, 2012, and the ten-day period for Williams to file a motion for costs and attorney's fees ended on February 20 or 22, 2012.[71] Williams did not file within that period. On March 1 Williams filed a motion for leave to enlarge time to file a motion for attorney's fees, asking the court to accept an attached motion for $469,331.[68] in attorney's fees and several exhibits. Williams argued that its failure to meet the ten-day deadline was the result of excusable neglect under Rule 6(b) because it did not know that Rule 82's requirements would apply to its motion for attorney's fees under the Dispute Resolution Agreement. Williams further argued that the delay "does not impact the judicial proceedings in this case and it does not prejudice ConocoPhillips." ConocoPhillips argued that an attorney's mistake as to the applicable rules in this context cannot constitute excusable neglect.

The superior court granted Williams's motion to enlarge time to file a motion for attorney's fees, finding "excusable neglect and no prejudice." The superior court explained that "[t]he court was inartful" in its Final Judgment, in which the court stated that "Williams may move the Court for an award of attorney fees" as the "prevailing party pursuant to the parties' Dispute Resolution Agreement." The superior court explained that it "should also have struck the 'pursuant to' clause, because the attorney fee entitlement is pursuant to ARCP 82."

On appeal, ConocoPhillips argues that the superior court abused its discretion when it "took the blame for Williams'[s] failure to timely file its motion." ConocoPhillips reasoned that there was no excusable neglect for the late motion because Rule 82(c)'s applicability to contract-based fee motions was clear on the face of the Rule and that nothing in the superior court's final judgment created ambiguity on that issue. ConocoPhillips also reasoned that the mere lack of prejudice to ConocoPhillips alone cannot sustain a finding of excusable neglect. We review

(case continues)

a trial court's disposition of a motion to enlarge time for abuse of discretion.[72]

We affirm the superior court's order granting Williams's motion to enlarge time to file a motion for attorney's fees. The superior court certainly did not abuse its discretion in this case. The delay of ten days in this case is well within the zone of permissible discretion suggested by our precedent. In *T & G Aviation, Inc. v. Footh*,[73] we held that the superior court did not abuse its discretion by allowing a party to file a motion for attorney's fees 70 days late, even in the absence of a persuasive explanation for the delay.[74] Indeed, when there is no showing of prejudice, it may be an abuse of discretion not to allow an untimely motion for attorney's fees on facts such as those presented in this case.[75] In short, Williams's neglect in failing to recognize the applicability of Rule 82(c)'s deadlines is "that type of excusable inadvertence or neglect common to all who share the ordinary frailties of [hu]mankind,"[76] and the superior court did not abuse its discretion by granting Williams's motion to enlarge time to file a motion for attorney's fees.

The superior court did not abuse its discretion by granting Williams additional time to file its motion for court costs

Alaska Civil Rule 79(b) requires[77] a prevailing party seeking to recover costs to "file and serve an itemized and verified cost bill, showing the date costs were incurred, within 10 days after the date shown in the clerk's certificate of distribution on the judgment or such additional time as the court may allow." The rule further specifies that "[f]ailure of a party to file and serve a cost bill will be construed as a waiver of the party's right to recover costs."[78] Just as discussed previously with regard to Rule 82(c) motions for attorney's fees, Rules 6(b) and 94 provide further discretionary flexibility on a showing of excusable neglect or when a strict adherence to the ten-day limit would "work injustice."[79]

Eight to ten days after it would have been due under Rule 79(b)'s ten-day period,[80] Williams filed a motion for leave to enlarge the time to file its motion for attorney's fees on March 1, 2012. Although this motion did not mention Civil Rule 79 by name, it clearly indicated that Williams was seeking compensation for court costs. Specifically, that motion mentioned the difficulty Williams experienced assessing fees and costs; included a costs calculation of $10,489.05 as an exhibit attached to the motion; included a section for the clerk's ruling on the cost bill and a separate line for "recoverable costs" of $10,489.05 in the attached motion for attorney's fees; and it concluded the motion for attorney's fees by asking for "$479,819.73 as reasonable attorney fees and court costs." ConocoPhillips argued that Williams had waived any right to costs because "[c]ost bills are considered by the clerk pursuant to a separate procedure, and Williams may not 'piggy-back' an untimely cost bill onto its attempt to file an untimely fee motion." The superior court granted Williams's motion for leave to enlarge time to file a motion for attorney's fees and also "deemed filed" the motion for attorney's fees as well as "exhibits supporting [Williams's motion for attorney's fees]," which included the cost bill.

Six months later, and eight months following the expiration of the ten-day period under Rule 79, the superior court ruled on Williams's motion for attorney's fees and awarded Williams full attorney's fees. In that order, the court also noted that "Williams should submit its cost bill to the Clerk of Court for a reasonableness review." ConocoPhillips objected that "[t]his *sua sponte* grant of an 8–month extension of time was improper" because Williams had never requested it and because Williams did not show excusable neglect. The Clerk of Court granted $6,441.70 in court costs to Williams, and the superior court rejected ConocoPhillips's motion for review of cost award. The superior court's final judgment on attorney's fees and costs included $6,441.70 of court costs.

ConocoPhillips argues that the superior court abused its discretion when it granted Williams an extension of time to file its cost bill. ConocoPhillips reasons that Rule 6(b) allows extension after the time period lapses only " 'upon motion' establishing that 'the failure to act was the result of excusable neglect.' "Under its view, neither condition was met here because the court awarded an extension sua sponte and because there was no showing of excusable neglect for such a long delay. Williams argues that it sought an extension of the Rule 79 deadline by including costs in its motion for leave to enlarge time to file a motion for attorney's fees and that this same motion showed excusable neglect. It argues that the superior court "deemed filed" its cost bill, as an attached exhibit, when it granted its motion for leave to enlarge time for filing a motion for attorney's fees, and that the court's subsequent invitation to file its cost bill with the Clerk of Court was within the court's discretionary authority.

We conclude that the superior court did not abuse its discretion in granting Williams leave to file a late cost bill with the Clerk of Court. In *Vazquez v. Campbell*,[81] we confronted a situation in which the prevailing plaintiff timely filed a sufficiently detailed cost bill, not as a cost bill presented to the Clerk

(*case continues*)

of Court as required by Rule 79(b), but rather as a motion to the superior court.[82] We held that the prevailing party had "substantially complied with the requirements of rule 79" because "[i]f the superior court had wished, it could have referred the question of costs to the clerk for an initial decision."[83] Unlike in *Vazquez*, Williams did not timely file its motion for court costs under Rule 79(b) (instead, it filed its cost bill with the Clerk of Court eight months late), and it is unclear on this record whether its cost accounting associated with its motion for leave to enlarge time to file a motion for attorney's fees was sufficiently detailed to meet the requirements of Rule 79. Nevertheless, we conclude that the superior court did not abuse its discretion in granting an extension to Williams to file its cost bill with the Clerk of Court. ConocoPhillips does not argue that it was prejudiced by the delay.[84] It had a chance to object when the final cost bill was submitted, and it even succeeded in reducing the bill significantly. In this case, because of the lack of prejudice and because the motion for leave to enlarge time to file a motion for attorney's fees had objective indications on its face that Williams was also seeking an extension of time to seek court costs, we conclude that the superior court did not abuse its discretion in granting Williams an extension of the Rule 79(b) deadline.

The superior court did not abuse its discretion by refusing to reduce the award of attorney's fees

This court reviews an award of attorney's fees for an abuse of discretion.[85] Under this standard, "[t]he trial court has broad discretion in awarding attorney's fees; this court will not find an abuse of discretion absent a showing that the award was arbitrary, capricious, manifestly unreasonable, or stemmed from improper motive."[86] When evaluating a motion for attorney's fees, "a court should carefully consider all factors relevant to reasonableness."[87] There is no exhaustive list of factors a court may consider to determine whether the attorney's fees claimed are objectively reasonable, but the factors listed in Rule 82(b)(3) may be instructive.[88] Those factors include "the reasonableness of the claims and defenses pursued by each side" and "vexatious or bad faith conduct."[89] This court reviews "a trial court's fact-based determinations regarding whether attorney's fees are reasonable for an abuse of discretion."[90]

After granting Williams's motion for enlargement of time to file a motion for attorney's fees, the superior court granted Williams's motion for attorney's fees in the full amount of $465,451. As relevant here, ConocoPhillips had argued that the superior court should reduce the attorney's fee award by 50% because Williams's legal arguments had been rejected by the superior court at every stage of litigation. ConocoPhillips also sought an additional reduction for fees spent relative to Williams's (unsuccessful) claim for $30 million in damages resulting from ConocoPhillips's alleged tortious conduct during litigation. The superior court rejected ConocoPhillips's requests for reductions in the award of attorney's fees. The superior court "decline[d] to adjust the fee merely because arguments were ultimately rejected," reasoning that it would be "unfair to reduce the Williams fee by 50 percent, given that it prevailed on the relief it sought" because "the case was very difficult" and "[t]he parties' briefing was high quality and helpful." The superior court noted that "if Williams strayed in its initial briefing, so too did Conoco." The superior court also rejected the request for a reduction in fees relative to the tort claim, reasoning that "[b]oth [parties] adopted aggressive positions," that "[n]either party spent great time or energy on these positions," and that it had already concluded that it would "decline to adjust the fee merely because arguments were ultimately rejected." ConocoPhillips raises three primary arguments on appeal.

First, ConocoPhillips argues that the superior court abused its discretion by not reducing the award of attorney's fees in light of the fact that the superior court resolved the dispute on different legal grounds than those advanced by the prevailing party. But ConocoPhillips cites no authority for the proposition that such a reduction should be forthcoming simply because the prevailing party advocates a legal position not adopted by the court. Indeed, ConocoPhillips states that this is an issue of first impression in this court. Whether or not this is truly an issue of first impression, we reject ConocoPhillips's proposed rule. Although the superior court ultimately rested its orders on grounds not directly advanced by Williams,[91] the superior court necessarily considered the issues raised in Williams's briefs in making its determinations.[92] And the superior court found that Williams's briefing was of "high quality and helpful." We conclude that the superior court did not abuse its discretion by refusing to reduce an award of attorney's fees when the court rested its orders on legal grounds not advanced by the prevailing party. Fee-shifting contracts and Rule 82 already create ex ante uncertainty about who will bear the ultimate burden of litigation expenses; we are unwilling to create additional uncertainty as to the ultimate size of litigation expenses by telling litigants that they must accurately predict the exact legal basis of the

(*case continues*)

court's holding in order to receive a full award as the prevailing party.

Second, ConocoPhillips argues that the superior court, in stating that "if Williams strayed in its initial briefing, so too did Conoco," abused its discretion by "obligat[ing] the losing party to identify the prevailing party's winning argument." But ConocoPhillips misinterprets the superior court's statement. The superior court did not give ConocoPhillips the burden of identifying the correct legal theory in order to prevail on its motion to reduce the award of attorney's fees for Williams's failure to identify the correct legal theory. Rather, the superior court merely used ConocoPhillips's parallel failure to do so as evidence that the theories advanced by Williams were not unreasonable such that no reduction in attorney's fees would be warranted. Accordingly, we reject ConocoPhillips's argument and conclude that the superior court did not abuse its discretion by relying on such a parallel failure as evidence supporting the reasonableness of the arguments advanced by the prevailing party.

Finally, ConocoPhillips argues that the superior court abused its discretion by refusing to reduce the award of attorney's fees by the amount Williams spent pursuing its unsuccessful tort claim: $14,888.96. ConocoPhillips reasons that its own litigation position (that no contract was formed and no interest credit was due) was reasonable and "*the central issue in the case*" while Williams's tort claim was "utterly unsupportable," such that the superior court made a clearly erroneous factual finding when it characterized both as "aggressive positions" that nonetheless were reasonable in the context of the litigation. (Emphasis in original.) But beyond its bare assertion that "Williams' [s] attempt to recover $30 million was utterly unsupportable," ConocoPhillips does not offer any reason to believe that the tort claim was frivolous or was "not reasonably intended to advance the litigation."[93] We conclude that ConocoPhillips has not met its burden of showing that the superior court's factual finding on this issue was clearly erroneous or that its order refusing to reduce attorney's fees was an abuse of discretion.

Conclusion

Because the superior court's decision on summary judgment was correct and should not have been rescinded on reconsideration, the initial grant of summary judgment is REINSTATED and AFFIRMED. Because we conclude that the superior court was right in its initial grant of summary judgment, we do not reach the UCC § 2–207(3) or quantum meruit holdings from its order on reconsideration. The superior court's rulings on attorney's fees and costs are AFFIRMED.

---

1. LIBOR, or the London Interbank Offered Rate, is the interest rate that large London banks charge each other for short-term loans.
2. The parties expected the FERC to impose interest on any retrospectively assessed degradation charges. The FERC rate imposed by regulation was expected to be substantially higher than the LIBOR rate.
3. In September 2007, the parties entered into a Quality Bank Interest Dispute Resolution Agreement in which the parties agreed to "jointly file for a Declaratory Judgment Order" and to limit discovery and briefing. As relevant to the attorney's fee dispute in this case, the parties also agreed that "[t]he prevailing Party in the Declaratory Judgment proceeding shall be entitled to recover reasonable attorney fees and court costs" to be "paid within twenty (20) days after receipt of an invoice for such costs containing documentation reasonably supporting the amounts."
4. Sections 2–207(1) & (2) of the Uniform Commercial Code, codified and slightly amended at Ohio Rev.Code Ann. § 1302.10(A) & (B) (West 2013), state:(1) A definite and seasonable expression of acceptance or a written confirmation which is sent within a reasonable time operates as an acceptance even though it states terms additional to or different from those offered or agreed upon, unless acceptance is expressly made conditional on assent to the additional or different terms.(2) The additional terms are to be construed as proposals for addition to the contract. Between merchants such terms become part of the contract unless:(a) the offer expressly limits acceptance to the terms of the offer;(b) they materially alter it; or(c) notification of objection to them has already been given or is given within a reasonable time after notice of them is received.
5. Section 2–207(3) of the UCC, codified and slightly amended at Ohio Rev.Code Ann. § 1302.10(C) (West 2013), states:(3) Conduct by both parties which recognizes the existence of a contract is sufficient to establish a contract for sale although the writings of the parties do not otherwise establish a contract. In such case the terms of the particular contract consist of those terms on which the writings of the parties agree, together with any supplementary terms incorporated under any other provisions of this Act.
6. *Witt v. State, Dep't of Corr.*, 75 P.3d 1030, 1033 (Alaska 2003). The same standard applies to orders granting, denying, and reconsidering summary judgment, all of which are presented on appeal in this case.
7. *Zeman v. Lufthansa German Airlines*, 699 P.2d 1274, 1280 (Alaska 1985).
8. *Kalenka v. Jadon, Inc.*, 305 P.3d 346, 349 (Alaska 2013) (quoting *Burnett v. Covell*, 191 P.3d 985, 990 (Alaska 2008)).
9. *Id.*
10. *Cf. L.D.G., Inc. v. Brown*, 211 P.3d 1110, 1118 (Alaska 2009) ("Where 'the admissibility of evidence turns on whether the trial court applied the correct legal standard, we review the [lower] court's decision using our independent legal judgment.' "(quoting *Marsingill v. O'Malley*, 128 P.3d 151, 155–56 (Alaska 2006))).

(case continues)

11. *Cf. id.* ("Issues regarding the constitutionality of statutes are questions of law that we review de novo. We review the interpretation of a statute de novo "(citing *Alaskans For Efficient Gov't, Inc. v. Knowles*, 91 P.3d 273, 275 (Alaska 2004); *State v. Alaska Civil Liberties Union*, 978 P.2d 597, 603 (Alaska 1999))).
12. *Villars v. Villars*, 277 P.3d 763, 768 (Alaska 2012) (citing *Burns v. Burns*, 157 P.3d 1037, 1039 (Alaska 2007)).
13. *Russell ex rel. J.N. v. Virg–In*, 258 P.3d 795, 802 (Alaska 2011) (quoting *Jacob v. State, Dep't of Health & Soc. Servs., Office of Children's Servs.*, 177 P.3d 1181, 1184 (Alaska 2008)) (internal quotation marks omitted).
14. OHIO REV.CODE ANN. § 1302.02 (West 2013) (codifying U.C.C. § 2–102).
15. *Id.* § 1309.109(A)(1) (codifying U.C.C. § 9–109).
16. The parties vigorously dispute this preliminary issue because of their perception that Article 2 and Article 9 differ substantially in how they would apply to this case. ConocoPhillips argues that Article 9 imposes no duty to give credit for interest on cash collateral absent any actual interest earned and that any agreement for interest would have to be established under traditional common law rules of offer and acceptance. Williams seeks to benefit from the relaxed contract-formation provisions of § 2–207 to find a contract for FERC interest resulting from the October 2002 correspondence. Because we hold in favor of Williams under § 2–207(1), we do not reach ConocoPhillips's argument about the outcome of the case under Article 9.
17. Five years later, ConocoPhillips continued to view the $31 million payment as an "advance," at least in an internal email.
18. *See, e.g., May Co. v. Trusnik*, 375 N.E.2d 72, 74–75 (Ohio App.1977) (holding that Article 2 governed an installment payment agreement modifying an original sales contract for consumer goods after the buyer defaulted under the original payment plan).
19. OHIO REV.CODE ANN. § 1302.12(A) (West 2013) (codifying U.C.C. § 2–209(1)).
20. *Id.* § 1302.12(B) (codifying U.C.C. § 2–209(2)).
21. *Id.* § 1302.12(D) (codifying U.C.C. § 2–209(4)).
22. RESTATEMENT (SECOND) OF CONTRACTS § 59 (1981); 1 JAMES J. WHITE, ROBERT S. SUMMERS & ROBERT A. HILLMAN, UNIFORM COMMERCIAL CODE § 2:9, at 79 (6th ed.2012).
23. OHIO REV.CODE ANN. § 1302.10(A) (codifying U.C.C. § 2–207(1)).
24. Williams argues that ConocoPhillips failed to make this argument to the superior court and thus should not be able to raise it for the first time in this court. But a review of the record reveals that ConocoPhillips did argue to the superior court in its motion for reconsideration that "UCC 2–209 preempts UCC 2–207" and styled its arguments about UCC § 2–207's application to this case in the alternative. Thus, the superior court was premature in stating in its order on motion for reconsideration that "Conoco and Williams now agree that UCC section 2–207 is applicable." We conclude that ConocoPhillips did not waive its § 2–209 argument.
25. ConocoPhillips presses this point because, in its view, § 2–209 and common law rules of acceptance would mean that "[e]ven if ConocoPhillips'[s] October 29 letter had assented to all terms of Williams' [s] October 18 letter except the FERC interest term, UCC § 2–209 would still require that the parties *expressly* assent to FERC interest." Because we hold that § 2–207 applies to the contract modification in this case, we do not address what the outcome would be under common law rules of contract formation and modification.
26. *See Energy Mktg. Servs., Inc. v. Homer Laughlin China Co.*, 186 F.R.D. 369, 375 (S.D.Ohio 1999) (applying the substantive contract law of Ohio and analyzing under UCC § 2–207 a non-mirroring acceptance of an offer to modify a preexisting contract), *aff'd*, 229 F.3d 1151 (6th Cir.2000).
27. *See, e.g., Step–Saver Data Sys., Inc. v. Wyse Tech.*, 939 F .2d 91, 98 (3d Cir.1991) ("In the absence of evidence demonstrating an express intent to adopt a writing as a final expression of, *or a modification to*, an earlier agreement, we find UCC § 2–207 to provide the appropriate legal rules for determining whether such an intent can be inferred from continuing with the contract after receiving a writing containing additional or different terms." (emphasis added)); *U.S. Surgical Corp. v. Orris, Inc.*, 5 F.Supp.2d 1201, 1206 (D.Kan.1998) (same), *aff'd sub nom. U.S. Surgical Corp. v. Lorris, Inc.*, 185 F.3d 885 (Fed.Cir.1999); *Ariz. Retail Sys., Inc. v. Software Link, Inc.*, 831 F.Supp. 759, 764 (D.Ariz.1993) (applying § 2–207 and § 2–209 to an attempted contract modification).
28. ConocoPhillips cites no authority for the proposition that § 2–209 displaces § 2–207 and requires that all modifications of preexisting contracts satisfy the old common law mirror-image rule. Those cases that ConocoPhillips does cite do not address this issue but rather establish a distinct proposition: because all modifications (like all contracts) require mutual assent, unilateral modification of a preexisting contract is impossible and mere silence in the face of an offer to modify a contract is ineffective to convey acceptance of the offered modification. *See U.S. Surgical Corp.*, 5 F.Supp.2d at 1206 (when seller attached a label to the packaging of surgical equipment purporting to limit the customer to a single use of the equipment the buyer had already purchased pursuant to contract, no contract modification occurred simply by performing the original agreement and opening the package); *Ariz. Retail Sys., Inc.*, 831 F.Supp. at 764 (when seller attached a shrink-wrap license to software packaging that buyer had already contracted to purchase, merely opening the package and continuing to perform the original contract did not function as a modification for lack of mutual assent); *Wachter Mgmt. Co. v. Dexter & Chaney, Inc.*, 144 P.3d 747, 752–55 (Kan.2006) (same); *Jones v. Best*, 950 P.2d 1, 5 (Wash.1998) (when a realtor and seller of real property had a preexisting contract for realty services, the realtor's proposed modification to his commission did not effect a modification because the seller's silence to the proposal did not manifest mutual assent); *Alaska Pac. Trading Co. v. Eagon Forest Prods., Inc.*, 933 P.2d 417, 420 (Wash.App.1997) (when seller sent a proposal for modification of preexisting contract to buyer and buyer did not respond, no contract modification occurred because modification requires mutual assent). These cases do not establish what *type* of mutual assent is required to effectuate a contract modification—mirror-image acceptance as under the common law or something less as permitted by § 2–207(1). Accordingly, ConocoPhillips's unsupported assertion that § 2–209 displaces § 2–207 with regard to contract modification does not affect our conclusion to the contrary, which is supported by the case law of Ohio and other jurisdictions as well as a commonsense reading of the statute.
29. OHIO REV.CODE ANN. § 1302.12(B) (West 2013) (codifying U.C.C. § 2–209(2)).
30. *Id.* § 1302.12(D) (codifying U.C.C. § 2–209(4)) ("Although an attempt at modification does not satisfy the [signed-writing] requirement of [subsection (2)] it can operate as a waiver.").
31. 652 N.E.2d 218, 225–26 (Ohio App.1994).
32. *Id.*
33. *Id.*

(case continues)

34. RESTATEMENT (SECOND) OF CONTRACTS § 59 (1981); 1 WHITE, SUMMERS & HILLMAN, *supra* note 22, § 2:9, at 79.
35. 1 WHITE, SUMMERS & HILLMAN, *supra* note 22, § 2:9, at 79. *See also* OHIO REV.CODE ANN. § 1302. 10 cmt. 1 (replicating U.C.C. § 2–207 cmt. 1) (indicating that this section was "intended to deal with" a situation in which "the seller's form contains terms different from or additional to those set forth in the buyer's form"); *Idaho Power Co. v. Westinghouse Elec. Corp.*, 596 F.2d 924, 926 (9th Cir.1979) ("Section 207 rejects the 'mirror image' rule, and converts a common law counteroffer into an acceptance even though it states additional or different terms.").
36. OHIO REV.CODE ANN. § 1302.10(A) (West 2013).
37. *Id.* cmt. 2 (replicating U.C.C. § 2–207 cmt. 2).
38. 1 WHITE, SUMMERS & HILLMAN, *supra* note 22, § 2:11, at 89; *see also id.* at 89 n. 1 (collecting cases).
39. OHIO REV.CODE ANN. § 1302.10(B) (codifying U.C.C. § 2–207(2)).
40. OHIO REV.CODE ANN. § 1302.01(A)(5) (codifying U.C.C. § 2–104(1)) (" 'Merchant' means a person who deals in goods of the kind or otherwise by the person's occupation holds the person out as having knowledge or skill peculiar to the practices or goods involved in the transaction").
41. *Id.* § 1302.10(B) (codifying U.C.C. § 2–207(2)).
42. The superior court's conclusion depended on six important facts, as summarized in its order on motion for reconsideration: 1. Contrary to Conoco's litigation position, Conoco's October 29 letter failed to state it was a rejection of and counteroffer to Williams's October 18 offer. 2. Conoco affirmatively indicated receipt and retention of the wire transfer, quoting Williams's specified means of acceptance. 3. Conoco stated that while it did not agree with all of Williams's proposed terms, no further negotiation was necessary. It thereby reasonably communicated its acceptance of all but the explicitly rejected joint-negotiation provision in the Williams counteroffer. 4. Conoco explicitly stated that it "received and retained the payment as a preliminary partial settlement" of Williams's contingent liability in the FERC proceeding. By this rhetoric, Conoco suggested that the matter was settled. This would only occur if Conoco accepted Williams's counteroffer. 5. Conoco stated no objection to Williams's interest provision. Conoco had previously proposed that the payment would accrue interest in its initial offer on October 17. 6. Conoco closed its letter by indicating satisfaction with Williams's proffered assurance and agreeing to continue to honor the exchange agreement, thereby lifting its threat to cease deliveries of crude oil to Williams's refinery. This language is inconsistent with a call for further negotiation.
43. We note that ConocoPhillips also sent a reply email on October 18 following receipt of the wire transfer and Williams's letter specifying the terms of the offer, in which ConocoPhillips acknowledged receipt and concluded that it could "now focus [its] efforts on getting [the FERC rate-making case] settled." We do not reach the issue of which reply led to contract formation under § 2–207(1): the email of October 18 or the subsequent letter of October 29. We follow the influential and persuasive authority of other jurisdictions in deciding that "[w]e *see* no need to parse the parties's [sic] various actions to decide exactly when the parties formed a contract" under § 2–207(1). *Step–Saver Data Sys., Inc. v. Wyse Tech.*, 939 F.2d 91, 98 (3d Cir.1991). Rather, the content of both documents informs the analysis and drives our conclusion that a contract was formed under § 2–207(1).
44. That ConocoPhillips considered the matter settled as per the October 18 letter is further supported by an email sent from ConocoPhillips to Williams on October 18: "We received your letter and our treasury guys just confirmed receipt of the funds. We can now focus our efforts on getting [the] Quality Bank [rate-making case] settled."
45. For the purposes of this analysis, we assume arguendo that ConocoPhillips actually rejected Williams's joint-negotiating term. However, on this record, that is far from certain. Williams had offered as a term in its letter of October 18 that "ConocoPhillips agrees that it will continue good faith efforts to resolve all Quality Bank issues through negotiated settlement and vigorous support of the Eight–Party Joint Defense Position before FERC and the RCA." In its reply letter of October 29, ConocoPhillips stated that it "is continuing 'good faith efforts to resolve all Quality Bank issues through negotiated settlement and vigorous support for the Eight–Party Joint Defense Position before FERC and the RCA,' "but it insisted that this obligation was "[c]ompletely independent of the Payment" and that "[t]here is no linkage whatsoever" between ConocoPhillips demanding adequate assurances and the joint-negotiating position in the rate-making case. We note that the superior court concluded that ConocoPhillips "rejected" the joint-negotiating term and are mindful of the need to make all reasonable inferences in favor of the non-moving party when considering a grant of summary judgment. *Witt v. State, Dep't of Corr.*, 75 P.3d 1030, 1033 (Alaska 2003). But we note that if the best view of the facts were that ConocoPhillips did *not* reject the joint-negotiating provision, our conclusion about contract formation under § 2–207(1) would be even stronger.
46. OHIO REV.CODE ANN. § 1302.10(A) (codifying U.C.C. § 2–207(1)).
47. *Id.* § 1302.10 cmt. 1 (replicating U.C.C. § 2–207 cmt. 1).
48. UCC § 2–207(2) governs when additional, non-mirroring terms from a return letter constituting an acceptance under § 2–207(1) will become part of the contract thus formed. UCC § 2–207(2)(b) indicates that, among merchants, non-mirroring terms automatically become part of the contract unless those terms "materially alter" the contract formed under § 2–207(1). *See also* 1 WHITE, SUMMERS & HILLMAN, *supra* note 22, § 2:10, at 83.
49. 1 WHITE, SUMMERS & HILLMAN, *supra* note 22, § 2:10, at 83 (emphasis added).
50. 477 N.E.2d 1206, 1211 (Ohio App.1984). *See also* 1 WHITE, SUMMERS & HILLMAN, *supra* note 22, § 2:17, at 112 ("Not all return documents are 2–207(1) 'acceptances.' If the return document diverges significantly as to a dickered term, it cannot be a 2–207(1) acceptance.").
51. *See* 477 N.E.2d at 1211 n. 5; 1 WHITE, SUMMERS & HILLMAN, *supra* note 22, § 2:17, at 112–13.
52. 477 N.E.2d at 1210. In that particular case, the delivery date appears to have been a crucial and hotly disputed term throughout negotiations. Indeed, the delivery date "appears to have been more important to the buyer than was the exact price" and "[t]he seller appeared to be just as adamant not to be bound to any particular date." *Id.*
53. The parties offer competing interpretations of the scope of the dickered-for exception, both of which we reject.Williams argues that a dickered-for term is one which is "both material and previously negotiated between the parties" and that the joint-negotiating provision cannot qualify because it was not negotiated prior to the October 18 letter. Not only does Williams not cite any authority for this proposition, but it also conflicts with the established example of a dickered-for term in the *Alliance Wall* case, where the court cited as an example of a dickered-for term a price change that had not previously been disputed by the parties. *See* 477 N.E.2d at 1211 n. 5. ConocoPhillips argues that dickered-for terms are defined in opposition to "standard boiler-plate terms" and encompass

(*case continues*)

all those terms "that are unique to each transaction such as price, quality, quantity, or delivery terms as compared to the usual unbargained terms on the reverse side [of a form] concerning remedies, arbitration, and the like[.]" (Alterations in original.) ConocoPhillips argues that "[i]n this case, *all* of the terms in the parties' correspondence were 'dickered for' terms." (Emphasis in original.) But a distinction between front-side terms and reverse-side or boilerplate terms is not useful in this context, where the parties have negotiated every provision of the contract rather than engaging in a traditional battle of the forms. Under ConocoPhillips's theory, § 2–207(1) has no application outside of the boilerplate context. Yet nothing in the text of § 2–207 would limit itself in such a way, and courts have often applied § 2–207 in situations not involving boilerplate forms but rather detailed negotiation among sophisticated parties, on the theory that § 2–207 applies whenever an acceptance does not mirror an offer. *See, e.g., Energy Mktg. Servs., Inc. v. Homer Laughlin China Co.*, 186 F.R.D. 369 (S.D.Ohio 1999) (stating that, as a matter of Ohio contract law, UCC § 2–207(1) applies "when an acceptance differs in terms from an offer," *id.* at 374, including where the parties had negotiated a contract amendment over the course of years, *id.* at 371–73), *aff'd*, 229 F.3d 1151 (6th Cir.2000). We reject any interpretation of the dickered-for terms exception that would swallow the more general § 2–207(1) rule and bring common law rules in through the back door.Accordingly, we reject both parties' proffered definitions of the scope of the dickered-for terms exception in favor of our formulation here of the outer bounds of the exception, whatever its precise definition.

54. The superior court concluded that "Conoco accepted the proffered $31 million and behaved as if a contract had in fact been formed."

55. In addition to ConocoPhillips's purported rejection of the joint-negotiating provision, ConocoPhillips also stated in its letter of October 29 that it "d[id] not agree with all of the terms stated in [Williams's] letter" but that it "also d[id] not believe it would prove productive to conduct a letter writing campaign as to what the Payment represents or specific terms and conditions associated with the Payment." In the words of the superior court in its order on motion for summary judgment, such "seemingly studied ambiguity" hinting at "undisclosed issues with at least one term of Williams' [s] counteroffer" cannot preclude the conclusion that there was a definite and seasonable expression of acceptance in this case. As the superior court properly concluded, "If Conoco perceived no need to further discuss the terms Williams proposed, but elected to retain the $31 million, the reasonable implication is that Conoco grudgingly but definitively assented to the Williams terms, except those explicitly rejected." Vague hints of disagreement combined with acceptance of payment in the form prescribed by the offer and explicit disagreement with one term cannot be allowed to convert an otherwise-definite expression of acceptance into an ineffective counteroffer. To hold to the contrary would be to undermine the guiding principle of interpretation of UCC § 2–207: preventing one party from obtaining an "unearned advantage." *See* 1 White, Summers & Hillman, *supra* note 22, § 2:9, at 81. In order for objections in a return letter to foreclose contract formation under § 2–207(1), those objections must be sufficiently explicit as to which provisions they pertain to, or sufficiently clear as to the respondent's intent to reject the offer in general. *See id.* § 2:11, at 89 (arguing that silence in a § 2–207(1) acceptance as to a term in the offer constitutes grudging acceptance of that term); *id.* at 89 n. 1 (collecting cases). Here, ConocoPhillips never characterized its letter of October 29 as a rejection in general, and the only specific term it registered disagreement with was the joint-negotiating provision. Accordingly, its exercise in studied ambiguity cannot succeed where its more specific objections failed. As the superior court correctly concluded, "Conoco grudgingly but definitively assented to the Williams terms, except those explicitly rejected."

56. *Idaho Power Co. v. Westinghouse Elec. Corp.*, 596 F.2d 924, 926 (9th Cir.1979).

57. *Dorton v. Collins & Aikman Corp.*, 453 F.2d 1161, 1168 (6th Cir.1972). Indeed, such a narrow interpretation is required by the nature of UCC § 2–207(1) as abrogating the mirror-image rule of the common law: If non-mirroring acceptances were construed too liberally as being conditioned on the assent of the offeror, the rigidity of the mirror-image rule would re-enter the Code through the back door of an exception to § 2–207(1).

58. 1 White, Summers & Hillman, supra note 22, § 2:11, at 89; *see also id.* at 89 n. 1 (collecting cases).

59. *Armco Steel Corp. v. Isaacson Structural Steel Co.*, 611 P.2d 507, 518 (Alaska 1980).

60. *See, e.g., Constr. Aggregates Corp. v. Hewitt–Robins, Inc.*, 404 F.2d 505, 510 (7th Cir.1968) (concluding that offeror "could reasonably have assumed that [offeree's] single objection was an acquiescence in the remaining terms of the counter offer"); *Earl M. Jorgensen Co. v. Mark Const., Inc.*, 540 P.2d 978, 983 (Haw.1975) (holding that "silence was not an effective rejection or a counteroffer" when an offer included a specific provision and the response otherwise indicated assent but omitted reference to the provision).

61. *See supra* note 28.

62. ConocoPhillips disagrees and argues that it would be unfair to credit interest at the administratively prescribed FERC rate rather than the "market rate" of LIBOR. ConocoPhillips argues that LIBOR is inherently fair because "[h]ad the parties proceeded on this basis, neither party would have gained or lost value" because "Williams would have lost the time value of its $31 million, but it would have received interest at a market rate from ConocoPhillips to make up for that time value loss." ConocoPhillips confuses the issue by hypothesizing a single market rate of interest and thus attempts to make Williams's demand for FERC interest seem unreasonable. But it is axiomatic that there is no single "market rate" of interest; rather, market rates of return depend on *which* market the investor chooses to enter and the concomitant risk the investor chooses to assume. *See, e.g.*, Edwin J. Elton & Martin J. Gruber, *Modern Portfolio Theory, 1950 to Date*, 21 J. Banking & Fin. 1743, 1744 (1997). If Williams knew it would be responsible for the higher FERC interest rate on retroactively assessed Quality Bank degradation charges, then it would be reasonable for Williams to attempt to earn FERC rates of interest on the principal it set aside for such charges by purchasing assets in a market with correspondingly high levels of risk and return. Accordingly, it might be reasonable for Williams to insist when it transferred ownership of the principal corpus to ConocoPhillips that ConocoPhillips agree to credit Williams with the FERC rate of interest Williams would have otherwise attempted to earn for itself. Indeed, in oral argument, counsel for Williams stated that this was precisely the rationale behind Williams's proposal for FERC interest. Thus, LIBOR interest is not the only " 'break even' point" in the transaction, ConocoPhillips's assertions to the contrary notwithstanding. Rather, the prospective time-value of money is an endogenous variable susceptible to influence by the actions of the person making investment decisions.

63. As an additional reason favoring its reconsideration of the grant of summary judgment, the superior court stated that its "characterization of Conoco's rejection of the joint-negotiating term fits

(*case continues*)

awkwardly within the actual wording of UCC section 2–207(B) [sic], which speaks of *additional* terms being construed as 'proposals for addition to the contract.' "(Emphasis in original.) The superior court's concerns were inapposite to the question before the court. UCC § 2–207(1) and (2) address two distinct issues: (1) addresses the issue of contract formation, while (2) addresses the issue of which additional terms from the non-mirroring acceptance come into the new contract. The § 2–207(2) question in this case—whether ConocoPhillips's apparent rejection of the joint-negotiating provision would cause that provision to fall out of the contract formed under § 2–207(1) or whether, in the alternative, the rejection of a term in the offer cannot be effective under § 2–207(2) because that section addresses only "additional" terms—has no bearing on the § 2–207(1) question in this case—whether the October 29 letter constitutes a definite expression of acceptance of Williams's October 18 offer.

64. Because we conclude that a contract for FERC interest was created in October 2002 under UCC § 2–207(1), we decline to reach other issues raised on appeal, including whether a contract for FERC interest was reached under § 2–207(3) and whether or at what rate Williams is owed interest on a theory of quantum meruit.
65. To the extent that the superior court was under the impression that a reply letter containing a mere "material" change to the contract could prevent contract formation under § 2–207(1), the court erred. UCC § 2–207(2)'s provisions governing which non-mirroring terms enter a contract formed under § 2–207(1) make clear that a materially different term in the reply letter can nonetheless result in contract formation. *See* Ohio Rev.Code Ann. § 1302.10(B)(2) (West 2013) (codifying U.C.C. § 2–207(2)(b)) (stating that, when the parties to a contract formed by acceptance under § 2–207(1) are merchants, non-mirroring terms in an acceptance do not automatically become part of the resulting contract where those terms "materially alter" the offer).
66. We ordinarily do not review denials of motions for summary judgment after a trial on the merits, "at least when the 'motions are denied on the basis that there are genuine issues of material fact.'" *Larson v. Benediktsson*, 152 P.3d 1159, 1169 (Alaska 2007) (quoting *Ondrusek v. Murphy*, 120 P.3d 1053, 1056 n. 2 (Alaska 2005)). We have reviewed denials of summary judgment after a trial on the merits when the order was entered on a legal ground that affected the subsequent trial. *Id.* at 1169 (citing *W. Pioneer, Inc. v. Harbor Enters., Inc.*, 818 P.2d 654, 658 (Alaska 1991)). But the situation before the court today is entirely different. Rather than seeking to roll back the tape to summary judgment after having proceeded through trial to resolve disputed facts, Williams seeks merely to roll back the tape to the initial grant of summary judgment under § 2–207(1) after we find that the order on reconsideration was error as a matter of law. Neither *Larson* nor any other precedent of this court prevents us from reviewing a prior motion for summary judgment in this procedural context. Indeed, *Larson* and *Western Pioneer* support the proposition that review in this context is proper because the error in the order on reconsideration was a legal error.
67. Alaska R. Civ. P. 82(c).
68. *Id.*
69. Alaska R. Civ. P. 6(b).
70. Alaska R. Civ. P. 94.
71. The parties disagree as to when the ten-day clock ran in this case. Williams argues that it filed its motion to enlarge time to file a motion for attorney's fees "eight days after it was due" on March 1, implying that the clock would have run on February 22. (2012 was a leap year.) ConocoPhillips argues that Williams's motion was due by Monday, February 20, 2012 and that its motion was ten days late. Neither party adequately explains the legal theory underlying these assertions. But we conclude that the two-day difference between being late by eight days (Williams's theory) and being late by ten days (ConocoPhillips's theory) would not change the outcome of our holding in this case.
72. *State v. 1.163 Acres, More or Less, Chuckwm, Inc.*, 449 P.2d 776, 779 (Alaska 1968); *see also Worland v. Worland*, 193 P.3d 735, 742 (Alaska 2008) (quoting *Estate of Lampert Through Thurston v. Estate of Lampert Through Stauffer*, 896 P.2d 214, 218 (Alaska 1995)) (holding that the "authority to enlarge the time allowable for an act pursuant to Rule 6(b) is a function addressed to the sound discretion of the trial court").
73. 792 P.2d 671 (Alaska 1990) (per curiam).
74. *Id.* at 672; *see also Alderman v. Iditarod Props., Inc.*, 32 P.3d 373, 397 (Alaska 2001) (holding it was not an abuse of discretion to allow a motion for attorney's fees filed 70 days late where there was no showing of prejudice).
75. *See Conger v. Conger*, 950 P.2d 119, 122–23 (Alaska 1997) (directing superior court to accept late-filed opposition to custody modification where delay was caused by a miscalculation of the due date).
76. *Id.* at 122 (quoting *Jenkins v. Arnold*, 573 P.2d 1013, 1016 (Kan.1978)).
77. We assume without deciding that Civil Rule 79(b) applies in this case, even though court costs were sought pursuant to contractual entitlement rather than Rule 79 itself. ConocoPhillips and Williams both couch their arguments as if Rule 79(b) provided the relevant deadlines for filing a cost bill. But we note sua sponte that Rule 79(b), unlike Rule 82(c), does not purport to require a cost bill filing for an award of court costs "under this rule or pursuant to contract." Alaska R. Civ. P. 82(c). Rather than purporting to apply specifically to contract-based awards of court costs, Rule 79(b) states flatly that "[t]o recover costs, the prevailing party must file and serve an itemized and verified cost bill within 10 days." Alaska R. Civ. P. 79(b). Whether Rule 79 applies to contractual court-cost awards, or whether its rules should apply only by analogy or by the adoption and stipulation of the parties, we leave for another day when that issue is presented to the court squarely. We hold today that, even if Rule 79's requirements apply in full force in this case, the superior court did not abuse its discretion in granting leave to Williams to file its cost bill late.
78. Alaska R. Civ. P. 79(b).
79. Rule 6(b) provides that, where the Alaska Civil Rules require an act "be done at or within a specified time, the court for cause shown may at any time in its discretion upon motion made after the expiration of the specified period permit the act to be done where the failure to act was the result of excusable neglect." Alaska R. Civ. P. 6(b). Rule 94 provides that the Civil Rules "are designed to facilitate business and advance justice" and they "may be relaxed or dispensed with by the court in any case where it shall be manifest to the court that a strict adherence to them will work injustice." Alaska R. Civ. P. 94.
80. *See supra* note 71.
81. 146 P.3d 1 (Alaska 2006).
82. *Id.* at 2.
83. *Id.* at 2–3.
84. This distinguishes this case from *Pruitt v. State, Department of Public Safety, Division of Motor Vehicles*, 825 P.2d 887 (Alaska 1992), in which we held that "the state's motion for attorney's fees, filed seven months after final judgment has

(case continues)

been entered, was not filed within a 'reasonable time.' "*Id.* at 896. Our holding in that case was influenced by the finding that the non-prevailing party "was prejudiced by the state's delay." *Id.*

85. *See Ware v. Ware*, 161 P.3d 1188, 1192 (Alaska 2007) (citing *United Servs. Auto. Ass'n v. Pruitt*, 38 P.3d 528, 531 (Alaska 2001)).
86. *Id.* (quoting *Power Constructors, Inc. v. Taylor & Hintze*, 960 P.2d 20, 44 (Alaska 1998)).
87. *Krone v. State, Dep't of Health & Soc. Servs.*, 222 P.3d 250, 258 (Alaska 2009).
88. *See Valdez Fisheries Dev. Ass'n v. Froines*, 217 P.3d 830, 833 & n. 17 (Alaska 2009).
89. Alaska R. Civ. P. 82(b)(3)(F) & (G).
90. *Valdez*, 217 P.3d at 832 (citations omitted).
91. The superior court rested its first grant of summary judgment on UCC § 2-207(1), an issue which Williams had not briefed, and the superior court rested its order on reconsideration on UCC § 2–207(3), even though Williams had supported the original grant of summary judgment under § 2–207(1).
92. The superior court must have been informed by Williams's initial argument that a contract had been formed under the common law in reaching its conclusion that UCC § 2–207(1) governed the case and displaced the common law, and the superior court necessarily considered Williams's argument on reconsideration that UCC § 2–207(1) governed the case before it held that summary judgment was improvidently granted under § 2–207(1) and instead granted summary judgment under § 2–207(3).
93. *Valdez*, 217 P.3d at 833.

CASE *The Catering Contract Debate*

United Airlines, Inc. v Good Taste, Inc. D/B/A Saucy Sisters Catering

3AN-91-4157 CI, 5139 July 9, 1999
Supreme Court of Alaska
Before: Matthews, Chief Justice, Compton, Eastaugh, Fabe, and Bryner, Justices
Opinion by, BRYNER, Justice

United Airlines terminated a catering contract with Saucy Sisters Catering in Anchorage. Saucy Sisters sued, claiming fraud, breach of contract, and breach of the implied covenant of good faith and fair dealing. The trial court dismissed the breach of contract claim but allowed the other claims to be tried. A jury, finding no fraud but a breach of the implied covenant, awarded Saucy Sisters damages. We hold that under Illinois law, which the parties agree governs, the contract could be terminated at will, and the implied covenant did not require United to have a legitimate business reason for termination. We therefore remand for entry of judgment for United.

Facts and Proceedings

The background facts are undisputed; the trial court summarized them concisely as follows:

In 1987, United contacted Saucy Sisters' President and invited her to bid on United's in-flight catering contract. Shortly after United's invitation, Saucy Sisters entered into discussions/negotiations with United regarding the particulars of the catering contract and the obligations of the parties. On March 14, 1988, United awarded Saucy Sisters the catering contract. As a result of being awarded the contract, and in order to meet United's operation requirements for contracting caterers, Saucy Sisters expanded its operation extensively, spending roughly one million dollars in the process. [Footnote omitted.] A "Catering Agreement" ("Agreement") was signed by the parties and was performed for approximately one year. On May 18, 1989, United gave Saucy Sisters a ninety (90) day notice of termination by which it notified Saucy Sisters that its performance under the Agreement would terminate as of August 15, 1989. The Agreement was terminated August 15, 1989.

United's ninety day termination notice was in accordance with a no-cause termination provision found in the Catering Agreement. The provision states:

Term: The term of this Agreement shall commence on May 1, 1988, and shall continue for a period of 3 years(s); provided, however, either party may terminate this Agreement upon ninety (90) days' prior written notice.

The facts surrounding this termination provision are at the center of this dispute. In its version of the facts, Saucy Sisters alleges that Roger Groth, United's contracting representative, assured Saucy Sisters that United had never used the ninety day termination provision in the past and that the provision existed only to provide United with an "out" in the event

(case continues)

United chose not to fly to Anchorage in the future. Saucy Sisters claims it would not have undertaken such a massive and expensive expansion effort at the risk of a no-cause, ninety day termination notice but for Roger Groth's allegedly fraudulent representations regarding the restrictions on the termination provision. United fails to dispute these facts anywhere in the record, but stated during oral argument that Roger Groth would testify that he never made such statements regarding the termination provision.

Saucy Sisters sued United, alleging wrongful termination of the Catering Agreement, fraud, and breach of the covenant of good faith and fair dealing. The parties filed opposing motions for summary judgment: United sought judgment on all three claims; Saucy Sisters moved for judgment on its claim of fraud. Superior Court Judge Brian C. Shortell ruled on these motions. Relying on Section 22 of the Agreement,[1] Judge Shortell initially found that Illinois law would apply to all claims. The judge went on to find: (1) that the facts surrounding the fraud claim were disputed and should go to the jury; (2) that the ninety-day termination clause was an unambiguous no-cause termination provision and that United did not breach the express terms of that clause; and (3) that a genuine factual dispute existed as to Saucy Sisters' covenant of good faith and fair dealing claim, which was permissible under Illinois law, despite existence of a no-cause termination clause. As to the implied covenant claim, the judge specifically stated:

Applied to the facts of the instant case, the covenant of good faith and fair dealing may impose limits on the manner in which either of the parties could exercise the broad discretion given them by the no-cause termination clause found in Section III.... *[A]lthough the implied covenant of good faith and fair dealing does not create an enforceable legal duty to be nice or to behave decently in a general way, it may require both United and Saucy Sisters to exercise the discretion afforded to them by the termination clause in a manner consistent with the reasonable expectation of both parties*. This means that even though United did not breach the express terms of Section III of the Catering Agreement, it might still be found to have breached the contract by breaching the implied covenant of good faith and fair dealing. Whether United acted in such a way as to breach that covenant is a question of fact to be decided at trial.

(Citation omitted.)

United unsuccessfully moved for reconsideration of this ruling. Later, at the close of evidence at trial, it unsuccessfully moved for a directed verdict on the covenant claim. The jury returned a verdict finding that United had not engaged in fraud but had breached the covenant of good faith and fair dealing. The jury awarded Saucy Sisters $1,541,000 in damages. After adding prejudgment interest, costs, and attorney's fees to the verdict, Judge Shortell entered judgment in Saucy Sisters' favor for $3,604,843.57. United moved for a judgment notwithstanding the verdict and, in the alternative, for a new trial. Judge Shortell denied these motions.

Discussion

United appeals, claiming that the superior court misconstrued Illinois law in denying United's motion for summary judgment on Saucy Sisters' claim for breach of the implied covenant of good faith and fair dealing. United further contends that the jury's award of damages also was contrary to Illinois law and that the court erred in applying Alaska law in awarding attorney's fees and prejudgment interest. Saucy Sisters cross-appeals, claiming that, because the Agreement was ambiguous and extrinsic evidence concerning its meaning differed, the trial court erred in granting summary judgment against Saucy Sisters on its breach of contract claim. For simplicity's sake, we consider Saucy Sisters' argument on cross-appeal before we take up United's direct appeal arguments.

Under Illinois Law, the Trial Court Properly Granted Summary Judgment to United on Saucy Sisters' Breach of Contract Claim

Saucy Sisters asserts that the Agreement's ninety-day termination clause was ambiguous and allowed for varying interpretations, one of which might have sustained a breach of contract claim. Saucy Sisters asserts that this ambiguity created a genuine issue of material fact as to its claim for breach of contract, precluding summary judgment and requiring the claim to be submitted to the jury.

This court reviews trial court orders granting summary judgment de novo, drawing all inferences in favor of the opposing party, to determine whether genuine issues of material fact exist and whether the moving party is entitled to judgment as a matter of law.[2] In the present case, the Agreement's ninety-day termination clause provided:

Term: The term of this Agreement shall commence on May 1, 1988, and shall continue for a period of 3 years(s); provided, however, either party may terminate this Agreement upon ninety (90) days' prior written notice.

The superior court found this provision clear and unambiguous, ruling that it "has only one reasonable interpreta tion, which is that the contract period is for three years unless one of the parties decides to take affirmative action to end it early." Accordingly, the

(case continues)

court determined as a matter of law that United did not breach the express terms of the contract when it terminated the catering contract upon ninety days' written notice.

Under Illinois law, the question of whether a contract is ambiguous is ordinarily one for the court to determine.[3] A disagreement as to contract terms does not in itself create an ambiguity; the reviewing court must initially seek to ascertain the meaning of the contract from the provisions of the contract itself.[4] Contract terms are to "be given their plain, ordinary, popular, and natural meaning."[5] And "[w]hen the language of a contract is unambiguous, the express provision governs and there is no need for construction or inquiry as to the intention of the parties."[6]

Here, the meaning of the disputed termination clause is clear and unambiguous on its face when its words are given "their plain, ordinary, popular, and natural meaning."[7] This provision clearly fixes the Agreement's term at three years, but allows each party to end it earlier by doing nothing more than giving the other party ninety days' notice. As the superior court aptly noted, such termination clauses are hardly uncommon:

Anyone familiar with real world business practices would instantly recognize this provision as a no-cause termination provision that is often used to limit an otherwise definite term. No-cause termination clauses like the one considered here are widely used, and this one in particular would not cause anyone to second-guess its clear and unambiguous terms.

Because the Agreement's no-cause termination provision was clear and unambiguous on its face, the trial court, applying Illinois law, had no occasion to consider extrinsic evidence supporting Saucy Sisters' assertion that it actually understood the provision to have a different meaning.[8] And because United undisputedly abided by the literal terms of the provision—terminating the Agreement upon ninety days' written notice to Saucy Sisters—the trial court properly concluded that no genuine issue of material fact existed and that United was entitled to summary judgment on Saucy Sisters' breach of contract claim.

Under Illinois Law, the Trial Court Erred in Denying United's Motion for Summary Judgment on Saucy Sisters' Covenant of Good Faith and Fair Dealing Claim

United asserts that Illinois law does not permit an implied covenant of good faith and fair dealing to supplant the clear language of a contract allowing termination without cause. According to United, because the disputed Agreement clearly and unambiguously allowed either party to terminate upon ninety days' notice and did not require good cause for termination, the trial court erred in finding the implied covenant applicable and in denying United summary judgment on this claim.

Saucy Sisters responds that the ninety-day termination clause gave both parties broad discretion to terminate their agreement. In such situations, Saucy Sisters argues, Illinois law applies the implied covenant of good faith and fair dealing as a limit on the permissible bounds of contractual discretion. Thus, in Saucy Sisters' view, the implied covenant applied in this case, and the trial court properly allowed this claim to go to the jury.

We review orders denying summary judgment de novo and affirm if we find that a genuine issue of material fact exists or that the moving party is not entitled to judgment as a matter of law.[9] In deciding if a genuine issue of material fact exists, we draw all reasonable inferences in favor of the non-moving party.[10] Here, the primary dispute concerning the trial court's summary judgment ruling centers on the correct interpretation of Illinois law. This is a purely legal question that we decide independently, based on our review and evaluation of applicable Illinois precedent.

The covenant of good faith and fair dealing is well accepted in Illinois, and its broad contours are firmly established: the covenant is implied in every contract.[11] The implied covenant guides the construction of contracts without creating independent duties for the contracting parties.[12] Its implied terms cannot modify the express terms of the contract.[13]

The covenant operates to define the intent of contracting parties when a contract is ambiguous or when it vests the parties with broad discretion as to its performance.[14] In cases involving unambiguous contracts that vest broad discretion in one of the parties, the covenant operates by constraining that party to exercise its discretion reasonably and fairly: "not arbitrarily, capriciously, or in a manner inconsistent with the reasonable expectation of the parties."[15]

Of course, a contractual no-cause termination clause may accurately be characterized as vesting the parties with broad discretion as to the termination of their contract; for this reason, it might be plausible to argue in the case of a no-cause termination clause that the implied covenant requires the parties to terminate reasonably—that is, for some legitimate reason. This is essentially the view that Saucy Sisters advocated at trial. And in denying United's pretrial motion for summary judgment on the implied covenant claim, the court adopted Saucy Sisters' theory:

(*case continues*)

[A]lthough the implied covenant of good faith and fair dealing does not create an enforceable legal duty to be nice or to behave decently in a general way, it may require both United and Saucy Sisters to exercise the discretion afforded to them by the termination clause in a manner consistent with the reasonable expectation of both parties.

Saucy Sisters thereafter relied on this theory at trial. It expressly argued to the jury that even if United made no misrepresentations concerning the ninety-day no-cause termination clause, the implied covenant prevented it from violating Saucy Sisters' reasonable expectation that the agreement would be terminated only for a legitimate business reason:

[Y]ou can't terminate for an arbitrary or capricious reason or to prevent the other party from obtaining reasonably anticipated benefits. You can't violate those reasonable expectations just because you find a better deal. Just because it's now in your financial interest to walk away from the agreement that you made.

Saucy Sisters invoked the same theme in opposing United's motions for judgment notwithstanding the verdict and a new trial on the implied covenant claim:

[T]he United catering contract gave both parties discretion. There was, however, no express provision saying either party could exercise that discretion unreasonably. Accordingly, the implied covenant of good faith and fair dealing was applicable, and neither party was permitted to terminate the contract for arbitrary and capricious reasons.

Applying this view of the law to the facts here, Saucy Sisters insisted that the jury's verdict on the implied covenant claim should be upheld because "reasonable jurors could have found that [Saucy Sisters] performed the contract properly, that any problems in performance were caused by United, and that United terminated the contract without any legitimate business reason whatsoever."

But as far as we can determine, Illinois courts have never held the implied covenant to require good cause or a legitimate business reason for terminating a contract with an express no-cause termination provision. To the contrary, Illinois courts seem to have recognized consistently that "terminable-at-will contracts are generally held to permit termination for any reason, good cause or not, or for no cause at all."[16] The courts have likewise recognized that applying the implied covenant to limit the terms of a no-cause termination provision would be "incongruous" with this general rule[17] and might "eviscerate the at will doctrine altogether."[18]

Several courts have reconciled this tension between no-cause termination clauses and the implied good faith covenant by explaining that parties to contracts with such clauses must reasonably expect the possibility of termination for any reason or no reason at all.[19] But in any event, the prevailing rule in Illinois, however rationalized, unmistakably favors the provisions of an express no-cause contract over potentially conflicting demands of the implied covenant: "[T]he duty of good faith and fair dealing does not override the clear right to terminate at will, since no obligation can be implied which would be inconsistent with and destructive of the unfettered right to terminate at will."[20]

To be sure, some Illinois precedent hints that the implied covenant might apply in particular at-will termination situations. In *Hentze v. Unverfehrt*, the Illinois Court of Appeals, finding bad faith conduct that amounted to "opportunistic advantage-taking," held the implied covenant applicable when a company terminated an at-will dealership contract and engaged in a variety of other bad-faith tactics specifically aimed at driving one of two competing dealers out of business.[21]

Saucy Sisters relies heavily on *Hentze*. It asserts that, as interpreted in *Hentze*, "[T]he covenant of good faith and fair dealing requires, at a minimum, a proper motive to exercise the power [of termination without cause]." Because, in Saucy Sisters' view, the evidence at trial supported the conclusion that United ended its catering contract to seek a more lucrative arrangement with a competing caterer (Marriott), Saucy Sisters asserts that United's action, under *Hentze's* approach, amounted to impermissible advantage-taking: "[A] party engages in opportunistic advantage- taking in Illinois when exercising the reserved power to terminate unreasonably and with an improper motive[.]"

But Saucy Sisters reads *Hentze* too broadly. The *Hentze* court took pains to acknowledge that, under the settled Illinois rule, the defendant company, DECO, "had the right to terminate the [dealership] contract for no reason at all."[22] So too, the *Hentze* court emphasized that, "[h]ad DECO merely ... sent Hentze a termination letter ... , we would be hard-pressed to find any absence of good faith."[23] The court thus made clear that its invocation of the implied covenant rested not on DECO's termination of the contract without, as Saucy Sisters puts it, "a proper motive to exercise the power," but rather on DECO's deliberate efforts to drive Hentze out of business by using other "tactics ... [that] went far beyond the intendments of any at- will clause."[24]

In short, the opportunistic advantage-taking described in *Hentze* was considerably more than an absence of the "legitimate business reason"

(*case continues*)

that Saucy Sisters insists is a necessary ingredient for a valid at-will termination under Illinois law; it was instead a subjectively improper purpose—the malicious goal of driving Hentze out of business—combined with a variety of objectively unfair tactics designed to achieve that goal.[25]

Stripped of its implied covenant trappings, Saucy Sisters' broad reading of *Hentze*—its contention that United could not act arbitrarily or capriciously, but instead was required to have a legitimate business reason for termination—amounts to a claim that United could terminate the catering contract only for cause. But, as we have seen, this claim cannot be countenanced under Illinois law. The settled rule in Illinois remains that a contract expressly terminable at will may be ended for any reason or no reason at all.[26] *Hentze* does indicate that Illinois law might provide a measure of protection against a termination specifically motivated by bad faith and accompanied by unfair tactics.[27] But Saucy Sisters neither alleged nor proved "opportunistic advantage-taking"[28] of this kind. To the contrary, Saucy Sisters' complaint alleged no ulterior motive or subjective bad faith on United's part for terminating the contract, and its evidence at trial suggested only that United might have ended the contract in order to strike a better bargain with Marriott, not—as United claimed—because of Saucy Sisters' poor performance.

United's alleged desire for a more advantageous arrangement with Marriott certainly might not amount to "good cause" for terminating Saucy Sisters' contract, and from Saucy Sisters' perspective termination for this reason might even amount to arbitrary or capricious conduct, carried out for no legitimate business reason. But under Illinois law, the goal of achieving higher profits from a lower-bidding supplier is not itself inherently impermissible and does not amount to opportunistic advantage-taking; neither does reliance on an express at-will termination clause to attain this goal evince subjective bad faith or amount to an objectively unfair tactic.

Citing *Dayan v. McDonald's Corporation*,[29] the dissent concludes that Illinois would invoke the implied covenant to preclude United from terminating its contract "in a manner inconsistent with the reasonable expectations of the parties."[30] But *Dayan* does not support this conclusion.[31] Instead, it narrowly limits its broad view of the implied covenant to franchise contracts, noting that this view reflects "judicial concern over longstanding abuses in franchise relationships, particularly contract provisions giving the franchisor broad unilateral powers of termination at will."[32] And even in franchise cases, *Dayan* seemingly would apply its broad interpretation of the good faith requirement only when "the exercise of discretion [is] vested in one of the parties to a contract."[33]

In fact, *Dayan* expressly recognizes that Illinois law applies a narrower interpretation of the implied covenant outside the area of franchise contracts. Dayan describes Illinois law as holding that the covenant protects at-will employees only when a termination is "inspired by an improper motive, such as a desire to deprive the employee of health or pension benefits[.]"[34] This is essentially the rule of law that we conclude Illinois would apply to the present case. As a matter of Illinois law, the appropriateness of this narrow view of the implied covenant—rather than *Dayan's* broader franchise rule—seems apparent given that the contract at issue here does not involve a franchise. Moreover, the contract's termination clause applied not just to United but to Saucy Sisters as well, giving both parties contractual discretion to terminate at will upon ninety days' notice.

That Illinois law would narrowly construe the implied covenant's effect on this contract seems unmistakable in light of *Jespersen v. Minnesota Mining and Manufacturing Co*.[35] The Illinois Court of Appeals there emphatically rejected a claim that the implied covenant barred termination of an at-will distributorship contract without good cause:

[T]erminable-at-will contracts are generally held to permit termination for any reason, good cause or not, or for no cause at all. Mindful that every contract carries the duty of good faith and fair dealing, as a matter of law, absent express disavowal by the parties, the duty of good faith and fair dealing does not override the clear right to terminate at will, since no obligation can be implied which would be inconsistent with and destructive of the unfettered right to terminate at will.[36] The Illinois Supreme Court recently affirmed the decision of the court of appeals, observing, "Both parties here enjoyed the right to terminate the agreement at will, which means they could terminate the agreement for any reason or no reason without committing a breach of contract."[37]

In sum, we conclude that the trial court was mistaken in ruling that the implied covenant of good faith and fair dealing might "require both United and Saucy Sisters to exercise the discretion afforded to them by the termination clause in a manner consistent with the reasonable expectation of both parties." Under Illinois law, Saucy Sisters could not reasonably expect something other than what it expressly bargained for: a contract expressly terminable for any cause or no cause upon ninety days' notice. Because we conclude that the court erred in submitting Saucy Sisters' implied covenant claim to the jury, we reverse the judgment against United.[38] Our

(*case continues*)

disposition makes it unnecessary to consider any other arguments raised on appeal or cross-appeal.

Conclusion

We AFFIRM the trial court's order granting United summary judgment on Saucy Sisters' breach of contract claim, but REVERSE its order denying United summary judgment on the implied covenant claim. Accordingly, we VACATE the judgment and REMAND for entry of judgment in favor of United.

MATTHEWS, Chief Justice, Dissenting

While I agree with the majority that Illinois law "favors the provisions of an express no-cause contract over potentially conflicting demands of the implied covenant [of good faith and fair dealing],"[1] that type of contract is not at issue in this case. If this contract creates a right to terminate for no cause, the right exists because of a legal inference, not because that right is explicitly stated. I believe that a different legal inference should be drawn: that either party could terminate the contract for no cause if the reason for termination was consistent with the parties' reasonable expectations.[2]

This reading is consistent with the implied covenant of good faith and fair dealing as expressed in section 205 of the Restatement (Second) of Contracts: "Every contract imposes upon each party a duty of good faith and fair dealing in its performance and enforcement." The Supreme Court of Illinois has adopted a similar rule: "Every contract implies good faith and fair dealing between the parties ...."[3] A review of Martindell and the Illinois Appellate Court cases cited in the majority opinion gives me no reason to think that Illinois law respecting the covenant of good faith and fair dealing is inconsistent with the Restatement's discussion of the covenant.

According to the Restatement, good faith enforcement "emphasizes faithfulness to an agreed common purpose and consistency with the justified expectations of the other party."[4] One type of violation recognized by the Restatement is the "abuse of a power ... to terminate the contract."[5] As authority for this comment the Restatement draws on various types of cases, including those involving franchise terminations.[6]

The covenant of good faith and fair dealing was discussed in *Dayan v. McDonald's Corp.*,[7] a franchise termination case involving Illinois law. The court reviewed its understanding of Illinois law regarding the covenant in terms materially indistinguishable from the Restatement:

As the above authorities demonstrate, the doctrine of good faith performance imposes a limitation on the exercise of discretion vested in one of the parties to a contract. In describing the nature of that limitation the courts of this state have held that a party vested with contractual discretion must exercise that discretion reasonably and with proper motive, and may not do so arbitrarily, capriciously, or in a manner inconsistent with the reasonable expectations of the parties.[8]

Dayan confirms my view that the termination clause in the present case—since it does not state that the contract may be canceled without cause—should be construed to incorporate the covenant. Quoting with approval from a Utah case which held that the implied covenant of good faith limited the power of the franchisor to terminate a franchise agreement without good cause where, by its terms, the franchise was terminable upon sixty days written notice to the franchisee, the court in Dayan stated:

When parties enter into a contract of this character, and there is no express provision that it may be cancelled without cause, it seems fair and reasonable to assume that both parties entered into the arrangement in good faith, intending that if the service is performed in a satisfactory manner it will not be cancelled arbitrarily.[9]

The parties in this case could have agreed on a termination provision which expressly stated that cancellation could be on any basis whatsoever, reasonable or unreasonable, just as they could have adopted a termination provision which required cause. They did neither. Instead, they left the provision open to differing interpretations. It is therefore logical to infer that the parties intended to operate in an atmosphere of good faith and fair dealing, and that the covenant applies.

The majority opinion dismisses the significance of *Dayan* by reading into it an artificial limitation.[10] But *Dayan* gives no indication that its holding is limited to cases involving franchises, and there is no logic to such a rule. Franchise cases are not a special subcategory of contract law, but merely a type of contract case that reflects an imbalance of power between contracting parties. The Restatement of Contracts uses franchise cases as appropriate examples to illustrate general rules of contract law.[11] Similarly, the "unilateral power" of the franchisor is not a significant distinguishing element. The problem is that the franchisee—the economically weaker party—must spend large amounts to begin business and then is at risk of losing the investment based on the decision of the franchisor—the economically stronger party. The problem is not solved by giving the weaker party a similar power

(*case continues*)

of termination. In other words, to use the *Dayan* parties as an example, Dayan's vulnerability to termination of his franchise by McDonald's is hardly changed by giving him the power to terminate the franchise. This is the situation in the present case.[12]

While it would be sufficient to end the analysis here, the following observations concerning the covenant's application to the facts of this case seem worth making.

Determining the reasonable expectations of contracting parties is not necessarily an easy task. Contract language must be considered along with the parties' discussions and the purposes of the contract.[13] And it may be useful to ask what the parties would have done had they considered the precise issue when the contract was formed. The Supreme Court of Delaware addressed this recently in *DuPont v. Pressman:*[14]

The Covenant is best understood as a way of "implying terms in the agreement." It is a way of "honoring the reasonable expectations created by the autonomous expressions of the contracting parties."

One method of analyzing the Covenant is to ask what the parties likely would have done if they had considered the issue involved. "[I]s it clear from what was expressly agreed upon that the parties who negotiated the express terms of the contract would have agreed to proscribe the act later complained of ... had they thought to negotiate with respect to that matter?" [T]he Covenant "is a stab at approximating the terms the parties would have negotiated had they foreseen the circumstances that have given rise to their dispute."

Both parties knew that Saucy Sisters must undergo expensive renovations in order to serve United. Saucy Sisters claims a cost of $600,000. We might ask what the parties would have done had Saucy Sisters asked United whether United could terminate the contract either soon after start up or at any time during the three-year term solely because a competitor offered better terms. I think the answer would have been that United would forego that power. Had United asserted the right to terminate to get better terms, there likely would have been no contract. Saucy Sisters would probably not have spent what for it was a small fortune had United overtly reserved the right to make a better deal during the three-year period.

Most cases invoking the obligation to perform in good faith can be synthesized using the following principle: a party performs in bad faith by using discretion in performance for reasons outside the justified expectations of the parties arising from their agreement. Distinguishing allowed from disallowed reasons—opportunities forgone from opportunities preserved on entering a contract—will often be easy. But the distinction will be difficult in some cases. Specific disallowed reasons may be inferred from the express contract terms in light of the ordinary course of business and customary practice, in accordance with the usual principles of contract interpretation. It is not hard to infer from a fixed contract price, for example, that the parties have forgone opportunities to take advantage of market price fluctuations.[15]

Thus, in my view, early termination by United motivated by a desire to contract with a competitor on better terms would have contradicted the justified expectations of Saucy Sisters.

In light of the foregoing, I believe that summary judgment in favor of United was therefore correctly denied. Whether particular conduct qualifies as good faith is a question of law for the court.[16] But whether United in fact acted with an impermissible motive was properly a question for the jury.[17] No question has been raised as to whether the jury was correctly instructed. I would therefore affirm the judgment on the question of liability.[18]

---

1. Section 22 of the Agreement provided that "any dispute arising under or in connection with this Agreement, including any action in tort, shall be governed by the laws of the State of Illinois."
2. *See West v. City of St. Paul*, 936 P.2d 136, 138 (Alaska 1997).
3. *See Newcastle Properties, Inc. v. Shalowitz*, 582 N.E.2d 1165, 1168 (Ill. App. 1991).
4. *See id.* at 1169.
5. *Id.* (quoting *Village of Glenview v. Northfield Woods Water & Util. Co.*, 576 N.E.2d 238 (Ill. App. 1991)).
6. *P.A. Bergner & Co. v. Lloyds Jewelers, Inc.*, 492 N.E.2d 1288, 1291 (Ill. 1986).
7. Newcastle, 582 N.E.2d at 1169.
8. *See id.*
9. *See Western Pioneer v. Harbor Enter.*, 818 P.2d 654, 656 n.3 (Alaska 1991).
10. *See Smith v. State*, 921 P.2d 632, 634 (Alaska 1996).
11. *See Martindell v. Lake Shore Nat'l Bank*, 154 N.E.2d 683, 690 (Ill. 1958).
12. *See Echo, Inc. v. Whitson Co.*, 121 F.3d 1099, 1105–06 (7th Cir. 1997); *Anderson v. Burton Assocs., Ltd.*, 578 N.E.2d 199, 203 (Ill. App. 1991); *see also Koroglugan v. Chicago Title & Trust Co.*, 572 N.E.2d 1154, 1161 (Ill. App. 1991).
13. *See Northern Trust Co. v. VIII South Mich. Assocs.*, 657 N.E.2d 1095, 1104 (Ill. App. 1995).
14. *See id.*
15. *Id.*
16. *Jespersen v. Minnesota Mining & Mfg. Co.*, 681 N.E.2d 67, 71 (Ill. App. 1997) (citing *Alderman Drugs, Inc. v. Metropolitan Life Ins. Co.*, 515 N.E.2d 689 (Ill. 1987)) (emphasis added), aff'd, 700 N.E.2d 1014 (Ill. 1998). *See also Digital Equip. Corp. v. Uniq Digital Tech., Inc.*, 73 F.3d 756, 759–60 (7th Cir. 1996)

(case continues)

(holding that a termination clause allowing for termination of a distributorship contract at the end of any year could not be modified by the duty of good faith even though the manufacturer relied on the contract and invested $1 million in facilitating the needs of the contract); *Gordon v. Matthew Bender & Co.*, 562 F. Supp. 1286, 1290 (N.D. Ill. 1983) (holding that if the implied obligation to deal in good faith were allowed to create a cause of action in an employment-at-will situation, it would "eviscerate the at will doctrine altogether"); *Harrison v. Sears, Roebuck & Co.*, 546 N.E.2d 248, 256 (Ill. App. 1989) (holding that putting implied restrictions on an employment-at-will contract would be inconsistent with the express terms of the contract which allowed for termination at any time).

17. *Harrison*, 546 N.E.2d at 256.
18. *Gordon*, 562 F. Supp. at 1290.
19. *See Beraha v. Baxter Health Care Corp.*, 956 F.2d 1436, 1444–45 (7th Cir. 1992); *Nichols Motorcycle Supply Inc. v. Dunlop Tire Corp.*, 913 F. Supp. 1088, 1143 (N.D. Ill. 1995) (vacated in part pursuant to settlement, September 18, 1995).
20. *Jespersen* [Fn. 39], 681 N.E.2d at 71.
21. 604 N.E.2d 536, 539–40 (Ill. App. 1992).
22. *Id.* at 540.
23. *Id.*
24. *Id.*
25. So described in *Hentze*, the practices prohibited by the implied covenant of good faith and fair dealing resemble the kind of opportunistic advantage-taking this court has recognized as impermissible under Alaska's law governing the implied covenant. See, e.g., *Mitford v. de Lasala*, 666 P.2d 1000, 1007 (Alaska 1983). And, like Illinois courts, we have recognized that this prohibition against subjectively improper opportunism does not convert an at-will contract into a contract requiring good cause for termination. *See Ramsey v. City of Sand Point*, 936 P.2d 126, 133 (Alaska 1997).
26. *See Jespersen*, 681 N.E.2d at 71.
27. *See Hentze*, 604 N.E.2d at 540.
28. *Id.* at 539.
29. 466 N.E.2d 958 (Ill. App. 1984).
30. Dissent at 2 (quoting *Dayan*, 466 N.E.2d at 972).
31. *Seegmiller v. Western Men, Inc.*, 437 P.2d 892 (Utah 1968), also mentioned by the dissent, fails to support the dissent's conclusion because, like *Dayan*, it involves a franchise contract. Moreover, because the franchise at issue in *Seegmiller* was terminated for good cause, *Seegmiller's* interpretation of the good faith covenant is dictum.
32. *Dayan*, 466 N.E.2d at 973.
33. *Id.* at 972 (emphasis added).
34. *Id.*
35. 681 N.E.2d 67 (Ill. App. 1997), aff'd, 700 N.E.2d 1014 (Ill. 1998).
36. *Id.* at 71 (citations omitted).
37. 700 N.E.2d at 1017.
38. Saucy Sisters asserts that United waived its right to appeal the implied covenant issue by failing to object to, or propose alternative versions of, the jury instruction concerning the covenant. But this instruction merely paraphrased Saucy Sisters' interpretation of Illinois law governing the implied covenant. The trial court expressly adopted this interpretation of Illinois law in denying United's pretrial motion for summary judgment on the implied covenant claim and tacitly adhered to it in summarily denying United's mid-trial motion for directed verdict on the claim; later, the court again tacitly adhered to this interpretation in denying United's post-trial motions for JNOV and a new trial. Given these circumstances, United did not waive its right to appeal by failing to object separately to the implied covenant instruction. *See Landers v. Municipality of Anchorage*, 915 P.2d 614, 617 (Alaska 1996); cf. *Brown v. Estate of Jonz*, 591 P.2d 532, 534 (Alaska 1979).
39. In October 1997 the Illinois Supreme Court allowed appeal of *Jespersen*; however, no decision has been issued. *See Jespersen v. Minnesota Min. and Mfg. Co.*, 686 N.E.2d 1162 (Ill. Oct 01, 1997) (Table, No. 83728).

Dissent

1. Slip Op. at 12–13.
2. *See* 3A Arthur Corbin, Corbin on Contracts sec. 654A, at 114 (1999 Supp.).
3. *Martindell v. Lake Shore Nat'l Bank*, 154 N.E.2d 683, 690 (Ill. 1958).
4. Restatement (Second) of Contracts sec. 205 cmt. a (1981).
5. *Id.* at cmt. e.
6. *See id.*, Reporter's Note to sec. 205, cmt. e.
7. 466 N.E.2d 958 (Ill. App. 1984).
8. *Id.* at 972 (citations omitted).
9. *Id.* (quoting *Seegmiller v. Western Men, Inc.*, 437 P.2d 892 (Utah 1968)).
10. Slip Op. at 16–17.
11. *See* Restatement (Second) of Contracts sec. 205, Reporter's Note to cmt. e (1981) (citing various franchise and non-franchise cases to illustrate concept of good faith in enforcement).
12. The court also dismisses the rule as described by *Seegmiller* as dictum. Slip Op. at 16 n.31. While it is true that the holding in Seegmiller rested on other grounds, the language does reflect the general rule accepted by Illinois courts.
13. *See* Steven J. Burton & Eric G. Andersen, Contractual Good Faith: Formation, Performance, Breach, Enforcement sec. 2.3 (1995).
14. 679 A.2d 436, 443 (Del. 1996) (citations omitted) (alteration in original).
15. Burton & Anderson, *supra*, sec. 2.3.3 at 57.
16. 3A Corbin on Contracts sec. 655B, at 116–17 (1999 Supp.).
17. *See id.*
18. United also raises a question as to whether the damage award is consistent with Illinois law. Given my dissenting position, I have not addressed this question.

CASE *Alaska Construction Law*

Philbin, D/B/A Philbin Construction, v. Matanuska-Sustina Borough

S-8573, November 19, 1999
Supreme Court of Alaska
Before: Matthews, Chief Justice, Eastaugh, Fabe, Bryner, and Carpeneti, Justices
Opinion by, EASTAUGH, Justice

Introduction

Before he was paid, a contractor signed a release. The superior court held that the release barred his breach of contract action. Because the contractor raised genuine material fact disputes about the intended effect of the release, we reverse the summary judgment entered against him.

Facts and Proceedings

Joseph Philbin, doing business as Philbin Construction, entered into a written contract with the Matanuska-Susitna Borough on October 6, 1995 to supply, load, haul, and deliver approximately 9,250 cubic yards of crushed gravel.[1] The gravel was to be overlaid on Beverly Lakes Road, Vine Extension Road, and Meadow Lakes Road, in that order. The borough issued Philbin a notice to proceed on October 10; work was to be completed by November 6.

Although Philbin thought he could complete the project within the time the contract allotted, by October 20 the project was behind schedule. Chuck Kaucic, a project manager at the borough's public works department, met that day with Philbin and discussed the project's status. At that meeting Kaucic gave Philbin a letter dated October 19 asking for a revised schedule of anticipated quantities and delivery times, through completion of the project.[2]

By October 24 Philbin had only completed the first, Beverly Lakes Road, portion of the contract. At the suggestion of the borough's construction inspector, on October 25 Philbin billed the borough $19,608 for that portion of the contract. Philbin blamed his lack of progress on deteriorating weather which made crushing rock difficult and caused equipment breakdowns. Moreover, cold weather caused the road surfaces to freeze, preventing installation of more rock.

In early November but before November 6, Kaucic and Philbin met and discussed the possibility of a winter shutdown. A winter shutdown would have allowed Philbin to carry the project over to the spring. Philbin testified that Kaucic instructed him to shut down due to the onset of winter, and that written notification of a winter shutdown would be forthcoming.[3] Kaucic denied telling Philbin to stop producing material. Rather, he testified that he spoke to Philbin *1265 about the possibility of shutting down and restarting in the spring if the freezing road conditions prevented further work in 1995.

Regardless of what was said at that meeting, the borough, by letter dated November 6, 1995, terminated the contract for nonperformance. The letter stated, in part:

> *This letter is to serve as official notification that the Matanuska-Susitna Borough is terminating the Load, Haul and Supply Gravel Agreement contract signed on October 6, 1995.... This agreement is being terminated under Section 10A which states "This Agreement may be terminated by the Borough if the Contractor fails to perform any obligation under this Agreement." You are in noncompliance....*
>
> *... As of today, 2,280 cubic yards of the 9,250 cubic yards specified in the agreement have been produced and hauled....*
>
> *... [I]t has been agreed that in the best public interest the Matanuska-Susitna Borough must terminate this agreement effective 12:01 a.m. November 7, 1995.*

On November 8 Philbin met with executives from the borough's public works department; they reiterated the borough's decision to terminate the contract. But they suggested that Philbin submit a written proposal regarding the possible purchase of crushed rock the following spring. Philbin testified that he declined that offer until he could speak to an attorney.

Philbin later executed an affidavit describing his discussions with the borough and his understanding based on the November 8 discussion of what the borough would do. We discuss that affidavit below in more detail.

(*case continues*)

On November 15 Philbin picked up a borough check for the Beverly Lakes Road portion of the contract. Before giving Philbin the check, the borough required him to sign a form entitled "CONTRACTOR'S RELEASE AND AFFIDAVIT OF PAYMENTS OF DEBTS AND CLAIMS." The form stated that "in consideration of the final payment ... the undersigned contractor ... releases and discharges the Matanuska-Susitna Borough ... from any and all further claim, debt, charge, demand, liability or other obligation whatsoever under or arising from said contract ...." By his handwritten reservation to the release on lines provided for the purpose, Philbin reserved claims to recover payments to individuals to whom he owed money for the rock-crushing equipment.

The following spring the borough refused to buy additional crushed rock from Philbin. In April 1997 Philbin sued the borough, alleging that the borough's refusal in the spring of 1996 to purchase the remaining "Contract material" from Philbin was a breach of contract. Philbin's complaint did not claim that the borough breached the contract by issuing the November 6, 1995 termination letter. The borough raised the release as an affirmative defense, and moved for summary judgment. Enforcing the release, the superior court granted the borough's motion. Philbin appeals.

Discussion

Standard of Review

We review a grant of summary judgment de novo.[4] Drawing all reasonable inferences in favor of the non-movant, we determine whether the parties genuinely dispute any facts material to a viable legal theory and, if not, whether the undisputed facts entitle the movant to judgment as a matter of law.[5] The moving party bears the initial burden of proving through admissible evidence (1) the absence of genuine fact disputes, and (2) its entitlement to judgment as a matter of law.[6] Once the *1266 moving party has established a prima facie case, "the non-movant is 'required, in order to prevent entry of summary judgment, to set forth specific facts showing that he could produce admissible evidence reasonably tending to dispute or contradict the movant's evidence, and thus demonstrate that a material issue of fact exists.'"[7]

Whether the trial court applied the law correctly is a question of law which we review de novo.[8] "Under this standard, it is our duty to adopt the rule of law that is most persuasive in light of precedent, reason, and policy."[9]

The Parties' Intentions and Understanding of the Release Document

Philbin first argues that the evidence demonstrated a factual dispute concerning the parties' intent when he signed the release. He also argues that there is a factual dispute as to whether factors exist sufficient to set aside the release, precluding summary judgment.[10] The borough argues that the release is clear and unambiguous, that Philbin has not established by clear and convincing evidence that the release should be set aside, and that Philbin's unilateral mistake in understanding the release cannot excuse its application to him.

In our prior cases we have used two approaches to determine whether a release is enforceable. Though consistent, they vary in their emphasis.

Under the first approach, a release is to be construed according to the parties' intent. This approach potentially raises questions of fact.[11] The parties' intent is determinative.[12] Accordingly, summary judgment is inappropriate if there is a genuine fact dispute as to the parties' intent.[13]

The second approach focuses on the aggrieved party's understanding of the nature of the instrument he or she has signed.[14] Under this approach, releases are presumptively valid and the releasor must show by clear and convincing evidence that the release should be set aside.[15] In addition, we have stated that "for a release to be effective it must be given with an understanding of what is being released."[16] But we have also stated that absent a showing of coercion or fraud, a mistaken understanding of the contents of a release is not sufficient to justify setting it aside.[17]

Under either approach, the focus is on what a reasonable person would have *1267 understood the release language to have meant.[18]

The evidence permits a reasonable inference that Philbin, based on his November 8 discussion with Kaucic, justifiably believed that the borough would purchase the remaining material, and that, notwithstanding the November 6 termination letter, the borough had not ruled out the possibility that Philbin could complete the contract in the spring of 1996. This evidence is found in part in two paragraphs of Philbin's affidavit opposing summary judgment:

> *6. I discussed with Borough personnel my intentions to complete the contract and produce all of the contract material prior to the time the Borough would need the material in the spring of 1996. It was my understanding from Project Manager Charles Kaucic that the Borough would purchase the remaining*

(*case continues*)

> *material from me in late spring 1996 after the sub-base had adequately thawed and could be properly prepared. At that time, no one told me that the material would not be purchased by the Borough from me in the spring.*
>
> . . . .
>
> *9. At the time that I signed the document, the Borough had not refused to purchase the additional material that had been produced under the contract and that was presently stockpiled and ready for use. Rather, Borough personnel were discussing with me the options of either the Borough purchasing the stockpiled material on hand at that time, or me continuing with production to produce all needed material by spring.*

Based on this understanding, Philbin would have had no reason to expect that the release he signed on November 15 would preclude him from asserting a breach of contract claim against the borough in the event the borough declined to purchase the remaining gravel and permit him to complete the contract.

Other evidence supports the reasonableness of this interpretation. Kaucic testified in deposition that as of November 2 or 3, a winter shutdown was necessary, and that he had informed Philbin that they could not continue because of the weather. His affidavit permits an inference that he talked with Philbin about completing the project in the spring if weather prevented further work in 1995. Although Kaucic characterized this as a "hypothetical" possibility, his testimony that freezing weather prevented continuation removes that factual contingency.

There is also some evidence that the borough itself did not consider the release, when Philbin signed it, to foreclose a breach of contract claim. First, it appears the borough had decided as of November 3 to obtain its standard "lien release" even before it issued the termination letter. There is evidence to the contrary, but given Philbin's assertions about a November 8 conversation with Kaucic, a fact finder could find that the borough had decided to require him to sign the standard release even before it decided to terminate the contract. Second, the form of the release suggests it was primarily intended to protect the borough from lien claims. The borough's Acting Director of Public Works referred to it on November 3 as a "lien release." And the claims Philbin excepted from the release were those of equipment suppliers, who might have asserted lien claims against the borough. Philbin's reading of the release form was therefore consistent with it being a "lien release." Philbin's theory that the release covered only that part of the contract relating to Beverly Lakes Road is also supported by the language of the payment request submitted by the public works department to the borough *1268 receiving department. That request sought "partial" payment under the contract and indicated that the contract performance was "incomplete."

Further, the borough could not have insisted that Philbin execute a complete release as a condition to payment for the initial gravel deliveries because that would have been coercive and in bad faith.[19] In other words, it could not have expected Philbin to give up any possible contract breach claim in exchange for paying him what he had already earned for his partial performance of the contract to date.[20] And the release form permitted the contractor to except from the release particular "specified claims." As the borough's counsel explained at oral argument, this would have permitted Philbin to except a breach of contract claim. Accepting this assertion at face value, it means that the borough, in demanding that Philbin sign the release, had no reasonable advance expectation that the release as finally executed would preclude a breach of contract claim. This implies that it did not intend the release to encompass a breach of contract claim.

Finally, it is significant that Philbin affined that the borough did not raise the release as a defense when, in the spring of 1996, Philbin broached the issue of the completion of the contract with the borough. Philbin also affied that the borough never mentioned "any 'release'" during the following year while Philbin attempted to negotiate with the borough "to resolve this matter short of litigation." The borough first raised the release as a defense to contract claims in May 1997, a year later. This implies that the borough never intended the release to cut off any breach of contract claim.

On the other hand, there is evidence to support the borough's interpretation of the release and its effect. And Philbin's testimony in his deposition and in another proceeding undercuts his affidavits. But this contrary evidence is not conclusive given the averments in Philbin's affidavit and the permissible inferences which we must draw in favor of the non-movant.[21]

The standard of proof for setting aside a release is clear and convincing evidence. But that standard only comes into play when a fact finder is called upon to consider the parties' reasonable expectations. Despite the borough's implied argument that we should apply that standard here, we refuse to do so. It has no direct application at the summary judgment stage.[22]

(case continues)

We conclude that summary judgment is improper, because there is a genuine fact dispute about what the parties intended when the borough paid Philbin for his partial performance of the contract and Philbin signed the release.

We do not agree with the borough's assertion that *Martech Construction Co. v. Ogden Environmental Services*[23] requires affirmance. We there held that a release barred suit, where (1) the release covered "claims of any nature whatsoever," (2) the settlement clearly "sought to resolve the entire transaction," and (3) the later dispute was "reasonably ascertainable" when the release was signed.[24] Although the release Philbin executed covers "any and all further claim[s] ... whatsoever," and the subsequent dispute might be described as "reasonably ascertainable," it is not clear that the settlement sought to resolve the entire transaction, for the reasons we noted above.

***1269 C. Effect of AS 45.01.107** Philbin argues that to read the release as the borough does would require a conclusion that he released all contract claims, even as to what he calls Phases II and III of the contract, without receiving any additional consideration.[25] The borough claims that AS 45.01.107, Alaska's codification of Uniform Commercial Code (UCC) § 1-107, applies, and that because Philbin executed the release after the borough allegedly breached the contract, no consideration was required. Alaska Statute 45.01.107 provides:

> Waiver or renunciation of claim or right after breach. *A claim or right arising out of an alleged breach can be discharged in whole or in part without consideration by a written waiver or renunciation signed and delivered by the aggrieved party.*

The UCC applies to a contract for the sale of gravel.[26]

The section headings are part of the code.[27] Philbin consequently argues that section 107 would not excuse the lack of consideration for a broad release, because he signed the release *before* the borough allegedly breached the contract by refusing in spring 1996 to purchase the remaining "Contract material." The borough claims that Philbin executed the release *after* the borough terminated the contract and canceled the purchase order.

Whether, for purposes of applying section 107, Philbin signed the release after a breach occurred is a fact question which remains to be determined. The superior court did not decide this issue, and we cannot say as a matter of law whether a breach occurred on November 6, or whether the borough breached the contract, as Philbin's complaint alleges, in spring 1996 when it refused to purchase the remaining material.

Consequently, we cannot say as a matter of law whether section 107 applies here and whether the release was valid despite the want of consideration. This question will be before the superior court on remand, subject to being mooted if that court concludes that the parties intended the release to apply only to the Beverly Lakes Road portion of the contract.

Philbin also argues that even if section 107 does apply, the borough did not act in good faith because it indicated to him that the contract was only shut down for the winter and would resume in the spring. He asserts that not until spring 1996 did he know that the borough had breached its contract. The official comment to the UCC provides that section 107 "must be read in conjunction with the section imposing an obligation of good faith. (Section 1-203)."[28] "Good faith" is defined as "honesty in fact in the conduct or transaction concerned."[29]

But we cannot say as a matter of law that the borough failed to act in good faith such that the release must be invalidated, and Philbin has not asked us to do so.

Admissibility Of Parol Evidence

As an alternative ground for affirming, the borough argues that the release was an integrated contract which must be enforced as a matter of law. It consequently reasons that Philbin's theory of asserted partial release and partial payment is inconsistent with the plain and unambiguous language of the release. *1270 Thus, the parol evidence rule would preclude evidence contradicting the parties' agreement.

The parol evidence rule states that an integrated written contract may not be varied or contradicted by prior negotiations or agreements.[30] Before the rule can be applied, three things must be determined: (1) whether the contract is integrated, (2) what the contract means, and (3) whether the prior agreement conflicts with the integrated agreement.[31] The superior court did not decide whether these three requirements of the rule were satisfied.

We agree with Philbin's argument that the release is not an integrated agreement. There is no evidence that the release memorialized terms of an agreement between Philbin and the borough; it appears simply to have been a standard form presented to Philbin when he went to pick up his check. The release contains no integration clause. The borough has not disputed that it owed Philbin the payment he received upon signing the release. That circumstance is

(*case continues*)

inconsistent with reading the release as having memorialized a previously reached agreement to waive all past, present, and future claims.

In any event, it is not apparent that the rule applies here. The parol evidence rule does not apply "where a contract has been formed as a result of misrepresentation or mutual mistake."[32] Philbin's purpose in offering evidence about what he was told by borough representatives on November 2, 3 or 8 was to show that the parties did not intend that the November 15 release had the meaning the borough ascribed to it, not to vary or contradict the terms of the written contract. This was a permissible use of extrinsic evidence to prove mutual mistake.

Philbin as "Commercially Sophisticated" Contractor

The borough argues that Philbin was a sophisticated contractor who must be deemed to have understood that the release barred all claims arising under the contract. The record does not establish that Philbin's experience was such that he was compelled to read the contract in the same way the borough does. We do not see this to be the determinative issue.

Conclusion

Because there are genuine issues of material fact as to the parties' understanding of the release, we REVERSE and REMAND for further proceedings.

CARPENETI, Justice, Dissenting

The court today concludes that a disputed issue of material fact exists as to what the parties intended when the Matanuska-Susitna Borough presented and Joseph Philbin signed the release in question. Because I believe that a reasonable person in Philbin's position, viewing the evidence in the light most favorable to Philbin, must have understood the release language to mean that Philbin "release[d] and discharge[d] the Mat-Su Borough from any and all further claim, debt, charge, demand or liability whatsoever under or arising from" the contract he had entered, I would affirm the decision of the superior court.

Our cases make clear, and the court today reiterates, that the legal standard is "what a reasonable person would have understood the release language to have meant."[1] I agree that this is the test. But none of the six reasons posited by the court to support its conclusion that there are material facts in dispute on this issue withstands scrutiny. For that reason, I dissent.

The court first relies on two paragraphs in Philbin's affidavit to support the proposition that "Philbin . . . justifiably believed that the borough would purchase the remaining material."[2] *1271 First, we have made clear that after-the-fact subjective assertions of intent in contract situations are entitled to no evidentiary weight:

> *Differences of opinion among the parties as to their subjective intent, expressed during the litigation, do not establish an issue of fact regarding the parties' reasonable expectations at the time they entered into the contract, since such self-serving statements are not considered to be probative.*[3]

Moreover, we have held that where the language of an agreement in a commercial context is clear on its face, and the releasor realizes he or she is signing a release, the conclusion that the release is enforceable may be compelled as a matter of law.[4] In *Ahwinona v. State*[5] we specifically rejected an argument based on the releasor's claim that he had not understood the release to preclude a later lawsuit: "Absent any showing of coercion or fraud, Ahwinona's mistaken understanding of the release is not sufficient to set it aside."[6] And in *Mitchell v. Mitchell* we said that the releasor's mistake was "legally irrelevant because the [settlement] clearly and unambiguously dismisses the entire lawsuit."[7] Finally, whether the borough and Philbin might reestablish a commercial relationship the following spring is not the issue. Even if Philbin believed a continuing relationship was possible, he could not have reasonably believed that such a relationship, if it did come about, would have been compelled by the contract which the borough clearly terminated several days earlier.

The court's second reason to reverse is Kaucic's deposition testimony that a winter shutdown was necessary as of November 2 or 3, and that he discussed this with Philbin, permitting an inference that Philbin might be allowed to complete the project in the spring.[8] There is no question that the borough and Philbin discussed that possibility before November 6. But there is likewise no question that the borough abandoned that approach when it unambiguously terminated the contract for nonperformance on November 6. The mere discussion of options cannot suffice to create a dispute of material fact when those discussions are followed by termination of the contract and an unambiguous release.[9]

The court's third reason" there is also some evidence that the borough itself did not consider the release, when Philbin signed it, to foreclose a breach of contract claim"[10] fails both legally and factually. Legally, we look to the language of the release and the parties' reasonable expectations concerning that language. The release's language is broad and all-encompassing: the contractor "releases and

(case continues)

discharges the Matanuska-Susitna Borough, its officers, agents and employees of and from any and all further claim, debt, charge, demand, liability or other obligation whatsoever under or arising from said contract, whether known or unknown and whether or not ascertainable at the time of the execution of this instrument except specified claims ...." Factually, it should be of little consequence that a borough employee referred to the release as a "lien release." *1272 Indeed, the only reasonable interpretation of the document is that it is a general release with a possible *exception* for lien and related claims.

The court's fourth rationale is that "Philbin's theory that the release covered only that part of the contract relating to Beverly Lakes Road is also supported by the language of the payment request submitted by the public works department to the borough receiving department. That request sought 'partial' payment under the contract and indicated that the contract performance was 'incomplete.'"[11] But this is irrelevant for several reasons. First, the request was an internal document, not communicated to Philbin. Second, the request was submitted on November 3, when the Borough had not yet announced its decision to terminate the contract; that announcement came three days later. As the Engineering Manager for the borough testified: "When this purchase order request for payment was received by borough purchasing personnel, they changed the 'P' [partial] to 'F' [full] on both lines, as *it was determined by that date* that this would definitely be a closed contract." (Emphasis added.) Finally, the release is clear on its face. How can an internal document, unseen by Philbin and subsequently properly modified to reflect the decision to terminate the contract, be used to justify a conclusion that Philbin's intent in signing the *release* is in dispute?

The court's fifth justification relies on the observation that "the Borough could not have insisted that Philbin execute a complete release as a condition to payment for the initial gravel deliveries because that would have been coercive and in bad faith."[12] I have no quarrel with this statement. But the borough did not do that. The release specifically allowed the releasor to except whatever claims he wished to except. Counsel for the borough properly admitted at oral argument that this would have allowed Philbin to except a breach of contract claim. The majority somehow turns this into the unwarranted conclusion that "[the borough] did not intend the release to encompass a breach of contract claim."[13] Philbin did not except any breach of contract claim, and the language of the release is otherwise extremely broad. Under these circumstances, the only reasonable interpretation of the release is that "any and all" claims, demands, or other obligations arising from the contract were released, unless specifically excepted.

The court last points to the borough's alleged failure to mention the release in subsequent negotiations when Philbin tried to resurrect the terminated contract the following spring. Using a party's negotiating technique in these circumstances as evidence of the party's intent in signing a document months earlier seems questionable. For one thing, the borough's reliance on the release in negotiations with Philbin would probably have been inconsistent with reaching a negotiated settlement of the dispute. For another, positions taken in settlement negotiations have never been relevant later when negotiations have proved unsuccessful.[14] I would give no weight to the borough's alleged failure to mention the release several months later in settlement negotiations when assessing the meaning of the release.

The court fails to set out[15] the compelling evidence that Philbin knew, when he signed the release, that the contract had been terminated and that he was releasing any and all claims arising under the contract (except *1273 those that he specifically excepted). While he now argues that the contract remained open and he therefore had no reason to understand that the release he signed actually was a release of all claims "arising under the contract," there is no doubt that he knew the contract was terminated. His own words prove it:

> *[F]our or five days [after the meeting with Mr. Kaucic] ... I got another letter ... stating that they've decided to terminate the contract, I was irate. I've never had that happen. You don't tell somebody you're going to make a winter shutdown, especially before the duration of the contract, and then let that time pass and then hand them a termination notice ...* I arranged a meeting with the Borough and I told them that within a two-week period come spring once the ground was thawed, I could absolutely guarantee that I could crush the material and well before the road restrictions lifted .... *I would like to go ahead and crush the material.* And they said no, they just didn't believe I could do it. *My record didn't look good because of this project.*

(Emphasis added.) This testimony was given in a related case pitting Philbin against an equipment supplier on the contract in this case. In the same case, Philbin testified that the proposed winter shutdown option had been discarded by the borough, a decision with which he heartily disagreed. Specifically,

(*case continues*)

he testified that he was "shocked" when he received the termination letter instead of a shut down order:

> *In the context of the conversation [on November 2 or 3, Chuck Kaucic] informed me that the road surfaces were too hard to blade and prepare to accept gravel and then if we put gravel down on it, it wouldn't bond, it would come off. And at that point I was glad to hear that because I wasn't getting any production out of the plant at all. The material was frozen, lumped up. It wouldn't process right.* And it came as a shock after he'dhe'd orally told me that to get this letter saying they terminated it. That it no longer was considering picking back up in the spring to let me finish it.

(Emphasis added.)

Given Philbin's own testimony, no reasonable fact-finder could conclude that, as of the time he signed the release, he reasonably believed that the road contract was still in effect, that he would resume work on it in the spring, and that the release only concerned the work already performed. A reasonable person in Philbin's position must have understood that he was releasing the borough from the claims he now seeks to pursue. Moreover, the law is clear that, absent coercion or fraud, even a mistaken understanding of the contents of a release is not sufficient to set it aside. Under these circumstances, and given the breadth of the release language, I believe that the superior court was correct when it found no material issues of fact in dispute. I would affirm that decision.

---

1. Because this case was dismissed on summary judgment, our description of the facts draws all permissible inferences in favor of the non-movant, Philbin. *See Maddox v. River & Sea Marine, Inc.*, 925 P.2d 1033, 1035 (Alaska 1996).
2. No such letter is in the record. *See infra* note 3.
3. Some months after Philbin so testified in his deposition in this case, he testified, at the trial of a related claim, that Kaucic in fact handed him a letter officially notifying him to stop producing crushed gravel. According to Philbin, the letter also indicated that he and the borough should discuss restarting in the spring. But no such letter is in the record in this appeal. It may be that this was the letter dated October 19 regarding a revised schedule that Kaucic hand delivered to Philbin on October 20. *See supra* note 2.
4. *See Arctic Tug & Barge, Inc. v. Raleigh, Schwarz & Powell*, 956 P.2d 1199, 1200 (Alaska 1998).
5. *See id*.
6. *See Shade v. Co & Anglo Alaska Serv. Corp.*, 901 P.2d 434, 437 (Alaska 1995).
7. *Jennings v. State*, 566 P.2d 1304, 1309 (Alaska 1977) (quoting *Howarth v. First Nat'l Bank*, 540 P.2d 486, 489–90 (Alaska 1975)) (internal brackets omitted).
8. *See Langdon v. Champion*, 752 P.2d 999, 1001 (Alaska 1988).
9. *Guin v. Ha*, 591 P.2d 1281, 1284 n. 6 (Alaska 1979).
10. Philbin also argues that a fact dispute exists as to whether the borough validly terminated the contract. But this question is only relevant to the extent it implicates Philbin's understanding and intent when he signed the release. Therefore, we will discuss it in context of that issue.
11. *See, e.g., Schmidt v. Lashley*, 627 P.2d 201, 203 n. 4 (Alaska 1981).
12. *See id*. at 204 n. 7.
13. *See Alaska Continental, Inc. v. Trickey*, 933 P.2d 528, 534 (Alaska 1997).
14. *See, e.g., Ahwinona v. State*, 922 P.2d 884, 887 (Alaska 1996); *Witt v. Watkins*, 579 P.2d 1065, 1067–68 (Alaska 1978).
15. *See Ahwinona*, 922 P.2d at 887 ("[O]nce the party relying on a release establishes that it was given with an understanding of the nature of the instrument, the burden is on the releasor to show by clear and convincing evidence that the release should be set aside."); *Mitchell v. Mitchell*, 655 P.2d 748, 751 (Alaska 1982); *Witt*, 579 P.2d at 1067–68.
16. *Alaska State Hous. Auth. v. Sipary*, 668 P.2d 824, 828 (Alaska 1983) (citing *Schmidt*, 627 P.2d at 204).
17. *See Ahwinona*, 922 P.2d at 887. *See also Mitchell*, 655 P.2d at 753 (refusing to set aside settlement, stating that releasor's mistake was "legally irrelevant because the [settlement] clearly and unambiguously dismisses the entire lawsuit").
18. *See Johnson v. Schaub*, 867 P.2d 812, 818 n. 12 (Alaska 1994). *Cf. Martech Constr. Co. v. Ogden Envtl. Serv., Inc.*, 852 P.2d 1146, 1150 n. 8 (Alaska 1993). In *Martech*, we considered the scope of a release that included "blatantly broad language to cover all possible causes of action." *Id.* at 1152. We upheld the application of the release to a later-arising dispute on grounds that the disputed claim was "reasonably ascertainable" at the time the release was executed. *Id.* at 1151–52.
19. *See* Restatement (Second) of Contracts § 175 (1981) ("If a party's manifestation of assent is induced by an improper threat by the other party that leaves the victim no reasonable alternative, the contract is voidable by the victim.").
20. Such a requirement could constitute economic duress. *See Totem Marine Tug & Barge, Inc. v. Alyeska Pipeline Serv. Co.*, 584 P.2d 15, 20–23 (Alaska 1978) (setting out elements of economic duress).
21. The testimony we refer to here includes the same testimony quoted at length by the dissent.
22. *See* Alaska R. Civ. P. 56(c); *Moffatt v. Brown*, 751 P.2d 939, 944 (Alaska 1988).
23. 852 P.2d 1146 (Alaska 1993).
24. *Id.* at 1151–52.
25. We addressed a roughly analogous situation in *Pride v. Harris*, 882 P.2d 381 (Alaska 1994). In that case, Pride obtained a judgment against a truck driver for property damage caused in a collision. *See id.* at 382. On the check tendered to Pride to satisfy the judgment were the words "For Full & Final Settlement of all claims." *Id.* The driver argued that in endorsing the check, Pride executed an accord and satisfaction of any personal injury claims he might have had. *See id.* at 384. We held that such an accord would be invalid for lack of consideration. *See id.*
26. *See A & G Constr. Co. v. Reid Bros. Logging Co.*, 547 P.2d 1207, 1211 (Alaska 1976).
27. *See* AS 45.01.109.
28. UCC § 1–107, 1 U.L.A. 57 (1989).
29. AS 45.01.201(20).
30. *See Alaska Diversified Contractors, Inc. v. Lower Kuskokwim Sch. Dist.*, 778 P.2d 581, 583 (Alaska 1989).
31. *See id*.

(case continues)

32. *Diagnostic Imaging Ctr. Assoc. v. H & P*, 815 P.2d 865, 867 (Alaska 1991).

CARPENETI, Justice, Dissenting

1. Op. at 1266.
2. *Id.*
3. *Peterson v. Wirum*, 625 P.2d 866, 870 (Alaska 1981).
4. *Ahwinona v. State*, 922 P.2d 884, 886 (Alaska 1996).
5. *Id.*
6. *Id.* at 887.
7. 655 P.2d 748, 752–53 (Alaska 1982).
8. Op. at 1267.
9. In this regard, the court's statement about the discussion is puzzling: "Although Kaucic characterized this as a 'hypothetical' possibility, his testimony that freezing weather prevented continuation removes that factual contingency." Op. at 1267. That freezing weather as of early November forced a shutdown did not preclude the borough from terminating the contract, because Philbin was significantly behind the contract's production schedule well before that date. The borough was free to offer a continuation of the contract, but it was not required to do so.
10. Op. at 1267–1268.
11. *Id.* at 1268.
12. Op. at 1268.
13. *Id.* at 1269.
14. *See* Alaska Rule of Evidence 408.
15. The court satisfies itself with the observation that this evidence "support[s] the borough's interpretation ... [b]ut ... is not conclusive given the averments in Philbin's affidavit" and the inferences which must be drawn in favor of the non-movant. Op. at 1268. This approach ignores our well-established rule that subjective statements made during litigation are entitled to no weight "since such self-serving statements are not considered to be probative." *Peterson v. Wirum*, 625 P.2d at 870.

CASE *Alaska Oil Regulation*

Tesoro Alaska Company v. Union Oil Company of California

3AN-08-05877 CI, 6802 July 26, 2013
Supreme Court of Alaska
Before: Carpeneti, Chief Justice, Fabe, Winfree, and Stowers, Justice
Opinion by, CARPENETI, Chief Justice

Introduction

In 2001 an oil producer on the Alaska North Slope entered into a contract to sell its oil to another oil company. Under the contract the buyer took title at the North Slope, but agreed to use a pipeline company associated with the supplier to transport the oil through the Trans-Alaska Pipeline. The price per barrel was calculated as the West Coast market price less marine transport and pipeline tariff. The contract made no mention of whether the pipeline tariff was tied to the ultimate destination of the oil. At the time, the interstate and intrastate pipeline tariffs were the same. The buyer shipped the oil to an in-state refinery and paid the tariff to the pipeline company. The supplier duly subtracted the tariff amount from the market price of the oil less marine transport and sent invoices to the buyer. Meanwhile, the buyer successfully challenged the intrastate tariff as unjust and unreasonable and the pipeline company issued a refund, including 10.5% interest. Then, the supplier claimed that it was entitled to the tariff refund under the contract. The superior court, on motions for summary judgment, awarded the principal amount of the refund to the supplier and the interest to the buyer.

Both parties appeal. The buyer claims that the reference to tariffs in the contract related to interstate tariffs because the price of the oil was a netback price to the Los Angeles market. The supplier asserts that the contractual reference to tariffs meant the actual tariff amount paid. In its cross-appeal, the supplier asserts that because it was awarded the principal amount, it should have received the statutory interest as well. We hold that the pricing term was a netback price to the Los Angeles market referencing the interstate tariff. Accordingly, we reverse the superior court's grant of summary judgment to the supplier and remand for entry of judgment in favor of the buyer. In light of our conclusion, we do not reach the issues raised in the cross-appeal.

Facts and Proceedings

Facts

Background and regulatory commission of alaska proceedings

This appeal concerns two crude oil purchase contracts between Tesoro Alaska Company (Tesoro) and Union Oil Company of California (Union Oil). Under

(case continues)

the contracts Tesoro agreed to purchase all of Union Oil's Alaska North Slope (ANS) crude oil production in 2000, 2001, and 2002. The first contract was executed in November 1999, covering January 1, 2000 through December 31, 2000. The second contract was executed in November 2000; it covered January 1, 2001 through December 31, 2002. Under the contracts, title and risk of loss transferred to Tesoro at the outlet flange of Pump Station No. 1[1] of the Trans-Alaska Pipeline System (TAPS). The price was set as follows:

> *The price ... shall be the average ANS [crude oil] closing price as quoted by Reuters and Telerate for each trading day of the month prior to the delivery ... less $1.35 per barrel for marine transportation less one of the following:*
>
> *a.) Tesoro will, at Unocal's direction, nominate and ship the Quantity of [crude oil] onto Unocal Pipeline space on TAPS and the Unocal [Pipeline] TAPS tariff shall apply to all [Union Oil] Crude shipped on Unocal [Pipeline] space. Tesoro agrees to pursue any such nomination diligently and absolutely until or unless prorated out of Unocal Pipeline space.*
>
> *b.) If not directed by Unocal, Tesoro shall use its best efforts to nominate and ship the Quantity of [crude oil] on the TAPS so as to minimize, to the extent practical, pipeline transportation costs. The weighted average tariff rates paid by Tesoro shall then apply.*

TAPS carries oil from the Alaska North Slope to Valdez. The owners of the pipeline are allocated space and share costs according to the portion of the pipeline owned. Some pipeline owners are affiliated with oil producers. Here, Unocal Pipeline was owned by the same parent company as Union Oil, Unocal Corporation. Pipeline owners are considered common carriers. Subject to regulatory oversight, each pipeline owner determines a tariff for oil shipped through its space. The pipeline tariffs are subject to different regulation depending upon whether the oil is ultimately shipped interstate or intrastate. The Federal Energy Regulatory Commission regulates interstate tariffs, while the Regulatory Commission of Alaska (RCA) regulates intrastate tariffs and is tasked with setting "just and reasonable rates." Throughout the duration of these contracts the intrastate and interstate tariffs were the same.

Tesoro challenged the TAPS intrastate tariffs, including that of Unocal Pipeline, in two RCA proceedings, one covering tariffs from 1997 to 2000 and another covering tariffs from 2001 to 2003. In December 1997, Unocal Corporation's counsel placed himself on the distribution list for matters concerning the tariff rate proceedings and received RCA orders. After Tesoro's challenge was initiated the RCA issued orders accepting the filed tariff rates as "temporary" and collectable but "subject to refund."

In the meantime, Union Oil delivered the oil and Union Oil's affiliated pipeline company, Unocal Pipeline Company, shipped it. Unocal Pipeline Company invoiced Tesoro using the published pipeline tariff rates for the duration of the contract. Tesoro paid all invoices. Ultimately, the RCA found that the intrastate tariffs were unjust and unreasonable.[2] In 2008, as a result of Tesoro's rate protest, Unocal Pipeline was required to issue a refund to Tesoro of over $24 million in principal and interest.

The first contract

Union Oil contracted with ARCO for the sale of Union Oil's ANS crude for 1998 and 1999. Under the contract ARCO was required to ship the oil on Unocal Pipeline space "so that [Unocal Pipeline] would be assured of at least some revenues to offset its ongoing TAPS expenses." The pricing mechanism on the ARCO contract was based on a West Coast delivery point. Therefore, although ARCO was required to take title and risk of loss at Pump Station No. 1 and ship on Unocal Pipeline space, according to Unocal, ARCO could deduct "the theoretical transportation cost of moving the ANS crude to Valdez" and the marine transport cost from Valdez to Los Angeles.

As the ARCO contract neared expiration Tesoro began negotiations with Union Oil. The contract between Union Oil and Tesoro was essentially the same contract that Union Oil had previously negotiated with ARCO. Point of sale was on the North Slope and title and risk of loss passed at Pump Station No. 1. Tesoro agreed to ship on Unocal Pipeline space if space was available and the tariff would be deducted from the price charged. The contract contained no mechanism for retroactive pricing adjustments and no definitions section. However, there was a reservation for retroactive adjustment of taxes.

When the contract circulated within Union Oil and was passed to Tesoro, there was no indication that either party discussed the meaning of the "Unocal [Pipeline] TAPS Tariff" term. Internal Union Oil emails do not indicate that Union Oil reserved the right to seek a refund; they also do not clarify whether the pricing mechanism was tied to the interstate tariff. The emails give an overview of the pricing mechanism and key contract terms, such as maintaining sale at Pump Station No. 1 and shipping on Unocal Pipeline space, and note the then-current interstate (and intrastate) tariff. A post-contract Unocal email refers to "netback" pricing stating, "[h]ere are the pipeline netback numbers you requested," and requests verification of the tariff amounts.

(*case continues*)

Union Oil claims that it understood the pricing mechanism as a "penny for penny pass-through payment," where Union Oil would reimburse Tesoro for the actual transportation costs; Tesoro claims that the pricing mechanism was a netback price[3] tied to the West Coast market, simply a convenient way to price crude oil purchased in an untraded market that was not tied to the actual transportation costs. A November 3, 1999 Union Oil email noting the successfully-negotiated deal with Tesoro refers to "our netback North Slope price."

Union Oil admits that it did not expressly state its intention that the price would reflect actual costs, but claims that it understood that Tesoro would be able to deduct no "more than the actual TAPS transportation cost it incurred." A Union Oil employee also admitted that "Tesoro ... would be allowed to deduct the theoretical transportation cost of moving ANS crude to Valdez, irrespective of the actual destination for the oil. The TAPS tariffs were selected as that was deemed to be the TAPS transportation cost that Tesoro would actually incur."

Tesoro's oil industry expert reviewed the contract and found that it contained a standard netback pricing mechanism. He testified that "[c]onsistent with industry practice, the [Union Oil] and Tesoro contracts agree to deduct the 'theoretical transportation costs,' " subtracting the interstate tariff rate regardless of where the oil shipped. The netback formula accounts for the fact that the seller did not bear the cost of shipping the oil to market; under the scheme the seller gets the net amount it would have gotten if it had shipped the oil to market and sold it there.

Union Oil submitted invoices using the base rate of the West Coast price and subtracting the marine transport and the weighted average TAPS rate (that is, the tariff). Tesoro paid the tariff to Unocal Pipeline or to other pipeline owners if shipped by another carrier. Neither party disputes that the invoices were paid as billed.

The second contract: 2001-2002

In 2000, the second contract was negotiated for 2001-2002. During negotiations, an internal Union Oil email provided an outline of the contract stating "Tesoro will ship on Unocal [Pipeline]'s space ... ([Union Oil] will reimburse Tesoro for pipeline tariff)." No mention of a reimbursement plan was made to Tesoro. There was no reservation for possible tariff refunds. In the end, the second contract was the same as the first except for a change in the date. As with the 2000 contract Union Oil invoiced Tesoro and the invoices were paid.

Proceedings

After Union Oil formally requested the RCA-ordered refunds, Tesoro filed a declaratory action to establish its rights. Union Oil counterclaimed, seeking the funds under the contracts.[4] Both parties filed cross-motions for summary judgment. The superior court granted summary judgment for Union Oil "as to refunds for tariffs paid on barrels of oil shipped intrastate." RCA-ordered tariff refunds have both a principal and a 10.5% interest rate component. The superior court awarded Union Oil the principal amount plus prejudgment interest based on a breach of contract theory but found that Union Oil was not entitled to the 10.5% statutory interest. Tesoro appealed, arguing that the contract's pricing mechanism was a netback price tied to interstate tariffs. Union Oil cross-appealed the superior court's conclusion that it was due only contract-based prejudgment interest rather than the 10.5% RCA-ordered interest.

Standard of Review

"We review a grant of summary judgment de novo."[5] All reasonable inferences are drawn in favor of the nonmoving party.[6] Summary judgment will be entered "if there is no genuine factual dispute and the moving party is entitled to judgment as a matter of law."[7] "The moving party has the initial burden of offering admissible evidence showing both the absence of any genuine dispute of fact and the legal right to a judgment."[8] Once that burden is satisfied, the non-moving party, to avoid summary judgment, must produce "admissible evidence reasonably tending to dispute or contradict the movant's evidence."[9] The non-moving party may not, however, "rest upon mere allegations, but must set forth specific facts showing that there is a genuine issue of material fact."[10] "To create a genuine issue of material fact there must be more than a scintilla of contrary evidence."[11]

Discussion

It Was Error to Grant Summary Judgment to Union Oil

The main issue in this case is which party is entitled to the RCA refunds. The key to this issue is the meaning of "Unocal [Pipeline] TAPS tariff" in the contract's pricing mechanism. Tesoro asserts that the contract used a netback pricing mechanism subtracting the filed interstate tariff (and marine transportation costs) reflecting the West Coast crude oil market price, fixed at delivery. In short, it is a theoretical market price not tied to any actual tariff paid on a particular barrel of oil. Union Oil asserts that the

(*case continues*)

term was defined by reference to the particular tariff applicable to a given barrel of oil, and that therefore any refund from TAPS would flow back to Union Oil. The superior court found that the contract was "ambiguous as to price" and ultimately agreed with Union Oil's interpretation.

When resolving disputes concerning the meaning of an agreement, we "begin by viewing the contract as a whole and the extrinsic evidence surrounding the disputed terms, in order to determine if those terms are ambiguous – that is, if they are reasonably subject to differing interpretation[s]."[12] Where an ambiguity exists, we resolve the ambiguity by determining "the reasonable expectations of the [contracting] parties" in light of the "language of any disputed provisions, other provisions, relevant extrinsic evidence, and case law interpreting similar provisions."[13]

We look first to the language of the contract itself. Tesoro argues that the language is a standard netback pricing [14] formula. Union Oil claims that while the pricing mechanism set out a pricing formula it did not fix the actual price. Neither interpretation is required by the contract language, and the contract does not illuminate the meaning of the term as there is no definition section or any direction for managing possible retroactive adjustments.

Other provisions in the contract are likewise inconclusive because, although they explicitly address retroactive adjustments, they do not resolve the issue before us. For example, one such provision in the contracts allows Union Oil to retroactively collect taxes. Tesoro argues that the existence of other provisions providing for retroactive adjustments proves that Union Oil did not intend to include the ability to retroactively adjust price under the maxim "expressio unius est exclusio alterius."[15] We are not convinced that these other provisions are helpful in this case. First, the maxim, while it may be used in contract interpretation, is not applicable here.[16] It applies when "parties list specific items in a document, [and instructs that] any item not so listed is typically thought to be excluded."[17] Second, although the existence of the provisions suggests that Union Oil could make retroactive contract adjustments, the omission of such a provision expressly related to tariffs does no more than show that Union Oil did not foresee a need for retroactive adjustment of tariffs. It does not resolve the underlying question, that is, "what does the term 'Unocal [Pipeline] TAPS tariff' mean in this contract?" Accordingly, we do not give much weight to the fact that the parties included other retroactive pricing adjustments.

The circumstances surrounding the adoption of the contract also are not useful in interpreting the term. Neither party paid much attention to the pricing mechanism; each simply adopted the pricing mechanisms in the original ARCO contract with an adjustment for marine transport cost. Further, internal emails from Union Oil suggest that netback pricing was contemplated, but they do not clarify whether the tariff deduction was tied to the ultimate destination of the oil. One email that announced the successful contract negotiations described the final "netback North Slope price" Union Oil could expect under the new contract. However, the email is silent on the issue of whether the tariff refers to interstate or intrastate tariffs. There simply is little indication that the parties considered a retroactive adjustment in the tariffs, either intrastate or interstate, at the time the contract was signed.

The objective of the contract, however, supports Tesoro's position. Union Oil argues that the contract's objective was to shift the cost of the tariff to it. Tesoro responds that the pricing term did not shift the cost of transportation, but rather sought to provide a netback price so Tesoro was paying a West Coast market price for the oil. The superior court found that the contract "neutralize[d] the tariff cost [so that] Tesoro ... was not actually affected by the unjust intrastate tariffs." It further found that because the contract was negotiated when the interstate and intrastate tariffs were identical, there was no need for the parties to differentiate between the two in the contract.

The contract's objective was to set a price for the oil that reflected the price that could be obtained in a widely-traded market. Union Oil's insistence that its affiliate pipeline be used to transport the oil does not change the fundamental goal of the contract's pricing term: setting a price for the oil. While Union Oil is correct that the contract shifts the cost of the tariff to it, that fact does not mean the contract was designed to insulate Tesoro from the tariffs. The parties were engaged in the buying and selling of oil. The focus of the contract and therefore its objective was necessarily the pricing of the oil. If the parties had intended the pricing scheme to provide reimbursement for the actual costs incurred by Unocal, the contract would have contemplated other actual costs associated with the transportation of oil. This would include the actual marine transportation costs (instead of setting a standard rate of $1.35/barrel throughout the life of the contract) and interstate tariffs that depend on the final destination of the oil.

Trade usage is extremely important in interpreting the pricing term. Tesoro presented an oil industry expert who stated that the contract pricing term was a netback designed to create a price for oil equivalent to that found in the West Coast market. The expert

(case continues)

stated that at the time the contracts were signed the "[standard] industry practice for a net back price would [be] the FERC interstate tariff plus the marine transportation price ... subtracted from the prior month's average Los Angeles basin posted prices to determine the contract price or net back to Pump Station #1." Union Oil did not present evidence to rebut this expert, although it argues that trade usage is not relevant because the contracts are "relatively unique."

We look to the "general and accepted usage of the trade or business involved" when interpreting contracts.[18] Trade usage and case law can be relevant in interpreting a contract because "[a] person entering into a contract in the ordinary course of business is presumed to have done so in reference to any existing general usage or custom relating to such business."[19] Trade usage is helpful because it "often establishes a special and unusual meaning definitely in conflict with the more common and ordinary usages."[20]

In this case, trade usage is persuasive and, importantly, is not disputed. Standard pricing for Alaskan oil, whether title is transferred at Pump Station No. 1 or Valdez, is a netback to another market because there is no widely-traded market in Alaska. Tesoro's oil expert's determination that the contract provided a netback pricing scheme is instructive because the parties are sophisticated players in the oil industry, and they are presumed to have entered into the contract with knowledge of established practices. Here, each is presumed to know that the standard method for pricing Alaskan oil is a netback pricing formula referencing the interstate tariffs. Further, the lack of attention paid to the pricing mechanism suggests that the parties shared a common understanding of the term that was based on this industry practice.

As noted above, the key to resolving contractual ambiguities is the parties' reasonable expectations.[21] At the time of contract formation, the two tariffs – interstate and intrastate – were the same, so neither party had a reason to indicate the destination of the oil for the purposes of calculating the deduction, and Union Oil sought to encourage shipping on its affiliated pipeline company to provide a revenue stream for the affiliate. However, the parties entered into the contract in the context of a highly-developed industry standard pricing model: netback pricing to a widely-traded market. The reasonable expectations of the parties align with the industry practice. Here, the widely-traded market is the West Coast market and the contract's pricing term provided a netback price referencing the interstate tariffs. The parties did not expect that the contract would be adjustable based on a change in the intrastate tariffs. Accordingly, we reverse the superior court's grant of summary judgment to Union Oil.

Tesoro is Entitled to Summary Judgment Because there is no Genuine Dispute of Material Fact that the Contracts Contained a Netback Pricing Term

Having determined that summary judgment was improvidently granted to Union Oil, we must consider Tesoro's claim that it is entitled to judgment. Specifically, is there more than a scintilla of evidence that "reasonably tend[s]" to dispute Tesoro's position, thus creating a genuine dispute of material fact to defeat its motion for summary judgment?[22] Remembering that the pricing scheme adopted in the contract – the netback approach – is not tied to actual costs, only TAPS tariffs, the question is whether any evidence raises a genuine issue of material fact as to Union Oil's argument on appeal. We have thoroughly reviewed the record and conclude that no such genuine dispute of material fact exists.[23] Union Oil meets none of Tesoro's trade usage evidence. Union Oil's position is heavily reliant on affidavits crafted after litigation began, which detailed the subjective statements of the involved negotiators and Union Oil executives. These affidavits do not create a genuine dispute of material fact because "[e]xtrinsic evidence of parties' subjective intent, expressed during the course of litigation, does not establish an issue of fact regarding the parties' reasonable expectations."[24] Rather these affidavits are merely a restatement of the parties' positions in litigation.

No contemporary expression supports Union Oil's suggested interpretation. After the original contract with Tesoro was fully performed, a single internal Union Oil email was sent during negotiations for the second contract. This internal Union Oil email provided an outline of the contract stating "Tesoro will ship on Unocal [Pipeline]'s space ... ([Union Oil] will reimburse Tesoro for pipeline tariff[.])" However, the email does not tend to reasonably dispute Tesoro's position that the term is a netback pricing term. First, it is an internal document that evidences only an employee's subjective view of the contract. Second, it is a late-arising outlier in conflict with every other Union Oil email referencing a netback pricing scheme. Third, it is silent as to whether the tariff referenced is the interstate or the intrastate tariff. This email is insufficient to create a genuine dispute of material fact as it is not more than a scintilla of

(case continues)

evidence.[25] Accordingly, Tesoro is entitled to judgment in its favor.

Conclusion

Because we find that there is no dispute of material fact that the contract employed a netback pricing scheme subtracting interstate tariffs (and marine transportation costs) from a West Coast price to establish a North Slope price for the oil, we REVERSE the grant of summary judgment to Union Oil and REMAND for entry of judgment in favor of Tesoro. Given our holding we do not reach Union Oil's cross-appeal regarding the RCA-ordered interest because Union Oil is not entitled to any part of the RCA-ordered refunds.

---

1. Pump Station No. 1 is the beginning of the Trans-Alaska Pipeline. The Center for Land Use Interpretation, The Trans-Alaska Pipeline, LAY OF THE LAND NEWSLETTER (Spring 2009), http://www.clui.org/newsletter/spring-2009/trans-alaskapipeline.
2. The pipeline companies appealed one of the orders, which was affirmed by this court in *Amerada Hess Pipeline Corp. v. Regulatory Comm'n of Alaska*, 176 P.3d 667, 669 (Alaska 2008). The pipeline companies declined to appeal the other order. In 2008 the pipeline companies issued appropriate refunds.
3. An expert for Tesoro testified that netback pricing is used in places like Alaska's North Slope where there is no widely-traded market for oil. It is a " 'theoretical' or surrogate price at Pump Station [No.] 1 net backed from a widely-traded market. A netback is the assumed final destination price less the assumed delivery charges to this hypothetical destination (e.g., the Los Angeles basin)."
4. As noted above, there are two contracts at issue in this appeal. Because the relevant provisions are identical in the two contracts, this opinion occasionally refers to "the contract."
5. *Anderson v. Alyeska Pipeline Serv. Co.*, 234 P.3d 1282 , 1286 (Alaska 2010) (citing *Parker v. Tomera*, 89 P.3d 761 , 765 (Alaska 2004)).
6. *Id.* (citing *Moore v. Allstate Ins. Co.*, 995 P.2d 231 , 233 (Alaska 2000)).
7. *Id.*
8. *Cikan v. ARCO Alaska, Inc.*, 125 P.3d 335 , 339 (Alaska 2005).
9. *Philbin v. Matanuska-Susitna Borough*, 991 P.2d 1263 , 1265-66 (Alaska 1999) (citing *Jennings v. State*, 566 P.2d 1304 , 1309 (Alaska 1977)).
10. *Cikan*, 125 P.3d at 339.
11. *Id.* (quoting *Martech Constr. Co. v. Ogden Envtl. Servs., Inc.*, 852 P.2d 1146 , 1149 n.7 (Alaska 1993)).
12. *Hartley v. Hartley*, 205 P.3d 342 , 347 (Alaska 2009) (quoting *Zito v. Zito*, 969 P.2d 1144 , 1147 n.4 (Alaska 1998)) (internal quotation marks omitted); *Rockstad v. Erikson*, 113 P.3d 1215, 1222 (Alaska 2005).
13. *Keffer v. Keffer*, 852 P.2d 394 , 397 (Alaska 1993) (internal citations omitted); *see Monzingo v. Alaska Air Grp.*, Inc., 112 P.3d 655 , 660 (Alaska 2005) ("Courts look to the language of the contract as a whole, the objects sought to be accomplished by the contract, the circumstances surrounding its adoption, and case law interpreting its provisions to ascertain the reasonable expectations of the parties." (citing *Craig Taylor Equip. Co. v. Pettibone Corp.*, 659 P.2d 594 , 597 (Alaska 1983))).
14. As noted above, a netback formula deducts from the assumed final destination price the assumed delivery charges to this hypothetical destination. *See supra* note 3. Here, the assumed final destination price was the monthly average of prices reported by Reuters and Telerate. The assumed delivery charges were comprised of a preset marine transportation charge ($1.35/barrel) and the applicable pipeline tariff.
15. Expressio unius est exclusio alterius instructs that when parties list specific items any item not so listed is excluded. *See Vanvelzor v. Vanvelzor*, 219 P.3d 184 , 188 (Alaska 2009) (citing *Ranney v. Whitewater Eng'g*, 122 P.3d 214, 218-19 (Alaska 2005)).
16. See, e.g., *Bentley Mall Assocs. v. ADC Distrib. Corp.*, Mem. Op. & J. No. 865, 1997 WL 33812770, at *1 (Alaska, Oct. 15, 1997).
17. *Id.*
18. *Chambers v. Scofield*, 247 P.3d 982, 987 (Alaska 2011) (quoting *Dominic Wenzell, D.M.D. P.C. v. Ingrim, D.M.D.*, 228 P.3d 103, 108 (Alaska 2010) (internal quotation marks omitted)).
19. *Graham v. Rockman*, 504 P.2d 1351, 1356 (Alaska 1972).
20. *Jowett, Inc. v. United States*, 234 F.3d 1365, 1369 (Fed. Cir. 2000) (quoting 3 ARTHUR L. CORBIN, CORBIN ON CONTRACTS § 555, at 233-34 (1960)).
21. *Keffer v. Keffer*, 852 P.2d 394, 397 (Alaska 1993).
22. *See Philbin v. Matanuska-Susitna Borough*, 991 P.2d 1263, 1265-66
23. We also note that Alaska Civil Rule 56(c) directs a party opposing summary judgment to provide "a concise 'statement of genuine issues' setting forth all material facts as to which it is contended there exists a genuine issue necessary to be litigated, and any other memorandum in opposition to the motion." (Emphasis added.) This did not occur in this case. Both parties submitted memoranda that supported their positions, but neither party submitted a concise statement of genuine issues. Although we have completed an extensive review of the record, the parties would have benefitted from submitting such a statement, as each could have directed the review to their specific interpretations of the factual dispute.
24. *Western Pioneer, Inc. v. Harbor Enters., Inc.*, 818 P.2d 654, 657 (Alaska 1991) (citing *Peterson v. Wirum*, 625 P.2d 866, 870 (Alaska 1981)).
25. *See DeNardo v. Bax*, 147 P.3d 672, 680-82 (Alaska 2006) (holding that evidence appellant presented, including deposition testimony and affidavits, that conflicted in several respects with appellee's claims that she was afraid for her safety, was insufficient to produce a genuine dispute of material fact); *Yurioff v. Am. Honda Motor Co.*, 803 P.2d 386, 389 (Alaska 1990) (holding that there was no genuine dispute of material fact where plaintiff presented only one piece of evidence, his own deposition testimony, that an accident occurred within the statute of limitations).

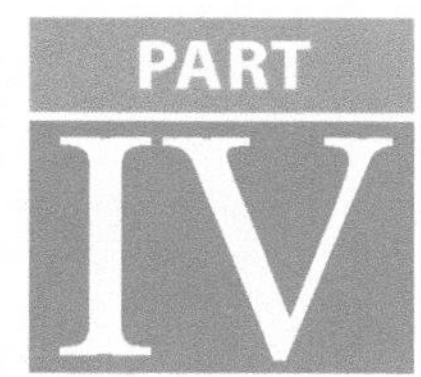

Sales and Lease Contracts and Warranties

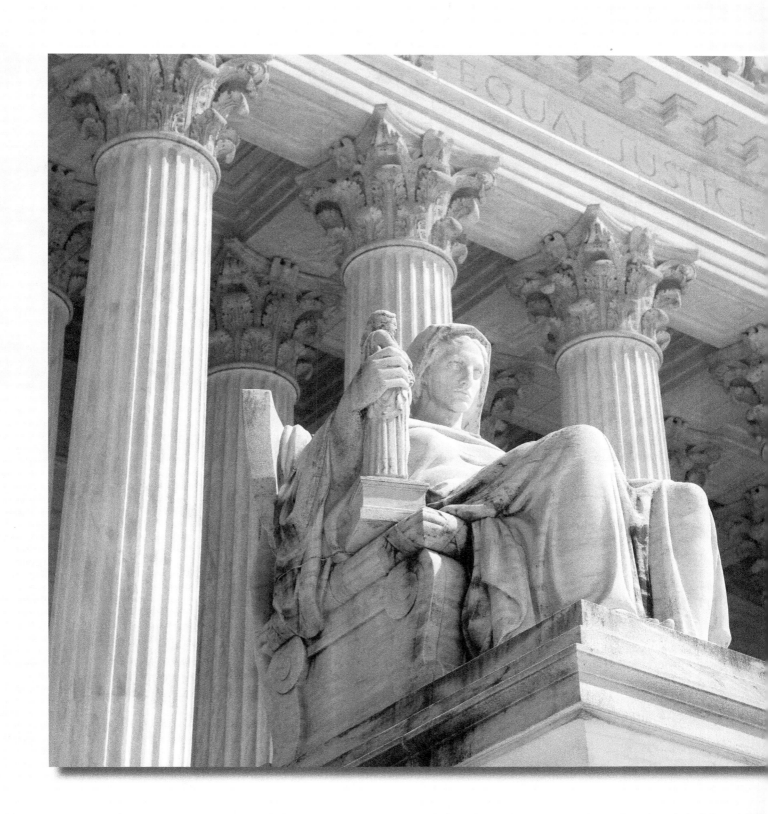

CHAPTER

18 Formation of Sales and Lease Contracts

EQUIPMENT

The sale and lease of goods—business equipment, automobiles, consumer goods, computers, electronics, and such—make up a considerable part of the U.S. economy. A special law—the Uniform Commercial Code (UCC)—contains rules that apply to contracts for the sale and lease of goods. The UCC is a model act that many states have adopted in whole or in part as their commercial code. Article 2 of the UCC covers sales of goods and Article 2A of the UCC covers the lease of goods.

Learning Objectives

After studying this chapter, you should be able to:

1. Describe sales contracts governed by Article 2 of the Uniform Commercial Code (UCC).
2. Describe lease contracts governed by Article 2A of the UCC.
3. Describe the formation of sales and lease contracts.
4. Define the UCC's *firm offer rule*, *additional terms rule*, and *written confirmation rule*.
5. Describe how Revised Article 2 (Sales) and Article 2A (Leases) permit electronic contracting.

Chapter Outline

Chapter Contents *(continued)*

> *"Commercial law lies within a narrow compass, and is far purer and freer from defects than any other part of the system."*
>
> —*Henry Peter Brougham*
> *House of Commons of the United Kingdom, February 7, 1828*

Introduction to Formation of Sales and Lease Contracts

Most tangible items—such as books, clothing, and tools—are considered *goods*. In medieval times, merchants gathered at fairs in Europe to exchange such goods. Over time, certain customs and rules evolved for enforcing contracts and resolving disputes. These customs and rules, which were referred to as the *Law Merchant*, were enforced by "fair courts" established by the merchants. Eventually, the customs and rules of the Law Merchant were absorbed into the common law.

Toward the end of the 1800s, England enacted a statute (the Sales of Goods Act) that codified the common law rules of commercial transactions. In the United States, laws governing the sale of goods also developed. In 1906, the **Uniform Sales Act** was promulgated in the United States and enacted in many states. It was quickly outdated, however, as mass production and distribution of goods developed in the twentieth century.

A lean agreement is better than a fat judgment.

Proverb

In 1949, the National Conference of Commissioners on Uniform State Laws promulgated a comprehensive statutory scheme called the *Uniform Commercial Code (UCC)*. The UCC covers most aspects of commercial transactions.

Article 2 (Sales) and *Article 2A (Leases)* of the UCC govern personal property sales and leases. These articles are intended to provide clear, easy-to-apply rules that place the risk of loss of the goods on the party most able either to bear the risk or insure against it. The common law of contracts governs whether either Article 2 or Article 2A is silent on an issue.

This chapter discusses the formation of sales and lease contracts. Subsequent chapters cover the performance, enforcement, breach, and remedies for the breach of sales and lease contracts as well as sales and lease contract warranties.

Uniform Commercial Code

One of the major frustrations of businesspeople conducting interstate business is that they are subject to the laws of each state in which they operate. To address this problem, in 1949, the National Conference of Commissioners on Uniform State Laws promulgated the **Uniform Commercial Code (UCC)**. The following feature discusses the UCC.

Uniform Commercial Code (UCC)
A model act that includes comprehensive laws that cover most aspects of commercial transactions. All the states have enacted all or part of the UCC as statutes.

Landmark Law

Uniform Commercial Code

The UCC is a *model act* drafted by the American Law Institute and the National Conference of Commissioners on Uniform State Laws. This model act contains uniform rules that govern commercial transactions. For the UCC or any part of the UCC to become law in a state, that state needs to enact the UCC as its commercial law statute. Every state (except Louisiana, which has adopted only parts of the UCC) has enacted the UCC or the majority of the UCC as a commercial statute.

The UCC is divided into articles, with each article establishing uniform rules for a particular facet of commerce in this country. The articles of the UCC are:

Article 1	General Provisions
Article 2	Sales
Article 2A	Leases
Article 3	Negotiable Instruments
Article 4	Bank Deposits
Article 4A	Funds Transfers
Article 5	Letters of Credit
Article 6	Bulk Transfers and Bulk Sales
Article 7	Warehouse Receipts, Bills of Lading, and Other Documents of Title
Article 8	Investment Securities
Article 9	Secured Transactions

The UCC is continually being revised to reflect changes in modern commercial practices and technology.

Article 2 (Sales)

Critical Legal Thinking

What is the benefit of states having similar or almost similar laws regarding transactions in goods? Should uniform laws also be adopted for the providing of services, sale of real estate, and other transactions?

Article 2 (Sales)
An article of the UCC that governs sale of goods.

sale
The passing of title of goods from a seller to a buyer for a price.

All states except Louisiana have adopted some version of **Article 2 (Sales)** of the UCC. Article 2 is also applied by federal courts to sales contracts governed by federal law.

What Is a Sale?

Article 2 of the UCC applies to transactions in goods [UCC 2-102]. All states have held that Article 2 applies to **sales contracts** for the sale of goods. A **sale** consists of the passing of title of goods from a seller to a buyer for a price [UCC 2-106(1)].

Example The purchase of an automobile (costing $500 or more) is a sale of a good subject to Article 2, whether the automobile was paid for using cash, credit card, or another form of consideration (see **Exhibit 18.1**).

Exhibit 18.1 SALES TRANSACTION

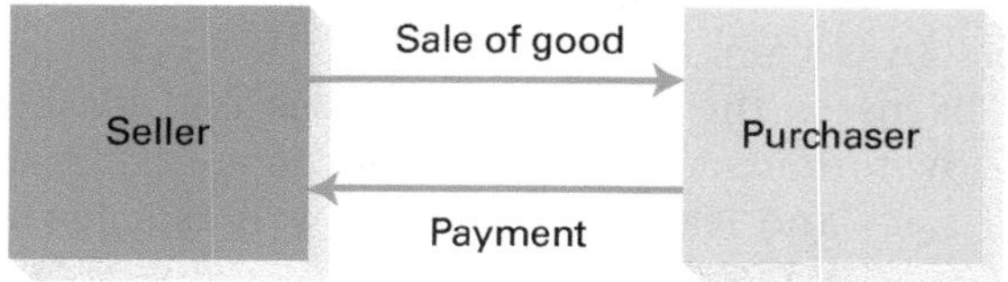

What Are Goods?

goods
Tangible items that are movable at the time of their identification to a contract.

Goods are defined as tangible items that are movable at the time of their identification to a contract [UCC 2-105(1)]. Specially manufactured goods and the unborn young of animals are examples of goods. Certain items are not considered goods and are not subject to Article 2. They include:

- Money and intangible items are not tangible goods.

  Examples Stocks, bonds, and patents are not tangible goods.

- Real estate is not a tangible good because it is not movable [UCC 2-105(1)]. However, minerals, structures, growing crops, and other items that are severable from real estate may be classified as goods subject to Article 2.

  Examples The sale and removal of a chandelier in a house is a sale of goods subject to Article 2 because its removal would not materially harm the real estate. The sale and removal of the furnace, however, would be a sale of real property because its removal would cause material harm [UCC 2-107(2)].

Goods Versus Services

Contracts for the provision of services—including legal services, medical services, and dental services—are not covered by Article 2. Sometimes, however, a sale involves both the provision of a service and a good in the same transaction. This sale is referred to as a **mixed sale**. Article 2 applies to mixed sales only if the goods are the predominant part of the transaction. Whether the sale of goods is the predominant part of a mixed sale is decided by courts on a case-by-case basis.

mixed sale
A sale that involves the provision of a service and a good in the same transaction.

In the following case, the court had to decide whether a sale was of a good or a service.

CASE 18.1 *STATE COURT CASE Good or Service*

Brandt v. Boston Scientific Corporation and Sarah Bush Lincoln Health Center

204 Ill.2d 640, 792 N.E.2d 296, 2003 Ill. Lexis 785 (2003)
Supreme Court of Illinois

"Where there is a mixed contract for goods and services, there is a transaction in goods only if the contract is predominantly for goods and incidentally for services."

—Garman, Justice

Facts

Brenda Brandt was admitted to Sarah Bush Lincoln Health Center (Health Center) to receive treatment for urinary incontinence. During the course of an operation, the doctor surgically implanted a Prote-Gen Sling (sling) in Brandt. Subsequently, the manufacturer of the sling, Boston Scientific Corporation, issued a recall of the sling because it was causing medical complications in some patients. Brandt suffered serious complications and had the sling surgically removed.

Brandt sued Boston Scientific Corporation and the Health Center for breach of the implied warranty of merchantability included in Article 2 (Sales) of the Uniform Commercial Code (UCC). Health Center filed a motion with the court to have the case against it dismissed. Health Center argued that it was a provider of services and not a merchant that sold goods, and because the UCC (Sales) applies to the sale of goods, Health Center was not subject to the UCC. The trial court agreed with Health Center, found that the transaction was predominantly the provision of services and not the sale of goods, and dismissed Brandt's case against Health Center. The appellate court affirmed the decision. Brandt appealed.

Issue

Is the transaction between Brandt and Health Center predominantly the provision of services or the sale of goods?

Language of the Court

Where there is a mixed contract for goods and services, there is a transaction in goods only if the contract is predominantly for goods and incidentally for services. In this case, Brandt's bill from the Health Center reflects that of the $11,174.50 total charge for her surgery, a charge of $1,659.50, or 14.9%, was for the sling and its surgical kit. The services, the medical treatment, were the primary purpose of the transaction between Brandt and the Health Center, and the purchase of the sling was incidental to the treatment. Only a small fraction

(case continues)

of the total charge was for the sling, the goods at issue in this case.

Decision

The supreme court of Illinois held that the provision of services and not the sale of goods was the predominant feature of the transaction between Brandt and Health Center and that Health Center was not liable under Article 2 (Sales) of the UCC. The supreme court of Illinois upheld the dismissal of the case against Health Center.

Note

Brandt can seek recovery from the manufacturer of the sling, Boston Scientific Corporation, based on product defect.

Ethics Questions

Based on the facts, did Brandt have a reasonable case against Health Center? Can Health Center recover its lawyers' fees in this case?

Who Is a Merchant?

Generally, Article 2 of the UCC applies to all sales contracts, whether they involve merchants or not. However, Article 2 contains several provisions that either apply only to merchants or impose a greater duty on merchants. UCC 2-104(1) defines a **merchant** as (1) a person who deals in the goods of the kind involved in the transaction or (2) a person who by his or her occupation holds him- or herself out as having knowledge or skill peculiar to the goods involved in the transaction.

merchant
A person who (1) deals in the goods of the kind involved in a transaction or (2) by his or her occupation holds him- or herself out as having knowledge or skill peculiar to the goods involved in the transaction.

Examples A sporting goods dealer is a merchant with respect to the sporting goods he or she sells. This sporting goods dealer is not a merchant concerning the sale of his or her lawn mower to a neighbor.

LEASED AUTOMOBILES
More than 20 percent of automobiles and other vehicles are leased. Such leases are subject to the provisions of Article 2A of the UCC.

Article 2A (Leases)

Personal property leases are a billion-dollar industry. Consumer leases of automobiles or equipment and commercial leases of items such as aircraft and industrial machinery fall into this category. **Article 2A (Leases)** of the UCC directly addresses personal property leases [UCC 2A-101]. It establishes a comprehensive, uniform law covering the formation, performance, and default of leases in goods [UCC 2A-102, 2A-103(h)].

Article 2A (Leases)
An article of the UCC that governs leases of goods.

Article 2A is similar to Article 2. In fact, many Article 2 provisions were simply adapted to reflect leasing terminology and practices that carried over to Article 2A.

Definition of *Lease*

A **lease** is a transfer of the right to the possession and use of named goods for a set term in return for certain consideration [UCC 2A-103(1)(i)(x)]. Leased goods can be anything from an automobile leased to an individual to a complex line of industrial equipment leased to a multinational corporation.

lease
A transfer of the right to the possession and use of named goods for a set term in return for certain consideration.

In a **lease contract**, the **lessor** is the person who transfers the right of possession and use of goods under the lease [UCC 2A-103(1)(p)]. The **lessee** is the person who acquires the right to possession and use of goods under a lease [UCC 2A-103(1)(n)].

lessor
A person who transfers the right of possession and use of goods under a lease.

lessee
A person who acquires the right to possession and use of goods under a lease.

Example Ingersoll-Rand Corporation, which manufactures robotic equipment, enters into a contract to lease robotic equipment to Dow Chemical. This is a lease contract. Ingersoll-Rand is the lessor, and Dow Chemical is the lessee (see **Exhibit 18.2**).

Exhibit 18.2 **LEASE**

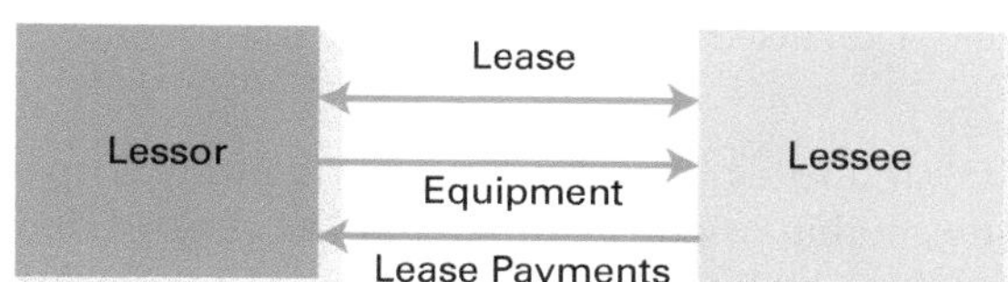

Finance Lease

A **finance lease** is a three-party transaction consisting of a lessor, a lessee, and a **supplier** (or vendor). The lessor does not select, manufacture, or supply the goods. Instead, the lessor acquires title to the goods or the right to their possession and use in connection with the terms of the lease [UCC 2A-103(1)(g)].

finance lease
A three-party transaction consisting of a lessor, a lessee, and a supplier.

Example JetGreen Airways, a commercial air carrier, decides to lease a new airplane that is manufactured by Boeing. To finance the airplane acquisition, JetGreen goes to City Bank. City Bank purchases the airplane from Boeing, and City Bank then leases the airplane to JetGreen. Boeing is the supplier, City Bank is the lessor, and JetGreen is the lessee. City Bank does not take physical delivery of the airplane; the airplane is delivered by Boeing directly to JetGreen (see **Exhibit 18.3**).

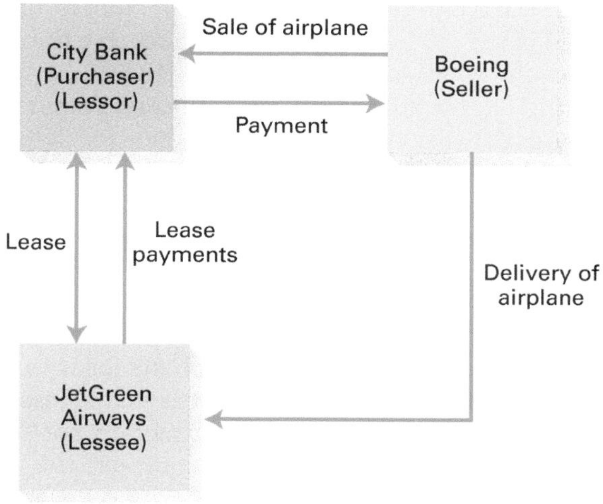

Exhibit 18.3 **FINANCE LEASE**

City Bank (Purchaser) (Lessor)
Sale of airplane
Payment
Boeing (Seller)
Lease
Lease payments
Delivery of airplane
JetGreen Airways (Lessee)

Formation of Sales and Lease Contracts: Offer

As with general contracts, the formation of sales and lease contracts requires an offer and an acceptance. The UCC-established rules for each of these elements often differ considerably from common law.

A contract for the sale or lease of goods may be made in any manner sufficient to show agreement, including conduct by both parties that recognizes the existence of a contract [UCC 2-204(1), 2A-204(1)]. Under the UCC, an agreement sufficient to constitute a contract for the sale or lease of goods may be found even though the moment of its making is undetermined [UCC 2-204(2), 2A-204(2)].

Open Terms

Sometimes the parties to a sales or lease contract leave open a major term in the contract. The UCC is tolerant of open terms. According to UCC 2-204(3) and 2A-204(3), a contract does not fail because of indefiniteness if (1) the parties intended to make a contract and (2) there is a reasonably certain basis for giving an appropriate remedy. In effect, certain **open terms** are permitted to be "read into" sales or lease contracts. This rule is commonly referred to as the **gap-filling rule**. Some examples of terms that are commonly left open are discussed in the following list:

gap-filling rule
A rule that says an open term can be "read into" a contract.

- **Open price term.** If a sales contract does not contain a specific price (**open price term**), a "reasonable price" is implied at the time of delivery.

  Example A contract may provide that a price is to be fixed by a market rate, such as a commodities market rate.

  Example A contract may provide that a price will be set or recorded by a third person or an agency, such as a government agency. For example, the federal government sets minimum prices for some agricultural products.

  A contract may provide that the price will be set by another standard, either on delivery or on a set date. If the agreed-on standard is unavailable when the price is to be set, a reasonable price is implied at the time of delivery of the goods [UCC 2-305(1)]. A seller or buyer who reserves the right to fix a price must do so in good faith [UCC 2-305(2)]. When one of the parties fails to fix an open price term, the other party may opt either (1) to treat the contract as canceled or (2) to fix a reasonable price for the goods [UCC 2-305(3)].

Laws made by common consent must not be trampled on by individuals.
George Washington (1732–1799)

- **Open payment term.** If the parties to a sales contract do not agree on payment terms, payment is due at the time and place at which the buyer is to receive the goods.

  If delivery is authorized and made by way of document of title, payment is due at the time and place at which the buyer is to receive the document of title, regardless of where the goods are to be received [UCC 2-310].
- **Open delivery term.** If the parties to a sales contract do not agree to the time, place, and manner of delivery of the goods, the place for delivery is the seller's place of business. If the seller does not have a place of business, delivery is to be made at the seller's residence.

  If identified goods are located at some other place and both parties know of this fact at the time of contracting, that place is the place of delivery [UCC 2-308].

  If goods are to be shipped but the shipper is not named, the seller is obligated to make the shipping arrangements. Such arrangements must be made in good faith and within limits of commercial reasonableness [UCC 2-311(2)].

The foundation of justice is good faith.
Cicero
De Officiis, book 1, chapter VII (44 BCE)

- **Open time term.** If the parties to a sales contract do not set a specific time of performance for any obligation under the contract, the contract must be performed within a reasonable time.

If a sales contract provides for successive performance over an unspecified period of time, the contract is valid for a reasonable time [UCC 2-309].

- **Open assortment term.** If the assortment of goods to a sales contract is left open, the buyer is given the option of choosing those goods. The buyer must make the selection in good faith and within limits set by commercial reasonableness (UCC 2-311(2)].

The following feature discusses a unique UCC rule.

Contemporary Environment

UCC Firm Offer Rule

Recall that the common law of contracts allows the offeror to revoke an offer any time prior to its acceptance. The UCC recognizes an exception to this rule, which is called the **firm offer rule**. This rule states that a *merchant* who (1) offers to buy, sell, or lease goods and (2) gives a written and signed assurance on a separate form that the offer will be held open cannot revoke the offer for the time stated or, if no time is stated, for a reasonable time. The maximum amount of time permitted under this rule is three months [UCC 2-205, 2A-205].

Example On June 1, Sophisticated LLC, a BMW automobile dealer, offers to sell a BMW M3 coupe to Mandy for $60,000. Sophisticated LLC signs a written assurance to keep that offer open to Mandy until July 15. On July 5, Sophisticated LLC sells the car to another buyer. On July 15, Mandy tenders $60,000 for the car. Sophisticated LLC is a merchant subject to the firm offer rule. Sophisticated LLC is liable to Mandy for breach of contract. Thus, if Mandy has to pay $70,000 for the car at another dealership, she can recover $10,000 from Sophisticated LLC.

Consideration

The formation of sales and lease contracts requires consideration. However, the UCC changes the common law rule that requires the modification of a contract to be supported by new consideration. An agreement modifying a sales or lease contract needs no consideration to be binding [UCC 2-209(1), 2A-208(1)].

Modification of a sales or lease contract must be made in good faith [UCC 1-203]. As in the common law of contracts, modifications are not binding if they are obtained through fraud, duress, extortion, and so on.

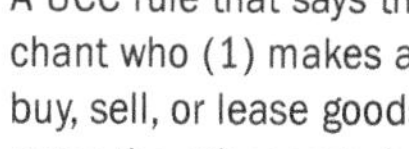

firm offer rule
A UCC rule that says that a merchant who (1) makes an offer to buy, sell, or lease goods and (2) assures the other party in a separate writing that the offer will be held open cannot revoke the offer for the time stated or, if no time is stated, for a reasonable time.

TRUCKING INDUSTRY
Goods subject to sales contracts are commonly transported by trucks across the United States.

Formation of Sales and Lease Contracts: Acceptance

Both common law and the UCC provide that a contract is created when the offeree (i.e., the buyer or lessee) sends an acceptance to the offeror (seller or lessor), not when the offeror receives the acceptance.

Examples A sales or lease contract is made when the acceptance letter is delivered to the post office. The contract remains valid even if the post office loses the letter. An e-contract is made when the offeree sends an e-mail or another electronic document to the offeror.

Method and Manner of Acceptance

Law must be stable and yet it cannot stand still.

Roscoe Pound
Interpretations of Legal History (1923)

Unless otherwise unambiguously indicated by language or circumstance, an offer to make a sales or lease contract may be accepted in any manner and by any reasonable medium of acceptance [UCC 2-206(1)(a), 2A-206(1)].

Example A seller sends a telegram to a proposed buyer, offering to sell the buyer certain goods. The buyer responds by mailing a letter of acceptance to the seller. In most circumstances, mailing the letter of acceptance would be considered reasonable. If the goods were extremely perishable or if the market for the goods were very volatile, however, a faster means of acceptance (e.g., a telegram) might be warranted.

If an order or other offer to buy goods requires prompt or current shipment, the offer is accepted if the seller (1) promptly promises to ship the goods or (2) promptly ships either conforming or nonconforming goods [UCC 2-206(1)(b)]. The shipment of conforming goods signals acceptance of the buyer's offer.

Acceptance of goods occurs after the buyer or lessee has a reasonable opportunity to inspect them and signifies that (1) the goods are conforming, (2) he or she will take or retain the goods despite of their nonconformity, or (3) he or she fails to reject the goods within a reasonable time after tender or delivery [UCC 2-513(1), 2A-515(1)].

additional terms
In certain circumstances, the UCC permits an acceptance of a sales contract to contain additional terms and to act still as an acceptance rather than a counteroffer.

The following feature discusses an area of the law where the UCC differs from the common law of contracts.

Contemporary Environment

UCC Permits Additional Terms

Under common law's **mirror image rule**, an offeree's acceptance must be on the same terms as the offer. The inclusion of **additional terms** in the acceptance is considered a **counteroffer** rather than an acceptance. Thus, a counteroffer extinguishes the offeror's original offer.

UCC 2-207(1) is more liberal than the mirror image rule. It permits definite and timely expression of acceptance or written confirmation to operate as an acceptance even though the contract contains terms that are additional to or different from the offered terms, unless the acceptance is expressly conditional on assent to such terms.

If one or both parties to a sales contract are *nonmerchants*, any additional terms are considered **proposed additions** to the contract. The proposed additions do not constitute a counteroffer or extinguish the original offer. If the offeree's proposed additions are accepted by the original offeror, they become part of the contract. If they are not accepted, the sales contract is formed on the basis of the terms of the original offer [UCC 2-207(2)].

Example A salesperson at a Lexus dealership offers to sell an automobile to a buyer for $65,000. The buyer replies, "I accept your offer, but I would like to have a satellite radio in the car." The satellite radio is a proposed addition to the contract. If the salesperson agrees, the contract between the parties consists of the terms of the original offer plus the additional term regarding the satellite radio. If the salesperson rejects the proposed addition, the sales contract consists of the terms of the original offer because the buyer made a definite expression of acceptance.

Accommodation Shipment

A shipment of nonconforming goods does not constitute an acceptance if the seller reasonably notifies the buyer that the shipment is offered only as an **accommodation** to the buyer [UCC 2-206(1)(b)].

accommodation
A shipment that is offered to a buyer as a replacement for the original shipment when the original shipment cannot be filled.

Example A buyer offers to purchase 500 red umbrellas from a seller. The seller's red umbrellas are temporarily out of stock. The seller sends the buyer 500 green umbrellas and notifies the buyer that these umbrellas are being sent as an accommodation. The accommodation is a counteroffer from the seller to the buyer. The buyer is free either to accept or to reject the counteroffer.

The following feature discusses how the UCC resolves a common problem that occurs between merchants.

Business Environment

UCC Battle of the Forms

When *merchants* negotiate sales contracts, they often exchange preprinted forms. These "boilerplate" forms usually contain terms that favor the drafter. Thus, an offeror who sends a standard form contract as an offer to the offeree may receive an acceptance drafted on the offeree's own form contract. This scenario—commonly called the **battle of the forms**—raises important questions: Is there a contract? If so, what are its terms? The UCC provides guidance in answering these questions.

Under UCC 2-207(2), if both parties are merchants, any additional terms contained in an acceptance become part of the sales contract unless (1) the offer expressly limits acceptance to the terms of the offer, (2) the additional terms materially alter the terms of the original contract, or (3) the offeror notifies the offeree that he or she objects to the additional terms within a reasonable time after receiving the offeree's modified acceptance.

In the battle of the forms, there is no contract if the additional terms so materially alter the terms of the original offer that the parties cannot agree on the contract. This fact-specific determination is made by the courts on a case-by-case basis.

UCC Statute of Frauds

The UCC includes Statute of Frauds provisions that apply to sales and lease contracts. The provisions of the **UCC Statute of Frauds** are as follows:

- All contracts for the *sale of goods* priced at *$500 or more* must be in writing [UCC 2-201(1)].
- *Lease* contracts requiring payments of *$1,000 or more* must be in writing (UCC 2A-201(1)].

Future amendments to the UCC may increase these dollar amounts.

The writing must be sufficient to indicate that a contract has been made between the parties. Except as discussed in the paragraphs that follow, the writing must be signed by the party against whom enforcement is sought or by his or her authorized agent or broker. If a contract falling within these parameters is not written, it is unenforceable.

Example A seller orally agrees to sell her computer to a buyer for $550. When the buyer tenders the purchase price, the seller asserts the Statute of Frauds and refuses to sell the computer to him. The seller is correct. The contract must be in writing to be enforceable because the contract price for the computer exceeds $499.99.

battle of the forms
A UCC rule stating that if both parties are merchants, then additional terms contained in the acceptance may become part of the sales contract if certain requirements are met.

Critical Legal Thinking

The UCC additional terms rule and UCC battle of the forms rule differs from the mirror image rule applicable to non-UCC contracts. Why are the UCC rules more liberal in allowing contracts to be formed?

UCC Statute of Frauds
A rule in the UCC that requires all contracts for the sale of goods costing $500 or more and lease contracts involving payments of $1,000 or more to be in writing.

Exceptions to the UCC Statute of Frauds

In three situations, a sales or lease contract that would otherwise be required to be in writing is enforceable even if it is not in writing [UCC 2-201(3), UCC 2A-201(4)]:

1. **Specially manufactured goods.** Buyers and lessees often order **specially manufactured goods**. If a contract to purchase or lease such goods is oral, the buyer or lessee may not assert the Statute of Frauds against the enforcement of the contract if (1) the goods are not suitable for sale or lease to others in the ordinary course of the seller's or the lessor's business and (2) the seller or lessor has made either a substantial beginning of the manufacture of the goods or commitments for their procurement.
2. **Admissions in pleadings or court.** If the party against whom enforcement of an oral sales or lease contract is sought admits in pleadings, testimony, or otherwise in court that a contract for the sale or lease of goods was made, the oral contract is enforceable against that party. However, the contract is enforceable only as to the quantity of goods admitted.
3. **Part acceptance.** An oral sales or lease contract that should otherwise be in writing is enforceable to the extent to which the goods have been received and accepted by the buyer or lessee.

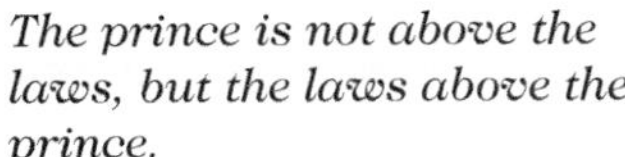

The prince is not above the laws, but the laws above the prince.

Pliny the Younger (Gaius Caecilius Secundus) (61-113 CE)

Example A lessor orally contracts to lease 20 automobiles to a lessee. The lessee accepts the first eight automobiles tendered by the lessor. This action is part acceptance. The lessee refuses to take delivery of the remaining 12 automobiles. Here, the lessee must pay for the eight automobiles it originally received and accepted. The lessee does not have to accept or pay for the remaining 12 automobiles.

The following feature discusses a unique UCC rule that applies to contracts between merchants.

Business Environment

UCC Written Confirmation Rule

Under the **written confirmation rule**, if both parties to an oral sales or lease contract are *merchants*, the Statute of Frauds writing requirement can be satisfied if (1) one of the parties to an oral agreement sends a written confirmation of the sale or lease within a reasonable time after contracting and (2) the other merchant does not give written notice of an objection to the contract within 10 days after receiving the confirmation. This situation is true even though the party receiving the written confirmation has not signed it. The only stipulations are that the confirmation is sufficient and that the party to whom it was sent has reason to know its contents [UCC 2-201(2)].

Example A merchant-seller in Chicago orally contracts by telephone to sell goods to a merchant-buyer in Phoenix for $100,000. Within a reasonable time after contracting, the seller sends a sufficient written confirmation to the buyer of the agreed-on transaction. The buyer, who has reason to know the contents of the written confirmation, fails to object to the contents of the confirmation in writing within 10 days after receiving it. Under the UCC, the Statute of Frauds has been met, and the buyer cannot thereafter raise it against enforcement of the contract.

When Written Modification Is Required

Oral modification of a contract is not enforceable if the parties agree that any modification of the sales or lease contract must be signed in writing [UCC 2-209(2), 2A-208(2)]. In the absence of such an agreement, oral modifications to sales and lease contracts are binding if they do not violate the Statute of Frauds. If the oral modification brings the contract within the Statute of Frauds, it must be in writing to be enforceable.

Example A lessor and lessee enter into an oral lease contract for the lease of goods at a rent of $450. Subsequently, the contract is modified by raising the rent to $550. Because the modified contract rent is more than $499.99, the contract comes under the UCC Statute of Frauds, and the modification must be in writing to be enforceable.

written confirmation rule
A rule stating that, if both parties to an oral sales or lease contract are merchants, the Statute of Frauds writing requirement can be satisfied if (1) one of the parties to an oral agreement sends a written confirmation of the sale or lease within a reasonable time after contracting and (2) the other merchant does not give written notice of an objection to the contract within 10 days after receiving the confirmation.

Parol Evidence Rule

The **parol evidence rule** states that when a sales or lease contract is evidenced by a writing that is intended to be a final expression of the parties' agreement or a confirmatory memorandum, the terms of the writing may not be contradicted by evidence of (1) a prior oral or written agreement or (2) a contemporaneous oral agreement (i.e., parol evidence) [UCC 2-202, 2A-202]. This rule is intended to ensure certainty in written sales and lease contracts.

parol evidence rule
A rule that says that if a written contract is a complete and final statement of the parties' agreement, any prior or contemporaneous oral or written statements that alter, contradict, or are in addition to the terms of the written contract are inadmissible in court regarding a dispute over the contract.

Occasionally, the express terms of a written contract are not clear on their face and must be interpreted. In such cases, reference may be made to certain sources outside the contract. These sources are construed together when they are consistent with each other. If that is unreasonable, they are considered in descending order of priority [UCC 2-208(2), 2A-207(2)]:

1. **Course of performance.** Conduct of the parties concerning the contract in question.
2. **Course of dealing.** Conduct of the parties in prior transactions and contracts.
3. **Usage of trade.** Any practice or method of dealing that is regularly observed or adhered to in a place, a vocation, a trade, or an industry.

Example A cattle rancher contracts to purchase 3,000 bushels of "corn" from a farmer. The farmer delivers feed corn to the rancher. The rancher rejects this corn and demands delivery of corn that is fit for human consumption. If the parties did not have any prior course of performance or course of dealing that would indicate otherwise, usage of trade would be used to interpret the word *corn*. Thus, the delivery of feed corn would be assumed and become part of the contract.

CONCEPT SUMMARY
COMPARISON OF CONTRACT LAW AND THE LAW OF SALES

Topic	Common Law of Contract	UCC Law of Sales
Definiteness	Contract must contain all the material terms of the parties' agreement.	The UCC gap-filling rule permits terms to be implied if the parties intended to make a contract and there is reasonably certain basis for giving an appropriate remedy [UCC 2-204].
Irrevocable offers	Option contracts.	Option contracts. Firm offers by merchants to keep an offer open are binding up to 3 months without any consideration [UCC 2-205].

(continued)

Topic	Common Law of Contract	UCC Law of Sales
Counteroffers	Acceptance must be a mirror image of the offer. A counteroffer rejects and terminates the offeror's original offer.	Additional terms of an acceptance become part of the contract if (1) they do not materially alter the terms of the offer and (2) the offeror does not object within a reasonable time after reviewing the acceptance [UCC 2-207].
Statute of Frauds	Writing must be signed by the party against whom enforcement is sought.	Writing may be enforced against a party who has not signed a contract if (1) both parties are merchants, (2) one party sends a written confirmation of oral agreement within a reasonable time after contracting, and (3) the other party does not give written notice of objection within 10 days after receiving the confirmation [UCC 2-201].
Modification	Consideration is required.	Consideration is not required [UCC 2-209].

Electronic Sales and Lease Contracts

Certain states have adopted provisions that recognize the importance of electronic contracting in sales and lease transactions. Most state laws recognize **electronic sales contracts (e-sales contracts)** and **electronic lease contracts (e-lease contracts)**. Following are some of the definitions for electronic commerce and their implications:

- **Electronic** means relating to technology having electrical, digital, magnetic, wireless, optical, electromagnetic, or similar capabilities. This term extends many of the provisions and rules of the UCC to cover electronic contracting of sales and lease contracts.
- **Electronic agent** means a computer program or an electronic or other automated means used independently to initiate an action or respond to electronic records or performances in whole or in part, without review or action by an individual. This definition allows for the contracting for the sale and lease of goods over the Internet, using websites to order or lease goods.
- **Electronic record (e-record)** means a record created, generated, sent, communicated, received, or stored by electronic means. This term is often used in addition to the words *writing* and *record* and thus recognizes that UCC contracts and other information may be sent or stored by electronic means rather than in tangible writings.
- **Electronic signature (e-signature)** means the signature of a person that appears on an electronic record and is recognized as a lawful signature. An electronic signature may also be that of a person's electronic agent.

These definitions expand the coverage of the provisions of UCC Article 2 and Article 2A to electronic contracting of sales and lease contracts.

The following feature discusses the use of letters of credit in international trade.

electronic agent
A computer program or an electronic or other automated means used independently to initiate an action or respond to electronic records or performances in whole or in part, without review or action by an individual.

electronic record (e-record)
A record created, generated, sent, communicated, received, or stored by electronic means.

letter of credit
A document that is issued by a bank on behalf of a buyer who purchases goods on credit from a seller that guarantees that if the buyer does not pay for the goods, then the bank will pay the seller.

Article 5 (Letters of Credit)
An article of the UCC that governs letters of credit.

Global Law

Letters of Credit and International Trade

SAUDI ARABIA
Letters of credit *support the sale of goods. If a buyer wishes to purchase goods on credit from a seller, the seller may require the buyer to obtain a letter of credit from a bank. A letter of credit guarantees the seller that if the buyer does not pay for the goods, then the bank will pay the seller. A buyer of a letter of credit must pay a bank a fee to write the letter of credit. Letters of credit are governed by* **Article 5 (Letters of Credit)** *of the Uniform Commercial Code (UCC). Letters of credit are of significant importance in supporting the international sale of goods. Often a seller located in one country will sell goods on credit to a buyer located in another country only if the buyer submits a letter of credit from a bank guaranteeing payment if the buyer does not pay. Many banks require that international letters of credit be governed by the* **Uniform Customs and Practices for Documentary Credits (UCP)**.

Key Terms and Concepts

Accommodation (411)
Additional terms (410)
Article 2 (Sales) (404)
Article 2A (Leases) (406)
Article 5 (Letters of Credit) (415)
Battle of the forms (411)
Counteroffer (410)
Course of dealing (413)
Course of performance (413)
Electronic (414)
Electronic agent (414)
Electronic lease contract (e-lease contract) (414)
Electronic record (e-record) (414)
Electronic sales contract (e-sales contract) (414)
Electronic signature (e-signature) (414)
Finance lease (407)
Firm offer rule (409)
Gap-filling rule (408)
Goods (404)
Lease (407)

Lease contract (407)
Lessee (407)
Lessor (407)
Letters of credit (415)
Merchant (406)
Mirror image rule (410)
Mixed sale (405)
Open assortment term (409)
Open delivery term (408)
Open payment term (408)
Open price term (408)
Open term (408)
Open time term (408)
Parol evidence rule (413)
Proposed additions (410)
Sale (404)
Sales contract (404)
Specially manufactured goods (412)
Supplier (407)
UCC Statute of Frauds (411)
Uniform Commercial Code (UCC) (403)
Uniform Customs and Practices for Documentary Credits (UCP) (415)
Uniform Sales Act (403)
Usage of trade (413)
Written confirmation rule (412)

Critical Legal Thinking Cases

18.1 Good or Service Mr. Gulash lived in Shelton, Connecticut. He wanted an aboveground swimming pool installed in his backyard. Gulash contacted Stylarama, Inc. (Stylarama), a company specializing in the sale and construction of pools. The two parties entered into a contract that called for Stylarama to "furnish all labor and materials to construct a Wavecrest brand pool, and furnish and install a pool with vinyl liners." The total cost for materials and labor was $3,690. There was no breakdown in the contract of costs between labor and materials. After the pool was installed, its sides began bowing out, the four-inch wooden supports for the pool rotted and misaligned, and the entire pool became tilted. Gulash brought suit, alleging that Stylarama had violated several provisions of Article 2 of the UCC. Is this transaction one involving goods, making it subject to Article 2? *Gulash v. Stylarama*, 33 Conn. Supp. 108, 364 A.2d 1221, 1975 Conn. Super. Lexis 209 (Superior Court of Connecticut)

18.2 Statute of Frauds St. Charles Cable TV (St. Charles) was building a new cable television system in Louisiana. It contacted Eagle Comtronics, Inc. (Eagle), by phone and began negotiating to buy descrambler units for its cable system. These units would allow St. Charles's customers to receive the programs they had paid for. Although no written contract was ever signed, St. Charles ordered several thousand descramblers. The descramblers were shipped to St. Charles, along with a sales acknowledgment form. St. Charles made partial payment for the descramblers before discovering that some of the units were defective. Eagle accepted a return of the defective scramblers. St. Charles then attempted to return all the descramblers, asking that they be replaced by a newer model. When Eagle refused to replace all the old descramblers, St. Charles stopped paying Eagle. Eagle sued St. Charles, claiming that no valid contract existed between the parties. Is there a valid sales contract? *St. Charles Cable TV v. Eagle Comtronics, Inc.*, 687 F.Supp. 820, 1988 U.S. Dist. Lexis 4566 (United States District Court for the Southern District of New York)

18.3 Battle of the Forms Dan Miller was a commercial photographer who had taken a series of photographs that appeared in *The New York Times*. *Newsweek* magazine wanted to use the photographs. When a *Newsweek* employee named Dwyer phoned Miller, Dwyer was told that 72 images were available. Dwyer said that he wanted to inspect the photographs and offered a certain sum of money for each photo *Newsweek* used. The photos were to remain Miller's property. Miller and Dwyer agreed to the price and the date for delivery. *Newsweek* sent a courier to pick up the photographs. Along with the photos, Miller gave the courier a delivery memo that set out various conditions for the use of the photographs. The memo included a clause that required *Newsweek* to pay $1,500 each if any of the photos were lost or destroyed. After *Newsweek* received the package, it decided it no longer needed Miller's work. When Miller called to have the photos returned, he was told that they had all been lost. Miller demanded that *Newsweek* pay him $1,500 for each of the 72 lost photos. Assume that the court finds Miller and *Newsweek* to be merchants. Are the clauses in the delivery memo part of the sales contract? *Miller v. Newsweek, Inc.*, 660 F.Supp. 852, 1987 U.S. Dist. Lexis 4338 (United States District Court for the District of Delaware)

18.4 Open Terms Alvin Cagle was a potato farmer in Alabama who had had several business dealings with the H. C. Schmieding Produce Co. (Schmieding). Several months before harvest, Cagle entered into an oral sales contract with Schmieding. The contract called for Schmieding to pay the market price at harvest time for all the red potatoes that Cagle grew on his 30-acre farm. Schmieding asked that the potatoes be delivered during the normal harvest months. As Cagle began harvesting his red potatoes, he contacted Schmieding to arrange delivery. Schmieding told the farmer that no contract had been formed because the terms of the agreement were too indefinite. Cagle demanded that Schmieding buy his crop. When Schmieding refused, Cagle sued to have the contract enforced. Has a valid sales contract been formed? *H. C. Schmieding Produce Co. v. Cagle*,

529 So.2d 243, 1988 Ala. Lexis 284 (Supreme Court of Alabama)

18.5 Statute of Frauds Collins was a sales representative of Donzi Marine Corp. (Donzi), a builder of light speedboats. Collins met Wallach, the owner of a retail boat outlet, at a marine trade show. Collins offered him a Donzi dealership, which would include the right to purchase and then market Donzi speedboats. Wallach tendered a check for $50,000 to Collins. Collins accepted the check, but neither party ever signed a written contract. Wallach ordered several boats. Donzi terminated the dealership because it had found another boat dealer willing to pay more for the franchise. Wallach sued Donzi for breach of contract. Is the contract enforceable under the UCC? *Wallach Marine Corp. v. Donzi Marine Corp.*, 675 F.Supp. 838, 1987 U.S. Dist. Lexis 11762 (United States District Court for the Southern District of New York)

18.6 Good or Service Frances Hector entered Cedars-Sinai Medical Center (Cedars-Sinai), Los Angeles, California, for a surgical operation on her heart. During the operation, a pacemaker was installed in Hector. The pacemaker, which was manufactured by American Technology, Inc., was installed at Cedars-Sinai Medical Center by Hector's physician, Dr. Eugene Kompaniez. The pacemaker was defective, causing injury to Hector. Hector sued Cedars-Sinai Medical Center under Article 2 (Sales) of the UCC to recover damages for breach of warranty of the pacemaker. Hector alleged that the surgical operation was primarily a sale of a good and therefore covered by the UCC. Cedars-Sinai Medical Center argued that the surgical operation was primarily a service and therefore the UCC did not apply. Who wins? *Hector v. Cedars-Sinai Medical Center*, 180 Cal. App.3d 493, 225 Cal. Rptr. 595, 1986 Cal. App. Lexis 1523 (Court of Appeal of California)

Ethical

Ethics Cases

18.7 Ethics Case Kurt Perschke was a grain dealer in Indiana. Perschke phoned Ken Sebasty, the owner of a large wheat farm, and offered to buy 14,000 bushels of wheat for $1.95 per bushel. Sebasty accepted the offer. Perschke said that he could send a truck for the wheat on a stated date six months later. On the day of the phone call, Perschke's office manager sent a memorandum to Sebasty, stating the price and quantity of wheat that had been contracted for. One month before the scheduled delivery, Perschke called Sebasty to arrange for the loading of the wheat. Sebasty stated that no contract had been made. When Perschke brought suit, Sebasty claimed that the contract was unenforceable because of the Statute of Frauds. Was it ethical for Sebasty to raise the Statute of Frauds as a defense? Assuming that both parties are merchants, who wins the suit? *Sebasty v. Perschke*, 404 N.E.2d 1200, 1980 Ind. App. Lexis 1489 (Court of Appeals of Indiana)

18.8 Ethics Case Gordon Construction Company (Gordon) was a general contractor in the New York City area. Gordon planned on bidding for the job of constructing two buildings for the Port Authority of New York. In anticipation of its own bid, Gordon sought bids from subcontractors. E. A. Coronis Associates (Coronis), a fabricator of structured steel, sent a signed letter to Gordon. The letter quoted a price for work on the Port Authority project and stated that the price could change based on the amount of steel used. The letter contained no information other than the price Coronis would charge for the job. One month later, Gordon was awarded the Port Authority project. Four days later, Coronis sent Gordon a telegram, withdrawing its offer. Gordon replied that it expected Coronis to honor the price that it had previously quoted to Gordon. When Coronis refused, Gordon sued. Gordon claimed that Coronis was attempting to withdraw a firm offer. Did Coronis act ethically in withdrawing its offer? Who wins? *E. A. Coronis Associates v. Gordon Construction Co.*, 90 N.J. Super. 69, 216 A.2d 246, 1966 N.J. Super. Lexis 368 (Superior Court of New Jersey)

Title to Goods and Risk of Loss

JERUSALEM, ISRAEL
Companies in Israel often use international sales contracts. Israel's major exports include high-tech goods, software, communications and space equipment, and agricultural products.

Learning Objectives

After studying this chapter, you should be able to:

1. Identify when title to goods passes in shipment and destination contracts.
2. Define *shipment* and *delivery terms*.
3. Describe who bears the risk of loss when goods are lost or damaged in shipment.
4. Identify who bears the risk of loss when goods are stolen and resold.
5. Define *good faith purchaser for value* and *buyer in the ordinary course of business*.

Chapter Outline

> *"A lawyer without history or literature is a mechanic, a mere working mason: if he possesses some knowledge of these, he may venture to call himself an architect."*
>
> —*Sir Walter Scott*
> *Guy Mannering, chapter 37 (1815)*

Introduction to Title to Goods and Risk of Loss

Under common law, the rights and obligations of the buyer, the seller, and third parties are determined based on who held technical title to the goods. Article 2 of the Uniform Commercial Code (UCC) establishes precise rules for determining the *passage of title* in sales contracts. Other provisions of Article 2 apply, irrespective of title, except as otherwise provided [UCC 2-401].

Common law placed the **risk of loss** to goods on the party who held title to the goods. Article 2 of the UCC rejects this notion and adopts concise rules for risk of loss that are not tied to title. It also gives the parties to a sales contract the right to *insure* the goods against loss if they have an "insurable interest" in the goods.

Agreement makes law.
Legal maxim

Article 2A (Leases) of the UCC establishes rules regarding title and risk of loss for leased goods. It also gives the parties to the lease contract the right to *insure* the goods against loss if they have an "insurable interest" in the goods.

Title, risk of loss, and insurable interest for the sale and lease of goods are discussed in this chapter.

Identification of Goods and Passage of Title

The *identification of goods* is rather simple. It means distinguishing the goods named in a contract from the seller's or lessor's other goods. The seller or lessor retains the risk of loss of the goods until he or she identifies them in a sales or lease contract. Further, UCC 2-401(1) and 2-501 prevent title to goods from passing from the seller to the buyer unless the goods are identified to the sales contract. In a lease transaction, title to the leased goods remains with the lessor or a third party. It does not pass to the lessee.

Decided cases are the anchors of the law, as laws are of the state.
Francis Bacon (1561-1626)

The identification of goods and passage of title are discussed in the following paragraphs.

Identification of Goods

Identification of goods can be made at any time and in any manner explicitly agreed to by the parties of a contract. In the absence of such an agreement, the UCC mandates when identification occurs [UCC 2-501(1), 2A-217]:

identification of goods
Distinguishing of the goods named in a contract from the seller's or lessor's other goods.

- Already existing goods are identified when a contract is made and names the specific goods sold or leased.

  Examples A piece of farm machinery, a car, or a boat is identified when its serial number is listed on a sales or lease contract.

- Goods that are part of a larger mass of goods are identified when the specific merchandise is designated.

  Example If a food processor contracts to purchase 150 cases of oranges from a farmer who has 1,000 cases of oranges, the buyer's goods are identified when the seller explicitly separates or tags the 150 cases for that buyer.

- **Future goods** are goods not yet in existence.

  Examples Unborn young animals (such as unborn cattle) are identified when the young are conceived. Crops to be harvested are identified when the crops are planted or otherwise become growing crops.

future goods
Goods not yet in existence (e.g., ungrown crops, unborn stock animals).

Future goods other than crops and unborn young are identified when the goods are shipped, marked, or otherwise designated by the seller or lessor as the goods to which the contract refers.

Passage of Title to Goods

Once the goods that are the subject of a contract exist and have been identified, title to the goods may be transferred from the seller to the buyer. Article 2 of the UCC establishes precise rules for determining the **passage of title** in sales contracts. (As mentioned earlier, lessees do not acquire title to the goods they lease.)

title
Legal, tangible evidence of ownership of goods.

Under UCC 2-401(1), **title** to goods passes from the seller to the buyer in any manner and on any conditions explicitly agreed on by the parties. If the parties do not agree to a specific time, title passes to the buyer when and where the seller's performance with reference to the physical delivery is completed. This point in time is determined by applying the rules discussed in the following paragraphs [UCC 2-401(2)].

Shipment and Destination Contracts

shipment contract
A contract that requires the seller to ship the goods to the buyer via a common carrier.

destination contract
A contract that requires the seller to deliver the goods either to the buyer's place of business or to another destination specified in the sales contract.

A **shipment contract** requires the seller to ship the goods to the buyer via a common carrier. The seller is required to (1) make proper shipping arrangements and (2) deliver the goods into the carrier's hands. Title passes to the buyer at the time and place of shipment [UCC 2-401(2)(a)].

A **destination contract** requires the seller to deliver the goods either to the buyer's place of business or to another destination specified in the sales contract. Title passes to the buyer when the seller tenders delivery of the goods at the specified destination [UCC 2-401(2)(b)].

Delivery of Goods Without Moving Them

document of title
An actual piece of paper, such as a warehouse receipt or bill of lading, that is required in some transactions of pickup and delivery.

Sometimes a sales contract authorizes goods to be delivered without requiring the seller to move them. In other words, the buyer might be required to pick up goods from the seller. In such situations, the time and place of the passage of title depends on whether the seller is to deliver a **document of title** (i.e., a warehouse receipt or bill of lading) to the buyer. If a document of title is required, title passes when and where the seller delivers the document to the buyer [UCC 2-401(3)(a)].

Example If the goods named in a sales contract are located at a warehouse, title passes when the seller delivers to the buyer a warehouse receipt representing the goods.

If (1) no document of title is needed and (2) the goods are identified at the time of contracting, title passes at the time and place of contracting [UCC 2-401(3)(b)].

Example If a buyer signs a sales contract to purchase bricks from a seller and the contract stipulates that the buyer will pick up the bricks at the seller's place of business, title passes when the contract is signed by both parties. This situation is true even if the bricks are not picked up until a later date.

The following feature discusses commonly used shipping terms.

Business Environment

Commonly Used Shipping Terms

Often, goods subject to a sales contract are shipped by a common carrier such as a trucking company, a ship, or a railroad. Many sales contracts contain **shipping terms** that have different legal meanings and consequences. The following are commonly used shipping terms:

- **Free on board (F.O.B.) point of shipment** requires the seller to arrange to ship the goods and put the goods in the carrier's possession. The buyer bears the shipping expense and risk of loss while the goods are in transit [UCC 2-319(1)(a)].

Example If a shipment contract specifies "F.O.B. Anchorage, Alaska," and the goods are shipped from New Orleans, Louisiana, the buyer bears the shipping expense and risk of loss while the goods are in transit to Anchorage, Alaska.

- **Free alongside ship (F.A.S.) port of shipment** or **Free alongside ship (F.A.S.) (vessel) port of shipment** requires the seller to deliver and tender the goods alongside the named vessel or on the dock designated and provided by the buyer. The seller bears the expense and risk of loss until this is done [UCC 2-319(2)(a)]. The buyer bears shipping costs and the risk of loss during transport.

  Example If a contract specifies "F.A.S. *The Gargoyle*, New Orleans," and the goods are to be shipped to Anchorage, Alaska, the seller bears the expense and risk of loss until it delivers the goods into the hands of the vessel *The Gargoyle* in New Orleans. Once this is done, the buyer pays the shipping costs, and the risk of loss passes to the buyer during transport to Anchorage, Alaska.

- **Cost, insurance, and freight (C.I.F.)** is a pricing term that means that the price includes the cost of the goods and the costs of insurance and freight. **Cost and freight (C.&F.)** is a pricing term that means that the price includes the cost of the goods and the cost of freight. In both cases, the seller must, at his or her own expense and risk, put the goods into the possession of a carrier. The buyer bears the risk of loss during transportation [UCC 2-320(1), (3)].

  Example If a contract specifies "C.I.F. *The Gargoyle*, New Orleans, Louisiana" or "C.&F. *The Gargoyle*, New Orleans, Louisiana," and the goods are to be shipped to Anchorage, Alaska, the seller bears the expense and risk of loss until it delivers the goods into the hands of the vessel *The Gargoyle* in New Orleans. Once this is done, the risk of loss passes to the buyer during transport from New Orleans to Anchorage, Alaska.

- **Free on board (F.O.B.) place of destination** requires the seller to bear the expense and risk of loss until the goods are tendered to the buyer at the place of destination [UCC 2-319(1)(b)].

  Example If a destination contract specifies "F.O.B. Anchorage, Alaska," and the goods are shipped from New Orleans, Louisiana, the seller bears the expense and risk of loss before and while the goods are in transit until the goods are tendered to the buyer at the port of Anchorage, Alaska.

- **Ex-ship (from the carrying vessel)** requires the seller to bear the expense and risk of loss until the goods are unloaded from the ship at its port of destination [UCC 2-322(1)(b)].

  Example If a contract specifies "Ex-ship, *The Gargoyle*, Anchorage, Alaska," and the goods are shipped from New Orleans, Louisiana, the seller bears the expense and risk of loss before and until the goods are unloaded from *The Gargoyle* at the port in Anchorage, Alaska.

- **No-arrival, no-sale contract** requires the seller to bear the expense and risk of loss of the goods during transportation. However, the seller is under no duty to deliver replacement goods to the buyer because there is no contractual stipulation that the goods will arrive at the appointed destination [UCC 2-324(a), (b)].

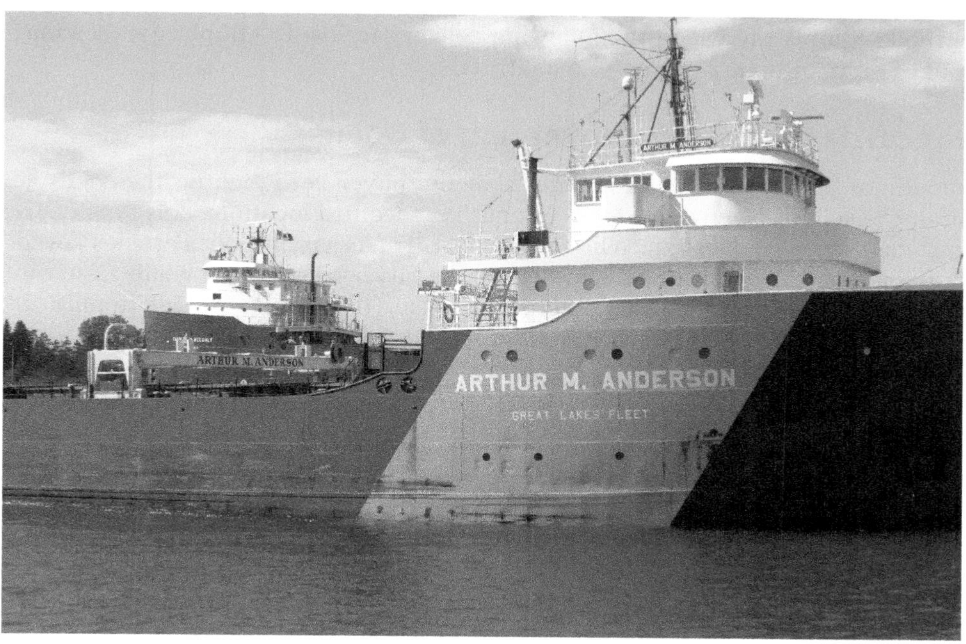

FREIGHTER
Common carriers, such as freighters and other ships, carry goods for buyers and sellers on the Great Lakes and other waterways in the United States and on oceans and other bodies on water worldwide. Risk of loss of the goods while in transit depends on the shipping terms used in the shipping or destination contract.

Risk of Loss Where There Is No Breach of the Sales Contract

Laws are not masters but servants, and he rules them who obeys them.

Henry Ward Beecher
Proverbs from Plymouth Pulpit (1887)

In the case of sales contracts, common law placed the risk of loss of goods on the party who had title to the goods. Article 2 of the UCC rejects this notion and allows the parties to a sales contract to agree among them who will bear the risk of loss if the goods subject to the contract are lost or destroyed. If the parties do not have a specific agreement concerning the assessment of the risk of loss, the UCC mandates who will bear the risk.

Where there has been no breach of the sales contract, the UCC provides the following rules regarding title and risk of loss.

Carrier Cases: Movement of Goods

Unless otherwise agreed, goods that are shipped via carrier (e.g., railroad, ship, truck) are considered to be sent pursuant to a *shipment contract* or a *destination contract*. Absent any indication to the contrary, sales contracts are presumed to be shipment contracts rather than destination contracts.

risk of loss in a shipment contract
The buyer bears the risk of loss during transportation.

A *shipment contract* requires the seller to deliver goods conforming to the contract to a carrier. The **risk of loss in a shipment contract** passes to the buyer when the seller delivers the conforming goods to the carrier. The buyer bears the risk of loss of the goods during transportation [UCC 2-509(1)(a)]. Shipment contracts are created in two ways. The first method requires the use of the term *shipment contract*. The second requires the use of one of the following delivery terms: F.O.B. point of shipment, F.A.S., C.I.F., or C.&F.

risk of loss in a destination contract
The seller bears the risk of loss during transportation.

A *destination contract* requires the seller to deliver conforming goods to a specific destination. The **risk of loss in a destination contract** is on the seller while the goods are in transport. Thus, except in the case of a no-arrival, no-sale contract, the seller is required to replace any goods lost in transit. The buyer does not have to pay for destroyed goods. The risk of loss does not pass until the goods are tendered to the buyer at the specified destination [UCC 2-509(1)(b)].

Unless otherwise agreed, destination contracts are created in two ways. The first method requires the use of the term *destination contract*. The alternative method requires the use of the following delivery terms: F.O.B. place of destination, ex-ship, or no-arrival, no-sale contract.

Noncarrier Cases: No Movement of Goods

The law is not a series of calculating machines where definitions and answers come tumbling out when the right levers are pushed.

William O. Douglas
The Dissent, A Safeguard of Democracy (1948)

Sometimes a sales contract stipulates that the buyer is to pick up the goods at either the seller's place of business or another specified location. This type of arrangement raises a question: Who bears the risk of loss if the goods are destroyed or stolen after the contract date but before the buyer picks up the goods from the seller? The UCC provides two different rules for this situation. One applies to *merchant-sellers* and the other to *nonmerchant-sellers* [UCC 2-509(3)]:

- **Merchant-seller.** If the seller is a merchant, the risk of loss does not pass to the buyer until the goods are received. In other words, a merchant-seller bears the risk of loss between the time of contracting and the time the buyer picks up the goods.
- **Nonmerchant-seller.** Nonmerchant-sellers pass the risk of loss to the buyer on "tender of delivery" of the goods. Tender of delivery occurs when the seller (1) places or holds the goods available for the buyer to take delivery and (2) notifies the buyer of this fact.

Goods in the Possession of a Bailee

bailee
A holder of goods who is not a seller or a buyer (e.g., a warehouse).

Goods sold by a seller to a buyer are sometimes in the possession of a **bailee** (e.g., a warehouse). If such goods are to be delivered to the buyer without the seller moving them, the risk of loss passes to the buyer when (1) the buyer receives a negotiable document of title (e.g., warehouse receipt, bill of lading) covering the goods, (2) the bailee acknowledges the buyer's right to possession of the goods, or (3) the buyer receives a nonnegotiable document of title or other written direction to deliver *and* has a reasonable time to present the document or direction to the bailee and demand the goods. If the bailee refuses to honor the document or direction, the risk of loss remains on the seller [UCC 2-509(2)].

Risk of Loss Where There Is a Breach of the Sales Contract

Special risk of loss rules apply to situations in which there has been a breach of a sales contract [UCC 2-510]. These rules are discussed in the following paragraphs.

Seller in Breach of a Sales Contract

A seller breaches a sales contract if he or she tenders or delivers nonconforming goods to the buyer. If the goods are so nonconforming that the buyer has the right to reject them, the risk of loss remains on the seller until (1) the defect or nonconformity is cured or (2) the buyer accepts the nonconforming goods.

Example A buyer orders 1,000 talking dolls from a seller. The contract is a shipment contract, which normally places the risk of loss during transportation on the buyer. However, the seller ships to the buyer totally nonconforming dolls that cannot talk. This switches the risk of loss to the seller during transit. The goods are destroyed in transit. The seller bears the risk of loss because he breached the contract by shipping nonconforming goods.

Buyer in Breach of a Sales Contract

A buyer breaches a sales contract if he or she (1) refuses to take delivery of conforming goods, (2) repudiates the contract, or (3) otherwise breaches the contract. A buyer who breaches a sales contract before the risk of loss would normally pass to him or her bears the risk of loss of any goods identified to the contract. The risk of loss rests on the buyer for only a commercially reasonable time. The buyer is liable only for any loss in excess of insurance recovered by the seller.

The following feature discusses a source of international contract law.

United Nations Convention on Contracts for the International Sale of Goods (CISG) A model act for international sales contracts that provides legal rules that govern the formation, performance, and enforcement of international sales contracts entered into between international businesses.

Global Law

United Nations Convention on Contracts for the International Sale of Goods

FINLAND

International contracts of companies located around the world are often governed by the **United Nations Convention on Contracts for the International Sale of Goods (CISG)**. *The CISG is a model act for international sales contracts. More than 75 countries are signatories to the CISG.*

The CISG provides legal rules that govern the formation, performance, and enforcement of international sales contracts entered into between international businesses. Many of its provisions are remarkably similar to those of the U.S. Uniform Commercial Code (UCC).

The CISG applies to contracts for the international sale of goods when the buyer and seller have their places of business in different countries. For the CISG to apply to an international sales contract, either (1) both of the nations must be parties to the convention or (2) the contract specifies that the CISG controls. The contracting parties may agree to exclude (i.e., opt out of) or modify the application of the CISG.

Risk of Loss in Conditional Sales

Sellers often entrust possession of goods to buyers on a trial basis. These transactions are classified as *sales on approval*, *sales or returns*, and *consignment* transactions [UCC 2-326]. Title and risk of loss in these types of **conditional sales** are discussed in the following paragraphs.

conditional sales
Type of sales where the seller entrusts possession of goods to a buyer on a trial basis.

Sale on Approval

sale on approval
A type of sale in which there is no actual sale unless and until the buyer accepts the goods.

In a **sale on approval**, there is no sale unless and until the buyer accepts the goods. A sale on approval occurs when a merchant allows a customer to take the goods for a specified period of time to see if they fit the customer's needs. The prospective buyer may use the goods to try them out during this time.

Acceptance of the goods occurs if the buyer (1) expressly indicates acceptance, (2) fails to notify the seller of rejection of the goods within the agreed-on trial period (or, if no time is agreed on, a reasonable time), or (3) uses the goods inconsistently with the purpose of the trial (e.g., a customer resells a computer to another person).

In a sale on approval, the risk of loss and title to the goods remain with seller. They do not pass to the buyer until acceptance [UCC 2-327(1)]. The goods are not subject to the claims of the buyer's creditors until the buyer accepts them.

Sale or Return

sale or return contract
A contract in which the seller delivers goods to a buyer with the understanding that the buyer may return the goods if they are not used or resold within a stated or reasonable period of time.

In a **sale or return contract**, the seller delivers goods to a buyer with the understanding that the buyer may return them if they are not used or resold within a stated period of time (or within a reasonable time, if no specific time is stated). The sale is considered final if the buyer fails to return the goods within the specified time or within a reasonable time, if no time is specified. The buyer has the option of returning all the goods or any commercial unit of the goods.

Example Louis Vuitton delivers 10 women's handbags to a Fashion Boutique Store on a sale or return basis. The boutique pays $10,000 ($1,000 per handbag). If Fashion Boutique Store sells six handbags but fails to sell the other four handbags within a reasonable time, such as three months, it may return the unsold handbags to Louis Vuitton and can recover the compensation it paid to Louis Vuitton for the four returned handbags ($4,000).

In a sale or return contract, the risk of loss and title to the goods pass to the buyer when the buyer takes possession of the goods [UCC 2-327(2)]. Goods sold pursuant to a sale or return contract are subject to the claims of the buyer's creditors while the goods are in the buyer's possession.

Example In the previous example, title and risk of loss transferred to Fashion Boutique Store when it took possession of the Louis Vuitton handbags. If the Louis Vuitton handbags are destroyed while in the possession of Fashion Boutique Store, the store is responsible for their loss. It cannot recover the value of the handbags from Louis Vuitton.

Consignment

consignment
An arrangement in which a seller (the consignor) delivers goods to a buyer (the consignee) to sell on his or her behalf.

In a **consignment**, a seller (the **consignor**) delivers goods to a buyer (the **consignee**) to sell on his or her behalf. The consignee is paid a fee if he or she sells the goods on behalf of the consignor.

A consignment is treated as a sale or return under the UCC; that is, title and risk of loss of the goods pass to the consignee when the consignee takes possession of the goods.

Whether goods are subject to the claims of a buyer's creditors usually depends on whether the seller files a financing statement, as required by Article 9 of the UCC.

If the seller files a financing statement, the goods are subject to the claims of the seller's creditors. If the seller fails to file such a statement, the goods are subject to the claims of the buyer's creditors [UCC 2-326(3)].

Risk of Loss in Lease Contracts

The parties to a lease contract are the party who leases the goods (the **lessor**) and the party who receives the goods (the **lessee**). The lessor and the lessee may agree about who will bear the risk of loss of the goods if they are lost or destroyed. If the parties do not so agree, the UCC provides the following risk of loss rules:

1. In the case of an **ordinary lease**, if the lessor is a merchant, the risk of loss passes to the lessee on the receipt of the goods [UCC 2A-219].
2. If the lease is a **finance lease** and the supplier is a merchant, the risk of loss passes to the lessee on the receipt of the goods [UCC 2A-219]. A finance lease is a three-party transaction consisting of a lessor, a lessee, and a supplier (or vendor).
3. If a tender of delivery of goods fails to conform to the lease contract, the risk of loss remains with the lessor or supplier until cure or acceptance [UCC 2A-220(1)(a)].

The following feature describes insuring goods against risk of loss.

Critical Legal Thinking

Can the parties to a sales or lease contract change the UCC risk of loss rules that would apply to their contract? If so, how?

Business Environment

Insuring Goods Against Risk of Loss

To protect against financial loss that would occur if goods were damaged, destroyed, lost, or stolen, the parties to sales and lease contracts should purchase insurance against such loss. If the goods are then lost or damaged, the insured party receives reimbursement from the insurance company for the loss.

To purchase insurance, a party must have an **insurable interest** in the goods. A seller has an insurable interest in goods as long as he or she retains title or has a security interest in the goods. A lessor retains an insurable interest in the goods during the term of the lease. A buyer or lessee obtains an insurable interest in the goods when they are identified in the sales or lease contract. Both the buyer and the seller or the lessee and the lessor can have an insurable interest in the goods at the same time [UCC 2-501, 2A-218].

Sale of Goods by Nonowners

Sometimes people sell goods even though they do not hold valid title to them. The UCC anticipated many of the problems this situation could cause and established rules concerning the title, if any, that could be transferred to purchasers.

Stolen Goods

In a case in which a buyer purchases goods or a lessee leases goods from a thief who has stolen them, the purchaser does not acquire title to the goods, and the lessee does not acquire any leasehold interest in the goods. The real owner can reclaim the goods from the purchaser or lessee [UCC 2-403(1)]. This is called **void title** or **void leasehold interest**.

void title
A situation in which a thief acquires no title to goods he or she steals.

Example Jack steals a truckload of Sony high-definition televisions that are owned by Electronics Store. The thief resells the televisions to City-Mart, which does not know that the goods were stolen. If Electronics Store finds out where the televisions are, it can reclaim them because the thief had no title in the goods, so title was not transferred to City-Mart. There is void title. City-Mart's only recourse is against the thief, if he or she can be found.

Fraudulently Obtained Goods

voidable title
A title that a purchaser has on goods obtained by (1) fraud, (2) a check that is later dishonored, or (3) impersonation of another person.

good faith purchaser for value
A person to whom good title can be transferred from a person with voidable title. The real owner cannot reclaim goods from a good faith purchaser for value.

buyer in the ordinary course of business
A person who, in good faith and without knowledge that the sale violates the ownership or security interests of a third party, buys goods in the ordinary course of business from a person in the business of selling goods of that kind. A buyer in the ordinary course of business takes the goods free of any third-party security interest in the goods.

entrustment rule
A rule stating that, when an owner *entrusts* the possession of his or her goods to a merchant who deals in goods of that kind, the merchant has the power to transfer all rights (including title) in the goods to a buyer in the ordinary course of business.

Critical Legal Thinking
Describe the buyer in the ordinary course of business rule. When does this rule apply? Is the result of this rule fair?

A seller or lessor has **voidable title** or **voidable leasehold interest** to goods if he or she obtained the goods through fraud, if his or her check for the payment of the goods or lease is dishonored, or if the seller or lessor impersonated another person.

A person with voidable title to goods can transfer good title to a **good faith purchaser for value** or a good leasehold interest to a **good faith subsequent lessee**. A good faith purchaser or lessee for value is someone who pays sufficient consideration or rent for the goods to the person he or she honestly believes has good title to or leasehold interest in those goods [UCC 2-201(1), 1-201(44)(d)]. The real owner cannot reclaim goods from such a purchaser or lessee [UCC 2-403(1)].

Example Max buys a Rolex watch from his neighbor Dorothy for nearly fair market value. It is later discovered that Dorothy obtained the watch from Jewelry Store with a bounced check—that is, a check for which there were insufficient funds to pay for the Rolex watch. Jewelry Store cannot reclaim the watch from Max because Max, the second purchaser, purchased the watch in good faith and for value.

Entrustment Rule

If an owner *entrusts* the possession of his or her goods to a merchant who deals in goods of that kind, the merchant has the power to transfer all rights (including title) in the goods to a **buyer in the ordinary course of business** [UCC 2-403(2)]. The real owner cannot reclaim the goods from this buyer. This is called the **entrustment rule**.

Example Kim brings her diamond ring to Ring Store to be repaired. Ring Store both sells and repairs jewelry. Kim leaves (entrusts) her diamond ring at the store until it is repaired. Ring Store sells Kim's ring to Harold, who is going to propose marriage to Gretchen. Harold, a buyer in the ordinary course of business, acquires title to the ring. Kim cannot reclaim her ring from Harold (or Gretchen). Her only recourse is to sue Ring Store.

The entrustment rule also applies to leases. If a lessor entrusts the possession of his or her goods to a lessee who is a merchant who deals in goods of that kind, the merchant-lessee has the power to transfer all the lessor's and lessee's rights in the goods to a buyer or sublessee in the ordinary course of business [UCC 2A-305(2)].

In the following case, the court had to decide whether a purchaser was a buyer in the ordinary course of business.

CASE 19.1 ***STATE COURT CASE Entrustment Rule***

Lindholm v. Brant

925 A.2d 1048, 2007 Conn. Lexis 264 (2007)
Supreme Court of Connecticut

"Any entrusting of possession of goods to a merchant who deals in goods of that kind gives him power to transfer all rights of the entruster to a buyer in ordinary course of business."

—Rogers, Justice

Facts

In 1962, Andy Warhol, a famous artist, created a silk-screen on canvas titled *Red Elvis*. Kerstin Lindholm was an art collector who, for thirty years, had been represented by Anders Malmberg, an art dealer. In

(case continues)

1987, with the assistance and advice of Malmberg, Lindholm purchased *Red Elvis* for $300,000.

In 2000, Malmberg told Lindholm that he could place *Red Elvis* on loan to the Louisiana Museum in Denmark if Lindholm agreed. By letter dated March 20, 2000, Lindholm agreed and gave permission to Malmberg to obtain possession of *Red Elvis*, which he did. Instead of placing *Red Elvis* on loan to the Louisiana Museum, Malmberg, claiming ownership to *Red Elvis*, immediately contracted to sell *Red Elvis* to Peter M. Brant, an art collector, for $2.9 million. Brant paid $2.9 million to Malmberg and received an invoice of sale and possession of *Red Elvis*.

Subsequently, Lindholm made arrangements to sell *Red Elvis* to a Japanese buyer for $4.6 million. Shortly thereafter, Lindholm discovered the fraud. Lindholm brought a civil lawsuit in the state of Connecticut against Brant to recover *Red Elvis*. Brant argued that he was a buyer in the ordinary course of business because he purchased *Red Elvis* from an art dealer to whom Lindholm had entrusted *Red Elvis*, and he had a claim that was superior to Lindholm's claim of ownership. The superior court of Connecticut issued a memorandum opinion that awarded *Red Elvis* to Brant.

Issue

Is Brant a buyer in the ordinary course of business who has a claim of ownership to *Red Elvis* that is superior to that of the owner Lindholm?

Language of the Court

Any entrusting of possession of goods to a merchant who deals in goods of that kind gives him power to transfer all rights of the entruster to a buyer in ordinary course of business. Once K. Lindholm entrusted Red Elvis to Malmberg she gave him the power to transfer all of her rights as the entruster to a buyer in the ordinary course. Accordingly, because Brant has proven his special defense of being a buyer in the ordinary course, judgment will enter in favor of the defendant on all counts.

Decision

The trial court held that Brant was a buyer in the ordinary course of business who obtained ownership to *Red Elvis* when he purchased the stolen *Red Elvis* from Malmberg.

Note

Lindholm appealed the decision of the trial court to the supreme court of Connecticut, which affirmed the decision of the trial court and awarded the *Red Elvis* to Brant. A court in Sweden convicted Malmberg of criminal fraud and sentenced him to three years in prison. A Swedish court awarded Lindholm $4.6 million in damages against Malmberg.

Ethics Questions

Did Malmberg act ethically in this case? Did he act criminally? Does Lindholm have some responsibility for her loss of the *Red Elvis*?

CONCEPT SUMMARY

PASSAGE OF TITLE BY NONOWNER THIRD PARTIES

Type of Transaction	Title Possessed by Seller	Innocent Purchaser	Purchaser Acquires Title to Goods
Goods acquired by theft are resold.	Void title	Good faith purchaser for value	No. Original owner may reclaim the goods.
Goods acquired by fraud or dishonored check are resold.	Voidable title	Good faith purchaser for value	Yes. Purchaser takes goods, free of claim of original owner.
Goods entrusted by owner to merchant who deals in that type of goods are resold.	No title	Buyer in the ordinary course of business	Yes. Purchaser takes goods, free of claim of original owner.

Critical Legal Thinking

Describe the good faith purchaser for value and the good faith subsequent lessee rules. When do these rules apply? Is the result of these rules fair?

Key Terms and Concepts

Bailee (422)
Buyer in the ordinary course of business (426)
Conditional sale (424)
Consignee (424)
Consignment (424)
Consignor (424)
Cost and freight (C.&F.) (421)
Cost, insurance, and freight (C.I.F.) (421)
Destination contract (420)
Document of title (420)
Entrustment rule (426)
Ex-ship (from the carrying vessel) (421)
Free alongside ship (F.A.S.) port of shipment (421)
Free alongside ship (F.A.S.) (vessel) port of shipment (421)
Finance lease (425)
Free on board (F.O.B.) place of destination (421)
Free on board (F.O.B.) point of shipment (420)
Future goods (419)
Good faith purchaser for value (426)
Good faith subsequent lessee (426)
Identification of goods (419)
Insurable interest (425)
Lessee (425)
Lessor (425)
No-arrival, no-sale contract (421)
Ordinary lease (425)
Passage of title (420)
Risk of loss (419)
Risk of loss in a destination contract (422)
Risk of loss in a shipment contract (422)
Sale on approval (424)
Sale or return contract (424)
Shipment contract (420)
Shipping terms (420)
Title (420)
United Nations Convention on Contracts for the International Sale of Goods (CISG) (423)
Void title (425)
Void leasehold interest (425)
Voidable title (426)
Voidable leasehold interest (426)

Critical Legal Thinking Cases

19.1 Conditional Sale Numismatic Funding Corporation (Numismatic), with its principal place of business in New York, sells rare and collector coins by mail throughout the United States. Frederick R. Prewitt, a resident of St. Louis, Missouri, responded to Numismatic's advertisement in the *Wall Street Journal*. Prewitt received several shipments of coins from Numismatic via the mails. These shipments were "on approval" for 14 days. Numismatic gave no instructions as to the method for returning unwanted coins. Prewitt kept and paid for several coins and returned the others to Numismatic, fully insured, via FedEx. Numismatic then mailed Prewitt 28 gold and silver coins worth over $60,000 on a 14-day approval. Thirteen days later, Prewitt returned all the coins via certified mail of the U.S. Postal Service and insured them for the maximum allowed, $400. Numismatic never received the coins. Numismatic sued Prewitt to recover for the value of the coins, alleging that Prewitt had an express or implied duty to ship the coins back to Numismatic by FedEx and fully insured. Prewitt argued that he was not liable for the coins because this was a sale or return contract. Who wins? *Prewitt v. Numismatic Funding Corporation*, 745 F.2d 1175, 1984 U.S. App. Lexis 17926 (United States Court of Appeals for the Eighth Circuit)

19.2 Identification of Goods The Big Knob Volunteer Fire Company (Fire Co.) agreed to purchase a fire truck from Hamerly Custom Productions (Hamerly), which was in the business of assembling various component parts into fire trucks. Fire Co. paid Hamerly $10,000 toward the price two days after signing the contract. Two weeks later, it gave Hamerly $38,000 more toward the total purchase price of $53,000. Hamerly bought an engine chassis for the new fire truck on credit from Lowe and Meyer Garage (Lowe and Meyer). After installing the chassis, Hamerly painted the Big Knob Fire Department's name on the side of the cab. Hamerly never paid for the engine chassis, and the truck was repossessed by Lowe and Meyer. Fire Co. sought to recover the fire truck from Lowe and Meyer. Although Fire Co. was the buyer of a fire truck, Lowe and Meyer questioned whether any goods had ever been identified in the contract. Are they? *Big Knob Volunteer Fire Co. v. Lowe and Meyer Garage*, 338 Pa. Super. 257, 487 A.2d 953, 1985 Pa. Super. Lexis 5540 (Superior Court of Pennsylvania)

19.3 Stolen Goods John Torniero was employed by Micheals Jewelers, Inc. (Micheals). During the course of his employment, Torniero stole pieces of jewelry, including several diamond rings, a sapphire ring, a gold pendant, and several loose diamonds. Over a period of several months, Torniero sold individual pieces of the stolen jewelry to G&W Watch and Jewelry Corporation (G&W). G&W had no knowledge of how Torniero obtained the jewels. Torniero was arrested when Micheals discovered the thefts. After Torniero admitted that he had sold the stolen jewelry to G&W, Micheals attempted to recover it from G&W. G&W claimed title to the jewelry as a good faith purchaser for value. Micheals challenged G&W's claim to title in court. Who wins? *United States v. Micheals Jewelers, Inc.*, 42 UCC Rep. Serv. 141, 1985 U.S. Dist. Lexis 15142 (United States District Court for the District of Connecticut)

19.4 Passage of Title J. A. Coghill owned a used Rolls Royce Corniche automobile, which he sold to a man claiming to be Daniel Bellman. Bellman gave Coghill a cashier's check for $94,500. When Coghill tried to cash the check, his bank informed him that the check had been forged. Coghill reported the vehicle as stolen. Subsequently, Barry Hyken responded to a newspaper ad listing a Rolls Royce Corniche for sale. Hyken went to meet the seller of the car, the man who claimed to be Bellman, in a parking lot. Hyken agreed to pay $62,000 for the car. When Hyken asked to see Bellman's identification, Bellman provided documents with two different addresses. Bellman explained that he was in the process of moving. Hyken took possession of the vehicle. Three weeks later, the Rolls Royce Corniche was seized by the police. Hyken sued to get it back. Who wins? *Landshire Food Service, Inc. v. Coghill*, 709 S.W.2d 509, 1986 Mo. App. Lexis 3961 (Court of Appeals of Missouri)

19.5 Entrustment Rule Fuqua Homes, Inc. (Fuqua), is a manufacturer of prefabricated houses. MMM, a dealer of prefabricated homes, was a partnership created by two men named Kirk and Underhill. On seven occasions before the disputed transactions occurred, MMM had ordered homes from Fuqua. MMM was contacted by Kenneth Ryan, who wanted to purchase a 55-foot modular home. MMM called Fuqua and ordered a prefabricated home that met Ryan's specifications. Fuqua delivered the home to MMM and retained a security interest in it until MMM paid the purchase price. MMM installed the house on Ryan's property and collected full payment from Ryan. Kirk and Underhill then disappeared, taking Ryan's money with them. Fuqua was never paid for the prefabricated home it had manufactured. Ryan had no knowledge of the dealings between MMM and Fuqua. Fuqua claimed title to the house based on its security interest. Who has title to the home? *Fuqua Homes, Inc. v. Evanston Bldg. & Loan Co.*, 52 Ohio App. 2d 399, 370 N.E.2d 780, 1977 Ohio App. Lexis 6968 (Court of Appeals of Ohio)

19.6 Risk of Loss All America Export-Import Corp. (All America) placed an order for several thousand pounds of yarn with A. M. Knitwear (Knitwear). On June 4, All America sent Knitwear a purchase order. The purchase order stated the terms of the sale, including language that stated that the price was F.O.B. the seller's plant. A truck hired by All America arrived at Knitwear's plant. Knitwear turned the yarn over to the carrier and notified All America that the goods were now on the truck. The truck left Knitwear's plant and proceeded to a local warehouse. Sometime during the night, the truck was hijacked, and all the yarn was stolen. All America had paid for the yarn by check but stopped payment on it when it learned that the goods had been stolen. Knitwear sued All America, claiming that it must pay for the stolen goods because it bore the risk of loss. Who wins? *A. M. Knitwear v. All America, Etc.*, 41 N.Y.2d 14, 359 N.E.2d 342, 390 N.Y.S.2d 832, 1976 N.Y. Lexis 3201 (Court of Appeals of New York)

Ethics Case

Ethical

19.7 Ethics Case Executive Financial Services, Inc. (EFS), purchased three tractors from Tri-County Farm Company (Tri-County), a John Deere dealership owned by Gene Mohr and James Loyd. The tractors cost $48,000, $19,000, and $38,000. EFS did not take possession of the tractors but instead left the tractors on Tri-County's lot. EFS leased the tractors to Mohr-Loyd Leasing (Mohr-Loyd), a partnership between Mohr and Loyd, with the understanding and representation by Mohr-Loyd that the tractors would be leased out to farmers. Instead of leasing the tractors, Tri-County sold them to three different farmers. EFS sued and obtained judgment against Tri-County, Mohr-Loyd, and Mohr and Loyd personally for breach of contract. Because that judgment remained unsatisfied, EFS sued the three farmers who bought the tractors to recover the tractors from them. Did Mohr and Loyd act ethically in this case? Who owns the tractors, EFS or the farmers? *Executive Financial Services, Inc. v. Pagel*, 238 Kan. 809, 715 P.2d 381, 1986 Kan. Lexis 290 (Supreme Court of Kansas)

Remedies for Breach of Sales and Lease Contracts

TRUCK UNLOADING GOODS
A seller or lessor is under a duty to deliver conforming goods, and the buyer or lessee is under a duty to pay for these goods. The Uniform Commercial Code (UCC) provides certain remedies to sellers and lessors and to the buyers and lessees if the other party does not perform his or her duties.

Learning Objectives

After studying this chapter, you should be able to:

1. Describe the performance of sales and lease contracts.
2. List and describe the seller's remedies for the buyer's breach of a sales contract.
3. List and describe the buyer's remedies for the seller's breach of a sales contract.
4. List and describe the lessor's remedies for the lessee's breach of a lease contract.
5. List and describe the lessee's remedies for the lessor's breach of a lease contract.

Chapter Outline

"*Trade and commerce, if they were not made of Indian rubber, would never manage to bounce over the obstacles which legislators are continually putting in their way.*"

—*Henry D. Thoreau*
Resistance to Civil Government (1849)

Introduction to Remedies for Breach of Sales and Lease Contracts

Usually, the parties to a sales or lease contract owe a duty to **perform the obligations** specified in their agreement [UCC 2-301, 2A-301]. The seller's or lessor's general obligation is to transfer and deliver the goods to the buyer or lessee. The buyer's or lessee's general obligation is to accept and pay for the goods.

The buyer needs a hundred eyes, the seller not one.

George Herbert
Jacula Prudentum (1651)

When one party **breaches** a sales or lease contract, the Uniform Commercial Code (UCC) provides the injured party with a variety of prelitigation and litigation remedies. These remedies are designed to place the injured party in as good a position as if the breaching party's contractual obligations were fully performed [UCC 1-106(1), 2A-401(1)]. The best remedy depends on the circumstances of the particular case.

obligation
An action a party to a sales or lease contract is required by law to carry out.

breach
Failure of a party to perform an obligation in a sales or lease contract.

The performance of obligations and remedies available for breach of sales and lease contracts are discussed in this chapter.

Seller and Lessor Performance

The seller's or lessor's basic obligation is the **tender of delivery**, or the transfer and delivery of goods to the buyer or lessee in accordance with a sales or lease contract [UCC 2-301]. Tender of delivery requires the seller or lessor to (1) put and hold conforming goods at the buyer's or lessee's disposition and (2) give the buyer or lessee any notification reasonably necessary to enable delivery of goods. The parties may agree as to the time, place, and manner of delivery. If there is no special agreement, tender must be made at a reasonable hour, and the goods must be kept available for a reasonable period of time.

tender of delivery
The obligation of a seller to transfer and deliver goods to the buyer or lessee in accordance with a sales or lease contract.

Example The seller cannot telephone the buyer at 12:01 A.M. and say that the buyer has 15 minutes to accept delivery [UCC 2-503(1), 2A-508(1).

Place of Delivery

Many sales and lease contracts state where the goods are to be delivered. Often, the contract will say that the buyer or lessee must pick up the goods from the seller or lessor. If the contract does not expressly state the **place of delivery**, the UCC stipulates place of delivery based on the following rules:

A legal decision depends not on the teacher's age, but on the force of his argument.

The Talmud

1. **Noncarrier cases.** Unless otherwise agreed, the place of delivery is the seller's or lessor's place of business. If the seller or lessor has no place of business, the place of delivery is the seller's or lessor's residence. If the parties have knowledge at the time of contracting that identified goods are located in some other place, that place is the place of delivery.

   Example If parties contract regarding the sale of wheat that is located in a silo, the silo is the place of delivery [UCC 2-308].

2. **Carrier cases.** Unless the parties have agreed otherwise, if delivery of goods to a buyer is to be made by carrier, the UCC establishes different rules for *shipment contracts* and *destination contracts*:

   a. **Shipment contract.** A sales contract that requires the seller to send the goods to the buyer but not to a specifically named destination is a

shipment contract
A sales contract that requires the seller to send the goods to the buyer but not to a specifically named destination.

destination contract
A sales contract that requires the seller to deliver the goods to the buyer's place of business or another specified destination.

shipment contract. Under such contracts, the seller must put the goods in the carrier's possession and contract for the proper and safe transportation of the goods and promptly notify the buyer of the shipment [UCC 2-504]. Delivery occurs when the seller puts the goods in the carrier's possession.

b. **Destination contract.** A sales contract that requires the seller to deliver goods to the buyer's place of business or another specified destination is a **destination contract**. Unless otherwise agreed, destination contracts require delivery to be tendered at the buyer's place of business or other location specified in the sales contract [UCC 2-503]. Delivery occurs when the goods reach this destination.

Perfect Tender Rule

perfect tender rule
A rule that says if the goods or tender of a delivery fail in any respect to conform to the contract, the buyer may opt (1) to reject the whole shipment, (2) to accept the whole shipment, or (3) to reject part and accept part of the shipment.

A seller or lessor is under a duty to deliver conforming goods. If the goods or tender of delivery fail in any respect to conform to the contract, the buyer or lessee may opt (1) to reject the whole shipment, (2) to accept the whole shipment, or (3) to reject part and accept part of the shipment. This option is referred to as the **perfect tender rule** [UCC 2-601, 2A-509]. If a buyer accepts nonconforming goods, the buyer may seek remedies against the seller.

Example A sales contract requires the Lawn Mower Company to deliver 100 lawn mowers to Outdoor Store. When the buyer inspects the delivered goods, it is discovered that 80 lawn mowers conform to the contract and that 20 lawn mowers do not conform. Pursuant to the perfect tender rule, the buyer Outdoor Store may reject the entire shipment of lawn mowers. In the alternative, the buyer Outdoor Store can accept the 80 conforming lawn mowers and reject the 20 nonconforming lawn mowers. As another alternative, the buyer Outdoor Store may accept the whole shipment, both the conforming and the nonconforming lawn mowers, and seek remedies from the seller Lawn Mower Company for the 20 nonconforming lawn mowers.

right to cure
An opportunity to repair or replace defective or nonconforming goods.

The UCC allows the parties to a sales or lease contract to limit the effect of the perfect tender rule. For example, they may decide that (1) only the defective or nonconforming goods may be rejected, (2) the seller or lessor may replace nonconforming goods or repair defects, or (3) the buyer or lessee will accept nonconforming goods with appropriate compensation from the seller or lessor [UCC 2-614(1)].

The following feature discusses the seller's and lessor's opportunity to cure the delivery of nonconforming goods under certain circumstances.

Contemporary Environment

Seller's and Lessor's Right to Cure

The UCC gives a seller or lessor who delivers nonconforming goods the **right to cure** the nonconformity. Although the term **cure** is not defined by the UCC, it generally means an opportunity to repair or replace defective or nonconforming goods [UCC 2-508, 2A-513].

A cure may be attempted if the time for performance has not expired and the seller or lessor notifies the buyer or lessee of his or her intention to make a conforming delivery within the contract time.

Example A lessee contracts to lease a BMW 750i automobile from a lessor for delivery on July 1. On June 15, the lessor delivers a BMW 550i to the lessee, and the lessee rejects it as nonconforming. The lessor has until July 1 to cure the nonconformity by delivering the BMW 750i specified in the contract.

A cure may also be attempted if the seller or lessor had reasonable grounds to believe the nonconforming delivery would be accepted. The seller or lessor may have a further reasonable time to substitute a conforming tender.

Example A buyer contracts to purchase 500 red dresses from a seller for delivery on July 1. On July 1, the seller delivers 100 blue dresses to the buyer. In the past, the buyer has accepted different-colored dresses than those ordered. This time, though, the buyer rejects the blue dresses as nonconforming. The seller has a reasonable time after July 1 to deliver conforming red dresses to the buyer.

Installment Contracts

An **installment contract** is a contract that requires or authorizes goods to be delivered and accepted in separate lots. Such a contract must contain a clause that states "each delivery in a separate lot" or equivalent language.

Example A contract in which the buyer orders 1,000 widgets to be delivered in four equal installments is an installment contract.

The UCC alters the perfect tender rule with regard to installment contracts. The buyer or lessee may reject the entire contract only if the nonconformity or default with respect to any installment or installments substantially impairs the value of the entire contract [UCC 2-612, 2A-510].

Destruction of Goods

The UCC provides that if goods identified in a sales or lease contract are totally destroyed without the fault of either party before the risk of loss passes to the buyer or the lessee, the contract is void. Both parties are then excused from performing the contract.

If the goods are only partially destroyed, the buyer or lessee may inspect the goods and then choose either to treat the contract as void or to accept the goods. If the buyer or lessee opts to accept the goods, the purchase price or rent will be reduced to compensate for damages [UCC 2-613, 2A-221].

Example A buyer contracts to purchase a sofa from a seller. The seller agrees to deliver the sofa to the buyer's home. The truck delivering the sofa is hit by an automobile, and the sofa is totally destroyed. Because the risk of loss has not passed to the buyer, the contract is voided, and the buyer does not have to pay for the sofa.

The following ethics feature discusses the concepts of good faith and reasonableness that the UCC imposes on parties.

good faith
Every contract or duty within this Act imposes an obligation of good faith in its performance or enforcement [UCC 1-203].

reasonableness
A term used throughout the UCC to establish the duties of performance by the parties to sales and lease contracts.

commercial reasonableness
The term that establishes certain duties of merchants under the UCC.

Critical Legal Thinking

Why does the UCC impose the duties of *good faith* and *reasonableness*? Are these concepts difficult to apply? Does this differ from the common law of contracts?

Ethics

UCC Imposes Duties of Good Faith and Reasonableness

Generally, the common law of contracts only obligates the parties to perform their contracts according to the **express terms** of their contract. There is no breach of contract unless the parties fail to meet these terms. However, the UCC adopts two broad principles that govern the performance of sales and lease contracts: **good faith** and **reasonableness**.

UCC 1-203 states, "Every contract or duty within this Act imposes an obligation of good faith in its performance or enforcement." Thus, both parties owe a duty of good faith to perform a sales or lease contract. Merchants are held to a higher standard of good faith than nonmerchants [UCC 2-103(1)(b)].

The words *reasonable* and *reasonably* are used throughout the UCC to establish the duties of performance by the parties to sales and lease contracts. In addition, the term **commercial reasonableness** is used to establish certain duties of merchants under the UCC.

Note that the concepts of good faith and reasonableness extend to the "spirit" of a contract as well as the contract terms. The underlying theory is that the parties are more apt to perform properly if their conduct is to be judged against these principles.

Ethics Questions Does the concept of *good faith* promote ethical behavior? Does the vagueness of such UCC terms as *good faith*, *reasonableness*, and *commercial reasonableness* serve a useful purpose when determining the legality of a party's actions?

Buyer and Lessee Performance

The buyer or lessee in a sales or lease contract owes certain duties of performance under the contract. These duties are either specified in the contract itself or are created by UCC Articles 2 and 2A. Once the seller or lessor has properly tendered delivery, the buyer or lessee is obligated to accept and pay for the goods in accordance with the sales or lease contract. If there is no agreement, the provisions of the UCC apply.

Right of Inspection

Unless otherwise agreed, the buyer or lessee has the **right to inspect** goods that are tendered, delivered, or identified in a sales or lease contract prior to accepting or paying for them. If the goods are shipped, the inspection may take place after their arrival. If the inspected goods do not conform to the contract, the buyer or lessee may reject the goods and not pay for the goods [UCC 2-513(1), 2A-515(1)]. If the goods are rejected for nonconformance, the cost of inspection can be recovered from the seller [UCC 2-513(2)].

The parties may agree as to the time, place, and manner of inspection. If there is no such agreement, the inspection must occur at a reasonable time and place and in a reasonable manner. Reasonableness depends on the circumstances of the case, common usage of trade, prior course of dealing between the parties, and such. If the goods conform to the contract, the buyer pays for the inspection.

Acceptance

acceptance
An act that occurs when a buyer or lessee takes either of the following actions after a reasonable opportunity to inspect the goods that are the subject of a contract: (1) signifies to the seller or lessor in words or by conduct that the goods are conforming or that the buyer or lessee will take or retain the goods despite their nonconformity or (2) fails to effectively reject the goods within a reasonable time after their delivery or tender by the seller or lessor. Acceptance also occurs if a buyer acts inconsistently with the seller's ownership rights in the goods.

Acceptance occurs when the buyer or lessee takes either of the following actions after a reasonable opportunity to inspect the goods: (1) signifies to the seller or lessor in words or by conduct that the goods are conforming or that the buyer or lessee will take or retain the goods despite their nonconformity or (2) fails to effectively reject the goods within a reasonable time after their delivery or tender by the seller or lessor. Acceptance also occurs if a buyer acts inconsistently with the seller's ownership rights in the goods. Acceptance occurs if the buyer resells the goods delivered by the seller [UCC 2-606(1), 2A-515(1)].

Buyers and lessees may only accept delivery of a *commercial unit*—a unit of goods that commercial usage deems is a single whole for purpose of sale. Acceptance of a part of any commercial unit is acceptance of the entire unit [UCC 2-606(2), 2A-515(2)].

Example A commercial unit may be a single article (e.g., a machine), a set of articles (e.g., a suite of furniture or an assortment of sizes), a quantity (e.g., a bale, a gross, or a carload), or any other unit treated in use or in the relevant market as a single whole.

Payment

A proceeding may be perfectly legal and may yet be opposed to sound commercial principles.

Lord Justice Lindley
Verner v. General and Commercial Trust (1894)

Goods that are accepted must be paid for [UCC 2-607(1)]. Unless the parties to a contract agree otherwise, **payment** is due from a buyer when and where the goods are delivered, even if the place of delivery is the same as the place of shipment. Buyers often purchase goods on credit extended by the seller. Unless the parties agree to other terms, the credit period begins to run from the time the goods are shipped [UCC 2-310]. A lessee must pay lease payments in accordance with the lease contract [UCC 2A-516(1)].

The goods can be paid for in any manner currently acceptable in the ordinary course of business (e.g., check, credit card) unless the seller demands payment in cash or unless the contract names a specific form of payment. If the seller requires cash payment, the buyer must be given an extension of time necessary to procure the cash. If the buyer pays by check, payment is conditional on the check being honored (paid) when it is presented to the bank for payment [UCC 2-511].

Revocation of Acceptance

A buyer or lessee who has accepted goods may subsequently revoke his or her acceptance if (1) the goods are nonconforming, (2) the nonconformity substantially impairs the value of the goods to the buyer or lessee, and (3) one of the following factors is shown: (a) the seller's or lessor's promise to timely cure of the nonconformity is not met, (b) the goods were accepted before the nonconformity was discovered and the nonconformity was difficult to discover, or (c) the goods were accepted before the nonconformity was discovered and the seller or lessor assured the buyer or lessee that the goods were conforming.

Revocation of acceptance is not effective until the seller or lessor is so notified. In addition, the revocation must occur within a reasonable time after the buyer or lessee discovers or should have discovered the grounds for the revocation. The revocation, which must be of a lot or commercial unit, must occur before there is any substantial change in the condition of the goods (e.g., before perishable goods spoil) [UCC 2-608(1), 2A-517(1)].

revocation of acceptance
Reversal of acceptance.

Seller and Lessor Remedies

Often, a buyer or lessee may breach a sales or lease contract. The UCC provides various remedies to sellers and lessors if a buyer or lessee *breaches a contract*. The remedies that are available to sellers and lessors if a buyer or lessee breaches a sales or lease contract are discussed in the following paragraphs.

Right to Withhold Delivery

A seller or lessor may withhold delivery of goods in his or her possession when the buyer or lessee breaches the contract. The **right to withhold delivery** is available if the buyer or lessee wrongfully rejects or revokes acceptance of the goods, fails to make a payment when due, or repudiates the contract. If part of the goods under the contract have been delivered when the buyer or lessee materially breaches the contract, the seller or lessor may withhold delivery of the remainder of the affected goods [UCC 2-703(a), 2A-523(1)(c)].

right to withhold delivery
The right of a seller or lessor to refuse to deliver goods to a buyer or lessee on breach of a sales or lease contract by the buyer or lessee or the insolvency of the buyer or lessee.

Right to Stop Delivery of Goods in Transit

Often, sellers and lessors employ common carriers and other bailees (e.g., warehouses) to hold and deliver goods to buyers and lessees. The goods are considered to be *in transit* while they are in possession of these carriers or bailees.

A seller or lessor has the **right to stop delivery of goods in transit** if while the goods are in transit (1) the buyer or lessee repudiates the contract, (2) the buyer or lessee fails to make payment when due, or (3) the buyer or lessee otherwise gives the seller or lessor some other right to withhold or reclaim the goods. In these circumstances, the delivery can be stopped only if it constitutes a carload, a truckload, a planeload, or a larger express or freight shipment [UCC 2-705(1), 2A-526(1)]. A seller or lessor who learns of the buyer's or lessee's insolvency while the goods are in transit has a right to stop delivery of the goods in transit, regardless of the size of the shipment.

right to stop delivery of goods in transit
The right of a seller or lessor to stop delivery of goods in transit if he or she learns of the buyer's or lessee's insolvency or if the buyer or lessee repudiates the contract, fails to make payment when due, or gives the seller or lessor some other right to withhold the goods.

Right to Reclaim Goods

In certain situations, a seller or lessor may demand the return of the goods it sold or leased that are already in the possession of the buyer or lessee. In a sale transaction, the seller or lessor has the **right to reclaim goods** in two situations. If the goods are delivered in a credit sale and the seller then discovers that the buyer was insolvent, the seller has 10 days to demand that the goods be returned [UCC 2-507(2)]. If the buyer misrepresented his or her solvency in writing within three months before delivery [UCC 2-702(2)] or paid for goods in a cash sale with a check that bounces [UCC 2-507(2))], the seller may reclaim the goods at any

right to reclaim goods
The right of a seller or lessor to demand the return of goods from the buyer or lessee under specified situations.

time. A lessor may reclaim goods in the possession of the lessee if the lessee is in default of the contract [UCC 2A-525(2)].

Right to Dispose of Goods

If a buyer or lessee breaches or repudiates a sales or lease contract before the seller or lessor has delivered the goods, the seller or lessor may resell or release the goods and recover damages from the buyer or lessee [UCC 2-703(d), 2-706(1), 2A-523(1)(e), 2A-527(1)]. The **right to dispose of goods** also arises if the seller or lessor has reacquired the goods after stopping them in transit.

right to dispose of goods
The right of a seller or lessor to dispose of goods in a good faith and commercially reasonable manner. A seller or lessor who is in possession of goods at the time the buyer or lessee breaches or repudiates a contract may in good faith resell, release, or otherwise dispose of the goods in a commercially reasonable manner and recover damages, including incidental damages, from the buyer or lessee.

The seller or lessor may recover any damages incurred on the disposition of the goods. In the case of a sales contract, damages are defined as the difference between the disposition price and the original contract price. In the case of a lease contract, damages are the difference between the disposition price and the rent the original lessee would have paid. Any profit made on the resale or release of the goods does not revert to the original buyer or lessee if the seller or lessor disposes of the goods at a higher price than the buyer or lessee contracted to pay.

The seller or lessor may also recover any **incidental damages** (reasonable expenses incurred in stopping delivery, transportation charges, storage charges, sales commission, and the like) [UCC 2-710, 2A-530] incurred on the disposition of the goods [UCC 2-706(1), 2A-527(2)].

Unfinished Goods

Sometimes a sales or lease contract is breached or repudiated before the goods are finished. In a case of **unfinished goods**, the seller or lessor may choose either (1) to cease manufacturing the goods and resell them for scrap or salvage value or (2) to complete the manufacture of the goods and resell, release, or otherwise dispose of them to another party [UCC 2-704(2), 2A-524(2)]. The seller or lessor may recover damages from the breaching buyer or lessee.

Right to Recover the Purchase Price or Rent

In certain circumstances, the UCC provides that a seller or lessor may sue the buyer or lessee to recover the purchase price or rent stipulated in a sales or lease contract. The seller or lessor has the **right to recover the purchase price or rent** in the following situations:

right to recover the purchase price or rent
The right of a seller or lessor to recover the contracted-for purchase price or rent from the buyer or lessee (1) if the buyer or lessee fails to pay for accepted goods, (2) if the buyer or lessee breaches the contract and the seller or lessor cannot dispose of the goods, or (3) if the goods are damaged or lost after the risk of loss passes to the buyer or lessee.

1. The buyer or lessee accepts the goods but fails to pay for them when the price or rent is due.
2. The buyer or lessee breaches the contract after the goods have been identified in the contract and the seller or lessor cannot resell or dispose of them.
3. The goods are damaged or lost after the risk of loss passes to the buyer or lessee [UCC 2-709(1), 2A-529(1)].

The seller or lessor may also recover incidental damages from the buyer or lessee.

Right to Recover Damages for Breach of Contract

right to recover damages for breach of contract
The right of a seller or lessor to recover damages measured as the difference between the contract price (or rent) and the market price (or rent) at the time and place the goods were to be delivered, plus incidental damages, from a buyer or lessee who repudiates the contract or wrongfully rejects tendered goods.

If a buyer or lessee repudiates a sales or lease contract or wrongfully rejects tendered goods, the seller or lessor has the **right to recover damages for breach of contract** caused by the buyer's or lessee's breach. Generally, the amount of damages is calculated as the difference between the contract price (or rent) and the market price (or rent) of the goods at the time and place the goods were to be delivered to the buyer or lessee plus incidental damages [UCC 2-708(1), 2A-528(1)].

If the preceding measure of damages will not put the seller or lessor in as good a position as performance of the contract would have, the seller or lessor has the **right to recover any lost profits** that would have resulted from the full performance of the contract plus an allowance for reasonable overhead and incidental damages [UCC 2-708(2), 2A-528(2)].

Right to Cancel a Contract

A seller or lessor has the **right to cancel a contract** if the buyer or lessee breaches the contract by rejecting or revoking acceptance of the goods, failing to pay for the goods, or repudiating all or any part of the contract. The cancellation may refer only to the affected goods or to the entire contract if the breach is material [UCC 2-703(f), 2A-523(1)(a)].

The following feature discusses the UCC rule that applies to a lost volume seller.

lost volume seller
A seller who can recover lost profits from a defaulting buyer even though the seller sold the item to another buyer, where the seller has other similar items and would have made two sales had the original buyer not defaulted.

Business Environment

Lost Volume Seller

Should a seller be permitted to recover the profits it lost on a sale to a defaulting buyer if the seller sold the goods to another buyer? It depends. If the seller had only one item or a limited number of items and could produce no more, the seller cannot recover lost profits from the defaulting buyer if the seller sold the one item to another buyer or sold the limited number of items to other buyers. This is because the seller made profits on the sale or sales.

If, however, the seller could have produced more of the item, the seller is a **lost volume seller**. In this situation, the seller can recover the profit it would have made on the sale to the defaulting buyer. This is because the seller has realized profits from the sales to the other buyers and would have also made a profit from the sale to the defaulting buyer.

Example Carpet Store purchases hundreds of oriental rugs from manufacturers that it sells to customers in its store. Mary contracts to purchase an oriental rug for $3,000 from Carpet Store. This rug cost Carpet Store $1,200. Mary defaults and does not take possession of the rug. Carpet Store sells the rug to another buyer for $3,000. Here, Carpet Store can recover lost profits from Mary because the buyer of the rug that Mary did not buy might have purchased a different rug from Carpet Store, and, therefore, Carpet Store would have had two sales if Mary had not breached the sales contract. Therefore, Carpet Store can recover $1,800 of lost profits from Mary.

CONCEPT SUMMARY

SELLER'S AND LESSOR'S REMEDIES

Possession of Goods at the Time of the Buyer's or Lessee's Breach	Seller's or Lessor's Remedies
Goods in the possession of the seller or lessor	1. Withhold delivery of the goods [UCC 2-703(a), 2A-523(1)(c)]. 2. Resell or release the goods and recover the difference between the contract or lease price and the resale or release price [UCC 2-706, 2A-527]. 3. Sue for breach of contract and recover as damages the difference between the market price and the contract price [UCC 2-708(1), 2A-528(1)]. 4. A lost volume seller can sue and recover lost profits [UCC 2-708(2), 2A-528(2)]. 5. Cancel the contract [UCC 2-703(f), 2A-523(1)(a)].
Goods in the possession of a common carrier or bailee	1. Stop goods in transit [UCC 2-705(1), 2A-526(1)]. a. Carload, truckload, planeload, or larger shipment if the buyer is solvent. b. Any size shipment if the buyer is insolvent.
Goods in the possession of the buyer or lessee	1. Sue to recover the purchase price or rent [UCC 2-709(1), 2A-529(1)]. 2. Reclaim the goods [UCC 2-507(2), 2A-525(2)].

Buyer and Lessee Remedies

Nobody has a more sacred obligation to obey the law than those who make the law.

Sophocles (496–406 BCE)

If a seller or lessor breaches a sales or lease contract, the UCC provides a variety of remedies to the buyer or lessee for the seller's or lessor's breach. These remedies are discussed in the following paragraphs.

Right to Reject Nonconforming Goods or Improperly Tendered Goods

right to reject nonconforming goods or improperly tendered goods
The right of a buyer or lessee to reject goods that do not conform to a contract. If the goods or the seller's or lessor's tender of delivery fails to conform to the contract, the buyer or lessee may (1) reject the whole, (2) accept the whole, or (3) accept any commercial unit and reject the rest.

If the contracted-for goods or the seller's or lessor's tender of delivery fails to conform to a sales or lease contract in any way, the buyer or lessee has the **right to reject nonconforming goods or improperly tendered goods** and may (1) reject the whole, (2) accept the whole, or (3) accept any commercial unit and reject the rest. Nonconforming or improperly tendered goods must be rejected within a reasonable time after their delivery or tender. The seller or lessor must be notified of the rejection. The buyer or lessee must hold any rightfully rejected goods with reasonable care for a reasonable time [UCC 2-602(2), 2A-512(1)].

If the buyer or lessee chooses to reject the goods, he or she must identify defects that are ascertainable by reasonable inspection [UCC 2-601, 2A-509]. Any buyer or lessee who rightfully rejects goods is entitled to reimbursement from the seller or lessor for reasonable expenses incurred in holding, storing, reselling, shipping, and otherwise caring for the rejected goods.

Right to Recover Goods from an Insolvent Seller or Lessor

right to recover goods from an insolvent seller or lessor
The right of a buyer or lessee who has wholly or partially paid for goods before they are received to recover the goods from a seller or lessor who becomes insolvent within 10 days after receiving the first payment; the buyer or lessee must tender the remaining purchase price or rent due under the contract.

If a buyer or lessee makes partial or full payment for goods before they are received and the seller or lessor becomes insolvent within 10 days after receiving the first payment, the buyer or lessee has the **right to recover the goods from the insolvent seller or lessor**. To do so, the buyer or lessee must tender the unpaid portion of the purchase price or rent due under the sales or lease contract. Only conforming goods that are identified in the contract may be recovered [UCC 2-502, 2A-522]. This remedy is often referred to as **capture**.

Right to Obtain Specific Performance

specific performance
A decree of the court that orders a seller or lessor to perform his or her obligations under the contract; this usually occurs when the goods in question are unique, such as art or antiques.

If goods are unique or the remedy at law is inadequate, a buyer or lessee has the **right to obtain specific performance** of a sales or a lease contract. A decree of **specific performance** orders the seller or lessor to perform the contract. Specific performance is usually used to obtain possession of works of art, antiques, rare coins, and other unique items [UCC 2-716(1), 2A-521(1)].

Example A buyer enters into a sales contract to purchase a specific Rembrandt painting from a seller for $25 million. When the buyer tenders payment, the seller refuses to sell the painting to the buyer. The buyer may bring an equity action to obtain a decree of specific performance from the court, which orders the seller to sell the painting to the buyer.

The following feature discusses a buyer's and lessee's UCC right to cover.

Contemporary Environment

Buyer's and Lessee's Right to Cover

A buyer or lessee has the **right to cover** by purchasing or renting substitute goods if the seller or lessor fails to make delivery of the goods or repudiates the contract or if the buyer or lessee rightfully rejects the goods or justifiably revokes their acceptance. The buyer's or lessee's **cover** must be made in good faith and without unreasonable delay. If the exact commodity is not available, the buyer or lessee may purchase or lease any commercially reasonable substitute.

A buyer or lessee who rightfully covers may sue the seller or lessor to recover as damages the difference between the cost of cover and the contract price or rent. The buyer or lessee may also recover incidental and consequential damages, less expenses saved (such as delivery costs) [UCC 2-712, 2A-518].

Example University contracts to purchase 1,000 electronic tablets from Orange Store for $300 each to be used by its faculty members. Orange Store breaches the contract and does not deliver the tablets to University. University covers and contracts with Apple Store to purchase 1,000 tablets at the price of $400 per tablet. Here, University may recover $100,000 from Orange Store ($400 cover price − $300 contract price = $100 × 1,000 tablets).

Failure of the buyer or lessee to cover does not bar the buyer from other remedies against the seller.

Right to Replevy Goods

A buyer or lessee has the **right to replevy (recover) goods** from a seller or lessor who is wrongfully withholding the goods. The buyer or lessee must show that he or she was unable to cover or that attempts at cover will be unavailing. Thus, the goods must be scarce but not unique. **Replevin** actions are available only as to goods identified in a sales or lease contract [UCC 2-716(3), 2A-521(3)].

right to cover
The right of a buyer or lessee to purchase or lease substitute goods if a seller or lessor fails to make delivery of the goods or repudiates the contract or if the buyer or lessee rightfully rejects the goods or justifiably revokes their acceptance.

replevin
An action by a buyer or lessor to recover scarce goods wrongfully withheld by a seller or lessor.

Right to Cancel a Contract

If a seller or lessor fails to deliver conforming goods or repudiates the contract, the buyer or lessee may cancel the sales or lease contract (**buyer's or lessee's cancellation**). The buyer or lessee can also cancel a sales or lease contract if the buyer or lessee rightfully rejects the goods or justifiably revokes acceptance of the goods. The contract may be canceled with respect to the affected goods, or if there is a material breach, the whole contract may be canceled. A buyer or lessee who rightfully cancels a contract is discharged from any further obligations on the contract and retains his or her rights to other remedies against the seller or lessor [UCC 2-711(1), 2A-508(1)(a)].

buyer's or lessee's cancellation
A buyer's or lessee's right to cancel a sales or lease contract if the seller or lessor fails to deliver conforming goods or repudiates the contract or if the buyer or lessee rightfully rejects the goods or justifiably revokes acceptance of the goods.

Right to Recover Damages for Nondelivery or Repudiation

If a seller or lessor fails to deliver the goods or repudiates the sales or lease contract, the buyer or lessee has the **right to recover damages for nondelivery or repudiation**. The measure of **damages** is the difference between the contract price (or original rent) and the market price (or rent) at the time the buyer or lessee learned of the breach. Incidental and consequential damages, less expenses saved, can also be recovered [UCC 2-713, 2A-519].

Example Fresh Foods Company contracts to purchase 10,000 bushels of soybeans from Sunshine Farms for $14 per bushel. Delivery is to occur on August 1. On August 1, the market price of soybeans is $24 per bushel. Sunshine Farms does not deliver the soybeans to Fresh Foods. Fresh Foods decides not to cover and to do without the soybeans. Fresh Foods sues Sunshine for market value minus the contract price damages. It can recover $100,000 ($24 market price − $14 contract price = $10 × 10,000 bushels) plus incidental damages less expenses saved because of Sunshine's breach. Fresh Foods cannot recover consequential damages because it did not attempt to cover.

damages
Damages a buyer or lessee recovers from a seller or lessor who fails to deliver the goods or repudiates a contract. Damages are measured as the difference between the contract price (or original rent) and the market price (or rent) at the time the buyer or lessee learned of the breach.

Right to Recover Damages for Accepted Nonconforming Goods

A buyer or lessee may accept nonconforming goods from a seller or lessor. Even with acceptance, the buyer or lessee still has the **right to recover damages for accepted nonconforming goods** and any loss resulting from the seller's or lessor's breach. Incidental and consequential damages may also be recovered. The buyer or lessee must notify the seller or lessor of the nonconformity within a reasonable time after the breach was or should have been discovered. Failure to do so bars the buyer or lessee from any recovery. If the buyer or lessee accepts nonconforming goods, he or she may deduct all or any part of damages resulting from the breach from any part of the purchase price or rent still due under the contract [UCC 2-714(1), 2A-516(1)].

This is the kind of order which makes the administration of justice stink in the nostrils of commercial men.

A. L. Smith
L. J. Graham v. Sutton, Carden & Company (1897)

Example Retail Clothing contracts to purchase 1,000 designer dresses for $500 per dress from Manhattan Loft, a women's clothes designer and manufacturer. Retail Clothing pays for the dresses prior to delivery. After the dresses are delivered, Retail Clothing discovers that 200 of the dresses have flaws in them. Retail Clothing may accept these nonconforming dresses and sue Manhattan Loft for reasonable damages resulting from the nonconformity.

CONCEPT SUMMARY
BUYER'S AND LESSEE'S REMEDIES

Situation	Buyer's or Lessee's Remedy
Seller or lessor refuses to deliver the goods or delivers nonconforming goods that the buyer or lessee does not want.	1. Reject nonconforming goods [UCC 2-601, 2A-509]. 2. Cover and recover damages [UCC 2-712, 2A-518]. 3. Sue for breach of contract and recover damages [UCC 2-713, 2A-519]. 4. Cancel the contract [UCC 2-711(1), 2A-508(1)(a)].
Seller or lessor tenders nonconforming goods, and the buyer or lessee accepts them.	1. Sue for ordinary damages [UCC 2-714(1), 2A-516(1)]. 2. Deduct damages from the unpaid purchase or rent price [UCC 2-714(1), 2A-516(1)].
Seller or lessor refuses to deliver the goods, and the buyer or lessee wants them.	1. Sue for specific performance [UCC 2-716(1), 2A-521(1)]. 2. Replevy the goods [UCC 2-716(3), 2A-521(3)]. 3. Recover the goods from an insolvent seller or lessor [UCC 2-502, 2A-522].

Additional Performance Issues

UCC Articles 2 (Sales) and 2A (Leases) contain several other provisions that affect the parties' performance of a sales or lease contract. These provisions are discussed in the following paragraphs.

Assurance of Performance

Each party to a sales or lease contract expects that the other party will perform his or her contractual obligations. If one party to a contract has reasonable grounds to believe that the other party either will not or cannot perform his or her contractual obligations, an **adequate assurance of performance** may be demanded in writing. If it is commercially reasonable to do so, the party making the demand may suspend his or her performance until adequate assurance of due performance is received from the other party [UCC 2-609, 2A-401].

adequate assurance of performance
Adequate assurance of performance from the other party if there is an indication that a contract will be breached by that party.

Example A buyer contracts to purchase 1,000 bushels of wheat from a farmer. The contract requires delivery on September 1. In July, the buyer learns that floods have caused substantial crop loss in the area of the seller's farm. The farmer receives the buyer's written demand for adequate assurance on July 15. The farmer fails to give adequate assurance of performance. The buyer may suspend performance and treat the sales contract as having been repudiated.

UCC statute of limitations
A rule that provides that an action for breach of any written or oral sales or lease contract must commence within four years after the cause of action accrues. The parties may agree to reduce the limitations period to one year.

Statute of Limitations

The **UCC statute of limitations** provides that an action for breach of any written or oral sales or lease contract must commence within four years after the legal claim accrues. The parties may agree to reduce the limitations period to one year, but they cannot extend it beyond four years.

Example A buyer contracts to purchase cattle from a seller with a delivery date of July 1, 2017. The seller breaches the contract and does not deliver the cattle on July 1, 2017. Under the UCC four-year statute of limitations, the buyer has until July 1, 2021, to bring a lawsuit against the seller for breach of contract. If the buyer waits until after this date has passed, then he or she loses the right to sue the seller. The parties could have included a provision in their contract to reduce the limitations period to one year, or July 1, 2018.

Agreements Affecting Remedies

The parties to a sales or lease contract may agree on remedies in addition to or in substitution for the remedies provided by the UCC. The parties may limit the buyer's or lessee's remedies to repair and replacement of defective goods or parts or to the return of the goods and repayment (refund) of the purchase price or rent.

Convenience is the basis of mercantile law.

Lord Mansfield
Medcalf v. Hall (1782)

The remedies agreed on by the parties are in addition to the remedies provided by the UCC unless the parties expressly provide that they are exclusive. If an exclusive remedy fails in its essential purpose (e.g., there is an exclusive remedy of repair, but there are no repair parts available), any remedy may be had, as provided in the UCC.

Liquidated Damages

The UCC permits parties to a sales or lease contract to establish in advance in their contract the damages that will be paid on a breach of the contract. Such pre-established damages, called **liquidated damages**, substitute for actual damages. In a sales or lease contract, liquidated damages are valid if they are reasonable in light of the anticipated or actual harm caused by the breach, the difficulties of proof of loss, and the inconvenience or nonfeasibility of otherwise obtaining an adequate remedy [UCC 2-718(1), 2A-504].

liquidated damages Damages that will be paid on a breach of contract that are established in advance.

The UCC doctrine of unconscionable contract is discussed in the following ethics feature.

Ethics

UCC Doctrine of Unconscionability

UCC Article 2 (Sales) and Article 2A (Leases) have adopted the equity doctrine of **unconscionability**. Under this doctrine, a court may determine as a matter of law that a contract is an **unconscionable contract**. To prove unconscionability, there must be proof that the parties had substantially unequal bargaining power, that the dominant party misused its power in contracting, and that it would be manifestly unfair or oppressive to enforce the contract. This sometimes happens where a dominant party uses a preprinted form contract and the terms of the contract are unfair or oppressive.

If a court finds that a contract or any clause in a contract is unconscionable, the court may refuse to enforce the contract, it may enforce the remainder of the contract without the unconscionable clause, or it may so limit the application of any unconscionable clause as to avoid any unconscionable result [UCC 2-302, 2A-108]. Unconscionability is sometimes found in a consumer lease if the consumer has been induced by unconscionable conduct to enter into the lease. The doctrine of unconscionability applies to online contracts as well as traditional contracts.

Ethics Questions Does the fact that the term *unconscionable* is somewhat vague serve any useful purpose? Does the doctrine of unconscionability encourage ethical behavior?

Key Terms and Concepts

Acceptance (434)
Adequate assurance of performance (440)
Breach (431)
Buyer's or lessee's cancellation (439)
Capture (438)
Commercial reasonableness (433)
Cover (438)
Cure (432)
Damages (439)
Destination contract (432)
Express terms (433)
Good faith (433)
Incidental damages (436)
Installment contract (433)
Liquidated damages (441)
Lost volume seller (437)
Obligation (431)
Payment (434)
Perfect tender rule (432)
Place of delivery (431)
Reasonableness (433)
Replevin (439)
Revocation of acceptance (435)
Right to cancel a contract (437)
Right to cover (438)
Right to cure (432)
Right to dispose of goods (436)
Right to inspect (434)
Right to obtain specific performance (438)
Right to reclaim goods (435)
Right to recover damages for accepted nonconforming goods (439)
Right to recover damages for breach of contract (436)
Right to recover damages for nondelivery or repudiation (439)
Right to recover goods from an insolvent seller or lessor (438)
Right to recover lost profits (436)
Right to recover the purchase price or rent (436)
Right to reject nonconforming goods or improperly tendered goods (438)
Right to replevy (recover) goods (439)
Right to stop delivery of goods in transit (435)
Right to withhold delivery (435)
Shipment contract (432)
Specific performance (438)
Tender of delivery (431)
UCC statute of limitations (440)
Unconscionability (441)
Unconscionable contract (441)
Unfinished goods (436)

Critical Legal Thinking Cases

20.1 Nonconforming Goods The Jacob Hartz Seed Company, Inc. (Hartz), bought soybeans for use as seed from E. R. Coleman. Coleman certified that the seed had an 80 percent germination rate. Hartz paid for the beans and picked them up from a warehouse in Card, Arkansas. After the seed was transported to Georgia, a sample was submitted for testing to the Georgia Department of Agriculture. When the department reported a germination level of only 67 percent, Coleman requested that the seed be retested. The second set of tests reported a germination rate of 65 percent. Hartz canceled the contract after the second test, and Coleman reclaimed the seed. Hartz sought a refund of the money it had paid for the seed, claiming that the soybeans were nonconforming goods. Who wins? *Jacob Hartz Seed Co. v. Coleman*, 271 Ark. 756, 612 S.W.2d 91, 1981 Ark. Lexis 1153 (Supreme Court of Arkansas)

20.2 Right to Cure Connie R. Grady purchased a new Chevrolet Chevette from Al Thompson Chevrolet (Thompson). Grady gave Thompson a down payment on the car and financed the remainder of the purchase price through General Motors Acceptance Corporation (GMAC). Grady picked up the Chevette. The next day, the car broke down and had to be towed back to Thompson. Grady picked up the repaired car one day later. The car's performance was still unsatisfactory in that the engine was hard to start, the transmission slipped, and the brakes had to be pushed to the floor to function. Two weeks later, Grady again returned the Chevette for servicing. When she picked up the car that evening, the engine started, but the engine and brake warning lights came on. This pattern of malfunction and repair continued for another two months. Grady wrote a letter to Thompson, revoking the sale. Thompson repossessed the Chevette. GMAC sued Grady to recover its money. Grady sued Thompson to recover her down payment. Thompson claimed that Grady's suit was barred because the company was not given adequate opportunity to cure. Who wins? *General Motors Acceptance Corp. v. Grady*, 27 Ohio App.3d 321, 501 N.E.2d 68, 1985 Ohio App. Lexis 10353 (Court of Appeals of Ohio)

20.3 Right to Resell Goods Meuser Material & Equipment Company (Meuser) was a dealer in construction equipment. Meuser entered into an agreement with Joe McMillan for the sale of a bulldozer to McMillan. The agreement called for Meuser to deliver the bulldozer to McMillan's residence in Greeley, Colorado. McMillan paid Meuser with a check. Before taking delivery, McMillan stopped payment on the check. Meuser entered into negotiations with McMillan in an attempt to get McMillan to abide by the sales agreement. During this period, Meuser paid for the upkeep of the bulldozer. When it became apparent that further negotiations would be fruitless, Meuser began looking for a new buyer. Fourteen months after the original sale was supposed to have taken place, the bulldozer was resold for less than the original contract price. Meuser sued McMillan to recover the difference between the contract price and the resale price as well as for the cost of upkeep on the bulldozer for 14 months. Who wins? *McMillan v. Meuser Material & Equipment*

Company, 260 Ark. 422, 541 S.W.2d 911, 1976 Ark. Lexis 1814 (Supreme Court of Arkansas)

20.4 Right to Recover Lost Profits Saber Energy, Inc. (Saber), entered into a sales contract with Tri-State Petroleum Corporation (Tri-State). The contract called for Saber to sell Tri-State 110,000 barrels of gasoline per month for six months. Saber was to deliver the gasoline through the colonial pipeline in Pasadena, Texas. The first 110,000 barrels were delivered on time. On August 1, Saber was informed that Tri-State was canceling the contract. Saber sued Tri-State for breach of contract and sought to recover its lost profits as damages. Tri-State admitted its breach but claimed that lost profits is an inappropriate measure of damages. Who wins? *Tri-State Petroleum Corporation v. Saber Energy, Inc.*, 845 F.2d 575, 1988 U.S. App. Lexis 6819 (United States Court of Appeals for the Fifth Circuit)

20.5 Specific Performance Dr. and Mrs. Sedmak (Sedmaks) were collectors of Chevrolet Corvettes. The Sedmaks saw an article in *Vette Vues* magazine concerning a new limited-edition Corvette. The limited edition was designed to commemorate the selection of the Corvette as the official pace car of the Indianapolis 500. Chevrolet was manufacturing only 6,000 of these pace cars. The Sedmaks visited Charlie's Chevrolet, Inc. (Charlie's), a local Chevrolet dealer. Charlie's was to receive only one limited-edition car, which the sales manager agreed to sell to the Sedmaks for the sticker price of $15,000. When the Sedmaks went to pick up and pay for the car, they were told that because of the great demand for the limited edition, it was going to be auctioned to the highest bidder. The Sedmaks sued the dealership for specific performance. Who wins? *Sedmak v. Charlie's Chevrolet, Inc.*, 622 S.W.2d. 694, 1981 Mo. App. Lexis 2911 (Court of Appeals of Missouri)

20.6 Right to Cover Kent Nowlin Construction, Inc. (Nowlin), was awarded a contract by the state of New Mexico to pave a number of roads. After Nowlin was awarded the contract, it entered into an agreement with Concrete Sales & Equipment Rental Company, Inc. (C&E). C&E was to supply 20,000 tons of paving material to Nowlin. Nowlin began paving the roads, anticipating C&E's delivery of materials. On the delivery date, however, C&E shipped only 2,099 tons of paving materials. Because Nowlin had a deadline to meet, the company contracted with Gallup Sand and Gravel Company (Gallup) for substitute material. Nowlin sued C&E to recover the difference between the higher price it had to pay Gallup for materials and the contract price C&E had agreed to. C&E claims that it is not responsible for Nowlin's increased costs. Who wins? *Concrete Sales & Equipment Rental Company, Inc. v. Kent Nowlin Construction, Inc.*, 106 N.M. 539, 746 P.2d 645, 1987 N.M. Lexis 3808 (Supreme Court of New Mexico)

Ethical

Ethics Case

20.7 Ethics Case Both Allsopp Sand and Gravel (Allsopp) and Lincoln Sand and Gravel (Lincoln) were in the business of supplying sand to construction companies. In March, Lincoln's sand dredge became inoperable. To continue in business, Lincoln negotiated a contract with Allsopp to purchase sand over the course of a year. The contract called for the sand to be loaded on Lincoln's trucks during Allsopp's regular operating season (March through November). Loading at other times was to be done by "special arrangement." By the following November, Lincoln had taken delivery of one-quarter of the sand it had contracted for. At that point, Lincoln requested that several trucks of sand be loaded in December. Allsopp informed Lincoln that it would have to pay extra for this special arrangement. Lincoln refused to pay extra, pointing out that the sand was already stockpiled at Allsopp's facilities. Allsopp also offered to supply an employee to supervise the loading. Negotiations between the parties broke down, and Lincoln informed Allsopp that it did not intend to honor the remainder of the contract. Allsopp sued Lincoln. Is it commercially reasonable for Lincoln to demand delivery of sand during December? Has Lincoln acted ethically in this case? *Allsopp Sand and Gravel v. Lincoln Sand and Gravel*, 171 Ill. App.3d 532, 525 N.E.2d 1185, 1988 Ill. App. Lexis 939 (Appellate Court of Illinois)

CHAPTER 21

Warranties

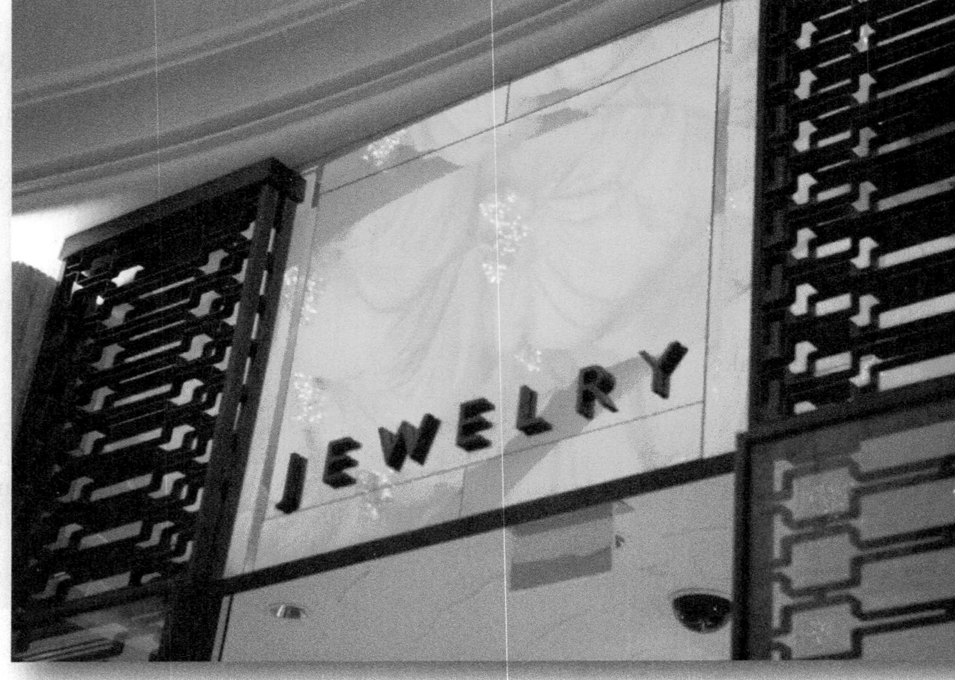

EXPRESS WARRANTY

The sellers of goods are liable for breach of warranties that they make. For example, when a jewelry store sells a diamond ring, it states the "four Cs" of the ring: cut, clarity, color, and carat weight. If a party purchases a ring but it does not meet the four Cs as stated by the seller, the seller has breached a warranty. The purchaser can sue the seller for breach of a warranty.

Learning Objectives

After studying this chapter, you should be able to:

1. Identify and describe express warranties.
2. Describe the implied warranty of merchantability.
3. Describe the implied warranty of fitness for a particular purpose.
4. Identify warranty disclaimers and determine when they are unlawful.
5. Describe the warranties of good title and no infringements.

Chapter Outline

"When a manufacturer engages in advertising in order to bring his goods and their quality to the attention of the public and thus to create consumer demand, the representations made constitute an express warranty running directly to a buyer who purchases in reliance thereon. The fact that the sale is consummated with an independent dealer does not obviate the warranty."

—*Francis, Justice*
Henningsen v. Bloomfield Motors, Inc. 161 A.2d 69, 1960 N.J. Lexis 213 (1960)

Introduction to Warranties

The doctrine of ***caveat emptor***—"let the buyer beware"—governed the law of sales and leases for centuries. Finally, the law recognized that consumers and other purchasers and lessees of goods needed greater protection. Article 2 of the Uniform Commercial Code (UCC), adopted in whole or in part by all 50 states, establishes certain warranties that apply to the sale of goods. In addition, Article 2A of the UCC, adopted in almost all states, establishes warranties that apply to lease transactions.

Warranties are favored in law, being a part of a man's assurance.

Sir Edward Coke (1552–1634)
First Institute of the Laws of England, Volume 2

Warranties are the buyer's or lessee's assurance that the goods meet certain standards. Warranties that are based on contract law may be either *expressly* stated or *implied* by law. If the seller or lessor fails to meet a warranty, the buyer or lessee can sue for breach of warranty.

warranty
A seller's or lessor's express or implied assurance to a buyer or lessee that the goods sold or leased meet certain quality standards.

Sales and lease warranties are discussed in this chapter.

Express Warranty

Express warranties are created when a seller or lessor affirms that the goods he or she is selling or leasing meet certain standards of quality, description, performance, or condition [UCC 2-313(1), 2A-210(1)]. Express warranties can be either written, oral, or inferred from the seller's conduct. It is not necessary to use formal words such as *warrant* or *guarantee* to create an express warranty. Express warranties can be made by mistake because the seller or lessor does not have to specifically intend to make the warranty [UCC 2-313(2), 2A-210(2)].

express warranty
A warranty created when a seller or lessor makes an affirmation that the goods he or she is selling or leasing meet certain standards of quality, description, performance, or condition.

Sellers and lessors are not required to make express warranties. Generally, express warranties are made to entice consumers and others to buy or lease their products. That is why these warranties are often found in advertisements, brochures, catalogs, pictures, illustrations, diagrams, blueprints, and so on. Buyers and lessees can recover for breach of an express warranty if the warranty induced the buyer to purchase the product or the lessee to lease the product.

Creation of an Express Warranty

An express warranty is created when a seller or lessor indicates that the goods will conform to the following:

1. All *affirmations of fact or promise* made about the goods

   Examples Promises are statements such as "This car will go 100 miles per hour" or "This house paint will last at least five years."

2. Any *description* of the goods

   Examples Descriptions of goods include terms such as *Idaho potatoes* and *Michigan cherries*.

3. Any *model* or *sample* of the goods

   Example A model of an oil-drilling rig or a sample of wheat taken from a silo creates an express warranty.

Buyers and lessees can recover for a breach of an express warranty if the warranty was a contributing factor that induced the buyer to purchase the product or the lessee to lease the product [UCC 2-313(1), 2A-210(1)]. Generally, a retailer is liable for the express warranties made by manufacturers of goods it sells. A manufacturer is not liable for express warranties made by wholesalers and retailers unless the manufacturer authorizes or ratifies a warranty.

Statement of Opinion

statement of opinion (puffing)
A commendation of goods, made by a seller or lessor, that does not create an express warranty.

Many express warranties arise during the course of negotiations between a buyer and a seller or a lessor and a lessee. A seller's or lessor's **statement of opinion** (i.e., **puffing**) or commendation of the goods does not create an express warranty. It is often difficult to determine whether a seller's statement is an affirmation of fact (which creates an express warranty) or a statement of opinion (which does not create a warranty). An affirmation of the *value* of goods does not create an express warranty [UCC 2-313(2), 2A-210(2)].

Examples A used car salesperson's says, "This is the best used car available in town," but this statement does not create an express warranty because it is an opinion and mere puffing. However, a statement such as "This car has been driven only 20,000 miles" is an express warranty because it is a statement of fact.

Examples Statements such as "This painting is worth a fortune" or "Others would gladly pay $20,000 for this car" do not create an express warranty because these are statements of value and not statements of fact.

Damages Recoverable for Breach of Warranty

compensatory damages
Damages that are generally equal to the difference between the value of the goods as warranted and the actual value of the goods accepted at the time and place of acceptance.

Where there has been a breach of warranty, the buyer or lessee may sue the seller or lessor to recover **compensatory damages**. The amount of recoverable compensatory damages is generally equal to the difference between (1) the value of the goods as warranted and (2) the actual value of the goods accepted at the time and place of acceptance [UCC 2-714(2), 2A-508(4)]. A purchaser or lessee can recover for personal injuries that are caused by a breach of warranty.

Example A used car salesperson warrants that a used car has been driven only 20,000 miles. If true, that would make the car worth $20,000. The salesperson gives the buyer a "good deal" and sells the car for $16,000. Unfortunately, the car was worth only $10,000 because it was actually driven 100,000 miles. The buyer discovers the breach of warranty and sues the salesperson for damages. The buyer can recover $10,000 ($20,000 warranted value minus $10,000 actual value). The contract price ($16,000) is irrelevant to this computation.

Implied Warranties

In addition to express warranties made by a manufacturer or seller, the law sometimes *implies* warranties in the sale or lease of goods. **Implied warranties** are not expressly stated in the sales or lease contract but instead are **implied by law**. The most common forms of implied warranties are the *implied warranty of merchantability*, the *implied warranty of fitness for human consumption*, and the *implied warranty of fitness for a particular purpose*. These warranties are discussed in the following paragraphs.

Implied Warranty of Merchantability

If a seller or lessor of a good is a *merchant* with respect to goods of that kind, the sales contract or lease contract contains an **implied warranty of merchantability** of the good unless this implied warranty is properly disclaimed [UCC 2-314(1), 2A-212(1)]. This implied warranty requires that the following standards be met:

implied warranty of merchantability
Unless properly disclosed, a warranty that is implied that sold or leased goods are fit for the ordinary purpose for which they are sold or leased, as well as other assurances.

1. The goods must be fit for the ordinary purposes for which they are used.

   Examples A chair must be able to safely perform the function of a chair. If a normal-sized person sits in a chair that has not been tampered with and the chair collapses, there has been a breach of the implied warranty of merchantability. If the same person is injured because he or she uses the chair as a ladder and it tips over, there is no breach of implied warranty because use as a ladder is not the ordinary purpose of a chair.

2. The goods must be adequately contained, packaged, and labeled.

   Example The implied warranty of merchantability applies to a milk bottle as well as to the milk inside the bottle.

3. The goods must be of an even kind, quality, and quantity within each unit.

   Example All the goods in a carton, package, or box must be consistent.

4. The goods must conform to any promise or affirmation of fact made on the container or label.

   Example The goods must be capable of being used safely in accordance with the instructions on the package or label.

5. The quality of the goods must pass without objection in the trade.

   Example The goods must be of such quality that other users of the goods would not object to their quality.

6. Fungible goods must meet a fair average or middle range of quality.

   Example To be classified as a certain grade, such as pearl millet grain (*Pennisetum glaucum*) or iron ore (magnetite Fe_3O_4), goods must meet the average range of quality of that grade.

Critical Legal Thinking

How do an express warranty and an implied warranty differ? What is the public policy for implying a warranty of merchantability?

Law should be like death, which spares no one.

Charles de Montesquieu (1689–1755)

In the following case, the court had to decide if the implied warranty of merchantability had been breached.

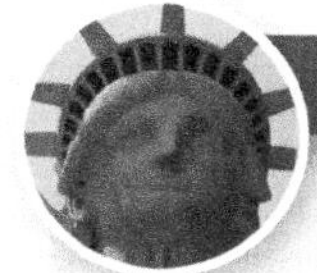

CASE 21.1 FEDERAL COURT CASE *Implied Warranty of Merchantability*

Osorio v. One World Technologies, Inc.

659 F.3d 81, 2011 U.S. App. Lexis 20174 (2011)
United States Court of Appeals for the First Circuit

"Manufacturers must design products so that they are fit for the ordinary purposes for which such goods are used."

—Torruella, Circuit Judge

Facts

Carlos Osorio worked at a construction site for his employer, a contractor who repairs and installs hardwood floors. The employer had purchased a Ryobi Model BTS 15 table saw at Home Depot for $179. The saw was manufactured by Ryobi Technologies, Inc. As Osorio was using the BTS 15 saw to make a cut along the length of a piece of wood, his left hand slipped and slid into the saw's blade, causing severe injury. Osorio sued Ryobi in U.S. district court, claiming breach of the implied warranty of merchantability. At trial, Osorio produced a witness, Dr. Stephen Gass, who invented "SawStop," a mechanism that allows

(*case continues*)

a table saw to sense when the blade comes into contact with flesh, immediately stops the blade from spinning, and causes the blade to retreat into the body of the saw. Dr. Gass testified that he presented the technology to Ryobi, but the company did not incorporate this technology into its saws. The jury held that Ryobi had breached the implied warranty of merchantability by not adopting the flesh-detection technology in its saws and awarded Osorio damages of $1.5 million. Ryobi appealed.

Issue

Did Ryobi breach the implied warranty of merchantability?

Language of the Court

Manufacturers must design products so that they are fit for the ordinary purposes for which such goods are used. It is the province of the jury to determine whether a product's design is unreasonable. Considering the evidence before it, the jury simply agreed with Osorio's case and found in his favor.

Decision

The U.S. court of appeals affirmed the U.S. district court's finding that Ryobi breached the implied warranty of merchantability.

Ethics Questions

Should Ryobi have adopted flesh-detection technology in its saws? What would be the impact on consumers if it did?

The implied warranty of merchantability does not apply to sales or leases by nonmerchants or casual sales.

Examples The implied warranty of merchantability applies to the sale of a lawn mower that is sold by a merchant who is in the business of selling lawn mowers. The implied warranty of merchantability does not apply when one neighbor sells a lawn mower to another neighbor.

The following critical legal thinking case discusses the implied warranty of merchantability.

Critical Legal Thinking Case

Implied Warranty of Merchantability

"Plaintiff introduced a Ford marketing manual that predicted many buyers would be attracted to the Bronco because utility vehicles were suitable to 'contemporary lifestyles' and were 'considered fashionable' in some suburban areas."

—Titone, Judge

Nancy Denny purchased a Bronco, a sport-utility vehicle (SUV) that was manufactured by Ford Motor Company. Denny testified that she purchased the Bronco for use on paved city and suburban streets and not for off-road use. When Denny was driving the vehicle on a paved road, she slammed on the brakes in an effort to avoid a deer that had walked directly into her SUV's path. The Bronco rolled over, and Denny was severely injured. Denny sued Ford Motor Company to recover damages for breach of the implied warranty of merchantability.

Denny alleged that the Bronco presented a significantly higher risk of occurrence of rollover accidents than did ordinary passenger vehicles. Denny introduced evidence at trial that showed the Bronco had a low stability index because of its high center of gravity, narrow tracks, shorter wheelbase, and the design of its suspension system.

Ford countered that the Bronco was intended as an off-road vehicle and was not designed to be used as a conventional passenger automobile on paved streets. However, the plaintiff introduced a Ford marketing manual that predicted that many buyers would be attracted to the Bronco because utility vehicles were suitable to "contemporary lifestyles" and were "considered fashionable" in some suburban areas. According to this manual, the sales presentation of the Bronco should take into account the vehicle's "suitability for commuting and for suburban and city driving."

The trial court found that Ford had violated the implied warranty of merchantability and awarded Denny $1.2 million. The court of appeals upheld this verdict. *Denny v. Ford Motor Company*, 87 N.Y.2d 248, 662 N.E.2d 730, 639 N.Y.S.2d 250, 1995 N.Y. Lexis 4445 (Court of Appeals of New York)

Critical Legal Thinking Questions
Why does the law recognize implied warranties? What public purpose is served by doing so? Did Ford act ethically in asserting the "off-road vehicle" defense?

Impiled Warranty of Fitness for Human Consumption

The common law implied a special warranty—the **implied warranty of fitness for human consumption**—to food products. The UCC incorporates this warranty within the implied warranty of merchantability, and it applies to food and drink consumed on or off the seller's premises. Restaurants, grocery stores, fast-food outlets, coffee shops, bars, vending machines, and other purveyors of food and drink are all subject to this warranty. States use one of the following two tests in determining whether there has been a breach of the implied warranty of fitness for human consumption:

implied warranty of fitness for human consumption
A warranty that applies to food or drink consumed on or off the premises of restaurants, grocery stores, fast-food outlets, coffee shops, bars, vending machines, and other purveyors of food and drink.

1. **Foreign substance test.** Under the **foreign substance test**, a food product is unmerchantable if a foreign object in that product causes injury to a person.

   Examples Under this test, the implied warranty would be breached if a person were injured by eating a nail in a cherry pie. This is because a nail is a foreign object in the cherry pie. The implied warranty would not be breached if a person were injured by eating a cherry pit in the pie. This is because the cherry pit is not a foreign object in the cherry pie.

foreign substance test
A test to determine merchantability based on foreign objects found in food.

2. **Consumer expectation test.** The majority of states have adopted the modern **consumer expectation test** to determine the merchantability of food products. Under this test, the court asks what a consumer would expect to find or not find in food or drink that he or she consumes.

   Examples Under this test, the implied warranty would be breached if a person were injured by a chicken bone while eating a chicken salad sandwich. This is because a consumer would expect that the food producer would have removed all bones from the chicken. Under this test, the implied warranty would not be breached if a person were injured by a chicken bone while eating fried chicken. This is because a consumer would expect to find bones in fried chicken.

consumer expectation test
A test to determine merchantability based on what the average consumer would expect to find in food products.

Implied Warranty of Fitness for a Particular Purpose

The UCC contains an **implied warranty of fitness for a particular purpose**. This implied warranty attaches to the sale or lease of goods if the seller or lessor has made statements that the goods will meet the buyer's or lessee's needs or purpose. This implied warranty is breached if the goods do not meet the buyer's or lessee's expressed needs. The warranty applies to both merchant and nonmerchant sellers and lessors.

implied warranty of fitness for a particular purpose
A warranty that arises when a seller or lessor warrants that the goods will meet the buyer's or lessee's expressed needs.

The warranty of fitness for a particular purpose is implied at the time of contracting if [UCC 2-315, 2A-213]:

- The seller or lessor has reason to know the particular purpose for which the buyer is purchasing the goods or the lessee is leasing the goods.
- The seller or lessor makes a statement that the goods will serve this purpose.

- The buyer or lessee relies on the seller's or lessor's skill and judgment and purchases or leases the goods.

Example Susan wants to buy lumber to build a small deck in her backyard. She goes to Joe's Lumber Yard to purchase the lumber and describes to Joe, the owner of the lumber yard, the size of the deck she intends to build. Susan also tells Joe that she is relying on him to select the right lumber for the project. Joe selects the lumber and states that the lumber will serve Susan's purpose. Susan buys the lumber and builds the deck. The deck collapses because the lumber was not strong enough to support it. Susan can sue Joe for breach of the implied warranty of fitness for a particular purpose.

CONCEPT SUMMARY
EXPRESS AND IMPLIED WARRANTIES

Type of Warranty	How Created	Description
Express warranty	Made by the seller or lessor	Affirms that the goods meet certain standards of quality, description, performance, or condition [UCC 2-313(1), 2A-210(1)].
Implied warranty of merchantability	Implied by law if the seller or lessor is a merchant	Implies that the goods: 1. Are fit for the ordinary purposes for which they are used. 2. Are adequately contained, packaged, and labeled. 3. Are of an even kind, quality, and quantity within each unit. 4. Conform to any promise or affirmation of fact made on the container or label. 5. Pass without objection in the trade. 6. Meet a fair, average, or middle range of quality for fungible goods [UCC 2-314(1), 2A-212(1)].
Implied warranty of fitness for human consumption	Implied by law	Implies that food is fit for human consumption. Each state has adopted one of the following standards: 1. Foreign substance test. 2. Consumer expectation test.
Implied warranty of fitness for a particular purpose	Implied by law	Implies that the goods are fit for the purpose for which the buyer or lessee acquires the goods if: 1. The seller or lessor has reason to know the particular purpose for which the goods will be used. 2. The seller or lessor makes a statement that the goods will serve that purpose. 3. The buyer or lessee relies on the statement and buys or leases the goods [UCC 2-315,UCC 2A-213].

Warranty Disclaimers

warranty disclaimer
A statement that negates express and implied warranties.

Warranties can be disclaimed, or limited. If an *express warranty* is made, it can be limited only if the **warranty disclaimer** and the warranty can be reasonably construed with each other. All implied warranties of quality may be disclaimed. The rules for disclaiming implied warranties are the following:

- **"As is" disclaimer.** Expressions such as *as is*, *with all faults*, or other language that makes it clear to the buyer that there are no implied warranties disclaims all implied warranties. An **"as is" disclaimer** is often included in sales contracts for used products.

- **Disclaimer of the implied warranty of merchantability.** If the "as is" type of disclaimer is not used, a **disclaimer of the implied warranty of merchantability** must specifically mention the term *merchantability* for the implied warranty of merchantability to be disclaimed. These disclaimers may be oral or written.
- **Disclaimer of the implied warranty of fitness for a particular purpose.** If the "as is" type of disclaimer is not used, a **disclaimer of the implied warranty of fitness for a particular purpose** may contain general language, without specific use of the term *fitness*. The disclaimer has to be in writing.

Conspicuous Display of Disclaimer

Written disclaimers must be conspicuously displayed to be valid. The courts construe **conspicuous** to mean noticeable to a reasonable person [UCC 2-316, 2A-214]. A heading printed in uppercase letters or a typeface that is larger or in a different style than the rest of the body of a sales or lease contract is considered to be conspicuous. Different-color type is also considered conspicuous.

conspicuous
A requirement that warranty disclaimers be noticeable to a reasonable person.

The following case addresses the issue of a warranty disclaimer.

CASE 21.2 *STATE COURT CASE Warranty Disclaimer*

Roberts v. Lanigan Auto Sales

406 S.W.3d 882, 2013 Ky. App. Lexis 4 (2013)
Court of Appeals of Kentucky

"A valid 'as is' agreement prevents a buyer from holding a seller liable if the thing sold turns out to be worth less than the price paid."
—Vanmeter, Judge

Facts

Evan Roberts purchased a used vehicle from Lanigan Auto Sales. The sales contract contained a clause stating that the vehicle was "sold as is." Subsequently, Roberts obtained a report that stated that the vehicle had previously been involved in an accident and suffered damage to the undercarriage of the vehicle. Roberts sued Lanigan for damages, alleging that Lanigan breached express and implied warranties by not disclosing the vehicle's prior damage and accident history. Lanigan maintained it had never represented the quality of the vehicle and filed a motion to dismiss Roberts's action. The trial court dismissed Roberts's action on the basis that the sales contract contained the express term that the vehicle was "sold as is." Roberts appealed.

Issue

Did the "sold as is" language of the sales contract bar Roberts' action?

Language of the Court

A valid "as is" agreement prevents a buyer from holding a seller liable if the thing sold turns out to be worth less than the price paid. Thus, by agreeing to purchase something "as is," a buyer agrees to make his or her own appraisal of the bargain and to accept the risk that he or she may be wrong, and the seller gives no assurances, express or implied, concerning the value or condition of the thing sold.

Decision

The court of appeals affirmed the trial court's decision that the "sold as is" language in the sales contract prevented Roberts from recovering damages from Lanigan Auto Sales. The supreme court of Kentucky affirmed the decision.

Ethics Questions

Why do sellers include "sold as is" clauses in sales contracts? Did Roberts act ethically in trying to avoid the "sold as is" clause of the sales contract?

Magnuson-Moss Warranty Act

Magnuson-Moss Warranty Act
A federal statute that regulates written warranties on consumer products.

The **Magnuson-Moss Warranty Act** is a federal statute that covers written warranties related to **consumer products**.[1] This act is administered by the Federal Trade Commission (FTC). *Consumer transactions* but not commercial and industrial transactions are governed by the act.

The act does not require a seller or lessor to make an *express* written warranty. However, sellers or lessors who do make express warranties are subject to the provisions of the act. If a warrantor chooses to make an express warranty, the Magnuson-Moss Warranty Act requires that the warranty be labeled as either "full" or "limited":

- **Full warranty.** For a warranty to qualify as a **full warranty**, the warrantor must guarantee that a defective product will be repaired or replaced free during the warranty period. The warrantor must indicate whether there is a time limit on the full warranty (e.g., "full 36-month warranty").
- **Limited warranty.** In a **limited warranty**, the warrantor limits the scope of the warranty in some way. A warranty that covers the costs of parts but not the labor to fix a defective product is a limited warranty.

Critical Legal Thinking
What does the Magnuson-Moss Warranty Act provide? What is the difference between a full warranty and a limited warranty?

Limited warranties are made more often by sellers and lessors than are full warranties. The act stipulates that sellers or lessors who make express written warranties related to *consumer products* are forbidden from disclaiming or modifying the implied warranties of merchantability and fitness for a particular purpose.

The act authorizes warrantors to establish an informal dispute-resolution procedure, such as arbitration. A successful plaintiff can recover damages, attorney's fees, and other costs incurred in bringing the action.

The following feature discusses warranty disclaimers in software licenses.

Digital Law

Warranty Disclaimers in Software Licenses

Most software companies license their software to users. A software license is a complex contract that contains the terms of the license. Most software licenses contain warranty disclaimer and limitation on liability clauses that limit the licensor's liability if the software malfunctions. Disclaimer of warranty and limitation on liability clauses that are included in a typical software license appear below.

SOFTWARE.COM, INC.
LIMITATION AND WAIVERS OF WARRANTIES, REMEDIES, AND CONSEQUENTIAL DAMAGES

Limited Warranty. Software.com, Inc. warrants that (a) the software will perform substantially in accordance with the accompanying written materials for a period of 90 days from the date of receipt, and (b) any hardware accompanying the software will be free from defects in materials and workmanship under normal use and service for a period of one year from the date of the receipt. Any implied warranties on the software and hardware are limited to 90 days and one (1) year, respectively. Some states do not allow limitations on duration of an implied warranty, so the above limitation may not apply to you.

Customer Remedies. Software.com, Inc.'s entire liability and your exclusive remedy shall be, at Software.com, Inc.'s option, either (a) return of the price paid or (b) repair or replacement of the software or hardware that does not meet Software.com, Inc.'s Limited Warranty and that is returned to Software.com, Inc. with a copy of your receipt. This Limited Warranty is void if failure of the software or hardware has resulted from accident, abuse, or misapplication. Any replacement software will be warranted for the remainder of the original warranty or 30 days, whichever is longer. These remedies are not available outside the United States of America.

No Other Warranties. Software.com, Inc. disclaims all other warranties, either express or implied, including but not limited to implied warranties of merchantability and fitness for a particular purpose, with respect to the software, the accompanying written materials, and any accompanying hardware. This Limited Warranty gives you specific legal rights. You may have others, which vary from state to state.

No Liability for Consequential Damages. In no event shall Software.com, Inc. or its suppliers be liable for any damages whatsoever (including, without limitation, damages for loss of business profits, business interruption, loss of business information, or other pecuniary loss) arising out of the use of or inability to use this Software.com, Inc. product, even if Software.com, Inc. has been advised of the possibility of such damages. Because some states do not allow the exclusion or limitation of liability for consequential or incidental damages, the above limitation may not apply to you.

Warranties of Title and Possession

The UCC imposes special warranties on sellers and lessors of goods. These include a *warranty of good title*, a *warranty of no security interests*, a *warranty against infringements*, and a *warranty of no interference*. These warranties are discussed in the following paragraphs.

Warranty of Good Title

Unless they properly disclaim warranties, sellers of goods warrant that they have valid title to the goods they are selling and that the transfer of title is rightful [UCC 2-312(1)(a)]. This is called the **warranty of good title**. Persons who transfer goods without proper title breach this warranty.

warranty of good title
A warranty in which the seller warrants that he or she has valid title to the goods he or she is selling and that the transfer of title is rightful.

Example Ingersoll-Rand owns a heavy-duty crane. A thief steals the crane and sells it to Turner Construction. Turner Construction does not know that the crane is stolen. If Ingersoll-Rand discovers that Turner Construction has the equipment, it can reclaim it. Turner Construction, in turn, can recover against the thief for breach of the warranty of title. This is because the thief impliedly warranted that he had good title to the equipment and that the transfer of title to Turner Construction was rightful.

Warranty of No Security Interests

Under the UCC, sellers of goods automatically warrant that the goods they sell are delivered free from any third-party security interests, liens, or encumbrances that are unknown to the buyer [UCC 2-312(1)(b)]. This is called the **warranty of no security interests**.

warranty of no security interests
A warranty in which sellers of goods warrant that the goods they sell are delivered free from any third-party security interests, liens, or encumbrances that are unknown to the buyer.

Example Albert purchases a refrigerator on credit from Appliance World, an appliance store. The store takes back a security interest in the refrigerator. Before completely paying off the refrigerator, Albert sells it to Monica for cash. Monica has no knowledge of the store's security interest in the refrigerator. After Albert misses several payments, the appliance store discovers that Monica has the refrigerator and repossesses the refrigerator. Monica can recover against Albert, based on his breach of warranty of no security interests in the goods [UCC 2-312(1)(b)].

The warranties of good title and no security interests may be excluded or modified by specific language [UCC 2-312(2)]. For example, specific language such as "seller hereby transfers only those rights, title, and interest as he or she has in the goods" is sufficient to disclaim these warranties. General language such as "as is" or "with all faults" is not specific enough to be a disclaimer to the warranties of good title and no security interests. The special nature of certain sales (e.g., sheriffs' sales) tells the buyer that the seller is not giving title warranties with the sale of the goods.

Warranty Against Infringements

Unless otherwise agreed, a seller or lessor who is a merchant regularly dealing in goods of the kind sold or leased automatically warrants that the goods are delivered free of any third-party patent, trademark, or copyright claim [UCC 2-312(3), 2A-211(2)]. This is called the **warranty against infringements**.

warranty against infringements
An automatic warranty provided by a seller or lessor who is a merchant who regularly deals in goods of the kind sold or leased that warrants that the goods are delivered free of any third-party patent, trademark, or copyright claim.

Example Adams Company, a manufacturer of machines that make shoes, sells a machine to Smith & Franklin, a shoe manufacturer. Subsequently, Nerdette claims that she has a patent on the machine. Nerdette proves her patent claim in court. Nerdette notifies Smith & Franklin that the machine can no longer be used without her permission and the payment of a fee to her. Smith & Franklin may rescind the sales contract with Adams Company, based on the breach of the warranty against infringement.

Warranty of No Interference

When goods are leased, the lessor warrants that no person holds a claim or an interest in the goods that arose from an act or omission of the lessor that will interfere with the lessee's enjoyment of his or her leasehold interest [UCC 2A-211(1)]. This is referred to as the **warranty of no interference**, or the **warranty of quiet possession**.

warranty of no interference (warranty of quiet possession)
A warranty in which the lessor warrants that no person holds a claim or an interest in the goods that arose from an act or omission of the lessor that will interfere with the lessee's enjoyment of his or her leasehold interest.

Example Occi-Petroleum, as lessor, leases a piece of heavy equipment to Aztec Drilling. Occi-Petroleum later gives a security interest in the equipment to City-Bank as collateral for a loan. If Occi-Petroleum defaults on the loan to CityBank and CityBank repossesses the equipment from Aztec, Aztec can recover damages from Occi-Petroleum for breach of the warranty of no interference.

Key Terms and Concepts

"As is" disclaimer (450)
Caveat emptor (445)
Compensatory damages (446)
Conspicuous (451)
Consumer expectation test (449)
Consumer products (452)
Disclaimer of the implied warranty of fitness for a particular purpose (451)
Disclaimer of the implied warranty of merchantability (451)
Express warranty (445)
Foreign substance test (449)
Full warranty (452)
Implied by law (446)
Implied warranty (446)
Implied warranty of fitness for a particular purpose (449)
Implied warranty of fitness for human consumption (449)
Implied warranty of merchantability (447)
Limited warranty (452)
Magnuson-Moss Warranty Act (452)
Statement of opinion (puffing) (446)
Warranty (445)
Warranty against infringements (453)
Warranty disclaimer (450)
Warranty of good title (453)
Warranty of no interference (warranty of quiet possession) (454)
Warranty of no security interests (453)

Critical Legal Thinking Cases

21.1 Express Warranty W. Hayes Daughtrey consulted Sidney Ashe, a jeweler, about the purchase of a diamond bracelet as a Christmas present for his wife. Ashe showed Daughtrey a diamond bracelet that he had for sale for $15,000. When Daughtrey decided to purchase the bracelet, Ashe completed and signed an appraisal form that stated that the diamonds were "H color and v.v.s. quality." (v.v.s. is one of the highest ratings in a jeweler's quality classification.) After Daughtrey paid for the bracelet, Ashe put the bracelet and the appraisal form in a box. Daughtrey gave the bracelet to his wife as a Christmas present. One year later, when another jeweler looked at the bracelet, Daughtrey discovered that the diamonds were of substantially lower grade than v.v.s. Daughtrey filed a specific performance suit against Ashe to compel him to replace the bracelet with one mounted with v.v.s. diamonds or pay appropriate damages. Has an express warranty been made by Ashe regarding the quality of the diamonds in the bracelet? Who wins? *Daughtrey v. Ashe*, 243 Va. 73, 413 S.E.2d 336, 1992 Va. Lexis 152 (Supreme Court of Virginia)

21.2 "As Is" Warranty Disclaimer Joseph Mitsch purchased a used Chevrolet Yukon SUV vehicle from Rockenbach Chevrolet. The Yukon was manufactured by General Motors Corporation (GMC). The Yukon had been driven over 36,000 miles. The purchase contract with Rockenbach Chevrolet contained the following disclaimer:

> *As is this used motor vehicle is sold as is. The purchaser will bear the entire expense of repairing or correcting any defects that presently exist or that may occur in the vehicle.*

Mitsch purchased GMC's extended service plan for the Yukon. During a period of approximately 18 months, Mitsch experienced problems with the Yukon's transmission, engine, suspension, and climate control.

All the repairs were made by GMC dealerships and paid for by the GMC extended service plan. Mitsch sued Rockenbach Chevrolet for breach of the implied warranty of merchantability and sought to rescind his acceptance of the Yukon. Rockenbach Chevrolet argued that the "as is" disclaimer barred Mitsch's claim. Mitsch alleged that the "as is" disclaimer was not conspicuous and should be voided. Is the "as is" disclaimer conspicuous, and does it therefore properly disclaim the implied warranty of merchantability? *Mitsch v. Rockenbach Chevrolet*, 359 Ill. App.3d 99, 833 N.E.2d 936, 2005 Ill. App. Lexis 699 (Appellate Court of Illinois, 2005)

Ethical

Ethics Case

21.3 Ethics Case Cole Energy Development Company (Cole Energy) wanted to lease a gas compressor for use in its business of pumping and selling natural gas and began negotiating with the Ingersoll-Rand Company (Ingersoll-Rand) for the lease of a gas compressor. The two parties entered into a lease agreement whereby Ingersoll-Rand leased a gas compressor to KOA. The lease agreement contained a section labeled "WARRANTIES." Part of the section read,

> *There are no implied warranties of merchantability or fitness for a particular purpose contained herein.*

The gas compressor that was installed failed to function properly. As a result, Cole Energy lost business. Cole Energy sued Ingersoll-Rand for the breach of an implied warranty of merchantability. Is Ingersoll-Rand liable? Has Cole-Energy acted ethically in bringing the lawsuit? Has Ingersoll-Rand acted ethically in denying liability for the failure of a product it sold? *Cole Energy Development Company v. Ingersoll-Rand Company*, 678 F.Supp. 208, 1988 U.S. Dist. Lexis 923 (United States District Court for the Central District of Illinois)

Note

1. 15 U.S.C. Sections 2301–2312.

CASE *Alaska Environmental Law*

Native Village of Point Hope, et al v. Sally Jewell, et al

12-35297, March 5, 2013
United States Court of Appeals for the Ninth Circuit
Before: Fernandez, Fletcher, and Rawlinson, Judges
Opinion by, FLETCHER, Judge

Summary

Environmental Law

The panel reversed the district court's summary judgment entered in favor of federal defendants in an action challenging the government's environmental impact statements analyzing the environmental effects of proposed leases for oil and gas development in the Chukchi Sea off the northwest coast of Alaska.

The panel held that the Final Environmental Impact Statement and Supplemental Environmental Impact Statement prepared by the federal defendants properly took account of incomplete or unavailable information. The panel held, however, that the reliance in the Final Environmental Impact Statement on a one billion barrel estimate of total economically recoverable oil was arbitrary and capricious. The panel remanded for further proceedings.

Judge Rawlinson concurred in part and dissented in part. Judge Rawlinson agreed with most of the majority opinion, but she did not agree that the federal Bureau of Ocean Energy Management, Regulation and Enforcement acted arbitrarily in selecting one billion barrels of oil as the benchmark for analyzing the environmental affects of the proposed leases.

Counsel

Erik Clifford Grafe (argued), Earthjustice, Anchorage, Alaska; Eric Paul Jorgensen, Earthjustice, Juneau, Alaska, for Plaintiffs-Appellants.

David C. Shilton (argued), United States Department of Justice, Washington, D.C., for Defendants-Appellees.

Kyle W. Parker (argued), Crowell & Moring LLP, Anchorage, Alaska; Jeffrey Wayne Leppo and Ryan P. Steen, Stoel Rives, LLP, Seattle, Washington; Ken Diemer and Rebecca Kruse, Office of Alaska Attorney General, Anchorage, Alaska; and James Leik, Perkins Coie LLP, Anchorage, Alaska, for Intervenor-Defendants-Appellees.

Opinion

W. FLETCHER, Circuit Judge:

The Bureau of Ocean Energy Management ("BOEM")[1] of the Department of the Interior has sought to lease "excellent prospects" for oil and gas development in the Chukchi Sea off the northwest coast of Alaska. The parcels available for lease are cumulatively known as Lease Sale 193. Pursuant to the National Environmental Policy Act ("NEPA"), BOEM prepared a Final Environmental Impact Statement ("FEIS") analyzing the environmental effects of the proposed leases. BOEM based its environmental analysis on the assumption that if oil development actually occurs, one billion barrels of oil will be economically recoverable.

Plaintiffs argued in the district court that BOEM abused its discretion by failing to account for essential missing information in the FEIS. Plaintiffs also argued that BOEM's estimate of one billion barrels is arbitrary and capricious. They contended that the potential economically recoverable oil from the lease sale is far higher than one billion barrels, and that BOEM had not given an adequate explanation for using its lower estimate. The district court initially rejected the FEIS for failing to account for the missing information. After remand, BOEM prepared a Supplemental EIS ("SEIS") addressing the missing information. Based on the FEIS and SEIS, the district court granted summary judgment to defendants.

We largely agree with the district court that the agency did not abuse its discretion in its analysis of the missing information. However, we agree with plaintiffs that the agency's estimate of one billion barrels was chosen arbitrarily, and that this arbitrary decision meant that the agency based its decision on inadequate information about the amount of oil to be produced pursuant to the lease sale.

Background

The Chukchi Sea is a southern arm of the Arctic Ocean between Alaska and Russia. The Sea contains a wide variety of animals, including bowhead whales, polar bears, pacific walrus, seals, fish, and birds. Some of these animals provide subsistence for native Inupiat communities along the Alaskan coast. Some of the animals are listed under the Endangered Species Act ("ESA") as endangered or threatened. Five exploratory wells were drilled in the Sea between 1989 and 1991. They had "positive shows" but did not lead to commercial production.

The Outer Continental Shelf Lands Act ("OCSLA") prescribes four steps the federal government must

(case continues)

take in order to pursue offshore oil and gas development: "'(1) formulation of a five year leasing plan by the Department of the Interior; (2) lease sales; (3) exploration by the lessees; [and] (4) development and production.'" *Edwardsen v. U.S. Dep't of the Interior*, 268 F.3d 781, 784 (9th Cir. 2001) (quoting Sec'y of the *Interior v. California*, 464 U.S. 312, 337 (1984)). At the "lease sale" stage, the Secretary of the Interior selects the parcels that will be offered for lease, accepts bids from parties, and collects funds from parties with winning bids. The Department of the Interior must review and approve specific exploration and development plans before winning bidders can "proceed with full exploration, development, or production" of oil or gas. *Sec'y of the Interior*, 464 U.S. at 339. However, successful bidders have the right to undertake "ancillary activities" in the field such as geological and geophysical surveys and studies that "model potential oil and hazardous substance spills." 30 C.F.R. § 550.207.

NEPA

NEPA "protect[s] the environment by requiring that federal agencies carefully weigh environmental considerations and consider potential alternatives to the proposed action before the government launches any major federal action." *Barnes v. U.S. Dep't of Transp.*, 655 F.3d 1124, 1131 (9th Cir. 2011) (internal quotation marks omitted). "'NEPA imposes procedural requirements designed to force agencies to take a "hard look" at environmental consequences'" of major federal action. *Id. (quoting Earth Island Inst. v. U.S. Forest Serv.*, 351 F.3d 1291, 1300 (9th Cir. 2003)). The statute requires federal agencies to "consider every significant aspect of the environmental impact of a proposed action" and to "inform the public that [they] ha[ve] indeed considered environmental concerns in [their] decisionmaking process." *Balt. Gas & Elec. Co. v. Natural Res. Def. Council, Inc.*, 462 U.S. 87, 97 (1983) (internal quotation marks omitted).

NEPA requires that federal agencies prepare an EIS for any "major Federal actions significantly affecting the quality of the human environment." 42 U.S.C. § 4332(2)(C). An agency must consider:

(i) the environmental impact of the proposed action,
(ii) any adverse environmental effects which cannot be avoided should the proposal be implemented,
(iii) alternatives to the proposed action,
(iv) the relationship between local short-term uses of man's environment and the maintenance and enhancement of long-term productivity, and
(v) any irreversible and irretrievable commitments of resources which would be involved in the proposed action should it be implemented.

Id. An agency must take into account all "reasonably foreseeable significant adverse effects" of the proposed action in its analysis of environmental effects. 40 C.F.R. § 1502.22; *see also id.* § 1508.7. NEPA also requires an agency to analyze missing and incomplete information. As we explain in greater detail below, an agency must either obtain information that is "essential to a reasoned choice among alternatives" or explain why such information was too costly or difficult to obtain. *Id.* § 1502.22.

An agency is required to comply with NEPA at various stages of the oil and gas development process. An agency is not required at the lease sale stage to analyze potential environmental effects on a site-specific level of detail. *N. Alaska Envtl. Ctr. v. Kempthorne*, 457 F.3d 969, 975–76 (9th Cir. 2006). To some degree, lease sale analyses may be based on information that is uncertain or missing at the time of the sale when that information can be obtained at a "later stage of the exploration process." *Tribal Vill. of Akutan v. Hodel*, 869 F.2d 1185, 1192 (9th Cir. 1988). At the same time, the agency cannot shirk its responsibility to "consider all foreseeable direct and indirect impacts" of the proposed action in its EIS. *N. Alaska Envtl. Ctr.*, 457 F.3d at 975 (internal quotation marks omitted). The agency also must "discuss ... adverse impacts" without "improperly minimiz[ing] negative side effects." *Id.*

Lease Sale 193

After completing a five-year leasing plan for the Chukchi Sea, BOEM decided to offer a large portion of the Sea for oil and gas leasing. The FEIS analyzed four alternatives for the lease sale: (1) a 34-million acre proposed lease option covering 6,156 blocks of the Chukchi Sea; (2) a no-lease option; (3) a proposed lease option excluding 1,765 blocks extending along a corridor about 60 miles from the Alaskan coast; and (4) a proposed lease option excluding 795 blocks extending along a corridor between 25 and 50 miles from the Alaskan coast.

The National Marine Fisheries Service recommended that the Secretary of the Interior select the third alternative, under which development would be farther from the coast, based on its conclusion that numerous endangered and threatened species living close to shore would be adversely affected by oil development. The Secretary of the Interior accepted BOEM's recommendation and selected the fourth alternative, under which development would be closer to the coast.

The lease sale occurred on February 6, 2008. The federal government collected over $2.6 billion from the winning bidders. At the time of the lease sale, there were no active leases in the Sea.

(case continues)

Procedural History

Plaintiffs filed suit, alleging seven deficiencies in the FEIS:

1. [The FEIS] does not adequately analyze and present the impacts of Lease Sale 193 on the environment and human communities;
2. [It] fails to include essential missing information about the Chukchi Sea and the potential impacts of the lease sale, or explain why excluding this information is justified;
3. [It] fails to adequately analyze the impact of the lease sale in the context of a warming climate;
4. [It] understates the potential impacts of oil and gas development pursuant to the leases by analyzing a limited development scenario;
5. [It] understates the risks of an oil spill;
6. [It] fails to fully analyze the cumulative impacts to threatened eiders of the lease sale and other oil and gas development in threatened eiders' Arctic habitat; and
7. [It] provides a misleading analysis of the effects of seismic surveying.

The parties cross-moved for summary judgment.

The district court agreed with defendants that much of the FEIS complied with NEPA, including the FEIS's assumption that there would be one billion barrels of economically recoverable oil. However, the court concluded that the FEIS's analysis was flawed in three respects: it "failed to analyze the environmental impact of natural gas development, despite industry interest and specific lease incentives for such development"; it "failed to determine whether missing information identified by the agency was relevant or essential under 40 C.F.R § 1502.22"; and it "failed to determine whether the cost of obtaining the missing information was exorbitant, or the means of doing so unknown." The district court granted in part plaintiffs' motion for summary judgment, issued a limited injunction, and remanded to BOEM for further proceedings.

After remand from the district court, BOEM prepared an SEIS. The SEIS analyzed the consequences of natural gas exploration and production. In the aftermath of the Deepwater Horizon oil spill in the Gulf Coast, it also analyzed the environmental impacts of a very large oil spill. Finally, BOEM prepared an appendix analyzing "whether the information gaps that were identified in the Sale 193 FEIS were relevant and necessary to evaluate reasonably foreseeable significant adverse effects." Based on the FEIS, now supplemented by the SEIS, the Secretary of Interior again chose the fourth alternative for oil and gas leasing.

Based on the FEIS and SEIS, the district court granted BOEM's motion for summary judgment. The court found that "BOEM has identified missing or incomplete information and has adequately evaluated it in a manner that is clearly sufficient at this stage of the development process to satisfy the requirements of 40 C.F.R. § 1502.22." The court gave "considerable deference ... to BOEM's expertise." Plaintiffs timely appealed.

Standard of Review

Our review of an EIS is governed by the Administrative Procedure Act ("APA"). "Under the APA, we may set aside an agency decision if it is 'arbitrary, capricious, an abuse of discretion, or otherwise not in accordance with law.'" *Native Ecosystems Council v. U.S. Forest Serv.*, 428 F.3d 1233, 1238 (9th Cir. 2005) (quoting 5 U.S.C. § 706(2)(A)). "Review under the arbitrary and capricious standard is narrow, and we do not substitute our judgment for that of the agency." *Lands Council v. McNair (Lands Council II)*, 537 F.3d 981, 987 (9th Cir. 2008) (en banc) (alterations and internal quotation marks omitted). However, an agency's decision can be set aside if:

> *the agency relied on factors Congress did not intend it to consider, entirely failed to consider an important aspect of the problem, or offered an explanation that runs counter to the evidence before the agency or is so implausible that it could not be ascribed to a difference in view or the product of agency expertise.*

Id. (internal quotation marks omitted). Such actions would be "clear error[s] of judgment that would render [the agency's] action arbitrary and capricious." *Id.* at 993 (internal quotation marks omitted).

We "may affirm a summary judgment only if, viewing the evidence in the light most favorable to the party against whom it is granted, we find no genuine issue of material fact, and we find that the prevailing party is clearly entitled to judgment as a matter of law." *California v. Watt*, 683 F.2d 1253, 1258 (9th Cir. 1982), *rev'd on other grounds sub nom. Sec'y of* the *Interior v. California*, 464 U.S. 312 (1984).

Discussion

On appeal, plaintiffs argue that BOEM abused its discretion in two respects. First, they argue that "essential" information is missing from the FEIS and SEIS, in violation of 40 C.F.R. § 1502.22. Second, they argue that the FEIS and SEIS underestimate the adverse environmental impact of the lease sale because they use an unrealistically low estimate of the economically recoverable oil. We disagree with plaintiffs' first argument, but agree with their second argument.

(case continues)

Essential Information

An agency's obligation with respect to incomplete or unavailable information is spelled out in 40 C.F.R. § 1502.22. The agency "shall always make clear that ... information is lacking." *Id.* If the missing information is "relevant to reasonably foreseeable significant adverse impacts" and is "essential to a reasoned choice among alternatives and the overall costs of obtaining it are not exorbitant," the agency must include that information in the EIS. *Id.* § 1502.22(a). If the missing information "cannot be obtained because the overall costs of obtaining it are exorbitant or the means to obtain it are not known," the agency must include the following in the EIS: (1) a statement that such information is "incomplete or unavailable"; (2) a statement of the "relevance of the incomplete or unavailable information to evaluating reasonably foreseeable significant adverse impacts on the human environment"; (3) a "summary of existing credible scientific evidence ... relevant to evaluating the reasonably foreseeable adverse impacts"; and (4) the agency's "evaluation of such impacts based upon theoretical approaches or research methods generally accepted in the scientific community." *Id.* § 1502.22(b). Section 1502.22(b) clarifies that reasonably foreseeable effects "include impacts which have catastrophic consequences, even if their probability of occurrence is low."

Much of the information missing from the EIS concerns animal populations potentially affected by oil exploration and production under the leases. The missing information concerns such things as population levels of various species of animals in the Chukchi Sea, including endangered or threatened animals; the locations of various animal populations during the year; the feeding and breeding habits of various animal populations; and the vulnerability of various animal populations to drilling and other exploration and production-related activities.

With respect to the potential environmental harm from a large oil spill, BOEM concluded that the missing information was not essential to a reasoned choice among the alternatives. It wrote in the SEIS, "[I]n the unlikely event of a large oil spill, it is well-understood that environmental impacts could be severe. The severity of potential impacts would be nearly identical under any action alternative; therefore, very specific types of information relevant to species, particular life history traits, or behavior do not help substantially in distinguishing among alternatives." With respect to other activities or events with potential adverse impacts on the animal populations in the Chukchi Sea, BOEM concluded that sufficient protections would be provided by the requirements of other environmental statutes, such as the Clean Air Act, the Marine Mammal Protection Act ("MMPA"), and the ESA, and by the requirement under NEPA to provide site-specific analyses at later stages of development.

Based on these conclusions, BOEM stated in the SEIS that it did not consider any of the incomplete or unavailable information at issue to be "essential to a reasoned choice among alternatives" at this stage of the development process. 40 C.F.R. § 1502.22(a). BOEM therefore did not determine whether the information was unobtainable "because the overall costs of obtaining it are exorbitant or the means to obtain it are not known." *Id.* § 1502.22(b). Nor did BOEM go through the steps required by § 1502.22(b) if it had found "essential" information to be unobtainable. Instead, BOEM specifically relied in the SEIS on what it characterized as its "understanding that certain items of presently missing or incomplete information will be known (and utilized to avoid or minimize adverse impacts) at a later stage of OCS Lands Act environmental review." BOEM promised in the SEIS that it "would thoroughly review specific development & production plans at Step 4 ['development and production'], if and when a project proponent actually submits a plan. Thus, while certain information may, in fact, be essential at a later stage of OCS Lands Act [review], such information may not be essential to a reasoned choice among alternatives at this lease sale stage."

In *Village of False Pass v. Clark*, 733 F.2d 605 (9th Cir. 1984), we reviewed an EIS of an oil and gas lease sale under OCSLA. The plaintiff had argued that the commitment made by the government when entering into leases under OCSLA is so substantial that a fully exhaustive environmental analysis under NEPA had to be performed at the lease sale stage. We disagreed, writing:

> *NEPA may require an environmental impact statement at each stage: leasing, exploration, and production and development. Furthermore, each stage remains separate. The completion of one stage does not entitle a lessee to begin the next.*

Id. at 614. We wrote to the same effect in *Northern Alaska Environmental Center*:

> *[P]rojects [for the development of oil and gas natural resources] generally entail separate stages of leasing, exploration and development. At the earliest stage, the leasing stage we have before us, there is no way of knowing what plans for development, if any, may eventually materialize.*

457 F.3d at 977.

A lease sale under OCSLA is analogous to a "programmatic" plan. The required level of analysis in an EIS is different for programmatic and site-specific

(case continues)

plans. We wrote in *Friends of Yosemite Valley v. Norton*, 348 F.3d 789 (9th Cir. 2003):

> *An agency's planning and management decisions may occur at two distinct administrative levels:*
>
> (1) the "programmatic level" at which the [agency] develops alternative management scenarios responsive to public concerns, analyzes the costs, benefits and consequences of each alternative in an [EIS], and adopts an amendable [management] plan to guide management of multiple use resources; and (2) the implementation stage during which individual site specific projects, consistent with the [management] plan, are proposed and assessed.
>
> Ecology Ctr., Inc. v. United States Forest Serv., *192 F.3d 922, 923, [n.2] (9th Cir. 1999). An EIS for a programmatic plan ... must provide 'sufficient detail to foster informed decision-making,' but 'site-specific impacts need not be fully evaluated until a critical decision has been made to act on site development.'* N. Alaska Envtl. Ctr. v. Lujan, *961 F.2d 886, 890–91 (9th Cir. 1992).*

Id. at 800 (alterations in original).

Regardless of whether a programmatic or site-specific plan is at issue, NEPA requires that an EIS analyze environmental consequences of a proposed plan as soon as it is "reasonably possible" to do so. We wrote in *Kern v. U.S. Bureau of Land Management*, 284 F.3d 1062 (9th Cir. 2002), with respect to a programmatic plan:

> *Once an agency has an obligation to prepare an EIS, the scope of its analysis of environmental consequences in that EIS must be appropriate to the action in question. NEPA is not designed to postpone analysis of an environmental consequence to the last possible moment. Rather, it is designed to require such analysis as soon as it can reasonably be done. If it is reasonably possible to analyze the environmental consequences in an EIS for [a Resource Management Plan], the agency is required to perform that analysis.*

Id. at 1072 (citation omitted); *see also Pac. Rivers Council v. U.S. Forest Serv.*, 689 F.3d 1012, 1025–27, 1029–30 (9th Cir. 2012), *dismissed as moot*, 133 S. Ct. 2843 (2013). This is not to say that an agency must provide the most extensive environmental analysis possible at the earliest possible moment, for an agency has some flexibility in deciding the level of analysis to be performed at a particular stage. We will defer to the agency's judgment about the appropriate level of analysis so long as the EIS provides as much environmental analysis as is reasonably possible under the circumstances, thereby "provid[ing] sufficient detail to foster informed decision-making" at the stage in question. *Friends of Yosemite Valley*, 348 F.3d at 800 (internal quotation marks omitted).

In the case before us, we conclude that BOEM has reasonably concluded that the missing information from the FEIS and SEIS is not "essential" to informed decisionmaking at the lease sale stage. We agree with BOEM that compliance with statutes such as the MMPA and the ESA will provide protection for animals covered by those statutes. The MMPA generally prohibits the "take" of marine mammals. 16 U.S.C. § 1371(a). A "take" encompasses any act of "torment" or "annoyance" that "has the potential to injure ... or ... disturb a marine mammal or marine mammal stock in the wild by causing disruption of natural behavioral patterns, including, but not limited to, migration, surfacing, nursing, breeding, feeding, or sheltering." *Id.* § 1362(13), (18)(A)(i)–(ii). Unlawful "takes" trigger civil and criminal penalties. *Id.* § 1375(a)(1), (b). Further, under the ESA § 7(a)(2), 16 U.S.C. § 1536(a)(2), BOEM must consult with the National Marine Fisheries Service and the U.S. Fish and Wildlife Service to "insure that any action authorized, funded, or carried out by such agency ... is not likely to jeopardize the continued existence of any endangered species or threatened species." If an action is likely to jeopardize a species, the acting agency must determine whether any "reasonable and prudent alternatives" exist that will avoid jeopardizing that species. 16 U.S.C. § 1536(b)(3)(A). We recognize that BOEM has already consulted with these agencies at the lease sale stage. It may well have to consult with them again at the development and production stage when specific plans have been proposed and site-specific activities are contemplated. (We note that it may also have to consult again at the lease sale stage, once it has performed a proper analysis of the estimated overall oil production.) Because these statutes provide additional protections for animals in the Chukchi Sea, they support BOEM's conclusion that missing information about these animals was not "essential" at this stage.

We also agree with BOEM that further environmental analysis will be appropriate at a later stage. In BOEM's words, "certain items of presently missing or incomplete information will be known (and utilized to avoid or minimize adverse impacts) at a later stage of OCS Lands Act environmental review." That is, "when a project proponent actually submits a plan," BOEM will be required under NEPA to perform a plan- or site-specific environmental analysis of that proposed plan. At that stage, missing or incomplete information that has not been "essential to

(case continues)

a reasoned choice among alternatives" at the lease sale stage may later become essential. If there is "essential" information at the plan- or site-specific development and production stage, BOEM will be required to perform the analysis under § 1502.22(b) that it has not performed in the FEIS and SEIS now before us.

Of course, we recognize that our discussion and decision in the next section regarding BOEM's one billion barrel estimate may have some effects upon the remainder of the FEIS. But we will not at this time speculate about the extent of those effects, if any. The Defendants are in the best position to analyze those effects, if any, and have the duty to analyze them in the first instance.

One Billion Barrel Estimate

Plaintiffs contend that BOEM chose an arbitrary number for the total barrels of economically recoverable oil from Lease Sale 193. The FEIS estimated the amount of recoverable oil by estimating production from the "first offshore oil field" that would be developed within the area of the leases. BOEM did not make any estimate of recoverable oil from additional fields that might be developed. The FEIS specified that the "recoverable oil resources from this field are assumed to be 1 billion barrels (Bbbl)." The FEIS then used the one billion barrel estimate as the basis for its environmental analysis.

We must determine whether BOEM has articulated a rational basis for its decision to use the one billion barrel estimate. *Mora-Meraz v. Thomas,* 601 F.3d 933, 939 (9th Cir. 2010). We must reverse a decision as arbitrary and capricious if

> *the agency relied on factors Congress did not intend it to consider, entirely failed to consider an important aspect of the problem, or offered an explanation that runs counter to the evidence before the agency or is so implausible that it could not be ascribed to a difference in view or the product of agency expertise.*

Lands Council II, 537 F.3d at 987 (internal quotation marks omitted). For the reasons that follow, we conclude that BOEM's one billion barrel estimate is arbitrary and capricious.

The selection of one billion barrels

BOEM first announced it was developing an EIS in preparation for Lease Sale 193 in July 2005. According to internal BOEM emails, BOEM analyst Jim Craig was assigned to provide "resource estimates and a scenario" which other BOEM scientists would use to analyze environmental effects. Craig emailed his supervisor, Deborah Cranswick, stating that he believed that "[t]he reasonably foreseeable scenario" should include "oil production from the first field only, not the full economic potential." Craig's reason for focusing on the first field production was practical; he would have to wait for about two months to have information that would allow him to develop a scenario for the entire area covered by the lease sale. Craig stated in his email, "You realize that we won't have the 2005 resource assessment numbers until Sept, so we must base the scenario on the 'first development' not the total economic potential." Craig also indicated that this emphasis on the first oil field was a "departure from previous work."

Craig asked Cranswick whether the scenario should employ a single estimate of oil production from that first field, or whether it should employ a range. Cranswick responded by email that she preferred a range. Craig then suggested, in a July 29 email, a range from 500 million barrels to 1.5 billion barrels. Craig emphasized in his email that the scenario should assume "equal probability for any volume within the range" so that one billion barrels "does not become the de facto most-likely" outcome. Craig's draft scenario also noted, with respect to recoverable oil in the Chukchi Sea, that "[o]ur current petroleum assessment indicates that recoverable oil resources could range from 3.6 to 11.8 billion barrels."

There is a gap in the email chain in our record, so we do not know Cranswick's next response to Craig. But we do know that in a subsequent email from Craig to Cranswick on August 2, Craig proposed a single one billion barrel estimate as an alternative to using a range that was "too broad":

> *Attached is a table with E&D data. If this represents too broad of a range, then I think we should fall back to a single volume (1.0 Bbbl) for the EIS analysis with a corresponding set of single E&D numbers. It's hard to have it both ways (very narrow range) when these figures are entirely speculative.*
>
> There are two clear options:
>
> 1) 500-1500 MMbbl, as a uniform distribution (every point in range is equally likely). This will require a low and high case analysis.
> 2) 1.0 Bbbl as a single point estimate with no confidence interval. This will require a mostly likely case analysis only.
>
> *Although it would be nice to propose a recoverable oil volume of 932 MMbbl +/– 134 MMbbl in a 90% confidence interval, we don't have any data to support it.*

(case continues)

Pick (1) *or* (2), but not (1) *and* (2).

On August 3, Cranswick emailed Craig a data chart reflecting Craig's second option. It contained only a single one billion barrel estimate.

On that same day, Craig emailed to Cranswick a draft scenario relying on the one billion barrel estimate of oil production. This draft explained:

> *The scenario assumed for environmental analysis involves the discovery, development, and production of the first oil field in the Chukchi sale area. Ultimately recoverable oil resources from this field are assumed to be 1 billion barrels (Bbbl). Smaller oil volumes are not likely to be economic to produce and single pools containing larger volumes are increasingly rare. If oil prices drop below $30.00 per barrel (they are above $50.00 when this scenario was written), exploration in the Chukchi OCS is expected to be minimal and oil discoveries may not be developed.*

The draft also pointed out that "the mean recoverable oil resource [in the Chukchi Sea] is 12 Bbbl with a 5% probability of 29 Bbbl." Craig also prepared a chart for Cranswick comparing the numbers Craig had selected for the Lease Sale 193 EIS to an EIS prepared for the Chukchi Sea and Hope Sea Basin for the 2002–2007 Five Year Oil and Gas Leasing Program. That previous EIS had estimated a range for economical oil production from 0.96 billion barrels to 2.42 billion barrels.

On August 10, Cranswick circulated the Lease Sale 193 EIS scenario to other BOEM scientists who would be working on the EIS. The scenario contained the one billion barrel estimate. Cranswick explained in an email that

> *[t]he scenario is based on a one mid-range economic resource number (note - this is* not *necessarily the most likely. A lower volume is more likely to occur but less likely to be developed from an economic standpoint; a higher volume is less likely to occur but more likely to be developed).*

Several BOEM employees expressed concern with the agency's proposed scenario. For example, one NEPA analyst employed by BOEM, Dee Williams, wrote, "I don't understand why [the agency] doesn't use their sophisticated assessment indices to impose a more definitive likely scenario. Clearly, it is impossible to predict 'with certainty', but the narrative needs to inspire greater public confidence by explaining the parameters of reasonable expectations." Williams further stated:

> *If it becomes economical to build one platform to produce an estimated 1 billion barrels, and there is between 12 and 29 billion barrels that are recoverable, why is the scenario not compelled to imagine more than one platform (i.e. is a single platform* always *the initial scenario, in which case maybe we should just explain that)?*

Cranswick responded that "the initial scenario is one platform because we can't have only a partial platform if that is all that the resource estimate support[s]." At the same time, Cranswick suggested that smaller oil developments would be associated with the first oil platform. "Once the first platform goes in, it is likely that additional satellite subsea completions would be developed before another host platform would be considered."

Once the draft EIS was completed, BOEM sought comments from other agencies and from the public. Numerous outside commentators expressed concern about the scenario BOEM had developed. For example, the Environmental Protection Agency wrote that

> *the hypothetical development scenario that is used in the document add[s] additional layers of uncertainty regarding the probabilities of exploration, production and development activities and the risks associated with those activities.... EPA is concerned that, overall, the depth and diversity of uncertainties presented in the document resulted in the lack of adequate support for many of the document's conclusions.*

The Division of Migratory Bird Management at the U.S. Fish and Wildlife Service ("FWS") similarly challenged the one billion barrel estimate as inaccurate:

> *The basic assumptions used in the analysis of effects are flawed with regards to the size of development scenarios. The [Draft EIS ("DEIS")] states that the current petroleum assessment indicates a mean recoverable oil resource of 12 billion barrels; yet all environmental analyses reported in the DEIS are based on a development of 1 billion barrels, thereby significantly underestimating likely scenarios.*

The Division recommended that BOEM not proceed with the lease sale until problems with the EIS were corrected. Public commentators similarly pointed to flaws in employing a one billion barrel production estimate, including that such an estimate was "based on a price of oil at half the current market value," that the estimate "severely understates the true cumulative impacts" of oil production, and that

(case continues)

it was "nowhere . . . justified with scientific analysis." Despite these criticisms, BOEM continued to rely on its one billion barrel estimate. The one billion barrel estimate was the basis for the entire FEIS, including its analysis of the risk of a large oil spill. For example, BOEM instructed the FWS to rely on that estimate in that agency's analysis of whether the lease sale would jeopardize listed threatened species such as the spectacled and Steller's eiders. Had FWS made a jeopardy finding, BOEM either would not have been able to proceed with the Lease Sale under the ESA or would have had to obtain an exemption from the "no jeopardy" rule. 16 U.S.C. § 1536(a)(2).

Arbitrary and Capricious

Plaintiffs contend that the one billion barrel estimate was chosen arbitrarily, and that BOEM did not provide an adequate explanation for its selection. We agree for three reasons.

First, BOEM has not justified its choice of the lowest possible amount of oil that was economical to produce as the basis for its analysis. The draft EIS scenario stated that the agency chose to focus on a one billion barrel estimate in part because any volume lower than one billion barrels would not be economical to produce. At the same time, BOEM was well aware that if any oil was produced from Lease Sale 193, the economically recoverable oil was very likely to exceed one billion barrels. In an August 18, 2005, email commenting on the in-progress draft EIS, Jim Craig wrote, "We assume 1 billion bbl for the first field, but there is another 11 Bbbl that is economic at $70." Craig attached a table to a December 2005 email, listing "Estimates for Speculative Oil and Gas Reserves," specifying a range between 1.0 and 6.1 billion barrels for the "Chukchi Shelf." Finally, in a May 2006 email Craig wrote, "The '1-billion barrel, first field' assumption is subjective ('for purposes of analysis') and represents only a fraction of the full economic resource potential in the Chukchi (which was recently published)."

The mean estimate of economical oil production, at the center of the distribution curve, is by definition a more likely occurrence than is the lowest estimate of viable oil production. Previous EISes in the Chukchi Sea had used the mean estimate of oil production as the basis for their analyses, and those EISes had also included low and high estimates. For example, BOEM previously leased portions of the Chukchi Sea in now-expired Lease Sale 109. The parcels leased in Lease Sale 109 overlap substantially with the parcels leased in Lease Sale 193. Documents prepared in advance of Lease Sale 109 stated that "[t]he mean resource estimate . . . is 2.68 billion barrels of oil with a 20 percent chance of a discovery of commercially recoverable oil." In estimating the effects of oil spills from Lease Sale 109, BOEM "assume[d] the full development of the resource estimate of 2.68 billion barrels." In contrast, while estimates in the record about the economically recoverable amount of oil from Lease Sale 193 vary, nowhere is the mean amount of economical production calculated to be less than 2.37 billion barrels. But the FEIS for Lease Sale 193 uses one billion rather than 2.37 billion barrels as the basis for its analysis of environmental consequences.

BOEM's primary explanation for using its low-end estimate for oil production is that this scenario overestimates the likely amount of production. BOEM emphasizes that because of the remoteness of the area and the risk of economic failure, any oil production activity is an unlikely result of the lease sale. More specifically, BOEM estimates that there is a less than 10 percent likelihood that oil development in the region will occur. Defendants argue that since the most likely foreseeable outcome is no oil development at all, one billion barrels of oil production is actually a generous estimate.

This analysis is flawed. The assumption that there is a 10 percent chance of commercial oil development is itself without a rational basis in the record. Jim Craig first developed the estimate "off the top of [his] head" in an email exchange. That calculation contradicts estimates used earlier in the EIS, as well as estimates used in past EISes for the Chukchi Sea. Further, BOEM conflates the likelihood of oil and gas production with the likelihood of environmental effects if such production occurs. Based on its responsibility to "'consider all foreseeable direct and indirect impacts'" of the proposed action, *N. Alaska Envtl.* Ctr., 457 F.3d at 975 (citation omitted), BOEM concluded that oil production was "reasonably foreseeable." There is a substantial basis for this in the record because, as noted by BOEM, "the area has high oil resource potential and there is existing transportation infrastructure to move oil from northern Alaska to distant markets." Once BOEM made the determination that production is reasonably foreseeable, it was required to consider the full cumulative impact of that production. See 40 C.F.R. § 1508.7. Put differently, BOEM might well be right that the most likely outcome is that there will be no oil development in the Chukchi Sea. But that fact should have made no difference to BOEM's analysis of the reasonably foreseeable environmental effects of oil development, if such development does occur.

Second, the FEIS did not take into account variation in oil prices in arriving at the estimate that one billion barrels of oil are economically recoverable. An assumption of stable prices ignores the fact that

(case continues)

the amount of economically recoverable oil varies substantially depending on oil prices. This may be seen, for example, in a 2006 report of the Minerals Management Service (a prior incarnation of BOEM), which estimated economically recoverable oil from the Chukchi Shelf at different prices. At $30 per barrel, the mean estimate was 0 barrels; at $46 per barrel, the mean estimate was 2.37 billion barrels; at $60 per barrel, the mean estimate was 8.38 billion barrels; at $80 dollars per barrel, the mean estimate was 12 billion barrels.

Third, BOEM has not provided an adequate explanation for its decision to base its EIS only on the amount of oil expected to be produced from the first field in the leased area of the Chukchi Sea. It is unclear from the record how BOEM initially estimated that the first field would produce one billion barrels of oil. Jim Craig himself suggested that his calculations regarding that first development were "entirely speculative." But even assuming that one billion barrels is an accurate estimate of the amount of oil to be produced from the first field, it is unclear why BOEM assumed that only one oil field would be developed in the lease area. The FEIS itself acknowledges that "[w]hen the first project overcomes the cost, logistical, and regulatory hurdles, more projects are ... likely to follow."

The FEIS explains that it is unlikely that "all economically viable resources will be developed" in the Sea due to the difficulties in operating in a frontier area of oil production. But the FEIS does not explain why production would be expected to stop if the first oil field is developed. The primary explanation for that assumption suggested by the record is that data to analyze "the full economic potential" of the lease sale would not be available until about two months after Jim Craig initially proposed an estimate based on the first field. Previous evaluations of Chukchi Sea oil development had assumed that multiple oil fields would develop once commercial development was viable. In a technology assessment of Chukchi Sea petroleum development performed in 1983 for BOEM, the Bureau of Land Management had used a 1.5 billion barrel estimate to measure prospects in "the central Chukchi shelf." That assessment assumed that two oil fields would be developed: one of one billion barrels and one of 0.5 billion barrels. On the record before us, it remains unclear why BOEM chose to analyze the lowest amount of oil that could be produced in the Chukchi Sea from the smallest number of oil fields that could be developed.

Defendants contend that any error resulting from using the one billion barrel estimate can be corrected through site-specific EISes later in the development process. We disagree. An agency is required to analyze the environmental effects in an EIS as soon as it is "reasonably possible" to do so. Kern, 284 F.3d at 1072. An appropriate time to estimate the total oil production from the lease sale is the time of the lease sale itself. Under NEPA, BOEM is required to take into account the full environmental effects of its actions when deciding whether and in what manner to pursue the lease sale. 42 U.S.C. § 4332(2)(C). A later project or site-specific environmental analysis is an inadequate substitute for an estimate of total production from the lease sale as a whole. It is only at the lease sale stage that the agency can adequately consider cumulative effects of the lease sale on the environment, including the overall risk of oil spills and the effects of the sale on climate change. It is also only at the lease sale stage that the agency can take into account the effects of oil production in deciding which parcels to offer for lease.

We also disagree with defendants that our decisions in *Akutan*, 869 F.2d at 1191–92, *False Pass*, 733 F.2d at 617, and *Watt,* 683 F.2d at 1267–68, compel a contrary result. In *False Pass*, plaintiffs challenged the agency for failing to consider the worst case scenario for oil development. 773 F.2d at 614. In the circumstances presented there, we held that there was a rational explanation for not considering the worst case at the lease sale stage. Here, in contrast, the BOEM considered only the *best* case scenario for environmental harm, assuming oil development. A best case scenario "skew[s]" the data toward fewer environmental impacts, and thus impedes a "full and fair discussion of the potential effects of the project." *Native Ecosystems Council v. U.S. Forest Serv.*, 418 F.3d 953, 965 (9th Cir. 2005) (citation and internal quotation marks omitted).

Unlike in *Akutan,* BOEM's estimate did not merely inform an assessment of the likelihood of an oil spill. 869 F.2d at 1192. Among other things, its estimate informed an assessment of seismic effects, habitat effects, oil production, and the cumulative effects of the sale on global warming. BOEM's estimate also informed FWS's determination that Lease Sale 193 would not jeopardize listed species. The record suggests that FWS was close to finding, even under the one billion barrel assumption, that the lease sale would jeopardize the spectacled and Steller's eiders. Had BOEM not selected the least amount of oil necessary for production, FWS may well have concluded that the listed species were in jeopardy. *See* 16 U.S.C. § 1536(a)(2).

(case continues)

Finally, the degree of error in the estimation of total oil production is greater here than in our earlier cases. In *Watt*, the agency was ready to publish its EIS when newly available figures suggested that oil reserves were "roughly twice those originally estimated." 683 F.2d at 1267. We held in *Watt* that the agency had acted reasonably when it decided not to supplement its EIS with last-minute analysis of the risk of an oil spill based on the new figures. *Id.* at 1267–68. In the case before us, BOEM was fully aware from the very beginning that if one billion barrels could be economically produced, many more barrels could also be economically produced. Indeed, at current oil prices, it would be economical to recover twelve times the one billion barrel estimate used by BOEM. This is a far more dramatic difference than in *Watt*.

We do not criticize BOEM's decision to estimate the total amount of economically recoverable oil from the lease sale. Given the uncertainties involved in the Chukchi Sea, BOEM had no choice but to make an estimate. But having decided that oil production was reasonably foreseeable, NEPA required BOEM to base its analysis on the full range of likely production if oil production were to occur. It did not do so here.

Conclusion

We conclude that the FEIS and SEIS properly took account of incomplete or unavailable information. However, we conclude that reliance in the FEIS on a one billion barrel estimate of total economically recoverable oil was arbitrary and capricious.

We REVERSE and REMAND to the district court for further proceedings consistent with this opinion.

RAWLINSON, Circuit Judge, concurring in part and dissenting in part:

I agree with most of the majority opinion, including that the missing information from the final environmental impact statement (FEIS) and the Supplemental Environmental Impact Statement (SEIS) is not essential to informed decisionmaking at the lease sale stage, and that further environmental analysis will be more appropriate at a later stage. However, I do not agree that the Bureau of Ocean Energy Management, Regulation and Enforcement (BOEM) acted arbitrarily in selecting one billion barrels of oil as the benchmark for analyzing the environmental effects of the proposed leases.

I begin with a reminder that our review of the agency's analysis of technical data is extremely limited. *See Lands Council v. McNair*, 537 F.3d 981, 987 (9th Cir. 2008) (en banc), *overruled on other grounds as recognized by Am. Trucking Ass'ns v. City of Los Angeles*, 559 F.3d 1046, 1052 (9th Cir. 2009) ("Review under the arbitrary and capricious standard is narrow, and we do not substitute our judgment for that of the agency. . . .") (citation, alteration and internal quotation marks omitted). We should also keep in mind that the National Environmental Policy Act (NEPA) "does not mandate particular results." Dep't of *Transp. v. Pub. Citizen*, 541 U.S. 752, 756 (2004). Rather, the statute "imposes only procedural requirements on federal agencies . . ." *Id.* Under NEPA, "[w]e review an [Environmental Impact Statement] under a rule of reason to determine whether it contains a reasonably thorough discussion" of the potential environmental effects of a planned federal action. *Edwardsen v. Department of the Interior*, 268 F.3d 781, 784 (9th Cir. 2001) (citation omitted).

The majority opinion takes issue with the agency's selection of one billion barrels of oil as the benchmark amount for assessing potential environmental effects of the oil leases. However, our review is at its most deferential when we consider a predictive estimate such as BOEM's estimate of the amount of oil recovery that should be included in the environmental effects analysis. See Lands Council, 537 F.3d at 993 ("[W]e are to conduct a particularly deferential review of an agency's predictive judgments about areas that are within the agency's field of discretion and expertise . . .) (citations and internal quotation marks omitted). Our task is only to ensure that the agency has not:

> *relied on factors which Congress has not intended it to consider, entirely failed to consider an aspect of the problem, offered an explanation for its decision that runs counter to the evidence before the agency, or an explanation that is so implausible that it could not be ascribed to a difference in view or the product of agency expertise.*

Id. (citations, alteration, and internal quotation marks omitted).

The majority does not intimate that BOEM relied on factors Congress did not intend it to consider, or that BOEM entirely failed to consider an aspect of the problem. The majority opinion also cannot be fairly read to describe BOEM's benchmark choice as so implausible that it could not be ascribed to a difference in view or the product of agency expertise. In fact, the majority opinion discusses the different views and agency expertise brought to bear on this issue. *See Majority Opinion*, pp. 21–26 (discussing the differing views from within and without the agency).

(case continues)

So it appears that the basis for the majority's ruling is that BOEM's benchmark estimate runs counter to the evidence before the agency. But it doesn't.

The potential size of commercially extractable oil deposits in the Chukchi Sea is a quintessential example of a predictive judgment uniquely within BOEM's area of expertise. Indeed, we have previously recognized that "[p]rior to exploration, it is difficult to make so much as an educated guess as to the volume of oil likely to be produced ... Without this information, an oil spill risk analysis can never be more than speculative, *regardless of what methodology is used.... " Tribal Village of Akutan v. Hodel*, 869 F.2d 1185, 1192 (9th Cir. 1989), *as amended*.

It is beyond dispute that the Chukchi Sea contains oil deposits well in excess of one billion barrels. But that is not the point. The point is whether the selection of one billion barrels as the benchmark was the product of agency expertise. *See Lands Council*, 537 F.3d at 993. After considering the available evidence, BOEM concluded that substantial obstacles to oil development in the region made it unlikely that future production would "ever reach the full economic potential" in the Chukchi Sea. Five explorations had already tested some of the largest prospective sites without discovering a "commercial-size" oil source. With these circumstances in mind, BOEM ultimately selected one billion barrels as the benchmark estimate because lower oil volumes were not likely to be economically feasible. Rather than relying on general resource assessments as was done previously, BOEM opted for the more "realistic" benchmark tied to the discovery/development of the initial commercially viable offshore oil field. BOEM explained that the unique, remote, and previously unexplored nature of the Chukchi region required analysis of the "statistically most-likely development activity associated with a reasonable range of resources ... given the uncertainties of geology, engineering, and economics that exist now" and the "streamlined" environmental impact statement (EIS) undertaken at the leasing stage of the process. *See Akutan*, 869 F.2d at 1192 ("We are the least troubled by what may seem to be incomplete or speculative data at the lease sale stage.... ").

The majority is of the view that BOEM's "analysis is flawed." *Majority Opinion*, p. 28. But we do not sit as a panel of super scientists to dissect the agency's analysis. Rather, we only review the process for reasonable thoroughness. *See Edwardsen*, 268 F.3d at 784 (establishing the role of the reviewing court to determine whether the agency's environmental impact statement "contains a reasonably thorough discussion"). Not only was BOEM's discussion of the selected benchmark "reasonably thorough," *id.*, its selection of the benchmark was within the range of alternatives contained in the record. As the majority opinion acknowledges, a previous EIS had estimated a range of economical oil production from 0.96 billion barrels to 2.42 billion barrels. *See Majority Opinion*, p. 24. One billion barrels is certainly within that range. The same is true for the "range between 1.0 and 6.1 billion barrels" referenced at page 27 of the Majority Opinion.

I readily acknowledge that there was disagreement in the scientific community concerning the selected benchmark. But disagreement does not render the chosen estimate irrational. Rather, it typifies the "difference in view" that we have established as a safe harbor against successful attack under NEPA. *See Lands Council*, 537 F.3d at 993. There is no such thing as a perfect estimate and BOEM was not required to adopt a different benchmark in the face of its critics. *See Environmental Defense Center, Inc. v. EPA*, 344 F.3d 832, 872 (9th Cir. 2003) ("We defer to an agency decision not to invest the resources necessary to conduct the perfect study..."). BOEM explained its reasons for selecting its benchmark estimate, and we are uniquely unqualified to second-guess that selection. As the D.C. Circuit recognized in *City of L.A. v. Dep't of Transp.*, 165 F.3d 972, 977 (D.C. Cir. 1999): "[That some or many [experts] would disapprove of [BOEM's] approach does not answer the question presented to us. In reviewing [BOEM's EIS], we do not sit as a panel of referees on a professional [scientific] journal, but as a panel of generalist judges obliged to defer to a reasonable judgment by an agency acting pursuant to congressionally delegated authority.... ") (citations omitted).

Because of the deference due the agency, and because BOEM's chosen benchmark was reasonably selected and adequately explained, our work here is done. We should afford BOEM's EIS the deference due and affirm the district court's order of dismissal.

I respectfully dissent.

---

* This summary constitutes no part of the opinion of the court. It has been prepared by court staff for the convenience of the reader.

1. Earlier incarnations of the agency have been the Minerals Management Service and the Bureau of Ocean Energy Management, Regulation and Enforcement. For simplicity, we refer to the agency, including its earlier incarnations, as BOEM.

PART

V

Negotiable Instruments, Banking, and Electronic Financial Transactions

CHAPTER 22 Creation of Negotiable Instruments

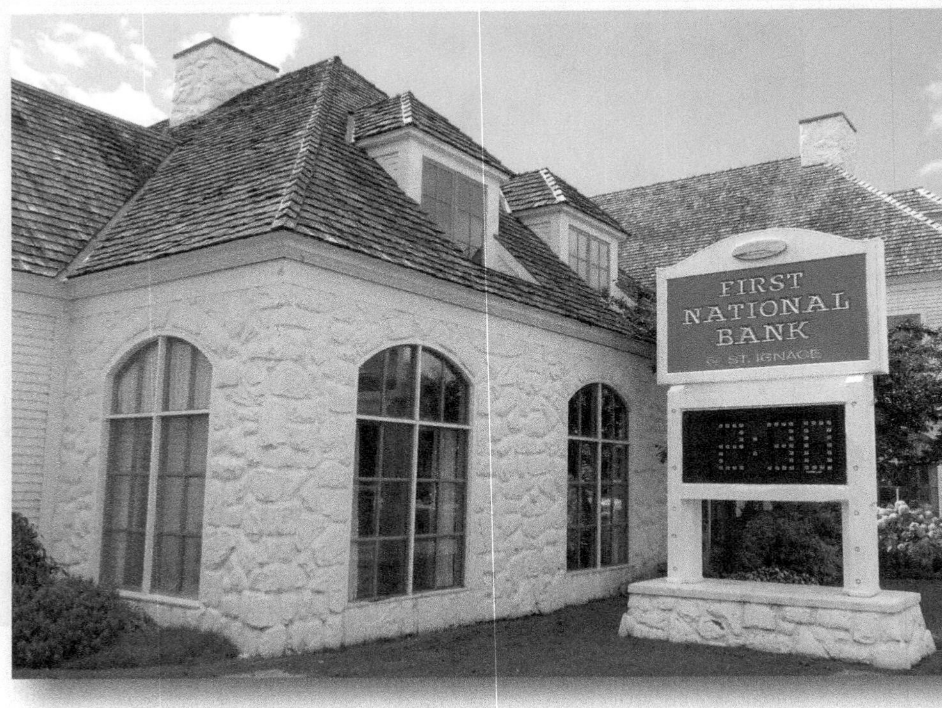

COMMUNITY BANK
Individuals and businesses have checking accounts at banks. A check qualifies as a negotiable instrument. Negotiable instruments are governed by Article 3 of the Uniform Commercial Code (UCC).

Learning Objectives

After studying this chapter, you should be able to:

1. Distinguish between negotiable and nonnegotiable instruments.
2. Describe drafts and checks and identify the parties to these instruments.
3. Describe promissory notes and certificates of deposit and identify the parties to these instruments.
4. List and describe the formal requirements of a negotiable instrument.
5. Distinguish between instruments payable to order and instruments payable to bearer.

Chapter Outline

"The great object of the law is to encourage commerce."

—*Judge Chamber*
Beale v. Thompson (1803)

Introduction to Creation of Negotiable Instruments

Negotiable instruments (or **commercial paper**) are important for the conduct of business and individual affairs. In this country, modern commerce could not continue without them. Examples of negotiable instruments include checks (e.g., a check used by a business to purchase equipment) and promissory notes (e.g., a note executed by a borrower of money to pay for tuition). The term *instrument* means negotiable instrument [UCC 3-104(b)]. These terms are often used interchangeably.

The types of negotiable instruments and their creation are discussed in this chapter.

negotiable instrument (commercial paper)
A special form of contract that satisfies the requirements established by Article 3 of the UCC.

Negotiable Instruments

To qualify as a negotiable instrument, a document must meet certain requirements established by Article 3 of the Uniform Commercial Code (UCC). If these requirements are met, a transferee who qualifies as a **holder in due course (HDC)** takes the instrument free of many defenses that can be asserted against the original payee. In addition, the document is considered an ordinary contract that is subject to contract law.

The concept of **negotiation** is important to the law of negotiable instruments. The primary benefit of a negotiable instrument is that it can be used as a substitute for money. As such, it must be freely transferable to subsequent parties. Technically, a negotiable instrument is negotiated when it is originally issued. The term *negotiation*, however, is usually used to describe the transfer of negotiable instruments to subsequent transferees.

A trader is trusted upon his character, and visible commerce, that credit enables him to acquire wealth.

The Earl of Mansfield
(1705–1793)
Lord Chief Justice of England

Article 3 of the UCC

Article 3 (Commercial Paper) of the UCC, which was promulgated in 1952, established rules for the creation of, transfer of, enforcement of, and liability on negotiable instruments. Most states and the District of Columbia have adopted Article 3 of the UCC.

In 1990, the American Law Institute and the National Conference of Commissioners on Uniform State Laws promulgated **Revised Article 3 (Negotiable Instruments) of the UCC**. The new article, which is called "Negotiable Instruments" instead of "Commercial Paper," is a comprehensive revision of Article 3. Revised Article 3 is used as the basis for this and the following chapters on negotiable instruments.

Article 3 (Commercial Paper)
A model code that establishes rules for the creation of, transfer of, enforcement of, and liability on negotiable instruments.

Revised Article 3 (Negotiable Instruments)
A comprehensive revision of the UCC law of negotiable instruments that reflects modern commercial practices.

Functions of Negotiable Instruments

Negotiable instruments serve the following functions:

1. **Substitute for money.** Merchants and consumers often do not carry cash for fear of loss or theft. Further, it would be almost impossible to carry enough cash for large purchases (e.g., a car, a house). Thus, certain forms of negotiable instruments—such as checks—serve as **substitutes for money**.
2. **Act as credit devices.** Some forms of negotiable instruments extend credit from one party to another. A seller may sell goods to a customer on a customer's

promise to pay for the goods at a future time, or a bank may lend money to a buyer who signs a note promising to repay the money. Both of these examples represent **extensions of credit**. Without negotiable instruments, the "credit economy" of the United States and other modern industrial countries would not be possible.

3. **Act as record-keeping devices.** Negotiable instruments often serve as **record-keeping devices**. Banks either return checks to checking-account customers each month or allow customers to view them online. These act as a record-keeping device for the preparation of financial statements, tax returns, and the like.

Types of Negotiable Instruments

The UCC recognizes four kinds of negotiable instruments: (1) *drafts*, (2) *checks*, (3) *promissory notes*, and (4) *certificates of deposit*. Each of these is discussed in the following paragraphs.

Draft

draft
A three-party instrument that is an unconditional written order by one party that orders a second party to pay money to a third party.

drawer of a draft
The party who writes an order for a draft.

drawee of a draft
The party who must pay the money stated in a draft. Also called the *acceptor* of a draft.

payee of a draft
The party who receives the money from a draft.

A **draft**, which is a three-party instrument, is an unconditional written order by one party (the **drawer of a draft**) that orders a second party (the **drawee of a draft**) to pay money to a third party (the **payee of a draft**) [UCC 3-104(e)]. The drawee is obligated to pay the drawer money before the drawer can order the drawee to pay this money to a third party (the payee).

For the drawee to be liable on a draft, the drawee must accept the drawer's written order to pay it. Acceptance is usually shown by the written word *accepted* on the face of the draft, along with the drawee's signature and the date. The *drawee* is called the acceptor of a draft because his or her obligation changes from having to pay the drawer to having to pay the payee. After the drawee accepts the draft, it is returned to the drawer or the payee. The drawer or the payee, in turn, can freely transfer it as a negotiable instrument to another party.

Example Mary owes Hector $1,000. Hector wants Mary to pay the money to Cindy instead of to him. Hector writes out a draft that orders Mary to pay the $1,000 to Cindy. Mary agrees to this change of obligation and writes the word "accepted" on the draft and signs the draft. Hector is the drawer, Mary is the drawee and acceptor of the draft, and Cindy is the payee. Mary is now obligated to pay Cindy $1,000.

time draft
A draft payable at a designated future date.

sight draft (demand draft)
A draft payable on sight.

A draft can be either a time draft or a sight draft. A **time draft** is payable at a designated future date. Language such as "pay on January 1, 2016" or "pay 120 days after date" creates a time draft (see **Exhibit 22.1**). A **sight draft** is payable on sight. A sight draft is also called a **demand draft**. Language such as "on demand pay" or "at sight pay" creates a sight draft. A draft can be both a time draft and a sight draft. Such a draft would provide that it is payable at a stated time after sight. This type of draft is created by language such as "payable 90 days after sight."

trade acceptance (bill of exchange)
A sight draft that arises when credit is extended (by a seller to a buyer) with the sale of goods. The seller is both the drawer and the payee, and the buyer is the drawee.

Trade Acceptance A **trade acceptance (bill of exchange)** is a sight draft that arises when credit is extended by the seller to the buyer with the sale of goods. With this type of draft, the seller is both the drawer and the payee. The buyer to whom credit is extended is the drawee. Even though only two actual parties are involved, it is considered a three-party instrument because three legal positions are involved. A trade acceptance is not countersigned by the drawee's bank, so it is only as good as the buyer–drawee's creditworthiness.

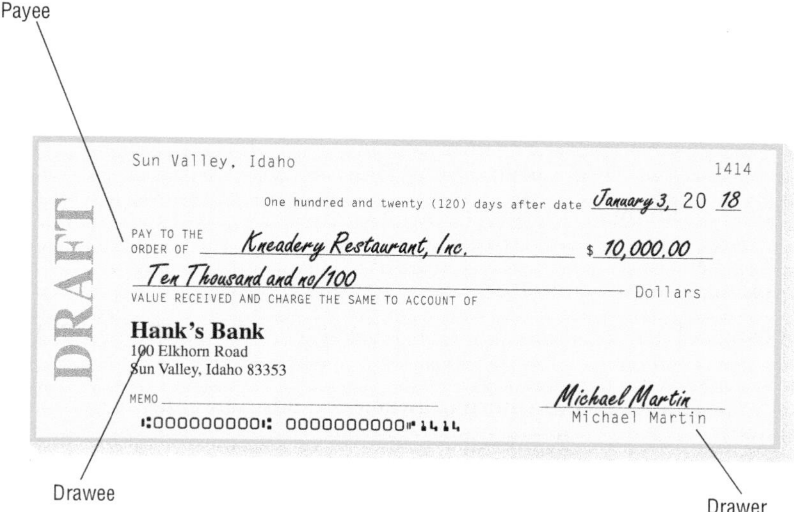

Exhibit 22.1 TIME DRAFT

Check

A **check** is a distinct form of draft. It is unique in that it is drawn on a financial institution (the drawee) and is payable on demand [UCC 3-104(f)]. In other words, a check is an *order to pay* (see **Exhibit 22.2**). Most businesses and many individuals have checking accounts at financial institutions. Like other drafts, a check is a three-party instrument. A customer who has a checking account and writes (draws) a check is the **drawer of a check**. The financial institution on which the check is written is the **drawee of a check**. And the party to whom the check is written is the **payee of a check**.

Example Justin has a checking account at Country Bank. When Justin purchases a car from Mary's Motors, a car dealership, Justin pays for the car by writing a check on the bank made payable to Mary's Motors. Here, Justin is the drawer, Country Bank is the drawee, and Mary's Motors is the payee.

check
A distinct form of draft drawn on a financial institution and payable on demand.

drawer of a check
The checking account holder and writer of a check.

drawee of a check
The financial institution where the drawer of a check has his or her account.

payee of a check
The party to whom a check is written.

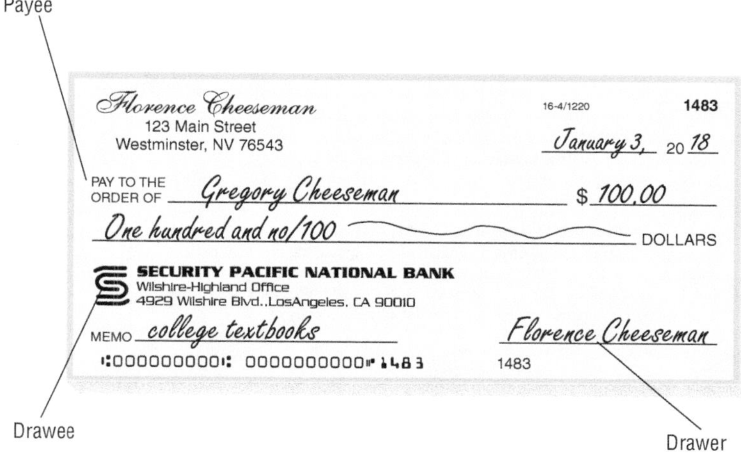

Exhibit 22.2 CHECK

CONCEPT SUMMARY
TYPES OF ORDERS TO PAY

Order to Pay	Parties	Description
Draft	Drawer	Person who issues a draft.
	Drawee	Person who owes money to a drawer; person who is ordered to pay a draft and accepts the draft.
	Payee	Person to whom a draft is made payable.
Check	Drawer	Owner of a checking account at a financial institution; person who issues a check.
	Drawee	Financial institution where drawer's checking account is located; party who is ordered to pay a check.
	Payee	Person to whom a check is made payable.

Promissory Note

promissory note (note) A two-party negotiable instrument that is an unconditional written promise by one party to pay money to another party.

maker of a note The party who makes a promise to pay (borrower).

payee of a note The party to whom a promise to pay is made (lender).

A **promissory note** (or **note**) is an unconditional written promise by one party to pay money to another party [UCC 3-104(e)]. It is a two-party instrument (see **Exhibit 22.3**), not an order to pay. Promissory notes usually arise when one party borrows money from another. The note is evidence of (1) the extension of credit and (2) the borrower's promise to repay the debt. A party who makes a promise to pay is the **maker of a note** (i.e., the borrower). The party to whom the promise to pay is made is the **payee of a note** (i.e., the lender). A promissory note is a negotiable instrument that the payee can freely transfer to other parties.

Example Andrew borrows $10,000 from Wei and signs a promissory note agreeing to pay Wei the principal and 10 percent annual interest over three years in equal monthly installments. Here, Andrew is the maker of the note, and Wei is the payee.

time note A note payable at a specific time.

demand note A note payable on demand.

The parties are free to design the terms of a note to fit their needs. Notes can be payable at a specific time (**time notes**) or on demand (**demand notes**). Notes can be made payable to a named payee or to "bearer." They can be payable in a

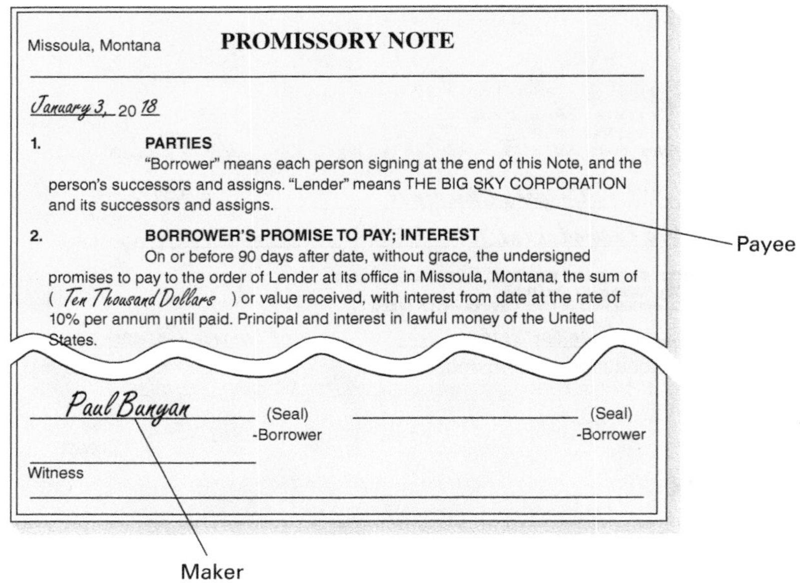
Missoula, Montana PROMISSORY NOTE

January 3, 2018

1. PARTIES
"Borrower" means each person signing at the end of this Note, and the person's successors and assigns. "Lender" means THE BIG SKY CORPORATION and its successors and assigns.

2. BORROWER'S PROMISE TO PAY; INTEREST
On or before 90 days after date, without grace, the undersigned promises to pay to the order of Lender at its office in Missoula, Montana, the sum of (Ten Thousand Dollars) or value received, with interest from date at the rate of 10% per annum until paid. Principal and interest in lawful money of the United States.

Paul Bunyan (Seal) -Borrower (Seal) -Borrower

Witness

Exhibit 22.3 **PROMISSORY NOTE**

single payment or in installments. The latter are called **installment notes**. Most notes require the borrower to pay interest on the principal.

Lenders sometimes require the maker of a note to post security for the repayment of the note. This security, which is called **collateral**, may be in the form of automobiles, houses, securities, or other property. If a maker fails to repay a note when it is due, the lender can foreclose and take the collateral as payment for the note. Notes are often named after the security that underlies the note. For example, notes that are secured by real estate are called **mortgage notes**, and notes that are secured by personal property are called **collateral notes**.

Certificate of Deposit

A **certificate of deposit (CD)** is a special form of note that is created when a depositor deposits money at a financial institution in exchange for the institution's promise to pay back the amount of the deposit plus an agreed-on rate of interest on the expiration of a set time period agreed on by the parties [UCC 3-104(j)].

The financial institution is the borrower (the **maker of a certificate of deposit**), and the depositor is the lender (the **payee of a certificate of deposit**). A CD is a two-party instrument (see **Exhibit 22.4**). Note that a CD is a promise to pay, not an order to pay. Unlike a regular passbook savings account, a CD is a negotiable instrument. CDs under $100,000 are commonly referred to as **small CDs**. CDs of $100,000 or more are usually called **jumbo CDs**.

certificate of deposit (CD)
A two-party negotiable instrument that is a special form of note created when a depositor deposits money at a financial institution in exchange for the institution's promise to pay back the amount of the deposit plus an agreed-on rate of interest on the expiration of a set time period agreed on by the parties.

maker of a certificate of deposit
The financial institution that issues a CD (borrower).

payee of a certificate of deposit
The party to whom a CD is made payable; usually the depositor (lender).

Example Millicent has $50,000 that she would like to invest and earn income on. Millicent goes into City Bank and deposits her money with the bank in exchange for a certificate of deposit (CD) that bears an annual interest rate of 7 percent. Here, City Bank is the maker of the CD (borrower), and Millicent is the payee (lender).

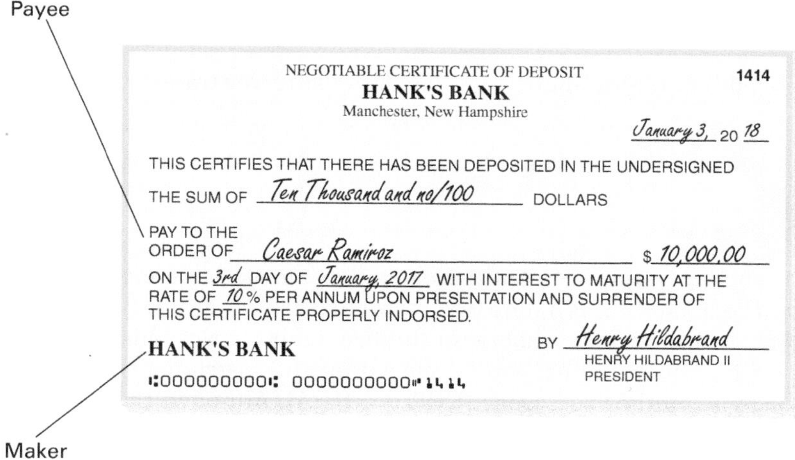

NEGOTIABLE CERTIFICATE OF DEPOSIT 1414
HANK'S BANK
Manchester, New Hampshire

January 3, 20 18

THIS CERTIFIES THAT THERE HAS BEEN DEPOSITED IN THE UNDERSIGNED
THE SUM OF Ten Thousand and no/100 DOLLARS
PAY TO THE ORDER OF Caesar Ramiroz $ 10,000.00
ON THE 3rd DAY OF January, 2017 WITH INTEREST TO MATURITY AT THE RATE OF 10 % PER ANNUM UPON PRESENTATION AND SURRENDER OF THIS CERTIFICATE PROPERLY INDORSED.

HANK'S BANK BY Henry Hildabrand
HENRY HILDABRAND II
PRESIDENT

⑆0000000000⑆ 0000000000⑈ 1414

Exhibit 22.4 CERTIFICATE OF DEPOSIT

CONCEPT SUMMARY

TYPES OF PROMISES TO PAY

Promise to Pay	Parties	Description
Promissory note	Maker	Party who issues a promissory note; this is usually the borrower.
	Payee	Party to whom a promissory note is made payable; this is usually the lender.
Certificate of deposit (CD)	Maker	Financial institution that issues a CD.
	Payee	Party to whom a CD is made payable; this is usually the depositor.

Requirements for Creating a Negotiable Instrument

According to UCC 3-104(a), a negotiable instrument must do the following:

1. Be in writing.
2. Be signed by the maker or drawer.
3. Be an unconditional promise or order to pay.
4. State a fixed amount of money.
5. Not require any undertaking in addition to the payment of money.
6. Be payable on demand or at a definite time.
7. Be payable to order or to bearer.

These requirements must appear on the *face* of the instrument. If they do not, the instrument does not qualify as negotiable. Each of these seven requirements is discussed in the paragraphs and sections that follow.

1. Be in Writing

Money speaks sense in a language all nations understand.

Aphra Behn
The Rover (1677)

A negotiable instrument must be (1) in writing and (2) permanent and portable. The **writing requirement** is met if the writing is on a preprinted form, but typewritten, handwritten, or other tangible agreements are also acceptable [UCC 1-201(46)]. The instrument can be a combination of different kinds of writing.

Example A check is often a preprinted form on which the drawer handwrites the amount of the check, the name of the payee, and the date of the check.

permanency requirement
A requirement of negotiable instruments that says they must be in a permanent state, such as written on ordinary paper.

Most writings on paper meet the **permanency requirement**. However, a writing that is on tissue paper would not meet this requirement because of its impermanence. Oral promises do not qualify as negotiable instruments because they are not clearly transferable in a manner that will prevent fraud. Tape recordings and videotapes are not negotiable instruments because they are not considered writings.

portability requirement
A requirement of negotiable instruments that says they must be able to be easily transported between areas.

The **portability requirement** is intended to ensure free transfer of an instrument.

Example A promise to pay chiseled in a tree would not qualify as a negotiable instrument because the tree is not freely transferable in commerce.

2. Be Signed by the Maker or the Drawer

signature requirement
A requirement that states that a negotiable instrument must be signed by the drawer or maker. Any symbol executed or adopted by a party with a present intent to authenticate a writing qualifies as his or her signature.

The UCC **signature requirement** indicates that a negotiable instrument must be *signed* by the maker if it is a note or CD and by the drawer if it is a check or draft. The maker or drawer is not liable on the instrument unless his or her signature appears on it. The signature can be placed on the instrument by the maker or drawer or by an authorized agent [UCC 3-401(a)]. Although the signature of the maker, drawer, or agent can be located anywhere on the face of the negotiable instrument, it is usually placed in the lower-right corner.

The UCC broadly defines **signature** as any symbol executed or adopted by a party with a present intent to authenticate the writing [UCC 1-201(39)]. A signature is made by the use of any name, including a trade or an assumed name, or by any word or mark used in lieu of a written signature [UCC 3-401(b)].

Examples The requisite signature can be the maker or drawer's formal name (Henry Richard Cheeseman), informal name (Hank Cheeseman), initials (HRC), or nickname (The Big Cheese).

Any other symbol or device (e.g., an *X*, a thumbprint) adopted by the signer as his or her signature also qualifies. The signer's intention to use the symbol as his or her signature is controlling. Typed, printed, lithographed, rubber-stamped, and other mechanical means of signing instruments are recognized as valid by the UCC.

Representative's Signature A maker or drawer can appoint an *agent* to sign a negotiable instrument on his or her behalf. In such circumstances, the **representative's signature** binds the maker or drawer.

Example Corporations and other organizations use agents, usually corporate officers or employees, to sign the corporation's checks and other negotiable instruments. Individuals can also appoint agents to sign their negotiable instruments.

A maker or drawer is liable on a negotiable instrument signed by an authorized agent. The agent is not personally liable on the negotiable instrument if his or her signature properly unambiguously discloses (1) his or her agency status and (2) the identity of the maker or drawer [UCC 3-402(b)]. In the case of an organization, the agent's signature is proper if the organization's name is preceded or followed by the name of the authorized agent.

3. Be an Unconditional Promise or Order to Pay

To be a negotiable instrument under the requirements of UCC 3-104, a writing must contain either an **unconditional order to pay** (draft or check) or an **unconditional promise to pay** (note or CD) a fixed amount of money on demand or at a definite time. The term *unconditional*, which is discussed in the following paragraphs, is one of the keys.

unconditional promise or order to pay requirement
A requirement that says a negotiable instrument must contain either an *unconditional promise to pay* (note or CD) or an *unconditional order to pay* (draft or check).

Order to Pay To be negotiable, a *draft* or *check* must contain the drawer's unconditional **order to pay** a payee. The language of the order must be precise and contain the word *pay*.

order to pay
A drawer's unconditional order to a drawee to pay a payee.

Examples The words *Pay to the order of* are usually used on a check or draft. The printed word *pay* on a check is a proper order that is sufficient to make a check negotiable.

An order can be directed to one or more parties jointly, such as "to A *and* B," or, in the alternative, such as "to A *or* B."

Promise to Pay To be negotiable, a *promissory note* must contain the maker's unconditional and affirmative **promise to pay**. The mere acknowledgment of a debt is not sufficient to constitute a negotiable instrument.

promise to pay
A maker's (borrower's) unconditional and affirmative undertaking to repay a debt to a payee (lender).

Examples The statement "I owe you $100" is merely an I.O.U. It acknowledges a debt, but it does not contain an express promise to repay the money. If the I.O.U. used language such as "I promise to pay" or "the undersigned agrees to pay," however, a negotiable instrument would be created because the note would contain an affirmative obligation to pay.

Certificates of deposit (CDs) are an exception to this rule. CDs do not require an express promise to pay because the bank's acknowledgment of the payee's bank deposit and other terms of the CD clearly indicate the bank's promise to repay the certificate holder. Nevertheless, most CDs contain an express promise to pay.

unconditional
Not conditional or limited. Promises to pay and orders to pay must be unconditional in order to be negotiable.

Unconditional To be negotiable, a promise or an order must be **unconditional** [UCC 3-104(a)]. A promise or an order that is **conditional** on another promise or event is not negotiable because the risk of the other promise or event not occurring would fall on the person who held the instrument. A conditional promise is not a negotiable instrument and is therefore subject to normal contract law.

Critical Legal Thinking
Why does the UCC require that the writing is an unconditional order to pay or an unconditional promise to pay to qualify as a negotiable instrument?

Example American Airlines buys a $50 million airplane from Boeing. American signs a promissory note that promises to pay Boeing if it is "satisfied" with the airplane. This promise is a conditional promise. The condition—that American is satisfied with the airplane—destroys the negotiability of the note.

A promise or an order is conditional and, therefore, not negotiable if it states (1) an express condition to payment, (2) that the promise or order is subject to or governed by another writing, or (3) the rights or obligations with respect to the promise or order are stated in another writing. The mere reference to a different writing does not make a promise or an order conditional [UCC 3-106(a)].

Examples Dow Chemical purchases equipment from Illinois Tool Works and signs a sales contract. Dow Chemical borrows the purchase price from Citibank and executes a promissory note evidencing this debt and promising to repay the borrowed money plus interest to Citibank. The note contains the following reference: "Sales contract—purchase of equipment." This reference does not affect the negotiability of the note. The note would not be negotiable, however, if the reference stated, "This note hereby incorporates by this reference the terms of the sales contract between Dow Chemical and Illinois Tool Works of this date."

A promise or an order remains unconditional even if it refers to a different writing for a description of rights to collateral, prepayment, or acceleration.

Example An unconditional promise or order might state, "See collateral agreement dated January 15, 2018."

A promise or an order may also stipulate that payment is limited to a particular fund or source and still remain unconditional [UCC 3-106(b)].

Example An unconditional promise or order might state, "Payable out of the proceeds of the Tower Construction Contract."

4. State a Fixed Amount of Money

fixed amount of money
A requirement that a negotiable instrument contain a promise or an order to pay a fixed amount of money.

To be negotiable, an instrument must contain a promise or an order to pay a **fixed amount of money** [UCC 3-104(a)].

Fixed Amount The fixed amount of money requirement ensures that the value of the instrument can be determined with certainty. The principal amount of the instrument must appear on the face of the instrument.

An instrument does not have to be payable with interest, but if it is, the amount of interest being charged may be expressed as either a *fixed* or *variable* rate. The amount or rate of interest may be stated or described in the instrument or may require reference to information not contained in the instrument. If an instrument provides for interest but the amount of interest cannot be determined from the description, interest is payable at the judgment rate (legal rate) in effect at the place of payment of the instrument [UCC 3-112].

Example A note that contains a promise to pay $10,000 in one year at a stated rate of 10 percent interest is a negotiable instrument because the value of the note can be determined at any time. A note that contains a promise to pay in goods or services is not a negotiable instrument because the value of the note would be difficult to determine at any given time.

money
A "medium of exchange authorized or adopted by a domestic or foreign government" [UCC 1-201(24)].

Payable in Money UCC 3-104(a) provides that the fixed amount of a negotiable instrument must be **payable in money**. The UCC defines **money** as a "medium of exchange authorized or adopted by a domestic or foreign government as part of its currency" [UCC 1-201(24)].

Examples An instrument that is "payable in $10,000 U.S. currency" is a negotiable instrument.

Instruments that are fully or partially payable in a medium of exchange other than money are not negotiable.

Examples An instrument that is "payable in $10,000 U.S. gold" is not negotiable. Although the stated amount is a fixed amount, it is not payable in a medium of exchange of the U.S. government.

Example Instruments that are payable in diamonds, commodities, goods, services, stocks, bonds, and such do not qualify as negotiable instruments.

Bad money drives out good money.

Sir Thomas Gresham (1560)

5. Not Require Any Undertaking in Addition to the Payment of Money

To qualify as a negotiable instrument, a promise or an order to pay cannot state any other undertaking by the person promising or ordering payment to do any act in addition to the payment of money [UCC 3-104(a)(3)].

Example If a note required the maker to pay a stated amount of money *and* perform some type of service, it would not be negotiable.

A promise or an order may include authorization or power to protect collateral, dispose of collateral, and waive any law intended to protect the obligee.

6. Be Payable on Demand or at a Definite Time

For an instrument to be negotiable, it is necessary to know when the maker, drawee, or acceptor is required to pay it. UCC 3-104(a)(2) requires the instrument to be either *payable on demand* or *payable at a definite time*, as noted on the face of the instrument.

payable on demand or at a definite time
A requirement that a negotiable instrument be payable either *on demand* or *at a definite time*.

Payable on Demand Instruments that are **payable on demand** are called **demand instruments**. Demand instruments are created by language such as "payable on demand," "payable at sight," or "payable on presentment" [UCC 3-108(a)]. By definition, checks are payable on demand [UCC 3-104(f)]. Other instruments, such as notes, CDs, and drafts, can be but are not always payable on demand.

demand instrument
An instrument payable on demand.

Payable at a Definite Time Instruments that are **payable at a definite time** are called **time instruments**. UCC 3-108(b) and 3-108(c) state that an instrument is payable at a definite time if it is payable as follows:

time instrument
An instrument payable (1) at a fixed date, (2) on or before a stated date, (3) at a fixed period after sight, or (4) at a time readily ascertainable when the promise or order is issued.

1. At a fixed date.

   Example An instrument is payable at a definite time if it says "Payable on January 1, 2020."

2. On or before a stated date.

   Example An instrument is payable at a definite time if it says "Payable on or before January 1, 2020." In this case, the maker or drawee has the option of paying the note before—but not after—the stated maturity date.

Instruments that are payable on an uncertain act or event are not negotiable.

Example Sarah's father executes a promissory note that states, "I promise to pay to the order of my daughter, Sarah, $100,000 on the date she marries Bobby Boggs." This note is nonnegotiable because the act and date of marriage are uncertain.

7. Be Payable to Order or to Bearer

The UCC requires that negotiable instruments be either **payable to order** or **payable to bearer** [UCC 3-104(a)(1)]. Promises or orders to pay that do not meet this requirement are not negotiable.

order instrument (order paper)
An instrument that is payable (1) to the order of an identified person or (2) to an identified person or order.

Payable to Order An instrument is an **order instrument** or **order paper** if it is payable (1) to the order of an identified person or (2) to an identified person or order [UCC 3-109(b)].

Example An instrument that states "payable to the order of IBM" or "payable to IBM or order" is a negotiable order instrument. It would not be negotiable if it stated either "payable to IBM" or "pay to IBM" because it is not payable to *order*.

An instrument can be payable to the order of the maker, the drawer, the drawee, the payee, or two or more payees together or, alternatively, to an office, an officer by his or her title, a corporation, a partnership, an unincorporated association, a trust, an estate, or another legal entity. A party to which an instrument is payable may be identified in any way, including by name, identifying number, office, or account number. An instrument is payable to the party intended by the signer of the instrument even if that party is identified in the instrument by a name or another identification that is not that of the intended party [UCC 3-110].

Examples An instrument made "payable to the order of Lovey" is negotiable. The identification of "Lovey" may be determined by evidence. On the other hand, an instrument made "payable to the order of my loved ones" is not negotiable because the payees are not ascertainable with reasonable certainty.

bearer instrument (bearer paper)
An instrument that is payable to anyone in physical possession of the instrument who presents it for payment when it is due.

Payable to Bearer A **bearer instrument** or **bearer paper** is payable to anyone in physical possession of the instrument who presents it for payment when it is due. The person in possession of the instrument is called the **bearer**. *Bearer paper* results when the drawer or maker does not make the instrument payable to a specific payee.

Examples An instrument is payable to bearer when any of the following language is used: "payable to the order of bearer," "payable to bearer," "payable to Google or bearer," "payable to cash," or "payable to the order of cash."

In addition, any other indication that does not purport to designate a specific payee creates bearer paper [UCC 3-109(a)].

Example An instrument "payable to my dog Fido" creates a bearer instrument.

In the following case, the court held that a gambling casino marker was a negotiable instrument.

CASE 22.1 *FEDERAL COURT CASE Negotiable Instrument*

Las Vegas Sands, LLC, dba Venetian Resort Hotel Casino v. Nehme

632 F.3d 526, 2011 U.S. App. Lexis 492 (2011)
United States Court of Appeals for the Ninth Circuit

"The marker therefore was valid and enforceable as a negotiable instrument under Nevada law."
—Bea, Circuit Judge

Facts

Amine T. Nehme, a California resident, is a repeat gambler at the Venetian, a licensed casino in Las Vegas, Nevada. The Venetian is owned by Las Vegas Sands, LLC. Nehme applied for a line of credit with the Venetian by completing a standard credit application form. The bottom of the credit application provided, "Before drawing on my line of credit, if granted, I agree to sign credit instruments in the amount of the draw. Each draw against my credit line constitutes a separate loan of money. I will sign a credit instrument in the amount of the loan." By signing the credit application, Nehme agreed to repay all loans and draws against his credit line.

The Venetian approved a credit line of $500,000 to Nehme. One day, while gambling at the Venetian, Nehme signed a casino marker for $500,000 payable to the Venetian. Nehme exchanged the marker for chips and lost all $500,000 worth of chips playing blackjack. Nehme then left the Venetian with the marker outstanding. The Venetian presented the $500,000 marker to Bank of America, the bank specified on the marker, but the marker was returned for insufficient funds. The Venetian sued Nehme for failure to pay a negotiable instrument.

(case continues)

Issue

Is the Venetian's casino marker signed by Nehme a negotiable instrument under the Nevada Uniform Commercial Code?

Language of the Court

Here, the marker is a negotiable instrument and a check because it provides a mechanism for payment of $500,000 from Bank of America to the order of the Venetian, is signed by Nehme, and is payable on demand because it states no time or date of payment. On the face of the marker, the order is unconditional and states no undertakings by Nehme other than to pay a specific sum of money. The marker therefore was valid and enforceable as a negotiable instrument under Nevada law.

Decision

The U.S. court of appeals held that the casino marker was a negotiable instrument. The court remanded the case for the determination of other issues involved in the case.

Ethics Questions

Did Nehme act ethically in trying not to pay his marker? Should gambling casinos advance credit to gamblers?

Prepayment, Acceleration, and Extension Clauses

The inclusion of *prepayment, acceleration,* or *extension clauses* in an instrument does not affect its negotiability. Such clauses are commonly found in promissory notes.

A **prepayment clause** permits the maker to pay the amount due prior to the due date of the instrument.

prepayment clause
A clause in an instrument that permits the maker to pay the amount due prior to the date of the instrument.

Example A person borrows money from a bank to purchase a house. The loan is a 30-year loan, with interest and principal to be paid in equal monthly installments. If the loan agreement contains a prepayment clause, the borrower can pay off the loan at any time during the 30-year period.

An **acceleration clause** allows the payee or holder to accelerate payment of the principal amount of an instrument, plus accrued interest, on the occurrence of an event, such as missing a loan payment.

acceleration clause
A clause in an instrument that allows the payee or holder to accelerate payment of the principal amount of the instrument, plus accrued interest, on the occurrence of an event.

Example A person borrows money from a bank to purchase an automobile. The loan is a five-year loan with interest and principal to be paid in equal monthly installments. After making payments for two years, the borrower misses a payment and defaults on the loan. If the loan agreement contains an acceleration clause, the entire amount of the loan, plus accrued interest, is due and payable at the time of default.

An **extension clause** is the opposite of an acceleration clause: It allows the date of maturity of an instrument to be extended to sometime in the future. An extension clause contains the terms for extension, such as setting the interest rate during the extension period.

extension clause
A clause in an instrument that allows the date of maturity of the instrument to be extended to sometime in the future.

Example A college student borrows money from her mother for college expenses. The loan agreement provides that the student will repay the loan five years after graduation from college. The loan agreement contains an extension clause that permits the graduate to extend the loan another two years if, at the end of five years, she wants extra time to pay the loan.

nonnegotiable contract
A contract that fails to meet the requirements of a negotiable instrument and, therefore, is not subject to the provisions of UCC Article 3.

Critical Legal Thinking
If the writing does meet the requirements to be a negotiable instrument, what is it? Is it still enforceable?

Nonnegotiable Contract

If a promise or an order to pay does not meet one of the previously discussed requirements of negotiability, it is a **nonnegotiable contract** and is therefore not subject to the provisions of UCC Article 3. A promise or an order that conspicuously states that it is not negotiable or is not subject to Article 3 is not a negotiable instrument [UCC 3-104(d)] and is therefore a nonnegotiable contract.

A nonnegotiable contract is not rendered either nontransferable or unenforceable. A nonnegotiable contract can be enforced under normal contract law. If the maker or drawer of a nonnegotiable contract fails to pay it, the holder of the contract can sue the nonperforming party for breach of contract.

Global Law

Negotiable Instruments Payable in Foreign Currency

SEOUL, SOUTH KOREA

The UCC expressly provides that an instrument may state that it is payable in foreign currency *[UCC 3-107].*

Key Terms and Concepts

Acceleration clause (479)
Article 3 (Commercial Paper) of the UCC (469)
Bearer (478)
Bearer instrument (bearer paper) (478)
Certificate of deposit (CD) (473)
Check (471)
Collateral (473)
Collateral note (473)
Conditional (475)
Demand draft (470)
Demand instrument (477)
Demand note (472)
Draft (470)
Drawee of a check (471)
Drawee of a draft (470)
Drawer of a check (471)
Drawer of a draft (470)
Extension clause (479)
Extension of credit (470)
Fixed amount of money (476)
Holder in due course (HDC) (469)

Installment note (473)
Jumbo CD (473)
Maker of a certificate of deposit (473)
Maker of a note (472)
Money (476)
Mortgage note (473)
Negotiable instrument (commercial paper) (469)
Negotiation (469)
Nonnegotiable contract (479)
Order instrument (order paper) (477)
Order to pay (475)
Payable at a definite time (477)
Payable in foreign currency (480)
Payable in money (476)
Payable on demand (477)
Payable to bearer (477)
Payable to order (477)
Payee of a certificate of deposit (473)
Payee of a check (471)
Payee of a draft (470)
Payee of a note (472)
Permanency requirement (474)
Portability requirement (474)
Prepayment clause (479)
Promise to pay (475)
Promissory note (note) (472)
Record-keeping device (470)
Representative's signature (475)
Revised Article 3 (Negotiable Instruments) of the UCC (469)
Sight draft (470)
Signature (474)
Signature requirement (474)
Small CD (473)
Substitute for money (469)
Time draft (470)
Time instrument (477)
Time note (472)
Trade acceptance (bill of exchange) (470)
Unconditional (475)
Unconditional order to pay (475)
Unconditional promise to pay (475)
Writing requirement (474)

Critical Legal Thinking Cases

22.1 Negotiable Instrument William H. Bailey, MD, executed a note payable to California Dreamstreet, a joint venture that solicited investments for a cattle breeding operation. Bailey's promissory note read, "Dr. William H. Bailey hereby promises to pay to the order of California Dreamstreet the sum of $329,800." Four years later, Dreamstreet negotiated the note to Cooperative Centrale Raiffeisen-Boerenleenbank B.A. (Cooperatieve), a foreign bank. A default occurred, and Cooperatieve filed suit against Bailey to recover on the note. Is the note executed by Bailey a negotiable instrument? *Cooperatieve Centrale Raiffeisen-Boerenleenbank B.A. v. Bailey*, 710 F.Supp. 737, 1989 U.S. Dist. Lexis 4488 (United States District Court for the Central District of California)

22.2 Formal Requirements Mr. Higgins operated a used car dealership in the state of Alabama. Higgins purchased a Chevrolet Corvette. He paid for the car with a draft on his account at the First State Bank of Albertville. Soon after, Higgins resold the car to Mr. Holsonback. To pay for the car, Holsonback signed a check that was printed on a standard-sized envelope. The reason the check was printed on an envelope is that this practice made it easier to transfer title and other documents from the seller to the buyer. The envelope on which the check was written contained a certificate of title, a mileage statement, and a bill of sale. Does a check printed on an envelope meet the formal requirements to be classified as a negotiable instrument under the UCC? *Holsonback v. First State Bank of Albertville*, 394 So.2d 381, 1980 Ala. Civ. App. Lexis 1208 (Court of Civil Appeals of Alabama)

22.3 Reference to Another Agreement Holly Hill Acres, Ltd. (Holly Hill), purchased land from Rogers and Blythe. As part of its consideration, Holly Hill gave Rogers and Blythe a promissory note and purchase money mortgage. The note read, in part, "This note with interest is secured by a mortgage on real estate made by the maker in favor of said payee. The terms of said mortgage are by reference made a part hereof." Rogers and Blythe assigned this note and mortgage to Charter Bank of Gainesville (Charter Bank) as security in order to obtain a loan from the bank. Within a few months, Rogers and Blythe defaulted on their obligation to Charter Bank. Charter Bank sued to recover on Holly Hill's note and mortgage. Does the reference to the mortgage in the note cause it to be nonnegotiable? *Holly Hill Acres, Ltd. v. Charter Bank of Gainesville*, 314 So.2d 209, 1975 Fla. App. Lexis 13715 (Court of Appeal of Florida)

Ethical

Ethics Case

22.4 Demand Instrument Stewart P. Blanchard borrowed $50,000 from Progressive Bank & Trust Company (Progressive) to purchase a home. As part of the transaction, Blanchard signed a note secured by a mortgage. The note provided for a 10 percent annual interest rate. Under the terms of the note, payment was "due on demand, if no demand is made, then $600 monthly" beginning at a specified date. Blanchard testified that he believed Progressive could demand immediate payment only if he failed to make the monthly installments. After one year, Blanchard received notice that the rate of interest on the note would rise to 11 percent. Despite the notice, Blanchard continued to make $600 monthly payments. One year later, Progressive notified Blanchard that the interest rate on the loan would be increased to 12.75 percent. Progressive requested that Blanchard sign a form consenting to the interest rate adjustment. When Blanchard refused to sign the form, Progressive demanded immediate payment of the note balance. Progressive sued Blanchard to enforce the terms of the note. Is the note a demand instrument? Did either party act unethically in this case? *Blanchard v. Progressive Bank & Trust Company*, 413 So.2d 589, 1982 La. App. Lexis 7213 (Court of Appeal of Louisiana)

CHAPTER

23 Holder in Due Course and Transferability

BANK
Checks are cleared using the banking system.

Learning Objectives

After studying this chapter, you should be able to:

1. Describe how negotiable instruments are indorsed and transferred.
2. Describe how order and bearer paper are negotiated.
3. Distinguish between blank, special, qualified, and restrictive indorsements.
4. Define *holder* and *holder in due course*.
5. Identify and apply the requirements for becoming a holder in due course.

Chapter Outline

"*A negotiable bill or note is a courier without luggage.*"

—*Chief Justice Gibson*
Overton v. Tyler 3 Pa. 346, 1846 Pa. Lexis 117 (1846)

Introduction to Holder in Due Course and Transferability

The borrower runs in his own debt.

Ralph Waldo Emerson
Essays, Vol. Compensation (1841)

Once created, a negotiable instrument can be transferred to subsequent parties by *negotiation*. This is accomplished by placing an *indorsement* on the instrument. There are several types of indorsements, each with its own requirements and effect.

Recall that the primary purpose of commercial paper is to act as a substitute for money. For this to occur, the holder of a negotiable instrument must qualify as a *holder in due course (HDC)*. Commercial paper held by an HDC is virtually as good as money because HDCs take an instrument free of all claims and most defenses that can be asserted by other parties.

This chapter discusses the negotiation of an instrument, types of indorsements, and the requirements that must be met to qualify as an HDC.

Transfer of a Nonnegotiable Contract by Assignment

assignment
The transfer of rights under a nonnegotiable contract. The transferor is the *assignor*, and the transferee is the *assignee*.

nonnegotiable contract
A contract that lacks one or more of the requirements to be a negotiable instrument.

An **assignment** is the transfer of rights under a contract. It transfers the rights of the transferor (**assignor**) to the transferee (**assignee**). Because normal contract principles apply, the assignee acquires only the rights that the assignor possessed. Thus, any defenses to the enforcement of the contract that could have been raised against the assignor can also be raised against the assignee.

A **nonnegotiable contract** is a contract that lacks one or more of the requirements to be a negotiable instrument. An assignment occurs when a nonnegotiable contract is transferred. In the case of a negotiable instrument, assignment occurs when the instrument is transferred but the transfer fails to qualify as a negotiation under Article 3 of the Uniform Commercial Code (UCC). In this case, the transferee is an *assignee* rather than a *holder*.

Example Sandra borrows $25,000 from Joshua at 5 percent interest and signs a promissory note agreeing to repay the principal and interest in equal monthly installments over five years. This promissory note would normally be a negotiable instrument. However, the note contains a reference to another document, and by doing so it becomes a nonnegotiable instrument. If Joshua transfers the note to Mabel, this is an assignment of rights—a transfer of a normal contract—and not a negotiation subject to Article 3 of the UCC. Joshua is the assignor, and Mabel is the assignee. Mabel can enforce the note against Sandra, but Sandra can raise many defenses she has against Joshua (e.g., fraud) against Mabel.

Transfer of a Negotiable Instrument by Negotiation

negotiation
The transfer of a negotiable instrument by a person other than the issuer to a person who thereby becomes a *holder*.

Negotiation is the transfer of a *negotiable instrument* by a person other than the issuer. The person to whom the instrument is transferred becomes the *holder* [UCC 3-201(a)]. The holder receives at least the rights of the transferor and may acquire even greater rights than the transferor if he or she qualifies as a holder in due course (HDC) [UCC 3-302]. An HDC has greater rights because he or she is not subject to some of the defenses that could otherwise have been raised against the transferor.

The proper method of negotiation depends on whether the instrument involved is *order paper* or *bearer paper*, as discussed in the following paragraphs.

Negotiating Order Paper

An instrument that is payable to a specific payee or indorsed to a specific indorsee is an **order instrument** or **order paper**. Order paper is negotiated by delivery with the necessary indorsement [UCC 3-201(b)]. Thus, for order paper to be negotiated there must be delivery and indorsement.

order instrument (order paper)
An instrument that is payable to a specific payee or indorsed to a specific indorsee. Order paper is negotiated by (1) delivery and (2) indorsement.

Example Sam Bennett receives a weekly payroll check from his employer, Ace Corporation, made "payable to the order of Sam Bennett." Sam takes the check to a local store, signs his name on the back of the check (indorsement), gives the check to the cashier (delivery), and receives cash for the check. Sam has negotiated the check to the store. Delivery and indorsement have occurred.

Critical Legal Thinking

What is order paper? What is bearer paper? What is the difference in the negotiation of order paper versus bearer paper?

Negotiating Bearer Paper

An instrument that is not payable to a specific payee or indorsee is a **bearer instrument** or **bearer paper**. Bearer paper is negotiated by *delivery*; indorsement is not necessary [UCC 3-201(b)]. Substantial risk is associated with the loss or theft of bearer paper.

bearer instrument (bearer paper)
An instrument that is not payable to a specific payee or indorsee. Bearer paper is negotiated by delivery; indorsement is not necessary.

Example Mary draws from her checking account a $1,500 check made out to "pay to cash" and gives it to Peter. This is a bearer instrument because the check has not been made out to a named payee. There has been a negotiation because Mary delivered a bearer instrument (the check) to Peter. Subsequently, Carmen steals the check from Peter. There has not been a negotiation because the check was not voluntarily delivered. But Carmen physically possesses the bearer instrument. The negotiation is complete if Carmen delivers the check to an innocent third party, Ida. Ida is a holder and may qualify as a holder in due course (HDC) with all the rights in the check [UCC 3-302]. If the holder, Ida, is an HDC, she can deposit the check in her account, and Mary's checking account will be debited $1,500. Peter's only recourse is to recover the $1,500 from Carmen, the thief.

The case that follows demonstrates the risk of bearer paper.

CASE 23.1 *STATE COURT CASE Bearer Paper*

Gerber & Gerber, P.C. v. Regions Bank

596 S.E.2d 174, 2004 Ga. App. Lexis 206 (2004)
Court of Appeals of Georgia

"Accordingly, when here the payees of the cashier's checks indorsed the checks in blank, the checks then became bearer paper and could—similar to cash—be transferred by possession alone."

—Miller, Judge

Facts

Cynthia Stafford worked as a real estate closing secretary for Gerber & Gerber, P.C. (G&G), a law firm. The law firm acted as a trustee for the closing of real estate transactions. Real estate buyers would write cashier's checks for the purchase price of the real estate and make these checks payable to the seller-payee. The seller-payee in turn indorsed these checks in blank to the law firm and gave the checks to the law firm to hold during the time period for closing of their real estate transactions. This created bearer paper. Over a period of two years, Stafford stole some of these blank-indorsed cashier's checks. Stafford then personally indorsed the cashier's checks in her possession and deposited them in her personal bank account at Regions Bank. The total loss was $180,000.

(*case continues*)

Stafford confessed to the theft. She pleaded guilty to criminal charges and received a five-year jail sentence. Stafford claimed to have spent the money. G&G sued Regions Bank to recover for the checks paid to Stafford, alleging that the bank was negligent in accepting the checks from Stafford. Regions Bank moved for summary judgment, arguing that it had acted properly under the Uniform Commercial Code (UCC) in accepting the bearer blank-indorsed checks from Stafford. The trial court granted Regions Bank summary judgment as to the bearer paper. G&G appealed.

Issue

Has Regions Bank properly accepted the blank-indorsed bearer cashier's checks from Stafford?

Language of the Court

Accordingly, when here the payees of the cashier's checks indorsed the checks in blank, the checks then became bearer paper and could—similar to cash—be transferred by possession alone. Thus, Regions Bank quite properly accepted the indorsed-in-blank cashier's checks from the person in possession of them and deposited the checks into that person's account.

Decision

The court of appeals held that Regions Bank was not negligent in accepting the blank-indorsed bearer cashier's checks from Stafford and placing the money in Stafford's personal account. The court of appeals upheld the trial court's grant of summary judgment to Regions Bank.

Ethics Questions

Did Stafford act ethically in this case? Did G&G act ethically in suing Regions Bank to recover for Stafford's thefts?

The following feature discusses how order and bearer paper can be converted from one to the other.

Contemporary Environment

Converting Order and Bearer Paper

An instrument can be converted from order paper to bearer paper and vice versa many times until the instrument is paid [UCC 3-109(c)]. The deciding factor is the type of indorsement placed on the instrument at the time of each subsequent transfer. Follow the indorsements in the example shown here to determine whether order or bearer paper has been created.

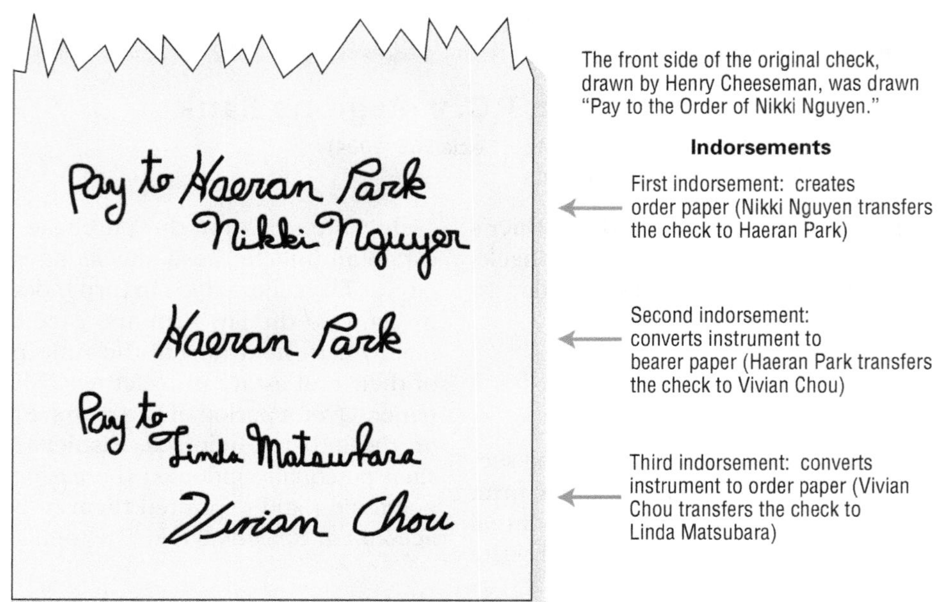

Pay to Haeran Park
Nikki Nguyen
Haeran Park
Pay to Linda Matsubara
Vivian Chou
The front side of the original check, drawn by Henry Cheeseman, was drawn "Pay to the Order of Nikki Nguyen."
Indorsements
First indorsement: creates order paper (Nikki Nguyen transfers the check to Haeran Park)
Second indorsement: converts instrument to bearer paper (Haeran Park transfers the check to Vivian Chou)
Third indorsement: converts instrument to order paper (Vivian Chou transfers the check to Linda Matsubara)

Transfer of a Negotiable Instrument by Indorsement

An **indorsement** is the signature of a signer (other than as a maker, a drawer, or an acceptor) that is placed on an instrument to negotiate it to another person. The signature may (1) appear alone, (2) name an individual to whom the instrument is to be paid, or (3) be accompanied by other words [UCC 3-204(2)]. The person who indorses an instrument is called the **indorser**. If the indorsement names a payee, this person is called the **indorsee**. Indorsements are required to negotiate order paper, but they are not required to negotiate bearer paper [UCC 3-201(b)].

indorsement
The signature (and other directions) written by or on behalf of the holder somewhere on an instrument.

An indorsement is usually placed on the reverse side of the instrument, such as on the back of a check (see **Exhibit 23.1**). If there is no room on the instrument, the indorsement may be written on a separate piece of paper called an **allonge**. The allonge must be affixed (e.g., stapled, taped) to the instrument [UCC 3-204(a)].

allonge
A separate piece of paper attached to an instrument on which an indorsement is written.

Exhibit 23.1 PLACEMENT OF AN ENDORSEMENT

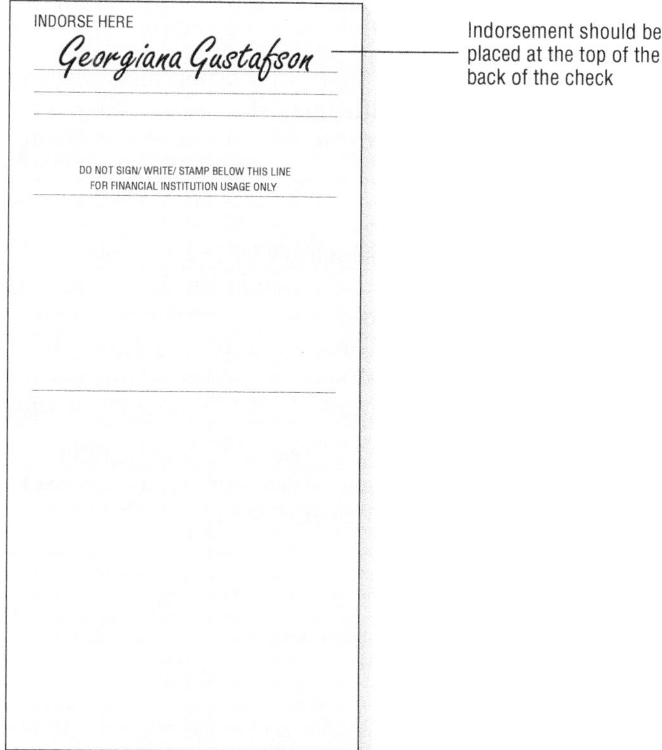

Types of Indorsements

There are four categories of indorsements:

1. Blank indorsement
2. Special indorsement
3. Qualified indorsement
4. Restrictive indorsement

These types of indorsements are discussed in the following paragraphs.

Blank Indorsement

A **blank indorsement** does not specify a particular indorsee. It may consist of just a signature [UCC 3-205(b)].

blank indorsement
An indorsement that does not specify a particular indorsee. It creates *bearer paper*.

Example Harold Green draws a check "pay to the order of Victoria Rudd" and delivers the check to Victoria. Victoria indorses the check in blank by writing her signature "Victoria Rudd" on the back of the check (see **Exhibit 23.2**).

Exhibit 23.2 BLANK INDORSEMENT

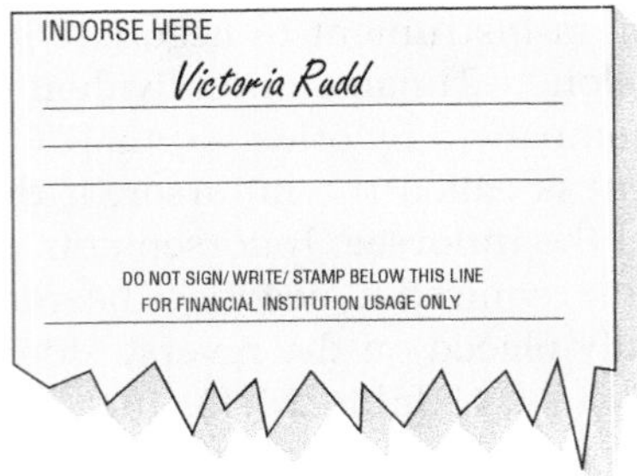

Order paper that is indorsed in blank becomes bearer paper. As mentioned earlier, bearer paper can be negotiated by delivery; indorsement is not required. Thus, a lost bearer paper can be presented for payment or negotiated to another holder.

Example In the prior example, assume that Victoria Rudd loses the check she has indorsed in blank and that Mary Smith finds the check. Mary Smith, who is in possession of bearer paper, can deliver it to another person without indorsing it.

Special Indorsement

special indorsement
An indorsement that contains the signature of the indorser and specifies the person (indorsee) to whom the indorser intends the instrument to be payable. It creates *order paper*.

A **special indorsement** contains the signature of the indorser and specifies the person (indorsee) to whom the indorser intends the instrument to be payable [UCC 3-205(a)]. Words of negotiation (e.g., "pay to the order of . . .") are not required for a special indorsement. Words such as "pay Emily Ingman" are sufficient to form a special indorsement. A special indorsement creates *order paper*. As mentioned earlier, order paper is negotiated by indorsement and delivery.

Example A special indorsement would be created if Betsy McKenny indorsed her check and then wrote "pay to Dan Jones" above her signature (see **Exhibit 23.3**). The check is negotiated when Betsy gives it to Dan.

Exhibit 23.3 SPECIAL INDORSEMENT

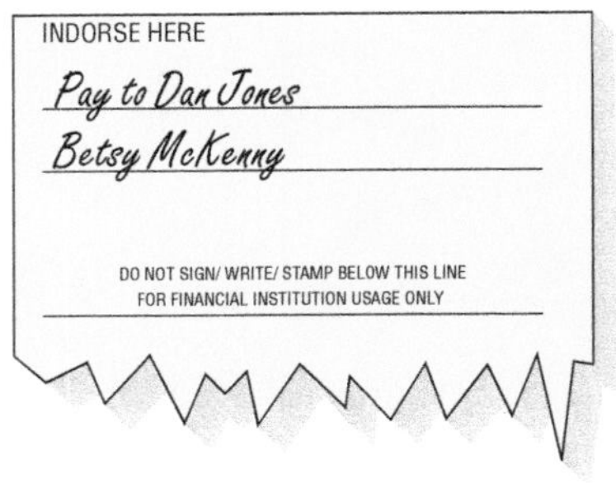

To prevent the risk of loss from theft, a special indorsement (which creates order paper) is preferred over a blank indorsement (which creates bearer paper). A holder can convert a blank indorsement into a special indorsement by writing contract instructions over the signature of the indorser [UCC 3-205(c)]. Words such as "pay to John Jones" written above the indorser's signature are enough to convert bearer paper to order paper.

Qualified Indorsement

Generally, an indorsement is a promise by the indorser to pay the holder or any subsequent indorser the amount of the instrument if the maker, drawer, or acceptor defaults on it. This promise is called an **unqualified indorsement**. Unless otherwise agreed, the order and liability of the indorsers is presumed to be the order in which they indorse the instrument [UCC 3-415(a)].

unqualified indorsement
An indorsement whereby the indorser promises to pay the holder or any subsequent indorser the amount of the instrument if the maker, drawer, or acceptor defaults on it.

Example Cindy draws a check payable to the order of John. John (indorser) indorses the check and negotiates it to Steve (indorsee). When Steve presents the check for payment, there are insufficient funds in Cindy's account to pay the check. John, as an **unqualified indorser**, is liable on the check. John can recover from Cindy.

The UCC permits **qualified indorsements**—that is, indorsements that disclaim or limit liability on the instrument. A **qualified indorser** does not guarantee payment of the instrument if the maker, drawer, or acceptor defaults on it. A qualified indorsement is created by placing a notation such as "without recourse" or other similar language that disclaims liability as part of the indorsement [UCC 3-415(b)]. A qualified indorsement protects only the indorser who wrote an indorsement on the instrument. A qualified indorsement is often used by persons who sign instruments in a representative capacity.

qualified indorsement
An indorsement that includes the notation "without recourse" or similar language that disclaims liability of the indorser.

Example Suppose an insurance company that is paying a claim makes out a check payable to the order of the attorney representing the payee. The attorney can indorse the check to his client (the payee) with the notation "without recourse." This notation ensures that the attorney is not liable as an indorser if the insurance company fails to pay the check.

A qualified indorsement can be either a special qualified indorsement or a blank qualified indorsement. A *special qualified indorsement* creates order paper that can be negotiated by indorsement and delivery. A *blank qualified indorsement* creates bearer paper that can be further negotiated by delivery without indorsement (see **Exhibit 23.4**).

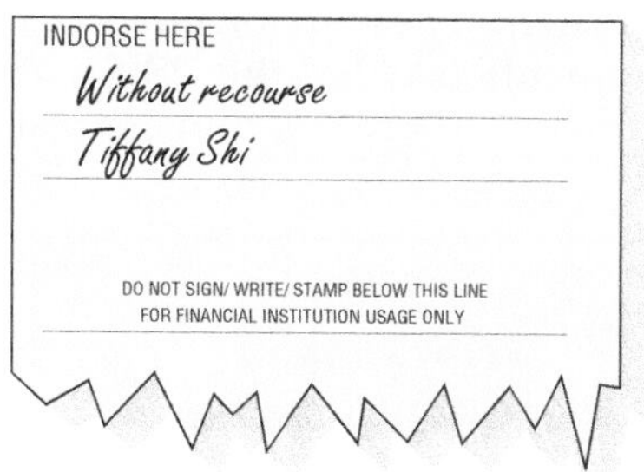

Exhibit 23.4 **QUALIFIED INDORSEMENT**

Restrictive Indorsement

Most indorsements are *nonrestrictive*. **Nonrestrictive indorsements** do not have any instructions or conditions attached to the payment of the funds.

nonrestrictive indorsement
An indorsement that has no instructions or conditions attached to the payment of the funds.

Example An indorsement is nonrestrictive if the indorsee merely signs his or her signature to the back of an instrument or includes a notation to pay a specific indorsee ("pay to Sam Smith").

Occasionally, an indorser includes some form of instruction in an indorsement. This instruction is called a **restrictive indorsement**. A restrictive indorsement restricts the indorsee's rights in some manner. An indorsement that purports to prohibit further negotiation of an instrument does not destroy the negotiability of the instrument.

restrictive indorsement
An indorsement that contains some sort of instruction from the indorser.

Example A check that is indorsed "pay to Sarah Stein only" can still be negotiated to other transferees. Because of its ineffectiveness, this type of restrictive indorsement is seldom used.

UCC 3-206 recognizes the following types of restrictive indorsements:

indorsement for deposit or collection
An indorsement that makes the indorsee the indorser's collecting agent (e.g., "For deposit only").

- **Indorsement for deposit or collection.** An indorser can indorse an instrument so as to make the indorsee his collecting agent. Such indorsement—called an **indorsement for deposit or collection**—is often done when an indorser deposits a check or another instrument for collection at a bank. Words such as *for collection*, *for deposit only*, and *pay any bank* create this type of indorsement. Banks use this type of indorsement in the collection process.

  Example Harriet Brown receives her paycheck from her employer. She indorses the back of the check "For deposit only" and signs her name under these words. Harriet deposits the check at an ATM of her bank. This is an indorsement for deposit or collection. Harriet's bank will send the check to the employer's bank for collection (see **Exhibit 23.5**).

Exhibit 23.5 RESTRICTIVE INDORSEMENT

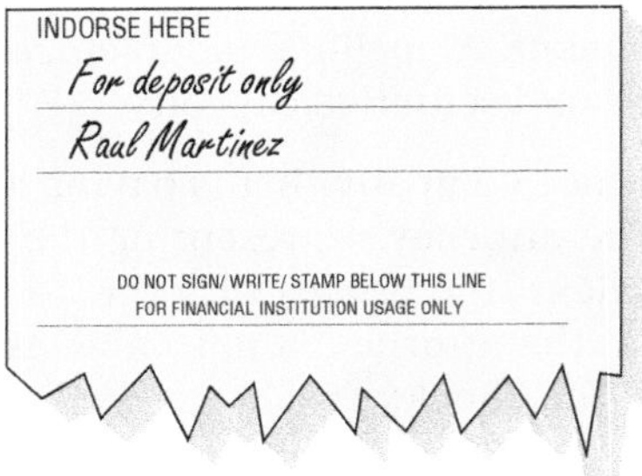

indorsement in trust (agency indorsement)
An indorsement that states that it is for the benefit or use of the indorser or another person.

- **Indorsement in trust.** An indorsement can state that it is for the benefit or use of the indorser or another person.

  Example Checks are often indorsed to attorneys, executors of estates, real estate agents, and other fiduciaries in their representative capacity for the benefit of clients, heirs, or others. These indorsements are called **indorsements in trust**, or **agency indorsements** (see **Exhibit 23.6**). The indorser is not personally liable on the instrument if there is a proper trust or agency indorsement.

Exhibit 23.6 TRUST INDORSEMENT

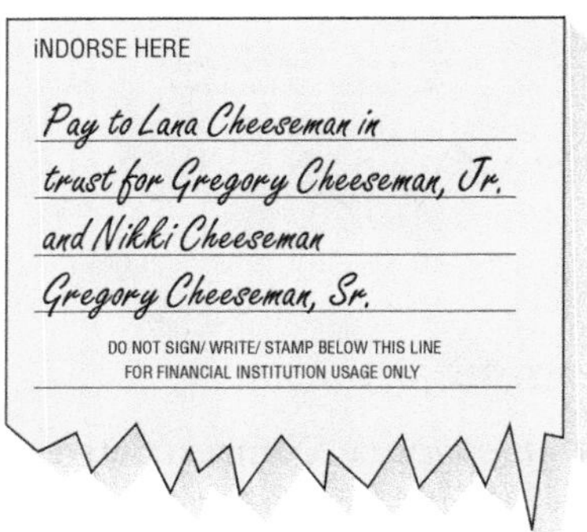

An indorsee who does not comply with the instructions of a restrictive indorsement is liable to the indorser for all losses that occur because of such noncompliance.

Example Suppose a check is drawn "payable to Anne Spencer, attorney, in trust for Joseph Watkins." If Spencer indorses the check to an automobile dealer in payment for a car that she purchases personally, the automobile dealer (indorsee) has not followed the instructions of the restrictive indorsement. The automobile dealer is liable to Joseph Watkins for any losses that arise because of the dealer's noncompliance with the restrictive indorsement.

CONCEPT SUMMARY
TYPES OF INDORSEMENTS

Type of Indorsement	Description
Blank	Does not specify a particular indorsee (e.g., /s/Mary Jones). This indorsement creates bearer paper.
Special	Specifies the person to whom the indorser intends the instrument to be payable (e.g., "Pay to the order of John Smith" /s/Mary Jones). This indorsement creates order paper. (If it is not payable to order [e.g., "Pay to John Smith" /s/Mary Jones], it can be converted to order paper [e.g., "Pay to the order of Fred Roe" /s/John Smith].)
Unqualified	Does not disclaim or limit liability. The indorsee is liable on the instrument if it is not paid by the maker, acceptor, or drawer.
Qualified	Disclaims or limits the liability of the indorsee. There are two types: 1. Special qualified indorsement (e.g., "Pay to the order of John Smith, without recourse" /s/Mary Jones). 2. Blank qualified indorsement (e.g., "Without recourse" /s/Mary Jones).
Nonrestrictive	No instructions or conditions are attached to the payment of funds (e.g., "Pay to John Smith or order" /s/Mary Jones).
Restrictive	Conditions or instructions restrict the indorsee's rights. There are three types: 1. Indorsement prohibiting further indorsement (e.g., "Pay to John Smith only" /s/Mary Jones). 2. Indorsement for deposit or collection (e.g., "For deposit only" /s/Mary Jones). 3. Indorsement in trust (e.g., "Pay to John Smith, trustee" /s/Mary Jones).

Misspelled or Wrong Name

Where the name of the payee or indorsee is misspelled in a negotiable instrument, the payee or indorsee can indorse the instrument using the misspelled name, the correct name, or both.

Example If Susan Worth receives a check payable to "Susan Wirth," she can indorse the check by signing "Susan Wirth" or "Susan Worth" or both. A person paying or taking the instrument for value or collection may require a signature in both the misspelled and the correct versions [UCC 3-204(d)].

Multiple Payees or Indorsees

Drawers, makers, and indorsers often make checks, promissory notes, and other negotiable instruments payable to two or more payees or indorsees. The question then arises: Can the instrument be negotiated by the signature of one payee or indorsee, or are both or all of their signatures required to negotiate the instrument?

Section 3-110(d) of Revised Article 3 of the UCC and cases that have interpreted that section establish the following rules:

- If an instrument is **payable jointly** using the word *and*, both persons' indorsements are necessary to negotiate the instrument.

  Example "Pay to Shou-Yi Kang and Min-Wer Chen." Here, the indorsement signatures of *both* Shou-Yi Kang and Min-Wer Chen are required to negotiate the instrument. The indorsement signature of only one of the named persons is not sufficient to negotiate the instrument.

- If the instrument is **payable in the alternative** using the word *or*, either person's indorsement signature alone is sufficient to negotiate the instrument.

  Example "Pay to Shou-Yi Kang or Min-Wer Chen." Here, *either* Shou-Yi Kang or Min-Wer Chen can individually indorse and negotiate the instrument without the other's signature.

- If a **virgule**—a slash mark (/)—is used, courts have held that the instrument is *payable in the alternative*—that is, the instrument is treated as if the / is an "or." Thus, if a virgule is used, either person may individually negotiate the instrument.

  Example "Pay to Shou-Yi Kang/Min-Wer Chen." Here, the virgule (/) is treated as an "or," and either Shou-Yi Kang or Min-Wer Chen can individually indorse and negotiate the instrument without the other's indorsement.

Holder in Due Course (HDC)

holder
A person who is in possession of a negotiable instrument that is drawn, issued, or indorsed to him or to his order, or to bearer, or in blank.

Two of the most important concepts of the law of negotiable instruments are the concepts of *holder* and *holder in due course*. A **holder** is a person in possession of an instrument that is payable to a bearer or an identified person who is in possession of an instrument payable to that person [UCC 1-201(20)]. A holder is subject to all the claims and defenses that can be asserted against the transferor.

The concept of *holder in due course (HDC)* is unique to the area of negotiable instruments. An HDC takes a negotiable instrument free of all claims and most defenses that can be asserted against the transferor of the instrument. Only *universal defenses*—and not *personal defenses*—may be asserted against an HDC. Thus, an HDC can acquire greater rights than a transferor.

Example John purchases an automobile from Shannen. At the time of sale, Shannen tells John that the car has had only one previous owner and has been driven only 20,000 miles. John, relying on these statements, purchases the car. He pays 10 percent down and signs a promissory note to pay the remainder of the purchase price, with interest, in 12 equal monthly installments. Shannen transfers the note to Patricia. Then John discovers that the car has actually had four previous owners and has been driven 100,000 miles. If Patricia were a holder (but not an HDC) of the note, John could assert Shannen's fraudulent representations against enforcement of the note by Patricia. John could rescind the note and refuse to pay Patricia. Patricia's only recourse would be against Shannen.

Example If in the prior example Patricia qualified as an HDC, the result would be different. John could not assert Shannen's fraudulent conduct against enforcement of the note by Patricia because this type of fraud is a *personal defense* that cannot be raised against an HDC. Therefore, Patricia could enforce the note against John. John's only recourse would be against Shannen, if she could be found.

Requirements for HDC Status

holder in due course (HDC)
A holder who takes a negotiable instrument for value, in good faith, and without notice that it is defective or overdue.

To qualify as a **holder in due course (HDC)**, a transferee must meet the requirements established by the Uniform Commercial Code (UCC): The person must be the *holder* of a negotiable instrument that was taken (1) for value; (2) in good faith; (3) without notice that it is overdue, dishonored, or encumbered in any way; and (4) bearing no apparent evidence of forgery, alterations, or irregularity [UCC 3-302]. These requirements are discussed in the paragraphs that follow. **Exhibit 23.7** illustrates the HDC doctrine.

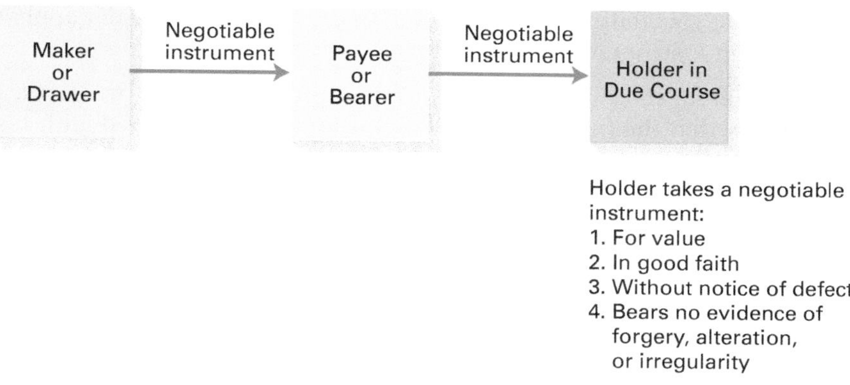

Exhibit 23.7 **HOLDER IN DUE COURSE**

1. Taking for Value

Under the UCC **taking for value requirement**, the holder must have *given value* for the negotiable instrument in order to qualify as an HDC [UCC 3-302(a)(2)(i)].

taking for value requirement
A requirement that says a holder must give value for a negotiable instrument in order to qualify as an HDC.

Example Ted draws a check "payable to the order of Mary Smith" and delivers the check to Mary. Mary indorses it and gives it as a gift to her daughter. Mary's daughter cannot qualify as an HDC because she has not given value for it. The purchaser of a limited interest in a negotiable instrument is an HDC only to the extent of the interest purchased.

Under the UCC, value has been given if the holder does the following [UCC 3-303]:

- Performs the agreed-on promise
- Acquires a security interest in or lien on the instrument
- Takes the instrument in payment of or as security for an antecedent claim
- Gives a negotiable instrument as payment
- Gives an irrevocable obligation as payment

If a person promises to perform but has not yet done so, no value has been given, and that person is not an HDC.

Example Karen executes a note payable to Fred for $3,000 for goods she purchased from him. Fred transfers the note to Amy, who pays $2,500 for the note. Amy has *given value* for the negotiable instrument and therefore meets this qualification for HDC status.

Example Ted draws a check "payable to the order of Mary Smith" and delivers the check to Mary. Mary indorses it and gives it as a gift to her daughter. Mary's daughter cannot qualify as an HDC because she has not given value for it.

2. Taking in Good Faith

Under the UCC **taking in good faith requirement**, a holder must *take* an instrument in *good faith* to qualify as an HDC [UCC 3-302(a)(2)(ii)]. **Good faith** means honesty in fact in the conduct or transaction concerned [UCC 1-201(19)]. *Honesty in fact* is a subjective test that examines the holder's actual belief. A holder's subjective belief can be inferred from the circumstances.

taking in good faith requirement
A UCC requirement that says a holder must take the instrument in good faith in order to qualify as an HDC.

good faith
Honesty in fact in the conduct or transaction concerned. The good faith test is subjective.

Example If a holder acquires an instrument from a stranger under suspicious circumstances and at a deep discount, it could be inferred that the holder did not take the instrument in good faith. A naive person who acquired the same instrument at the same discount, however, may be found to have acted in good faith and thereby qualify as an HDC. Each case must be reviewed individually.

Note that the good faith test applies only to the holder. It does not apply to the transferor of an instrument.

Example A thief steals a negotiable instrument and transfers it to Harry. Harry does not know that the instrument is stolen. Harry meets the good faith test and qualifies as an HDC.

3. Taking Without Notice of Defect

taking without notice of defect requirement
A UCC requirement that says a person cannot qualify as an HDC if he or she has notice that the instrument is defective in certain ways.

Under the UCC **taking without notice of defect requirement**, a person cannot qualify as an HDC if he or she has notice that the instrument is defective in any of the following ways [UCC 3-302(a)(2)]:

- It is overdue.
- It has been dishonored.
- It contains an unauthorized signature or has been altered.
- There is a claim to it by another person.
- There is a defense against it.

time instrument
An instrument that specifies a definite date for payment of the instrument.

Overdue Instruments A **time instrument** is an instrument with an express due date. If a time instrument is not paid on its expressed due date, it becomes overdue the next day. This is called an **overdue time instrument**. When an instrument is not paid when due, there is some defect to its payment.

Example Suppose a promissory note is due June 15, 2020. To qualify as an HDC, a purchaser must acquire the note by 11:59 P.M. June 15, 2020. A purchaser who acquires the note on June 16, 2020, or thereafter, is only a holder and not an HDC.

dishonored instrument
An instrument that is presented for payment and payment is refused.

Dishonored Instruments An instrument is *dishonored* when it is presented for payment and payment is refused. This is called a **dishonored instrument**. A holder who takes such an instrument with notice of its dishonor cannot qualify as an HDC.

Example A person who takes a check that has been marked by the payer bank "payment refused—not sufficient funds" cannot qualify as an HDC.

taking where there is no evidence of forgery, alteration, or irregularity requirement
A requirement that says a holder cannot become an HDC to an instrument that is apparently forged or altered or is so otherwise irregular or incomplete as to call into question its authenticity.

shelter principle
A principle that says a holder who does not qualify as a holder in due course in his or her own right becomes a holder in due course if he or she acquires an instrument through a holder in due course.

4. Taking Where There Is No Evidence of Forgery, Alteration, or Irregularity

The UCC imposes a taking where there is **no evidence of forgery, alteration, or irregularity requirement**. Under this rule, a holder does not qualify as an HDC if at the time the instrument was issued or negotiated to the holder, it bore apparent evidence of forgery or alteration or was otherwise so irregular or incomplete as to call into question its authenticity [UCC 3-302(a)(1)].

Clever and undetectable forgeries and alterations are not classified as obvious irregularities. Determining whether a forgery or an alteration is apparent and whether the instrument is so irregular or incomplete that its authenticity should be questioned are issues of fact that must be decided on a case-by-case basis.

The following feature discusses a special UCC rule.

Contemporary Environment

Shelter Principle

A holder who does not qualify as a holder in due course in his or her own right becomes a holder in due course if he or she acquires the instrument through a holder in due course. This is called the **shelter principle**.

Example Jason buys a used car from Debbie. He pays 10 percent down and signs a negotiable promissory note, promising to pay Debbie the remainder of the purchase price, with interest, in 36 equal monthly installments.

At the time of sale, Debbie materially misrepresented the mileage of the automobile. Later, Debbie negotiates the note to Eric, who has no notice of the misrepresentation. Eric, an HDC, negotiates the note to Jaime. Assume that Jaime does not qualify as an HDC in her own right. She becomes an HDC, however, because she acquired the note through an HDC (Eric). Jaime can enforce the note against Jason.

Key Terms and Concepts

Allonge (487)
Assignee (484)
Assignment (484)
Assignor (484)
Bearer instrument (bearer paper) (485)
Blank indorsement (487)
Dishonored instrument (494)
Good faith (493)
Holder (492)
Holder in due course (HDC) (492)
Indorsee (487)
Indorsement (487)
Indorsement for deposit or collection (490)
Indorsement in trust (agency indorsement) (490)
Indorser (487)
Negotiation (484)
Nonnegotiable contract (484)
Nonrestrictive indorsement (489)
Order instrument (order paper) (485)
Overdue time instrument (494)
Payable in the alternative (492)
Payable jointly (491)
Qualified indorsement (489)
Qualified indorser (489)
Restrictive indorsement (489)
Shelter principle (494)
Special indorsement (488)
Taking for value requirement (493)
Taking in good faith requirement (493)
Taking where there is no evidence of forgery, alteration, or irregularity requirement (494)
Taking without notice of defect requirement (494)
Time instrument (494)
Unqualified indorsement (489)
Unqualified indorser (489)
Virgule (492)

Critical Legal Thinking Cases

23.1 Payable Jointly Murray Walter, Inc. (Walter, Inc.) was a general contractor for the construction of a waste treatment plant in New Hampshire. Walter, Inc., contracted with H. Johnson Electric, Inc. (Johnson Electric), to install the electrical system in the treatment plant. Johnson Electric purchased its supplies for the project from General Electric Supply (G.E. Supply). Walter, Inc., issued a check payable to "Johnson Electric and G.E. Supply" in the amount of $54,900, drawn on its account at Marine Midland Bank (Marine Midland). Walter, Inc., made the check payable to both the subcontractor and its material supplier, to be certain that the supplier was paid by Johnson Electric. Despite this precautionary measure, Johnson Electric negotiated the check without G.E. Supply's indorsement, and the check was paid by Marine Midland. Johnson Electric never paid G.E. Supply. G.E. Supply then demanded payment from Walter, Inc. When Walter, Inc. learned that Marine Midland had paid the check without G.E. Supply's indorsement, it demanded to be reimbursed. When Marine Midland refused, Walter, Inc., sued Marine Midland to recover for the check. Was Johnson Electric's indorsement sufficient to legally negotiate the check to Marine Midland Bank? *Murray Walter, Inc. v. Marine Midland Bank*, 103 A.D.2d 466, 480 N.Y.S.2d 631, 1984 N.Y. App. Div. Lexis 19962 (Supreme Court of New York)

23.2 Assignment FFP Operating Partners, L.P. (FFP Operating) operates a number of convenience stores and gas stations. FFP Operating executed 31 promissory notes in favor of Franchise Mortgage Acceptance Company (FMAC). In connection with the notes, FFP Marketing Company, Inc. (FFP Marketing), executed guaranties of payment in favor of FMAC for all 31 notes. Loan and security agreements were also executed in connection with all 31 transactions. The promissory notes incorporated by reference the loan, security, and guaranty agreements, which included waivers, consents, and acknowledgments. Long Lane Master Trust IV (LLMT) became a successor in interest to FMAC with respect to the promissory notes, guaranties, and associated loan documents.

FFP Operating failed to make payments on the notes to LLMT. LLMT gave notice to FFP Operating of the default, accelerated the obligations under the promissory notes, and demanded payment. The notes went unpaid. The outstanding principal of the notes was $13,212,199, with unpaid interest of $1,488,899. LLMT filed suit against FFP Operating and FFP Marketing. LLMT filed a motion for summary judgment on its claim of default under the 31 promissory notes and guaranties for the amount due. FFP Operating declared bankruptcy and was dismissed from this case. The trial court entered summary judgment in favor of LLMT against FFP Marketing. FFP Marketing appealed.

Why does LLMT want the notes to be found to be negotiable instruments? Are the 31 promissory notes negotiable instruments that can be enforced against FFP Marketing? *FFP Marketing Company, Inc. v. Long Lane Master Trust IV*, 169 S.W.3d 402, 2005 Tex. App. Lexis 5277 (Court of Appeals of Texas, 2005)

Ethical

Ethics Case

23.3 Ethics Case Samuel C. Mazilly wrote a personal check that was drawn on Calcasieu-Marine National Bank of Lake Charles, Inc. (CMN Bank). The check was made payable to the order of Lee St. Mary and was delivered to him. St. Mary indorsed the check in blank and delivered it to Leland H. Coltharp Sr. in payment for some livestock. Coltharp accepted the check and took it to the City Savings Bank & Trust Company (City Savings) to deposit it. He indorsed the check as follows: "Pay to the order of City Savings Bank & Trust Company, DeRidder, Louisiana." City Savings accepted the check and forwarded it to CMN Bank for payment. The check never arrived at CMN Bank. Some unknown person stole the check while it was in transit and presented it directly to CMN Bank for payment. The teller at CMN Bank cashed the check without indorsement of the person who presented it. When CMN Bank accepts the check, is it order or bearer paper? Has the person cashing the check acted unethically and has he acted illegally? *Caltharp v. Calcasieu-Marine National Bank of Lake Charles, Inc.*, 199 So.2d 568, 1967 La. App. Lexis 5203 (Court of Appeal of Louisiana)

Liability, Defenses, and Discharge

HONG KONG
Hong Kong is one of the world's greatest banking centers. Hong Kong is home to large domestic banks and offices of foreign banks from around the world. Banks in Hong Kong provide a wide range of financial services, including retail banking, deposit taking, trade financing, interbank wholesale transfer, and foreign exchange.

Learning Objectives

After studying this chapter, you should be able to:

1. Describe the signature liability of makers, drawers, drawees, acceptors, and accommodation parties for negotiable instruments.
2. List the transfer and presentment warranties and describe the liability of parties breaching them.
3. Identify the universal (real) defenses that can be asserted against a holder in due course.
4. Describe the Federal Trade Commission rule that limits holder in due course status in consumer transactions.
5. Describe how parties are discharged from liability on negotiable instruments.

Chapter Outline

"If one wants to know the real value of money, he needs but to borrow some from his friends."

—*Confucius*
Analects (ca. 500 BCE)

Introduction to Liability, Defenses, and Discharge

If payment is not made on a negotiable instrument when it is due, the holder can use the court system to enforce the instrument. Various parties, including both signers and nonsigners, may be liable on it. Some parties are primarily liable on the instrument, while others are secondarily liable. Accommodation parties (i.e., guarantors) can also be held liable.

Once a holder qualifies as a holder in due course (HDC), the HDC takes an instrument free of most defenses that can be asserted against other parties. However, several defenses, called *universal defenses*, can be raised against the payment of the instrument to the HDC. The Uniform Commercial Code (UCC) also specifies when and how certain parties are discharged from liability on negotiable instruments.

This chapter discusses the liability of parties to pay a negotiable instrument, the defenses that can be raised against an HDC, and the discharge of liability on a negotiable instrument.

Signature Liability for Negotiable Instruments

A person cannot be held contractually liable on a negotiable instrument unless his or her signature appears on it [UCC 3-401(a)]. Therefore, this type of liability is often referred to as **signature liability**, or **contract liability**. A signature on a negotiable instrument identifies who is obligated to pay it. The signature on a negotiable instrument can be any name, word, or mark used in lieu of a written signature [UCC 3-401(b)].

signature liability (contract liability)
Liability in which a person cannot be held contractually liable on a negotiable instrument unless his or her signature appears on the instrument.

Signers of instruments sign in many different capacities: as makers of notes or certificates of deposit, drawers of drafts or checks, drawees who certify or accept checks or drafts, indorsers who indorse instruments, agents who sign on behalf of others, and accommodation parties. The location of the signature on an instrument generally determines the signer's capacity.

signer
A person signing an instrument who acts in the capacity of (1) a maker of notes or certificates of deposit, (2) a drawer of drafts or checks, (3) a drawee who certifies or accepts checks or drafts, (4) an indorser who indorses an instrument, (5) an agent who signs on behalf of others, or (6) an accommodation party.

Examples A signature in the lower-right corner of a check indicates that the signer is the drawer of the check. A signature in the lower-right corner of a promissory note indicates that the signer is the maker of the note. The signature of the drawee named in a draft on the face of the draft or another location on the draft indicates that the signer is an acceptor of the draft.

Most indorsements appear on the back or reverse side of an instrument. Unless an instrument clearly indicates that such a signature is made in some other capacity (e.g., agents who properly sign the instrument), it is presumed to be that of the indorser. Every party that signs a negotiable instrument (except qualified indorsers and agents who properly sign the instrument) is either primarily or secondarily liable on the instrument.

Signature Defined

The **signature** on a negotiable instrument can be any name, word, or mark used in lieu of a written signature [UCC 3-401(b)]. In other words, a signature is any symbol that is (1) handwritten, typed, printed, stamped, or made in almost any other manner and (2) executed or adopted by a party to authenticate a writing [UCC 1-201(39)]. This rule permits trade names and other assumed names to be used as signatures on negotiable instruments.

signature
Any name, word, or mark used in lieu of a written signature; any symbol that is (1) handwritten, typed, printed, stamped, or made in almost any other manner and (2) executed or adopted by a party to authenticate a writing.

The unauthorized signature of a person on an instrument is ineffective as that person's signature. It is effective as the signature of the unauthorized signer in favor of an HDC, however. A person who forges a signature on a check may be held liable to an HDC. An unauthorized signature may be ratified [UCC 3-403(a)].

Primary Liability for Negotiable Instruments

Makers of promissory notes and certificates of deposit have **primary liability** for the instruments. On signing a promissory note, the maker unconditionally promises to pay the amount stipulated in the note when it is due. A maker is absolutely liable to pay the instrument, subject only to certain universal (real) defenses. The holder need not take any action to give rise to this obligation. Generally, the maker is obligated to pay a note according to its original terms. If the note was incomplete when it was issued, the maker is obligated to pay the note as completed, as long as he or she authorized the terms as they were filled in [UCC 3-412].

primary liability
Absolute liability to pay a negotiable instrument, subject to certain universal (real) defenses.

A draft or a check is an order from a drawer to pay the instrument to a payee (or other holder) according to its terms. No party is primarily liable when the draft or check is issued because such instruments are merely orders to pay. Thus, a drawee that refuses to pay a draft or a check is not liable to the payee or holder. If there has been a wrongful dishonor of the instrument, the drawee may be liable to the drawer for certain damages.

On occasion, a drawee is requested to accept a draft or check. Acceptance of a draft occurs when the drawee writes the word *accepted* across the face of the draft. The acceptor—that is, the drawee—is primarily liable on the instrument. A check, which is a special form of draft, is accepted when it is certified by a bank. The bank's certification discharges the drawer and all prior indorsers from liability on the check. Note that the bank may choose to refuse to certify the check without liability. The issuer of a cashier's check is also primarily liable on the instrument [UCC 3-411].

The great source of the flourishing state of this kingdom is its trade, and commerce, and paper currency, guarded by proper regulations and restrictions, is the life of commerce.

Justice Ashhurst
Jordaine v. Lashbrooke (1798)

Secondary Liability for Negotiable Instruments

Under the UCC's *indorsers' liability* rules, drawers of checks and drafts and unqualified indorsers of negotiable instruments have **secondary liability** on the instruments. This liability is similar to that of a guarantor of a simple contract. It arises when the party primarily liable on the instrument defaults and fails to pay the instrument when due.

secondary liability
Liability on a negotiable instrument that is imposed on a party only when the party primarily liable on the instrument defaults and fails to pay the instrument when due.

If an unaccepted draft or check is dishonored by the drawee or acceptor, the drawer is obliged to pay it according to its terms, either when it is issued or, if incomplete when issued, when it is properly completed [UCC 3-414(a)].

Example Elliot draws a check on his checking account at City Bank "payable to the order of Phyllis Jones." When Phyllis presents the check for payment, City Bank refuses to pay it. Phyllis can collect the amount of the check from Elliot because Elliot—the drawer—is secondarily liable on the check when it is dishonored.

Unqualified Indorser

An **unqualified indorser** has secondary liability on negotiable instruments. In other words, he or she must pay any dishonored instrument to the holder or to any subsequent indorser according to its terms, when issued or properly completed. Unless otherwise agreed, indorsers are liable to each other in the order in which they indorsed the instrument [UCC 3-415(a)].

unqualified indorsers
Those who are secondarily liable on negotiable instruments they endorse.

Example Dara borrows $10,000 from Todd and signs a promissory note, promising to pay Todd this amount plus 10 percent interest in one year. Todd indorses the note and negotiates it to Frank. Frank indorses the note and negotiates it to Linda. Linda presents the note to Dara for payment when the note is due. Dara refuses to pay the note. Because Frank became secondarily liable on the note when he indorsed it to Linda, he must pay the amount of the note—$11,000—to Linda. Frank can then require Todd to pay the note to Frank because Todd (as payee) became secondarily liable on the note when he indorsed it to Frank. Todd can then enforce the note against Dara. Linda could have skipped over Frank and required the payee, Todd, to pay the note. In this instance, Frank would have been relieved of any further liability because he indorsed the instrument after the payee.

Qualified Indorser

qualified indorser
One who disclaims liability and is not secondarily liable on instruments they endorse.

A **qualified indorser** (i.e., an indorser who indorses instruments "without recourse" or similar language that disclaims liability) is not secondarily liable on an instrument because he or she has expressly disclaimed liability [UCC 3-415(b)]. The drawer can disclaim all liability on a draft (but not a check) by drawing the instrument "without recourse." In this instance, the drawer becomes a qualified drawer [UCC 3-414(e)]. Many payees, however, will not accept a draft or check that has been drawn without recourse.

Requirements for Imposing Secondary Liability

A party is secondarily liable on a negotiable instrument only if the following requirements are met:

presentment
A demand for acceptance or payment of an instrument made on the maker, acceptor, drawee, or other payer by or on behalf of the holder.

- **The instrument is properly presented for payment. Presentment** is a demand for acceptance or payment of an instrument made on the maker, acceptor, drawee, or other payer by or on behalf of the holder. Presentment may be made by any commercially reasonable means, including oral, written, or electronic communication. Presentment is effective when it is received by the person to whom presentment is made [UCC 3-501].
- **The instrument is dishonored.** An instrument is a **dishonored instrument** when acceptance or payment of the instrument is refused or cannot be obtained from the party required to accept or pay the instrument within the prescribed time after presentment is duly made [UCC 3-502].
- **Notice of the dishonor is timely given to the person to be held secondarily liable on the instrument.** A secondarily liable party cannot be compelled to accept or pay an instrument unless proper **notice of dishonor** has been given. Notice may be given by any commercially reasonable means. The notice must reasonably identify the instrument and indicate that it has been dishonored. Return of an instrument given to a bank for collection is sufficient notice of dishonor. Banks must give notice of dishonor before midnight of the next banking day following the day that presentment is made. Others must give notice of dishonor within 30 days following the day on which the person receives notice of dishonor [UCC 3-503].

notice of dishonor
The formal act of letting the party with secondary liability to pay a negotiable instrument know that the instrument has been dishonored.

Liability of an Accommodation Party

accommodation party
A party who signs an instrument and lends his or her name (and credit) to another party to the instrument.

A party who signs an instrument for the purpose of lending his or her name (and credit) to another party to the instrument is the **accommodation party**. The accommodation party, who may sign an instrument as maker, drawer, acceptor, or indorser, is obliged to *pay* the instrument in the capacity in which he or she signs [UCC 3-419(a),(b)]. An accommodation party who pays an instrument can recover reimbursement from the accommodated party and enforce the instrument against him or her [UCC 3-419(e)].

There are two types of liability of an accommodation party:

guarantee of payment
A form of accommodation in which the accommodation party guarantees *payment* of a negotiable instrument; the accommodation party is *primarily liable* on the instrument.

1. **Guarantee of payment.** An accommodation party who signs an instrument **guaranteeing payment** is *primarily liable* on the instrument. This party is

called an **accommodation maker**. That is, the debtor can seek payment on the instrument directly from the accommodation maker without first seeking payment from the maker.

Example Sonny, a college student, wants to purchase an automobile on credit from ABC Motors. He does not have a sufficient income or credit history to justify the extension of credit to him alone. Sonny asks his mother to cosign the note to ABC Motors, which she does. Sonny's mother is an accommodation maker and is primarily liable on the note.

2. **Guarantee of collection.** An accommodation party may sign an instrument **guaranteeing collection** rather than guaranteeing payment of an instrument. This party is called an **accommodation indorser**. In this situation, the accommodation indorser is only *secondarily liable* on the instrument. To reserve this type of liability, the signature of the accommodation party must be accompanied by words indicating that he or she is guaranteeing collection rather than payment of the obligation. An accommodation party who guarantees collection is obliged to pay the instrument only if (1) execution of judgment against the other party has been returned unsatisfied, (2) the other party is insolvent or in an insolvency proceeding, (3) the other party cannot be served with process, or (4) it is otherwise apparent that payment cannot be obtained from the other party [UCC 3-419(d)].

guarantee of collection
A form of accommodation in which the accommodation party guarantees *collection* of a negotiable instrument; the accommodation party is *secondarily liable* on the instrument.

CONCEPT SUMMARY

LIABILITY OF ACCOMODATION MAKER AND ACCOMODATION INDORSER COMPARED

Accommodation Party	Contract Liability
Accommodation maker	Primarily liable on the instrument
Accommodation indorser	Secondarily liable on the instrument

Agent's Signature

A person may either sign a negotiable instrument him- or herself or authorize a representative to sign the instrument on his or her behalf [UCC 3-401(a)]. The representative is the **agent**, and the represented person is the **principal**. The authority of an agent to sign an instrument is established under general agency law. No special form of appointment is necessary. If an authorized agent signs an instrument with either the principal's name or the agent's own name, the principal is bound as if the signature were made on a simple contract. It does not matter whether the principal is identified in the instrument [UCC 3-402(2)].

agent
A person who has been authorized to sign a negotiable instrument on behalf of another person.

principal
A person who authorizes an agent to sign a negotiable instrument on his or her behalf.

Example Suppose Anderson is the agent for Puttkammer. The following signatures on a negotiable instrument would bind Puttkammer on the instrument:

1. Puttkammer, by Anderson, agent
2. Puttkammer
3. Puttkammer, Anderson
4. Anderson

An authorized agent's personal liability on an instrument he or she signs on behalf of a principal depends on the information disclosed in the signature. The agent has no liability if the signature shows unambiguously that it is made on behalf of a principal who is identified in the instrument [UCC 3-402(b)(1)].

Example Signature number 1 ("Puttkammer, by Anderson, agent") satisfies this requirement.

If an authorized agent's signature does not show unambiguously that the signature was made in a representative capacity and the agent cannot prove that the original parties did not intend him or her to be liable, the agent is liable (1) to an HDC who took the instrument without notice that the agent was not intended to be liable on the instrument and (2) to any other person other than an HDC [UCC 3-402(b)(2)].

Examples Signature number 2 ("Puttkammer") does not show unambiguously that the signature was made in a representative capacity. Signatures number 3 ("Puttkammer, Anderson") and 4 ("Anderson") place the agent at risk of personal liability to an HDC that does not have notice that the agent was not intended to be liable on the instrument. To avoid liability to a non-HDC for these signatures, the agent would have to prove that the third-party non-HDC did not intend to hold the agent liable on the instrument.

There is one exception to these rules: If an agent signs his or her name as the drawer of a check without indicating the agent's representative status and the check is payable from the account of the principal who is identified on the check, the agent is not liable on the check [UCC 3-402(c)].

Unauthorized Signature

unauthorized signature
A signature made by a purported agent without authority from the purported principal.

An **unauthorized signature** is a signature made by a purported agent without authority from the purported principal. Such a signature arises if (1) a person signs a negotiable instrument on behalf of a person for whom he or she is not an agent or (2) an authorized agent exceeds the scope of his or her authority. An unauthorized signature by a purported agent does not act as the signature of the purported principal. The purported agent is liable to any person who in good faith pays the instrument or takes it for value [UCC 3-403(a)]. The purported principal is liable if he or she ratifies the unauthorized signature [UCC 3-403(a)].

Example Max, a purported agent, signs a contract and promissory note to purchase a building for ViVi, a purported principal. Suppose that ViVi, the purported principal, likes the deal and accepts it. ViVi has ratified the transaction and is liable on the note.

Forged Indorsements

forged indorsement
The forged signature of a payee or holder on a negotiable instrument.

Article 3 of the UCC establishes certain rules for assessing liability when a negotiable instrument has been paid over a **forged indorsement**. Generally, an unauthorized indorsement is wholly inoperative as the indorsement of the person whose name is signed [UCC 3-401(a)]. Where an indorsement on an instrument has been forged or is unauthorized, the loss falls on the party who first takes the forged instrument after the forgery.

imposter rule
A rule that states that if an imposter forges the indorsement of the named payee, the drawer or maker is liable on the instrument to any person who, in good faith, pays the instrument or takes it for value or for collection.

Example Andy draws a check payable to the order of Mallory. Leslie steals the check from Mallory, forges Mallory's indorsement, and cashes the check at a liquor store. The liquor store is liable. Andy, the drawer, is not. The liquor store can recover from Leslie, the forger (if she can be found).

There are two exceptions to this general rule: the (1) *imposter rule* and (2) *fictitious payee rule*. These rules are discussed in the following two ethics features.

Ethics

Imposter Rule

An *imposter* is someone who impersonates a payee and induces the maker or drawer to issue an instrument in the payee's name and give the instrument to the imposter. If the imposter forges the indorsement of the named payee, the drawer or maker is liable on the instrument to any person who, in good faith, pays the instrument or takes it for value or for collection [UCC 3-404(a)]. This rule is called the **imposter rule**.

Example Fred purchases goods by telephone from Cynthia. Fred has never met Cynthia. Beverly goes to Fred and pretends to be Cynthia. Fred draws a check payable to the order of Cynthia and gives the check to Beverly, believing her to be Cynthia. Beverly forges Cynthia's indorsement and cashes the check at a liquor store. Under the imposter rule, Fred is liable and the liquor store is not because Fred was in the best position to have prevented the forged indorsement.

Ethics Questions Does an imposter act ethically? What is the public policy underlying the imposter rule?

Ethics

Fictitious Payee Rule

A drawer or maker is liable on a forged or unauthorized indorsement under the **fictitious payee rule**. This rule applies when a person signing as or on behalf of a drawer or maker intends the named payee to have no interest in the instrument or when the person identified as the payee is a fictitious person [UCC 3-404(b)].

Example Marcia is the treasurer of Weld Corporation. As treasurer, Marcia makes out and signs the payroll checks for the company. Marcia draws a payroll check payable to the order of her neighbor Harold Green, who does not work for the company. Marcia does not intend Harold to receive this money. She indorses Harold's name on the check and names herself as the indorsee. She cashes the check at a liquor store. Under the fictitious payee rule, Weld Corporation is liable because it was in a better position than the liquor store to have prevented the fraud.

Ethics Questions Does a fictitious payee act ethically? What is the public policy underlying the fictitious payee rule?

Warranty Liability for Negotiable Instruments

In addition to signature liability, transferors can be held liable for breaching certain **implied warranties** when negotiating instruments. **Warranty liability** is imposed whether or not the transferor signed the instrument. Note that a transferor makes an implied warranty; implied warranties are not made when a negotiable instrument is originally issued.

There are two types of implied warranties: *transfer warranties* and *presentment warranties*. Transfer and presentment warranties shift the risk of loss to the party who was in the best position to prevent the loss. This party is usually the one who dealt face-to-face with the wrongdoer. These implied warranties are discussed in the paragraphs that follow.

fictitious payee rule
A rule that states that a drawer or maker is liable on a forged or unauthorized indorsement if the person signing as or on behalf of a drawer or maker intends the named payee to have no interest in the instrument or when the person identified as the payee is a fictitious person.

implied warranties
Certain warranties that the law implies on transferors of negotiable instruments. There are two types of implied warranties: transfer and presentment warranties.

transfer
Any passage of an instrument other than its issuance and presentment for payment.

Transfer Warranties

Any passage of an instrument other than its issuance and presentment for payment is considered a **transfer**. Any person who transfers a negotiable instrument for consideration makes the following five **transfer warranties** to the transferee. If the transfer is by indorsement, the transferor also makes these warranties to any subsequent transferee [UCC 3-416(a)]:

1. The transferor has good title to the instrument or is authorized to obtain payment or acceptance on behalf of one who does have good title.

transfer warranties
The following five implied warranties made by any person who transfers a negotiable instrument for consideration to a transferee who took the instrument in good faith: (1) The transferor has good title to the instrument or is authorized to obtain payment or acceptance on behalf of one who does have good title, (2) all signatures are genuine or authorized, (3) the instrument has not been materially altered, (4) no defenses of any party are good against the transferor, and (5) the transferor has no knowledge of any insolvency proceeding against the maker, the acceptor, or the drawer of an unaccepted instrument.

2. All signatures are genuine or authorized.
3. The instrument has not been materially altered.
4. No defenses of any party are good against the transferor.
5. The transferor has no knowledge of any insolvency proceeding against the maker, the acceptor, or the drawer of an unaccepted instrument.

Transfer warranties cannot be disclaimed with respect to checks, but they can be disclaimed with respect to other instruments. An indorsement that states "without recourse" disclaims the transfer warranties [UCC 3-419(c)]. A transferee who took the instrument in good faith may recover damages for breach of transfer warranty from the warrantor equal to the loss suffered. The amount recovered cannot exceed the amount of the instrument plus expenses and interest [UCC 3-416(b)].

Example Jill signs a promissory note to pay $1,000 to Adam. Adam cleverly raises the note to $10,000 and negotiates the note to Nick. Nick indorses the note and negotiates it to Matthew. When Matthew presents the note to Jill for payment, she has to pay only the original amount of the note, $1,000. Matthew can collect the remainder of the note ($9,000) from Nick, based on a breach of the transfer warranty. If Nick is lucky, he can recover the $9,000 from Adam.

Presentment Warranties

presentment warranties
Three implied warranties that a person who presents a draft or check for payment or acceptance makes to a drawee or an acceptor who pays or accepts the instrument in good faith: (1) The presenter has good title to the instrument or is authorized to obtain payment or acceptance of the person who has good title, (2) the instrument has not been materially altered, and (3) the presenter has no knowledge that the signature of the maker or drawer is unauthorized.

Any person who presents a draft or check for payment or acceptance makes the following **presentment warranties** to a drawee or an acceptor who pays or accepts the instrument in good faith [UCC 3-417(a)]:

1. The presenter has good title to the instrument or is authorized to obtain payment or acceptance of the person who has good title.
2. The instrument has not been materially altered.
3. The presenter has no knowledge that the signature of the maker or drawer is unauthorized.

A drawee who pays an instrument may recover damages for breach of presentment warranty from the warrantor. The amount that can be recovered is limited to the amount paid by the drawee less the amount the drawee received or is entitled to receive from the drawer because of the payment plus expenses and interest [UCC 3-147(b)].

Example Maureen draws a $1,000 check on City Bank "payable to the order of Paul." Paul cleverly raises the check to $10,000 and indorses and negotiates the check to Neal. Neal presents the check for payment to City Bank. As the presenter of the check, Neal makes the presentment warranties of UCC 3-417(a) to City Bank. City Bank pays the check as altered ($10,000) and debits Maureen's account. When Maureen discovers the alteration, she demands that the bank recredit her account, which the bank does. City Bank can recover against the presenter (Neal), based on breach of the presentment warranty that the instrument was not altered when it was presented. Neal can recover against the wrongdoer (Paul), based on breach of the transfer warranty that the instrument was not altered.

Defenses to Payment of Negotiable Instruments

The creation of negotiable instruments may give rise to defenses against their payment. Many of these defenses arise from the underlying transactions. There are two general types of defenses: (1) *universal (real) defenses* and (2) *personal defenses*. A **holder in due course (HDC)** (or a holder through an HDC) takes an instrument free from personal defenses but not universal defenses. Personal and universal defenses can be raised against a normal **holder** of a negotiable instrument. Universal defenses and personal defenses are discussed in the following paragraphs.

Universal (Real) Defenses

Universal defenses (also called **real defenses**) can be raised against both ordinary *holders* and *holders in due course (HDCs)* to deny the payment of negotiable instruments [UCC 3-305(b)]. If a universal defense is proven, the holder or HDC cannot recover on the negotiable instrument. The most important universal defenses are the following:

universal defense (real defense)
A defense that can be raised against both holders and HDCs.

1. **Minority.** A **minor** who does not misrepresent his or her age can disaffirm negotiable instruments that he or she has issued if state law permits the minor to disaffirm simple contracts under the **infancy doctrine** [UCC 3-305(a)(1)(i)].
2. **Extreme duress.** **Extreme duress** requires force or violence. If extreme duress was used to have a negotiable instrument issued (e.g., a promissory note was signed at gunpoint), then it is unenforceable [UCC 3-305(a)(1)(ii)]. (Ordinary duress is a personal defense.)
3. **Mental incapacity.** A person **adjudicated mentally incompetent** by a court or other appropriate government agency cannot issue a negotiable instrument; the instrument is *void* and therefore unenforceable from its inception [UCC 3-305(a)(1)(ii)]. (Nonadjudicated mental incompetence is a personal defense.)
4. **Illegality.** If an instrument arises out of an **illegal transaction**, it is unenforceable if the law declares the instrument void [UCC 3-305(a)(1)(ii)].

   Example Assume that a state's law declares gambling to be illegal and gambling contracts to be void. Gordon wins $5,000 from Jerry in an illegal poker game. Jerry, who does not have cash to immediately cover his debt, signs a promissory note promising to pay Gordon this amount plus 10 percent interest in 30 days. Gordon negotiates this note to Dawn, an HDC. When Dawn presents the note to Jerry for payment, Jerry can raises the universal defense of illegality against the enforcement of the note by Dawn. Dawn's only recourse is against Gordon.

Critical Legal Thinking

What is a universal (real) defense? What are the consequences to a holder in due course (HDC) if a universal defense is proven? Can HDCs protect themselves from universal defenses?

5. **Discharge in bankruptcy.** Bankruptcy law is designed to relieve debtors of burdensome debts, including paying negotiable instruments. Negotiable instruments **discharged in bankruptcy** are thereafter unenforceable [UCC 3-305(a)(1)(iv)].
6. **Fraud in the inception.** If a person is deceived into signing a negotiable instrument, thinking that it is something else, this is **fraud in the inception** (also called **fraud in the factum** or **fraud in the execution**). An instrument obtained by fraud in the inception is unenforceable [UCC 3-305(a)(1)(iii)].
7. **Forgery.** **Forgery** occurs where a party places the unauthorized signature of a maker, a drawer, or an indorser on an instrument. Because the signature is wholly inoperative as that of the person whose name is signed, the instrument is unenforceable [UCC 3-403(a)]. A forged signature operates as the signature of the forger, who is liable on the instrument.
8. **Material alteration.** **Material alteration** consists of adding to any part of a signed instrument, removing any part of a signed instrument, or making changes to the dollar amount of the instrument. An instrument that has been fraudulently and materially altered cannot be enforced by an ordinary holder. HDCs cannot enforce such an instrument if the alteration is apparent or obvious [UCC 3-407(b)].

One cannot help regretting that where money is concerned it is too much the rule to overlook moral obligations.

Vice Chancellor Malins
Ellis v. Houston (1878)

Personal Defenses

Personal defenses can be raised against *ordinary holders* to deny the payment of negotiable instruments [UCC 3-305(b)]. Thus, if a personal defense is proven, the holder cannot recover on the negotiable instrument. However, personal defenses

personal defense
A defense that can be raised against enforcement of a negotiable instrument by an ordinary holder but not against an HDC.

cannot be raised against *HDCs* to deny the payment of negotiable instruments [UCC 3-305(b)]. Thus, even if a personal defense is proven, the HDC can still recover on the negotiable instrument. The most important personal defenses are the following:

1. **Breach of contract.** If a negotiable instrument arises from a transaction where there has been a **breach of contract**, the negotiable instrument is unenforceable by a holder but is enforceable by an HDC.

   Example Brian purchases a used car from Karen and signs a promissory note promising to pay Karen the purchase price plus interest over three years. Karen, the seller, warrants that the car is in perfect working condition. A month later, the car's engine's fails; the cost of repair is $5,000. Brian can raise the defense of breach of contract against Karen's attempt to enforce the negotiable instrument against him. However, if Karen negotiated the promissory note to Max, an HDC, Brian could not raise Karen's breach of warranty against Max, and Brian would have to pay the amount of the promissory note to Max. Brian's only recourse then would be to seek recovery for breach of warranty against Karen.

Critical Legal Thinking

What is a personal defense? What are the consequences to a holder in due course (HDC) if a personal defense is proven? Compare this to the consequence of finding a universal defense.

2. **Fraud in the inducement.** **Fraud in the inducement** occurs when a wrongdoer makes a false statement to another person to lead that person to enter into a contract with the wrongdoer and issue a negotiable instrument. Fraud in the inducement makes a negotiable instrument unenforceable by an ordinary holder but enforceable by an HDC.

   Example Heather represents to potential investors that if they give her money she will invest it for them and pay them interest on their investment. Heather, however, plans to use the money for her personal means. John draws a $50,000 check payable to Heather. John learns of Heather's plan and stops payment on the check. Here, Heather is only a holder, so John can raise the defense of fraud in the inception and not pay the check. However, if Heather negotiated the check to Max, an HDC, John could not raise Heather's fraud in the inception against Max, and John would have to pay the amount of the check to Max. John's only recourse then would be to seek recovery against Heather.

3. **Mental illness that makes a contract voidable instead of void.** If mental illness is found that makes a contract *voidable* rather than void—because the drawer or maker is mentally ill but has not been adjudicated mentally ill (**nonadjudicated mentally incompetent**)—then the negotiable instrument is unenforceable by a holder but is enforceable by an HDC.
4. **Illegality of a contract that makes the contract voidable instead of void.** If a contract is found to be illegal but the illegality makes the contract only *voidable* rather than void, then the negotiable instrument is unenforceable by a holder but is enforceable by an HDC.
5. **Ordinary duress or undue influence.** If a person is wrongfully influenced or threatened to enter into a negotiable instrument but the pressure is only **ordinary duress or undue influence** and does not amount to extreme duress, it is unenforceable by a holder but is enforceable by an HDC [UCC 3-305(a)(1)(ii)].
6. **Discharge of an instrument by payment or cancellation.** If an instrument is discharged by payment or cancellation, it is unenforceable by a holder but is enforceable by an HDC.

In the following case, the court had to decide if a defense could be asserted against an HDC.

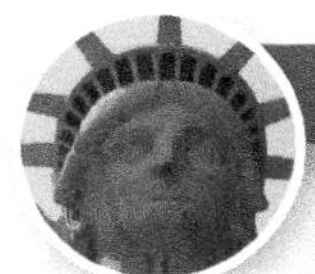

CASE 24.1 FEDERAL COURT CASE Holder in Due Course

Bank of Colorado v. Berwick

2011 U.S. Dist. Lexis 34373 (2011)
United States District Court for the District of Colorado

"The Court finds that Las Vegas Sands was a holder in due course."

—Arguello, District Judge

Facts

Ron Bryant wanted money to obtain promotional premiums from the Venetian Resort Hotel Casino located in Las Vegas, Nevada. The Venetian is owned by Las Vegas Sands, LLC (Sands). James Berwick agreed to supply the funds to Bryant in return for a promise by Bryant to repay Berwick the next day. On October 29, 2008, Berwick purchased a cashier's check (check) in the amount of $250,000 from Bank of Colorado made payable to Ron Bryant. Thus, Bank of Colorado held $250,000 of Berwick's money until the check was presented for payment, at which time it would pay the check. Berwick transferred the check to Bryant.

The next day, October 30, Bryant presented the check to the Sands, who paid him the $250,000 value of the check. On the following day, October 31, Bryant did not repay Berwick the $250,000. On November 3, unbeknownst to the Sands, Berwick stopped payment on the check, alleging to Bank of Colorado that the check had been lost. Berwick knew that the check had not been lost. Berwick filed a police report with the Las Vegas Metro Police Department stating that Bryant had misappropriated the $250,000.

On November 8, the Sands deposited the check at its bank, but when the check was presented to the Bank of Colorado for payment, it refused to pay the check because of Berwick's stop-payment order. In a lawsuit in the U.S. district court, both Berwick and the Sands claimed the right to be paid the funds. The Bank of Colorado agreed to hold the funds until the court determined whom the funds should be paid. The Sands alleged that it was a holder in due course and that Bryant's fraud on Berwick was fraud in the inducement, a personal defense that could not be raised against an HDC. Berwick claimed that he was due the funds because of his stop-payment order.

Issue

Is Sands an HDC against whom the personal defense of fraud in the inducement cannot be raised?

Language of the Court

The Court finds that Las Vegas Sands was a holder in due course. The Court finds that Las Vegas Sands is entitled to the amount of the check because it received the check in good faith and for value, without knowledge of Bryant's alleged fraudulent scheme against Berwick. Therefore, the loss must fall on Berwick; his recourse is against Bryant, who defrauded him.

Decision

The U.S. district court held that Las Vegas Sands was a holder in due course and that Bryant's fraud on Berwick was fraud in the inducement, a personal defense that could not be raised against an HDC.

Ethics Questions

Did Bryant act ethically? Did Berwick act ethically in trying to place his loss on the Sands?

The following feature discusses a federal consumer protection rule that affects negotiable instruments.

Contemporary Environment

FTC Rule Limits HDC Status in Consumer Transactions

In certain situations, the HDC rule can cause a hardship for consumers who sign negotiable instruments, usually promissory notes, in conjunction with the purchase of goods. If the consumer has a legitimate claim against the seller of a defective product who has negotiated the promissory note to another party, the consumer cannot raise this claim against an HDC seeking enforcement on the negotiable instrument.

(continued)

To correct this harsh result, the **Federal Trade Commission (FTC)**, a federal administrative agency in charge of consumer protection, adopted the **FTC HDC rule** pursuant to its federal statutory powers. The FTC rule eliminates HDC status with regard to negotiable instruments arising out of certain *consumer* credit transactions.[1] This federal law takes precedence over any state's UCC.

Example Greg, a consumer, purchases a television on credit from Lou's Electronics. He signs a note, promising to pay the purchase price plus interest to Lou's Electronics in 12 equal monthly installments. Lou's Electronics immediately negotiates the note at a discount to City Bank for cash. City Bank is an HDC. The television is defective. Greg would like to stop paying for it, but under the UCC Greg cannot assert the personal defense of the defectiveness of a product against City Bank, an HDC, from collecting on the note. Under the UCC, Greg's only recourse is to sue Lou's Electronics. However, this is often an unsatisfactory result because Greg has no leverage against Lou's Electronics, and bringing a court action is expensive and time consuming. However, because the FTC HDC rule eliminates HDC status for negotiable instruments arising out of consumer transactions, Greg can assert the otherwise personal defense of the defectiveness of the product against enforcement of the promissory note by City Bank, an HDC.

FTC HDC rule
A rule adopted by the Federal Trade Commission (FTC) that eliminates HDC status with regard to negotiable instruments that arise out of certain consumer credit transactions.

Critical Legal Thinking
How does the FTC HDC rule affect the rights of a holder in due course (HDC)? What public policy supports this rule?

discharge
Actions or events that relieve certain parties from liability on negotiable instruments. There are three methods of discharge: (1) payment of the instrument, (2) cancellation, and (3) impairment of the right of recourse.

Discharge of Liability

The UCC specifies when and how certain parties are **discharged** (relieved) from liability on negotiable instruments. Generally, all parties to a negotiable instrument are discharged from liability if (1) the party primarily liable on the instrument pays it in full to the holder of the instrument or (2) a drawee in good faith pays an unaccepted draft or check in full to the holder. When a party other than a primary obligor (e.g., an indorser) pays a negotiable instrument, that party and all subsequent parties to the instrument are discharged from liability [UCC 3-602].

The holder of a negotiable instrument can discharge the liability of any party to the instrument by **cancellation** [UCC 3-604]. Cancellation can be accomplished by (1) any manner apparent on the face of the instrument or the indorsement (e.g., writing *canceled* on the instrument) or (2) destruction or mutilation of a negotiable instrument with the intent of eliminating the obligation.

Intentionally striking out the signature of an indorser cancels that party's liability on the instrument and the liability of all subsequent indorsers. Prior indorsers are not discharged from liability. The instrument is not canceled if it is destroyed or mutilated by accident or by an unauthorized third party. The holder can bring suit to enforce the destroyed or mutilated instrument.

A party to a negotiable instrument sometimes posts collateral as security for the payment of the obligation. Other parties (e.g., holders, indorsers, accommodation parties) look to the credit standing of the party primarily liable on the instrument, the collateral (if any) that is posted, and the liability of secondary parties for the payment of the instrument when it is due. A holder owes a duty not to impair the rights of others when seeking recourse against the liable parties or the collateral. Thus, a holder who either (1) releases an obligor from liability or (2) surrenders the collateral without the consent of the parties who would benefit thereby discharges those parties from their obligation on the instrument [UCC 3-605(e)]. This discharge is called **impairment of the right of recourse**.

Key Terms and Concepts

Accommodation maker (501)
Accommodation indorser (501)
Accommodation party (500)
Adjudicated mentally incompetent (505)
Agent (501)
Breach of contract (506)
Cancellation (508)
Discharge in bankruptcy (505)
Discharged (508)
Dishonored instrument (500)
Extreme duress (505)
Federal Trade Commission (FTC) (508)
Fictitious payee rule (503)

Forged indorsement (502)
Forgery (505)
Fraud in the inception (fraud in the factum or fraud in the execution) (505)
Fraud in the inducement (506)
FTC HDC rule (508)
Guarantee of collection (501)
Guarantee of payment (500)
Holder (504)
Holder in due course (HDC) (504)
Illegal transaction (505)
Impairment of the right of recourse (508)
Implied warranties (503)
Imposter rule (503)
Infancy doctrine (505)
Material alteration (505)
Minor (505)
Nonadjudicated mentally incompetent (506)
Notice of dishonor (500)
Ordinary duress or undue influence (506)
Personal defense (505)
Presentment (500)
Presentment warranty (504)
Primary liability (499)
Principal (501)
Qualified indorser (500)
Secondary liability (499)
Signature liability (contract liability) (498)
Signature (498)
Signer (498)
Transfer (503)
Transfer warranty (503)
Unauthorized signature (502)
Universal defense (real defense) (505)
Unqualified indorser (499)
Warranty liability (503)

Critical Legal Thinking Cases

24.1 Transfer Warranty David M. Fox was a distributor of tools manufactured and sold by Matco Tools Corporation (Matco). Cox purchased tools from Matco, using a credit line that he repaid as the tools were sold. The credit line was secured by Cox's Matco tool inventory. In order to expedite payment on Cox's line of credit, Matco decided to authorize Cox to deposit any customer checks that were made payable to "Matco Tools" or "Matco" into Cox's own account. Matco's controller sent Cox's bank, Pontiac State Bank (Pontiac), a letter stating that Cox was authorized to make such deposits. Several years later, some Matco tools were stolen from Cox's inventory. The Travelers Indemnity Company (Travelers), which insured Cox against such a loss, sent Cox a settlement check in the amount of $24,960. The check was made payable to "David M. Cox and Matco Tool Co." Cox indorsed the check and deposited it in his account at Pontiac. Pontiac forwarded the check through the banking system for payment by the drawee bank. Cox never paid Matco for the destroyed tools. Matco sued Pontiac for accepting the check without the proper indorsements. Is Pontiac liable? *Matco Tools Corporation v. Pontiac State Bank*, 614 F.Supp. 1059, 1985 U.S. Dist. Lexis 17234 (United States District Court for the Eastern District of Michigan)

24.2 Presentment Warranty John Waddell Construction Company (Waddell) maintained a checking account at the Longview Bank & Trust Company (Longview Bank). Waddell drafted a check from this account made payable to two payees, Engineered Metal Works (Metal Works) and E. G. Smith Construction (Smith Construction). The check was sent to Metal Works, which promptly indorsed the check and presented it to the First National Bank of Azle (Bank of Azle) for payment. The Bank of Azle accepted the check with only Metal Works's indorsement and credited Metal Works's account. The Bank of Azle subsequently presented the check to Longview Bank through the Federal Reserve System. Longview Bank accepted and paid the check. When Waddell received the check along with its monthly checking statements from Longview Bank, a company employee noticed the missing indorsement and notified Longview Bank. Longview Bank returned the check to the Bank of Azle, and the Bank of Azle's account was debited the amount of the check at the Federal Reserve. Has the Bank of Azle breached its warranty of good title? *Longview Bank & Trust Company v. First National Bank of Azle*, 750 S.W.2d 297, 1988 Tex. App. Lexis 1377 (Court of Appeals of Texas)

Ethical

Ethics Case

24.3 Ethics Case The Grand Island Production Credit Association (Grand Island) is a federally chartered credit union. Carl M. and Beulah C. Humphrey, husband and wife, entered into a loan arrangement with Grand Island for a $50,000 line of credit. Mr. and Mrs. Humphrey signed a line of credit promissory note that provided, in part, "As long as the Borrower is not in default, the Association will lend to the Borrower, and the Borrower may borrow and repay and reborrow at any time from date of said 'Line of Credit' Promissory Note in accordance with the terms thereof and prior to maturity thereof, up to an aggregate maximum amount of principal at any one time outstanding of $50,000."

Mr. Humphrey borrowed money against the line of credit to purchase cattle. Two months later, Mrs. Humphrey went to Grand Island's office and told the loan officer that she had left Mr. Humphrey and filed for divorce. She told the loan officer not to advance any more money to Mr. Humphrey for his cattle purchases. When the Humphreys failed to pay the outstanding balance on the line of credit, Grand Island sued Mr. and Mrs. Humphrey to recover the unpaid balance of $13,936.71. Is Mrs. Humphrey a co-maker of the line of credit promissory note and, therefore, primarily liable for the outstanding principal balance of the note, plus interest? Is it ethical for Mrs. Humphrey to deny liability on the promissory note in this case? *Grand Island Production Credit Association v. Humphrey*, 388 N.W.2d 807, 1986 Neb. Lexis 1185 (Supreme Court of Nebraska)

Note

1. 16 C.F.R. 433.2 (1987).

Banking System and Electronic Financial Transactions

AUTOMATIC TELLER MACHINE
Automatic teller machines (ATMs) permit the withdrawal of cash from bank accounts, provide cash advances against credit cards, accept deposits to banking accounts, allow payments of bank loans, and permit other banking services. ATMs are located at banks and other establishments.

Learning Objectives

After studying this chapter, you should be able to:

1. Describe the difference between certified and cashier's checks.
2. Describe the system of processing and collecting checks through the banking system.
3. Describe electronic banking and e-money.
4. Define *commercial wire transfer* and describe the use of wire transfers in commerce.
5. Describe the banking reform provisions of the Dodd-Frank Wall Street Reform and Consumer Protection Act.

Chapter Outline

Chapter Outline *(continued)*

Bank Reform

LANDMARK LAW *Dodd-Frank Wall Street Reform and Consumer Protection Act*

GLOBAL LAW *Hiding Money in Offshore Banks*

"*Bankers have no right to establish a customary law among themselves, at the expense of other men.*"

—*Justice Foster*
Hankey v. Trotman (1746)

Introduction to the Banking System and Electronic Financial Transactions

Money is a good servant, but a dangerous master.

Dominique Bouhours (1628–1702)

Checks are the most common form of negotiable instrument used in this country. Checks act both as substitutes for money and as record-keeping devices. There are many special forms of checks, including certified checks and cashier's checks.

The banking system is made up of international, national, regional, and community banks. Banks are highly regulated financial institutions. Banks, with the assistance of the Federal Reserve System, process checks.

In addition, many banking transactions now occur online and electronically. These include wire transfers of money, interbank transfers, and electronic consumer transactions. This is often referred to as e-money transactions.

This chapter discusses checks, the banking system, electronic financial transactions, the regulation of financial institutions, and bank reform.

The Bank–Customer Relationship

creditor–debtor relationship
A relationship that is created when a customer deposits money into the bank; the customer is the creditor, and the bank is the debtor.

When a customer makes a deposit into a bank, a **creditor–debtor relationship** is formed. The customer is the *creditor* and the bank is the *debtor*. In effect, the customer is loaning money to the bank.

A **principal–agent relationship** is created if (1) the deposit is a check that the bank must collect for the customer or (2) the customer writes a check against his or her account. The customer is the *principal* and the bank is the *agent*. The bank is obligated to follow the customer's order to collect or pay the check. The rights and duties of a bank and a checking account customer are contractual. The signature card and other bank documents signed by the customer form the contract.

Uniform Commercial Code Governs Checks and Banking

Article 3 (Commercial Paper)
An article of the UCC that sets forth the requirements for negotiable instruments, including checks.

Revised Article 3 (Negotiable Instruments)
A revision of Article 3 of the UCC.

Various articles of the **Uniform Commercial Code (UCC)** establish rules for creating, collecting, and enforcing checks and wire transfers. These articles are the following:

- **Article 3 (Commercial Paper).** **Article 3 (Commercial Paper)** establishes the requirements for negotiable instruments. Because a check is a negotiable instrument, the provisions of Article 3 apply. **Revised Article 3 (Negotiable Instruments)** was promulgated in 1990. The provisions of Revised Article 3 serve as the basis of the discussion of Article 3 in this chapter.

- **Article 4 (Bank Deposits and Collections).** **Article 4 (Bank Deposits and Collections)** establishes the rules and principles that regulate bank deposit and collection procedures for checking accounts offered by commercial banks and check-like accounts offered by other financial institutions. Article 4 was substantially amended in 1990. The amended Article 4 serves as the basis of the discussion of Article 4 in this chapter.
- **Article 4A (Funds Transfers).** **Article 4A (Funds Transfers)** establishes rules that regulate the creation and collection of and liability for wire transfers. Article 4A was added to the UCC in 1989.

Article 4 (Bank Deposits and Collections)
An article of the UCC that establishes the rules and principles that regulate bank deposit and collection procedures.

Article 4A (Funds Transfers)
An article is the UCC that establishes rules regulating the creation and collection of and liability for wire transfers.

Ordinary Checks

Most adults and businesses have at least one checking account at a bank. A customer opens a checking account by going to a bank, completing the necessary forms (including a signature card), and making a **deposit** to the account. The bank issues checks to the customer. The customer then uses the checks to purchase goods and services.

Parties to a Check

UCC 3-104(f) defines a **check** as an order by the drawer to the drawee bank to pay a specified sum of money from the drawer's checking account to the named payee (or holder). There are three parties to an **ordinary check**:

1. **Drawer.** The **drawer of a check** is the customer who maintains the checking account and writes (draws) checks against the account.
2. **Drawee (or payer bank).** The **drawee of a check** is the bank on which a check is drawn.
3. **Payee.** The **payee of a check** is the party to whom a check is written.

Example The Kneadery Restaurant, Inc., has a checking account at Mountain Bank. Mike Martin, the president of the Kneadery Restaurant, writes a check for $1,000 from this account, payable to Sun Valley Bakery, to pay for food supplies. The Kneadery Restaurant is the drawer, Mountain Bank is the drawee, and Sun Valley Bakery is the payee. Mountain Bank is obligated to pay the check when it is presented for payment if the Kneadery Restaurant's checking account has sufficient funds to cover the amount of the check at the time of presentment (see **Exhibit 25.1**).

ordinary check
An order by a drawer to a drawee bank to pay a specified sum of money from the drawer's checking account to the named payee (or holder).

drawer of a check
The checking account holder and writer of a check.

drawee of a check
The bank where a check drawer has his or her account.

payee of a check
The party to whom a check is written.

Exhibit 25.1 ORDINARY CHECK

Special Types of Checks

If a payee fears that there may be insufficient funds in the drawer's account to pay a check when it is presented for payment or that the drawer has stopped payment of the check, the payee may be unwilling to accept an ordinary check from the drawer. However, the payee might be willing to accept a **bank check**—that is, a *certified check* or a *cashier's check*. These types of checks are usually considered "as good as cash" because the bank is solely or primarily liable for payment. These forms of checks are discussed in the following paragraphs.

bank check
A certified check or a cashier's check, the payment for which a bank is solely or primarily liable.

Certified Checks

Men such as they are, very naturally seek money or power; and power because it is as good as money.

Ralph Waldo Emerson (1803–1882)

When a bank *certifies a check*, it agrees in advance (1) to accept the check when it is presented for payment and (2) to pay the check from funds set aside from the customer's account and either placed in a special certified check account or held in the customer's account. Certified checks do not become stale. Thus, they are payable at any time from the date they are issued.

A check is a **certified check** when the bank writes or stamps the word *certified* across the face of an ordinary check. The certification should also contain the date, the amount being certified, and the name and title of the person at the bank who certifies the check. Note that a bank is not obligated to certify a check. A bank's refusal to do so is not a dishonor of a check [UCC 3-409(d)]. The drawer cannot stop payment on a certified check (see **Exhibit 25.2**).

certified check
A type of check for which a bank agrees in advance (*certifies*) to accept the check when it is presented for payment.

Exhibit 25.2 CERTIFIED CHECK

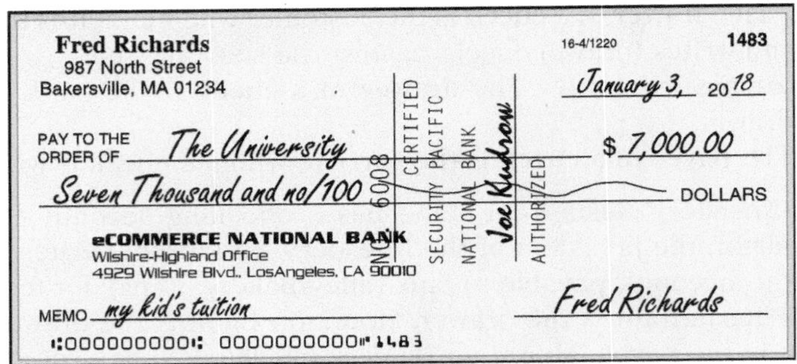
Fred Richards
987 North Street
Bakersville, MA 01234
16-4/1220 1483
January 3, 2018
PAY TO THE ORDER OF The University $ 7,000.00
Seven Thousand and no/100 DOLLARS
CERTIFIED
SECURITY PACIFIC
NATIONAL BANK
Joe Kudrow
AUTHORIZED
NO. 6008
eCOMMERCE NATIONAL BANK
Wilshire-Highland Office
4929 Wilshire Blvd. LosAngeles, CA 90010
MEMO my kid's tuition
Fred Richards
⑆000000000⑆ 0000000000⑈ 1483

Cashier's Checks

A person can purchase a **cashier's check** from a bank by paying the bank the amount of the check plus a fee for issuing the check. Usually, a specific payee is named. The purchaser does not have to have a checking account at the bank.

A cashier's check is a two-party check for which (1) the issuing bank serves as both the drawer and the drawee and (2) the holder serves as payee [UCC 3-104(g)]. The bank, which has been paid for the check, guarantees its payment. When the check is presented for payment, the bank debits its own account [UCC 3-412] (see **Exhibit 25.3**).

cashier's check
A check issued by a bank for which the customer has paid the bank the amount of the check and a fee. The bank guarantees payment of the check.

Exhibit 25.3 CASHIER'S CHECK

eCOMMERCE NATIONAL BANK
Bank Check Accounting Services
Brea, California 92621-6398
10341504 16-4/1220
OFFICE NUMBER 142
DATE: January 3, 2018
PAY TO THE ORDER OF *********** HELEN PITTS *********** $ 1,000.00
EXACTLY 1,000 AND 00 DOLLARS
($100,000 AND OVER REQUIRES TWO SIGNATURES)
CASHIER'S CHECK
Dg Lotten
AUTHORIZED SIGNATURE
Kerry Fields
AUTHORIZED SIGNATURE
⑈10341504⑈ ⑆122000043⑆928⑈917016⑈

Honoring Checks

When a customer opens a checking account at a bank, the customer impliedly agrees to keep sufficient funds in the account to pay any checks written against it. Thus, when the drawee bank receives a properly drawn and payable check, the bank is under a duty to **honor** the check and charge (debit) the drawer's account the amount of the check if there are sufficient funds in the customer's checking account at the bank [UCC 4-401(a)].

honor
To pay a drawer's properly drawn check.

Stale Checks

Occasionally, a payee or another holder in possession of a check fails to present the check immediately to the payer bank for payment. A check that has been outstanding for more than six months is considered stale, and the bank is under no obligation to pay it. A bank that pays a **stale check** in good faith may charge the drawer's account [UCC 4-404].

stale check
A check that has been outstanding for more than six months.

Incomplete Checks

Drawers sometimes write checks that omit certain information, such as the amount of the check or the payee's name, either on purpose or by mistake. These are called **incomplete checks**. In such cases, the payee or any holder can complete the check, and the payer bank that in good faith makes payment on the completed check can charge the customer's account the amount of the completed check unless it has notice that the completion was improper [UCC 3-407(c), 4-401(d)(2)]. The UCC places the risk of loss of an incomplete item on the drawer.

Example Richard, who owes Sarah $500, draws a check payable to Sarah on his checking account at City Bank. Richard signs the check but leaves the amount blank. Sarah fraudulently fills in $1,000 and presents the check to City Bank, which pays it. City Bank can charge Richard's account $1,000. Richard's only recourse is to sue Sarah.

The love of money is the root of all evil.

I Timothy 6:10
The Bible

Postdated Checks

On occasion, a drawer of a check does not want a check he or she writes to be cashed until sometime in the future. This is called a **postdated check**. Under UCC 4-401(c), to require a bank to abide by a postdated check, the drawer must take the following steps:

1. The drawer must postdate the check to some date in the future.
2. The drawer must give *separate written notice* to the bank, describing the check with reasonable certainty and notifying the bank not to pay the check until the date on the check.

If these steps are taken and the bank pays the check before its date, the bank is liable to the drawer for any losses resulting from its act.

postdated check
A check that a drawer does not want cashed until sometime in the future.

Stop-Payment Orders

A **stop-payment order** is an order by a drawer of a check to the payer bank not to pay or certify a check. Only the drawer can order a stop-payment order. A stop-payment order can be given orally or in writing. An *oral order* is binding on the bank for only 14 calendar days, unless confirmed in writing during this time. A *written order* is effective for six months. It can be renewed in writing for additional six-month periods [UCC 4-403]. If the payer bank fails to honor a valid stop-payment order, it must recredit the customer's account.

stop-payment order
An order by a drawer of a check to the payer bank not to pay or certify a check.

Overdrafts

overdraft
The amount of money a drawer owes a bank after it has paid a check despite the drawer's account having insufficient funds.

If the drawer does not have enough money in his or her account when a properly payable check is presented for payment, the payer bank can either (1) dishonor the check or (2) honor the check and create an **overdraft** in the drawer's account [UCC 4-401(a)].

If a bank dishonors a check, the bank notifies the drawer of the dishonor and returns the check to the holder, marked **insufficient funds**. The holder often resubmits the check to the bank, hoping that the drawer has deposited more money into the account and the check will clear. If the check does not clear, the holder's recourse is against the drawer of the check.

A banker so very careful to avoid risk would soon have no risk to avoid.
Lord MacNaghten
Bank of England v. Vaglliano Brothers (1891)

If the bank chooses to pay the check even though there are insufficient funds in the drawer's account, it can later charge the drawer's account for the amount of the overdraft [UCC 4-401(a)]. If the drawer does not fulfill this commitment, the bank can sue him or her to recover payment for the overdrafts and overdraft fees. Many banks offer optional expressly agreed-on overdraft protection to their customers.

Wrongful Dishonor

wrongful dishonor
A situation in which there are sufficient funds in a drawer's account to pay a properly payable check, but the bank does not do so.

If a bank does not honor a check when there are sufficient funds in the drawer's account to pay a properly payable check, it is liable for **wrongful dishonor**. The payer bank is liable to the drawer for damages proximately caused by the wrongful dishonor as well as for consequential damages, damages caused by criminal prosecution, and so on. A payee or holder cannot sue the bank for damages caused by the wrongful dishonor of a drawer's check. The only recourse for the payee or holder is to sue the drawer to recover the amount of the check [UCC 4-402].

The following ethics feature discusses federal currency reporting law.

Ethics

Federal Currency Reporting Law

The federal **Bank Secrecy Act**[1] requires financial institutions and other entities (such as retailers, car and boat dealers, antiques dealers, jewelers, and real estate brokers) to file a **Currency Transaction Report (CTR)** with the Internal Revenue Service (IRS), reporting the following:

- The receipt in a single transaction or a series of related transactions of cash in an amount greater than $10,000 (daily aggregate amount). "Cash" is not limited to currency but includes cashier's checks, bank drafts, traveler's checks, and money orders (but not ordinary checks).
- Suspected criminal activity by bank customers involving a financial transaction of $1,000 or more in funds.

The law also stipulates that it is a crime to structure or assist in structuring any transaction for the purpose of evading these reporting requirements. Financial institutions and entities may be fined for negligent violations of the currency reporting requirements. Fines may be levied for a pattern of negligent violations. Willful violations may subject the violator to civil money penalties, charges of aiding and abetting the criminal activity, and prosecution for violating money-laundering statutes.

Ethics Questions Why were the reporting requirements adopted? Do you think that many transactions are structured to avoid the reporting statute?

Bank Secrecy Act
A federal law that requires financial institutions and other entities to report to the Internal Revenue Service (IRS) the receipt of a transaction or series of transactions in an amount greater than $10,000 in cash and suspected criminal activity involving a financial transaction of $1,000 or more in funds.

Forged Signatures and Altered Checks

Major problems associated with checks and other negotiable instruments are that (1) signatures are sometimes forged and (2) the instrument itself may have been altered prior to presentment for payment. The UCC rules that apply to these situations are discussed in the following paragraphs. These rules apply to all types of negotiable instruments but are particularly important concerning checks.

Forged Signature of the Drawer

When a check is presented to the payer bank for payment, the bank is under a duty to verify the drawer's signature. This is usually done by matching the signature on the signature card on file at the bank to the signature on the check.

A check with a *forged drawer's signature* is called a **forged instrument**. A forged signature is wholly inoperative as the signature of the drawer. The check is not properly payable because it does not contain an order of the drawer. The payer bank cannot charge the customer's account if it pays a check over the forged signature. If the bank has charged the customer's account, it must recredit the account, and the forged check must be dishonored [UCC 3-401].

forged instrument
A check with a forged drawer's signature on it.

The bank can recover from the party who presented the check to it for payment only if that party had knowledge that the signature of the drawer on the check was unauthorized [UCC 3-417(a)(3)]. The forger is liable on the check because the forged signature acts as the forger's signature [UCC 3-403(a)]. Although the payer bank can sue the forger, the forger usually cannot be found or is **judgment proof**; that is, he does not have funds or assets to pay the judgment.

Example Gregory has a checking account at Country Bank. Mildred steals one of Gregory's checks, completes it by writing in $10,000 as the amount of the check, adding her name as the payee, and forges Gregory's signature. Mildred indorses the check to Sam, who knows that Gregory's signature has been forged. Sam indorses the check to Barbara, who is innocent and does not know of the forgery. Barbara presents the check to Country Bank, the payer bank, which pays the check. Country Bank may recover from the original forger, Mildred, and from Sam, who knew of the forgery. It cannot recover from Barbara because she did not have knowledge of the forgery.

Critical Legal Thinking
What is a forged check? Explain the liability of the following parties where there has been a forged check: (1) drawer, (2) payor bank, (3) presenter of the check, and (4) forger.

Altered Checks

Sometimes a check is altered before it is presented for payment. This is an unauthorized change in the check that modifies the legal obligation of a party [UCC 3-407(a)]. The payer bank can dishonor an **altered check** if it discovers the alteration. If the payer bank pays the altered check, it can charge the drawer's account for the **original tenor** of the check but not the altered amount [UCC 3-407(c), 4-401(d)(1)].

altered check
A check that has been altered without authorization and thus modifies the legal obligation of a party.

original tenor
The original amount for which the drawer wrote a check.

If the payer bank has paid the altered amount, it can recover the difference between the altered amount and the original tenor from the party who presented the altered check for payment. This is because the presenter of the check for payment and each prior transferor *warrant* that the check has not been altered [UCC 3-417(a)(2)]. If there has been an alteration, each party in the chain of collection can recover from the preceding transferor based on a breach of this warranty. The ultimate loss usually falls on the party that first paid the altered check because that party was in the best position to identify the alteration. The forger is liable for the difference between the original tenor and the altered amount—if he or she can be found and is not judgment proof.

Example Father draws a $100 check on City Bank made payable to his daughter. The daughter alters the check to read "$1,000" and cashes the check at a liquor store. The liquor store presents the check for payment to City Bank. City Bank pays the check. Father is liable only for the original tenor of the check ($100), and City Bank can charge the father's account this amount. City Bank is liable for the $900 difference, but it can recover this amount from the liquor store for breach of presentment warranty. This is because the liquor store was in the best position to identify the alteration. The liquor store can seek to recover the $900 from the daughter.

Critical Legal Thinking
What is an altered check? Explain the liability of the following parties where there has been an altered check: (1) drawer, (2) payor bank, (3) presenter of the check, and (4) forger.

One-Year Rule

The drawer's failure to report a forged or altered check to the bank within *one year* of receiving the bank statement and canceled checks containing it relieves the bank of any liability for paying the instrument [UCC 4-406(3)]. Thus, the payer bank is not required after this time to recredit the customer's account for the amount of the forged or altered check, even if the customer later discovers the forgery or alteration. This is called the **one-year rule**.

one-year rule
A rule that states that if a drawer fails to report a forged or altered check to the bank within *one year* of receiving the bank statement and canceled checks containing it, the bank is relieved of any liability for paying the instrument.

Series of Forgeries

If the same wrongdoer engages in a **series of forgeries or alterations** on the same account, the customer must report that to the payer bank within a reasonable period of time, not exceeding 30 days from the date that the bank statement was made available to the customer [UCC 4-406(d)(2)]. The customer's failure to do so discharges the bank from liability on all similar forged or altered checks after this date and prior to notification.

The Federal Bureau of Investigation (FBI) is authorized to investigate forgeries, bank fraud, and other financial crimes.

In the following case, the court held that a checking account holder failed to review its bank statements as required by law to catch a series of forgeries by an employee.

CASE 25.1 *STATE COURT CASE Series of Forgeries of Checks*

Spacemakers of America, Inc. v. SunTrust Bank

609 S.E.2d 683, 2005 Ga. App. Lexis 43 (2005)
Court of Appeals of Georgia

"In this case, the undisputed evidence showed that Spacemakers hired as a bookkeeper a twice-convicted embezzler who was on probation, then delegated the entire responsibility of reviewing and reconciling its bank statements to her while failing to provide any oversight on these essential tasks."

—Ellington, Judge

Facts

Spacemakers of America, Inc. hired Jenny Triplett as its bookkeeper. Spacemakers did not inquire about any prior criminal record or conduct a criminal background check of Triplett. If it had taken those steps, it would have discovered that Triplett was on probation for 13 counts of forgery and had been convicted of theft by deception. All convictions were the result of Triplett forging checks of previous employers.

Spacemakers delegated to Triplett sole responsibility for maintaining the company's checkbook, reconciling the checkbook with monthly bank statements, and preparing financial reports. Triplett also handled the company's accounts payable and regularly presented checks to Dennis Rose, the president of Spacemakers, so he could sign them.

Just weeks after starting her job at Spacemakers, Triplett forged Rose's signature on a check for $3,000 made payable to her husband's company, Triple M Entertainment Group, which was not a vendor for Spacemakers. By the end of the first full month of employment, Triplett had forged five more checks totaling $22,320, all payable to Triple M. Over the next nine months, Triplett forged 59 more checks totaling approximately $475,000. All checks were drawn against Spacemakers's bank account at SunTrust Bank. No one except Triplett reviewed the company's bank statements.

Subsequently, a SunTrust employee visually inspected a $30,670 check. She became suspicious of the signature and called Rose. The SunTrust employee faxed a copy of the check to Rose, which was made payable to Triple M. Rose knew that Triple M was not one of the company's vendors, and a Spacemakers employee reminded Rose that Triplett's husband owned Triple M. Rose immediately called the police, and Triplett was arrested.

Spacemakers sent a letter to SunTrust Bank, demanding that the bank credit $523,106 to its account for the forged checks. The bank refused, contending that Spacemakers's failure to provide the bank with timely notice of the forgeries barred Spacemakers's claim. Spacemakers sued SunTrust for negligence and unauthorized payment of forged items. The trial court granted SunTrust's motion for summary judgment. Spacemakers appealed.

Issue

Did Spacemakers's failure to uncover the forgeries and failure to provide SunTrust with timely notice of the forgeries bar its claim against SunTrust?

(case continues)

Language of the Court

In this case, the undisputed evidence showed that Spacemakers hired as a bookkeeper a twice-convicted embezzler who was on probation, then delegated the entire responsibility of reviewing and reconciling its bank statements to her while failing to provide any oversight on these essential tasks. There is every reason to believe that, if Spacemakers had simply reviewed its bank statements, it would have discovered the forgeries. Accordingly, we find that Spacemakers is precluded as a matter of law from asserting claims based upon the forgeries in this case.

Decision

The court of appeals held that Spacemakers was barred from recovering the value of the forged checks from SunTrust. The court of appeals affirmed the trial court's grant of summary judgment to SunTrust.

Ethics Questions

Did Triplett act ethically in this case? Did Spacemakers act ethically when it sued SunTrust to try to recover its losses caused by the forgeries?

The Collection Process

A bank is under a duty to accept deposits into a customer's account. This includes collecting checks that are drawn on other banks and made payable or indorsed to the depositor. The **collection process**, which may involve several banks, is governed by Article 4 of the UCC.

When a payee or holder receives a check, he or she can either go to the drawer's bank (the **payer bank**) and present the check for payment in cash or—as is more common—deposit the check into a bank account at his or her own bank, called the **depository bank**. (The depository bank may also serve as the payer bank if both parties have accounts at the same bank.)

The depository bank must present a check to the payer bank for collection. At this point in the process, the Federal Reserve System and other banks may be used in the collection of a check. The depository bank and these other banks are called **collecting banks**. Banks in the collection process that are not the depository or payer bank are called **intermediary banks**. A bank can have more than one role during the collection process [UCC 4-105]. The check collection process is illustrated in **Exhibit 25.4**.

payer bank
The bank where the drawer has a checking account and on which a check is drawn.

depository bank
The bank where the payee or holder has an account.

collecting bank
The depository bank and other banks in the collection process (other than the payer bank).

intermediary bank
A bank in the collection process that is not the depository bank or the payer bank.

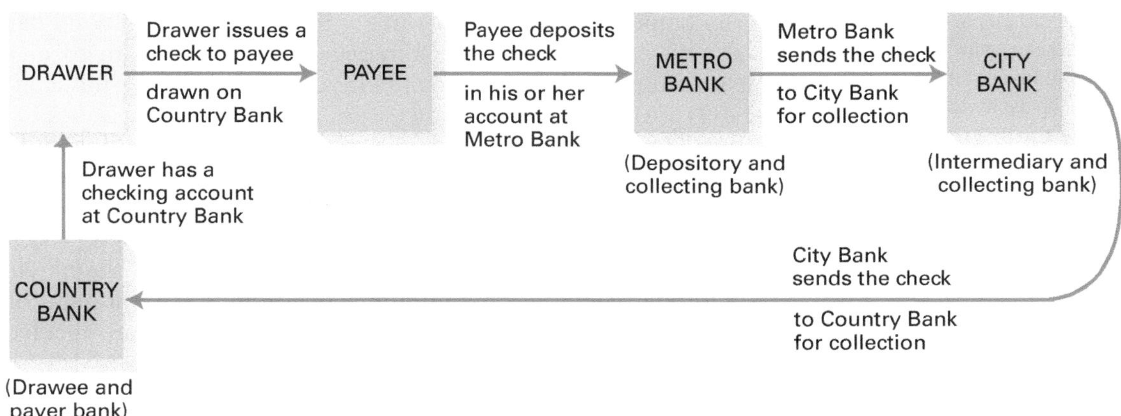

Exhibit 25.4 **CHECK COLLECTION PROCESS**

Federal Reserve System

Federal Reserve System
A system of 12 regional Federal Reserve banks that assist other banks in the collection of checks.

The **Federal Reserve System** (also known as the **Federal Reserve**) was created by Congress as the central bank of the United States. The Federal Reserve has many functions, including being a check-clearing system for banks and other depository institutions. The Federal Reserve consists of 12 regional Federal Reserve banks located in major cities in different geographical areas of the country.

Most banks in this country have accounts at regional Federal Reserve banks. Rather than send a check directly to another bank for collection, member banks may submit paid checks to the Federal Reserve banks for collection. The Federal Reserve banks debit and credit the accounts of these banks daily to reflect the collection and payment of checks. Banks pay the Federal Reserve banks a fee for this service. In large urban areas, private clearinghouses may provide similar check collection services [UCC 4-110, 4-213(a)].

Bank Payment Rules

The federal government has established rules for the payment of checks by banks and other depository institutions. The following are the major time rules that apply to depository institutions for the payment of checks.

Deferred Posting

deferred posting rule
A rule that allows banks to fix an afternoon hour of 2:00 P.M. or later as a cutoff hour for the purpose of processing items.

The **deferred posting rule** allows banks to fix an afternoon hour of 2:00 P.M. or later as a cutoff hour for the purpose of processing checks and deposits. Any check or deposit of money received after this cutoff hour is treated as being received on the next banking day [UCC 4-108]. Saturdays, Sundays, and holidays are not banking days unless the bank is open to the public for carrying on substantially all banking functions [UCC 4-104(a)(3)].

Settlement

A check is finally paid when the payer bank (1) pays the check in cash, (2) settles for the check without having a right to revoke the settlement, or (3) fails to dishonor the check within certain statutory time periods. These time periods are as follows:

A man is usually more careful of his money than he is of his principles.

Ralph Waldo Emerson (1803–1882)

"on us" item
A check that is presented for payment where the depository bank is also the payer bank. That is, the drawer and payee or holder have accounts at the same bank.

"on them" item
A check presented for payment by a payee or holder where the depository bank and the payer bank are not the same bank.

midnight deadline
The midnight of the next banking day following the banking day on which the bank received an "on them" check for collection.

1. **Deposit of cash.** A **deposit of cash** to an account becomes available for withdrawal at the opening of the next banking day following the deposit [UCC 4-215(a)].
2. **"On us" Items.** If the drawer and the payee or holder has accounts at the *same* bank, the depository bank is also the payer bank. The check is called an **"on us" item** when it is presented for payment by the payee or holder. In this case, the bank has until the opening of business on the second banking day following the receipt of the check to dishonor it. If it fails to do so, the check is considered paid. The payee or holder can withdraw the funds at this time [UCC 4-215(e)(2)].
3. **"On them" Items.** If a drawer and a payee or holder have accounts at *different* banks, the payer bank and depository bank are not the same bank. In this case, the check is called an **"on them" item.**

   Except for the collecting bank, each bank in the collection process, including the payer bank, must take proper action on an "on them" check prior to its midnight deadline. The **midnight deadline** is the midnight of the next banking day following the banking day on which the bank received an "on them" check for collection [UCC 4-104(a)(10)].

   This deadline is of particular importance to the payer bank: If the payer bank does not dishonor a check by its midnight deadline, the bank is *accountable* (liable) for the face amount of the check. It does not require that the check be properly payable or not [UCC 4-302(a)].

4. **Presentment across the counter.** Instead of depositing an "on them" check for collection, a depositor can physically present the check for payment at the payer bank. This is called **presentment across the counter**. In this case, the payer bank has until the end of that banking day to dishonor the check. If it fails to do so, it must pay the check [UCC 4-301(a)].

presentment across the counter
A situation in which a depositor physically presents a check for payment at the payer bank instead of depositing an "on them" check for collection.

The following feature discusses insured deposits at banks.

Contemporary Environment

FDIC Insurance of Bank Deposits

The **Federal Deposit Insurance Corporation (FDIC)** is a federal government agency that insures deposits at most banks and savings institutions in the United States. Each insured bank pays assessed yearly premiums based on the size of its deposits to the FDIC. If an FDIC-insured bank fails and the insured bank does not have sufficient assets to pay its depositors back their money, the FDIC will pay the depositors their lost deposits, up to certain limits.

FDIC insurance covers savings accounts, checking accounts, money market accounts, certificates of deposit, IRAs and retirement accounts, and other types of deposits received at an insured bank. To show whether it is covered by FDIC insurance, a bank or savings institution will display the official FDIC sign.

FDIC insurance per insured bank is set at (1) $250,000 per single account owned by one person, (2) $250,000 per co-owner for joint accounts owned by two or more persons, and (3) $250,000 per corporation, partnership, and unincorporated association accounts. IRAs and other retirement accounts are insured up to $250,000 per owner. Accounts at separate banks are each insured to these amounts. However, funds deposited in separate branches of the same bank are not separately insured.

Example Henry has $250,000 on deposit at the First National Bank and another $250,000 on deposit at Central Savings Bank. Each deposit is insured.

Example Kerry is married to Patricia. Kerry has $250,000 on deposit at the Second National Bank, Patricia has $250,000 on deposit at the bank, Kerry and Patricia have a $250,000 joint account at the bank, and Kerry's law firm (under a limited liability partnership entity) has $250,000 on deposit at the bank. Each deposit is insured.

If the FDIC is unable to cover the insured deposits, the *full faith and credit* of the U.S. government backs the FDIC. Thus, if there are major failures of many banks and the FDIC insurance fund is insufficient to cover all of the depositors' losses, then the U.S. government will pay the depositors the money owed by the FDIC.

Electronic Banking and E-Money

Computer and electronic technology have made it possible for banks to offer electronic deposit, withdrawal, payment, and collection services to bank customers. This technology is collectively referred to as the **electronic funds transfer system (EFTS)**. EFTS is supported by contracts among and between customers, banks, private clearinghouses, and other third parties. Some of the major forms of electronic banking services are discussed in the following paragraphs.

Federal Deposit Insurance Corporation (FDIC)
The Federal Deposit Insurance Corporation (FDIC) is a government agency that insures deposits at most banks and savings institutions ("insured bank") in the United States.

electronic funds transfer system (EFTS)
Computer and electronic technology that makes it possible for banks to offer electronic deposit, withdrawal, payment, and collection services to bank customers.

Automated Teller Machine

An **automated teller machine (ATM)** is an electronic machine that is located either on a bank's premises or at some other convenient location, such as a shopping center or supermarket. These devices are connected online to the bank's computers and permit the withdrawal of cash from bank accounts, provide cash advances against credit cards, accept deposits to banking accounts, allow payment of bank loans (e.g., mortgage payments), and permit other banking services. Each bank customer is issued a secret personal identification number (PIN) to access his or her bank accounts through ATMs.

Debit Cards

Many banks issue **debit cards** to customers. Debit cards are electronically connected to a bank account of the holder of the debit card. Debit cards are often

debit card
A card that is issued to a holder of a bank account that permits purchases of goods and services and withdrawals of cash by deducting the amount of the purchase or withdrawal from the card holder's bank account.

used by holders to make purchases or make withdrawals of cash. No credit is extended. Instead, the customer's bank account is immediately debited for the amount of a purchase. Debit cards can be used at merchants that have a point-of-sale terminal or other similar electronic device. These terminals are connected online to a bank's computers. To make a purchase or withdrawal, a customer inserts a debit card into the appropriate electronic device for the amount of the purchase. If there are sufficient funds in the customer's account, the transaction will debit the customer's account and credit the merchant's account for the amount of the purchase. If there are insufficient funds in the customer's account, the purchase is rejected unless the customer has overdraft protection. At many electronic terminals, customers can also obtain cash using their debit card.

Electronic Funds Transfer Act
A federal statute that regulates *consumer* electronic funds transfers.

The following feature discusses federal law that governs debit cards and *consumer* electronic funds transfers.

Digital Law

Consumer Electronic Funds Transfers

Computers have made it much easier and faster for banks and their customers to conduct banking transactions. The U.S. Congress enacted the **Electronic Fund Transfer Act**[2] to regulate *consumer* electronic funds transfers. The Federal Reserve Board adopted **Regulation E** to further interpret the act. The Electronic Funds Transfer Act and Regulation E establish the following consumer rights:

- **Unsolicited debit cards.** A bank can send unsolicited EFTS debit cards to a consumer only if the cards are not valid for use. Unsolicited cards can be validated for use by a consumer's specific request.
- **Lost or stolen debit cards.** Debit cards are sometimes lost or stolen. If a customer notifies the issuing bank within two days of learning that his or her debit card has been lost or stolen, the customer is liable for only $50 for unauthorized use. If a customer does not notify the bank within this two-day period, the customer's liability increases to $500. If the customer fails to notify the bank within 60 days after an unauthorized use appears on the customer's bank statement, the customer can be held liable for more than $500.
- **Evidence of transaction.** Other than for a telephone transaction, a bank must provide a customer with a written receipt of a transaction made through a computer terminal or electronic device. This receipt is *prima facie* evidence of the transaction. The receipt can be provided electronically by the bank.
- **Bank statements.** A bank must provide a monthly statement to an electronic funds transfer customer at the end of the month in which the customer conducts a transaction. The statement must include the date and amount of the transfer, the name of the retailer, the location and identification of the terminal, and the fees charged for the transaction. Bank statements must also contain the address and telephone number where inquiries or errors can be reported. The statement can be provided electronically by the bank.

A bank is liable for wrongful dishonor when it fails to pay an electronic funds transfer when there are sufficient funds in the customer's account to do so.

Direct Deposit and Withdrawal

Many banks provide the service of paying recurring payments and crediting recurring deposits on behalf of customers. Direct recurring payments are commonly to pay utility bills, insurance premiums, mortgage payments, and the like. Social Security checks, wages, and dividend and interest checks are examples of recurring direct deposits.

online banking
Electronic system that permit bank customers to check their bank statements online and pay bills from their bank accounts by using personal computers and other electronic devices.

Online Banking

Many banks permit customers to check their bank statements online and pay bills from their bank accounts by using personal computers and other electronic devices. This is referred to as **online banking**. To engage in online banking, a customer must enter his or her PIN and account name or number, the amount of the bill to be paid, and the account number of the payee to whom the funds are to be transferred.

Smart phones and other electronic devices can now be used by bank account holders to deposit checks into their account by taking photographs of the check, to pay for goods and services by placing the phone on a device at a merchant's store, and for completing other electronic banking transactions. Internet banking is increasing dramatically.

The following feature discusses federal law that governs *commercial* electronic funds transfers.

Dodd-Frank Wall Street Reform and Consumer Protection Act
A federal statute that reforms many aspects of the banking system.

Digital Law

Commercial Electronic Wire Transfers

Commercial wire transfers, or **wholesale wire transfers**, are electronic transfers of funds from a bank to another party. They are often used to transfer payments between businesses and financial institutions. A customer of a bank may request the bank to pay another party by wiring funds (money) to the other party's bank account. UCC Article 4A (Funds Transfers) governs *commercial wire transfers*. Article 4A applies only to **commercial electronic funds transfers**; consumer electronic funds transfers are not subject to Article 4A. The customer is liable to pay the bank for any properly paid funds transfer [UCC 4A-103(a)].

Example Boeing Aircraft Corporation wants to pay Pittsburgh Steel Company for supplies it purchased. Instead of delivering a check to Pittsburgh Steel, Boeing instructs its bank, Washington Bank, to wire the funds to Pittsburgh Steel's bank, Liberty Bank, with instructions to credit Pittsburgh Steel's account.

Trillions of dollars are transferred each day using wire transfers. A wire transfer often involves a large amount of money (multi-million-dollar transactions are common). The benefit of using wire transfers is their speed—most transfers are completed on the same day.

Bank Reform

After the country suffered a major financial and economic depression in the mid-2000s, Congress decided that the bank system needed to be reformed. To accomplish this, Congress passed the **Dodd-Frank Wall Street Reform and Consumer Protection Act**.[3]

Landmark Law

Dodd-Frank Wall Street Reform and Consumer Protection Act

The most important provisions of the Dodd-Frank Wall Street Reform and Consumer Protection Act are the following:

- **Bank regulation.** The act reorganized and streamlined the federal government agencies that regulate the banking industry and increased the powers and strengthened bank regulatory oversight by federal agencies.
- **Lending regulation.** The act requires mortgage lenders to make a reasonable and good faith determination that a borrower has the ability to repay the loan. This must be based on the verified and documented income and assets of the proposed borrower. In a foreclosure action brought by a lender, a borrower may assert a violation of this standard as a defense to the lender recovering money from the borrower.
- **Consumer Financial Protection Bureau.** The act created the **Consumer Financial Protection Bureau (CFPB)**, a new federal regulatory agency. This agency has broad authority to regulate consumer financial products and services, including requiring increased disclosure of credit terms and risk to consumers. The agency can adopt rules to regulate the activities of banks, financial institutions, payday lenders, debt counselling firms, and other entities.

The act is discussed in the following feature.

Global Law

Hiding Money in Offshore Banks

THE BAHAMAS

This office building is located in the Bahamas. There are many offices in this building that act as "banks" for offshore money. This is primarily because the Bahamas offers bank secrecy laws and tax shelter laws. There are other bank secrecy hideouts and tax-evasion haven countries around the world, including Bermuda in the Caribbean, the countries of Liechtenstein and Monaco in Europe, the Isle of Man off of Great Britain, the micro-islands of Niue and Vanuatu in the South Pacific, and the Philippines, just to name a few. Tax evaders, money launderers, drug cartels, criminal organizations, corrupt government officials, white-collar criminals, terrorist groups, and others who want anonymity use these offshore banking countries to hide their money.

Key Terms and Concepts

Altered check (517)
Article 3 (Commercial Paper) (512)
Article 4 (Bank Deposits and Collections) (513)
Article 4A (Funds Transfers) of the UCC (513)
Automated teller machine (ATM) (521)
Bank check (514)
Bank Secrecy Act (516)
Cashier's check (514)
Certified check (514)
Check (513)
Collecting bank (519)
Collection process (519)
Commercial electronic funds transfers (523)
Commercial wire transfer (wholesale wire transfer) (523)
Consumer Financial Protection Bureau (CFPB) (523)
Creditor–debtor relationship (512)
Currency Transaction Report (CTR) (516)
Debit card (521)

Deferred posting rule (520)
Deposit (513)
Deposit of cash (520)
Depository bank (519)
Dodd-Frank Wall Street Reform and Consumer Protection Act (523)
Drawee of a check (513)
Drawer of a check (513)
Electronic Fund Transfer Act (EFTA) (522)
Electronic funds transfer system (EFTS) (521)
Federal Deposit Insurance Corporation (FDIC) (521)
Federal Reserve System (Federal Reserve) (520)
Forged instrument (517)
Honor (515)
Incomplete check (515)
Insufficient funds (516)
Intermediary bank (519)
Judgment proof (517)
Midnight deadline (520)
"On them" item (520)
"On us" item (520)
One-year rule (518)
Online banking (522)
Ordinary check (513)
Original tenor (517)
Overdraft (516)
Payee of a check (513)
Payer bank (519)
Postdated check (515)
Presentment across the counter (521)
Principal–agent relationship (512)
Regulation E (522)
Revised Article 3 (Negotiable Instruments) (512)
Series of forgeries or alterations (518)
Stale check (515)
Stop-payment order (515)
Uniform Commercial Code (512)
Wrongful dishonor (516)

Critical Legal Thinking Cases

25.1 Cashier's Check Dr. Graham Wood purchased a cashier's check in the amount of $6,000 from Central Bank of the South (Bank). The check was made payable to Ken Walker and was delivered to him. Eleven months later, Bank's branch manager informed Wood that the cashier's check was still outstanding. Wood subsequently signed a form, requesting that payment be stopped and a replacement check issued. He also agreed to indemnify Bank for any damages resulting from the issuance of the replacement check. Bank issued a replacement check to Wood. Seven months later, Walker deposited the original cashier's check in his bank, which was paid by Bank. Bank requested that Woods repay the bank $6,000. When he refused, Bank sued Woods to recover this amount. Who wins? *Wood v. Central Bank of the South*, 435 So.2d 1287, 1982 Ala. Civ. App. Lexis 1362 (Court of Civil Appeals of Alabama)

25.2 Overdraft Louise Kalbe maintained a checking account at the Pulaski State Bank (Bank) in Wisconsin. Kalbe made out a check for $7,260, payable in cash. Thereafter, she misplaced it but did not report the missing check to the bank or stop payment on it. One month later, some unknown person presented the check to a Florida bank for payment. The Florida bank paid the check and sent it to Bank for collection. Bank paid the check even though it created a $6,542.12 overdraft in Kalbe's account. Bank requested Kalbe pay this amount. When she refused, Bank sued Kalbe to collect the overdraft. Who wins? *Pulaski State Bank v. Kalbe*, 122 Wis.2d 663, 364 N.W.2d 162, 1985 Wisc. App. Lexis 3034 (Court of Appeals of Wisconsin)

25.3 Wrongful Dishonor Larry J. Goodwin and his wife maintained a checking and savings account at City National Bank of Fort Smith (Bank). Bank also had a customer named Larry K. Goodwin. Two loans of Larry K. Goodwin were in default. Bank mistakenly took money from Larry J. Goodwin's checking account to pay the loans. At the end of the month, the Goodwins received written notice that four of their checks, which were written to merchants, had been dishonored for insufficient funds. When the Goodwins investigated, they discovered that their checking account balance was zero and that the bank had placed their savings account on hold. After being informed of the error, Bank promised to send letters of apology to the four merchants and to correct the error. Bank, however, subsequently "bounced" several other checks of the Goodwins. Eventually, Bank notified all the parties of its error. One month later, the Goodwins closed their accounts at Bank and were paid the correct balances due. They sued the bank for consequential and punitive damages for wrongful dishonor. Who wins? *City National Bank of Fort Smith v. Goodwin*, 301 Ark. 182, 783 S.W.2d 335, 1990 Ark. Lexis 49 (Supreme Court of Arkansas)

25.4 Stale Check Charles Ragusa & Son (Ragusa), a partnership consisting of Charles and Michael Ragusa, issued a check in the amount of $5,000, payable to Southern Masonry, Inc. (Southern). The check was drawn on Community State Bank (Bank). Several days later, Southern informed Ragusa that the check had been lost. Ragusa issued a replacement check for the same amount and sent it to Southern, and that check was cashed. At the same time, Ragusa gave a verbal stop-payment order to Bank regarding the original check. Three years later, the original check was deposited by Southern into its account at the Bank of New Orleans. When the check was presented to Bank, it paid it and charged $5,000 against Ragusa's account. The partnership was not made aware of this transaction until one month later, when it received its monthly bank statement. Ragusa demanded that Bank recredit its account $5,000. When Bank refused to do so, Ragusa sued. Who wins? *Charles Ragusa & Son v. Community State Bank*, 360 So.2d 231, 1978 La. App. Lexis 3435 (Court of Appeal of Louisiana)

25.5 Postdated Check David Siegel maintained a checking account with the New England Merchants National Bank (Bank). On September 14, Siegel drew and delivered a $20,000 check payable to Peter Peters. The check was dated November 14. Peters immediately deposited the check in his own bank, which forwarded it for collection. On September 17, Bank paid the check and charged it against Siegel's account. Siegel discovered that the check had been paid when another of his checks was returned for insufficient funds. Siegel informed Bank that the check to Peters was postdated November 14 and requested that the bank return the $20,000 to his account. When Bank refused, Siegel sued for wrongful debit of his account. Must Bank recredit Siegel's account? *Siegel v. New England Merchants National Bank*, 386 Mass. 672, 437 N.E.2d 218, 1982 Mass. Lexis 1559 (Supreme Judicial Court of Massachusetts)

25.6 Stop Payment Dynamite Enterprises, Inc. (Dynamite), a corporation doing business in Florida, maintained a checking account at Eagle National Bank of Miami (Bank). Dynamite drew a check on this account, payable to one of its business associates. Before the check had been cashed or deposited, Dynamite issued a written stop-payment order to Bank. Bank informed Dynamite that it would not place a stop-payment order on the check because there were insufficient funds in the account to pay the check. Several weeks later, the check was presented to Bank for payment. By this time, sufficient funds had been deposited in the account to pay the check. Bank paid the check and charged Dynamite's account. When Dynamite learned that the check had been paid, it requested Bank to recredit its account. When Bank refused, Dynamite sued to recover the amount of the check. Who wins? *Dynamite Enterprises, Inc. v. Eagle National Bank of Miami*, 517 So.2d 112, 1987 Fla. App. Lexis 11791 (Court of Appeal of Florida)

Ethical

Ethics Case

25.7 Ethics Case Mr. Gennone maintained a checking account at Peoples National Bank & Trust Company of Pennsylvania (Bank). Gennone noticed that he was not receiving his bank statements and canceled checks. When Gennone contacted Bank, he was informed that the statements had been mailed to him. Bank agreed to hold future statements so that he could pick them up in person. Gennone picked up the statements but did not reconcile the balance of the account. As a result, it was not until two years later that he discovered that beginning more than one year earlier, his wife had forged his signature on 25 checks. Gennone requested Bank to reimburse him for the amount of these checks. When Bank refused, Gennone sued Bank to recover. Did Gennone act ethically in suing the bank? Who wins? *Gennone v. Peoples National Bank & Trust Co.*, 9 U.C.C. Rep. Serv. 707, 1971 Pa. Dist. & Cnty. Dec. Lexis 551, 51 Pa. D. & C.2d 529 (Common Pleas Court of Montgomery County, Pennsylvania)

Notes

1. 31 U.S.C. 5311 et seq.
2. 15 U.S.C. 1693 et seq.
3. Public Law 111-203.

CASE *Uniform Commercial Code in Alaska*

National Bank of Alaska v. Univentures 1231 and State of Alaska, Department of Administration

3AN-88-278 Civil, 3799 January 24, 1992
Supreme Court of Alaska
Before: Rabinowitz, Chief Justice, Burke, Matthews, Compton, and Moore, Justices
Opinion by, MOORE, Justice

National Bank of Alaska (NBA) brought an action against the State of Alaska, Univentures 1231 (Univentures), Charles D. LeViege, and Lee D. Garcia to recover the amount which NBA paid on a warrant issued by the state. The superior court held that the warrant is not a negotiable instrument under the Uniform Commercial Code as enacted in Alaska, and that NBA therefore could not recover as a holder in due course under the code. NBA appeals. The sole issue on appeal is whether the superior court was correct in finding that the state treasury warrant is a non-negotiable instrument under Article III of the Uniform Commercial Code. We reverse.

I

The State of Alaska is a tenant in a large office building which is owned by Univentures. On November 24, 1987, the state made a lease payment of $28,143.47 to Univentures with state treasury warrant No. 21045102. Charles LeViege, the managing partner of Univentures, assigned the warrant on behalf of Univentures to Lee Garcia.

As a result of a dispute which arose among the partners of Univentures, the state was notified on November 25, 1987 that it should no longer pay Charles LeViege the monthly rent due the partnership. The state was directed to hold the rent in abeyance pending the naming of a court-appointed receiver. On November 27, 1987, the state treasury placed a stop-payment order on warrant No. 21045102.

Garcia presented the warrant to NBA, the state's clearing bank, on November 30, 1987. NBA paid Garcia $28,143.47 on the warrant but did not debit the state's account because of the stop-payment order. On January 14, 1988, NBA filed an action against the State of Alaska, Charles LeViege, and Lee Garcia, to recover the sum of $28,143.47 which NBA had paid to Lee Garcia in exchange for the warrant. The state deposited an equivalent sum with the court and moved to join Univentures as a party. Samuel and Catherine LeViege answered on behalf of Univentures.

NBA moved for summary judgment claiming that it is a holder in due course under AS 45.03.302(a). NBA argued that the warrant is a negotiable instrument and that it paid the warrant in good faith, without knowledge of facts which would indicate the instrument may not be payable as its terms provide. As such, NBA maintained that it took the warrant free from the defenses presented by Univentures and the state. The state and Univentures opposed NBA's motion, arguing that NBA is not a holder in due course because the warrant is not a negotiable instrument, and because NBA had notice of the stop-payment order when it paid Garcia on the warrant. Univentures filed a cross-motion for summary judgment.

The superior court granted Univentures' cross-motion for summary judgment and denied NBA's motion for summary judgment. Judge Ripley, in ruling for Univentures, specifically found that the warrant is not a negotiable instrument and that NBA therefore is not a holder in due course. Pursuant to the parties' stipulation, $16,000.00 of the money deposited with the court was immediately disbursed to Univentures and NBA in equal amounts. The court ordered that the remaining $12,143.47 be held by the court pending appeal of the court's determination that the warrant is not negotiable. This appeal followed.

II

Article III of the Uniform Commercial Code provides that the holder in due course of an instrument takes the instrument free of all but a very limited class of defenses that the original payor might have against the original payee. AS 45.03.305.[1] The code defines a holder in due course as one who takes a negotiable instrument for value, in good faith, and "without notice that [the instrument] is overdue or has been dishonored or of any defense against or claim to it on the part of any person." AS 45.03.302(a). If a holder of an instrument is not a holder in due course, the holder takes the instrument subject to all valid claims to the instrument, as well as subject to several classes of defenses. AS 45.03.306.[2]

(case continues)

The superior court held that NBA was not a holder in due course because the state treasury warrant involved is not a negotiable instrument to which the Uniform Commercial Code applies.[3] As a result, the superior court concluded that NBA took the warrant subject to the state's defense that it had issued a valid stop-payment order pursuant to AS 45.04.403(a).[4] NBA argues that the warrant is a negotiable instrument, and that NBA is therefore a holder in due course. Whether the warrant is a negotiable instrument is a question of law, which we examine de novo. *See Hicklin v. Orbeck*, 565 P.2d 159, 163 n.6 (Alaska 1977) rev'd on other grounds, 437 U.S. 518 (1978).

Alaska Statute 45.03.104(a) provides that for a writing to be a negotiable instrument it must:

> *(1) be signed by the maker or drawer;*
> *(2) contain an unconditional promise or order to pay a sum certain in money and no other promise, order, obligation, or power given by the maker or drawer except as authorized by this chapter;*
> *(3) be payable on demand or at a definite time, and*
> *(4) be payable to order or to bearer.*

Alaska Statute 45.01.102(a) provides that the Code is to be "liberally construed and applied to promote the underlying purposes and policies." The underlying purposes and policies of the Uniform Commercial Code are:

> *(1) to simplify, clarify, and modernize the law governing commercial transactions;*
> *(2) to permit the continued expansion of commercial practices through custom, usage, and agreement of the parties;*
> *(3) to make uniform the law among the various jurisdictions.*

AS 45.01.102(b).

Warrant No. 21045102 satisfies all four elements of the definition of a negotiable instrument. First, the warrant is signed by the maker, Governor Steve Cowper. Second, the warrant contains an unconditional promise or order to pay a sum certain of $28,143.47. A promise or order otherwise unconditional is not made conditional by the fact that the instrument is limited to payment out of a particular fund if the instrument is issued by a government or governmental agency or unit. AS 45.03.105(a)(7). Third, the warrant is payable at a definite time. Although the warrant states that it "will be deemed paid unless redeemed within two years after the date of issue," AS 45.03.109 provides that an instrument is payable at a definite time if by its terms it is payable on or before a stated date. AS 45.03.109(a)(1). Finally, the warrant clearly indicates that it is payable to the order of Univentures. An "instrument is payable to order if by its terms it is payable to the order or assigns of a person specified in the instrument with reasonable certainty." AS 45.03.110(a). Because the warrant meets the statutory definition in AS 45.03.104, we hold that the warrant is a negotiable instrument.[5]

The purposes for which the Uniform Commercial Code was enacted support the conclusion that warrants which satisfy the statutory definition of negotiability must be deemed negotiable. Univentures claims that state warrants should be deemed non-negotiable because the state must retain its rights to assert the defenses of a maker in order to maintain and protect its fiscal policies, practices, and procedures. This argument is directly contrary to the Code's policy of promoting commercial transactions by allowing a party to ascertain the negotiability of an instrument from its face. 5 R. Anderson, Uniform Commercial Code, 3-104:4 (1984) ("The whole idea of the facilitation of easy transfer of notes and instruments requires that a transferee be able to trust what the instrument says, and be able to determine the validity of the note and its negotiability from the language in the note itself."). To carve out an exception to the statutory definition of negotiability would jeopardize Article III's purposes of clarifying and modernizing commercial transactions by allowing reliance on written instruments. The transferee of an instrument must be able to rely on the negotiability of the instrument as evidenced by the instrument's terms, so that the transaction is not stalled while the transferee verifies its rights on the instrument.[6]

No Alaska case law addresses the issue of whether a state treasury warrant constitutes a negotiable instrument. Prior to the enactment of the Uniform Commercial Code, warrants issued by states, local governments, and municipalities were almost universally deemed non-negotiable. *See, e.g.*, Negotiability of County, Municipal, School, State, or Town Warrants, 36 A.L.R. 949, 949 (1925); Hamilton Nat'l *Bank v. Pool*, 144 S.W.2d 670, 671 (Tex. App. 1940); *State v. Liberty Nat'l Bank & Trust Co.*, 414 P.2d 281, 283 (Okla. 1966). The drafters of the Uniform Commercial Code apparently intended to change this body of law, however, as evidenced by the Official Code Comment to 3-105. 5 R. Anderson, Uniform Commercial Code, 3-105:1, at 228 (1984)("[Section 3-105(1)(g)] will permit some municipal warrants to be negotiable if they are in proper form.").[7]

Those courts which have considered the negotiability of government warrants have generally found

(case continues)

those warrants to be negotiable so long as they satisfy the Code's requirements. The Louisiana Court of Appeals held that a warrant issued by a levee district to pay a construction company was a negotiable instrument. *St. James Bank & Trust Co. v. Board of Comm'rs*, 354 So. 2d 233 (La. App. 1978). The construction company in that case had negotiated the warrant to a bank. After the levee's Board of Commissioners stopped payment on the warrant, the warrant was returned to the bank unpaid. The court found that the warrant was a negotiable instrument because it satisfied the requirements of 10:3-104 of the Louisiana statutes. That section is identical to AS 45.03.104. *Id.* at 234.

Similarly, the Supreme Court of Nebraska held that a warrant issued by a county sanitary and improvement district was a negotiable instrument. *Sanitary & Improvement Dist. v. Continental Western*, 343 N.W.2d 314 (Neb. 1983). In that case, the sanitary and improvement district which had issued capital and improvement warrants sought a judicial declaration of the invalidity of the warrants. After examining the warrants in light of 3-104 of the Nebraska Uniform Commercial Code, which is almost identical to AS 45.03.104, the Supreme Court of Nebraska held that they were negotiable instruments.

We are mindful of a 1987 attorney general opinion which concluded that state treasury warrants are not negotiable. While attorney general opinions are entitled to some deference in matters of statutory construction, they are not always correct.[8] In this instance we are unconvinced by the attorney general's opinion. It fails to consult the language and policies of the Uniform Commercial Code, and it relies mainly on cases examining the negotiability of warrants arising prior to the enactment of the Uniform Commercial Code.

The decision of the superior court is REVERSED. The $12,143.47 on deposit with the court is awarded to NBA.[9]

---

1. AS 45.03.305 provides:
   To the extent that a holder is a holder in due course the holder takes the instrument free from
   (1) all claims to it on the part of any person; and
   (2) all defenses of any party to the instrument with whom the holder has not dealt except
   (A) infancy, to the extent that it is a defense to a simple contract;
   (B) such other incapacity, or duress, or illegality of the transaction as renders the obligation of the party a nullity;
   (C) such misrepresentation as has induced the party to sign the instrument with neither knowledge nor reasonable opportunity to obtain knowledge of its character or its essential terms;
   (D) discharge in solvency proceedings; and
   (E) any other discharge of which the holder has notice when the holder takes the instrument.
2. AS 45.03.306 provides:
   Unless the person has the rights of a holder in due course, a person takes the instrument subject to
   (1) all valid claims to it on the part of any person;
   (2) all defenses of a party which would be available in an action on a simple contract;
   (3) the defenses of want or failure of consideration, nonperformance of a condition precedent, nondelivery, or delivery for a special purpose (AS 45.03.408); and
   (4) the defense that the person or a person through whom the person holds the instrument acquired it by theft, or that payment or satisfaction to the holder would be inconsistent with the terms of a restrictive endorsement; the claim of a third person to the instrument is not otherwise available as a defense to a party liable on the instrument unless the third person personally defends the action for the party.
3. Univentures argued in its cross-motion for summary judgment that even if the warrant is a negotiable instrument, NBA is not a holder in due course because NBA had notice of the stop-payment order when it paid Garcia on the warrant. Univentures claimed that NBA was given notice of the stop-payment order on November 27, 1987, in its role as the clearing bank for state treasury warrants. The superior court apparently found that NBA did not have knowledge of the stop-payment order when it accepted the warrant, for the final judgment provides that NBA is entitled to the funds on deposit with the court if this court determines warrant No. 21045102 is a negotiable instrument. We do not consider whether NBA had knowledge of the stop-payment order, for that issue is not a stated point on appeal, and was not briefed by either party.
4. AS 45.04.403(a) provides:

   A customer may, by order to the bank, stop payment of an item payable for the customer's account, but the order must be received at a time and in a manner which afford the bank a reasonable opportunity to act on it before an action by the bank with respect to the item described in AS 45.04.303.

5. AS 45.03.104(b) classifies certain writings which satisfy the definition of "negotiable instrument" as drafts, checks, certificates of deposit, and notes. We reject the state's argument that an instrument must fit within one of these categories before it can qualify as a negotiable instrument. Negotiability is determined by the four-pronged test of AS 45.03.104, not by the name affixed to a particular writing. If it were necessary to categorize the warrant at issue in this case, it would be a draft. An instrument is a draft if it is an order. AS 45.03.104(b)(1).
6. If the state truly believes that the non-negotiability of treasury warrants is essential to maintain and protect its fiscal policies, the state could make its warrants non-negotiable simply by printing "non-negotiable" on the face of the warrants.
7. All of the cases cited by Univentures and the state are distinguishable from the present case for the reason that all were based upon the "law merchant" which has now been replaced in Alaska by the Uniform Commercial Code. *See Prince v.*

(case continues)

LeVan, 486 P.2d 959, 962 (Alaska 1971) ("By legislative declaration the code is the law, and if general principles appear inconsistent, they must be considered displaced under [this section]. Moreover, even where inconsistency does not exist, the code must be regarded as supreme; general principles even when consistent with the code are merely supplementary.").

8. *Carney v. State Board of Fisheries*, 785 P.2d 544, 548 (Alaska 1990) ("Opinions of the attorney general, while not controlling on matters of statutory interpretation, are entitled to some deference."); *Girves v. Kenai Peninsula Borough*, 536 P.2d 1221, 1225 (Alaska 1975) ("We hold that the 1962 Attorney General's opinion is in error insofar as it concludes that the territorial government of Alaska had no power to accept the right-of-way granted in 43 U.S.C. 932 (1964).").

9. NBA and Univentures stipulated that if we reverse the superior court's determination that the warrant is not a negotiable instrument, Univentures waives all other claims to the interpled money against NBA and the state, including the claim that NBA was not a holder in due course of the instrument.

CASE *Breach of Contract*

Wing v. Schaub

1389, S-13508, July 27, 2011
Supreme Court of Alaska
Before: Carpeneti, Chief Justice, Fabe, Winfree, Christen, and Stowers, Justices

Introduction

Gregory Wing and Kirk Schaub were owners of Body Tech Gym (Body Tech), a small neighborhood gym in Anchorage. For most of the time they owned the company, Schaub acted as manager of the gym. In August 2004 Body Tech lost its lease, and in November 2004 Wing agreed to purchase Schaub's share of the company. Under the purchase agreement, Wing agreed to pay Schaub $20,000 in cash and to sign a $50,000 promissory note due in January 2005. Schaub agreed to relinquish his share of the company and to assist Wing in the transfer of assets into his name. Wing relocated Body Tech after he purchased Schaub's share of the gym.

Wing did not pay the $50,000 promissory note and Schaub sued to enforce the note. Wing raised several counterclaims, including claims that Schaub breached the purchase agreement and the covenant of good faith and fair dealing, that Schaub made fraudulent misrepresentations during the negotiations, and that Schaub breached his fiduciary duty to Wing by making unauthorized withdrawals from Body Tech's accounts. At the end of a six-day trial, the superior court entered judgment in Schaub's favor, concluding that Wing owed Schaub pursuant to the promissory note and that Wing had not proven his counterclaims. Wing appeals.

We hold that it was error for the superior court to conclude that Schaub did not breach the purchase agreement and the covenant of good faith and fair dealing. We therefore reverse that part of the superior court's decision determining that Schaub did not breach the purchase agreement, did not breach the covenant of good faith and fair dealing, and did not convert Wing's property. We affirm that part of the superior court's decision determining that Wing did not prove his breach of employment contract, breach of fiduciary duty, and fraud claims. We vacate the superior court's attorney's fee award and remand for: (1) a determination of whether Schaub's breaches were material and therefore excused Wing's failure to pay the promissory note, and (2) a calculation of any damages that may have resulted from Schaub's breaches.

Facts and Proceedings

Body Tech Gym

In July 2002 Gregory Wing, Kirk Schaub, and Tim Sweeny purchased Body Tech Gym, a small neighborhood gym. At the time of the purchase Wing lived in Anchorage, and Schaub lived in Florida and worked for Anheuser-Busch. The investors intended for Schaub eventually to serve as manager of Body Tech after he moved from Florida to Anchorage. In July 2003 Schaub returned to Alaska to take over as manager of the gym; he would hold the position until November 2004.

In addition to managing the gym, Schaub took clients as a personal trainer at Body Tech. Schaub was also an Alaska distributor for Cytosport products, distributing the products to other vendors in the Anchorage area. Schaub also sold Cytosport products at Body Tech.

At trial the parties presented conflicting testimony on what Schaub's compensation was for managing

(case continues)

Body Tech. Schaub testified that they had agreed that he would receive $5,000 a month, all sales from his Cytosport distribution business (including 100% of profits from Body Tech's Cytosport sales), and all of his personal training fees. Wing testified that they had agreed that Schaub would receive ten percent of gross sales from the gym, all proceeds from Cytosport sales outside the gym, and all of his personal training fees.

While Schaub managed Body Tech he did not segregate his personal finances from the business's finances. He used the company accounts to pay his bills, his mortgage, and other expenses. He used his personal credit card for company expenses. Schaub also deposited the money that he received from personal training fees and product sales into the company accounts.

During Schaub's tenure as manager, Body Tech contracted with Cornerstone Credit Services (Cornerstone) to provide two forms of services. First, Body Tech contracted with Cornerstone to act as a collections agency for past-due accounts. Cornerstone would send Body Tech money that it recovered from delinquent members. Second, Body Tech contracted with Cornerstone to process electronic funds transfers (EFTs). Cornerstone provided a computer program to Body Tech that would allow the gym to track billing and payments via credit card. The program would gather all the monthly credit card transactions and send them to Cornerstone to process. Cornerstone would then deposit the funds from the transactions into a Body Tech checking account.

Body Tech had a main checking account at Northrim Bank to which both Wing and Schaub had access. On July 26, 2004, Wing froze Schaub's access to the Northrim bank account. In response, Schaub opened a second Body Tech checking account at Northern Skies Federal Credit Union on July 30, 2004. That same day, Wing restored Schaub's access to the Northrim bank account. After Wing restored his access to the Northrim account, Schaub continued to use the Northern Skies bank account for deposits and to pay business and personal obligations.

On August 2, 2004, Schaub received notice that Body Tech was going to lose its lease and that the gym had to move or shut down. Schaub informed Wing of the notice around August 23, and they obtained an extension on the lease until November 17 to find a place to relocate the gym.

Negotiation of the Purchase Agreement

Wing and Schaub could not agree on where to relocate Body Tech and on November 2, 2004 began negotiations regarding which of them would purchase the other's interest in the gym. Wing offered to sell his interest to Schaub, but Schaub declined the offer. The parties engaged in two days of negotiation over a purchase price for Wing to buy Schaub's share of the gym. Wing and Schaub documented their negotiations primarily through several handwritten sheets of paper that they introduced in evidence at trial.

During the negotiations, Schaub told Wing that he had loaned Body Tech $9,900 in August 2004. Schaub also told Wing how much he had withdrawn from Body Tech accounts during his tenure as manager. According to Wing, Schaub stated that he withdrew a total of $63,090. According to Schaub, the amount he had taken out was $97,863 in total draws. One section of the negotiation document that seems to address Schaub's withdrawals states "[check] acct draws 63090." It also states "$ draw 6000."

Wing decided to buy Schaub's interest and continue operating the gym as "World Gym." On November 10, 2004, the parties signed the purchase agreement under which Schaub would sell Wing his share of Body Tech for an up-front payment of $20,000 cash and a promissory note for $50,000 payable on January 15, 2005. Schaub was to retain $12,000 worth of equipment. The promissory note further stated that "[i]f any suit or action is instituted to collect this Note . . . [Wing] . . . agrees to pay . . . a reasonable sum as attorney fees in such action or suit."

Body Tech after the Purchase Agreement

Schaub's transfer of body tech financial information and accounts to wing

Under the purchase agreement, Wing was to receive Body Tech's records, financial accounts, and customer membership information. Wing also was to receive Body Tech's phone number and all accounts receivable earned before the sale.

At the time of the purchase, Wing had access to Body Tech's Northrim bank account, but Schaub was the sole signer on Body Tech's Northern Skies bank account. Wing did not learn of the Northern Skies bank account until after the sale, and he had to go through his lawyer to gain access to the account. The Northern Skies bank account was not transferred into Wing's name until December 6, 2004.

On the day the purchase agreement was signed, Schaub recorded a message on Body Tech's answering machine instructing callers to "please contact [him] directly" if they had "questions regarding Body Tech effective November 10." Although Wing changed the phone number into his name approximately five days later, Wing did not realize that Schaub had recorded the message for several weeks. Schaub had not given

(case continues)

Wing the passwords to change the message. Wing eventually changed the message after he sent proof of corporate ownership to the phone company.

After he signed the purchase agreement, Wing asked Schaub where the customer billing information was; Schaub replied it was on the computer. But the customer billing information, including past billing information, was missing from the computer.

Schaub did not tell Wing about Body Tech's contracts with Cornerstone. Wing did not learn about Body Tech's EFT contract with Cornerstone until trial in January 2009. Because Wing did not have access to the EFT account information through Cornerstone or on the computer, he had to recreate the billing accounts and manually charge Body Tech members' credit cards.

Wing did not learn about Body Tech's accounts receivable collections contract with Cornerstone until several months after the sale. Schaub also did not inform Cornerstone that he had sold his stake in Body Tech to Wing. Cornerstone's records show that Cornerstone received a call from Schaub on March 14, 2005 regarding the buy out of Body Tech by World Gym, and a note in Cornerstone's file memorializing the call states: "[T]he collection accounts were not part of the sale agreement, leave the address the way it is, refer World Gym to Kirk, do not disclose anything." Wing eventually gained access to the account.

Between November 2004 and March 2005, Cornerstone sent several Body Tech collections checks to Schaub's personal post office box. Schaub did not turn over these checks, which totaled approximately $2,800, to Wing until April 2005.

Later developments

On November 15, 2004, five days after Wing and Schaub signed the purchase agreement, Body Tech closed at its original location. On November 29, 2004, Schaub sent a letter to all Body Tech gym members without Wing's knowledge. The letter stated that "BodyTech has closed." The letter also stated that the members had "the option to continue training at World Gym who has offered to honor existing BodyTech member contracts if you choose to train at the World Gym facility." Schaub testified that he sent the letter to describe what happened to the gym to those members who did not regularly visit the gym. After Schaub sent the letter, he received e-mails and letters from members who interpreted his letter as giving the members an option to cancel their contracts. Schaub did not respond to these e-mails or forward them to Wing.

Wing eventually relocated Body Tech to a nearby location, spending over $98,000 in the process. After moving Body Tech, Wing operated Body Tech as a World Gym franchise for two years before selling the gym to the Alaska Club. He testified that the gym averaged a loss of approximately $3,000 per month during this two-year period.

Wing never paid Schaub $50,000 as required by the promissory note and the purchase agreement.

Procedural History

On March 24, 2005, Schaub sued Wing in superior court, claiming that Wing had failed to pay the promissory note. In response, Wing raised six counterclaims, including: (1) breach of contract; (2) breach of the covenant of good faith and fair dealing; (3) breach of fiduciary duty; (4) restitution; (5) fraud; and (6) conversion. A six-day trial on the claims began on January 26, 2009.

On March 18, 2009, the superior court issued its Decision and Order. The court found that Wing had failed to pay the note and that Schaub's case was therefore "virtually stipulated." It held that Wing had failed to prove his case on all of his counterclaims, and ruled in favor of Schaub overall. The superior court awarded Schaub full attorney's fees under the attorney's fee provision in the promissory note, omitting only a small portion of the fees attributable to Sweeny as an intervenor.[1]

Wing appeals.

Discussion

Standard of Review

We apply our independent judgment when reviewing the trial court's interpretation of a contract.[2] We review the trial court's findings of fact, including those on the credibility of witnesses, for clear error.[3] We will find clear error only if, after a thorough review of the record, we come to a "definite and firm conviction that a mistake has been made."[4] We review factual findings in the light most favorable to the prevailing party below.[5]

Whether a party breached a contract or the covenant of good faith and fair dealing is a question for the trier of fact.[6] However, we may review the application of legal doctrine to undisputed facts without the usual deference to the superior court.[7] Thus, we may review de novo the court's determination that these undisputed facts do not prove a breach of the contract or the covenant of good faith and fair dealing.[8]

Schaub Breached the Purchase Agreement and the Covenant of Good Faith and Fair Dealing

At trial, Wing presented several claims for breach of contract and breach of the covenant of good faith and

(case continues)

fair dealing. The superior court held that Schaub did not breach the contract or violate the duty of good faith and fair dealing. Wing argues that the superior court erred in holding that he did not prove six of his claims. Wing argues that he suffered significant damages due to Schaub's breaches and that Schaub's breaches should excuse Wing's failure to pay the promissory note.

Schaub's November 2004 letter and Schaub's answering machine message

Wing argues that Schaub "clearly intended to get as many members as possible to cancel their contracts" by sending the November 2004 letter to Body Tech members, a violation of the subjective prong of the covenant of good faith and fair dealing. He similarly argues that Schaub violated the covenant of good faith and fair dealing by recording a message on Body Tech's answering machine instructing customers to contact Schaub directly.[9]

The superior court concluded that Schaub did not breach the purchase agreement or the covenant of good faith and fair dealing by sending the November 2004 letter, noting that the letter was an "accurate description of what had happened" because "[i]t correctly set out the options for the customers." The superior court also concluded that the answering machine message was "not a breach of contract and the fact that Mr. Wing was slow to deal with the message merely reflects a pattern of ineffectiveness he demonstrated as a businessman."

We have held that:

> *The covenant of good faith and fair dealing is implied in every contract to give effect to the reasonable expectations of the parties, preventing each party from interfering with another party's right to receive the benefits of the agreement. The implied covenant has both a subjective and an objective prong. The subjective prong prohibits one party from acting to deprive the other of the benefits of the contract. The objective prong requires both parties to act in a way that a reasonable person would consider fair.*[10]

It was error to conclude that Schaub did not breach the covenant of good faith and fair dealing by sending the November 2004 letter.[11] We base our holding not to transfer the number to his name five days after signing the agreement. Schaub did not breach section 1(d) of the purchase agreement. on the fact that the November 2004 letter "could have been worded more perfectly" when it stated that Body Tech was "closed," but on the fact that it was deceptively worded. Schaub's letter was perhaps true in the most literal sense because Body Tech was losing its lease at its then-current location and would be temporarily shut down. But the letter was false in the most commonly understood sense: as Schaub knew, Body Tech gym would continue to be open under new management at a new location.

The letter's misrepresentation, that the gym was permanently closed instead of merely relocating, is important because every Body Tech member's contract had an "opt-out" clause that allowed the member to cancel the contract if the gym closed. The letter therefore seems to instruct its recipients that they could cancel their Body Tech contracts. The letter reinforces this implied meaning by stating that members had the "option" to continue training at another gym. Schaub's message did not go unnoticed; several members contacted Schaub and Wing in response to the letter to request cancellation of their Body Tech memberships. Schaub did not forward to Wing any of the e-mails or letters he received from Body Tech members in response to his November 2004 letter. Even if Schaub did not intend to sabotage the contracts by sending the letter, as he claims, it is clear to us that the letter had the effect of sabotaging Wing's business. We therefore hold that the trial court's factual finding on the letter's accuracy was clearly erroneous.

It was also error to conclude that Schaub did not breach the covenant of good faith and fair dealing by leaving a message on Body Tech's answering machine directing customers to contact him directly. Schaub does not dispute the facts relevant to Wing's claim. Schaub changed the message on Body Tech's answering machine on the evening that he sold his share of Body Tech to Wing. The new message directed Body Tech customers to contact Schaub directly. Schaub did not tell Wing about the existence of the message, and did not give Wing the passwords to change the message. We therefore hold that the trial court's finding that Schaub's conduct was not a breach of the covenant of good faith and fair dealing was unsupported by the record and thus clearly erroneous.

Cornerstone collection accounts

Wing also argues that the superior court erred in concluding that Schaub did not breach sections 1(h)[12] and 4.6[13] of the contract when he failed to give Wing access to Body Tech's collections account with Cornerstone and possession of the Cornerstone collection checks. Section 1(h) of the purchase agreement states that Wing "will retain and collect all cash and accounts receivable" earned before the execution of the agreement. Section 4.6 of the purchase

(case continues)

agreement states: "Seller agrees . . . to do all things that are reasonabl[y] necessary for the vesting and transfer of assets to the Purchaser."

It was error to hold that Schaub did not breach the purchase agreement by failing to tell Wing about the Cornerstone collections account. It was also error to hold that Schaub did not breach the purchase agreement by failing to promptly turn over the Cornerstone collections checks. Both the superior court's written findings and the record support our conclusion.

The superior court ruled that Schaub had not breached the contract by failing to give Wing information about the Cornerstone collections contract or by failing to give Wing the collections checks. But the court also found that "[t]he fact that [Schaub] initially didn't want to share information about the funds to be collected does suggest that at least momentarily he had larceny in his heart." This finding irreconcilably conflicts with the court's legal conclusion. If Schaub did not tell Wing about the Cornerstone contract, he necessarily breached his duty under section 4.6 to assist Wing in transferring Body Tech assets. It is inconsistent to say that Schaub was "assisting" Wing while he simultaneously withheld vital information about Body Tech's contracts and assets. Likewise, if Schaub failed to hand over the collections checks with "larceny in his heart," he necessarily breached his duty under section 1(h) to hand over Body Tech's accounts receivable, and section 4.6's requirement that he was "to do all things reasonabl[y] necessary" to transfer the gym's assets to Wing.

The record supports the superior court's finding that Schaub did not turn over the information about the contract or the checks. Wing testified that Schaub never informed him of the Cornerstone collections account; he only learned of the account when Cornerstone called Body Tech expecting to talk to Schaub, but Wing answered the phone. Schaub did not present any evidence showing that he told Wing about the Cornerstone collections account. Additionally, the record shows Schaub called Cornerstone and stated that the collection accounts were not part of the purchase agreement, and instructed Cornerstone not to disclose anything to Wing. Wing undisputedly did not receive access to the Cornerstone collections account until March 2005. Finally, Schaub did not turn over several collections checks he received from Cornerstone until April 2005. Under our de novo review of the undisputed facts, we hold that Schaub breached both the contract and the covenant of good faith and fair dealing by actively impeding Wing's ability to collect Body Tech's accounts receivable in violation of sections 1(h) and 4.6 of the purchase agreement.

Cornerstone EFT account

Wing argues the superior court erred in failing to hold that Schaub breached sections 1(g), 1(h), and 4.6 of the purchase agreement by failing to tell Wing about Body Tech's EFT contract with Cornerstone. The superior court did not make findings on Wing's claim that Schaub breached the purchase agreement by not telling Wing about the EFT account.

Under section 1(h) of the purchase agreement, Schaub agreed to "assist [Wing] with the orderly transfer of the Electronic Fund Transfers ("EFT") for Body Tech's members." Likewise, under section 4.6, Schaub agreed to "do all things reasonabl[y] necessary for the . . . transfer of the EFT's." We interpret these provisions of the purchase agreement to impose an affirmative duty on Schaub to inform Wing about the existence of the Cornerstone EFT contract. Wing testified that he did not receive any information about the EFTs from Schaub, and that he was not even aware of the existence of the Cornerstone contract until the trial. Schaub did not dispute either of these assertions at trial and does not address the issue on appeal. We therefore hold that Schaub breached sections 1(h) and 4.6 of the contract and the covenant of good faith and fair dealing by failing to inform Wing of the existence of the Cornerstone EFT contract.

Northern Skies bank account

Finally Wing argues that Schaub breached section 1(g)[14] of the purchase agreement by failing to immediately transfer Body Tech's Northern Skies bank account into his name. The superior court did not make findings on Wing's claim that Schaub breached the purchase agreement by failing to turn over the bank account.

Section 1(g) of the purchase agreement states that "bank records . . . are property of the Purchaser and must be turned over upon execution of the Agreement." Wing testified, and Schaub does not dispute, that Wing did not know about the Northern Skies account at the time they signed the purchase agreement. Instead, Wing did not receive access to the account until December 6, 2004, nearly a month after his purchase of Body Tech. We therefore hold that Schaub breached section 1(g) of the purchase agreement and the covenant of good faith and fair dealing by failing to turn over the bank account immediately.

Summary

In conclusion, we hold that Schaub breached the purchase agreement and the covenant of good faith and fair dealing by sending the November 2004 letter.

(case continues)

Wing testified that Body Tech's member contracts were the primary assets that he purchased. The record supports Wing's assertion: Body Tech gym had few other assets because it was about to lose its lease and its gym equipment was encumbered by loans. Schaub's November 2004 letter, besides being objectively unfair, deprived Wing of some of the member contracts that he had purchased; several members cancelled their contracts in response to the letter.

We likewise hold that Schaub breached the purchase agreement and the covenant of good faith and fair dealing by failing to assist Wing in the transfer of the EFT accounts. The purchase agreement specifically required Schaub to assist Wing in transferring the EFTs for Body Tech members in sections 1(h) and 4.6.

Finally we hold that Schaub breached the purchase agreement and the covenant of good faith and fair dealing by failing to: (1) inform Wing about the Cornerstone collection account; (2) turn over approximately $2,800 in Cornerstone collections checks immediately; and (3) turn over access to the Northern Skies bank account immediately. The record shows that Wing, as the sole owner of Body Tech, was in a precarious financial position at the time of the purchase agreement. Body Tech was about to lose its lease and would have to relocate. Wing eventually incurred more than $98,000 in costs associated with relocating the gym, and had an upcoming obligation to pay Schaub the $50,000 promissory note.

We therefore reverse the superior court's conclusion that Schaub's actions did not constitute a breach of either the purchase agreement or the covenant of good faith and fair dealing and the court's conclusion that Wing breached the purchase agreement by failing to pay the promissory note, and we remand for a determination of whether Schaub's actions constituted a material breach.[15] On remand, the superior court should consider what both parties contemplated at the time of contract formation and determine what damages, if any, Wing suffered through Schaub's breaches of both the purchase agreement and the covenant of good faith and fair dealing.[16] The court should also determine the extent to which Schaub's breaches and related torts excused Wing's payments under the note. The court has the discretion to reopen evidence on remand, especially given Wing's undisputed claim that he did not know of the existence of the EFT account until the second day of trial.[17]

Wing's other Arguments

Wing's conversion claim

The superior court held that Wing "failed to prove conversion of corporate or personal money or property." It stated that "[t]here is no proof related to Mr. Schaub's handling of Mr. Wing's money." Wing argues that the superior court erred in holding that Schaub did not convert his property.

Conversion is "an intentional exercise of dominion or control over a chattel which so seriously interferes with the right of another to control it that the actor may justly be required to pay the other the full value of the chattel."[18]

As discussed above, the Cornerstone collection checks were Wing's property after the execution of the purchase agreement. Schaub does not dispute that it was several months before he turned over some of the collection checks to Wing. We therefore conclude, on the undisputed facts, that Schaub interfered with Wing's possession of his property.[19] Furthermore, although "ultimately the funds of the corporation still to be collected were paid" to Wing, the return of the converted property does not absolve a tortfeasor of liability.[20] Instead, the tortfeasor's return of the property diminishes the damages recoverable for the conversion.[21]

We hold that it was legal error to conclude that Schaub did not convert Wing's property. On remand, the superior court should determine any damages Wing suffered due to Schaub's conversion.

Wing's breach of employment contract, breach of fiduciary duty, and fraud claims

Wing raises several arguments regarding Schaub's actions before their execution of the purchase agreement. He argues that Schaub breached his employment agreement by withdrawing more than his management fee from company funds. He also argues that Schaub breached his fiduciary duty to Wing by making these unauthorized withdrawals from Body Tech's funds. Wing argues that Schaub committed fraud by representing during the purchase negotiations that he had withdrawn $63,090 in total draws when he had actually withdrawn more than $110,000.[22]

The superior court concluded that Wing had not proved that Schaub breached his employment contract or his fiduciary duty to Wing. It also concluded that Wing had not proved his fraud claims. The superior court seems to have implicitly found that Schaub withdrew the amount of money he was authorized to withdraw under his employment contract. It also seems to have implicitly found that Schaub did not make fraudulent statements during the negotiations.

While they ostensibly organized Body Tech as a corporation, neither Wing nor Schaub followed any corporate formalities. Schaub's employment contract was an oral contract, and Body Tech's records under his tenure as manager consisted mostly of

(case continues)

handwritten notes that are difficult to decipher. The parties presented conflicting testimony on how much Schaub would be paid for managing the gym, and the amount that Schaub withdrew from Body Tech accounts. Wing and Schaub's negotiation document is difficult to understand, but the document appears to support Schaub's testimony regarding his withdrawals.[23] Given the conflicting testimony presented at trial, we defer to the superior court's factual findings on these claims. We cannot say the superior court clearly erred in its implicit findings, and we affirm the court's conclusion that Wing did not prove his claims.

Attorney's fees

After entering its order in Schaub's favor, the superior court awarded Schaub full attorney's fees under the promissory note's "reasonable attorney fee" enforcement provision. Because we hold that Schaub breached the covenant of good faith and fair dealing and the purchase agreement, we also vacate the superior court's attorney's fee award.

Conclusion

For the reasons described above, we REVERSE that part of the superior court's decision determining that Schaub did not breach the purchase agreement, did not breach the covenant of good faith and fair dealing, and did not convert Wing's property. We AFFIRM that part of the superior court's decision determining that Wing did not prove his breach of employment contract, breach of fiduciary duty, and fraud claims. We VACATE the superior court's attorney's fee award, and we REMAND for further proceedings consistent with this opinion.

---

* Entered pursuant to Appellate Rule 214.

1. Tim Sweeny was a minority owner of the gym. Schaub purchased Sweeny's 10% ownership of the gym in July 2003. Sweeny participated in the suit as an intervenor, but was ultimately dismissed from the case.
2. *N. Pac. Processors, Inc. v. City & Borough of Yakutat*, 113 P.3d 575, 579 (Alaska 2005).
3. *Romero v. Cox*, 166 P.3d 4, 7 (Alaska 2007) (citing *Soules v. Ramstack*, 95 P.3d 933, 936-37 (Alaska 2004)).
4. *Id.* at 8.
5. *Id.* (citing *N. Pac. Processors, Inc.*, 113 P.3d at 579).
6. *See Rockstad v. Erikson*, 113 P.3d 1215, 1219 (Alaska 2005); *Luedtke v. Nabors Alaska Drilling, Inc.*, 834 P.2d 1220, 1223 (Alaska 1992).
7. *Id.* (citing *Foss Alaska Line, Inc. v. Northland Servs., Inc.*, 724 P.2d 523, 526 (Alaska 1986)).
8. *Id.*
9. Wing also argues that Schaub breached section 1(d) of the purchase agreement by changing the Body Tech answering machine message. Section 1(d) of the purchase agreement states: "Seller shall retain the rights to use the name Body Tech. . . . However, the rights to the phone number 338-2639 shall pass to Purchaser under this Agreement." But Wing received the rights to the phone number and was able
10. *Hawken Nw., Inc. v. State, Dep't of Admin.*, 76 P.3d 371, 381 (Alaska 2003) (quoting *McConnell v. State, Dep't of Health & Soc. Servs.*, 991 P.2d 178, 184 (Alaska 1999)) (internal quotation marks omitted).
11. Wing also argues that Schaub breached section 4.6 of the purchase agreement by sending the November 2004 letter and recording his message on Body Tech's answering machine. Section 4.6 of the purchase agreement states: "Seller agrees . . . to do all things that are reasonabl[y] necessary for the vesting and transfer of assets to the Purchaser." We interpret Schaub's promise to "do all things reasonabl[y] necessary" to include, by negative implication, a promise *not* to do things that impede the transfer of assets to Wing. As we discuss below, the November 2004 letter misrepresented Body Tech's relocation and enabled members to cancel their contracts. We therefore hold that Schaub's November 2004 letter also breached his duties under section 4.6 of the purchase agreement and therefore constituted a breach of the covenant of good faith and fair dealing.
12. Section 1(h) of the purchase agreement states: "Purchaser will retain and collect all cash and accounts receivable . . . . Seller further agrees to cooperate and assist Purchaser with the orderly transfer of the Electronic Fund Transfers ("EFT") for Body Tech's members."
13. The relevant language of section 4.6 is set out in footnote 11.
14. Section 1(g) of the purchase agreement states in relevant part: "Seller . . . acknowledges and agrees that all records of Body Tech, its members, bank records, accounts, etc., are property of the Purchaser and must be turned over upon execution of this Agreement."
15. Wing argues that Schaub's breaches of the purchase agreement and the covenant of good faith and fair dealing excuse Wing's failure to pay the $50,000 promissory note. Every breach of contract gives rise to a claim for damages, *Alaska Energy Auth. v. Fairmont Ins. Co.*, 845 P.2d 420, 423 n.3 (Alaska 1993) (quoting RESTATEMENT (SECOND) OF CONTRACTS § 236 cmt. b (1981)), and all material breaches justify the injured party's temporary suspension of performance. RESTATEMENT (SECOND) OF CONTRACTS § 242 cmt. a (1981). But only an uncured material breach will discharge the injured party's remaining duty of performance. *Id.* A breach is material if it goes to the "essence" of the contract or if it is "of such a nature as to defeat the object of the parties in making the contract." 14 RICHARD A. LORD, WILLISTON ON CONTRACTS § 43.6, at 578-79 (4th ed. 2000); *see Estate of Lampert ex rel. Thurston v. Estate of Lampert ex rel. Stauffer*, 896 P.2d 214, 219 (Alaska 1995) (holding that plaintiff may be entitled to rescission if defendant's actions "destroyed the 'essence' of the bargain." (citing RESTATEMENT (SECOND) OF CONTRACTS §§ 372-73 (1981))). Because the materiality of a breach is a question of fact reserved for the trial court, *see Wirum & Cash, Architects v. Cash*, 837 P.2d 692, 708 (Alaska 1992); *see also Hensley v. E. R. Carpenter Co., Inc.*, 633 F.2d 1106, 1109-10 (5th Cir. 1980) (remanding to trial court to determine if breach was material), we remand for a determination of whether Schaub's breach excused Wing's failure to pay the promissory note. It will be up to the trial court to determine whether, given the importance of the EFTs, Schaub's failure to assist Wing in transferring the EFTs went to the "essence" of the contract. Likewise, it is up to the trial court to determine whether, given Body Tech's precarious financial condition—of which Schaub was clearly

(case continues)

aware—Schaub's failure to disclose the Cornerstone account and hand over Body Tech's assets went to the "essence" of the purchase agreement. *See* 14 RICHARD A. LORD, WILLISTON ON CONTRACTS § 43.6, at 578-79 (4th ed. 2000) ("[W]hether a nonperformance is sufficiently material [to suspend or discharge the other party's duty to perform] is a question of fact. . . . Generally, such nonperformance will attain this level of materiality only when it goes to the . . . essence of the contract or is of such a nature as to defeat the object of the parties. . . . ").

16. For instance, Wing should be due damages from any contracts that Body Tech members cancelled because of Schaub's November 2004 letter. At minimum, Wing should be due damages equal to the interest on the collection checks Schaub did not turn over.

17. *See, e.g., Oberhansly v. Oberhansly*, 798 P.2d 883, 888 (Alaska 1990).

18. RESTATEMENT (SECOND) OF TORTS § 222A (1965).

19. *See K&K Recycling, Inc. v. Alaska Gold Co.*, 80 P.3d 702, 717 (Alaska 2003).

20. RESTATEMENT (SECOND) OF TORTS § 922 (1965).

21. *Id.*

22. Wing also argues Schaub committed fraud by representing that he had loaned the company $9,900. Schaub testified that the money was a loan from his father that he deposited in Body Tech's accounts. Wing presented evidence that the money was actually cash from Body Tech's daily sales. The superior court did not clearly err in crediting Schaub's testimony over Wing's testimony.

23. The negotiations document states "[check] acct draws 63090." It also states "$ draw 6000." This evidence reinforces the superior court's findings because Schaub probably would not have told Wing during negotiations that he had withdrawn $63,090 in "total" draws when the negotiations document also states that he withdrew $63,090 in "checking account" draws and that he withdrew the additional "cash" draws listed on the sheet.

CASE *Alaska Fur Gallery*

Alaska Fur Gallery, Inc v. First National Bank Alaska

3AN-06-06120 CI, 6986 March 13, 2015
Before: Stowers and Bolger, Justices, and Eastaugh, Senior Justice
Opinion by, BOLGER, Justice

Introduction

A family of business owners obtained a bank loan to invest in a fledgling hotel project. The family later sued the bank, alleging that one of its loan officers fraudulently induced them to invest in the project. This appeal concerns numerous aspects of the resulting superior court proceedings. In particular, the family claims that the bank committed a fraud upon the court through inaccurate and inconsistent portrayals of the loan officer's conduct. We conclude that although some testimony offered by the bank may have been misleading, it was not sufficiently egregious as to constitute fraud upon the court. We therefore affirm.

Facts and Proceedings

William McGrew, now deceased, was a loan officer and the senior vice president for commercial lending at First National Bank Alaska (the Bank). Among the Bank's corporate customers were Alaska Fur Gallery, Inc. and Hernandez & Associates, LLC. Both entities are owned and operated by members of the Hernandez family, and we refer to these entities collectively as "the Hernandezes" unless context requires otherwise.

The Hernandezes borrowed money from the Bank to invest in a hotel project, the Inn at Whittier, LLC (the Inn). But according to the Hernandezes, McGrew used his position of trust to induce unwise investments in the Inn and, when trouble arose, assured the Hernandezes that he would relieve them of their financial liability by finding replacement financing, which never came to fruition. The Hernandezes filed suit, alleging both common law tort claims and Alaska Securities Act[1] violations.

The case was originally tried in 2008, but for reasons not relevant to this appeal, the superior court ordered a new trial. This second trial, conducted in 2010, resulted in an award for the Hernandezes on their common law negligence claim only. The jury found that the Hernandezes had suffered $675,000 in damages but determined that the Bank was only partially at fault. The jury concluded that another investor, Edward Cronick, also contributed to the Hernandezes' loss, and that the Hernandezes themselves were negligent and unreasonably failed to avoid damages. The jury allocated 45% of the fault to the Hernandezes, 41% to Cronick, and 14% to the Bank.

Based on the jury's verdict, the superior court entered judgment against the Bank in the amount of $94,500 in damages, plus interest. The court also awarded the Hernandezes attorney's fees and costs.

(case continues)

The Hernandezes' appeal and the Bank's cross-appeal involve multiple rulings at various stages of the superior court proceedings. These specific rulings and the underlying facts are detailed in the discussion below.

Standard of Review

A superior court's determination as to whether fraud upon the court has occurred is reviewed for abuse of discretion.[2] "In reviewing the denial of a motion for directed verdict or [judgment notwithstanding the verdict (JNOV)], we apply an objective test to determine whether the evidence, when viewed in the light most favorable to the non-moving party, is such that reasonable [persons] could not differ in their judgment."[3] "We review denial of a new trial under an abuse of discretion standard wherein we disturb the trial court's discretion only in the most exceptional circumstances to prevent a miscarriage of justice."[4]

A superior court's decision to admit or exclude evidence is reviewed for abuse of discretion, and "will be upset only if we find there has been an error which affected the substantial rights of a party."[5] "We review jury instructions de novo when a timely objection is made."[6] Absent a timely objection, we review only for plain error.[7] Whether equitable estoppel applies is a question of law that this court reviews de novo.[8]

"We review the decision to award attorney's fees for abuse of discretion and [will] overturn it only where the award is manifestly unreasonable."[9] Here, the Bank asks for de novo review of the Hernandezes' enhanced attorney's fees award since the judge who made that award had not been present at the two trials. The Bank argues that since the awarding judge did not have the benefit of observing the proceedings, the rationale for the more deferential standard of review does not apply.[10]

We have never reviewed an award of attorney's fees with less deference where a new superior court judge has been assigned to a case, and we decline to do so here. Alaska Civil Rule 82(b)(3) gives the superior court significant discretion to "vary an attorney's fee award" based on the consideration of various factors, and makes no distinction between a judge sitting at trial versus a judge later assigned to a matter. Even a superior court judge who did not preside over the trial in a case may have a more current perspective through which to evaluate some of the Rule 82(b)(3) factors, such as "the reasonableness of the attorneys' hourly rates and the number of hours expended"; "the reasonableness of the number of attorneys used"; or an attorney's "efforts to minimize fees."[11] We therefore review the award of enhanced attorney's fees to the Hernandezes for abuse of discretion.

A superior court's prevailing party determination for purposes of attorney's fees is similarly reviewed for abuse of discretion.[12] Whether an offer of judgment complies with Alaska Civil Rule 68, however, is a question of law to which we apply independent judgment.[13] Similarly, we interpret the civil rules de novo,[14] and apply our independent judgment to the interpretation of contracts.[15]

Discussion

Although the Bank's Litigation Conduct Supports the Award of Enhanced Attorney's Fees for the First Trial, the Superior Court did not Err by Finding no Fraud upon the Court

Before the second trial in this case commenced, the Hernandezes filed a motion seeking to establish the Bank's liability on the grounds that the Bank perpetrated a "fraud upon the court" during the first trial.[16] The Hernandezes argued that Bank officers, despite their knowledge that McGrew had in fact violated bank policy and may have violated federal or state laws, presented testimony and "directed a litigation defense" based on the claim that McGrew had never committed any wrongdoing. As evidence, the Hernandezes pointed to alleged inconsistencies between the Bank's testimony in their case (*AFG*) and a separate case involving McGrew's conduct with respect to a different Bank client, Todd Christianson (*Christianson*).[17]

The superior court concluded that the Hernandezes "failed to demonstrate, by clear and convincing evidence, conduct by [the Bank] egregious enough to support a finding of fraud upon the court." The court also noted that the verdict from the first trial had already been vacated; thus the Hernandezes would have an opportunity at the second trial to "examine the bank officers about their knowledge of McGrew's conduct." Finally, the order made clear that the Hernandezes could later seek attorney's fees incurred during the first trial if they could "show new evidence elucidated at the upcoming trial that [would] justify a finding of misconduct by [the Bank] or fraud upon the court."

Upon conclusion of the second trial, the Hernandezes filed a renewed fraud upon the court motion, which was similarly denied. However, the superior court noted it would "consider the actions of the defense and their witnesses in conjunction with the anticipated motion for attorney's fees," and the court ultimately awarded the Hernandezes enhanced fees for hours spent on the first trial and on the motion for a new trial. The court found that the Bank's "litigation conduct prior to the first trial was not undertaken in good faith and, at times, was unreasonable" and that "testimony given in the *Christianson* matter was at odds with testimony presented in this litigation." But with regard to the second trial, the court found that the Hernandezes were able to present "whatever evidence

(case continues)

[they] deemed relevant and probative" and that no enhanced fees were warranted. The Bank appeals the award of enhanced attorney's fees for the first trial,[18] and the Hernandezes contend that enhanced fees should have been awarded for both trials.

The Hernandezes also appeal the denial of their fraud upon the court motions and further contend the Bank has committed a fraud upon *this* court. A typical remedy for fraud upon the court is to vacate the fraudulently obtained judgment.[19] Here, however, the Hernandezes seek an alternative remedy, which is for this court to direct judgment in their favor and remand solely for determination of damages.

Fraud upon the court may only be found in the most egregious circumstances involving the corruption of the judicial process

"Fraud upon the court" is an equitable doctrine that allows a court to set aside a judgment obtained as a result of fraudulent conduct.[20] It is an exception to the general rule that courts "[will] not alter or set aside their judgments after the expiration of the term at which the judgments were finally entered."[21] In Alaska, the doctrine is codified in Alaska Civil Rule 60(b), whereby a court has the power "to set aside a judgment for fraud upon the court."[22] "[T]he party claiming a fraud on the court bears the burden of proving the claim by clear and convincing evidence."[23]

We have noted that "specific attempts to define fraud on the court are not particularly helpful,"[24] but "have nevertheless consistently recognized that [a] fraud upon the court may only be found in the most egregious circumstances involving a corruption of the judicial process itself."[25] Similarly, we have adopted the view that the drafters of Rule 60(b) viewed fraud upon the court as referring "to very unusual cases involving far more than an injury to a single litigant."[26]

On the other hand, we have "declined to hold that an intent to defraud must invariably be proved to establish a fraud on the court" and have found recklessness to be sufficient.[27] In *Mallonee v. Grow*, for example, a party filed for a writ of execution that "grossly overstated" the amount a judgment debtor owed him, used the writ to levy upon property that the debtor did not actually own, and failed to serve legally required notice of the motion to confirm the property's sale.[28] Although we recognized that neither the party nor his attorney had "an actual intent to defraud," we nonetheless concluded that "the court has the same duty to rectify the wrong" "[w]hether the deprivation of a party's rights . . . [is] attributable to a willful intent to defraud or a reckless disregard of rules or statutory provisions."[29]

Finally, fraud upon the court may be found even in the absence of trial counsel's involvement. In *Pumphrey v. K.W. Thompson Tool Co.*, the Ninth Circuit Court of Appeals held that a gun manufacturer's in-house counsel perpetrated a fraud upon the court when he failed to present evidence of a video-recorded test he had observed during which a gun fired when dropped on the ground.[30] The in-house counsel also neglected to raise the issue when the person who had conducted the experiment testified that the gun had never fired when dropped during testing.[31] Although the in-house counsel did not represent the gun manufacturer at trial, the court nonetheless concluded that he "engaged in a scheme to defraud."[32] Nevertheless, the general rule is that a witness's perjury, if "unassisted by the party in interest or by counsel, . . . does not amount to fraud upon the court."[33]

The trial court did not err in denying the Hernandezes' original fraud upon the court motion

As the superior court noted, the Hernandezes' fraud upon the court claim requires "a factual inquiry into whether [Bank officers] were aware of any wrongdoing by McGrew, if so, when they became aware of it, and if their testimony and pretrial discovery square with those factual findings." We review the outcome of that inquiry for abuse of discretion.[34]

The Bank's alleged knowledge of McGrew's wrongdoing

As evidence that the Bank already knew of McGrew's wrongdoing during the first *AFG* trial in June 2008, the Hernandezes presented testimony given by Bank officials during the *Christianson* litigation. Although these statements were not made until after the conclusion of the first *AFG* trial, they nonetheless shed light on knowledge the Bank may have gained about McGrew's lending practices before the first *AFG* trial.

Most notably, the Hernandezes highlighted deposition testimony from Bank senior vice president and general counsel David Lawer suggesting that Lawer knew of McGrew's improper practices as early as 2005. When Lawer was asked when he had discovered that McGrew "had violated the bank's rules," he answered, "With—within the year 2005." Lawer also described his conclusion that McGrew was "making loans [and] renewing loans at maturity to avoid identification of a borrower or borrowers who were unable to pay prior credit obligations and who currently were not creditworthy and . . . not worthy of further loans." Lawer stated that he reached this conclusion based on a review of numerous loan files—a process that may have been completed before the first *AFG* trial.[35] The Bank admits that repeated loan extensions to a borrower who is not creditworthy would, "absent some justification," violate bank policy.

(case continues)

The Hernandezes also highlighted the statements of Bank senior vice president David Stringer, who learned about some of McGrew's loan practices after McGrew's death in December 2004. Stringer testified that he received multiple reports from some of McGrew's former customers, who claimed they had been given loans "for the purposes of the proceeds being distributed for [someone else's] benefit." Such loans, which have their proceeds distributed to a third party rather than to the borrower, are sometimes referred to as "nominee loans," and McGrew's former customers told Stringer he should look to the third-party beneficiaries for repayment. Stringer testified that he "probably" received these reports between 2005 and 2007 and that he relayed them to Bank president Dan Cuddy as they arose.

Stringer also testified about information he and Cuddy acquired regarding McGrew's dealings with a particular Bank client, Kaylen LeBaron, who appeared to be receiving the proceeds from some of these nominee loans. Stringer testified that after McGrew's death, LeBaron requested a meeting with Cuddy.[36] According to Stringer's testimony, LeBaron admitted at the meeting that he was the beneficiary of numerous loans taken out on his behalf.

The Bank's testimony and pre-trial disclosures

The Hernandezes argue that the Bank's testimony in *Christianson* reveals its representations during the first *AFG* trial to be fraudulent. But the superior court could reasonably conclude that the Bank's alleged misrepresentations, when viewed in context, did not constitute "the most egregious circumstances involving a corruption of the judicial process itself."[37]

We turn first to what is arguably the Hernandezes' most persuasive evidence of fraudulent conduct: direct discrepancies between Lawer's testimony in the *AFG* and Christianson cases. During a 2007 deposition before the *AFG* trial, Lawer was asked whether, "as the bank compliance officer, [he] believe[d] [McGrew] did his job relative to lending within the parameters of federal, [s]tate, and bank rules[.]" Lawer answered, "Yes, as far as I know." Yet Lawer later testified in *Christianson* that he acquired knowledge about McGrew's bank rule violations in 2005.

Nevertheless, we agree with the superior court that Lawer's 2007 deposition testimony, while misleading and potentially false, was not sufficiently egregious to find fraud upon the court. We have expressed caution in finding fraud upon the court based purely on the after-discovered perjury of a witness.[38] And although the Ninth Circuit has found fraud upon the court based solely on the conduct of a party's general counsel, Lawer's conduct was distinguishable from the concealment of pivotal evidence at issue in *Pumphrey*.[39] Even if Lawer misrepresented McGrew's general track record at the Bank, the misrepresentation did not directly relate to McGrew's transactions with the Hernandezes. The superior court could reasonably conclude that Lawer's testimony did not constitute a corruption of the judicial process itself.[40]

The Hernandezes also argued that Bank officials' in-court testimony misrepresented McGrew's history at the Bank. For instance, Cuddy testified that he could not think of any reason why the Hernandezes should not have trusted McGrew. Cuddy also answered affirmatively when asked if, as far as he knew, "McGrew's conduct [was] lawful in all respects." Cuddy went on to state that McGrew "was well respected in [the] bank and . . . [had] done a good job for . . . 25 years." Lawer testified at trial that he thought Cuddy had testified accurately, with the exception of one unrelated issue, and further characterized McGrew as a "very successful" Bank employee.

The Hernandezes contrast Cuddy's *AFG* testimony with Stringer's statements in *Christianson* that Cuddy knew about McGrew's nominee loans as early as 2005, when Cuddy began receiving Stringer's reports and met with LeBaron. The Hernandezes argue that McGrew's use of nominee loans violated both bank policy and federal law, contradicting Cuddy's characterization of McGrew's conduct as lawful. However, the Bank contends that nominee loans are "not uncommon" and are only illegal if done in a way that deceives a bank or its examiners. Because of this dispute over the legality of nominee loans, it is possible that at the time of the first *AFG* trial the Bank still lacked reason to believe that McGrew's lending practices were illegal.

Moreover, there were other reasons to discount the Hernandezes' fraud upon the court claim. Even if Cuddy's answer that McGrew's conduct was lawful in all respects was misleading, its impact on the court was lessened by Cuddy's disclaimer that he had not familiarized himself with the Hernandezes' case. Likewise, the Bank's general defenses of McGrew's character were largely subjective and likely had little impact. And because the superior court had vacated the first jury verdict on other grounds, the Hernandezes had already received the presumptive remedy for fraud upon the court: relief from judgment.[41] The superior court correctly noted that the second trial would provide the Hernandezes with "the opportunity to examine the bank officers about their knowledge of McGrew's conduct."

For the reasons above, the court could reasonably conclude that the alleged inconsistencies in the Bank's testimony did not rise to "clear and convincing" evidence of fraud upon the court.

(case continues)

The trial court did not err in awarding the Hernandezes enhanced attorney's fees

While the Bank's conduct during the first *AFG* trial may not have been sufficiently egregious to constitute fraud upon the court, the superior court could reasonably conclude that testimony from the Bank's corporate officers was a bad faith attempt to minimize McGrew's misconduct, warranting enhanced attorney's fees. This court reviews "the decision to award attorney's fees for abuse of discretion and [will] overturn it only where the award is manifestly unreasonable."[42]

In particular, Lawer's 2007 deposition testimony that McGrew had done his job "within the parameters" of Bank rules may have prevented the plaintiffs from discovering the extent of McGrew's wrongdoing. And it is difficult to reconcile Lawer's 2007 testimony with his later statement that "within the year 2005" he came to "know" that McGrew had violated those rules.

As the superior court noted, "It is clear from Lawer's testimony in his *Christianson* deposition that he found out sometime in 2005 from Stringer that bank customers were making allegations against McGrew regarding nominee loans . . . " Lawer countered in an affidavit that merely hearing "allegations by a few defaulting debtors" was insufficient to support a "reasonable belief" that McGrew had committed wrongdoing. While this reasoning may, standing alone, be sensible, it does not explain Lawer's testimony in *Christianson* that he came to "know" in 2005 that McGrew violated Bank rules.

The Bank argues that in awarding the Hernandezes enhanced attorney's fees, the superior court did not sufficiently "specify its reasons in the record."[43] We disagree. The court specifically found that "testimony given in the *Christianson* matter was at odds with testimony presented in this litigation." The court could reasonably conclude that the Bank had not adequately explained this inconsistency. Accordingly, the court did not abuse its discretion in awarding the plaintiffs their full fees for the first trial.

Nor did the court abuse its discretion in restricting its award of enhanced fees to those the Hernandezes incurred for the first trial. The superior court could reasonably conclude that the second trial offered the Hernandezes an opportunity to "present whatever evidence [they] deemed relevant and probative" regarding the Bank officers' testimony in prior proceedings. Accordingly, the Hernandezes had a chance to remedy any obfuscation resulting from the Bank's testimony in the first trial. As discussed below, moreover, the evidence that the Bank engaged in fraudulent or even misleading conduct is less compelling with respect to the second trial.

The trial court did not err in denying the Hernandezes' renewed motion for fraud upon the court

The inconsistencies the Hernandezes rely on from the second trial are much less serious than those alleged in their original fraud upon the court motion. These inconsistencies did not require the superior court to direct judgment in their favor.

In their renewed motion, the Hernandezes highlighted the Bank's alleged knowledge of McGrew's wrongdoing by the time the second *AFG* trial commenced in November 2010. They pointed first to a report the Bank commissioned for its defense in the *Christianson* litigation, authored by Burton McCullough (the McCullough Report). The report is dated June 2009, and opines that McGrew issued illegal "nominee loans" for Christianson's benefit. The Bank intimated during the second *AFG* trial that it did not consider the report credible.

The Hernandezes next pointed to a superior court order issued in the *Christianson* case, finding that McGrew "had established a practice of using one bank customer to help the troubled loans and financial problems of other bank customers." The order also found, "Much of this lending was granted to customers who did not qualify for the loans and whose ability to pay was questionable." However, these findings did not relate to McGrew's interactions with the Hernandezes, nor did they specifically determine that McGrew acted in contravention of law or bank policy. This order may illustrate the Bank's knowledge of McGrew's misconduct with respect to Christianson by the time of the second *AFG* trial, but the superior court could reasonably conclude that such knowledge was tangential to the question of whether there was wrongdoing with respect to the Hernandezes.

The Hernandezes argue that the Bank's defense in the second *AFG* trial was nonetheless inconsistent with its admission of McGrew's wrongdoing in *Christianson*. For example, the Hernandezes cited the Bank's opening statement in *AFG*, purportedly describing "McGrew's unwillingness to engage in fraudulent conduct." Yet in this same opening statement, the Bank admitted McGrew "ben[t]" the Bank's policies and procedures in order "to give a borrower a break." This kind of admission is inconsistent with conduct "involving a corruption of the judicial process itself."[44]

The Hernandezes also highlighted Stringer's testimony during the second *AFG* trial. In particular, Stringer testified that he had "never been aware of [Bank] policies that . . . Mr. McGrew was violating," and he opined that McGrew would not have told customers that they were not required to pay back

(case continues)

"nominee loans" for which they were the named beneficiaries. These claims were arguably inconsistent with Stringer's testimony in *Christianson* that, beginning in 2005, he began receiving reports from customers claiming that McGrew had given them nominee loans and assured them they would not be responsible for repayment. Yet even if Stringer's statements during the second *AFG* trial were inaccurate, his misrepresentations about whether he personally believed McGrew engaged in prohibited practices were not sufficiently egregious to compel a finding of fraud upon the court.

Nor did Lawer's in-court testimony during the second *AFG* trial warrant such a finding. Lawer denied having personal knowledge that McGrew contravened legal rules or Bank policies in his dealings with the Hernandezes, but conceded that McGrew might have violated Bank policies with respect to Christianson. Lawer testified that giving illegal nominee loans would be "out of character" for McGrew, but offered only equivocal statements as to whether McGrew may have engaged in criminal activity.

Unlike the Bank officers' testimony during the first *AFG* trial, these statements largely avoided sweeping pronouncements that McGrew had a blemish-free record at the Bank. And when Bank officers did testify about McGrew's general track record, they entertained the possibility that McGrew's lending practices might have violated the law or Bank policy. Accordingly, the superior court could reasonably conclude that the Bank did not commit a fraud upon the court during the second *AFG* trial.

The Bank has not committed a fraud upon this court

The Hernandezes argue that the Bank's "misrepresentations of McGrew's conduct and presentation of false evidence" constitutes a fraud upon *this* court. The Hernandezes point out that the Bank asserted in its *Christianson* appellate briefing that McGrew had engaged in criminal conduct, contradicting the Bank's prior denials of McGrew's wrongdoing. But the Bank has not asserted to *this* court that McGrew never committed a crime, and the Hernandezes do not point to particular statements in the Bank's briefing that are fraudulent. Accordingly, we conclude the Bank has not committed a fraud upon this court.

The Superior Court did not Err in Denying the Hernandezes' Motions for Directed Verdict and JNOV on the Issue of Whether McGrew Acted Solely as a "Finder"

Among the determinations the jury was asked to make in the underlying case was whether McGrew had acted solely as a "finder" with respect to the Hernandezes' investments in the Inn. As the jury instructions provided, "A national bank that acts as a finder may identify potential parties, make inquiries as to interest, introduce or arrange contacts or meetings of interested parties, act as an intermediary between interested parties, and otherwise bring parties together for a transaction that the parties themselves negotiate and consummate."[45] The instruction also listed five illustrative examples of what a finder could not engage in:

1) Be an agent of one party or another;
2) Broker a deal while representing only one party;
3) Make false representations as to the value or the quality of the investment;
4) Make false recommendations as to the amount that should be invested;
5) Make false representations about the success of the investment.

Finally, the instructions advised the jurors that if they found the Bank or McGrew to have acted only as a "finder," they must find for the Bank on all of the securities claims.[46] At the conclusion of trial, the Hernandezes moved for a directed verdict that McGrew had engaged in activities that were forbidden for a "finder"; the superior court denied the directed verdict motion.

In reviewing this issue, "we apply an objective test to determine—whether the evidence, when viewed in the light most favorable to the non-moving party, is such that reasonable [persons] could not differ in their judgment.'"[47] The Hernandezes assert that the "uncontested record" illustrates that McGrew engaged in activities forbidden for a finder. Specifically, they point to statements made by various witnesses that, in their view, tend to show McGrew made false representations as to the quality of the Inn as an investment opportunity. But even if these statements were uncontradicted, as the Hernandezes assert, the jurors were nonetheless free to disbelieve such testimony[48] or conclude that the alleged conduct fell within the parameters of permitted "finder" activities.

Moreover, there was substantial testimony suggesting that McGrew acted only as a finder, including expert testimony from one of the Bank's witnesses, Professor Theresa Gabaldon. At trial, Gabaldon stated, "Everything I have reviewed is entirely consistent with . . . my conclusion that [McGrew] was acting as a finder, as understood for purposes of federal banking law." Testimony from the Inn's original investors, Kirk Loeffler and Edward Cronick, provided further evidence favoring the Bank on this issue. According to Loeffler, McGrew informed him

(case continues)

that while he could provide the contact information of potential investors, Loeffler would need to actually "sell the project" to these contacts. Cronick similarly testified that McGrew gave "suggestions" of potential investors and that the Inn was not using McGrew "as a sales agent." In light of this evidence, reasonable jurors could have reached differing conclusions on whether McGrew acted solely as a "finder."[49]

The Hernandezes argue that the prejudice they suffered from the denial of their motion for directed verdict was exacerbated by the absence of a "curative" jury instruction "that McGrew's use of nominee loans was felonious conduct." In view of our disposition on the "finder" issue, however, the jury would have been precluded from finding the Bank liable on the plaintiffs' securities claims in any event. And the Hernandezes do not show how an instruction regarding nominee loans would have been relevant to their non-securities claims.[50] Accordingly, we are not required to decide whether the judge should have given a jury instruction regarding the legality of nominee loans.

Similarly, we need not reach the issue of whether the superior court erred in denying the Hernandezes' motion for JNOV finding certain outstanding debts to the Bank non-collectible under AS 45.55.930(g). Under this statutory provision, a person cannot sue to enforce a contract if that person had knowledge of facts which rendered the making or performance of the contract a violation of the Alaska Securities Act.[51] But the jury's conclusion that McGrew was only a "finder" relieved the Bank of liability under the Securities Act.

The Superior Court Did Not Abuse Its Discretion In Limiting The Evidence Concerning The McCullough Report

The Hernandezes argue that the superior court erred in excluding the McCullough Report from evidence and limiting McCullough's testimony. As discussed above, the Bank retained McCullough to prepare a report for its defense in the *Christianson* litigation, and the report opined that McGrew had engaged in illegal lending activity with respect to Bank client Todd Christianson. In this case, the Bank argued that the McCullough Report was irrelevant to McGrew's interactions with the Hernandezes, and even if it were relevant for some limited purpose, the report's assertion that McGrew engaged in criminal wrongdoing with respect to Christianson was highly prejudicial.

The court ultimately excluded the McCullough Report and limited McCullough's testimony. Specifically, McCullough was allowed to testify that he had provided the Bank with a report concluding that McGrew had repeatedly violated both banking regulations and the Bank's policies and procedures. But he was not allowed to state his conclusion that McGrew's conduct described in *Christianson* was felonious.

A trial court's decision to admit or exclude evidence is reviewed for abuse of discretion and for prejudice to the opposing party.[52] The Hernandezes argue that the trial court was compelled to admit the McCullough Report based on our holding in *Fred Meyer of Alaska, Inc. v. Bailey*.[53] But our analysis in *Fred Meyer* did not implicate the key issue on which the trial court based its decision to limit McCullough's testimony: relevance.[54]

In *Fred Meyer*, the superior court was tasked with determining whether the defendant-employer had acted in good faith in classifying an employee as exempt from overtime under the Alaska Wage and Hour Act (AWHA).[55] In a previous lawsuit, the employer had commissioned an expert report concluding that the plaintiff-employee's job position should be classified as non-exempt.[56] Because this arguably put the employer on notice of its AWHA violation, the report was directly relevant to evaluating the employer's defense that the misclassification was in good faith.[57]

The contents of the McCullough Report, in contrast, raise relevance problems not present in *Fred Meyer*. First, the Bank did not receive the McCullough Report until 2009—well after the events relevant to the Hernandezes' claims took place. Moreover, the report was limited to McGrew's misconduct relating to Christianson's loans and did not discuss possible misconduct with respect to the Hernandezes' transactions. According to McCullough, none of the materials he reviewed in preparing his report related to McGrew's interactions with the Hernandezes or the Inn's other investors, Cronick and Loeffler.

The superior court could therefore reasonably conclude that the report was not directly relevant to McGrew's conduct with respect to the plaintiffs. The court had considerable discretion, moreover, to limit McCullough's testimony about McGrew's criminal misconduct to avoid unfair prejudice.[58] The limitations on McCullough's testimony were not unreasonable in view of the other evidence that the court admitted regarding McGrew's wrongdoing in the Christianson matter.

No Plain Error Resulted from the Special Verdict Form

The Hernandezes argue that the questions on the special verdict form led the jury to "unknowingly make a double reduction" of the Hernandezes' damage award. Absent a timely objection, we review the propriety of the special verdict form and the associated jury instructions for plain error.[59]

The special verdict form contained two questions that the Hernandezes claim may have confused the

(case continues)

jury. Question 6 asked the jury "[w]hat amount of damages, if any, was legally caused by the [Bank's] negligence," and the jury answered "$675,000." And Question 25 asked the jury to determine the percentage of fault assigned to the Hernandezes, the Bank, and Cronick, who settled with the Hernandezes out of court. The jury determined the Bank to be 14% at fault. The Hernandezes argue that the jury understood the $675,000 figure to be *solely* attributable to the Bank's negligence and did not realize that the allocation of fault in Question 25 would reduce the amount of damages ultimately owed to the Hernandezes.

The Hernandezes are correct that Question 6 could have been framed more clearly to emphasize that it referred to their total damages. But any ambiguity in the question was directly addressed at trial, when subsequent requests for clarification confirmed that the jury correctly understood what was asked of them. First, the jury responded in the affirmative to the question, "Does your answer to Question No. 6 [damages caused by the Bank's negligence] reflect the damages you awarded to Plaintiff *before* you made any deduction based upon your answer to Question No. 25 [allocation of fault among the Bank, Cronick, and the Hernandezes]?"[60] A second request asked the jury to re-examine its apportionment of fault "[i]n light of [its] decision that Plaintiffs are only entitled to damages based upon their claim of negligence." The request further instructed the jury to "consider the nature of [the Bank's, Cronick's, and the Hernandezes'] conduct and the extent of the causal relationship between the conduct and any damages" the jury had identified. The jury returned the same apportionment as in their original verdict.

These interrogatories show that in answering the special verdict form, the jury properly calculated the amount of the Hernandezes' loss and then apportioned fault to take into account the degree to which the Bank, the Hernandezes, and Cronick contributed to that loss. In light of this clarification, we conclude that no plain error resulted from the special verdict form.

The Hernandezes' Common Law Tort Claims are Not Barred by the Statute of Limitations

The Hernandezes' common law tort claims are governed by a two-year statute of limitations.[61] "Although a cause of action generally accrues when the plaintiff incurs an injury, accrual can be delayed under . . . [the] common-law discovery rule."[62] "[T]he discovery rule may provide different possible dates on which a statute of limitations can begin to run."[63] Generally, however, the operative date is "when the plaintiff has information which is sufficient to alert a reasonable person to begin an inquiry to protect his rights"—often referred to as inquiry notice.[64] Here, the Hernandezes conceded "that as of October of 2003 [they] were on—inquiry notice' . . . as to their common law misrepresentation claims." However, the Hernandezes did not file their complaint until March 2006, after the two-year period had run.

But we have held that "[a] party who fraudulently conceals from a plaintiff the existence of a cause of action may be estopped to plead the statute of limitation if the plaintiff's delay in bringing suit was occasioned by reliance on the false or fraudulent representation."[65] Specifically, a plaintiff must show: "(1) fraudulent conduct, which may take the form of either an affirmative misrepresentation or a failure to disclose facts where there is a duty to do so; (2) justifiable reliance; and (3) damage."[66]

In the proceedings below, the Bank filed a motion for summary judgment, arguing that the Hernandezes' common law tort claims were barred by the statute of limitations. In opposition, the Hernandezes pleaded equitable estoppel, citing McGrew's alleged assurances that he would find other investors or arrange for alternative financing to get the Hernandezes out of their investment in the Inn. The court denied the Bank's motion, finding there were issues of fact "as to whether it was utterly unreasonable for Plaintiffs to not be fully aware of the falsity of McGrew's alleged misrepresentation . . . until informed so by [Bank] Vice President Stringer after McGrew's death in January 2005."

The Bank later filed a motion for directed verdict on the same grounds, which the court similarly denied, first noting that it is the judge who determines whether the elements of estoppel have been satisfied, acting "as a factfinder in determining the applicability of the statute of limitations." The court found that McGrew made misrepresentations to the Hernandezes and that the Bank "knew about the weaknesses of the project" but did nothing to stop McGrew from refinancing it. Accordingly, the court concluded that the Hernandezes' reliance on McGrew's misrepresentations was not "utterly unreasonable." The Bank filed a motion for JNOV on the same grounds, which the court summarily denied.

The superior court applied the correct burden of proof to determine the elements of equitable estoppel

The Bank contends the superior court should have required the Hernandezes to prove each element of equitable estoppel by "clear and convincing

(case continues)

evidence." But the Bank relies on our application of this standard in real estate cases where the application of equitable estoppel divests title from one party and transfers it to another.[67] Where title to land is at issue, the stricter standard serves to "foster reliance on record title and enhance marketability."[68] But these policy concerns do not apply here, and we have never required "clear and convincing evidence" to prove equitable estoppel in the context of a statute of limitations defense. We decline to do so now.

The Bank also takes issue with the superior court's application of the "utterly unreasonable" standard this court articulated in *Palmer v. Borg-Warner Corporation*.[69] As we have noted, "a party should be charged with knowledge of the fraudulent misrepresentation or concealment only when it would be utterly unreasonable for the party not to be aware of the deception."[70] Once it is utterly unreasonable not to know about the deception, the plaintiff must take timely action or risk losing the protection of equitable estoppel.[71]

The Bank contends that the "utterly unreasonable" standard is only applicable "in cases of fraudulent concealment of a claim." Yet the "utterly unreasonable" standard as we have articulated it expressly applies to "fraudulent misrepresentation,"[72] which is precisely what the Hernandezes alleged. We conclude that the superior court correctly applied the "utterly unreasonable" standard in this case.

The superior court reasonably concluded that the Bank's defense was barred by equitable estoppel

The issue of whether equitable estoppel applies is a question of law that we review de novo.[73] However, the elements of equitable estoppel involve questions of fact,[74] which we review for clear error.[75]

The Bank asserts there was insufficient evidence to support the superior court's finding that "McGrew failed to adequately make necessary disclosures and made misrepresentations to [the Hernandezes], such that they continued to work with him and [the Bank]." But the Hernandezes attested that "[e]ach time McGrew advanced funds to the Hernandez family members he would repeat that this was going to work and that as soon as the hotel was finished he could find other investors to take the Hernandez family completely out." McGrew allegedly made such representations in October and December of 2003, and in January, April, May, and October of 2004. According to the Hernandezes, McGrew also stated that he would combine the Hernandezes' various loans into a single "wrap around" loan secured by the completed Inn.

The Bank does not appear to argue on appeal that the Hernandezes' recounting of their conversations with McGrew is inaccurate. Rather, the Bank contends that these statements were not "misrepresentations," but merely promises that were never performed. We have noted that "[a] statement made as to future intentions and actions is not a misrepresentation if it is accurate when it is made, even if future events render it inaccurate."[76] But the Bank does not point to any evidence that McGrew intended to perform on his promise, such as an indication that McGrew was actively searching for another investor or had the capacity to divest the Hernandezes of their responsibility for the project. The Bank does point out that the Hernandezes *believed* McGrew was seeking replacement financing, but this does not show that McGrew actually intended to do so. Accordingly, it was not clearly erroneous for the superior court to conclude that McGrew's reassurances were "misrepresentations."

The Bank also makes two arguments as to why, as a matter of law, McGrew's statements could not be considered misrepresentations. The first is that McGrew's promise to divest the Hernandezes of their investment was unenforceable under the Statute of Frauds, since certain types of financing or loans in excess of $50,000 must be in writing.[77] But the provision the Bank cites applies only to "an agreement to lend . . . or to grant or extend credit"[78] and therefore does not apply to McGrew's promises to *divest* the Hernandezes of their financial responsibility for existing loans. The Bank also argues that McGrew's assurances were merely speculative promises regarding a third party's actions and thus could not have been misleading as a matter of law. However, McGrew also allegedly told the Hernandezes that if they helped him finish building the Inn, *he* would help them by "find[ing] an investor to take over the project." Thus, McGrew was taking personal responsibility for an outcome he failed to provide, and accordingly, such a promise could constitute a misrepresentation.

In its order denying the Bank's motion for directed verdict, the superior court also found that "in light of the bank's tacit support of McGrew's actions," the Hernandezes were not "utterly unreasonable" in relying on McGrew's "continued misrepresentations to allay their suspicions."

As an initial matter, the Bank argues that the Hernandezes have never provided evidence that they *actually* relied on McGrew's assurances. But the Hernandezes' reliance may be inferred from the nature of McGrew's assurances and evidence that the Hernandezes continued to sign loan documents after their discussions with McGrew.

The Bank also argues that reliance on McGrew's assurances would have been unreasonable. In

(case continues)

particular, the Bank asserts it was unreasonable for the Hernandezes to rely on statements about potential financing that contained no details regarding amount, source, or terms. As the superior court noted, however, McGrew was a "long-time friend and trusted loan officer." And even testimony from the Bank's own officers confirmed that the Hernandezes should have had no reason not to trust McGrew. Accordingly, it was not "utterly unreasonable" for the Hernandezes to rely on McGrew's assurances that he would secure new financing for the Inn.

The Issue of Whether an Interest in an LLC is a Security is Moot

The Bank argues that the superior court erred in ruling that the Hernandezes acquired a "security" interest in the Inn, within the meaning of the Alaska Securities Act. The court made this finding when it denied the Bank's motion for summary judgment on the Hernandezes' securities claims. But the jury ultimately found that McGrew acted only as a "finder," thus relieving the Bank of any liability under the Alaska Securities Act.[79] Therefore our determination of this issue would have no direct bearing on the outcome of this litigation.

"Under ordinary circumstances, we will refrain from deciding questions where events have rendered the legal issue moot. A claim is moot if it is no longer a present, live controversy, and the party bringing the action would not be entitled to relief, even if it prevails."[80] But under the collateral consequences exception, we may decide a case that is otherwise moot where "a judgment may carry indirect consequences in addition to its direct force, either as a matter of legal rules or as a matter of practical effect."[81]

The Bank contends that the superior court's security interest finding has "important collateral consequences" for the Bank. Because its insurer withdrew coverage and defense since its policy did not cover "any claims arising out of efforts to promote the sale of a security," and because policy disputes under the insurance policy are submitted for binding arbitration, the Bank claims that the superior court's decision may "unfairly prejudice the arbitrators" or be considered dispositive in the future coverage dispute.

We disagree. The mere possibility of "unfairly prejudic[ing] the arbitrators" is insufficient to compel resolution of an otherwise moot issue. And the Bank presents no legal authority explaining how the superior court's interlocutory finding would preclude an arbitration panel from reaching its own independent conclusion on this question of law. A court's resolution of an issue has preclusive effect only if that issue is essential to the final judgment, and other courts are not bound by interlocutory findings that are not essential to a final judgment.[82] Accordingly, the superior court's finding that the Hernandezes acquired a security interest in the Inn will not be controlling in the Bank's insurance coverage arbitration because that finding was not essential to the final judgment.

We therefore conclude that this issue is moot and that the collateral consequences exception does not apply.

The Superior Court did not Err in Determining that the Hernandezes Were Entitled to Attorney's Fees and Costs

In the proceedings below, the superior court determined that the Hernandezes were the prevailing party and awarded them attorney's fees and costs. The Bank appeals this award on several grounds.

The Bank's deeds of trust did not preclude the superior court from awarding attorney's fees to the Hernandezes

The Bank first argues that the award of attorney's fees and costs in this case was governed by contract—namely, the deeds of trust securing the Bank's loans to the Hernandezes. The Bank points to the following provision in its deeds of trust:

> *If [the Bank] institutes any suit or action to enforce any of the terms of this Deed of Trust, [the Bank] shall be entitled to recover such sum as the court may adjudge reasonable as attorneys' fees at trial and upon any appeal. Whether or not any court action is involved or pending, and to the extent not prohibited by law, all reasonable expenses [the Bank] incurs that in [the Bank's] opinion are necessary at any time for the protection of its interest or the enforcement of its rights shall become a part of the indebtedness payable on demand and shall bear interest at the Note rate . . . .*

The Bank contends this suit required it to "protect and enforce" its right to repayment of the Hernandezes' loans, and the superior court was therefore required to grant the Bank attorney's fees and costs for its defense.

We have held that "where a contract between the parties allows for one party to recover attorney's fees in the event of litigation, the contract provision must prevail" over the general rule that the prevailing party in a civil case is awarded attorney's fees.[83] Accordingly, an attorney's fees provision in the Bank's deeds of trust would arguably govern here. We interpret the relevant contract provision applying our independent judgment.[84] "In interpreting a contract, the object is to give effect to the reasonable expectations of the parties. To ascertain these

(case continues)

expectations, the court looks to the language of the disputed provision, the language of other provisions of the contract, relevant extrinsic evidence, and case law interpreting similar provisions."[85]

The first sentence of the excerpt above states only that the Bank will be entitled to reasonable fees in any suit the Bank "institutes" to enforce the deed of trust. But this suit was brought by the Hernandezes, and the Bank did not bring a counterclaim to enforce the deed of trust. Therefore, this provision is inapplicable.

The Bank seems to rely on the second sentence of the quoted language, which allows "all reasonable expenses" necessary to protect the Bank's interest to be added to the note by "becom[ing] a part of the indebtedness payable on demand," "[w]hether or not any court action is involved or pending." Accordingly, the Bank may indeed be entitled to add certain litigation expenses to the indebtedness owed on the Hernandezes' notes. But the Bank did not counterclaim to enforce its notes, nor are we reviewing any judicial or nonjudicial proceeding to collect on the "indebtedness payable." It would therefore defy the "reasonable expectations" of the parties[86] to grant the Bank its litigation expenses outside of a proceeding to collect on the Hernandezes' notes.

Because the attorney's fees provision in the parties' contractual agreement is inapplicable to the present dispute, the civil rules control.

The superior court did not err in finding that the Bank's offers of judgment were invalid under Civil Rule 68

The Bank argues that it made valid offers of judgment that were significantly higher than the Hernandezes' recovery at trial, thus rendering the Bank the prevailing party under Civil Rule 68. Rule 68 encourages settlement[87] by providing that if a party makes an offer of judgment that is rejected, the rejecting party must pay attorney's fees and costs if the final judgment "is at least 5 percent less favorable" than the rejected offer.[88] However, "[a]n offer not in compliance with Rule 68 may not be considered in determining costs and attorney's fees."[89] "Whether an offer of judgment complies with Civil Rule 68 is a question of law that we review using the independent judgment standard."[90]

The Bank's offer presented two recovery options to the Hernandezes: (1) the sum of $230,000, plus interest; or (2) 105% of $212,167.67, Alaska Civil Rule 79 costs, and interest. Under either of these two options, however, $100,000 of this amount was to "be paid by offset against the principal of one or more" of three loans owed to the Bank: one belonging solely to Alaska Fur Gallery, one shared between Alaska Fur Gallery and Hernandez & Associates, and one shared between Alaska Fur Gallery and the Inn. Additionally, the offer provided that, with the exception of one particular loan, the Hernandezes would be "discharged from their payment guarantees" for the Inn's outstanding loans. However, the offer also listed four loans that would be "confirmed as being valid and enforceable liabilities of the plaintiffs." In total, the principal on these loans exceeded $5 million.

We agree with the superior court that this offer was invalid. First, both options were joint offers, which are usually invalid as Rule 68 offers of judgment due to apportionment difficulties.[91] In determining whether a joint offer may nonetheless be valid, we consider two factors: (1) whether "[t]he settlement offer clearly indicated all claims between the parties would be resolved if the offer were accepted"; and (2) whether apportionment difficulty actually exists.[92]

While the Bank's offer may satisfy the first factor in that it would have resolved all of the plaintiffs' claims, "apportionment difficulty" indeed exists here. The Bank points out that Alaska Fur Gallery and Hernandez & Associates are both owned by members of the Hernandez family, who stated during trial that they did not see the two entities as "distinct." But the offer of judgment not only required a lump sum to be apportioned between these two plaintiffs, but also implicated several different loans—one of which was held jointly by Alaska Fur Gallery and the Inn. Accordingly, it was not clear how the $100,000 "offset" against the loan principal would be apportioned or which of the three plaintiffs would reap the benefit of that principal reduction.[93]

Finally, even if the Bank's offer were valid under Rule 68, it is unclear that it is a better offer than what the Hernandezes received from the final judgment. The offer contains a condition that the plaintiffs confirm the validity of over five million dollars in loans. The litigation did not satisfy that condition: while the final judgment in this case may not have relieved the Hernandezes of their debt obligations, it did not affirmatively confirm their loans as "valid and enforceable liabilities." In this sense, it would be incorrect to say that the Bank's offer—"confirming" millions of dollars in debt liability with approximately $230,000 in compensation—was better than the plaintiffs' recovery at trial.

The superior court did not abuse its discretion by concluding that the Hernandezes were the prevailing party

The Bank argues that it was the prevailing party, based on its defeat of numerous claims and the small size of the Hernandezes' award compared to the total damages sought. A superior court's prevailing party determination is reviewed for abuse of discretion.[94]

(case continues)

As we have held,

> *For purposes of awarding fees pursuant to Civil Rule 82, the general rule is that the prevailing party is the one who has successfully prosecuted or defended against the action, the one who is successful on the main issue of the action and in whose favor the decision or verdict is rendered and the judgment entered.*[95]

"[A] party does not have to prevail on all the issues in the case to be a—prevailing party.'"[96] "With few exceptions, the party who obtains an affirmative recovery is considered prevailing."[97]

Here, the Hernandezes prevailed on their negligence claim, and recovered $94,500 in damages, plus interest. Based on this affirmative recovery, the superior court could reasonably conclude that the Hernandezes were the prevailing party.

The superior court did not err by declining to apportion costs

The Bank argues that the superior court erred in awarding the Hernandezes 100% of their costs, given the jury's verdict that the Bank was only 14% at fault for the Hernandezes' damages. The Bank requested a modified cost bill that would have apportioned only 14% of the Hernandezes' costs to the Bank, but the superior court denied that request. The court concluded, and the Hernandezes argue on appeal, that Civil Rule 79(h) only applies to apportionment among multiple non-prevailing parties. Because this issue involves the interpretation of the civil rules, we review this question de novo.[98]

Civil Rule 79(h) states: "In a case in which damages are apportioned among the parties under AS 09.17.080, costs must be apportioned and awarded according to the provisions of Civil Rule 82(e)." Rule 82(e) provides: "In a case in which damages are apportioned among the parties under AS 09.17.080, the [attorney's] fees awarded to the plaintiff under (b)(1) of this rule must also be apportioned among the parties according to their respective percentages of fault." And the fee schedule in Rule 82(b)(1) requires the court to calculate attorney's fees based on the judgment and, if awarded, the prejudgment interest.

We have previously held that "the fit between Rule 79(h) and Rule 82(e) is snug."[99] When "Rule 82(e) does not apply with regard to attorney's fees, . . . the same conclusion must follow with respect to Rule 79(h) costs."[100] And because Rule 82(b)(1) calculates attorney's fees based on the final judgment awarded to the prevailing party—not the claimant's total injury before apportionment—attorney's fees calculated under Rule 82(b)(1) will already have been reduced to reflect any fault attributed to the plaintiff or to non-parties. Where there is only one non-prevailing party, no further reduction is necessary. Accordingly, Rule 82(e) apportionment should only occur if there are multiple non-prevailing parties to the litigation.

Here, although the jury found that the Hernandezes, the Bank, and Cronick all shared fault to the varying degrees, the Bank was the only non-prevailing party, and the final judgment against the Bank reflected the Bank's percentage of fault: 14%. Because the Bank was the only non-prevailing party against whom the jury awarded damages, the court correctly determined that Rule 82(e) did not apply; further apportionment of the attorney's fee award would result in a double reduction to that award. And because Rule 82(e) did not apply, Rule 79(h) was also inapplicable. We therefore conclude that the superior court did not err by declining to apportion costs.

Conclusion

We AFFIRM the superior court's judgment in all respects.

---

1. AS 45.55.010-.55.995.
2. *Mallonee v. Grow*, 502 P.2d 432, 439 (Alaska 1972) (citing *Erick Rios Bridoux v. E. Air Lines*, 214 F.2d 207, 207-10 (D.C. Cir. 1954)).
3. *Turner v. Municipality of Anchorage*, 171 P.3d 180, 185 (Alaska 2007) (quoting *Wal-Mart, Inc. v. Stewart*, 990 P.2d 626, 631-32 (Alaska 1999)) (internal quotation marks omitted).
4. *Id.* (second alteration in original) (quoting *Bierria v. Dickinson Mfg. Co.*, 36 P.3d 654, 656 (Alaska 2001)) (internal quotation marks omitted).
5. *Cartee v. Cartee*, 239 P.3d 707, 712 (Alaska 2010) (citing *Dobos v. Ingersoll*, 9 P.3d 1020, 1023 (Alaska 2000)).
6. *Cummins, Inc. v. Nelson*, 115 P.3d 536, 541 (Alaska 2005) (citing *Reich v. Cominco Alaska, Inc.*, 56 P.3d 18, 25 (Alaska 2002)).
7. *Id.* (citing *Manes v. Coats*, 941 P.2d 120, 125 (Alaska 1997)).
8. *Ogar v. City of Haines*, 51 P.3d 333, 335 (Alaska 2002) (citing *Hubbard v. Hubbard*, 44 P.3d 153, 155 (Alaska 2002)).
9. *Williams v. GEICO Cas. Co.*, 301 P.3d 1220, 1225 (Alaska 2013) (citing *DeNardo v. Cutler*, 167 P.3d 674, 677-78 (Alaska 2007)).
10. *See, e.g., Valdez Fisheries Dev. Ass'n, Inc. v. Froines*, 217 P.3d 830, 833 (Alaska 2009) ("The purpose of conferring discretion on the trial court to determine reasonable actual attorney's fees is to allow it to use its greater familiarity with the details of the case to perform an objective inquiry into these questions [of reasonable litigation expenses] and their like." (internal quotation marks omitted)).
11. Alaska R. Civ. Pr. 82(b)(3)(C)-(E).
12. *Progressive Corp. v. Peter ex rel. Peter*, 195 P.3d 1083, 1092 (Alaska 2008) (citing *Interior Cabaret, Hotel, Rest. & Retailers Ass'n v. Fairbanks N. Star Borough*, 135 P.3d 1000, 1002 (Alaska 2006)).
13. *Anderson v. Alyeska Pipeline Serv. Co.*, 234 P.3d 1282, 1286 (Alaska 2010) (citing *Ellison v. Plumbers & Steam Fitters Union Local 375*, 118 P.3d 1070, 1073-74 (Alaska 2005)).

(case continues)

14. *Ford v. Municipality of Anchorage*, 813 P.2d 654, 655 (Alaska 1991).
15. *Casey v. Semco Energy, Inc.*, 92 P.3d 379, 382 (Alaska 2004) (citing *Old Harbor Native Corp. v. Afognak Joint Venture*, 30 P.3d 101, 104 (Alaska 2001)).
16. The Hernandezes' motion sought a finding of "Contempt Upon This Court (Similar To Fraud Upon the Court)," which the superior court analyzed under Alaska's "fraud upon the court" law. The Hernandezes do not appear to dispute this interpretation.
17. *See Christianson v. First Nat'l Bank Alaska*, Mem. Op. & J. No. 1445, 2012 WL 6062124 (Alaska Dec. 5, 2012).
18. The Bank raises additional issues regarding attorney's fees and costs that are unrelated to its alleged litigation conduct. These are addressed separately in subpart IV.G.
19. *See* Alaska R. Civ. P. 60(b); *see also Higgins v. Municipality of Anchorage*, 810 P.2d 149, 154 (Alaska 1991) (concluding that this court's prior judgment "should be set aside for fraud upon the court"); *Mallonee v. Grow*, 502 P.2d 432, 440 (Alaska 1972) (affirming a superior court's decision to set aside its prior order based on a finding of fraud upon the court).
20. *Murray v. Ledbetter*, 144 P.3d 492, 497 (Alaska 2006) (citing *Hazel-Atlas Glass Co. v. Hartford-Empire Co.*, 322 U.S. 238, 244-45 (1944)).
21. *Hazel-Atlas Glass Co.*, 322 U.S. at 244.
22. *See Murray*, 144 P.3d at 497.
23. *Id.* at 498.
24. *Id.* at 499 (quoting *Allen v. Bussell*, 558 P.2d 496, 500 (Alaska 1976)) (internal quotation marks omitted).
25. *Id.* (alteration in original) (quoting *Lowe v. Lowe*, 817 P.2d 453, 457 n.9 (Alaska 1991)) (internal quotation marks omitted).
26. *Id.* (quoting *Allen*, 558 P.2d at 500) (internal quotation marks omitted).
27. *Id.* (citing *Mallonee v. Grow*, 502 P.2d 432, 438-39 (Alaska 1972); *Higgins v. Municipality of Anchorage*, 810 P.2d 149, 154 (Alaska 1991)).
28. 502 P.2d at 438-39.
29. *Id.*
30. 62 F.3d 1128, 1129-31 (9th Cir. 1995).
31. *Id.* at 1132.
32. *Id.* at 1131-32.
33. *State v. Alaska Cont'l Dev. Corp.*, 630 P.2d 977, 991 (Alaska 1980) (internal quotation marks omitted).
34. *Mallonee v. Grow*, 502 P.2d 432, 439 (Alaska 1972).
35. Lawer testified on March 31, 2009, that he had completed his review of McGrew's loans before "the last year or so." The first *AFG* trial took place in June 2008.
36. Although the Hernandezes did not attribute an exact date to this meeting, LeBaron testified that he received a loan resulting from this meeting "four or five" months following McGrew's death in December 2004.
37. *See Murray v. Ledbetter*, 144 P.3d 492, 499 (Alaska 2006) (quoting *Lowe v. Lowe*, 817 P.2d 453, 457 n.9 (Alaska 1991)) (internal quotation marks omitted).
38. *See Alaska Cont'l Dev. Corp.*, 630 P.2d at 991 ("While perjury by a witness is always a cause for concern, we do not believe, even if we were to accept the state's argument that [the opposing party's witness] committed perjury, that in this case it would rise to the level of—the most egregious conduct involving a corruption of the judicial process itself,' that we have required for a finding of—fraud upon the court' in past cases." (quoting *Allen v. Bussell*, 558 P.2d 496, 500 (Alaska 1976))).
39. *See* 62 F.3d 1128, 1129-31 (9th Cir. 1995).
40. See Murray, 144 P.3d at 499.
41. *See* Alaska R. Civ. P. 60(b) (noting the "power of a court to entertain an independent action to relieve a party from a judgment, order or proceeding . . . or to set aside a judgment for fraud upon the court").
42. *Williams v. GEICO Cas. Co.*, 301 P.3d 1220, 1225 (Alaska 2013) (citing *DeNardo v. Cutler*, 167 P.3d 674, 677-78 (Alaska 2007)).
43. *See Taylor Constr. Servs., Inc. v. URS Co.*, 758 P.2d 99, 102-03 (Alaska 1988) (2-2 decision) (opinion of Rabinowitz, C.J.) ("We have repeatedly recognized the trial court's broad discretion in awarding attorney's fees. We have required only that the trial court specify its reasons in the record when it departs from the fee schedule of Rule 82(a)." (citations omitted)).
44. *See Murray*, 144 P.3d at 499 (quoting *Lowe v. Lowe*, 817 P.2d 453, 457 n.9 (Alaska 1991)) (internal quotation marks omitted).
45. *See* 12 C.F.R. § 7.1002 (2014).
46. The Hernandezes' securities claims were based on the Alaska Securities Act. Federal regulations expressly permit a national bank to act as a finder, and state law may not "prevent or significantly interfere with the national bank's exercise of its powers." *Gutierrez v. Wells Fargo Bank, NA*, 704 F.3d 712, 722 (9th Cir. 2012) (quoting *Barnett Bank of Marion Cnty., N.A. v. Nelson*, 517 U.S. 25, 33 (1996)) (internal quotation marks omitted); 12 C.F.R. § 7.1002(a) ("It is part of the business of banking under 12 U.S.C. 24(Seventh) for a national bank to act as a finder, bringing together interested parties to a transaction."); *see also Rose v. Chase Bank USA, N.A.*, 513 F.3d 1032, 1037 (9th Cir. 2008) ("[T]he usual presumption against federal preemption of state law is inapplicable to federal banking regulation." (citations and internal quotation marks omitted)).
47. *Turner v. Municipality of Anchorage*, 171 P.3d 180, 185 (Alaska 2007) (alteration in original) (quoting *Wal-Mart, Inc. v. Stewart*, 990 P.2d 626, 631-32 (Alaska 1999)).
48. The jury was instructed, "You may believe all or none of the testimony of any witness. You need not believe a witness even if the witness'[s] testimony is uncontradicted."
49. The superior court also denied the Hernandezes' subsequent motion for JNOV on the "finder" issue and in the alternative, a new trial on several issues, including the securities claims. We conclude that for the same reasons as articulated above, the superior court did not err in denying this motion.
50. The Hernandezes do contend that the absence of an instruction regarding nominee loans "allowed jurors to more easily accept [the Bank's] repeated claims . . . that McGrew's wrongful conduct was merely minor and was undertaken only in an attempt to assist his clients." But they do not appear to argue that such an impression would have affected the jury's consideration of the non-securities claims.
51. AS 45.55.930(g).
52. *Cartee v. Cartee*, 239 P.3d 707, 712 (Alaska 2010) (citing *Dobos v. Ingersoll*, 9 P.3d 1020, 1023 (Alaska 2000)).
53. 100 P.3d 881 (Alaska 2004).
54. *See id.* at 888. In *Fred Meyer*, we discussed three evidentiary objections to the admission of an expert report: 1) that the report violated the rule limiting an opposing party's access to non-testifying expert witnesses; 2) that the report's author lacked the requisite personal knowledge for a lay witness; and 3) that the report was inadmissable hearsay. *Id.*
55. *Id.* at 882, 887.
56. *Id.* at 888.
57. *See id.* ("[The plaintiff] did not offer the report for the truth of the matters stated; rather he offered it to show that Fred Meyer had notice of its potential violations of Alaska law." (footnote omitted)).
58. *See Cartee v. Cartee*, 239 P.3d 707, 712 (Alaska 2010) ("A trial court's decision to admit or exclude evidence is reviewed

(case continues)

by us for abuse of discretion, and will be upset only if we find there has been an error which affected the substantial rights of a party." (citing *Dobos v. Ingersoll*, 9 P.3d 1020, 1023 (Alaska 2000))).

59. *See Cummins, Inc. v. Nelson*, 115 P.3d 536, 541 (Alaska 2005) ("Without a timely objection, we will only review [jury] instructions for plain error. A special verdict form is a type of jury instruction subject to the same standard of review." (footnote omitted)). We note that when a timely objection has been made, we review jury instructions de novo. *Id.* Here, however, the Hernandezes point to no objection raised below, never argue that we should apply our independent judgment, and expressly assert that the trial court committed "plain error."
60. Emphasis added.
61. *See* AS 09.10.070(a).
62. *Gefre v. Davis Wright Tremaine, LLP*, 306 P.3d 1264, 1274 (Alaska 2013).
63. *Id.* at 1275.
64. *Id.* (quoting *Cameron v. State*, 822 P.2d 1362, 1366 (Alaska 1991)) (internal quotation marks omitted).
65. *Palmer v. Borg-Warner Corp.*, 838 P.2d 1243, 1247 (Alaska 1992) (quoting *Sharrow v. Archer*, 658 P.2d 1331, 1333 (Alaska 1983)) (internal quotation marks omitted).
66. *Gefre*, 306 P.3d at 1277 (quoting *Williams v. Williams*, 129 P.3d 428, 432 (Alaska 2006)) (internal quotation marks omitted).
67. *See, e.g., Dressel v. Weeks*, 779 P.2d 324, 329 (Alaska 1989).
68. *See Curran v. Mount*, 657 P.2d 389, 391 (Alaska 1982) (adopting the clear and convincing standard for adverse possession cases).
69. 838 P.2d at 1251.
70. *Id.; see also Waage v. Cutter Biological Div. of Miles Labs., Inc.*, 926 P.2d 1145, 1149 (Alaska 1996).
71. *Palmer*, 838 P.2d at 1251.
72. *Waage*, 926 P.2d at 1149.
73. *Ogar v. City of Haines*, 51 P.3d 333, 335 (Alaska 2002) (citing *Hubbard v. Hubbard*, 44 P.3d 153, 155 (Alaska 2002)).
74. *See, e.g., Palmer*, 838 P.2d at 1251 ("The determination of when a fraudulent misrepresentation or concealment should have been discovered is a question of fact for the trial court to decide." (citing *Carter v. Hoblit*, 755 P.2d 1084, 1087 (Alaska 1988))).
75. *Shumway v. Betty Black Living Trust*, 321 P.3d 372, 375 (Alaska 2014).
76. *Valdez Fisheries Dev. Ass'n v. Alyeska Pipeline Serv. Co.*, 45 P.3d 657, 672 (Alaska 2002).
77. *See* AS 09.25.010(a)(13).
78. *Id.*
79. *See* 12 C.F.R. § 7.1002(a) ("It is part of the business of banking under 12 U.S.C. 24(Seventh) for a national bank to act as a finder, bringing together interested parties to a transaction."); *see also Gutierrez v. Wells Fargo Bank, NA*, 704 F.3d 712, 722 (9th Cir. 2012) (noting that state law may not "prevent or significantly interfere with the national bank's exercise of its powers." (citation and internal quotation marks omitted)).
80. *Fairbanks Fire Fighters Ass'n, Local 1324 v. City of Fairbanks*, 48 P.3d 1165, 1167 (Alaska 2002) (alteration omitted) (quoting *Gerstein v. Axtell*, 960 P.2d 599, 601 (Alaska 1998)) (internal quotation marks omitted).
81. *In re Mark V.*, 324 P.3d 840, 843 (Alaska 2014) (quoting *In re Joan K.*, 273 P.3d 594, 598 (Alaska 2012)) (internal quotation marks omitted).
82. *See* RESTATEMENT (SECOND) OF JUDGMENTS § 27 cmt. h (1982) ("If issues are determined but the judgment is not dependent upon the determinations, relitigation of those issues in a subsequent action between the parties is not precluded. Such determinations have the characteristics of dicta, and may not ordinarily be the subject of an appeal by the party against whom they were made.").
83. *O'Connell v. Will*, 263 P.3d 41, 47 (Alaska 2011) (quoting *Rockstad v. Erikson*, 113 P.3d 1215, 1224 (Alaska 2005)) (internal quotation marks omitted); *see also* Alaska R. Civ. P. 82(a) ("Except as otherwise provided by law or agreed to by the parties, the prevailing party in a civil case shall be awarded attorney's fees calculated under this rule.").
84. *See Casey v. Semco Energy, Inc.*, 92 P.3d 379, 382 (Alaska 2004) (citing *Old Harbor Native Corp. v. Afognak Joint Venture*, 30 P.3d 101, 104 (Alaska 2001)).
85. *Peterson v. Wirum*, 625 P.2d 866, 872 n.10 (Alaska 1981) (citation omitted).
86. *See id.*
87. *Pagenkopf v. Chatham Elec., Inc.*, 165 P.3d 634, 644 (Alaska 2007).
88. Alaska R. Civ. P. 68(a), (b). If there are multiple defendants, the threshold is ten percent rather than five percent. Alaska R. Civ. P. 68(b).
89. *Grow v. Ruggles*, 860 P.2d 1225, 1227 (Alaska 1993).
90. *Anderson v. Alyeska Pipeline Serv. Co.*, 234 P.3d 1282, 1286 (Alaska 2010).
91. *See Brinkerhoff v. Swearingen Aviation Corp.*, 663 P.2d 937, 943 (Alaska 1983).
92. *John's Heating Serv. v. Lamb*, 46 P.3d 1024, 1042 & n.85 (Alaska 2002) (alteration in original) (citation and internal quotation marks omitted).
93. The Bank contends that the Inn should not be considered a plaintiff for purposes of the Rule 68 offer because it had no individual claim aside from those raised by the Hernandezes, and because the court instructed the jury that the word "plaintiff" or "plaintiffs" in the instructions referred to Alaska Fur Gallery and Hernandez & Associates. However, the Bank itself referred to the Inn as a separate party in its offer of judgment, and the Bank provides no authority as to why the Inn is not a relevant party for Rule 68 purposes.
94. *Progressive Corp. v. Peter ex rel. Peter*, 195 P.3d 1083, 1092 (Alaska 2008) (citing *Interior Cabaret, Hotel, Rest. & Retailers Ass'n v. Fairbanks N. Star Borough*, 135 P.3d 1000, 1002 (Alaska 2006)).
95. *Day v. Moore*, 771 P.2d 436, 437 (Alaska 1989) (quoting *Adoption of V.M.C.*, 528 P.2d 788, 795 n.14 (Alaska 1974)) (internal quotation marks omitted).
96. *Id.* (quoting *Malvo v. J.C. Penney Co.*, 512 P.2d 575, 586 (Alaska 1973)).
97. *Alaska Ctr. for the Env't v. State*, 940 P.2d 916, 921 (Alaska 1997) (citing *Hillman v. Nationwide Mut. Fire Ins. Co.*, 855 P.2d 1321, 1327-28 (Alaska 1993)).
98. *See E.P. v. Alaska Psychiatric Inst.*, 205 P.3d 1101, 1106 (Alaska 2009) ("We . . . review questions of statutory interpretation *de novo*."); *City of Kodiak v. Parish*, 986 P.2d 201, 202 (Alaska 1999) (applying independent judgment to the interpretation of Rule 82(e)); *Ford v. Municipality of Anchorage*, 813 P.2d 654, 655 (Alaska 1991) ("Since this case involves the interpretation of a civil rule, we exercise our independent judgment.").
99. *Parish*, 986 P.2d at 204.
100. *Id.*

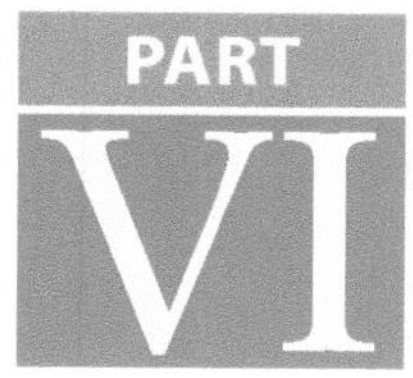

Credit, Secured Transactions, and Bankruptcy

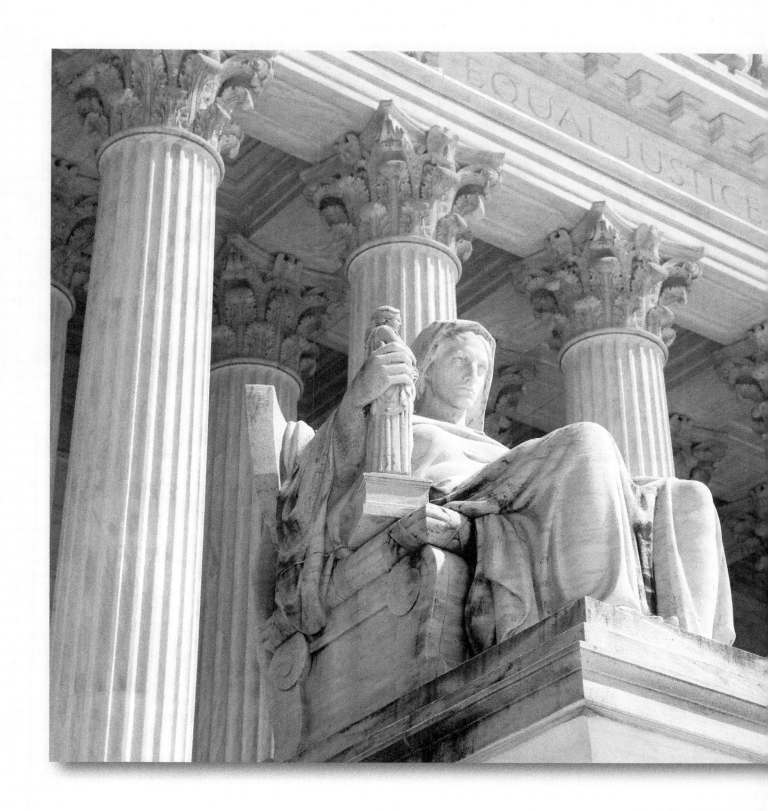

CHAPTER 26 Credit, Real Property Financing, and Debtor's Rights

HOUSE

A house is often a person's most valuable asset. Homeowners often borrow money to help provide the funds to purchase a house. Usually, the lender takes back a mortgage that secures the house as collateral for the repayment of the loan. If the borrower defaults, the lender can bring a foreclosure proceeding to recover the collateral.

Learning Objectives

After studying this chapter, you should be able to:

1. Distinguish between unsecured and secured credit.
2. Describe security interests in real property, such as mortgages and deeds of trust.
3. Compare surety and guaranty arrangements.
4. Describe the provisions of the Consumer Financial Protection Act of 2010, Mortgage Reform and Anti-Predatory Lending Act of 2010, and Credit CARD Act of 2009.
5. Describe the Consumer Financial Protection Bureau.

Chapter Outline

Introduction to Credit, Real Property Financing, and Debtor's Rights

Credit

Unsecured Credit

Secured Credit

Real Property Financing

CASE 26.1 *Old Republic National Title Insurance Company v. Fifth Third Bank*

BUSINESS ENVIRONMENT *Construction Liens on Real Property*

Security and Guaranty Arrangements

Collection Remedies

Consumer Financial Protection

CONTEMPORARY ENVIRONMENT *Consumer Financial Protection Bureau*

ETHICS *Credit CARD Act*

BUSINESS ENVIRONMENT *Dodd-Frank Wall Street Reform and Consumer Protection Act*

"Creditors have better memories than debtors."

—Benjamin Franklin
Poor Richard's Almanack (1758)

Introduction to Credit, Real Property Financing, and Debtor's Rights

The U.S. economy is a credit economy. Consumers borrow money to make major purchases (e.g., homes, automobiles, appliances) and use credit cards (e.g., Visa, MasterCard) to purchase goods and services at clothing stores, restaurants, and other businesses. Businesses use credit to purchase equipment, supplies, and other goods and services.

Words pay no debts.

William Shakespeare
Troilus and Cressida, act III (ca. 1602)

Because lenders are sometimes reluctant to lend large sums of money simply on the borrower's promise to repay, many of them take a *security interest* in the property purchased or some other property of the debtor. The property in which the security interest is taken is called *collateral*. If the debtor does not pay the debt, the creditor can foreclose on and recover the collateral.

A lender who is unsure whether a debtor will have sufficient income or assets to repay a loan may require another person to guarantee payment. If the borrower fails to repay the loan, the person who agreed to guarantee the loan is responsible for paying it.

In addition, governments have enacted consumer financial protection laws that protect consumer-debtors in credit transactions.

This chapter discusses unsecured credit, secured credit, mortgages and other security interests in real property, guaranty and surety arrangements, and consumer-debtor financial protection laws.

Credit

credit
Occurs when one party makes a loan to another party.

creditor (lender)
The lender in a credit transaction.

debtor (borrower)
The borrower in a credit transaction.

In a transaction involving the extension of **credit** (either unsecured or secured), there are two parties. The party extending the credit, the **lender**, is called the **creditor**. The party borrowing the money, the **borrower**, is called the **debtor** (see **Exhibit 26.1**).

Exhibit 26.1 RELATIONSHIP BETWEEN DEBTOR AND CREDITOR

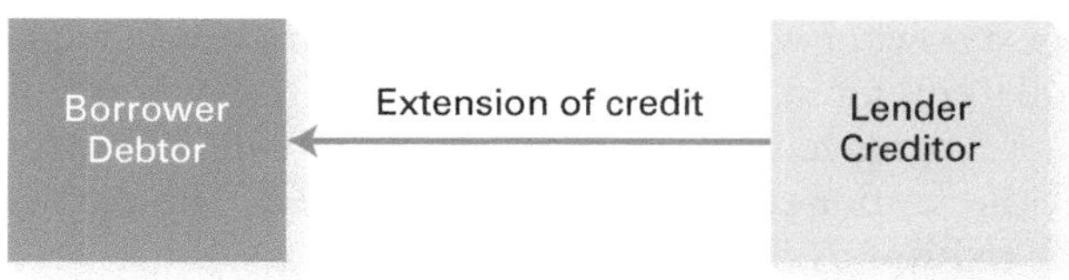

Example Prima Company goes to Urban Bank and borrows $100,000. In this case, Prima Company is the *borrower-debtor*, and Urban Bank is the *lender-creditor*.

Credit may be extended on either an *unsecured* or a *secured* basis. The following paragraphs discuss these types of credit.

Unsecured Credit

unsecured credit
Credit that does not require any security (collateral) to protect the payment of the debt.

Unsecured credit does not require any security (collateral) to protect the payment of the debt. Instead, the creditor relies on the debtor's promise to repay the principal (plus any interest) when it is due. The creditor is called an **unsecured creditor**. In deciding whether to make the loan, the unsecured creditor considers the debtor's credit history, income, and other assets. If the debtor fails to make the payments, the creditor may bring legal action and obtain a judgment against him or her. If the debtor is **judgment proof** (i.e., has little or no property or no income that can be garnished), the creditor may never collect.

Example Arnold borrows $15,000 from Mary. Mary lends the money to Arnold without taking an interest in collateral for the loan. This is an unsecured loan. Mary is relying on Arnold's credit standing when she makes the loan. If Arnold defaults on the loan, Mary has no collateral to foreclose on. Mary's recourse is to sue Arnold to recover the unpaid loan amount.

Secured Credit

secured credit
Credit that requires security (collateral) that secures payment of the loan.

To minimize the risk associated with extending unsecured credit, a creditor may require a security interest in the debtor's property (**collateral**). The collateral secures payment of the loan. This type of credit is called **secured credit**. The creditor who has a security interest in collateral is called a **secured creditor**, or **secured party**. Security interests may be taken in real, personal, intangible, and other property. If the debtor fails to make the payments when due, the collateral may be repossessed to recover the outstanding amount. Generally, if the sale of the collateral is insufficient to repay the loan plus interest, the creditor may bring a lawsuit against the debtor to recover a deficiency judgment for the difference.

Rather go to bed supperless than rise in debt.
Benjamin Franklin
(1706–1790)

Example Sarah purchases an automobile from a car dealership. She borrows part of the purchase price from a lender. The lender requires Sarah to give it a security interest in the automobile to secure the loan. This is a secured credit transaction with the automobile being collateral for the loan. If Sarah defaults and fails to make the required payments, the lender can repossess the automobile.

Real Property Financing

mortgage
An arrangement where an owner of real property borrows money from a lender and pledges the real property as collateral to secure the repayment of the loan.

Owners of real estate can create **security interests in real property**. This occurs if an owner borrows money from a lender and pledges real estate as security for repayment of the loan.

Mortgage

mortgagor (owner-debtor)
The owner-debtor in a mortgage transaction.

mortgagee (creditor)
The creditor in a mortgage transaction.

A person who owns a piece of real property has an ownership interest in that property. A property owner who borrows money from a creditor may use his or her real estate as collateral for repayment of the loan. This type of collateral arrangement, known as a **mortgage**, is a *two-party instrument*. The **owner-debtor** is the **mortgagor**, and the **lender-creditor** is the **mortgagee**. The parties to a mortgage are illustrated in **Exhibit 26.2**.

Exhibit 26.2 PARTIES TO A MORTGAGE

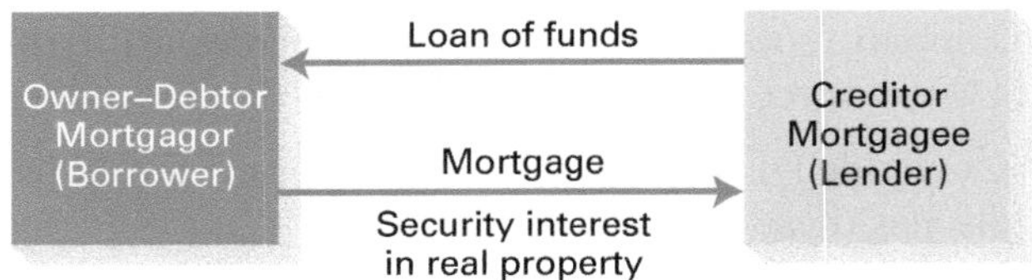

Example General Electric purchases a manufacturing plant for $10 million, pays $2 million cash as a down payment, and borrows the remaining $8 million from City Bank. General Electric is the debtor, and City Bank is the creditor. To secure the loan, General Electric gives a mortgage on the plant to City Bank. This is a secured loan, with the plant being collateral for the loan. General Electric is the mortgagor, and City Bank is the mortgagee. If General Electric defaults on the loan, the bank may take action under state law to foreclose and take the property.

When a mortgage is repaid in full, the lender files a written document called a **reconveyance**, sometimes referred to as **satisfaction of a mortgage**, with the county recorder's office which is proof that the mortgage has been paid.

Note and Deed of Trust

Some states' laws provide for the use of a *deed of trust and note* in place of a mortgage. The **note** is the instrument that is evidence of the borrower's debt to the lender; the **deed of trust** is the instrument that gives the creditor a security interest in the debtor's property that is pledged as collateral.

note
An instrument that is evidence of a borrower's debt to the lender.

deed of trust
An instrument that gives a creditor a security interest in the debtor's real property that is pledged as collateral for a loan.

A deed of trust is a *three-party instrument*. Under it, legal title to the real property is placed with a **trustee** (usually a trust corporation) until the amount borrowed has been paid. The **owner-debtor** is called the **trustor**. Although legal title is vested in the trustee, the trustor has full legal rights to possession of the real property. The **lender-creditor** is called the **beneficiary**. **Exhibit 26.3** illustrates the relationship between the parties.

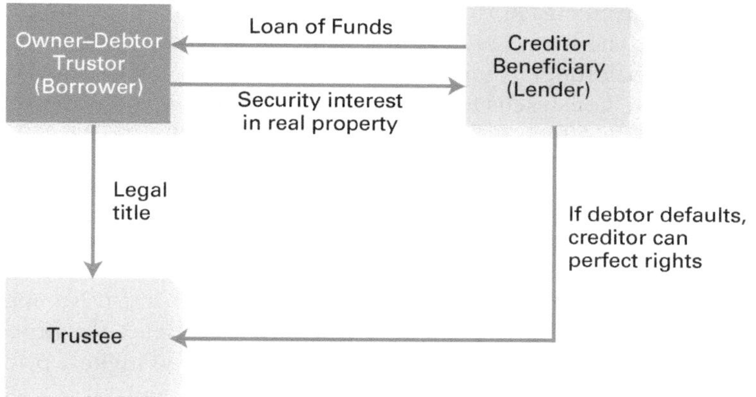

Exhibit 26.3 **PARTIES TO A NOTE AND DEED OF TRUST**

When the loan is repaid, the trustee files a written document called a *reconveyance* with the county recorder's office, which transfers title to the real property to the borrower-debtor.

Debt is the prolific mother of folly and of crime.

Benjamin Disraeli
Henrietta Temple (1837)

Recording Statute

Most states have enacted **recording statutes** that require a mortgage or deed of trust to be recorded in the **county recorder's office** in the county in which the real property is located. These filings are public record and alert the world that a mortgage or deed of trust has been recorded against the real property. This record gives potential lenders or purchasers of real property the ability to determine whether there are any existing liens (mortgages) on the property.

recording statute
A statute that requires a mortgage or deed of trust to be recorded in the county recorder's office of the county in which the real property is located.

The **nonrecordation of a mortgage** or deed of trust does not affect either the legality of the instrument between the mortgagor and the mortgagee or the rights and obligations of the parties. In other words, the mortgagor is obligated to pay the amount of the mortgage according to the terms of the mortgage, even if the document is not recorded. However, an improperly recorded document is not effective against either (1) subsequent purchasers of the real property or (2) other mortgagees or lienholders who have no notice of the prior mortgages.

Example Eileen purchases a house for $500,000. She borrows $400,000 from Boulevard Bank and gives the bank a mortgage on the house for this amount. Boulevard Bank fails to record the mortgage. Eileen then applies to borrow $400,000 from Advance Bank. Advance Bank reviews the real estate recordings and finds no mortgage recorded against the property, so it lends Eileen $400,000.

By no means run in debt.

George Herbert
The Temple (1633)

Advance Bank records its mortgage. Later, Eileen defaults on both loans. In this case, Advance Bank can foreclose on the house because it recorded its mortgage. Boulevard Bank, even though it made the first loan to Eileen, does not get the house and can only sue Eileen to recover the unpaid loan.

Foreclosure Sale

foreclosure sale
A legal procedure by which a secured creditor causes the judicial sale of the secured real estate to pay a defaulted loan.

A debtor that does not make the required payments on a secured real estate transaction is in **default**. All states permit **foreclosure sales**. Under this method, the debtor's default may trigger a legal court action for **foreclosure**. Any party having an interest in the property—including owners of the property and other mortgagees or lienholders—must be named as defendants. If the mortgagee's case is successful, the court will issue a judgment that orders the real property to be sold at a judicial sale. The procedures for a foreclosure action and sale are mandated by state statute. Any surplus must be paid to the mortgagor.

Example Christine borrows $500,000 from Country Bank to buy a house. Christine (mortgagor) gives a mortgage to Country Bank (mortgagee), making the house collateral to secure the loan. Later, Christine defaults on the loan. Country Bank can foreclose on the property and follow applicable state law to sell the house at a judicial sale. If the house sells for $575,000, the bank keeps $500,000 and must remit $75,000 to Christine. Most state statutes permit the mortgagee-lender to recover the costs of the foreclosure and judicial sale from the sale proceeds before remitting the surplus to the mortgagor-borrower.

power of sale
A power stated in a mortgage or deed that permits foreclosure without court proceedings and sale of the property through an auction.

Most states permit foreclosure by **power of sale**, although this must be expressly conferred in the mortgage or deed of trust. Under a power of sale, the procedure for that sale is provided in the mortgage or deed of trust itself. No court action is necessary. Some states have enacted statutes that establish the procedure for conducting the sale. Such a sale must be by auction for the highest price obtainable. Any surplus must be paid to the mortgagor.

In the following case, the courts had to decide the priority of mortgages and a lien on a piece of real property.

CASE 26.1 ***STATE COURT CASE Mortgages and Liens***

Old Republic National Title Insurance Company v. Fifth Third Bank

2008 Ohio App. Lexis 4423 (2008)
Court of Appeals of Ohio

"The recording statute sets forth the general rule that the first mortgage recorded shall have preference over subsequently recorded mortgages."

—Dinkelacker, Judge

Facts

James and Heather McCarthy (McCarthy) owned a house in Cincinnati, Ohio. The house was purchased with a mortgage loan from Countrywide Home Loans, which recorded its mortgage in the appropriate county recorder's office. Subsequently, the following events occurred:

- March 10—McCarthy borrowed money from Fifth Third Bank and gave the bank a mortgage on their house. Fifth Third Bank did not record the mortgage.
- March 10—McCarthy went to Centex Home Equity Company to refinance the original mortgage loan from Countrywide.
- March 19—Centex's title search revealed Countrywide's loan but did not reveal Fifth Third's unrecorded mortgage.
- March 24—The law firm of Santen and Hughes recorded a lien judgment on McCarthy's house for failure to pay for legal services.

(case continues)

- April 1—McCarthy closed on the Centex loan. Centex was not informed that McCarthy had previously obtained a loan from Fifth Third. Centex did not conduct a new title search, so it was not aware of the law firm's recorded lien. The proceeds from Centex's loan were used to pay off Countrywide's mortgage. Centex notified its agent, Buckeye Title Company (Buckeye), to record Centex's mortgage within 24 hours. Buckeye failed to record Centex's mortgage.
- April 15—Fifth Third recorded its mortgage.
- May 2—Centex recorded its mortgage.

When Santen and Hughes commenced a foreclosure action against McCarthy's house, Fifth Third and Centex were brought into the suit. The trial court held that the Santen and Hughes' lien had first priority. As to the mortgages, the court applied the doctrine of equity and ruled that Centex's first-in-time but later recorded mortgage had priority over Fifth Third's later made but previously recorded mortgage. Fifth Third appealed.

Issue

What is the priority of the lien and two mortgages on McCarthy's house?

Language of the Court

Under Ohio law, lien priority is determined by the time of filing. The recording statute sets forth the general rule that the first mortgage recorded shall have preference over subsequently recorded mortgages. Lien priority in this case is hereby established as follows: the Santen and Hughes lien has first priority, the Fifth Third mortgage has second priority, and the Centex mortgage has third priority.

Decision

The court of appeals reversed the decision of the trial court and ruled that the priority of the security interests on McCarthy's house were by the recording date: first, Santen and Hughes; second, Fifth Third; and third, Centex.

Ethics Questions

Was it ethical for Centex to argue that its unrecorded mortgage should take priority over Fifth Third's prior recorded mortgage?

Deficiency Judgment

Some states permit a mortgagee to bring a separate legal action to recover a deficiency from the mortgagor. If the mortgagee is successful, the court will award a **deficiency judgment** that entitles the mortgagee to recover the amount of the judgment from the mortgagor's other property.

deficiency judgment
A judgment of a court that permits a secured lender to recover other property or income from a defaulting debtor if the collateral is insufficient to repay the unpaid loan.

Example Kaye buys a house for $800,000. She puts $200,000 down and borrows $600,000 from a bank, which takes a mortgage on the property to secure the loan. Kaye defaults, and when the bank forecloses on the property, it is worth only $500,000. There is a deficiency of $100,000 ($600,000 loan − $500,000 foreclosure sale price). The bank can recover the $100,000 deficiency from Kaye's other property. The bank has to bring a legal action against Kaye to do so.

Antideficiency Statutes

Several states have enacted statutes that prohibit deficiency judgments regarding certain types of mortgages, such as loans for the original purchase of residential property. These statutes are called **antideficiency statutes**. Antideficiency statutes usually apply only to **first purchase money mortgages** (i.e., mortgages that are taken out to purchase houses). Second mortgages and other subsequent mortgages, even mortgages that refinance the first mortgage, usually are not protected by antideficiency statutes.

antideficiency statute
A statute that prohibits deficiency judgments regarding certain types of mortgages, such as those on residential property.

Example Assume that a house is located in a state that has an antideficiency statute. Qian buys the house for $800,000. She puts $200,000 down and borrows $600,000 of the purchase price from First Bank, which takes a mortgage on the property to secure the loan. This is a first purchase money mortgage. Subsequently, Qian borrows $100,000 from Second Bank and gives a second mortgage to Second Bank to secure the loan. Qian defaults on both loans, and when she defaults, the house is worth only $500,000. Both banks bring foreclosure proceedings to recover the house. First Bank can recover the house worth $500,000 at foreclosure. However, First Bank has a deficiency of $100,000 ($600,000 loan − $500,000 foreclosure sale price). Because of the state's antideficiency statute, First Bank cannot recover this deficiency from Qian; First Bank can recover only the house in foreclosure and must write off the $100,000 loss. Second Bank's loan, a second loan, is not covered by the antideficiency statute. Therefore, Second Bank can sue Qian to recover its $100,000 deficiency from Qian's other property.

right of redemption
A right that allows the mortgagor to redeem real property after default and before foreclosure. It requires the mortgagor to pay the full amount of the debt incurred by the mortgagee because of the mortgagor's default.

construction lien (mechanic's lien)
A contractor's, laborer's, supplier's, or design professional's statutory lien that makes the real property to which services or materials have been provided security for the payment of the services and materials.

lien release
A written document signed by a contractor, subcontractor, laborer, or material person, waiving his or her statutory lien against real property.

Right of Redemption

The common law and many state statutes give the mortgagor the right to redeem real property after default and before foreclosure. This right, called the **right of redemption**, requires the mortgagor to pay the full amount of the debt—that is, principal, interest, and other costs—incurred by the mortgagee because of the mortgagor's default. Redemption of a partial interest is not permitted. On redemption, the mortgagor receives title to the property, free and clear of the mortgage debt. Most states allow the mortgagor to redeem real property for a specified period (usually six months or one year) after foreclosure. This is called the **statutory period of redemption**.

The following feature describes liens that contractors and laborers can obtain on real property.

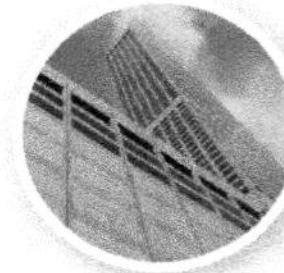

Business Environment

Construction Liens on Real Property

Owners of real property often hire contractors, architects, and laborers (e.g., painters, plumbers, roofers, bricklayers, furnace installers) to make improvements to the real property. The contractors and laborers expend the time to provide their services as well as money to provide the materials for the improvements. Their investments are protected by state statutes that permit them to file a **construction lien** (also known as a **mechanic's lien**) against the improved real property. Construction liens are often called by more specific names, such as a supplier's lien (also called material person's lien) for those parties supplying materials, laborer's lien for persons providing labor, and design professional's lien for those parties providing architectural and design services.

The lienholder must file a **notice of lien** with the county recorder's office in the county in which the real property subject to the lien is located. When a lien is properly filed, the real property to which the improvements have been made becomes security for the payment of these services and materials. In essence, the lienholder has the equivalent of a mortgage on the property. If the owner defaults, the lienholder may foreclose on the lien, sell the property, and satisfy the debt plus interest and costs out of the proceeds of the sale. Any surplus must be paid to the owner-debtor. Mechanic's liens are usually subject to the debtor's right of redemption.

Most state statutes permit an owner of real property to have subcontractors, laborers, and material persons who will provide services or materials to a real property project to sign a written **release of lien** contract (also called a **lien release**) releasing any lien they might otherwise assert against the property. A lien release can be used by the property owner to defeat a statutory lienholder's attempt to obtain payment.

Example Landowner, which owns an undeveloped piece of property, hires General Contractor, a general contractor, to build a house on the property. General Contractor hires Roofing Company, a roofer, as a subcontractor to put the roof on the house. When the house is complete, Landowner pays General Contractor the full contract price for the house but has failed to obtain a lien release from Roofing Company. General Contractor fails to pay Roofing Company for the roofing work. Roofing Company files a mechanic's lien against the house and demands payment from Landowner. Here, Landowner must pay Roofing Company for the roofing work; if Landowner does not, Roofing Company can foreclose on the house, have it sold, and satisfy the debt out of the proceeds of the sale. To prevent foreclosure, Landowner must pay Roofing Company for its work. Landowner ends up paying twice for the roofing work—once to General Contractor, the general contractor, and a second time to Roofing Company, the subcontractor. Landowner's only recourse is to sue General Contractor to recover its payment.

Example Suppose in the preceding example that Landowner obtained a lien release from Roofing Company, the subcontractor, before or at the time Landowner paid General Contractor, the general contractor. If General Contractor fails to pay Roofing Company, the subcontractor, then Roofing Company could not file a lien against Landowner's house because it had signed a lien release. In this situation, Roofing Company's only recourse would be to sue General Contractor to recover payment for its services.

LAND SALES CONTRACT
Most states permit the transfer and sale of real property pursuant to a **land sales contract**. *In this contract, the owner of real property agrees to sell the property to a purchaser, who agrees to pay the purchase price to the owner-seller over an agreed-on period of time. Often, making such a loan is referred to as "carrying the paper." Land sales contracts are often used to sell undeveloped property, farms, and the like. If the purchaser defaults, the seller may declare forfeiture and retake possession of the property.*

Surety and Guaranty Arrangements

Sometimes a creditor refuses to extend credit to a debtor unless a third person agrees to become liable on the debt. The third person's credit becomes the security for the credit extended to the debtor. This relationship may be either a *surety arrangement* or a *guaranty arrangement*. These arrangements are discussed in the following paragraphs.

land sales contract
An arrangement in which the owner of real property sells property to a purchaser and extends credit to the purchaser.

Surety Arrangement

In a strict **surety arrangement**, a third person—known as the **surety**, or **co-debtor**—promises to be liable for the payment of another person's debt. A person who acts as a surety is commonly called an **accommodation party**, or **co-signer**. Along with the principal debtor, the surety is **primarily liable** for paying the principal debtor's debt when it is due. The principal debtor does not have to be in default on the debt, and the creditor does not have to have exhausted all its remedies against the principal debtor before seeking payment from the surety.

surety arrangement
An arrangement in which a third party promises to be *primarily liable* with the borrower for the payment of the borrower's debt.

Example Ivy, a college student, wants to purchase a new BMW automobile. She goes to Auto Dealer and finds exactly the car she wants, and she wants to finance the car. Auto Dealer will not sell the car to Ivy on credit based on her own credit standing. Auto Dealer requires Ivy to find a co-signer on the purchase and credit contract. Ivy asks her mother to co-sign on the agreement. When Ivy's mother signs as a co-signer, she is now a surety. Ivy's mother is equally bound by the contract with Ivy. Ivy's mother is *primarily liable* with Ivy on the loan. Usually, if Ivy does not pay, Auto Dealer will immediately bring legal action against Ivy's mother for payment. Auto Dealer does not have to sue Ivy first.

Guaranty Arrangement

guaranty arrangement
An arrangement in which a third party promises to be *secondarily liable* for the payment of another's debt.

In a **guaranty arrangement**, a third person, the **guarantor**, agrees to pay the debt of the principal debtor if the debtor defaults and does not pay the debt when it is due. In this type of arrangement, the guarantor is **secondarily liable** on the debt. In other words, the guarantor is obligated to pay the debt if the principal debtor defaults on the debt and the creditor has not been able to collect the debt from the debtor.

Example Ivan, a college student, wants to purchase a new computer, printer, and other electronic equipment on credit from Electronics Retail, Inc. Electronics will not sell the computer and other equipment to Ivan unless he can get someone to guarantee the payment. Ivan asks his roommate, Edward, to guarantee the payment. Edward agrees, and he is placed on the credit agreement as a guarantor. Edward is *secondarily liable*: If Ivan fails to make the necessary payment, Electronics must first attempt unsuccessfully to recover the payments from Ivan before taking legal action against Edward to recover payment.

Defenses of a Surety or Guarantor

Generally, the defenses the principal debtor has against the creditor may also be asserted by a surety or guarantor.

Example If credit has been extended for the purchase of a piece of machinery that proves to be defective, both the debtor and the surety can assert the defect as a defense to liability. The defenses of fraudulent inducement to enter into the surety or guaranty agreement and duress may also be cited as personal defenses to liability.

CONCEPT SUMMARY
SURETY AND GUARANTY CONTRACTS

Type of Arrangement	Party	Liability
Surety contract	Surety	Primarily liable. The surety is a co-debtor who is liable to pay the debt when it is due.
Guaranty contract	Guarantor	Secondarily liable. The guarantor is liable to pay the debt if the debtor defaults and the creditor has been unsuccessful in collecting the debt from the debtor.

Collection Remedies

Once a creditor has obtained a judgment against a debtor, the creditor can petition the court for a *postjudgment order* to obtain property in possession of the debtor or a third party to satisfy the judgment. In some occasions, a court can issue a *prejudgment order* to tie up property of the debtor during the court proceedings. The most common **collection remedies** are discussed in the following paragraphs:

Writ of Attachment

Attachment is a **prejudgment court order** that permits the seizure of a debtor's property that is in the debtor's possession while a lawsuit against the debtor is pending. To obtain a **writ of attachment**, a creditor must follow the procedures of state law, give the debtor notice, and post a bond with the court.

writ of attachment
A prejudgment court order that permits the seizure of a debtor's property while a lawsuit is pending.

Example Taryn sues Justin for fraud. Taryn lost a large sum of money to Justin when she invested in what she alleges was a fraudulent investment scheme. Because it may take more than one year before the case is heard, Taryn is afraid that Justin will transfer any money or property he has to avoid having to pay a judgment if he loses at trial. Taryn can immediately make a motion to the court to have the court issue a writ of attachment ordering the seizure of Justin's property, pending the outcome of the lawsuit. The court will do so if it determines that there is some merit to Taryn's claim against Justin and there is justification to believe that Justin might dispose of his property prior to the trial.

Writ of Execution

Execution is a **postjudgment court order** that permits the seizure of the debtor's property that is in the possession of the debtor. Certain property is exempt from levy (e.g., tools of trade, clothing, homestead exemption). A **writ of execution** is a court order directing the sheriff or other government officials to seize the debtor's property in the debtor's possession and authorizes a judicial sale of that property. The proceeds are used to pay the creditor the amount of the final judgment. Any surplus must be paid to the debtor.

writ of execution
A postjudgment court order that permits the seizure of the debtor's property that is in the possession of the debtor.

Example Aamir wins a $25,000 judgment against Nicole. Nicole refuses to pay the amount of the judgment to Aamir. Aamir can obtain a postjudgment writ of execution from the court whereby the court directs the sheriff to seize Nicole's automobile and other property and have them sold at public auction to satisfy the judgment she owes Aamir.

Writ of Garnishment

Garnishment is a *postjudgment court order* that permits the seizure of a debtor's property that is in the possession of third parties. The creditor (also known as the **garnishor**) must go to court to seek a **writ of garnishment**. A third party in this situation is called a **garnishee**. Common garnishees are employers who possess wages due a debtor, banks in possession of funds belonging to the debtor, and other third parties in the possession of property of the debtor.

writ of garnishment
A postjudgment court order that permits the seizure of a debtor's property that is in the possession of third parties.

Example Yuming wins a $30,000 judgment against Lisa. Lisa refuses to pay the amount of the judgment to Yuming. Lisa works for E-Communications Company. Yuming obtains a postjudgment writ of garnishment from the court whereby the court orders E-Communications Company to pay 25 percent of Lisa's weekly disposable earnings (after taxes) directly to Yuming. Thus, after receiving this writ of garnishment, E-Communications Company must deduct the amount of the garnishment from Lisa's wages before she is paid and remit this amount to Yuming until the judgment is paid.

To protect debtors from abusive and excessive garnishment actions by creditors, Congress enacted **Title III of the Consumer Credit Protection Act**.[1] This federal law allows debtors who are subject to a writ of garnishment to retain the greater of (1) 75 percent of their weekly disposable earnings (after taxes) or (2) an amount equal to 30 hours of work paid at federal minimum wage. State law limitations on garnishment control are often more stringent than federal law.

Title III of the Consumer Credit Protection Act
A federal law that permits debtors who are subject to a writ of garnishment to retain a specified percentage or amount of their earnings.

CONCEPT SUMMARY
COLLECTION REMEDIES

Type of Collection Remedy	Period When Collection Remedy Occurs	Debtor's Property in the Possession of This Party
Attachment	Prejudgment	Debtor
Execution	Postjudgment	Debtor
Garnishment	Postjudgment	Third party

Consumer Financial Protection

Consumer Financial Protection Bureau (CFPB) A federal administrative agency that is responsible for enforcing federal consumer financial protection statutes.

In many consumer credit transactions, the lender is an institution or party that has greater leverage than the borrower. In the past, this sometimes led to lenders taking advantage of debtors. To rectify this problem, the federal government has enacted many consumer financial protection statutes that protect debtors from abusive, deceptive, and unfair credit practices. Many of these **consumer financial protection** laws are discussed in the following paragraphs.

Contemporary Environment

Consumer Financial Protection Bureau

In 2010, Congress created a new federal government agency called the **Consumer Financial Protection Bureau (CFPB)**. The bureau has authority to supervise all participants in the consumer finance and mortgage area, including depository institutions, such as commercial and savings banks, and nondepository parties, such as insurance companies, mortgage brokers, credit-counseling firms, debt collectors, and debt buyers. The bureau provides uniform model forms that covered parties may use to make required disclosures.

The bureau has authority to prohibit unfair, deceptive, or abusive acts or practices regarding consumer financial products and services. The bureau is a watchdog over credit cards, debit cards, mortgages, payday loans, and other consumer financial products and services. The automobile industry is exempt from bureau supervision and is subject to oversight by the Federal Trade Commission (FTC).

The bureau has authority to enforce federal consumer financial protection laws. The bureau is authorized to adopt rules to interpret and enforce the provisions of the acts it administers. The bureau has investigative and subpoena powers and may refer matters to the U.S. attorney general for criminal prosecution.

Truth-in-Lending Act

Truth-in-Lending Act (TILA) A federal statute that requires creditors to make certain disclosures to debtors in consumer transactions and real estate loans on the debtor's principal dwelling.

The **Truth-in-Lending Act (TILA)**[2] is one of the first federal consumer protection statutes enacted by Congress. The TILA, as amended, requires creditors to make certain disclosures to debtors in consumer transactions (e.g., retail installment sales, automobile loans) and real estate loans on the debtor's principal dwelling. The TILA covers only creditors that regularly (1) extend credit for goods or services to consumers or (2) arrange such credit in the ordinary course of their business. **Consumer credit** is defined as credit extended to natural persons for personal, family, or household purposes.

Regulation Z A regulation that sets forth detailed rules for compliance with the TILA.

Regulation Z **Regulation Z**, an administrative agency regulation, sets forth detailed rules for compliance with the TILA.[3] The TILA and Regulation Z require the creditor to disclose the following information to the consumer-debtor:

- Cash price of the product or service
- Down payment and trade-in allowance
- Unpaid cash price

- Finance charge, including interest, points, and other fees paid for the extension of credit
- **Annual percentage rate (APR)** of the finance charges
- Charges not included in the finance charge (such as appraisal fees)
- Total dollar amount financed
- Date the finance charge begins to accrue
- Number, amounts, and due dates of payments
- Description of any security interest
- Penalties to be assessed for delinquent payments and late charges
- Prepayment penalties
- Comparative costs of credit (optional)

The uniform disclosures required by the TILA and Regulation Z are intended to help consumers shop for the best credit terms.

Consumer Leasing Act

Consumers often opt to lease consumer products, such as automobiles, rather than purchase them. The **Consumer Leasing Act (CLA)**[4] is a federal statute that extends the TILA's coverage to lease terms in consumer leases. The CLA applies to lessors who engage in leasing or arranging leases for consumer goods in the ordinary course of their business. Casual leases (such as leases between consumers) are not subject to the CLA. Creditors that violate the CLA are subject to the civil and criminal penalties provided in the TILA.

Consumer Leasing Act (CLA)
A federal statute that extends the TILA's coverage to lease terms in consumer leases.

Fair Credit Billing Act

The **Fair Credit Billing Act (FCBA)**[5] is a federal statute that regulates billing errors involving consumer credit. The act requires that creditors promptly acknowledge in writing consumer billing complaints and investigate billing errors. The act prohibits creditors from taking actions that adversely affect the consumer's credit standing until the investigation is completed. The act affords other protection during disputes. The amendment requires creditors to promptly post payments to the consumer's account and either refund overpayments or credit them to the consumer's account.

Fair Credit Billing Act
A federal statute that requires that creditors promptly acknowledge in writing consumer billing complaints and investigate billing errors and affords consumer-debtors other protection during billing disputes.

The following ethics feature discusses the Credit CARD Act of 2009.

Ethics

Credit CARD Act

Credit-card companies, including banks and other issuers of credit cards, have long engaged in unfair, abusive, deceptive, and unethical practices that took advantage of consumer-debtors. Most of the practices did not, however, violate the law. This changed when Congress enacted the **Credit Card Accountability Responsibility and Disclosure Act of 2009**, more commonly referred to as the **Credit CARD Act.**[6]

Some of the main provisions of the Credit CARD Act are the following:

- Requires that the terms of the credit-card agreement must be written in plain English and in no less than 12-point font (thus avoiding "legalese" and fine-print agreements).
- Credit cards cannot be issued to anyone under the age of 21 (used to be 18) unless they have a co-signer (e.g., parent) or they can prove they have the means to pay credit-card expenses.
- Requires that payments above the minimum payment be applied to pay higher-interest balances first (previously issuers applied payments to lower-interest balance first). The minimum payment can be applied to pay off lowest-interest-rate balances first.
- Prevents card companies from retroactively increasing interest rates on existing balances.
- Provides that if a cardholder cancels a card, he or she has the right to pay off existing balances at the existing interest rate and existing payment schedule (e.g., current minimum monthly payment).
- Provides that cardholders who have been subject to an interest rate increase because of default but then

(continued)

pay on time for six months must have the interest rate returned to the rate prior to the rate increase.

- Prohibits the application of the "universal default" rule from being applied retroactively to existing balances that the cardholder has on his or her credit cards. The **universal default rule** (which was used extensively by credit-card companies prior to the act) allowed *all* credit-card companies with whom a cardholder had a credit card to raise the interest rate on his or her card, including on the existing balances, if the cardholder was late in making a payment to *any* credit-card company. The act does not eliminate the universal default rule but only permits credit-card companies to apply the rule to future balances.
- Requires card companies to place a notice on each billing statement that notifies the cardholder how long it would take to pay off the existing balance plus interest if the cardholder were to make minimum payments on the card.
- Requires card companies to place a notice on each billing statement that notifies the cardholder what monthly payment would be necessary for the cardholder to pay off the balance plus interest in 36 months.

The Credit CARD Act does not limit how high an interest rate can be charged on a credit card. The act does not apply to commercial or business credit cards. Violations of the act are subject to criminal prosecution and civil lawsuits.

Ethics Questions Have credit-card companies acted unethically in the past? Is the universal default rule justified? Or was it just greed of the credit-card companies?

Credit Card Accountability Responsibility and Disclosure Act of 2009 (Credit CARD Act)
A federal statute that requires disclosures to consumers concerning credit-card terms, adds transparency to the creditor–debtor relationship, and eliminates many of the abusive practices of credit-card issuers.

Fair Credit Reporting Act (FCRA)
A federal statute that protects a consumer who is the subject of a credit report by setting rules for credit bureaus to follow and permitting consumers to obtain information from credit reporting businesses.

credit report
Information about a person's credit history that can be secured from a credit reporting agency.

Fair Debt Collection Practices Act (FDCPA)
A federal act that protects consumer-debtors from abusive, deceptive, and unfair practices used by debt collectors.

Fair Credit Reporting Act

The **Fair Credit Reporting Act (FCRA)**[7] is a federal statute that regulates credit reporting companies. This act protects a consumer who is the subject of a **credit report** by setting rules for consumer reporting agencies—that is, credit bureaus that compile and sell credit reports for a fee. A consumer may request the following information at any time: (1) the nature and substance of all the information in his or her credit file, (2) the sources of this information, and (3) the names of recipients of his or her credit report.

If a consumer challenges the accuracy of pertinent information contained in a credit file, the agency may be compelled to reinvestigate. If the agency cannot find an error, despite the consumer's complaint, the consumer may file a 100-word written statement of his or her version of the disputed information. If a consumer reporting agency or user violates the FCRA, the injured consumer may bring a civil action against the violator and recover actual damages. The FCRA also provides for criminal penalties.

The **Fair and Accurate Credit Transactions Act**[8] gives consumers the right to obtain one free credit report once every 12 months from the three nationwide credit reporting agencies (Equifax, Experian, TransUnion). Consumers may purchase for a reasonable fee their credit score and how the credit score is calculated. The act permits consumers to place fraud alerts on their credit files.

Fair Debt Collection Practices Act

The **Fair Debt Collection Practices Act (FDCPA)**[9] is a federal statute that protects consumer-debtors from abusive, deceptive, and unfair practices used by **debt collectors**. The FDCPA expressly prohibits debt collectors from using certain practices: (1) harassing, abusive, or intimidating tactics (e.g., threats of violence, obscene or abusive language); (2) false or misleading misrepresentations (e.g., posing as a police officer or an attorney); and (3) unfair or unconscionable practices (e.g., threatening the debtor with imprisonment).

A debt collector is not allowed to contact a debtor in some circumstances, including the following:

1. At any inconvenient time. The FDCPA provides that convenient hours are between 8:00 A.M. and 9:00 P.M., unless this time is otherwise inconvenient for the debtor (e.g., the debtor works a night shift and sleeps during the day).
2. At inconvenient places, such as at a place of worship or social events.
3. At the debtor's place of employment, if the employer objects to such contact.

4. If the debtor is represented by an attorney.
5. If the debtor gives a written notice to the debt collector that he or she refuses to pay the debt or does not want the debt collector to contact him or her again.

The FDCPA limits the contact that a debt collector may have with third persons other than the debtor's spouse or parents. Such contact is strictly limited. Unless the court has given its approval, third parties can be consulted only for the purpose of locating a debtor, and a third party can be contacted only once. A debt collector may not inform a third person that a consumer owes a debt that is in the process of collection. A debtor may bring a civil action against a debt collector for intentionally violating the FDCPA.

Equal Credit Opportunity Act

The **Equal Credit Opportunity Act (ECOA)**[10] is a federal statute that prohibits discrimination in the extension of credit based on sex, marital status, race, color, national origin, religion, age, or receipt of income from public assistance programs. The ECOA applies to all creditors that extend or arrange credit in the ordinary course of their business, including banks, savings-and-loan associations, automobile dealers, real estate brokers, credit-card issuers, and the like.

The creditor must notify the applicant within 30 days regarding the action taken on a credit application. If the creditor takes an *adverse action* (i.e., denies, revokes, or changes the credit terms), the creditor must provide the applicant with a statement containing the specific reasons for the action. If a creditor violates the ECOA, the consumer may bring a civil action against the creditor and recover actual damages (including emotional distress and embarrassment).

Equal Credit Opportunity Act (ECOA)
A federal statute that prohibits discrimination in the extension of credit based on sex, marital status, race, color, national origin, religion, age, or receipt of income from public assistance programs.

Fair Credit and Charge Card Disclosure Act

The **Fair Credit and Charge Card Disclosure Act**[11] is a federal statute that requires disclosure of credit terms on credit-card and charge-card solicitations and applications. The regulations adopted under the act require that any direct written solicitation to a consumer display, in tabular form, the following information: (1) the APR, (2) any annual membership fee, (3) any minimum or fixed finance charge, (4) any transaction charge for use of the card for purchases, and (5) a statement that charges are due when the periodic statement is received by the debtor.

Violations of consumer financial protection statutes are subject to fines, criminal prosecution, and civil lawsuits.

The following feature discusses the Dodd-Frank Wall Street Reform and Consumer Protection Act.

Fair Credit and Charge Card Disclosure Act
An amendment to the TILA that requires disclosure of certain credit terms on credit-card and charge-card solicitations and applications.

Dodd-Frank Wall Street Reform and Consumer Protection Act
A federal statute that regulates the financial industry and provides protection to consumers regarding financial products and services.

Business Environment

Dodd-Frank Wall Street Reform and Consumer Protection Act

In 2010, Congress enacted the **Dodd-Frank Wall Street Reform and Consumer Protection Act (Dodd-Frank Act)**.[12] The act is the most sweeping financial reform law enacted since the Great Depression in the 1930s. Major goals of the act are to regulate consumer credit and mortgage lending. Two main provisions of the act that affect consumer financial protection are the following:

- **Consumer Financial Protection Act of 2010.** **Title X of the Dodd-Frank Act**, which is titled the **Consumer Financial Protection Act of 2010**, is designed to increase relevant disclosure regarding consumer financial products and services and to eliminate deceptive and abusive loan practices. The act is also designed to prevent hidden fees and charges. The new law requires disclosure of relevant information to consumers in plain language that permits consumers to understand the costs, benefits, and risks associated with consumer financial products and services.

(continued)

- **Mortgage Reform and Anti-Predatory Lending Act. Title XIV of the Dodd-Frank Act**, which is titled the **Mortgage Reform and Anti-Predatory Lending Act**, is designed to eliminate many abusive loan practices and mandates new duties and disclosure requirements for mortgage lenders. The act requires that mortgage originators and lenders verify the assets and income of prospective borrowers, their credit history, employment status, debt-to-income ratio, and other relevant factors when making a decision to extend credit. The act puts the burden on lenders to verify that a borrower can afford to repay the loan for which he or she has applied. The act provides civil remedies for borrowers to sue lenders for engaging in deceptive and predatory practices and for violating the provisions of the act. The act provides civil remedies for borrowers to sue lenders for engaging in deceptive and predatory practices.

Key Terms and Concepts

Accommodation party (surety or co-debtor) (559)
Annual percentage rate (APR) (563)
Antideficiency statute (557)
Attachment (561)
Beneficiary (creditor) (555)
Collateral (554)
Collection remedies (560)
Construction lien (mechanic's lien) (558)
Consumer credit (562)
Consumer financial protection (562)
Consumer Financial Protection Bureau (CFPB) (562)
Consumer Financial Protection Act of 2010 (565)
Consumer Leasing Act (CLA) (563)
County recorder's office (555)
Credit (553)
Credit Card Accountability Responsibility and Disclosure Act of 2009 (Credit CARD Act) (563)
Credit report (564)
Creditor (lender) (553)
Debt collectors (564)
Debtor (borrower) (553)
Deed of trust (564)
Default (556)
Deficiency judgment (557)
Dodd-Frank Wall Street Reform and Consumer Protection Act (565)
Equal Credit Opportunity Act (ECOA) (565)
Execution (561)
Fair and Accurate Credit Transactions Act (564)
Fair Credit and Charge Card Disclosure Act (565)
Fair Credit Billing Act (FCBA) (563)
Fair Credit Reporting Act (FCRA) (564)
Fair Debt Collection Practices Act (FDCPA) (564)
First purchase money mortgage (557)
Foreclosure (556)
Foreclosure sale (556)
Garnishee (561)
Garnishment (561)
Garnishor (561)
Guarantor (560)
Guaranty arrangement (560)
Judgment proof (554)
Land sales contract (559)
Lien release (release of lien) (558)
Mortgage (554)
Mortgage Reform and Anti-Predatory Lending Act (566)
Mortgagee (creditor) (554)
Mortgagor (owner-debtor) (554)
Nonrecordation of a mortgage (555)
Note (555)
Notice of lien (558)
Postjudgment court order (561)
Power of sale (556)
Prejudgment court order (561)
Primarily liable (559)
Reconveyance (satisfaction of a mortgage) (555)
Recording statute (555)
Regulation Z (562)
Right of redemption (558)
Secondarily liable (560)
Secured credit (554)
Secured creditor (secured party) (554)
Security interests in real property (554)
Statutory period of redemption (558)
Surety (co-debtor) (559)
Surety arrangement (559)
Title III of the Consumer Credit Protection Act (561)
Trustee (555)
Trustor (owner-debtor) (555)
Truth-in-Lending Act (TILA) (562)
Universal default rule (564)
Unsecured credit (553)
Unsecured creditor (553)
Writ of attachment (561)
Writ of execution (561)
Writ of garnishment (561)
Title X of the Dodd-Frank Act (565)
Title XIV of the Dodd-Frank Act (566)

Critical Legal Thinking Cases

26.1 Lien Ironwood Exploration, Inc. (Ironwood) owned a lease on oil and gas property located in Duchesne County, Utah. Ironwood contracted to have Lantz Drilling and Exploration Company, Inc. (Lantz), drill an oil well on the property. Thereafter, Lantz rented equipment from Graco Fishing and Rental Tools, Inc. (Graco), for use in drilling the well. Graco billed Lantz for these rentals, but Lantz did not pay. Graco filed a notice of a lien on the well in the amount of $19,766. Ironwood, which had paid Lantz, refused to pay Graco. Graco sued to foreclose on its lien. Who wins? *Graco Fishing and Rental Tools, Inc. v. Ironwood Exploration, Inc.*, 766 P.2d 1074, 1988 Utah Lexis 125 (Supreme Court of Utah)

26.2 Foreclosure Atlantic Ocean Kampgrounds, Inc. (Atlantic) borrowed $60,000 from Camden National Bank (Camden National) and executed a note and mortgage on property located in Camden, Maine, securing that amount. Maine permits strict foreclosure. Atlantic defaulted on the loan, and Camden commenced strict foreclosure proceedings pursuant to state law. After the one-year period of redemption, Camden National sold the property to a third party in an amount in excess of the mortgage and costs of the foreclosure proceeding. Atlantic sued to recover the surplus from Camden National. Who wins? *Atlantic Ocean Kampgrounds, Inc. v. Camden National Bank*, 473 A.2d 884, 1984 Me. Lexis 666 (Supreme Judicial Court of Maine)

26.3 Redemption Elmer and Arletta Hans, husband and wife, owned a parcel of real property in Illinois. They borrowed $100,000 from First Illinois National Bank (First Illinois) and executed a note and mortgage to First Illinois, making the real estate security for the loan. The security agreement authorized First Illinois to take possession of the property on the occurrence of a default and required the Hanses to execute a quitclaim deed in favor of First Illinois. The state of Illinois recognizes the doctrine of redemption. When the Hanses defaulted on the loan, First Illinois filed a lawsuit, seeking an order requiring the Hanses to immediately execute a quitclaim deed to the property. Must the Hanses execute the quitclaim deed before the foreclosure sale? *First Illinois National Bank v. Hans*, 493 N.E.2d 1171, 1986 Ill. App. Lexis 2287 (Appellate Court of Illinois)

26.4 Deficiency Judgment Sally Fitch obtained a loan from Buffalo Federal Savings and Loan Association (Buffalo Federal). She signed a promissory note for $130,000 with interest at 17 percent. The loan was secured with a real estate mortgage on property owned by Fitch located in Johnson County, Wyoming. Wyoming did not have an antideficiency statute. Four years later, Fitch was in default on the note. When she was unable to pay the loan to current status, Buffalo Federal sent her a notice of foreclosure. After publication of proper public notice, the sheriff conducted the sale as advertised on the steps of the Johnson County Courthouse. The property sold for a high bid of $66,000. Buffalo Federal applied the $66,000 to the $150,209 balance on the note and sued Fitch to recover a judgment for the deficiency of $84,209. Who wins? *Fitch v. Buffalo Federal Savings and Loan Association*, 751 P.2d 1309, 1988 Wyo. Lexis 27 (Supreme Court of Wyoming)

Ethical

Ethics Cases

26.5 Ethics Case Jessie Lynch became seriously ill and needed medical attention. Her sister, Ethel Sales, took her to the Forsyth Memorial Hospital in North Carolina for treatment. Lynch was admitted for hospitalization. Sales signed Lynch's admission form, which included the following section:

> *The undersigned, in consideration of hospital services being rendered or to be rendered by Forsyth County Memorial Hospital Authority, Inc., in Winston-Salem, N.C., to the above patient, does hereby guarantee payment to Forsyth County Hospital Authority, Inc., on demand all charges for said services and incidentals incurred on behalf of such patient.*

Lynch received care and services rendered by the hospital until her discharge more than 30 days later. The total bill during her hospitalization amounted to $7,977. When Lynch refused to pay the bill, the hospital instituted an action against Lynch and Sales to recover the unpaid amount. Is Sales liable? Did Sales act ethically in denying liability? Did she have a choice when she signed the contract? *Forsyth County Memorial Hospital Authority, Inc. v. Sales*, 346 S.E.2d 212, 1986 N.C. App. Lexis 2432 (Court of Appeals of North Carolina)

26.6 Ethics Case Elizabeth Valentine purchased a home in Philadelphia, Pennsylvania. She applied for and received a home loan from Salmon Building and Loan Association (Salmon) for the purpose of paneling the cellar walls and redecorating the house. Salmon took a security interest in the house as collateral for the loan. Although Salmon gave Valentine a disclosure document, nowhere on the document were finance charges disclosed. The document did notify Valentine that Salmon had a security interest in the house. More than two years later, Valentine sued Salmon (which had since merged with Influential Savings and Loan Association) to rescind the loan. Who wins? Did Salmon act ethically in this case? *Valentine v. Influential Savings and Loan Association*, 572 F.Supp. 36, 1983 U.S. Dist. Lexis 15884 (United States District Court for the Eastern District of Pennsylvania)

Notes

1. 15 U.S.C. Sections 1671 et seq.
2. 15 U.S.C. Sections 1601–1667.
3. 12 C.F.R. 226.
4. 15 U.S.C. Sections 1667–1667f.
5. 15 U.S.C. Sections 1666–1666j.
6. Public Law 24, 123 Stat. 1734–1766.
7. 15 U.S.C. Sections 1681–1681u.
8. 15 U.S.C. Sections 1681–1681x.
9. 15 U.S.C. Sections 1692–1692o.
10. 15 U.S.C. Sections 1691–1691f.
11. 15 U.S.C. Sections 1637c–g.
12. Public Law 111-203 (2010).

CHAPTER

27 Secured Transactions

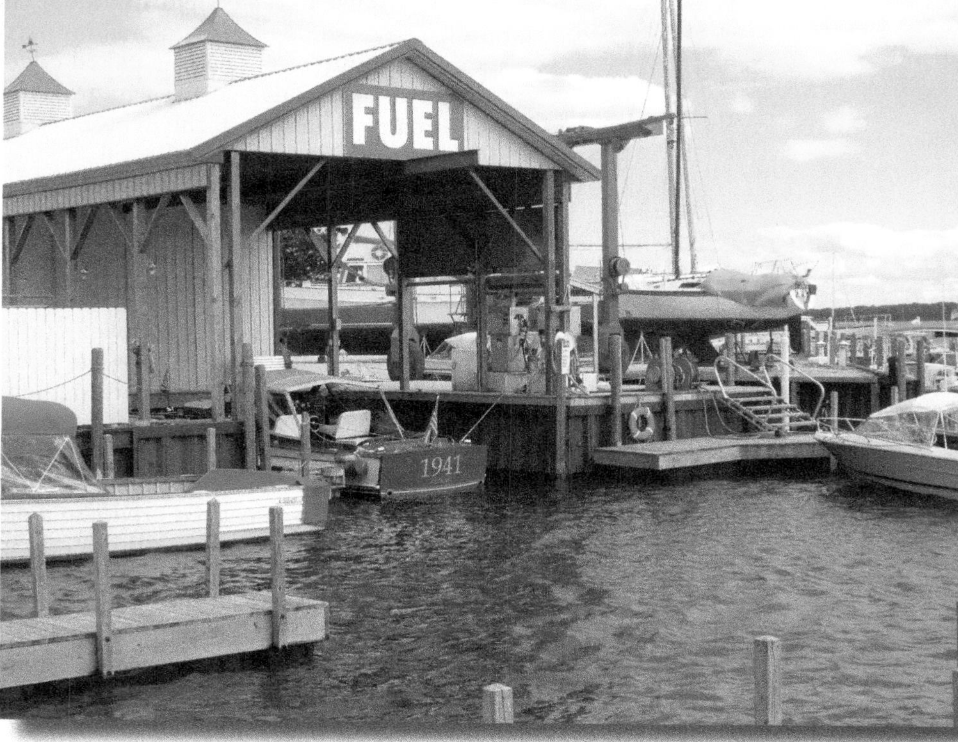

BOATS
People often purchase boats, automobiles, motorcycles, farm equipment, and other items using credit that is extended by banks, the seller, or other lenders. Often, the lender takes back a security interest in the property, which becomes collateral for the loan. This is a secured transaction that is governed by Article 9 of the Uniform Commercial Code (UCC).

Learning Objectives

After studying this chapter, you should be able to:

1. Describe the scope of Revised Article 9 of the UCC.
2. Describe how a security interest in personal property is created.
3. Describe the perfection of a security interest through the filing of a financing statement.
4. Explain the UCC rule for determining priority among conflicting claims.
5. Describe the electronic filing of financing statements and records.

Chapter Outline

"Debtors are liars."

—*George Herbert*
Jacula Prudentum (1651)

Introduction to Secured Transactions

Never spend your money before you have it.
Thomas Jefferson (1743–1826)

Many items of *personal property* are purchased with credit rather than cash. Because lenders are reluctant to lend large sums of money simply on the borrower's promise to repay, many of them take a *security interest* in either the item purchased or some other personal property of the debtor. The property in which a security interest is taken is called *collateral*. When a creditor extends credit to a debtor and takes a security interest in some property of the debtor, it is called a *secured transaction*. If the debtor does not pay the debt, the creditor can foreclose on and recover the collateral.

This chapter discusses secured transactions in personal property.

Secured Transactions in Personal Property

personal property
Tangible property, such as equipment, vehicles, furniture, and jewelry, as well as intangible property, such as securities, patents, trademarks, and copyrights.

Individuals and businesses purchase or lease various forms of tangible and intangible **personal property**. *Tangible personal property* includes equipment, vehicles, furniture, computers, clothing, jewelry, and the like. *Intangible personal property* includes securities, patents, trademarks, and copyrights.

Personal property is often sold on credit. This means the purchaser-debtor borrows money from a lender-creditor to purchase the personal property. Sometimes a lender extends *unsecured credit* to a debtor to purchase personal property. In this case, the creditor takes no interest in any collateral to secure the loan but bases the decision to extend credit on the credit standing of the debtor. If the debtor defaults on the loan, the creditor must sue the debtor to try to recover the unpaid loan amount.

In some credit transactions, particularly those involving large or expensive items, a creditor may agree to extend credit only if the purchaser pledges some personal property as collateral for the loan. This is called *secured credit*. If the debtor defaults on the loan, the creditor may seek to recover the collateral under a lawful foreclosure action.

Revised Article 9—Secured Transactions

Article 9 (Secured Transactions) of the Uniform Commercial Code (UCC) governs secured transactions where personal property is used as collateral for a loan or the extension of credit.

Revised Article 9 (Secured Transactions)
An article of the Uniform Commercial Code that governs secured transactions in personal property.

In 2001, after years of study and debate, the National Conference of Commissioners on Uniform State Laws and the American Law Institute issued **Revised Article 9 (Secured Transactions)** of the UCC. Since its release, all states have enacted Revised Article 9 (Secured Transactions) as a UCC statute within their states.

Revised Article 9 includes modern and efficient rules that govern secured transactions in personal property. Revised Article 9 contains many new provisions that recognize the importance of electronic commerce, including rules for the creation, filing, and enforcement of electronic secured transactions.

The material in this chapter that covers secured transactions is based on the provisions of Revised Article 9.

Secured Transaction

When a creditor extends credit to a debtor and takes a security interest in some personal property of the debtor, it is called a **secured transaction**. The **secured party** is the seller, lender, or other party in whose favor there is a security interest. If the debtor defaults and does not repay the loan, generally the secured party can foreclose and recover the collateral.

Definitions important to secured transactions are listed in **Exhibit 27.1**.

secured transaction
A transaction that is created when a creditor makes a loan to a debtor in exchange for the debtor's pledge of personal property as security.

1. **Debtor.** A person who has an ownership or other interest in the collateral and owes payment of a secured obligation [Revised UCC 9-102(a)(28)].

   Example A farmer who purchases a large John Deere tractor from a retail dealer on credit and gives the secured creditor an interest in the collateral is the debtor.
2. **Secured party.** A person in whose favor a security interest is created or provided under a security agreement [Revised UCC 9-102(a)(72)].

   Example In the previous example, the John Deere retail dealer is the secured creditor. The secured party can be the seller (e.g., the John Deere retail dealer), another lender (e.g., a bank), or buyer of accounts (e.g., an investor who purchases the security interest).
3. **Security interest.** An interest in the collateral, such as personal property or fixtures, that secures payment or performance of an obligation [UCC 1-201(b)(35)].

   Example In the previous example, the debtor-farmer gave the retail dealer-secured creditor a security interest in the John Deere tractor.
4. **Security agreement.** An agreement that creates or provides for a security interest [Revised UCC 9-102(a)(73)].

   Example In the prior example, when the farmer purchased the John Deere tractor from the retail dealer on credit, the retail dealer may require, as a condition of the sale, that the farmer sign a security agreement giving the retail dealer a secured interest in the tractor. If this is done and the farmer defaults on the payments, the John Deere retail dealer can foreclose on its security agreement and recover the tractor.
5. **Collateral.** The property that is subject to a security agreement [Revised UCC 9-102(a)(12)].

   Example In the previous example, the John Deere tractor is the collateral for the security agreement.
6. **Financing statement.** The record of an initial financing statement or filed record relating to the initial financing statement [Revised UCC 9-1 02(a)(39)]. This is *Form UCC 1 (UCC Financing Statement)*. The financing statement is usually filed with the appropriate state office to give public notice of the secured party's security interest in the collateral.

   Example In the previous example, if the retail dealer (the secured creditor) files a financing statement, it has given public notice of its secured interest in the collateral, the John Deere tractor.

Exhibit 27.1 **DEFINITIONS USED IN SECURED TRANSACTIONS**

Two-Party Secured Transaction

Exhibit 27.2 illustrates a **two-party secured transaction**. Such transactions occur, for example, when a seller sells goods to a buyer on credit and retains a security interest in the goods.

two-party secured transaction
Occurs when a seller sells goods to a buyer on credit and retains a security interest in the goods.

Exhibit 27.2 TWO-PARTY SECURED TRANSACTION

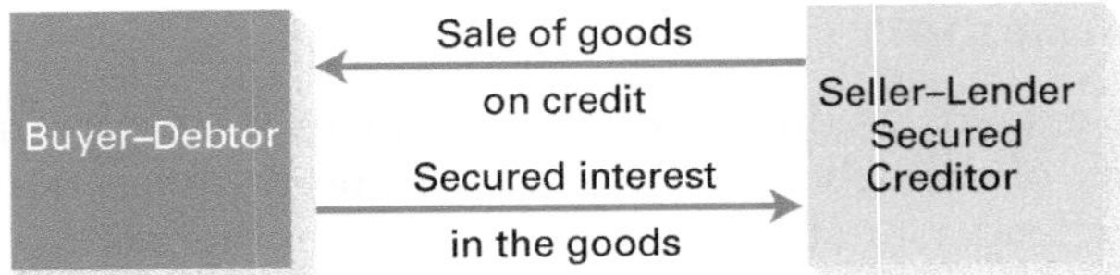

Example A farmer purchases equipment on credit from a farm equipment dealer. The dealer retains a security interest in the farm equipment that becomes collateral for the loan. This is a two-party secured transaction. The farmer is the buyer-debtor, and the farm equipment dealer is the seller-lender-secured creditor.

Three-Party Secured Transaction

three-party secured transaction
Occurs when a seller sells goods to a buyer who has obtained financing from a third-party lender who takes a security interest in the goods sold.

A three-party secured transaction arises when a seller sells goods to a buyer who has obtained financing from a third-party lender (e.g., a bank) and the **third-party lender** takes a security interest in the goods. **Exhibit 27.3** illustrates a **three-party secured transaction**.

Exhibit 27.3 THREE-PARTY SECURED TRANSACTION

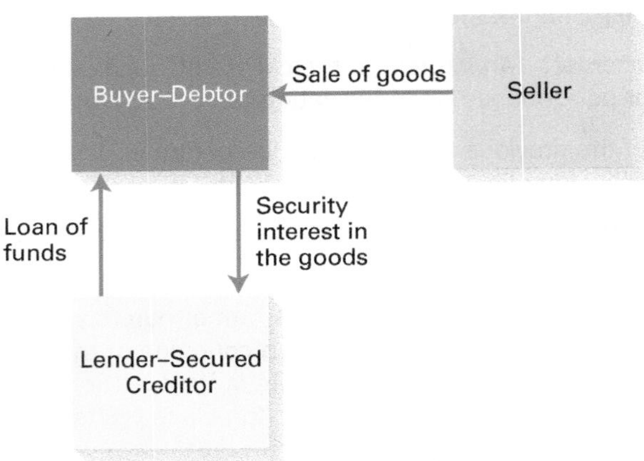

Example A business purchases an airplane from an airplane manufacturer. The business obtains a loan to purchase the airplane from a bank, which obtains a security interest in the airplane. The airplane manufacturer is paid for the airplane out of the proceeds of the loan. This is a three-party secured transaction. The airplane manufacturer is the seller, the purchasing business is the buyer-debtor, and the bank is the lender-secured creditor.

Personal Property Subject to a Security Agreement

collateral
Personal property that is subject to a security agreement.

A security interest may be given in various types of personal property that becomes **collateral** for the loan. This includes *tangible personal property* and *intangible personal property* [Revised UCC 9-102(a)(12)].

Tangible Personal Property

All things that are movable when a security interest attaches are called **tangible personal property** [Revised UCC 9-102(a)(44)]. Tangible personal property that can be used as collateral for a secured transaction is listed in **Exhibit 27.4**.

1. **Accessions** that are goods that are physically united with other goods in such a manner that the identity of the original goods is not lost [Revised UCC 9-102(a)(1)].

   Example A GPS system that is installed in an automobile.

2. **Consumer goods** bought or used primarily for personal, family, or household purposes [Revised UCC 9-102(a)(23)].

   Examples Household televisions, furniture, and furnishings.

3. **Equipment** bought or used primarily for business [Revised UCC 9-102(a)(33)].

   Examples Business trucks, moving cranes, and assembly line equipment.

4. **Farm products**, including crops, aquatic goods, livestock, and supplies produced in farming operations [Revised UCC 9-102(a)(34)].

   Examples Wheat, fish, cattle, milk, apples, and unborn calves.

5. **Inventory** held for sale or lease, including work in progress and materials [Revised UCC 9-102(a)(48)].

   Example Raw materials used in production of goods.

Exhibit 27.4 **TANGIBLE PERSONAL PROPERTY**

Intangible Personal Property

All things that are *nonphysical* personal property when a security interest attaches are called **intangible personal property**. Intangible personal property that can be used as collateral for a secured transaction is listed in **Exhibit 27.5**.

1. **Accounts** that include a right to payment of a monetary obligation for personal or real property sold or leased, services rendered, and policies of insurance [Revised UCC 9-102(a)(1)].

2. **Chattel paper**, which is a record that evidences both a monetary obligation and a security interest in specific goods [Revised UCC 9-102(a)(11)]. **Tangible chattel paper** is inscribed on a tangible medium [Revised UCC 9-102(a)(78)]. **Electronic chattel paper** is evidenced by information stored in an electronic medium [Revised UCC 9-102(a)(31)].

3. **Deposit accounts** [Revised UCC 9-102(a)(29)].

   Examples Demand, time, savings, passbook, or similar accounts maintained at banks and other financial institutions.

4. **General intangibles** [Revised UCC 9-102(a)(42)].

   Examples Patents, copyrights, royalties, and the like.

5. **Instruments** [Revised UCC 9-102(a)(47)].

   Examples Negotiable instruments such as checks and notes, stocks, bonds, and other investment securities [Revised UCC 9-102(a)].

   Revised Article 9 of the UCC does not apply to transactions involving real estate mortgages, landlord's liens, artisan's or mechanic's liens, liens on wages, judicial liens, and the like. These types of liens are usually covered by other laws.

Exhibit 27.5 **INTANGIBLE PERSONAL PROPERTY**

Creating a Security Agreement

Revised Article 9 sets forth the requirements that must be met to create a security interest in personal property. These requirements are discussed in the following paragraphs.

Security Agreement

security agreement
A written document signed by a debtor that creates a security interest in personal property.

Unless the creditor has possession of the collateral, there must be a **security agreement** signed by the debtor that creates a **security interest in personal property** to a creditor [Revised UCC 9-102(a)(73)]. A security agreement must (1) describe the collateral clearly so that it can be readily identified; (2) contain the debtor's promise to repay the creditor, including terms of repayment (e.g., interest rate, time of payment); (3) set forth the creditor's rights on the debtor's default; and (4) be signed by the debtor.

attachment
A situation in which a creditor has an enforceable security interest against a debtor and can satisfy the debt out of the designated collateral.

The debtor must have a current or future legal right in or the right to possession of the collateral. The rights of the secured party attach to the collateral. **Attachment** means that the creditor has an enforceable security interest against the debtor and can satisfy the debt out of the designated collateral [Revised UCC 9-203(a)].

The Floating Lien Concept

floating lien
A security interest in property that was not in the possession of the debtor when the security agreement was executed.

A security agreement may provide that the security interest attaches to property that was not originally in the possession of the debtor when the agreement was executed. This interest is usually referred to as a **floating lien**. A floating lien can attach to *after-acquired property*, *sale proceeds*, and *future advances*. These are discussed in the following paragraphs.

After-Acquired Property

after-acquired property
Property that a debtor acquires after a security agreement is executed.

Many security agreements contain a clause that gives the secured party a security interest in **after-acquired property** of the debtor. After-acquired property is property that the debtor acquires after the security agreement is executed [Revised UCC 9-204(a)].

Example Manufacturing Corporation borrows $100,000 from First Bank and gives the bank a security interest in both its current and after-acquired inventory. If Manufacturing Corporation defaults on its loan to First Bank, the bank can claim any available original inventory as well as enough after-acquired inventory to satisfy its secured claim.

Sale Proceeds

sale proceeds
The resulting assets from the sale, exchange, or disposal of collateral subject to a security agreement.

Unless otherwise stated in a security agreement, if a debtor sells, exchanges, or disposes of collateral subject to such an agreement, the secured party automatically has the right to receive the **sale proceeds** of the sale, exchange, or disposition [Revised UCC 9-102(a)(64), 9-203(f), 9-315(a)].

Example Zip, Inc., is a retail automobile dealer. To finance its inventory of new automobiles, Zip borrows money from First Bank and gives the bank a security interest in the inventory. Zip sells an automobile that is subject to the security agreement to Phyllis, who signs an installment sales contract, agreeing to pay Zip for the car in 24 equal monthly installments. If Zip defaults on its payment to First Bank, the bank is entitled to receive the remaining payments from Phyllis.

Future Advances

A debtor may establish a continuing or revolving line of credit at a bank. Certain personal property of the debtor is designated as collateral for future loans from the line of credit. A maximum limit that the debtor may borrow is set, but the debtor can draw against the line of credit at any time. Any **future advances** made against the line of credit are subject to the security interest in the collateral. A new security agreement does not have to be executed each time a future advance is taken against the line of credit [Revised UCC 9-204(c)].

future advances
Funds advanced to a debtor from a line of credit secured by collateral. Future advances are future withdrawals from a line of credit.

Example A technology company establishes a $1 million line of credit at a bank and pledges its patents as security for loans taken against the line of credit. The company borrows $600,000 against the line of credit. The loan is secured by the patents. The technology company pays back the $600,000. Subsequently, the company borrows $500,000 against the line of credit. This loan is secured by the patents.

Perfecting a Security Interest

The concept of **perfection of a security interest** establishes the right of a secured creditor against other creditors who claim an interest in the collateral. Perfection is a legal process. The three main methods of perfecting a security interest under the UCC are (1) perfection by filing a *financing statement*, (2) perfection by possession of collateral, and (3) perfection by a purchase money security interest in consumer goods. These three main methods of perfecting a security interest are discussed in the following paragraphs.

perfection of a security interest
A process that establishes the right of a secured creditor against other creditors who claim an interest in the collateral.

Perfection by Filing a Financing Statement

Often, a creditor's physical possession of collateral is impractical because it would deprive the debtor of use of the collateral (e.g., farm equipment, industrial machinery, consumer goods). At other times, it is simply impossible (e.g., accounts receivable).

A creditor filing a **financing statement** in the appropriate government office is the most common method of perfecting a creditor's security interest in collateral [Revised UCC 9-501]. This is called **perfection by filing a financing statement.**

financing statement
A document filed by a secured creditor with the appropriate government office that constructively notifies the world of his or her security interest in personal property.

The person who files the financing statement should request the filing officer to note on his or her copy of the document the file number, date, and hour of filing. A uniform financing statement form, **UCC Financing Statement (Form UCC-1)**, is used in all states [Revised UCC 9-521(a)]. A financing statement can be filed electronically [Revised UCC 9-102(a)(18)].

UCC Financing Statement (Form UCC-1)
A uniform financing statement form that is used in all states.

To be enforceable, a financing statement must contain the name of the debtor, the name and address of the secured party or a representative of the secured party, and the collateral covered by the financing statement [Revised UCC 9-502(a)]. The secured party can file the security agreement as a financing statement. A financing statement that provides only the debtor's trade name does not provide the name of the debtor sufficiently [Revised UCC 9-503(c)].

Critical Legal Thinking
What is a financing statement? What does the proper filing of a financing statement accomplish? What are the consequences if a financing statement is filed improperly?

State law specifies where a financing statement must be filed. A state may choose either the **secretary of state** or the **county recorder's office** in the county of the debtor's residence or, if the debtor is not a resident of the state, in the county where the goods are kept or in another county office or both. Most states require financing statements covering farm equipment, farm products, accounts, and consumer goods to be filed with the county clerk [Revised UCC 9-501].

Financing statements are available for review by the public. They serve as *constructive notice* to the world that a creditor claims an interest in a property. Financing statements are effective for five years from the date of filing [Revised UCC 9-515(a)]. A **continuation statement** may be filed up to six months prior to the expiration of a financing statement's five-year term. Such statements are effective for a new five-year term. Succeeding continuation statements may be filed [Revised UCC 9-515(d), 9-515(e)].

In the following case, the court had to determine whether the filing of a financing statement was effective.

CASE 27.1 STATE COURT CASE Filing a Financing Statement

Pankratz Implement Company v. Citizens National Bank

130 P.3d 57 2006 Kan. Lexis 141 (2006)
Supreme Court of Kansas

"Thus, Pankratz' financing statement using the misspelled name of the debtor, while prior in time, was seriously misleading, . . ."

—Davis, Justice

Facts

Rodger House purchased a tractor on credit from Pankratz Implement Company. House signed a note and security agreement that made the tractor collateral for the repayment of the debt. The creditor filed a financing statement with the Kansas secretary of state using the misspelled name of the debtor, "Roger House," rather than the correct name of the debtor, "Rodger House." One year later, House obtained a loan from Citizens National Bank (CNB). House gave a security interest to CNB by pledging all equipment that he owned and that he may own in the future as collateral for the loan. CNB filed a financing statement with the Kansas secretary of state using the correct name of the debtor, "Rodger House."

Several years later, while still owing money to Pankratz and CNB, House filed for bankruptcy. Pankratz filed a lawsuit in Kansas trial court to recover the tractor. CNB challenged the claim, alleging that it should be permitted to recover the tractor. The trial court found that Pankratz's misspelling of the debtor's first name on its financing statement was a minor error and granted summary judgment to Pankratz. The court of appeals held that Pankratz's misspelling of House's first name was seriously misleading and held in favor of CNB. Pankratz appealed.

Issue

Is Pankratz's filing of the financing statement under the wrong first name of the debtor seriously misleading?

Language of the Court

Because the primary purpose of a financing statement is to provide notice to third parties that the creditor has an interest in the debtor's property and the financing statements are indexed under the debtor's name, it is particularly important to require exactness in the name used, the debtor's legal name. We conclude that Pankratz' filed financing statement was "seriously misleading."

Decision

The supreme court of Kansas held that the misspelling of the debtor's name mislad creditors and was therefore ineffectual in giving CNB notice of Pankratz's security interest in the tractor. The state supreme court affirmed the court of appeals judgment in CNB's favor.

Ethics Questions

Did either party act unethically in this case? Or was this a legitimate legal dispute?

Perfection by Possession of Collateral

perfection by possession of collateral
A rule stating that, if a secured creditor has physical possession of the collateral, no financing statement has to be filed; the creditor's possession is sufficient to put other potential creditors on notice of the creditor's secured interest in the property.

No financing statement has to be filed if the creditor has physical possession of the collateral. This is known as **perfection by possession of collateral**. The rationale behind this rule is that if someone other than the debtor is in possession of the property, a potential creditor is on notice that another may claim an interest in the debtor's property. A secured creditor who holds the debtor's property as collateral must use reasonable care in its custody and preservation [Revised UCC 9-310, 9-312(b), 9-313].

Example Karen borrows $3,000 from Alan and gives her motorcycle to him as security for the loan. Alan does not file a financing statement. Another creditor obtains a judgment against Karen. This creditor cannot recover the motorcycle from Alan. Even though Alan has not filed a financing statement, his security interest in the motorcycle is perfected because he has possession of the motorcycle.

Perfection by a Purchase Money Security Interest in Consumer Goods

Sellers and lenders often extend credit to *consumers* to purchase consumer goods. **Consumer goods** include furniture, televisions, home appliances, and other goods used primarily for personal, family, or household purposes.

A creditor who extends credit to a consumer to purchase a consumer good under a written security agreement obtains a **purchase money security interest** in the consumer good. The agreement automatically perfects the creditor's security interest at the time of the sale. This is called **perfection by a purchase money security interest in consumer goods**. The creditor does not have to file a financing statement or take possession of the goods to perfect his or her security interest. This interest is called **perfection by attachment**, or the **automatic perfection rule** [Revised UCC 9-309(1)].

purchase money security interest
An interest a creditor automatically obtains when he or she extends credit to a consumer to purchase consumer goods.

Example Marcia buys a $2,000 television for her home on credit extended by the seller, Television Store. Television Store requires Marcia to sign a security agreement. Television Store has a purchase money security interest in the television that is automatically perfected at the time of the credit sale.

CONCEPT SUMMARY

METHODS OF PERFECTING A SECURITY INTEREST

Perfection Method	How Created
Financing statement	Creditor files a financing statement with the appropriate government office.
Possession of collateral	Creditor obtains physical possession of the collateral.
Purchase money security interest	Creditor extends credit to a debtor to purchase consumer goods and obtains a security interest in the goods.

Termination Statement

When a secured consumer debt is paid, the secured party must file a **termination statement** with each filing officer with whom the financing statement was filed. The termination statement must be filed within one month after the debt is paid or 20 days after receipt of the debtor's written demand, whichever occurs first [Revised UCC 9-513(b)]. If the affected secured party fails to file or send the termination statement as required, the secured party is liable for any other losses caused to the debtor.

termination statement
A document filed by a secured party that ends a secured interest because the debt has been paid.

Priority of Claims

Two or more creditors often claim an interest in the same collateral or property. The priority of the claims is determined according to (1) whether the claim is unsecured or secured and (2) the time at which secured claims were attached or perfected. The UCC establishes rules for determining **priority of claims** of creditors. The UCC rules for establishing priority of claims are as follows:

1. **Secured versus unsecured claims.** A creditor who has the only secured interest in the debtor's collateral has priority over unsecured interests.
2. **Competing unperfected security interests.** If two or more secured parties claim an interest in the same collateral but neither has a perfected claim, the first to attach has priority [Revised UCC 9-322(a)(3)].
3. **Perfected versus unperfected claims.** If two or more secured parties claim an interest in the same collateral but only one has perfected his or her security interest, the perfected security interest has priority [Revised UCC 9-322(a)(2)].

priority of claims
The order in which conflicting claims of creditors in the same collateral are solved.

Critical Legal Thinking
What could be the consequences if a secured creditor does not file a financing statement or otherwise perfect their security interest in personal property? Explain.

4. **Competing perfected security interests.** If two or more secured parties have perfected security interests in the same collateral, the first to perfect (e.g., by filing a financing statement, by taking possession of the collateral) has priority [Revised UCC 9-322(a)(1)].
5. **Perfected secured claims in fungible, commingled goods.** If a security interest in goods is perfected but the goods are later commingled with other goods in which there are also perfected security interests and the goods become part of a product or mass and lose their identity, the security interests rank equal and according to the ratio that the original cost of goods of each security interest bears to the cost of the total product or mass [Revised UCC 9-336].

Buyers in the Ordinary Course of Business

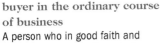

buyer in the ordinary course of business
A person who in good faith and without knowledge of another's ownership or security interest in goods buys the goods in the ordinary course of business from a person in the business of selling goods of that kind.

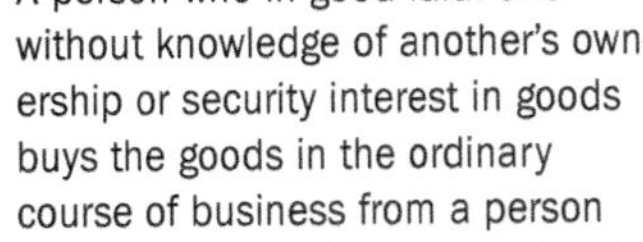

A **buyer in the ordinary course of business** who purchases goods from a merchant takes the goods free of any perfected or unperfected security interest in the merchant's inventory, even if the buyer knows of the existence of the security interest. This rule is necessary because buyers would be reluctant to purchase goods if a merchant's creditors could recover the goods if the merchant defaulted on loans owed to secured creditors [Revised UCC 9-320(a), UCC 1-201(9)].

A buyer in the ordinary course of business is a person who buys goods in good faith, without knowledge that the sale violates the rights of another person in the goods. The buyer purchases the goods in the ordinary course from a person in the business of selling goods of that kind.

Critical Legal Thinking
What is the public policy for having the buyer in the ordinary course of business rule? What would be the consequences if such a rule did not exist?

Example Central Car Sales, Inc. (Central), a new car dealership, finances all its inventory of new automobiles at First Bank. First Bank takes a security interest in Central's inventory of cars and perfects this security interest. Kim, a buyer in the ordinary course of business, purchases a car from Central for cash. The car cannot be recovered from Kim even if Central defaults on its payments to the bank.

The following feature describes how Revised Article 9 recognizes electronic financing statements and records.

Digital Law

Electronic Financing Statements and Records

Revised Article 9 (Secured Transactions) contains provisions that recognize the importance of electronic records. Revised Article 9 provides rules for the creation, filing, and enforcement of **electronic secured transactions**, or **e-secured transactions**, in personal property. Some of the definitions for electronic commerce and their implications are discussed here:

- **Record** means information that is inscribed on a tangible medium or that is stored in an electronic or other medium and is retrievable in perceivable form [Revised UCC 9-102(a)(69)]. The term *record* is now used in many of the provisions of Revised Article 9 in place of the term *writing*, further recognizing the importance of electronic commerce.
- **Electronic chattel paper** means chattel paper evidenced by a record or records consisting of information stored in an electronic medium [Revised UCC 9-102(a)(31)]. This includes records initially created and executed in electronic form and tangible writings that are converted to electronic form (e.g., electronic images created from a signed writing).
- **Financing statement** means a record composed of an initial financing statement and any filed record related to the initial financing statement [Revised UCC 9-102(a)(39)]. Thus, financing statements may be in electronic form and filed and stored as electronic records. Most states permit or require the filing of **electronic financing statements**, or **e-financing statements**.

These provisions of Revised Article 9 (Secured Transactions) recognize the importance of electronic transactions and records that are used in today's commercial environment.

Default and Remedies

Article 9 of the UCC defines the rights, duties, and remedies of the secured party and the debtor in the event of **default**. The term *default* is not defined. Instead, the parties are free to define it in their security agreement. Events such as failing to make scheduled payments when due, bankruptcy of the debtor, breach of the warranty of ownership as to the collateral, and other such events are commonly defined in security agreements as default.

default
Failure to make scheduled payments when due, bankruptcy of the debtor, breach of the warranty of ownership as to the collateral, and other events defined by the parties in a security agreement.

On default by a debtor, the secured party may reduce his or her claim to judgment, foreclose, or otherwise enforce his or her security interest by any available judicial procedure [Revised UCC 9-601(a)]. The UCC provides the secured party with the remedies discussed in the following paragraphs.

Take Possession of the Collateral

Most secured parties seek to cure a default by **taking possession of the collateral**. This taking is usually done by **repossession** of the goods from the defaulting debtor. A secured party may repossess the collateral pursuant to judicial process or without judicial process if the self-help repossession of the collateral does not breach the peace [Revised UCC 9-609(b)].

repossession
A right granted to a secured creditor to take possession of the collateral on default by the debtor.

After repossessing the goods, the secured party can either (1) retain the collateral, or (2) sell, lease, license, or otherwise dispose of it and satisfy the debt from the proceeds of the sale or disposition. There is one caveat: The secured party must act in good faith, with commercial reasonableness, and with reasonable care to preserve the collateral in his or her possession [Revised UCC 9-603, 9-610(a), 9-620].

Example Western Drilling, Inc. purchases a piece of oil-drilling equipment on credit from Halliburton, Inc. Halliburton files a financing statement covering its security interest in the equipment. If Western Drilling fails to make the required payments, Halliburton can foreclose on its lien and repossess the equipment.

Retention of the Collateral

In the event of a debtor's default, a secured creditor who repossesses collateral may propose to **retain the collateral** in satisfaction of the debtor's obligation. Notice of the proposal must be sent to the debtor unless he or she has signed a written statement renouncing this right. In the case of consumer goods, no other notice need be given [Revised UCC 9-620(a)].

retention of collateral
A secured creditor's repossession of collateral on a debtor's default and proposal to retain the collateral in satisfaction of the debtor's obligation.

Dispose of the Collateral

In the event of a debtor's default, a secured party who chooses not to retain the collateral may sell, lease, or otherwise **dispose of the collateral** in its current condition or following any commercially reasonable preparation or processing. Disposition of collateral may be by public or private proceeding. The method, manner, time, place, and terms of the disposition must be commercially reasonable [Revised UCC 9-610].

disposition of collateral
A secured creditor's repossession of collateral on a debtor's default and selling, leasing, or otherwise disposing of it in a commercially reasonable manner.

The secured party must notify the debtor in writing about the time and place of any public or private sale or any other intended disposition of the collateral unless the debtor has signed a statement renouncing or modifying his on her rights to receive such notice. In the case of consumer goods, no other notification need be sent.

The proceeds from a sale, a lease, or another disposition are applied to pay reasonable costs and expenses, satisfy the balance of the indebtedness, and pay subordinate (junior) security interests. The debtor is entitled to receive any surplus that remains [Revised UCC 9-608].

Deficiency Judgment

Unless otherwise agreed, after a debtor's default, if the proceeds from the disposition of collateral are not sufficient to satisfy the debt to the secured party, the debtor is personally liable to the secured party for the payment of the deficiency. The secured party may bring an action to recover a **deficiency judgment** against the debtor [Revised UCC 9-608(a)(4)].

deficiency judgment
A judgment of a court that permits a secured lender to recover other property or income from a defaulting debtor if the collateral is insufficient to repay the unpaid loan.

Example Sean borrows $15,000 from First Bank to purchase a new automobile. He signs a security agreement, giving First Bank a purchase money security interest in the automobile. Sean defaults after making payments that reduce the debt to $13,250. First Bank repossesses the automobile and sells it at a public auction for $11,000. The selling expenses and sales commission are $1,250. This amount is deducted from the proceeds. The remaining $9,750 is applied to the $13,250 balance of the debt. Sean remains personally liable to First Bank for the $3,500 deficiency ($13,250 balance − $9,750 proceeds).

Redemption Rights

In the event of a debtor's default, the debtor or another secured party may redeem the collateral before the priority lienholder has disposed of it, entered into a contract to dispose of it, or discharged the debtor's obligation by having exercised a right to retain the collateral. The **right of redemption** may be accomplished by payment of all obligations secured by the collateral, all expenses reasonably incurred by the secured party in retaking and holding the collateral, and any attorneys' fees and other legal expenses provided for in the security agreement and not prohibited by law [Revised UCC 9-623].

Relinquishing the Security Interest and Proceeding to Judgment on the Underlying Debt

When a debtor defaults, instead of repossessing the collateral, a secured creditor may relinquish his or her security interest in the collateral and proceed to **judgment** against the debtor to recover the underlying debt. This course of action is rarely chosen unless the value of the collateral has been reduced below the amount of the secured interest and the debtor has other assets from which to satisfy the debt [Revised UCC 9-601(a)].

judgment
A right granted to a secured creditor to relinquish his or her security interest in the collateral and sue a defaulting debtor to recover the amount of the underlying debt.

Example Suppose Jack borrows $100,000 from First Bank to purchase a piece of equipment, and First Bank perfects its security interest in the equipment for this amount. Jack defaults on the loan when he owes $80,000 on the loan. If the equipment has gone down in value to $60,000 at the time of default but Jack has other personal assets to satisfy the debt, it may be in the bank's best interest to relinquish its security interest, sue Jack, and proceed to judgment on the underlying debt.

artisan's lien
A statutory lien given to workers on personal property to which the workers furnish services or materials in the ordinary course of business.

If the secured creditor obtains a judgment against the debtor but the debtor has no money to pay the judgment, the secured creditor can proceed to take possession of the collateral.

The following feature discusses artisan's liens in personal property.

Business Environment

Artisan's Liens on Personal Property

If a worker in the ordinary course of business furnishes services or materials to someone with respect to goods and receives a lien on the goods by statute, this **artisan's lien** prevails over all other security interests in the goods unless a statutory lien provides otherwise. Thus, such liens are often called **super-priority liens**. An artisan's lien is possessory; that is, the artisan must be in possession of the property in order to affect an artisan's lien.

Example Janice borrows money from First Bank to purchase an automobile. First Bank has a purchase money security interest in the car and files a financing statement. The automobile is involved in an accident, and Janice takes the car to Joe's Repair Shop (Joe's) to be repaired. Joe's retains an artisan's lien on the car for the amount of the repair work. When the repair work is completed, Janice refuses to pay. She also defaults on her payments to First Bank. If the car is sold to satisfy the liens, the artisan's lien is paid in full from the proceeds before First Bank is paid anything.

Key Terms and Concepts

Accessions (573)
Accounts (573)
After-acquired property (574)
Article 9 (Secured Transactions) of the Uniform Commercial Code (UCC) (570)
Artisan's lien (581)
Attachment (574)
Buyer in the ordinary course of business (578)
Chattel paper (573)
Collateral (571)
Consumer goods (573)
Continuation statement (575)
County recorder's office (575)
Debtor (571)
Default (579)
Deficiency judgment (580)
Deposit accounts (573)
Disposition of collateral (579)
Electronic financing statement (e-financing statement) (578)
Electronic secured transaction (e-secured transaction) (578)
Electronic chattel paper (573)
Equipment (573)
Farm products (573)
Financing statement (571)
Floating lien (574)
Future advances (575)
General intangibles (573)
Instruments (573)
Intangible personal property (573)
Inventory (573)
Judgment (580)
Perfection by a purchase money security interest in consumer goods (577)
Perfection by attachment (automatic perfection rule) (577)
Perfection by filing a financing statement (575)
Perfection by possession of collateral (576)
Perfection of a security interest (575)
Personal property (570)
Priority of claims (577)
Purchase money security interest (577)
Record (578)
Repossession (579)
Retention of collateral (579)
Revised Article 9 (Secured Transactions) (570)
Right of redemption (580)
Sale proceeds (574)
Secretary of state (575)
Secured party (571)
Secured transaction (571)
Security agreement (571)
Security interest (571)
Security interest in personal property (574)
Super-priority lien (581)
Taking possession of collateral (579)
Tangible personal property (572)
Tangible chattel paper (573)
Termination statement (577)
Third-party lender (572)
Three-party secured transaction (572)
Two-party secured transaction (571)
UCC Financing Statement (Form UCC-1) (575)

Critical Legal Thinking Cases

27.1 Financing Statement PSC Metals, Inc. (PSC) entered into an agreement whereby it extended credit to Keystone Consolidated Industries, Inc., and took back a security interest in personal property owned by Keystone. PSC filed a financing statement with the state, listing the debtor's trade name, "Keystone Steel & Wire Co.," rather than its corporate name, "Keystone Consolidated Industries, Inc." When Keystone went into bankruptcy, PSC filed a motion with the bankruptcy court to obtain the personal property securing its loan. Keystone's other creditors and the bankruptcy trustee objected, arguing that because PSC's financing statement was defectively filed, PSC did not have a perfected security interest in the personal property. If this were true, then PSC would become an unsecured creditor in Keystone's bankruptcy proceeding. Is the financing statement filed in the debtor's trade name, rather than in its corporate name, effective? *In re FV Steel and Wire Company*, 310 B.R. 390, 2004 Bankr. Lexis 748 (United States Bankruptcy Court for the Eastern District of Wisconsin, 2004)

27.2 Financing Statement C&H Trucking, Inc. (C&H) borrowed $19,747.56 from S&D Petroleum Company, Inc. (S&D). S&D hired Clifton M. Tamsett to prepare a security agreement naming C&H as the debtor and giving S&D a security interest in a new Mack truck. The security agreement prepared by Tamsett declared that the collateral also secured

> *any other indebtedness or liability of the debtor to the secured party direct or indirect, absolute or contingent, due or to become due, now existing or hereafter arising, including all future advances or loans which may be made at the option of the secured party.*

Tamsett failed to file a financing statement or the executed agreement with the appropriate government office. C&H subsequently paid off the original debt, and S&D continued to extend new credit to C&H. Two years later, when C&H owed S&D more than $17,000, S&D learned that (1) C&H was insolvent, (2) the Mack truck had been sold, and (3) Tamsett had failed to file the security agreement. Does S&D have a security interest in the Mack truck? Is Tamsett liable to S&D? *S&D Petroleum Company, Inc. v. Tamsett*, 144 A.D.2d 849, 534 N.Y.S.2d 800, 1988 N.Y. App. Div. Lexis 11258 (Supreme Court of New York)

27.3 Floating Lien Joseph H. Jones and others (debtors) borrowed money from Columbus Junction State Bank (Bank) and executed a security agreement in favor of Bank. Bank perfected its security interest by filing financing statements covering "equipment, farm products, crops, livestock, supplies, contract rights, and all accounts and proceeds thereof" with the Iowa secretary of state. Four years and 10 months later, Bank filed a continuation statement with the Iowa secretary of state. Four years and 10 months after that, Bank filed a second continuation statement with the Iowa secretary of state. Two years later, the debtors filed for Chapter 7 liquidation bankruptcy. The bankruptcy trustee collected $10,073 from the sale of the debtors' crops and an undetermined amount of soybeans harvested on farmland owned by the debtors. The bankruptcy trustee claimed the funds and soybeans on behalf of the bankruptcy estate. Bank claimed the funds and soybeans as a perfected secured creditor. Who wins? *In re Jones*, 79 B.R. 839, 1987 Bankr. Lexis 1825 (United States Bankruptcy Court for the Northern District of Iowa)

27.4 Purchase Money Security Interest Prior Brothers, Inc. (PBI) began financing its farming operations through Bank of California, N.A. (Bank). Bank's loans were secured by PBI's equipment and after-acquired property. Bank immediately filed a financing statement, perfecting its security interest. Two years later, PBI contacted the International Harvester dealership in Sunnyside, Washington, about the purchase of a new tractor. A retail installment contract for a model 1066 International Harvester tractor was executed. PBI took delivery of the tractor "on approval," agreeing that if it decided to purchase the tractor, it would inform the dealership of its intention and would send a $6,000 down payment. The dealership received a $6,000 check. The dealership immediately filed a financing statement concerning the tractor. Subsequently, when PBI went into receivership, the dealership filed a complaint, asking the court to declare that its purchase money security interest in the tractor had priority over Bank's security interest. Does the dealership's purchase money security interest in the tractor have priority over Bank's security interest? *In the Matter of Prior Brothers, Inc.*, 632 P.2d 522, 1981 Wash. App. Lexis 2507 (Court of Appeals of Washington)

27.5 Buyer in the Ordinary Course of Business Heritage Ford Lincoln Mercury, Inc. (Heritage) was in the business of selling new cars. Heritage entered into an agreement with Ford Motor Credit Company (Ford) whereby Ford extended a continuing line of credit to Heritage to purchase vehicles. Heritage granted Ford a purchase money security interest in all motor vehicles it owned and thereafter acquired and in all proceeds from the sale of such motor vehicles. Ford immediately filed its financing statement with the secretary of state. When the dealership experienced financial trouble, two Heritage officers decided to double finance certain new cars by issuing dealer papers to themselves and obtaining financing for two new cars from First National Bank & Trust Company of El Dorado (Bank). The loan proceeds were deposited in the dealership's account to help with its financial difficulties. The cars were available for sale. When the dealership closed its doors and turned over the car inventory to Ford, Bank alleged that it had priority over Ford because the Heritage officers were buyers in the ordinary course of business. Who wins? *First National Bank and Trust Company of El Dorado v. Ford Motor Credit Company*, 646 P.2d 1057, 1982 Kan. Lexis 280 (Supreme Court of Kansas)

Ethical

Ethics Cases

27.6 Ethics Case Mike Thurmond operated Top Quality Auto Sales, a used car dealership. Top Quality financed its inventory of vehicles by obtaining credit under a financing arrangement with Indianapolis Car Exchange (ICE). ICE filed a financing statement that listed Top Quality's inventory of vehicles as collateral for the financing. Top Quality sold a Ford truck to Bonnie Chrisman, a used car dealer, who paid Top Quality for the truck. Chrisman in turn sold the truck to Randall and Christina Alderson, who paid Chrisman for the truck. When Chrisman filed to retrieve the title to the truck for the Aldersons, it was discovered that Top Quality had not paid ICE for the truck. ICE requested that the Indiana Bureau of Motor Vehicles place a lien in its favor on the title of the truck. When ICE refused to release the lien on the truck, the Aldersons sued ICE to obtain title to the truck. The Aldersons asserted that Chrisman, and then they, were buyers in the ordinary course of business and therefore acquired the truck free of ICE's financing statement. ICE filed a counterclaim to recover the truck from the Aldersons. Are Chrisman and the Aldersons buyers in the ordinary course of business who took the truck free from ICE's security interest in the truck? Did ICE have a legitimate claim in this case? *Indianapolis Car Exchange v. Alderson*, 910 N.E.2d 802, 2009 Ind. App. Lexis (Court of Appeals of Indiana, 2009)

27.7 Ethics Case Harder & Sons, Inc., an International Harvester dealership in Ionia, Michigan, sold a used International Harvester 1066 diesel tractor to Terry Blaser on an installment contract. Although the contract listed Blaser's address as Ionia County, Blaser informed Harder at the time of purchase that he was going to work and live in Barry County. Blaser took delivery of the tractor at his Ionia County address three days later. On that same day, Harder filed a financing statement, which was executed by Blaser with the installment contract, in Barry County. The State of Michigan UCC requires an Article 9 financing statement to be filed in the debtor's county of residence. The contract and security agreement were immediately assigned to International Harvester Credit Corporation (International Harvester).

Blaser subsequently moved to Barry County for about three months, then to Ionia County for a few months, then to Kent County for three weeks, and then to Muskegon County, where he sold the tractor to Jay and Dale Vos. At the time of sale, Blaser informed the Vos brothers that he owned the tractor. He did not tell them that it was subject to a lien. The Vos brothers went to First Michigan Bank & Trust Company (Bank) to obtain a loan to help purchase the tractor. When the Bank checked the records of Ionia County and found that no financing statement was filed against the tractor, it made a $7,000 loan to the Vos brothers to purchase the tractor. About six months later, International Harvester filed suit to recover the tractor from the Vos brothers on the grounds that it had a prior perfected security interest. Did Blaser act ethically in this case? Who wins? *International Harvester Credit Corporation v. Vos*, 290 N.W.2d 401, 1980 Mich. App. Lexis 2430 (Michigan Court of Appeals)

Chapter 28 Bankruptcy and Reorganization

OUT OF BUSINESS
Businesses that run into hard economic times often go out of business.

Learning Objectives

After studying this chapter, you should be able to:

1. Identify and describe the changes to federal bankruptcy law made by the Bankruptcy Abuse Prevention and Consumer Protection Act of 2005.
2. Describe bankruptcy procedures and the provisions of a Chapter 7 liquidation bankruptcy.
3. Describe a Chapter 13 adjustment of debts of an individual with regular income bankruptcy.
4. Describe how businesses are reorganized in Chapter 11 bankruptcy.
5. Identify fraudulent transfers of property and cases of financial abuse that violate bankruptcy law.

Chapter Outline

"A trifling debt makes a man your debtor, a large one makes him your enemy."

—*Lucius Annaeus Seneca*
Epistulae Morales ad Lucilium (ca. 65)

Introduction to Bankruptcy and Reorganization

The extension of credit from creditors to debtors in commercial and personal transactions is important to the viability of the U.S. and world economies. On occasion, however, borrowers become overextended and are unable to meet their debt obligations. The founders of our country thought that the plight of debtors was so important that they included a provision in the U.S. Constitution giving Congress the authority to establish uniform federal bankruptcy laws. Congress has enacted bankruptcy laws pursuant to this power. The goal of bankruptcy laws is to balance the rights of debtors and creditors and provide methods for debtors to be relieved of some debt in order to obtain a **fresh start**.

I will pay you some, and, as most debtors do, promise you indefinitely.

William Shakespeare
Henry IV, part 2
(ca. 1596–1599)

fresh start
The goal of federal bankruptcy law to grant a debtor relief from some of his or her burdensome debts while protecting creditors by requiring the debtor to pay more of his or her debts than would otherwise have been required prior to the 2005 act.

Prior to 2005, the most recent overhaul of federal bankruptcy law occurred in 1978. The 1978 law was structured to make it easier for debtors to be relieved of much of their debt by declaring bankruptcy; it was deemed "debtor friendly" because it allowed many debtors to escape their unsecured debts.

After a decade of lobbying by credit-card companies and banks, Congress enacted the *Bankruptcy Abuse Prevention and Consumer Protection Act of 2005*. The 2005 act makes it much more difficult for debtors to escape their debts under federal bankruptcy law. The 2005 act has been criticized by consumer groups for being too "creditor friendly."

During the past decade, because of national and personal economic problems, many persons who had purchased homes by borrowing money from banks and other financial institutions found it difficult the make payments on the loans. Congress enacted the *Helping Families Save Their Homes Act of 2009* to provide ways for some home owners to qualify to have their loans modified so that they could more easily retain their homes and prevent foreclosure.

This chapter discusses federal bankruptcy law, bankruptcy procedure, the different types of bankruptcy, and how the provisions of the Bankruptcy Abuse Prevention and Consumer Protection Act of 2005 and the Helping Families Save Their Homes Act have changed bankruptcy law.

Bankruptcy Law

Article I, section 8, clause 4 of the U.S. Constitution states, "The Congress shall have the power . . . to establish . . . uniform laws on the subject of bankruptcies throughout the United States." Bankruptcy law is exclusively federal law; there are no state bankruptcy laws. Congress enacted the original federal Bankruptcy Act in 1878.

Types of Bankruptcy

The Bankruptcy Code is divided into chapters. Chapters 1, 3, and 5 set forth definitions and general provisions that govern case administration. The provisions of these chapters generally apply to all forms of bankruptcy.

Bankruptcy Reform Act of 1978
A federal act that substantially changed federal bankruptcy law. The act made it easier for debtors to file for bankruptcy and have their unpaid debts discharged. This act was considered debtor friendly.

Bankruptcy Abuse Prevention and Consumer Protection Act of 2005
A federal act that substantially amended federal bankruptcy law. This act makes it more difficult for debtors to file for bankruptcy and have their unpaid debts discharged.

Bankruptcy Code
The name given to federal bankruptcy law, as amended.

Four special chapters of the Bankruptcy Code provide different types of bankruptcy under which individual and business debtors may be granted remedy. They are as follows:

Chapter	Type of Bankruptcy
Chapter 7	Liquidation
Chapter 11	Reorganization
Chapter 12	Adjustment of Debts of a Family Farmer or Fisherman with Regular Income
Chapter 13	Adjustment of Debts of an Individual with Regular Income

Approximately 1.5 million debtors file for personal bankruptcy and approximately 40,000 businesses file for business bankruptcy each year. The filing fees for filing a Chapter 7, Chapter 12, or Chapter 13 bankruptcy is approximately $300. The filing fee for a Chapter 11 bankruptcy is approximately $1,200. Bankruptcy petitions may be filed by the debtor without the assistance of an attorney or filing service. If the debtor uses an attorney or filing service, their fees must be paid.

The following feature discusses a landmark change in federal bankruptcy law.

Landmark Law

Bankruptcy Abuse Prevention and Consumer Protection Act of 2005

Over the years, Congress has adopted various bankruptcy laws. Federal **bankruptcy law** was completely revised by the **Bankruptcy Reform Act of 1978.**[1] The 1978 act substantially changed—and eased—the requirements for filing bankruptcy. The 1978 act made it easier for debtors to rid themselves of unsecured debt, primarily by filing for Chapter 7 liquidation bankruptcy.

For more than a decade before 2005, credit-card companies, commercial banks, and other businesses lobbied Congress to pass a new bankruptcy act that would reduce the ability of some debtors to relieve themselves of unwanted debt through bankruptcy. In response, Congress enacted the **Bankruptcy Abuse Prevention and Consumer Protection Act of 2005.**[2] The 2005 act substantially amended federal bankruptcy law, making it much more difficult for debtors to escape unwanted debt through bankruptcy.

Federal bankruptcy law, as amended, is called the **Bankruptcy Code**, which is contained in Title 11 of the U.S. Code. The Bankruptcy Code establishes procedures for filing for bankruptcy, resolving creditors' claims, and protecting debtors' rights.

The changes made by the 2005 act are integrated throughout this chapter.

Bankruptcy Courts

U.S. bankruptcy courts
Special federal courts that hear and decide bankruptcy cases.

U.S. Trustee
A federal government official who is responsible for handling and supervising many of the administrative tasks of a bankruptcy case.

Congress created a system of federal bankruptcy courts. These special **U.S. bankruptcy courts** are necessary because the number of bankruptcies would overwhelm the federal district courts. The bankruptcy courts are part of the federal court system, and one bankruptcy court is attached to each of the 94 U.S. district courts in the country. Bankruptcy judges, specialists who hear bankruptcy proceedings, are appointed for 14-year terms. The relevant district court has jurisdiction to hear appeals from bankruptcy courts.

Federal law establishes the office of the **U.S. Trustee**. A U.S. Trustee is a federal government official who has responsibility for handling and supervising many of the administrative tasks associated with a bankruptcy case.[3] A U.S. Trustee is empowered to perform many of the tasks that the bankruptcy judge previously performed.

Bankruptcy Procedure

The Bankruptcy Code requires that certain procedures be followed for the commencement and prosecution of a bankruptcy case. These procedures are discussed in the following paragraphs.

Prepetition and Postpetition Counseling

The 2005 act added a new provision that requires an individual filing for bankruptcy to receive **prepetition counseling** and **postpetition counseling**. A debtor must receive prepetition credit counseling within 180 days prior to filing his or her petition for bankruptcy. This includes counseling on types of credit, the use of credit, and budget analysis. The counseling is to be provided by not-for-profit credit counseling agencies approved by the U.S. Trustee.

In addition, the 2005 act requires that before an individual debtor receives a discharge in a Chapter 7 or Chapter 13 bankruptcy, the debtor must attend a personal financial management course approved by the U.S. Trustee. This course is designed to provide the debtor with information on responsible use of credit and personal financial planning.

Filing a Bankruptcy Petition

A bankruptcy case is commenced when a **petition** is filed with a bankruptcy court. Two types of petitions can be filed:

1. **Voluntary petition.** A **voluntary petition** is a petition filed by the debtor. A voluntary petition can be filed by the debtor in Chapter 7 (liquidation), Chapter 11 (reorganization), Chapter 12 (family farmer or fisherman), and Chapter 13 (adjustment of debts) bankruptcy cases. The petition has to state that the debtor has debts.
2. **Involuntary petition.** An **involuntary petition** is a petition that is filed by a creditor or creditors and places the debtor into bankruptcy. An involuntary petition can be filed in Chapter 7 (liquidation) and Chapter 11 (reorganization) cases; an involuntary petition cannot be filed in Chapter 12 (family farmer or fisherman) or Chapter 13 (adjustment of debts) cases.

petition
A document filed with a bankruptcy court that starts a bankruptcy proceeding.

voluntary petition
A petition filed by a debtor that states that the debtor has debts.

involuntary petition
A petition filed by creditors of a debtor that alleges that the debtor is not paying his or her debts as they become due.

An individual debtor must submit the following **schedules** on filing a voluntary petition: a list of secured and unsecured creditors, with addresses; a list of all property owned; a statement of the financial affairs of the debtor; a statement of the debtor's monthly income; current income and expenses; evidence of payments received from employers within 60 days prior to the filing of the petition; and a copy of the debtor's federal income tax return for the most recent year ending prior to the filing of the petition. In addition, an individual debtor must file a certificate stating that he or she has received the required prepetition credit counseling. All forms must be sworn under oath and signed by the debtor.

Bankruptcy petitions, along with supporting documents, may be filed electronically with bankruptcy courts.

A man may be a bankrupt, and yet be honest, for he may become so by accident, and not of purpose to deceive his creditors.

Roll, Chief Justice
Rooke v. Smith (1651)

Attorney Certification

The 2005 act requires an **attorney certification** whereby an attorney who represents a client in bankruptcy must certify the accuracy of the information contained in the bankruptcy petition and the schedules, under penalty of perjury. If any factual discrepancies are found, the attorney is subject to monetary fines and sanctions.

If an attorney represents a debtor in bankruptcy, the attorney has to conduct a thorough investigation of the debtor's financial position and schedules to determine the accuracy of the information contained in the petition and schedules.

WEB EXERCISE
Go to **www.uscourts.gov/uscourts/RulesAndPolicies/rules/BK_Forms_Official_201/B_001_0410.pdf**. Read the Voluntary Petition for Bankruptcy Form 1.

Order for Relief

order for relief
An order that occurs on the filing of either a voluntary petition or an unchallenged involuntary petition or an order that is granted after a trial of a challenged involuntary petition.

The filing of either a voluntary petition or an unchallenged involuntary petition constitutes an **order for relief**. If the debtor challenges an involuntary petition, a trial is held to determine whether an order for relief should be granted. If an order is granted, the case is accepted for further bankruptcy proceedings. In the case of an involuntary petition, the debtor must file the same schedules filed by voluntary petition debtors.

Meeting of the Creditors

meeting of the creditors (first meeting of the creditors)
A meeting of the creditors in a bankruptcy case must occur within a reasonable time after an order for relief. The debtor must appear at this meeting.

Within a reasonable time after the court grants an order for relief (not less than 10 days or more than 30 days), the court must call a **meeting of the creditors** (also called the **first meeting of the creditors**). The bankruptcy judge cannot attend the meeting. The debtor must appear and submit to questioning, under oath, by creditors. Creditors may ask questions regarding the debtor's financial affairs, disposition of property prior to bankruptcy, possible concealment of assets, and such. The debtor may have an attorney present at this meeting.

Proof of Claim and Proof of Interest

proof of claim
A document required to be filed by a creditor that states the amount of his or her claim against the debtor.

A creditor must file a **proof of claim** stating the amount of his or her claim against the debtor. The document for filing a proof of claim is provided by the court. The proof of claim must be timely filed, which generally means within six months of the first meeting of the creditors. A secured creditor whose claim exceeds the value of the collateral may submit a proof of claim and become an unsecured claimant as to the difference. An equity security holder (e.g., a shareholder of a corporation) must file a **proof of interest**.

proof of interest
A document required to be filed by an equity security holder that states the amount of his or her interest against the debtor.

Bankruptcy Trustee

bankruptcy trustee
A legal representative of the debtor's estate.

A **bankruptcy trustee** must be appointed in Chapter 7 (liquidation), Chapter 12 (family farmer or family fisherman), and Chapter 13 (adjustment of debts) bankruptcy cases. A trustee may be appointed in a Chapter 11 (reorganization) case on a showing of fraud, dishonesty, incompetence, or gross mismanagement of the affairs of the debtor by current management. Trustees, who are often lawyers, accountants, or business professionals, are entitled to receive reasonable compensation for their services and reimbursement for expenses. Once appointed, a trustee becomes the legal representative of the debtor's estate and has the power to sell and buy property, invest money, and the like.

Automatic Stay

automatic stay
The suspension of certain legal actions by creditors against a debtor or the debtor's property.

The filing of a voluntary or an involuntary petition automatically *stays*—that is, suspends—certain legal actions by creditors against the debtor or the debtor's property. This is called an **automatic stay**. The stay, which applies to collection efforts of secured and unsecured creditors, is designed to prevent a scramble for the debtor's assets in a variety of court proceedings. The following creditor actions are stayed:

- Instituting or maintaining legal actions to collect prepetition debts
- Enforcing judgments obtained against the debtor
- Obtaining, perfecting, or enforcing liens against the property of the debtor
- Nonjudicial collection efforts, such as self-help activities (e.g., repossession of an automobile)

Actions to recover domestic support obligations (e.g., alimony, child support), the dissolution of a marriage, and child custody cases are not stayed in bankruptcy. Criminal actions against the debtor are also not stayed.

Discharge of Debts

In Chapter 7 (liquidation), Chapter 11 (reorganization), Chapter 12 (family farmer and family fisherman), and Chapter 13 (adjustment of debts) bankruptcies, if the requirements are met, the court grants the debtor a **discharge** of all or some of his, her, or its debts. When discharge is granted, the debtor is relieved of responsibility to pay the discharged debts. In other words, the debtor is no longer legally liable to pay the discharged debts. Discharge is one of the primary reasons a debtor files for bankruptcy. The specifics of discharge under each type of bankruptcy are discussed in this chapter.

discharge
A court order that relieves a debtor of the legal liability to pay his or her debts that were not paid in the bankruptcy proceeding.

Critical Legal Thinking
What is the public policy that allows debtors to discharge debts in bankruptcy? When a discharge is granted, does any party suffer a detriment?

Certain debts are not dischargeable in bankruptcy. Creditors who have nondischargeable claims against the debtor may participate in the distribution of the bankruptcy estate. The creditor may pursue the nondischarged balance against the debtor after bankruptcy. Debts that are not discharged in bankruptcy are listed and described in **Exhibit 28.1**.

The following debts are not dischargeable in bankruptcy:

- Claims for income or gross receipts taxes owed to federal, state, or local governments accrued within three years prior to the filing of the petition for bankruptcy
- Certain fines and penalties payable to federal, state, and local governmental units
- Claims based on the debtor's liability for causing willful or malicious injury to a person or property
- Claims arising from fraud, larceny, or embezzlement by the debtor while acting in a fiduciary capacity
- Domestic support obligations and alimony, maintenance, and child support payments resulting from a divorce decree or separation agreement
- Unscheduled claims
- Claims based on a consumer-debtor's purchase of luxury goods or services of more than $650 from a single creditor on or within 90 days of the order for relief
- Cash advances in excess of $925 obtained by a consumer-debtor by use of a revolving line of credit or credit cards on or within 70 days of the order for relief
- Judgments and consent decrees against the debtor for liability incurred as a result of the debtor's operation of a motor vehicle, a vessel, or an aircraft while legally intoxicated
- A debt that would result in a benefit to the debtor that outweighs the detrimental consequences to a spouse, former spouse, or child of the debtor
- An amount owed to a pension, profit-sharing, or stock bonus plan and loans owed to employee retirement plans

Exhibit 28.1 **DEBTS THAT CANNOT BE DISCHARGED IN BANKRUPTCY**

In the following case, the court had to decide if a debt was dischargeable.

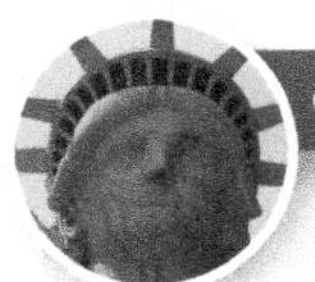

CASE 28.1 *FEDERAL COURT CASE Bankruptcy Discharge*

Speedsportz v. Lieben

2013 Bankr. Lexis 3783 (2013)
United States Bankruptcy Court for the Northern District of Georgia

"'Dear Thief,' she wrote in her diary, 'I'm writing this letter to understand you better and ask why you're such a dominant archetype in my life.'"
—Bankruptcy Judge

Facts

John Reaves is the sole owner and president of a small business called Speedsportz, LLC, which is in the business of refurbishing exotic automobiles. Reaves

(case continues)

had been in this business for about 30 years when he met Angela Lieben. Shortly after meeting, they started dating, and Lieben moved in with Reaves, who hired her as his company's office manager and bookkeeper. Lieben's duties included paying bills, reconciling bank statements, and entering information in the company's accounting software. Several years later, Reaves ended their relationship and terminated Lieben's employment. Reaves then discovered irregularities in the company's bank statements, checks that were written by unauthorized and forged signatures, cash that was missing, and unauthorized ATM withdrawals. Evidence showed that Lieben had previously been convicted of forgery. Lieben subsequently filed for personal bankruptcy. Speedsportz and Reaves filed appropriate documents with the bankruptcy court, alleging that Lieben's debt from her defalcations was not dischargeable in bankruptcy because they had been committed by fraud or embezzlement.

Issue

Did debtor Lieben's defalcations result from fraud or embezzlement and were therefore not dischargeable in bankruptcy?

Language of the Court

"Dear Thief," she wrote in her diary, "I'm writing this letter to understand you better and ask why you're such a dominant archetype in my life." Debtor Angela Lieben says this was just part of a fictional short story she was writing. Plaintiff John Reaves claims this letter was evidence that his former live-in girlfriend and bookkeeper stole money from him. Entries in Lieben's diaries and personal e-mails implicate her generally in this type of conduct against Reaves. The court finds that Lieben is liable to Speedsportz for the unauthorized transactions and concludes that these debts are nondischargeable because she committed fraud and embezzlement.

Decision

The U.S. bankruptcy court held that Lieben had committed fraud and embezzlement and is liable to Speedsportz for $49,232. The bankruptcy court ruled that this amount owed to Speedsportz cannot be discharged in Lieben's bankruptcy.

Ethics Questions

Did Lieben act ethically in this case? Could Reaves have prevented the fraud and embezzlement by keeping better track of his company's financial affairs?

Reaffirmation Agreement

reaffirmation agreement
An agreement entered into by a debtor with a creditor prior to discharge whereby the debtor agrees to pay the creditor a debt that would otherwise be discharged in bankruptcy. Certain requirements must be met for a reaffirmation agreement to be enforced.

A debtor and a creditor can enter into a **reaffirmation agreement**, whereby the debtor agrees to pay the creditor for a debt that is dischargeable in bankruptcy. This might occur if the debtor wishes to repay a debt to a family member, to a bank, or to another party. A reaffirmation agreement must be entered into before discharge is granted. A reaffirmation agreement must be filed with the court. Approval by the court is required if the debtor is not represented by an attorney. If the debtor is represented by an attorney, the attorney must certify that the debtor voluntarily entered into the reaffirmation agreement and understands the consequences of the agreement. Even if the debtor is represented by an attorney, court approval is required if the agreement will cause undue hardship on the debtor or his or her family.

Bankruptcy Estate

bankruptcy estate
The debtor's property and earnings that comprise the estate of a bankruptcy proceeding.

The **bankruptcy estate** is created on the commencement of a bankruptcy case. It includes all the debtor's legal and equitable interests in real, personal, tangible, and intangible property, wherever located, that exist when the petition is filed, and all interests of the debtor and the debtor's spouse in community property. Certain *exempt property* (as discussed later in this section) is not part of the bankruptcy estate.

Gifts, inheritances, life insurance proceeds, and property from divorce settlements that the debtor is entitled to receive within 180 days after the petition is filed are part of the bankruptcy estate. Earnings from property of the estate—such as rents, dividends, and interest payments—are property of the estate.

Earnings from services performed by an individual debtor are not part of the bankruptcy estate in a Chapter 7 liquidation bankruptcy. However, the 2005 act provides that a certain amount of postpetition earnings from services performed by the debtor that are earned for up to five years after the order for relief may be required to be paid as part of the completion of Chapter 12 (family farmer or family fisherman), Chapter 11 (reorganization), and Chapter 13 (adjustment of debts) cases.

fraudulent transfer
A transfer of a debtor's property or an obligation incurred by a debtor within two years of the filing of a petition, where (1) the debtor had actual intent to hinder, delay, or defraud a creditor or (2) the debtor received less than a reasonable equivalent in value.

The following ethics feature discusses debtors' fraudulent transfers of property prior to declaring bankruptcy.

Ethics

Fraudulent Transfer of Property Prior to Bankruptcy

The 2005 act gives the bankruptcy court the power to void certain **fraudulent transfers** of a debtor's property made by the debtor within two years prior to filing a petition for bankruptcy. To void a transfer or an obligation, the court must find that (1) the transfer was made or the obligation was incurred by the debtor with the actual intent to hinder, delay, or defraud a creditor or (2) the debtor received less than a reasonable equivalent in value.

Example Kathy owes her unsecured creditors $100,000. On February 9, Kathy knows that she is insolvent. Kathy owns a Mercedes-Benz automobile that is worth $55,000. On February 9, Kathy sells her Mercedes-Benz automobile to her friend, Wei, for $35,000. Wei is a bona fide purchaser who does not know of Kathy's financial situation. On July 1, Kathy files for Chapter 7 liquidation bankruptcy while still owing the $100,000 to her unsecured creditors. The court can void Kathy's sale of her automobile to Wei as a fraudulent transfer because it occurred within two years of the petition and Kathy received less than a reasonable equivalent in value. Because Wei was a bona fide purchaser, the court must repay Wei the purchase price of $35,000 to recover the automobile from her.

Ethics Questions Do you think there are many fraudulent transfers by debtors prior to their filing of bankruptcy petitions? What items or assets are likely to be involved in fraudulent transfers prior to bankruptcy?

The following case involves bankruptcy fraud.

CASE 28.2 *FEDERAL COURT Bankruptcy Fraud*

In Re Hoang

2012 Bankr. Lexis 4355 (2012)
United States Bankruptcy Court for the District of Maryland

"Here, the trustee seeks turnover of the diamonds."
—Catliota, Bankruptcy Judge

Facts

Minh Vu Hoang (Hoang) owned businesses and purchased and sold real estate. When she filed for bankruptcy, she listed ownership interests in ten business entities and five parcels of real estate. A bankruptcy trustee was appointed who in turn hired a forensic accountant to determine if Hoang had interests in any other properties. It was discovered that Hoang owned interests in dozens of businesses and real estate properties that were not disclosed in her bankruptcy schedules. These properties were owned in fictitious names, alter-ego entities, slush funds, and agents' names. In more than 60 adversarial proceedings, many of these properties were acquired for the bankruptcy estate. The forensic accountant identified that Hoang had used cash proceeds from the sale of a piece of real property that should have been an asset of the bankruptcy estate to purchase 48 carats of diamonds worth $171,000. These diamonds had not been disclosed or turned over to the

(case continues)

bankruptcy trustee. The bankruptcy trustee made a motion to the bankruptcy court to recover the diamonds as assets of the bankruptcy estate.

Issue

Are the diamonds considered property of the bankruptcy estate?

Language of the Court

The Bankruptcy Code provides a trustee with powers to obtain property of the estate. Here, the trustee seeks turnover of the diamonds. Hoang does not admit she acquired the diamonds, but she asserted her Fifth Amendment right and did not testify. The cash used by Hoang to purchase the diamonds was proceeds of property of the estate and thus the diamonds are proceeds from property of the estate and therefore property of the estate.

Decision

The bankruptcy court entered an order that required Hoang to turn over the diamonds to the bankruptcy trustee. The U.S. district court affirmed the bankruptcy court's decision.

Ethics Questions

Why did Hoang conceal her ownership interests in the undisclosed businesses, real property, and diamonds? Did Hoang's activities warrant the criminal proceeding?

Exempt Property

exempt property
Property that may be retained by the debtor pursuant to federal or state law that does not become part of the bankruptcy estate.

Because the Bankruptcy Code is not designed to make the debtor a pauper, certain property is exempt from the bankruptcy estate. **Exempt property** is property of the debtor that he or she can keep and that does not become part of the bankruptcy estate. The creditors cannot claim the property.

The Bankruptcy Code establishes a list of property and assets that a debtor can claim as exempt property. The federal exemptions, with the dollar limits, are listed in **Exhibit 28.2**.[4] Federal exemptions are adjusted every three years to reflect changes in the consumer price index.

The following debts are not dischargeable in bankruptcy:

1. Interest up to $22,975 in equity in property used as a residence and burial plots (called the "homestead exemption")
2. Interest up to $3,675 in value in one motor vehicle
3. Interest up to $575 per item in household goods and furnishings, wearing apparel, appliances, books, animals, crops, or musical instruments, up to an aggregate value of $12,250 for all items
4. Interest in jewelry up to $1,550
5. Interest in any property the debtor chooses (including cash) up to $1,225, plus up to $12,250 of any unused portion of the homestead exemption
6. Interest up to $2,300 in value in implements, tools, or professional books used in the debtor's trade
7. Any unmatured life insurance policy owned by the debtor
8. Professionally prescribed health aids
9. Many government benefits, regardless of value, including Social Security benefits, welfare benefits, unemployment compensation, veteran's benefits, disability benefits, and public assistance benefits
10. Certain rights to receive income, including domestic support payments (e.g., alimony, child support), certain pension benefits, profit sharing, and annuity payments
11. Interests in wrongful death benefits and life insurance proceeds to the extent necessary to support the debtor or his or her dependents
12. Personal injury awards up to $22,975
13. Retirement funds that are in a fund or an account that is exempt from taxation under the Internal Revenue Code, except that an exemption for individual retirement accounts (IRAs) shall not exceed $1,245,475 for an individual unless the interests of justice require this amount to be increased

Exhibit 28.2 FEDERAL EXEMPTIONS FROM THE BANKRUPTCY ESTATE

State Exemptions

The Bankruptcy Code permits states to enact their own exemptions. States that do so may (1) give debtors the option of choosing between federal and state exemptions or (2) require debtors to follow state law. The exemptions available under state law are often more liberal than those provided by federal law.

WEB EXERCISE
Go to **www.filing-bankruptcy-form.com/bankruptcy-exemptions.html**. Click on your state. What are the bankruptcy exemptions of your state?

Homestead Exemption

The federal Bankruptcy Code permits home owners to claim a **homestead exemption** of $22,975 in their principal residence. If the debtor's equity in the property (i.e., the value above the amount of mortgages and liens) exceeds the exemption limits, the trustee may sell the property to realize the excess value for the bankruptcy estate.

homestead exemption
Equity in a debtor's home that the debtor is permitted to retain.

Example Assume that a debtor owns a principal residence worth $500,000 that is subject to a $400,000 mortgage and the debtor therefore owns $100,000 of equity in the property. The debtor files a petition for Chapter 7 liquidation bankruptcy. The trustee may sell the home, pay off the mortgage, pay the debtor $22,975 (applying the federal exemption), and use the remaining proceeds of $77,025 for distribution to the debtor's creditors.

The following ethics feature discusses how the 2005 act limits homestead exemptions.

Ethics

Abusive Homestead Exemptions

The Bankruptcy Code's federal homestead exemption is $22,975. Homestead exemptions under many state laws are usually higher than the federal exemption. Most states exempt between $20,000 and $100,000 of equity in a debtor's principal residence from the bankruptcy estate.

Florida and Texas have no dollar amount limit on their homestead exemptions, although they do limit the size of the real property that qualifies for the homestead exemption. These states have been known as "debtor's havens" for wealthy debtors who file for bankruptcy. Prior to the 2005 act, many wealthy debtors from other states moved their money into principal residences in Florida and Texas to benefit from these generous homestead exemptions. Other states that allow debtors to protect an unlimited amount of equity from claims of creditors are Iowa, Kansas, and South Dakota.

The 2005 act limits **abusive homestead exemptions**. The 2005 act provides that a debtor may not exempt an amount greater than $155,675 if the property was acquired by the debtor within 40 months before the filing of the petition for bankruptcy.

Ethics Questions Why do some states adopt generous homestead exemptions for a debtor's bankruptcy estate? Will the federal limits on homestead exemptions reduce abusive bankruptcy behavior by wealthy debtors?

Chapter 7—Liquidation

Chapter 7—Liquidation (also called **straight bankruptcy**) is a familiar form of bankruptcy.[5] In this type of bankruptcy proceeding, the debtor is permitted to keep a substantial portion of his or her assets (exempt assets); the debtor's nonexempt property is sold for cash, and the cash is distributed to the creditors; any of the debtor's unpaid debts are discharged. The debtor's future income, even if he or she becomes rich, cannot be reached to pay the discharged debt. Thus, a debtor would be left to start life anew, without the burden of his or her prepetition debts.

WEB EXERCISE
Go to **http://www.lawfirms.com/resources/bankruptcy/chapter7/exemptions-to-liquidation.htm**. What is the homestead exemption for your state?

Example Annabelle finds herself overburdened with debt, particularly credit-card debt. Assume that Annabelle qualifies for Chapter 7 bankruptcy. At the time

Chapter 7—Liquidation (straight bankruptcy)
A form of bankruptcy in which the debtor's nonexempt property is sold for cash, the cash is distributed to the creditors, and any unpaid debts are discharged.

she files for Chapter 7 bankruptcy, her unsecured credit is $100,000. Annabelle has few assets, and most of those are exempt property (e.g., her clothes, some furniture). Her nonexempt property is $10,000, which will be sold to raise cash. The $10,000 in cash will be distributed to her debtors on a pro rata basis—that is, each creditor will receive 10 cents for every dollar of debt owed. The other $90,000 is *discharged*—that is, the creditors have to absorb this loss. Annabelle is free from this debt forever. Annabelle is given a fresh start, and her future earnings are hers.

Qualifications for Chapter 7 Bankruptcy

One of the purposes of the 2005 act's changes to Chapter 7 is to force many debtors out of Chapter 7 liquidation bankruptcy and into Chapter 13 debt adjustment bankruptcy, which requires debtors to pay some of their future income to pay off prepetition debts. Thus, the 2005 act reduces the number of debtors who qualify for Chapter 7 liquidation bankruptcy. To accomplish this, the 2005 act added two tests, the *median income test* and the *means test*, to determine whether a debtor qualifies to obtain a discharge of debts under Chapter 7:

median income test
A bankruptcy rule that states that if a debtor's median family income is at or below the state's median family income for a family the same size as the debtor's family, the debtor can receive Chapter 7 relief.

WEB EXERCISE
Go to **www.census.gov/hhes/www/income/data/statemedian/index.html**, which is a website of the U.S. Census Bureau. What is the median income for a family of four in your state?

- **Test 1: Median Income Test.** The first step in determining whether a debtor qualifies for Chapter 7 relief is to apply the **median income test**. A **state's median income** is defined as that income where half of the state's families of a specified size have incomes above that figure and half of the state's families of that size have incomes below that figure. The median income for a family of two will differ from the median income for a family of three and so on.

  If a family has median family income *equal to or below* the state's median family income for the size of the debtor's family, the debtor qualifies for Chapter 7 bankruptcy. The debtor may proceed with his or her Chapter 7 case and be granted discharge of his or her unsecured debts. Thus, for debtors at or below the state median income, the 2005 act makes no changes in the ability to obtain Chapter 7 relief.

  Example Assume that a state's median income for a family of four is $75,000. If the median income of the debtor's family of four is $60,000, the debtor qualifies for Chapter 7 bankruptcy relief.

  If a family has median family income that is *higher* than the state's median family income for the size of the debtor's family, the debtor does not automatically qualify for a Chapter 7 bankruptcy. A second test, the *means test*, is applied to see if the debtor qualifies for Chapter 7 bankruptcy.

means test
A bankruptcy rule that applies to a debtor who has a median family income that exceeds the state's median family income for families the same size as the debtor's family. A debtor in this category qualifies for Chapter 7 bankruptcy if he or she has disposable income below an amount determined by bankruptcy law but does not qualify for Chapter 7 bankruptcy if he or she has disposable income above an amount determined by bankruptcy law.

- **Test 2: Means Test.** The **means test** is a calculation that establishes a bright-line test to determine whether the debtor has sufficient *disposable income* to pay prepetition debts out of postpetition income. **Disposable income** is determined by taking the debtor's actual income and subtracting expenses for a typical family the same size as the debtor's family. Income is the actual income of the debtor. However, expenses are determined by using preestablished government tables and not the actual expenses of the family. A complicated formula is used to calculate the debtor's disposable income and thus determine whether the debtor qualifies for Chapter 7 bankruptcy.

  If, because of the application of the means test, a debtor is determined to have a sufficient amount of disposable income as determined by bankruptcy law, the debtor does not qualify for Chapter 7 bankruptcy. His or her petition for Chapter 7 bankruptcy will be denied by the bankruptcy court. Usually, these debtors will file for Chapter 13 bankruptcy (discussed later in this chapter).

If, however, using the means test calculation a debtor is determined to have an insufficient amount of disposable income as determined by bankruptcy law, the debtor qualifies for Chapter 7 bankruptcy. These debtors may be granted Chapter 7 discharge of debts.

Thus, some of the debtors that have income above the state's median income for the debtor's size of family will qualify for Chapter 7, and some will not.

Statutory Distribution of Property

If a debtor qualifies for a Chapter 7 liquidation bankruptcy, the **nonexempt property** of the bankruptcy estate must be distributed to the debtor's secured and unsecured creditors pursuant to statutory priority established by the Bankruptcy Code. The claims of secured creditors to the debtor's nonexempt property have priority over the claims of unsecured creditors.

With regard to secured creditors, the following two situations can result:

1. **Oversecured secured creditor.** If the value of the collateral securing the secured loan exceeds the secured interest, the secured creditor is an **oversecured creditor**. In this case, the property is usually sold, and the secured creditor is paid the amount of its secured interest (i.e., principal and accrued principal and interest) and reasonable fees and costs resulting from the debtor's default. The excess becomes available to satisfy the claims of the debtor's unsecured creditors.
2. **Undersecured secured creditor.** If the value of the collateral securing the secured loan is less than the secured interest, the secured creditor is an **undersecured creditor**. In this case, the property is usually awarded to the secured creditor. The secured creditor then becomes an unsecured creditor as to the amount still owed to it, which consists of unpaid principal and interest and reasonable fees and costs of the debtor's default.

It is the policy of the law that the debtor be just before he be generous.

Justice Finch
Hearn 45 St. Corp. v. Jano (1940)

The 2005 act added a new provision regarding **secured personal property**. Under the 2005 act, if personal property of an individual debtor secures a claim or is subject to an unexpired lease (e.g., an automobile lease) and is not exempt property, the debtor must (1) surrender the personal property, (2) redeem the property by paying the secured lien in full, or (3) assume the unexpired lease.

Unsecured claims are to be satisfied out of the bankruptcy estate in the order of their statutory priority, as established by the Bankruptcy Code. The **statutory priority of unsecured claims**, including the changes made by the 2005 act, is set forth in **Exhibit 28.3**.

Small debts are like small shot; they are rattling on every side, and can scarcely be escaped without a wound; great debts are like cannon; of loud noise, but little danger.

Samuel Johnson
Letters to Joseph Simpson (1759)

Exhibit 28.3 PRIORITY OF UNSECURED CREDITOR CLAIMS

1. Unsecured claims for domestic support obligations owed to a spouse, former spouse, or child of the debtor.
2. Fees and expenses of administering the estate, including court costs, trustee fees, attorney's fees, appraisal fees, and other costs of administration.
3. In an involuntary bankruptcy, secured claims of "gap" creditors who sold goods or services on credit to the debtor in the ordinary course of the debtor's business between the date of the filing of the petition and the date of the appointment of the trustee or issuance of the order for relief (whichever occurred first).
4. Unsecured claims for wages, salary, commissions, severance pay, and sick leave pay earned by the debtor's employees within 180 days immediately preceding the filing of the petition, up to $12,475 per employee.
5. Unsecured claims for contributions to employee benefit plans based on services performed within 180 days immediately preceding the filing of the petition, up to $12,475 per employee, but

(Continued)

Exhibit 2.2 **(CONTINUED)**

only to the extent that payments under item 4 above have not reached $12, 475. Thus, the payments under items 4 and 5 can total only $12,475.

Examples If an employee is owed $7,000 of unpaid priority benefits but has been paid $12,475 for priority unpaid wages, the employee receives no priority payment for unpaid benefits. He or she is still owed $7,000 for unpaid benefits, but the $7,000 becomes a nonpriority unsecured claim. If an employee has been paid $5,000 for priority unpaid wages, he or she can recover up to $7,475 of priority benefits owed to him or her.

6. Farm producers and fishermen against debtors who operate grain storage facilities or fish storage or processing facilities, respectively, up to $6,150 per claim.
7. Unsecured claims for cash deposited by a consumer with the debtor prior to the filing of the petition in connection with the purchase, lease, or rental of property or the purchases of services that were not delivered or provided by the debtor, up to $2,775 per claim.
8. Unsecured claims for unpaid income and gross receipts taxes owed to governments incurred during the three years preceding the bankruptcy petition and unpaid property taxes owed to governments incurred within one year preceding the bankruptcy petition.
9. Commitment by the debtor to maintain the capital of an insured depository institution, such as a commercial bank or savings bank.
10. Claims against the debtor for personal injuries or death caused by the debtor while he or she was intoxicated from using alcohol or drugs.

The 2005 act stipulates that a debtor can be granted Chapter 7 relief only after eight years following Chapter 7 or Chapter 11 relief and only after six years following Chapter 12 or Chapter 13 relief.

Chapter 7 Discharge

In a Chapter 7 bankruptcy, the property of the estate is sold, and the proceeds are distributed to satisfy allowed claims. The remaining unpaid debts that the debtor incurred prior to the date of the order for relief are discharged. *Discharge* means that the debtor is no longer legally responsible for paying those claims. The major benefit of a **Chapter 7 discharge** is that it is granted quite soon after the petition is filed. The individual debtor is not responsible for paying prepetition debts out of postpetition income, as would be required in other forms of bankruptcy.

Chapter 7 discharge
The termination of the legal duty of an individual debtor to pay unsecured debts that remain unpaid on the completion of a Chapter 7 proceeding.

Example Suppose that at the time that Eric is granted Chapter 7 relief, he still owes $50,000 of unsecured debt that there is no money in the bankruptcy estate to pay. This debt is composed of credit-card debt, an unsecured loan from a friend, and unsecured credit from a department store. This $50,000 of unsecured credit is discharged. This means that Eric is relieved of this debt and is not legally liable for its repayment. The unsecured creditors must write off this debt.

Acts That Bar Discharge

Any party of interest may file an objection to the discharge of a debt. The court then holds a hearing. Discharge of unsatisfied debts is denied if the debtor:

- Made false representations about his or her financial position when he or she obtained an extension of credit.
- Transferred, concealed, removed, or destroyed property of the estate with the intent to hinder, delay, or defraud creditors within one year before the date of the filing of the petition.
- Falsified, destroyed, or concealed records of his or her financial condition.
- Failed to account for any assets.
- Failed to submit to questioning at the meeting of the creditors (unless excused).
- Failed to complete an instructional course concerning personal financial management, as required by the 2005 act (unless excused).

Beggars can never be bankrupt.

Thomas Fuller
Gnomologia (1732)

If a discharge is obtained through fraud of the debtor, any party of interest may bring a motion to have the bankruptcy revoked. The bankruptcy court may revoke a discharge within one year after it is granted.

As the following feature shows, special rules apply for the discharge of student loans in bankruptcy.

Contemporary Environment

Discharge of Student Loans in Bankruptcy

Until their graduation from college and professional schools, many students have borrowed money to pay tuition and living expenses. At this point in time, when a student might have large student loans and very few assets, he or she might be inclined to file for bankruptcy in an attempt to have his or her student loans discharged.

To prevent such abuse of bankruptcy law, Congress amended the Bankruptcy Code to make it more difficult for students to have their **student loans** discharged in bankruptcy. Student loans are defined to include loans made by or guaranteed by governmental units; loans made by nongovernmental commercial institutions such as banks; as well as funds for scholarships, benefits, or stipends granted by educational institutions.

The Bankruptcy Code now states that student loans cannot be discharged in any form of bankruptcy unless their nondischarge would cause an **undue hardship** to the debtor and his or her dependents. Undue hardship is construed strictly and is difficult for a debtor to prove unless he or she can show severe physical or mental disability or that he or she is unable to pay for basic necessities, such as food or shelter, for his or her family.

Co-signers (e.g., parents who guarantee their child's student loan) must also meet the heightened undue hardship test to discharge their obligation.

Chapter 13—Adjustment of Debts of an Individual with Regular Income

Chapter 13—Adjustment of Debts of an Individual with Regular Income is a rehabilitation form of bankruptcy for individuals.[6] Chapter 13 permits a qualified debtor to propose a plan to pay all or a portion of the debts he or she owes in installments over a specified period of time, pursuant to the requirements of Chapter 13. The bankruptcy court supervises the debtor's plan for the payment.

Chapter 13—Adjustment of Debts of an Individual with Regular Income
A rehabilitation form of bankruptcy that permits bankruptcy courts to supervise the debtor's plan for the payment of unpaid debts in installments over the plan period.

The debtor has several advantages under Chapter 13. These include avoiding the stigma of Chapter 7 liquidation, retaining more property than is exempt under Chapter 7, and incurring fewer expenses than in a Chapter 7 proceeding. The creditors have advantages, too: They may recover a greater percentage of the debts owed them than they would recover under a Chapter 7 bankruptcy.

Chapter 13 petitions are usually filed by individual debtors who do not qualify for Chapter 7 liquidation bankruptcy and by home owners who want to protect nonexempt equity in their residence. Chapter 13 enables debtors to catch up on secured credit loans, such as home mortgages, and avoid repossession and foreclosure.

Filing a Chapter 13 Petition

A Chapter 13 proceeding can be initiated only through the voluntary filing of a petition by an individual debtor with regular income. A creditor cannot file an involuntary petition to institute a Chapter 13 case. An **individual with regular income** is an individual whose income is sufficiently stable and regular to enable such individual to make payments under a Chapter 13 plan. Regular income may be from any source, including wages, salary, commissions, and from investments, Social Security income, pension income, or public assistance. The debts of the individual debtor must be primarily consumer debt. **Consumer debt** means debts incurred by an individual for personal, family, or household purposes. The petition must be filed in good faith.[7]

individual with regular income
An individual whose income is sufficiently stable and regular to enable the individual to make payments under a Chapter 13 plan.

The petition must state that the debtor desires to obtain an extension or a composition of debts, or both.

extension
Provides a longer period of time for the debtor to pay his or her debts.

An **extension** provides for a longer period of time for the debtor to pay his or her debts.

Example A debtor who is obligated to pay a debt within one year petitions the bankruptcy court to extend the time in which he has to pay the debt to three years.

composition
Provides for the reduction of a debtor's debts.

A **composition** provides for the reduction of a debtor's debts.

Example A debtor who owes an unsecured creditor $10,000 petitions the court to reduce the unsecured debt that he owes the creditor to $7,000.

Limitations on Who Can File for Chapter 13 Bankruptcy

The 2005 act establishes dollar limits on the secured and unsecured debt that a debtor may have in order to qualify to file for Chapter 13 bankruptcy. Only an individual with regular income alone or with his or her spouse who owes individually or with his or her spouse (1) noncontingent, liquidated, unsecured debts of not more than $383,175 and (2) secured debts of not more than $1,149,525 may file a petition for Chapter 13 bankruptcy. Individual debtors who exceed these dollar limits do not qualify for Chapter 13 bankruptcy. Sole proprietorships, because they are owned by individuals, may file for Chapter 13 bankruptcy.

Property of a Chapter 13 Estate

Debt rolls a man over and over, binding him hand and foot, and letting him hang upon the fatal mesh until the long-legged interest devours him.

Henry Ward Beecher
Proverbs from Plymouth Pulpit (1887)

The property of a Chapter 13 estate consists of all nonexempt property of the debtor at the commencement of the case and nonexempt property acquired after the commencement of the case but before the case is closed. In addition, the property of the estate includes earnings and future income earned by the debtor after the commencement of the case but before the case is closed. This ensures that prepetition creditors receive payments from the debtor's postpetition earnings and income.

The debtor remains in possession of all of the property of the estate during the completion of the plan except as otherwise provided by the plan. If the debtor is self-employed, the debtor may continue to operate his or her business. Alternatively, the court may order that a trustee operate the business, if necessary.

Chapter 13 Plan of Payment

The debtor's **Chapter 13 plan of payment** must be filed not later than 90 days after the order for relief. The debtor must file information about his or her finances, including a budget of estimated income and expenses during the period of the plan. The Chapter 13 plan may be either up to three years or up to five years, depending on a complicated calculation specified in the 2005 act.

The plan must be submitted to secured and unsecured creditors for acceptance. The plan is confirmed as to a secured creditor or an unsecured creditor if that creditor accepts the plan. If a secured creditor does not accept the plan, the court may still confirm the plan if the secured creditor will be paid in full, including arrearages, during the course of the plan. If an unsecured creditor objects to the plan, the court may still confirm the plan if the debtor agrees to commit all of his or her disposable income during the plan period to pay his or her unsecured creditors. However, during the plan period, unsecured creditors might not receive full payment of the debt owed to them.

Disposable income is defined as current monthly income less amounts reasonably necessary to be spent for the maintenance or support of the debtor and the debtor's dependents. Expenses include amounts necessary to pay domestic support obligations and charitable donations that do not exceed 15 percent of the debtor's gross income for the year the charitable donations are made. If a debtor earns more than the median income of the state, his or her expenses are determined by the objective Internal Revenue Service (IRS) standards.

Confirmation of a Chapter 13 Plan of Payment

The court can confirm a Chapter 13 plan of payment if the prior requirements are met and if (1) the plan was proposed in good faith, (2) the plan passes the feasibility test (e.g., the debtor must be able to make the proposed payments), (3) the plan is in the best interests of the creditors (i.e., the present value of the payments must equal or exceed the amount that the creditors would receive in a Chapter 7 liquidation proceeding), (4) the debtor has paid all domestic support obligations owed, and (5) the debtor has filed all applicable federal, state, and local tax returns.

The debtor must begin making the planned installment payments to the trustee. The trustee is responsible for remitting these payments to the creditors. The trustee is paid for administering the plan. Payments under the plan must be made in equal monthly installments.

A Chapter 13 plan may be modified if the debtor's circumstances materially change. For example, if the debtor's income subsequently decreases, the court may decrease the debtor's payments under the plan.

Chapter 13 Discharge

The court grants an order discharging the debtor from all unpaid unsecured debts covered by the plan after all the payments required under the plan are completed (which could be up to three years or up to five years). This is called a **Chapter 13 discharge**. The debtor must certify that all domestic support payments have been paid before discharge is granted. Most unpaid taxes are not discharged.

A debtor cannot be granted Chapter 13 discharge if the debtor has received discharge under Chapter 7, 11, or 12 within the prior four-year period or Chapter 13 relief within the prior two-year period of the order for relief in the current Chapter 13 case.

Chapter 13 discharge
A discharge in a Chapter 13 case that is granted to the debtor after the debtor's plan of payment is completed (which could be up to three or up to five years).

Chapter 11—Reorganization

Chapter 11—Reorganization of the Bankruptcy Code provides a method for reorganizing a debtor's financial affairs under the supervision of the bankruptcy court.[8] The goal of Chapter 11 is to reorganize the debtor with a new capital structure so that the debtor emerges from bankruptcy as a viable concern. This option, which is referred to as **reorganization bankruptcy**, is often in the best interests of the debtor and its creditors.

Chapter 11 is available to partnerships, corporations, limited liability companies, and other business entities. The majority of Chapter 11 proceedings are filed by corporations and other businesses that want to reorganize their capital structure by receiving discharge of a portion of their debts, obtaining relief from burdensome contracts, and emerge from bankruptcy as *going concerns*. Chapter 11 is also filed by wealthy individual debtors who do not qualify for Chapter 7 or Chapter 13 bankruptcy.

Chapter 11—Reorganization
A bankruptcy method that allows the reorganization of the debtor's financial affairs under the supervision of the bankruptcy court.

Debtor-in-Possession

In most Chapter 11 cases, the debtor is left in place to operate the business during the reorganization proceeding. In such cases, the debtor is called a **debtor-in-possession**. The court may appoint a trustee to operate the debtor's

debtor-in-possession
A debtor who is left in place to operate the business during the reorganization proceeding.

business only on a showing of cause, such as fraud, dishonesty, or gross mismanagement of the affairs of the debtor by current management.

The debtor-in-possession is empowered to operate the debtor's business during the bankruptcy proceeding. This power includes authority to enter into contracts, purchase supplies, incur debts, and so on. Credit extended by postpetition unsecured creditors in the ordinary course of business is given automatic priority as an administrative expense in bankruptcy.

Creditors' Committees

creditors' committee
A committee of unsecured creditors that is appointed by the court to represent the class of unsecured claims. The court can also appoint committees for secured creditors and for equity holders.

After an order for relief is granted, the court appoints a **creditors' committee** composed of representatives of the class of unsecured claims. The court may also appoint a committee of secured creditors and a committee of equity holders. Generally, the parties holding the seven largest creditor claims or equity interests are appointed to their requisite committees. Committees may appear at bankruptcy court hearings, participate in the negotiation of a plan of reorganization, assert objections to proposed plans of reorganization, and the like.

Automatic Stay in Chapter 11

Poor bankrupt.
William Shakespeare
Romeo and Juliet (ca. 1594)

The filing of a Chapter 11 petition stays (suspends) actions by creditors to recover the debtor's property. This automatic stay suspends certain legal actions against the debtor or the debtor's property, including the ability of creditors to foreclose on assets given as collateral for their loans to the debtor. This automatic stay is extremely important to a business trying to reorganize under Chapter 11 because the debtor needs to keep its assets to stay in business.

Example Big Oil Company owns a manufacturing plant and has borrowed $50 million from a bank and used the plant as collateral for the loan. If Big Oil Company files for Chapter 11 bankruptcy, the automatic stay prevents the bank from foreclosing and taking the property. Once out of bankruptcy, Big Oil Company must pay the bank any unpaid arrearages and begin making the required loan payments again.

Executory Contracts and Unexpired Leases in Chapter 11

A major benefit of Chapter 11 bankruptcy is that the debtor is given the opportunity to accept or reject certain executory contracts and unexpired leases. **Executory contracts** or **unexpired leases** are contracts or leases that have not been fully performed.

executory contract or **unexpired lease**
A contract or lease that has not been fully performed. With the bankruptcy court's approval, a debtor may reject executory contracts and unexpired leases in bankruptcy.

A contract to purchase goods or supply goods at a later date is an executory contract. A 20-year office lease that has eight years left until it is completed is an unexpired lease. Other executory contracts and unexpired leases may include consulting contracts, contracts to purchase or provide services, equipment leases, warehouse leases, automobile and equipment leases, leases for office and commercial space, and such.

Under the Bankruptcy Code, a debtor-in-possession (or trustee) in a Chapter 11 proceeding is given authority to assume or reject executory contracts. In general, the debtor rejects unfavorable executory contracts and assumes favorable executory contracts. The debtor is not liable for damages caused by the rejection of executory contracts and unexpired leases in bankruptcy.

Examples Big Oil Company enters into a contract to sell oil to another company, and the contract has two years remaining when the oil company files for Chapter 11 bankruptcy. This is an *executory contract*. Big Oil Company has leased an office building for 20 years from a landlord to use as its headquarters, and it has 15 years left on the lease when it declares bankruptcy. This is an *unexpired lease*. In the Chapter 11 reorganization proceeding, Big Oil Company can reject (get out of) either the executory contract or the unexpired lease without any liability; it can keep either one if doing so is its best interests.

Labor Union and Retiree Benefits Contracts Debtors that file for Chapter 11 reorganization sometimes have collective bargaining agreements with labor unions that require the payment of agreed-on wages and other benefits to union member-employees for some agreed-on period in the future. Debtors also often have contracts to pay union and nonunion retired employees and their dependents' medical, surgical, hospitalization, dental, and death benefits (retiree benefits). In a Chapter 11 case, union members and union retirees are represented by the responsible labor union. The court appoints a committee to represent nonunion retirees.

Critical Legal Thinking

What is the public policy that allows businesses to file for Chapter 11 bankruptcy? Who benefits from Chapter 11 bankruptcy?

The debtor and the representatives of the union members and retirees can voluntarily agree to modification of the union collective bargaining agreement and retiree benefits. If such an agreement is not reached, the debtor must confer in good faith with the union and retirees' representative, but if a settlement cannot be reached, the debtor can petition the bankruptcy court to reject the union agreement or to modify retiree benefits. The court can reject a union contract or modify retirees' benefits if the court finds that the "balance of equities" favors rejection or modification and the rejection or modification is necessary to the debtor's reorganization.

Discharge of Debts

In its bankruptcy reorganization, the debtor usually proposes to reduce its *unsecured debt* so that it can come out of bankruptcy with fewer debts to pay than when it filed for bankruptcy. The bankruptcy court permits the debtor to *discharge* the amount of unsecured credit that would make its plan of reorganization feasible. Unsecured credit is discharged on a pro rata basis.

Example Big Oil Company has $100 million in secured debts (e.g., real estate mortgages, personal property secured transactions) and $100 million in unsecured credit when it files for Chapter 11 bankruptcy. In its plan of reorganization, Big Oil Company proposes to eliminate 60 percent—$60 million—of its unsecured credit. If the court approves, then Big Oil will emerge from bankruptcy owing only $40 million of prepetition unsecured debt. The other $60 million is discharged, and the creditors can never recover these debts in the future.

Chapter 11 Plan of Reorganization

The debtor has the exclusive right to file a **Chapter 11 plan of reorganization** with the bankruptcy court within the first 120 days after the date of the order for relief. Under the 2005 act, this period may be extended up to 18 months. The debtor has the right to obtain creditor approval of the plan, but if the debtor fails to do so, any party of interest (e.g., a trustee, a creditor, an equity holder) may propose a plan.

Chapter 11 plan of reorganization
A plan that sets forth a proposed new capital structure for a debtor to assume when it emerges from Chapter 11 reorganization bankruptcy.

The plan of reorganization sets forth the proposed new financial structure of the debtor. This includes the portion of the unsecured debts proposed to be paid by the debtor and the unsecured debt the debtor proposes to have discharged. The plan must specify the executory contracts and unexpired leases that the debtor proposes to reject that have not previously been rejected in the bankruptcy proceeding. The plan also designates how equity holders are to be treated, describes any new equity investments that are to be made in the debtor, and includes other relevant information.

The debtor must supply the creditors and equity holders with a *disclosure statement* that contains adequate information about the proposed plan of reorganization so that they can make an informed judgment about the plan.

Confirmation of a Chapter 11 Plan of Reorganization

confirmation of a Chapter 11 plan of reorganization
The bankruptcy court's approval of a plan of reorganization.

acceptance method
A method whereby the court confirms a plan of reorganization if the creditors accept the plan and if other requirements are met.

cram-down provision
A provision whereby the court confirms a plan of reorganization over an objecting class of creditors if certain requirements are met.

There must be **confirmation of a Chapter 11 plan of reorganization** by the bankruptcy court for the debtor to be reorganized under Chapter 11. The bankruptcy court confirms a plan of reorganization under the **acceptance method** if (1) the plan is in the best interests of the creditors because the creditors would receive at least what they would receive in a Chapter 7 liquidation bankruptcy, (2) the plan is feasible (i.e., the new reorganized company is likely to succeed), and (3) each class of creditors accepts the plan (i.e., at least one-half the number of creditors who represent at least two-thirds of the dollar amount of the debt vote to accept the plan).

If a class of creditors does not accept the plan, the plan can be confirmed by the court by using the Bankruptcy Code's **cram-down provision**. In order for the court to confirm a plan over the objection of a class of creditors, at least one class of creditors must have voted to accept the plan.

Example The BigDotCom Corporation has financial difficulties and has filed for Chapter 11 reorganization. At the time of filing for Chapter 11, the corporation has $100 million of secured credit, $100 million of unsecured credit, and common stockholders whose equity securities are now worthless. The corporation files a plan of reorganization whereby the corporation (1) keeps the secured assets for the business, pays the secured creditors any arrearages owed, and has the secured creditors retain their secured interests in the secured assets; (2) reduces unsecured debt by $45 million and discharges $55 million of unsecured debt; (3) eliminates the interests of the equity holders; (4) rejects specified executory contracts and unexpired leases; (5) eliminates several unprofitable product lines; (6) provides for the payment of required unpaid taxes; and (7) accepts the investment of $30 million in capital from an investment bank that wants to invest in the corporation. If this plan is approved by the court, $55 million of the corporation's unsecured debt is discharged. The corporation emerges from Chapter 11 as a reorganized going concern.

With money in your pocket you are wise, you are handsome, and you sing well too.

Proverb

The following feature discusses the Chapter 11 bankruptcy of the General Motors Corporation.

Business Environment

General Motors Bankruptcy

"Because for years I thought what was good for the country was good for General Motors, and vice versa."

—Charles Erwin Wilson, president of General Motors Corporation
Comment before a committee of the U.S. Senate, 1953

General Motors Corporation (GM) originally started in 1908 and grew to be the world's largest corporation. From the 1950s through the 1980s were profitable times for GM as it expanded operations in the United States and worldwide. Beginning in the 1970s, however, foreign competition began to make inroads into the U.S. automobile market. By the end of the first decade of the twenty-first century, GM was losing billions of dollars each year. This led GM to consider a once inconceivable solution: declare bankruptcy.

Luckily for GM, the U.S. federal government decided that GM was "too big to fail." The federal government thus provided GM with a bailout of taxpayers' money. In 2009, GM filed Chapter 11 bankruptcy and reorganized its financial structure and operations. At the time of the bankruptcy filing, GM had liabilities of $172 billion and assets of $82 billion. The GM bankruptcy was one of the largest bankruptcies in U.S. history.

The results of GM's bankruptcy were the following:

- The U.S. government provided more than $50 billion of taxpayer bailout money to GM. In exchange for the bailout, the federal government—the U.S. taxpayers—received 60 percent of the new GM stock.
- The Canadian federal and provincial governments, which provided more than $8 billion of bailout money, received 12 percent of GM stock.
- The United Auto Workers (UAW), a labor union that represents the majority of GM's nonmanagement workforce,

agreed to concessions of lower wages and benefits in exchange for a 17.5 percent ownership interest in GM.

- GM bondholders, who held more than $27 billion of GM bonds, were converted from bondholders to stockholders and given stock worth only a fraction of their original investment.
- GM shed more than two-thirds of its debt, reducing its prebankruptcy debt of $54 billion to only $17 billion. In exchange, the unsecured creditors were given 10 percent ownership of GM.
- GM's shareholders at the time of bankruptcy had the value of their investments wiped out.
- GM closed dozens of manufacturing and assembly plants and other operations in the United States.
- GM shed more than 20,000 blue-collar jobs through buyouts, early-retirement offers, and layoffs. After the bankruptcy, GM employed approximately 40,000 hourly workers in the United States.
- GM canceled more than 2,000 of its 6,000 dealership licenses.
- GM eliminated its Pontiac, Saturn, Hummer, and Saab brand names. GM pared down to four brand-name vehicles—Chevrolet, Cadillac, Buick, and GMC.

In addition to the bailout money, GM received $15 billion of tax benefits from the federal government. Subsequently, GM issued stock in a public offering, and the federal government sold its stock in GM. In total, including unpaid bailout money and the tax benefits given to GM, the American taxpayers lost approximately $35 billion on the GM bailout. *In re General Motors Corporation*, Chapter 11 Case No. 09-50026 (REG) (United States Bankruptcy Court for the Southern District of New York)

Critical Legal Thinking Questions

What is the public policy that allows companies to file for Chapter 11 reorganization bankruptcy? Are any parties hurt by a Chapter 11 bankruptcy? Should the federal government follow the axiom that some companies are "too big to fail"? Does GM owe an ethical duty to pay the government the money that the taxpayers lost on the bailout?

Small Business Bankruptcy

The Bankruptcy Code permits a "small business," defined as one with total debts of less than $2,490,925, to use a simplified, fast-track form of Chapter 11 reorganization bankruptcy. **Small business bankruptcy** provides an efficient and cost-saving method for small businesses to reorganize under Chapter 11.

CHAPTER 12 BANKRUPTCY

This is a farm in the state of Idaho. ***Chapter 12—Adjustment of Debts of a Family Farmer or Fisherman with Regular Income***[9] *of the federal Bankruptcy Code contains special provisions for the reorganization bankruptcy of family farmers and family fishermen. Under Chapter 12, only the debtor may file a voluntary petition for bankruptcy. To qualify, a family farmer cannot have debt that exceeds $4,031,575, and a family fisherman cannot have debt that exceeds $1,868,200. The debtor files a plan of reorganization.*

The plan may modify secured and unsecured credit and assume or reject executory contracts and unexpired leases. The plan period is usually three years, although a court may increase the period to up to five years, based on showing of cause. To confirm a plan of reorganization, the bankruptcy court must find the plan to be feasible. During the plan period, the debtor makes the debt payments required by the plan. When the family farmer or family fisherman has completed making the payments required by the plan, the bankruptcy court grants the debtor discharge of all the debts provided for by the plan.

Key Terms and Concepts

Abusive homestead exemption (593)
Acceptance method (602)
Article I, section 8, clause 4 of the U.S. Constitution (585)
Attorney certification (587)
Automatic stay (588)
Bankruptcy Abuse Prevention and Consumer Protection Act of 2005 (586)
Bankruptcy Code (586)
Bankruptcy estate (592)
Bankruptcy law (586)
Bankruptcy Reform Act of 1978 (586)
Bankruptcy trustee (588)
Chapter 7 discharge (598)
Chapter 7—Liquidation (straight bankruptcy) (593)
Chapter 11 plan of reorganization (601)
Chapter 11—Reorganization (599)
Chapter 12—Adjustment of Debts of a Family Farmer or Fisherman with Regular Income (603)
Chapter 13—Adjustment of Debts of an Individual with Regular Income (597)
Chapter 13 discharge (599)
Chapter 13 plan of payment (598)
Composition (598)
Confirmation of a Chapter 11 plan of reorganization (602)
Consumer debt (597)
Cram-down provision (602)
Creditors' committee (600)
Debtor-in-possession (599)
Discharge (589)
Disposable income (594)
Executory contract (600)
Exempt property (592)
Extension (598)
Fraudulent transfer (591)
Fresh start (585)
Homestead exemption (293)
Individual with regular income (597)
Involuntary petition (587)
Means test (594)
Median income test (594)
Meeting of the creditors (first meeting of the creditors) (588)
Nonexempt property (595)
Order for relief (588)
Oversecured creditor (595)
Petition (587)
Postpetition counseling (587)
Prepetition counseling (587)
Proof of claim (588)
Proof of interest (588)
Reaffirmation agreement (590)
Reorganization bankruptcy (599)
Schedules (587)
Secured personal property (595)
Small business bankruptcy (603)
State median income (594)
Statutory priority of unsecured claims (595)
Student loan (597)
Undersecured creditor (595)
Undue hardship (597)
Unexpired lease (600)
U.S. bankruptcy courts (586)
U.S. Trustee (586)
Voluntary petition (587)

Critical Legal Thinking Cases

28.1 Bankruptcy Estate Dr. Morris Lebovitz and Kerrye Hill Lebovitz, husband and wife, were residents of the state of Tennessee. Dr. Lebovitz filed for bankruptcy protection as a result of illness. Mrs. Lebovitz (Debtor) filed for bankruptcy because she had co-signed on a large loan with Dr. Lebovitz. The Debtor is the owner of the following pieces of jewelry: a Tiffany five-carat diamond engagement ring (purchase price $40,000 to $50,000), a pair of diamond stud earrings of approximately one carat each, a diamond drop necklace of approximately one carat, and a Cartier watch. All of these items were gifts from Dr. Lebovitz.

Tennessee opted out of the federal bankruptcy exemption provisions and adopted its own bankruptcy exemption provisions. Tennessee does not provide for an exemption for jewelry. Tennessee does provide for an exemption for "necessary and proper wearing apparel." Debtor claimed that her jewelry was necessary and proper wearing apparel and was therefore exempt property from the bankruptcy estate. The bankruptcy trustee filed an objection to the claim of exemption, arguing that the Debtor's jewelry does not qualify for an exemption and should be part of the bankruptcy estate. Does Debtor's jewelry qualify as necessary and proper wearing apparel, and should it thus be exempt property from the bankruptcy estate? *In re Lebovitz*, 344 B.R. 556, 2006 Bankr. Lexis 1044 (United States Bankruptcy Court for the Western District of Tennessee, 2006)

28.2 Petition Daniel E. Beren, John M. Elliot, and Edward F. Mannino formed Walnut Street Four, a general partnership, to purchase and renovate an office building in Harrisburg, Pennsylvania. They borrowed more than $200,000 from Hamilton Bank to purchase the building and begin renovation. Disagreements among the partners arose when the renovation costs exceeded their estimates. When Beren was unable to obtain assistance from Elliot and Mannino regarding obtaining additional financing, the partnership quit paying its debts. Beren filed an involuntary petition to place the partnership into Chapter 7 bankruptcy. The other partners objected to the bankruptcy filing. At the time of the filing, the partnership owed debts of more than $380,000 and had approximately $550 in the partnership bank account. Should the petition for involuntary bankruptcy be granted? *In re Walnut Street Four*, 106 B.R. 56, 1989 Bankr. Lexis 1806 (United States Bankruptcy Court for the Middle District of Pennsylvania)

28.3 Automatic Stay James F. Kost filed a voluntary petition for relief under Chapter 11 of the Bankruptcy Code. First Interstate Bank of Greybull (First Interstate) held a first mortgage on the debtor's residence near Basin, Wyoming. Appraisals and other evidence showed that the house was worth $116,000. The debt owed to First Interstate was almost $103,000 and was increasing at a rate of $32.46 per day. The debtor had only an 11.5 percent equity cushion in the property. Further evidence showed that (1) the Greybull/Basin area was suffering from tough economic times, (2) there were more than 90 homes available for sale in the area, (3) the real estate market in the area was declining, (4) the condition of the house was seriously deteriorating and the debtor was not financially able to make the necessary improvements, and (5) the insurance on the property had lapsed. First Interstate moved for a relief from stay so that it could foreclose on the property and sell it. Should the motion be granted? *In re Kost*, 102 B.R. 829, 1989 U.S. Dist. Lexis 8316 (United States District Court for the District of Wyoming)

28.4 Student Loan Donald Wayne Doyle (Debtor) obtained a guaranteed student loan to enroll in a school for training truck drivers. Due to his impending divorce, Debtor never attended the program. The first monthly installment of approximately $50 to pay the student loan became due. Two weeks later, Debtor filed a voluntary petition for Chapter 7 bankruptcy. Debtor was a 29-year-old man who earned approximately $1,000 per month at an hourly wage of $7.70 as a truck driver, a job that he had held for 10 years. Debtor resided on a farm where he performed work in lieu of paying rent for his quarters. Debtor was paying monthly payments of $89 on a bank loan for his former wife's vehicle, $200 for his truck, $40 for health insurance, $28 for car insurance, $120 for gasoline and vehicular maintenance, $400 for groceries and meals, and $25 for telephone charges. In addition, a state court had ordered Debtor to pay $300 per month to support his children, ages four and five. Debtor's parents were assisting him by buying him $130 of groceries per month. Should Debtor's student loan be discharged in bankruptcy? *In re Doyle*, 106 B.R. 272, 1989 Bankr. Lexis 1772 (United States Bankruptcy Court for the Northern District of Alabama)

28.5 Discharge Margaret Kawaauhau sought treatment from Dr. Paul Geiger for a foot injury. Dr. Geiger examined Kawaauhau and admitted her to the hospital to attend to the risks of infection. Although Dr. Geiger knew that intravenous penicillin would have been a more effective treatment, he prescribed oral penicillin, explaining that he thought that his patient wished to minimize the cost of her treatment. Dr. Geiger then departed on a business trip, leaving Kawaauhau in the care of other physicians. When Dr. Geiger returned, he discontinued all antibiotics because he believed that the infection had subsided. Kawaauhau's condition deteriorated over the next few days, requiring the amputation of her right leg below the knee. Kawaauhau and her husband sued Dr. Geiger for medical malpractice. The jury found Dr. Geiger liable and awarded the Kawaauhaus $355,000 in damages. Dr. Geiger, who carried no malpractice insurance, filed for bankruptcy in an attempt to discharge the judgment. Is a debt arising from a medical malpractice judgment that is attributable to negligent or reckless conduct dischargeable in bankruptcy? *Kawaauhau v. Geiger*, 523 U.S. 57, 118 S.Ct. 974, 1998 U.S. Lexis 1595 (Supreme Court of the United States)

28.6 Executory Contract The Record Company, Inc. (The Record Company), entered into a purchase agreement to buy certain retail record stores from Bummbusiness, Inc. (Bummbusiness). All assets and inventory were included in the deal. The Record Company agreed to pay Bummbusiness $20,000 and to pay the $380,000 of trade debt owed by the stores. In exchange, Bummbusiness agreed not to compete with the new buyer for two years within a 15-mile radius of the stores and to use its best efforts to obtain an extension of the due dates for the trade debt. The Record Company began operating the stores but shortly thereafter filed a petition for Chapter 11 bankruptcy. At the time of the bankruptcy filing, (1) The Record Company owed Bummbusiness $10,000 and owed the trade debt of $380,000, and (2) Bummbusiness was obligated not to compete with The Record Company. Can The Record Company reject the purchase agreement? *In re The Record Company*, 8 B.R. 57, 1981 Bankr. Lexis 5157 (United States Bankruptcy Court for the Southern District of Indiana)

Ethics Cases

Ethical

28.7 Ethics Case Peter and Geraldine Tabala (Debtors), husband and wife, purchased a house in Clarkstown, New York. They purchased a Carvel ice cream business for $70,000 with a loan obtained from People's National Bank. In addition, the Carvel Corporation extended trade credit to Debtors. Two years after getting the bank loan, Debtors conveyed their residence to their three daughters, ages 9, 19, and 20, for no consideration. Debtors continued to reside in the house and to pay maintenance expenses and real estate taxes due on the property. On the date of transfer, Debtors owed obligations in excess of $100,000. Five months after conveying their residence to their daughters, Debtors filed a petition for Chapter 7 bankruptcy. The bankruptcy trustee moved to set aside Debtors' conveyance of their home to their daughters as a fraudulent transfer. Did the Debtors act ethically in this case? Who wins? *In re Tabala*, 11 B.R. 405, 1981 Bankr. Lexis 3663 (United States Bankruptcy Court for the Southern District of New York)

28.8 Ethics Case UAL Corporation is the parent company of United Airlines, which was the largest scheduled passenger commercial airline in the world. On a daily basis, the airline offered more than 1,500 flights to 26 countries. The airline also offered regional service to domestic hubs through United Express carriers. Eventually, low-cost airlines such as Southwest Airlines began taking business from United. In response, United lowered fares to compete with the low-cost airlines. However, United's cost structure could not support its new strategy, and the company began losing substantial money on its operations.

UAL filed for Chapter 11 reorganization bankruptcy. At the time of filing the petition, UAL owned or leased airplanes, equipment, trucks and other vehicles, docking space at airports, warehouses, office space, and other assets. In many cases, UAL had borrowed the money to purchase or lease these assets. Most of the lenders took back mortgages or security interests in the assets for which they had loaned money to UAL to purchase or lease. In addition, UAL owed unsecured creditors money that it could not repay, and it had executory contracts and unexpired leases that it also could not pay. What should UAL propose to do in its plan of reorganization that it files with the bankruptcy court? *In re UAL Corporation*

Notes

1. 11 U.S.C. Sections 101–1330.
2. Public Law 109-8, 119 Stat. 23 (2005).
3. 28 U.S.C. Sections 586–589b.
4. 11 U.S.C. Section 522d.
5. 11 U.S.C. Sections 701–784.
6. 11 U.S.C. Sections 1301–1330.
7. Public Law 111-22.
8. 11 U.S.C. Sections 1101–1174.
9. 11 U.S.C. Sections 1201–1231.

CASE *United States Bankruptcy Court for the District of Alaska*

In re AVERY Case No. A06-00455-DMD, Adversary

A 08-90039-DMD March 31, 2011
United States Bankruptcy Court for the District of Alaska
MacDONALD IV, Bankruptcy Judge

Summary Judgment Memorandum

This is an action for recovery of damages of $150,000.00 based upon a variety of state and federal law theories. It is a core proceeding as to the plaintiffs' counts which allege violations of federal bankruptcy law. The plaintiffs' state law claims are not core proceedings, but the defendant has consented to the bankruptcy court's jurisdiction to enter orders and judgments regarding such claims.[1] Jurisdiction arises pursuant to 11 U.S.C. § 1334(b), the district court's order of reference and the consent of the parties.

The plaintiffs' amended complaint alleges nine causes of action: (1) professional negligence; (2) breach of fiduciary duty; (3) unjust enrichment; (4) conversion; (5) actual fraudulent conveyance - § 548(a)(1)(A); (6) actual fraudulent conveyance - AS 34.40.010; (7) constructive fraudulent conveyance - § 548(a)(1)(B); (8) constructive fraudulent conveyance - § 548(a)(1)(B)(IV);[2] and (9) violation of automatic stay and avoidance of post-petition transfers - §§ 362 and 549. The plaintiffs have filed a motion for summary judgment as to the following counts: (1) breach of fiduciary duty, (2) unjust enrichment, (3) conversion, (4) constructive fraudulent conveyance, and (5) illegal post-petition transfers. I will grant partial summary judgment to the plaintiffs on their count for conversion and full summary judgment on their count for illegal post-petition transfers. The balance of the plaintiffs' motion will be denied.

The defendant has filed a cross-motion for partial summary judgment as to the plaintiffs' claim for unjust enrichment. The defendant's cross-motion for partial summary judgment will be granted. Further, this court will grant summary judgment to the defendant on the plaintiffs' second cause of action–breach of fiduciary duty.

Background[3]

Debtor Mark Avery is the son of the late Luther Avery, a prominent San Francisco trust attorney. Luther was one of three named trustees for various trusts set up by Stanley Smith, a wealthy Australian mining magnate, and his wife, May Wong Smith. Stanley Smith died in 1968 but his wife continued to live long after his death. The trusts the Smiths established had substantial assets. The May and Stanley Smith Charitable Trust had assets of $350 million and the May Smith Trust had assets of $150 million.

When Luther Avery died in 2001, Mark Avery ("Avery") succeeded to his position as trustee of the Smith trusts. Avery, an attorney and former prosecutor, earned $600,000.00 a year as a trustee. He was also entitled to bill the trusts for legal services. After becoming trustee, Avery bought an expensive home in Eagle River in 2004. Around the time of this purchase, he met Robert Kane through Kane's mother, a real estate broker. With Kane's assistance, Avery moved May Smith from the Island of Guernsey, off the coast of France, to the Bahamas. May Smith suffered from dementia and needed full-time care. Yet she remained a trustee of her trust along with Avery and two other trustees, John Collins and Dale Matheny. All of the assets of the May Smith Trust were held by Avenco Ltd., a Bahamian Corporation. Avery, Collins and Matheny were the sole shareholders of Avenco.

After May Smith was relocated to the Bahamas, Avery, Collins and Matheny began to investigate options for providing reliable air transportation services for May Smith in case she needed to be moved from the Bahamas for medical treatment or other emergencies. In early May of 2005, Avery approached his co-trustees about a prospective business arrangement with Douglas Gilliland and his company, World Air, Inc. Under the proposal, Gilliland would use the assets of Avenco to secure a line of credit for the purchase of two to three long-range aircraft for use with a government contract. It was contemplated that the aircraft would also be available to provide any needed air transportation for May Smith.

On May 11, 2005, the trustees met in San Francisco and considered Avery's proposal. They agreed to make $50 million in trust assets available to use as collateral for the purchase of the aircraft. Avery was put in charge of making all the arrangements. Instead of utilizing the trust assets for the Gilliland venture, however, Avery used the assets for his own purposes. He opened a margin account in Avenco's name and immediately began taking massive draws on the account. On June 7, 2005, he directed $15 million from the margin account to an account belonging to

(case continues)

one of his wholly owned businesses, Avery & Associates. From June 16 through October 5, 2005, he directed an additional $37.125 million from the margin account to an account belonging to Regional Protective Services, another entity he controlled.

Avery went on a wild spending spree with the trust money. He spent nearly $10 million to acquire Security Aviation, Medic Air, Premier Aviation and Medical Training Institute. These entities were all established businesses at the time of purchase. Avery purchased a wide variety of fixed and rotor-wing aircraft, including Czech L-39 fighters, with over $28.2 million in disbursements from the Avery & Associates and Regional Protective Services accounts. Avery also purchased numerous costly personal assets, including a $500,000.00 mooseboat, a yacht, several vehicles, and motorhomes for himself and Kane.

Around the same time the Czech fighters were purchased, Security Aviation bought some rocket launchers to install on these aircraft. The FBI raided Security Aviation's offices and seized documents concerning the rocket launchers and the fighters. Federal criminal charges were filed against Robert Kane and Security Aviation for possession of unregistered destructive devices on February 22, 2006. Paul Stockler was retained as a criminal defense attorney for Kane. Wells Fargo pulled its line of credit for Security Aviation. Avery, after receiving $52 million from the May Smith Trust just months before, was broke. He had to liquidate aircraft to pay for the cost of defending against the criminal charges. Between April 17 and July 27, 2006, $8,442,351.05 of the proceeds from the sale of aircraft was transferred to Stockler's trust and e-trade accounts.

Security Aviation retained the law firm of Dorsey & Whitney to represent it in the criminal case. Dorsey & Whitney received a retainer of $400,000.00 from Avery's law firm, Avery and Associates, on February 2, 2006.[4] Kane retained Kevin Fitzgerald, an attorney in the firm of defendant Ingaldson, Maasen & Fitzgerald ("IMF"), to assist Stockler during the criminal trial.[5] Dorsey & Whitney transferred a portion of their retainer, $50,000.00, to IMF for IMF's representation of Kane during the criminal trial. The payment was made on February 24, 2006.[6]

Shortly after the criminal charges were brought against Kane and Security Aviation, the May Smith Trust retained the California firm of Townsend, Townsend & Crew to represent it in its efforts to obtain an accounting and recovery of the $52 million from Avery and Security Aviation. On March 9, 2006, Maureen Sheehy, an attorney in this firm, wrote a letter to Security Aviation's counsel, Robert Bundy at Dorsey & Whitney, to confirm recent phone conversations in which she had requested an accounting of trust assets from Avery and Security Aviation.[7] Sheehy also advised that until such an accounting was made, none of the property purchased with funds from the trust was to be sold without the written consent of the trust. The letter was sent via facsimile to Dorsey & Whitney the same day it was written.

Five days after Sheehy's letter was sent, on March 14, 2006, Security Aviation entered into an agreement for floor plan with Bell Aviation, Inc., for the sale of a S-550 Citation (N460-M).[8] This agreement provided $1,450,000 to Security Aviation for interim financing. These funds went to Stockler's trust account on March 22, 2006.[9] IMF received $150,000.00 from Stockler's trust account on April 13, 2006.[10] Avery testified at his § 341 meeting that proceeds from the sale of Security Aviation's aircraft were placed in Stockler's accounts in order to protect them, and that he believed the funds were being held in trust for Security Aviation.[11]

The criminal trial ran from May 15 to 26, 2006. Fitzgerald and Stockler represented Kane at the trial, and Robert Bundy represented Security Aviation. The jury acquitted Kane and Security Aviation of all charges. At the conclusion of the trial, IMF applied a portion of its retainer against its fees and costs. A balance of $100,302.92 remained in its trust account as of June 11, 2006.[12]

Two days before the jury entered its verdict, Louise Ma, another attorney with the California firm representing the May Smith Trust, wrote a letter to Robert Bundy regarding several issues.[13] First, she advised that the trust had decided it would oversee the care of May Smith, in place of Regional Protective Services, another Avery entity. Second, she noted that Avery had not yet responded to the firm's earlier requests for an accounting, and demanded repayment of the $52.125 million that Avery had received from the trust. Finally, she informed Bundy that Avery would no longer serve as counsel to the trust, and demanded return of any trust files in Avery's possession.

Ma wrote a second letter to Bundy on June 9, 2006.[14] In this letter, she stated, "As you know, [Avery] personally committed to repay [the $52 million] by March 31, 2006. To date, none of the principal has been paid and [Avery] has continued to refuse to address these issues."[15] Bundy wrote to Ma on June 29, 2006, to inform her that Dorsey & Whitney would no longer be representing Avery or his associated companies.[16] He indicated that Ma should direct all future correspondence to Fitzgerald.

On July 11, 2006, Fitzgerald wrote a letter to both Avery and Kane to confirm the understanding reached

(case continues)

between them regarding his representation of Avery "in the present misunderstanding and/or dispute with the other trustees [of the May Smith Trust]."[17] Fitzgerald was to address the "problem of the deteriorating relationship between [Avery] and the other two trustees" of the May Smith Trust, an effort which he said "ultimately may serve in [Kane's] best interests" as well.[18] The next day, July 12, 2006, Fitzgerald sent a letter to Louise Ma in which he advised that he represented "Avery and his associated companies in a limited manner with regard to matters involving the May Smith Trust."[19] In the letter, Fitzgerald indicated that he was aware of the trust's request for an accounting, but questioned whether the trust documents imposed any obligation upon Avery to provide one. He also indicated that Avery couldn't perform an accounting because his records had been seized by the federal government. Fitzgerald suggested that a meeting be scheduled between the parties on August 11, 2006 to "discuss a variety of issues."[20]

Ma responded to Fitzgerald's letter on July 26, 2006.[21] She confirmed that the May Smith Trust had made repeated requests of Avery for an accounting. She clarified for Fitzgerald that Avery, in his capacity as a trustee, had a fiduciary duty to provide an accounting of trust assets, and noted that Avery was well aware of these duties, as he had advertised himself as an attorney with expertise in representing trust fiduciaries. She reiterated that Avery was not to sell any property which he had purchased with trust assets, without the trust's written consent. Ma declined to schedule a meeting because she felt it would not be productive until Avery had supplied an accounting of the trust monies.

On July 27, 2006, the May Smith Trust filed suit against Avery in the California Superior Court in San Francisco.[22] Ma filed the verified petition on behalf of Collins and Matheny, the other two trustees of the May Smith Trust. The petition sought to remove Avery as a trustee and recover the $52.125 million he had taken. Avery was served with a copy of the complaint on July 28, 2006.[23] Fitzgerald was personally served with the complaint on the same date.[24] The suit was filed just 16 days after Fitzgerald had informed Ma that he represented Avery. In its answer, IMF admits that it was served with a copy of the California petition, but says that to the extent it was listed as Avery's counsel, this was done without its consent or authority.[25] Ma states that IMF never informed her firm that it was no longer representing Avery.[26]

The California court entered an order granting the trustees' petition and requiring the surrender of all trust property on August 2, 2006.[27] Avery and all companies he directly or indirectly controlled, including Security Aviation, were prohibited from making any kind of transfer of property that had been acquired from assets belonging to the May Smith Trust. Copies of the August 2, 2006, order were sent to Avery's California counsel, Armon Cooper, and Kevin Fitzgerald in Alaska on August 3, 2006.[28]

The May Smith Trust took the deposition of Dave Kurtz, Security Aviation's chief mechanic, on August 16, 2006. Paul Stockler appeared on behalf of Security Aviation at the deposition. Kurtz testified that $7.7 million in proceeds from sales of Security Aviation aircraft had been deposited into accounts belonging to Stockler.[29] $1,450,000.00 from the sale of one aircraft, an S-550 Citation (N460-M), was placed into Stockler's trust account on March 22, 2006. The proceeds from this sale funded the $150,000.00 retainer to IMF, as will be discussed in more detail below.

IMF was not a named defendant in the California litigation. It ignored the order which the California Superior Court had issued. IMF continued to apply its fees against the funds in its trust account from September of 2006 through March of 2007.[30] These fees were in excess of $43,000.00.[31] IMF also paid Kane a total of $47,500.00 between September and December, 2006, from its trust account.[32]

Avery filed a chapter 7 petition on October 23, 2006.[33] William Barstow was appointed chapter 7 trustee and, on December 11, 2006, he obtained court authority to operate Security Aviation.[34] Barstow also initiated an adversary proceeding against Stockler to recover funds that Avery or any of his entities had placed into Stockler's accounts.[35] On December 22, 2006, Barstow obtained a preliminary injunction which prohibited Stockler from disposing of any funds received from Avery entities without court approval.[36] The injunction also applied to Stockler's transfers of cash or property received from Robert Kane and any Kane entity.[37] Cam Rader, an attorney with IMF, attended the preliminary injunction hearings on behalf of Kane.

After assuming management of Security Aviation, Barstow placed this entity in chapter 11 on December 21, 2006.[38] He sold most of Security Aviation's assets to Stephen Kapper for $3.4 million on May 9, 2007.[39] A liquidating plan of reorganization was confirmed on May 19, 2008. Under Security Aviation's confirmed plan of liquidation, claims existing on the date of confirmation were transferred to the Avery bankruptcy estate.[40]

On March 5, 2007, the United States filed criminal charges against Mark Avery for five counts of wire fraud and ten counts of money laundering arising out of his transactions with the May Smith Trust. Avery immediately pled guilty to the charges. In his

(case continues)

plea agreement, he stipulated that he had abused his position as trustee to acquire more than $52 million dollars "through an ambiguous arrangement which used the assets of the May Smith Trust as collateral," that he placed his personal financial interests above those of the trust, and that he used the trust's funds for his benefit and did not repay them.[41] Avery also stipulated that he provided a fraudulent justification to acquire funds from the trust,[42] and that the assets and businesses he acquired with those funds benefitted him, personally, and not the trust.[43] On April 19, 2008, District Court Judge Ralph Beistline sentenced Avery to 102 months in prison followed by 36 months of supervised release.[44] Restitution of $52.125 million to the May Smith Trust was also imposed as a monetary penalty.[45]

Barstow initiated this adversary proceeding on October 22, 2008, in two capacities: as chapter 7 trustee of the Avery chapter 7 case and as successor in interest to Security Aviation, through the provisions of its confirmed chapter 11 plan. His motion for summary judgment was filed on October 5, 2010. IMF filed its motion for partial summary judgment on November 15, 2010. After oral argument on the motions, held December 13, 2010, the court permitted limited additional briefing. Both motions are now ripe for adjudication.

Summary Judgment

Fed. R. Civ. P. 56, which is applicable to adversary proceedings,[46] provides, in part:

(a) **Motion for Summary Judgment or Partial Summary Judgment.** A party may move for summary judgment, identifying each claim or defense–or the part of each claim or defense–on which summary judgment is sought. The court shall grant summary judgment if the movant shows that there is no genuine dispute as to any material fact and the movant is entitled to judgment as a matter of law. The court should state on the record the reasons for granting or denying the motion.

. . . .

(c) Procedures.

(1) ***Supporting Factual Positions.*** A party asserting that a fact cannot be or is genuinely disputed must support the assertion by:

(A) citing to the particular parts of materials in the record, including depositions, documents, electronically stored information, affidavits or declarations, stipulations (including those made for purposes of the motion only), admissions, interrogatory answers, or other materials; or

(B) showing that the materials cited do not establish the absence or presence of a genuine dispute, or that an adverse party cannot produce admissible evidence to support the fact.

(2) ***Objection That a Fact Is Not Supported by Admissible Evidence.*** A party may object that the material cited to support or dispute a fact cannot be presented in a form that would be admissible in evidence.

(3) ***Materials Not Cited.*** The court need consider only the cited materials, but it may consider other materials in the record.

(4) ***Affidavits or Declarations.*** An affidavit or declaration used to support or oppose a motion must be made on personal knowledge, set out facts that would be admissible in evidence, and show that the affiant or declarant is competent to testify on the matters stated.

. . . .

(e) **Failing to Properly Support or Address a Fact.** If a party fails to properly support an assertion of fact or fails to properly address another party's assertion of fact as required by Rule 56(c), the court may:

(1) give an opportunity to properly support or address the fact;

(2) consider the fact undisputed for purposes of the motion;

(3) grant summary judgment if the motion and supporting materials–including the facts considered undisputed–show the movant is entitled to it; or

(4) issue any other appropriate order.[47]

When considering a motion for summary judgment, all reasonable inferences supported by the evidence are drawn in favor of the party opposing a motion for summary judgment.[48] But such inferences may be drawn "only if they are rational, reasonable and otherwise permissible in light of the governing substantive law and substantive evidentiary burden."[49] A mere scintilla of evidence will not create a genuine issue of material fact.[50] "There must be evidence on which a jury could reasonably find for the plaintiff.[51] Finally, conclusory affidavits do not establish an issue

(case continues)

of fact for purposes of opposing a motion for summary judgment.[52] To defeat a motion for summary judgment, the non-moving party must establish the existence of material factual issues by producing evidence that would support a jury verdict in its favor.[53]

Summary judgment must be entered, "after adequate time for discovery and upon motion, against a party who fails to make a showing sufficient to establish the existence of an element essential to that party's case, and on which that party will bear the burden of proof at trial."[54] The Court may *sua sponte* enter summary judgment in favor of a non-moving party when the moving party has had a full and fair opportunity to ventilate the issues and under the facts it appears that the moving party could not prevail even if a trial were held.[55]

State Law

When interpreting state law, this Court is bound by the decisions of the state's highest court.[56] In the absence of a decision by the highest state court, this Court "must predict how the highest state court would decide the issue using intermediate appellate court decisions, decisions from other jurisdictions, statutes, treatises, and restatements as guidance."[57]

Source of the Retainers

In his summary judgment motion, the trustee seeks to recover both the $50,000.00 and $150,000.00 retainers that IMF received. Both transfers were made indirectly to IMF. It received an initial retainer of $50,000.00 from Dorsey & Whitney's trust account on February 24, 2006.[58] The source of these funds was Avery and Associates, which had transferred $400,000.00 to Dorsey & Whitney on February 2, 2006 as a retainer for its representation of Security Aviation in the criminal trial.[59] The trustee contends that payments from IMF's trust account to its operating account in March, April and May of 2006, which practically consumed the entirety of the initial $50,000.00 retainer, were transfers within the broad meaning of § 101(54). In his pending motion, the trustee seeks to recover these funds under his constructive fraudulent conveyance count.

I agree that the $50,000.00 retainer was an indirect transfer from Avery and Associates to IMF. But the trustee never alleged that these funds were recoverable by the estate in the amended complaint.[60] His fraudulent transfer counts are limited to the $150,000.00 retainer IMF received from Stockler's trust account. His other counts request relief in a lesser sum, e.g., the $100,302.92 IMF held in its trust account as of June 11, 2006, or the $35,764.42 IMF held in its trust account as of the date Security Aviation filed its chapter 11 petition. The amended complaint asserts no claim whatsoever as to the $50,000.00 retainer.[61] Summary judgment can only be made on a claim.[62] Accordingly, the court will make no determination on the $50,000.00 retainer here.

As to the second retainer received by IMF, the trustee's entire case rests upon his assertion that the $150,000.00 retainer was the property of Security Aviation. IMF disputes this, arguing that the funds belonged instead to Kane. IMF received $150,000.00 from Stockler's trust account on May 10, 2006.[63] The trustee contends these funds were proceeds from the sale of an S-550 Citation (N460-M) which belonged to Security Aviation. He supports this contention with two pieces of evidence: an accounting that IMF prepared in December of 2006 and the testimony and documentary evidence provided at the deposition of Dave Kurtz, taken August 16, 2006. The trustee says IMF's accounting shows that "the only funds available to fund the $150,000 retainer were the $1,450,000 received from the sale of the Citation."[64] I agree with the trustee on this point. IMF's accounting summarizes "the Avery entity transactions with Paul Stockler."[65] It reflects that a "Fedwire deposit" of $1,450,000.00 was made to Stockler's trust account on March 22, 2006.[66] The source of the deposit is not identified. The accounting also shows that a check from Stockler's trust account to IMF, in the sum of $150,000.00, was written on April 13, 2006.[67] There are no intervening deposits between March 22, 2006, and April 13, 2006, when the $150,000.00 check to IMF was issued. The trustee has established that the source of IMF's retainer was the $1.45 million Fedwire deposit into Stockler's trust account.

But how did the trustee match the $1.45 million deposit with the sale of the Citation? Regional Protective Services, the Avery entity that received $37.125 million of the May Smith Trust's monies, paid $1,850,565.00 for this aircraft on August 9, 2005.[68] The trustee alleges that it was placed in the name of Security Aviation. Documents attached to the deposition of Dave Kurtz reflect one of the aircraft owned by Security Aviation was an S-550 Citation (N460-M).[69] Security Aviation entered into an agreement for floor plan with Bell Aviation, Inc. on the Citation dated March 14, 2006.[70] This agreement provided $1,450,000.00 to Security Aviation for interim financing. Within days of entering into the floor plan agreement, Stockler's trust account was $1.45 million richer.[71] As noted earlier, Kurtz had testified that $7.7 million in proceeds from sales of Security Aviation aircraft had been deposited into accounts belonging to Stockler.[72]

Given the trustee's specific and meticulous documentation as to the source of the $150,000.00

(case continues)

retainer, IMF's responsive affidavits are entirely inadequate. Fitzgerald asserts that he "was informed by both Mr. Kane and Mr. Stockler that these monies were Mr. Kane's. This was consistent with Mr. Avery's later testimony as well as my own independent due diligence."[73] Fitzgerald doesn't describe the steps he took to perform his own "due diligence," and his assertions regarding Avery's later testimony are inaccurate.[74] His allegations as to statements made by Kane and Stockler are inadmissable hearsay under Rules 801 and 802 of the Fed. R. Evid. and Rule 56(c)(4) of the Fed. R. Civ. P. Further, Stockler's own testimony conflicts with Fitzgerald's statement as to Kane's ownership of the money. On January 4, 2007, Stockler testified that he didn't expect all the funds in his accounts were Kane's money,[75] that the money in his trust account was to fund the criminal trial,[76] and that he didn't know the source of the funds that were wired into his trust accounts, specifically, he didn't know "whether they were transferred from Avery & Associates, RPS, or Security Aviation."[77] However, Stockler confirmed that 99% of all the money placed into his accounts came from some "Avery entity."[78]

Fitzgerald's affidavit fails to address the evidence the trustee has presented as to the true source of the funds. Simply put, he does not have personal knowledge of the facts surrounding the initial transfer of funds into Stockler's account. He is not a competent witness on this point. His subjective and erroneous views as to the source of the retainer do not create a genuine dispute as to this material issue of fact.

The affidavit of Cam Rader also fails to rebut the evidence the trustee has presented. Rader supplies a copy of minutes purportedly from a meeting of the trustees of the May Smith Trust in which the trust authorized Avery to "employ a margin loan of up to 450,000" against certain trust investments "for purposes of acquiring and operating 'Security Aviation.'"[79] Further, Rader states that:

> *in addition to the trustee's unanimous approval [that Avery purchase Security Aviation], we were informed by Mr. Kane, Mr. Avery and counsel such as Paul Stockler, that Mr. Kane was a legitimate employee of Security Aviation and that he was paid money for his services, and indeed, that he was owed compensation by the company. We had good reason to believe, in good faith, that the legal fees paid to IMF came from the lawful monies authorized to Security Aviation, and its employees, such as Mr. Kane.*[80]

Rader's affidavit has the same failings as Fitzgerald's. Additionally, rather than supporting IMF's contention that the source of the retainer was Kane's property, his affidavit indicates that IMF may have known from the outset that its retainer came from "lawful monies authorized to Security Aviation." Further, even assuming Kane was owed money by Avery or Security Aviation, the purpose of the funds placed into Stockler's and then IMF's trust accounts was not for repayment of a debt, but to cover Kane's legal fees in the criminal trial.[81] The plaintiffs have thoroughly rebutted IMF's contentions to the contrary.[82]

Neither Fitzgerald's nor Rader's affidavit provides sufficient evidence to establish an issue of material fact as to the source of IMF's $150,000.00 retainer. Accordingly, based upon the trustee's evidence, and pursuant to Fed. R. Civ. P. 56(g), I find the following are material facts, not genuinely in dispute, which the court will treat as established in this case:

1) The S-550 Citation (N460-M) belonged to Security Aviation;
2) The source of the $1.45 million wired to Stockler's trust account on March 22, 2006, was from the sale of the Citation;
3) IMF's $150,000.00 retainer came out of the $1.45 million that had been wired to Stockler's trust account and was, therefore, attributable to the sale funds received for the Citation; and
4) Security Aviation had an interest in the $1.45 million wired to Stockler and, consequently, IMF's $150,000.00 retainer.[83]

Nature of Client Trust Account

Another issue that must be determined before reaching the meat of the plaintiffs' motion is the nature of the $150,000.00 while it was held in IMF's trust account. Resolution of this issue requires an analysis of the rights in an attorney's client trust account under Alaska law, including the Alaska Rules of Professional Conduct. As does the Alaska Supreme Court,[84] this Court will also look to the Restatement (Third) of the Law Governing Lawyers for guidance.

"A lawyer shall deposit funds received for future fees and expenses into a client trust account, *to be withdrawn by the lawyer only as fees are earned or expenses are incurred*."[85] Subject to specified exceptions, an attorney must deliver to the client or, as in this case, the nonclient so entitled, all funds in the attorney's possession belonging to the client or nonclient.[86] However, an attorney may retain the funds in his trust account if "there are substantial grounds for dispute as to the person entitled to the property," or "delivering the property to the client or nonclient would violate a court order or other legal obligation of the lawyer."[87] Finally,

(case continues)

> *[w]hen in the course of representation a lawyer is in possession of property in which both the lawyer and another person claim interests, the property shall be kept separate by the lawyer until there is an accounting and severance of their interests. If a dispute arises concerning their respective interests, the portion in dispute shall be kept separate by the lawyer until the dispute is resolved.*[88]

The initial purpose of the retainers paid to IMF were to fund Kane's defense in the criminal trial. Those funds were, however, subject to Security Aviation's right to request that the unearned portion of the funds be refunded.[89] By way of analogy, the transfer and deposit of funds into IMF's client trust account was similar to the deposit of funds with a bank in a demand account, albeit with a somewhat different method of withdrawal by Security Aviation. As in a bank demand account, the funds on deposit in IMF's client trust account remained the property of Security Aviation subject to disbursement at the direction of Security Aviation. Similarly, the right of IMF to withdraw the funds to pay its fees as earned and its expenses incurred in the defense of Kane is analogous to the right of a bank to debit a demand bank account for the agreed upon bank charges. Further, once IMF became aware that there was a dispute regarding who was entitled to receive the funds in its trust account, it was required to retain those funds until the dispute was resolved. These are the constraints under which IMF held the $150,000.00 in its trust account.

Breach of Fiduciary Duty

The trustee seeks summary judgment on the second cause of action stated in his amended complaint: breach of fiduciary duty. He argues that, once IMF agreed to represent Avery and his associated companies, the firm was in a sensitive position because it represented clients with conflicting claims: Avery and his companies on the one hand and Kane on the other. He says IMF knew or should have known, no later than August 16, 2006, that there were competing claims to the funds IMF held in its trust account. He pins IMF's knowledge to this date because it is the date on which Security Aviation's chief mechanic was deposed. Dave Kurtz's deposition was taken on the morning of August 15, 2006, in connection with the civil action the May Smith Trust had initiated against Avery.[90] Kurtz testified that he wired funds from the sale of Security Aviation aircraft, including the Citation, into Stockler's trust account. Stockler attended this deposition on behalf of Avery.[91] IMF's itemized billing statements reflect that Fitzgerald had extended conferences with Stockler, Kane and Avery the same day to discuss a variety of matters, including the "civil lawsuit."[92] IMF also billed for conferences with Kane and Avery on August 18, 2006, regarding "trust matters," and on August 23, 2006, IMF billed for a conference with Avery "regarding bankruptcy lawyers."[93]

In support of his motion on the breach of fiduciary count, the trustee cites *Willner's Fuel Distributors, Inc. v. Noreen*.[94] In *Willner's*, Fairbanks attorney Robert Noreen represented Thomas Rosson individually as well as Rosson's solely owned corporation, Rosson, Inc. Noreen placed both in bankruptcy in 1986. Willner's Fuel Distributors, Inc., was listed as a creditor in both bankruptcy cases.

Both bankruptcy petitions were dismissed on April 9, 1988. One day earlier, Rosson and his corporation filed suit against the Fairbanks North Star Borough and other entities for breach of contract and negligence. The claim arose from a contract that had been awarded to Rosson, Inc. On May 9, 1988, Willner's filed suit against Rosson and Rosson, Inc., for $20,212.17. After learning that Rosson, Inc., had been involuntarily dissolved in 1985, it moved for default against the corporation. In March of 1989, Rosson's claim against the Fairbanks North Star Borough was settled for $100,000.00. According to Noreen, Rosson settled in his individual capacity and as past president or assignee of the dissolved corporation. The settlement checks were made payable jointly to Rosson and Noreen, only. They were deposited in Noreen's trust account on March 28, 1989. That same day, a default judgment was entered against Rosson, Inc., in Willner's civil action.

The timing of events thereafter was disputed. Noreen said he deposited the settlement funds in his trust account on the morning of March 28. He directed the bank to make a cashier's check for $80,000.00 payable to Rosson individually. He then wrote a check to himself for $20,000.00 and deposited it in his business account. These two transactions spent the entirety of the settlement proceeds. Noreen alleged that Willners served him with a levy against his trust account on the afternoon of March 28, after the settlement funds had been disbursed. He responded to the levy by advising that he had no funds belonging to Rosson, Inc., under his control. Willners sued Noreen and Rosson, and alleged that Noreen had violated AS 09.40.040 for wrongfully disbursing funds of an insolvent, dissolved corporation. Willners moved for summary judgment and Noreen filed a cross-motion, contending that he owed no fiduciary duty to Willners.

The lower court granted Noreen's motion, but the Alaska Supreme Court reversed and remanded the case, finding that there were disputed facts regarding

(case continues)

the timing of the disbursals authorized by Noreen. The court discussed the fiduciary responsibilities arising upon the dissolution and insolvency of a corporation. It concluded that Rosson, in his capacity as director of a dissolved corporation, had a fiduciary responsibility to corporate creditors to preserve its assets for their benefit.[95]

The court also commented on the fiduciary responsibilities of Noreen. It noted that Noreen represented clients with conflicting interests–Rosson, who wanted to maximize his individual claim in the settlement proceeds, and Rosson, Inc., which wanted to maximize its share of the proceeds so it could disburse these funds to its creditors–and that an attorney in such a situation might be liable for breach of his fiduciary responsibilities to either client.[96] The court also found that Noreen had a fiduciary duty to the creditors of the dissolved corporation. "Just as creditors may sue directors on behalf of a dissolved corporation, creditors may maintain similar actions against the attorney of the dissolved corporation for breach of the attorney's fiduciary duties."[97]

> *By way of summation, we hold that if an attorney represents both a dissolved or insolvent corporation and a director or officer of that firm, and if the attorney controls corporate assets, then the attorney must protect the financial rights of creditors to these assets, where he or she knows or should know that the director or officer intends to interfere with creditors' claims through an improper distribution of these assets. To do otherwise would sanction a class of wrongs without a remedy.*[98]

The trustee argues that *Willner's* is applicable here and that he is entitled to the value of trust account funds held and disbursed by IMF following the Alaska criminal trial. I respectfully disagree. IMF did represent Avery "and his associated companies" for a limited period of time.[99] However, when IMF agreed to this representation, Fitzgerald advised both Avery and Kane that the two of them had a "potential conflict" and if an actual conflict did arise, IMF would represent Kane, not Avery.[100] In other words, the potential conflict was not between Avery and his corporate entity, Security Aviation, but between Avery and his related entities, on the one hand, and Kane, who purported to be a creditor of both.

IMF did control corporate assets, consisting of the $150,000.00 in Security Aviation proceeds placed in its trust account. IMF's disbursal of these funds after August 16, 2006, preferred IMF and Kane over the rights of the May Smith Trust, which was the largest creditor of both Avery and his related entity, Security Aviation. Further, IMF knew about the May Smith Trust's claims against Avery; the very purpose of its limited representation of Avery was to assist him "in the present misunderstanding and/or dispute with the other trustees" of the May Smith Trust.[101] After receipt of an injunction which prohibited Avery and his related entities from making any transfer of property acquired through the disposition of trust property, IMF continued to disburse funds from its trust account to itself and to Kane without regard to the rights of the May Smith Trust.

There are a number of similarities between *Willner's* and the case at bar. However, the May Smith Trust is not a party to this adversary proceeding. Barstow, as a chapter 7 trustee, has succeeded only to the rights of Avery, and his related entities, including Security Aviation. I conclude that the trustee and Security Aviation lack standing to assert a claim for breach of fiduciary duty against IMF under the rationale stated in *Willner's*. As the court made clear, the *creditor* of a dissolved corporation may maintain an action against the corporation's attorney for breach of fiduciary duty.[102] The trustee simply does not stand in these shoes. Further, the trustee cannot pursue this claim on behalf of the trust on the theory that it is an asset of either Avery's or Security Aviation's bankruptcy estate. The May Smith Trust is a creditor in both bankruptcies.

For these reasons, the trustee's motion for summary judgment on the issue of breach of fiduciary duty will be denied. Further, as noted above, the court may grant summary judgment *sua sponte* when, under the facts, it appears that the moving party could not prevail even if a trial were held.[103] Because the plaintiffs are not entitled to summary judgment on their second cause of action as a matter of law, IMF is entitled to summary judgment in its favor.

Conversion and Unlawful Post-Petition Transfer

The plaintiffs argue that IMF wrongfully converted funds remaining in its trust account after the conclusion of the criminal trial by paying Kane a total of $47,500.00 and paying its own legal bills for work it performed that was unrelated to the criminal trial.[104] The plaintiff's conversion count is the fourth cause of action in the amended complaint. It alleges damages in the sum of $92,810.31 under this theory.[105]

Conversion is a common law remedy governed by otherwise applicable state law. "The tort of conversion is 'an intentional exercise of dominion and control over a chattel which so seriously interferes with the right of another to control it that the actor may justly be required to pay the other the full value of the chattel.'"[106] As the Alaska Supreme Court has noted:

(case continues)

> *To establish a claim for conversion, the plaintiff must prove (1) that she had a possessory interest in the property; (2) that the defendant interfered with the plaintiff's right to possess the property; (3) that the defendant intended to interfere with plaintiff's possession; and (4) that the defendant's act was the legal cause of the plaintiff's loss of her property.*[107]

Did Security Aviation have a possessory interest in IMF's trust account funds as of June 11, 2006? Many courts have adopted a view that a plaintiff must either be in possession or entitled to immediate possession of the property in question at the time of the wrongful act to maintain an action for conversion. The Alaska Supreme Court has, however, rejected that view, instead holding that a future possessory interest is sufficient to maintain an action for conversion.[108]

As noted above, the funds held in IMF's client trust account were subject to the right of Security Aviation to request the unearned portion of the funds be refunded. Therefore, I find that Security Aviation had a sufficient future possessory interest in the funds transferred to IMF that were deposited in the IMF client trust account to support an action for conversion.

The second question is: did the post-June 11, 2006, disbursements by IMF interfere with Security Aviation's future possessory interest? To answer this question requires that the transfers be broken into two groups–transfers to Kane and transfers to IMF. Further, the transfers to IMF must be broken down further into transfers made in payment of its fees before and after Security Aviation filed its chapter 11 petition.

As noted above, the mere *retention* by IMF of the funds in its client trust account did not in any way interfere with Security Aviation's future possessory interest. The transfers, however, present an entirely different picture. Unless those transfers fell within one of the exceptions to the obligation of IMF to deliver the funds held in its trust account funds to Security Aviation upon its request, the transfers clearly interfered with Security Aviation's future possessory interest. Here, the only exceptions that would be applicable would be transfers which were made with the consent of Security Aviation or transfers made to satisfy a valid attorney's lien.[109] Under Alaska law, an attorney has a lien for compensation "upon money in the possession of the attorney belonging to the client."[110] Here, although the funds were subject to Security Aviation's future possessory interest, they were placed in IMF's trust account for the purpose of providing legal services to Kane. Additionally, IMF also represented Avery for a limited period before his bankruptcy petition was filed, and the retainer was applied against Avery's fees, as well. Thus, the transfer of funds from IMF's trust account did not interfere with Security Aviation's future possessory interest in those funds to the extent that IMF had a valid attorney's lien for fees earned or expenses incurred representing Kane and/or Avery. With respect to the prepetition transfers made to pay IMF's fees and expenses, I find that IMF had a valid, existing attorney's lien for the fees it had earned or the expenses it had incurred.[111] That lien extinguished Security Aviation's extant possessory interest and IMF was entitled to enforce its lien against the funds held in its client trust account for that purpose.

The post-petition transfers to IMF, however, present a different picture. A review of IMF's fee itemizations from December, 2006, forward indicate that all its post-petition work was performed on behalf of Kane.[112] After Security Aviation filed its chapter 11 petition, any attorney's lien IMF might assert for such services could not trump Security Aviation's possessory interest in the remainder of IMF's trust account.[113] There are two reasons for this. First, after Security Aviation filed bankruptcy, the balance of IMF's retainer become property of the bankruptcy estate. Prior approval from the court must be obtained before a creditor may acquire a post-petition security interest in property of the estate to secure obligations incurred by the debtor.[114] Even if Security Aviation had consented to IMF's post-petition representation of Kane, IMF could not assert a post-petition lien for such services against the funds in its trust account because it did not obtain prior approval from this court. Nor did IMF seek court approval of its employment as counsel for Security Aviation, which also required approval by this Court.[115]

Second, the filing of a petition in bankruptcy automatically stays "any act to create, perfect, or enforce any lien against property of the estate."[116] IMF did not obtain relief from the automatic stay before making the post-petition transfers to itself. Consequently, even if IMF might have otherwise held a lien, the post-petition transfers to itself in payment of its fees constituted acts to enforce a lien against property of the estate. Such acts violate the automatic stay and are void.[117]

The transfers to Kane present a different picture. Absent prior authorization or consent by Security Aviation, these transfers constituted conversion.[118] IMF does not contend that the $13,500.00 transferred post-petition was authorized by Security Aviation as the debtor in possession. With respect to the $34,000.00 transferred to Kane pre-petition, IMF has proffered no evidence that Security Aviation authorized the transfer to Kane.[119] And, as noted above, there is no evidence that these funds belonged to

(case continues)

Kane. There being no triable issue of fact, the entire $47,500 transferred by IMF to Kane constituted conversion, for which IMF is liable, as a matter of law.

The third question goes to the intent of IMF in making the transfers. Under Alaska law, an "intentional act" is defined to encompass either an intent to interfere with property or an act done with knowledge on the part of the defendant "that the act or omission would result in such interference."[120] Furthermore, an act may be intentional even if the defendant mistakenly believed that he or she had a right to interfere with the property, or was unaware of the rights of the plaintiff in the property.[121] In this case, the evidence supports but one logical, reasonable inference: IMF intended to deprive Security Aviation of the monies it held in its trust account. That the fourth element, that the conversion by IMF caused the loss to Security Aviation, is satisfied is self-evident and requires no further discussion.

I find that the following transfers by IMF from its client trust account constituted an intentional exercise of dominion or control over the funds that so seriously interfered with the rights of Security Aviation to control those funds that IMF may justly be required to repay those funds:

Date	Transferee	Amount
September 21, 2006	Robert Kane	$9,000.00
September 25, 2006	Robert Kane	$6,000.00
October 3, 2006	Robert Kane	$9,500.00
October 3, 2006	Robert Kane	$9,500.00
January 12, 2007	Robert Kane	$13,500.00
January 17, 2007	IMF	$6,328.08
February 8, 2007	IMF	$10,530.84
March 9, 2007	IMF	$1,110.25
April 10, 2007	IMF	$4,295.25
	Total	$69,764.42

These are material facts, not genuinely in dispute, which the court will treat as established in this case.[122] These transfers constituted a conversion of Security Aviation's property. Further, although the plaintiffs are not entitled to full summary judgment on their conversion theory, as to *all* transfers made by IMF from its trust account after June 11, 2006, I will grant partial summary judgment on their conversion claim, to the extent of the $69,764.42 in transfers shown above.

Additionally, the plaintiffs will be granted summary judgment on their claim for unlawful post-petition transfers. As explained above, the transfers IMF made from its trust account after Security Aviation filed its bankruptcy petition were in violation of 11 U.S.C. §§ 364, 327, and 362(a)(4). Summary judgment will be entered on the plaintiffs' ninth cause of action, in the sum of $35,764.42.

Fraudulent Transfers

The plaintiffs' seventh cause of action seeks to recover $130,596.14 from IMF on a fraudulent transfer theory under 11 U.S.C. § 548(a)(1)(B).[123] This figure represents the total of IMF's transfers from its trust account to pay for its legal fees, and includes the initial three transfers from March 15, 2006, through May 10, 2006, which consumed the $50,000.00 retainer IMF received from Dorsey & Whitney. As noted above, the $50,000.00 retainer will not be considered in the context of the plaintiffs' summary judgment motion because their amended complaint encompasses only the $150,000.00 retainer that IMF received from Stockler. Further, the plaintiffs' motion does *not* seek to recover any of the transfers from IMF's trust account to Kane as a fraudulent transfer.[124]

The transfers IMF made in payment of its fees, which arose *after* IMF's receipt of the Security Aviation funds from Stockler but *before* the filing of Security Aviation's chapter 11 petition, occurred from June 11, 2006, through December 14, 2006. In all, there were eight transfers, which totaled $80,909.05.125 These are the transfers which the court will evaluate here.

This court has already concluded that Security Aviation had an interest in the $150,000.00 IMF placed into its trust account. Under § 548(a)(1)(B), a trustee may avoid any transfer of an interest in property of the debtor which was incurred by the debtor within two years of the filing of the petition, if the debtor:

> *(B)(i) received less than a reasonably equivalent value in exchange for such transfer or obligation; and*
>
> *(ii) (I) was insolvent on the date that such transfer was made or such obligation was incurred, or became insolvent as a result of such transfer or obligation[.]*[126]

The term "transfer" includes "each mode, direct or indirect, absolute or conditional, voluntary or involuntary, of disposing of or parting with property; or an interest in property."[127] "The Bankruptcy Code's definition of "transfer' is *extremely* broad."[128] Further, the plain language of § 101(54) "makes clear that the transfer need not be made directly by the debtor."[129]

Looking first to the issue of insolvency, the plaintiffs' have presented credible evidence that Security Aviation was insolvent during the time the transfers to IMF were made. Mr. Minkemann, the trustee's C.P.A., has established that Security Aviation was insolvent throughout 2006 on a balance sheet

(case continues)

basis.[130] IMF's evidence to the contrary, consisting of the Rader affidavit, is wholly conjectural and has no evidentiary value on this issue. It fails to apply the balance sheet test for determining insolvency found in 11 U.S.C. § 101(32). I find that Security Aviation was insolvent in 2006 when the transfers were made from IMF's trust account to pay for its legal fees.

Did Security Aviation receive reasonably equivalent value for the transfers made to IMF?

> *Whether value has been given for a transfer depends on all the circumstances surrounding the transaction. Thus, whether a release of rights under a contract or the surrender of a lease is made for value must depend upon whether a good bargain is being given up or a burdensome obligation is being discharged. Whether the transfer is for "reasonably equivalent value" in every case is largely a question of fact, as to which considerable latitude must be given the trier of the facts. In order to determine whether a fair economic exchange has occurred . . . the bankruptcy court must analyze all the circumstances surrounding the transfer in question . . . Because the ultimate issue is the impact of the transfer on the debtor's estate, the court must thus determine whether the debtor, as opposed to some other entity, received such value. The analysis in such cases is similar to that of cases under the UFCA which held that a debtor did not receive reasonably equivalent value if its transfer was in exchange for a benefit to a third party.*[131]

The determination of "reasonably equivalent value" does not contain a good faith component.[132]

Both sides take broad strokes on the issue of reasonably equivalent value. The plaintiffs argue that *all* transfers from IMF's trust account to pay fees incurred after the criminal trial were made in payment for the debt of another, Kane, and therefore such payments provided no value to Security Aviation. They say that these miscellaneous fees, including those incurred on Kane's behalf in conjunction with the Avery bankruptcy, provided no value to Security Aviation. IMF argues that its fees did give value to Security Aviation, because Avery and Kane had identical interests and that its fees provided benefit to both. I feel there is a grey area in between these two positions. On the one hand, the interests of Kane, Avery and Security Aviation appear to have been so intertwined, with respect to the criminal charges, that IMF's services in the criminal case arguably benefitted the interests of all three of these parties. Additionally, a review of IMF's fee itemization for services rendered post-trial indicate that it dealt with residual issues related to the criminal charges after the trial concluded. Further, a portion of IMF's post-trial fees were incurred on Avery's behalf and paid out of the retainer. However, to the extent that fees were incurred exclusively for the benefit of Kane, particularly with regard to representing his interests in the Avery and Security Aviation bankruptcies, these fees would provide no value to Security Aviation.

These issues cannot be determined in the summary judgment context. There are disputed issues of fact that must be resolved by the trier of facts, the jury. Summary judgment for the plaintiffs on their seventh cause of action will therefore be denied.

Unjust Enrichment

The plaintiffs' motion seeks summary judgment on their third cause of action: unjust enrichment. IMF filed a cross-motion for partial summary judgment on this count. To establish a claim for unjust enrichment, the plaintiffs must show:

> *(1) a benefit conferred upon the defendant by the plaintiff;*
>
> *(2) appreciation by the defendant of such benefit; and*
>
> *(3) acceptance and retention by the defendant of such benefit under such circumstances that it would be inequitable for him to retain it without paying the value thereof.*[133]

The retainer received by IMF conferred a potential benefit of $150,000.00 to the firm. The plaintiffs only seek damages of $92,810.31, representing disbursements IMF made from its trust account after August 14, 2006.[134] Of this sum, $47,500.00 was paid directly to Kane. IMF clearly appreciated no benefit from the funds transferred to Kane, and the plaintiffs' unjust enrichment claim fails as to these transfers. That leaves at issue the sum of $45,310.31 which IMF charged for its attorney's fees and expenses.

The Alaska Supreme Court has found that the doctrine of unjust enrichment is not, in itself, a theory of recovery, but is "a prerequisite for the enforcement of the doctrine of restitution; that is, if there is no unjust enrichment, there is no basis for restitution."[135] Further, restitution is not a cause of action but a remedy for various causes of action, including quasi-contract, or contracts implied in law.[136]

> *The courts are in accord in stressing that the most significant requirement for recovery in quasi-contract is that the enrichment of the defendant must be unjust; that is, the defendant must receive a true windfall or "something for nothing." Where a defendant has given fair consideration or value to a third*

(case continues)

party in exchange for the benefits conferred by the plaintiff, there is no windfall and no recovery will lie.[137]

Here, IMF gave fair consideration or value to Robert Kane for the legal services it performed on his behalf. It did not receive a windfall. Neither the trustee nor Security Aviation have a valid claim for unjust enrichment.[138] Partial summary judgment for IMF is warranted.

Conclusion

The court finds that the following material facts, not genuinely in dispute, are established in this case pursuant to Fed. R. Civ. P. 56(g):

1) The S-550 Citation (N460-M) belonged to Security Aviation;
2) The source of the $1.45 million wired to Stockler's trust account on March 22, 2006, was from the sale of the Citation;
3) IMF's $150,000.00 retainer came out of the $1.45 million that had been wired to Stockler's trust account and was, therefore, attributable to the sale funds received for the Citation;
4) Security Aviation had an interest in the $1.45 million wired to Stockler and, consequently, IMF's $150,000.00 retainer.
5) The following transfers by IMF from its client trust account constituted an intentional exercise of dominion or control over the funds that so seriously interfered with the rights of Security Aviation to control those funds that IMF may justly be required to repay those funds:

Date	Transferee	Amount
September 21, 2006	Robert Kane	$9,000.00
September 25, 2006	Robert Kane	$6,000.00
October 3, 2006	Robert Kane	$9,500.00
October 3, 2006	Robert Kane	$9,500.00
January 12, 2007	Robert Kane	$13,500.00
January 17, 2007	IMF	$6,328.08
February 8, 2007	IMF	$10,530.84
March 9, 2007	IMF	$1,110.25
April 10, 2007	IMF	$4,295.25
	Total	$69,764.42

The plaintiffs' motion for summary judgment will be granted, in part, and denied, in part, as follows:

1) Partial summary judgment is granted on the plaintiffs' fourth cause of action, conversion, in the sum of $69,764.42.
2) Summary judgment is granted on the plaintiffs' ninth cause of action, for violation of the automatic stay and unlawful post-petition transfers, in the sum of $35,764.42.
3) Summary judgment is denied as to the remainder of the counts encompassed in the plaintiffs' motion (breach of fiduciary duty, unjust enrichment, and constructive fraudulent conveyance).

The defendant's cross-motion for partial summary judgment on the issue of unjust enrichment will be granted and the plaintiffs' third cause of action will be dismissed, with prejudice. Further, summary judgment will be entered in favor of IMF on the plaintiffs' count for breach of fiduciary duty, and the plaintiffs' second cause of action will be dismissed, with prejudice.

An order will be entered consistent with this memorandum.

DATED: March 31,2011.

DONALD MacDONALD IV
United States Bankruptcy Judge

---

1. Def.'s Answer to Am. Compl., filed Dec. 3, 2008 (Docket No. 8), ¶ 2.
2. This reference should probably be to § 548(a)(1)(B)(ii)(IV).
3. Some of the background facts in this memorandum are from this court's earlier Memorandum Regarding Substantive Consolidation, filed in the main case, *In re Avery*, Case No. A09-00455-DMD, on September 14, 2007 (Docket No. 136).
4. Decl. of Russell Minkemann, filed Oct. 5, 2010 (Docket No. 25), ¶ 5.
5. Decl. of Gary Spraker, filed Oct. 5, 2010 (Docket No. 26), Ex. C.
6. *Id.*, Ex. B at 5.
7. Spraker Decl. (Docket No. 26), Ex. E.
8. Spraker Decl. (Docket No. 26), Ex. S (Kurtz Dep.). The "Agreement for Floor Plan" between Security Aviation and Bell Aviation is the first attachment to this deposition excerpt.
9. Stockler's receipt of this sum was established in a prior adversary proceeding. *See Barstow v. Stockler*, Adv. No. A06-90059-DMD (Docket No. 13 –Mem. in Supp. of Mot. for Reconsid., Ex. 2).
10. Def.'s Answer to Am. Compl. (Docket No. 8), ¶ 29; Def.'s Opp'n to Mot. for Partial Summ. J., filed Nov. 15, 2010 (Docket No. 36), Ex. G.
11. Spraker Decl. (Docket No. 26), Ex. D, 105:13 - 106:3, 223:24 - 224:4.
12. Spraker Decl. (Docket No. 26), Ex. B.
13. *Id.*, Ex. H.
14. *Id.*, Ex. I.
15. *Id.*, Ex. I at 1.
16. Spraker Decl. (Docket No. 26), Ex. J.
17. *Id.*, Ex. K.
18. *Id.*
19. *Id.*, Ex. L.
20. *Id.*
21. Spraker Decl. (Docket No. 26), Ex. M.
22. *Id.*, Ex. N.
23. Aff. of Louise Ma, filed Dec. 8, 2010 (Docket No. 48), Ex. D.

(case continues)

24. Spraker Decl. (Docket No. 26), Ex. P; Aff. of Louise Ma (Docket No. 48), Ex. D.
25. Def.'s Answer to Am. Compl. (Docket No. 8), ¶ 37.
26. Aff. of Louise Ma, filed Dec. 8, 2010 (Docket No. 48),
27. Aff. of Louise Ma (Docket No. 48), ¶ 10.
28. Spraker Decl. (Docket No. 26), Ex. O; Aff. of Louise Ma (Docket No. 48), ¶ 13 and Ex. G. The order was sent via Federal Express overnight courier to Mr. Fitzgerald.
29. Spraker Decl. (Docket No. 26), Ex. S.
30. *Id.*, Ex. B.
31. *Id.*
32. *Id.*
33. *In re Avery*, Case No. A06-00455-DMD, Docket No. 1 (Petition). Nine entities associated with Avery were substantively consolidated with his bankruptcy individual case on September 14, 2007. *Id.*, Docket No. 137 (Order Granting, in Part, and Denying, in Part, Trustee's Mot. for Substantive Consolidation). The consolidation was *nunc pro tunc* to the date Avery's petition had been filed.
34. *Id.*, Docket No. 66 (Order Granting Trustee's App. to Settle Preference Claims re: Security Aviation, Inc., and App. to Operate Business).
35. *Barstow v. Stockler*, Adv. No. 06-90059-DMD.
36. *Id.*, Docket No. 10 (Prelim. Inj.). Kane moved for reconsideration. After a hearing, there were no material modifications of the original preliminary injunction. *Id.*, Docket No. 19 (Order re: Mot. for Recons. and Mot. to Compel).
37. *Id.*
38. *In re Security Aviation, Inc.*, Case No. A06-00559-DMD, filed Dec. 21, 2006, Docket No. 1 (Petition). IMF had $35,764.42 in its trust account at this time. Spraker Decl. (Docket No. 26), Ex. B.
39. *In re Security Aviation, Inc.*, Case No. A06-00559-DMD, Docket No. 115 (Revised Order Granting Mot. for Authority to Sell Assets Free and Clear of Liens and Assume and Assign Exec. Contracts). A second revised order was entered on September 25, 2007 (Docket No. 198) solely for the purpose of attaching an exhibit which was omitted from the May 9th order.
40. *Id.*, Docket No. 289 (Order Confirming Debtor's Plan of Liquidation).
41. Spraker Decl. (Docket No. 26), Ex. R at 9–10.
42. *Id.*, Ex. R at 10.
43. *Id.*, Ex. R at 12–13.
44. *United States v. Avery*, Case No. 3:07-CR-00028-RRB, Docket No. 71.
45. *Id.*
46. Fed. R. Bankr. P. 7056.
47. Fed. R. Civ. P. 56 (effective Dec. 1, 2010)(emphasis in text). Although the plaintiffs' and defendant's motions were filed prior to the effective date of amended Rule 56, under 28 U.S.C. § 2074(a) and the Order of the United States Supreme Court dated April 28, 2010, the amended rule applies to proceedings pending at the time the rule became effective, "insofar as just and practicable." *See* Order of the Supreme Court of the United States, dated April 28, 2010, regarding amendments to the Federal Rules found at http://www.uscourts.gov/RulesAndPolicies/FederalRulemaking/Overview/RulesForms120110.aspx.
48. *Ballen v. City of Redmond*, 466 F.3d 736, 741 (9th Cir. 2006).
49. *Bathony v. Transamerica Occidental Life Ins. Co.*, 795 F. Supp. 296, 298 (D. Alaska 1992).
50. *Anderson v. Liberty Lobby, Inc.*, 477 U.S. 242, 252 (1986).
51. *Id.*
52. *Shane v. Greyhound Lines, Inc.*, 868 F.2d 1057, 1061 (9th Cir. 1989) (conclusory affidavits not backed up by statements of fact cannot defeat a motion for summary judgment); *see also* Fed. R. Civ. P. 56(c)(4).
53. *Anderson v. Liberty Lobby, Inc.*, 477 U.S. 242, 256 (1986).
54. *Celotex Corp. v. Catrett*, 477 U.S. 317, 322 (1986).
55. *Cool Fuel, Inc. v. Connett*, 685 F.2d 309, 311–12 (9th Cir. 1982); Fed. R. Civ. P. 56(f).
56. *West v. Amer. Tel. &Tel. Co.*, 311 U.S. 223, 236 (1940) ("[T]he highest court of the state is the final arbiter of what is state law. When it has spoken, its pronouncement is to be accepted by federal courts as defining state law.").
57. *S.D. Myers, Inc. v. City and County of San Francisco*, 253 F.3d 461, 473 (9th Cir. 2001); *Paulman v. Gateway Ventures Partners III L.P. (In re Filtercorp, Inc.)*, 163 F.3d 570, 578 (9th Cir. 1998).
58. Spraker Decl. (Docket No. 26), Ex. B.
59. Minkemann Decl. (Docket No. 25), ¶ 5.
60. Am. Complaint, filed Oct. 23, 2008 (Docket No. 2).
61. *Id.*
62. Fed. R. Civ. P. 56(a).
63. Answer of Defendant IMF, paragraph 29, Docket No. 8.
64. Pls.' Reply to Def.'s Opp'n to Mot. for Summ. J., filed Dec. 8, 2010 (Docket No. 43), at 7.
65. Second Decl. of Spraker, filed Dec. 8, 2010 (Docket No. 44), Ex. DD at 2.
66. *Id.*, Ex. DD at Ex. 2, p. 1.
67. *Id.*
68. Second Decl. of Minkemann, filed Dec. 8, 2010 (Docket No. 45), ¶ 5.
69. Spraker Decl. (Docket No. 26), Ex. S (Dep. of Dave Kurtz).
70. *Id.* The "Agreement for Floor Plan" is the first documentary exhibit included with the excerpts of the Kurtz deposition found at Ex. S.
71. Second Decl. of Spraker, filed Dec. 8, 2010 (Docket No. 44), Ex. DD at Ex. 2, p. 1.
72. Spraker Decl. (Docket No. 26), Ex. S.
73. Aff. of Kevin Fitzgerald, filed Dec. 17, 2010 (Docket No. 52), at 2, ¶ 3.
74. Avery never testified that the $150,000.00 retainer was property of Kane. He stated that the money belonged to Security Aviation, the Mary C. Avery Trust or LACO. *See* Second Spraker Decl. (Docket No. 44), Ex. Z at 64:3–7. He also testified that the money which was put into Stockler's account belonged to Security Aviation and was placed with Stockler to protect it. Spraker Decl. (Docket No. 26), Ex. D at 105:13 - 106:3.
75. Second Decl. of Gary Spraker, filed Dec. 8, 2010 (Docket No. 44), Ex. AA at 36:3. Cam Rader attended the hearing in which Stockler provided this testimony, on behalf of Kane.
76. *Id.*, Ex. AA at 36:25–37:1.
77. *Id.*, Ex. AA at 39:11–17.
78. *Id.* at 39:20–24.
79. Aff. of Stuart "Cam" Rader, filed Nov. 15, 2010 (Docket No. 37), Ex. 2. The affidavit of Louise Ma notes that Rader has never attended any trust meetings or spoken with the other trustees of the May Smith Trust and his statements on this point lack any foundational support. Ma Aff. (Docket No. 48), at 2, ¶ 4. Further, as noted above, Avery admitted, in his plea agreement, that he had defrauded the trust and that any businesses he acquired with trust money were for his own benefit, rather than the trust's. Spraker Decl. (Docket No. 26), Ex. R at 10.
80. Rader Aff. (Docket No. 37), at 3, ¶ 4.
81. Second Decl. of Gary Spraker, filed Dec. 8, 2010 (Docket No. 44), Ex. AA at 36:25–37:1.
82. *See* Pls.' Reply to Def.'s Opp. to Mot. for Summ. J., filed Dec. 8, 2010 (Docket No. 43), at 5–13.
83. *Begier v. I.R.S.*, 496 U.S. 53, 58–59 (1990) ("property of the debtor" consists of "property that would have been part of the [bankruptcy estate] had it not been transferred before the commencement of bankruptcy proceedings."]

(case continues)

84. *See, e.g., Weiner v. Burr, Pease & Kurtz, P.C.*, 221 P.3d 1, 8 (Alaska 2009); *Compton v. Kittleson*, 171 P.3d 172, 177 (Alaska 2007); *Pederson v. Barnes*, 139 P.3d 552, 557 (Alaska 2006).
85. Rule 1.15(c), Alaska R. Prof. Conduct (in effect in 2006) (emphasis added). The current version of Rule 1.15(c) is identical.
86. Restatement (Third) of Law Governing Lawyers § 45(1) ("Except as provided in Subsection (2), a lawyer must promptly deliver, to the client or nonclient so entitled, funds or other property in the lawyer's possession belonging to a client or nonclient.").
87. Restatement (Third) of Law Governing Lawyers § 45(2)(d), (e).
88. Rule 1.15 (c), Alaska R. Prof. Conduct (in effect in 2006). This requirement is now found in Rule 1.15 (e), Alaska R. Prof. Conduct, but now clarifies that a lawyer must keep separate property in which "two or more persons (one of whom may be the lawyer), claim conflicting interests." *See also* Restatement (Third) of Law Governing Lawyers § 44 cmt. g (if a lawyer is in possession of property of "a person claiming that property deposited with the lawyer by the client was taken or withheld unlawfully from that person," the lawyer must safeguard the contested property until the dispute is resolved.)
89. *See* Rule 1.16(d), Alaska R. Prof. Conduct (in effect in 2006) ("Upon termination of representation, a lawyer shall . . . refund any advance payment of fee or expense that has not been earned or incurred."). The current version of Rule 1.16(d) contains essentially the same provision.
90. Spraker Decl. (Docket No. 26), Ex. S.
91. *Id.*
92. Def.'s Opp'n to Mot. for Summ. J., filed Nov. 15, 2010 (Docket No. 36), Ex. O at 1.
93. Spraker Decl. (Docket No. 26), Ex. B - IMF's Sept. 13, 2006 billing statement.
94. 882 P.2d 399 (Alaska 1994).
95. *Id.* at 404–05.
96. *Id.* at 405.
97. *Id.*
98. *Willner's Fuel Distrib.*, 882 P.2d at 406.
99. Spraker Decl. (Docket No. 26), Ex. L (Fitzgerald's June 12, 2006, letter advising Ma that he represented "Avery and his associated companies in a limited manner with regard to matters involving the May Smith Trust.")
100. Spraker Decl. (Docket No. 26), Ex. J.
101. *Id.*
102. *Willner's Fuel Distrib.*, 882 P.2d at 405 (emphasis added).
103. *Cool Fuel*, 685 F.2d at 311–12; Fed. R. Civ. P. 56(f).
104. Pls.' Mot. for Summ. J., filed Oct. 5, 2010 (Docket No. 24), at 21–22.
105. *See* Am. Complaint (Docket No. 2), at 15, ¶ 93. The plaintiffs' amended complaint contains a discrepancy regarding the amount remaining in IMF's trust account after the criminal trial. Their fourth cause of action states that this amount was $92,810.31, while ¶ 33 generally alleges that the balance after the trial concluded was $100,302.92. This discrepancy is not relevant to the court's analysis here.
106. *K & K Recycling, Inc. v. Alaska Gold, Inc.*, 80 P.3d 702, 717 (Alaska 2003) (quoting *Carver v. Quality Inspection & Testing, Inc.*, 946 P.2d 450, 456 (Alaska 1997)); *see also Dressel v. Weeks*, 779 P.2d 324, 328 (Alaska 1989)(conversion of specifically identified currency).
107. *Silvers v. Silvers*, 999 P.2d 786, 793 (Alaska 2000) (footnote omitted); *see also K & K Recycling, Inc.*, 80 P.3d at 717 (citing *Silvers*).
108. *McKibben v. Mohawk Oil Co., Ltd.*, 667 P.2d 1223, 1228–29 (Alaska 1983), *overruled on other grounds by Wien Air Alaska v. Bubbel*, 723 P.2d 627 (Alaska 1986).
109. Restatement (Third) of Law Governing Lawyers § 45(2)(a), (c).
110. AS § 34.35.430(a)(2).
111. It is uncontested that Security Aviation authorized the payment of IMF's fees from the $150,000.00. The plaintiffs do not contend, nor have they shown, that IMF did not earn the fees or properly incurr the expenses for which IMF reimbursed itself from the client trust account. However, while IMF's attorney's lien negates the plaintiffs' conversion claim, as to the pre-petition transfers, it does not affect the plaintiffs' fraudulent conveyance claims, which are based upon different legal principles.
112. Def.'s Mot. for Partial Summ. J., filed Nov. 15, 2010 (Docket No. 35), Ex. O, 9–12.
113. IMF does not contend the post-petition payments were authorized by Security Aviation as debtor in possession. Consequently, Security Aviation is also entitled to recover the funds transferred from the IMF client trust account as unauthorized post-petition transfers. 11 U.S.C. §§ 549, 550.
114. 11 U.S.C. § 364.
115. 11 U.S.C. § 327.
116. 11 U.S.C. § 362(a)(4).
117. *Kalb v. Feurerstein*, 308 U.S. 433, 438–39 (1940); *Gruntz v. County of Los Angeles (In re Gruntz)*, 202 F.3d 1074, 1082 (9th Cir. 2000) (en banc); *Schwartz v. United States (In re Schwartz)*, 954 F.2d 569, 571 (9th Cir. 1992).
118. Restatement (Second) of Torts § 228 ("One who is authorized to make a particular use of a chattel, and uses it in a manner exceeding the authorization, is subject to liability for conversion to another whose right to control the use of the chattel is thereby seriously violated.").
119. As noted above, this Court rejected IMF's argument that the monies deposited were Kane's property.
120. *Shields v. Cape Fox Corp.*, 42 P.3d 1083, 1088 n.12 (Alaska 2002).
121. *Id.*
122. Fed. R. Civ. P. 56(g).
123. The plaintiffs do not seek summary judgment on their other fraudulent conveyance counts, found in their fifth, sixth and eighth causes of action. The fifth count seeks relief under 11 U.S.C. § 548(A)(1)(A), the sixth under AS 34.40.010, and the eighth under § 548(a)(1)(B)(i)(IV).
124. *See* Pls.' Mot. for Summ. J. (Docket No. 24), at 22–23; Pls.' Response to Def.'s Sur-Reply, filed Jan. 10, 2011 (Docket No. 56), at 6.
125. Spraker Decl. (Docket No. 26), Ex. B.
126. 11 U.S.C. § 548(a)(1)(B).
127. 11 U.S.C. § 101(54)(D).
128. *Bernard v. Scheaffer (In re Bernard)*, 96 F.3d 1279, 1282 (9th Cir. 1996) (emphasis in original).
129. *Fursman v. Ulrich (In re First Prot., Inc.)*, 440 B.R. 821, 828 (B.A.P. 9th Cir. 2010).
130. *See* Second Minkemann Decl. (Docket No. 45) and Ex. D thereto, found at Docket No. 49 (Notice of Lodging Exs. to Second Minkemann Decl.).
131. 5 *Collier on Bankruptcy* ¶ 548.05[1][b] (Alan N. Resnick and Henry J. Sommer eds., 16th ed.) (footnotes omitted).
132. *Id.*, ¶ 548.05[1][b].
133. *Beluga Mining Co. v. State Dept. of Natural Res.*, 973 P.2d 570, 579 (Alaska 1999) (footnote omitted).
134. Am. Complaint (Docket No. 2), at 15.
135. *Alaska Sales and Serv., Inc. v. Millet*, 735 P.2d 743, 746 (Alaska 1978).
136. *Id.*
137. *Id.* (citations omitted).
138. As with the discussion on the conversion claim, because the legal principles differ, this holding does not affect the question of whether Security Aviation received reasonably equivalent value in the context of the fraudulent conveyance claims.